OPERATIONS MANAGEMENT

SPORTS AND GAMES

Practical Management Science

TITLES OF RELATED INTEREST

2ND EDITION

Practical Management Science

WAYNE L. WINSTON

Kelley School of Business, Indiana University

S. CHRISTIAN ALBRIGHT

Kelley School of Business, Indiana University

With Case Studies by
MARK BROADIE

Graduate School of Business, Columbia University

DUXBURY
—————★—————™
THOMSON LEARNING

Australia • Canada • Mexico • Singapore • Spain • United Kingdom • United States

DUXBURY

THOMSON LEARNING

Sponsoring Editor: *Curt Hinrichs*	Cover Illustration: *Todd Damen*
Marketing Representative: *Tom Ziolkowski*	Interior Illustration: *Lori Heckelman*
Assistant Editor: *Seema Atwal*	Photo Editor: *Jennifer Mackres*
Editorial Assistant: *Emily Davidson*	Photo Research: *Pat Quest*
Production Editor: *Janet Hill*	Print Buyer: *Jessica Reed*
Production Service: *Susan L. Reiland*	Typesetting: *Eigentype Compositors*
Interior Design: *Carolyn Deacy Design*	Cover Printing: *Phoenix Color Corporation*
Cover Design: *Vernon T. Boes*	Printing/Binding: *Quebecor World, Taunton*

COPYRIGHT © 2001 by Brooks/Cole
Duxbury is an imprint of Brooks/Cole, a division of Thomson Learning
Thomson Learning™ is a trademark used herein under license.

For more information about this or any other Duxbury product, contact:
DUXBURY
511 Forest Lodge Road
Pacific Grove, CA 93950 USA
www.duxbury.com
1-800-423-0563 Thomson Learning Academic Resource Center

Printed in the United States of America
10 9 8 7 6 5 4 3 2 1

Library of Congress Cataloging-in-Publication Data

Winston, Wayne L.
    Practical management science / Wayne L. Winston, S. Christian Albright; with case studies by Mark Broadie.
          p.   cm.
    Includes bibliographical references and index.
    ISBN 0-534-37135-3
    1. Management science—Computer simulation.   2. Management science—Mathematical models.   3. Electronic spreadsheets.   I. Albright, S. Christian.   II. Broadie, Mark Nathan.   III. Title.
T57.62. W55 2000
658'.001'13–dc21   00-033737

Photo Credits: *Page 1,* © EyeWire; *27,* © Artville; *67,* © Jean Luc Wang/Superstock; *111,* © EyeWire; *191,* Illustration/Lisa Torri; *275,* © EyeWire; *337,* © Artville; *399,* © EyeWire; *449,* © EyeWire; *493,* © Tony Stone Images; *563,* © EyeWire; *617,* © EyeWire; *715,* © Artville; *769,* © PhotoDisk, Inc.; *823,* © Artville; *887,* © Artville.

ABOUT THE AUTHORS

WAYNE WINSTON

Wayne L. Winston is Professor of Operations & Decision Technologies in the Kelley School of Business at Indiana University, where he has taught since 1975. Wayne received his B.S. degree in mathematics from MIT and his Ph.D. degree in operations research from Yale. He has written the successful textbooks *Operations Research: Applications and Algorithms, Mathematical Programming: Applications and Algorithms, Simulation Modeling Using @RISK, Data Analysis and Decision Making,* and *Financial Models Using Simulation and Optimization.* Wayne has published over 20 articles in leading journals and has won many teaching awards, including the schoolwide MBA award four times. He has taught classes at Microsoft, GM, Ford, Eli Lilly, Bristol-Myers Squibb, Arthur Andersen, Roche, PriceWaterhouseCoopers, and NCR. His current interest is in showing how spreadsheet models can be used to solve business problems in all disciplines, particularly in finance and marketing.

Wayne enjoys swimming and basketball, and his passion for trivia won him an appearance several years ago on the television game show *Jeopardy*, where he won two games. He is married to the lovely and talented Vivian. They have two children, Gregory and Jennifer.

S. CHRISTIAN ALBRIGHT

Chris Albright got his B.S. degree in Mathematics from Stanford in 1968 and his Ph.D. in Operations Research from Stanford in 1972. Since then he has been teaching in the Operations & Decision Technologies Department in the Kelley School of Business at Indiana University. He has taught courses in management science, computer simulation, and statistics to all levels of business students: undergraduates, MBAs, and doctoral students. In addition, he has recently taught simulation modeling at General Motors and Whirlpool. He has published over 20 articles in leading operations research journals in the area of applied probability, and he has authored the books *Statistics for Business and Economics, Student Execustat 3.0 MiniGuide, VBA for Modelers,* and *Data Analysis and Decision Making.* He also is working with the Palisade Corporation on a statistical software package. His current interests are in spreadsheet modeling and the development of VBA applications in Microsoft® Excel and Access.

On the personal side, Chris has been married for 28 years to his wonderful wife, Mary, who has somehow endured teaching 7th graders all of that time. They have one son, Sam, who is currently working in New York City in the music business and is playing saxophone with a rock band on the side. Chris has many interests outside the academic area. They include activities with his family (especially traveling with Mary), going to cultural events at Indiana University, playing golf and tennis, running and power walking, and reading. And, although he earns his livelihood from statistics and management science, his *real* passion is for playing the piano and listening to classical music.

DEDICATION

TO MY WONDERFUL FAMILY

Vivian, Jennifer, Gregory

W. L. W

TO MY MAIN SUPPORTERS

Mary, Sam, Tami, Ruth, and, of course, Charlie. And to Sam Senior, who is up there watching it all.

S. C. A.

BRIEF CONTENTS

CONTENTS

CHAPTER 4

Linear Programming Models 111

CHAPTER 5

Network Models 191

CHAPTER 6

Linear Optimization Models with Integer Variables 275

CHAPTER 7

Nonlinear Optimization Models 337

CHAPTER 8

Evolutionary Solver: An Alternative Optimization Procedure 399

CHAPTER 9

Multi-Objective Decision Making 449

CHAPTER 10

Decision Making Under Uncertainty 493

CHAPTER 11

Introduction to Simulation Modeling 563

CHAPTER 12

Simulation Models 617

CHAPTER 13

Inventory Models 715

CHAPTER 14

Queueing Models 769

CHAPTER 15

Regression Analysis 823

CHAPTER 16

Time Series Analysis and Forecasting 887

References 943

Index 947

PREFACE

Practical Management Science, Second Edition, provides a spreadsheet-based, example-driven approach to management science. Our initial objective in writing the book was to reverse negative attitudes about the course by making the subject relevant to students. We intended to do this by imparting valuable modeling skills that students can appreciate and take with them into their careers. We are very gratified by the success of the first edition. The book has done a lot to meet our initial objectives in our own courses. We are especially pleased to hear about the success of the book at many other colleges and universities around the world. The latest information is that over 200 schools are using the book in the United States alone. This has motivated us to revise the book and make it even better, by incorporating our own teaching experience and many user comments and suggestions. We believe this second edition is a significant improvement over the first. We hope you agree.

When we wrote the first edition, management science courses were regarded as irrelevant or uninteresting to many business students, and the use of spreadsheets in management science was in its first stages of development. Much has changed since the first edition was published in 1996, and we believe that these changes are for the better. We have learned a lot about the "best practices" of spreadsheet modeling for clarity and communication. We have also developed better ways of teaching the materials, and we understand more about where students tend to have difficulty with the concepts. Finally, we have had the opportunity to teach this material at several Fortune 500 companies (including Eli Lilly, Price Waterhouse Coopers, General Motors, Microsoft, and Intel). These companies, through their enthusiastic support, have further enhanced the realism of the models included in this book.

The success of the book outside of the classroom motivated our approach in the second edition. While we have retained many of the features that have made this book a bestseller, we have enhanced the coverage to make it more relevant and more accessible to students of varying backgrounds. Throughout the book, you will find many new models that are based on real problems, and you will find a much clearer presentation of the modeling, solution, and interpretation of the problems. Indeed, we have found that professionals, like students, have differing backgrounds in terms of mathematics and Excel, yet they both desire skills and knowledge that they can immediately apply to their own real problems. Those of you who are sympathetic to this approach will find this second edition better suited to these needs.

Why We Wrote This Book

Our initial objectives in writing the first edition were very simple. We wanted to make management science relevant and practical to students and professionals. There are four fundamental ways in which this book distinguishes itself relative to other texts.

- **Teach by Example.** We believe that the best way to learn modeling concepts is by working through examples and completing plenty of problems. This active learning approach is not new, but we believe this book has more fully developed this approach than any book in the field. The feedback we have received from many of you has appeared to confirm the success of this pedagogical approach for management science.

- **Integrate Modeling with Finance, Marketing, and Operations Management.** We integrate modeling into all functional areas of business. This is an important feature because the majority of students are majoring in finance and marketing. Almost all competing textbooks emphasize operations-management-related examples. While these examples are important, and many are included in the book, the application of modeling to problems in finance and marketing is too important to ignore. Throughout the book, we use real examples from all functional areas of business to illustrate the power of spreadsheet modeling to all of these areas. At our school, this has led to the development of special team-taught advanced electives in finance and marketing that build upon the content in this book. The inside front cover of the book illustrates the integrative applications contained in the book.

- **Teach Modeling and Not Just Models.** Poor attitudes among students in past management science courses can be attributed to the way in which they were taught: emphasis on algebraic formulations and memorization of models. (In fact, we hear of courses that continue to use this approach.) We believe that students gain more insight into the power of management science by developing skills in modeling. Throughout the book, we stress the logic associated with model development and formulation, and we discuss the solution in this context. Because real problems and real models often include limitations or alternatives, we include many "Modeling Issues" sections to discuss these important matters. Finally, we have included "Modeling Problems" in most chapters to help develop these skills.

- **Provide Numerous Problems and Cases.** While all textbooks contain problem sets for students to practice, we have spent an enormous amount of time crafting the problems and cases contained in this book. This new edition contains many new problems and cases. Each chapter contains four types of problems: Skill-Building Problems, Skill-Extending Problems, Modeling Problems, and Cases. We have attempted to grade these problems carefully within each section and at the conclusion of each chapter. Selected solutions appear on the accompanying CD-ROM and are denoted in the book by the color numbering of the problem. Solutions for all of the problems and cases are provided to adopting instructors. In addition, shell files (templates) are available for most of the problems (again, to adopting instructors). The shell files contain the basic structure of the problem with the relevant formulas omitted. By adding or omitting hints in individual solutions, instructors can tailor these shell files for their own purposes.

Enhancements to the Second Edition

Our experience over the past four years has taught us much about teaching a spreadsheet-based course in management science, and we have incorporated many suggestions from users of the first edition to improve the book. In addition, there have been several advances in spreadsheet-based technology in recent years. The accompanying software includes the most extensive and valuable suite of tools ever available in a management science textbook. The significant changes to the Second Edition include the following.

- **Improved Spreadsheet Readability and Documentation.** Many professionals we have taught instinctively document their spreadsheet models for the purpose of sharing them with colleagues or communicating them in presentations and reports. We believe this is an important element of good spreadsheet modeling, and the second edition does much more to emphasize this.

  Furthermore, grading homework assignments and exams can be a very time-consuming chore if students are permitted to construct their models in any form. Therefore, we place early and consistent emphasis on good spreadsheet habits. This should benefit both students and instructors. Although we try not to force any one approach on everyone, we do suggest some good habits that should lead to better spreadsheet models.

  To achieve this goal of better readability and documentation, we have completely reworked the examples in the chapters, and we have incorporated our new habits in the many new examples. This is especially important because this edition continues to be example-oriented; its most important feature is the set of examples. For users of the first edition, the changes will sometimes appear quite subtle, but we believe they will make a significant difference pedagogically. Improved readability and documentation are reflected in the following changes to the new edition.

- **Range Names.** We use range names in place of cell references whenever possible. We believe that nothing makes a formula more readable than the use of range names. The formula =SUMPRODUCT(Flows,UnitCosts) is certainly much easier to read (and grade) than =SUMPRODUCT(C15:C30,E15:E30). Range names are particularly helpful in Solver models. If the Solver dialog box has changing cells like AmtSold and constraints like Used <= Available, rather than obscure cell addresses, your grading will be much easier. Of course, naming ranges can be overdone, and it takes time. Arguably, we have possibly overdone it in some of our examples, and you might want to caution students not to name every single cell or range used in a model. However, in our experience, students *like* to name ranges, and they pick up on the habit very quickly.

- **Lists of Range Names.** We always list the range names and corresponding addresses we have used in a text box. This is a pedagogical tool used to make the *book* more readable. However, it is also a good practice for you and your students to use. (Alternatively, you can let Excel do it for you, by selecting the Insert/Names/Paste menu item and clicking on the Paste List button.)

- **Labels, Comments, Text Boxes.** We use labels, cell comments, and text boxes to document the logic behind the models wherever it is appropriate. One short sentence can be all it takes to let the reader know how or why you have done something in a certain way. There is no sense in keeping your logic a mystery to others.

- **Color Coding.** While it might not be apparent from the two-color format of the book, the accompanying example files contain color-coding that helps clarify the models. All decision variable cells (changing cells for Solver models) are in a red border, all input cells are in a blue border and shaded, and the target cell for Solver models is in a double-black border. The designation of input cells, whether in a blue border with shading or by some other means, is particularly important. When you look at someone else's model, you want to know immediately which cells are the inputs and which are calculated from them.

- **New Introductory Modeling Chapter 2.** Although students entering this course are becoming increasingly proficient in their Excel skills, many still need a "jump start" in the spreadsheet modeling process. Therefore, we have included a new introductory chapter that walks them through this process with relatively simple, but far from trivial, business examples. Important Excel tools included in this chapter include data tables for sensitivity analysis, trend lines on scatterplots, Goal Seek, the auditing toolbar, conditional formatting, and various "advanced" Excel functions, such as IF, SUMPRODUCT, VLOOKUP, and NPV. This chapter provides a "gentle" introduction to spreadsheet modeling, so that students will be better prepared for the Solver optimization chapters, beginning with Chapter 3. For those who are relatively new to Excel, we have also included an Excel tutorial file that can be used to get up to speed in basic Excel proficiency.

■ **New Evolutionary Solver Chapter 8.** If you have ever used Excel's Solver for optimization, you realize that it cannot handle certain types of nonlinearities, at least not without tricks that are difficult to teach. This is particularly true for problems that are modeled most naturally with IF, MAX, MIN, ABS, and several other functions. Fortunately, genetic algorithms are often able to solve these models with ease, provided that the software is available. It is *not* available with the standard Solver that ships with Excel, but we have been able to include a special version of the Solver developed by Frontline System (the developer of Excel's Solver) on the CD-ROM that accompanies the book. This version, called Premium Solver for Education, performs genetic algorithms with its "Evolutionary Solver." We exploit its capabilities in a new chapter to solve a number of interesting problems that could not, at least not easily, be solved with the standard Solver. By the way, the Premium Solver is easy to install, and, with a simple toggle, can be made to behave exactly like the Solver you are used to. We explain this in an appendix to Chapter 3.

■ **Improved Sensitivity Analysis.** Sensitivity analysis for optimization models is limited in Excel. To address this problem, we have included a unique new add-in called SolverTable that makes this important component of optimization much more intuitive. SolverTable is introduced in Chapter 3 and is used in succeeding optimization chapters. It makes Excel a much more powerful tool for sensitivity analysis.

■ **Reorganized and Streamlined Coverage.** After using the book for four years, we found that there was room for improvement in organization and coverage of the book. Specifically, several revisions were made to improve the focus of certain chapters and to provide additional discussions and practical examples where necessary.

■ **Simulation.** We were never satisfied with the organization of the two simulation chapters in the first edition. They were organized around the idea that some users have the @Risk add-in and others do not. This led us to write a chapter for each audience. In this edition we have included @Risk on the accompanying CD-ROM (as part of the Palisade Decision Tools suite), so we now know that *everyone* who uses this book has @Risk. This has allowed us to reorganize the two simulation chapters (Chapters 11 and 12) in a much more natural way. Chapter 11 introduces the basic concepts of simulation, and it illustrates how to use @Risk to create and run simulation models. Given this basic knowledge, Chapter 12 then presents a wide variety of simulation examples from different business areas. All of these take advantage

of @Risk. In fact, they use the newest version of @Risk, version 4.0, which was just released as we were writing this edition. This version takes some getting used to if you are an experienced @Risk user, but we believe you will appreciate its features very quickly.

■ **Inventory Models.** We have reorganized the inventory models so that they now appear in a single chapter. Most of the material from the first edition is still included, but because this chapter follows the simulation chapters, we are now able to include examples of inventory simulation models. This chapter also includes a new example of a supply chain model, currently one of the hottest topics in management science and in business.

■ **Queueing Models.** The queueing chapter (Chapter 14) now has less coverage of analytical models and more coverage of queueing simulation models. We have tried to make this chapter less mathematical, and we have placed more emphasis on the *insights* that can be obtained from a queueing model—either analytical or simulation.

■ **Regression and Forecasting.** Based on suggestions from several users, we have split the regression and forecasting chapter into two separate chapters, one on regression and one on time series analysis and forecasting. These chapters contain more material than in the first edition, particularly in the regression chapter.

■ **New Modeling Approaches.** There are at least two places where we have changed our approach to modeling certain problems. The first is in general network flow models in Chapter 5. We now develop virtually all network models in a standard way, using one range for information about arcs and another range for the node balance constraints. (We thank Cliff Ragsdale for this idea. We assume he was the first to develop it.) This approach appears to be more natural (for example, it does not require the obscure dummy nodes), and it is efficient in the sense of using the least number of changing cells. The second change is in the examples of project scheduling. In the first edition, we used an activity-on-arc approach in one chapter and an activity-on-node approach in another. While we still get arguments as to which approach is better or easier to teach, we believe it is better to be consistent. Therefore, we now use an activity-on-arc approach throughout.

■ **New Models and Problems.** Throughout the book we have added many new example models. These include pricing models, a supply chain model, break-even analysis, a hedging model with put options, and others. We have also added many new problems. These include the problems in the new Chapters 2 and 8, many problems that deal with SolverTable, and others throughout the book. As before, there is a CD-ROM available to all adopting instructors that contains solutions to all of the problems and cases in Excel format. (Many of these have been reworked, either because of bugs in the original solutions or because we discovered better solution methods.) In addition, because we have gotten numerous requests from nonacademic readers for problem solutions, we have included solutions to a few designated problems in the CD-ROM that accompanies this book. (These problems are designated by problem numbers printed in color in the chapters themselves.)

Contents of the Accompanying CD-ROM

We are very excited about offering the most comprehensive suite of software ever available with a management science textbook. The commercial value of the enclosed software exceeds $1000 if purchased directly. This software is for students only, and requires online registration within 30 days of installing it to activate the software for its full one-year license. Professionals may use the software for 30 days but will need to contact the software vendors directly to obtain licensed versions. The following software is included on the accompanying CD-ROM.

Palisade's **DecisionTools**™ **Suite,** including the award-winning **@Risk, PrecisionTree, BestFit, TopRank,** and **RiskView.** This software is not available with any competing textbook. Although @Risk was featured in the first edition of the text, the software was not included. The addition of the software in this edition makes the simulation chapters (Chapters 11 and 12) very useful without having to obtain a special license for the software. The PrecisionTree is used extensively for decision making under uncertainty in Chapter 10. It replaces the TreePlan add-in that was used for decision trees in the first edition. For more information about the Palisade Corporation and the DecisionTools Suite, visit Palisade's Web site at www.palisade.com.

Frontline Systems' **Premium Solver**™ **for Education** is included in the second edition and is utilized in the new Chapter 8 on Evolutionary Solvers. Premium Solver uses genetic algorithms to solve nonlinear optimization problems. For more information on Premium Solver or Frontline Systems, visit Frontline's Web site at www.frontsys.com.

Also available from Palisade Corporation is **StatPro**™, an Excel add-in for data analysis. StatPro is featured in the regression and forecasting chapters (Chapters 15 and 16). It performs many useful statistical operations, from creating simple charts and calculating basic summary measures to more complex techniques such as discriminant analysis and logistic regression. Much of this add-in is not necessary for this book, but the regression and forecasting tools are very useful in the final two chapters.

To make sensitivity analysis useful and intuitive, we provide **SolverTable**, which we have developed. SolverTable provides data-table-like output that is easy to interpret. In the first edition we tried our best to skirt around the difficult issue of interpreting the Solver's sensitivity reports for linear programming models. We believed then, and we believe even more strongly now, that these reports are too confusing to incorporate into a spreadsheet-based course. Admittedly, they sometimes provide useful information, but many times the information they provide is virtually impossible to untangle. The SolverTable add-in works much like Excel's data tables. You specify one or two input cells, a range of values for these cells that you want to test, and one or more output cells that you want to keep track of. Then SolverTable runs Solver repeatedly with your varying inputs and reports the corresponding outputs. It is the most intuitive way we have found of conducting sensitivity analysis in optimization models, and students can learn it almost immediately.

The CD-ROM also contains the **Excel workbooks** that are used in the examples, the **data files** required for a number of problems and cases, and the **solutions** to selected problems in the book. The problems with solutions on the enclosed CD-ROM are denoted with color numbering in the chapters. These are the only solutions that are available to students and professionals.

Companion VBA Book

Soon after the first edition appeared, we began using Visual Basic for Applications (VBA), the programming language for Excel, in our management science courses. VBA allows us to develop decision support systems around the spreadsheet models. (An example appears at the end of Chapter 3.) This use of VBA has been popular with our students, and many instructors have expressed interest in learning how to do it. Therefore, one of the authors (Albright) has written a companion book, *VBA for Modelers*. It assumes no prior experience in computer programming, but it progresses rather quickly to the development of interesting and nontrivial applications. The second edition of *Practical Management Science* depends in no way on this companion VBA book, but we expect that many instructors will want to incorporate some VBA into their management science courses.

Ancillary Materials

Besides the CD-ROM that accompanies this disk, the following materials are available.

For Instructors:

- **The Instructor's Suite** CD-ROM contains the solutions in Excel format for every problem and case study throughout the book. In addition, the CD-ROM contains shell files for every problem and case study. Shell files are partially completed solutions with formulas and other information removed. We have used these shell files in large classes where students might benefit from additional help.

- **PowerPoint presentation files** for all of the examples in the book.

- **A Test Items file** is under development. In teaching a spreadsheet-based management course, we have found testing and assessment to be the most challenging aspects of delivering a successful course. We are pleased that Christopher Zappe of Bucknell University is preparing a test item file that is especially suited to our approach.

For Students:

- **A Study Guide** for students assists them in successfully mastering the art of spreadsheet modeling by working through the examples from the textbook.

- *VBA for Modelers* is a stand-alone book, as previously described.

Acknowledgments

The authors would like to thank those people who helped make this book a reality. We are indebted to Mark Broadie of the Graduate School of Business, Columbia University, for contributing the excellent Cast Studies that appear throughout the book. Our special thanks to Jim Orlin of MIT for his vital ideas and suggestions regarding SolverTable.

This book has gone through several stages of reviews, and it is a much better product because of them. The majority of the reviewers' suggestions were very good ones, and we have attempted to incorporate them. Thanks to Sudhakar D. Deshmukh, Kellogg School of Management, Northwestern University; James Morris, University of Wisconsin; Stephen Powell, Tuck School, Dartmouth College; and Thomas J. Schriber, University of Michigan. Our thanks to the first-edition reviewers, whose suggestions helped lead this book to success: Aaron Paul Blossom, Grand Valley State University; Richard E. Crandall, Appalachian State University; Roger B. Grinde, University of New Hampshire; Jerrold H. May, University of Pittsburgh; James G. Morris, University of Wisconsin–Madison; Danny Myers, Bowling Green State University; James B. Orlin, Massachusetts Institute of Technology; Gary Reeves, University of South Carolina; Timothy A. Riggle, Baldwin-Wallace College; and David Schilling, Ohio State University. We thank also the first-edition adopters who have added so much to the second edition through their suggestions.

We would also like to thank two special people. First, we want to thank our editor Curt Hinrichs for continuing to be the guiding light on this project. Throughout the development of both editions, Curt has kept up incredible enthusiasm for this new approach to teaching management science. He is truly a visionary in this area, and his ideas have shaped much of what we have done here. If the new edition continues to be a success, it is due in large part to Curt's efforts. We also want to thank our production editor, Susan Reiland. She has been wonderful to work with. Any management science book is bound to contain a lot of details, and one based on spreadsheets has even more details. Trying to get all of these details correct is a difficult task—to say the least—and Susan has had the patience and the perfectionist attitude to help us "get it right."

In addition, we would like to thank Peter Vacek and William Baxter for their devoted work in the production of the book. Few people know how much work it takes to make a book *look* good, with tables placed properly, headings sized correctly, and numerous other details. Peter and William have been invaluable in this task.

We are grateful to the bookteam of professionals who worked behind the scenes at Duxbury to make this book a success: Emily Davidson, Editorial Assistant; Seema Atwal, Assistant Editor; Janet Hill, Production Editor; Vernon Boes, Cover Designer; Tom Ziolkowski, Marketing; Laura Hubrich and Samantha Cabaluna, Marketing Communications; and Jessica Reed, Manufacturing.

We would also enjoy hearing from you—we can be reached by e-mail. And please visit our Web site at www.duxbury.com and go to the online Book Companion link for more information and occasional updates.

Wayne L. Winston
winston@indiana.edu

S. Christian Albright
albright@indiana.edu

Practical Management Science

## CHAPTER 1

Introduction to Modeling

ALGORITHMS SOLVE COMPLEX REAL-WORLD PROBLEMS

As you embark on your study of management science, you might question the usefulness of quantitative methods to the "real world." A front-page article in the December 31, 1997, edition of *USA Today* entitled "Higher Math Delivers Formula for Success" provides some convincing evidence of the applicability of the methods you will be learning. The subheading of the article, "Businesses turn to algorithms to solve complex problems," says it all. Today's business problems tend to be very complex. In the past, many managers and executives used a "seat of the pants" approach to solve problems—that is, they used their business experience, their intuition, and some thoughtful guesswork to obtain solutions. But common sense and intuition go only so far in the solution of the complex problems businesses now face. This is where management science models—and the algorithms mentioned in the title of the article—are so useful. When the methods in this book are implemented in user-friendly computer software packages and are then applied to complex problems, the results can be amazing. Robert Cross, whose company, DFI Aeronomics, sells algorithm-based systems to airlines, states it succinctly: "It's like taking raw information and spinning money out of it."

The power of the methods in this book is that they are applicable to so many problems and environments. The article mentions the following "success stories" where management science has been applied; others will be discussed throughout this book. (1) United Airlines installed one of DFI's systems, which cost between $10 million and $20 million. United expects the system to add $50 million to $100 million *annually* to its revenues. (2) The Gap clothing chain uses management science to determine exactly how many employees should staff each store during the Christmas rush. (3) Management science has helped medical researchers test potentially dangerous drugs on fewer people with better results. (4) IBM obtained a $93 million contract to build a computer system for the Department of Energy that would do a once-impossible task: make exact real-time models of atomic blasts. It won the contract—and convinced the DOE that its system was cost-effective—only by developing management science models that would cut the processing time by half. (5) Hotels, airlines, and television broadcasters all use management science to implement a new method called "yield management." In this method, different prices are charged to different customers, depending on their willingness to pay. The effect is that more customers are attracted, and revenues increase.

The article concludes by stating that Microsoft's Excel spreadsheet software has a built-in optimization program called Solver. This is a key statement. Many of the algorithms that enable the successes discussed in the article are very complex mathematically. They are well beyond the grasp of the typical user, including most readers of this book. However, users no longer need to understand all of the details behind the algorithms. They need only to know (1) how to model business problems so that appropriate algorithms can be applied and (2) how to apply these algorithms with user-friendly software. We will see in Chapters 3–9 how to apply Excel's Solver to a variety of complex problems. You will not learn the intricacies of how Solver does its optimization, but you *will* learn how to use Solver very productively. The same statement applies to the other methods discussed in this book. You might not understand exactly what is happening in the computer's "black box" as it performs its calculations, but you will learn how to become very effective problem solvers by taking advantage of powerful software. ■

1.1 INTRODUCTION

The purpose of this of this book is to expose you to a variety of problems that have been solved successfully with management science methods and to give you experience in modeling these problems in the Excel spreadsheet package. The subject of management science has evolved for over 50 years and is now a mature field within the broad category of applied mathematics. Our intent in this book is to emphasize both the applied and mathematical aspects of management science. Beginning in this chapter and continuing throughout the rest of the book, we will discuss many successful management science applications, where teams of highly trained people have implemented solutions to the problems faced by major companies and have saved these companies millions of dollars. Many airlines and oil companies, for example, could hardly operate as they do today without the support of management science. In this book we will lead you through the solution procedure of many interesting and realistic problems, and you will experience firsthand what is required to solve these problems successfully. We recognize that most of you are not highly trained in mathematics. Therefore, we will utilize spreadsheets to solve problems, which makes the quantitative analysis much more understandable and intuitive.

The key to virtually every management science application is a **mathematical model**. In simple terms, a mathematical model is a quantitative representation, or approximation, of a real problem. This representation might be phrased in terms of mathematical expressions (equations and inequalities) or as a series of interrelated cells in a spreadsheet. We prefer the latter, especially for teaching purposes, and we will concentrate primarily on spreadsheet models in this book. However, in either case the purpose of a mathematical model is to represent the essence of a problem in a concise form. This has several advantages. First, it enables an analyst to understand the problem better. In particular, it helps to define the scope of the problem, the possible solutions, and the data requirements. Second, it allows the analyst to employ a variety of the mathematical solution procedures that have been developed over the past half-century. These solution procedures are often very computer intensive, but with today's cheap and abundant computing power, they are usually feasible. Finally, the modeling process itself, if it is done correctly, often helps to "sell" the solution to the people who must work with the system that is eventually implemented.

In this chapter we will introduce the concept of a mathematical model with a relatively simple example. Then we will discuss the difference between modeling and a collection of models, and we will describe a seven-step model-building process that should be followed—in essence if not in strict conformance—in all management science applications. Next, we will describe three successful applications of management science. For all three of these applications, we will illustrate how the seven-step model-building process was followed. Finally, we will discuss why the study of management science is valuable, not only to large corporations, but also to students like yourselves who are about to enter the business world.

1.2 A WAITING-LINE EXAMPLE

As indicated earlier, a mathematical model is a set of mathematical relationships that represent, or approximate, a real situation. Some models simply describe a situation. Such models are called **descriptive** models. Other models suggest a desirable course of action. Such models are called **prescriptive**, or **optimization**, models. To get us started, we discuss the following simple example of a mathematical model. It begins as a descriptive model, but we then expand it to become an optimization model.

Consider a 7–Eleven store with a single cash register. The manager of the store suspects that customers might be waiting too long in line at the checkout register and that these excessive waiting times might be hurting business. Customers who have to wait a long time might not come back, and potential customers who see a long line might not enter the store at all. Therefore, the manager wants to build a mathematical model to help understand the problem. The manager wants to build a model that reflects the current situation at the store but that will also be able to improve the current situation if possible.

A Descriptive Model

This example is a typical waiting line, or **queueing**, problem. (Such problems will be studied in detail in Chapter 14.) As mentioned earlier, the manager first wants to build a model that reflects the *current* situation at the store. Later he will alter the model to predict what might make the situation better. To describe the current situation, the manager realizes that there are two important *inputs* to the problem: (1) the arrival rate of potential customers to the store and (2) the rate at which customers can be served by the single cashier. It is intuitively clear that as the arrival rate increases and/or the service rate decreases, the waiting line will tend to increase and each customer will tend to wait longer in line. In addition, it is likely that more potential customers will decide not to enter at all. It is common to refer to these latter quantities (length of waiting line, time in line per customer, fraction of customers who don't enter) as *outputs*. The manager believes he has some understanding of the relationship between the inputs and the outputs, but he is not at all sure of the *exact* relationship between them.

This is where a mathematical model is useful. By making several simplifying assumptions about the nature of the arrival and service process at the store (as will be discussed in Chapter 14), we can relate the inputs to the outputs. In some cases, when the model is sufficiently simple, we can write an *equation* for an output in terms of the inputs. For example, in one of the simplest queueing models, if we let A be the arrival rate of customers per minute, S be the service rate of customers per minute, and W be the average time a typical customer waits in line (assuming that all potential customers enter the store), then the following relationship can be derived mathematically:

$$W = \frac{A}{S(S - A)} \tag{1.1}$$

This relationship is intuitive in one sense. It correctly predicts that as the service rate S increases, the average waiting time W will decrease, and as the arrival rate A increases, the average waiting time W will increase. Also, if the arrival rate is just barely less than the service rate—that is, $S - A$ is positive but very small—the average waiting time will become quite large. [This model requires that the arrival rate is *less than* the service rate; otherwise, equation (1.1) makes no sense.]

In many other models there is no such "closed-form" relationship between inputs and outputs (or if there is, it is too complex for the level of this book). Nevertheless, there may still be a mathematical procedure for calculating outputs from inputs, and it may be possible to implement this procedure in Excel. This is the case for the 7–Eleven problem. Again, by making certain simplifying assumptions, including the assumption that potential customers will not enter if the waiting line is sufficiently long, we can develop a spreadsheet model of the situation at the store.

Before presenting it, however, we need to discuss how the manager can obtain the inputs he needs for the spreadsheet model. There are actually three inputs: the arrival rate A, the service rate S, and the number in the store, labeled N, that will induce future customers not to enter. The first two of these can be measured with a stopwatch. For example, the manager can request an employee to measure the times between customer arrivals. Let's say the employee does this for several hours, and the average time between arrivals is observed to be 2 minutes. Then the arrival rate can be estimated as $A = 1/2 = 0.5$ (1 customer every 2 minutes). Similarly, the employee can record the times it takes the cashier to serve successive customers. If the average of these times (taken over many customers) is, say, 2.5 minutes, then the service rate

FIGURE 1.1
Descriptive Queueing
Model for 7-Eleven
Store

	A	B
1	**Descriptive queueing model for 7-Eleven**	
2		
3	**Inputs**	
4	Arrival rate (customers per minute)	0.5
5	Service rate (customers per minute)	0.4
6	Maximum customers (before others go elsewhere	5
7		
8	**Outputs**	
9	Average number in line	2.22
10	Average time (minutes) spent in line	6.09
11	Percentage of potential arrivals who don't enter	27.1%

can be estimated as $S = 1/2.5 = 0.4$ (1 customer every 2.5 minutes). Finally, if the manager notices that potential customers tend to take their business elsewhere when there are 5 customers in line, then he can let $N = 5$.

These input estimates can now be entered in the spreadsheet model shown in Figure 1.1. Don't worry about the details of this spreadsheet—they will be covered in Chapter 14. Just trust us that the formulas built into this spreadsheet reflect an adequate approximation of the 7–Eleven store's situation. For now, the important thing is that this model allows the manager to enter any values for the inputs in cells B4–B6 and observe the resulting outputs in cells B9–B11. The input values in Figure 1.1 represent the store's current input values. These values indicate that on average there are slightly more than 2 customers waiting in line, an average customer waits slightly more than 6 minutes in line, and about 27% of all potential customers do not enter the store at all (due to the perception that waiting times will be long).

The information in Figure 1.1 may not be all that useful to the manager. After all, he probably already has a sense of how long waiting times are and how many customers are being lost. The power of the model is that it allows the manager to ask many what-if questions. For example, what if he could somehow speed up the cashier, say, from 2.5 minutes per customer to 1.8 minutes per customer? He might guess that since the average service time has decreased by 28%, all of the outputs should also decrease by 28%. Is this the case? Evidently not, as shown in Figure 1.2. The average line length decreases to 1.41, a 36% decrease; the average waiting time decreases to 3.22, a 47% decrease; and the percentage of customers who do not enter decreases to 12.6%, a 54% decrease. To illustrate an even more extreme change, suppose the manager could cut the service time in half, from 2.5 minutes to 1.25 minutes. The spreadsheet in Figure 1.3 (page 6) shows that the average number in line decreases to 0.69, a 69% decrease

FIGURE 1.2
Queueing Model with
a Faster Service Rate

	A	B
1	**Descriptive queueing model for 7-Eleven**	
2		
3	**Inputs**	
4	Arrival rate (customers per minute)	0.5
5	Service rate (customers per minute)	0.556
6	Maximum customers (before others go elsewhere	5
7		
8	**Outputs**	
9	Average number in line	1.41
10	Average time (minutes) spent in line	3.22
11	Percentage of potential arrivals who don't enter	12.6%

FIGURE 1.3

Queueing Model with
an Even Faster
Service Rate

	A	B
1	**Descriptive queueing model for 7-Eleven**	
2		
3	**Inputs**	
4	Arrival rate (customers per minute)	0.5
5	Service rate (customers per minute)	0.8
6	Maximum customers (before others go elsewhere	5
7		
8	**Outputs**	
9	Average number in line	0.69
10	Average time (minutes) spent in line	1.42
11	Percentage of potential arrivals who don't enter	3.8%

from the original value; the average waiting time decreases to 1.42, a 77% decrease; and the percentage of customers who do not enter decreases to 3.8%, a whopping 86% decrease. The important lesson to be learned from the spreadsheet model is that as the manager increases the service rate, the output measures improve more than he might have expected.

In reality, the manager would attempt to validate the spreadsheet model before trusting its answers to these what-if questions. At the very least, the manager should examine the reasonableness of the assumptions. For example, one assumption is that the arrival rate remains *constant* for the time period under discussion. If the manager intends to use this model—with the *same* input parameters—during periods of time when the arrival rate varies quite a lot (such as peak lunchtime traffic followed by slack times in the early afternoon), then he is almost certainly asking for trouble. Besides determining whether the assumptions are reasonable, the manager can also check the outputs predicted by the model when the current inputs are used. For example, Figure 1.1 predicts that the average time a customer waits in line is approximately 6 minutes. At this point, the manager could ask his employee to use a stopwatch again to time customers' waiting times. If they average close to 6 minutes, then the manager can put more confidence in the model. However, if they average much more or much less than 6 minutes, then the manager probably needs to search for a new model.

An Optimization Model

As the model stands so far, it fails to reflect any *economic* information such as the cost of speeding up service, the cost of making customers wait in line, or the cost of losing customers. Given the spreadsheet model developed above, however, it is relatively straightforward to incorporate economic information and then make rational choices. To make this example simple, we will assume that the manager can do one of three things: (1) leave the system as it is, (2) hire a second person to help the first cashier process customers more quickly, or (3) lease a new model of cash register that will speed up the service process significantly. The effect of (2) is to decrease the average service time from 2.5 to 1.8 minutes. The effect of (3) is to decrease the service time from 2.5 to 1.25 minutes. What should the manager do?

He needs to examine three types of costs. The first is the cost of hiring the extra person or leasing the new cash register. We assume that these costs are known. For example, we will assume that the hourly wage for the extra person is $5 and the cost to lease a new cash register (converted to a per-hour rate) is $8 per hour. The second cost is the "cost" of making a person wait in line. Although this is not an out-of-pocket cost to the store, it does represent the cost of potential future business—a customer who has to wait a long time might not return. This cost is difficult to estimate on a per-minute or per-hour basis, but we will make a rough estimate of it as $10 per customer per hour in line.[1] Finally, there is the opportunity cost for customers who decide not to enter the store. The store loses not only their current revenue but also potential future revenue if they decide not to return. Again, this is a difficult cost to measure, but we will assume it is $20 per lost customer.

The next step in the modeling process is to combine these costs for each possible decision. Let's find the total cost per hour for decision (3), where the new cash register is leased. The lease cost is $8 per hour. From Figure 1.3 we see there is, on average, 0.69 customer in line at any time. Therefore, the average waiting cost per hour is 0.69($10) = $6.90. (This is because 0.69 customer-hour is spent in line each hour on average.) Finally, from Figure 1.3 we see that the average number of potential arrivals per hour is 60(1/2) = 30, and 3.8% of them do not enter. Therefore, the average cost per hour from lost customers is 0.038(30)($20) = $22.80. The combined cost for decision (3) is $8 + $6.90 + $22.80 = $37.70 per hour.

The spreadsheet model in Figure 1.4 incorporates these calculations and similar calculations for the other two decisions. (The discrepancy between the $37.70 above and the $37.67 in cell D24 is due to roundoff error.) As we see from row 24, the option to lease the new cash register is the clear winner from a cost standpoint. However, if the manager wants to see how sensitive these cost figures are to the rather uncertain input costs we assessed for waiting time and lost customers, it is simple to enter new values in rows 10 and 11 and see how the "bottom lines" in row 24 change. This flexibility represents the power of spreadsheet models. They not only allow us to build realistic and complex models, but they also allow us to answer many what-if questions simply by changing input values.

FIGURE 1.4
Queueing Model with Alternative Decisions

	A	B	C	D
1	Decision queueing model for 7-Eleven			
2				
3	Inputs	Decision 1	Decision 2	Decision 3
4	Arrival rate (customers per minute)	0.5	0.5	0.5
5	Service rate (customers per minute)	0.4	0.556	0.8
6	Maximum customers (before others go elsewhere	5	5	5
7				
8	Cost of extra person per hour	$0	$5	$0
9	Cost of leasing new cash register per hour	$0	$0	$8
10	Cost per customer per hour waiting in line	$10	$10	$10
11	Cost per customer who doesn't enter the store	$20	$20	$20
12				
13	Outputs			
14	Average number in line	2.22	1.41	0.69
15	Average time (minutes) spent in line	6.09	3.22	1.42
16	Percentage of potential arrivals who don't enter	27.1%	12.6%	3.8%
17				
18	Cost information			
19	Cost of extra person per hour	$0	$5	$0
20	Cost of leasing new cash register per hour	$0	$0	$8
21	Cost per hour of waiting time	$22.20	$14.08	$6.85
22	Cost per hour of lost customers	$162.63	$75.61	$22.82
23				
24	Total cost per hour	$184.84	$94.70	$37.67

[1] Here we are charging only for time in the queue. An alternative model is to charge for time in the queue *and* for time in service.

1.3 MODELING VERSUS MODELS

Management science, at least as it has been taught in most traditional courses, has evolved as a collection of mathematical models. These include various linear programming models (the transportation model, the diet model, the shortest route model, and others), inventory models, queueing models, and so on. Much time has been devoted to teaching (and learning) the intricacies of these particular models as an end in itself. Management science *practitioners*, on the other hand, have justifiably criticized this emphasis on specific models. They argue that the majority of real-world problems that can be solved by management science methods cannot be neatly categorized as one of the handful of models typically included in a management science textbook. That is, there is often no "off-the-shelf" model that can be used, without modification, to solve a company's real problem. Unfortunately, management science students have gotten the impression that all problems must be "shoe-horned" into one of the textbook models if they are to be solved at all.

The good news is that this emphasis on specific models has been changing in the past decade, and our goal in this book is to continue this change. Specifically, we plan to stress *modeling*, not models. Although the distinction between modeling and models is probably not clear at this point, it will become clearer as you proceed through the book. Learning specific models is generally more of a memorization process—memorizing the details of a particular model such as the transportation model, and possibly learning how to "trick" other problems into looking like a transportation model. Modeling, on the other hand, is more of a *process*, where we abstract the essence of a real problem into a model, spreadsheet or otherwise. Although the problems we will tackle fall naturally into several categories, we do not try to shoe-horn each problem into one of a small number of well-studied models. Instead, we treat each problem on its own merits and model it appropriately, using whatever logical, analytical, or spreadsheet skills we have at our disposal—and, of course, drawing analogies from previous models we have discussed whenever they are relevant. This way, if you come across a problem that does not look exactly like anything you studied in your management science course, you will still have the skills and flexibility to model it successfully.

This does not mean that we will not cover the "classical" models from management science. We will indeed discuss the transportation model in linear programming, the $M/M/1$ model in queueing, the EOQ model in inventory, and others. These are important models and should not be ignored. However, we certainly do not emphasize the memorization of these specific models. They are simply a few of the many models we will learn how to develop. The real emphasis throughout is on the modeling process—how a real-world problem is abstracted into a spreadsheet model of that problem. We discuss this modeling process in more detail in the following section.

1.4 THE SEVEN-STEP MODELING PROCESS

The discussion of the queueing problem in Section 1.2 presented some of the basic principles of management science modeling. In this section we will further explain these ideas by characterizing the modeling process as a seven-step procedure.

1. **Define the Problem** The management scientist first defines the organization's problem. Defining the problem includes specifying the organization's objectives and the parts of the organization that must be studied before the problem can

be solved. In our simple queueing model the organization's problem was how to minimize the total costs associated with the operation of the store's cash register.

2. **Observe the System and Collect Data**   After defining the problem, the analyst collects data to estimate the value of parameters that affect the organization's problem. These estimates are used to develop (in step 3) a mathematical model of the organization's problem and predict solutions (step 4). In the 7–Eleven queueing example, the manager would need to observe the arrivals and the checkout process to estimate the arrival rate and the service rate, A and S.

3. **Formulate a Model**   In the third step the analyst develops a model of the problem. In this book we will describe many methods that can be used to model systems.[2] Models such as equation (1.1), where we use an equation to relate parameters such as A and S to quantities of interest such as W, are called **analytic models**. Most realistic applications are so complex, however, that an analytic model does not exist or is too complex to work with. For example, if the 7–Eleven store had more than one register and customers were allowed to join any line or jump from one line to another, there would be no analytic model—no equation or system of equations—that could be used to determine W from knowledge of A, S, and the number of lines. When no tractable analytic model exists, we often rely instead on a **simulation model**, which enables a computer to approximate the behavior of the actual system. We will discuss simulation models in Chapters 11 and 12.

4. **Verify the Model and Use the Model for Prediction**   The management scientist now tries to determine whether the model developed in the previous step is an accurate representation of reality. A first step in determining how well the model fits reality is to check whether the model is valid for the current situation. As we discussed earlier, to validate equation (1.1) the manager might observe actual customer waiting times for several hours. As we have already seen, equation (1.1) predicts that when $A = 0.5$ and $S = 0.4$, the average customer spends 6.09 minutes in line. Now suppose the manager observes that 120 customers spend a total of 750 minutes in line. This indicates an average of $750/120 = 6.25$ minutes in line per customer. Because 6.25 is reasonably close to 6.09, the manager's observations would appear to lend credibility to the model. In contrast, if the 120 customers had spent 1200 minutes total in line, for an average of 10 minutes per customer, this would not agree very well with the model's prediction of 6.09 minutes, and we would doubt the validity of the model.

5. **Select a Suitable Alternative**   Given a model and a set of alternatives, the management scientist must now choose the alternative that best meets the organization's objectives. For example, the model represented by equation (1.1) allowed us to determine the service rate that would minimize cost. In many situations, however, the organization has more than one objective. For example, a firm considering the purchase of a microcomputer might want to buy the computer that best satisfies the following criteria: (1) it is economical, (2) it is easy to use, (3) it can run useful software, and (4) it is fast. It is likely that no single computer will be the best with respect to all four criteria. So which computer should the company purchase? This question can be answered with one of the multi-objective decision-making procedures that we will discuss in Chapter 9.

---

[2]All of these models can generically be called **mathematical models**. However, because we will implement them in spreadsheets, we will generally refer to them as **spreadsheet models.**

6. **Present the Results of the Study to the Organization**   In this step the analyst presents the model and the recommendations from the previous step to the organization. In some situations the analyst might present several alternatives and let the organization choose the one that best meets its needs.

7. **Implement and Evaluate Recommendations**   If the organization has accepted the validity and usefulness of the study, the analyst then helps to implement its recommendations. The implemented system must be monitored constantly (and updated dynamically as the environment changes) to ensure that the model enables the organization to meet its objectives.

The flowchart in Figure 1.5 illustrates this seven-step process. As the arrows back to the left indicate, there is room for feedback in the process. For example, at various steps the analyst might realize that the current model is not capturing some key aspects of the real problem. In this case the analyst might need to revise the problem definition or develop a new model.

FIGURE 1.5
Flowchart for
Seven-Step Process

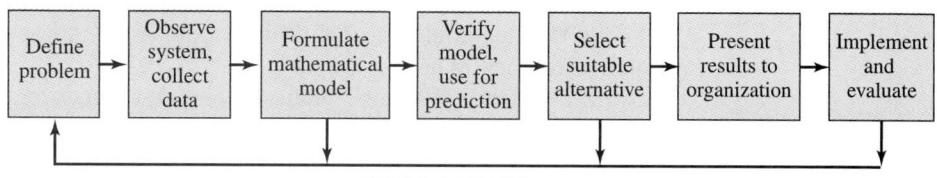

Possible feedback loops

Discussion of the Seven Steps

Now that we have defined the seven steps of model building, we discuss them in more detail.

1. **Problem Definition**   Typically, a management science model is commissioned when an organization believes it has a problem. Perhaps the company is losing money, perhaps its market share is declining, perhaps its customers are waiting too long for service—any number of problems might be evident. The organization (which we will refer to as the client) calls in a management scientist (the analyst) to solve this problem. In such cases the problem has probably already been defined by the client, and the client hires the analyst to solve *this particular problem*. As Miser (1993) and Volkema (1995) point out, however, the analyst should do some investigating before accepting the client's claim that the problem is already well defined. Failure to do so could mean solving the wrong problem and wasting valuable time and energy.

   For example, Miser cites the experience of an analyst who was hired by the military to investigate overly long turnaround times between fighter planes' landing and taking off again to rejoin the battle. The military (the client) was convinced that the problem was caused by inefficient ground crews—if they were sped up, turnaround times would decrease. The analyst nearly accepted this statement of the problem and was about to do classical time-and-motion studies on the ground crew to pinpoint the sources of their inefficiency. However, by snooping around he found that the problem obviously lay elsewhere. It seems that the trucks that refueled the planes were frequently late, which in turn was due to the inefficient way they were refilled from storage tanks at another location. Once this latter problem was solved—and its solution was embarrassingly simple—the turnaround times decreased to an acceptable level without any changes on the part of the ground crews. If the analyst had accepted the client's statement of the problem, the *real* problem might never have been located or solved.

The moral of this story is clear: If an analyst defines a problem incorrectly or too narrowly, the best solution to the real problem might never emerge. In his article, Volkema (1995) advocates spending as much time thinking about the problem and defining it properly as modeling and solving it. This is undoubtedly good advice, especially in real-world applications where problem boundaries are often difficult to define.

2. **Data Collection**   This crucial step in the process is often the most tedious. All organizations keep track of various data on their operations, but these data might not be in the form the analyst requires. They also might be scattered in different places throughout the organization, in all kinds of different formats. Therefore, one of the first jobs of the analyst is to gather exactly the right data and put the data into the appropriate form required by the model. This typically requires asking questions of key people (such as the accountants) throughout the organization, studying existing organizational databases, and performing time-consuming observational studies of the organization's processes. In short, it usually entails a lot of leg work.

In this book, as in most management science textbooks, we tend to shield you from this data-collection process by supplying the appropriate data to formulate and solve a model. Although this makes the overall modeling process seem easier than it really is, it is simply not practical in most class settings to have students go out to companies and gather data. (In many cases it would not even be allowed for proprietary reasons.) Nevertheless, in several examples we provide some insight into where the required data might come from, and in several exercises we ask you to list the types of data you would need to model a given problem successfully.

3. **Model Formulation**   This step (along with step 5) is where the management scientist brings his or her special skills into play. After defining the client's problem and gathering the necessary data, the analyst must formulate a model of the problem. Several properties are desirable for a good model. First, it should represent the client's real problem accurately. If it uses a linear (straight-line) function for costs when the real cost function is highly nonlinear (curved), the recommendations of the model could be very misleading. Similarly, if it ignores an important constraint such as an upper bound on capacity, its recommendations might not be possible to implement.

On the other hand, the model should be as simple as possible. Most good models (where "good" really means *useful*) capture the essence of the problem without getting bogged down in minor details. They should be *approximations* of the real world, not mirror images in every last detail. Overly complex models are often of little practical use. First, overly complex models are sometimes too difficult to solve with the solution algorithms and computers available. Second, complex models tend to be incomprehensible to clients. As you can imagine, if a client cannot understand a thing about a model, the chances are not too good that the model's recommendations will ever be implemented. Therefore, the skill in model formulation lies in being able to achieve the right balance between too simplistic and too complex.

4. **Model Verification**   This step is particularly important in real management science applications. A client is much more likely to accept an analyst's model if the analyst can provide some type of verification. This verification might take several forms. For example, the analyst could use the model with the company's current values of the *input* parameters. If the model's outputs are then in line with the *outputs* currently observed by the client, the analyst has at least shown that the

model can duplicate the current situation. We mentioned earlier how this could be done in the 7–Eleven queueing example. That is, if the model represented by equation (1.1) is able to predict the current average waiting time, given the current arrival rate and service rate as inputs, then it has passed the first test, and it *might* be able to predict the average waiting time for new inputs.

A second way to verify a model is to enter a number of sets of input parameters (even if they are not the company's current inputs) and see whether the outputs from the model are reasonable. One common approach is to use extreme values of the inputs to see whether the outputs behave as they should. For example, for the 7–Eleven queueing model we could enter an extremely large service rate or a service rate just barely above the arrival rate in equation (1.1). In the first case we would expect the average waiting time to approach 0, whereas in the latter case we would expect it to become very large. You can use equation (1.1) to see that this is exactly what happens. Therefore, we have another piece of evidence that this model is reasonable.

What if certain inputs are entered in the model, and the model's outputs are *not* as expected? There could be two causes. First, the model could simply be a poor representation of the actual situation. In this case it is up to the analyst to refine the model until it lines up more accurately with reality. The second possible cause is that the model is fine but our intuition is not very good. That is, when asked what we think would happen if the inputs were set equal to certain values, we might provide totally wrong predictions. In this case the fault lies with us, not the model.

A typical example of this occurs with random sequences of zeros and ones, such as might occur with successive flips of a fair coin. Most people guess that heads and tails will alternate and that there will be very few sequences of, say, four or more heads (or tails) in a row. However, a perfectly accurate simulation model of these flips will show, contrary to what most people expect, that fairly long runs of heads or tails are not at all uncommon. In fact, one or two long runs should be *expected* if there are enough flips.

Actually, the fact that outcomes sometimes defy intuition is an important reason why mathematical models have been, and continue to be, important. Such models prove that people's ability to predict outcomes in complex environments is often not very good. Nevertheless, if a model's predictions are not in line with what the client expects, it may be difficult for the analyst to explain that it is the client, not the model, who is in error!

5. **Selection of an Alternative**   Once the problem has been defined, the data have been collected, and the model has been formulated and verified, it is time to use the model to recommend decisions or strategies. In the majority of management science models this requires the optimization of an objective function, such as maximizing profit or minimizing cost. As we mentioned earlier, it can also mean finding the alternatives that best achieve multiple objectives, as we will discuss in Chapter 9.

The optimization phase is typically the most difficult phase from a mathematical standpoint. Indeed, much of the management science literature (mostly from academics) has focused on complex solution algorithms for various classes of models. Fortunately for all of us, this research has led to a number of solution algorithms—and computer packages that incorporate these algorithms—that can now be used to solve real problems. Undoubtedly the most famous of these is the simplex algorithm that spreadsheet Solvers and other commercial software packages use on a daily basis to solve companies' linear programming models.

Not all solution procedures find the optimal solution to a problem. Many models are too large or complex to be solved exactly. Therefore, many complex problems use **heuristic** methods to locate "good" solutions. A heuristic is a solution method that is guided by common sense, intuition, and trial and error to achieve a good, but probably not optimal, solution. Some heuristics are "quick and dirty," whereas others are quite sophisticated. As models become larger and more complex, good heuristics are sometimes the best that can be achieved—and frequently they are perfectly adequate.

For years optimization algorithms (and some heuristics) formed the basis for courses in management science. For example, all students were required to learn the inner workings of the simplex method. This focus on algorithms is now being deemphasized, and we will say very little about algorithms in this book. Many instructors (and certainly most students!) agree that this is the proper way to proceed, arguing by analogy that an automobile driver does not need to know how everything under the hood works to drive the car successfully. We buy this analogy—to a point. In contrast to most of us, race car drivers who drive cars for a living *do* need to know what is going on under the hood to achieve their best performance. In the same way, professional management scientists, the analysts who solve real companies' problems, must understand the algorithms that are being used to solve their models. Admittedly, most of you will not be professional management scientists, but you should appreciate that a few people out there have to understand how the computerized "black boxes" really work!

6. **Presentation of the Results** Sooner or later, the analyst must communicate the model and its recommendations to the client. To appreciate this step, you must appreciate the large gap that typically exists between the technical analyst and the managers of the organization. Managers know their business but often do not understand much about mathematics and mathematical models—or even spreadsheet implementations of these models. The burden is therefore on the analyst to present the model in terms that nonmathematical people can understand; otherwise, a perfectly good model might never see the light of day. The best strategy for successful presentation is to involve key people in the organization, including top executives, in the project *from the beginning*. If these people have been working with the analyst, helping to supply appropriate data and helping the analyst to understand the way the organization really works, they are much more likely to accept the eventual model. Step 6, therefore, should really occur throughout the modeling process, not just toward the end.

The analyst should also try to make the model as intuitive and as user-friendly as possible. Clients appreciate menu-driven systems with plenty of graphics. They also appreciate the ability to ask what-if questions and obtain answers quickly and in a form that is easy to understand. This is one reason for favoring spreadsheet models. While not all models can be developed on spreadsheets, due to size and/or complexity, we believe the spreadsheet approach in this book is an excellent choice whenever possible because most business people are comfortable with spreadsheets. Spreadsheet packages support the use of graphics, customized menus and toolbars, data tables and other tools for what-if analyses, and even macros (that can be made transparent to the users) for running complex programs.

7. **Implementation of the Model** A real management science application is not complete until it has been implemented. A successful implementation can occur only when step 6 has been accomplished. That is, the analyst must demonstrate the model to the client, and the client must be convinced that the model adds real value and that it can be used by the people who will have to use it. For this reason,

the analyst's job is not really complete until the system is up and running on a daily basis. To achieve a successful implementation, it is not just sufficient for upper management to accept the model; the people who will run it every day must be thoroughly trained in its use. At the very least, they should understand how to enter appropriate inputs, run what-if analyses, and interpret the model's outputs correctly. If they conclude that the model is more trouble than it's worth, they may simply refuse to use it, and the whole exercise will have been a waste of time.

It is interesting to observe how many successful management science applications take a life of their own after the initial implementation. Once an organization sees the benefits of a useful model (and of management science in general), it is likely to expand the model or create new models for uses beyond those originally intended. Knowing that this is often the case, the best analysts design models that can be expanded. They try to anticipate problems the organization might face besides the current problem. Also, they stay in contact with the organization after the initial implementation, just in case the organization needs their guidance in expanding the scope of the model.

This discussion of the seven-step modeling process has taken an optimistic point of view. We have assumed that a successful study will employ these seven steps, in approximately this chronological order, and everything will go smoothly. It does not always work out this way. Numerous potential applications are never implemented even though the *technical* aspects of the models are perfectly correct. Probably the most frequent cause is a failure to communicate. The analyst builds a complex mathematical model, but the people in the organization don't understand how it works and hence are reluctant to use it. Also, company politics can be a model's downfall if the model recommends a course of action that top management simply does not want to follow— for whatever reasons.

Even for applications that are eventually implemented, the analyst might not proceed through the seven steps exactly as described above. He or she might backtrack considerably throughout the process. For example, based on a tentative definition of the problem, a model is built and demonstrated to management. Management says that the model is impressive, but it doesn't really solve the company's problem. Therefore, the analyst goes back to step 1, redefines the problem, and builds a new model (or modifies the original model). In this way, the analyst might generate several iterations of some or all of the seven steps before the project is considered complete.

1.5   SUCCESSFUL MANAGEMENT SCIENCE APPLICATIONS

I n this section we discuss three successful management science applications. We will provide a detailed (but nonquantitative) description of each application. We will tie our discussion of each application to the seven-step model-building process discussed in the previous section.

Citgo Petroleum

Klingman et al. (1987) applied a variety of management science techniques to Citgo Petroleum. Their work saved the company an estimated $70 million per year, making this study one of the most successful applications of management science. Citgo is an oil refining and marketing company that was purchased in 1983 by Southland Corporation, the 7–Eleven convenience store giant. Southland's goal was to make

Citgo as successful in the downstream petroleum business (refining and marketing) as Southland was in the convenience store industry, while supplying Southland's 7–Eleven stores with quality motor fuels. Until that time, Citgo had concentrated primarily on its oil refinery operations and had paid too little attention to the downstream market. As a result, it was losing money—a pretax loss of over $50 million in 1984. Southland called in a management science team headed by Darwin Klingman to turn things around. The results were extremely impressive, as demonstrated by Citgo's pretax profit of over $70 million in 1985.

We will focus on two aspects of the study. The first, referred to as model 1, is a mathematical model that has been used to optimize the operations of Citgo's refineries. The second, referred to as model 2 (or SDM by the authors), is a mathematical model that has been used to develop a multiweek supply, distribution, and marketing plan for the entire business. In each case we will go through the seven-step process that made this study a huge success.

Model 1: Optimizing Refinery Operations

1. Klingman's team first concentrated on oil refinery operations at Citgo's Lake Charles refinery. Because of various changes that were occurring in the oil industry and because of some obvious inefficiencies the team spotted at Citgo's operations, it became apparent that Citgo had a multifaceted problem. It was not taking advantage of available cost-saving opportunities; it wasn't making the correct mix of products; it wasn't using its resources (equipment, labor, and energy) efficiently; and its data-gathering mechanism needed updating.

2. The Lake Charles, Louisiana, refinery was closely observed in an attempt to estimate key data and relationships such as
   - How the cost of producing each of Citgo's products (motor fuel, number 2 fuel oil, turbine fuel, naphtha, and several blended motor fuels) depends on the inputs used to produce each product
   - The amount of energy needed to produce each product (which required the installation of a new metering system)
   - The yield associated with each input–output combination
   - Maintenance costs and their relationship to parts inventories and equipment breakdowns

   Obtaining accurate data required the installation of a new database management system and an integrated maintenance information system. A process-control system was also installed to accurately monitor the inputs and resources used to manufacture each product.

3. A large, complex linear programming model was developed to optimize refinery operations. The model determines the cost-minimizing method for mixing or blending available inputs to produce desired outputs. The model contains constraints to ensure that inputs are blended in such a way that each output is of sufficiently high quality. The model also ensures that plant capacities are not exceeded and allows for the fact that each refinery can carry an inventory of each end-product. (We will discuss similar models in Chapter 4.)

4. To validate the model, inputs and outputs from the Lake Charles refinery were collected for one month. Given the actual inputs used at the refinery during the month, the actual outputs were compared to the outputs predicted by the model. After several modifications, the revised model did indeed predict outputs that were sufficiently close to the actual outputs.

5. Although Citgo had been using a linear programming model prior to the study, Klingman's team replaced Citgo's linear programming software package with the

most powerful package then available to solve the model in a more timely manner. This package was able to solve the model on a daily basis and suggest detailed strategies for running the refinery. For example, the model might recommend producing 400,000 gallons of turbine fuel by blending 300,000 gallons of crude 1 and 100,000 gallons of crude 2.

6. The linear programming software package implemented in the previous step was not only more powerful, but it was also much more user-friendly. This made it possible for Klingman's team to demonstrate the model's capabilities to Citgo staff in a way they could understand and trust.

7. Once the database and process control were in place, the model was used to guide day-to-day refinery operations. Citgo staff were immediately impressed with its versatility and flexibility in demonstrating how large cost-saving improvements could be made in refinery yields, labor efficiency, maintenance of equipment, and other areas. As further proof of its effects, Citgo had voluntarily participated, *before* the study, in an independent refinery evaluation with 75 other companies. Citgo's rankings on six key measures of performance varied from 38th to 58th, placing it in the middle of the third quartile. A similar evaluation in 1985, *after* implementation of the model, placed Citgo in the upper half of the second quartile of competing refineries. Such a jump, together with clear dollar cost savings of up to $50 million annually, could not help but convince management of the model's worth.

Model 2: The Supply Distribution Marketing (SDM) System

1. Prior to the study, Citgo had concentrated primarily on its refinery operations. Southland wanted Citgo to become more aware of its downstream marketing operations. Specifically, Southland wanted Citgo to change its mindset from trying to produce as much volume at its refinery as possible—even if this meant losing money overall—to a profit-maximization focus. This new focus generated such questions as
   - Where should crude oil be purchased?
   - Where should products be sold?
   - What price should Citgo charge for its products?
   - How much of each product should Citgo hold in inventory?
   Citgo had largely ignored these questions in the past, and it could not afford to do so in the future if it wanted to remain a viable business within Southland.

2. A database was developed to keep track of sales, inventory, and trades and exchanges of all refined products. Also, regression analysis (discussed in Chapter 15) was used to develop forecasts for wholesale prices and wholesale demand for each of Citgo's products. Klingman's team realized that this was a time (in the mid-1980s) when more and more data were becoming available. The trick was to gather the correct data, put them into a usable form, and take advantage of them in appropriate mathematical models.

3. The team developed a "minimum cost network flow" model (as discussed in Chapter 5) to determine an 11-week supply, marketing, and distribution strategy. This model was characterized by many algebraic equations, but it could also be portrayed graphically as a network, where goods are shipped from one location to another. This network representation had the advantage that it was more intuitive to most people. The model addressed all of the concerns discussed in step 1.

4. The forecasting modules were continuously evaluated to ensure that they provided accurate forecasts.

5. Besides being more intuitive, the network nature of the model had the advantage that it was easier to solve. The solution procedure made use of special algorithms and computer software. Impossible problems became possible, and hard problems became easy. For example, a typical run of the model involving 3000 equations and 15,000 decision variables required only 30 seconds on an IBM mainframe computer. This not only enabled real-time solutions, but it allowed the model to be run repeatedly to answer what-if questions.

6. Klingman's team was able to demonstrate the benefits of the integrated database management system, the forecasting models, and the optimization models to Southland and Citgo top management. The benefits included better communication and coordination between supply, distribution, marketing, and refining groups; improved data; reduced inventories; added insights into pricing policies; better forecasts; and, of course, lower costs.

7. Probably the most important key to the success of the project was the support of the organization's top executives from the start. The president and CEO of Citgo, the chairman of the board of Southland, and the CEO of Southland created the management science team and were receptive to its needs and recommendations throughout the process. In addition, the project benefited from the enthusiastic and dedicated support of many operational managers during the process. Implementing the SDM required several organizational changes. A new vice president was appointed to coordinate the operation of the SDM and the linear programming refinery model. The product supply and product scheduling departments were combined to improve communication and information flow.

San Francisco Police Scheduling

In the late 1980s Taylor and Huxley (1989) developed the Police Patrol Scheduling System (PPSS) for the San Francisco Police Department (SFPD). It is estimated that PPSS created an extra 170,000 productive hours per year, thereby saving the city of San Francisco $5.2 million annually. PPSS enabled SFPD to make strategic changes (such as adopting the 4/10 work schedule described below) that made officers happier and increased productivity. Response times to calls decreased by 20% after PPSS was adopted. All San Francisco precincts now use PPSS to schedule their officers. Other cities (Virginia Beach, Virginia, and Richmond, California) have also adopted PPSS. We now see how the seven-step process made this success possible.

1. For years the SFPD had scheduled its officers manually to various shifts. Because of the large size of the police force (about 1900 officers), the process was very complex, and the SFPD had no idea whether the manual scheduling procedure was producing good schedules. The SFPD had three main goals: (1) to have enough officers on duty to ensure citizens' safety at all times of day, (2) to keep costs low, and (3) to keep officer morale high. This involved difficult trade-offs, and the decisions were becoming even more difficult with increased demand for police services and decreasing budgets. Beyond this, the SFPD wanted a method for evaluating two new proposals that might or might not improve efficiency. The first was a change in shift schedules from the traditional 5/8 shift (five days a week, eight hours per day) to a 4/10 shift (four days a week, ten hours per day), the latter of which was favored by the police officers. The second proposal was to convert some of the traditional two-officer cars into one-officer cars.

   Believing that a computerized scheduling system was necessary, the SFPD appointed a task force from its staff to locate existing software that would solve the problem. No such software was found, so the task force hired Taylor and Huxley to develop a scheduling model.

2. The SFPD already had a sophisticated computer-aided dispatch (CAD) system. CAD kept track of all calls for police help, police travel time, police response time, and other pertinent data. Because the SFPD wanted each officer to be busy on calls approximately the same percentage of his or her shift, it was relatively straightforward, using CAD, to determine the number of officers needed each hour. For example, if each officer ought to be busy about 80% of the time and CAD indicates that 30 hours worth of work is generated from 1 to 2 A.M. on a Sunday morning, then approximately 38 officers are required during this time period ($0.8 \times 38 \approx 30$ hours).

3. The SFPD wanted a method to schedule officers in each precinct that would quickly (in less than one hour) produce a schedule and graphically display the schedule. The program needed to determine the staffing requirements for each hour of the week (as discussed in step 2). For example, 38 officers might be needed between 1 and 2 A.M. Sunday morning, but only 14 officers might be needed between 4 and 5 A.M. Sunday morning. Officers needed to be scheduled to minimize the sum, over each hour of the week, of the shortages and surpluses relative to the required number of officers. For example, if 20 officers were assigned to the 12 to 8 A.M. Sunday morning shift, there would be a shortage of 18 officers ($= 38 - 20$) from 1 to 2 A.M. and a surplus of 6 officers ($= 20 - 14$) from 4 to 5 A.M. The program needed to minimize the maximum of the hourly shortages. This is because a shortage of 10 officers during a single hour is far more serious than a shortage of one officer during 10 different hours. The SFPD further wanted a model that would make it easy for precinct captains to fine-tune the optimal schedule to account for last-minute occurrences.

   The analysts developed a linear programming model to solve the scheduling problem. (We develop a scaled-down version of such a scheduling model in Chapter 4.) The primary objective was to minimize the sum of hourly shortages and surpluses. The constraints in the PPSS model reflected the limited number of officers available and the relationship of the number of officers working each hour to the shortages and surpluses for that hour. At first, they allowed only 5/8 shifts and only three shift starting times (such as 6 A.M., 2 P.M., and 10 P.M.). Eventually, they modified the model to allow for more possibilities, including 4/10 shifts and more than three possible starting times.

   The primary purpose of the PPSS model was to decide how many officers should start work at each possible shift time. For example, PPSS might recommend that 20 officers should start work at 6 A.M. Monday (working 6 A.M. to 2 P.M. Monday through Friday), 30 officers should start work at 2 P.M. Saturday (working 2 P.M. to 10 P.M. Saturday through Wednesday), and so on. The analysts also expanded the capabilities of the model so that a scheduling person could, for example, see the effect of adding an officer to any schedule, opening a new starting time or closing an old one, or increasing or decreasing the percentage of one-officer cars.

4. Prior to implementing PPSS, the SFPD tested the PPSS schedules against manually created schedules. PPSS produced approximately a 50% reduction in both surpluses and shortages. The outputs from these tests convinced the SFPD that PPSS was not only working correctly, but that it could greatly improve overall efficiency.

5. Given the starting times for shifts and the type of work schedule (5/8 or 4/10), PPSS was able to produce a nearly optimal schedule within a matter of minutes on

a PC. More importantly, PPSS was designed so that it could be used to experiment with shift times and work rules. Specifically, PPSS was able to show that if only three shift times were allowed, a 5/8 schedule would be superior to a 4/10 schedule, whereas if five shift times were allowed, a 4/10 schedule would be superior to a 5/8 schedule. This finding was of critical importance because it enabled the SFPD to achieve two objectives at once: more efficiency in covering workloads and higher morale by instituting the 4/10 schedules favored by police officers. PPSS also enabled the SFPD to experiment with a mix of one-officer and two-officer patrol cars. This analysis convinced them to use several one-officer cars during certain times of the day.

6. Because the SFPD task force worked closely with the management science team of Taylor and Huxley from the start of the project, ease of use and flexibility of the model were always priorities. The resulting model allowed users to ask many kinds of what-if questions. The answers were obtained quickly, the data displays were easy to view and understand, and many graphical views were available. In short, the PPSS was very user-friendly, and this feature enabled it to gain immediate acceptance by the SFPD.

7. Certain implementation issues had to be ironed out. For example, the model recommended several one-officer patrol cars, which needed to be purchased. Management anticipated a problem convincing the city to fund these additional vehicles. However, after testing the model at one particular police station and demonstrating the effectiveness of the new scheduling system at this site, the city was persuaded to allocate an initial sum of $470,000 for additional cars.

   Despite some minor problems, implementation was not difficult. The user-friendly features of the PPSS made it possible for police officers to learn the system in an average of two days. The graphical displays assisted in this training since they explained why a given schedule was good or bad. Also, the system provided an environment where trainees could learn by challenging the system to see whether they could do better. The officers quickly learned to use the many features of the system and to trust the value of its recommendations.

GE Capital

GE Capital, a subsidiary of the General Electric Company's financial services business, provides credit card service to 50 million accounts. The average total outstanding balance exceeds $12 billion. GE Capital, led by Makuch et al. (1992), developed the PAYMENT system to reduce delinquent accounts and the cost of collecting from delinquent accounts.

1. At any time, GE Capital has over $1 billion in delinquent accounts. The company spends $100 million annually processing these accounts. Each day employees contact over 200,000 delinquent credit card holders with letters, taped phone messages, or live phone calls. However, there was no real scientific basis for the methods used to collect on various types of accounts. For example, GE Capital had no idea whether a two-month due account should receive a taped phone message, a live phone call, some combination of these, or no contact at all. The company's goal was to reduce delinquent accounts and the cost of processing these accounts, but it was not sure how to accomplish this goal. Therefore, GE Capital's retail financial services component, together with management scientists and statisticians from GE's corporate research and development group, analyzed the problem and eventually developed a model called PAYMENT. The purpose of

this model was to assign the most cost-effective collection methods to delinquent accounts.

2. The key data requirements for modeling delinquent accounts are **delinquency movement matrices** (DMMs). A DMM shows how the probability of the payment on a delinquent account depends on the collection action taken (no action, live phone call, taped message, or letter), the size of the unpaid balance, and the account's performance score. (The higher the performance score associated with a delinquent account, the more likely the account is to be collected.) For example, if a $250 account is two months delinquent, has a high performance score, and is contacted with a phone message, then certain events might occur with certain probabilities. The events and the probabilities listed in Table 1.1 illustrate one possibility. The key is to estimate these probabilities for each possible collection action and each account type.

TABLE 1.1 **Sample DMM Entries**

Event	Probability
Account completely paid off	0.30
One month is paid off	0.40
Nothing is paid off	0.30

Fortunately, because GE Capital had millions of delinquent accounts, plenty of data was available to estimate the DMMs accurately. To illustrate, suppose there are 1000 two-month delinquent accounts, each with balances under $300 and a high performance score. Also, suppose that each of these is contacted with a phone message. If 300 of these accounts are completely paid off by the next month, then an estimate of the probability of an account being completely paid off by next month is 0.30 (= 300/1000). By collecting the necessary data to estimate similar probabilities for all account types and collection actions, GE Capital finally had the basis for seeing which collection strategies were most cost-effective.

3. After collecting the required data and expressing it in the form of DMMs, the company needed to discover which collections worked best in which situations. Specifically, they wanted to maximize the expected delinquent accounts collected during the following six months. However, they realized that this is a **dynamic** decision problem. For example, one strategy is called **creaming**. In this strategy, most collection resources are concentrated on live phone calls to the delinquent accounts classified as most likely to pay up—the best customers. This creaming strategy is attractive because it is likely to generate short-term cash flows from these customers. However, it has two negative aspects. First, it is likely to cause a loss of goodwill among the best customers. Second, it gains nothing in the long run from the customers who are most likely to default on their payments. Therefore, the analysts developed the PAYMENT model to find the best **decision strategy**, a contingency plan for each type of customer that specifies which collection strategy to use at each stage of the account's delinquency. The constraints in the PAYMENT model ensure that available resources are not overused.

4. A key aspect of GE Capital's problem is uncertainty. When the PAYMENT model specifies the collection method to use for a certain type of account, it implies that the probability of collecting on this account with this collection method is relatively high. However, there is still a chance that the collection method will fail. With this high degree of uncertainty, it is difficult to convince skeptics that the

model will work as advertised until it has been demonstrated in an actual environment. This is exactly what GE Capital did. It piloted the PAYMENT model on a $62 million portfolio for a single department store chain. To see the real effect of PAYMENT's recommended strategies, the pilot study used manager-recommended strategies for some accounts and PAYMENT-recommended strategies for others. (They referred to this as the "champion" versus the "challenger.") The challenger (PAYMENT) strategies were the clear winners, with an average monthly improvement of $185,000 over the champion strategies during a five-month period. In addition, because the PAYMENT strategies included more "no contact" actions (don't bother the customer this month), they led to lower collection costs and greater customer goodwill. This demonstration was very convincing. In no time, other account managers wanted to take advantage of PAYMENT.

5. As described in step 3, the output from the PAYMENT model is a contingency plan. The model uses a very complex optimization scheme, along with the DMMs from step 2, to decide what collection strategy to use for each type of delinquent account at each stage (month) of its delinquency. At the end of each month, after the appropriate collection methods have been used and the results (actual payments) have been observed, the model then uses the status of each account to recommend the collection method for the next month. In this way, the model is used dynamically through time.

6. In general, the management scientist demonstrates the model to the client in step 6. In this application, however, the management science team members were GE's own people—they came from GE Capital and the GE corporate research and development group. Throughout the model-building process, the team of analysts strived to understand the requirements of the collection managers and staff—the end users—and tried to involve them in shaping the final system. This early and continual involvement, plus the impressive performance of PAYMENT in the pilot study, made it easy to "sell" the model to the people who would have to use it.

7. After the pilot study, PAYMENT was applied to the $4.6 billion Montgomery Ward department store portfolio with 18 million accounts. Compared to the collection results from a year earlier, PAYMENT increased collections by $1.6 million per month, or over $19 million per year. (This is actually a conservative estimate of the benefit obtained from PAYMENT, because PAYMENT was first applied to the Montgomery Ward portfolio during the depths of a recession, when it is much more difficult to collect delinquent accounts.) Since then, PAYMENT has been applied to virtually all of GE Capital's accounts, with similar success. Overall, GE Capital estimates that PAYMENT has increased collections by $37 million per year and uses less resources than previous strategies. The model is now being expanded in several directions. For example, the original model assumed that collection resources (such as the amount available for live phone calls) were fixed. The model has since been expanded to treat these resource levels as decision variables in a more encompassing optimization model.

1.6 WHY STUDY MANAGEMENT SCIENCE?

After reading the previous section, you should be convinced that management science is an important area and that highly trained analysts are needed to solve the large and complex problems faced by the business world. However, unless you are one of the relatively few students who intends to become a professional management scientist, you are probably wondering why you need to study management science. This is a legitimate concern. Indeed, for many years we in the field of management science education have received criticism from students and educators that management science courses were irrelevant to the majority of students who were required to take them. Looking back, it is difficult to argue with these critics. Typical management courses were centered primarily around a collection of very specific models and, worse, a collection of mind-numbing mathematical solution techniques—techniques that students were often required to implement *by hand*! (Some courses are probably still taught this way, but we hope the number is decreasing rapidly.)

There are two forces that have helped to change this tendency toward irrelevance. First, the many vocal critics have motivated many of us to examine our course materials and teaching methods. Certain topics have been eliminated and replaced by material that is more relevant and interesting to students. The second force is the emergence of powerful personal computers (PCs) and the accompanying easy-to-use software, especially spreadsheet software. With the availability of computers to do the number crunching, there is no need—except in very advanced courses—to delve into the mathematical details of the solution techniques. We can delegate this task to machines that are far better at it than we humans are. We can now use the time formerly spent on such details to develop modeling skills that are valuable to a wide audience.

Our intent in this book is not just to cover specific models and specific approaches to these models, but to teach a more general approach to the model-building process. Furthermore, we believe the spreadsheet approach is the best way to do this and appeals to the largest audience. We have been teaching our own courses with this spreadsheet-modeling approach for several years—to a wide range of business students—and we have received very few complaints about irrelevance. Indeed, many students have said openly that this is one of the most valuable business courses they have ever taken. The following are some of the reasons for this new-found relevance.

1. The modeling approach emphasized throughout this book is an important way to think about problems in general, not just the specific problems we discuss. This approach forces you to think logically. You must discover how given data can be used (or, as in some of the "modeling" problems, which data are necessary), you must determine the elements of the problem that you can control (the "decision variables"), and you must determine how the elements of the problem are logically related. Students realize that these logical thinking skills will be valuable in their careers, regardless of the specific careers they enter.

2. Management science is admittedly built around *quantitative* skills—it deals primarily with numbers and relationships between numbers. Some critics object that not everything in the real world can be reduced to numbers, but as one of our reviewers correctly pointed out, "a great deal that is of importance can." As you work through the many models in this book, your quantitative skills will be sharpened immensely. In a business world driven increasingly by numbers, quantitative skills are an obvious asset.

3. When you enter this course, your spreadsheet abilities might not be very good. By the time this course is over, however, we can promise you that you will be a proficient spreadsheet user. We deliberately chose the spreadsheet package Excel, which is arguably the most widely used package (other than word-processing packages) in the business world today. Many of our students have told us that the facility they gained in Excel was worth the price of the course. We do not mean to imply that this is a course in spreadsheet fundamentals and neat tricks, although you will undoubtedly pick up a few useful tricks along the way. A great spreadsheet package—and we strongly believe that Excel is the greatest

spreadsheet package written to date—gives you complete control over your model. You can apply spreadsheets to an endless variety of problems. Spreadsheets give you the flexibility to work in a way that suits *your* style best, and spreadsheets present results (and often catch errors) almost immediately. As you succeed with relatively easy problems, your confidence will build, and before long you will be able to tackle more difficult problems successfully. In short, spreadsheets enable everyone, not just technical people, to develop and use their quantitative skills.

4. Management science modeling helps you to develop your intuition, and it also indicates where intuition alone sometimes fails. When you confront a problem, you often make an educated (or maybe not so educated) guess at the solution. If the problem is sufficiently complex, as most of the problems in this book are, this guess will frequently be wide of the mark. In this sense the study of management science can be a humbling experience—you find that your unaided intuition is often not very good. But by studying many models and examining their solutions, you can sharpen your intuition considerably. This might be called the "Aha!" effect. All of a sudden, you see why a certain solution is best. The chances are that when you originally thought about the problem, you forgot to consider an important constraint or a key relationship, and this caused the poor initial guess. Presumably, the more problems you analyze, the better you become at recognizing the critical elements of new problems. Experienced management scientists tend to have excellent intuition, that is, the ability to see through to the essence of a problem almost immediately. However, they are not born with this talent; it comes through the kind of analysis you will be performing as you work through this book.

1.7 SOFTWARE INCLUDED IN THIS BOOK

Very few business problems are small enough to be solved with pencil and paper. They require powerful software. The software included in this book, together with Microsoft® Excel, provides you with a powerful software combination that you will not use for one course and then discard. It is software that is being used—and will continue to be used—by leading companies all over the world to solve large, complex problems. We firmly believe that the experience you obtain with this software, through working the examples and problems in this book, will give you a key competitive advantage in the marketplace.

It all begins with Excel. All of the quantitative methods that we discuss are implemented in Excel. It is impossible to forecast the state of computer software into the long-term or even medium-term future, but as we are writing this book, Excel is *the* most heavily used spreadsheet package on the market, and there is every reason to believe that this state will persist for at least several years. Most companies use Excel, most employees and most students have been trained in Excel, and Excel is a *very* powerful, flexible, and easy-to-use package.

Although Excel has a huge set of tools for performing numerical analysis, we have included several add-ins with this book (available on the accompanying CD-ROM) that make Excel even more powerful. We discuss these briefly here and in much more depth in specific chapters where they apply. Throughout the text, you will see where each of these add-ins is used, as denoted by the icon next to each description.

Premium Solver

Excel has a built-in add-in called Solver that was developed by Frontline Systems. This add-in will be used extensively throughout the book to find optimal solutions to spreadsheet models. The version of Solver that ships with Excel is quite powerful and suffices for the majority of the optimization models we will discuss. However, Frontline Systems has developed several other versions of Solver for the commercial market, and one of these, called Premium Solver, is included in this book. The primary advantage of Premium Solver is that it enables us to solve some problems with a kind of algorithm (called a genetic algorithm) that is quite different from the algorithms used by the built-in Solver. Only a small percentage of all optimization models require a genetic algorithm, but in Chapter 8 we will illustrate several very interesting models that take good advantage of genetic algorithms and hence the Premium Solver. These models could either not be solved with the built-in Solver, or they would require non-obvious modeling tricks to make them amenable to the built-in Solver.

Palisade Software

The Palisade Corporation has developed several powerful add-ins to Excel that we have included in this book. These are slightly scaled-down versions of commercial software packages used widely in the business world. We describe them briefly here.

Decision Tools® Suite

This is a collection of add-ins that Palisade sells separately or as a suite. All items in this suite are Excel add-ins—so the learning curve is not very steep. There are five separate add-ins in this suite: @Risk, PrecisionTree, TopRank, BestFit, and RiskView. The first two are the most important for our purposes, but all are useful for certain tasks.

@Risk The @Risk add-in is extremely useful for the development and analysis of spreadsheet simulation models. First, it provides a number of probability functions that enable us to build uncertainty explicitly into Excel models. Then when we run a simulation, @Risk automatically keeps track of any outputs we select, it displays the results in a number of tabular and graphical forms, and it enables us to perform sensitivity analyses, so that we can see which inputs have the most effect on the outputs.

PrecisionTree® The PrecisionTree add-in is used in Chapter 10 to analyze decision problems with uncertainty. The primary tool for performing this type of analysis is a decision tree. Decision trees are inherently graphical, and they have always been difficult to implement in spreadsheets, which are based on rows and columns. However, PrecisionTree does this in a very clever and intuitive way. Equally important, once the basic decision tree has been built, PrecisionTree makes it easy to perform sensitivity analyses on the model inputs.

TopRank® Although we will not use the other Palisade add-ins as extensively as @Risk and PrecisionTree, they are all worth investigating. TopRank is the most general of these. It starts with any spreadsheet model, where a set of inputs are used, together with spreadsheet formulas, to produce one or more outputs. TopRank then performs sensitivity analyses to see which inputs have the largest effects on the outputs. For example, it might tell us which affects after-tax profit the most: the tax rate, the risk-free rate for investing, the inflation rate, or the price charged by a competitor. Unlike @Risk, TopRank is used when uncertainty is not *explicitly* built into a spreadsheet model. However, it considers uncertainty implicitly by performing sensitivity analyseis on the important model inputs.

BestFit® BestFit is used to determine the most appropriate probability distribution for a spreadsheet model when we have data on some uncertain quantity. For example, a simulation might model each week's demand for a product as a random variable. What probability distribution should we use for weekly demand: the well-known normal distribution or possibly some skewed distribution? If we have historical data on weekly demands for the product, we can feed them into BestFit and let it recommend the distribution that best fits the data. This is a very useful tool in real applications. Instead of guessing a distribution that we think might be relevant, we can let BestFit point us to a distribution that fits historical data well.

RiskView™ RiskView is a drawing tool that complements @Risk. A number of probability distributions are available with @Risk that can be used in simulations. Each has an associated @Risk function, such as RiskNormal, RiskBinomial, and so on. Before selecting any of these distributions, however, it is useful (especially for beginners) to see what these distributions look like. RiskView performs this task easily. For any selected probability distribution (and any selected parameters of this distribution), it creates a graph of the distribution.[3]

StatPro™

Palisade has also developed a statistics add-in, called StatPro, that enhances the statistical capabilities of Excel. Excel's built-in statistical tools are rather limited. It has several functions such as AVERAGE and STDEV for summarizing data, and it includes the Analysis ToolPak, an add-in that was developed by a third party. However, these tools are not sufficiently powerful or flexible for the "heavy-duty" statistical analysis that is sometimes required. StatPro provides a collection of tools that help to fill the gap. Admittedly, this is not a *statistics* book, but the StatPro tools will come in particularly handy in Chapters 15 and 16, when we study regression analysis and forecasting.

Together with Excel and the add-ins included in this book, you have a wealth of software at your disposal. The examples and step-by-step instructions throughout this book will help you to become a power user of this software. This takes plenty of practice and a willingness to experiment, but it is certainly within your grasp. When you are finished, we will not be surprised if you rate improved software skills as the most valuable thing you have learned from this book.

1.8 CONCLUSION

In this chapter we have introduced the field of management science and the process of mathematical modeling. To provide a more concrete understanding of these concepts, we described a simple queueing model and chronicled three very successful management science applications. We also emphasized a seven-step model-building

---

[3]BestFit and RiskView were originally developed by Palisade as stand-alone software pacakages, and they are still available in this form. However, the newest version of @Risk, the version included in this book, incorporates the functionality of BestFit and RiskView into the simulation add-in in a very impressive and useful manner.

process that begins with problem definition and proceeds through final implementation. Finally, we discussed why the study of management science is a valuable experience, even if you do not intend to pursue a professional career in this field.

Don't worry if you didn't understand some of the terms such as *linear programming* or *regression analysis* that were used in this chapter. Although the seven-step process is not too difficult to comprehend, especially when it is discussed in the context of real applications, it typically entails some rather complex logical relationships and mathematical concepts. These ideas will be presented in much greater detail in the rest of this book. Specifically, you will learn how to build spreadsheet models in Excel, how to use them to answer what-if questions, and how to find optimal solutions with the help of a spreadsheet Solver. For practical reasons most of your work will take place in the classroom or in front of your own PC as you work through the examples and problems we have provided. The primary emphasis of this book, therefore, is on steps 3 through 6, that is, model formulation, testing the model with different inputs, optimizing the model, and presenting (and interpreting) your results to a client—probably your instructor.

It is nevertheless important to keep in mind that with real problems there are crucial steps you must take before and after the procedures you'll be practicing in this book. Because real problems don't come as nicely packaged as those we will study and because the necessary data are seldom given to you on a platter, you will have to wrestle with the problem's scope and its precise data requirements when you solve problems in a real setting. (We have included several "modeling problems" at the end of most chapters. These problems are not as well structured as the "skill" problems, so the burden is on you to determine an appropriate structure and decide which data are needed.) Also, because a mathematically accurate model does not necessarily result in a successful implementation, your work is not necessarily over once the numbers check out. To gain acceptance for a model, an analyst must have the right combination of technical skills *and* people skills. Try to keep this in mind as you write up your solutions to the problems in this book. Don't just hand in a mass of numbers with little or no explanation. *Sell* your solution!

## CHAPTER 2

Introductory Spreadsheet Modeling

ANALYSIS OF HIV/AIDS

Many of management science's most successful applications are in traditional functional areas of business, including operations management, logistics, finance, and marketing. Indeed, we will analyze many such applications in this book. However, another area where management science has had a strong influence over the past decade has been the analysis of the worldwide HIV/AIDS epidemic. Not only have theoretical models been developed, but even more important, they have been *applied* to help understand the epidemic and reduce its spread. To highlight the importance of management science modeling in this area, an entire special issue (May–June 1998) of *Interfaces*, the journal that reports successful management science applications, was recently devoted to HIV/AIDS models. Although many of the details of the articles in this issue are mathematically complex, we will discuss some of the highlights here, just so that you can get an idea of what management science has to offer in this important area.

Kahn et al. (1998) provide an overview of the problem. They discuss how governments, public-health agencies, and health-care providers must determine how best to allocate scarce resources for HIV treatment and prevention among different programs and populations. They discuss in some depth how management science models have influenced, and will continue to influence, AIDS policy decisions. Other articles in the issue discuss more specific problems. Caulkins et al. (1998) analyze whether the distribution of difficult-to-reuse syringes would reduce the spread of HIV among injection drug users. Based on their model, they conclude that the extra expense of these types of syringes would not be worth the marginal benefit they might provide. Paltiel and Freedberg (1998) investigate the costs and benefits of developing and administering treatments for cytomegalovirus (CMV), an infection to which HIV carriers are increasingly explosed. (Retinitis, CMV's most common manifestation, is associated with blindness and sometimes death.) Their model suggests that the costs compare unfavorably with alternative uses of scarce resources. Owens et al. (1998) analyze the effect of women's relapse to high-risk sexual and needle-sharing behavior on the costs and benefits of a voluntary program to screen women of childbearing age for HIV. They find, for example, that the effect of relapse to high-risk behaviors on screening program costs and benefits can be substantial, suggesting that behavioral interventions that produce sustained reductions in risk behavior, even if expensive, could be cost-saving. Bernstein et al. (1998) compared three intervention strategies for preventing heterosexual transmission of HIV using management science models. Their comparison was based on parameters estimated from a severely affected east African city. They found, for example, that the most effective intervention was reducing the number and rate of change of sex partners, followed by increased condom use and treatment for sexually transmitted diseases.

The important point is that these articles (and others not mentioned here) base their results on rigorous mathematical models of the HIV/AIDS phenomenon. In addition, they are backed up with real data. They are not simply opinions of the authors. ■

2.1 INTRODUCTION

This book is all about spreadsheet modeling. By the time we are finished, we will have covered some reasonably difficult and complex—and realistic—models. We will also have transformed many of you into Excel "power" users. However, from our experience in teaching this material, there is a danger of starting too quickly or assuming too much background from our audience. We have found that many students have trouble either with the modeling aspects or the Excel aspects or a combination of the two. We will try to remedy this problem in two ways. First, for those of you who need some practice getting up to speed with basic Excel features, we have included an Excel tutorial in the CD-ROM that accompanies this book. You can work through this tutorial at your own speed and cover the topics you need help with. Even if you have used Excel somewhat extensively, we urge you to give this tutorial a look. You might be surprised how some of our tips can improve your productivity.

Second, we have written this chapter to give you a gentle start in Excel modeling. This chapter will illustrate some interesting but relatively simple models, and we will step you through the modeling process. As we do so, we will cover some of the less well-known, but extremely valuable, Excel tools that are available. These include data tables, Goal Seek, trend curves, lookup tables, and auditing commands. Keep in mind, however, that our objective is not the same as that of the many "how-to" Excel books on the market. Specifically, we are not teaching Excel just for the sake of its many interesting features. Rather, we plan to *use* these features to provide insight into real business problems. In other words, we regard Excel as a problem-solving tool, not an end in itself.

2.2 BASIC SPREADSHEET MODELING CONCEPTS

Most mathematical models, including spreadsheet models, involve **inputs**, **decision variables**, and **outputs**. The model inputs are given values that are fixed, at least for the purposes of the model. The decision variables are values that a decision maker has control over. The model outputs are the ultimate values of interest; they are determined by the inputs and decision variables. A typical example is the following. Suppose a manager needs to place an order for a certain product. This product will go out of date fairly soon, so this is the only order that will be made for the product. The inputs are then the fixed cost of the order, the unit variable cost of each item ordered, the price charged for each item sold, and the "salvage" value for each item, if any, left in inventory after the product has gone out of date. The decision variable is the number of items to order. Finally, the main output is the profit (or loss) from the product. We might also break this "ultimate" output into the outputs that contribute to it: the total ordering cost, the revenue from sales, and the salvage value from any leftover items. We will certainly have to calculate these outputs to obtain profit.

Spreadsheet modeling is the process of entering the inputs and decision variables into a spreadsheet and then relating them appropriately, by means of formulas, to obtain the outputs. Once we have done this, we can then proceed in several directions. We might want to perform a sensitivity analysis to see how one or more outputs change as selected inputs or decision variables change. We might want to find the values of the decision variable(s) that minimize or maximize a particular output, possibly subject to certain constraints. We might also want to create charts that show graphically how certain parameters of the model are related.

We will illustrate these operations with several examples in this chapter. Indeed, getting all of the spreadsheet logic correct and producing useful results is a big part of the battle. However, we want to go further—we want to stress good spreadsheet modeling *habits*. The chances are that you will not be developing spreadsheet models for your own use. You will probably be sharing these with colleagues or even a boss (or an instructor). The point is that other people will probably be reading and trying to make sense out of your spreadsheet models. Therefore, it is imperative that you construct your spreadsheet models with *readability* in mind. Several features that can improve readability include:

- A clear, logical layout to the overall model
- Separation of different parts of a model across multiple worksheets
- Clear headings for different sections of the model and for all inputs, decision variables, and outputs
- Liberal use of range names
- Liberal use of boldface, italics, larger font size, coloring, indentation, and other formatting features

- Liberal use of cell comments
- Liberal use of text boxes for assumptions, lists, or any explanations

Obviously, the formulas and logic in any spreadsheet model must be correct, and this is where we will place most emphasis throughout this book. However, correctness will not take you very far if no one can understand what you have done. Much of the power of spreadsheets comes from their flexibility. When you open a blank spreadsheet, it is like a big blank canvas waiting for you to enter useful data and formulas. Practically anything is allowed. However, this power can be abused if you do not have an overall plan as to what should go where. So we urge you to plan ahead, before diving in. And if your plan does not look good once you start filling in the spreadsheet, do not hesitate to revise your plan.

We will not say any more in this section about the specifics of "best spreadsheet practices." We believe an abstract discussion of this topic at this point would not be very meaningful to readers without much spreadsheet modeling experience—the majority of you. Rather, we believe the best way to learn how to make your spreadsheet models more readable is to study how others have constructed their models. In particular, we have tried to set a good example throughout this book by incorporating all of the bulleted points above. This is not necessarily easy. It has often required us to revise our models several times, sometimes radically, until we were satisfied. Of course, there is more than one way to make a spreadsheet model readable, just as there is more than one way to write a memo or give a speech. Our style is not the only good style, and we encourage you to develop your own style. But just as a writing teacher stresses the importance of editing, editing, and more editing in writing, we stress the importance of editing your spreadsheet models for improved readability.

Because we place such emphasis on good spreadsheet style, we have included an appendix to this chapter that discusses a few tools for editing and documenting your spreadsheet models. We recommend that you try these tools right away. They will be very useful as you progress through the book.

2.3 MODELING EXAMPLES

We strongly believe in example-based learning. We think we can teach better, and you can learn better, if we cover modeling concepts and spreadsheet features in the context of examples rather than in the abstract. Therefore, we will proceed directly to examples for the rest of this chapter. As we discuss these examples, we will introduce several important modeling concepts (such as sensitivity analysis), several important Excel features (such as data tables), and even some important business concepts (such as net present value). We will also discuss good spreadsheet habits—why we did something in a certain way. To get the most from these examples, you should follow along at your own PC, starting with a blank spreadsheet. It is one thing to read about spreadsheet modeling; it is quite another to *do* it!

Finding a Breakeven Point

Many business problems are concerned with finding the appropriate level of some activity. This might be the level that maximizes profit (or minimizes cost), or it might be the level that allows a company to break even—no profit, no loss. We will discuss a typical breakeven analysis in the following example.

EXAMPLE 2.1

BREAKEVEN ANALYSIS AT GREAT THREADS

The Great Threads Company sells hand-knit sweaters. Great Threads is planning to print a catalog of its products and undertake a direct mail campaign. The cost of printing the catalog is $20,000 plus $0.10 per catalog. The cost of mailing each catalog (including postage, order forms, and buying of names from a mail-order database) is $0.15. In addition, the company will include direct reply envelopes in its mailings. It incurs $0.20 in extra costs for each direct mail envelope that is used by a respondent. The average size of a customer order is $40, and the company's variable cost per order (due primarily to labor and material costs) averages around 80% of the order's value. The company plans to mail 100,000 catalogs. It wants to develop a spreadsheet model to answer the following questions:

1. How does a change in the response rate affect profit?
2. For what response rate does the company break even?
3. If the company estimates a response rate of 3%, should it proceed with the mailing?
4. How does the presence of uncertainty affect the usefulness of the model?

Solution

The completed model appears in Figure 2.1. (See the file GREATTHREADS.XLS.[1]) First, note the clear layout of the model. The input cells are outlined (in blue on a color screen) and shaded, they are separated from the outputs, there are boldfaced headings, several headings are indented, numbers are formatted appropriately, and there is a text box to the right that spells out all range names we have used.

FIGURE 2.1
Great Threads
Model

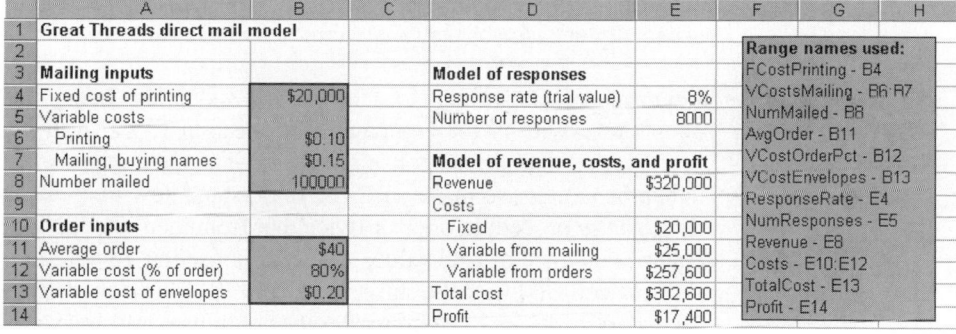

	A	B	C	D	E	F	G	H
1	Great Threads direct mail model							
2								
3	**Mailing inputs**			**Model of responses**		Range names used:		
4	Fixed cost of printing	$20,000		Response rate (trial value)	8%	FCostPrinting - B4		
5	Variable costs			Number of responses	8000	VCostsMailing - B6:B7		
6	Printing	$0.10				NumMailed - B8		
7	Mailing, buying names	$0.15		**Model of revenue, costs, and profit**		AvgOrder - B11		
8	Number mailed	100000		Revenue	$320,000	VCostOrderPct - B12		
9				Costs		VCostEnvelopes - B13		
10	**Order inputs**			Fixed	$20,000	ResponseRate - E4		
11	Average order	$40		Variable from mailing	$25,000	NumResponses - E5		
12	Variable cost (% of order)	80%		Variable from orders	$257,600	Revenue - E8		
13	Variable cost of envelopes	$0.20		Total cost	$302,600	Costs - E10:E12		
14				Profit	$17,400	TotalCost - E13		
						Profit - E14		

DEVELOPING THE SPREADSHEET MODEL

To create this model, proceed through the following steps.

❶ Enter headings and range names. Obviously, we have named a lot of cells, more than you might want to name, but you will see their value when we start entering formulas. (In general, we strongly support range names, but we caution you not to go

---

[1] The CD-ROM accompanying this book includes completed or partially completed files for all examples in this book. However, especially in this chapter, we suggest that you start with a blank spreadsheet and follow our step-by-step instructions on your own.

overboard. You can waste a lot of time naming ranges that do not *really* need to be named.)

❷ Enter input values. Enter these values and format them appropriately. We have put a blue border around all input cells (and because color doesn't show in the book, we have shaded them) to distinguish them as *input* cells. This is just one possible way to distinguish input cells, and we follow it throughout this book. We urge you to follow our example or at least develop a consistent system of your own.

❸ Model the responses. We have not specified the response rate to the mailing, so enter *any* reasonable value, such as 8%, in the ResponseRate cell—we will perform sensitivity on this value later on—and enter the formula

=NumMailed*ResponseRate

in the NumResponses cell. (Do you see the advantage of named ranges?)

❹ Model the revenue, costs, and profits. Enter the formula

=NumResponses*AvgOrder

in the Revenue cell, enter the formulas

=FCostPrinting
=SUM(VCostsMailing)*NumMailedand
=NumResponses*(AvgOrder*VCostOrderPct+VCostEnvelopes)

in the Costs cells (E10, E11, and E12), enter the formula

=SUM(Costs)

in the TotalCost cell, and enter the formula

=Revenue-TotalCost

in the Profit cell. (Note that the cost of envelopes in cell B13 is incurred only for customers who respond to the mailing.) These formulas should all be self-explanatory, especially because of the range names we have used.

Forming a Data Table Now that a basic model has been created, we can answer the questions posed by the company. For question 1, we form a data table to show how profit varies with the response rate. This data table appears in Figure 2.2. We will use data tables often, so make sure you understand how to create them. We will walk you through the procedure once or twice, but from then on, you will be on your own. First, enter a sequence of trial values of the response rate in column A, and enter a "link" to profit in cell B20 with the formula **=Profit**. (We have shaded this cell for emphasis, but this is not necessary.) In general, other outputs could be part of the table, in columns C, D, and so on. There would be a link to each output in row 20. Finally, highlight the entire table range, A20:B30, and select the Data/Table menu item to bring up the dialog box in Figure 2.3. It should be filled in as shown to indicate that the only input, ResponseRate, is listed along a column. (You can enter either a range name or a cell address in this dialog box.) When you click on OK, Excel substitutes each response rate value in the table into the ResponseRate cell, recalculates profit, and reports it in the table. For a final touch, we have created a scatterplot (or in Excel's terminology, an X-Y chart) of the values in the data table.

FIGURE 2.2
Data Table for Profit

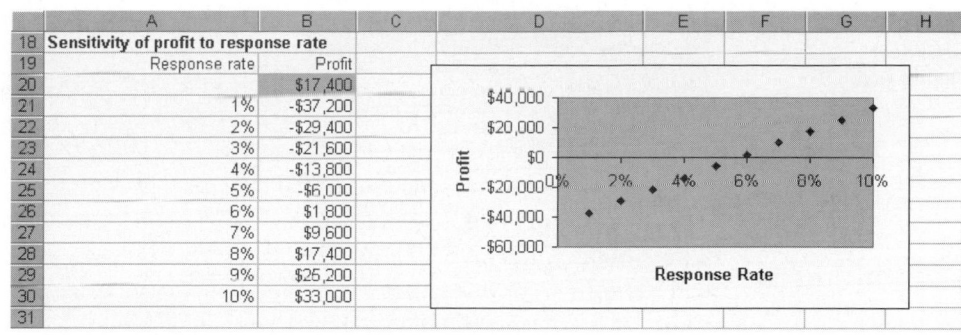

FIGURE 2.3
Data Table
Dialog Box

Clearly, profit increases in a linear manner as response rate varies. More specifically, a 1% increase in the response rate always increases profit by $7800. Here is the reasoning. Each 1% increase in response rate results in $100,000(0.01) = 1000$ more orders. Each order yields an average revenue of $40 but incurs a variable cost of $40(80\%) = \$32$ and a $0.20 envelope cost. The net gain in profit is $7.80 per order, or $7800 for 1000 orders.

USING GOAL SEEK

From the data table, we see that profit changes from negative to positive when the response rate is somewhere between 5% and 6%. Question 2 asks for the exact breakeven point. This could be found by trial and error, but it is easy with Excel's Goal Seek tool. Essentially, Goal Seek is useful for solving a *single* equation in a *single* unknown. Here, the equation is **Profit=0**, and the single unknown is the response rate. In Excel terminology, the unknown is called the **changing cell** because we are allowed to change it to make the equation true. To implement Goal Seek, select the Tools/Goal Seek menu item and fill in the resulting dialog box as shown in Figure 2.4 (page 34). (In general, range names or cell addresses can be used in the top and bottom boxes, but a *value* must be entered in the middle box.) After you click on OK, the ResponseRate and Profit cells have values 5.77% and $0.[2] In words, if the response rate is 5.77%, Great Threads breaks even. If the response rate is greater than 5.77%, the company makes money; otherwise, it loses money.

---

[2]Sometimes Goal Seek stops when the Set cell is close, but not exactly equal to, the desired value. To improve Goal Seek's accuracy, select the Tools/Options menu item and click on the Calculation tab. Then check the Iteration box and reduce Maximum change to any desired level of precision—we chose a precision level of 0.000001. For this level of precision, Goal Seek searches until profit is within 0.000001 of the desired value ($0).

FIGURE 2.4
Goal Seek
Dialog Box

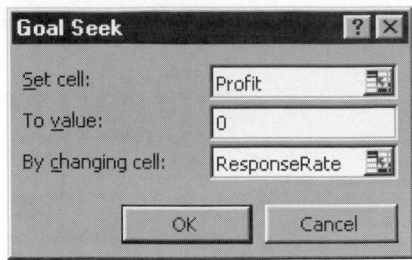

Limitations of the Model Question 3 asks whether the company should proceed with the mailing if the response rate is only 3%. From the data table, the apparent answer is "no" because profit is negative—a loss. However, like many U.S. companies, we are taking the short-term view with this reasoning. We should realize that many customers who respond to direct mail will *reorder* in the future. The company makes $7.80 per order. If each of the respondents ordered two more times, say, the company would earn $3000($7.80)(2) = \$46,800$ more than appears in the model, and profit would then be positive. The moral is that we must look at the long-term impact of our decisions. However, if we want to incorporate the long term explicitly into the model, we must build a more complex model.

Finally, question 4 asks about the impact of uncertainty in the model. We would be kidding ourselves to think that all model inputs are known with certainty. For example, the size of an order is not always $40—it might be, say, from $10 to $100. When there is a high degree of uncertainty about model inputs, it makes little sense to talk about *the* profit level or *the* breakeven response rate. It makes much more sense to talk about the *probability* that profit will have a certain value or the *probability* that the company will break even. It is too early to discuss this topic right now, but in Chapters 11 and 12 we will discuss in detail how simulation can be used to factor uncertainty into the analysis.

Using the Auditing Tool The model in this example is fairly small and simple. Even so, it is useful to illustrate a little-known Excel feature to see how all of the parts fit together. This is the Auditing tool, available from the Auditing toolbar (also available from the Tools menu). See Figure 2.5. This toolbar is not even on the list of toolbars you see if you right-click on any visible toolbar (or use the View/Toolbars menu item), but you can find it as follows. Right-click on any toolbar, select the Customize item, and click on the Toolbars tab. Now the Auditing toolbar *is* on the list, so you can check its box to make it visible. You might even like it well enough to keep it visible *all* the time.

FIGURE 2.5
Auditing Toolbar

The first and third buttons from the left (Trace Precedents and Trace Dependents) are probably the most useful buttons on this toolbar. To see which formulas have direct links to the NumResponses cell, select this cell and click on the Trace Dependents button. Arrows are drawn to each cell that directly depends on the NumResponses, as shown in Figure 2.6. In the other direction, to see which cells are used to create the formula in the Revenue cell, select this cell and click on the Trace Precedents button.

FIGURE 2.6
Dependents of
NumResponses Cell

	A	B	C	D	E
1	Great Threads direct mail model				
2					
3	Mailing inputs			Model of responses	
4	Fixed cost of printing	$20,000		Response rate (trial value)	8%
5	Variable costs			Number of responses	● 8000
6	Printing	$0.10			
7	Mailing, buying names	$0.15		Model of revenue, costs, and profit	
8	Number mailed	100000		Revenue	$320,000
9				Costs	
10	Order inputs			Fixed	$20,000
11	Average order	$40		Variable from mailing	$25,000
12	Variable cost (% of order)	80%		Variable from orders	$257,600
13	Variable cost of envelopes	$0.20		Total cost	$302,600
14				Profit	$17,400

FIGURE 2.7
Precedents of
Revenue Cell

	A	B	C	D	E
1	Great Threads direct mail model				
2					
3	Mailing inputs			Model of responses	
4	Fixed cost of printing	$20,000		Response rate (trial value)	8%
5	Variable costs			Number of responses	● 8000
6	Printing	$0.10			
7	Mailing, buying names	$0.15		Model of revenue, costs, and profit	
8	Number mailed	100000		Revenue	$320,000
9				Costs	
10	Order inputs			Fixed	$20,000
11	Average order	● $40		Variable from mailing	$25,000
12	Variable cost (% of order)	80%		Variable from orders	$257,600
13	Variable cost of envelopes	$0.20		Total cost	$302,600
14				Profit	$17,400

Now you will see that the AvgOrder and NumResponses cells were used directly to calculate Revenue, as shown in Figure 2.7. Using these two buttons, you can trace your logic (or someone else's logic) as far backward or forward as you like. When you are finished, just click on the Remove All Arrows button (fifth from the left).

Other Modeling Issues Is the layout in Figure 2.1 the best possible layout? This question is probably not too crucial for this model because this model is so small. However, we have put all of the inputs together (usually a good practice), and we have put all of the outputs together in a logical order. You might want to put the answers to questions 1 and 2 on separate sheets, but with such a small model, it is probably better to keep everything on a single sheet. We generally use separate sheets only when things start getting bigger and more complex. One final issue is placement of the chart. As you probably know from using the Chart Wizard, the last step of the wizard allows you to select whether you want to place the chart on the worksheet (floating above the cells) or on a separate "chart sheet" that has no rows or columns. This choice depends on your personal preference—neither choice is necessarily better than the other—but for this small model, we believe once again that everything on a single sheet provides the best layout. ■

Estimating the Relationship Between Price and Demand

The following example illustrates a very important modeling concept: estimating relationships between variables by **curve fitting**. We will study this topic in much more depth when we study regression in Chapter 15, but we can illustrate the ideas at a relatively low level by taking advantage of some of Excel's useful features.

EXAMPLE | **2.2**

ESTIMATING SENSITIVITY OF DEMAND TO PRICE AT LINKS

The Links Company sells its golf clubs at golf outlet stores throughout the United States. The company knows that demand for its clubs varies considerably with price. In fact, the price has varied over the past 12 months, and the demand at each price level has been observed. The data are in the Data sheet of the file GOLFCLUBS.XLS. (See Figure 2.8.) For example, during the last month, when the price was $390, 68,000 sets of clubs were sold. (The demands in column C are in thousands of units. The cell comment in cell C3 reminds us of this.) The company would like to estimate the relationship between demand and price. Then it would like to use this estimated relationship to answer the following questions:

1. Assuming the unit cost of producing a set of clubs is $250 and the price must be a multiple of $10, what price should Links charge to maximize its profit?
2. How does the optimal price depend on the unit cost of producing a set of clubs?
3. Is the model an accurate representation of reality?

Solution

We divide this example into two parts: estimating the relationship between price and demand, and creating the profit model. We begin with the estimation problem.

Estimating the Relationship Between Price and Demand A scatterplot of demand versus price appears in Figure 2.9. (This can be created in the usual way with Excel's Chart Wizard and the X-Y chart option, or it can be done even more easily with StatPro's StatPro/Charts/Scatterplot menu item.) Obviously, demand decreases as price increases, but we want to be more specific. Therefore, after creating this chart, select the Chart/Add Trendline menu item to bring up the dialog box in Figure 2.10 (page 38). This allows you to superimpose several different curves (including a straight line) onto the scatterplot. We will consider the **linear**, **power**, and **exponential** curves, defined by the general equations below (where y and x, a general output and input, correspond to demand and price for this example):

- Linear: $y = a + bx$
- Power: $y = ax^b$
- Exponential: $y = ae^{bx}$

Before proceeding, we describe some general properties of these three functions because of their widespread applicability. The linear function is the easiest. Its graph is a straight line. When x changes by 1 unit, y changes by b units. The constant a is called the intercept, and b is called the slope.

FIGURE 2.8
Demand and Price
Data for Golf Clubs

	A	B	C
1	Demand for golf clubs		
2			
3	Month	Price	Demand
4	1	450	45
5	2	300	103
6	3	440	49
7	4	360	86
8	5	290	125
9	6	450	52
10	7	340	87
11	8	370	68
12	9	500	45
13	10	490	44
14	11	430	58
15	12	390	68

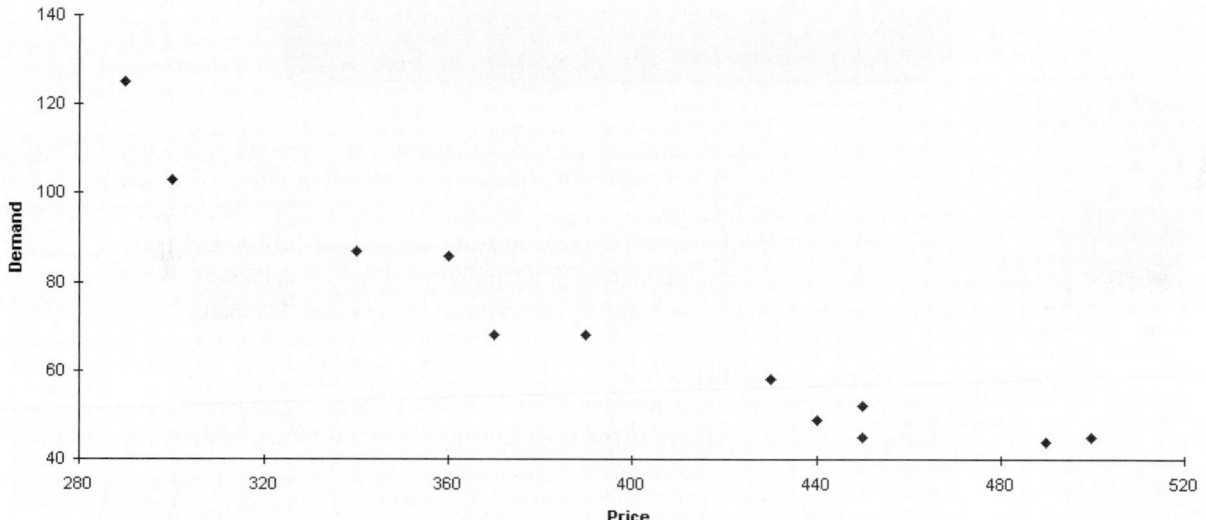

FIGURE 2.9 Scatterplot of Demand Versus Price

The power function is a curve except in the special case where the exponent b is 1. (Then it is a straight line.) The shape of this curve depends primarily on the exponent b. If $b > 1$, y increases at an increasing rate as x increases. If $0 < b < 1$, y increases, but at a decreasing rate, as x increases. Finally, if $b < 0$, y decreases as x increases. An important property of the power curve is that when x changes by 1%, y changes by a constant percentage, and this percentage is approximately equal to b%. For example, if we find that $y = 100x^{-2.35}$, then every 1% increase in x leads to an approximate 2.35% decrease in y.

The exponential function also represents a curve whose shape depends primarily on the constant b in the exponent. If $b > 0$, y increases as x increases; if $b < 0$, y decreases as x increases. An important property of the exponential function is that if x changes by 1 unit, y changes by a constant percentage, and this percentage is approximately equal to $100 \times b$%. For example, if we find that $y = 100e^{-0.014x}$, then whenever x increases by 1 unit, y decreases by approximately 1.4%. By the way, e is the special number 2.7182..., and e to any power can be calculated in Excel with the EXP function. For example, we can calculate $e^{-0.014}$ with the formula =EXP(-.014).

FIGURE 2.10
Add Trendline
Dialog Box

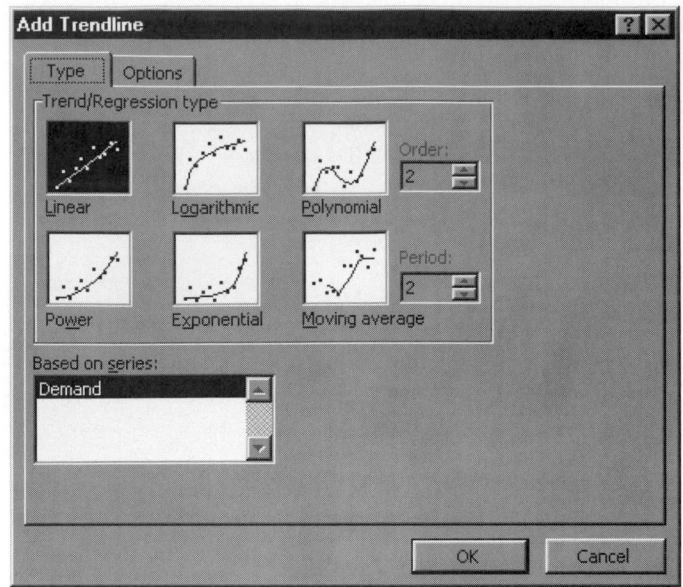

Returning to the example, if we superimpose any of these curves on the scatterplot of demand versus price, Excel will choose the best-fitting curve of that type. Better yet, if we click on the Options tab of the dialog in Figure 2.10 and check the Display Equation on Chart option, we see the equation of this best-fitting curve. Doing this for each type of curve, we obtain the results in Figures 2.11, 2.12, and 2.13. (The equations will not appear exactly as in the figures. However, they can be resized and reformatted to appear as shown.)

Each of these curves provides the best-fitting member of its "family" to the de-mand/price data, but which of these three is best overall? We answer this question by finding the **mean absolute percentage error** (MAPE) for each of the three curves. To

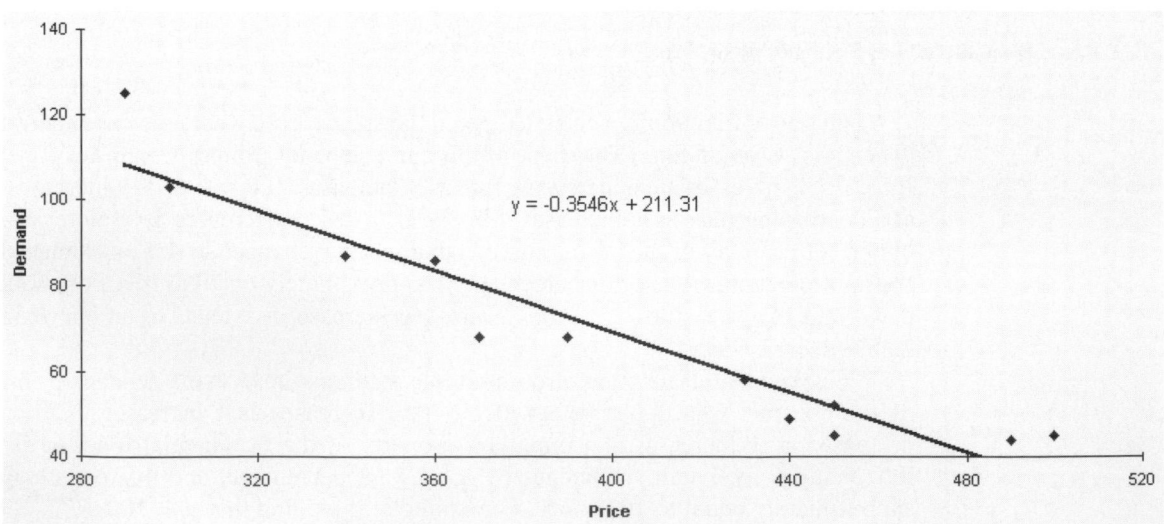

FIGURE 2.11 Best-Fitting Straight Line

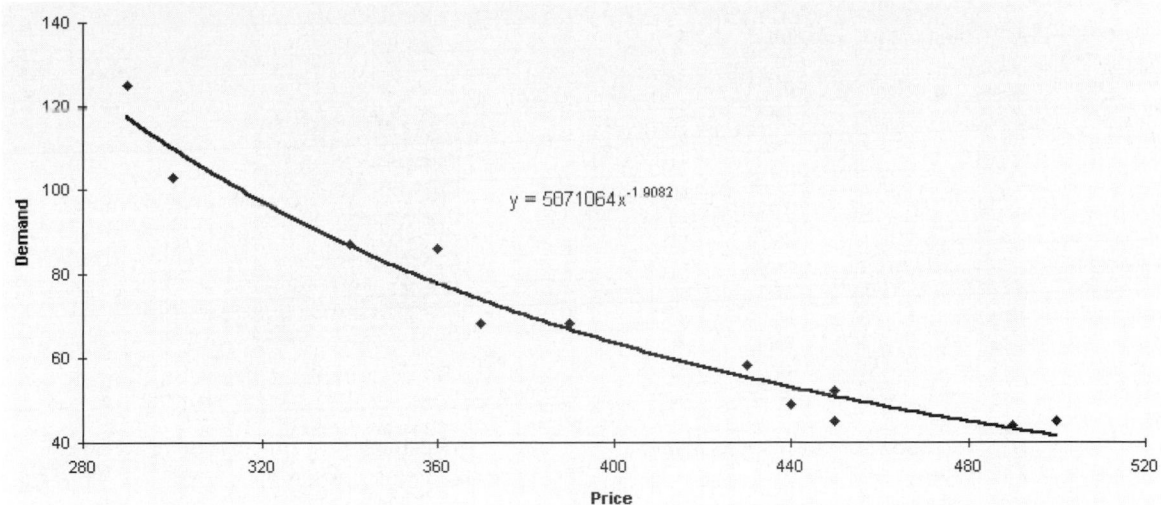

FIGURE 2.12 Best-Fitting Power Curve

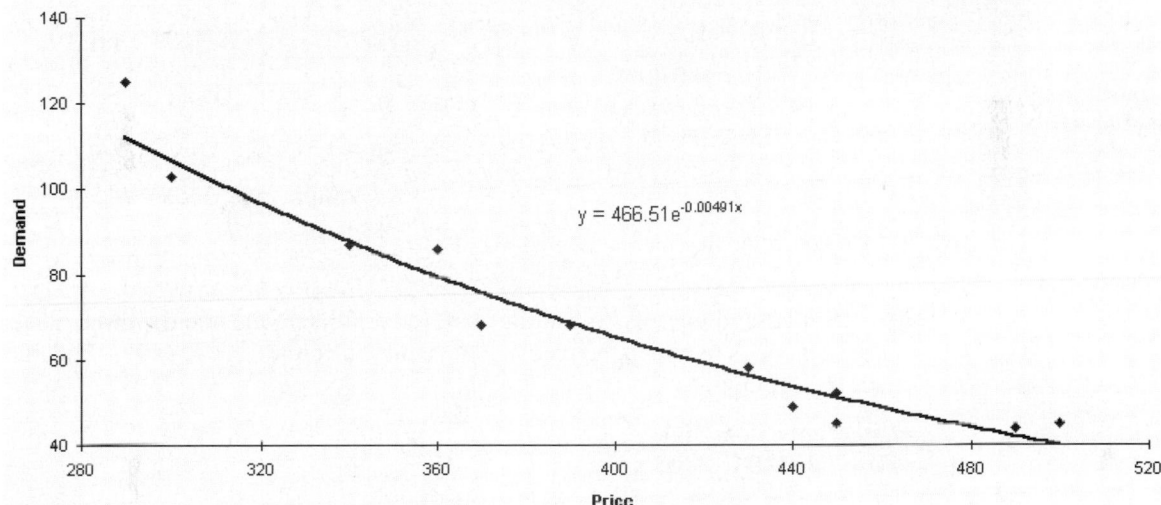

FIGURE 2.13 Best-Fitting Exponential Curve

do this, for any price in the data set and any of the three curves, we first predict demand by substituting the given price into the equation for the curve. The predicted demand will typically not be the same as the observed demand, so we calculate the absolute percentage error (APE) with the general formula

$$\text{APE} = \frac{|\text{Observed demand} - \text{Predicted demand}|}{\text{Observed demand}} \tag{2.1}$$

Then we average these values of APE for any curve to get its MAPE. We will consider the curve with the smallest MAPE as the best fit overall.

The calculations appear in Figure 2.14 (page 40). After (manually) entering the parameters of the equations from the scatterplots into column B and giving them the range names shown, proceed as follows.

	A	B	C	D	E	F	G	H	I	J
1	**Demand for golf clubs**									
2										
3	Month	Price	Demand							
4	1	450	45							
5	2	300	103				Range names			
6	3	440	49				used:			
7	4	360	86				Intercept - B19			
8	5	290	125				Slope - B20			
9	6	450	52				PowConst - B22			
10	7	340	87				PowExpon - B23			
11	8	370	68				ExpConst - B25			
12	9	500	45				ExpExpon - B26			
13	10	490	44							
14	11	430	58							
15	12	390	68							
16										
17	**Parameters of best-fitting curves**				**Predictions**			**Absolute percentage error**		
18	Linear				Linear	Power	Exponential	Linear	Power	Exponential
19	Intercept	211.31			51.74	50.80	51.20	14.98%	12.89%	13.78%
20	Slope	-0.3546			104.93	110.12	106.94	1.87%	6.91%	3.83%
21	Power				55.29	53.02	53.78	12.83%	8.21%	9.75%
22	Constant	5871064			83.65	77.76	79.65	2.73%	9.58%	7.38%
23	Exponent	-1.9082			108.48	117.48	112.32	13.22%	6.01%	10.14%
24	Exponential				51.74	50.80	51.20	0.50%	2.31%	1.53%
25	Constant	466.51			90.75	86.73	87.87	4.31%	0.32%	1.00%
26	Exponent	-0.00491			80.11	73.80	75.84	17.81%	8.53%	11.52%
27					34.01	41.55	40.06	24.42%	7.67%	10.99%
28					37.56	43.18	42.07	14.65%	1.86%	4.38%
29					58.83	55.40	56.49	1.43%	4.48%	2.61%
30					73.02	66.75	68.74	7.38%	1.84%	1.09%
31							MAPEs ->	9.68%	5.88%	6.50%

FIGURE 2.14 Finding the Best-Fitting Curve Overall

❶ **Predicted demands.** Substitute observed prices into the linear, power, and exponential functions to obtain the predicted demands in columns E, F, and G. Specifically, enter the formulas

=Intercept+Slope*B4
=PowConst*B4^PowExpon

and

=ExpConst*EXP(ExpExpon*B4)

in cells E19, F19, and G19, and copy them down their respective columns.

❷ **Average percentage errors.** Apply equation (2.1) to calculate APEs in columns H, I, and J. Specifically, enter the general formula

=ABS($C4-E19)/$C4

in cell H19 and copy it to the range H19:J30. (Do you see why column C is made absolute?)

❸ **MAPE.** Average the APEs in each column with the AVERAGE function to get the MAPEs in row 31.

Evidently, the power curve provides the best fit, with a MAPE of 5.88%. In words, its predictions are off, on average, by 5.88%. This power curve predicts that each 1% increase in price leads to an approximate 1.9% decrease in demand. (Economists would call this relationship very elastic—demand is very sensitive to price.)

DEVELOPING THE PROFIT MODEL

Now we move to the profit model, using the best-fitting power curve to predict demand from price. The model appears in Figure 2.15. Note there is now one input variable, unit variable cost, and one decision variable, unit price. (We put a red border around the decision variable to distinguish it as such. This is another convention we will continue throughout the book.) The profit model is straightforward to develop using the following steps.

❶ Predicted demand. Calculate the *predicted* demand in the PredDemand cell with the formula

=PowConst*UnitPrice$^\wedge$PowExpon

This uses the power function we estimated earlier.

❷ Revenue, cost, profit. Enter the following formulas in the TotRev, TotCost, and Profit:

=UnitPrice*PredDemand
=UnitCost*PredDemand

and

=TotRev-TotCost

Here we assume that the company produces exactly enough sets of clubs to meet customer demand.

FIGURE 2.15
Profit Model

	A	B	C	D	E	F
1	Profit model, using best fitting power curve for estimating demand					
2						
3	**Monetary inputs**			**Range names used:**		
4	Unit cost to produce	$250		UnitCost - B4		
5				UnitPrice - B7		
6	**Decision variable**			PredDemand - B10		
7	Unit price (trial value)	$400		TotRev - B11		
8				TotCost - B12		
9	**Profit model**			Profit B13		
10	Predicted demand	63.601		MaxProfit - B16		
11	Total revenue	$25,441		Prices - A22:A71		
12	Total cost	$15,900		Profits - B22:B71		
13	Profit	$9,540				

Maximizing Profit To see which price maximizes profit, we build the data table shown in Figure 2.16 (page 42). Here, the column input cell is UnitPrice and the "linking" formula in cell B21 is **=Profit**. The corresponding chart (a line chart) shows that profit first increases, then decreases. We can find the maximum profit and corresponding price in at least three ways. First, we can attempt to read them from the chart. Second, we can scan down the data table for the maximum profit, which we indicate in the figure. The following Excel tip describes a third method that uses some of Excel's more exotic features.

Excel Tip: Conditional Formatting We colored cell B49 in Figure 2.16 because it corresponds to the maximum profit in the column, but Excel's Conditional Formatting tool can do this for you—automatically.[3] First, enter the formula **=MAX(Profits)** in

---

[3]The value in cell B48 also appears to be the maximum, but to two decimals, it is slightly lower.

FIGURE 2.16
Profit as a Function
of Price

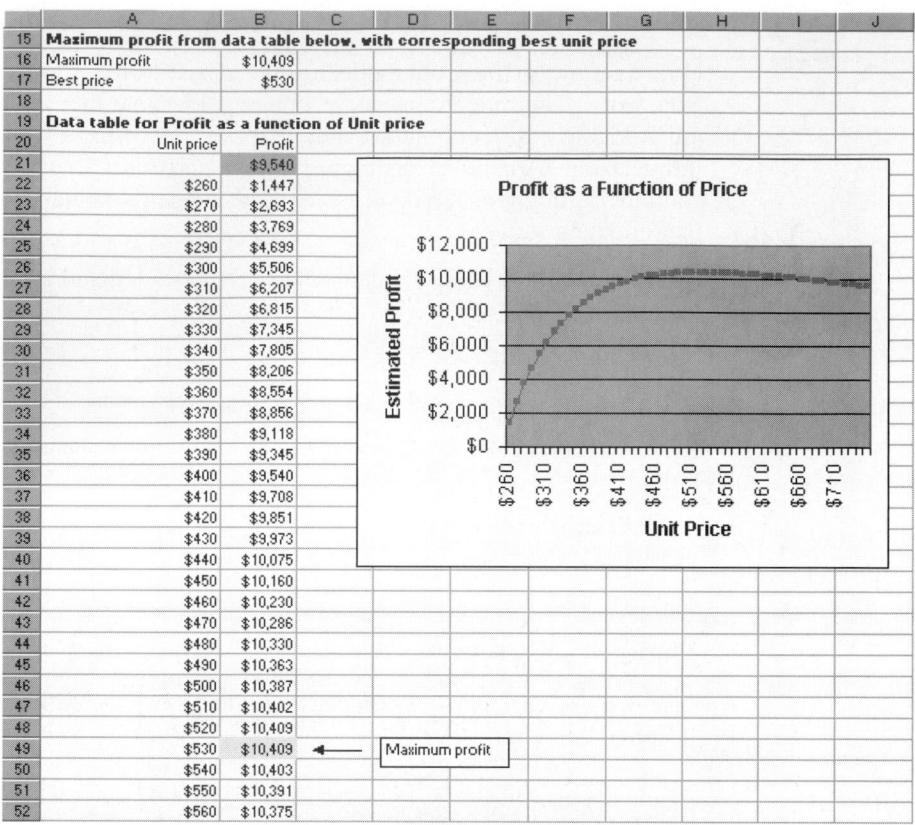

	A	B	C	D	E	F	G	H	I	J
15	**Maximum profit from data table below, with corresponding best unit price**									
16	Maximum profit	$10,409								
17	Best price	$530								
18										
19	**Data table for Profit as a function of Unit price**									
20	Unit price	Profit								
21		$9,540								
22	$260	$1,447								
23	$270	$2,693								
24	$280	$3,769								
25	$290	$4,699								
26	$300	$5,506								
27	$310	$6,207								
28	$320	$6,815								
29	$330	$7,345								
30	$340	$7,805								
31	$350	$8,206								
32	$360	$8,554								
33	$370	$8,856								
34	$380	$9,118								
35	$390	$9,345								
36	$400	$9,540								
37	$410	$9,708								
38	$420	$9,851								
39	$430	$9,973								
40	$440	$10,075								
41	$450	$10,160								
42	$460	$10,230								
43	$470	$10,286								
44	$480	$10,330								
45	$490	$10,363								
46	$500	$10,387								
47	$510	$10,402								
48	$520	$10,409								
49	$530	$10,409	←		Maximum profit					
50	$540	$10,403								
51	$550	$10,391								
52	$560	$10,375								

FIGURE 2.17
Conditional
Formatting Dialog
Box

Conditional Formatting ? ×

Condition 1
| Cell Value Is ▾ | equal to ▾ | =$B$16 |

Preview of format to use
when condition is true: AaBbCcYyZz   Format...

[?]   Add >>   Delete...   OK   Cancel

cell B16 to find the maximum profit from the data table. Next, highlight the range of profits (B22:B71), select the Format/Conditional Formatting menu item to bring up the dialog box in Figure 2.17, and fill it in as shown. Excel will scan the range you selected and apply the selected format (we chose a pale blue cell background) to every cell that meets the condition—the cell value is equal to the maximum value in cell B16—in the top line of the dialog box. You can even base the formatting on more than one condition (up to three) by clicking on the Add button. This is a great tool!

What about the corresponding best price, shown in cell B17 of Figure 2.16? You could enter this manually, but wouldn't it be nice if you could get Excel to find the maximum profit in the data table, determine the price in the cell to its left, and report it in cell B17, all automatically? There *is* a way—just enter the formula

=INDEX(Prices,MATCH(MaxProfit,Profits,0),1)

in cell B17, and the best price appears. This formula uses two Excel functions, MATCH and INDEX. MATCH compares the first argument (the MaxProfit cell) to the range specified in the second argument (the Profits range), and returns the index of the cell where a match appears. (The third argument, 0, specifies that we want an *exact* match.) In this case, the MATCH function returns 28 because the maximum profit is in the 28th cell of the Profits range. Then the INDEX function is called effectively as **=INDEX(Prices,28,1)**. The first argument is the Prices range, the second is a row index, and the third is a column index. Very simply, this function says to return the value in the 28th row and first column of the Prices range.

How do we learn about such exotic functions? We clicked on the Paste Function button (the f_x button) on the top toolbar and examined the functions in the Lookup & Reference category. After experimenting, we found that the INDEX and MATCH combination would solve our problem. We are not necessarily suggesting that you should memorize these functions, although this combination really does come in handy. Rather, our point is that you can often solve a problem by investigating some of Excel's less well-known features. You do not even need a manual—everything is there in online help.

Sensitivity to Variable Cost We now return to question 2 in the example: How does the best price change as the unit variable cost changes? We can answer this question with a **two-way data table**. This is a data table with two inputs, one along the left side and the other across the top row, and a single output. The two inputs for our problem are unit variable cost and unit price, and the single output is profit. The corresponding data table is in the range A80:F165, the top part of which appears in Figure 2.18. To develop this table, enter desired inputs in column A and row 80, enter the "linking" formula **=Profit** in cell A80 (it always goes in the top left corner of a two-way data table), highlight the entire table, select the Data/Table menu item, and enter UnitCost as the Row Input Cell and UnitPrice as the Column Input Cell.

As before, you can scan the columns of the data table for the maximum profits and enter them (manually) in rows 75 and 76. (Alternatively, you can use the more

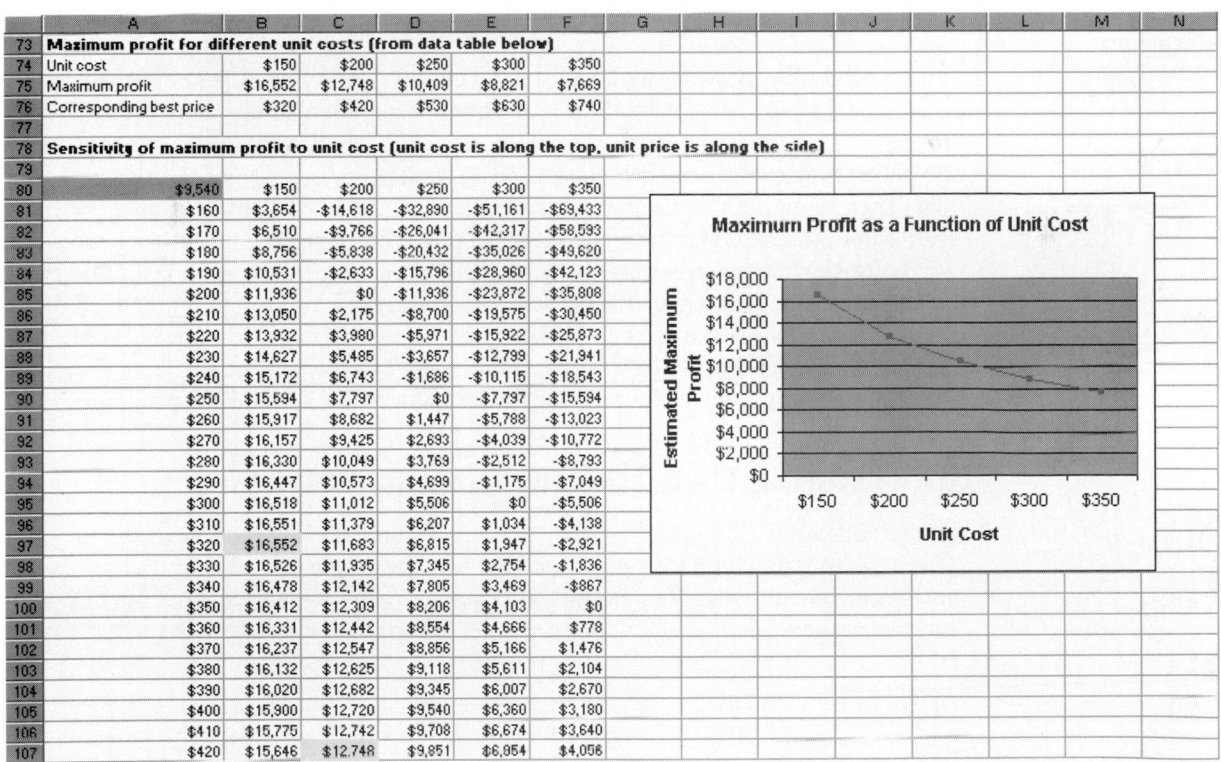

	A	B	C	D	E	F
73	Maximum profit for different unit costs (from data table below)					
74	Unit cost	$150	$200	$250	$300	$350
75	Maximum profit	$16,552	$12,748	$10,409	$8,821	$7,669
76	Corresponding best price	$320	$420	$530	$630	$740
77						
78	Sensitivity of maximum profit to unit cost (unit cost is along the top, unit price is along the side)					
79						
80	$9,540	$150	$200	$250	$300	$350
81	$160	$3,654	-$14,618	-$32,890	-$51,161	-$69,433
82	$170	$6,510	-$9,766	-$26,041	-$42,317	-$58,593
83	$180	$8,756	-$5,838	-$20,432	-$35,026	-$49,620
84	$190	$10,531	-$2,633	-$15,796	-$28,960	-$42,123
85	$200	$11,936	$0	-$11,936	-$23,872	-$35,808
86	$210	$13,050	$2,175	-$8,700	-$19,575	-$30,450
87	$220	$13,932	$3,980	-$5,971	-$15,922	-$25,873
88	$230	$14,627	$5,485	-$3,657	-$12,799	-$21,941
89	$240	$15,172	$6,743	-$1,686	-$10,115	-$18,543
90	$250	$15,594	$7,797	$0	-$7,797	-$15,594
91	$260	$15,917	$8,682	$1,447	-$5,788	-$13,023
92	$270	$16,157	$9,425	$2,693	-$4,039	-$10,772
93	$280	$16,330	$10,049	$3,769	-$2,512	-$8,793
94	$290	$16,447	$10,573	$4,699	-$1,175	-$7,049
95	$300	$16,518	$11,012	$5,506	$0	-$5,506
96	$310	$16,551	$11,379	$6,207	$1,034	-$4,138
97	$320	$16,552	$11,683	$6,815	$1,947	-$2,921
98	$330	$16,526	$11,935	$7,345	$2,754	-$1,836
99	$340	$16,478	$12,142	$7,805	$3,469	-$867
100	$350	$16,412	$12,309	$8,206	$4,103	$0
101	$360	$16,331	$12,442	$8,554	$4,666	$778
102	$370	$16,237	$12,547	$8,856	$5,166	$1,476
103	$380	$16,132	$12,625	$9,118	$5,611	$2,104
104	$390	$16,020	$12,682	$9,345	$6,007	$2,670
105	$400	$15,900	$12,720	$9,540	$6,360	$3,180
106	$410	$15,775	$12,742	$9,708	$6,674	$3,640
107	$420	$15,646	$12,748	$9,851	$6,954	$4,056

FIGURE 2.18 Profit as a Function of Unit Cost and Unit Price

exotic Excel features described in the previous Excel tip to accomplish these tasks. Take a look at the GOLFCLUBS.XLS file for details.) Then you can create a chart of maximum profit (or best price) versus unit cost. The chart in Figure 2.18 shows that the maximum profit decreases, but at a decreasing rate, as unit cost increases.

Limitations of the Model Question 3 asks us to step back from all of these details and evaluate whether the model is realistic. First, there is no real reason why golf club prices should be restricted to be multiples of $10. We required this only so we could use a data table to find the profit-maximizing price. Ideally, we would like to have a way to search over *all* possible prices to find the profit-maximizing price. Fortunately, Excel's built-in Solver tool enables us to accomplish this task fairly easily. The problem of finding a profit-maximizing price is an example of an **optimization model**. In optimization models we try to maximize or minimize a specified output cell by changing the values of the decision variable cells. Chapters 3–9 contain a detailed discussion of optimization models.

A second possible limitation of our model is the implicit assumption that price is the *only* factor that influences demand. In reality, other factors such as advertising, the state of the economy, competitors' prices, strength of competition, and promotional expenses also influence demand. In Chapter 15 we will learn how to use multiple regression to analyze the dependence of one variable on two or more other variables. This technique would allow us to incorporate other factors into the model for profit.

A final limitation of our model is that demand might not *equal* sales. For example, if actual demand for golf clubs during a year is 70,000 but the company's annual capacity is only 50,000, the company would observe sales of only 50,000. This would cause us to underestimate *actual* demand, and our curve fitting method would produce biased predictions. (Can you guess the probable effect on pricing decisions?)

As these comments indicate, most models are not perfect, but we have to start somewhere!

Other Modeling Issues The layout of the GOLFCLUBS.XLS file is fairly straightforward. However, we note that there are five sheets, not a single sheet. This is partly for logical purposes and partly to reduce clutter. There are two worksheets, one for the estimation model and one for the profit model. It seems logical to separate the two. Then there are three separate chart sheets for the linear, power, and exponential scatterplots. These could have been superimposed on the estimation model sheet, but we prefer separate chart sheets—it is basically a matter of taste. One last issue is the placement of the data tables for the sensitivity analysis. You might be inclined to put these on a separate Sensitivity sheet. However, Excel will not allow you to build a data table on one sheet that uses a row or column input cell from *another* sheet. Therefore, we are practically forced to put the data tables on the same sheet as the profit model. ■

An Ordering Decision with Quantity Discounts

In the following example we again attempt to find the appropriate level of some activity—how much of a product to order when customer demand for the product is uncertain. Two important features of this example are the presence of quantity discounts and the explicit use of probabilities to model uncertain demand.

EXAMPLE 2.3

ORDERING WITH QUANTITY DISCOUNTS AT SAM'S BOOKSTORES

Sam's Bookstore, with many locations across the United States, places orders for all of the latest books and then distributes them to its individual bookstores. Sam's needs a model to help it order the appropriate number of any title. For example, it plans to order a popular new hardback novel, which it will sell for $30. It can purchase any number of this book from the publisher, but due to quantity discounts, the unit cost for *all* books it orders depends on the number ordered. Specifically, if the number ordered is less than 1000, the unit cost is $24. After each 1000, the unit cost drops: to $23 for at least 1000 copies, to $22.25 for at least 2000, to $21.75 for at least 3000, and to $21.30 (the lowest possible unit cost) for at least 4000. For example, if Sam's orders 2500 books, its total cost is $22.25(2500) = $55,625. Sam's is very uncertain about the demand for this book—it estimates that demand could be anywhere from 500 to 4500. Also, as with most hardback novels, this one will eventually come out in paperback. Therefore, if Sam's has any hardbacks left when the paperback comes out, it will put them on sale for $10, at which price it believes all leftovers will be sold. How many copies of this hardback novel should Sam's order from the publisher?

Solution

We will first develop a model to calculate Sam's profit for any order quantity and any possible demand. Then we will perform a sensitivity analysis to see how profit depends on these two quantities. Finally, we will indicate one possible method Sam's might use to choose the "best" order quantity.

DEVELOPING THE SPREADSHEET MODEL

The profit model appears in Figure 2.19 (page 46). (See the file QUANTITYDIS-COUNT.XLS.) Note that the order quantity and demand in the OrderQuan and Demand cells are "trial" values. We can put any values in these cells, just to test the logic of the model. Also, note how we have used a table to indicate the quantity discounts for ordering. After entering the inputs and trial values of order quantity and demand, use the following steps to complete the model.

❶ **Revenues.** Sam's can sell only what it has, and it will sell any leftovers at the discounted sale price. Therefore, enter the formulas

=MIN(OrderQuan,Demand)
=IF(OrderQuan>Demand,OrderQuan-Demand,0)

and

=SoldReg*UnitPrice+SoldSale*SalePrice

in the SoldReg, SoldSale, and Revenue cells. The logic in the first two of these cells is necessary to account correctly for the case when the order quantity is greater than demand and its opposite.

❷ **Total ordering cost.** Depending on the order quantity, we find the appropriate unit cost from the unit cost table and multiply it by the order quantity to obtain the

	A	B	C	D	E	F	G	H	I
1	Ordering decision with quantity discounts								
2									
3	Inputs			Unit cost as a function of quantity ordered					
4	Unit cost - see table to right			At least	Unit cost				
5	Unit price	$30		0	$24.00		Range names used:		
6	Sale price for leftovers	$10		1000	$23.00		UnitPrice - B5		
7				2000	$22.25		SalePrice - B6		
8	Order quantity (trial value)	2500		3000	$21.75		CostLookup - D5:E9		
9				4000	$21.30		OrderQuan - B8		
10	Profit model						Demand - B11		
11	Demand (trial value)	2000					SoldReg - B12		
12	Units sold at regular price	2000					SoldSale - B13		
13	Units sold at sale price	500					Revenue - B14		
14	Revenue	$65,000					Cost - B15		
15	Cost	$55,625					Profit - B16		
16	Profit	$9,375					Probabilities - B32:J32		

FIGURE 2.19 Sam's Profit Model

total ordering cost. This could be accomplished with a complex nested IF formula, but a much better way is to use the VLOOKUP function. Specifically, enter the formula

=VLOOKUP(OrderQuan,CostLookup,2)*OrderQuan

in the Cost cell. The VLOOKUP part of this formula says to compare the order quantity to the first (leftmost) column of the table in the CostLookup range and return the corresponding value in the second column (because the last argument is 2). Here, "compare" means to scan down the leftmost column of the table and find the first entry greater than or equal to the order quantity. In general, there are two important things to remember about lookup tables: (1) the leftmost column is always the column used for comparison, and (2) the entries in this column must be arranged in increasing order from top to bottom.

❸ Profit. Calculate the profit with the formula

=Revenue-Cost

The next step is to create a data table for profit as a function of the order quantity and demand. This appears in Figure 2.20. (We will not spell out the details of creating the data table. We'll simply remind you that the Row Input Cell is Demand, the Column Input Cell is OrderQuan, and the linking formula in cell A19 is **=Profit**.) We have used the same values for both order quantity and demand, from 500 to 4500 in increments of 500. This is not necessary—we could let demand change in increments of 100 or even 1, for instance—but it is reasonable. Perhaps Sam's is required by the publisher to order in multiples of 500. This data table shows that profit depends heavily on both order quantity and demand, and (by scanning across rows) how higher demands lead to larger profits. But it is still far from clear which order quantity Sam's should select. Remember that Sam's has complete control over the order quantity (it can choose the *row* of the data table), but it has no direct control over demand (it cannot choose the column).

The ordering decision depends not only on which demands are *possible*, but on which demands are *likely* to occur. The usual way to express this information is with a set of probabilities that sum to 1. We show one possible set in Figure 2.21. Sam's would need to estimate these probabilities, possibly on the basis of other similar books it has sold in the past. The ones shown indicate that Sam's believes the most likely demands are 2000 and 2500, with other values on both sides less likely. Now we can use these probabilities to find an *expected* profit for each order quantity. This expected profit is a

	A	B	C	D	E	F	G	H	I	J
18	Data table of profit as a function of order quantity (along side) and demand (along top)									
19	$9,375	500	1000	1500	2000	2500	3000	3500	4000	4500
20	500	$3,000	$3,000	$3,000	$3,000	$3,000	$3,000	$3,000	$3,000	$3,000
21	1000	-$3,000	$7,000	$7,000	$7,000	$7,000	$7,000	$7,000	$7,000	$7,000
22	1500	-$9,500	$500	$10,500	$10,500	$10,500	$10,500	$10,500	$10,500	$10,500
23	2000	-$14,500	-$4,500	$5,500	$15,500	$15,500	$15,500	$15,500	$15,500	$15,500
24	2500	-$20,625	-$10,625	-$625	$9,375	$19,375	$19,375	$19,375	$19,375	$19,375
25	3000	-$25,250	-$15,250	-$5,250	$4,750	$14,750	$24,750	$24,750	$24,750	$24,750
26	3500	-$31,125	-$21,125	-$11,125	-$1,125	$8,875	$18,875	$28,875	$28,875	$28,875
27	4000	-$35,200	-$25,200	-$15,200	-$5,200	$4,800	$14,800	$24,800	$34,800	$34,800
28	4500	-$40,850	-$30,850	-$20,850	-$10,850	-$850	$9,150	$19,150	$29,150	$39,150

FIGURE 2.20 Profit as a Function of Order Quantity and Demand

	A	B	C	D	E	F	G	H	I	J
30	Model of expected demands									
31	Demand	500	1000	1500	2000	2500	3000	3500	4000	4500
32	Probability	0.025	0.05	0.15	0.25	0.25	0.15	0.07	0.04	0.015
33								Sum of probabilities -->		1
34	Order quantity	Expected profit								
35	500	$3,000								
36	1000	$6,750								
37	1500	$9,500		Order 2000 to						
38	2000	$12,250 ←		maximize the						
39	2500	$11,375		expected profit.						
40	3000	$9,500								
41	3500	$4,875								
42	4000	$1,350								
43	4500	-$4,150								

FIGURE 2.21 Comparison of Expected Profits

weighted average of the profits in any row in the data table, using the probabilities as the weights. The easiest way to do this is to enter the formula

=SUMPRODUCT(B20:J20,Probabilities)

in cell B35 and copy it down to cell B43. The SUMPRODUCT function takes two range arguments, which must be *exactly the same size and shape*, and sums the products of the corresponding cell values in these two ranges. It is an extremely useful function, and we will use it repeatedly throughout this book.

The largest of the expected profits, $12,250, corresponds to an order quantity of 2000, so we would recommend that Sam's order 2000 copies of the book. This does not guarantee that Sam's will make a profit of $12,250—the actual profit depends on the eventual demand—but it represents a reasonable way to proceed in the face of uncertain demand. We will have much more to say about making decisions under uncertainty and the expected value criterion in Chapter 10.

Other Modeling Issues Remember that when you develop a spreadsheet model, you start with a blank sheet. You can put anything anywhere you want. So why, for example, did we put order quantities along the side and demands along the top in the data table in Figure 2.20? There is no good reason; we could have switched them with no negative effects. However, once we do it this way, it is important to be consistent later on. Specifically, when entering the information in Figure 2.21, we keep demands *across a row* and order quantities *down a column*. This is not only logical, but it generally allows us to simplify and copy formulas—a great benefit in the model development process. (Examine the formula in cell B35 carefully to see how our model layout allows us to use a simple SUMPRODUCT formula and to copy this formula down.) ■

An Option Model for Hedging Investment Risk

The financial travails of Orange County, California, Barings Bank, and Long-Term Capital Management testify to the increased volatility in today's financial markets. It is important for any investor (personal or corporate) to understand the fundamental ideas of hedging. The next example provides a simple example of how to hedge equity (or stock market) risk.

Before introducing this example, we need several definitions. First, the **return** from any portfolio of investments is given by the formula

$$\text{Return} = \frac{\text{Amount received} - \text{Amount invested}}{\text{Amount invested}} \qquad \textbf{(2.2)}$$

This can be expressed as a percentage or a decimal (for example, 5% or 0.05). Second, a **European option** on a stock is a contract that gives the owner of the option the right to buy (if the option is a **call** option) or the right to sell (if the option is a **put** option) one share of the stock for a particular price (called the **exercise price**) on a particular date in the future (called the **exercise date**). The price of any option is determined by the famous Black–Scholes formula, a formula that was developed by academics in the 1970s but is now used every day in the financial world. (We will examine this formula in more detail when we study simulation in Chapters 11 and 12.)

The following example shows how spreadsheet models can be used to construct best-case and worst-case scenarios for alternative courses of action.

EXAMPLE   2.4

HEDGING RISK WITH PUT OPTIONS

On June 30, 1998, Harry Rockefeller purchases one share of Dell Computer stock for $94.25. However, Harry is worried about the possibility of Dell's price falling, so he decides to buy some European puts (expiring in 145 days, on November 22, 1998) with an exercise price of $80. Each put is priced at $5.25. As a function of the number of puts purchased, construct a worst-case and best-case scenario for the return earned on Harry's portfolio between June 30, 1998, and November 22, 1998, assuming that he sells his stock on the latter date. How does the analysis change if Harry purchases 100 shares rather than a single share?

Solution

First, because you might not have encountered options before, we provide some intuition. The key is why Harry is considering put options. He believes the price of the stock is going to *fall*. Therefore, he stands to lose on the stock he owns, and he wants to hedge this loss. Now consider what will happen if he purchases puts on the stock. If the stock price falls below the exercise price of $80, say, to $75—and he evidently considers this a possibility—then he can sell a share of stock in November for $80, buy it back right away for $75 (this is called "covering his position"), and make $5. (Of course, this does not take into account the $5.25 cost of the put.) So puts are the appropriate hedging vehicle if the owner of a stock believes the price is about to fall.

To model Harry's problem, we must make some assumptions about the possible price of Dell stock on November 22, 1998. We assume that the price on this date will be between $40 and $150. Next, we need to determine the value of the put at expiration. Recall that a put gives Harry the right to sell a share of stock for $80 on November 22, 1998. If the price of Dell stock on this date is $80 or more, no value can be obtained by selling a share of Dell for $80, so Harry will let his option expire—its value will be 0. However, if the price of Dell on November 22, 1998, is less than $80—say, $75—then we saw that Harry can make $5 by exercising the put.

DEVELOPING THE SPREADSHEET MODEL

The spreadsheet model in Figure 2.22 formalizes this logic. After entering the appropriate inputs, naming ranges, entering *any* trial values for the number of puts purchased and the future stock price, we can develop the model as follows.

❶ **Amount invested.** The total amount invested is the June price of one share of the stock plus the cost of the puts, so enter the formula

=CurrPrice+NumPuts*PutPrice

in the AmtInvested cell.

❷ **Amounts received.** In November, Harry will sell his one share of stock at the going price, and he will exercise his option if the November price is below $80. Therefore, enter the formulas

=FutPrice
=NumPuts*IF(FutPrice>ExerPrice,0,ExerPrice-FutPrice)

and

=SUM(B14:B15)

in cells B14, B15, and B16. The IF function in cell B15 indicates that Harry can earn money by exercising his put(s) only if the future price is less than the exercise price.

❸ **Return.** We use equation (2.2) to calculate the return from Harry's portfolio. The appropriate formula is

=(AmtReceived-AmtInvested)/AmtInvested

which we format as a percentage.

FIGURE 2.22
Hedging Model of
Portfolio Return

	A	B	C	D	E	F
1	**Dell risk hedging model using put options**					
2						
3	**Inputs**					
4	Current price of stock	$94.25				
5	Price per put	$5.25		**Range names used:**		
6	Exercise price	$80.00		CurrPrice - B4		
7				PutPrice - B5		
8	**Decision variable**			ExerPrice - B6		
9	Number of puts to purchase	3		NumPuts - B9		
10				AmtInvested - B12		
11	**Model of portfolio return**			FutPrice - B13		
12	Amount invested	$110.00		AmtReceived - B16		
13	Future stock price (trial value)	$60.00		Return - B17		
14	Amount received from stock	$60.00				
15	Amount received from puts	$60.00				
16	Total amount received	$120.00				
17	Return	9.09%				

The model shows a *positive* 9.09% return, but this is clearly a function of the number of puts Harry purchases and the future price of the stock. To examine this dependency more closely, we use a two-way data table to determine the portfolio return for each stock price between $40 and $150 and each number of puts from 0 to 5. (By now, you should be able to create this table without our help.) Figure 2.23 shows the first few rows of this table. Because it is difficult to digest this many numbers, we create the line chart in Figure 2.24, with a line for each column in the data table. This chart clearly shows how puts shield Harry from risk if the price of the stock falls precipitously. In fact, the more puts he buys, the more he stands to *gain* if the price falls significantly. If the price stays about the same or increases, he loses slightly by

	A	B	C	D	E	F	G	H
19	**Worst and best case returns from data table below for each number of puts purchased**							
20	Number of puts	0	1	2	3	4	5	
21	Worst return	-57.56%	-19.60%	-23.63%	-27.27%	-30.59%	-33.61%	
22	Best return	59.15%	50.75%	43.20%	45.45%	73.54%	99.17%	
23								
24	**Data table of return as a function of future price (along side) and puts purchased (along top)**							
25	9.09%	0	1	2	3	4	5	
26	$40	-57.56%	-19.60%	14.56%	45.45%	73.54%	99.17%	
27	$41	-56.50%	-19.60%	13.60%	43.64%	70.93%	95.85%	
28	$42	-55.44%	-19.60%	12.65%	41.82%	68.33%	92.53%	
29	$43	-54.38%	-19.60%	11.69%	40.00%	65.73%	89.21%	
30	$44	-53.32%	-19.60%	10.74%	38.18%	63.12%	85.89%	
31	$45	-52.25%	-19.60%	9.79%	36.36%	60.52%	82.57%	
32	$46	-51.19%	-19.60%	8.83%	34.55%	57.92%	79.25%	
33	$47	-50.13%	-19.60%	7.88%	32.73%	55.31%	75.93%	
34	$48	-49.07%	-19.60%	6.92%	30.91%	52.71%	72.61%	
35	$49	-48.01%	-19.60%	5.97%	29.09%	50.11%	69.29%	
36	$50	-46.95%	-19.60%	5.01%	27.27%	47.51%	65.98%	
37	$51	-45.89%	-19.60%	4.06%	25.45%	44.90%	62.66%	
38	$52	-44.83%	-19.60%	3.10%	23.64%	42.30%	59.34%	
39	$53	-43.77%	-19.60%	2.15%	21.82%	39.70%	56.02%	
40	$54	-42.71%	-19.60%	1.19%	20.00%	37.09%	52.70%	
41	$55	-41.64%	-19.60%	0.24%	18.18%	34.49%	49.38%	
42	$56	-40.58%	-19.60%	-0.72%	16.36%	31.89%	46.06%	
43	$57	-39.52%	-19.60%	-1.67%	14.55%	29.28%	42.74%	

FIGURE 2.23 Return as a Function of Future Price and Puts Purchased

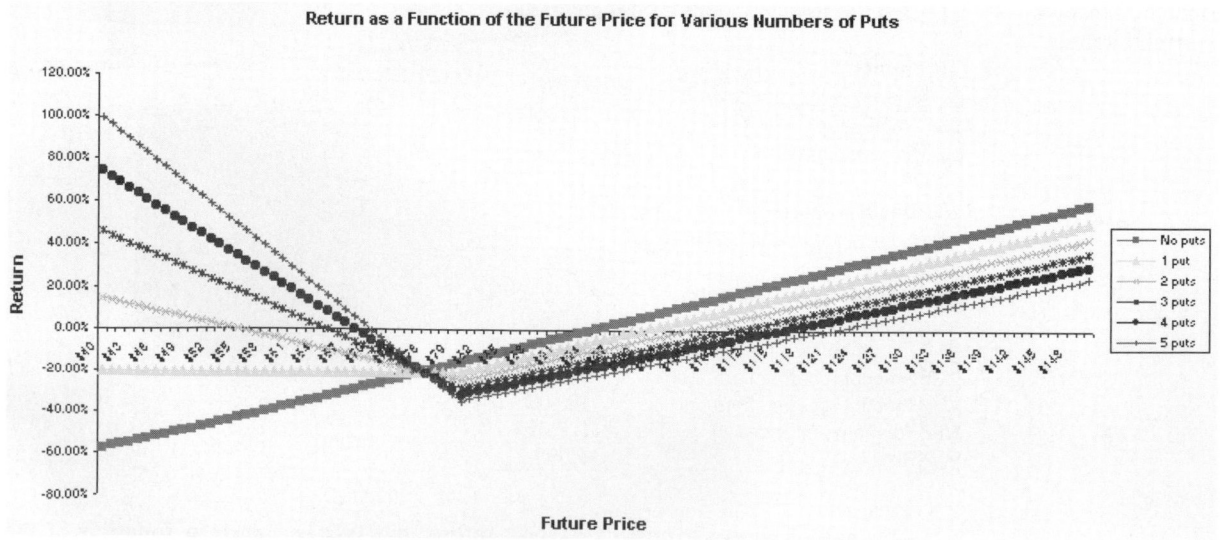

FIGURE 2.24 Return as a Function of Future Price

buying more puts (relative to buying fewer), but the difference is fairly minor. This is illustrated in rows 21 and 22 of Figure 2.23, where we use the MIN and MAX functions on the columns in the data table to find the worst-case and best-case returns. Harry could gain considerably more by purchasing a lot of puts, and his downside risk from doing so is fairly minimal.

Note that if Harry buys no puts, his worst case is a 57.56% loss, whereas if he buys a single put, his worst case is only a 19.6% loss. Here is the reason. With no puts, each $1 decrease in Dell's price decreases his return by $1/94.25 = 1.06\%$. If he owns one put, then any decrease in Dell's price below $80 costs him $1 (because he owns the stock), but this is offset by a $1 increase in the cash flow from the put. Thus, purchasing one put makes him immune to decreases in Dell's stock price below $80. Of course, there is no "free lunch." By purchasing one put, he caps his maximum return at 50.75%. If he buys no puts, his maximum return is 59.15%. The put strategy has a lower upside because the investment in the put suffers a complete loss if Dell's price increases. In effect, the put is portfolio insurance that hedges Harry's downside risk (risk due to decline in stock price) but limits his upside benefits. It is interesting to note that buying many puts (say, five) actually makes Harry's worst case inferior to purchasing one put. The reason is that if Dell drops to $80, Harry loses money on the stock, *and* his investment in five puts is a complete washout!

Nevertheless, it is still not clear how many puts Harry should purchase. As in the previous example, this depends on the probability distribution of the future stock price. It also depends on Harry's attitude toward risk. Does he mind taking risks, or does he avoid them whenever possible? We will investigate these aspects of decision making in more detail in Chapter 10. We will also show how to model the uncertainty of future stock prices when we study simulation in Chapters 11 and 12.

Other Modeling Issues Fortunately, it is easy to "scale" this type of model. If Harry purchases 100 shares of stock rather than one, we simply multiply the appropriate quantities in the model by 100. Specifically, his purchase amount for the stock and the amount he receives by selling the stock both increase by a factor of 100. Of course, if he decides to buy, say, three puts to hedge the risk from owning one share of stock, he will probably buy 300 puts if he owns 100 shares. ∎

Decisions Involving the Time Value of Money

In many business situations, cash flows are received at different points in time, and a company must determine a course of action that maximizes the "value" of cash flows. Here are some examples:

- Should a company buy a more expensive machine that lasts for 10 years or a less expensive machine that lasts for 5 years?

- What level of plant capacity is best for the next 20 years?

- A company needs to market one of several midsize cars. Which car should it market?

To make decisions when cash flows are received at different points in time, we need to understand that the later a dollar is received, the less valuable the dollar is. For example, suppose we can invest money at a 10% annual interest rate. Then $1 received now is essentially equivalent to $1.10 a year from now. The reason is that if we have $1 now, we could invest it and gain $0.10 in interest by next year. We can write this as

$$\$1 \text{ now} = \$1.10 \text{ a year from now} \tag{2.3}$$

Dividing both sides of equation (2.3) by $1 + r$, where $r = 0.1$ is the interest rate (expressed as a decimal), we can rewrite it as

$$\frac{\$1}{1 + r} \text{ now} = \$1 \text{ a year from now} \qquad \textbf{(2.4)}$$

In general, if money can be invested at rate r per year, then \$1 received t years from now has the same value as $1/(1 + r)^t$ dollars received today. If we value a cash flow received t years from now as $1/(1 + r)^t$, then the total value of all cash flows over all years is called the **net present value** (**NPV**) of our cash flows. Basic financial theory tells us that projects with positive NPVs increase the value of the company, whereas projects with negative NPVs decrease the value of the company. The rate r (usually called the **discount rate**) used by major corporations generally comes from some version of the **capital asset pricing model**. Most companies use a discount rate ranging from 10% to 20%. The following example illustrates how spreadsheet models and the time value of money can be used to make complex business decisions.

EXAMPLE 2.5

CALCULATING NPV AT ACRON

Acron is a large drug company. One of its new drugs, Niagara, is coming to market and Acron needs to determine how much annual production capacity to build for this drug. Government regulations make it difficult to add capacity at a later date, so Acron must determine a capacity recommendation *before* the drug comes to market. The drug will be sold for 20 years before it comes off patent. After 20 years, the rights to produce the drug are virtually worthless. Acron has made the following assumptions:

- Year 1 demand will be 10,000 units.
- During years 2–6, annual growth of demand will be 15%.
- During years 7–20, annual growth of demand will be 5%.
- It costs \$6, payable at the end of year 1, to build each unit of annual production capacity. The cost of building capacity is depreciated on a straight-line 5-year basis.
- During year 1, Niagara will sell for \$8 per unit and will incur a variable cost of \$5 to produce.
- The cost of maintaining a unit of capacity during year 1 is \$1.
- The unit price, unit variable cost, and unit capacity maintenance cost will increase by 5% per year.
- Profits are taxed at 40%.
- All cash flows are assumed to occur at the end of each year, and the corporate discount rate is 10%.

Acron wants to develop a spreadsheet model of its 20-year cash flows. Then it wants to answer the following questions:

1. What capacity level should be chosen?
2. How does a change in the discount rate affect the optimal capacity level?
3. How realistic is the model?

Solution

The model of Acron's cash flows appears in Figure 2.25. As with many financial spreadsheet models that extend over a multiyear period, this model is not as bad as it looks. Usually, we enter "typical" formulas in the first year or two and then copy this logic across to all years. For copying purposes, however, it is useful to divide the screen horizontally into two panes so that we can see the first and last years, as shown in the figure. To do this, click on the "separator" just to the right of the horizontal scrollbar at the bottom of the screen and drag it to the left. (There is a similar separator just above the vertical scrollbar for dividing the screen vertically.)

	A	B	C	D	E	F	G		T	U
1	**Drug Company planning with net present value**									
2										
3	**Inputs**			Range names used:						
4	Year 1 demand	10000		Demand1 - B4						
5	Annual demand growth			DemGrowth2_6 - B6						
6	Years 2 to 6	15%		DemGrowth7_20 - B7						
7	Years 7 to 20	5%		UnitCapCost - B8						
8	Unit cost of production capacity	$6		DeprecRate - B9						
9	Depreciation rate	20%		UnitPrice1 - B11						
10	Year 1 monetary values			UnitVCost - B12						
11	Unit price	$8		UnitMaintCost - B13						
12	Unit variable cost	$5		InflRate - B14						
13	Unit capacity maintenance cost	$1		TaxRate - B15						
14	Inflation rate	5%		DiscRate - B16						
15	Tax rate	40%		Capacity - B19						
16	Discount rate	10%		BuildingCost - B22						
17				FreeCashFlow - B39:U39						
18	**Decision variable**			NPV - B41						
19	Capacity level (trial value)	15000								
20										
21	**Model of net present value (NPV)**									
22	Year	1	2	3	4	5	6		19	20
23	Building cost	$90,000								
24	Depreciation	$18,000	$18,000	$18,000	$18,000	$18,000				
25										
26	Demand	10000	11500	13225	15209	17490	20114		37927	39823
27	Units sold	10000	11500	13225	15000	15000	15000		15000	15000
28										
29	Unit price	$8.00	$8.40	$8.82	$9.26	$9.72	$10.21		$19.25	$20.22
30	Unit variable cost	$5.00	$5.25	$5.51	$5.79	$6.08	$6.38		$12.03	$12.63
31	Unit maintence cost	$1.00	$1.05	$1.10	$1.16	$1.22	$1.28		$2.41	$2.53
32										
33	Revenue	$80,000	$96,600	$116,645	$138,915	$145,861	$153,154		$288,794	$303,234
34	Variable cost	$50,000	$60,375	$72,903	$86,822	$91,163	$95,721		$180,496	$189,521
35	Maintenance cost	$15,000	$15,750	$16,538	$17,364	$18,233	$19,144		$36,099	$37,904
36										
37	Pretax profit	-$3,000	$2,475	$9,204	$16,729	$18,465	$38,288		$72,199	$75,809
38	After tax profit	-$3,000	$1,485	$5,523	$10,037	$11,079	$22,973		$43,319	$45,485
39	Free cash flow	-$75,000	$19,485	$23,523	$28,037	$29,079	$22,973		$43,319	$45,485
40										
41	NPV	$146,107								

FIGURE 2.25 Drug Company Model of 20-Year NPV

DEVELOPING THE SPREADSHEET MODEL

To create the model, enter the given data in the input section, enter *any* trial value for the capacity decision in the Capacity cell, name ranges, and complete the following steps.

❶ **Building cost and depreciation.** Enter the total building cost in the BuildingCost cell with the formula

=Capacity*UnitCapCost

Then enter the depreciation over the first 5 years by entering the formula

=BuildingCost*DeprecRate

in cell B24 and copying it across to cell F24.

❷ **Demand and units sold.** The demand is governed by the percentage rate increases assumed by Acron. However, the number of units that can be sold is limited by building capacity. (Also, we assume Acron will produce only what it can sell, so that there is never any leftover inventory.) Therefore, enter the formula

=Demand1

in cell B26, enter the formula

=B26*(1+DemGrowth2_6)

in cell C26 and copy it across to cell G26, enter the formula

=G26*(1+DemGrowth7_20)

in cell H26, and copy it across to cell U26. These formulas ensure that demand will grow as specified each year. (Don't forget the "1+" parts of these formulas. They are easy to forget!) Then enter the formula

=MIN(B26,Capacity)

in cell B27 and copy it across to cell U27. By the way, an easy way to copy to a large range, assuming the first and last cells of the range are visible, is to select the first cell, then, with your finger on the Shift key, select the last cell. This selects the entire range and certainly beats scrolling.

❸ **Unit prices and costs.** The unit price and unit costs all grow by the *same* inflation factor. To calculate them for year 1, enter the formulas =UnitPrice1, =UnitVCost1, and =UnitMaintCost1 in cells B29, B30, and B31. Then for all other years, enter the formula

=B29*(1+InflRate)

in cell C29 and copy it to the range C29:U31.

❹ **Revenues and costs.** The revenues and variable costs depend on the number of units sold, so enter the formula

=B\$27*B29

in cell B33 and copy it to the range B33:U34. (Make sure you understand why we made an absolute reference to row 27.) Then to calculate the maintenance cost, enter the formula

=Capacity*B31

in cell B35 and copy it across to cell U35.

⑤ Pretax profits, after-tax profits, and free cash flows. This part is a bit tricky, especially if you are not an accountant. For tax purposes, depreciation is deducted from the difference between revenue and (nonbuilding) costs. Therefore, to obtain pretax profit, the amount on which taxes are based, enter the formula

=B33-B34-B35-B24

in cell B37 and copy it across. Next, subtract taxes to obtain after-tax profits, but keep in mind that there is no tax if there is a loss. This implies the formula

=IF(B37<0,B37,B37*(1-TaxRate))

in cell B38, which can then be copied across. Finally, the free cash flow, the "real" profit after taxes, is found by adding back the depreciation but subtracting the building cost in year 1. To obtain this, enter the formula

=B38+B24-B23

in cell B39 and copy it across. (We could specialize this formula for the first 5 years, since these are the only years when building costs and depreciation occur, but it doesn't hurt to add and subtract 0's in the other columns.)

⑥ Net present value. The NPV is based on the sequence of cash flows in row 39. From our general discussion of NPV, the value in cell B39 should be multiplied by $1/(1+r)^1$, the value in cell C39 should be multiplied by $1/(1+r)^2$, and so on, and these quantities should be summed to obtain the NPV. (Here, $r = 0.1$ is the discount rate.) Fortunately, however, Excel has a built-in NPV function to accomplish this calculation. To use it, enter the formula

=NPV(DiscRate,FreeCashFlow)

in the NPV cell. This NPV function takes two arguments: the discount rate and a range of cash flows. Furthermore, it assumes that the first cell of this range is the cash flow at the *end* of year 1, the second cell is the cash flow at the end of year 2, and so on. If we had assumed building costs were payable at the *beginning* of year 1, we would have excluded the building costs from the formula in cell B39, and the NPV formula would instead be

=BuildingCost+NPV(DiscRate,FreeCashFlow)

That is, any cash flow at the beginning of year 1 must be placed outside of the NPV function.

To get some understanding of NPV, note that the *sum* of the cash flows in row 39 is slightly more than $520,000, but the NPV is only about $146,000. In this sense, values farther into the future are discounted. For example, the $45,485 cash flow in year 20 is equivalent to only $45,485[1/(1+0.1)^{20}] = \$6,761$ now!

Deciding on Capacity To determine how much capacity Acron should build, it is useful to create the data table and corresponding chart in Figure 2.26 (page 56). This shows how NPV varies for different levels of capacity. More specifically, it indicates that Acron can maximize its NPV by using a capacity level of 21,000 units. It is probably intuitively clear why NPV is small for low capacity levels—the company is losing potential revenue from demand it cannot satisfy. But why is there a steep decrease in NPV for high capacity levels? First, note that year 20 demand is approximately 40,000 units. (This is why we limited capacity to 40,000 in the data table.) Now, the main effect of more capacity past a certain level is increased building and maintenance costs. The extra capacity is hardly ever needed (except in the last few years, when revenues are discounted heavily anyway), so it becomes much too expensive to build and maintain.

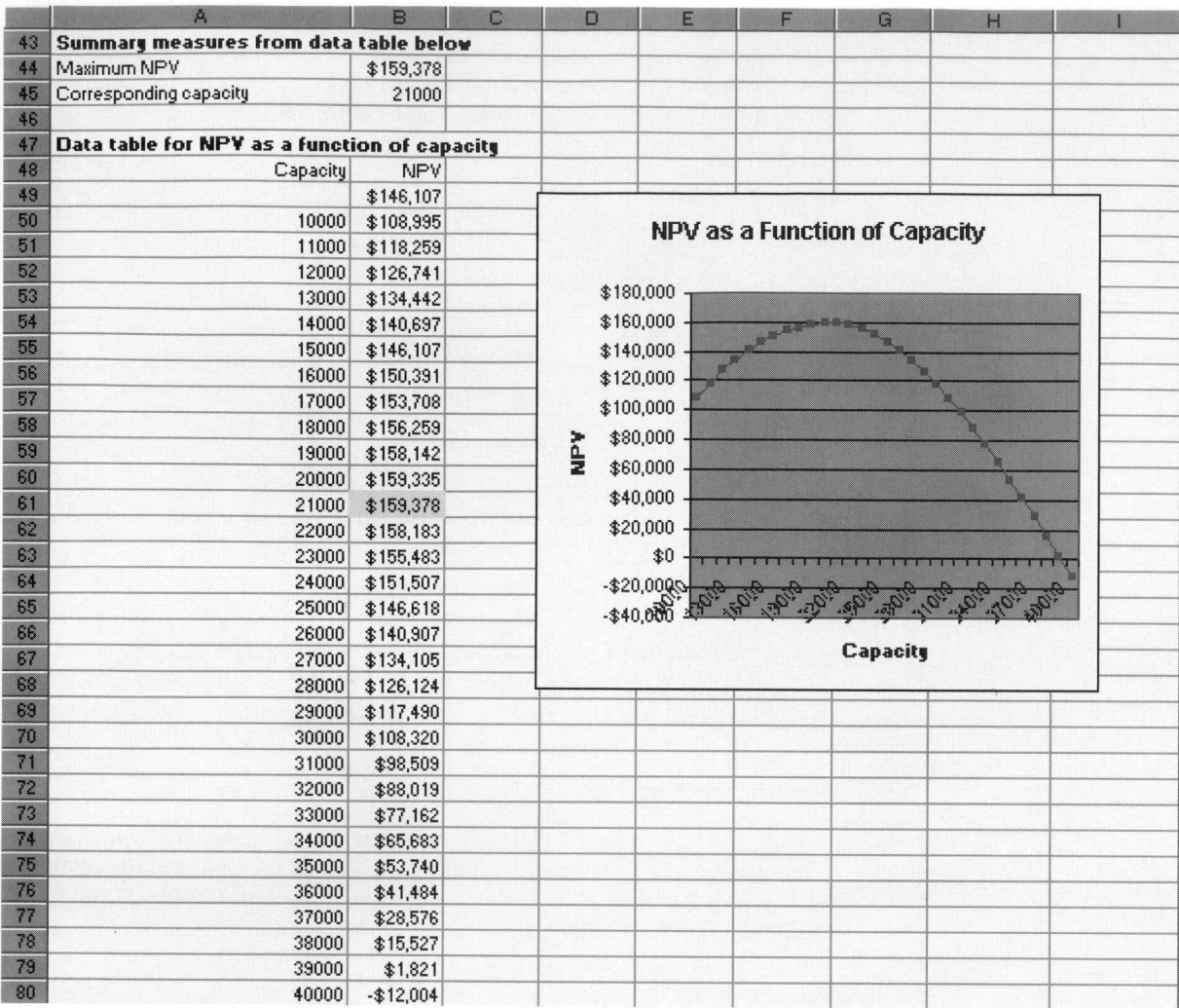

	A	B	C	D	E	F	G	H	I
43	**Summary measures from data table below**								
44	Maximum NPV	$159,378							
45	Corresponding capacity	21000							
46									
47	**Data table for NPV as a function of capacity**								
48	Capacity	NPV							
49		$146,107							
50	10000	$108,995							
51	11000	$118,259							
52	12000	$126,741							
53	13000	$134,442							
54	14000	$140,697							
55	15000	$146,107							
56	16000	$150,391							
57	17000	$153,708							
58	18000	$156,259							
59	19000	$158,142							
60	20000	$159,335							
61	21000	$159,378							
62	22000	$158,183							
63	23000	$155,483							
64	24000	$151,507							
65	25000	$146,618							
66	26000	$140,907							
67	27000	$134,105							
68	28000	$126,124							
69	29000	$117,490							
70	30000	$108,320							
71	31000	$98,509							
72	32000	$88,019							
73	33000	$77,162							
74	34000	$65,683							
75	35000	$53,740							
76	36000	$41,484							
77	37000	$28,576							
78	38000	$15,527							
79	39000	$1,821							
80	40000	-$12,004							

FIGURE 2.26 NPV as a Function of Building Capacity

Sensitivity to the Discount Rate Question 2 asks about the effect of the discount rate on optimal capacity. This is an important question for two reasons. First, it is often difficult for a company to determine the appropriate discount rate, and second, the NPV is typically quite sensitive to the discount rate. To answer the question, we build the two-way data table and corresponding chart in Figures 2.27 and 2.28. For each discount rate (each column of the table), we locate the maximum NPV and corresponding capacity level and record them in rows 84 and 85.[4] The chart is then based on the values in row 85. As we see, larger discount rates typically result in lower NPVs because future cash flows are discounted more heavily. Beyond this, the chart shows how the optimal capacity *decreases* as the discount rate increases. The reasoning is basically that "bad" things, especially building costs, tend to occur early, whereas "good" things (high revenues) tend to occur later on. A higher discount rate magnifies the bad things relative to the good things, so it induces the company to build less capacity.

[4]Actually, we used the Conditional Formatting tool and the MATCH and INDEX functions discussed in Example 2.2 to color the maxima in the table and find the values in row 85.

	A	B	C	D	E	F	G		O	P	Q
82	**Summary measures from data table below**										
83	Discount rate index	1	2	3	4	5	6		14	15	16
84	Discount rate	5%	6%	7%	8%	9%	10%		18%	19%	20%
85	Maximum NPV	$334,863	$287,519	$247,388	$213,504	$184,323	$159,378		$55,839	$49,572	$43,995
86	Corresponding capacity	24000	23000	23000	22000	21000	21000		14000	14000	13000
87											
88	**Data table for NPV as a function of capacity (along side) and discount rate (along top)**										
89	$146,107	5%	6%	7%	8%	9%	10%		18%	19%	20%
90	10000	$192,210	$170,843	$152,209	$135,905	$121,595	$108,995		$47,530	$42,958	$38,818
91	11000	$209,717	$186,229	$165,747	$147,829	$132,104	$118,259		$50,757	$45,741	$41,200
92	12000	$226,366	$200,774	$178,460	$158,943	$141,816	$126,741		$53,306	$47,857	$42,926
93	13000	$242,159	$214,478	$190,348	$169,246	$150,734	$134,442		$55,176	$49,305	$43,995
94	14000	$256,318	$226,589	$200,682	$178,033	$158,170	$140,697		$55,839	$49,572	$43,908
95	15000	$269,558	$237,796	$210,127	$185,946	$164,748	$146,107		$55,756	$49,104	$43,095
96	16000	$281,442	$247,698	$218,315	$192,647	$170,157	$150,391		$54,822	$47,813	$41,488
97	17000	$292,233	$256,534	$225,463	$198,335	$174,577	$153,708		$53,082	$45,733	$39,108
98	18000	$302,068	$264,457	$231,737	$203,186	$178,196	$156,259		$50,790	$43,122	$36,217
99	19000	$311,061	$271,576	$237,245	$207,305	$181,116	$158,142		$48,028	$40,061	$32,894
100	20000	$319,261	$277,924	$242,003	$210,695	$183,327	$159,335		$44,706	$36,454	$29,039
101	21000	$325,941	$282,836	$245,404	$212,801	$184,323	$159,378		$40,630	$32,131	$24,503
102	22000	$330,916	$286,152	$247,308	$213,504	$184,002	$158,183		$35,791	$27,086	$19,286
103	23000	$333,810	$287,519	$247,388	$212,496	$182,076	$155,483		$30,015	$21,157	$13,232
104	24000	$334,863	$287,180	$245,883	$210,017	$178,782	$151,507		$23,496	$14,529	$6,522
105	25000	$334,484	$285,534	$243,185	$206,446	$174,489	$146,618		$16,512	$7,474	-$584
106	26000	$332,771	$282,680	$239,391	$201,881	$169,293	$140,907		$9,133	$55	-$8,021
107	27000	$329,379	$278,289	$234,190	$196,025	$162,910	$134,105		$1,164	-$7,912	-$15,970
108	28000	$324,046	$272,147	$227,407	$188,737	$155,229	$126,124		-$7,379	-$16,407	-$24,406
109	29000	$317,516	$264,948	$219,687	$180,619	$146,813	$117,490		-$16,184	-$25,137	-$33,053
110	30000	$309,983	$256,865	$211,189	$171,815	$137,790	$108,320		-$25,197	-$34,053	-$41,865
111	31000	$301,221	$247,707	$201,748	$162,182	$128,040	$98,509		-$34,450	-$43,182	-$50,867
112	32000	$291,092	$237,362	$191,277	$151,654	$117,509	$88,019		-$43,940	-$52,520	-$60,054
113	33000	$280,210	$226,368	$180,244	$140,639	$106,556	$77,162		-$53,554	-$61,966	-$69,335
114	34000	$268,019	$214,249	$168,243	$128,791	$94,885	$65,683		-$63,369	-$71,588	-$78,771
115	35000	$254,802	$201,256	$155,498	$116,307	$82,670	$53,740		-$73,326	-$81,333	-$88,313
116	36000	$240,897	$187,678	$142,253	$103,397	$70,090	$41,484		-$83,377	-$91,160	-$97,926
117	37000	$225,486	$172,830	$127,936	$89,579	$56,742	$28,576		-$93,612	-$101,145	-$107,875
118	38000	$209,742	$157,702	$113,384	$75,564	$43,227	$15,527		-$103,887	-$111,164	-$117,452
119	39000	$192,408	$141,247	$97,721	$60,618	$28,930	$1,821		-$114,334	-$121,330	-$127,356
120	40000	$174,772	$124,542	$81,851	$45,499	$14,490	-$12,004		-$124,811	-$131,520	-$137,280

FIGURE 2.27 NPV as a Function of Capacity Level and Discount Rate

FIGURE 2.28
Optimal Capacity
Level Versus
Discount Rate

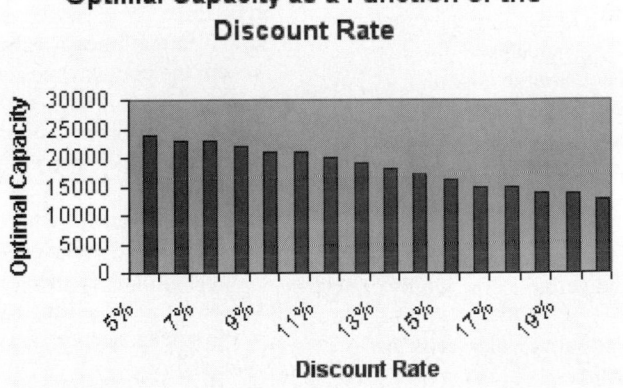

Optimal Capacity as a Function of the Discount Rate

Limitations of the Model Probably the major flaw in this model is that we have ignored uncertainty. It is clear that demand, future prices, and future costs are highly uncertain. We will discuss how to incorporate uncertainty into this type of model when we discuss simulation in Chapters 11 and 12. Of course, there are almost always ways to make *any* model more realistic—at the cost of increased complexity. For example, we could model the impact of competition on Niagara's profitability. We could also realize that Acron's pricing policy is not set in stone and the price it charges will influence the likelihood that competition will enter the market. Finally, Acron could probably add capacity in the future if it is experiencing larger-than-expected demand. However, it is important to realize that future flexibility in decision making has an impact on the correct decision for today. In Chapter 10 we will learn how to model decision making under uncertainty in situations where our future decision strategy impacts today's decision. ∎

2.4 CONCLUSION

The examples in this chapter have provided a glimpse of things to come in later chapters. We have illustrated the spreadsheet modeling approach to realistic business problems, we have discussed how to design spreadsheet models for readability, and we have illustrated some of Excel's powerful tools, especially data tables. In addition, at least three important themes have emerged from these examples: optimization, the role of uncertainty, and relationships between variables. Although we have not yet learned the tools to explore these themes fully, we will do so before long. Indeed, these themes will occupy us for most of the rest of this book.

PROBLEMS

Skill-Building Problems

1. Julie James is opening up a lemonade stand. She believes the fixed cost per week of running the stand is $50.00. Her best guess is that she can sell 300 cups per week at $0.50 per cup. The variable cost of producing a cup of lemonade is $0.20.
   a. Given her other assumptions, what level of sales volume will enable Julie to break even?
   b. Given her other assumptions, discuss how a change in sales volume affects profits.
   c. Given her other assumptions, discuss how a change in sales volume and variable cost jointly affect profits.
   d. Use Excel's auditing tool to show which cells in your spreadsheet affect profit.
2. We are thinking of opening a Broadway play, "I Love You, You're Mediocre, Now Get Better!" It will cost $5 million to develop the show. There are eight shows per week and we project the show will run for 100 weeks. It costs $1000 to open up the theatre each night. Tickets sell for $50.00 and we earn an average

of $1.50 profit per ticket holder from concessions. The theatre holds 800 and we expect 80% of the seats to be full.
   a. Given our other assumptions, how many weeks will the play have to run for us to earn a 100% return on the play's development cost?
   b. Given our other assumptions, how does an increase in the percentage of seats full affect profit?
   c. Given our other assumptions, determine how a joint change in the average ticket price and number of weeks the play runs influence profit.
   d. Use Excel's auditing tool to show which cells in the spreadsheet are affected by the percentage of seats full.
3. We are thinking of opening a small copy shop. It costs us $5000 to rent a copier for a year. It costs us $0.03 per copy to operate the copier. Other fixed costs of running the store amount to $400 per month. We charge an average of $0.10 per copy. We are open 365 days per year. Each copier can make up to 100,000 copies per year.

a. For 1–5 copiers rented and daily demands of 500, 1000, 1500, and 2000 copies per day, compute annual profit. That is, compute annual profit for *each* of these combinations of copiers rented and daily demand.

b. If we rent three copiers, what daily demand for copies will allow us to break even?

c. Graph profit as a function of the number of copiers for a daily demand of 500 copies; for a daily demand of 2000 copies. Interpret your graphs.

4. Georgia Mcbeal is trying to save for her retirement. She believes she can earn 10% on average each year on her retirement fund. Suppose at the beginning of each of the next 40 years Georgia will allocate x dollars to her retirement fund. If at the beginning of a year Georgia has y dollars in her fund, by the end of the year, it will grow to $1.1y$ dollars. How much should Georgia allocate to her retirement fund each year to ensure that she would have $1 million at the end of 40 years? What key factors are being ignored in our analysis of the amount saved for retirement?

5. A European call option on a stock earns the owner an amount equal to the price at expiration minus the exercise price, if the price of the stock on which the call is written exceeds the exercise price. Otherwise, the call pays nothing. A European put option earns the owner an amount equal to the exercise price minus the price at expiration, if the price at expiration is less than the exercise price. Otherwise the put pays nothing. The file P2_05.XLS contains a template that computes (based on the well-known Black–Scholes formula) the price of a European call and put based on the following inputs: today's stock price, the duration of the option (in years), the option's exercise price, the risk-free rate of interest (per year), and the annual volatility in stock price. For example, a 40% volatility means approximately that the standard deviation of annual percentage changes in the stock price are 40%.

a. Consider a 6-month European call option with exercise price $40. Assume a current stock price of $35, a risk-free rate of 5%, and an annual volatility of 40%. Determine the price of the call option.

b. Use a data table to show how a change in volatility changes the value of the option. Give an intuitive explanation for your results.

c. Use a data table to show how a change in today's stock price changes the option's value. Give an intuitive explanation for your results.

d. Use a data table to show how a change in the option's duration changes the option's value. Give an intuitive explanation for your results.

6. Repeat parts **a–d** of the previous problem for a 6-month European put option with exercise price $40. Again, assume a current stock price of $35, a risk-free rate of 5%, and an annual volatility of 40%.

7. Microsoft is trying to determine whether to give a $10 rebate, a $6 price cut, or have no price change on

a software product. Currently 40,000 units of the product are sold each week for $45. The variable cost of the product is $5. The most likely case appears to be that a $10 rebate will increase sales 30% and half of all people will claim the rebate. For the price cut, the most likely case is that sales will increase 20%.

a. Given all other assumptions, what increase in sales from the rebate would make the rebate and price cut equally desirable?

b. Microsoft does not really know the increase in sales that will result from a rebate or price cut. However, it is quite sure that the rebate will increase sales by between 15% and 40% and that the price cut will increase sales by between 10% and 30%. Perform a sensitivity analysis that could be used to help determine Microsoft's course of action.

8. Table 2.1 lists sales (in millions of dollars) of Dell Computer during the period 1987–1997 (where year 1 corresponds to 1987).

a. Fit a power and an exponential trend curve to these data. Which fits the data better?

b. Use your part **a** answer to predict 1999 sales for Dell.

c. Use your part **a** answer to describe how the sales of Dell have grown from year to year.

TABLE 2.1	Dell Sales
Year	**Sales**
1	69
2	159
3	258
4	389
5	546
6	890
7	2014
8	2873
9	3475
10	5296
11	7759

9. The file P2_09.XLS gives the annual sales for Microsoft (in millions of dollars) for the years 1984–1993, where 1984 = year 1.

a. Fit an exponential curve to these data.

b. By what percentage do you estimate that Microsoft will grow each year?

c. Why can't a high rate of exponential growth continue for a long time?

d. Rather than an exponential curve, what curve might better represent the growth of a new technology?

10. Assume that the number of units sold of a product is given by $100 - 0.5P + 26\sqrt{A}$, where P is the price (in dollars) charged for product and A is the amount spent on advertising (in thousands of dollars). Each unit of the product costs $5 to produce. What combination of price and advertising will maximize profit?

11. You are given the data on the price of new Taurus sedans and used Taurus sedans in Table 2.2. All used prices are in amounts paid in 1995. For example, a new Taurus bought in 1985 cost $11,790 and the wholesale used price of that car in 1995 was $1700. A new Taurus bought in 1994 cost $18,680 and sold used in 1995 for $12,600.

TABLE 2.2	Taurus Data		
Year Bought	Age When Sold	Resale Price	New Price
1985	10	1700	11,790
1986	9	2125	12,688
1987	8	2525	13,280
1988	7	3475	13,544
1989	6	4450	14,722
1990	5	5525	14,990
1991	4	7125	15,290
1992	3	8575	16,656
1993	2	10,450	17,220
1994	1	12,600	18,680

a. You want to predict the resale value (as a percentage of the original price of the vehicle) as a function of the vehicle's age. Develop an equation to do this. You should try two different curves and choose the one that fits best.

b. Suppose all police cars are Ford Tauruses. If you were the business manager for the New York Police Department, what use would you make of the information from part **a**?

12. I own 1000 shares of Microsoft stock and the price of the stock on December 27, 1999, is $116. I can buy any number of 1-year puts on Microsoft stock, each with an exercise price of $90, for a cost of $4.51 per put. Show how the percentage return on my portfolio varies as a function of the number of puts purchased and the price of Microsoft stock in one year. Assume that Microsoft stock will sell between $50 and $200 in one year. How might you determine how many puts to purchase?

13. The yield of a chemical reaction is defined as the ratio (expressed as a percentage) of usable output to the amount of raw material input. Suppose the yield of a chemical reaction is found to depend on the length of time the process is run and the temperature at which the process is run. The yield can be expressed as follows:

$$\text{Yield} = 90.79 - 1.095x_1 - 1.045x_2$$
$$-2.781x_1^2 - 2.524x_2^2 - 0.775x_1x_2$$

Here $x_1 = (\text{Temperature} - 125)/10$ and $x_2 = (\text{Time} - 300)/30$, where temperature is measured in degrees Fahrenheit and time is measured in seconds. Find the temperature and time settings that maximize the yield of this process.

14. The file P2_14.XLS gives the data bits power (in millions of chips) for several years in the 1980s and 1990s.

a. Fit an exponential curve to these data.

b. Give a prediction for data bits per chip in 2001–2003.

c. By what percentage do you estimate that data bits power per chip is improving per year? (The result of this problem is known as Moore's law. This exponential improvement in processing power has driven the success of semiconductor manufacturers such as Intel.)

15. A bond is currently selling for $1040. It pays the amounts listed in Table 2.3 at the end of the next six years. The yield of the bond is the interest rate that would make the NPV of the bond's payments equal to the bond's price. Use Excel's Goal Seek tool to find the yield of the bond.

TABLE 2.3	Bond Data
Year	Payment
1	$100
2	$100
3	$100
4	$100
5	$100
6	$1100

16. Assume the demand for the drug Wozac during the current year is 50,000, and assume demand will grow at 5% a year. If we build a plant that can produce x units of Wozac per year, it will cost us $16x$. Each unit of Wozac is sold for $3. Each unit of Wozac produced incurs a variable production cost of $0.20. It costs $0.40 per year to operate a unit of capacity. Determine how large a Wozac plant to build to maximize expected profit over the next ten years.

17. Consider a project with the following cash flows: year 1: −$400, year 2: $200, year 3: $600, year 4: −$900, year 5: $1000, year 6: $250, year 7: $230. Assume a discount rate of 15% per year.

a. Compute the project's NPV if cash flows occur at the ends of the respective years.

b. Compute the project's NPV if cash flows occur at the beginnings of the respective years.

c. Compute the project's NPV if cash flows occur at the middles of the respective years.

18. The payback of a project is the number of years it takes before the project's total cash flow is positive. Payback ignores the time value of money. It is interesting, however, to see how differing assumptions on project growth impact payback. Suppose, for example, that a project requires a $300 million investment at year 0 (right now). The project yields cash flows for ten years, and the year 1 cash flow will be between $30 million and $100 million. The annual cash flow growth will be between 5% and 25% per year. (Assume that this growth is the *same* each year.) Use a data table to see how the project payback depends on the year 1 cash flow and the cash flow growth rate.

19. A software company is considering translating its program into French. Each unit sold of the program sells for $50 and incurs a variable cost of $10 to produce. Currently the size of the market for the product is 300,000 units per year and the English version of the software has a 30% share of the market. The company estimates that the market size is growing at 10% a year for the next five years, and at 5% per year after that. It will cost the company $6 million to create a French version of the program. The translation will increase its market share to 40%. Given a 10-year planning horizon, for what discount rates is it profitable to create the French version of the software?

Skill-Extending Problems

20. We are entering the widget business. It costs $500,000, payable in year 1, to develop a prototype. This cost can be depreciated on a straight-line basis during years 1–5. Each widget sells for $40 and incurs a variable cost of $20. During year 1 the market size is 100,000, and the market is growing at 10% per year. We believe we will attain a 30% market share. Profits are taxed at 40%, but there are no taxes on *negative* profits.

a. Given our other assumptions, what market share is needed to ensure a total free cash flow (FCF) of $0 over years 1–5? *Note*: FCF during a year equals after-tax profits plus depreciation minus fixed costs (if any).

b. Explain how an increase in market share changes profit.

c. Explain how an increase in market size growth changes profit.

d. Use Excel's auditing tool to show how the market growth assumption influences your spreadsheet.

21. Suppose we are borrowing $25,000 and making monthly payments with 1% interest. Show that the monthly payments should equal $556.11. The key relationships are that for any month t

- (Ending month t balance) = (Ending month $t - 1$ balance) − ((Monthly payment) − (Month t interest))

- (Month t interest) = (Beginning month t balance) $*$ (Monthly interest rate)

    Of course, the ending month 60 balance must equal 0.

22. You are thinking of starting Peaco, which will produce Peakbabies, a product that competes with Ty's Beanie Babies. In year 0 (right now) you will incur costs of $4 million to build a plant. In year 1 you expect to sell 80,000 Peakbabies for a unit price of $25. The price of $25 will remain unchanged through years 1–5. Unit sales are expected to grow by the same percentage (g) each year. During years 1–5 Peaco incurs two types of costs: variable costs and SG&A costs. Each year variable costs equal half of revenue. During year 1, SG&A costs equal 40% of revenue. This percentage is assumed to drop 2% per year, so during year 2, SG&A costs will equal 38% of revenue, and so on. Peaco's goal is to have profits for years 0–5 sum to 0 (ignoring the time value of money). This will ensure that the $4 million investment in year 0 is "paid back" by the end of year 5. What annual percentage growth rate g does Peaco require to "pay back" the plant cost by the end of year 5?

23. The file P2_23.XLS contains the number of fax machines produced in the United States during the years 1982–1988 and the unit cost of producing a fax during each of these years.

a. Fit a power curve that can be used to determine how the cost of producing a fax depends on the number of faxes already produced. (This is an example of a learning curve.)

b. Given that 1,000,000 fax machines will be produced in 1989, develop a forecast for the cost of producing a fax during 1989.

c. If the cumulative number of faxes produced doubles, by how much will per-unit cost of making a fax decrease?

24. The file P2_24.XLS contains the cumulative number of bits (in trillions) of DRAM (a type of computer memory) produced and the price per bit (in thousandths of a cent).

a. Fit a power curve that can be used to show how price per bit drops with increased production. This relationship is known as the learning curve.

b. Suppose the cumulative number of bits doubles. Create a prediction for the price per bit. Does the change in the price per bit depend on the current price?

25. Suppose the demand (in thousands) for a toaster is given by $100p^{-2}$, where p is the price in dollars charged for the toaster.
   a. If the variable cost of producing a toaster is $10, what price will maximize profit?
   b. The elasticity of demand is defined by the percentage change in demand created by a 1% change in price. Show that the demand for toasters appears to have constant elasticity of demand. Would this be true if the demand for toasters were linear?

26. A large U.S. drug company, Pharmco, has 100 million yen coming due in one year. Currently the yen is worth $0.01. Because the value of the yen in U.S. dollars in one year is unknown, the value of this 100 million yen in U.S. dollars is highly uncertain. To hedge its risk, Pharmco is thinking of buying one-year put options on the yen with an exercise price of $0.008. For example, if the yen falls in value a year from now to $0.007, then the owner of the put receives $0.001. The price of such a put is $0.00007. Show how the dollar value of Pharmco's receipts and hedging expenses depends on the number of puts purchased and the final $/yen exchange rate. Assume final exchange rates between 0.006 $/yen and 0.015 $/yen are possible.

27. How could you determine a discount rate that makes two projects have the same NPV?

28. The internal rate of return (IRR) is the discount rate r that makes a project have an NPV of $0. You can find IRR in Excel with the built-in IRR function, using the syntax =IRR(range of cash flows). However, it can be tricky. In fact, if the IRR is not near 10%, this function might not find an answer and you will get an error message. Then you must try the syntax = IRR(range of cash flows, guess), where "guess" is your best guess for the IRR. It is best to try a range of guesses (say, −90% to 100%). Find the IRR of the project described in Problem 17.

29. A project does not necessarily have a unique IRR. (Refer to the previous problem for more information on IRR.) Show that a project with the following cash flows has two IRRs: year 1: −$20, year 2: $82, year 3: −$60, year 4: $2. (*Note:* It can be shown that if a project's cash flows changes sign only once, the project is guaranteed to have a unique IRR.)

30. How could you use Goal Seek to find a project's IRR? (Refer to problem 28 for more information on IRR.)

APPENDIX: TIPS FOR EDITING AND DOCUMENTING SPREADSHEETS

We have stressed the importance of editing and documenting your spreadsheet models. The following tips will make it much easier to do so.

❶ Format appropriately. Appropriate formatting can make a spreadsheet model much easier to read. To boldface, for example, select one or more cells and click on the **B** button on the formatting toolbar (or press Ctrl-b). Similarly, to italicize, indent, increase or decrease the number of decimal places, right-justify, or perform other common formatting tasks, use the buttons on the formatting toolbar. (See Figure 2.29.)

❷ Use range names. It takes time to name ranges, but it can make formulas much easier to read and understand. To enter a range name, highlight any cell or range of cells and enter a name for the range in the Name Box (just above the upper left corner of the worksheet). If you want to edit or delete range names, you must do so from the Insert/Name/Define menu item. Here are some other things you can do from the Insert/Name menu item.

- Once you have named some ranges, you might want a list of them in your spreadsheet. To obtain such a list, place the cursor at the top of the range where you want the list to be placed, select the Insert/Name/Paste menu item, and click on the Paste List button.

FIGURE 2.29 Excel Formatting Toolbar

- Suppose you have labels such as FixedCost, VarCost, Revenue, and Profit in the range A3:A6, with their values next to them in column B. You would like to name the cells in column B with the labels in column A. This is easy. Highlight the range A3:B6, select the Insert/Name/Create menu item, and make sure the Left Column box is checked. This creates the range names you want.

- If you have a formula such as =SUM(A10:A20) and then name the range A10:A20 as Costs, say, the formula will *not* change automatically to =SUM(Costs). However, you can make it adapt to your new range name by using the Insert/Name/Apply menu item.

3 **Use Text Boxes.** Text boxes are very useful for documenting your work. To enter an explanation, a list of range names, or any other text into a text box, make sure the Drawing toolbar is visible (right-click on any toolbar and check its box to make it visible), click on the Text Box button, and start typing.

4 **Use Cell Comments.** Cell comments provide another great way to document your work. To enter a comment in a cell, select the cell and right-click. This brings up the dialog box in Figure 2.30 (which is also useful for tasks other than entering comments). Click on the Insert Comment item to enter a comment. If there is already a comment in the cell, this menu will have Edit Comment and Delete Comment items. The cells with comments should have small red triangles up their corners. If they don't, select the Tools/Options menu item, click on the View tab, and make sure the Comment Indicator Only button is selected.

5 **Modify Toolbars.** You might think you are stuck with the built-in Excel toolbars, but you are not. Try the following. Right-click on any toolbar, select the Customize option, and click on the Commands tab. Under the various categories, you will see a lot of built-in toolbar buttons that come with Excel. Click on any of these to see a short description of the button's functionality. If you see any you like, simply drag them up to an existing toolbar—*any* toolbar. They will stay there until you open Customize again and drag them off. In fact, once Customize is open, you can drag *any* toolbar buttons off existing toolbars to get rid of them. Why clutter up toolbars with buttons you never use?

This is just the beginning. You might not want to become a programmer, but we will show you how to improve your productivity immensely without any *real* programming at all. Suppose you want to perform a task such as putting a blue border

FIGURE 2.30
Popup Dialog Box for Cells or Ranges

around a selected range and shading it gray. This is not difficult, but if you need to do it repeatedly, it becomes a real bother. We will show you how to record a **macro**—the programming part—to do such a task and then create your own toolbar with buttons that run the macros you recorded. From then on, if you want to perform the task, just click on a button! Here are the steps for creating a blue border with gray shading. You can modify these steps for any other routine task.

1. **Record the macro.** Highlight a range where you want the border and select the Tools/Macro/Record New Macro menu item. Fill out the resulting dialog as shown in Figure 2.31. Specifically, enter a descriptive name in the Macro Name box, and select Personal Macro Workbook from the pulldown menu. This latter setting will store your macro in a special hidden file called PERSONAL.XLS that opens every time you open Excel.[5] This means that your favorite macros will always be available to you, regardless of which files you have open. When you click on OK, the Stop Recording toolbar will appear. It indicates (like a tape recorder) that anything you do is being recorded until you click on the Stop Recording button (the blue square). Now create the blue border and shading. (Use the Format/Cells menu item with the Border tab for borders. Actually, we suggest that you practice doing this *before* turning on the recorder, just as you would practice a speech before turning on the tape recorder and doing it for real!) Once you have created the border and shading, click on the Stop Recording button to stop recording. If anything goes wrong, just do it all over again, using the same macro name to record over your messed-up version.

FIGURE 2.31
Record Macro
Dialog Box

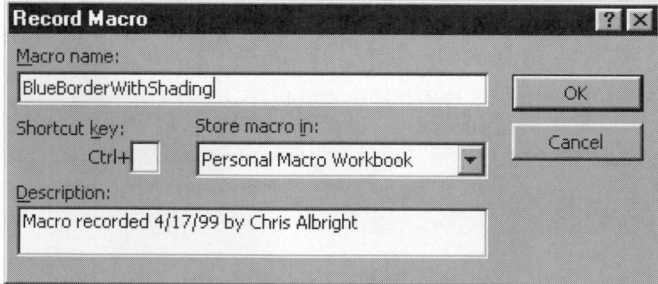

2. **Create your own toolbar.** Right-click on any toolbar and select the Customize item. (As before, this is the first step in *any* toolbar customizing you might want to do.) Click on the Toolbars tab, click on the New button, and then enter any name such as MyOwnToolbar. You now have your own toolbar, but nothing is on it yet. You can "populate" it with buttons in two ways: by dragging prebuilt buttons to it (from the list you see when you click on the Commands tab) or by creating your own buttons for it. We discuss the latter option in the next step.

3. **Create a button for your macro on the new toolbar.** Still within the Customize dialog box, click on the Commands tab and select the Macros item from the Categories list. In the right pane, you will see a "generic" button with a happy face. Drag it to your new toolbar. To operationalize the button, right-click on it to bring up the menu in Figure 2.32. The most important item on this menu is the Assign

---

[5]This will work on your own PC, but it might not work in your school's lab PCs. They might not give you access to a PERSONAL.XLS file.

FIGURE 2.32
Properties Menu for a
Toolbar Button

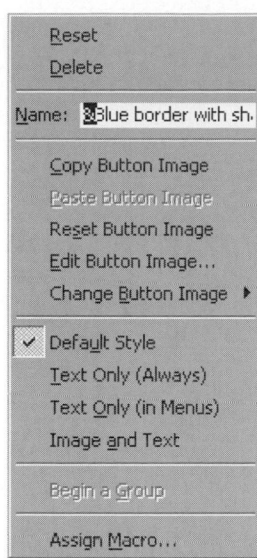

Macro item. Click on it and select the name of the macro you recorded. The rest is cosmetic. You can enter a description in the Name box, which will appear when you place the cursor above this button. (This is called a "toolbar tip.") You can also experiment with the "button image" items to change the happy face to something more suggestive, such as a picture of a blue border.

## CHAPTER 3

Introduction to Optimization Modeling

DIET MODELS

O ne of the many classic applications of linear programming is the "diet problem." This problem appears, often in a somewhat humorous guise, as a prototype linear programming example in almost all management science (MS) textbooks. Basically, it involves finding a group of foods—a diet—that meets all daily nutritional requirements at minimum cost. These textbook examples may or may not have any relevance to real meal planning. However, the problem is important in many real settings, as outlined by Lancaster (1992). A number of versions of this model have actually been used by institutions such as hospitals, nursing homes, schools, prisons, and other food-systems operations. In many of these applications, the computer-generated menus have provided a 10% to 30% cost savings, the nutritional requirements are guaranteed (in contrast to menus generated by traditional, non-MS methods), and, surprisingly, the acceptance of the menus by consumers has been very high.

This problem provides a good example of how to distinguish between good models and poor models. In the simplified diet problems in most textbooks, it is easy to develop a model that satisfies the conditions of low cost and minimal daily nutritional requirements but is so bland (or weird) that no one would eat it. The trick is to incorporate suitable "constraints" (mathematical equations or inequalities) that rule out unappetizing menus. For example, the applications cited in the article obtained more acceptable diets in one of two ways. Either they included a separation constraint (such as requiring at least three days between successive servings of mashed potatoes) or a frequency constraint (such as requiring that mashed potatoes can be served at most three times per week). By adding enough of these types of constraints, they obtained optimal menus that people were perfectly willing to eat.

A related article by Dantzig (1990) illustrates the humorous side of the problem. When Dantzig (one of the founders of linear programming) was developing his famous solution technique for linear programming in the late 1940s, he decided to use it to solve his *own* diet problem, one that would prescribe what he would actually eat each day. Even he was surprised by the outcome. His first solution called for various amounts of "normal" foods, plus 500 gallons of vinegar—he had forgotten a constraint! So he reformulated the problem, and his next solution called for 200 bouillon cubes per day. Still not (too) discouraged, he reformulated the problem (with an upper limit on bouillon cubes) and his resulting solution called for two pounds of bran per day. After an upper limit on bran was imposed, his next diet called for two pounds of blackstrap molasses. By this time, he started to get the point: It is possible to generate a low-cost, nutritional, and tasty diet using management science techniques, but it's not as easy as it appears! ■

3.1   INTRODUCTION

In this chapter we introduce spreadsheet optimization, one of the most powerful and flexible methods of quantitative analysis. The specific type of optimization we will discuss is **linear programming** (LP). LP is used in all types of organizations, often on a daily basis, and it is used to solve an extremely wide variety of problems. These include problems in human resource scheduling, inventory management, selection of advertising media, bond trading, management of cash flows, operation of an electrical utility's hydroelectric system, routing of delivery vehicles, blending in oil refineries, hospital staffing, and many others. The goal of this chapter is to introduce the basic elements of LP: the types of problems it can solve, how LP problems can be modeled in Excel, and how Excel's powerful add-in, the Solver, can be used to find optimal solutions. Then in the next several chapters we will examine a variety of LP applications, and we will also look at applications of integer and nonlinear programming, two important extensions of LP.

3.2   A BRIEF HISTORY OF LINEAR PROGRAMMING

A brief history of linear programming is enlightening. Mathematically, every LP problem involves optimizing a linear function subject to several linear constraints, expressed as linear inequalities or equalities. For example, the objective might be profit, and the constraints might be upper limits on resource availabilities. Until World War II, mathematicians knew a great deal, at least theoretically, about systems of linear equations and inequalities. They realized that a huge number of arithmetic operations are necessary to solve such systems, and without computing power, humans are not able to perform the required calculations in a reasonable amount of time. Therefore, no one seriously considered their potential usefulness.

During World War II, however, two things fortuitously came together. First, complex military logistics problems arose that could be modeled as LP problems (although the name "linear programming" did not yet exist). Second, computers were just being developed. All that was needed was a method for solving this new class of problem—a method that could take advantage of computer power. Fortunately, a young mathematician, George Dantzig, developed a method he called the **simplex method**. It involved a systematic, arithmetic-intensive search through the set of all possible solutions for the solution that optimized a given objective. It appeared to work efficiently on the problems he tried, and it was not too difficult to program on a computer.

The surprising thing is that Dantzig's method, with relatively minor modifications, is still the most important solution method for LP problems. For reasons that are not entirely understood even by mathematicians, it works quickly on problems that are orders of magnitude larger than any problems Dantzig could have imagined in the early days, and all large companies now own (or have access to) a commercial version of the simplex computer code. Recently, an entirely different type of solution method developed by Narendra Karmarkar at Bell Labs has emerged as a competitor to the simplex method, particularly for extremely large problems, but the simplex method is still comfortably in first place.

3.3   INTRODUCTION TO LP MODELING

We will not learn the simplex method. Instead, we will learn how to formulate problems as LP models. Once a problem is properly formulated, we will see that it is fairly easy to solve it on a computer and interpret the resulting solution. Actually, there are two ways to formulate an LP problem, the traditional algebraic way and the more recent spreadsheet way. We will illustrate both methods in this chapter, just for comparison. However, in the later chapters we will focus exclusively on spreadsheet formulations.

The first problem we will examine is often considered the prototype LP problem. The basic problem is to select the optimal mix of products to produce to maximize profit. We will refer to it as the **product mix** problem.

EXAMPLE   **3.1**

PRODUCING FRAMES AT MONET

The Monet Company produces four types of picture frames, which we label 1, 2, 3, and 4. The four types of frames differ with respect to size, shape, and materials used. Each type requires a certain amount of skilled labor, metal, and glass, as shown in Table 3.1 (page 70). This table also lists the unit selling price Monet charges for each type of frame. During the coming week, Monet can purchase up to 4000 hours of skilled labor, 6000 ounces of metal, and 10,000 ounces of glass. The unit costs are $8.00 per labor hour, $0.50 per ounce of metal, and $0.75 per ounce of glass. Also,

TABLE 3.1	Data for Monet Picture Frame Example			
	Skilled Labor	**Metal**	**Glass**	**Selling Price**
Frame 1	2	4	6	$28.50
Frame 2	1	2	2	$12.50
Frame 3	3	1	1	$29.25
Frame 4	2	2	2	$21.50

market constraints are such that it is impossible to sell more than 1000 type 1 frames, 2000 type 2 frames, 500 type 3 frames, and 1000 type 4 frames. The company wants to maximize its weekly profit.

Solution

In the traditional algebraic solution method, we first identify the decision variables. In this small problem they are the numbers of frames of types 1, 2, 3, and 4 to produce. We label these x_1, x_2, x_3, and x_4 (although any other labels would do). Next, we write total profit and the constraints in terms of the x's. Finally, since only nonnegative amounts can be produced, we add explicit constraints to ensure that the x's are nonnegative. The resulting algebraic formulation is shown below:

$$\text{maximize } 6x_1 + 2x_2 + 4x_3 + 3x_4 \quad \text{(profit objective)}$$
$$\text{subject to } 2x_1 + x_2 + 3x_3 + 2x_4 \leq 4000 \text{ (labor constraint)}$$
$$4x_1 + 2x_2 + x_3 + 2x_4 \leq 6000 \text{ (metal constraint)}$$
$$6x_1 + 2x_2 + x_3 + 2x_4 \leq 10{,}000 \text{ (glass constraint)}$$
$$x_1 \leq 1000 \text{ (frame 1 sales constraint)}$$
$$x_2 \leq 2000 \text{ (frame 2 sales constraint)}$$
$$x_3 \leq 500 \text{ (frame 3 sales constraint)}$$
$$x_4 \leq 1000 \text{ (frame 4 sales constraint)}$$
$$x_1, x_2, x_3, x_4 \geq 0 \text{ (nonnegativity constraints)}$$

To understand this formulation, consider the profit objective first. The profit from x_1 frames of type 1 is $6x_1$ because each frame contributes $6 to profit. This $6 is calculated as the unit selling price minus the cost of the inputs that go into a single type 1 frame:

$$\text{Unit profit} = 28.50 - [2(8.00) + 4(0.50) + 6(0.75)] = \$6$$

Profits for the other three types of frames are obtained similarly. Their unit profits are $2.00, $4.00, and $3.00, respectively. Then the total profit is the sum of the profits from the four products.

Next, consider the skilled labor constraint. The right side, 4000, is the number of hours available. On the left side, each type 1 frame uses 2 hours of labor, so x_1 units require $2x_1$ hours of labor. Similar statements hold for the other three products, and the total number of labor hours used is the sum over the four products. Then the constraint states that the number of hours used cannot exceed the number of hours available. The constraints for metal and glass are similar. Finally, the maximum sales constraints and the nonnegativity constraints put upper and lower limits on the quantities that can be produced.

For many years all LP problems were formulated this way. Thus, many commercial LP computer packages are written to accept LP problems in essentially this format. For example, in a popular package called LINDO, we would type in almost exactly what is shown above. In the past decade, however, a more intuitive method of expressing LP problems has emerged. This method takes advantage of the power and flexibility of spreadsheets. Actually, LP problems could always be *formulated* on spreadsheets, but now with the addition of Solver add-ins, spreadsheets have the capability of *solving* (that is, optimizing) LP problems as well. Specifically, Microsoft® Excel, Lotus® 1-2-3®, and Corel® Quattro® Pro all have built-in Solvers, and there is an LP add-in called What's Best! that can be used with all three. All examples in this book will be illustrated with Excel's Solver.[1]

There are many ways to develop an LP spreadsheet model. Everyone has his or her own preferences for arranging the data in the various cells. We will not give any exact prescriptions, but we will present enough examples to help you develop good habits. The common elements in all LP spreadsheet models are the following.

Spreadsheet Elements

1. **Inputs.** All numerical **inputs**—that is, the data needed to form the objective and the constraints—must appear somewhere in the spreadsheet. Although it is not absolutely necessary, our convention is to enclose all inputs in a blue border with shading. We try to put most of the inputs in the upper left section of the spreadsheet. However, we sometimes violate this convention when certain inputs fit more naturally somewhere else.

2. **Changing cells.** Instead of using variable names, such as x's, spreadsheet models use a set of designated cells that play the role of the decision variables. The values in these cells can be changed to optimize the objective. In Excel these cells are called the **changing cells**. To designate them clearly, our convention is to enclose the changing cells within a red border.

3. **Target (objective) cell.** One cell, called the **target** or **objective cell**, contains the value of the objective. The Solver systematically varies the values in the changing cells to optimize the value in the target cell. Our convention is to enclose the target cell within a black double-line border.[2]

4. **Constraints.** Excel does not show the constraints directly on the spreadsheet. Instead, we specify constraints in a Solver dialog box. For example, we might designate a set of related constraints by

   B15:D15<=B16:D16

   This implies three separate constraints. The value in B15 must be less than or equal to the value in B16, the value in C15 must be less than or equal to the value in C16, and the value in D15 must be less than or equal to the value in D16. In almost all cases we will assign range names to ranges that appear in the constraints. Then a typical constraint might be specified as

   Used<=Available

   This is much easier to read and understand.

---

[1] This Solver add-in is built into Microsoft Excel, but it has been developed by a third-party software company, Frontline Systems. We provide more discussion of Solver software offered by Frontline in the appendix to this chapter.
[2] Our red–blue–black color scheme shows up very effectively on a color monitor. The shading (for input cells) and double-line border (for the target cell) are used for clarification on the printed page.

5. **Nonnegativity.** Normally we want the decision variables—that is, the values in the changing cells—to be nonnegative. Except for Excel 95 and earlier versions of Excel, these constraints do not need to be written explicitly; we simply check a box to indicate that we want nonnegative changing cells. (Note, however, that if any *other* cells need to be constrained to be nonnegative, we need to specify these constraints explicitly.)

In general, the complete solution of a problem involves three stages. The first stage is to enter all of the inputs, trial values for the changing cells, and formulas relating these in a spreadsheet. We call this *developing the model*. This stage is the most crucial because it is here that all of the "ingredients" of the model are included and related appropriately. In particular, the spreadsheet *must* include a formula that relates the objective to the changing cells, either directly or indirectly, so that if the values in the changing cells vary, the objective value varies accordingly. Similarly, the spreadsheet must include expressions for the various constraints (usually their left sides) that are related appropriately to the changing cells.

After the model is developed, we can proceed to the second stage—invoking the Solver. At this point, we formally designate the objective cell, the changing cells, the constraints, and selected options, and we tell the Solver to find the *optimal* solution. If the first stage has been done correctly, the second stage is usually very straightforward.

The third stage is **sensitivity analysis**. In most model formulations of real problems, we make "best guesses" for the numerical inputs to the problem. There is typically some uncertainty about quantities such as unit prices, forecasted demands, and resource availabilities. When we use the Solver to solve the problem, we use our best estimates of these quantities to obtain an optimal solution. However, it is then important to see how the optimal solution changes (if at all) as we vary selected inputs. Also, a sensitivity analysis often gives us important insights about how the model works.

DEVELOPING THE SPREADSHEET MODEL

The spreadsheet in Figure 3.1 illustrates the solution procedure for Monet's product mix problem. (See the file PRODUCTMIX.XLS.) The first stage is to develop the spreadsheet, as explained in step-by-step fashion below.

❶ **Inputs.** Enter the various inputs in the shaded ranges. Again, remember that our convention is to shade all input cells (and enclose them in a blue border). Enter only *numbers*, not formulas, in input cells. They should always be numbers straight from the problem statement.

❷ **Production levels.** Enter *any* four values in the range we have named Produced.[3] These do *not* have to be the values shown in Figure 3.1. These cells are the changing cells—that is, the cells where the decision variables are placed. Any trial values can be used initially; the Solver will eventually find the *optimal* values. Note that the four values shown in Figure 3.1 cannot be optimal because they do not satisfy all of the constraints. Specifically, this plan uses more labor hours and metal than are available, and it produces more type 4 frames than can be sold. However, we do not need to worry about satisfying constraints at this point; the Solver will take care of this later.

❸ **Resources used.** Enter the formula

=SUMPRODUCT(B9:E9,Produced)

---

[3]As in the previous chapter, we frequently use descriptive range names for selected ranges, shown in the box in the figure. These are not necessary, but they make the model easier to understand and explain.

FIGURE 3.1
An Initial Solution
for Product Mix
Model

	A	B	C	D	E	F	G	H
1	**Product Mix Problem**							
2								
3	**Input data**							
4	Hourly wage rate	$8.00						
5	Cost per oz of metal	$0.50						
6	Cost per oz of glass	$0.75						
7								
8	Frame type	1	2	3	4		Range names:	
9	Labor hours per frame	2	1	3	2		Available: D21:D23	
10	Metal (oz.) per frame	4	2	1	2		MaxSales: B18:E18	
11	Glass (oz.) per frame	6	2	1	2		Produced: B16:E16	
12	Unit selling price	$28.50	$12.50	$29.25	$21.50		TotProfit: F32	
13							Used: B21:B23	
14	**Production plan**							
15	Frame type	1	2	3	4			
16	Frames produced	500	800	400	1500			
17		<=	<=	<=	<=			
18	Maximum sales	1000	2000	500	1000			
19								
20	**Constraints on inpu**	Used		Available				
21	Labor hours	6000	<=	4000				
22	Metal (oz.)	7000	<=	6000				
23	Glass (oz.)	8000	<=	10000				
24								
25	**Revenue, cost summary**							
26	Frame type	1	2	3	4	Totals		
27	Revenue	$14,250	$10,000	$11,700	$32,250	$68,200		
28	Costs of inputs							
29	Labor	$8,000	$6,400	$9,600	$24,000	$48,000		
30	Metal	$1,000	$800	$200	$1,500	$3,500		
31	Glass	$2,250	$1,200	$300	$2,250	$6,000		
32	Profit	$3,000	$1,600	$1,600	$4,500	$10,700		

in cell B21 and copy it to the rest of the Used range. These formulas calculate the units of labor, metal, and glass used by the current product mix. The SUMPRODUCT function is especially useful in LP models. Here it means to multiply each value in the range B9:E9 by the corresponding value in the Produced range and then sum these products.

❹ Revenues, costs, and profits. The area from row 25 down shows the summary of monetary values. Actually, all we need is the total profit in cell F32, but it is useful to calculate the revenues and costs associated with each product. To obtain the revenues, enter the formula

=B12*B16

in cell B27 and copy this to the range C27:E27. For the costs, enter the formula

=$B4*B$16*B9

in cell B29 and copy this to the range B29:E31. (Note how the mixed absolute and relative references enable copying to the entire range.) Then calculate profits for each product by entering the formula

=B27-SUM(B29:B31)

in cell B32 and copy this to the range C32:E32. Finally, calculate the totals in column F by summing across each row with the SUM function.

The next step is to specify the changing cells, the objective cell, and the constraints in a Solver dialog box and then instruct the Solver to find the optimal solution. However, before we do this, it is useful to try a few "guesses" in the changing cells. There are two reasons for doing so. First, by entering different sets of values in the changing cells, we can confirm that the formulas in the other cells are working correctly.

The second reason for trying a few guesses is to provide a better understanding of the model. For example, it is tempting to guess that the frame types with the highest profit margins should be produced to the greatest extent possible. To try this out, begin by entering 0's in the Produced range. When we produce nothing, we earn zero profit. Next, because frame 1 has the highest profit margin ($6) and its market constraint permits at most 1000 frames, enter 1000 in cell B16. Note that none of the resources are yet used up completely. Therefore, we can make some type 3 frames, the type with the next highest profit margin. Because the type 3 market constraint permits at most 500 frames, enter 500 in cell D16. There is still some availability of each resource. This allows us to make some type 4 frames, the type with the next largest profit margin. However, the most we can make is 250 type 4 frames, because at that point we completely exhaust the available labor hours. The resulting solution appears in Figure 3.2. Its corresponding profit is $8750.

We have now produced as much as possible of the three frame types with the three highest profit margins. Does this guarantee that this solution is the best possible product mix? Unfortunately, it does not! The solution in Figure 3.2 is *not* optimal. Even in this small model it is difficult to guess the optimal solution, even when we use a relatively intelligent trial-and-error procedure. The problem is that a frame type with a high profit margin can use up a lot of the resources and preclude other profitable frames from being produced. So although it is instructive and sometimes enlightening to try guessing the optimal solution, we might never find it. This is where the Solver enters the picture.

FIGURE 3.2
Another Possible Solution for Product Mix Model

	A	B	C	D	E	F	G	H
1	**Product Mix Problem**							
2								
3	**Input data**							
4	Hourly wage rate	$8.00						
5	Cost per oz of metal	$0.50						
6	Cost per oz of glass	$0.75						
7								
8	Frame type	1	2	3	4		Range names:	
9	Labor hours per frame	2	1	3	2		Available: D21:D23	
10	Metal (oz.) per frame	4	2	1	2		MaxSales: B18:E18	
11	Glass (oz.) per frame	6	2	1	2		Produced: B16:E16	
12	Unit selling price	$28.50	$12.50	$29.25	$21.50		TotProfit: F32	
13							Used: B21:B23	
14	**Production plan**							
15	Frame type	1	2	3	4			
16	Frames produced	1000	0	500	250			
17		<=	<=	<=	<=			
18	Maximum sales	1000	2000	500	1000			
19								
20	**Constraints on inpu**	Used		Available				
21	Labor hours	4000	<=	4000				
22	Metal (oz.)	5000	<=	6000				
23	Glass (oz.)	7000	<=	10000				
24								
25	**Revenue, cost summary**							
26	Frame type	1	2	3	4	Totals		
27	Revenue	$28,500	$0	$14,625	$5,375	$48,500		
28	Costs of inputs							
29	Labor	$16,000	$0	$12,000	$4,000	$32,000		
30	Metal	$2,000	$0	$250	$250	$2,500		
31	Glass	$4,500	$0	$375	$375	$5,250		
32	Profit	$6,000	$0	$2,000	$750	$8,750		

USING THE SOLVER

To invoke Excel's Solver, select the Tools/Solver menu item. (If there is no such menu item on your PC, see the appendix to this chapter.) The dialog box in Figure 3.3 appears. It has three important sections that you must fill in: the target cell, the changing cells, and the constraints. For the product mix problem, we can fill these in by typing cell references or we can point, click, and drag the appropriate ranges in the usual way. Also, if we have named any of the ranges, we can use these range names instead of cell addresses. (If you decide to point, click, and drag, you might need to move the Solver dialog box so that it isn't in the way of the cells you want to select. The Solver in Excel 97 and later versions has a great feature for getting the dialog box out of the way while pointing—just click on the right edge of the cell reference box.)

FIGURE 3.3
Solver Dialog Box
for Product Mix
Model

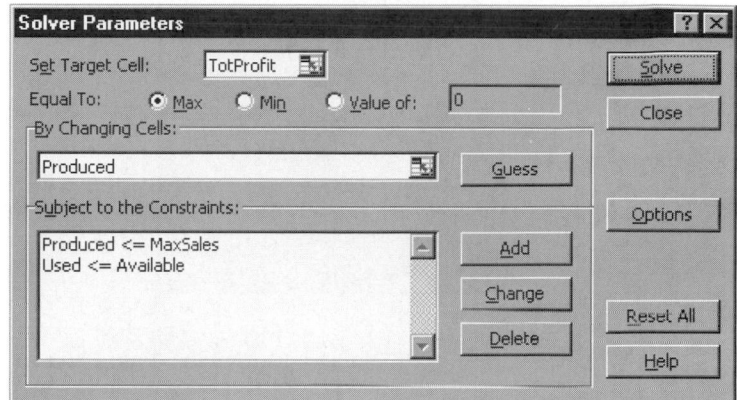

❶ Objective. Select the TotProfit cell as the target cell, and click on the Maximize button.

❷ Changing cells. Select the Produced range, the numbers of frames to produce, as the changing cells.

❸ Constraints. Click on the Add button to add the following constraints:

Used <=Available
Produced <=MaxSales

The first constraint says to use no more of each resource than is available. The second constraint says to produce no more of each product than can be sold. *Note*: The <= signs in column C and row 17 (see Figure 3.1 or 3.2) are *not* a necessary part of the Excel model. They are entered simply as *labels* in the spreadsheet and have no effect on any calculations. However, they help to document the model, so we include them in all of the examples. You are not required to do so when you formulate your own models, but we believe it is a good habit to develop.

❹ Nonnegativity. Because negative production quantities make no sense, we must tell the Solver *explicitly* to make the changing cells nonnegative. There are two ways to do this. First, we can add another constraint as in step 3:

Produced>=0

In fact, before Excel 97, this was the only way to specify nonnegativity constraints. However, with the Solver in Excel 97 or later versions, we can click on the Options button in Figure 3.3 and check the Assume Non-Negative box in the resulting dialog box. (See Figure 3.4.) This automatically ensures that *all* changing cells are nonnegative.

⑤   Linear model. There is one last step before clicking on the Solve button. The Solver uses one of several numerical methods to solve various types of models. The models discussed in this chapter are all *linear* models. (We will discuss the properties of linear models shortly.) Linear models can be solved most efficiently by the simplex method. To instruct Excel to use this method, we also check the Assume Linear Model in the Solver options dialog box shown in Figure 3.4.

FIGURE 3.4
Solver Options
Dialog Box

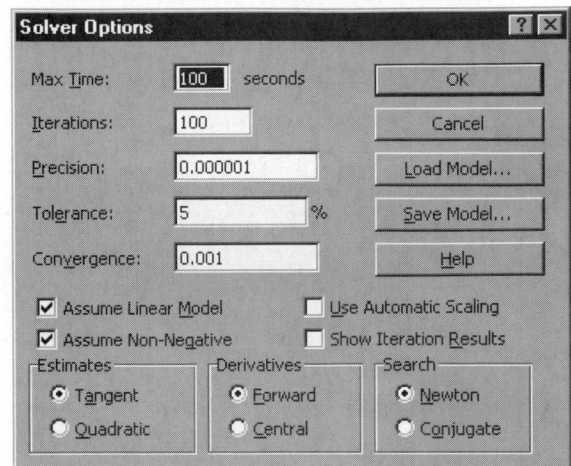

⑥   Optimize. Click on the Solve button in the dialog box in Figure 3.3.

At this point, the Solver searches through a number of possible solutions until it finds the optimal solution. (You can watch the progress on the lower left of the screen.) When it finishes, it displays the message in Figure 3.5. You can then tell it to return the values in the changing cells to their original (probably nonoptimal) values or retain the optimal values found by the Solver. In most cases you will choose the latter. (Actually, this is the message we hope for. However, in some cases the Solver is *not* able to find an optimal solution, in which case one of several error messages will appear. We will discuss some of these later in this chapter.) For now, click on the OK button to keep the Solver solution. You should see the solution shown in Figure 3.6.

FIGURE 3.5
Solver Message That
Optimal Solution
Has Been Found

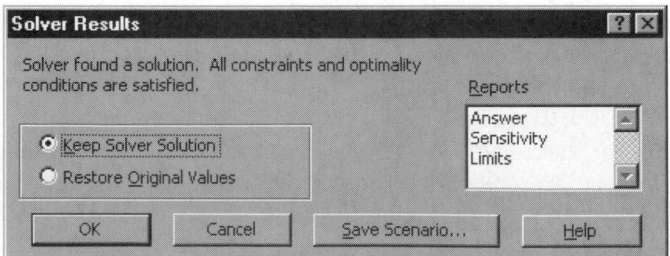

The optimal plan is to produce 1000 type 1 frames, 800 type 2 frames, 400 type 3 frames, and no type 4 frames. This is close to the production plan from Figure 3.2, but the current plan earns $450 more profit. Also, it uses all of the available labor hours and metal, but only 8000 of the 10,000 available ounces of glass. Finally, in terms of maximum sales, the optimal plan could produce more of frame types 2, 3, and 4 (if there were more skilled labor and/or metal available). This is typical of an LP solution. Some of the constraints are met exactly—that is, as equalities—whereas

FIGURE 3.6
Optimal Solution for
Product Mix Model

	A	B	C	D	E	F	G	H
1	**Product Mix Problem**							
2								
3	**Input data**							
4	Hourly wage rate	$8.00						
5	Cost per oz of metal	$0.50						
6	Cost per oz of glass	$0.75						
7								
8	Frame type	1	2	3	4	**Range names:**		
9	Labor hours per frame	2	1	3	2	Available: D21:D23		
10	Metal (oz.) per frame	4	2	1	2	MaxSales: B18:E18		
11	Glass (oz.) per frame	6	2	1	2	Produced: B16:E16		
12	Unit selling price	$28.50	$12.50	$29.25	$21.50	TotProfit: F32		
13						Used: B21:B23		
14	**Production plan**							
15	Frame type	1	2	3	4			
16	Frames produced	1000	800	400	0			
17		<=	<=	<=	<=			
18	Maximum sales	1000	2000	500	1000			
19								
20	**Constraints on inpu**	Used		Available				
21	Labor hours	4000	<=	4000				
22	Metal (oz.)	6000	<=	6000				
23	Glass (oz.)	8000	<=	10000				
24								
25	**Revenue, cost summary**							
26	Frame type	1	2	3	4	Totals		
27	Revenue	$28,500	$10,000	$11,700	$0	$50,200		
28	Costs of inputs							
29	Labor	$16,000	$6,400	$9,600	$0	$32,000		
30	Metal	$2,000	$800	$200	$0	$3,000		
31	Glass	$4,500	$1,200	$300	$0	$6,000		
32	Profit	$6,000	$1,600	$1,600	$0	$9,200		

others contain a certain amount of "slack." The constraints that hold as equalities are called **binding** constraints, and the ones with slack are called **nonbinding**. You can think of the binding constraints as the "bottlenecks." They are the constraints that prevent Monet from earning even higher profits.

Experimenting with New Inputs If we want to experiment with different inputs to this problem—the unit revenues or resource availabilities, for example—we can simply change the inputs and then rerun the Solver. The second time we use the Solver, we do not have to respecify the target and changing cells or the constraints. Excel remembers all of these settings, and it saves them when we save the file.

As a simple what-if example, consider the modified model in Figure 3.7 (page 78). Here the unit selling price for frame type 4 has increased from $21.50 to $26.50, and all other inputs have remained the same. By making type 4 frames more profitable, we might expect them to enter the optimal mix. This is exactly what happens. The new optimal plan discontinues production of frame types 2 and 3 and instead calls for production of 1000 units of frame type 4. This solution increases the total profit to $14,000.

There is one technical note we should mention. Because of the way numbers are stored and calculated on a computer, the optimal values in the changing cells and elsewhere can contain small roundoff errors. For example, the value that really appeared in cell E16 (in Figure 3.6) on our PC was 8.731E-09, a very small number (0.000000008731). For all practical purposes, this number can be treated as 0, and we have formatted it as such in Figure 3.6.

FIGURE 3.7
Solution to Product
Mix Model with
New Inputs

	A	B	C	D	E	F	G	H
1	**Product Mix Problem**							
2								
3	**Input data**							
4	Hourly wage rate	$8.00						
5	Cost per oz of metal	$0.50						
6	Cost per oz of glass	$0.75						
7								
8	Frame type	1	2	3	4			
9	Labor hours per frame	2	1	3	2			
10	Metal (oz.) per frame	4	2	1	2			
11	Glass (oz.) per frame	6	2	1	2			
12	Unit selling price	$28.50	$12.50	$29.25	$26.50			
13								
14	**Production plan**							
15	Frame type	1	2	3	4			
16	Frames produced	1000	0	0	1000			
17		<=	<=	<=	<=			
18	Maximum sales	1000	2000	500	1000			
19								
20	**Constraints on inputs**	Used		Available				
21	Labor hours	4000	<=	4000				
22	Metal (oz.)	6000	<=	6000				
23	Glass (oz.)	8000	<=	10000				
24								
25	**Revenue, cost summary**							
26	Frame type	1	2	3	4	Totals		
27	Revenue	$28,500	$0	$0	$26,500	$55,000		
28	Costs of inputs							
29	Labor	$16,000	$0	$0	$16,000	$32,000		
30	Metal	$2,000	$0	$0	$1,000	$3,000		
31	Glass	$4,500	$0	$0	$1,500	$6,000		
32	Profit	$6,000	$0	$0	$8,000	$14,000		

Range names:
Available: D21:D23
MaxSales: B18:E18
Produced: B16:E16
TotProfit: F32
Used: B21:B23

3.4 SENSITIVITY ANALYSIS AND THE SOLVERTABLE ADD-IN

Now that we have solved Monet's product mix problem, it might appear that we are finished. But in real LP applications the solution to a *single* model is hardly ever the end of the analysis. It is almost always useful to perform a sensitivity analysis to see how (or if) the optimal solution changes as we change one or more model inputs. We will illustrate a systematic way of doing so in this section.

The Solver dialog box in Figure 3.5 indicates one possible approach. By checking the Sensitivity Report option, we obtain a new sheet with a lot of information about the model's sensitivity to various inputs. This report is based on a very well developed theory of sensitivity in LP models. Unfortunately, this report is based on an *algebraic* approach to LP modeling that requires us to adhere to certain conventions. The problem is that there is no real need to adhere to these conventions in spreadsheet modeling. The effect is that the Solver's sensitivity report is sometimes very useful but sometimes virtually impossible to unravel. We believe it is more likely to confuse than to enlighten.

Nevertheless, sensitivity analysis is too important to neglect. Therefore, we have written an add-in to Excel called SolverTable that makes sensitivity analysis much more straightforward. This add-in is contained on the CD that comes with this book. To install it, simply run the Setup program on this CD-ROM and choose the SolverTable option. You can then check that it is installed by selecting the Tools/Add-Ins menu item in Excel. There should be a SolverTable item in the resulting list of add-ins. To actually add SolverTable in (load it into memory), just check its box in this list. To unload it from memory, just uncheck its box.

Using the SolverTable Add-in

The SolverTable add-in was developed to mimic Excel's built-in Data Table feature. Recall that data tables allow you to vary one or two inputs in a spreadsheet model and see how selected outputs change. SolverTable is similar except that now the Solver is rerun for every new input (or pair of inputs). There are two ways it can be used, as described below.

1. **One-way table.** A "one-way" table means that there is a *single* input cell and *any number of* output cells. That is, there can be a single output cell or as many output cells as you like.

2. **Two-way table.** A "two-way" table means that there are *two* input cells and one or more outputs. (You might recall that an Excel two-way data table allows only one output. The SolverTable add-in allows more than one. It then creates a separate table for each output as a function of the two inputs.)

We illustrate some of the possibilities in the following continuation of the product mix example.

EXAMPLE 3.1 (CONTINUED)

PRODUCING FRAMES AT MONET

Check how sensitive the optimal profit and the optimal product mix are to (1) changes in the number of labor hours available and (2) the cost per ounce of metal. Then check how sensitive the optimal profit is to simultaneous changes in the hourly labor cost and the total labor hours available.

Solution

We assume that the product mix model has been formulated and optimized (as shown in Figure 3.6) and that the SolverTable add-in has been installed. Then the solution to question (1) is shown in Figure 3.8. To obtain this output (the part in the range A37:F48), we use the Data/SolverTable menu item, select a one-way table in the first dialog box, and fill in the second dialog box as shown in Figure 3.9 (page 80). (Note that ranges can be entered as cell addresses or range names. Also, multiple ranges in the Outputs box should be separated by commas. If you like to *drag* multiple output ranges, the trick is is keep your finger on the Ctrl key as you perform the dragging. This will automatically enter the separating comma(s) for you.) When we click on

FIGURE 3.8
Sensitivity to Available Labor Hours

	A	B	C	D	E	F	G
34	**Sensitivity of optimal solution to number of labor hours**						
35			Frames produced				
36	Labor hours	1	2	3	4	Total profit	Increase
37		$B$16	$C$16	$D$16	$E$16	$F$32	
38	2500	1000	500	0	0	$7,000	
39	2750	1000	750	0	0	$7,500	$500
40	3000	1000	1000	0	0	$8,000	$500
41	3250	1000	950	100	0	$8,300	$300
42	3500	1000	900	200	0	$8,600	$300
43	3750	1000	850	300	0	$8,900	$300
44	4000	1000	800	400	0	$9,200	$300
45	4250	1000	750	500	0	$9,500	$300
46	4500	1000	500	500	250	$9,750	$250
47	4750	1000	250	500	500	$10,000	$250
48	5000	1000	0	500	750	$10,250	$250

FIGURE 3.9
SolverTable Dialog
Box for One-Way
Table

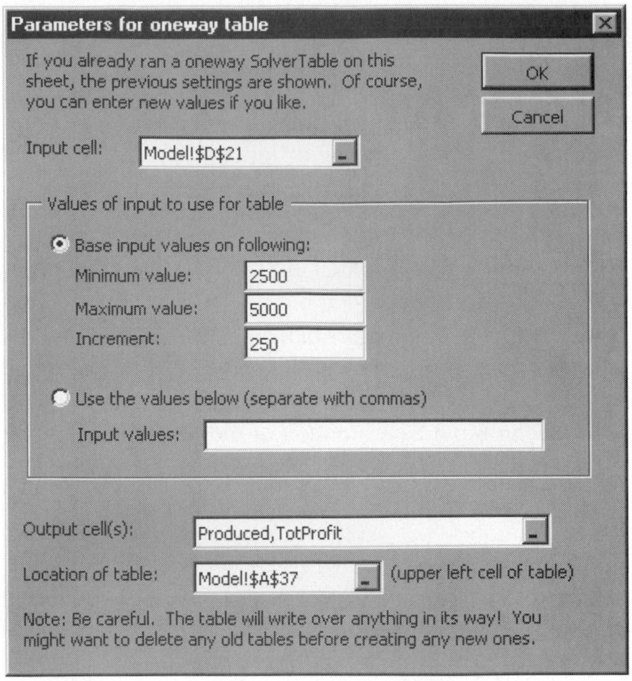

OK, the Solver solves a separate optimization problem for each of the 11 rows of the table and then reports the requested outputs (frames produced and total profit) in the table. It might take a while, depending on the speed of your PC, but everything is automatic. However, if you want to update this table—by using new labor hour values in column A, for example—you must repeat the procedure. Note that SolverTable enters comments (indicated by the small red triangles) in several cells to help you interpret the output.

There are several ways to interpret the output from this sensitivity analysis. First, we can look at columns B–E to see how the product mix changes as more labor hours become available. For example, frames of type 4 are finally produced when 4500 labor hours are available, and frames of type 2 are discontinued in the final row. Second, we can see how extra labor hours add to the total profit. We show this numerically in column G, where each value is the increase in profit from the previous row. (Column G is not produced by SolverTable; we created it manually.) Note exactly what this increased profit means. For example, when labor hours increase from 2500 to 2750, the model requires that we *pay* $8 apiece for these extra hours (if we use them). But the *net* effect is that profit increases by $500. In other words, the labor cost increases by $2000 [= $8(250)], but this is more than offset by the increase in revenue that comes from having the extra labor hours.

As column G illustrates, it is worthwhile to obtain extra labor hours, even though we have to pay for them, because profit increases. However, the increase in profit per extra labor hour, called the **shadow price** of labor hours, is not constant. We see that it decreases as more labor hours are already owned. An extra 250 labor hours first results in $500 more profit, then $300, and then only $250. This is typical of shadow prices for scarce resources in LP models.

We can also chart the optimal profit values in column F (or any other quantities from a SolverTable output). The line chart in Figure 3.10 illustrates how the shadow price (slope of the line) decreases as more labor hours are already owned. (The first decrease in slope is perceptible; the second is hard to see in the chart.)

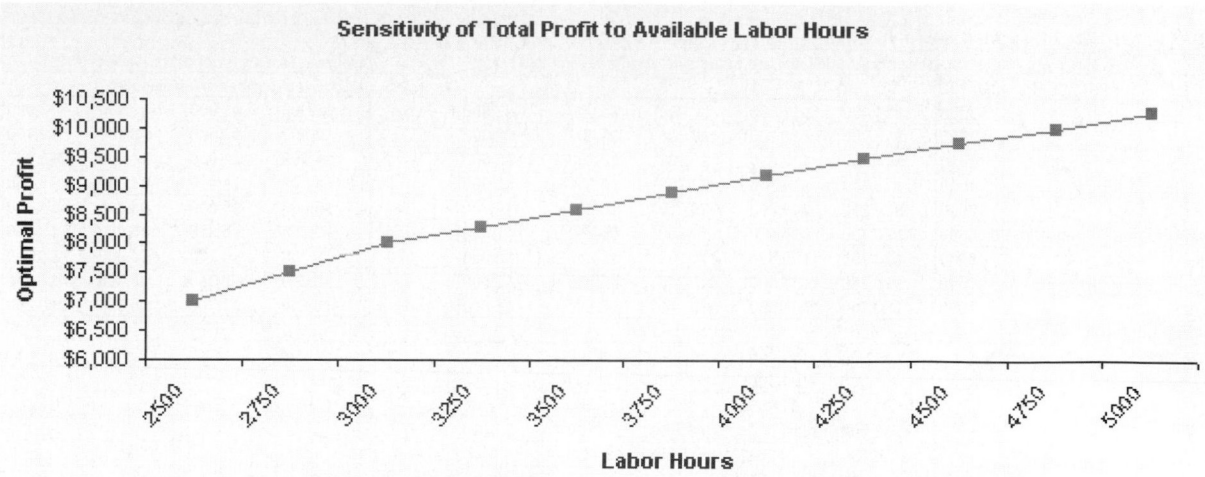

FIGURE 3.10 Sensitivity of Optimal Profit to Labor Hours

FIGURE 3.11
Sensitivity of Optimal
Solution to Cost of
Metal

	A	B	C	D	E	F	G
50	Sensitivity of optimal solution to unit cost of metal (per oz.)						
51		Frames produced					
52	Cost (per oz.) of metal	1	2	3	4	Total profit	Decrease
53		$B$16	$C$16	$D$16	$E$16	$F$32	
54	$0.30	1000	800	400	0	$10,400	
55	$0.50	1000	800	400	0	$9,200	$1,200
56	$0.70	1000	800	400	0	$8,000	$1,200
57	$0.90	1000	500	500	0	$6,800	$1,200
58	$1.10	1000	0	500	250	$5,750	$1,050
59	$1.30	1000	0	500	250	$4,750	$1,000

The answer to the sensitivity question (2) is similar and appears in Figure 3.11. We used the SolverTable exactly as before; only the input cell and input values differ. Note how the optimal product mix remains unchanged for a cost of metal in the $0.30 to $0.70 range. Within this range, the only thing that changes is the profit, and it decreases only because metal gets more expensive. Outside of this range, however, we change the product mix (and obtain less profit). Intuitively, once metal becomes expensive enough, products that use metal most heavily become less attractive. They will then be produced at lower levels or dropped from the mix all together.

Finally, we answer sensitivity question (3) with a two-way table, as shown in the range A63:F72 of Figure 3.12 (page 82). Now the values of the two inputs, hourly labor cost and labor hours available, are listed along the top and left-hand side, and the address of the single output, total profit, is placed in the upper left cell of the table. To produce this table, we fill in SolverTable's second dialog box as shown in Figure 3.13. Now the Solver must solve 9(5) = 45 separate problems, one for each combination of input values, so it can take a few seconds or more. However, the optimal profits are eventually listed in the table. From these, we can see how total profit *decreases* in each row as the hourly labor cost increases (see the range H64:K72, produced manually) and how it *increases* in each column as the available labor hours increase (see the range B74:F81, also produced manually). We can also chart the profits in the table. Figure 3.14 shows one possibility.

	A	B	C	D	E	F	G	H	I	J	K
61	Sensitivity of optimal profit to changes in labor hours available and hourly labor cost										
62	(Labor costs are along top, labor hours available are along side, profits are in table body)							Decreases as a function of labor cost for			
63	$F$32	6	7	8	9	10		each fixed number of labor hours			
64	3000	$14,000	$11,000	$8,000	$5,000	$2,000		$3,000	$3,000	$3,000	$3,000
65	3500	$15,600	$12,100	$8,600	$5,100	$2,000		$3,500	$3,500	$3,500	$3,100
66	4000	$17,200	$13,200	$9,200	$5,200	$2,000		$4,000	$4,000	$4,000	$3,200
67	4500	$18,750	$14,250	$9,750	$5,250	$2,000		$4,500	$4,500	$4,500	$3,250
68	5000	$20,250	$15,250	$10,250	$5,250	$2,000		$5,000	$5,000	$5,000	$3,250
69	5500	$20,750	$15,500	$10,250	$5,250	$2,000		$5,250	$5,250	$5,000	$3,250
70	6000	$20,750	$15,500	$10,250	$5,250	$2,000		$5,250	$5,250	$5,000	$3,250
71	6500	$20,750	$15,500	$10,250	$5,250	$2,000		$5,250	$5,250	$5,000	$3,250
72	7000	$20,750	$15,500	$10,250	$5,250	$2,000		$5,250	$5,250	$5,000	$3,250
73											
74	Increases as a function	$1,600	$1,100	$600	$100	$0					
75	of labor hours for each	$1,600	$1,100	$600	$100	$0					
76	fixed labor cost	$1,550	$1,050	$550	$50	$0					
77		$1,500	$1,000	$500	$0	$0					
78		$500	$250	$0	$0	$0					
79		$0	$0	$0	$0	$0					
80		$0	$0	$0	$0	$0					
81		$0	$0	$0	$0	$0					

FIGURE 3.12 Sensitivity of Optimal Profit to Labor Hour Cost and Availability

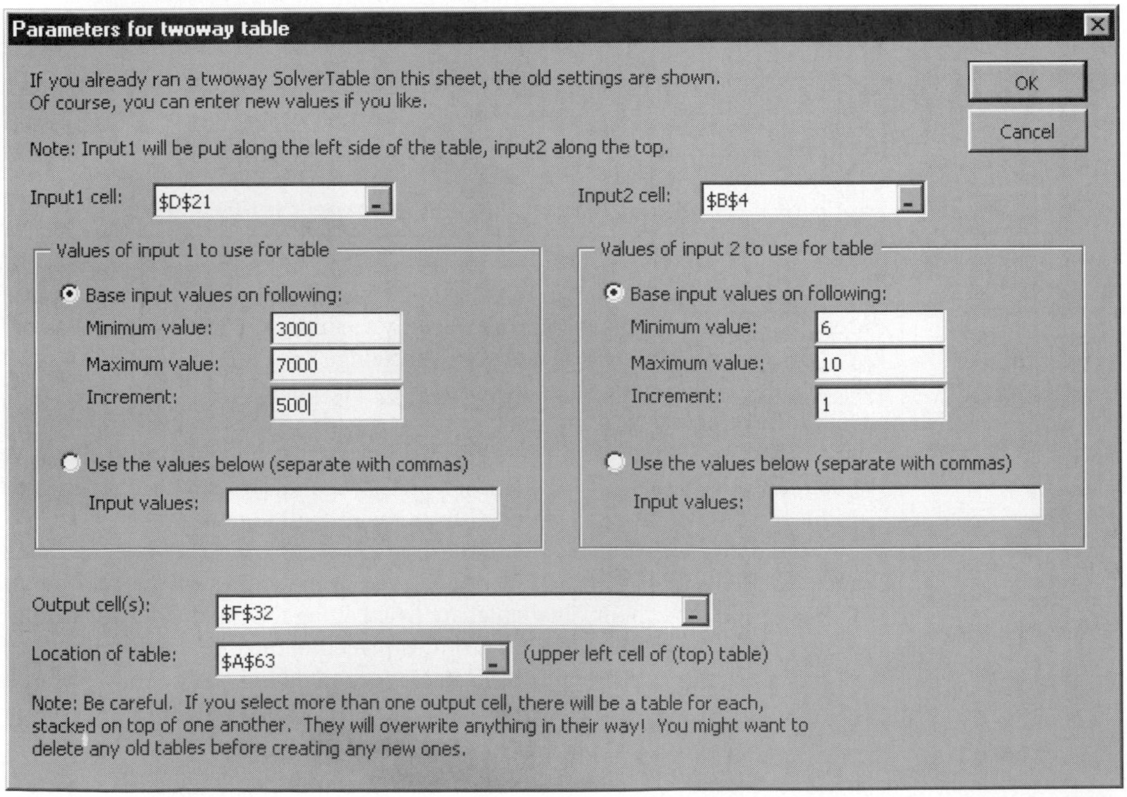

FIGURE 3.13 SolverTable Dialog Box for Two-Way Table

FIGURE 3.14
Bar Chart of
Optimal Profit

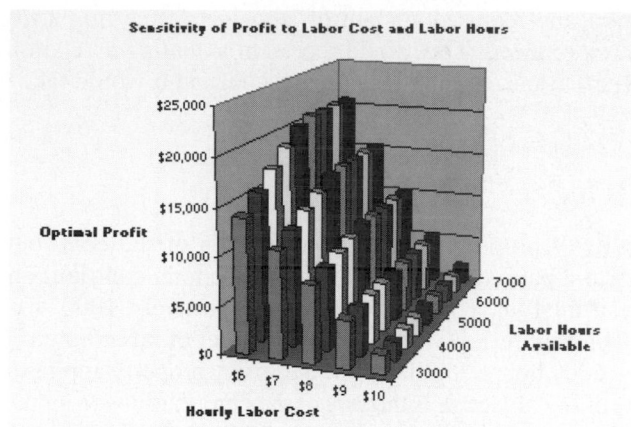

It is always possible to run a sensitivity analysis by changing inputs directly in the spreadsheet model and rerunning the Solver. The advantages of the SolverTable add-in, however, are that it enables us to perform a *systematic* sensitivity analysis for any selected inputs and outputs, and it keeps track of the results in a table. Then if we like, we can show these results in graphical form. We will see other applications of this useful add-in in this and later chapters.

3.5 THE LINEAR ASSUMPTIONS

Linear programming is an important subset of a larger class of models called **mathematical programming models**.[4] All such models select the levels of various activities that can be performed, subject to a set of constraints, to maximize or minimize an objective such as total profit or total cost. In Monet's product mix example, the activities are the production of the four frame types, and the purpose of the model is to find the levels of these activities that maximize total profit subject to specified constraints.

In terms of this general setup—selecting the optimal levels of activities—there are three important properties that LP models possess that distinguish them from general mathematical programming models: **proportionality**, **additivity**, and **divisibility**. We discuss these properties briefly in this section.

Proportionality

Proportionality means that if the level of any activity is multiplied by a constant factor, then the contribution of this activity to the objective, or to any of the constraints in which the activity is involved, is multiplied by the same factor. For example, suppose that the production of type 1 frames is cut from its optimal value of 1000 (see Figure 3.6) to 500—that is, it is multiplied by 0.5. Then the amounts of labor, metal, and glass consumed by type 1 frames are all cut in half, and the profit contribution from type 1 frames is also cut in half. In contrast, suppose that certain efficiencies could be gained by producing type 1 frames in larger quantities. Then, contrary to the proportionality

---

[4] The word *programming* in linear programming or mathematical programming has nothing to do with computer programming. It originated with the British term *programme*, which is essentially a plan or a schedule of operations.

assumption, the required amount of labor per frame might *decrease* as more type 1 frames are produced. This would represent a *nonlinear* relationship between the level of the type 1 frame activity and labor usage, and it would take us outside of the linear realm.

Additivity

The additivity property implies that the sum of the contributions from the various activities to a particular constraint equals the total contribution to that constraint. For example, if the four types of frames use, respectively, 1000, 800, 1200, and 3000 labor hours (as in Figure 3.1), then the total number of labor hours used is the *sum* of these amounts, 6000 hours. Similarly, the additivity property applies to the objective. That is, the value of the objective is the *sum* of the contributions from the various activities. The additivity property implies that the contribution of any decision variable to the objective or to any constraint is *independent* of the levels of the other decision variables.

Divisibility

The divisibility property simply means that we allow both integer and noninteger levels of the activities. In the product mix example, it fortunately turned out that the optimal quantities of frame types 1 through 4 were all integers. However, it is more frequent that the optimal quantities are nonintegers, such as 47.53. In LP models we allow such values. In reality, however, they might not make physical sense. For example, if product 1 is a refrigerator, it makes no sense to make 47.53 refrigerators. On the other hand, there are products, such as salt measured in pounds, where 47.53 units makes sense. If we want the levels of some activities to be integer values, there are two possible approaches: (1) We can solve the LP model without integer constraints, and if the solution turns out to have noninteger values, we can attempt to round them to integer values, or (2) we can explicitly constrain certain changing cells to contain integer values. The latter approach, however, takes us into the realm of *integer programming*, a much more difficult class of problems than LP problems. (We will study integer programming models in Chapter 6.)

Whenever we model a real problem, we usually make some simplifying assumptions. This is certainly the case with LP models. The world is frequently *not* linear, which means that an entirely realistic model will typically violate some or all of the three properties just discussed. However, many successful applications of LP have demonstrated the usefulness of linear models, even if they are only approximations of reality. If we suspect that the violations are serious enough to invalidate a linear model, then we should use an integer or nonlinear model, as we illustrate with several examples in later chapters.

In terms of Excel's Solver, if the model is linear—that is, if it satisfies the proportionality, additivity, and divisibility properties—then we should check the Assume Linear Model box that appears in the Solver Options dialog box. Then the Solver will use the simplex method, which is the most efficient method for a linear model, to solve the problem. Actually, we can check the Assume Linear Model box even if the divisibility property is violated—that is, for linear models with integer variables—but the Solver will use a method other than the simplex method in its solution procedure.

Linear Models and Scaling

In some cases you might be sure that a model is linear, but when you check the Assume Linear Model box, you get a message from the Solver that "the conditions for Assume Linear Model are not satisfied." This can indicate a logical error in your formulation, so that at least one of the proportionality, additivity, and divisibility conditions is indeed not satisfied. However, it can also indicate that the Solver erroneously *thinks* the linearity conditions are not satisfied, which is typically due to roundoff error in its calculations. If the latter occurs, and you are convinced that the formulation is correct, you can try *not* checking the Assume Linear Model box and see if that works. If it does not, consult your instructor. It is possible that the nonlinear algorithm employed by the Solver when this box is not checked simply cannot find the solution to your problem.

In any case, it helps to have a *well-scaled* model. In a well-scaled model, all of the numbers are roughly the same magnitude. If the model contains some very large numbers—100,000 or more, say—and some very small numbers—0.001 or less, say—it is *poorly scaled* for the methods used by the Solver, and roundoff error is far more likely to cause problems, not only in the Solver's test for linearity conditions but in all of its algorithms.

If you believe your model is poorly scaled, there are two possible remedies. The first is to check the Use Automatic Scaling box in the Solver Options dialog box (see Figure 3.4). This might help and it might not—we have had mixed success. (Frontline Systems has told us that the only drawback to checking this box is that the solution procedure could take a second or two longer.) The second option is to redefine the units in which the various quantities are defined. For example, in the Monet product mix model a natural rescaling would be to:

- Define the changing cells as the number of frames of each type produced *in thousands*.
- Define maximum sales limitations *in thousands*.
- Define profit *in thousands of dollars*.
- Define resource availabilities *in thousands of units* (labor hours or ounces of glass or metal).

If we rescale according to the steps above, the solution in Figure 3.15 (page 86) results. (Actually, all we had to do was rescale the inputs in B18:E18 and D21:D23 and rerun the Solver.) Now all of the model quantities are of similar magnitude.

Manually rescaling takes time, and it introduces the possibility of errors from converting units incorrectly in your formulas. However, in a few of the models we have developed, we have found it to be the best way to guarantee a correct Solver solution.

FIGURE 3.15
Product Mix Model
with Rescaled Values

	A	B	C	D	E	F	G	H
1	**Product Miz Problem**							
2								
3	**Input data**							
4	Hourly wage rate	$8.00						
5	Cost per oz of metal	$0.50						
6	Cost per oz of glass	$0.75						
7								
8	Frame type	1	2	3	4			
9	Labor hours per frame	2	1	3	2			
10	Metal (oz.) per frame	4	2	1	2			
11	Glass (oz.) per frame	6	2	1	2			
12	Unit selling price	$28.50	$12.50	$29.25	$21.50			
13								
14	**Production plan**							
15	Frame type	1	2	3	4			
16	Frames produced (1000s)	1.00	0.80	0.40	0.00			
17		<=	<=	<=	<=			
18	Maximum sales (1000s)	1	2	0.5	1			
19								
20	**Constraints on inputs**	Used		Available				
21	Labor hours (1000s)	4.0	<=	4				
22	Metal (1000s of oz.)	6.0	<=	6				
23	Glass (1000s of oz.)	8.0	<=	10				
24								
25	**Revenue, cost summary (all values in $1000s)**							
26	Frame type	1	2	3	4	Totals		
27	Revenue	$28.5	$10.0	$11.7	$0.0	$50.2		
28	Costs of inputs							
29	Labor	$16.0	$6.4	$9.6	$0.0	$32.0		
30	Metal	$2.0	$0.8	$0.2	$0.0	$3.0		
31	Glass	$4.5	$1.2	$0.3	$0.0	$6.0		
32	Profit	$6.0	$1.6	$1.6	$0.0	$9.2		

Range names:
Available: D21:D23
MaxSales: B18:E18
Produced: B16:E16
TotProfit: F32
Used: B21:B23

3.6 GRAPHICAL SOLUTION METHOD

Once LP problems are formulated, they are almost always solved numerically with computer software. The amount of computation makes manual calculation prohibitive for realistically sized problems. However, it is instructive to look at a graphical solution procedure for models with only two decision variables. Admittedly, almost no real problems have only two decision variables, but the graphical solution is useful for the insights it provides, even for larger problems.

EXAMPLE 3.2

A GRAPHICAL SOLUTION TO MONET'S PROBLEM

To illustrate the graphical approach, we will use a slightly different, scaled-down version of Monet's product mix problem. Now there are only two frame types, 1 and 2, and only two scarce resources, labor hours and metal. The algebraic model is given below:

$$\max\ 2.25x_1 + 2.60x_2 \quad \text{(profit objective)}$$
$$\text{subject to } 2x_1 + x_2 \le 4000 \quad \text{(labor constraint)}$$
$$x_1 + 2x_2 \le 5000 \quad \text{(metal constraint)}$$
$$x_1, x_2 \ge 0 \quad \text{(nonnegativity constraints)}$$

The objective implies that each type 1 frame contributes a profit of $2.25, whereas each type 2 frame contributes a profit of $2.60. The first constraint is a labor hour constraint. There are 4000 hours available. Each type 1 frame requires 2 labor hours, and each type 2 frame requires 1 labor hour. Similarly, the second constraint is a metal constraint. There are 5000 ounces of metal available. Each type 1 frame requires 1 ounce of metal, and each type 2 frame requires 2 ounces of metal. Find the optimal product mix graphically.

Solution

The idea is to graph the constraints on a two-dimensional graph to see which points (x_1, x_2) satisfy all of the constraints. This set of points is labeled the **feasible region**. Then we see which point in the feasible region provides the largest profit.

The graphical solution appears in Figure 3.16. To produce this graph, we first locate the lines where the constraints hold as equalities. For example, the line for labor hours is $2x_1 + x_2 = 4000$. The easiest way to graph this line is to find the two points where it crosses the axes. It crosses the x_1-axis when $x_2 = 0$, that is, at $x_1 = 4000/2 = 2000$. Similarly, it crosses the x_2-axis when $x_1 = 0$, that is, at $x_2 = 4000$. Joining the points (0, 4000) and (2000, 0), we get the line where the labor constraint is satisfied exactly, that is, as an equality. All points below and to the left of this line are also feasible; these are the points where less than the maximum of 4000 labor hours are used. [To see this, try the point (0, 0). It obviously satisfies the labor hour constraint, so it must be on the feasible side of the line. If (0, 0) did not satisfy the constraint, then the feasible side would be the side *not* including (0, 0).] We indicate the feasible side of the line by the short arrows pointing down to the left from the labor constraint line.

Similarly, the metal constraint line crosses the axes at the points (0, 2500) and (5000, 0), so we join these two points to find the line where all 5000 ounces of metal are used. Then all points below this line, indicated by the short arrows, use less than

FIGURE 3.16
Graphical Solution for Two-Variable Model

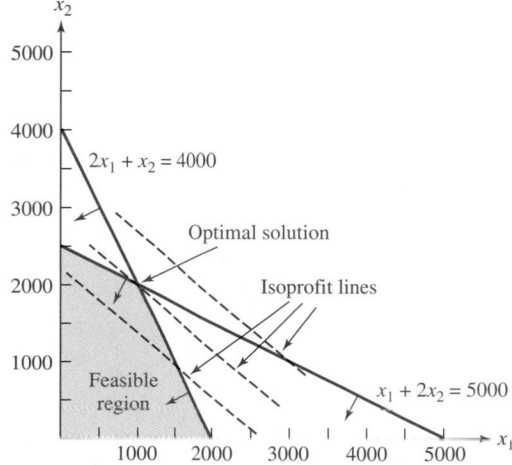

5000 ounces of metal. Finally, the points on or below both of these lines constitute the feasible region. These are the points below the heavy lines, as indicated in Figure 3.16. (Of course, the feasible region includes only points to the right of the vertical axis and above the horizontal axis, because negative production quantities are impossible.) You can think of the feasible region as all points on or inside the figure formed by four points: (0, 0), (0, 2500), (2000, 0), and the point where the labor hour and metal constraint lines intersect.

The next step is to bring profit into the picture. We do this by constructing "isoprofit" lines—that is, lines where total profit is a constant. Any such line can be written as

$$2.25x_1 + 2.60x_2 = P$$

where P is a constant profit level. Solving for x_2, we can put this equation in slope–intercept form:

$$x_2 = P/2.60 - (2.25/2.60)x_1$$

This shows that any isoprofit line has slope $-2.25/2.60$, and it crosses the vertical axis at the value $P/2.60$. Three of these isoprofit lines appear in Figure 3.16 as dashed lines. As the dashed line moves up and to the right, the profit P increases. Therefore, to maximize profit, we want to move the dashed line up and to the right until it just barely touches the feasible region. Graphically, we can see that the last feasible point it will touch is the "Optimal solution" point indicated in the figure, where the labor hour and metal constraint lines cross. (The corresponding isoprofit line is the middle dashed line.) We can then solve two equations in two unknowns to find the coordinates of this point. They are $x_1 = 1000$ and $x_2 = 2000$, with a corresponding profit of $P = \$7450$.

Note that if the slope of the isoprofit lines were much steeper, then the optimal point would be (2000, 0). On the other hand, if the slope were much *less* steep, the optimal point would be (0, 2500). These statements make intuitive sense. If the isoprofit lines are steep, it is because the unit profit from frame type 1 is large relative to the unit profit from frame type 2. If there is a large enough disparity, Monet will produce only frame type 1 and none of frame type 2. The opposite statement is true if the isoprofit lines are much less steep, inducing Monet to produce only frame type 2 and none of type 1. The crucial point, however, is that only three points can be optimal: (2000, 0), (0, 2500), or (1000, 2000), the three "corner" points [other than (0, 0)] in the feasible region.[5] The best of these depends on the relative slopes of the constraint lines and isoprofit lines in the graph. ∎

This graphical approach is virtually never used to solve real problems, but it does provide important insights into LP in general. Namely, all linear programming problems have feasible regions that can be thought of as multidimensional polygons (figures with straight edges). The only points that can be optimal (except in the case of multiple optimal solutions) are the corner points of this polygon. To see which corner point is optimal, we move an isoprofit line as far as possible in the desired direction (the direction that improves the objective function) until it just barely intersects with the feasible region. The corner point that is touched last is then the optimal solution. The simplex method—the method Excel's Solver uses for LP problems—is really just an efficient method of searching through the thousands (or millions) of corner points that occur in realistic problems.

---

[5] This is not quite true. If the slope of the isoprofit lines is *exactly* the same as the slope of one of the constraint lines, then a whole line segment can be optimal. We call this the **multiple optimal solution case**—the case of ties. Even in the case of ties, however, we can still restrict the search for optimal solutions to corner points.

PROBLEMS

Skill-Building Problems

1. Leary Chemical manufactures three chemicals: A, B, and C. These chemicals are produced via two production processes: 1 and 2. Running process 1 for an hour costs $4 and yields 3 units of A, 1 unit of B, and 1 unit of C. Running process 2 for an hour costs $1 and yields 1 unit of A and 1 unit of B. To meet customer demands, at least 10 units of A, 5 units of B, and 3 units of C must be produced daily.
   a. Use Solver to determine a daily production plan that minimizes the cost of meeting Leary's daily demands.
   b. Confirm graphically that the daily production plan from part **a** minimizes the cost of meeting Leary's daily demands.

2. Starting with the optimal solution to the previous problem, use the SolverTable add-in to see what happens to the decision variables and the total cost when the hourly processing cost for process 2 increases in increments of $0.50. How large must this cost increase be before the decision variables change? What happens when it continues to increase beyond this point?

3. Furnco manufactures desks and chairs. Each desk uses 4 units of wood, and each chair uses 3 units of wood. A desk contributes $40 to profit, and a chair contributes $25. Marketing restrictions require that the number of chairs produced be at least twice the number of desks produced. There are 20 units of wood available.
   a. Use Solver to maximize Furnco's profit.
   b. Confirm graphically that the solution in part **a** maximizes Furnco's profit.

4. Starting with the optimal solution to the previous problem, use the SolverTable add-in to see what happens to the decision variables and the total profit when the availability of wood varies from 10 to 30 in 1-unit increments. Based on your findings, how much would Furnco be willing to pay for each extra unit of wood over its current 20 units? How much profit would Furnco lose if it lost any of its current 20 units?

5. A farmer in Iowa owns 45 acres of land. She is going to plant each acre with wheat or corn. Each acre planted with wheat yields $200 profit; each with corn yields $300 profit. The labor and fertilizer used for each acre are given in Table 3.2. One hundred workers and 120 tons of fertilizer are available.

TABLE 3.2	Data for Farmer Problem	
	Wheat	**Corn**
Labor	3 workers	2 workers
Fertilizer	2 tons	4 tons

   a. Use Solver to help the farmer maximize the profit from her land.
   b. Confirm graphically that the solution from part **a** maximizes the farmer's profit from her land.

6. Starting with the optimal solution to the previous problem, use the SolverTable add-in to see what happens to the decision variables and the total profit when the availability of fertilizer varies from 20 tons to 220 tons in 10-ton increments.
   a. When does the farmer discontinue producing wheat? When does she discontinue producing corn?
   b. How does the profit change for each 10-ton increment? Make this more obvious by creating a line chart of profit (vertical axis) versus fertilizer availability.

Skill-Extending Problem

7. Truckco manufactures two types of trucks, types 1 and 2. Each truck must go through the painting shop and the assembly shop. If the painting shop were completely devoted to painting type 1 trucks, 800 per day could be painted, whereas if the painting shop were completely devoted to painting type 2 trucks, 700 per day could be painted. If the assembly shop were completely devoted to assembling truck 1 engines, 1500 per day could be assembled, and if the assembly shop were completely devoted to assembling truck 2 engines, 1200 per day could be assembled. It is possible, however, to paint *both* types of trucks in the painting shop. Similarly, it is possible to assemble both types in the assembly shop. Each type 1 truck contributes $300 to profit; each type 2 truck contributes $500. Use Solver to maximize Truckco's profit. (*Hint*: One approach, but not the only approach, is to try a graphical procedure first and then deduce the constraints from the graph.)

3.7 INFEASIBILITY AND UNBOUNDEDNESS

In this section we discuss two of the things that can go wrong when we invoke the Solver. Both of these might indicate that there is a mistake in the formulation. Therefore, because mistakes are common in LP formulations, you should be aware of the error messages you might encounter.

Infeasibility

The first problem is infeasibility. If a solution satisfies all of the constraints, we say that it is **feasible**. Among all of the feasible solutions, we are looking for the one that optimizes the objective. Now, it is possible that there are no feasible solutions to the model. There are generally two possible reasons for this: (1) There is a mistake in the formulation (an input entered incorrectly, such as a $\geq$ instead of a $\leq$) or (2) the problem has been so constrained that there are no solutions left! In the former case, a careful check of the formulation should find the error. In the latter case, the analyst might need to change, or even eliminate, some of the constraints.

To show how an infeasible problem could occur, suppose in Monet's product mix problem that we incorrectly enter the maximum sales constraints with the wrong inequality: Produced>=MaxSales instead of Produced<=MaxSales. Now Monet must produce *at least* as much as the maximum sales values. If the constraint is changed this way and the Solver is then used, the message in Figure 3.17 appears, indicating that the Solver cannot find a feasible solution. The reason is clear: There is no way, given the resource availabilities, that the company can meet these production constraints. If we are observant, we will notice the error in the formulation, change the direction of the inequality, and proceed. However, there is no foolproof way to find the problem when a "no feasible solution" message appears. Careful checking and rethinking are required.

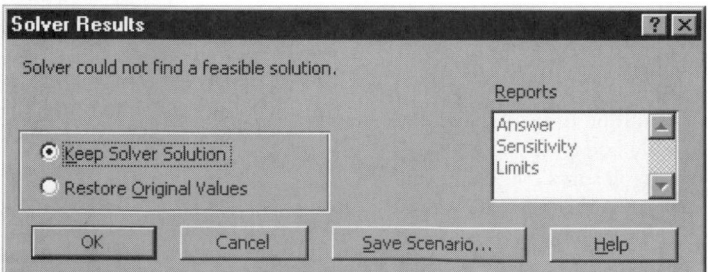

Unboundedness

A second type of problem is **unboundedness**. In this case, the model has been formulated in such a way that the objective is unbounded—that is, it can be made as large (or as small, for minimization problems) as we like. If this occurs, we have probably entered a wrong input or forgotten some constraints. To see how this could occur in the product mix problem, suppose that we enter both the maximum sales constraints and the resource constraints with $\geq$ instead of $\leq$. Now there is no upper bound on how much of each product Monet can make because there is no upper bound on the amount of the resources available. Because each frame generates a profit, the total profit is unlimited. If we make these changes in the formulation and then use the Solver, the message in Figure 3.18 appears, stating that the target cell does not converge. In other words, the total profit is growing without bound.

Infeasibility and unboundedness are quite different in a practical sense. It is quite possible for a reasonable model to have no feasible solutions. For example, the marketing department might impose several constraints, the production department might add some more, the engineering department might add some more, and so on. Together, they might constrain the problem so much that there are no feasible solutions left. The only way out is to change or eliminate some of the constraints. An unboundedness problem is quite different. There is no way a realistic model can have an unbounded solution. If we get the message in Figure 3.18, then we must have made a mistake—either we made an input error or we omitted one or more constraints.

FIGURE 3.18
Solver Dialog Box
Indicating an
Unbounded Solution

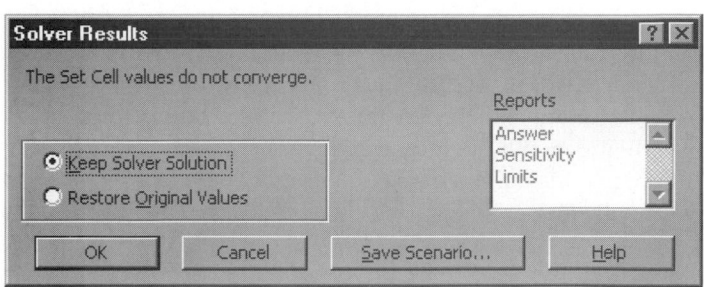

3.8 A MULTIPERIOD PRODUCTION PROBLEM

The product mix example illustrates a typical LP model. However, LP models come in many forms. For variety, we will now illustrate a quite different type of problem that can also be solved with LP. (In the next few chapters we will illustrate many other examples, linear and otherwise.) The distinguishing feature of the following problem is that it relates decisions made in several time periods. This type of problem occurs when a company must make a decision now that will have ramifications in the future. The company does not want to focus completely on the near future and forget about the long run.

EXAMPLE 3.3

PRODUCING FOOTBALLS AT PIGSKIN

The Pigskin Company produces footballs. Pigskin must decide how many footballs to produce each month. It has decided to use a 6-month planning horizon. The forecasted demands for the next 6 months are 10,000, 15,000, 30,000, 35,000, 25,000, and 10,000. Pigskin wants to meet these demands on time, knowing that it currently has 5000 footballs in inventory and that it can use a given month's production to help meet the demand for that month. (For simplicity, we assume that production occurs during the month, and demand occurs at the end of the month.) During each month there is enough production capacity to produce up to 30,000 footballs, and there is enough storage capacity to store up to 10,000 footballs at the end of the month, after demand has occurred. The forecasted production costs per football for the next 6 months are $12.50, $12.55, $12.70, $12.80, $12.85, and $12.95, respectively. The holding cost per football held in inventory at the end of any month is figured at 5% of the production cost for that month. (This cost includes the cost of storage and also the cost of money tied up in inventory.) The selling price for footballs is not considered relevant to the production decision because Pigskin will satisfy all customer demand exactly when it occurs—at whatever the selling price is. Therefore, Pigskin wants to determine the production schedule that minimizes the total production and holding costs.

Solution

In the traditional algebraic formulation, the decision variables are the production quantities for the 6 months, labeled P_1 through P_6. It is also convenient to let I_1 through I_6 be the corresponding end-of-month inventories (after demand has occurred). For example, I_3 is the number of footballs left over at the end of month 3. Therefore, the obvious constraints are on production and inventory storage capacities: $P_j \leq 300$ and $I_j \leq 100$ for each month j, $1 \leq j \leq 6$. (From here on, to minimize the number of zeros shown, we will express all quantities in *hundreds* of footballs.)

In addition to these constraints, we need **balance** constraints that relate the P's and I's. In any month the inventory from the previous month plus the current production must equal the current demand plus leftover inventory. If D_j is the forecasted demand for month j, then the balance equation for month j is

$$I_{j-1} + P_j = D_j + I_j$$

The first of these constraints, for month $j = 1$, uses the known beginning inventory, 50, for the previous inventory (the I_{j-1} term). By putting all variables (P's and I's) on the left and all known values on the right (a standard LP convention), we can write these balance constraints as

$$
\begin{aligned}
P_1 - I_1 &= 100 - 50 \\
I_1 + P_2 - I_2 &= 150 \\
I_2 + P_3 - I_3 &= 300 \\
I_3 + P_4 - I_4 &= 350 \\
I_4 + P_5 - I_5 &= 250 \\
I_5 + P_6 - I_6 &= 100
\end{aligned}
\tag{3.1}
$$

As usual, we impose nonnegativity constraints: All P's and I's must be nonnegative. What about meeting demand on time? This requires that, in each month, the inventory from the preceding month plus the current production must be at least as large as the current demand. But take a look, for example, at the balance constraint for month 3. By rearranging it slightly, we can write it as

$$I_3 = I_2 + P_3 - 300$$

Now, the nonnegativity constraint on I_3 implies that the right side of this equation, $I_2 + P_3 - 300$, is also nonnegative. But this implies that demand in month 3 is covered—the beginning inventory in month 3 plus month 3 production is at least 300. Therefore, the nonnegativity constraints on the I's *automatically* guarantee that all demands will be met on time, and no other constraints are needed. Alternatively, we could write directly that $I_2 + P_3 \geq 300$. In words, the amount on hand after production in month 3 is at least as large as the demand in month 3. We will take advantage of this interpretation in the spreadsheet model.

Finally, the objective is the sum of unit production costs multiplied by P's, plus unit holding costs multiplied by I's.

DEVELOPING THE SPREADSHEET MODEL

The spreadsheet model of Pigskin's production problem appears in Figure 3.19. (See the file PIGSKIN1.XLS.) The main feature that distinguishes this model from the product mix model is that some of the constraints, namely, the balance constraints (3.1), are built into the spreadsheet itself by means of formulas. In other words, the only changing cells are the production quantities. The ending inventories shown in row 20 are *determined* by the production quantities and equations (3.1). To form the spreadsheet model in Figure 3.19, proceed as follows.

❶ Inputs. Enter the inputs in the shaded ranges. Again, these are all entered as *numbers* straight from the problem statement. (Unlike some spreadsheet modelers who prefer to put all inputs in the upper left corner of the spreadsheet, we have entered the inputs wherever they fit most naturally. Of course, this takes some planning and experimenting.)

❷ Production quantities. Enter *any* values in the range Produced as production quantities. As always, you can enter values that you believe are good, maybe even optimal. This is not crucial, however, because the Solver will eventually find the optimal production quantities.

❸ On-hand inventory. Enter the formula

=InitInv+B12

in cell B16. This calculates the first month on-hand inventory after production (but before demand). Then enter the "typical" formula

=B20+C12

	A	B	C	D	E	F	G	H	I	J
1	**Multiperiod production model**									
2										
3	**Input data**									
4	Initial inventory (100s)	50								
5	Holding cost as % of prod cost	5%								
6										
7	Month	1	2	3	4	5	6	**Range names used:**		
8	Production cost/unit	$12.50	$12.55	$12.70	$12.80	$12.85	$12.95	InitInv - B4		
9								HoldPct - B5		
10	**Production plan (all quantities are in 100s of footballs)**							Produced - B12:G12		
11	Month	1	2	3	4	5	6	ProdCap - B14:G14		
12	Units produced	150	150	300	300	250	100	OnHand - B16:G16		
13		<=	<=	<=	<=	<=	<=	Demand - B18:G18		
14	Production capacity (100s)	300	300	300	300	300	300	EndInv - B20:G20		
15								StoreCap - B22:G22		
16	On hand after production	200	250	400	400	300	150	TotCost - H28		
17		>=	>=	>=	>=	>=	>=			
18	Demand	100	150	300	350	250	100			
19										
20	Ending inventory	100	100	100	50	50	50			
21		<=	<=	<=	<=	<=	<=			
22	Storage capacity	100	100	100	100	100	100			
23										
24	**Summary of costs (all costs are in hundreds of dollars)**									
25	Month	1	2	3	4	5	6	Totals		
26	Production costs	$1,875.00	$1,882.50	$3,810.00	$3,840.00	$3,212.50	$1,295.00	$15,915.00		
27	Holding costs	$62.50	$62.75	$63.50	$32.00	$32.13	$32.38	$285.25		
28								$16,200.25		

FIGURE 3.19 Nonoptimal Solution to Pigskin's Production Model

for on-hand inventory after production in month 2 in cell C16 and copy it across row 16. In multiperiod problems, we often need a slightly different formula for the first period than for all other periods.

❹   Ending inventories. Enter the formula

=B16-B18

for ending inventory in cell B20 and copy it to the rest of the EndInv range. This formula calculates ending inventory in the current month as on-hand inventory before demand minus the demand in that month.

❺   Production and holding costs. Enter the formula

=B8*B12

in cell B26 and copy it across to cell G26 to calculate the monthly production costs. Then enter the formula

=HoldPct*B8*B20

in cell B27 and copy it across to cell G27 to calculate the monthly holding costs. Note that these are based on monthly ending inventories. Finally, calculate the cost totals in column H by summing with the SUM function.

The logic behind the constraints is now straightforward. All we have to guarantee is that (1) the production quantities are nonnegative and do not exceed the production capacities, (2) the on-hand inventories after production are at least as large as demands, and (3) ending inventories do not exceed storage capacities.

USING THE SOLVER

To use the Solver, fill out the dialog boxes as follows and then click on Solve.

❶   Model. Fill out the Solver dialog box as in Figure 3.20. Of course, if we didn't use range names, we would refer directly to the corresponding cell addresses.

❷   Options. In the Solver Options dialog box, check the Assume Linear Model and Assume Non-Negative boxes. Note that the latter ensures only that the *changing* cells are nonnegative. If we wanted to explicitly constrain the ending inventory cells to be nonnegative, we would have to add an extra constraint in Figure 3.20.

The Solver solution appears in Figure 3.21. This solution is also represented graphically in Figure 3.22. We can interpret the solution by comparing production quantities with demands. (Also, remember that all quantities are in units of 100 footballs.) In month 1 Pigskin should produce just enough to meet month 1 demand (taking into account the initial inventory of 5000). In month 2 it should produce 5000 more footballs than month 2 demand, and then in month 3 it should produce just enough to meet month 3 demand, still carrying the extra 5000 footballs in inventory from month 2 production. In month 4 Pigskin should finally use these 5000 footballs, along with the maximum production amount, 30,000, to meet month 4 demand. Then in months 5 and 6 it should produce exactly enough to meet these months' demands. The total cost is $1,535,563, most of which is production cost. (This total cost is expressed in actual dollars. The value in the spreadsheet is in hundreds of dollars). Don't feel sorry for Pigskin, however. Remember that we ignored the selling price. The revenues from these sales should make Pigskin a handsome profit.

Could you have guessed that this is the optimal solution? Upon some reflection, it makes perfect sense. Because the monthly holding costs are large relative to the differences in monthly production costs, there is little incentive to produce footballs

FIGURE 3.20
Solver Dialog Box
for Production Model

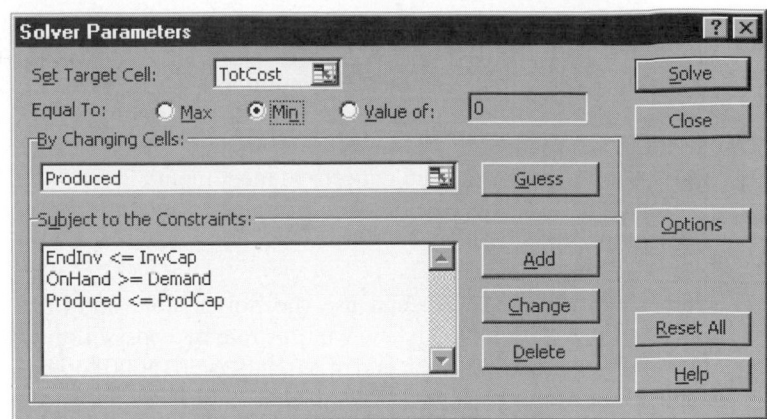

	A	B	C	D	E	F	G	H	I	J
1	**Multiperiod production model**									
2										
3	**Input data**									
4	Initial inventory (100s)	50								
5	Holding cost as % of prod cost	5%								
6										
7	Month	1	2	3	4	5	6	**Range names used:**		
8	Production cost/unit	$12.50	$12.55	$12.70	$12.80	$12.85	$12.95	InitInv - B4		
9								HoldPct - B5		
10	**Production plan (all quantities are in 100s of footballs)**							Produced - B12:G12		
11	Month	1	2	3	4	5	6	ProdCap - B14:G14		
12	Units produced	50	200	300	300	250	100	OnHand - B16:G16		
13		<=	<=	<=	<=	<=	<=	Demand - B18:G18		
14	Production capacity (100s)	300	300	300	300	300	300	EndInv - B20:G20		
15								StoreCap - B22:G22		
16	On hand after production	100	200	350	350	250	100	TotCost - H28		
17		>=	>=	>=	>=	>=	>=			
18	Demand	100	150	300	350	250	100			
19										
20	Ending inventory	0	50	50	0	0	0			
21		<=	<=	<=	<=	<=	<=			
22	Storage capacity	100	100	100	100	100	100			
23										
24	**Summary of costs (all costs are in hundreds of dollars)**									
25	Month	1	2	3	4	5	6	Totals		
26	Production costs	$625.00	$2,510.00	$3,810.00	$3,840.00	$3,212.50	$1,295.00	$15,292.50		
27	Holding costs	$0.00	$31.38	$31.75	$0.00	$0.00	$0.00	$63.13		
28								$15,355.63		

FIGURE 3.21 Optimal Solution for Production Model

FIGURE 3.22
Graphical
Representation of
Optimal Production
Schedule

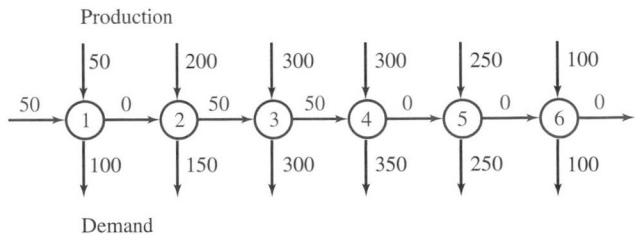

Months are in circles.
Inventory levels are on horizontal arrows.

before they are needed to take advantage of a "cheap" production month. Therefore, the Solver tells Pigskin to produce footballs in the month in which they are needed—when this is possible. The only exception to this rule is the 20,000 footballs produced during month 2 when only 15,000 are needed. The extra 5000 units produced during month 2 are needed, however, to meet month 4's demand of 35,000, because month 3 production capacity is used entirely to meet month 3 demand. Thus month 3 capacity is not available to meet month 4 demand, and 5000 units of month 2 capacity are used to meet month 4 demand.

Sensitivity Analysis We can use the SolverTable add-in to perform a number of interesting sensitivity analyses. We illustrate two possibilities. First, note that the most inventory ever carried at the end of a month is 50 (5000 footballs), although the storage capacity each month is 100. Perhaps this is because the holding cost percentage, 5%, is fairly large. Would more ending inventory be carried if this holding cost percentage were reduced? Or would even less be carried if it were increased? We check this with the SolverTable output shown in Figure 3.23. Now the single input cell is the HoldPct cell, and the *single* output we keep track of is the maximum ending inventory ever held, which we calculate in cell B31 with the formula

=MAX(EndInv)

As we see, only when the holding cost percentage decreases to 1% do we reach the storage capacity limit. (From this output we cannot tell which month or how many months the ending inventory will be at this upper limit.) On the other side, even when the holding cost percentage reaches 10%, we still continue to hold a maximum ending inventory of 50.

FIGURE 3.23
Sensitivity of
Maximum Ending
Inventory to Holding
Cost Percentage

	A	B	C	D	E	F
30	Sensitivity of maximum amount of ending inventory to holding cost percentage					
31	Output formula	100				
32						
33	Holding cost percentage	MaxEndInv				
34		$B$31				
35	1%	100				
36	2%	50				
37	3%	50				
38	4%	50				
39	5%	50				
40	6%	50				
41	7%	50				
42	8%	50				
43	9%	50				
44	10%	50				

A second possible sensitivity analysis is suggested by the way the optimal production schedule would probably be implemented. The optimal solution to Pigskin's model specifies the production level for each of the next 6 months. In reality, however, the company might implement the model's recommendation only for the *first* month. Then at the beginning of the second month, it will gather new forecasts for the *next* 6 months, months 2 through 7, solve a new 6-month model, and again implement the model's recommendation for the first of these months, month 2. If the company continues in this manner, we say that it is following a 6-month **rolling planning horizon**.

The question then is whether the assumed demands (really, forecasts) toward the end of the planning horizon have much effect on the optimal production quantity in month 1. We would hope not because these forecasts could be quite inaccurate.

	A	B	C	D	E	F
46	**Sensitivity of month 1 production quantity to demands in months 5 and 6**					
47	Month 5 demand is along side, month 6 demand is along top					
48	$B$12	100	200	300		
49	100	50	50	50		
50	200	50	50	50		
51	300	50	50	50		

The two-way Solver table in Figure 3.24 shows how the optimal month 1 production quantity varies with the assumed demands in months 5 and 6. As we see, if the assumed month 5 and 6 demands remain fairly small, the optimal month 1 production quantity remains at 50. This is good news. It means that the optimal production quantity in month 1 is fairly insensitive to the possibly inaccurate forecasts for months 5 and 6. ■

MODELING ISSUES

We assume that Pigskin uses a 6-month planning horizon. Why 6 months? In multi-period models such as this, the company has to make forecasts about the future, such as the level of customer demand. Therefore, the length of the planning horizon is usually the length of time for which the company can make reasonably accurate forecasts. Here, Pigskin evidently believes that it can forecast up to 6 months from now, so it uses a 6-month planning horizon. ■

PROBLEMS

Skill-Building Problems

8. A customer requires during the next 4 months, respectively, 50, 65, 100, and 70 units of a commodity, and no backlogging is allowed (that is, the customer's requirements must be met on time). Production costs are $5, $8, $4, and $7 per unit during these months. The storage cost from one month to the next is $2 per unit (assessed on ending inventory). It is estimated that each unit on hand at the end of month 4 could be sold for $6. Determine how to minimize the net cost incurred in meeting the demands for the next 4 months.

9. Starting with the optimal solution to the previous problem, use the SolverTable add-in to see what happens to the decision variables and the total cost when the initial inventory varies from 0 (the implied value in the previous problem) to 100 in 10-unit increments. How much lower would the total cost be if the company started with 10 units in inventory, rather than none? Would this same cost decrease occur for *every* 10-unit increase in initial inventory?

10. A company faces the following demands during the next 3 weeks: week 1, 20 units; week 2, 10 units; week 3, 15 units. The unit production costs during each week are as follows: week 1, $13; week 2, $14;

week 3, $15. A holding cost of $2 per unit is assessed against each week's ending inventory. At the beginning of week 1, the company has 5 units on hand. In reality, not all goods produced during a month can be used to meet the current month's demand. To model this fact, we assume that only half of the goods produced during a week can be used to meet the current week's demands. Determine how to minimize the cost of meeting the demand for the next 3 weeks.

11. Revise the model for the previous problem so that the demands are of the form $D_t + k\Delta_t$, where D_t is the original demand (from the previous problem) in month t, k is a factor, and Δ_t is an amount of change in month t demand. Formulate the model in such a way that you can use the SolverTable add-in to analyze changes in the amounts produced and the total cost when k varies from 0 to 10 in 1-unit increments, for any fixed values of the Δ_t's. For example, try this when $\Delta_1 = 2$, $\Delta_2 = 5$, and $\Delta_3 = 3$. Describe the behavior you observe in the table. Can you find any "reasonable" Δ_t's that induce *positive* production levels in week 3?

12. James Beerd bakes cheesecakes and Black Forest cakes. During any month he can bake at most 65 cakes. The costs per cake and the demands for cakes, which must be met on time, are listed in Table 3.3. It costs $0.50 to hold a cheesecake and $0.40 to hold a Black Forest cake in inventory for a month. Determine how to minimize the total cost of meeting the next three months' demands.

13. Revise the model for the previous problem so that the unit production costs are of the form $c_t(1 + \Delta_t)^k$ in month t, where c_t is the original unit cost (from the previous problem) in month t, Δ_t is an amount of change in month t, and k is an exponent. The c_t's

and Δ_t's for cheesecakes can differ from those for Black Forest cakes, but k should be the same for both. Formulate the model so that you can use the SolverTable add-in to investigate changes in the production quantities and total cost when k varies from 0 to 4 in 1-unit increments. You can try any reasonable values for the Δ_t's, such as $\Delta_1 = 0.1$, $\Delta_2 = 0.15$, and $\Delta_3 = 0.2$ for cheesecakes, and $\Delta_1 = 0.05$, $\Delta_2 = 0.1$, and $\Delta_3 = 0.15$ for Black Forest cakes. Write a short report on your findings.

TABLE 3.3	Data for Cake Problem					
	Month 1		Month 2		Month 3	
	Demand	Cost/Cake	Demand	Cost/Cake	Demand	Cost/Cake
Cheesecake	40	$3.00	30	$3.40	20	$3.80
Black Forest	20	$2.50	30	$2.80	10	$3.40

3.9 A DECISION SUPPORT SYSTEM

If your job is to develop an LP spreadsheet model to solve a problem such as Pigskin's production problem, then you will be considered the "expert" in LP. Many people who need to use such models, however, are *not* experts. They might understand the basic ideas behind LP and the types of problems it is intended to solve, but they will not know the details. In this case it is useful to provide these users with a **decision support system** (DSS) that can help them solve problems without having to worry about technical details.

We will not teach you in this book how to build a full-scale DSS, but we will indicate what they look like and what they can do.[6] (We will consider only DSSs built around spreadsheets. There are many other platforms for developing DSSs that we will not consider.) Basically, a spreadsheet-based DSS contains a spreadsheet model of a problem, such as the one in Figure 3.21. However, the users might never even see this model. Instead, they see a "front end" and a "back end." The front end allows them to select input values for their particular problem. The user interface for this front end can include several features, such as buttons, dialog boxes, toolbars, and menus—the things we are used to seeing in Windows applications. The back end then produces a report that explains the optimal policy in nontechnical terms.

We illustrate a DSS for a slight variation of the Pigskin problem in the file PIGSKIN2.XLS. This file has three sheets. When you open the file, you see the Explanation sheet. (See Figure 3.25.) It contains two buttons, one for setting up the problem (getting the user's inputs) and one for solving the problem (running the Solver). When you press the Set Up Problem button, you are asked for a series of inputs: the initial inventory, the number of months in the planning horizon, the forecasted demands for each month, and others. An example appears in Figure 3.26, where you must enter information about the holding costs. These input boxes should be self-explanatory, so that all you need to do is enter the values you want to try. After you have entered all

---

[6] For readers interested in learning more about spreadsheet DSSs, we provide a companion booklet with several applications and instructions for creating them with VBA.

FIGURE 3.25
Explanation Sheet for
DSS

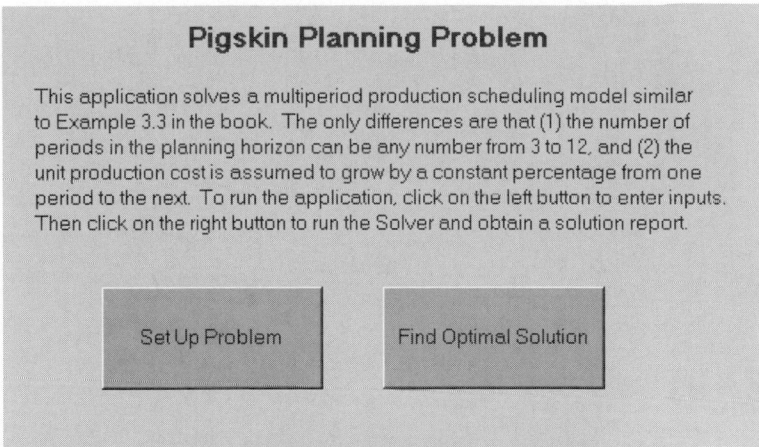

FIGURE 3.26
Input Dialog Box for
Holding Cost
Percentage

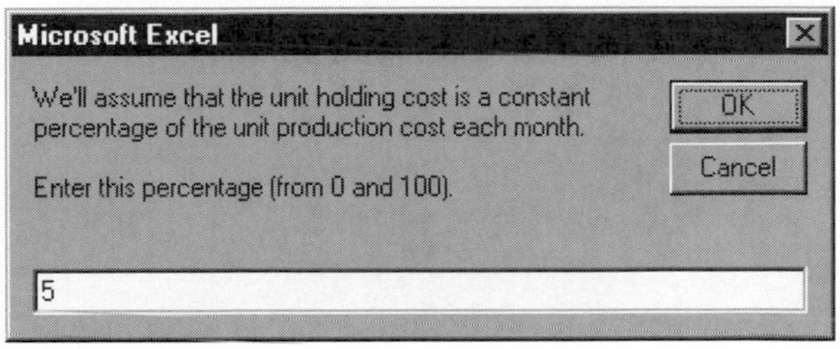

of these inputs, take a look at the Formulation sheet. This sheet contains a spreadsheet model similar to the one we saw earlier in Figure 3.21, but with the inputs you just entered. (However, the nontechnical user would never see this sheet.)

Now go back to the Explanation sheet and press the Find Optimal Solution button. This automatically sets up the Solver dialog box and runs the Solver. There are two cases. First, it is possible that there is no feasible solution to the problem with the inputs you entered. In this case you will see a message to this effect. (See Figure 3.27.) In most cases, however, the problem will have a feasible solution. In this case you will see the Report sheet, which summarizes the optimal solution in nontechnical terms. (See Figure 3.28 (page 100), which presents a solution for a 4-month planning horizon.) After studying this report, you are then allowed to click on the Solve Another Problem button, which takes you back to the Explanation sheet so that you can solve a new problem.

All of this is done automatically with Excel macros. These macros use Microsoft's Visual Basic for Applications (VBA) programming language to automate various tasks. We will not explain any of the details of this language, but you are encouraged to look at the code in the Visual Basic Editor (or the module sheets in Excel 95 or Excel 5) to get some sense of what it is doing. (Press Alt-F11 to get into the Visual Basic Editor.) In most professional applications, the Formulation sheet and programming code would be hidden and protected from the end user. These nontechnical people need only to enter inputs and look at reports.

FIGURE 3.27
No Solution Message

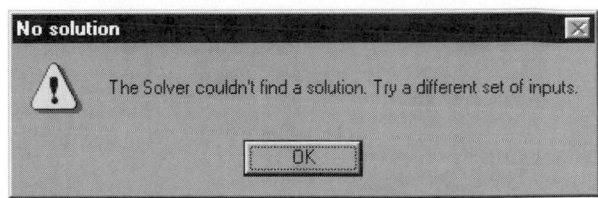

FIGURE 3.28
Report Sheet for DSS

Summary of optimal solution

Planning horizon (months)	4
Total production cost	$10,839.00
Total holding cost	$63.44
Total cost	$10,902.44

[Solve Another Problem]

Monthly schedule (scroll down to see more)

Month 1

Units		Dollars	
Start with	50		
Produce	50	Production cost	$625.00
Demand is	100		
End with	0	Holding cost	$0.00

Month 2

Units		Dollars	
Start with	0		
Produce	200	Production cost	$2,525.00
Demand is	150		
End with	50	Holding cost	$31.57

Month 3

Units		Dollars	
Start with	50		
Produce	300	Production cost	$3,825.39
Demand is	300		
End with	50	Holding cost	$31.88

Month 4

Units		Dollars	
Start with	50		
Produce	300	Production cost	$3,863.64
Demand is	350		
End with	0	Holding cost	$0.00

3.10 CONCLUSION

This chapter has provided a good start in LP modeling. We learned how to develop two basic LP spreadsheet models, how to use the Solver to find their optimal solutions, and how to use the SolverTable add-in to perform sensitivity analyses. We also saw how to recognize whether a mathematical programming model satisfies the linear assumptions. In the next few chapters we will discuss a variety of other optimization models, some considerably more complex than the ones in this chapter, but the three basic steps of model development, Solver optimization, and sensitivity analysis will remain the same.

PROBLEMS

Skill-Building Problems

14. Peg and Al Fundy have a limited food budget, so Peg is trying to feed the family as cheaply as possible. However, Peg still wants to make sure her family members meet their daily nutritional requirements. Peg can buy two foods. Food 1 sells for $7 per pound, and each pound contains 3 units of vitamin A and 1 unit of vitamin C. Food 2 sells for $1 per pound, and each pound contains 1 unit of each vitamin. Each day, the family needs at least 12 units of vitamin A and 6 units of vitamin C.

    a. Verify that Peg should purchase 12 units of food 2 each day and thus oversatisfy the vitamin C requirement by 6 units.

    b. Al has put his foot down and demanded that Peg fulfill the family's daily nutritional requirement exactly by obtaining precisely 12 units of vitamin A and 6 units of vitamin C. The optimal solution to the new problem will involve ingesting less vitamin C, but it will be more expensive. Why?

15. Starting with the optimal solution to the previous problem, use the SolverTable add-in to see what happens to the total cost when the vitamin A and vitamin C requirements both vary (independently) from 3 to 18 in 3-unit increments. That is, form a two-way table. Describe the behavior you observe. In particular, are the changes in total cost the *same* as you look across each row of the table? Are they the same as you look down each column of the table?

16. Bloomington Brewery produces beer and ale. Beer sells for $5 per barrel, and ale sells for $2 per barrel. Producing a barrel of beer requires 5 pounds of corn and 2 pounds of hops. Producing a barrel of ale requires 2 pounds of corn and 1 pound of hops. The brewery has 60 pounds of corn and 25 pounds of hops.
    a. Use Solver to maximize Bloomington Brewery's revenue.
    b. Confirm graphically that the solution in part **a** maximizes Bloomington Brewery's revenue.

17. Starting with the optimal solution to the previous problem, use the SolverTable add-in to either substantiate or refute the following statements: The availability of corn can decrease by any amount (up to 60 pounds), and each unit decrease will cost Bloomington Brewery the same amount in terms of lost revenue. On the other hand, increases in the availability of corn do *not* have a constant effect on total revenue; the first few extra units have a larger effect than subsequent units.

18. A gourmet cook bakes two types of cake (chocolate and vanilla) to supplement her income. Each chocolate cake can be sold for $12, and each vanilla cake can be sold for $9. Each chocolate cake requires 20 minutes of baking time and uses 4 eggs. Each vanilla cake requires 40 minutes of baking time and uses 1 egg. The baker has 8 hours of baking time and 30 eggs.
    a. Use Solver to determine how the cook can maximize her profit.
    b. Confirm graphically that the solution in part **a** maximizes the cook's profit.

19. Revise the model for the previous problem so that the baking times for both types of cake can increase by a factor $1 + k$. Formulate the model so that you can use the SolverTable add-in to investigate changes in the numbers of cakes produced and the total profit as k varies from 0 to 0.5 in increments of 0.05. Explain the behavior you observe. In particular, are the changes in optimal profit *linear* with respect to changes in k? If not, indicate how they behave. (*Note*: If you like, you can constrain the numbers of cakes to be integers. However, if you do so, you might run into a problem we observed—the Solver states that at least one of the

problems has no feasible solution even though they are all clearly feasible.)

20. For a telephone survey, a marketing research group needs to contact at least 150 wives, 120 husbands, 100 single adult males, and 110 single adult females. It costs $2 to make a daytime call and (because of higher labor costs) $5 to make an evening call. Table 3.4 lists the results that can be expected. For example, 30% of all daytime calls are answered by a wife, and 15% of all evening calls are answered by a single male. Because of a limited staff, at most half of all phone calls can be evening calls. Determine how to minimize the cost of completing the survey.

TABLE 3.4	Data for Phone Problem	
Person Responding	Percentage of Daytime Calls	Percentage of Evening Calls
Wife	30	30
Husband	10	30
Single male	10	15
Single female	10	20
None	40	5

21. Starting with the optimal solution to the previous problem, use the SolverTable add-in to investigate changes in the unit cost of either type of call. Specifically, investigate changes in the cost of a daytime call, with the cost of an evening call fixed, to see when (if ever) *only* daytime calls or *only* evening calls will be made. Then repeat the analysis by changing the cost of an evening call and keeping the cost of a daytime call fixed.

22. Woodco manufactures tables and chairs. Each table and chair must be made entirely out of oak or entirely out of pine. A total of 150 board feet of oak and 210 board feet of pine are available. A table requires either 17 board feet of oak or 30 board feet of pine, and a chair requires either 5 board feet of oak or 13 board feet of pine. Each table can be sold for $40, and each chair for $15. Determine how Woodco can maximize its revenue.

23. Referring to the previous problem, suppose you want to investigate the effects of simultaneous changes in the selling prices of the products. Specifically, you want to see what happens to the total revenue when the selling prices of oak products change by a factor $1 + k_1$ and the selling prices of pine products change by a factor $1 + k_2$. Revise your model from the previous problem so that you can use the SolverTable add-in to investigate changes in total revenue as k_1 and k_2 both vary from -0.3 to 0.3 in increments of 0.1. Would you conclude that total revenue changes *linearly* within this range?

24. Alden Enterprises produces two products. Each product can be produced on either of two machines. The time (in hours) required to produce each product on each machine is shown in Table 3.5. Each month, 500 hours of time are available on each machine. Each month, customers are willing to buy up to the quantities of each product at the prices also given in Table 3.5. The company's goal is to maximize the revenue obtained from selling units during the next 2 months. Determine how it can meet this goal. Assume that Alden will not produce any units in either month that it cannot sell in that month.

TABLE 3.5	Machine Times for Alden Problem	
	Machine 1	**Machine 2**
Product 1	4	3
Product 2	7	4

25. Referring to the previous problem, suppose Alden wants to see what will happen if customer demands for each product in each month simultaneously change by a factor $1 + k$. Revise the model so that you can use the SolverTable add-in to investigate the effect of this change on total revenue as k varies from -0.3 to 0.3 in increments of 0.1. Does revenue change in a linear manner over this range? Can you explain intuitively why it changes in the way it does?

26. There are three factories on the Momiss River: 1, 2, and 3. Each emits two types of pollutants, labeled P1 and P2, into the river. If the waste from each factory is processed, the pollution in the river can be reduced. It costs $15 to process a ton of factory 1 waste, and each ton processed reduces the amount of P1 by 0.10 ton and the amount of P2 by 0.45 ton. It costs $10 to process a ton of factory 2 waste, and each ton processed will reduce the amount of P1 by 0.20 ton and the amount of P2 by 0.25 ton. It costs $20 to process a ton of factory 3 waste, and each ton processed will reduce the amount of P1 by 0.40 ton and the amount of P2 by 0.30 ton. The state wants to reduce the amount of P1 in the river by at least 30 tons and the amount of P2 by at least 40 tons.

a. Use Solver to determine how to minimize the cost of reducing pollution by the desired amounts.
b. Do you think that the LP assumptions (proportionality, additivity, and divisibility) are reasonable for this problem?

27. Referring to the previous problem, suppose you want to investigate the effects of increases in the minimal reductions required by the state. Specifically, you want to see what happens to the amounts of waste processed at the three factories and the total cost if both requirements (currently 30 and 40 tons, respectively) are increased by the *same* percentage. Revise your model so that you can use the SolverTable add-in to investigate these changes when the percentage increase varies from 10% to 100% in increments of 10%. Do the amounts processed at the three factories and the total cost change in a linear manner?

Skill-Extending Problems

28. U.S. Labs manufactures mechanical heart valves from the heart valves of pigs. Different heart operations require valves of different sizes. U.S. Labs purchases pig valves from three different suppliers. The cost and size mix of the valves purchased from each supplier are given in Table 3.6. Each month, U.S. Labs places an order with each supplier. At least 500 large, 300 medium, and 300 small valves must be purchased each month. Because of limited availability of pig valves, at most 500 valves per month can be purchased from each supplier. Use Solver to determine how U.S. Labs can minimize the cost of acquiring the needed valves.

29. Referring to the previous problem, suppose U.S. Labs wants to investigate the effect on total cost of increasing its minimal purchase requirements each month. Specifically, it wants to see how total cost changes as the minimal purchase requirements of large, medium, and small valves all increase from their values in the previous problem by the *same* percentage. Revise your model so that the SolverTable add-in can be used to investigate these changes when the percentage increase varies from 2% to 20% in increments of 2%. Explain intuitively what happens when this percentage is at least 16%.

TABLE 3.6	Data for U.S. Labs Problem			
	Cost per Valve	**Percentage Small**	**Percentage Medium**	**Percentage Large**
Supplier 1	$5	40	40	20
Supplier 2	$4	30	35	35
Supplier 3	$3	20	20	60

30. Sailco Corporation must determine how many sailboats to produce during each of the next four quarters. The demand during each of the next four quarters is as follows: first quarter, 40 sailboats; second quarter, 60 sailboats; third quarter, 75 sailboats; fourth quarter, 25 sailboats. Sailco must meet demands on time. At the beginning of the first quarter, Sailco has an inventory of 10 sailboats. At the beginning of each quarter, Sailco must decide how many sailboats to produce during that quarter. For simplicity, we assume that sailboats manufactured during a quarter can be used to meet demand for that quarter. During each quarter, Sailco can produce up to 40 sailboats with regular-time labor at a total cost of $400 per sailboat. By having employees work overtime during a quarter, Sailco can produce additional sailboats with overtime labor at a total cost of $450 per sailboat. At the end of each quarter (after production has occurred and the current quarter's demand has been satisfied), a holding cost of $20 per sailboat is incurred. Determine a production schedule to minimize the sum of production and inventory holding costs during the next four quarters.

31. Referring to the previous problem, suppose Sailco wants to see whether any changes in the $20 holding cost per sailboat could induce the company to carry more or less inventory. Revise your model so that the SolverTable add-in can be used to investigate the effects on ending inventory during the 4-month interval of systematic changes in the unit holding cost. (Assume that even though the unit holding cost changes, it is still constant over the 4-month interval.) Are there any (nonnegative) unit holding costs that would induce Sailco to hold *more* inventory than it holds when the holding cost is $20? Are there any unit holding costs that would induce Sailco to hold *less* inventory than it holds when the holding cost is $20?

32. During the next 2 months General Cars must meet (on time) the following demands for trucks and cars: month 1, 400 trucks and 800 cars; month 2, 300 trucks and 300 cars. During each month at most 1000 vehicles can be produced. Each truck uses 2 tons of steel, and each car uses 1 ton of steel. During month 1, steel costs $400 per ton; during month 2, steel costs $600 per ton. At most 2500 tons of steel can be purchased each month. (Steel can be used only during the month in which it is purchased.) At the beginning of month 1, 100 trucks and 200 cars are in inventory. At the end of each month, a holding cost of $150 per vehicle is assessed. Each car gets 20 mpg, and each truck gets 10 mpg. During each month, the vehicles produced by the company must average at least 16 mpg. Determine how to meet the demand and mileage requirements at minimum total cost.

33. Referring to the previous problem, check how sensitive the total cost is to the 16 mpg requirement by using the SolverTable add-in. Specifically, let this requirement vary from 14 mpg to 18 mpg in increments of 0.25 mpg, and write a short report of your results. In your report, explain intuitively what happens when the requirement is greater than 17 mpg.

34. The Deckers Clothing Company produces shirts and pants. Each shirt requires 2 square yards of cloth, and each pair of pants requires 3 square yards of cloth. During the next 2 months the following demands for shirts and pants must be met (on time): month 1, 1000 shirts and 1500 pairs of pants; month 2, 1200 shirts and 1400 pairs of pants. During each month the following resources are available: month 1, 9000 square yards of cloth; month 2, 6000 square yards of cloth. (Cloth that is available during month 1 and is not used can be used during month 2.) During each month it costs $4 to make an article of clothing with regular-time labor and $8 with overtime labor. During each month a total of at most 2500 articles of clothing can be produced with regular-time labor, and an unlimited number of articles of clothing can be produced with overtime labor. At the end of each month, a holding cost of $3 per article of clothing is assessed. Determine how to meet demands for the next 2 months (on time) at minimum cost. Assume that at the beginning of month 1, 100 shirts and 200 pairs of pants are available.

35. Referring to the previous problem, use the SolverTable add-in to investigate the effect on total cost of two *simultaneous* changes. The first change is to allow the ratio of overtime to regular time production cost (currently $8/$4 = 2) to decrease from 20% to 80% in increments of 20%, while keeping the regular time cost at $4. The second change is to allow the production capacity *each* month (currently 2500) to decrease from 10% to 50% in increments of 10%. The idea here is that less regular time capacity is available, but overtime is becoming relatively cheaper. Is the net effect on total cost positive or negative?

36. Each year, Comfy Shoes faces demands (which must be met on time) for pairs of shoes as shown in Table 3.7. Workers work three consecutive quarters and then receive one quarter off. For example,

TABLE 3.7	Demands for Comfy Shoes Problem	
		Demand
Quarter 1		6000
Quarter 2		3000
Quarter 3		8000
Quarter 4		1000

a worker might work during quarters 3 and 4 of one year and quarter 1 of the next year. During a quarter in which a worker works, he or she can produce up to 500 pairs of shoes. Each worker is paid $5000 per quarter. At the end of each quarter, a holding cost of $10 per pair of shoes is assessed. Determine how to minimize the cost per year (labor plus holding) of meeting the demands for shoes. To simplify matters, assume that at the end of each year, the ending inventory is zero. (*Hint*: You may assume that a given worker will get the *same* quarter off during each year.)

37. Referring to the previous problem, suppose Comfy Shoes can pay a flat fee for a training program that will increase the productivity of all of its workers. Use the SolverTable add-in to see how much the company would be willing to pay for a training program that increases worker productivity from 500 pairs to shoes per quarter to P pairs of shoes per quarter, where P varies from 525 to 700 in increments of 25.

38. A company must meet (on time) the following demands: quarter 1, 3000 units; quarter 2, 2000 units; quarter 3, 4000 units. Each quarter, up to 2700 units can be produced with regular-time labor, at a cost of $40 per unit. During each quarter, an unlimited number of units can be produced with overtime labor, at a cost of $60 per unit. Of all units produced, 20% are unsuitable and cannot be used to meet demand. Also, at the end of each quarter, 10% of all units on hand spoil and cannot be used to meet any future demands. After each quarter's demand is satisfied and spoilage is accounted for, a cost of $15 per unit is assessed against the quarter's ending inventory. Determine how to minimize the total cost of meeting the next 3 quarters' demands. Assume that 1000 usable units are available at the beginning of quarter 1.

39. Referring to the previous problem, the company wants to know how much money it would be worth to decrease the percentage of unsuitable items and/or the percentage of items that spoil. Write a short report that provides relevant information. Base your report on three uses of the SolverTable add-in: one where the percentage of unsuitable items decreases and the percentage of items that spoil stays at 10%; one where the percentage of unsuitable items stays at 20% and the percentage of items that spoil decreases; and one where both percentages decrease. Does the sum of the separate effects on total cost from the first two tables equal the combined effect from the third table? Include an answer to this question in your report.

40. Money manager Boris Milkem deals with French currency (the franc) and American currency (the dollar). At midnight, he can buy francs by paying 0.25 dollar per franc, and he can buy dollars by paying 3 francs per dollar. Assume that both types of transactions take place simultaneously and the only constraint is that Boris must have a nonnegative number of francs and dollars at 12:01 A.M.

   a. Formulate a model to maximize the number of dollars Boris can obtain after all transactions are completed. When you run Solver, you should get a "does not converge" message. Has Solver made an error, or is there a logical reason for the message?

   b. Use the SolverTable add-in to investigate changes in the decision variables and the objective value when the cost in dollars of purchasing francs varies from 0.30 dollar to 0.50 dollar in increments of a nickel. Explain the behavior you observe in the resulting table.

41. A pharmaceutical company manufactures two drugs at Los Angeles and Indianapolis. The cost of manufacturing a pound of each drug depends on the location, as indicated in Table 3.8. The machine time (in hours) required to produce a pound of each drug at each city is also shown in this table. The company needs to produce at least 1000 pounds per week of drug 1 and at least 2000 pounds per week of drug 2. It has 500 hours per week of machine time at Indianapolis and 400 hours per week at Los Angeles.

   a. Determine how the company can minimize the cost of producing the required drugs.

   b. Use SolverTable to determine how much the company would be willing to pay to purchase a combination of A extra hours of machine time at Indianapolis and B extra hours of machine time at Los Angeles, where A and B can be any positive multiples of 10 up to 50.

42. A company produces two products on two machines. The number of hours of machine time and labor depends on the machine and product as shown in Table 3.9. The cost of producing a unit of each product depends on which machine produces it. These unit costs appear in Table 3.10. There are 200 hours available on each of the two machines, and there are 400 labor hours available. This month at least 200 units of product 1 and at least 240 units of product 2 must be produced. Also, at least half of the product 1 requirement must be produced on machine 1, and at least half of the product 2 requirement must be made on machine 2.

   a. Determine how the company can minimize the cost of meeting this month's requirements.

   b. Use SolverTable to see how much the "at least half" requirements are costing the company. Do this by changing *both* of these requirements from "at least half" to "at least x percent," where x can be any multiple of 5% from 0% to 50%.

TABLE 3.8   Unit Costs and Machine Requirements

	Drug 1		Drug 2	
	Indianapolis	**Los Angeles**	**Indianapolis**	**Los Angeles**
Unit cost	$4.10	$4.00	$4.50	$5.20
Machine time	0.20	0.24	0.30	0.33

TABLE 3.9   Machine and Labor Requirements

	Product 1		Product 2	
	Machine 1	**Machine 2**	**Machine 1**	**Machine 2**
Machine time	0.70	0.80	0.75	0.9
Labor	0.75	1.20	0.75	1.0

TABLE 3.10   Unit Costs

	Product 1		Product 2	
	Machine 1	**Machine 2**	**Machine 1**	**Machine 2**
Unit cost	$1.50	$2.20	$0.40	$4.00

APPENDIX: INFORMATION ON SOLVERS

Microsoft Office (or Excel) ships with a built-in version of Solver. This version and all other versions of Solver have been developed by Frontline Systems, not Microsoft. When you install Office (or Excel), you have the option of installing or not installing Solver. In fact, a "typical" install might *not* install Solver. To check whether Solver is installed on your system, open Excel and select the Tools menu. If there is a Solver menu item, then Solver has been installed. Otherwise, you need to run the Office Setup program with the Add/Remove feature to install Solver.

The built-in version of Solver is able to solve most problems you are likely to encounter. However, it does have two limitations you should be aware of. First, it allows only 200 changing cells. This might sound like plenty, but many real-world problems go well beyond 200 changing cells. If you want to solve larger problems, you will need to purchase one of Frontline's commercial versions of Solver. Second, the built-in Solver is not able to handle several functions, including IF, ABS, MAX, MIN, and several others.[7] If you want to use these functions to make your model easier to read and understand, the best option is to use Frontline's Evolutionary Solver. This Solver uses a different kind of algorithm, called a genetic algorithm, that can handle models the built-in Solver cannot handle. We discuss such models in Chapter 8.

Normally, the only way to obtain the Evolutionary Solver is to purchase a package that Frontline calls its Premium Solver. This package includes the standard linear and nonlinear algorithms available in the built-in Solver, plus the Evolutionary Solver.

---

[7]To be more exact, Solver cannot handle these functions if they involve, either directly or indirectly, the changing cells.

Fortunately, we have been able to include an educational version of Premium Solver on the CD-ROM in this book. It has the following features:

- There is still the same limit of 200 changing cells as in the built-in Solver.
- The only advantage to the Premium Solver is that it provides the Evolutionary Solver, that is, the genetic algorithm. Its linear and nonlinear algorithms are virtually identical to those in the built-in Solver.
- The educational version has been developed so that you can easily toggle back and forth between the built-in Solver and the Premium Solver. Assuming you have installed the Premium Solver from our CD-ROM, when you choose the Tools/Solver menu item, you will see a dialog box as in Figure 3.29. This is virtually the same as the dialog box for the built-in Solver except that it has a Premium button. This button indicates that you are using the built-in Solver, but if you want to switch to the Premium Solver, you need only click on this button. If you do so, you obtain the dialog box in Figure 3.30. Now the button has changed to Standard, indicating that you can switch back to the built-in Solver by clicking on this button again. While using the Premium Solver, you can click on the drop-down arrow in Figure 3.30 to obtain the algorithm options shown in Figure 3.31. If you have a linear model, you would choose the Standard Simplex LP option. (This is equivalent to checking the Assume Linear Model box in the built-in Solver.) If you have a nonlinear model, you would choose the Standard GRG Nonlinear option. (This is equivalent to *not* checking the Assume Linear Model box in the built-in Solver.) Finally, you would choose the Standard Evolutionary option to use a genetic algorithm for the types of models we discuss in Chapter 8.

FIGURE 3.29
Dialog Box When Built-In Solver Is Active

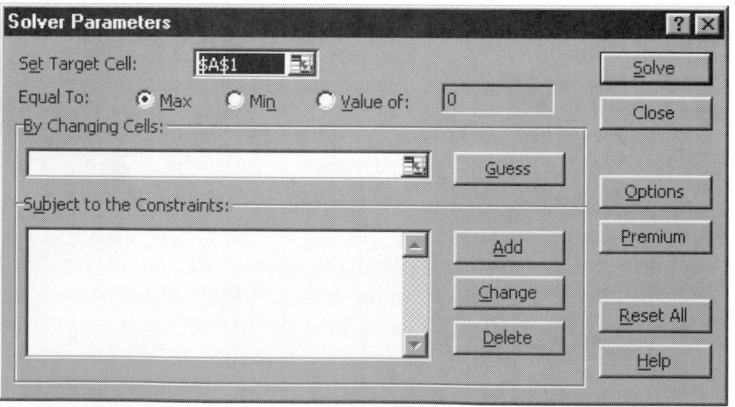

FIGURE 3.30
Dialog Box When Premium Solver Is Active

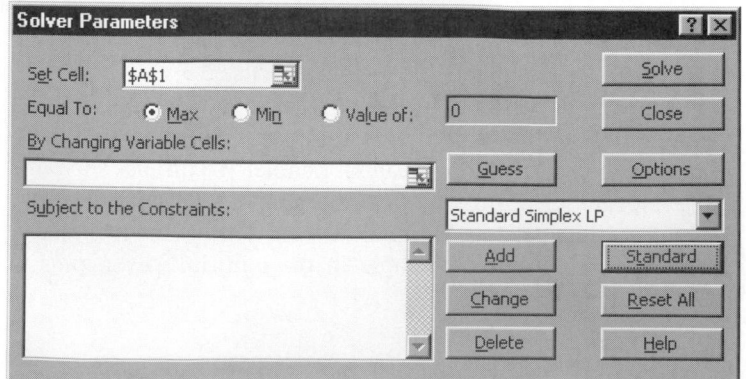

FIGURE 3.31
Premium Solver
Algorithm Options

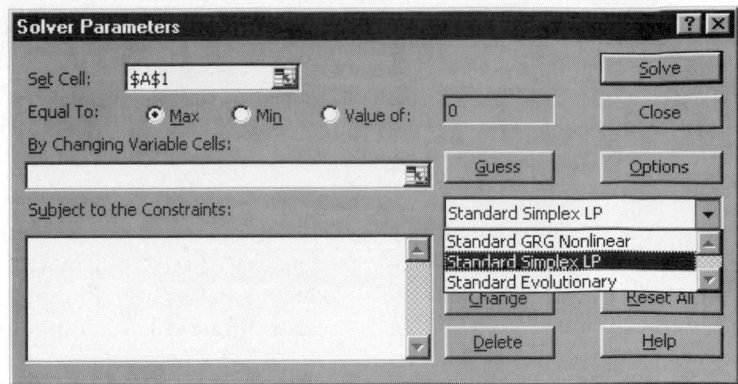

- To install the Premium Solver, simply run the Setup program on the CD-ROM in this book and choose the Premium Solver option.

Shelby Shelving

helby Shelving is a small company that manufactures two types of shelves for grocery stores. Model S is the standard model, and model LX is a heavy-duty model. Shelves are manufactured in three major steps: stamping, forming, and assembly. In the stamping stage, a large machine is used to stamp, i.e., cut, standard sheets of metal into appropriate sizes. In the forming stage, another machine bends the metal into shape. Assembly involves joining the parts with a combination of soldering and riveting. Shelby's stamping and forming machines work on both models of shelves. Separate assembly departments are used for the final stage of production.

The file SHELBY.XLS contains relevant data for Shelby. (See Figure 3.32.) The hours required on each machine for each unit of product are shown in the range B5:C6 of the AccountingData sheet. For example, the production of one model S shelf requires 0.25 hour on the forming machine. Both the stamping and forming machines can operate for 800 hours each month. The model S assembly department has a monthly capacity of 1900 units.

The model LX assembly department has a monthly capacity of only 1400 units. Currently Shelby is producing and selling 400 units of model S and 1400 units of model LX per month.

Model S shelves are sold for $1800, and model LX shelves are sold for $2100. Shelby's operation is fairly small in the industry, and management at Shelby believes it cannot raise prices beyond these levels because of the competition. However, the marketing department feels that Shelby can sell as much as it can produce at these prices. The costs of production are summarized in the AccountingData sheet. As usual, values in blue borders are given, whereas other values are calculated from these.

Management at Shelby just met to discuss next month's operating plan. Although the shelves are selling well, the overall profitability of the company is a concern. The plant's engineer suggested that the current production of model S shelves be cut back. According to him, "Model S shelves are sold for $1800 per unit, but our costs are $1839. Even though we're only selling 400 units a month, we're losing money on each one. We should decrease production

FIGURE 3.32 Accounting Data for Shelby

	A	B	C	D	E	F	G	H	I
1	**Shelby Shelving Data for Current Production Schedule**								
2									
3	Machine requirements (hours per unit)					Given monthly overhead cost data			
4		Model S	Model LX				Fixed	Variable S	Variable LX
5	Stamping	0.3	0.3			Stamping	$125,000	$80	$90
6	Forming	0.25	0.5			Forming	$95,000	$120	$170
7						Model S Assembly	$80,000	$165	$0
8		Model S	Model LX			Model LX Assembly	$85,000	$0	$185
9	Current monthly production	400	1400						
10						Standard costs of the shelves -- *based on the current production levels*			
11	Hours spent in departments							Model S	Model LX
12		Model S	Model LX	Totals		Direct materials		$1,000	$1,200
13	Stamping	120	420	540		Direct labor:			
14	Forming	100	700	800		Stamping	$35	$35	
15						Forming	$60	$90	
16	Percentages of time spent in departments					Assembly	$80	$85	
17		Model S	Model LX			Total direct labor		$175	$210
18	Stamping	22.2%	77.8%			Overhead allocation			
19	Forming	12.5%	87.5%			Stamping	$149	$159	
20						Forming	$150	$229	
21						Assembly	$365	$246	
22						Total overhead		$664	$635
23						Total cost		$1,839	$2,045

of model S." The controller disagreed. He said that the problem was the model S assembly department trying to absorb a large overhead with a small production volume. "The model S units are making a contribution to overhead. Even though production doesn't cover all of the fixed costs, we'd be worse off with lower production."

Your job is to complete the formulation of an LP model on the LP sheet (of the SHELBY.XLS file), then run the Solver, and finally make a recommendation to Shelby management, with a short verbal argument supporting the engineer or the controller.

Notes on AccountingData calculations: The fixed overhead is distributed using activity-based costing principles. For example, at current production levels, the forming machine spends 100 hours on model S shelves and 700 hours on model LX shelves. The forming machine is used 800 hours of the month, of which 12.5% of the time is spent on model S shelves and 87.5% is spent on model LX shelves. The $95,000 of fixed overhead in the forming department is distributed as $11,875 ($= 95,000 \times 0.125$) to model S shelves and $83,125 ($= 95,000 \times 0.875$) to model LX shelves. The fixed overhead per unit of output is allocated as $29.69 ($= 11,875/400$) for model S and $59.38 ($= 83,125/1400$) for model LX. In the calculation of the standard overhead cost, the fixed and variable costs are added together, so that the overhead cost for the forming department allocated to a model S shelf is $149.69 ($= 29.69 + 120$, shown rounded up to $150). Similarly, the overhead cost for the forming department allocated to a model LX shelf is $229.38 ($= 59.38 + 170$, shown rounded down to $229).

## CHAPTER 4

Linear Programming Models

GLASS MANUFACTURING AT LIBBEY-OWENS-FORD

As we saw in the previous chapter, linear programming (LP) can be used for product mix decisions and inventory planning. This was the case at Libbey-Owens-Ford (LOF), a large plate glass company with 9000 employees and annual sales of $900 million. In the article "Integrated Production, Distribution, and Inventory Planning at Libbey-Owens-Ford," Martin, Dent, and Eckhart (1993) describe the process of building and implementing a large-scale LP model of the plate glass production and distribution process at LOF. The model (named FLAGPOL for *FLAt Glass Products Optimization ModeL*) deals with four manufacturing plants, over 200 separate glass products, and over 40 demand centers in a 12-month planning horizon. The development of the model took over 2 years to complete, but since then it has resulted in annual savings of over $2 million.

The production of plate glass is an extremely complex manufacturing process. The glass is produced in large batches, each batch producing a certain color or tint of glass. The batches are large because the time required to change from one tint to another is very long (on the order of 2 to 4 days). Therefore, production occurs in cycles of approximately 10 months, and a particular tint is produced only once during a cycle. Given these long cycles, inventory planning is crucial. The production quantity of a particular tint in a cycle must be large enough to cover orders, both planned and forecasted, for a long period of time. Another complication is the cutting process. The glass is produced in long "ribbons" that can be cut to various dimensions. If the cuts are made during the production processing, yields tend to be higher than if they are made off-line, after processing. However, off-line cuts are sometimes necessary when orders arrive for nonstandard dimensions of glass.

The management at LOF decided that the complexity of the entire process necessitated a formal model. Therefore, the company appointed a task force to develop an LP model of the process. Since the task force included staff members from finance, marketing, MIS, materials management, transportation, production planning, and representatives from the plants, the scope of the resulting model became very broad. The first step was to develop the database that would support the model. This was a major undertaking since data were required on market demand and selling prices, freight rates, production rates and yields, manufacturing costs, inventory levels, and interplant rail schedules. Once these data were available, the FLAGPOL model was built, tested, and finally implemented. The implementation process itself took about 9 months. During this time, several changes to the original model were required. For example, the company realized that differences in the cost accounting systems of the various plants needed to be addressed. Also, the model's reports were redesigned to make them more useful and comprehensible to the eventual users.

Now that FLAGPOL is fully implemented, it is run 10 to 20 times each month for short-run tactical plans, as well as for longer-range strategic decisions. At the tactical level, the model recommends how much of each product to produce at each plant each month, how much of each product to ship between plants each month, how much of each product to cut off-line at each plant each month, and how much inventory to hold of each product at each plant each month. At the strategic level, FLAGPOL has been used to address such issues as (1) planning the transition from a two-plant operation to a four-plant operation, (2) introducing new products or eliminating existing products from plants, (3) developing schedules for major construction and plant maintenance, and (4) analyzing possible locations and sizing for new facilities. Management at LOF now considers FLAGPOL an integrated part of the company's planning process. It helps the company to reduce costs, increase profits, and enhance overall customer service. ■

4.1 INTRODUCTION

I n a survey of Fortune 500 firms, 85% of those responding said that they used linear programming. In this chapter we will discuss some of the LP models that are most often applied to real-world applications. In the chapter's examples and problems, you will discover how to

- schedule bank clerks for check encoding
- optimize the operation of an oil refinery
- plan dairy production at a creamery

- schedule production of fiberglass products at Owens-Corning Fiberglass
- optimize a Wall Street firm's bond portfolio

Actually, these problems are just a sampling of the many problems we will model with LP in this chapter. There are two basic goals in this chapter. The first is to illustrate some of the many real applications that can take advantage of LP. You'll see that these applications cover a wide range, from oil production to worker scheduling to cash management. The second goal is to increase your facility in modeling LP problems on a spreadsheet. We will present a few principles that will help you model a wide variety of problems. The best way to learn, however, is to see many examples and work through numerous problems. In short, mastering the art of LP spreadsheet modeling takes hard work and practice. You will have plenty of opportunity to do each with the material in this chapter.

4.2 STATIC WORKFORCE SCHEDULING MODELS

Many organizations must determine how to schedule employees to provide adequate service. The following example illustrates how LP can be used to schedule employees.

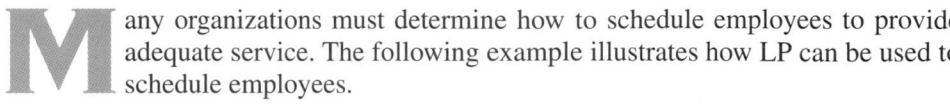

EXAMPLE 4.1

POSTAL EMPLOYEE SCHEDULING

A post office requires different numbers of full-time employees on different days of the week. The number of full-time employees required each day is given in Table 4.1. Union rules state that each full-time employee must work 5 consecutive days and then receive 2 days off. For example, an employee who works Monday to Friday must be off on Saturday and Sunday. The post office wants to meet its daily requirements using only full-time employees. Its objective is to minimize the number of full-time employees that must be hired.

TABLE 4.1	Employee Requirements for Post Office
	Minimum Employees Required
Monday	17
Tuesday	13
Wednesday	15
Thursday	19
Friday	14
Saturday	16
Sunday	11

Solution

To model the post office problem with a spreadsheet, we must keep track of the following:

- number of employees starting work on each day of the week
- number of employees working each day
- total number of employees

It is important to keep track of the number of employees starting work each day, because this is the only way to incorporate the fact that workers work 5 consecutive days. If you don't believe this, try solving the problem by just keeping track of the total number of employees and the number of employees working each day.

DEVELOPING THE SPREADSHEET MODEL

The spreadsheet model for this problem appears in Figure 4.1. (See the file POSTAL. XLS.) To form this spreadsheet, proceed as follows.

❶ Daily requirements. Enter the number of employees needed on each day of the week (from Table 4.1) in the MinReqd range.

❷ Employees beginning each day. Enter *any* trial values for the number of employees beginning work on each day of the week in the Starting range. (The one shown here is *not* optimal.)

❸ Employees on hand each day. The important key to this solution is to realize that the numbers in the Starting range do not represent the number of workers who will show up each day. As an example, the number who start on Monday (in cell B4) work Monday through Friday. Therefore, enter the formula

=$B$4

in cell B14 and copy it across to cell F14. Proceed similarly for rows 15–20, being careful to take "wrap arounds" into account. For example, the workers starting on Thursday

FIGURE 4.1
Postal Scheduling Model with a Nonoptimal Solution

	A	B	C	D	E	F	G	H
1	Post Office scheduling model - nonoptimal solution shown							
2								
3	Number starting their five-day shift on various days				Range names used:			
4	Mon	5			Starting - B4:B10			
5	Tue	5			Available - B21:H21			
6	Wed	5			MinReqd - B23:H23			
7	Thu	5			TotEmployees - B25			
8	Fri	5						
9	Sat	5						
10	Sun	5						
11								
12	Number working on various days (along top) who started their shift on various days (along side)							
13		Mon	Tue	Wed	Thu	Fri	Sat	Sun
14	Mon	5	5	5	5	5		
15	Tue		5	5	5	5	5	
16	Wed			5	5	5	5	5
17	Thu	5			5	5	5	5
18	Fri	5	5			5	5	5
19	Sat	5	5	5			5	5
20	Sun	5	5	5	5			5
21	Available	25	25	25	25	25	25	25
22		>=	>=	>=	>=	>=	>=	>=
23	Min required	17	13	15	19	14	16	11
24								
25	Total employees	35						

work Thursday through Sunday, plus Monday. Then calculate the total number who show up on each day by entering the formula

=SUM(B14:B20)

in cell B21 and copying it across to cell H21. (*Note*: You'll be doing this—entering a "typical" formula into a cell and then copying it across—many times throughout this book. Here is an efficiency tip. First, highlight the entire range, here B21:H21. Then enter the typical formula, here **=SUM(B14:B20)**, and press **Ctrl-Enter**. As you'll see, this has the same effect as copying, but we find it much quicker.)

❹ Total employees. Calculate the total number of employees in cell B25 with the formula

=SUM(Starting)

At this point, you might want to try rearranging the numbers in the Starting range to see if you can "guess" an optimal solution. It's not that easy! Each worker who starts on a given day works the next 4 days as well, so when you find a solution that meets the minimal requirements for the various days, you usually have many more workers available on some days than are needed.

USING SOLVER

Now invoke the Solver and specify the following:

❶ Objective. Choose the TotEmployees cell as the target cell to minimize.

❷ Changing cells. Choose the Starting range as the changing cells.

❸ Daily requirement constraint. Enter the constraint Avail>=MinReqd. This constraint ensures that enough people are working each day. After completing these steps, the Solver dialog box should appear as shown in Figure 4.2.

FIGURE 4.2
Solver Dialog Box
for Postal Model

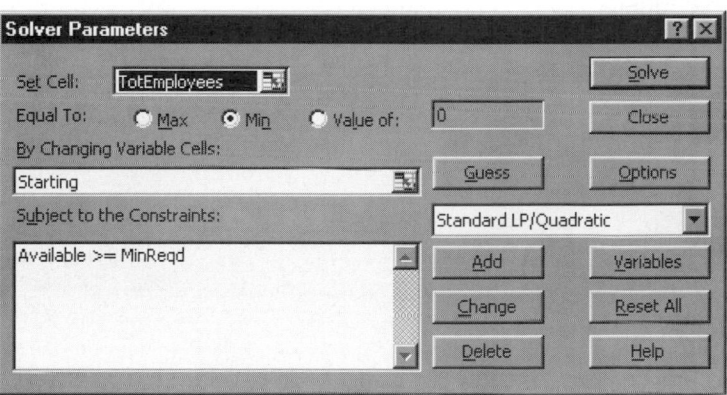

❹ Specify nonnegativity and optimize. Under Solver Options, check the nonnegativity box, and use the LP algorithm to obtain the optimal solution shown in Figure 4.3 (page 116).

This optimal solution requires the number of employees starting work on some days to be a fraction. Because part-time employees are not allowed, this solution is unrealistic. We will now show how to solve the post office model when the number of employees beginning work each day must be an integer.

FIGURE 4.3
Optimal
(Non-Integer)
Solution to Postal
Model

	A	B	C	D	E	F	G	H
1	**Post Office scheduling model - optimal noninteger solution**							
2								
3	Number starting their five-day shift on various days				**Range names used:**			
4	Mon	6.33				Starting - B4:B10		
5	Tue	5.00				Available - B21:H21		
6	Wed	0.33				MinReqd - B23:H23		
7	Thu	7.33				TotEmployees - B25		
8	Fri	0.00						
9	Sat	3.33						
10	Sun	0.00						
11								
12	Number working on various days (along top) who started their shift on various days (along side)							
13		Mon	Tue	Wed	Thu	Fri	Sat	Sun
14	Mon	6.33	6.33	6.33	6.33	6.33		
15	Tue		5.00	5.00	5.00	5.00	5.00	
16	Wed			0.33	0.33	0.33	0.33	0.33
17	Thu	7.33			7.33	7.33	7.33	7.33
18	Fri	0.00	0.00			0.00	0.00	0.00
19	Sat	3.33	3.33	3.33			3.33	3.33
20	Sun	0.00	0.00	0.00	0.00			0.00
21	Available	17.00	14.67	15.00	19.00	19.00	16.00	11.00
22		>=	>=	>=	>=	>=	>=	>=
23	Min required	17	13	15	19	14	16	11
24								
25	Total employees	22.33						

Using Solver with Integer Constraints In the Solver dialog box, add the constraint Starting=Integer. To do this, simply select "int" instead of <=, =, or >= in the Add Constraint dialog. Now when you solve, you obtain the solution in Figure 4.4. As we see, the post office needs to hire 23 full-time employees. This solution reveals an aspect of some modeling problems. Because of the irregular daily requirements and the constraint on consecutive days off, no solution can exactly match available workers to daily requirements. All solutions have surplus workers some days. Sometimes the optimal solution to a modeling problem is not the "perfect" solution you were hoping for.

FIGURE 4.4
Optimal Integer
Solution to Postal
Model

	A	B	C	D	E	F	G	H
1	**Post Office scheduling model**							
2								
3	Number starting their five-day shift on various days				**Range names used:**			
4	Mon	6				Starting - B4:B10		
5	Tue	6				Available - B21:H21		
6	Wed	0				MinReqd - B23:H23		
7	Thu	7				TotEmployees - B25		
8	Fri	0						
9	Sat	4						
10	Sun	0						
11								
12	Number working on various days (along top) who started their shift on various days (along side)							
13		Mon	Tue	Wed	Thu	Fri	Sat	Sun
14	Mon	6	6	6	6	6		
15	Tue		6	6	6	6	6	
16	Wed			0	0	0	0	0
17	Thu	7			7	7	7	7
18	Fri	0	0			0	0	0
19	Sat	4	4	4			4	4
20	Sun	0	0	0	0			0
21	Available	17	16	16	19	19	17	11
22		>=	>=	>=	>=	>=	>=	>=
23	Min required	17	13	15	19	14	16	11
24								
25	Total employees	23						

By the way, if you solve this problem on your computer, you may get a different schedule that is still optimal (uses 23 employees total and meets all constraints). This is a case of **multiple optimal solutions** and is not at all uncommon in LP problems.

As we see in this postal example, it is easy to add integer constraints to an LP model. However, you should be aware that this makes the problem *much* more difficult to solve mathematically. In fact, Solver uses a different algorithm called **branch and bound** for integer models. For small models, you will probably not see much increase in the time to find the optimal solution, but we warn you that solution times can increase *significantly* with more complex models. Our advice is to use integer constraints sparingly. For example, if changing cells specify how many radios to produce, and the expected quantities are in the hundreds or thousands, ignore integer constraints. What is the difference, after all, between producing 970 and 971 radios?

Solver Tolerance Setting One other comment about integer constraints concerns Solver's **Tolerance** setting. The idea is as follows. As Solver searches for the best integer solution, it is often able to find "good" solutions fairly quickly, but it often has to spend a lot of time finding slightly better solutions. A nonzero tolerance setting allows it to quit early. The default tolerance setting is 0.05. This means that if Solver finds a feasible solution that is guaranteed to have an objective value no more than 5% from the optimal value, it will quit and report this "good" solution (which might even be the optimal solution). Therefore, if you accept this default value, your integer solutions will sometimes not be optimal, but they will be close. If you want to ensure the optimal solution, just change the Solver tolerance value to 0. (For the Solver that accompanies this book, you can find this setting by clicking on the Solver Options button, then on the Integer Options button. For the standard Solver that accompanies Excel, it is directly under the Solver Options.)

Sensitivity Analysis The most obvious type of sensitivity analysis involves examining how the work schedule and the total number of employees change as the number of employees required each day changes. Suppose the number of employees needed on each day of the week increases by 2, 4, or 6. How does this change the total number of employees needed? We can answer this by using the SolverTable add-in, but we first have to alter the model slightly, as shown in Figure 4.5 (page 118). The problem is that we want to increase *each* of the daily minimal required values by the same amount. Therefore, we move the original requirements up to row 12, enter a trial value for the extra number required per day in the Extra cell, and enter the formula

=B12+Extra

in cell B25, which is then copied across. Now we can use the one-way SolverTable option, using the Extra cell as the single input, letting it vary from 0 to 6 in increments of 2, and specifying the TotEmployees cell as the single output cell.

The results appear in rows 32–35 of Figure 4.5. When the requirement increases by 2 each day, only 2 extra employees are necessary (scheduled appropriately). However, when the requirement increases by 4 each day, *more* than 4 extra employees are necessary. The same is true when the requirement increases by 6 each day. This might surprise you at first, but there is an intuitive explanation—each extra worker works only 5 days of the week.

Creating a "Fair" Schedule for Employees The Solver solution to the post office model shown in Figure 4.4 requires 6 employees to start work on Monday, 6 on Tuesday, 7 on Thursday, and 4 on Saturday. Certainly the 4 employees who begin work on Saturday will be unhappy, because they never get a weekend off! The Solver

Post Office scheduling model

	A	B	C	D	E	F	G	H	I	J	K	L
1	**Post Office scheduling model**											
2												
3	Number starting their five-day shift on various days					Range names used:						
4	Mon	6				Starting - B4:B10						
5	Tue	6				Extra - J12						
6	Wed	0				Available - B23:H25						
7	Thu	7				MinReqd - B27:H27						
8	Fri	0				TotEmployees - B27						
9	Sat	4										
10	Sun	0										
11										Extra per day (for sensitivity)		
12	Min required	17	13	15	19	14	16	11		0		
13												
14	Number working on various days (along top) who started their shift on various days (along side)											
15		Mon	Tue	Wed	Thu	Fri	Sat	Sun				
16	Mon	6	6	6	6	6						
17	Tue		6	6	6	6	6					
18	Wed			0	0	0	0	0				
19	Thu	7			7	7	7	7				
20	Fri	0	0			0	0	0				
21	Sat	4	4	4			4	4				
22	Sun	0	0	0	0			0				
23	Available	17	16	16	19	19	17	11				
24		>=	>=	>=	>=	>=	>=	>=				
25	Final min required	17	13	15	19	14	16	11				
26												
27	Total employees	23										
28												
29	**Sensitivity of total number of employees to extra required each day**											
30		Extra	Total									
31			$B$27									
32		0	23									
33		2	25									
34		4	28									
35		6	31									

FIGURE 4.5 Sensitivity Analysis for Postal Model

solution can be used to implement a "fairer" schedule that treats all employees in an equal fashion. We simply rotate the schedules of the employees over a 23-week period. To see how this is done, consider the following schedule:

- Weeks 1–6: Start on Monday
- Weeks 7–12: Start on Tuesday
- Weeks 13–19: Start on Thursday
- Weeks 20–23: Start on Saturday

Employee 1 follows this schedule for a 23-week period. Employee 2 starts with week 2 of this schedule (start on Monday) and follows the schedule through week 23. For the last week of the 23-week period, employee 2 follows week 1 of the schedule (starts on Monday). We continue in this fashion to generate a 23-week schedule for each employee. For example, employee 11 will have the following schedule:

- Weeks 1–2: Start on Tuesday
- Weeks 3–9: Start on Thursday
- Weeks 10–13: Start on Saturday
- Weeks 14–19: Start on Monday
- Weeks 20–23: Start on Tuesday

This method of scheduling treats each employee equally. ∎

MODELING ISSUES

1. The postal employee scheduling example is called a **static** scheduling model, because we assume that the post office faces the same situation each week. In reality, demands change over time, workers take vacations in the summer, and so on, so the post office does not face the same situation each week. **Dynamic** scheduling models are discussed in the next two sections.

2. If you wanted to set up a weekly scheduling model for a supermarket or a fast-food restaurant, the number of variables could be very large and the computer might have difficulty finding an exact solution. In this situation, *heuristic* methods can be used to find a good solution to the problem. See Love and Hoey (1990) for an example of how this can be done.

3. Our model can easily be expanded to handle part-time employees, the use of overtime, and alternative objective functions such as maximizing the number of weekend days off received by employees. (See Problems 1, 3, and 4.)

4. How did we determine the number of workers needed each day? Perhaps the post office wants to have enough employees to ensure that 95% of all letters are sorted within an hour. To determine the number of employees needed to provide adequate service, the post office would need to use queueing theory, which we discuss in Chapter 14, and forecasting, which we discuss in Chapter 16. ■

ADDITIONAL APPLICATIONS

Encoder Scheduling at Ohio National Bank

Krajewski, Ritzman, and McKenzie (1980) used linear programming to schedule clerks who process checks at Ohio National Bank. Their model determined the minimum cost combination of part-time employees, full-time employees, and overtime labor needed to complete the processing of the checks received each day by the end of the workday (10 P.M.). The major input to their model was a forecast of the number of checks arriving at the bank each hour. This forecast was generated with a multiple regression model (see Chapter 15). The major output of the LP was a work schedule. For example, the LP might suggest that 2 full-time employees work daily from 11 A.M. to 8 P.M., 33 part-time employees work every day from 1 P.M. to 6 P.M., and 27 part-time employees work from 6 P.M. to 10 P.M. on Monday, Tuesday, and Friday.

The LP approach to scheduling encoder clerks saved an estimated $80,000 per year in labor costs. The LP approach also resulted in faster processing of the checks. Before LP was used to schedule encoder clerks, the day's checks were rarely processed by the end of the day, whereas after LP was used, the day's checks were processed by the end of the day 98% of the time! (For a simplified version of encoder scheduling, see Problem 97.) ■

Skill-Building Problems

1. In the post office example, suppose that each full-time employee works 8 hours per day. Thus, Monday's requirement of 17 workers can be viewed as a requirement of 8(17) = 136 hours. The post office can meet its daily labor requirements by using both full-time and part-time employees. During each week a full-time employee works 8 hours a day for 5 consecutive days, and a part-time employee works 4 hours a day for 5 consecutive days. A full-time employee costs the post office $15 per hour, whereas a part-time employee (with reduced fringe benefits) costs the post office only $10 per hour. Union requirements limit part-time labor to 25% of weekly labor requirements.
   a. Use Solver to minimize the post office's weekly labor costs.
   b. Use SolverTable to determine how a change in the part-time labor limitation (currently 25%) influences the optimal solution.
2. During each 4-hour period, the Smalltown police force requires the following number of on-duty police officers: 8 from midnight to 4 A.M.; 7 from 4 A.M. to 8 A.M.; 6 from 8 A.M. to noon; 6 from noon to 4 P.M.; 5 from 4 P.M. to 8 P.M.; and 4 from 8 P.M. to midnight. Each police officer works 2 consecutive 4-hour shifts.

   a. Determine how to minimize the number of police officers needed to meet Smalltown's daily requirements.
   b. Use SolverTable to see how the number of police officers changes as the number of officers needed from midnight to 4 A.M. changes.

Skill-Extending Problems

3. In the post office example, suppose that the post office can force employees to work 1 day of overtime each week. For example, an employee whose regular shift is Monday to Friday can also be required to work on Saturday. Each employee is paid $50 a day for each of the first 5 days worked during a week and $62 for the overtime day (if any).
   a. Determine how the post office can minimize the cost of meeting its weekly work requirements.
   b. Suppose the Tuesday and Wednesday requirements *each* change by the same amount. Use SolverTable to investigate how the total cost changes.
4. Suppose the post office has 25 full-time employees and is not allowed to hire or fire any employees. Determine a schedule that maximizes the number of weekend days off received by the employees.

4.3 AGGREGATE PLANNING MODELS

I n this section we extend the inventory model discussed in the previous chapter to include a situation where the number of workers available influences the possible production levels. We allow the workforce level to be modified each period through the hiring and firing of workers. We also allow demand to be backlogged, that is, demand need not be met on time. **Aggregate planning models** can accommodate workforce variability and backlogging. We will discuss several such models in this section.

EXAMPLE 4.2

WORKER AND PRODUCTION PLANNING AT SURESTEP

During the next 4 months the SureStep Company must meet (on time) the following demands for pairs of shoes: 3000 in month 1; 5000 in month 2; 2000 in month 3; and 1000 in month 4. At the beginning of month 1, 500 pairs of shoes are on hand, and SureStep has 100 workers. A worker is paid $1500 per month. Each worker can work up to 160 hours a month before he or she receives overtime. A worker may be forced to work up to 20 hours of overtime per month and is paid $13 per hour for overtime labor. It takes 4 hours of labor and $15 of raw material to produce a pair of shoes. At the beginning of each month, workers can be hired or fired. Each hired worker costs $1600, and each fired worker costs $2000. At the end of each month, a holding cost of $3 per pair of shoes left in inventory is incurred. Production in a given month can be used to meet that month's demand. SureStep wants to use linear programming to determine its optimal production schedule and labor policy.

Solution

To model SureStep's problem, we need to keep track of the following:

- the number of workers hired, fired, and available during each month
- the number of pairs of shoes produced each month with regular time and overtime labor
- the number of overtime hours used each month
- the beginning and ending inventory of shoes each month
- the monthly costs and the total cost

DEVELOPING THE SPREADSHEET MODEL

The spreadsheet model appears in Figure 4.6 (page 122).[1] (See the file SURESTEP1. XLS.) It can be developed as follows.

❶   Inputs. Enter the input data in the range B4:B14 and (for monthly demands) in the Demand range.

❷   Production, hiring and firing plan. Enter *any* trial values for the number of pairs of shoes produced each month in the Produced range, the overtime hours used each month in the OTHrs range, the workers hired each month in the Hired range, and the workers fired each month in the Fired range. These four ranges comprise the changing cells.

If we define A_t as the number of available workers in month t, after hiring and firing, and we let H_t and F_t be the numbers of workers hired and fired, respectively, at the beginning of month t, then A_0 is given as 100 (the value in the InitWorkers cell), and for any month $t \geq 1$, we have the "balance" equation

$$A_t = A_{t-1} + H_t - F_t \qquad (4.1)$$

This is the rationale behind the next step.

❸   Workers available each month. In cell B17 enter the initial number of workers available with the formula

=InitWorkers

Because the number of workers available at the beginning of any other month (before hiring and firing) is equal to the number of workers from the previous month, enter the formula

=B20

in cell C17 and copy it to the range D17:E17. Then in cell B20 calculate the number of workers available in month 1 (after hiring and firing) with the formula

=B17+B18–B19

[1]From here on, to save space we will show only the model with the *optimal* solution. However, when you set up the model on your own, you can enter *any* initial values in the changing cells.

FIGURE 4.6
SureStep Aggregate
Planning Model

	A	B	C	D	E	F	G	H
1	**SureStep aggregate planning model**							
2								
3	**Input data**					**Range names used:**		
4	Initial inventory of shoes	500				InitInv - B4		
5	Initial number of workers	100				InitWorkers - B5		
6	Regular hours/worker/month	160				StdRTHrs - B6		
7	Maximum overtime hours/worker/month	20				MaxOTHrs - B7		
8	Hiring cost/worker	$1,600				UnitHireCost - B8		
9	Firing cost/worker	$2,000				UnitFireCost - B9		
10	Regular wages/worker/month	$1,500				RTWageRate - B10		
11	Overtime wage rate/hour	$13				OTWageRate - B11		
12	Labor hours/pair of shoes	4				HrsPerPair - B12		
13	Raw material cost/pair of shoes	$15				UnitMatCost - B13		
14	Holding cost/pair of shoes in inventory/month	$3				UnitHoldCost - B14		
15						Hired - B18:E18		
16	**Worker plan**	Month 1	Month 2	Month 3	Month 4	Fired - B19:E19		
17	Workers from previous month	100	94	93	50	OTHrs - B23:E23		
18	Workers hired	0	0	0	0	OTAvailable - B25:E25		
19	Workers fired	6	1	43	0	Produced - B30:E30		
20	Workers available after hiring and firing	94	93	50	50	ProdCap - B32:E32		
21						OnHand - B34:E34		
22	Regular-time hours available	15040	14880	8000	8000	Demand - B36:E36		
23	Overtime labor hours used	0	80	0	0	TotCost - F46		
24		<=	<=	<=	<=			
25	Maximum overtime labor hours available	1880	1860	1000	1000			
26								
27	Total hours for production	15040	14960	8000	8000			
28								
29	**Production plan**	Month 1	Month 2	Month 3	Month 4			
30	Shoes produced	3760	3740	2000	1000			
31		<=	<=	<=	<=			
32	Production capacity	3760	3740	2000	2000			
33								
34	Inventory after production	4260	5000	2000	1000			
35		>=	>=	>=	>=			
36	Demand	3000	5000	2000	1000			
37	Ending inventory	1260	0	0	0			
38								
39	**Summary of costs**	Month 1	Month 2	Month 3	Month 4	Totals		
40	Hiring cost	$0	$0	$0	$0	$0		
41	Firing cost	$12,000	$2,000	$86,000	$0	$100,000		
42	Regular-time wages	$141,000	$139,500	$75,000	$75,000	$430,500		
43	Overtime wages	$0	$1,040	$0	$0	$1,040		
44	Raw material cost	$56,400	$56,100	$30,000	$15,000	$157,500		
45	Holding cost	$3,780	$0	$0	$0	$3,780		
46	Totals	$213,180	$198,640	$191,000	$90,000	$692,820		

and copy this formula to the range C20:E20 for months 2 through 4. This formula is based on equation (4.1).

❹ Overtime capacity. Because each available worker can work up to 20 hours of overtime in a month, enter the formula

=MaxOTHrs*B21

in cell B25 and copy it to the range C25:E25 to compute the overtime hours capacity for months 2 through 4.

❺ Production capacity. Because each worker can work 160 regular-time hours per month, calculate the regular-time hours available in month 1 in cell B22 with the formula

=StdRTHrs*B21

and copy it to the range C22:E22 for the other months. Then calculate the total hours available for production in cell B27 with the formula

=SUM(B23:B24)

and copy it to the range C27:E27 for the other months. Finally, because it takes 4 hours of labor to make a pair of shoes, calculate the production capacity for month 1 by entering the formula

=B27/HrsPerPair

in cell B32, and copy it to the range C32:E32.

❻ Inventory each month. Calculate the inventory after production in month 1 (which is available to meet month 1 demand) by entering the formula

=InitInv+B30

in cell B34. For any other month, the inventory after production is the previous month's ending inventory plus that month's production, so enter the formula

=B37+C30

in cell C34 and copy it to the range D34:E34. Then calculate the month 1 ending inventory in cell B37 with the formula

=B34-B36

and copy it to the range C37:E37.

❼ Monthly costs. Calculate the various costs shown in rows 40 through 45 for month 1 by entering the formulas

=UnitHireCost*B18
=UnitFireCost*B19
=RTWageRate*B20
=OTWageRate*B23
=UnitMatCost*B30
=UnitHoldCost*B37

in cells B40 through B45. Then copy the range B40:B45 to the range C40:E45 to calculate these costs for the other months.

❽ Totals. In row 46 and column F, use the SUM function to calculate cost totals, with the value in F46 being the overall total cost.

USING SOLVER

The Solver dialog box should appear as shown in Figure 4.7. To accomplish this, proceed as follows.

FIGURE 4.7
Solver Dialog Box
for SureStep Model

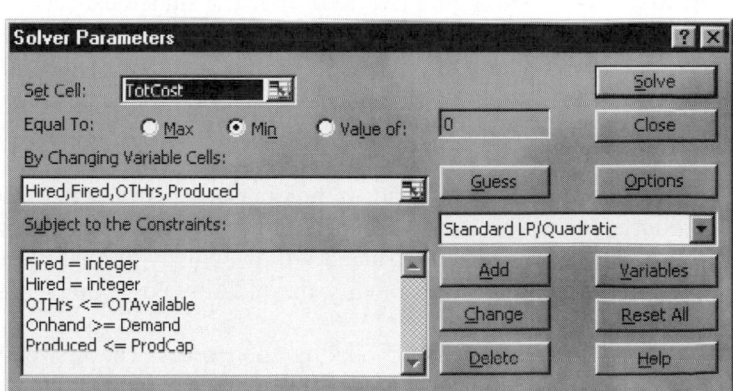

➊ Objective. Select the TotCost cell as the target cell to minimize.

➋ Changing cells. Select the ranges Hired, Fired, Production, and OTHrs as changing cells. *Note:* As shown in Figure 4.7, the way to select multiple ranges is to enter the first range, type a comma, enter the second range, type a comma, and so on.

➌ Overtime constraint. Add the constraint OTHrs<=OTAvailable. This ensures that overtime hours during each month do not exceed the allowable amount.

➍ Production capacity constraint. Enter the constraint Produced<=ProdCap. This ensures that each month's production does not exceed the limit set by the number of available hours.

➎ Demand constraint. Enter the constraint OnHand>=Demand. This ensures that each month's demand is met on time.

➏ Integer constraints. Although this is optional, we decided to constrain the number hired and fired to be integers. We could also have constrained the Production range to be integers. However, integer constraints typically require longer solution times. Therefore, it is often best to ignore such constraints, especially when the optimal values are fairly large, as are the production quantities in this model. If the solution then has noninteger values, we can usually round them to integers for a solution that is at least close to the optimal integer solution.

➐ Specify nonnegativity and optimize. Under Solver Options, check the nonnegativity box, and use the LP algorithm to obtain the optimal solution shown in Figure 4.6. Observe that SureStep should never hire any workers, and it should fire 6 workers in month 1, 1 worker in month 2, and 43 workers in month 3. Eighty hours of overtime are used, but only in month 2. The company produces over 3700 pairs of shoes during each of the first 2 months, 2000 pairs in month 3, and 1000 pairs in month 4. A total cost of $692,820 is incurred.

Again, we would probably not force the number of pairs of shoes produced each month to be an integer. It makes little difference whether the company produces 3760 or 3761 pairs of shoes during a month, and forcing each month's shoe production to be an integer can greatly increase the time the computer needs to find an optimal solution. On the other hand, it is somewhat more important to ensure that the number of workers hired and fired each month is an integer, given the small numbers of workers involved.

Finally, if you want to ensure that Solver finds the optimal solution in a problem where some or all of the changing cells must be integers, it is a good idea to go into Options (in the Solver dialog box), then into Integer Options, and set the tolerance to 0. Otherwise, Solver might stop when it finds a solution that is *close* to optimal.

Model with Backlogging Allowed In many situations, backlogging is allowed—that is, customer demand can be met later than it occurs. We now show how to modify the SureStep formulation to include the option of backlogged demand. We assume that at the end of each month a cost of $20 is incurred for each unit of demand that remains unsatisfied at the end of the month. This is easily modeled by allowing a month's ending inventory to be negative. For example, if month 1's ending inventory is −10, a shortage cost of $200 (and no holding cost) is incurred. To ensure that SureStep produces any shoes at all, we constrain month 4's ending inventory to be nonnegative. This also ensures that all demand will eventually be met by the end of the 4-month horizon. We now need to modify the monthly cost computations to incorporate the costs due to shortages.

We actually show two modeling approaches. The first is the more "natural," but it results in a nonlinear model. It appears in Figure 4.8 (page 125). (See the file SURESTEP2_NONLINEAR.XLS.) To begin, we enter the per-unit monthly shortage

FIGURE 4.8
Nonlinear SureStep
Model with
Backlogging

	A	B	C	D	E	F
1	SureStep model with backlogging - a "natural" but nonlinear formulation					
2						
3	**Input data**					
4	Initial inventory of shoes	500				
5	Initial number of workers	100	Additional range names:			
6	Regular hours/worker/month	160	UnitShortCost - B15			
7	Maximum overtime hours/worker/month	20	LastOnhand - E35			
8	Hiring cost/worker	$1,600	LastDemand - E37			
9	Firing cost/worker	$2,000	EndInv - B43:E43			
10	Regular wages/worker/month	$1,500				
11	Overtime wage rate/hour	$13				
12	Labor hours/pair of shoes	4				
13	Raw material cost/per of shoes	$15				
14	Holding cost/pair of shoes in inventory/month	$3				
15	Shortage cost/pair of shoes/month	$20				
16						
17	**Worker plan**	Month 1	Month 2	Month 3	Month 4	
18	Workers from previous month	100	94	93	38	
19	Workers hired	0	0	0	0	
20	Workers fired	6	1	55	0	
21	Workers available after hiring and firing	94	93	38	38	
22						
23	Regular-time hours available	15040	14880	6080	6080	
24	Overtime labor hours used	0	0	0	0	
25		<=	<=	<=	<=	
26	Maximum overtime labor hours available	1880	1860	760	760	
27						
28	Total hours for production	15040	14880	6080	6080	
29						
30	**Production plan**	Month 1	Month 2	Month 3	Month 4	
31	Shoes produced	3760	3720	1520	1500	
32		<=	<=	<=	<=	
33	Production capacity	3760	3720	1520	1520	
34						
35	Inventory after production	4260	4980	1500	1000	
36					>=	
37	Demand	3000	5000	2000	1000	
38	Ending inventory	1260	-20	-500	0	
39						
40	**Summary of costs**	Month 1	Month 2	Month 3	Month 4	Totals
41	Hiring cost	$0	$0	$0	$0	$0
42	Firing cost	$12,000	$2,000	$110,000	$0	$124,000
43	Regular-time wages	$141,000	$139,500	$57,000	$57,000	$394,500
44	Overtime wages	$0	$0	$0	$0	$0
45	Raw material cost	$56,400	$55,800	$22,800	$22,500	$157,500
46	Holding cost	$3,780	$0	$0	$0	$3,780
47	Shortage cost	$0	$400	$10,000	$0	$10,400
48	Totals	$213,180	$197,700	$199,800	$79,500	$690,180

cost in the UnitShortCost cell. Note in row 38 how the ending inventory in months 1–3 can be positive (leftovers) or negative (shortages). We can account correctly for the resulting costs with IF functions in rows 46 and 47. For holding costs, enter the formula

=IF(B38>0,UnitHoldCost*B38,0)

in cell B46 and copy it across. For shortage costs, enter the formula

=IF(B38<0,-UnitShortCost*B38,0)

in cell B47 and copy it across. (The minus sign makes this a *positive* cost.)

While these formulas accurately compute holding and shortage costs, the IF functions make the objective function nonlinear, and we must use Solver's Standard GRG

Nonlinear algorithm, as shown in Figure 4.9. Even so, this algorithm is not guaranteed to find the optimal solution. It might succeed for some starting solutions and not for others, or it might fail to obtain an optimal solution to the problem. Alternatively, we could try Solver's Evolutionary algorithm (available with the Solver included in this book, but not with the standard Solver included in Excel). The Evolutionary Solver uses **genetic algorithms** to solve optimization problems. For most problems, genetic algorithms are slower than the "standard" Solver algorithms. However, their advantage is that they can handle *any* spreadsheet model. We will discuss them in Chapter 8.

FIGURE 4.9
Setup for Standard GRG Nonlinear Algorithm

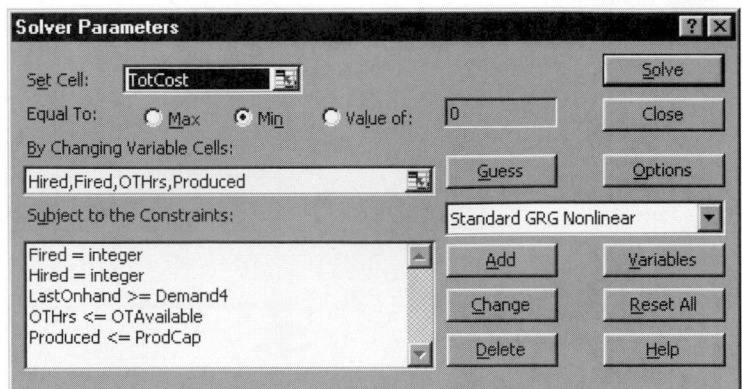

Although this nonlinear model is "natural," the fact that it is not guaranteed to find the optimal solution is disturbing. We can, however, handle shortages and maintain a *linear* formulation. The method is illustrated in Figure 4.10. (See the file SURESTEP2_LINEAR.XLS.) To develop this modified spreadsheet model, starting from the original model in the SURESTEP1.XLS file, proceed as follows.

❶ **Enter shortage cost.** Insert a new row below row 14 and enter the shortage cost per pair of shoes per month in the UnitShortCost cell.

❷ **Rows for amounts held and short.** Insert 5 new rows (which will now be rows 38 through 42) between the Demand and Ending inventory rows. The range B39:E40 will be changing cells. The Excess range in row 39 contains the amounts left in inventory (if any), whereas the Shortage range in row 40 contains the shortages (if any). Enter *any* values in these ranges.

❸ **Ending inventory (positive or negative).** The key observation is the following. Let L_t be the amount of leftover inventory at the end of month t, and let S_t be the amount short at the end of month t. Then $L_t = 0$ if $S_t \geq 0$, and $S_t = 0$ if $L_t \geq 0$. So if we allow ending inventory to be negative (meaning that there is a shortage), then for each month we have

$$I_t = L_t - S_t$$

For example, if $I_2 = 6$, then $L_2 = 6$ and $S_2 = 0$, indicating that SureStep has 6 pairs of shoes left over at the end of month 2. But if $I_2 = -3$, then $L_2 = 0$ and $S_2 = 3$, indicating that SureStep has a shortage of 3 pairs of shoes at the end of month 2. To incorporate this into the spreadsheet, enter the formula

=B39–B40

in cell B41 and copy it to the range C41:E41.

FIGURE 4.10
Linear Formulation
of SureStep Model
with Backlogging

	A	B	C	D	E	F
1	**SureStep model with backlogging - a linear formulation**					
2						
3	**Input data**					
4	Initial inventory of shoes	500				
5	Initial number of workers	100	**Additional range names:**			
6	Regular hours/worker/month	160	UnitShortCost - B15			
7	Maximum overtime hours/worker/month	20	LastOnhand - E35			
8	Hiring cost/worker	$1,600	LastDemand - E37			
9	Firing cost/worker	$2,000	Excess - B39:E39			
10	Regular wages/worker/month	$1,500	Shortage - B40:E40			
11	Overtime wage rate/hour	$13	Net - B41:E41			
12	Labor hours/pair of shoes	4	EndInv - B43:E43			
13	Raw material cost/pair of shoes	$15				
14	Holding cost/pair of shoes in inventory/month	$3				
15	Shortage cost/pair of shoes/month	$20				
16						
17	**Worker plan**	Month 1	Month 2	Month 3	Month 4	
18	Workers from previous month	100	94	93	38	
19	Workers hired	0	0	0	0	
20	Workers fired	6	1	55	0	
21	Workers available after hiring and firing	94	93	38	38	
22						
23	Regular-time hours available	15040	14880	6080	6080	
24	Overtime labor hours used	0	0	0	0	
25		<=	<=	<=	<=	
26	Maximum overtime labor hours available	1880	1860	760	760	
27						
28	Total hours for production	15040	14880	6080	6080	
29						
30	**Production plan**	Month 1	Month 2	Month 3	Month 4	
31	Shoes produced	3760	3720	1520	1500	
32		<=	<=	<=	<=	
33	Production capacity	3760	3720	1520	1520	
34						
35	Inventory after production	4260	4980	1500	1000	
36					>=	
37	Demand	3000	5000	2000	1000	
38						
39	Excess	1260	0	0	0	
40	Shortage	0	20	500	0	
41	Net (excess minus shortage)	1260	-20	-500	0	
42		=	=	=	=	
43	Ending inventory	1260	-20	-500	0	
44						
45	**Summary of costs**	Month 1	Month 2	Month 3	Month 4	Totals
46	Hiring cost	$0	$0	$0	$0	$0
47	Firing cost	$12,000	$2,000	$110,000	$0	$124,000
48	Regular-time wages	$141,000	$139,500	$57,000	$57,000	$394,500
49	Overtime wages	$0	$0	$0	$0	$0
50	Raw material cost	$56,400	$55,800	$22,800	$22,500	$157,500
51	Holding cost	$3,780	$0	$0	$0	$3,780
52	Shortage cost	$0	$400	$10,000	$0	$10,400
53	Totals	$213,180	$197,700	$199,800	$79,500	$690,180

❹ Monthly costs. Insert a new row (which will be row 52) below the holding cost row. Modify the holding cost for month 1 by entering the formula **=UnitHoldCost*B39** in cell B51. Calculate the shortage cost for month 1 in cell B52 with the formula

=UnitShortCost*B40

Then copy the range B51:B52 to the range C51:E52 for the other months. Make sure the totals in row 53 and column F are updated to include the shortage costs.

Using Solver for the Backlog Model The changes from the original Solver setup are as follows.

①   **Extra changing cells.** Add the Excess and Shortage ranges as changing cells. This allows the Solver to adjust each month's amount left over and amount short to be consistent with the desired ending inventory for the month.

②   **Constraint on last month's inventory.** Change the constraints that were previously listed as Onhand>=Demand to LastOnhand>=LastDemand. This allows months 1 through 3 to have negative ending inventory, whereas it ensures that all demand is met by the end of month 4.

③   **Logical constraint on ending inventory.** Add the constraints Net=EndInv. If you study the model closely, you will notice that we have calculated ending inventory in two different ways (in rows 41 and 43). This constraint ensures that both ways produce the same values.

④   **Optimize.** Make sure the LP algorithm is selected, and click on Solve to obtain the optimal solution shown in Figure 4.10.

Note that this solution is the same as the one in Figure 4.8 that was obtained with the nonlinear algorithm. So this time it worked, but it might not always work. This solution is quite similar to the solution with no backlogging allowed, but now SureStep fires more workers in month 3 than before, and it purposely incurs shortages in months 2 and 3. With more options—it can now backlog demand if it desires—the company's total cost cannot be any more than when backlogging was not allowed. However, the decrease is a rather minor one, from $692,820 to $690,180.

Sensitivity Analysis There are many sensitivity analyses we could perform on this final SureStep model. We illustrate one of them, where we see how the total cost and the shortages SureStep is willing to incur in months 1–3 vary with the unit shortage cost. The model is all set up to handle this analysis. All we need to do is invoke SolverTable, specify a one-way table, specify UnitShortCost as the input cell, enter a range such as $0 to $35 in increments of $5 for the input cell, and specify the TotCost cell and the range B40:D40 as the output cells. The results appear in Figure 4.11. As we see, when the unit shortage cost is below $20, SureStep is willing to incur large shortages—at a significantly lower total cost. However, shortages become much less attractive when the unit shortage cost increases, and no shortages are incurred at all when this unit cost is above $25. In this case, we get the *same* solution as when shortages are disallowed.

The Rolling Planning Horizon Approach In reality, an aggregate planning model is usually implemented via a rolling planning horizon. To illustrate, we assume that SureStep works with a 4-month planning horizon. To implement the SureStep model in the rolling planning horizon context, we view the "demands" as forecasts and solve a 4-month model with these forecasts. However, we implement only the month 1 production and work scheduling recommendation. Thus (assuming that the numbers of workers hired and fired in a month must be integers and that shortages are allowed)

FIGURE 4.11
Sensitivity to Unit
Shortage Cost

	A	B	C	D	E	F
55	**Sensitivity of shortages in the first three months and total cost to unit shortage cost**					
56	Unit shortage cost	Shortage1	Shortage2	Shortage3	TotalCost	
57		$B$40	$C$40	$D$40	$F$53	
58	0	0	2280	1640	$621,740	
59	5	0	2220	1580	$640,920	
60	10	0	2220	1580	$659,920	
61	15	0	2220	1580	$678,920	
62	20	0	20	500	$690,180	
63	25	0	20	20	$692,780	
64	30	0	0	0	$692,820	
65	35	0	0	0	$692,820	

SureStep should hire no workers, fire 6 workers, and produce 3760 pairs of shoes with regular time labor in month 1. Next, we observe month 1's actual demand. Suppose it is 2950. Then SureStep begins month 2 with 1310 (= 4260 − 2950) pairs of shoes and 94 workers. We would now enter 1310 in cell B4 and 94 in cell B5 (referring to Figure 4.10). Then we would replace the demands in the Demand range with the updated forecasts for the *next* 4 months. Now we would rerun Solver and use the production levels and hiring and firing recommendations in column B as the production level and workforce policy for month 2. Just like the caissons, the planning horizon goes rolling along! ■

MODELING ISSUES

1. Hiring costs include training costs as well as the cost of decreased productivity due to the fact that a new worker must learn his or her job (the "learning curve" effect).

2. Firing costs include severance costs and costs due to loss of morale.

3. Silver et al. (1998) recommend that when demand is seasonal, the planning horizon should extend beyond the next seasonal peak.

4. Beyond a certain point, the cost of using extra hours of overtime labor increases because workers become less efficient. We haven't modeled this type of behavior because it would make the model nonlinear. ■

ADDITIONAL APPLICATIONS

Multiproduct Production Scheduling at Owens-Corning Fiberglass

Oliff and Burch (1985) developed an aggregate planning LP model that is used to schedule production of fiberglass products at Owens-Corning Fiberglass. Their model minimizes the sum of direct payroll costs, overtime costs, hiring and firing costs, and inventory holding costs. They also take into account (using integer programming; see Chapter 6) the cost (due to lost production time) incurred when a machine changes from making one product to making a different product. Their model has saved Owens-Corning over $100,000 per year. (See Problem 12 for a simplified version of this situation.) ■

PROBLEMS

Skill-Building Problems

5. Mondo Motorcycles is determining its production schedule for the next 4 quarters. Demands for motorcycles are forecasted to be 40 in quarter 1; 70 in quarter 2; 50 in quarter 3; 20 in quarter 4. Mondo incurs four types of costs:
   - It costs Mondo $400 to manufacture each motorcycle.

- At the end of each quarter, a holding cost of $100 per motorcycle left in inventory is incurred.
- Increasing production from one quarter to the next incurs costs for training employees. It is estimated that a cost of $700 per motorcycle is incurred if production is increased from one quarter to the next.
- Decreasing production from one quarter to the next incurs costs for severance pay, decreasing

morale, and so forth. It is estimated that a cost of $600 per motorcycle is incurred if production is decreased from one quarter to the next.

All demands must be met on time, and a quarter's production can be used to meet demand for the current quarter (as well as future quarters). During the quarter immediately preceding quarter 1, 50 Mondos were produced. Assume that at the beginning of quarter 1, no Mondos are in inventory.

  a. Determine how to minimize Mondo's total cost during the next 4 quarters.

  b. Use SolverTable to determine how Mondo's optimal production schedule would be affected by a change in the cost of increasing production from one quarter to the next.

  c. Use SolverTable to determine how Mondo's optimal production schedule would be affected by a change in the cost of decreasing production from one quarter to the next.

6. Referring to the previous problem, suppose that Mondo no longer must meet demands on time. For each quarter that demand for a motorcycle is not met, a shortage cost of $110 per motorcycle short is assessed. Thus, demand can now be backlogged. All demands must be met, however, by the end of quarter 4. Determine the optimal solution to this modified problem.

7. A bus company believes that it will need the following numbers of bus drivers during each of the next 5 years: 60 drivers in year 1; 70 drivers in year 2; 50 drivers in year 3; 65 drivers in year 4; 75 drivers in year 5. At the beginning of each year, the bus company must decide how many drivers to hire or fire. It costs $4000 to hire a driver and $2000 to fire a driver. A driver's salary is $10,000 per year. At the beginning of year 1 the company has 50 drivers. A driver hired at the beginning of a year can be used to meet the current year's requirements and is paid full salary for the current year.

  a. Determine how to minimize the bus company's salary, hiring, and firing costs over the next 5 years.

  b. Use SolverTable to determine how the total number hired, total number fired, and total cost change as the unit hiring and firing costs *each* increase by the same percentage.

8. Shoemakers of America forecasts the following demand for the next 6 months: 5000 pairs in month 1; 6000 pairs in month 2; 5000 pairs in month 3; 9000 pairs in month 4; 6000 pairs in month 5; 5000 pairs in month 6. It takes a shoemaker 15 minutes to produce a pair of shoes. Each shoemaker works 150 hours per month plus up to 40 hours per month of overtime. A shoemaker is paid a regular salary of $2000 per month plus $50 per hour for overtime. At the beginning of each month, Shoemakers can either hire or fire workers. It costs the company $1500 to hire a

worker and $1900 to fire a worker. The monthly holding cost per pair of shoes is 3% of the cost of producing a pair of shoes with regular-time labor. The raw materials in a pair of shoes cost $10. At the beginning of month 1, Shoemakers has 13 workers. Determine how to minimize the cost of meeting (on time) the demands of the next 6 months.

Skill-Extending Problems

9. Clothco manufactures pants. During each of the next 6 months, Clothco can sell up to the numbers of pants given in Table 4.2. Demand that is not met during a month is lost (not backlogged). A pair of pants sells for $40, requires 2 hours of labor, and uses $10 of raw material. At the beginning of month 1, Clothco has 4 workers. A worker can sew pants for up to 200 hours per month and is paid $2000 per month (regardless of how many hours he or she works). At the beginning of each month workers can be hired and/or fired. It costs $1500 to hire a worker and $1000 to fire a worker. A holding cost of $5 per pair of pants is assessed against each month's ending inventory. Determine how Clothco can maximize its profit for the next 6 months.

TABLE 4.2	Demand for Clothco Problem
Maximum Demand	
Month 1	500
Month 2	600
Month 3	300
Month 4	400
Month 5	300
Month 6	800

10. During the next 4 quarters, Dorian Auto must meet (on time) the following demands for cars: 4000 in quarter 1; 2000 in quarter 2; 5000 in quarter 3; 1000 in quarter 4. At the beginning of quarter 1, there are 300 autos in stock. The company has the capacity to produce at most 3000 cars per quarter. At the beginning of each quarter, the company can change production capacity. It costs $100 to increase quarterly production capacity by one unit. For example, it would cost $10,000 to increase capacity from 3000 to 3100. It also costs $50 per quarter to maintain each unit of production capacity (even if it is unused during the current quarter). The variable cost of producing a car is $2000. A holding cost of $150 per car is assessed against each quarter's ending inventory. It is required that at the end of quarter 4, plant capacity must be at least 4000 cars.

a. Determine how to minimize the total cost incurred during the next 4 quarters.

b. Use SolverTable to determine how much the total cost increases as the required capacity at the end of quarter 4 increases (from its current value of 4000).

11. Carco uses robots to manufacture cars. The following demands for cars must be met (not necessarily on time, but all demands must be met by end of quarter 4): 600 in quarter 1; 800 in quarter 2; 500 in quarter 3; 400 in quarter 4. At the beginning of the year, Carco has 2 robots. Robots can be purchased at the beginning of each quarter, but a maximum of 2 per quarter can be purchased. Each robot can build up to 200 cars per quarter. It costs $5000 to purchase a robot. Each quarter a robot incurs $500 in maintenance costs (even if it is not used to build any cars). Robots can also be sold at the beginning of each quarter for $3000. At the end of each quarter, a holding cost of $200 per car left in inventory is incurred. If any demand is backlogged, a cost of $300 per car is incurred for each quarter the shortage lasts. At the end of quarter 4, Carco must have at least 2 robots. Determine how to minimize the total cost incurred in meeting demand for the next 4 quarters.

12. Owens-Wheat uses 2 production lines to produce 3 types of fiberglass mat. The demand requirements (in tons) for each of the next 4 months are shown in Table 4.3. If it were dedicated entirely to the production of one product, a line 1 machine could produce either 20 tons of type 1 mat or 30 tons of

TABLE 4.3	**Demands for Owens-Wheat Problem**		
	Type 1	**Type 2**	**Type 3**
Month 1	200	300	400
Month 2	300	100	300
Month 3	200	400	200
Month 4	300	200	100

type 2 mat during a month. Similarly, a line 2 machine could produce either 25 tons of type 2 mat or 28 tons of type 3 mat. It costs $5000 per month to operate a machine on line 1 and $5500 per month to operate a machine on line 2. A cost of $2000 is incurred each time a new machine is purchased, and a cost of $1000 is incurred if a machine is retired from service. At the end of each month, Owens would like to have at least 50 tons of each product in inventory. At the beginning of month 1, Owens has 5 machines on line 1 and 8 machines on line 2. Assume the per-ton cost of holding either product in inventory for one month is $5.

a. Determine a minimum cost production schedule for the next 4 months.

b. There is an important aspect of this situation that cannot be modeled by linear programming. What is it? (*Hint*: If Owens makes product 1 and product 2 on line 1 during a month, is this as efficient as making just product 1 on line 1?)

4.4 DYNAMIC WORKFORCE PLANNING MODELS

We have already discussed how to adjust workforce levels in our discussion of the aggregate planning model. Here is another example.

EXAMPLE 4.3

TRAINING EMPLOYEES AT CYBERLINKS

CyberLinks is a chain of computer stores. During the next 5 months, the following numbers of skilled repair hours will be needed: 6000 in January; 7000 in February; 8000 in March; 9500 in April; 11,000 in May. At the beginning of January, CyberLinks employs 50 skilled technicians. Each skilled technician can work up to 160 hours per month. To meet future demands, new technicians must be trained. It takes 1 month to train a new technician. During the month of training, a trainee must be supervised for 50 hours by an experienced technician. Experienced technicians are paid $2000 per month and trainees are paid $1000 per month during their month of training. Historical data indicate that 5% of the company's skilled technicians quit each month. CyberLinks wants to use linear programming to determine a training schedule that minimizes the cost of meeting the demands for the next 5 months.

Solution

To model the company's situation, we must keep track of the following:

- the number of workers trained each month
- the number of experienced workers on hand each month
- the number of skilled hours available to meet each month's needs
- the monthly and total costs

DEVELOPING THE SPREADSHEET MODEL

The spreadsheet model for CyberLinks's problem appears in Figure 4.12. (See the file CYBERLINKS.XLS.) To develop this spreadsheet, proceed as follows.

1 **Inputs.** Enter all of the relevant data in the range B4:B9 and (for the number of repair hours required each month) in the HrsReqd range.

2 **Number of trainees each month.** The only decision CyberLinks must make is the number of trainees to hire each month. This will automatically determine the number of skilled technicians needed (and available) each month. Therefore, enter *any* trial values for trainees in the Trainees range.

3 **Skilled technicians available each month.** In cell B14 enter the formula

=InitTechs

This corresponds to the 50 workers available at the beginning of January. Now, let S_t, Q_t, and T_t be, respectively, the number of skilled workers available in month t, the

	A	B	C	D	E	F	G	H	I
1	**CyberLinks workforce training model**								
2									
3	**Inputs**						Range names used:		
4	January skilled technicians	50					InitTechs - B4		
5	Hours/month/skilled technician	160					HrsPerTech - B5		
6	Supervision hours/trainee/month	50					HrsPerTrainee - B6		
7	Monthly pay/skilled technician	$2,000					UnitTechCost - B7		
8	Monthly pay/trainee	$1,000					UnitTraineeCost - B8		
9	Percentage quitters/month	5%					PctQuitters - B9		
10							Trainees - B13:F13		
11	**Planning schedule**						Technicians - B14:F14		
12	Month	1	2	3	4	5	HrsAvailable - B18:F18		
13	# of trainees	0	8.45	11.45	9.52	0	HrsReqd - B20:F20		
14	# of skilled technicians	50	47.5	53.58	62.35	68.75	TechCost - B23		
15	# of quitters at end of month	2.5	2.38	2.68	3.12	3.44	TraineeCost - B24		
16							TotCost - B25		
17	**Constraints on hours**								
18	Available hours for repair	8000	7177.34	8000	9500	11000			
19		>=	>=	>=	>=	>=			
20	Required hours for repair	6000	7000	8000	9500	11000			
21									
22	**Cost summary**								
23	Skilled technician costs	$564,355							
24	Trainee costs	$29,421							
25	Total cost	$593,777							

FIGURE 4.12 CyberLinks Workforce Training Model

number of quitters at the end of month t, and the number of trainees in month t. Then we have the following balance equation:

$$S_t = S_{t-1} - Q_{t-1} + T_{t-1}$$

This follows because all of the trainees in month $t - 1$ are skilled by month t, and all but the quitters come back the following month. Use this relationship to compute the number of skilled technicians available during February by entering the formula

=B13+B14–B15

in cell C14. Then copy this formula to the range D14:F14 for the other months.

4 **Quitters each month.** Calculate the number who quit at the end of month 1 in cell B15 with the formula

=PctQuitters*B14

and copy this to the range C15:F15 for the quitters in the other months.

5 **Hours available for repair each month.** Let H_t be the number of hours available for repair in month t. Then the following equation relates the number of hours available for repair to the number of skilled workers and the number of trainees:

$$H_t = 160S_t - 50T_t$$

Use this relationship to compute the available repair hours for January in cell B18 with the formula

=HrsPerTech*B14–HrsPerTrainee*B13

Then copy this formula to the range C18:F18 for the other months.

6 **Payroll costs.** Compute the total payroll costs for skilled technicians and trainees in cells B23 and B24 with the formulas

=UnitTechCost*SUM(Technicians)

and

=UnitTraineeCost*SUM(Trainees)

Then sum these to get the total cost in the TotCost cell.

USING SOLVER

To use Solver to solve CyberLinks's problem, proceed as follows. (When you are finished, the Solver dialog box should appear as shown in Figure 4.13.)

FIGURE 4.13
Solver Dialog Box for CyberLinks Model

① **Objective.** Select the TotCost cell as the target cell to minimize.

② **Changing cells.** Select the Trainees range as the changing cells.

③ **Skilled technician hour constraint.** Enter the constraint HrsAvailable>= HrsReqd. This ensures that enough skilled technician hours are available each month to meet requirements.

④ **Specify nonnegativity and optimize.** Under Solver Options, check the nonnegativity box, and use the LP algorithm to obtain the optimal solution shown in Figure 4.12. We see that a minimum cost of $593,777 is obtained by the following training schedule: train 0 in January, 8.45 in February, 11.45 in March, 9.52 in April, and 0 in May.

If the number of trainees during each month is required to be an integer, then we can add the constraint that the Trainee range be integers. Unfortunately, there is still a problem—the number of skilled technicians during each month is still fractional because of the quitters. When we multiply the number of skilled trainees by 0.05, we typically do not get integers. One possible remedy is to assume that *approximately* 5% quit, and implement this with Excel's ROUND function. Specifically, enter the formula

=ROUND(PctQuitters*B14,0)

in cell B15 and copy it across row 15. This rounds the first argument to 0 decimals. But life is never this easy. The model is now nonlinear, as Solver will remind you if you try to use the LP algorithm. The logical solution is to use the GRG nonlinear algorithm. Although it is not always guaranteed to work with models using the ROUND function, it does work here, giving the solution in Figure 4.14. Note that this solution costs a little over $2000 more than the solution without integer constraints. Extra constraints always cost money!

Sensitivity Analysis One interesting sensitivity analysis is to see how the number of trainees and the total cost vary with the percentage of quitters. We tried this by using SolverTable on the model that includes the ROUND function and integer constraints, letting the percentage of quitters vary from 0% to 10% in increments of 1%. (Remember

	A	B	C	D	E	F	G	H	I
1	CyberLinks workforce training model with integer constraints								
2									
3	**Inputs**						**Range names used:**		
4	January skilled technicians	50					InitTechs - B4		
5	Hours/month/skilled technician	160					HrsPerTech - B5		
6	Supervision hours/trainee/month	50					HrsPerTrainee - B6		
7	Monthly pay/skilled technician	$2,000					UnitTechCost - B7		
8	Monthly pay/trainee	$1,000					UnitTraineeCost - B8		
9	Percentage quitters/month	5%					PctQuitters - B9		
10							Trainees - B13:F13		
11	**Planning schedule**						Technicians - B14:F14		
12	Month	1	2	3	4	5	HrsAvailable - B18:F18		
13	# of trainees	0	9	12	9	0	HrsReqd - B20:F20		
14	# of skilled technicians	50	47	54	63	69	TechCost - B23		
15	# of quitters at end of month	3	2	3	3	3	TraineeCost - B24		
16							TotCost - B25		
17	**Constraints on hours**								
18	Available hours for repair	8000	7070.00	8040	9630	11040			
19		>=	>=	>=	>=	>=			
20	Required hours for repair	6000	7000	8000	9500	11000			
21									
22	**Cost summary**								
23	Skilled technician costs	$566,000							
24	Trainee costs	$30,000							
25	Total cost	$596,000							

FIGURE 4.14 Optimal Integer Solution to CyberLinks Model

to enter *decimals* in the SolverTable dialog box for these input percentages.) The results appear in the top half of Figure 4.15. The values in column H are the increases in total cost as the percentage of quitters increases. Do you believe these "bumpy" results? We didn't. We thought it strange that total cost would first increase by $4000, then by $0, then by $4000, and so on. Therefore, we ran Solver "manually" on each of these problems, inputting each percentage of quitters in the PctQuitters cell. The results in the bottom half of Figure 4.15 are similar, but not identical, to the results from SolverTable. Why the inconsistency?

Sooner or later, inconsistent results such as these will probably happen to you, so be ready and willing to do some detective work. We thought the problem was probably with Solver's nonlinear algorithm not liking the ROUND function. However, this was not it. Upon more careful inspection, we found that SolverTable (for reasons we still do not understand) uses input values that are slightly off from those specified, at least when the specified values involve decimals. For example, the value in cell A32 is 0.999999977648258%, not exactly 1%. When we entered the former value into the PctQuitters cell and ran Solver, we obtained the solution shown in row 32—a *different* solution from row 45 where 1% is used. Inconsistencies like these can be a source of frustration or a learning experience. We favor the latter. Specifically, we learn how sensitive integer models can be to slight changes in inputs. Evidently, the model is on the edge of rounding up or down. In one case it evidently rounds down, and in the other it evidently rounds up.

FIGURE 4.15
Inconsistent
Solutions

	A	B	C	D	E	F	G	H
27	**Sensitivity of number of trainees and total cost to percentage of quitters**							
28	**SolverTable results**							
29	PctQuitters			Number of trainees			Total cost	
30		$B$13	$C$13	$D$13	$E$13	$F$13	$B$25	Change
31	0%	0	3	9	7	0	$587,000	
32	1%	0	4	9	8	0	$591,000	$4,000
33	2%	0	6	9	8	0	$591,000	$0
34	3%	0	6	11	8	0	$595,000	$4,000
35	4%	0	8	11	9	0	$596,000	$1,000
36	5%	0	8	12	9	0	$597,000	$1,000
37	6%	0	10	12	10	0	$598,000	$1,000
38	7%	3	9	12	10	0	$606,000	$8,000
39	8%	2	11	12	11	0	$606,000	$0
40	9%	2	11	14	11	0	$610,000	$4,000
41	10%	3	12	14	11	0	$612,000	$2,000
42	**Results from doing it manually**							
43		$B$13	$C$13	$D$13	$E$13	$F$13	$B$25	Change
44	0%	0	3	9	7	0	$587,000	
45	1%	0	5	9	8	0	$590,000	$3,000
46	2%	0	6	9	8	0	$591,000	$1,000
47	3%	0	7	11	8	0	$594,000	$3,000
48	4%	0	8	11	9	0	$596,000	$2,000
49	5%	0	9	12	9	0	$596,000	$0
50	6%	0	10	12	10	0	$598,000	$2,000
51	7%	2	10	12	10	0	$604,000	$6,000
52	8%	2	11	12	11	0	$606,000	$2,000
53	9%	3	11	14	11	0	$611,000	$5,000
54	10%	3	12	15	11	0	$613,000	$2,000

Skill-Building Problems

13. An insurance company believes that it will require the following numbers of personal computers during the next 6 months: January, 9; February, 5; March, 7; April, 9; May, 10; June, 5. Computers can be rented for a period of 1, 2, or 3 months at the following unit rates: 1-month rate, $200; 2-month rate, $350; 3-month rate, $450.

   a. Determine how to minimize the cost of renting the required computers. You can assume that if a machine is rented for a period of time extending beyond June, the cost of the rental is prorated. For example, if a computer is rented for 3 months at the beginning of May, then a rental fee of $(2/3)450 = \$300$ is assessed.

   b. A key factor in determining the optimal rental policy is the ratio of the 2-month rental cost to the 1-month cost and the ratio of the 3-month rental cost to the 2-month rental cost. Use SolverTable to determine how simultaneous changes in these ratios affect the total rental cost.

14. The Internal Revenue Service (IRS) has determined that during each of the next 12 months it will need the numbers of supercomputers given in Table 4.4. To meet these requirements, the IRS rents supercomputers for a period of 1, 2, or 3 months. It costs $100 to rent a supercomputer for 1 month, $180 for 2 months, and $250 for 3 months. At the beginning of month 1, the IRS has no supercomputers.

TABLE 4.4	Computer Requirements for IRS Problem
	Computer Requirements
Month 1	800
Month 2	1000
Month 3	600
Month 4	500
Month 5	1200
Month 6	800
Month 7	800
Month 8	600
Month 9	400
Month 10	500
Month 11	800
Month 12	600

   a. Determine the rental plan that meets the requirements for the next 12 months at minimum cost. You can assume that fractional rentals are allowed. Thus, if your solution says to rent 140.6 computers for one month, you can round this up to 141 or down to 140 without much effect on the total cost.

   b. Suppose the monthly requirement increases anywhere from 10% to 50% each month. (Assume that whatever the percentage increase is, it is the *same* each month.) Use SolverTable to see whether the total rental cost increases by this same percentage.

Skill-Extending Problems

15. You own a wheat warehouse with a capacity of 20,000 bushels. At the beginning of month 1, you have 6000 bushels of wheat. Each month wheat can be bought and sold at the prices per 1000 bushels shown in Table 4.5.

TABLE 4.5	Selling and Purchasing Prices for Wheat Problem	
	Selling Price	**Purchase Price**
Month 1	$3	$8
Month 2	$6	$8
Month 3	$7	$2
Month 4	$1	$3
Month 5	$4	$4
Month 6	$5	$3
Month 7	$5	$3
Month 8	$1	$2
Month 9	$3	$5
Month 10	$2	$5

The sequence of events during each month is as follows:

- You observe your initial stock of wheat.
- You can sell any amount of wheat up to your initial stock at the current month's selling price.
- You can buy as much wheat as you want, subject to the warehouse size limitation.

   a. Determine how to maximize the profit earned over the next 10 months.

   b. Use SolverTable to determine how a change in the capacity of the warehouse affects the optimal solution.

16. In the CyberLinks computer example, suppose it takes 2 months to train a technician. Also, suppose that during the second month of training, each trainee requires 10 hours of experienced technician time. Modify the formulation in the text to account for these changes.

4.5 BLENDING MODELS

In many situations various inputs must be blended together to produce desired outputs. In many of these situations linear programming can find the optimal combination of outputs as well as the "mix" of inputs that are used to produce the desired outputs. Some examples of blending problems follow:

Inputs	Outputs
Meat, filler, water	Different types of sausage
Various types of oil	Heating oil, gasolines, aviation fuels
Carbon, iron, molybdenum	Different types of steel
Different types of pulp	Different kinds of recycled paper

The following example illustrates how to model a typical blending problem on a spreadsheet. Although this example is small relative to blending problems in real applications, we think you will agree that it is fairly complex. If you are able to guess the optimal solution, your intuition is much better than ours!

EXAMPLE 4.4

BLENDING AT CHANDLER OIL

Chandler Oil has 5000 barrels of crude oil 1 and 10,000 barrels of crude oil 2 available. Chandler sells gasoline and heating oil. These products are produced by blending together the two crude oils. Each barrel of crude oil 1 has a "quality level" of 10 and each barrel of crude oil 2 has a quality level of 5. Gasoline must have an average quality level of at least 8, whereas heating oil must have an average quality level of at least 6. Gasoline sells for $25 per barrel and heating oil sells for $20 per barrel. The advertising cost to sell one barrel of gasoline is $0.20 and the advertising cost to sell one barrel of heating oil is $0.10. We assume that demand for heating oil and gasoline is unlimited, so that all of Chandler's production can be sold. Chandler wants to maximize its profit.

Solution

To model Chandler's problem with a spreadsheet, we must keep track of the following:

- the number of barrels of gasoline and heating oil produced (the outputs)
- the number of barrels of each crude oil (the inputs) used to produce each output
- the quality levels of the inputs used to make the outputs
- the total profit earned

DEVELOPING THE SPREADSHEET MODEL

The spreadsheet model for this problem appears in Figure 4.16. (See the file BLEND-ING.XLS.) To set it up, proceed as follows.

❶ Monetary and quality inputs. Enter the unit profit contributions and advertising costs in the SellingPrices and UnitAdCosts ranges. Enter the quality levels for crude oils in the QualityLevels range and the quality standards for the outputs in the range B13:C13. (See, we don't name *all* of the ranges!) Enter the barrels available in the Available range.

❷ Inputs blended into each output. Although it may not be immediately apparent, the quantities Chandler must choose to specify any solution are the barrels of each input used to produce each output. Therefore, enter *any* trial values for these quantities in the BlendPlan range. For example, the value in cell B17 is the amount of crude oil 1 used to make gasoline and the value in cell C17 is the amount of crude oil 1 used to make heating oil. The BlendPlan range will be the changing cell range.

❸ Inputs used and outputs sold. We need to calculate the row sums (in column D) and column sums (in row 19) of the BlendPlan range. This is a common operation, so it is worth knowing an easy way of doing it. Just highlight both the Used and Sold ranges (highlight one, then hold down the Ctrl key and highlight the other), and click on the Summation (Σ) button on the main Excel toolbar. This creates SUM formulas in each highlighted cell.

❹ Quality achieved. Keeping track of the quality level of gasoline and heating oil in the QualityObtained range is tricky. Begin by calculating for each output the number of quality points (QP) in the inputs used to produce this output:

$$QP \text{ in gasoline} = 10 * (\text{Oil 1 in gasoline}) + 5 * (\text{Oil 2 in gasoline})$$
$$QP \text{ in heating oil} = 10 * (\text{Oil 1 in heating oil}) + 5 * (\text{Oil 2 in heating oil})$$

FIGURE 4.16
Chandler Oil
Blending Model

	A	B	C	D	E	F
1	**Chandler blending model**					
2					**Range names used:**	
3	**Monetary inputs**	Gasoline	Heating oil		SellingPrices - B4:C4	
4	Selling price/barrel	$25.00	$20.00		UnitAdCosts - B5:C5	
5	Advertising cost/barrel	$0.20	$0.10		QualityLevels - B8:B9	
6					BlendPlan - B17:C18	
7	**Quality level per barrel of crudes**				Used - D17:D18	
8	Crude oil 1	10			Available - F17:F18	
9	Crude oil 2	5			Sold - B19:C19	
10					QualityObtained - B23:C23	
11	**Required quality level per barrel of product**				QualityReqd - B25:C25	
12		Gasoline	Heating oil		Revenue - B28	
13		8	6		AdCost - B29	
14					Profit - B30	
15	**Blending plan (barrels of crudes in each product)**					
16		Gasoline	Heating oil	Barrels used		Barrels available
17	Crude oil 1	3000	2000	5000	<=	5000
18	Crude oil 2	2000	8000	10000	<=	10000
19	Barrels sold	5000	10000			
20						
21	**Constraints on quality**					
22		Gasoline	Heating oil			
23	Quality "points" obtained	40000	60000			
24		>=	>=			
25	Quality "points" required	40000	60000			
26						
27	**Monetary summary**					
28	Revenue	$325,000				
29	Advertising cost	$2,000				
30	Profit	$323,000				

For the gasoline produced to have a quality level of at least 8, we must have

$$\text{QP in gasoline} \geq 8 * \text{Gasoline sold} \qquad \textbf{(4.2)}$$

For the heating oil produced to have a quality level of at least 6, we must have

$$\text{QP in heating oil} \geq 6 * \text{Heating oil sold} \qquad \textbf{(4.3)}$$

To implement inequalities (4.2) and (4.3), calculate the QP for gasoline in cell B23 with the formula

=SUMPRODUCT(B17:B18,QualityLevels)

Then copy this formula to cell C23 to generate the QP for heating oil.

❺   Quality required. Calculate the required quality points for gasoline and heating oil in the QualityReqd range. Specifically, in cell B25 determine the required quality points for gasoline with the formula

=B13*B19

Then copy this formula to cell C25 to calculate the required quality points for heating oil.

❻   Revenue, cost, and profit. Calculate the total revenue, total advertising cost, and total profit in the Revenue, AdCost, and Profit cells with the formulas

=SUMPRODUCT(SellingPrices,Sold)
=SUMPRODUCT(UnitAdCosts,Sold)

and

=Revenue-AdCost

USING SOLVER

To solve Chandler's problem with Solver, proceed as follows. When you are finished, the Solver dialog box should appear as shown in Figure 4.17.

❶   Objective. Maximize profit by choosing the Profit cell as the target cell.

❷   Changing cells. Select the BlendPlan range as the changing cells.

❸   Crude oil availability constraint. Enter the constraint Used<=Available. This ensures that no more of any oil is used than is available.

❹   Quality constraint. Enter the constraint QualityObtained>=QualityReqd. This ensures that the gasoline and heating oil produced are of acceptable quality.

FIGURE 4.17
Solver Dialog Box
for Blending Model

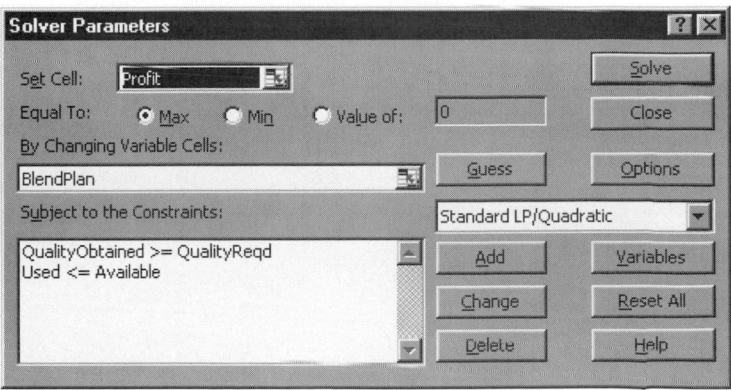

⑤ Specify nonnegativity and optimize. Under Solver Options, check the non-negativity box, and use the LP algorithm to obtain the optimal solution shown in Figure 4.16.

The solution implies that Chandler should make 5000 barrels of gasoline with 3000 barrels of crude oil 1 and 2000 barrels of crude oil 2. It should also make 10,000 barrels of heating oil with 2000 barrels of crude oil 1 and 8000 barrels of crude oil 2. With this blend, Chandler will earn a profit of $323,000.

As stated earlier, we believe this problem is sufficiently complex to defy intuition. Clearly, gasoline is more profitable per barrel than heating oil, but given the crude availability and the quality constraints, it turns out that Chandler should sell twice as much heating oil as gasoline. This would have been very difficult to guess ahead of time.

Sensitivity Analysis We perform two typical sensitivity analyses on the Chandler blending model. In each, we see how profit and the amounts of the outputs produced (and sold) vary. In the first analysis, we use the unit selling price of gasoline as the input and let it vary from $20 to $80 in increments of $5. The SolverTable results appear in Figure 4.18. Two things are of interest. First, as the price of gasoline increases, Chandler produces more gasoline and less heating oil, exactly as we would expect. Second, the profit never decreases, as the changes in column E indicate.

In the second sensitivity analysis, we vary the availability of crude 1 from 2000 barrels to 20,000 barrels in increments of 1000 barrels. The resulting SolverTable output appears in Figure 4.19. These results make sense if we analyze them carefully. First, the profit increases, but at a decreasing rate, as more crude 1 is available. This is a common occurrence in LP models. As more of a resource is made available, profit can only increase, but each extra unit of the resource produces less (or at least no more) profit than the previous unit. Second, the amount of gasoline produced increases while the amount of heating oil produced decreases. Here is the reason. Crude 1 has higher quality than crude 2, and gasoline requires higher quality. Gasoline also sells for a higher price. Therefore, as more crude 1 is available, Chandler can produce more gasoline, receive more profit, and still meet quality standards.

FIGURE 4.18
Sensitivity to the Selling Price of Gasoline

	A	B	C	D	E
32	Sensitivity of profit and outputs sold to the selling price of gasoline				
33	Price of gasoline	Gasoline	Heating oil	Profit	
34		$B$19	$C$19	$B$30	Increase
35	20	0	15000	$298,500	
36	25	5000	10000	$323,000	$24,500
37	30	5000	10000	$348,000	$25,000
38	35	5000	10000	$373,000	$25,000
39	40	5000	10000	$398,000	$25,000
40	45	5000	10000	$423,000	$25,000
41	50	5000	10000	$448,000	$25,000
42	55	5000	10000	$473,000	$25,000
43	60	8333	0	$498,333	$25,333
44	65	8333	0	$540,000	$41,667
45	70	8333	0	$581,667	$41,667
46	75	8333	0	$623,333	$41,667
47	80	8333	0	$665,000	$41,667

FIGURE 4.19
Sensitivity to
the Availability of
Crude 1

	A	B	C	D	E
49	Sensitivity of profit and outputs sold to the availability of crude 1				
50	Availability of crude 1	Gasoline	Heating oil	Profit	
51		$B$19	$C$19	$B$30	Increase
52	2000	0	10000	$199,000	
53	3000	1000	12000	$263,600	$64,600
54	4000	3000	11000	$293,300	$29,700
55	5000	5000	10000	$323,000	$29,700
56	6000	7000	9000	$352,700	$29,700
57	7000	9000	8000	$382,400	$29,700
58	8000	11000	7000	$412,100	$29,700
59	9000	13000	6000	$441,800	$29,700
60	10000	15000	5000	$471,500	$29,700
61	11000	17000	4000	$501,200	$29,700
62	12000	19000	3000	$530,900	$29,700
63	13000	21000	2000	$560,600	$29,700
64	14000	23000	1000	$590,300	$29,700
65	15000	25000	0	$620,000	$29,700
66	16000	26000	0	$644,800	$24,800
67	17000	27000	0	$669,600	$24,800
68	18000	28000	0	$694,400	$24,800
69	19000	29000	0	$719,200	$24,800
70	20000	30000	0	$744,000	$24,800

MODELING ISSUES

1. We used inequality (4.2) as the quality constraint for gasoline. It might appear more natural to write the constraint in terms of average quality points by dividing through by Gasoline sold:

$$(\text{QP in gasoline})/(\text{Gasoline sold}) \geq 8 \qquad (4.4)$$

Although this is logically correct, we prefer inequality (4.2) for two reasons. First, it is conceivable that no gasoline should be sold. In this case we would be dividing by 0 in inequality (4.4), which would certainly cause a problem for Excel. The second reason is that inequality (4.4) is technically nonlinear, as the Solver will inform you if you try to use the LP algorithm. The lesson, therefore, is to "clear denominators" in blending problem constraints.

2. We have assumed that the quality level of a mixture is a *linear* function of the fraction of each input used in the mixture. For example, we have assumed that if gasoline is made with a fraction 3/5 of crude oil 1 and 2/5 of crude oil 2 (as in the optimal solution), then

$$\text{Quality Level for Gasoline} = (3/5) * \text{Quality Level for Oil 1}$$
$$+ (2/5) * \text{Quality Level for Oil 2}$$

If the quality level of the output is not a linear function of the fraction of each input used in the mixture, then we no longer have a linear model; we have a *non*linear model. For example, let g_i be the fraction of gasoline made with crude oil i. Suppose that

$$\text{Quality Level for Gasoline} = \sqrt{g_1} * \text{Quality Level for Oil 1}$$
$$+ \sqrt{g_2} * \text{Quality Level for Oil 2}$$

Then we do not have an LP model because the quality level of gasoline is not a linear function of g_1 and g_2. We will discuss nonlinear models in Chapter 7.

3. In reality, a company using a blending model would run the model periodically (each day, say) and set production on the basis of the current inventory of inputs and the current demand forecasts. Then the forecasts and the input levels would be updated, and the model would be run again to determine the next day's production. ■

Blending at Texaco

Texaco [see DeWitt et al. (1989)] uses a nonlinear programming model (OMEGA) to plan and schedule its blending applications. Their model is nonlinear because blend volatilities and octanes are nonlinear functions of the amount of each input used to produce a particular gasoline.

Blending in the Steel Industry

Fabian (1958) describes a complex LP model that can be used to optimize the production of iron and steel. For each product produced there are several blending constraints. For example, basic pig iron must contain at most 1.5% silicon, at most 0.05% sulfur, between 0.11% and 0.90% phosphorus, between 0.4% and 2% manganese, and between 4.1% and 4.4% carbon. See Problem 57 for a simple example of blending in the steel industry.

Blending in the Oil Industry

Many oil companies use LP to optimize their refinery operations. Problem 30 contains an example [based on Magoulas and Marinos-Kouris (1988)] of a blending model that can be used to maximize a refinery's profit. ■

PROBLEMS

Skill-Building Problems

17. NewAge Pharmaceuticals produces the drug NasaMist from four chemicals. Today the company must produce 1000 pounds of the drug. The three active ingredients in NasaMist are A, B, and C. By weight, at least 8% of NasaMist must consist of A, at least 4% of B, and at least 2% of C. The cost per pound of each chemical and the amount of each active ingredient in 1 pound of each chemical are given in Table 4.6. It is necessary that at least 100 pounds of chemical 2 be used.
   a. Determine the cheapest way of producing today's batch of NasaMist.
   b. Use SolverTable to see how much the percentage of requirement of A is really costing NewAge. Let the percentage required vary from 6% to 12%.

TABLE 4.6	Costs and Ingredients for NewAge Problem			
	Cost/Pound	A	B	C
Chemical 1	$8	0.03	0.02	0.01
Chemical 2	$10	0.06	0.04	0.01
Chemical 3	$11	0.10	0.03	0.04
Chemical 4	$14	0.12	0.09	0.04

18. You have decided to enter the candy business. You are considering producing two types of candies: Slugger candy and Easy Out candy, both of which consist solely of sugar, nuts, and chocolate. At present you have in stock 10,000 ounces of sugar, 2000 ounces of nuts, and 3000 ounces of chocolate. The mixture used to make Easy Out candy must

contain at least 20% nuts. The mixture used to make Slugger candy must contain at least 10% nuts and 10% chocolate. Each ounce of Easy Out candy can be sold for $0.50, and each ounce of Slugger candy for $0.40.

   a. Determine how you can maximize your revenue from candy sales.

   b. Use SolverTable to determine how changes in the price of Easy Out change the optimal solution.

   c. Use SolverTable to determine how changes in the amount of available sugar change the optimal solution.

19. Sunblessed Juice Company sells bags of oranges and cartons of orange juice. Sunblessed grades oranges on a scale of 1 (poor) to 10 (excellent). At present, Sunblessed has 100,000 pounds of grade 9 oranges and 120,000 pounds of grade 6 oranges on hand. The average quality of oranges sold in bags must be at least 7, and the average quality of the oranges used to produce orange juice must be at least 8. Each pound of oranges that is used for juice yields a revenue of $1.50 and incurs a variable cost (consisting of labor costs, variable overhead costs, inventory costs, and so on) of $1.05. Each pound of oranges sold in bags yields a revenue of $1.50 and incurs a variable cost of $0.70.

   a. Determine how Sunblessed can maximize its profit.

   b. Use SolverTable to determine how a change in the cost per bag of oranges changes the optimal solution.

   c. Use SolverTable to determine how a change in the amount of grade 9 oranges available affects the optimal solution.

   d. Use SolverTable to determine how a change in the required average quality required for juice changes the optimal solution.

20. A bank is attempting to determine where its assets should be invested during the current year. At present, $500,000 is available for investment in bonds, home loans, auto loans, and personal loans. The annual rates of return on each type of investment are known to be the following: bonds, 10%; home loans, 16%; auto loans, 13%; personal loans, 20%. To ensure that the bank's portfolio is not too risky, the bank's investment manager has placed the following three restrictions on the bank's portfolio:

   ■ The amount invested in personal loans cannot exceed the amount invested in bonds.

   ■ The amount invested in home loans cannot exceed the amount invested in auto loans.

   ■ No more than 25% of the total amount invested may be in personal loans.

   Help the bank maximize the annual return on its investment portfolio.

21. Young MBA Erica Cudahy can invest up to $1000 in stocks and loans. Each dollar invested in stocks yields $0.10 profit, and each dollar invested in a loan yields $0.15 profit. At least 30% of all money invested must be in stocks, and at least $400 must be in loans. Determine how Erica can maximize the profit earned on her investments.

22. Bullco blends silicon and nitrogen to produce two types of fertilizers. Fertilizer 1 must be at least 40% nitrogen and sells for $70 per pound. Fertilizer 2 must be at least 70% silicon and sells for $40 per pound. Bullco can purchase up to 8000 pounds of nitrogen at $15 per pound and up to 10,000 pounds of silicon at $10 per pound.

   a. Assuming that all fertilizer produced can be sold, determine how Bullco can maximize its profit.

   b. Use SolverTable to explore the effect on profit of changing the minimum percentage of nitrogen required in fertilizer 1.

   c. Suppose the availabilities of nitrogen and silicon both increase by the same percentage from their current values. Use SolverTable to explore the effect of this change on profit.

23. Eli Daisy uses chemicals 1 and 2 to produce two drugs. Drug 1 must be at least 70% chemical 1, and drug 2 must be at least 60% chemical 2. Up to 4000 ounces of drug 1 can be sold at $6 per ounce; up to 3000 ounces of drug 2 can be sold at $5 per ounce. Up to 4500 ounces of chemical 1 can be purchased at $6 per ounce, and up to 4000 ounces of chemical 2 can be purchased at $4 per ounce. Determine how to maximize Daisy's profit.

24. Hiland's TV-Radio Store must determine how many TVs and radios to keep in stock. A TV requires 10 square feet of floor space, whereas a radio requires 4 square feet; 5000 square feet of floor space is available. A TV sale results in an $80 profit, and a radio earns a profit of $20. The store stocks only TVs and radios. Marketing requirements dictate that at least 60% of all appliances in stock be radios. Finally, a TV ties up $200 in capital, and a radio $50. Hiland wants to have at most $60,000 worth of capital tied up at any time.

   a. Determine how to maximize Hiland's profit.

   b. Use SolverTable to explore how much profit the minimum percentage of radio requirement is costing Hiland's.

   c. Use SolverTable to explore how much profit the upper limit on capital being tied up is costing Hiland's.

25. Linear programming models are used by many Wall Street firms to select a desirable bond portfolio. The following is a simplified version of such a model. Solodrex is considering investing in four bonds; $1 million is available for investment. The expected annual return, the worst-case annual return on each bond, and the "duration" of each bond are given in Table 4.7 (page 144). (The duration of a bond is a measure of the bond's sensitivity to interest

TABLE 4.7	Bond Returns and Durations for Solodrex Problem		
	Expected Return	Worst-Case Return	Duration
Bond 1	13%	6%	3
Bond 2	8%	8%	4
Bond 3	12%	10%	7
Bond 4	14%	9%	9

rates.) Solodrex wants to maximize the expected return from its bond investments, subject to three constraints:

- The worst-case return of the bond portfolio must be at least 8%.
- The average duration of the portfolio must be at most 6. For example, a portfolio that invests $600,000 in bond 1 and $400,000 in bond 4 has an average duration of

$$[600,000(3) + 400,000(9)]/1,000,000 = 5.4$$

- Because of diversification requirements, at most 40% of the total amount invested can be invested in a single bond.

  Determine how Solodrex can maximize the expected return on its investment.

26. Coalco produces coal at three mines and ships it to four customers. The cost per ton of producing coal, the ash and sulfur content (per ton) of the coal, and the production capacity (in tons) for each mine are given in Table 4.8. The number of tons of coal demanded by each customer is given in Table 4.9. The cost (in dollars) of shipping a ton of coal from a mine to each customer is given in Table 4.10. The total amount of coal shipped must contain at most 6% ash and at most 3.5% sulfur. Show Coalco how to minimize the cost of meeting customer demands.

TABLE 4.8	Cost and Other Data for Coalco Problem			
	Production Cost	Capacity	Ash Content	Sulfur Content
Mine 1	$50	120	0.08 ton	0.05 ton
Mine 2	$55	100	0.06 ton	0.04 ton
Mine 3	$62	140	0.04 ton	0.03 ton

TABLE 4.9	Customer Demand for Coalco Problem			
	Customer 1	Customer 2	Customer 3	Customer 4
Demand	80	70	60	40

TABLE 4.10	Shipping Costs for Coalco Problem			
	Customer 1	Customer 2	Customer 3	Customer 4
Mine 1	4	6	8	12
Mine 2	9	6	7	11
Mine 3	8	12	3	5

Skill-Extending Problems

27. Sunco Oil manufactures three types of gasoline (gas 1, gas 2, and gas 3). Each type is produced by blending three types of crude oil (crude 1, crude 2, and crude 3). The selling price per barrel of gasoline and the purchase price per barrel of crude oil are given in Table 4.11. Sunco can purchase up to 5000

TABLE 4.11	Selling and Purchase Prices for Sunco Problem		
	Selling Price per Barrel		Purchase Price per Barrel
Gas 1	$70	Crude 1	$45
Gas 2	$60	Crude 2	$35
Gas 3	$50	Crude 3	$25

barrels of each type of crude oil daily. The three types of gasoline differ in their octane rating and sulfur content. The crude oil blended to form gas 1 must have an average octane rating of at least 10 and contain at most 1% sulfur. The crude oil blended to form gas 2 must have an average octane rating of at least 8 and contain at most 2% sulfur. The crude oil blended to form gas 3 must have an octane rating of at least 6 and contain at most 1% sulfur. The octane rating and the sulfur content of the three types of oil are given in Table 4.12. It costs $4 to transform one barrel of oil into 1 barrel of gasoline, and Sunco's refinery can produce up to 14,000 barrels of gasoline daily. Sunco's customers require the following amounts of each gasoline: gas 1, 3000 barrels per day; gas 2, 2000 barrels per day; gas 3, 1000 barrels per day. The company considers it an obligation to meet these demands.

TABLE 4.12	Octane Rating and Sulfur Content for Sunco Problem	
	Octane Rating	Sulfur Content
Crude 1	12	0.5%
Crude 2	6	2.0%
Crude 3	8	3.0%

Sunco also has the option of advertising to stimulate demand for its products. Each dollar spent daily in advertising a particular type of gas increases the daily demand for that type of gas by 10 barrels. For example, if Sunco decides to spend $20 daily in advertising gas 2, the daily demand for gas 2 will increase by 200 barrels. Determine how Sunco can maximize its profit.

28. The risk index of an investment can be obtained by taking the absolute values of percentage changes in the value of the investment for each year and averaging them. Suppose you are trying to determine what percentage of your money you should invest in T-bills, gold, and stocks. Table 4.13 lists the annual returns (percentage changes in value) for these investments for the years 1968–1988. Let the risk index of a portfolio be the weighted average of the risk indices of these investments, where the weights are the fractions of the portfolio assigned to the investments. Suppose that the amount of each investment must be between 20% and 50% of the total invested. You would like the risk index of your portfolio to equal 0.15, and your goal is to maximize the expected return on your portfolio. Determine the maximum expected return on your portfolio, subject to the stated constraints. Use the average return earned by each investment during the years 1968–1988 as your estimate of expected return.

29. The owner of Sunco (see Problem 27) does not believe that our optimal LP solution will maximize the company's daily profit. He reasons, "We have 14,000 barrels of daily refinery capacity, but your optimal solution produces only 13,500 barrels. Therefore, it cannot be maximizing profit." How would you respond?

30. Based on Magoulas and Marinos-Kouris (1988). Oilco produces two products: regular and premium gasoline. Each product contains 0.15 gram of lead per liter. The two products are produced from six inputs: reformate, fluid catalytic cracker gasoline (FCG), isomerate (ISO), polymer (POL), MTBE, and butane (BUT). Each input has four attributes: research octane number (RON), RVP, ASTM volatility at 70 degrees Celsius, and ASTM volatility at 130 degrees Celsius. The attributes and daily availability (in liters) of each input are given in Table 4.14. The requirements for each output are given in Table 4.15 (page 146). The daily demand (in thousands of liters) for each product must be met, but more can be produced if desired. The RON

TABLE 4.13	Returns for Investment Problem						
	1968	**1969**	**1970**	**1971**	**1972**	**1973**	**1974**
Stocks	11	−9	4	14	19	−15	−27
Gold	11	8	−14	44	44	66	64
T-bills	5	7	7	4	4	7	8
	1975	**1976**	**1977**	**1978**	**1979**	**1980**	**1981**
Stocks	37	24	−7	7	19	33	−5
Gold	0	−22	18	31	59	99	−25
T-bills	6	5	5	7	10	11	15
	1982	**1983**	**1984**	**1985**	**1986**	**1987**	**1988**
Stocks	22	23	6	32	19	5	17
Gold	4	−11	−15	−12	16	22	−2
T-bills	11	9	10	8	6	5	6

TABLE 4.14	Inputs for Oilco Problem				
	Availability	**RON**	**RVP**	**ASTM (70)**	**ASTM (130)**
Reformate	15,572	98.9	7.66	−5	46
FCG	15,434	93.2	9.78	57	103
ISO	6,709	86.1	29.62	107	100
POL	1,190	97.0	14.51	7	73
MTBE	748	117.0	13.45	98	100
BUT	unlimited	98.0	166.99	130	100

and ASTM requirements are minimums; the RVP requirement is a maximum. Regular gasoline sells for $0.2949 per liter, premium gasoline for $0.3143. Before each product is ready for sale, 0.15 gram per liter of lead must be removed. The cost of removing 0.1 gram per liter is $0.085. At most 38% of each type of gasoline can consist of FCG. Show Oilco how to maximize its daily profit.

TABLE 4.15	Output Requirements for Oilco Problem				
	Demand	RON	RVP	ASTM (70)	ASTM (130)
Regular	9.8	90	21.18	10	50
Premium	30.0	96	21.18	10	50

4.6 PRODUCTION PROCESS MODELS

Linear programming is often used to determine the optimal method of operating a production process. In particular, many oil refineries use LP to manage their production operations. [For example, see Garvin et al. (1957).] The following example shows how spreadsheets can be used to optimize production processes.

EXAMPLE 4.5

DRUG PRODUCTION AT REPCO

Repco produces three drugs, A, B, and C, and can sell these drugs in unlimited quantities at unit prices $8, $70, and $100, respectively. Producing a unit of A requires 1 hour of labor. Producing a unit of B requires 2 hours of labor and 2 units of A. Producing 1 unit of C requires 3 hours of labor and 1 unit of B. Any product A that is used to produce B cannot be sold, and any product B that is used to produce C cannot be sold. A total of 40 hours of labor are available. Repco wants to use linear programming to maximize its sales revenue.

Solution

To model Repco's operations, we need to keep track of the following:

- the number of units produced of each product
- the number of units sold of each product
- the number of units of A and B used to produce other products
- the number of labor hours used
- the revenue received

DEVELOPING THE SPREADSHEET MODEL

The key to developing the spreadsheet model is that everything that is produced must be used in some way. Either it must be used as an input to the production of some other product, or it must be sold. Therefore, we have the "balance" equation for each product:

Amount produced = Amount used to produce other products + Amount sold   (4.5)

We will implement this "balance" equation by designating *both* the amounts produced and the amounts sold as changing cells. Then we will impose a constraint that equation (4.5) must be satisfied.

The spreadsheet model for Repco appears in Figure 4.20. (See the file REPCO. XLS.) To proceed, carry out the following steps.

1 **Inputs.** Enter the number of labor hours needed to produce a unit of each product in the HrsReqd range and enter the number of units of each product needed to manufacture each other product in the range B7:D9. For example, the 2 in cell C7 indicates that 2 units of product A are needed to produce each unit of product B. Then enter the unit selling prices for the products in the UnitPrices range and enter the available labor hours in the HrsAvailable cell.

2 **Units produced.** Enter *any* trial values for the number of units produced and sold in the UnitsProduced and UnitsSold ranges.

3 **Units used to make other products.** In the range G16:I18, calculate the total number of units of each product that are used to produce other products. Begin by calculating the amount of A used to produce A in cell G16 with the formula

=B7*B$16

and copy this formula to the range G16:I18 for the other combinations of products. Then calculate the row totals in column J with the SUM function. For example, the 20 in cell J16 indicates that all 20 units produced of product A are being used to make other products (specifically, product B). It is convenient to "transfer" these sums in column J to the B18:D18 range. This is easy, using Excel's TRANSPOSE function. (This function creates a row from a column or vice versa.) Highlight the B18:D18 range, type the formula

=TRANSPOSE(UnitsUsedAsInputs)

and press Ctrl-Shift-Enter (all at once).

	A	B	C	D	E	F	G	H	I	J	K	L
1	Repco production model											
2												
3	Inputs used (along side) to make one unit of product (along top)					Range names used:						
4		Product A	Product B	Product C		HrsReqd - B5:D5						
5	Labor hours	1	2	3		UnitPrices - B12:D12						
6						UnitsProduced - B16:D16						
7	Product A	0	2	0		UnitsUsedAsInputs - J16:J18						
8	Product B	0	0	1		UnitsSold - B19:D19						
9	Product C	0	0	0		UnitsUsedTotal - B25:D25						
10						HrsUsed - B28						
11	Unit selling price	Product A	Product B	Product C		HrsAvailable - D28						
12		$8	$70	$100		Revenue - B30						
13												
14	Production and sales plan					Units of products used (along side) to make products (along top)						
15		Product A	Product B	Product C			Product A	Product B	Product C	Total used		
16	Units produced	20	10	0		Product A	0	20	0	20		
17						Product B	0	0	0	0		
18	Units used in production	20	0	0		Product C	0	0	0	0		
19	Units leftover and sold	0	10	0								
20												
21	Balance constraint on products											
22		Product A	Product B	Product C								
23	Produced	20	10	0								
24		=	=	=								
25	Used (for production or sales)	20	10	0								
26												
27	Labor hour constraint	Used		Available								
28		40	<=	40								
29												
30	Revenue from sales	$700										

FIGURE 4.20 Repco Production Model

④ Units used total. Referring to equation (4.5), we want to force the units produced of each product to equal the units used total (as inputs or for sales) of each product. We do this in rows 23 through 25. For row 23, enter the formula

=B16

in cell B23 and copy it to the range C23:D23. For row 25, enter the formula

=B18+B19

in cell B25 and copy it to the range C25:D25. (Now do you see why we used the TRANSPOSE function? It allows us to copy across row 25 easily.)

⑤ Labor hours used. Calculate the total number of labor hours used in the HrsUsed cell with the formula

=SUMPRODUCT(HrsReqd,UnitsProduced)

⑥ Total revenue. Calculate Repco's revenue from sales in the Revenue cell with the formula

=SUMPRODUCT(UnitPrices,UnitsSold)

USING SOLVER

To use Solver to maximize Repco's revenue, proceed as follows. When you are finished, your Solver dialog box should appear as shown in Figure 4.21.

① Objective. Select the Revenue cell as the target cell to maximize.

② Changing cells. Select the UnitsProduced and UnitsSold ranges as the changing cells.

③ Labor availability constraint. Enter the constraint HrsUsed<=HrsAvailable. This ensures that at most 40 hours of labor are used.

④ Product balance constraint. Enter the constraint UnitsProduced=UnitsUsedTotal to ensure that production matches usage for each product.

⑤ Specify nonnegativity and optimize. Under Solver Options, check the nonnegativity box, and use the LP algorithm to obtain the optimal solution shown in Figure 4.20.

We see that Repco obtains a revenue of $700 by producing 20 units of product A, which are then used to produce 10 units of product B. All units of product B produced are sold. Even though product C has the highest selling price, Repco produces none of product C because of the large labor requirement for product C.

FIGURE 4.21
Solver Dialog Box for Repco Model

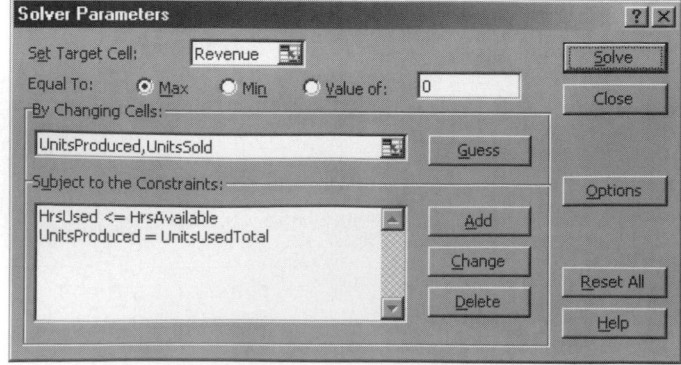

Sensitivity Analysis We saw that product C is not produced at all, even though its selling price is by far the highest. How high would this selling price have to be to induce Repco to produce any of product C? We use SolverTable to answer this, using product C selling price as the input variable, letting it vary from $100 to $200 in increments of $10, and keeping track of the total revenue, the units produced of each product, and the units used (row 18) of each product. The results appear in Figure 4.22.

As we see, until the product C selling price gets to $130, Repco uses the same solution as above. However, when it increases to $130 and beyond, 5.714 units of C are produced. This in turn requires 5.714 units of product B, which requires 11.429 units of product A, but only product C is actually sold. Of course, Repco would like to produce even more of product C (which would require more production of products A and B), but the labor hour constraint does not allow it. Therefore, further increases in the selling price of product C have no effect on the solution—other than increasing revenue.

Because available labor imposes an upper limit on the production of product C, even when it is very profitable, it is interesting to see what happens when the selling price of product C *and* the labor hours available both increase. Here we use the two-way SolverTable option, selecting selling price of product C and labor hour availability as the two inputs with appropriate values, and selecting the amount produced of product C as the single output. (We could choose more than one output. This would result in multiple tables.) The results from SolverTable appear in Figure 4.23.

This table again shows that no product C is produced, regardless of labor hour availability, until the selling price of C is $130. (Of course, the actual breakpoint might be *between* $120 and $130. We can't tell from the grid of input values used in the table.) The effect of increases in labor hour availability is to let Repco produce more

	A	B	C	D	E	F	G	H
32	Sensitivity of revenue, units produced, and units used as inputs to product C selling price							
33	Product C selling price	A produced	B produced	C produced	A used	B used	C used	Revenue
34		$B$16	$C$16	$D$16	$B$18	$C$18	$D$18	$B$30
35	100	20	10	0	20	0	0	$700
36	110	20	10	0	20	0	0	$700
37	120	20	10	0	20	0	0	$700
38	130	11.429	5.714	5.714	11.429	5.714	0	$743
39	140	11.429	5.714	5.714	11.429	5.714	0	$800
40	150	11.429	5.714	5.714	11.429	5.714	0	$857
41	160	11.429	5.714	5.714	11.429	5.714	0	$914
42	170	11.429	5.714	5.714	11.429	5.714	0	$971
43	180	11.429	5.714	5.714	11.429	5.714	0	$1,029
44	190	11.429	5.714	5.714	11.429	5.714	0	$1,086
45	200	11.429	5.714	5.714	11.429	5.714	0	$1,143

FIGURE 4.22 Sensitivity to Selling Price of Product C

	A	B	C	D	E	F	G	H	I
47	Sensitivity of amount of C produced to selling price of C (along side) and labor hour availability (along top)								
48	$D$16	40	50	60	70	80	90	100	
49	100	0	0	0	0	0	0	0	
50	110	0	0	0	0	0	0	0	
51	120	0	0	0	0	0	0	0	
52	130	5.714	7.143	8.571	10.000	11.429	12.857	14.286	
53	140	5.714	7.143	8.571	10.000	11.429	12.857	14.286	
54	150	5.714	7.143	8.571	10.000	11.429	12.857	14.286	
55	160	5.714	7.143	8.571	10.000	11.429	12.857	14.286	
56	170	5.714	7.143	8.571	10.000	11.429	12.857	14.286	
57	180	5.714	7.143	8.571	10.000	11.429	12.857	14.286	
58	190	5.714	7.143	8.571	10.000	11.429	12.857	14.286	
59	200	5.714	7.143	8.571	10.000	11.429	12.857	14.286	

FIGURE 4.23 Sensitivity to Price of C and Labor Hour Availability

of product C. Specifically, Repco will produce as much of C as possible, given that 1 unit of B, and hence 2 units of A, are required for each unit of C.

Before leaving this example, we provide some further insight into the sensitivity behavior in Figure 4.22. Specifically, why should Repco start producing product C when its unit selling price increases to some value between $120 and $130? We can provide a straightforward answer to this question because there is a *single* resource constraint, the labor hour constraint. (The analysis would be significantly more complicated with multiple resources.) Consider the production of 1 unit of product B. It requires 2 labor hours plus 2 units of A, each of which requires 1 labor hour, for a total of 4 labor hours, and it returns $70 in revenue. Therefore, revenue per labor hour when producing product B is $17.50. To be eligible as a "winner," product C has to beat this. Note that each unit of product C requires 7 labor hours (3 for itself and 4 for the unit of B it requires). To beat the $17.50 revenue per labor hour of product B, product C's unit selling price must be at least $122.50 ($= 17.50 \times 7$). If its selling price is below this, such as $120, Repco will sell all product B and no product C. If its selling price is above this, such as $130, Repco will sell all product C and no product B. As this analysis illustrates, we can sometimes—but not always—unravel the information obtained by SolverTable. ■

ADDITIONAL APPLICATIONS

Production Process Modeling for a Creamery

Sullivan and Secrest (1985) developed a linear programming model to aid Dairyman's Cooperative Creamery Association in its production of dairy products. Each day their program took as input the amount of available raw milk and cream. As an output, the LP told the creamery how much sour cream, raw milk, buttermilk, and cottage cheese to produce. The problem was complicated by the relationships between the products. For example, if cottage cheese is produced, then whey is produced as a by-product. Then the whey is used to produce cream, which is used in other products. The model has increased the creamery's profit by $48,000 per year. (See Problem 38 for a simplified version of this model.) ■

PROBLEMS

Skill-Building Problems

31. Rylon Corporation manufactures Brute and Chanelle perfumes. The raw material needed to manufacture each type of perfume can be purchased for $3 per pound. Processing 1 pound of raw material requires 1 hour of laboratory time. Each pound of processed raw material yields 3 ounces of Regular Brute perfume and 4 ounces of Regular Chanelle perfume. Regular Brute can be sold for $7 per ounce and Regular Chanelle for $6 per ounce. Rylon also has the option of further processing Regular Brute and Regular Chanelle to produce Luxury Brute, sold at $18 per ounce, and Luxury Chanelle, sold at $14 per ounce. Each ounce of Regular Brute processed

further requires an additional 3 hours of laboratory time and a $4 processing cost and yields 1 ounce of Luxury Brute. Each ounce of Regular Chanelle processed further requires an additional 2 hours of laboratory time and a $4 processing cost and yields 1 ounce of Luxury Chanelle. Each year Rylon has 6000 hours of laboratory time available and can purchase up to 4000 pounds of raw material.

a. Determine how Rylon can maximize its profit. Assume that the cost of the laboratory hours is a fixed cost (so that it can be ignored for this problem).

b. Suppose that 1 pound of raw material can be used to produce either 3 ounces of Brute or

4 ounces of Chanelle. How does your answer to part **a** change?

  c. Use SolverTable to determine how a change in the price of Luxury Chanelle changes the optimal profit.

  d. Use SolverTable to determine how simultaneous changes in lab time and raw material availability change the optimal profit.

  e. Use SolverTable to determine how a change in the lab time required to process Luxury Brute changes the optimal profit.

32. Sunco Oil has three different processes that can be used to manufacture various types of gasoline. Each process involves blending oils in the company's catalytic cracker. Running process 1 for an hour costs $5 and requires 2 barrels of crude oil 1 and 3 barrels of crude oil 2. The output from running process 1 for an hour is 2 barrels of gas 1 and 1 barrel of gas 2. Running process 2 for an hour costs $4 and requires 1 barrel of crude 1 and 3 barrels of crude 2. The output from running process 2 for an hour is 3 barrels of gas 2. Running process 3 for an hour costs $1 and requires 2 barrels of crude 2 and 3 barrels of gas 2. The output from running process 3 for an hour is 2 barrels of gas 3. Each week 200 barrels of crude 1, at $2 per barrel, and 300 barrels of crude 2, at $3 per barrel, can be purchased. All gas produced can be sold at the following per-barrel prices: gas 1, $9; gas 2, $10; gas 3, $24. Determine how to maximize Sunco's profit (revenues less costs). Assume that only 100 hours of time on the catalytic cracker are available each week.

33. Furnco manufactures tables and chairs. A table requires 40 board feet of wood, and a chair requires 30 board feet of wood. Wood can be purchased at a cost of $1 per board foot, and 40,000 board feet of wood are available for purchase. It takes 2 hours of skilled labor to manufacture an unfinished table or an unfinished chair. Three more hours of skilled labor will turn an unfinished table into a finished table, and 2 more hours of skilled labor will turn an unfinished chair into a finished chair. A total of 6000 hours of skilled labor are available (and have already been paid for). All furniture produced can be sold at the following unit prices: an unfinished table, $70; a finished table, $140; an unfinished chair, $60; a finished chair, $110.

  a. Determine how to maximize Furnco's profit from manufacturing tables and chairs.

  b. Use a two-way SolverTable to see how the numbers of unfinished products (both chairs and tables) sold depend on the selling prices of these unfinished products. Of course, neither unfinished selling price should be as large as the corresponding finished selling price.

34. Chemco produces three products, 1, 2, and 3. Each pound of raw material costs $25. The raw material undergoes processing and yields 3 ounces of product 1 and 1 ounce of product 2. It costs $1 and takes 2 hours of labor to process each pound of raw material. Each ounce of product 1 can be used in one of three ways. First, it can be sold for $10 per ounce. Second, it can be processed into 1 ounce of product 2. This requires 2 hours of labor and costs $1. Third, it can be processed into 1 ounce of product 3. This requires 3 hours of labor and costs $2. Each ounce of product 2 can be used in one of two ways. First, it can be sold for $20 per ounce. Second, it can be processed into 1 ounce of product 3. This requires 1 hour of labor and costs $6. Product 3 is sold for $30 per ounce. The maximum numbers of ounces of products 1, 2, and 3 that can be sold are, respectively, 5000, 5000, and 3000. A maximum of 25,000 hours of labor are available.

  a. Determine how Chemco can maximize its profit.

  b. Use SolverTable to determine how a change in the demand for each product changes the optimal profit.

  c. Use SolverTable to determine how a change in raw material cost changes the optimal profit.

  d. Use SolverTable to determine how a change in the selling price of product 1 changes the optimal profit.

35. A company produces three products, A, B, and C, and can sell these products in unlimited quantities at the following unit prices: A, $10; B, $56; C, $100. Producing a unit of A requires 1 hour of labor; a unit of B, 2 hours of labor plus 2 units of A; and a unit of C, 3 hours of labor plus 1 unit of B. Any A that is used to produce B cannot be sold. Similarly, any B that is used to produce C cannot be sold. A total of 40 hours of labor are available. Determine how to maximize the company's revenue.

36. Abotte Products produces three products, A, B, and C. The company can sell up to 300 pounds of each product at the following prices (per pound): product A, $10; product B, $12; product C, $20. Abotte purchases raw material at $5 per pound. Each pound of raw material can be used to produce either 1 pound of A or 1 pound of B. For a cost of $3 per pound processed, product A can be converted to 0.6 pound of product B and 0.4 pound of product C. For a cost of $2 per pound processed, product B can be converted to 0.8 pound of product C. Determine how Abotte can maximize its profit.

Skill-Extending Problems

37. Capsule Drugs manufactures two drugs, 1 and 2. The drugs are produced by blending two chemicals, 1 and 2. By weight, drug 1 must contain at least 65% chemical 1, and drug 2 must contain at least 55% chemical 1. Drug 1 sells for $6 per ounce, and drug 2 sells for $4 per ounce. Chemicals 1 and 2 can be produced by one of two production processes. Running process 1 for an hour requires 7 ounces of raw material and 2 hours skilled labor and yields 3 ounces of each chemical. Running process 2 for an hour requires 5 ounces of raw material and 3 hours of skilled labor and yields 3 ounces of chemical 1 and 1 ounce of chemical 2. A total of 120 hours of skilled labor and 100 ounces of raw material are available. Determine how to maximize Capsule's sales revenues.

38. Based on Sullivan and Secrest (1985). Lizzie's Dairy produces cream cheese and cottage cheese. Milk and cream are blended to produce these two products. Both high-fat and low-fat milk can be used to produce cream cheese and cottage cheese. High-fat milk is 60% fat; low-fat milk is 30% fat. The milk used to produce cream cheese must average at least 50% fat; for cottage cheese, at least 35% fat. At least 40% of the inputs (by weight) to cream cheese and at least 20% of the inputs (by weight) to cottage cheese must be cream.

   Both cottage cheese and cream cheese are produced by putting milk and cream through the cheese machine. It costs $0.40 to process 1 pound of inputs into a pound of cream cheese. It costs $0.40 to produce 1 pound of cottage cheese, but every pound of input for cottage cheese yields 0.9 pound of cottage cheese and 0.1 pound of waste.

   Cream can be produced by evaporating high-fat and low-fat milk. It costs $0.40 to evaporate 1 pound of high-fat milk. Each pound of high-fat milk that is evaporated yields 0.6 pound of cream. It costs $0.40 to evaporate 1 pound of low-fat milk. Each pound of low-fat milk that is evaporated yields 0.3 pound of cream.

   Each day up to 3000 pounds of input can be sent through the cheese machine. Each day at least 1000 pounds of cottage cheese and 1000 pounds of cream cheese must be produced. Up to 1500 pounds of cream cheese and 2000 pounds of cottage cheese can be sold each day.

   Cottage cheese is sold for $2.10 per pound and cream cheese for $2.50 per pound. High-fat milk is purchased for $0.80 per pound and low-fat milk for $0.40 per pound. The evaporator can process at most 2000 pounds of milk daily. Determine how to maximize Lizzie's daily profit.

39. Flexco produces six products in the following manner. Each unit of raw material purchased yields 4 units of product 1, 2 units of product 2, and 1 unit of product 3. Up to 1200 units of product 1 can be sold, and up to 300 units of product 2 can be sold. Demand for products 3 and 4 is unlimited. Each unit of product 1 can be sold or processed further. Each unit of product 1 that is processed further yields 1 unit of product 4. Each unit of product 2 can be sold

or processed further. Each unit of product 2 that is processed further yields 0.8 unit of product 5 and 0.3 unit of product 6.

   Up to 1000 units of product 5 can be sold, and up to 800 units of product 6 can be sold. Up to 3000 units of raw material can be purchased at $6 per unit. Leftover units of products 5 and 6 must be destroyed. It costs $4 to destroy each leftover unit of product 5 and $3 to destroy each leftover unit of product 6. Ignoring raw material purchase costs, the unit price and production cost for each product are shown in Table 4.16. Determine a profit-maximizing production schedule for Flexco.

TABLE 4.16   **Prices and Costs for Flexco Problem**

	Selling Price	Production Cost
Product 1	$7	$4
Product 2	$6	$4
Product 3	$4	$2
Product 4	$3	$1
Product 5	$20	$5
Product 6	$35	$5

40. Each week Chemco can purchase unlimited quantities of raw material at $6 per pound. Each pound of purchased raw material can be used to produce either input 1 or input 2. Each pound of raw material can yield 2 ounces of input 1, requiring 2 hours of processing time and incurring $2 in processing costs. Each pound of raw material can yield 3 ounces of input 2, requiring 2 hours of processing time and incurring $4 in processing costs.

   Two production processes are available. It takes 2 hours to run process 1, requiring 2 ounces of input 1 and 1 ounce of input 2. It costs $1 to run process 1. Each time process 1 is run, 1 ounce of product A and 1 ounce of liquid waste are produced. Each time process 2 is run requires 3 hours of processing time, 2 ounces of input 2, and 1 ounce of input 1. Each process 2 run yields 1 ounce of product B and 0.8 ounce of liquid waste. Process 2 incurs $8 in costs. Chemco can dispose of liquid waste in the Port Charles River or use the waste to produce product C or product D. Government regulations limit the amount of waste Chemco is allowed to dump into the river to 1000 ounces per week.

   One ounce of product C costs $4 to produce and sells for $11. One hour of processing time, 2 ounces of input 1, and 0.8 ounce of liquid waste are needed to produce an ounce of product C. One ounce of product D costs $5 to produce and sells for $7. One hour of processing time, 2 ounces of input 2, and 1.2

TABLE 4.17   **Prices and Other Data for Limeco Problem**

	Grade					
	1	**2**	**3**	**4**	**5**	**6**
Unit price	$12	$14	$10	$18	$20	$25
Amount produced	2	2	3	1	1.5	2
Maximum demand	20	30	40	35	25	50
Disposal cost	$3	$2	$3	$2	$4	$2

ounces of liquid waste are needed to produce an ounce of product D. At most 5000 ounces of product A and 5000 ounces of product B can be sold each week, but weekly demand for products C and D is unlimited. Product A sells for $18 per ounce and product B sells for $24 per ounce. Each week 6000 hours of processing time are available. Determine how Chemco can maximize its weekly profit.

41. Limeco owns a lime factory and sells six grades of lime (grades 1 through 6). The selling price per pound of each grade is given in Table 4.17. Lime is produced by kilns. If a kiln is run for an 8-hour shift, the amounts (in pounds) of each grade of lime given in Table 4.17 are produced. It costs $150 to run a kiln for an 8-hour shift. Each day the factory believes it can sell up to the amounts (in pounds) of lime given in Table 4.17. Lime that is produced by the kiln can be reprocessed by using any one of the five processes described in Table 4.18. For example, at a cost of $1 per pound, a pound of grade 4 lime can be transformed into 0.5 pound of grade 5 lime and 0.5 pound of grade 6 lime. Any extra lime left over at the end of each day must be disposed of, with the disposal costs (per pound) given in

TABLE 4.18   **Input and Output Data for Limeco Problem**

Input	Cost	Output
1 lb of grade 1	$2	0.3 lb of grade 3
		0.2 lb of grade 4
		0.3 lb of grade 5
		0.2 lb of grade 6
1 lb of grade 2	$1	1.0 lb of grade 6
1 lb of grade 3	$1	0.8 lb of grade 4
1 lb of grade 4	$1	0.5 lb of grade 5
		0.5 lb of grade 6
1 lb of grade 5	$2	0.9 lb of grade 6

Table 4.17. Determine how Limeco can maximize its daily profit. (You may assume that the number of 8-hour shifts used can be fractional, or you can constrain it to be an integer.)

42. Molecular Products produces 3 chemicals, B, C, and D. The company begins by purchasing chemical A for a cost of $6 per 100 liters. For an additional cost of $3 and the use of 3 hours of skilled labor, 100 liters of A can be transformed into 40 liters of C and 60 liters of B. Chemical C can either be sold or processed further. It costs $1 and 1 hour of skilled labor to process 100 liters of C into 60 liters of D and 40 liters of B. For each chemical the selling price per 100 liters and the maximum amount (in 100s of liters) that can be sold are given in Table 4.19. A maximum of 200 labor hours are available. Determine how Molecular can maximize its profit.

TABLE 4.19   **Prices and Demands for Molecular Problem**

	B	**C**	**D**
Unit price	$12	$16	$26
Maximum demand	30	60	40

43. Bexter Labs produces three products: A, B, and C. Bexter can sell up to 30 units of product A, up to 20 units of product B, and up to 20 units of product C. Each unit of product C uses 2 units of A and 3 units of B and incurs $5 in processing costs. Products A and B are produced from either raw material 1 or raw material 2. It costs $6 to purchase and process 1 unit of raw material 1. Each processed unit of raw material 1 yields 2 units of A and 3 units of B. It costs $3 to purchase and process a unit of raw material 2. Each processed unit of raw material 2 yields 1 unit of A and 2 units of B. The unit prices for the products are: A, $5; B, $4; C, $25. The quality levels of each product are: A, 8; B, 7; C, 6. The average quality level of the units sold must be at least 7. Determine how to maximize Bexter's profit.

4.7 DYNAMIC FINANCIAL MODELS

ften a company must determine the optimal level of investment and/or borrowing at different points in time. In this section we show how linear programming can be used to model such situations.

EXAMPLE 4.6

FINANCIAL PLANNING AT FUNTOYS

A small toy store, FunToys, projects the monthly cash inflows listed in Table 4.20 (in thousands of dollars) during the year 2000. A negative cash flow means that cash outflows exceed cash inflows to the business. To pay its bills, FunToys will need to borrow money early in the year. The company can borrow money in two ways: (1) It can obtain a long-term 1-year loan and receive the total amount in January. Beginning in February 2000, 1% interest will be charged each month on this loan. The loan must be paid back by the beginning of January 2001. (2) Each month FunToys can borrow money from a short-term bank line of credit with a monthly interest rate of 1.5%. All short-term loans must be paid off by the beginning of January 2001. At the end of each month excess cash earns 0.4% interest. FunToys wants to use LP to either maximize its cash position at the beginning of January 2001 or minimize the total amount of interest it pays on its loans. It has $6500 in cash at the beginning of January 2000, and its policy is to have a cash balance of at least $5000 at the end of each month.

TABLE 4.20 **Cash Inflows for FunToys**

	Cash Inflow		Cash Inflow
January	−12	July	−7
February	−10	August	−2
March	−8	September	15
April	−10	October	12
May	−4	November	−7
June	5	December	45

Solution

To model FunToys's problem, we must keep track of the following:

- the amount of the long-term loan
- the amount of the short-term loan each month
- the monthly interest and paybacks on the loans
- the cash balance at the beginning of each month (including interest on excess cash)
- the cash balance at the end of each month
- the cash balance at the end of the problem (the beginning of January 2001)
- the total interest paid on loans

This problem is a challenging modeling exercise, and there are probably several "reasonable" solutions, depending on your interpretation of the problem statement. We will discuss these below. There are several key points to consider when modeling this problem. First, FunToys can take out a short-term loan each month and close out the short-term loan at the beginning of the next month. Second, letting CB_t be the cash balance at the end of month t, note that

$$\begin{aligned}
CB_t = \ &\text{Cash balance from month } t - 1 \\
&+ \text{Interest on cash balance from month } t - 1 \\
&+ \text{Loan(s) received during month } t \\
&+ \text{Cash inflow in month } t \\
&- \text{Interest paid on long-term loan during month } t \\
&- \text{Interest paid on month } t - 1 \text{ short-term loan} \\
&- \text{Long-term loan payback (only in January 2001)} \\
&- \text{Payback of month } t - 1 \text{ short-term loan} \quad \textbf{(4.6)}
\end{aligned}$$

Third, all bills will have been paid on time only if each month's ending cash balance is nonnegative. However, FunToys requires more than nonnegativity; it requires an ending cash balance of at least $5000 each month. This will certainly guarantee that all bills are paid on time.

One crucial consideration in this type of multiperiod model is the timing of events. Here we have to make some modeling decisions. First, when does FunToys obtain interest on excess cash, and on what amount is this interest based? We will assume it is based on the ending cash balance in any month and is realized in next month's beginning cash balance. For example, if the ending June balance is $7000, then the July beginning balance will be $7028 (= 7000 × 1.004). Second, what about the timing of loan (and loan interest) paybacks? We might assume that these must be made at the *beginning* of each month, whereas the cash inflows and outflows in Table 4.20 occur later each month. If this is the case, we need to ensure that FunToys has a large enough cash balance at the beginning of the month, including any income from *new* loans, to cover these paybacks. We will handle this with an extra constraint.

Finally, the problem statement mentions *two* possible objectives: maximizing the final cash in January 2001 and minimizing total interest paid on loans. To allow for either possibility, we will simply calculate each of these quantities. Then, depending on which we want to optimize, we will specify it as the target cell in the Solver settings. For example, if we decide to maximize final cash, total interest paid will basically "come along for the ride"—we will calculate it, but we will not base any decisions on it.

DEVELOPING THE SPREADSHEET MODEL

The spreadsheet model for FunToys's problem appears in Figure 4.24 (page 156). (See the file CASHBALANCE1.XLS.) To set up this spreadsheet, proceed as follows.

 Inputs. Enter the relevant interest rates in the range B9:B11, the minimum cash balance and initial cash in the range B14:B15, and the monthly cash inflows/outflows in the range B28:M28. Note that all monetary values from row 19 down are expressed in thousands of dollars. This avoids large numbers and decreases the chance that Solver will report that this is not a linear model (when in fact it is).

2 **Loan amounts.** Enter *any* trial values in the LTLoan and STLoan ranges.

3 **Beginning cash balance each month.** Row 19 is used to keep track of the cash balance, plus interest, from the previous month. Enter the formula

=InitCash/1000

	Jan	Feb	Mar	Apr	May	Jun	Jul	Aug	Sep	Oct	Nov	Dec	Jan
FunToys cash balance model													
Assumptions:													
At the beginning of any month, loans are received and loans are paid back with interest (see note below row 26).													
At the end of each month, after bills or revenues occur, the balance must be at least some minimal amount.													
The objective is to maximize total cash at end (or possibly to minimize total interest paid).													

Range names used:
- LTRate - B10
- STRate - B11
- IntRate - B12
- MinCashBal - B14
- InitCash - B15
- LTLoan - B21
- STLoan - B22:M22
- BalAfterLoan - B26:N26
- EndBal - B29:M29
- MinBal - B31:M31
- TotIntPaid - B34
- FinalBal - B35

Monthly rates
Long-term loan	1.0%
Short-term loan	1.5%
Excess cash	0.4%

Other inputs
Min ending cash balance	$5,000
Initial cash carried over	$6,500

Financial calculations - all values in $1000s

	Jan	Feb	Mar	Apr	May	Jun	Jul	Aug	Sep	Oct	Nov	Dec	Jan
Beginning balance	6.500	24.944	14.699	6.421	5.020	5.020	5.020	5.020	5.020	15.060	12.303	5.020	49.915
Cash inflows from loans													
Long-term loan	30.344												
Short-term loan	0.000	0.000	0.000	8.882	13.299	8.782	16.197	18.724	14.288	0.000	0.000	0.000	
Cash outflows from loans													
Long-term interest/payback		0.303	0.303	0.303	0.303	0.303	0.303	0.303	0.303	0.303	0.303	0.303	30.648
Short-term interest/payback		0.000	0.000	0.000	9.016	13.498	8.914	16.440	19.004	14.502	0.000	0.000	0.000
Balance after loan activities	36.844	24.640	14.396	15.000	9.000	0.000	12.000	7.000	0.000	0.254	12.000	4.717	19.267

Depending on model assumptions, may want to constrain this row to be nonnegative.

	Jan	Feb	Mar	Apr	May	Jun	Jul	Aug	Sep	Oct	Nov	Dec
Cash inflow/outflow	-12.000	-10.000	-8.000	-10.000	-4.000	5.000	-7.000	-2.000	15.000	12.000	-7.000	45.000
Balance at end of month	24.844	14.640	6.396	5.000	5.000	5.000	5.000	5.000	15.000	12.254	5.000	49.717
	>=	>=	>=	>=	>=	>=	>=	>=	>=	>=	>=	
Minimal balance	5.000	5.000	5.000	5.000	5.000	5.000	5.000	5.000	5.000	5.000	5.000	5.000

Possible objectives
Min total interest paid	4.844
Max final balance	19.267

FIGURE 4.24 FunToys Cash Balance Model

in cell B19. (Do you see why we divide by 1000? Always be careful about the units in which values are expressed.) Then enter the formula

=B29*(1+IntRate)

in cell C19 and copy it across row 19.

❹ **Loan (and loan interest) paybacks.** Rows 21 and 22 are used to keep track of the loan and loan interest paybacks, starting in February 2000. Note that FunToys repays each short-term loan, with interest, in the month after the loan is made. Interest on the long-term loan must be made each month, but the loan payback occurs only in the last month, January 2001. Therefore, enter the formula

=LTLoan*LTRate+IF(C18="Jan",LTLOAN)

in cell C24 and copy it across row 24. (The IF function guarantees that the loan payback will occur only in January 2001.) Then enter the formula

=B22*(1+STRate)

in cell C25 and copy it across row 25.

❺ **Balance after loan activities.** After new loans have been made and old loans have been paid back (with interest), it might be a good idea to calculate the cash balance. Then, as the above discussion and the text box in the spreadsheet indicate, we can constrain this balance to be nonnegative if loan payments must be covered prior to cash inflow/outflows. Therefore, enter the formula

=SUM(B19:B22)-SUM(B24:B25)

in cell B26 and copy it across row 26.

6 **Ending balances.** Row 29 is used to calculate the ending balance each month. To do so, enter the formula

=B26+B28

in cell B29 and copy it across row 29. Similarly, to show the minimal required balance in row 31, enter the formula

=MinCashBal/1000

in cell B31 and copy it across row 31.

7 **Possible objectives.** Calculate the total interest paid and the final cash balance in the "objective" cells. Specifically, enter the formula

=12*LTLoan*LTRate+STRate*SUM(STLoan)

in the TotIntPaid cell, and enter the formula

=N26

in the FinalBal cell.

USING SOLVER

To solve the FunToys problem with Solver, proceed as follows. (When you are finished, the Solver dialog box should appear as shown in Figure 4.25. This is only one version of the model, as we will discuss.)

1 **Objective.** Select the FinalBal cell as the target cell to maximize.

2 **Changing cells.** Select the LTLoan and STLoan ranges as the changing cells.

3 **Ending cash balance constraint.** Add the constraint EndBal>=MinBal. This ensures that there is at least $5000 in cash at the end of each month.

4 **Constraint on balance after loan activities.** Add the constraint BalAfterLoan >=0. Although this constraint might not be necessary, depending on how we interpret FunToys's problem, we have added it here under the assumption that FunToys must have enough cash to cover its loan paybacks early in each month.

5 **Specify nonnegativity and optimize.** Under Solver Options, check the non-negativity box, and use the LP algorithm to obtain the optimal solution shown in Figure 4.24.

FIGURE 4.25
Solver Dialog Box
for FunToys Cash
Balance Model

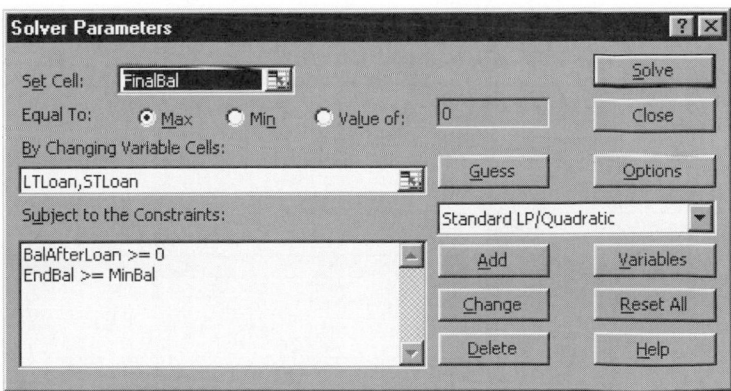

The solution recommends a long-term loan of $30,344 along with short-term loans of various amounts during the 6 months from April to September. At the beginning of January 2001, FunToys's final cash balance will be $19,267, it will have paid back all of its loans, and it will have paid $4,844 in interest.

Sensitivity Analysis   Our earlier discussion suggests several obvious sensitivity analyses. First, what happens if we change the objective to a minimization of total interest paid? We simply select the TotIntPaid cell as the target cell in the Solver settings and click on Solve. (One other thing—don't forget to click on the Minimize option!) The new solution appears in Figure 4.26. It is very similar to the previous solution. As we would expect, total interest paid is now a bit better (lower) and the final cash balance is a bit worse (lower). Also, the long-term loan is lower, and more short-term loans are made.

Second, we can drop the nonnegativity constraint on the balance after loan activities if we can assume this is not a financial requirement for FunToys. Its omission should provide more flexibility, so that the objective (whichever objective we choose) should improve. After deleting this constraint, choosing to maximize the final cash balance,

17 Financial calculations - all values in $1000s													
18	Jan	Feb	Mar	Apr	May	Jun	Jul	Aug	Sep	Oct	Nov	Dec	Jan
19 Beginning balance	6.500	23.526	13.289	5.020	5.020	5.020	5.020	5.020	5.020	15.060	12.048	5.020	48.469
20 Cash inflows from loans													
21 Long-term loan	28.932												
22 Short-term loan	0.000	0.000	0.000	10.269	14.693	10.182	17.604	20.138	15.709	1.174	1.433	0.000	
23 Cash outflows from loans													
24 Long-term interest/payback		0.289	0.289	0.289	0.289	0.289	0.289	0.289	0.289	0.289	0.289	0.289	29.221
25 Short-term interest/payback		0.000	0.000	0.000	10.423	14.913	10.335	17.869	20.440	15.945	1.192	1.455	0.000
26 Balance after loan activities	35.432	23.236	13.000	15.000	9.000	0.000	12.000	7.000	0.000	0.000	12.000	3.276	19.248
27 *Depending on model assumptions, may want to constrain this row to be nonnegative.*													
28 Cash inflow/outflow	-12.000	-10.000	-8.000	-10.000	-4.000	5.000	-7.000	-2.000	15.000	12.000	-7.000	45.000	
29 Balance at end of month	23.432	13.236	5.000	5.000	5.000	5.000	5.000	5.000	15.000	12.000	5.000	48.276	
30	>=	>=	>=	>=	>=	>=	>=	>=	>=	>=	>=		
31 Minimal balance	5.000	5.000	5.000	5.000	5.000	5.000	5.000	5.000	5.000	5.000	5.000		
33 **Possible objectives**													
34 Min total interest paid	4.840												
35 Max final balance	19.248												

FIGURE 4.26 Minimizing the Total Interest Paid on Loans

17 Financial calculations - all values in $1000s													
18	Jan	Feb	Mar	Apr	May	Jun	Jul	Aug	Sep	Oct	Nov	Dec	Jan
19 Beginning balance	6.500	24.834	14.589	6.312	5.020	5.020	5.020	5.020	5.020	5.020	12.302	5.020	49.917
20 Cash inflows from loans													
21 Long-term loan	30.235												
22 Short-term loan	0.000	0.000	0.000	8.990	13.407	8.891	16.307	18.833	4.398	0.000	0.000	0.000	
23 Cash outflows from loans													
24 Long-term interest/payback		0.302	0.302	0.302	0.302	0.302	0.302	0.302	0.302	0.302	0.302	0.302	30.537
25 Short-term interest/payback		0.000	0.000	0.000	9.125	13.608	9.024	16.551	19.116	4.464	0.000	0.000	0.000
26 Balance after loan activities	36.735	24.531	14.287	15.000	9.000	0.000	12.000	7.000	-10.000	0.253	12.000	4.718	19.380
27 *Depending on model assumptions, may want to constrain this row to be nonnegative.*													
28 Cash inflow/outflow	-12.000	-10.000	-8.000	-10.000	-4.000	5.000	-7.000	-2.000	15.000	12.000	-7.000	45.000	
29 Balance at end of month	24.735	14.531	6.287	5.000	5.000	5.000	5.000	5.000	5.000	12.253	5.000	49.718	
30	>=	>=	>=	>=	>=	>=	>=	>=	>=	>=	>=		
31 Minimal balance	5.000	5.000	5.000	5.000	5.000	5.000	5.000	5.000	5.000	5.000	5.000		
33 **Possible objectives**													
34 Min total interest paid	4.691												
35 Max final balance	19.380												

FIGURE 4.27 Model with Nonnegativity Constraint Omitted

and using Solver, we obtain the solution in Figure 4.27. It shows that the increased flexibility—taken advantage of only in September (see cell J26)—nets only about $100 in extra final cash compared to the original solution.

We can also use SolverTable to perform interesting sensitivity analyses. We illustrate one of these, where one of the inputs to be varied is the *ratio* of the short-term rate to the long-term rate, currently 1.5. This requires some modification of the original model, as shown in Figure 4.28. (See the file CASHBALANCE2.XLS.) We create a Ratio cell, cell D9, and we substitute the *value* in the STRate cell with the *formula* **=LTRate*Ratio**. Given this modification, we now use the two-way SolverTable option to see how the long-term loan and the *largest* short-term loan vary with two inputs: the ratio of the short-term rate to the long-term rate and the long-term rate. For reasonable values of these inputs, the results appear in Figure 4.29. (This solution is for the model with final cash as the objective and the nonnegativity constraint included.)

FIGURE 4.28
Modification of Model to Account for Ratio of Rates

	A	B	C	D	E	F
8	**Monthly rates**			Ratio of ST to LT		
9	Long-term loan	1.0%		1.5		
10	Short-term loan	1.5%				
11	Excess cash	0.4%				

First, note that because there was no formula for the largest short-term loan, we had to create one in cell B37 with the formula **=MAX(STLoan)**. This is always possible when using SolverTable. If the output of interest does not appear explicitly in the model, just create it with a new formula. The SolverTable results are interesting. We see in the top table that if the short-term rate is lower than the long-term rate—the ratio is less than 1—FunToys should not take out a long-term loan at all. However, if the ratio is fixed at 1.5 and the long-term rate increases, the optimal long-term loan actually *increases*. This is surprising, but don't forget that with a fixed ratio, the short-term rate is also increasing. In the bottom table, we see that as the ratio increases, the largest short-term loan decreases. Also, for a fixed ratio, the largest short-term loan increases as the long-term rate increases. This is again somewhat surprising because the short-term rate is also increasing in this situation. ∎

	A	B	C	D	E	F	G	H	I	J	K	L	M
37	Maximum ST loan	18.724											
38													
39	Sensitivity of LT loan (top table) and maximum ST loan (bottom table) to LT rate (along side) and ratio of ST rate to LT rate (along top)												
40	$B$21	0.5	0.75	1	1.25	1.5							
41	1.0%	0.000	0.000	10.500	28.932	30.344							
42	1.1%	0.000	0.000	10.500	28.991	30.790							
43	1.2%	0.000	0.000	10.500	29.050	31.240							
44	1.3%	0.000	0.000	10.500	29.109	31.338							
45	1.4%	0.000	0.000	10.500	29.168	31.761							
46	1.5%	0.000	0.000	10.500	27.784	32.189							
47													
48	$B$37	0.5	0.75	1	1.25	1.5							
49	1.0%	47.483	48.055	38.133	20.004	18.724							
50	1.1%	47.597	48.228	38.366	20.223	18.572							
51	1.2%	47.711	48.401	38.601	20.443	18.419							
52	1.3%	47.826	48.575	38.836	20.665	18.622							
53	1.4%	47.940	48.750	39.072	20.889	18.502							
54	1.5%	48.055	48.925	39.310	22.553	18.380							

FIGURE 4.29 SolverTable Results

1. In reality, we do not know future short-term interest rates and future cash needs; we must forecast them using the forecasting methods discussed in Chapter 16.

2. As in Section 4.3, FunToys's model would be implemented with a rolling planning horizon. ■

ADDITIONAL APPLICATIONS

Using LP to Optimize Bond Portfolios

Many Wall Street firms buy and sell bonds. Rohn (1987) discusses a bond selection model that maximizes profit from bond purchases and sales subject to constraints that minimize the firm's risk exposure. The method used to model this situation is closely related to the method we used to model the FunToys problem. (See Problem 47 for a simplified version of this model.) ■

PROBLEMS

Skill-Building Problems

44. Finco Investment Corporation must determine an investment strategy for the firm for the next 3 years. At present (time 0), $100,000 is available for investment. Investments A, B, C, D, and E are available. The cash flow associated with investing $1 in each investment is given in Table 4.21. For example, $1 invested in investment B requires a $1 cash outflow at time 1 and returns $0.50 at time 2 and $1 at time 3. To ensure that the company's portfolio is diversified, Finco requires that at most $75,000 be placed in any single investment. In addition to investments A through E, Finco can earn interest at 8% per year by keeping uninvested cash in money market funds. Returns from investments can be reinvested immediately. For example, the positive cash flow received from investment C at time 1 can be reinvested immediately in investment B. Finco

cannot borrow funds, so the cash available for investment at any time is limited to cash on hand.
  a. Determine how to maximize cash on hand at time 3.
  b. Use SolverTable to determine how a change in the limit placed on each investment influences the optimal solution to the problem.
  c. Use SolverTable to determine how a change in the yield of investment E changes the optimal solution to the problem.

45. Moneyco has $1000 to invest at time 1 (the beginning of year 1). The cash flows associated with the five available investments are described in Table 4.22. For example, every dollar invested in A at time 1 yields $1.40 at time 4. In addition to these investments, Moneyco can invest as much money each year as it wants in CDs, which pay 6% interest. The company wants to maximize its available cash at time 4. Assuming it can put no more than $500 in any investment, formulate an LP model to help Moneyco achieve its goal.

TABLE 4.21	Cash Flows for Finco Problem			
	Cash Flow at Time			
	0	**1**	**2**	**3**
Investment A	−$1.00	$0.50	$1.00	$0.00
Investment B	$0.00	−$1.00	$0.50	$1.00
Investment C	−$1.00	$1.20	$0.00	$0.00
Investment D	−$1.00	$0.00	$0.00	$1.90
Investment E	$0.00	$0.00	−$1.00	$1.50

TABLE 4.22	Cash Flows for Moneyco Problem				
	A	**B**	**C**	**D**	**E**
Time 1	−1.00	−1.00	−1.00		
Time 2		+1.15			−1.00
Time 3			+1.28	−1.00	
Time 4	+1.40			+1.15	+1.32

46. At time 0 you have $10,000. Investments A and B are available; their cash flows are shown in Table 4.23. Assume that any money not invested in A or B earns interest at an annual rate of 8%.

TABLE 4.23	Cash Flows for Investment Problem	
	A	**B**
Time 0	−$1.00	$0.00
Time 1	$0.20	−$1.00
Time 2	$1.50	$0.00
Time 3	$0.00	$1.90

a. Determine how to maximize your cash on hand at time 3.
b. Use SolverTable to determine how a change in the year 2 yield for investment A changes the optimal solution to the problem.
c. Use SolverTable to determine how a change in the yield of investment B changes the optimal solution to the problem.

Skill-Extending Problems

47. Broker Sonya Wong is currently trying to maximize her profit in the bond market. Four bonds are available for purchase and sale at the bid and ask prices shown in Table 4.24. Sonya can buy up to 1000 units of each bond at the ask price or sell up to 1000 units of each bond at the bid price. During each of the next 3 years, the person who sells a bond will pay the owner of the bond the cash payments shown in Table 4.25. Sonya's goal is to maximize her revenue from selling bonds minus her payment for buying bonds, subject to the constraint that after each year's payments are received, her current cash position (due only to cash payments from bonds and not purchases or sales of bonds) is nonnegative. Note that her current cash position can depend on past coupons and that cash accumulated at the end of each year earns 11.111% annual interest.

TABLE 4.24	Bid and Ask Prices for Bond Problem	
	Bid Price	**Ask Price**
Bond 1	980	990
Bond 2	970	985
Bond 3	960	972
Bond 4	940	954

TABLE 4.25	Cash Payments for Bond Problem			
	Bond 1	**Bond 2**	**Bond 3**	**Bond 4**
Year 1	100	80	70	60
Year 2	110	90	80	50
Year 3	1100	1120	1090	1110

Determine how to maximize net profit from buying and selling bonds, subject to the constraints previously described. Why do you think we limit the number of units of each bond that can be bought or sold?

48. Consider the FunToys example with the following modification. Each month FunToys can delay payments on some or all of the cash owed for the current month. (This is possible only for months where cash is due, indicated by negative amounts in row 29 of Figure 4.24.) This is called **stretching payments**. Payments can be stretched for only one month, and a 1% penalty is charged on the amount stretched. For example, if FunToys stretches its payments on $10,000 of the $12,000 cash owed in January, it must pay $10,100 (=10,000×1.01) in February. With this modification, determine how FunToys can maximize its final cash balance in January 2001.

49. You are managing a company pension fund. The fund needs to make the payments shown in Table 4.26 (in thousands) on the first day of each year. You are going to finance these payments by buying bonds. Three bonds are available for purchase on January 1, 1995. The price and coupons for each bond are as follows. (All coupon payments are received on January 1 and arrive in time to meet cash demands for the date on which they arrive.)
- Bond 1 costs $980 and yields a $60 coupon in 1996–1999 and a $1060 payment in year 2000.
- Bond 2 costs $970 and yields a $65 coupon in 1996–2005 and a $1065 payment in 2006.
- Bond 3 costs $1050 and yields a $75 coupon in 1996–2008 and a $1075 payment in 2009.

TABLE 4.26	Payments for Pension Problem				
	Payment		**Payment**		**Payment**
1995	11	2000	18	2005	25
1996	12	2001	20	2006	30
1997	14	2002	21	2007	31
1998	15	2003	22	2008	31
1999	16	2004	24	2009	31

On January 1, 1995, you purchase bonds and then meet your demand of $11,000. During each year your cash on hand earns 4% interest. You must determine the bonds that should be purchased to minimize the January 1, 1995, investment needed to meet the 1995–2009 cash requirements. You may assume that fractional numbers of bonds can be purchased.

4.8 DATA ENVELOPMENT ANALYSIS (DEA)

Often we wonder whether a university, hospital, restaurant, or other business is operating efficiently. The **data envelopment analysis** (DEA) method can be used to answer this question. Specifically, DEA can be used by inefficient organizations to benchmark efficient and "best-practice" organizations. We quote from a paper by Sherman and Ladino (1995):

> Many managers of service organizations would describe benchmarking and best-practice analysis as basic, widely accepted concepts already used in their businesses. Closer examination indicates that the traditional techniques used to identify and promulgate best practices are not very effective, largely because the operations of these service organizations are too complex to allow them to identify best practices accurately. DEA provides an objective way to identify best practices in these service organizations and has consistently generated new insights that lead to substantial productivity gains that were not otherwise identifiable.

The following example illustrates DEA. It is based on Callen (1991). See also Norton (1994).

EXAMPLE 4.7

DEA IN THE HOSPITAL INDUSTRY

Consider a group of three hospitals. To simplify matters, we assume that each hospital "converts" two inputs into three different outputs. (In a real DEA, there might be many more inputs and outputs.) The two inputs used by each hospital are

- input 1 = capital (measured by hundreds of hospital beds)
- input 2 = labor (measured by thousands of labor hours used in a month)

The outputs produced by each hospital are

- output 1 = hundreds of patient-days during month for patients under age 14
- output 2 = hundreds of patient-days during month for patients between 14 and 65
- output 3 = hundreds of patient-days for patients over 65

The inputs and outputs for these hospitals are given in Table 4.27. Which of these three hospitals is efficient in terms of using its inputs and producing outputs?

TABLE 4.27		Input and Output for Hospital Example			
	Inputs		**Outputs**		
	1	**2**	**1**	**2**	**3**
Hospital 1	5	14	9	4	16
Hospital 2	8	15	5	7	10
Hospital 3	7	12	4	9	13

Solution

The idea is that if we focus on any particular hospital, we want to show it in the "best possible light." That is, we want to value the inputs and outputs in such a way that this hospital looks as good as possible relative to the other hospitals. More specifically, to determine whether a hospital is efficient, we define a price per unit of each output and a cost per unit of each input. Then the efficiency of a hospital is defined to be

$$\text{Efficiency of hospital} = \frac{\text{Value of hospital's outputs}}{\text{Value of hospital's inputs}}$$

The DEA approach uses the following four ideas to determine whether a hospital is efficient.

1. No hospital can be more than 100% efficient. Therefore, the efficiency of each hospital is constrained to be less than or equal to 1. To make this a *linear* constraint, we express it in this form:

$$\text{Value of hospital's outputs} \leq \text{Value of hospital's inputs}$$

2. When we are trying to determine whether a hospital is efficient, it simplifies matters to scale input prices so that the value of the hospital's inputs equals 1. Any other value would suffice, but using 1 causes the efficiency of the hospital to be equal to the value of the hospital's outputs.

3. If we are interested in evaluating the efficiency of a hospital, we attempt to choose input and output prices that maximize this hospital's efficiency. If the hospital's efficiency equals 1, then the hospital is efficient; if the hospital's efficiency is less than 1, then the hospital is inefficient.

4. All input costs and output prices must be nonnegative.

DEVELOPING THE SPREADSHEET MODEL

Figure 4.30 (page 164) contains the DEA spreadsheet model used to determine the efficiency of hospital 1. (See the file HOSPITALDEA.XLS) To develop this model, proceed as follows.

❶ **Input given data.** Enter the input and output information for each hospital in the ranges B6:C8 and F6:H8.

❷ **Selected hospital.** Enter 1, 2, or 3 in cell B3, depending on which hospital you want to analyze.

❸ **Unit input costs and output prices.** Enter *any* trial values for the input costs and output prices in the UnitInputCosts and UnitOutputPrices ranges.

	A	B	C	D	E	F	G	H
1	DEA model for checking efficiency of a selected hospital							
2					Run Solver			
3	Selected hospital	1						
4								
5	Inputs used	Input 1	Input 2		Outputs produced	Output 1	Output 2	Output 3
6	Hospital 1	5	14		Hospital 1	9	4	16
7	Hospital 2	8	15		Hospital 2	5	7	10
8	Hospital 3	7	12		Hospital 3	4	9	13
9								
10	Unit costs of inputs	0.000	0.071		Unit prices of outputs	0.0857	0.0571	0.000
11								
12	Constraints that input costs must cover output values							
13		Hospital	Input costs		Output Values	Range names used:		
14		1	1.000	>=	1.000	SelectedHospital - B3		
15		2	1.071	>=	0.829	UnitInputCosts - B10:C10		
16		3	0.857	>=	0.857	UnitOutputPrices - F10:H10		
17						InputCosts - B14:B16		
18	Constraint that selected hospital's input cost must equal a nominal value of 1					OutputValues - D14:D16		
19	Selected hospital input cost	1.000	=	1		LTable - A14:D16		
20						SelectedInputCost - B19		
21	Maximize selected hospital's output value (to see if it is 1, hence efficient)					SelectedOutputValue - B22		
22	Selected hospital output value	1.000						

FIGURE 4.30 DEA Model for Hospital 1

❹ Total input costs and output values. In the InputCosts range, calculate the cost of the inputs used by each hospital. To do this, enter the formula

=SUMPRODUCT(UnitInputCosts,B6:C6)

in cell B14 for hospital 1, and copy this to the rest of the InputCosts range for the other hospitals. Similarly, calculate the output values by entering the formula

=SUMPRODUCT(UnitOutputPrices,F6:H6)

in cell D14 and copying it to the rest of the OutputValues range. Note that even though we are focusing on hospital 1's efficiency, we still calculate input costs and output values for the other hospitals so that we have something to compare hospital 1 to.

❺ Total input cost and output value for selected hospital. In row 19 we want to constrain the total input cost of the *selected* hospital to be 1. To do this, enter the formula

=VLOOKUP(SelectedHospital,LTable,2)

in the SelectedInputCost cell, and enter a 1 in cell D19. Similarly, enter the formula

=VLOOKUP(SelectedHospital,LTable,4)

in the SelectedOutputValue cell. (Make sure you understand how these VLOOKUP functions work.) Remember that because the selected hospital's input cost is constrained to be 1, its output value in cell B22 is automatically its efficiency.

USING SOLVER TO DETERMINE WHETHER HOSPITAL 1 IS EFFICIENT

To see whether hospital 1 is efficient, use Solver as follows. (When you are finished, the Solver dialog box should appear as shown in Figure 4.31.)

❶ Objective. Select the SelectedOutputValue cell as the target cell to maximize. Because the cost of hospital 1 inputs is constrained to be 1, this will cause Solver to maximize the efficiency of hospital 1.

FIGURE 4.31
Solver Dialog Box
for DEA Model

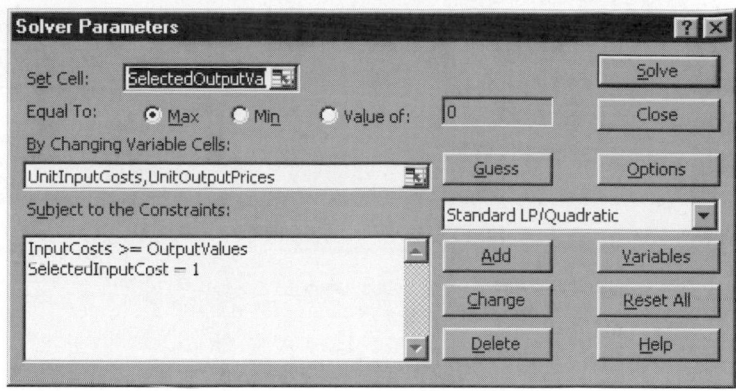

2 **Changing cells.** Choose the UnitInputCosts and UnitOutputPrices ranges as the changing cells.

3 **Selected hospital's input cost constraint.** Add the constraint SelectedInput-Cost=1. This sets the value of hospital 1 inputs equal to 1.

4 **Efficiency constraint.** Add the constraint InputCosts>=OutputValues. This ensures that no hospital is more than 100% efficient.

5 **Specify nonnegativity and optimize.** Under Solver Options, check the nonnegativity box, and use the LP algorithm to obtain the optimal solution shown in Figure 4.30.

The 1 in cell B22 of this solution means that hospital 1 *is* efficient. In words, we have been able to find a set of unit costs for the inputs and the unit prices for the outputs such that the total value of hospital 1's outputs equals the total cost of its inputs.

Determining Whether Hospitals 2 and 3 Are Efficient To determine whether hospital 2 is efficient, we simply replace the value in cell B3 by 2 and rerun Solver. The Solver settings do not need to be modified. (In fact, we have included a button on the spreadsheet that runs a macro to run Solver. It's simply a convenience.) The optimal solution appears in Figure 4.32. From the value of 0.773 in cell B22, we see that

	A	B	C	D	E	F	G	H
1	DEA model for checking efficiency of a selected hospital							
2								
3	Selected hospital	2			**Run Solver**			
4								
5	Inputs used	Input 1	Input 2		Outputs produced	Output 1	Output 2	Output 3
6	Hospital 1	5	14		Hospital 1	9	4	16
7	Hospital 2	8	15		Hospital 2	5	7	10
8	Hospital 3	7	12		Hospital 3	4	9	13
9								
10	Unit costs of inputs	0.000	0.067		Unit prices of outputs	0.0800	0.0533	0.000
11								
12	Constraints that input costs must cover output values							
13		Hospital	Input costs		Output Values		Range names used:	
14		1	0.933	>=	0.933		SelectedHospital - B3	
15		2	1.000	>=	0.773		UnitInputCosts - B10:C10	
16		3	0.800	>=	0.800		UnitOutputPrices - F10:H10	
17							InputCosts - B14:B16	
18	Constraint that selected hospital's input cost must equal a nominal value of 1						OutputValues - D14:D16	
19	Selected hospital input cost	1.000	=	1			LTable - A14:D16	
20							SelectedInputCost - B19	
21	Maximize selected hospital's output value (to see if it is 1, hence efficient)						SelectedOutputValue - B22	
22	Selected hospital output value	0.773						

FIGURE 4.32 DEA Model for Hospital 2

	A	B	C	D	E	F	G	H
1	DEA model for checking efficiency of a selected hospital							
2					Run Solver			
3	Selected hospital	3						
4								
5	Inputs used	Input 1	Input 2		Outputs produced	Output 1	Output 2	Output 3
6	Hospital 1	5	14		Hospital 1	9	4	16
7	Hospital 2	8	15		Hospital 2	5	7	10
8	Hospital 3	7	12		Hospital 3	4	9	13
9								
10	Unit costs of inputs	0.000	0.083		Unit prices of outputs	0.1000	0.0667	0.000
11								
12	Constraints that input costs must cover output values							
13		Hospital	Input costs		Output Values	Range names used:		
14		1	1.167	>=	1.167	SelectedHospital - B3		
15		2	1.250	>=	0.967	UnitInputCosts - B10:C10		
16		3	1.000	>=	1.000	UnitOutputPrices - F10:H10		
17						InputCosts - B14:B16		
18	Constraint that selected hospital's input cost must equal a nominal value of 1					OutputValues - D14:D16		
19	Selected hospital input cost	1.000	=	1		LTable - A14:D16		
20						SelectedInputCost - B19		
21	Maximize selected hospital's output value (to see if it is 1, hence efficient)					SelectedOutputValue - B22		
22	Selected hospital output value	1.000						

FIGURE 4.33 DEA Model for Hospital 3

hospital 2 is *not* efficient. Similarly, we can determine that hospital 3 *is* efficient by replacing the value in cell B3 by 3 and rerunning Solver. See Figure 4.33.

In summary, we have found that hospitals 1 and 3 are efficient, but hospital 2 is inefficient.

What Does It Mean to Be Efficient or Inefficient? This idea of efficiency or inefficiency might still be a mystery, so we will attempt to shed some more light on it. A hospital is efficient if we can price the inputs and outputs in such a way that this hospital gets out all of the value that it puts in. The pricing scheme will depend on the hospital. Each hospital will try to price inputs and outputs so as to put its operations in the best possible light. In our example, hospital 1 attaches 0 prices to input 1 (hospital beds) and output 3 (patient-days for patients over 65), and it attaches positive prices to the rest. This makes hospital 1 look efficient. Hospital 3, which is also efficient, also attaches 0 prices to input 1 and output 3, but its prices for the others are somewhat different from hospital 1's prices.

If DEA finds that a hospital is inefficient, then there is no pricing scheme where that hospital can recover its entire input costs in output values. Actually, it can be shown that if a hospital is inefficient, then a "combination" of the efficient hospitals can be found that uses no more inputs than the inefficient hospital, yet produces at least as much of each output as the inefficient hospital. It is in this sense that the inefficient hospital is inefficient.

To see how this combination can be found, consider the spreadsheet model in Figure 4.34. We begin by entering any positive weights in the Weights range. For any such weights (they don't even need to sum to 1), we consider the combination hospital as a fraction of hospital 1 and another fraction of hospital 3. For example, with the weights shown, the combination hospital uses 26% of the inputs, and produces 26% of the outputs, of hospital 1, and it uses 66% of the inputs, and produces 66% of the outputs, of hospital 3. When we combine these in row 28 with the SUMPRODUCT function [for example, the formula in cell C28 is **=SUMPRODUCT(Weights,C26:C27)**], we find the quantities of inputs this combination hospital uses and the quantities of outputs it produces. To find weights where the combination hospital is better than hospital 2, we find any *feasible* solution to the inequalities indicated in rows 28–30 by using the Solver setup in Figure 4.35. (The weights in Figure 4.34 do the job.) Note that there

FIGURE 4.34
Illustrating How
Hospital 2 Is
Inefficient

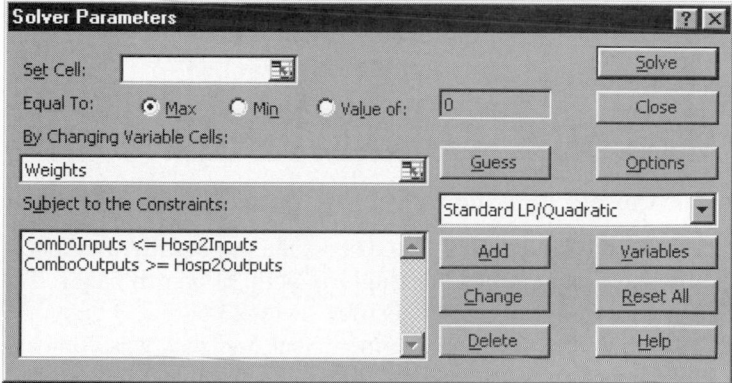

	A	B	C	D	E	F	G	H
24	**Comparing combination of hospitals 1 and 3 to inefficient hospital 2**							
25		Weight	Input1	Input2		Output 1	Output 2	Output 3
26	Hospital 1	0.28	5	14		9	4	16
27	Hospital 3	0.66	7	12		4	9	13
28	Combination		5.9	11.6		5.0	7.0	12.8
29			<=	<=		>=	>=	>=
30	Hospital 2		8	15		5	7	10
31								
32			Extra range names used:					
33			Weights - B26:B27					
34			ComboInputs - C28:D28					
35			ComboOutputs - F28:H28					
36			Hosp2Inputs - C30:D30					
37			Hosp2Outputs - F30:H30					

FIGURE 4.35
Solver Setup for
Finding an
Inefficiency

is no objective to maximize or minimize; all we want is a solution that satisfies the constraints. Furthermore, we know there will be a feasible solution because we have already identified hospital 2 as being inefficient.

In reality, once DEA analysis identifies an organizational unit as being inefficient, this unit should consider benchmarking itself relative to its competition to see where it might make more efficient use of its inputs. ■

MODELING ISSUES

1. The ratio (input i price)/(input j price) can be interpreted as the marginal rate of substitution (at the optimal solution) of input i for input j. That is, the same level of outputs can be maintained if we decrease the use of input i by a small amount Δ and increase the use of input j by [(input i price)/(input j price)]Δ. For example, for hospital 2, (input 2 price/input 1 price) = 6700. This implies that if the use of input 2 were decreased a small amount Δ, hospital 2 could maintain its current output levels if the usage of input 1 were increased by 6700Δ.

2. The ratio (output i price)/(output j price) can be interpreted as the marginal rate of substitution (at the optimal solution) of output i for output j. That is, the same level of input usage can be maintained if we decrease the production of output i by a small amount Δ and increase the production of output j by [(output i price)/(output j price)]Δ. For example, for hospital 2, (output 2 price)/(output 1 price) = 0.67. This implies that if the use of output 2 were decreased a small amount Δ, hospital 2 could maintain its current resource usage if the production of output 1 were increased by 0.67Δ.

3. Sexton et al. (1994) used DEA to evaluate the efficiency of school bus transportation for the counties of North Carolina. For each county they used two inputs: buses used and total operating expense. They used a single output: pupils transported per day. However, they noted a problem with "traditional" DEA. Consider two counties (county 1 and county 2) that use exactly the same inputs and produce the same outputs. Suppose that county 1 is very sparsely populated and county 2 is densely populated. Then it is clear that county 1 is transporting pupils more efficiently than county 2, but a DEA conducted by the method we have described will not show this. Realizing this, the authors developed a method to adjust the output of county 2 downward and the output of county 1 upward to compensate for this problem. The North Carolina Department of Education penalized the inefficient counties by reducing their budgetary appropriations. Since the time DEA was performed, most counties have greatly increased their efficiency. ∎

ADDITIONAL APPLICATIONS

DEA in the Banking Industry

Sherman and Ladino (1995) discuss the use of DEA in identifying the most and least efficient branches in a banking firm with 33 branch banks. They found efficiency ratings that varied from 37% to 100%, with 23 of the 33 branches rated below 100% and 10 below 70%. Each of the inefficient branches was compared to a reference set of "best-practice" branches—efficient branches that offered the same types of services as the inefficient branch. This allowed them to make specific suggestions as to how the inefficient branches could improve. For example, they showed that branch 1 should be able to provide its current level and mix of services with 4.5 fewer customer-service personnel, 1.8 fewer sales service personnel, 0.3 fewer managers, $222,928 less in operating expenses, and 1304 fewer square feet. They also indicated the added amount of service that the inefficient branches could provide, in addition to resource savings, if these branches could become as efficient as the best-practice branches. For example, branch 1 could handle (per year) about 15,000 additional deposits, withdrawals, and checks cashed, 2000 added bank checks, bonds, and travelers' checks, and eight additional night deposits, while reducing the resources needed if it attained the efficiency level of the best-practice branches. See the May–June 1999 issue of *Interfaces* for more applications of DEA in the banking industry. ∎

PROBLEMS

Skill-Building Problems

50. The Salem Board of Education wants to evaluate the efficiency of the town's four elementary schools. The three outputs of the schools are
   - output 1 = average reading score
   - output 2 = average mathematics score
   - output 3 = average self-esteem score

The three inputs to the schools are
   - input 1 = average educational level of mothers (defined by highest grade completed: 12 = high school graduate; 16 = college graduate, and so on)
   - input 2 = number of parent visits to school (per child)
   - input 3 = teacher-to-student ratio

TABLE 4.28	Input/Output Table for School Problem					
	Inputs			**Outputs**		
	1	**2**	**3**	**1**	**2**	**3**
School 1	13	4	0.05	9	7	6
School 2	14	5	0.05	10	8	7
School 3	11	6	0.06	11	7	8
School 4	15	8	0.08	9	9	9

The relevant information for the four schools is given in Table 4.28. Determine which (if any) schools are inefficient.

51. Pine Valley Bank has three branches. You have been asked to evaluate the efficiency of each. The following inputs and outputs are to be used for the study:
   - input 1 = labor hours used (hundreds per month)
   - input 2 = space used (in hundreds of square feet)
   - input 3 = supplies used per month (in dollars)
   - output 1 = loan applications per month
   - output 2 = deposits processed per month (in thousands)
   - output 3 = checks processed per month (in thousands)

   The relevant information is given in Table 4.29. Use these data to determine whether any bank branches are inefficient.

TABLE 4.29	Input/Output Table for Bank Problem					
	Input			**Output**		
	1	**2**	**3**	**1**	**2**	**3**
Bank 1	15	20	50	200	15	35
Bank 2	14	23	51	220	18	45
Bank 3	16	19	51	210	17	40

52. You have been asked to evaluate the efficiency of the Port Charles Police Department. Three precincts are to be evaluated. The inputs and outputs for each precinct are as follows:
   - input 1 = number of policemen
   - input 2 = number of vehicles used
   - output 1 = number of patrol units responding to service requests (thousands per year)
   - output 2 = number of convictions obtained each year (in hundreds)

   You are given the data in Table 4.30. Use this information to determine which precincts, if any, are inefficient.

TABLE 4.30	Input/Output Table for Police Problem			
	Input		**Output**	
	1	**2**	**1**	**2**
Precinct 1	200	60	6	8.0
Precinct 2	300	90	8	9.5
Precinct 3	400	120	10	11.0

53. You have been commissioned by Indiana University to evaluate the relative efficiency of four degree-granting units: Business, Education, Arts and Sciences, and Health, Physical Education, and Recreation (HPER). You are given the information in Table 4.31. Use DEA to identify all inefficient units.

TABLE 4.31	Input/Output Table for University Problem				
	Faculty	**Support Staff**	**Supply Budget (in millions)**	**Credit Hours (in thousands)**	**Research Publications**
Business	150	70	5	15.0	225
Education	60	20	3	5.4	70
Arts & Sciences	800	140	20	56.0	1300
HPER	30	15	1	2.1	40

4.9 CONCLUSION

I n this chapter we have formulated linear programming spreadsheet models of many diverse situations. There is no standard procedure that can be used to attack all problems. However, there are several keys to most formulations.

1. First, determine the changing cells. For example, in blending problems it is vital to realize that the changing cells are the amount of each input used to produce each output, or, as in the post office scheduling example, the changing cells are the number of people who start work each day of the week.

2. Set up the spreadsheet so that you can easily compute what you wish to maximize or minimize (usually profit or cost). For example, in the aggregate planning model, an easy way to compute total cost is to compute the monthly cost of operation in each row.

3. Set up the spreadsheet so that the relationships between the cells in the spreadsheet and the problem constraints are readily apparent. For example, in the post office scheduling example, it is convenient to compute the number of people working each day of the week near the number of people needed for each day of the week.

4. Make your spreadsheet readable. Use range names liberally, and think about your model layout before you dive in. This might not be important for small, straightforward models, but it is crucial for large, complex models.

5. LP models tend to fall into categories, but they are definitely not all alike. For example, a problem might involve a combination of the ideas discussed in the inventory scheduling, blending, and production process examples of this chapter. Many of the review problems are not strictly analogous to any of the models we have discussed. However, spreadsheets provide the flexibility to model just about any problem. All it takes is practice and perseverance!

PROBLEMS

Skill-Building Problems

54. You now have $10,000, and the following investments are available to you during the next 3 years:
    - Investment A: Every dollar invested now yields $0.10 a year from now and $1.30 three years from now.
    - Investment B: Every dollar invested now yields $0.20 a year from now and $1.10 two years from now.
    - Investment C: Every dollar invested a year from now yields $1.50 three years from now.
    During each year, you can place uninvested cash in money market funds that yield 6% interest per year. However, you can invest at most $5000 in any one of A, B, or C. Determine how to maximize your cash on hand 3 years from now.

55. Sunco processes oil into aviation fuel and heating oil. It costs $40 to purchase each 1000 barrels of oil, which is then distilled and yields 500 barrels of aviation fuel and 500 barrels of heating oil. Output from the distillation can be sold directly or processed in the catalytic cracker. If sold after distillation without further processing, aviation fuel sells for $60 per 1000 barrels, and heating oil sells for $40 per 1000 barrels. It takes 1 hour to process 1000 barrels of aviation fuel in the catalytic cracker, and these 1000 barrels can be sold for $130. It takes 45 minutes to process 1000 barrels of heating oil in the cracker, and these 1000 barrels can be sold for $90. Each day at most 20,000 barrels of oil can be purchased, and 8 hours of cracker time are available. Determine how to maximize Sunco's profit.

56. The following investments are available to Finco:
    - Investment 1: For each dollar invested at time 0, Finco receives $0.10 at time 1 and $1.30 at time 2 (where time 0 = now, time 1 = one year from now, and so on).

- Investment 2: For each dollar invested at time 1, Finco receives $1.60 at time 2.
- Investment 3: For each dollar invested at time 2, Finco receives $1.20 at time 3.

At any time, leftover cash can be invested in T-bills, which pay 10% per year. At time 0, Finco has $10,000. At most $5000 can be invested in any one of investments 1, 2, or 3. Determine how to maximize Finco's cash on hand at time 3.

57. All steel manufactured by Steelco must meet the following requirements: between 3.2% and 3.5% carbon; between 1.8% and 2.5% silicon; between 0.9% and 1.2% nickel; tensile strength of at least 45,000 pounds per square inch (psi). Steelco manufactures steel by combining two alloys. The cost and properties of each alloy are given in Table 4.32. Assume that the tensile strength of a mixture of the two alloys can be determined by averaging the tensile strength of the alloys that are mixed together. For example, a 1-ton mixture that is 40% alloy 1 and 60% alloy 2 has a tensile strength of $0.4(42,000) + 0.6(50,000)$. Determine how to minimize the cost of producing a ton of steel.

TABLE 4.32	Requirements for Steelco Problem	
	Alloy 1	**Alloy 2**
Cost per ton	$190	$200
Percent silicon	2%	2.5%
Percent nickel	1%	1.5%
Percent carbon	3%	4.0%
Tensile strength	42,000 psi	50,000 psi

58. Steelco manufactures two types of steel at three different steel mills. During a given month, each steel mill has 200 hours of blast furnace time available. Because of differences in the furnaces at each mill, the time and cost to produce a ton of steel differ for each mill, as shown in Table 4.33. Each month Steelco must manufacture at least 500 tons of steel 1 and 600 tons of steel 2. Determine how Steelco can minimize the cost of manufacturing the desired steel.

59. Based on Heady and Egbert (1964). Walnut Orchard has two farms that grow wheat and corn. Because of differing soil conditions, there are differences in the yields and costs of growing crops on the two farms. The yields and costs are shown in Table 4.34. Each farm has 100 acres available for cultivation; 11,000 bushels of wheat and 7000 bushels of corn must be grown.

TABLE 4.34	Yields and Costs for Walnut Orchard Problem	
	Farm 1	**Farm 2**
Corn yield per acre	500 bushels	650 bushels
Cost per acre of corn	$100	$120
Wheat yield per acre	400 bushels	350 bushels
Cost per acre of wheat	$90	$80

a. Determine a planting plan that will minimize the cost of meeting these requirements.
b. Use SolverTable to see how the total cost changes if the requirements for wheat and corn both change by the *same* percentage, where this percentage change can be as low as −50% or as high as +50%.

60. Candy Kane Cosmetics (CKC) produces Leslie Perfume, which requires chemicals and labor. Two production processes are available. Process 1 transforms 1 unit of labor and 2 units of chemicals into 3 ounces of perfume. Process 2 transforms 2 units of labor and 3 units of chemicals into 5 ounces of perfume. It costs CKC $3 to purchase a unit of labor and $2 to purchase a unit of chemicals. Each year up to 20,000 units of labor and 35,000 units of chemicals can be purchased. In the absence of advertising, CKC believes it can sell 1000 ounces of perfume. To stimulate demand for Leslie, CKC can hire the lovely model Jenny Nelson. Jenny is paid $100 per hour. Each hour Jenny works for the company is estimated to increase the demand for Leslie Perfume by 200 ounces. Each ounce of Leslie Perfume sells for $5. Determine how CKC can maximize its profit.

TABLE 4.33	Times and Costs for Steelco Problem			
	Steel 1		**Steel 2**	
	Cost	**Time (minutes)**	**Cost**	**Time (minutes)**
Mill 1	$10	20	$11	22
Mill 2	$12	24	$9	18
Mill 3	$14	28	$10	30

61. Carco has a $150,000 advertising budget. To increase its automobile sales, the firm is considering advertising in newspapers and on television. The more Carco uses a particular medium, the less effective each additional ad is. Table 4.35 shows the number of new customers reached by each ad. Each newspaper ad costs $1000 and each television ad costs $10,000. At most 30 newspaper ads and 15 television ads can be placed. How can Carco maximize the number of new customers created by advertising?

TABLE 4.35	Ad Exposures for Carco Problem	
	Number of Ads	**New Customers**
Newspaper	1–10	900
	11–20	600
	21–30	300
Television	1–5	10,000
	6–10	5,000
	11–15	2,000

62. Sunco Oil has refineries in Los Angeles and Chicago. The Los Angeles refinery can refine up to 2 million barrels of oil per year, and the Chicago refinery up to 3 million. Once refined, oil is shipped to two distribution points, Houston and New York City. Sunco estimates that each distribution point can sell up to 5 million barrels per year. Because of differences in shipping and refining costs, the profit earned (in dollars) per million barrels of oil shipped depends on where the oil was refined and on the point of distribution. This information is listed in Table 4.36. Sunco is considering expanding the capacity of each refinery. Each million barrels of annual refining capacity that is added will cost $120,000 for the Los Angeles refinery and $150,000 for the Chicago refinery. Determine how Sunco can maximize its profit (including expansion costs) over a 10-year period.

TABLE 4.36	Profits for Sunco Problem	
	Profit per Million Barrels	
	To Houston	**To New York**
From Los Angeles	$20,000	$15,000
From Chicago	$18,000	$17,000

63. Feedco produces two types of cattle feed, both consisting totally of wheat and alfalfa. Feed 1 must contain at least 80% wheat, and feed 2 must contain at least 60% alfalfa. Feed 1 sells for $1.50 per pound, and feed 2 sells for $1.30 per pound. Feedco can purchase up to 1000 pounds of wheat at $0.50 per pound and up to 800 pounds of alfalfa at $0.40 per pound. Demand for each type of feed is unlimited. Determine how to maximize Feedco's profit.

64. Feedco (from the preceding problem) has decided to give its customer a quantity discount. (Assume that it has only one customer.) If the customer purchases over 300 pounds of feed 1, each pound over the first 300 will sell for only $1.25 per pound. Similarly, if the customer purchases more than 300 pounds of feed 2, each pound over the first 300 will sell for $1.00 per pound. Determine how to maximize Feedco's profit.

65. Dexter Chemical produces two compounds, A and B. These compounds are produced via two manufacturing processes. Process 1 requires 2 hours of labor and 1 pound of raw material to produce 2 ounces of A and 1 ounce of B. Process 2 requires 3 hours of labor and 2 pounds of raw material to produce 3 ounces of A and 2 ounces of B. Sixty hours of labor and 40 pounds of raw material are available. Demand for A is unlimited, but only 20 ounces of B can be sold. Compound A sells for $16 per ounce, and B sells for $14 per ounce. Any B that is unsold must be disposed of at a cost of $2 per ounce. Determine how to maximize Dexter's revenue less disposal costs.

66. Natural Furniture manufactures tables and chairs. Each table and chair must be made entirely out of oak or entirely out of pine. A total of 1500 board feet of oak and 2100 board feet of pine are available. A table requires either 17 board feet of oak or 30 board feet of pine, and a chair requires either 5 board feet of oak or 13 board feet of pine. Each table can be sold for $40, and each chair for $15. Determine how Natural can maximize its revenue.

67. Carrington Oil produces two types of gasoline: gas 1 and gas 2 from two types of crude oil: crude 1 and crude 2. Gas 1 is allowed to contain up to 4% impurities, and gas 2 is allowed to contain up to 3% impurities. Gas 1 sells for $8 per barrel, while gas 2 sells for $12 per barrel. Up to 4200 barrels of gas 1 and up to 4300 barrels of gas 2 can be sold. The cost per barrel of each crude, availability, and the level of impurities in each crude are listed in Table 4.37. Before blending the crude oil into gas, any amount of each crude can be "purified" for a cost of $0.50 per barrel. Purification eliminates half of the impurities in the crude oil.

   a. Determine how to maximize profit.

   b. Use SolverTable to determine how an increase in the availability of crude 1 affects the optimal profit.

TABLE 4.37   Data for Crude Oils

Oil	Cost per Barrel	Impurity Level	Availability
Crude 1	$6	10%	5000
Crude 2	$8	2%	4500

   c. Use SolverTable to determine how an increase in the availability of crude 2 affects the optimal profit.

   d. Use SolverTable to determine how a change in the profitability of gas 2 changes profitability and the types of gas produced.

68. A company produces two products: A and B. Product A sells for $11 per unit and product B sells for $23.00 per unit. To produce a unit of product A requires 2 hours on assembly line 1 and 1 unit of raw material. To produce a unit of product B requires 2 units of raw material, 1 unit of A, and 2 hours on assembly line 2. There are 1300 hours of time available on line 1 and 500 hours on line 2. A unit of raw material can be bought (for $5 a unit) or produced (at no cost) by using 2 hours of time on line 1.

   a. Determine how to maximize profit.

   b. The company will stop buying raw material when the price of raw material increases to above what value? (Use SolverTable.)

69. Pear produces low budget cars. Each car is sold for $790. The raw material in a car costs $600. Labor time and robot time are needed to produce cars. A worker can do the needed labor on at most 100 cars per month and a robot can complete the needed work on at most 200 cars per month. Initially Pear has 4 workers. Each worker receives a monthly salary of $6000. It costs $2500 to hire a worker and $1000 to fire a worker. Hired workers are fully productive during the month they are hired. Robots must be bought at the beginning of month 1 at a cost of $15,000 per robot. The (assumed known) demand for cars is listed in Table 4.38. At the end of each month Pear incurs a holding cost of $50 per car. How can Pear maximize the profit earned during the next 6 months?

TABLE 4.38   Demand for Pear Cars

Month	Demand
1	600
2	500
3	400
4	800
5	300
6	600

70. The ZapCon Company is considering investing in three projects. If it fully invests in a project, the realized cash flows (in millions of dollars) will be as listed in Table 4.39. For example, project 1 requires cash outflow of $3 million today and returns $5.5 million 3 years from now. Today ZapCon has $2 million in cash. At each time point (0, 0.5, 1, 1.5, 2, and 2.5 years from today) the company can, if desired, borrow up to $2 million at 3.5% (per 6 months) interest. Leftover cash earns 3% (per 6 months) interest. For example, if after borrowing and investing at time 0, ZapCon has $1 million, it would receive $30,000 in interest at time 0.5 year. The company's goal is to maximize cash on hand after cash flows 3 years from now are accounted for. What investment and borrowing strategy should it use? Assume that the company can invest in a fraction of a project. For example, if it invests in 0.5 of project 3, it has, for example, cash outflows of −$1 million at times 0 and 0.5.

TABLE 4.39   Cash Flow Data

Time (years)	Project 1 Cash Flow	Project 2 Cash Flow	Project 3 Cash Flow
0	−3.0	−2.0	−2.0
0.5	−1.0	−0.5	−2.0
1.0	−1.8	1.5	−1.8
1.5	0.4	1.5	1.0
2.0	1.8	1.5	1.0
2.5	1.8	0.2	1.0
3.0	5.5	−1.0	6.0

71. You are a CFA (chartered financial analyst). Madonna has come to you because she needs help paying off her credit card bills. She owes the amounts on her credit cards listed in Table 4.40. Madonna is willing to allocate up to $5000 per month to pay off these credit cards. All cards must be paid off within 36 months. Madonna's goal is to minimize the total of all her payments. To solve this problem, you must understand how interest on a loan works. To illustrate, suppose Madonna pays $5000 on Saks during month 1. Then her Saks balance at the beginning of month 2 is $20,000 − [5000 − 0.005(20,000)]$. This

TABLE 4.40   Madonna's Credit Card Bills

Credit Card	Balance	Monthly Rate
Saks Fifth Avenue	$20,000	0.5%
Bloomingdale's	$50,000	1.0%
Macy's	$40,000	1.5%

follows because Madonna incurs 0.005(20,000) in interest charges on her Saks card during Month 1. Help Madonna solve her problem. Once you have solved this problem, give an intuitive explanation of the solution found by Solver.

72. Aluminaca produces 100-foot, 200-foot, and 300-foot long ingots for customers. This week's demand for ingots is listed in Table 4.41. Aluminaca has four furnaces in which ingots can be produced. During a week each furnace can be operated for 50 hours. Because ingots are produced by cutting up long strips of aluminum, longer ingots take less time to produce than shorter ingots. If a furnace is devoted completely to producing one type of ingot, the number it can produce in a week is as listed in Table 4.42. For example, furnace 1 could produce 350 300-foot ingots per week. The material in an ingot costs $10 per foot. A customer who wants a 100-foot or 200-foot ingot will accept an ingot of that length or longer. How can Aluminaca minimize the material costs incurred in meeting required weekly demands?

TABLE 4.41	Ingot Demand
Ingot Length	**Demand**
100-foot	700
200-foot	300
300-foot	150

TABLE 4.42	Production Data		
Furnace	**100-foot**	**200-foot**	**300-foot**
1	230	340	350
2	230	260	280
3	240	300	310
4	200	280	300

Skill-Extending Problems

73. Based on Franklin and Koenigsberg (1973). The city of Busville contains three school districts. The numbers of minority and nonminority students in each district are given in Table 4.43. The local court has decided that each of the town's two high schools (Cooley High and Walt Whitman High) must have approximately the same percentage of minority students (within 5%) as the entire town. The distances (in miles) between the school districts and the high schools are given in Table 4.44. Each high school must have an enrollment of 300 to 500 students. Determine an assignment of students to schools that minimizes the total distance students must travel to school.

TABLE 4.43	Student Counts for Busville Problem	
	Students	**Students**
District 1	50	200
District 2	50	250
District 3	100	150

TABLE 4.44	Distances for Busville Problem	
	Cooley High	**Walt Whitman High**
District 1	1	2
District 2	2	1
District 3	1	1

74. Based on Carino and Lenoir (1988). Brady Corporation produces cabinets. Each week, Brady requires 90,000 cubic feet of processed lumber. The company can obtain lumber in two ways. First, it can purchase lumber from an outside supplier and then dry it at the Brady kiln. Second, Brady can chop down trees on its land, cut them into lumber at its sawmill, and then dry the lumber at its kiln. The company can purchase grade 1 or grade 2 lumber. Grade 1 lumber costs $3 per cubic foot and when dried yields 0.7 cubic foot of useful lumber. Grade 2 lumber costs $7 per cubic foot and when dried yields 0.9 cubic foot of useful lumber. It costs the company $3 to chop down a tree. After being cut and dried, a log yields 0.8 cubic feet of lumber. Brady incurs costs of $4 per cubic foot of lumber it dries. It costs $2.50 per cubic foot of logs sent through the sawmill. Each week the sawmill can process up to 35,000 cubic feet of lumber. Each week up to 40,000 cubic feet of grade 1 lumber and up to 60,000 cubic feet of grade 2 lumber can be purchased. Each week 40 hours of time are available for drying lumber. The time it takes to dry 1 cubic foot of lumber is as follows: grade 1, 2 seconds; grade 2, 0.8 second; log, 1.3 seconds. Determine how Brady can minimize the weekly cost of meeting its demand for processed lumber.

75. Based on Cheung and Auger (1976). The Canadian Parks Commission controls two tracts of land. Tract 1 consists of 300 acres and tract 2, 100 acres. Each acre of tract 1 can be used for spruce trees, hunting, or both. Each acre of tract 2 can be used for spruce trees, camping, or both. The capital (in hundreds of dollars) and labor (in worker-days) required to maintain 1 acre of each tract and the profit (in thousands of dollars) per acre for each possible use of land are given in Table 4.45. Capital of $150,000

TABLE 4.45	Data for Canadian Parks Problem			
		Capital	Labor	Profit
Tract 1	Spruce	3	0.10	0.20
	Hunting	3	0.20	0.04
	Both	4	0.20	0.05
Tract 2	Spruce	1	0.05	0.06
	Camping	30	5.00	0.09
	Both	10	1.01	1.10

and 200 worker-days of labor are available. How should the land be allocated to various uses to maximize profit received from the two tracts?

76. Based on Dobson and Kalish (1988). Chandler Enterprises produces two competing products, A and B. The company wants to sell these products to two groups of customers, group 1 and group 2. The values each customer places on a unit of A and B are shown in Table 4.46. Each customer will buy either product A or product B, but not both. A customer is willing to buy product A if she believes that

Premium of product A $\geq$ Premium of product B

and

Premium of product A ≥ 0

Here, the "premium" of a product is its value minus its price. Similarly, a customer is willing to buy B if she believes

Premium of product B $\geq$ Premium of product A

and

Premium of product B ≥ 0

Group 1 has 1000 members, and group 2 has 1500 members. Chandler wants to set prices for each product to ensure that group 1 members purchase product A and group 2 members purchase product B. Determine how Chandler can maximize its revenue.

TABLE 4.46	Customers' Values for Chandler Problem	
	Group 1 Customer	Group 2 Customer
Value of A	$10	$12
Value of B	$8	$15

77. Juiceco manufactures two products, premium orange juice and regular orange juice. Both products are made by combining two types of oranges,

grade 6 and grade 3. The oranges in premium juice must have an average grade of at least 5; those in regular juice, at least 4. During each of the next 2 months, Juiceco can sell up to 1000 gallons of premium juice and up to 2000 gallons of regular juice. Premium juice sells for $1.00 per gallon, and regular juice sells for $0.80 per gallon. At the beginning of month 1, Juiceco has 3000 gallons of grade 6 oranges and 2000 gallons of grade 3 oranges. At the beginning of month 2, Juiceco can purchase additional grade 3 oranges for $0.40 per gallon and additional grade 6 oranges for $0.60 per gallon. Juice spoils at the end of the month, so Juiceco cannot make extra juice during month 1 to help meet month 2 demand. Oranges left over at the end of month 1 can be used to produce juice for month 2. At the end of month 1, a holding cost of $0.05 is assessed against each gallon of leftover grade 3 oranges, and $0.10 against each gallon of leftover grade 6 oranges. In addition to the cost of the oranges, it costs $0.10 to produce each gallon of (regular or premium) juice. Determine how Juiceco can maximize its profit during the next 2 months.

78. Each day Eastinghouse produces capacitors during three shifts: 8 A.M. to 4 P.M., 4 P.M. to midnight, and midnight to 8 A.M. The hourly salary paid to the employees on each shift, the price charged for each capacitor made during each shift, and the number of defects in each capacitor produced during a given shift are shown in Table 4.47. The company can employ up to 25 workers, and each worker can be assigned to one of the three shifts. A worker produces 10 capacitors during a shift, but due to machinery limitations, no more than 10 workers can be assigned to any shift. Each capacitor produced can be sold, but the average number of defects per capacitor for the day's production cannot exceed 3. Determine how Eastinghouse can maximize its daily profit.

TABLE 4.47	Data for Eastinghouse Problem		
	Hourly Salary	Defects per Capacitor	Price
8 A.M. to 4 P.M.	$12	4	$18
4 P.M. to midnight	$16	3	$22
Midnight to 8 A.M.	$20	2	$24

79. During the next 3 months, Airco must meet (on time) the following demands for air conditioners: month 1, 300; month 2, 400; month 3, 500. Air conditioners can be produced in either New York or Los Angeles. It takes 1.5 hours of skilled labor to

produce an air conditioner in Los Angeles, and 2 hours in New York. It costs $400 to produce an air conditioner in Los Angeles, and $350 in New York. During each month each city has 420 hours of skilled labor available. It costs $100 to hold an air conditioner in inventory for a month. At the beginning of month 1, Airco has 200 air conditioners in stock. Determine how Airco can minimize the cost of meeting air conditioner demands for the next 3 months.

80. During the next 3 months, Steelco faces the following demands for steel: month 1, 100 tons; month 2, 200 tons; month 3, 50 tons. During any month a worker can produce up to 15 tons of steel. Each worker is paid $5000 per month. Workers can be hired or fired at a cost of $3000 per worker fired and $4000 per worker hired. The cost of holding a ton of steel in inventory for 1 month is $100. Demand can be backlogged at a cost of $70 per ton per month. For example, if 1 ton of month 1 demand is met during month 3, a backlogging cost of $140 is incurred. At the beginning of month 1, Steelco has 8 workers. During any month, at most 2 workers can be hired. All demand must be met by the end of month 3. The raw material used to produce a ton of steel costs $300. Determine how to minimize Steelco's costs.

81. Gotham City National Bank is open Monday through Friday from 9 A.M. to 5 P.M. From past experience, the bank knows that it needs the numbers of tellers shown in Table 4.48. Gotham City Bank hires two types of tellers. Full-time tellers work 9 A.M. to 5 P.M. 5 days a week, with 1 hour off each day for lunch. The bank determines when a full-time employee takes his or her lunch hour, but each teller must go between noon and 1 P.M. or between 1 P.M. and 2 P.M. Full-time employees are paid (including fringe benefits) $8 per hour, which includes payment for lunch hour. The bank can also hire part-time tellers. Each part-time teller must work exactly 3 consecutive hours each day. A

part-time teller is paid $5 per hour and receives no fringe benefits. To maintain adequate quality of service, the bank has decided that at most 5 part-time tellers can be hired. Determine how to meet the bank's teller requirements at minimum cost.

82. Based on Rothstein (1973). The Springfield City Police Department employs 30 police officers. Each officer works 5 days per week. The crime rate fluctuates with the day of the week, so the number of police officers required each day depends on the day of the week: Saturday, 28; Sunday, 18; Monday, 18; Tuesday, 24; Wednesday, 25; Thursday, 16; Friday, 21. The police department wants to schedule police officers to minimize the number whose days off are *not* consecutive. Determine how to accomplish this goal.

83. Based on Charnes and Cooper (1955). Alex Cornby makes his living buying and selling corn. On January 1 he has 50 tons of corn and $1000. On the first day of each month Alex can buy corn at the following prices per ton: January, $300; February, $350; March, $400; April, $500. On the last day of each month, Alex can sell corn at the following prices per ton: January, $250; February, $400; March, $350; April, $550. Alex stores his corn in a warehouse that can hold at most 100 tons of corn. He must be able to pay cash for all corn at the time of purchase. Determine how Alex can maximize his cash on hand at the end of April.

84. Based on Robichek et al. (1965). At the beginning of month 1, Finco has $400 in cash. At the beginning of months 1, 2, 3, and 4, Finco receives certain revenues, after which it pays bills. (See Table 4.49.) Any money left over can be invested for 1 month at the interest rate of 0.1% per month; for 2 months at 0.5% per month; for 3 months at 1% per month; or for 4 months at 2% per month. Determine an investment strategy that maximizes cash on hand at the beginning of month 5.

TABLE 4.49	Data for Finco Problem	
	Revenues	Bills
Month 1	$400	$600
Month 2	$800	$500
Month 3	$300	$500
Month 4	$300	$250

85. City 1 produces 500 tons of waste per day, and city 2 produces 400 tons of waste per day. Waste must be incinerated at incinerator 1 or 2, and each incinerator can process up to 500 tons of waste per day. The cost to incinerate waste is $40 per ton at

TABLE 4.48	Teller Requirements for Gotham Bank Problem
Time Period	Tellers Required
9–10	4
10–11	3
11–noon	4
Noon–1	6
1–2	5
2–3	6
3–4	8
4–5	8

incinerator 1 and $30 per ton at incinerator 2. Incineration reduces each ton of waste to 0.2 ton of debris, which must be dumped at one of two landfills. Each landfill can receive at most 200 tons of debris per day. It costs $3 per mile to transport a ton of material (either debris or waste). Distances (in miles) between locations are shown in Table 4.50. Determine how to minimize the total cost of disposing of the waste from both cities.

TABLE 4.50	Distances for Landfill Problem	
	Incinerator 1	Incinerator 2
City 1	30	5
City 2	36	42
Landfill 1	5	9
Landfill 2	8	6

86. Based on Smith (1965). Silicon Valley Corporation (Silvco) manufactures transistors. An important aspect of the manufacture of transistors is the melting of the element germanium (a major component of a transistor) in a furnace. Unfortunately, the melting process yields germanium of highly variable quality. Two methods can be used to melt germanium. Method 1 costs $50 per transistor, and method 2 costs $70 per transistor. The qualities of germanium obtained by methods 1 and 2 are

TABLE 4.51	Germanium Qualities for Silvco Problem	
	Yield (percent)	
	Method 1	Method 2
Defective	30	20
Grade 1	30	20
Grade 2	20	25
Grade 3	15	20
Grade 4	5	15

shown in Table 4.51. Silvco can refire melted germanium in an attempt to improve its quality. It costs $25 to refire the melted germanium for one transistor. The results of the refiring process are shown in Table 4.52. For example, if grade 3 germanium is refired, half of the resulting germanium will be grade 3 and the other half will be grade 4. Silvco has sufficient furnace capacity to melt or refire germanium for at most 20,000 transistors per month. Silvco's monthly demands are for 1000 grade 4 transistors, 2000 grade 3 transistors, 3000 grade 2 transistors, and 3000 grade 1 transistors. Determine how to minimize the cost of producing the needed transistors.

87. The Wild Turkey Company produces two types of turkey cutlets for sale to fast-food restaurants. Each type of cutlet consists of white meat and dark meat. Cutlet 1 sells for $4 per pound and must consist of at least 70% white meat. Cutlet 2 sells for $3 per pound and must consist of at least 60% white meat. At most 50 pounds of cutlet 1 and 30 pounds of cutlet 2 can be sold. The two types of turkey used to manufacture the cutlets are purchased from the GobbleGobble Turkey Farm. Each type 1 turkey costs $10 and yields 5 pounds of white meat and 2 pounds of dark meat. Each type 2 turkey costs $8 and yields 3 pounds of white meat and 3 pounds of dark meat. Determine how to maximize Wild Turkey's profit.

88. The production line employees at Grummins Engine work 4 days a week, 10 hours a day. Each day of the week, the following minimum numbers of line employees are needed: Monday through Friday, 7 employees; Saturday and Sunday, 3 employees. Grummins employs 11 line employees. Determine how to maximize the number of consecutive days off received by these employees. For example, a worker who gets Sunday, Monday, and Wednesday off receives 2 consecutive days off.

89. Based on Lanzenauer et al. (1987). To process income tax forms, the Internal Revenue Service (IRS) first sends each form through the data preparation (DP) department, where information is coded for computer entry. Then the form is sent to data entry (DE), where it is entered into the

TABLE 4.52	Refiring Results for Silvco Problem				
	Yield from Refiring (percent)				
	Defective	Grade 1	Grade 2	Grade 3	Grade 4
Defective	30	25	15	20	10
Grade 1	0	30	30	20	20
Grade 2	0	0	40	30	30
Grade 3	0	0	0	50	50

computer. During the next 3 weeks, the following numbers of forms will arrive: week 1, 40,000; week 2, 30,000; week 3, 60,000. All employees work 40 hours per week and are paid $500 per week. Data preparation of a form requires 15 minutes, and data entry of a form requires 10 minutes. Each week an employee is assigned to either data entry or data preparation. The IRS must complete processing all forms by the end of week 5 and wants to minimize the cost of accomplishing this goal. Assume that all workers are full-time employees and that the IRS will have the same number of employees each week. Assume all employees are capable of performing data preparation and data entry. Determine how many workers should be working and how the workers should allocate their hours during the next 5 weeks.

90. The mayor of Llanview is trying to determine the number of judges needed to handle the judicial caseload. The estimated numbers of judicial hours needed during each month of the year are given in Table 4.53.

TABLE 4.53   Hours for Judicial Problem

	Hours		Hours
January	400	July	200
February	300	August	400
March	200	September	300
April	600	October	200
May	800	November	100
June	300	December	300

a. Suppose each judge works all 12 months and can handle up to 120 hours per month of casework. To avoid creating a backlog, all cases must be handled by the end of December. Determine how many judges Llanview needs.

b. If each judge receives 1 month of vacation each year, how does your answer change?

91. Based on Robichek et al. (1965). The Korvair Department Store has $100,000 in available cash. At the beginning of each of the next 6 months, Korvair will receive revenues and pay bills as shown in Table 4.54. It is clear that Korvair will have a short-term cash flow problem until the store receives revenues from the Christmas shopping season. To solve this problem, Korvair must borrow money. At the beginning of July, the company takes out a 6-month loan. Any money borrowed for a 6-month period must be paid back at the end of December along with 9% interest (early payback does not reduce the total interest of the loan). Korvair can also meet cash needs through month-to-month

TABLE 4.54   Revenues and Bills for Korvair Problem

	Revenues	Bills
July	$100,000	$500,000
August	$200,000	$500,000
September	$200,000	$600,000
October	$400,000	$200,000
November	$700,000	$200,000
December	$900,000	$100,000

borrowing. Any money borrowed for a 1-month period incurs an interest cost of 4% per month. Determine how Korvair can minimize the cost of paying its bills on time.

92. Based on Garvin et al. (1957). Ole Oil produces three products: heating oil, gasoline, and jet fuel. The average octane levels must be at least 4.5 for heating oil, 8.5 for gas, and 7.0 for jet fuel. To produce these products Ole purchases two types of oil: crude 1 (at $12 per barrel) and crude 2 (at $10 per barrel). Each day at most 10,000 barrels of each type of oil can be purchased. Before crude can be used to produce products for sale, it must be distilled. Each day at most 15,000 barrels of oil can be distilled. It costs $0.10 to distill a barrel of oil. The result of distillation is as shown in Table 4.55. Distilled naphtha can be used only to produce gasoline or jet fuel. Distilled oil can be used to produce heating oil or it can be sent through the catalytic cracker (at a cost of $0.15 per barrel). Each day at most 5000 barrels of distilled oil can be sent through the cracker, with the results as shown in Table 4.56. Cracked oil can be used to produce gasoline and jet fuel but not heating oil. The

TABLE 4.55   Distillation Results for Ole Oil Problem

	Yield (in barrels)		
	Naphtha	Distilled 1	Distilled 2
Crude 1	0.6	0.3	0.1
Crude 2	0.4	0.2	0.4

TABLE 4.56   Catalytic Cracker Results for Ole Oil Problem

	Yield (in barrels)	
	Cracked 1	Cracked 2
Distilled 1	0.8	0.2
Distilled 2	0.7	0.3

octane level of each type of oil is as follows: naphtha, 8; distilled 1, 4; distilled 2, 5; cracked 1, 9; cracked 2, 6.

All heating oil produced can be sold at $14 per barrel; all gasoline produced, $18 per barrel; all jet fuel produced, $16 per barrel. Marketing considerations dictate that at least 3000 barrels of each product must be produced daily. Determine how Ole can maximize its profit.

93. Mackk Engine produces diesel trucks. New government emission standards have dictated that the average pollution emissions of all trucks produced in the next 3 years cannot exceed 10 grams per truck. Mackk produces two types of trucks. Each type 1 truck sells for $20,000, costs $15,000 to manufacture, and emits 15 grams of pollution. Each type 2 truck sells for $17,000, costs $14,000 to manufacture, and emits 5 grams of pollution. Production capacity limits total truck production during each year to at most 320 trucks. The maximum numbers of each truck type that can be sold during each of the next 3 years are given in Table 4.57. Demand can be met from previous production or the current year's production. It costs $2000 to hold one truck (of any type) in inventory for 1 year. Determine how Mackk can maximize its profit during the next 3 years.

TABLE 4.57	Demand for Mackk Problem	
	Type 1	Type 2
Year 1	100	200
Year 2	200	100
Year 3	300	150

94. Priceler manufactures sedans and wagons. The numbers of vehicles that can be sold in each of the next 3 months are listed in Table 4.58. Each sedan sells for $13,000, and each wagon sells for $11,500. It costs $9000 to produce a sedan and $8500 to produce a wagon. To hold a vehicle in inventory for 1 month costs $250 per sedan and $200 per wagon. During each month at most 1500 vehicles can be produced. Production line restrictions dictate that during month 1, at least two-thirds of all cars

TABLE 4.58	Demands for Priceler Problem	
	Sedans	Wagons
Month 1	1100	600
Month 2	1500	700
Month 3	1200	500

produced must be sedans. At the beginning of month 1, 200 sedans and 100 wagons are available. Determine how to maximize Priceler's profit during the next 3 months.

95. Each day, workers at the Gotham City Police Department work two 6-hour shifts chosen from midnight to 6 A.M., 6 A.M. to noon, noon to 6 P.M., and 6 P.M. to midnight. The following numbers of workers are needed during each shift: 15 from midnight to 6 A.M.; 5 from 6 A.M. to noon; 12 from noon to 6 P.M.; and 6 from 6 P.M. to midnight. Workers whose two shifts are consecutive are paid $12 per hour, whereas workers whose shifts are not consecutive are paid $18 per hour. Determine how to minimize the cost of meeting the daily workforce demands of the Gotham City Police Department.

96. During each 6-hour period of the day, the Bloomington Police Department needs at least the number of police officers shown in Table 4.59. Police officers can be hired to work either 12 consecutive hours or 18 consecutive hours. Police officers are paid $4 per hour for each of the first 12 hours they work in a day and $6 per hour for each of the next 6 hours they work in a day. Determine how to minimize the cost of meeting Bloomington's daily police requirements.

TABLE 4.59	Requirements for Bloomington Police Problem
Time Period	Police Officers Required
Midnight to 6 A.M.	12
6 A.M. to noon	8
Noon to 6 P.M.	6
6 P.M. to midnight	15

97. Each hour from 10 A.M. to 7 P.M., Bank One receives checks and must process them. Its goal is to process all checks the same day they are received. The bank has 13 check processing machines, each of which can process up to 500 checks per hour. It takes one worker to operate each machine. Bank One hires both full-time and part-time workers. Full-time workers work either 10 A.M. to 6 P.M., 11 A.M. to 7 P.M., or noon to 8 P.M. and are paid $160 per day. Part-time workers work either 2 P.M. to 7 P.M. or 3 P.M. to 8 P.M. and are paid $75 per day. The numbers of checks received each hour are shown in Table 4.60 (page 180). In the interest of maintaining continuity, Bank One believes that it must have at least 3 full-time workers under contract. Develop a work schedule that processes all checks by 8 P.M. and minimizes daily labor costs.

TABLE 4.60	Checks Received for Bank One Problem		
	Checks Received		**Checks Received**
10 A.M.	5000	3 P.M.	3000
11 A.M.	4000	4 P.M.	4000
Noon	3000	5 P.M.	4500
1 P.M.	4000	6 P.M.	3500
2 P.M.	2500	7 P.M.	3000

98. Based on Glassey and Gupta (1978). A paper recycling plant processes box board, tissue paper, newsprint, and book paper into pulp that can be used to produce three grades of recycled paper (grades 1, 2, and 3). The prices per ton and the pulp contents of the four inputs are shown in Table 4.61.

TABLE 4.61	Data for Paper Problem	
	Cost	**Pulp Content**
Box board	$5	15%
Tissue paper	$6	20%
Newsprint	$8	30%
Book paper	$10	40%

Two methods, de-inking and asphalt dispersion, can be used to process the four inputs into pulp. It costs $20 to de-ink a ton of any input. The process of de-inking removes 10% of the input's pulp, leaving 90% of the original pulp. It costs $15 to apply asphalt dispersion to a ton of material. The asphalt dispersion process removes 20% of the input's pulp. At most 3000 tons of input can be run through the asphalt dispersion process or the de-inking process. Grade 1 paper can be produced only with newsprint or book paper pulp; grade 2 paper, only with book paper, tissue paper, or box board pulp; and grade 3 paper, only with newsprint, tissue paper, or box board pulp. To meet its current demands, the company needs 500 tons of pulp for grade 1 paper, 500 tons of pulp for grade 2 paper, and 600 tons of pulp for grade 3 paper. Determine how to minimize the cost of meeting the demands for pulp.

99. At the beginning of month 1, GE Capital has 50 million accounts. Of these, 40 million are paid up (0-due), 4 million are 1 month overdue (1-due), 4 million are 2 months overdue (2-due), and 2 million are 3 months overdue (3-due). Once an account is more than 3 months overdue, it is written off as a bad debt. For each overdue account, GE Capital can either phone the cardholder, send a letter, or do nothing. A letter requires an average of 0.05 hour of labor, whereas a phone call requires an average of 0.10 hour of labor. Each month 500,000 hours of labor are available. We assume that the average amount of a monthly payment is $30. Thus, if a 2-due account remains 2-due, it means that 1 month's payment ($30) has been received, and if a 2-due account becomes 0-due, it means that 3 months' payments ($90) have been received. On the basis of thousands of accounts, DMMs (Delinquency Movement Matrices), shown in Tables 4.62, 4.63, and 4.64, have been estimated. For example, the top left 0.60 entry in Table 4.62 means that 60% of all 1-due accounts that receive a letter become 0-due by the next month. The 0.10 and 0.30 values in this same row mean that 10% of all 1-due accounts remain 1-due after receiving a letter, and 30% of all 1-due accounts become 2-due after receiving a letter. Your goal is to determine how to allocate your workforce over the next 4 months to maximize the expected collection revenue received during that time. (*Note*: 0-due accounts are never contacted, which accounts for the lack of 0-due rows in Tables 4.62 and 4.63.)

100. You have been put in charge of the Melrose oil refinery. The refinery produces gas and heating oil from crude oil. Gas sells for $8 per barrel and must have an average "grade level" of at least 9. Heating oil sells for $6 a barrel and must have an average "grade level" of at least 7. At most 2000 barrels of gas and at most 600 barrels of heating oil can be sold. Incoming crude can be processed by one of three methods. The per-barrel yield and per-barrel cost of each processing method are listed in Table 4.65. For example, if we refine 1 barrel of incoming crude by method 1, it costs us $3.40 and

TABLE 4.62	DMM If Account Receives a Letter				
	0-Due	**1-Due**	**2-Due**	**3-Due**	**Bad Debt**
1-Due	0.60	0.10	0.30	0.00	0.00
2-Due	0.15	0.15	0.40	0.30	0.00
3-Due	0.00	0.00	0.20	0.60	0.20
Bad debt	0.00	0.00	0.00	0.00	1.00

TABLE 4.63　DMM If Account Receives a Phone Call

	0-Due	1-Due	2-Due	3-Due	Bad Debt
1-Due	0.70	0.20	0.10	0.00	0.00
2-Due	0.30	0.25	0.30	0.15	0.00
3-Due	0.00	0.00	0.50	0.40	0.10
Bad debt	0.00	0.00	0.00	0.00	1.00

TABLE 4.64　DMM for Do-Nothing Action

	0-Due	1-Due	2-Due	3-Due	Bad Dept
0-Due	0.90	0.10	0.00	0.00	0.00
1-Due	0.20	0.25	0.55	0.00	0.00
2-Due	0.10	0.10	0.20	0.60	0.00
3-Due	0.00	0.00	0.10	0.40	0.50
Bad debt	0.00	0.00	0.00	0.00	1.00

TABLE 4.65　Crude Processing Data

Method	Grade 6	Grade 8	Grade 10	Cost
1	0.2	0.2	0.6	$3.40
2	0.3	0.3	0.4	$3.00
3	0.4	0.4	0.2	$2.60

TABLE 4.66　Water Inflows and Requirements

Month	Inflow	Requirement
1	80	120
2	120	90
3	120	130
4	130	140
5	200	110
6	90	100
7	100	120
8	80	90
9	100	110
10	90	80
11	80	90
12	70	70

yields 0.2 barrel of grade 6, 0.2 barrel of grade 8, and 0.6 barrel of grade 10. Before being processed into gas and heating oil, processed grades 6 and 8 can be sent through the catalytic cracker to improve their quality. For $1.30 per barrel, a barrel of grade 6 can be "cracked" into a barrel of grade 8. For $2.00 per barrel, a barrel of grade 8 can be cracked into a barrel of grade 10. Any leftover processed and/or cracked oil that cannot be used for heating oil or gas must be disposed of at a cost of $0.20 per barrel. Determine how to maximize the refinery's profit.

101. You have been assigned to manage a reservoir near Hoover Dam that is used to supply hydroelectric power. Based on past weather patterns, you believe the number of barrels (in millions) of water listed in Table 4.66 will flow into the reservoir during the next 12 months. Based on electric power demands, you believe the water requirements (in millions of barrels of water) during each of the next 12 months will be those listed in Table 4.66. At the beginning of the current month the reservoir has 40 million barrels of water. The reservoir can hold (at end of any month) at most 80 million barrels of water. You are to determine the outflow from the reservoir during each of the next 12 months. Your goal is to match as closely as possible the monthly outflows

to the monthly requirements. Assume that all inflows occur at the beginning of the month, so the inflow during a month may be used as an outflow. For example, during month 1 you can have an outflow of between 40 and 120 million barrels.

102. It is February 15, 2000. Three bonds, as listed in Table 4.67 (page 182), are for sale. Each bond has a face value of $100. Every 6 months, starting 6 months from the current date and ending at the expiration date, each bond pays 0.5 * (coupon rate) * (Face value). At the expiration date the face value is paid. For example, the second bond pays
- $2.75 on 8/15/00
- $102.75 on 2/15/01

TABLE 4.67	Bond Data		
Bond	Current Price	Expiration Date	Coupon Rate
1	$101.625	8/15/2000	6.875
2	$101.5625	2/15/2001	5.5
3	$103.80	2/15/2001	7.75

Given the current price structure, the question is whether there is a way to make an infinite amount of money. To answer this, we look for an arbitrage. An arbitrage exists if there is a combination of bond sales and purchases today that yields

- a positive cash flow today
- nonnegative cash flows at all future dates

If such a strategy exists, then it is possible to make an infinite amount of money. For example, if buying 10 units of bond 1 today and selling 5 units of bond 2 today yielded, say, $1 today and nothing at all future dates, then we could make k by purchasing $10k$ units of bond 1 today and selling $5k$ units of bond 2 today. We would also be able to cover all payments at future dates from money received on those dates. Clearly, we expect that bond prices at any point in time will be set so that no arbitrage opportunities exist.

a. Show that an arbitrage opportunity exists for the bonds in Table 4.67. (*Hint*: Set up an LP that maximizes today's cash flow subject to constraints that cash flow at each future date is nonnegative. You should get a "no convergence" message from Solver.)

b. Usually bonds are bought at an ask price and sold at a bid price. Consider the same three bonds listed in Table 4.67 and suppose the ask and bid prices are as listed in Table 4.68. Show that these bond prices admit no arbitrage opportunities.

TABLE 4.68	Bid and Ask Prices	
Bond	Ask Price	Bid Price
1	$101.6563	$101.5938
2	$101.5938	$101.5313
3	$103.7813	$103.7188

103. Suppose you borrow $1000 at 12% annual interest with 60 monthly payments. Assume equal payments are made at the ends of months 1–60. By entering the function =PMT(.01,60,1000) in Excel, you find directly that the monthly payment is $22.24. However, it is instructive to find this from

"first principles"—without the PMT function. Each month you owe an interest payment of 0.01 times the current unpaid balance. The remainder of the monthly payment is used to reduce the unpaid balance. For example, suppose you pay $30 each month. At the beginning of month 1, your unpaid balance is $1000, so $10 of your month 1 payment goes to interest and $20 to paying off the unpaid balance. Then you would begin month 2 with an unpaid balance of $980. Use Solver to determine the monthly payment that will pay off the loan at the end of month 60. (*Hint*: There is no objective to maximize or minimize, but Solver can also be used to solve equations.)

104. Widgetco produces widgets by combining processed elements A and B. At most 15,000 widgets per week can be sold for $20 per widget. Machine 1 processes 5 pounds of A and 6 pounds of B per hour. Machine 1 costs $40,000 to rent and costs $2.50 per hour to operate. Unlimited amounts of unprocessed A and B can be purchased at a cost of $2 per pound for A and $3 per pound for B. Processed A and B can be turned into widgets by using either machine 2 or machine 3. Each machine 2 costs $30,000 per year to rent and costs $3.50 per hour to operate. Each minute that machine 2 is operated, it uses 2 pounds of processed A and 1.5 pounds of processed B to produce a widget. Each machine 3 costs $25,000 per year to rent and $2.20 per hour to operate. Every 1.5 minutes that machine 3 is operated, it uses 1.5 pounds of processed A and 1.4 pounds of processed B to produce a widget. Widgets cannot be stored, so each week the company will produce the same number of widgets and operate machines for the same number of hours. Also, any processed A and B coming out of machine 1 that is not used to produce widgets must be disposed of at a cost of $0.35 per pound. Each machine can be operated up to 40 hours per week. Machines must be rented for the whole year and widgets are sold by the pound, so a fractional number of widgets can be produced each week. The number of machines of each type rented must be an integer. How can Widgetco maximize its weekly (or annual) profit?

Modeling Problems

105. You have been assigned to develop a model that can be used to schedule employees at a local fast-food restaurant. Assume that computer technology has advanced to the point where very large problems can be solved on a PC at the restaurant.

a. What data would you collect as inputs to your model?

b. Describe in words several appropriate objective functions for your model.

c. Describe in words the constraints needed for your model.

106. You have been assigned to develop a model that can be used to schedule the nurses working in a maternity ward.

a. What data would you collect as inputs to your model?

b. Describe in words several appropriate objective functions for your model.

c. Describe in words the constraints needed for your model.

107. Keefer Paper produces recycled paper from paper purchased from local offices and universities. The company sells three grades of paper: high-brightness paper, medium-brightness paper, and low-brightness paper. The high-brightness paper must have a brightness level of at least 90, the medium-brightness paper must have a brightness level of between 80 and 90, and the low-brightness paper must have a brightness level no greater than 80. Discuss how Keefer might use a blending model to maximize its profit.

108. In this chapter we give you the cost of producing a product and other inputs that are used in the analysis. Do you think that it is easy for most companies to determine the cost of producing a product? What difficulties might arise?

109. Discuss how the aggregate planning model could be extended to handle a company that produces several products on several types of machines. What information would you need to model this type of problem?

110. Explain how FunToys (in Example 4.6) could use a rolling planning horizon to implement its borrowing strategy.

111. A banking firm has many branch banks located throughout the state. You have been asked to determine which of these are operating inefficiently and why.

a. What information would you collect and how would you use it?

b. Would you have any reservations about using DEA in this situation?

112. A large CPA firm currently has 100 junior staff members and 20 partners. In the long run—say, 20 years from now—the firm would like to consist of 130 junior staff members and 20 partners. During a given year, 10% of all partners and 30% of all junior staff members leave the firm. The firm can control the number of hires each year and the fraction of junior employees who are promoted to partner each year. Can you develop a personnel strategy that would meet the CPA firm's goals?

113. Bed T. Rock owns a small company that produces three grades of rocks at two quarries. Five major customers purchase the different grades of rocks. How could you use linear programming to help Bed T. Rock schedule his monthly production?

114. Ann and Ben are getting divorced, and they want to determine how to divide up their joint property: retirement account, home, summer cottage, investments, and miscellaneous assets. To determine how much value they place on these assets, Ann and Ben are asked to allocate 100 total points to the assets. Their allocations appear in Table 4.69. Assuming that all assets are divisible (that is, a fraction of each asset can be given to each person), how should the assets be allocated? Two criteria appear reasonable:

- Each person should end up with the same number of points. This prevents Ann from envying Ben and vice versa.

- The total number of points received by Ann and Ben should be maximized.

If one or more of the assets could *not* be split between the two people, how would you modify your solution?

TABLE 4.69	**Allocation Preferences**	
Item	**Ann's Points**	**Ben's Points**
Retirement account	50	40
Home	20	30
Summer cottage	15	10
Investments	10	10
Miscellaneous	5	10

Lakefield Corporation's Oil Trading Desk

Lakefield Corporation's oil trading desk buys and sells oil products (crude oil and refined fuels), options, and futures in international markets. The trading desk is responsible for buying raw material for Lakefield's refining and blending operations and for selling final products. In addition to trading for the company's operations, the desk also takes speculative positions. In speculative trades, the desk attempts to profit from its knowledge and information about conditions in the global oil markets.

One of the traders, Lisa Davies, is responsible for transactions in the cash market (as opposed to the futures or options markets). Lisa has been trading for several years and has seen the prices of oil-related products fluctuate tremendously. Figure 4.36 shows the prices of heating oil #2 and unleaded gasoline from January 1986 through July 1992. While excessive volatility of oil prices is undesirable for most businesses, Lakefield's oil trading desk often makes substantial profits in periods of high volatility.

The prices of various oil products tend to move together over long periods of time. Since finished oil products are refined from crude oil, the prices of all finished products will tend to rise if the price of crude increases. Because finished oil products are not perfect substitutes, the prices of individual products do not move in lockstep. Indeed, over short time periods, the price movements of two products can have a low correlation. For example, in late 1989 and early 1990, there was a severe cold wave in the northeastern United States. The price of heating oil rose from $0.60 per gallon to over $1 per gallon. In the same time period, the price of gasoline rose just over $0.10 per gallon.

Lisa Davies believes that some mathematical analysis might be helpful to spot trading opportunities in the cash markets. The next section provides background about a few important characteristics of fuel oils. The properties of blended fuels and some implications for pricing are then discussed.

FIGURE 4.36
Price of Heating Oil #2 and Unleaded Gasoline

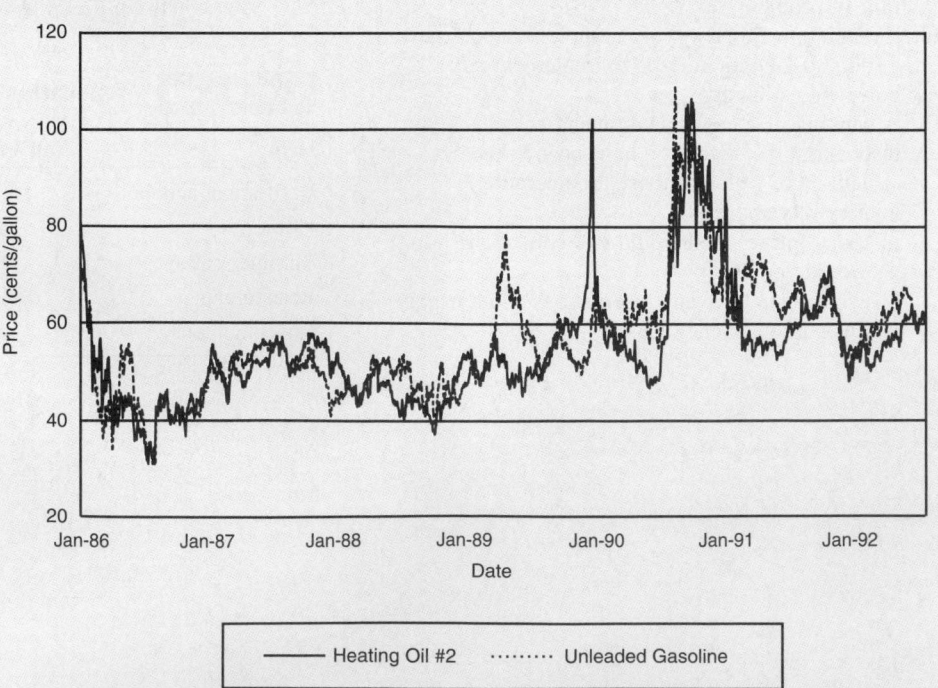

Characteristics of Hydrocarbon Fuels

The many varieties of hydrocarbon fuels include heating oil, kerosene, gasoline, and diesel oil. Each type of fuel has many characteristics, e.g., heat content, viscosity, freeze point, luminosity, volatility (speed of vaporization), and so on. The relative importance of each characteristic depends on the intended use of the fuel. For example, octane rating is one of the most important characteristics of gasoline. Octane is a measure of resistance to ignition under pressure. An engine burning low-octane fuel is susceptible to "engine knock," which reduces its power output. Surprisingly, octane rating is more important than heat content for gasoline. In contrast, the most important characteristic of kerosene jet fuel is its heat content, but viscosity is also important. High viscosity fuels do not flow as smoothly through fuel lines.

For the types of fuels Lisa Davies usually trades, the most important characteristics are density, viscosity, sulfur content, and flash point, which will be described below. When trading and blending other fuels, characteristics besides these four are important to consider.

Density The density of a substance is its mass per unit volume (e.g., grams per cubic centimeter). The density of water is 1 g/cc. A related measure is American Petroleum Institute gravity (API), which is measured in degrees. API is related to density by

$$\text{API} = \frac{141.5}{D} - 131.5$$

where D is density measured in g/cc. Water has an API of 10°. Note that density and API are *inversely* related.

The specifications for kerosene jet fuel are nearly identical for all civilian airlines worldwide. Kerosene jet fuel should have an API gravity between 37° and 51°. Diesel fuel and heating oil are required to have an API not less than 30°. API is important for controlling the flow of fuel in a combustion engine. It can also be used to limit the concentration of heavy hydrocarbon compounds in the fuel.

Viscosity Viscosity refers to the resistance of a liquid to flow. A highly viscous liquid, such as ketchup or molasses, does not pour easily. Viscosity is measured by the amount of time a specified volume of liquid takes to flow through a tube of a certain

diameter. It is commonly measured in units of centistokes (hundredths of stokes). Most fuel specifications place upper limits on viscosity. Less viscous fuel flows easily through lines and atomizes easily for efficient combustion. More viscous fuels must be heated initially to reduce viscosity.

Sulfur Content The content of sulfur is measured in percentage of total sulfur by weight. For example, a fuel with 2% sulfur content has 2 grams of sulfur for every 100 grams of fuel. Sulfur causes corrosion and abrasion of metal surfaces. Low sulfur content is important for maintaining the proper operation of equipment.

Flash Point The flash point of a substance is the lowest temperature at which the substance ignites when exposed to a flame. The product description of kerosene jet fuel from the American Society for Testing and Materials specifies a flash point of at least 100°F. The New York Mercantile Exchange futures contract for heating oil #2 specifies a flash point of at least 130°F. Flash-point restrictions are often prescribed for safety reasons.

Table 4.70 (page 186) gives a description of some fuels and their prices on a given day. In Table 4.70 the units of viscosity are centistokes, sulfur is given in percentage by weight, and flash point is in degrees Fahrenheit. For convenience, all prices in Table 4.70 are given in dollars per barrel. In practice, the prices of heating oil, gasoline, and kerosene jet fuel are typically quoted in cents per gallon. (There are 42 gallons in a barrel.)

Blending Fuels

Since hydrocarbon fuels are made of similar compounds and have similar characteristics, there is a certain degree of substitutability among fuels. Different fuels can also be blended to form a new fuel. Next we describe how the characteristics of the individual fuels combine in the blended fuel.

Sulfur combines linearly by weight. This means, for example, that mixing equal weights of a 1% sulfur oil with a 3% sulfur oil produces a 2% sulfur oil. To a close approximation, sulfur combines linearly by volume (because the densities of oils are not very different). That is, combining 0.5 barrel of 1% sulfur oil with 0.5 barrel of 3% sulfur oil gives 1 barrel of very nearly 2% sulfur oil.

TABLE 4.70	**Description of Available Fuels**					
	Fuel 1 **1% Sulfur** **Fuel Oil**	**Fuel 2** **3% Sulfur** **Fuel Oil**	**Fuel 3** **0.7% Sulfur** **Fuel Oil**	**Fuel 4** **Heating** **Oil**	**Fuel 5** **1% Vacuum** **Gas Oil**	**Fuel 6** **2% Vacuum** **Gas Oil**
API	10.50	10.50	10.50	34.00	25.00	25.00
Viscosity	477.00	477.00	477.00	3.50	25.00	25.00
Sulfur	1.00	3.00	0.70	0.20	1.00	2.00
Flash point	140.00	140.00	140.00	130.00	200.00	200.00
Price	16.08	13.25	17.33	24.10	20.83	20.10
	Fuel 7 **0.5% Vacuum** **Gas Oil**	**Fuel 8** **Straight Run** **(Low Sulfur)**	**Fuel 9** **Straight Run** **(High Sulfur)**	**Fuel 10** **Kerosene** **Jet Fuel**	**Fuel 11** **Diesel** **Fuel**	**Fuel 12** **Slurry**
API	25.00	21.00	17.00	46.000	35.00	−4.50
Viscosity	25.00	212.00	212.00	1.500	2.50	261.00
Sulfur	0.50	0.30	2.75	0.125	0.20	2.37
Flash point	200.00	250.00	250.00	123.000	150.00	109.00
Price	21.46	21.00	20.00	25.520	24.30	11.50

In general, to say that a certain property of oil combines linearly (by volume) means the following: Suppose x_j barrels of oil j (for $j = 1, 2, \ldots, n$) are blended together to form one barrel of oil. That is, $\sum_{j=1}^{n} x_j = 1$. Also suppose that c_j is the measure of the property of oil j. Then if the property combines linearly, the measure of the property for the blended oil is a linear combination of the c_j's, that is, $\sum_{j=1}^{n} c_j x_j$.

API gravity does not combine linearly, but density does combine linearly. For example, consider blending 0.5 barrel of oil that has a density of 0.8 g/cc with 0.5 barrel of oil with a density of 1.2 g/cc. The resulting barrel of oil has a density of 1.0 (= 0.8[0.5] + 1.2[0.5]). The 0.8 g/cc density oil has an API of 45.38° and the 1.2 g/cc density oil has an API of −13.58°. If API combined linearly, the blended barrel of oil would have an API of 15.90° (= 45.38°[0.5] − 13.58°[0.5]). However, an API of 15.90° corresponds to a density of 0.96 g/cc, not 1.0 g/cc.[2]

Viscosity, measured in centistokes, does not combine linearly. However, chemical engineers have determined that viscosity can be transformed to another measure, called linear viscosity, that (nearly) combines linearly.[3] Similarly, flash points measured in degrees Fahrenheit do not combine linearly. But chemical engineers defined a new measure, termed linear flash point, that does combine linearly.[4] Table 4.71 summarizes the properties of the twelve fuels measured in units that combine linearly.

Implications for Pricing

Sulfur in oil is a contaminant. Therefore, oil with a low sulfur content is more valuable than oil with a higher sulfur content, all other characteristics being equal. This relationship can be seen in Table 4.70 by comparing the prices of fuels 1, 2, and 3 and fuels

---

[3] Let vs represent viscosity measured in centistokes. Then linear viscosity, denoted v, is defined $v = \ln(\ln[vs + 0.08])$.
[4] Let fp denote flash point measured in degrees Fahrenheit. Then linear flash point is defined $f = 10^{42}(fp + 460)^{-14.286}$. Empirical analysis of oil blending data confirms that the measure f combines nearly linearly.

---

[2] To convert API to density use $D = 141.5/(API + 131.5)$.

TABLE 4.71 **Properties of Available Fuels Measured in Units That Combine Linearly**

	Fuel 1 1% Sulfur Fuel Oil	Fuel 2 3% Sulfur Fuel Oil	Fuel 3 0.7% Sulfur Fuel Oil	Fuel 4 Heating Oil	Fuel 5 1% Vacuum Gas Oil	Fuel 6 2% Vacuum Gas Oil
Density	0.996	0.996	0.996	0.855	0.904	0.904
Linear visc.	1.819	1.819	1.819	0.243	1.170	1.170
Sulfur	1.000	3.000	0.700	0.200	1.000	2.000
Linear flash	204.800	204.800	204.800	260.400	52.500	52.500
Price	16.080	13.250	17.330	24.100	20.830	20.100

	Fuel 7 0.5% Vacuum Gas Oil	Fuel 8 Straight Run (Low Sulfur)	Fuel 9 Straight Run (High Sulfur)	Fuel 10 Kerosene Jet Fuel	Fuel 11 Diesel Fuel	Fuel 12 Slurry
Density	0.904	0.928	0.953	0.797	0.850	1.114
Linear visc.	1.170	1.678	1.678	−.782	−.054	1.716
Sulfur	0.500	0.300	2.750	0.125	0.200	2.370
Linear flash	52.500	18.500	18.500	308.800	161.700	437.000
Price	21.460	21.000	20.000	25.520	24.300	11.500

5, 6, and 7. Lower-density oils are generally preferred to higher-density oils, because energy per unit mass is higher for low-density fuels, which reduces the weight of the fuel. Lower-viscosity oils are preferred because they flow more easily through fuel lines than oils with higher viscosities. High flash points are preferred for safety reasons. However, since flash point and linear flash point are inversely related, this means that oils with lower linear flash point are preferred to oils with higher linear flash point.

That fuels can be blended cheaply to form new fuels affects price as well. For example, fuel 2 and fuel 3 from Table 4.70 can be blended to form a fuel with the same API, viscosity, sulfur, and flash point as fuel 1. In particular, 0.1304 barrel of fuel 2 and 0.8696 barrel of fuel 3 can be blended to form 1 barrel of a new fuel, which, in terms of the four main characteristics, is identical to fuel 1. Since the cost of blending is quite small, prices combine nearly linearly. The cost to create the blended fuel is $16.80 per barrel ($16.80 = 0.1304[13.25] + 0.8696[17.33]). If the price of fuel 1 were greater than $16.80, say $17.10, Lisa Davies could create an arbitrage. She could buy fuels 2 and 3 in the appropriate proportions, Lakefield Corporation could blend them together, and Lisa could sell the blend at the price of fuel 1. The profit would be $0.30 per barrel minus any blending and transaction costs. However, the actual price of fuel 1 is $16.08, so this plan does not represent an arbitrage opportunity.

The *no-arbitrage pricing principle* is simply a generalization of the previous example. No arbitrage means that the price of any fuel must be less than or equal to the cost of any blend of fuels of equal or better quality. As mentioned above, better means larger API, lower viscosity, lower sulfur content, and higher flash point. In terms of linear properties, better means lower density, lower linear viscosity, lower sulfur content, and lower linear flash point. Any number of fuels (not just two) can be blended together.

Lisa Davies would like to develop a system that automatically checks the no-arbitrage pricing condition for all of the fuels. If the condition is violated, she would like to know the appropriate amounts of the fuels to buy to create the arbitrage, the profit per barrel of the blended fuel, and the characteristics of the blended fuel.

Questions

1. Suppose that 0.3 barrel of fuel 2, 0.3 barrel of fuel 3, and 0.4 barrel of fuel 4 are blended together. What is the cost of the blended fuel? What are the (linear) properties of the blended

fuel (i.e., density, linear viscosity, sulfur content, and linear flash point)?

2. Using the data from Table 4.71, check whether any of the fuels violate the no-arbitrage pricing condition. If no fuel violates the condition, which fuel's price comes the closest to the no-arbitrage upper bound? If there is a violation, give the explicit recipe.

3. What modifications would you make to the analysis to account for blending costs?

4. What would be the important issues or steps involved in creating a real system for this problem?

Foreign Currency Trading

Daily trading volume in the foreign exchange markets often exceeds $1 trillion. Participants trade in the spot currency markets, forward markets, and futures markets. In addition, currency options, currency swaps, and other derivative contracts are traded. For simplicity, we focus on the spot currency market only.

A spot currency transaction is simply an agreement to buy some amount of one currency using another currency.[5] For example, a British company might need to pay a Japanese supplier 150 million yen. Suppose that the spot yen/pound rate is 154.7733. Then the British company could use the spot currency market to buy 150 million yen at a cost of 969,159.41 (= 150,000,000/154.7733) British pounds. A sample of today's cross-currency spot rates is given in Table 4.72.

To continue the example, suppose the company canceled the order from the supplier and wanted to convert the 150 million yen back into British pounds. From Table 4.72 the pound/yen spot rate is 0.00645. So the company could use the 150 million yen to buy 967,500 (= 150,000,000 × 0.00645) pounds. Notice that the 967,500 pounds is less than the original 969,159.41 pounds. The difference is the result

of the bid-offer spread: The price to buy yen (the bid price) is greater than the price to sell yen (the offer price). The bid-offer spread represents a transaction cost to the company.

Occasionally market prices may become "out of line" in the sense that there are arbitrage opportunities. In this context, arbitrage means that there is a set of spot currency transactions that creates positive wealth but does not require any funds to initiate, i.e., it is a "money pump." When such pure arbitrage opportunities exist, supply and demand forces will generally move prices to eliminate the opportunities. Hence, it is desirable to be able to quickly identify arbitrage opportunities when they do exist and to take advantage of them to the greatest extent possible.

Questions

1. Formulate a decision model to determine whether there are any arbitrage opportunities with the spot currency rates given in Table 4.72. Note that an arbitrage opportunity could involve several currencies. If there is an arbitrage opportunity, your model should specify the exact set of transactions to achieve it.

2. Find the cross-currency rates in a recent paper— for example, in the *Wall Street Journal*. (Note that the meaning of the entries could be the opposite of that in Table 4.72.) Check the numbers for an arbitrage opportunity. If you find one, do you think it represents a real arbitrage opportunity? Why or why not?

[5]A spot transaction agreed to today is *settled* (i.e., the money changes hands) two business days from today. By contrast, a three-month forward transaction agreed to today is settled (approximately) three months from today.

TABLE 4.72	**Cross-Currency Spot Rates**				
		To			
		US Dollar	Pound	FFranc	DMark	Yen
From	US Dollar	—	0.63900	5.37120	1.57120	98.8901
	Pound	1.56480	—	8.43040	2.45900	154.7733
	FFranc	0.18560	0.11860	—	0.29210	18.4122
	DMark	0.63610	0.40630	3.42330	—	62.9400
	Yen	0.01011	0.00645	0.05431	0.01588	—

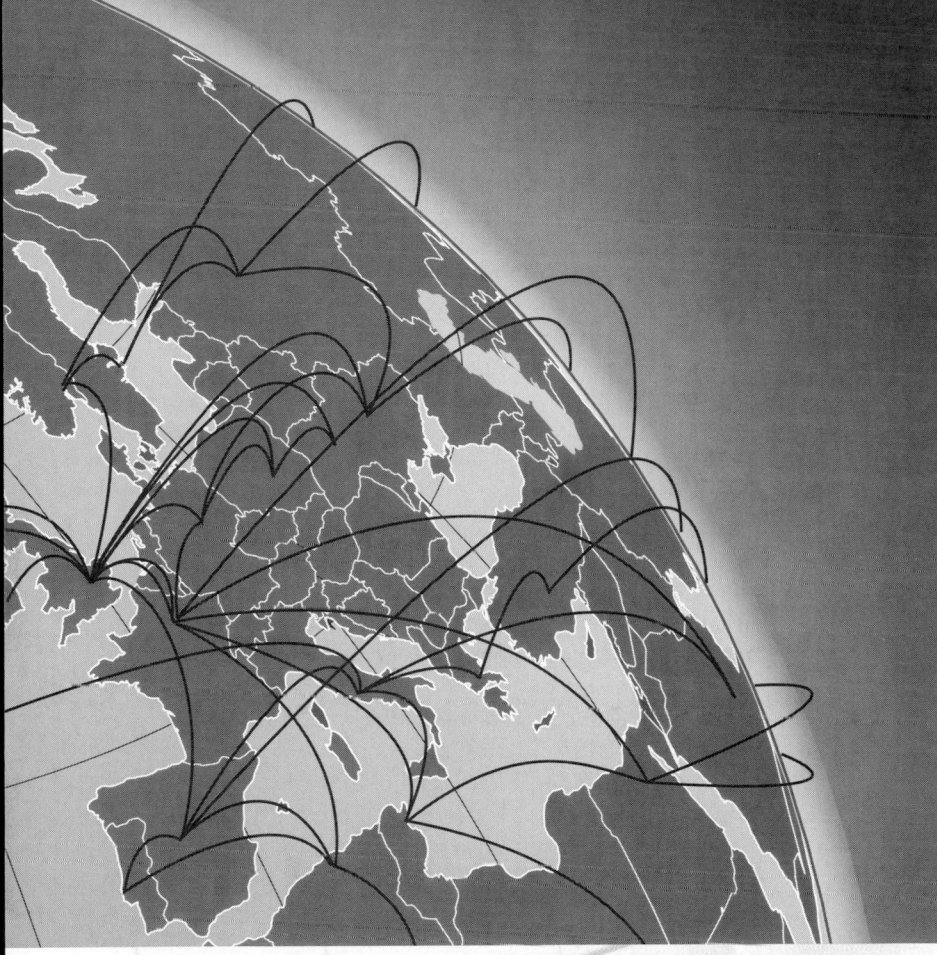

Network Models

DEC GLOBAL SUPPLY CHAIN MANAGEMENT

Many of the models in this chapter can be characterized as **logistics problems**—that is, problems of finding the least expensive way to transport products from their origin to their destination. In addition, real logistics problems are often coupled with manufacturing or plant location decisions; a company must decide where to locate its manufacturing plants and what products to produce at each plant. Computer manufacturer Digital Equipment Corporation (DEC) faced such a problem, as reported by Arntzen et al. (1995) in "Global Supply Chain Management at Digital Equipment Corporation." DEC faces a huge global manufacturing and distribution problem with its wide range of products (mainframe computers, minicomputers, PCs, and many types of computer parts and peripherals). It must decide where (or whether) to manufacture these products and how to get them to its customers around the world in the most economical manner.

Until the late 1980s DEC specialized primarily in mainframes and minicomputers, using a manufacturing and distribution system that had proved very successful for over 20 years. But as PCs revolutionized the industry, DEC realized that it had to change—quickly and radically—if it wanted to remain a thriving company. It had too many plants and too much overhead, and too many groups within DEC were making decisions without central coordination. In 1989 the company began to redesign its supply and delivery network and to reengineer its manufacturing and logistics processes. A key step in these corporate changes was the development of the Global Supply Chain Model (GSCM), an extremely complex linear programming model.[1] Since that time, DEC has used GSCM to perform thousands of optimizations in scores of studies.

The typical models run with GSCM are huge. They generally contain from 2000 to 6000 constraints and from 5000 to 20,000 decision variables. (They are *not* suitable for spreadsheets!) The objective typically minimizes total cost, where total cost includes production costs, inventory holding costs, facility material handling costs, taxes, facility fixed charges, production line fixed costs, transportation costs, and duty costs.

The constraints include customer demand requirements, "balance" constraints for production and inventory, limits on the weight of products through the facilities, production capacities, storage capacities, and others. Also, the models become even more complicated because of multiple products, multiple time periods (planning for four consecutive quarters, for example), and the complexities of international trade. Nevertheless, by taking advantage of the special structure of these models and the advanced software that is now available, DEC is able to solve these models routinely.

To illustrate, DEC ran a large study during 1992 to determine the optimal supply chain design for all of DEC's manufacturing. The study recommended an 18-month plan to restructure the manufacturing infrastructure completely to cut costs. Specifically, it recommended that the number of worldwide plants be reduced from 33 to 12, it called for the three basic customer regions (Pacific Rim, Americas, and Europe) to be served primarily by plants within their own regions, and it included a quarter-by-quarter implementation plan. This 18-month plan has since been implemented. By spring 1994 it led to a decrease of $167 million in manufacturing costs (with another $160 million by June 1995) and a decrease of over $200 million in logistics costs. This is quite impressive considering that the number of units manufactured and shipped increased dramatically during this same time period. ∎

5.1 INTRODUCTION

Many important optimization models have a natural graphical network representation. In this chapter we will consider several specific examples of network models. These include the transportation model, the maximum flow model, the shortest route model, and others. All of these models are special cases of the **minimum cost network flow model** (MCNFM), which we will also discuss. There are several reasons for distinguishing network models from other LP models. First, many companies have real problems, often extremely large problems, that can be formulated as network models. For example, Delta Airlines has recently developed a network model to schedule its entire fleet of passenger airplanes. Second, the network structure of these models allows us to represent them graphically in a way that is intuitive to users. We can then use this graphical representation as an aid in

---

[1]The GSCM is actually more than an LP model; it is a mixed-integer model with 0–1 (binary) variables for the plant location decisions. We will study problems with binary variables in the next chapter.

the spreadsheet model formulation. Finally, specialized solution techniques have been developed specifically for network models. Although we will not discuss the details of these solution techniques, they are extremely important because they allow companies to solve huge problems that could not be solved by the usual LP algorithms.

5.2 TRANSPORTATION MODELS

In many situations a company produces products at locations called **supply points** and ships these products to customer locations called **demand points**. Typically, each supply point has a limited amount that it can ship, and each customer must receive a required quantity of the product. Spreadsheet solvers can be used to determine the minimum-cost shipping method for satisfying customer demands.

A Shipping Model

For now we assume that the only possible shipments are those directly from a supply point to a demand point. That is, no shipments between supply points or between demand points are possible. This problem has been studied extensively by management scientists. In fact, it was one of the first management science models developed, over a half century ago. It is generally called the **transportation model**.

EXAMPLE 5.1

SUPPLYING POWER AT MIDWEST ELECTRIC

Midwest Electric has three electric power plants that supply the power needs of four cities. Each power plant can supply the amounts shown in Table 5.1 (in millions of kilowatt-hours of electricity). The peak power demand (again in millions of kwh) at each city is given in Table 5.2. Finally, the cost (in dollars) of sending a million kwh from each plant to each city is given in Table 5.3. Midwest Electric wants to find the lowest-cost method for meeting the demand of the four cities.

TABLE 5.1 Plant Supplies in Midwest Electric Example

	Supply
Plant 1	35
Plant 2	50
Plant 3	40

TABLE 5.2 City Requirements for Midwest Electric Example

	Demand
City 1	45
City 2	20
City 3	30
City 4	30

TABLE 5.3 Shipping Costs for Midwest Electric Example

	City 1	City 2	City 3	City 4
Plant 1	8	6	10	9
Plant 2	9	12	13	7
Plant 3	14	9	16	5

Solution

To set up a spreadsheet model for Midwest Electric's problem, we need to keep track of the following:

- the power shipped (in millions of kwh) from each plant to each city
- the total power shipped out of each plant
- the total power received by each city
- the total shipping cost incurred

DEVELOPING THE SPREADSHEET MODEL

The spreadsheet model is shown in Figure 5.1. (See the file TRANSPORT1.XLS.) To develop this model, perform the following steps.

	A	B	C	D	E	F	G	H	I
1	Midwest Electric transportation model								
2									
3	Unit shipping costs						Range names used:		
4			To				UnitCosts: C6:F8		
5			City 1	City 2	City 3	City 4	Shipped: C13:F15		
6	From	Plant 1	$8	$6	$10	$9	ShippedOut: G13:G15		
7		Plant 2	$9	$12	$13	$7	Capacities: I13:I15		
8		Plant 3	$14	$9	$16	$5	ShippedIn: C16:F16		
9							Demands: C18:F18		
10	Shipments						TotalCost: B20		
11			To						
12			City 1	City 2	City 3	City 4	Total shipped		Capacity
13	From	Plant 1	0	10	25	0	35	<=	35
14		Plant 2	45	0	5	0	50	<=	50
15		Plant 3	0	10	0	30	40	<=	40
16		Total received	45	20	30	30			
17			>=	>=	>=	>=			
18		Demand	45	20	30	30			
19									
20	Total cost	$1,020							

FIGURE 5.1 Transportation Model

1 Inputs. Enter the unit shipping costs for each plant to each city in the UnitCosts range, the plant capacities in the Capacities, and the cities' demands in the Demands range.

2 Amounts shipped. Enter *any* trial values for the shipments from each plant to each city in the Shipped range. These are the changing cells.

3 Amounts shipped out of plants. To ensure that a plant does not ship more than its available supply, we need to calculate the amount shipped out of each plant. In cell G13 calculate the amount shipped out of plant 1 with the formula

=SUM(C13:F13)

and copy this formula to the range G14:G15 for the other plants.

4 Amounts received by cities. To ensure that each city receives the needed power, we keep track of the power received by each city. Calculate the power received by city 1 in cell C16 with the formula

=SUM(C13:C15)

and copy this to the range D16:F16 for the other cities.

⑤ Total shipping cost. Calculate the total cost of shipping power from the plants to the cities in the TotalCost cell with the formula

=SUMPRODUCT(UnitCosts,Shipped)

This formula sums all products of unit shipping costs and amounts shipped.

USING SOLVER

Now invoke Solver with the following specifications. The completed Solver dialog box should appear as in Figure 5.2.

FIGURE 5.2
Solver Dialog Box
for Transportation
Model

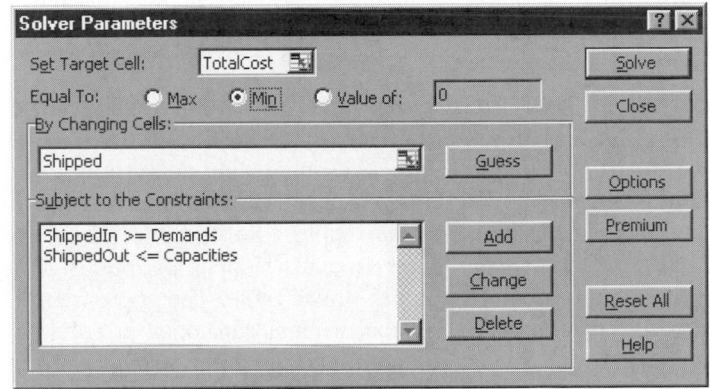

① Objective. Select the TotalCost cell as the objective to minimize.

② Changing cells. Select the Shipped range as the changing cells. These cells correspond to the amounts shipped from each plant to each city.

③ Supply constraints. Add the constraints ShippedOut<=Capacities. These constraints (called **supply constraints**) ensure that no plant ships an amount of power exceeding its capacity.

④ Demand constraints. Add the constraints ShippedIn> =Demands. These constraints (called **demand constraints**) ensure that each city receives enough power.

⑤ Specify nonnegativity and optimize. Under Solver Options, check the nonnegativity box, and use the LP algorithm to obtain the optimal solution shown in Figure 5.1.

The Solver solution is illustrated graphically in Figure 5.3. A minimum cost of $1020 is incurred by using the shipments listed in Figure 5.3. Except for the six routes shown, no other routes are used. Note that all available capacity is used. The reason is that total demand and total capacity are both equal to 125, so that the entire capacity is required to meet demand.

FIGURE 5.3
Graphical
Representation of
Transportation
Model

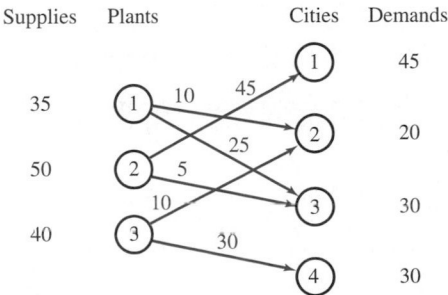

When total demand equals total supply, we call this a **balanced** model. If total capacity is greater than total demand, then some of the capacity will go unused, but the formulation does not need to be changed. On the other hand, if total capacity is less than total demand, we need to change the model, for in this case there is no way to meet total demand—Solver will report "no feasible solution." We need to drop the "greater than or equal to" demand constraints and probably include unit penalty costs for not meeting demand at the various cities. A formulation along these lines appears in Figure 5.4, with the completed Solver dialog box shown in Figure 5.5. Here we treat the unmet demand in row 21 as an extra set of changing cells, we add a constraint that requires the sums (of cells in rows 20 and 21) in row 22 to *equal* demand, and we account for the penalty cost of unmet demand in the total cost. The optimal solution trades off shipping costs with the penalties from unmet demand. In this case, the least-cost solution meets all demand except at city 3.

Sensitivity analysis There are many sensitivity analyses we could perform on the basic transportation model. We could vary one (or two) shipping costs, or we could vary capacities or demands. One interesting analysis is to keep shipping costs and demands constant and allow *all* of the capacities to increase by a certain percentage. This percentage becomes the input to SolverTable. Then we can keep track of the total cost and any particular amounts shipped of interest. The key is to modify the model slightly before running SolverTable. The appropriate modifications appear in Figure 5.6. Now we store the original capacities in column K, we enter a percent increase in the PctIncrease cell, and we enter *formulas* in the Capacities range. For example, the formula in cell I13 is **=K13*(1+PctIncrease)**. Then we run SolverTable with the PctIncrease cell as the single input cell, allowing it to vary from 0% to 50% in increments of 10%, and we keep track of total cost, as well as the shipments out of plant 1. (We could also keep track of other shipments if desired.)

	A	B	C	D	E	F	G	H	I	J
1	Midwest Electric unbalanced transportation model									
2										
3	Unit shipping costs							Range names used:		
4			To					UnitCosts: C6:F8		
5			City 1	City 2	City 3	City 4		UnitPenaltyCosts: C12:F12		
6	From	Plant 1	$8	$6	$10	$9		Shipped: C17:F19		
7		Plant 2	$9	$12	$13	$7		ShippedOut: G17:G19		
8		Plant 3	$14	$9	$16	$5		Capacities: I17:I19		
9								ShippedIn: C20:F20		
10	Penalty costs per unit of unmet demand							UnmetDemand: C21:F21		
11			City 1	City 2	City 3	City 4		ShippedInOrUnmet: C22:F22		
12			$20	$25	$22	$35		Demands: C24:F24		
13								TotalCost: B28		
14	Shipments									
15			To							
16			City 1	City 2	City 3	City 4	Total shipped		Capacity	
17	From	Plant 1	0	20	15	0	35	<=	35	
18		Plant 2	50	0	0	0	50	<=	50	
19		Plant 3	0	5	0	35	40	<=	40	
20		Total received	50	25	15	35				
21		Unmet demand	0	0	20	0				
22		Sum	50	25	35	35				
23			=	=	=	=				
24		Demand	50	25	35	35				
25										
26	Shipping cost	$940								
27	Penalty cost	$440								
28	Total cost	$1,380								

FIGURE 5.4 Transportation Model with Insufficient Capacity

FIGURE 5.5 Solver Dialog Box for Unbalanced Model

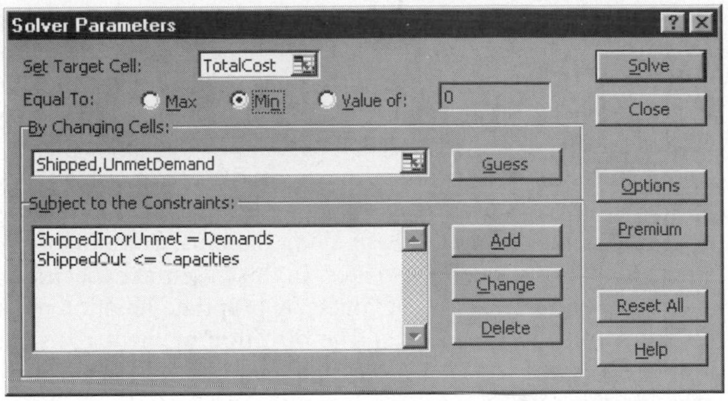

The results are possibly surprising. Because total demand is not changing, the extra capacity does *not* imply that we will ship more units total—there is no incentive to send more than the demands require. However, the increased capacity gives us more flexibility to use lower-cost shipping routes. As we see, the total cost steadily decreases as more capacity is available, and we tend to take more advantage of the routes out of plant 1. This sensitivity analysis demonstrates that even though transportation models are among the simplest of all LP models to formulate, their optimal solutions can have somewhat unintuitive properties.

An alternative formulation The transportation model formulation in Figure 5.1 is a very natural one. If we consider the graphical representation in Figure 5.3, we note that all "flows" go from left to right, from suppliers to demanders. Therefore, the rectangular range of shipments allows us to calculate shipments out of plants as row sums and shipments into cities as column sums. In anticipation of later models in this

	A	B	C	D	E	F	G	H	I	J	K
1	**Midwest Electric transportation model**										
2											
3	**Unit shipping costs**										
4			To								
5			City 1	City 2	City 3	City 4					
6	From	Plant 1	$8	$6	$10	$9					
7		Plant 2	$9	$12	$13	$7					
8		Plant 3	$14	$9	$16	$5					
9											
10	**Shipments**										
11			To								
12			City 1	City 2	City 3	City 4	Total shipped		Capacity		Original capacity
13	From	Plant 1	0	10	25	0	35	<=	38.50		35
14		Plant 2	45	0	5	0	50	<=	55.00		50
15		Plant 3	0	10	0	30	40	<=	44.00		40
16		Total received	45	20	30	30					
17			>=	>=	>=	>=					Percent increase
18		Demand	45	20	30	30					10%
19											
20	**Total cost**	$1,020									
21											
22	**Sensitivity of total cost and amounts shipped out of plant 1 to percent increase**										
23			$B$20	$C$13	$D$13	$E$13	$F$13				
24		0%	$1,020	0	10	25	0				
25		10%	$1,010	0	8.5	30	0				
26		20%	$999	0	12	30	0				
27		30%	$989	0	20	25.5	0				
28		40%	$978	0	20	29	0				
29		50%	$973	2.5	20	30	0				

Range names used:
UnitCosts: C6:F8
Shipped: C13:F15
ShippedOut: G13:G15
Capacities: I13:I15
ShippedIn: C16:F16
Demands: C18:F18
TotalCost: B20
PctIncrease: K18

FIGURE 5.6 Sensitivity to Extra Capacity

chapter, however, where the graphical network can be more complex, we present an alternative formulation of the transportation model. (See the file TRANSPORT2.XLS.)

First, it is useful to introduce some standard network terminology. When we represent a network model graphically, as in Figure 5.3, we generally connect circles with arrows. The circles are called **nodes**. They generally represent cities, warehouses, manufacturing plants, or other locations. The arrows are called **arcs**. They generally represent routes, such as roads, train tracks, or rivers. The numbers on the arcs represent **flows**, the numbers of units sent along the arcs. Sometimes arcs have **capacities**, the upper limits of flows on these arcs. In this case the capacities are often shown on the arcs, along with the flows. Of course, appropriate notation must be used to distinguish the flows from the capacities. The direction of the arrows indicates which way the flows are allowed to travel. An arc pointed into a node is called an **inflow**, whereas an arrow pointed out of a node is called an **outflow**. In the basic transportation model, all outflows originate from suppliers, and all inflows go toward demanders. However, general networks can have both inflows and outflows corresponding to any given node.

With this general structure in mind, the typical network model has one changing cell per arc. It indicates how much (if any) to send along that arc (in the direction of the arrow). Therefore, it is often useful to model network problems by listing all of the arcs and their corresponding flows in one long list. Then we can deal with constraints in a separate section of the spreadsheet. Specifically, for each node in the network there will be a **flow balance constraint.** These flow balance constraints for the basic transportation model are simply the supply and demand constraints we have already discussed, but they can be more general for other network models, as we will discuss in later sections.

The alternative formulation of the Midwest Electric model appears in Figure 5.7. In the range A12:B23, we manually enter the plant and city indices. Each of these corresponds to a given route—that is, an arc in the network. For example, row 19 corresponds to the route from plant 2 to city 4. In column C we enter the unit shipping costs. If they have already been entered in a rectangular range, as in the CostMatrix range, we can easily "transfer" them to the appropriate cells in the UnitCosts range by entering the formula

=INDEX(CostMatrix,A12,B12)

in cell C12 and copying it down. (This INDEX function can be quite useful. It has the general form

$$=INDEX(Range, Row, Column)$$

where *Range* is any rectangular range, and *Row* and *Column* are row and column indices for this range. The INDEX function simply returns the element of the range in the specified row and column.) Then we enter a column of changing cells for the flows in column D.

The flow balance constraints are conceptually straightforward. Each cell in the Outflows and Inflows ranges contains the appropriate sum of changing cells. For example, cell G13 represents the sum of cells D12 through D15, whereas cell G19 represents the sum of cells D12, D16, and D20. But is there an *easy* way to take advantage of copying when entering these formulas?[2] Fortunately, the answer is "yes." We use Excel's built-in SUMIF function, in the form

$$=SUMIF(Range, Criteria, SumRange)$$

---

[2]Try entering these formulas manually, even for a 3×4 transportation model, and you will see why we asked this question!

Midwest Electric transportation model: an alternative formulation

Unit shipping costs

From	Plant	City 1	City 2	City 3	City 4
From	1	$8	$6	$10	$9
	2	$9	$12	$13	$7
	3	$14	$9	$16	$5

Range names used:
CostMatrix - C6:F8
Origins - A12:A23
Dests - B12:B23
UnitCosts - C12:C23
Flows - D12:D23
Outflows - G13:G15
Capacities - I13:I15
Inflows - G19:G22
Demands - I19:I22
TotalCost - B25

Network formulation

Origin	Destination	Unit cost	Flow
1	1	8	0
1	2	6	10
1	3	10	25
1	4	9	0
2	1	9	45
2	2	12	0
2	3	13	5
2	4	7	0
3	1	14	0
3	2	9	10
3	3	16	0
3	4	5	30

Flow balance constraints

Capacity constraints

Plant	Outflow		Capacity
1	35	<=	35
2	50	<=	50
3	40	<=	40

Demand constraints

City	Inflow		Demand
1	45	>=	45
2	20	>=	20
3	30	>=	30
4	30	>=	30

Total Cost $1,020

FIGURE 5.7 Alternative Formulation of the Transportation Model

For example, the formula in cell G13 is

=SUMIF(Origins,F13,Flows)

This compares the plant number in cell F13 to the Origins range in column A and sums all flows where they are equal—that is, it sums all flows out of plant 1. By copying this down, we obtain the flows out of the other plants. For flows into cities, we enter the similar formula

=SUMIF(Dests,F19,Flows)

in cell G19 to sum all flows into city 1, and we copy it down for flows into the other cities. In general, the SUMIF function finds all cells in the first argument that satisfy the criteria in the second argument and then sums the corresponding cells in the third argument—a *very* handy function.

This use of the SUMIF function, along with the list of origins, destinations, unit costs, and flows in columns A–D, is the key to the network formulation. From there on, the model is straightforward. We calculate the total cost as the SUMPRODUCT of UnitCosts and Flows, and we set up the Solver dialog box exactly as before. We will see many similar formulations throughout this chapter. To a certain extent, this makes all network models look alike. There is an additional benefit from this model formulation. Suppose that, for whatever reason, flows from certain plants to certain cities are not allowed. (Maybe no roads exist.) It is not easy to disallow such routes in the original formulation. The usual trick is to allow the "disallowed" routes but impose extremely large unit shipping costs on them. This works, but it is wasteful because it adds changing cells that do not really belong in the model. However, the current formulation simply omits arcs that are not allowed. For example, if the route from plant 2 to city 4 is not allowed, the data in the range A19:D19 are omitted. This creates a model with exactly as many changing cells as allowable arcs. This additional benefit can be very valuable when the number of potential arcs in the network is huge, even though the vast majority of them are disallowed—and this is exactly the situation is most large network models. ■

1. If all the supplies and demands for a transportation problem are integers, then the optimal Solver solution will automatically have integer-valued shipments.

2. Shipping costs are often nonlinear due to quantity discounts. For example, if it costs $3 per item to ship up to 100 items between cities and $2 per item for each additional item, the proportionality assumption of LP is violated and the transportation model we have developed is not valid. Shipping problems that involve quantity discounts are generally quite difficult to solve.

3. Spreadsheet Solvers solve transportation problems by the simplex method. There is a simplified version of the simplex method, called the **transportation simplex method**, that is much more efficient than the ordinary simplex method for transportation problems. Large transportation problems are usually solved with the transportation simplex method or the network simplex method (briefly discussed in the next section). See Winston (1994) for a discussion of the transportation and network simplex methods. ■

ADDITIONAL APPLICATIONS

Allocating Electric Power in Norway

The Midwest Electric example is based on Aarvik and Randolph (1975). Their work was used to allocate electric power in Norway. They solved transportation problems having up to 75 supply and up to 92 demand points. ■

A Dynamic Inventory Model

It is possible to formulate some problems that do not involve shipping goods as transportation models. We illustrate one such example, a dynamic inventory model. (Compare this to the solution of similar inventory models in Sections 3.8 and 4.3.)

EXAMPLE 5.2

MANUFACTURING SAILBOATS AT SAILCO

Sailco manufactures sailboats. During the next 4 months the company must meet (on time) the demand for sailboats listed in Table 5.4. At the beginning of month 1, Sailco has 10 boats in inventory. Each month it must determine how many boats to produce. During any month Sailco can produce up to 40 boats with regular-time labor and an

TABLE 5.4	Demand for Sailco Example
	Demand
Month 1	40
Month 2	60
Month 3	75
Month 4	25

unlimited number of boats with overtime labor. Boats produced with regular-time labor cost $400 to produce, and boats produced with overtime labor cost $450 to produce. It costs $20 to hold a sailboat in inventory at the end of any month. Sailco wants to find a production and inventory schedule that minimizes the cost of meeting the next 4 months' demands on time.

Solution

Although this problem can be solved much like the Pigskin problem in Chapter 3, an alternative is to model it as a transportation problem. The key idea is to define the supply and demand points appropriately. The supply points are the initial inventory, each month's regular time production, and each month's overtime production. The demand points are the demands for each month. A "shipment" from a supply point to a demand point specifies how much of a given type of supply is used to meet a given month's demand. For example, "shipping" 5 units from initial inventory to month 3 demand means that 5 units of the initial inventory are used to meet month 3 demand. We describe the details of this procedure next.

DEVELOPING THE SPREADSHEET MODEL

We set up Sailco's problem as a transportation model (the alternative version, as described earlier) in Figure 5.8 (page 202). (See the file SAILCO.XLS.) The steps are as follows.

❶ **Inputs.** Enter the given inputs in the shaded cells.

❷ **Cost matrix.** It is useful to set up a matrix of unit costs first. To understand the logic, consider meeting a demand of one boat in month 4 from regular-time production in month 2. The production cost is $400, and the boat is held in inventory at the ends of months 2 and 3, for a total holding cost of 2($20) = $40. This explains the $440 unit cost in cell F16. To generate the costs in this matrix quickly, enter 0 in cell C13, enter the formula

=RTUnitCost

in cells C14, D16, E18, and F20, and enter the formula

=OTUnitCost

in cells C15, D17, E19, and F21. Finally, to fill in all of the remaining unit costs, enter the formula

=C15+UnitHoldCost

in cell D15, and copy it to all of the other (nonblank) cells in the CostMatrix range. The reason is that each of these costs is the same as the cost to its left, except that an extra month's holding cost is incurred.

❸ **Origin and destination indices.** Starting in row 25, enter *indices* for the supply and demand points corresponding to each nonblank cell in the CostMatrix range. The supply points are indexed 1 to 9, while the demand points are indexed 1 to 4. For example, the indices 3 and 2 in row 34 correspond to the arc in the network from the third supply point (overtime production in month 1) to the second demand point (demand in month 2).

❹ **Costs on arcs.** To obtain the corresponding costs for these arcs from the Cost-Matrix, enter the formula

Sailco production problem modeled as a transportation model

	A	B	C	D	E	F	G	H	I	J
1	Sailco production problem modeled as a transportation model									
2										
3	**Input data**						Range names used:			
4	Initial inventory	10					InitInv - B4			
5	Regular-time capacity	40					RTCap - B5			
6	Regular-time cost/boat	$400					RTUnitCost - B6			
7	Overtime cost/boat	$450					OTUnitCost - B7			
8	Holding cost/boat/month	$20					UnitHoldCost - B8			
9							CostMatrix - C13:F21			
10	**Unit "shipping" costs**						Origins - A25:A48			
11			To				Dests - B25:B48			
12			Demand, month 1	Demand, month 2	Demand, month 3	Demand, month 4	Costs - C25:C48			
13	**From**	Initial inventory	$0	$20	$40	$60	Flows - D25:D48			
14		RT, month 1	$400	$420	$440	$460	Outflows - H26:H30			
15		OT, month 1	$450	$470	$490	$510	Capacities - J26:J30			
16		RT, month 2		$400	$420	$440	Inflows - H34:H37			
17		OT, month 2		$450	$470	$490	Reqts - J34:J37			
18		RT, month 3			$400	$420	TotCost - B50			
19		OT, month 3			$450	$470				
20		RT, month 4				$400				
21		OT, month 4				$450				
22										
23	**Network formulation**						Flow balance constraints			
24		OriginIndex	DestIndex	Cost	Flow		Capacity constraints			
25		1	1	0	0		Source	OriginIndex	Outflow	Capacity
26		1	2	20	10		Initial inventory	1	10	<=	10
27		1	3	40	0		RT, month 1	2	40	<=	40
28		1	4	60	0		RT, month 2	4	40	<=	40
29		2	1	400	40		RT, month 3	6	40	<=	40
30		2	2	420	0		RT, month 4	8	25	<=	40
31		2	3	440	0					
32		2	4	460	0		Demand constraints			
33		3	1	450	0		Demand	DestIndex	Inflow	Required
34		3	2	470	0		Month 1	1	40	=	40
35		3	3	490	0		Month 2	2	60	=	60
36		3	4	510	0		Month 3	3	75	=	75
37		4	2	400	40		Month 4	4	25	=	25
38		4	3	420	0					
39		4	4	440	0					
40		5	2	450	10					
41		5	3	470	0					
42		5	4	490	0					
43		6	3	400	40					
44		6	4	420	0					
45		7	3	450	35					
46		7	4	470	0					
47		8	4	400	25					
48		9	4	450	0					
49										
50	**Total cost**	$78,450								

FIGURE 5.8 Sailco Transportation Model

=INDEX(CostMatrix,A25,B25)

in cell C25, and copy it down.

❺ **Flows on arcs.** Enter *any* trial values in the Flows range. (Although we call these "flows," they are actually production quantities.)

❻ **Node balance constraints.** There are two types of node balance constraints, capacity and demand. For capacity, we cannot allocate more of the initial inventory than there is, and we cannot use more regular-time capacity than there is. The relevant supply points are 1, 2, 4, 6, and 8, so enter these in the range G26:G30. To get the flows out of these points, enter the formula

=SUMIF(Origins,G26,Flows)

in cell H26, and copy it down. Then enter links to initial inventory and regular-time production to fill the Capacities range. For the demands, we need the inflows to the demand points, so enter the formula

=SUMIF(Dests,G34,Flows)

in cell H34, and copy it down.

7 **Total cost.** Enter the formula

=SUMPRODUCT(Costs,Flows)

to calculate the total of all production and holding costs in the TotCost cell.

Using the Solver The Solver dialog box should be filled in as shown in Figure 5.9. We minimize the total cost, with the flows on the arcs as the changing cells. The constraints are that capacities cannot be exceeded, and demands must be met on time. (The Assume Linear Model and Assume Non-Negative boxes should also be checked.)

FIGURE 5.9
Solver Dialog Box
for Sailco Model

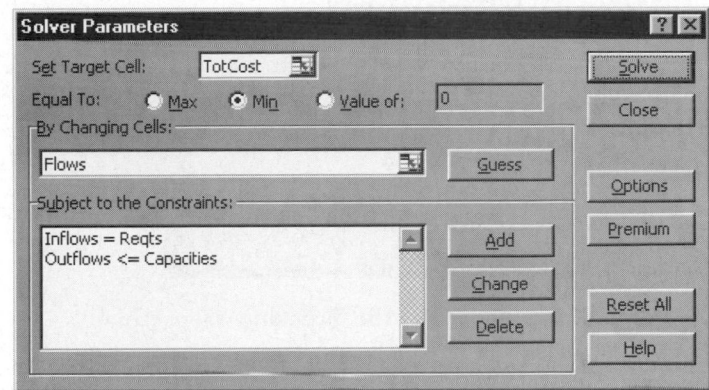

The optimal solution in Figure 5.8 shows that Sailco can meet its demands at a minimum cost of $78,450. By examining the flows column, we see that month 1 demand is met with 40 units of month 1 regular-time production. Month 2 demand is met with 10 units of initial inventory, 40 units of month 2 regular-time production, and 10 units of month 2 overtime production. Month 3 demand is met with 40 units of month 3 regular-time production and 35 units of month 3 overtime production. Month 4 demand is met with 25 units of month 4 regular-time production.[3] This solution is represented graphically in Figure 5.10.

This solution makes intuitive sense. Sailco wishes to avoid expensive holding costs and overtime costs and to take advantage of relatively cheap regular-time production costs whenever possible. This is exactly what this solution allows Sailco to do. Of course, some overtime is required to meet demand.

FIGURE 5.10
Graphical
Representation of
Sailco Solution

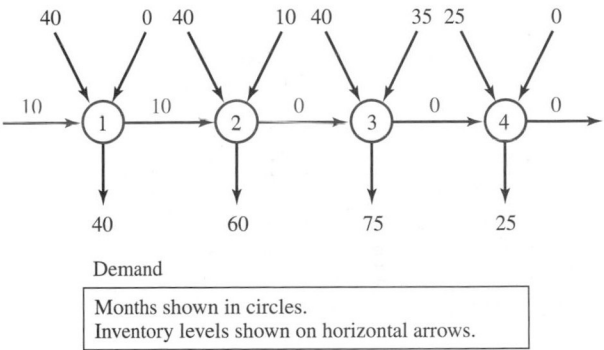

[3]As you can probably tell, there are multiple optimal solutions to this model, and you might obtain one of them. But your total cost should be the same as ours.

Is this "transportation model" of Sailco's problem any better than the more standard way of modeling it, similar to the Pigskin model in Chapter 3? This is for you to decide. We would not argue with the claim that the Pigskin type of formulation is more straightforward and easier to understand. However, an important theme of this chapter is that many real-world (and large) problems that do not *look* like network problems can be *modeled* as such. This provides an alternative way of thinking about these problems, and it often allows us to use a more efficient algorithm to solve them.

MODELING ISSUES

This model can easily be extended to handle backlogged demand, lost sales, and purchasing from a subcontractor—the make or buy decision. See Problem 77 for an example. ■

ADDITIONAL APPLICATIONS

Merging Data Records at the Treasury Department

The U.S. Treasury Department maintains two huge data files: the Current Population Survey and Statistics of Income. The Current Population Survey contains demographic data concerning U.S. families. A typical record in this survey might state that 1000 Jewish families with two children are headed by white males. A typical record in the Statistics of Income file might state that 10,000 families with three members make an income of $22,000 per year. To analyze the effects of changes in government policy, information from both files is needed. This necessitates merging information from the two files. Merging the files necessitates that some information will be lost. Glover and Klingman (1977) devised a transportation model whose solution described how to merge the records and minimize the resulting information loss. See Problem 12 for an example. Using computing power available in 1977, they solved a transportation model with 2500 supply and 2500 demand constraints! ■

PROBLEMS

Skill-Building Problems

1. Transportco supplies goods to three customers, who each require 30 units. The company has two warehouses. In warehouse 1, 40 units are available, and in warehouse 2, 30 units are available. The costs of shipping one unit from each warehouse to each customer are shown in Table 5.5. There is a penalty for each unsatisfied customer unit of demand—with customer 1 a penalty cost of $90 is incurred; with customer 2, $80; and with customer 3, $110.
   a. Determine how to minimize the sum of penalty and shipping costs.
   b. Use SolverTable to see how a change in customer 3's unit penalty cost affects the optimal cost.

TABLE 5.5	Shipping Costs for Transportco Problem		
		To	
From	Customer 1	Customer 2	Customer 3
Warehouse 1	$15	$35	$25
Warehouse 2	$10	$30	$40

   c. Use SolverTable to see how a change in the capacity of warehouse 2 affects the optimal cost.
2. Referring to the previous problem, suppose that Transportco can purchase and ship extra units to either warehouse for a total cost of $100 per unit and

that all customer demand must be met. Determine how to minimize the sum of purchasing and shipping costs.

3. The Wingtip shoe company forecasts the following demands during the next 6 months: month 1, 200; month 2, 260; month 3, 240; month 4, 340; month 5, 190; month 6, 150. It costs $7 to produce a pair of shoes with regular-time labor (RT) and $11 with overtime labor (OT). During each month, regular-time production is limited to 200 pairs of shoes, and overtime production is limited to 100 pairs. It costs $1 per month to hold a pair of shoes in inventory. Determine how Wingtip can minimize the total cost of meeting the next 6 months' demand on time.

4. Steelco manufactures three types of steel at different plants. The time required to manufacture one ton of steel (regardless of type) and the costs at each plant are shown in Table 5.6. Each week, 100 tons of each type of steel (1, 2, and 3) must be produced. Each plant is open 40 hours per week. Determine how to minimize the cost of meeting Steelco's weekly requirements.

TABLE 5.6 **Times and Costs for Steelco Problem**

| | Cost | | | Time |
	Steel 1	Steel 2	Steel 3	(minutes)
Plant 1	$60	$40	$28	20
Plant 2	$50	$30	$30	16
Plant 3	$43	$20	$20	15

5. In the previous problem suppose that the time required to produce one ton of steel depends on the type of steel as well as on the plant at which it is produced. (See Table 5.7.) Can a transportation problem still be formulated?

TABLE 5.7 **Plant-Dependent Times for Steelco Problem**

| | Time (minutes) | | |
	Steel 1	Steel 2	Steel 3
Plant 1	15	12	15
Plant 2	15	15	20
Plant 3	10	10	15

6. A hospital needs to purchase 3 gallons of a perishable medicine for use during the current month and 4 gallons for use during the next month. Because the medicine is perishable, it can be used only during the

month of purchase. Two companies (Daisy and Laroach) sell the medicine, which is in short supply. Thus, during the next 2 months the hospital is limited to buying at most 5 gallons from each company. The companies charge the prices shown in Table 5.8. Determine how to minimize the cost of purchasing the needed medicine.

TABLE 5.8 **Prices for Hospital Problem**

| | Price/Gallon | |
	Current Month	Next Month
Daisy	$800	$720
Laroach	$710	$750

7. Bankco has two check processing sites. Site 1 can process 10,000 checks per day, and site 2 can process 6000 checks per day. The bank processes three types of checks: vendor, salary, and personal. The processing cost per check depends on the site, as listed in Table 5.9. Each day 5000 checks of each type must be processed. Determine how to minimize the daily cost of processing checks.

TABLE 5.9 **Processing Costs for Bankco Problem**

Check Type	Site 1	Site 2
Vendor	$0.05	$0.03
Salary	$0.04	$0.04
Personal	$0.02	$0.05

8. The government is auctioning off oil leases at two sites: 1 and 2. At each site 100,000 acres of land are to be auctioned. Cliff Ewing, Blake Barnes, and Alexis Pickens are bidding for the oil. Government rules state that no bidder can receive more than 40% of the land being auctioned. Cliff has bid $1000 per acre for site 1 land and $2000 per acre for site 2 land. Blake has bid $900 per acre for site 1 land and $2200 per acre for site 2 land. Alexis has bid $1100 per acre for site 1 land and $1900 per acre for site 2 land.
   a. Determine how to maximize the government's revenue.
   b. Use SolverTable to see how changes in the government's rule on 40% of all land being auctioned affect the optimal revenue. Why can the optimal revenue not decrease if this percentage required increases? Why can the optimal revenue not increase if this percentage required decreases?

9. The Amorco Oil Company controls two oil fields. Field 1 can produce up to 40 million barrels of oil per day, and field 2 can produce up to 50 million barrels of oil per day. At field 1 it costs $3 to extract and refine a barrel of oil; at field 2 the cost is $2. Amorco sells oil to two countries: United Kingdom and Japan. The shipping costs per barrel are shown in Table 5.10. Each day the United Kingdom is willing to buy up to 40 million barrels (at $6 per barrel), and Japan is willing to buy up to 30 million barrels (at $6.50 per barrel). Determine how to maximize Amorco's profit.

TABLE 5.10 — **Shipping Costs for Amorco Oil Problem**

From	U.K.	Japan
Field 1	$1	$2
Field 2	$2	$1

To

10. Touche Young has three auditors. Each can work up to 160 hours during the next month, during which time three projects must be completed. Project 1 takes 130 hours, project 2 takes 140 hours, and project 3 takes 160 hours. The amount per hour that can be billed for assigning each auditor to each project is given in Table 5.11. Determine how to maximize total billings during the next month.

TABLE 5.11 — **Billing Costs for Auditing Problem**

	Project 1	Project 2	Project 3
Auditor 1	$120	$150	$190
Auditor 2	$140	$130	$120
Auditor 3	$160	$140	$150

Skill-Extending Problems

11. Based on Glassey and Gupta (1978). Paperco recycles newsprint, uncoated paper, and coated paper into recycled newsprint, recycled uncoated paper, and recycled coated paper. Recycled newsprint can be produced by processing newsprint or uncoated paper. Recycled coated paper can be produced by recycling any type of paper. Recycled uncoated paper can be produced by processing uncoated paper or coated paper. The process used to produce recycled newsprint removes 20% of the input's pulp, leaving 80% of the input's pulp for recycled paper. The process used to produce recycled coated paper removes 10% of the input's pulp. The process used to produce recycled uncoated paper removes 15% of the input's pulp. The purchasing costs, processing costs, and availability of each type of paper are shown in Table 5.12. To meet demand, Paperco must produce at least 250 tons of recycled newsprint pulp, at least 300 tons of recycled uncoated paper pulp, and at least 150 tons of recycled coated paper pulp. Determine how to minimize the cost of meeting Paperco's demands.

12. Based on Glover and Klingman (1977). The government has many computer files that must be merged frequently. For example, consider the Survey of Current Income (SCI) and the Consumer Price Service (CPS) files, which keep track of family income and family size. The breakdown of records in each file is given in Table 5.13. SCI and CPS files contain other pieces of data, but the only variables common to the two files are income and family size. Suppose that the SCI and CPS files must be merged to create a file that will be used for an important analysis of government policy. How should the files be merged? We would like to lose as little information as possible in merging the records. For example, merging an SCI record for a family with income $25,000 and family size 2 with a CPS record for a family with income $26,000 and family size 2 results in a smaller loss of information than if an SCI record for a family with income $25,000 and family size 2 is merged with a CPS record for a family with income $29,000 and family size 3. Let the "cost" of merging an SCI record with a CPS record be

$$|I_{SCI} - I_{CPS}| + |FS_{SCI} - FS_{CPS}|$$

where I_{SCI} and I_{CPS} are the incomes from the SCI and CPS records, and FS_{SCI} and FS_{CPS} are the family sizes. Determine the least expensive way to merge the SCI and CPS records.

13. Bloomington has two hospitals. Hospital 1 has four ambulances, and hospital 2 has two ambulances. Ambulance service is deemed adequate if there is only a 10% chance that no ambulance will be available when an ambulance call is received by a hospital. The average length of an ambulance service call is 20 minutes. Given this information, queueing theory tells us that hospital 1 can be assigned up to 4.9 calls per hour and that hospital 2 can be assigned up to 1.5 calls per hour. Bloomington has been divided into 12 districts. The average number of calls per hour emanating from each district is given in Table 5.14. This table also shows the travel time (in minutes) needed to travel from each district to each hospital. The objective is to minimize the average travel time needed to respond to a call. Determine the proper assignment of districts to hospitals. (*Hint:* Be careful about defining the supply points!)

TABLE 5.12 Data for Paperco Problem

	Purchase Cost per Ton of Pulp	Processing Cost per Ton of Input	Availability (tons)
Newsprint	$10		500
Coated paper	$9		300
Uncoated paper	$8		200
NP used for RNP		$3	
NP used for RCP		$4	
UCP used for RNP		$4	
UCP used for RUP		$1	
UCP used for RCP		$6	
CP used for RUP		$5	
CP used for RCP		$3	

TABLE 5.13 Data for Computer Files Problem

File	Income	Family Size	Number of Records
SCI	$20,000	4	10,000
SCI	$24,000	3	6,000
SCI	$25,000	2	8,000
CPS	$26,000	2	3,000
CPS	$27,000	1	5,000
CPS	$29,000	3	4,000
CPS	$22,000	2	12,000

TABLE 5.14 Data for Ambulance Problem

	Calls/Hour	Time to Hospital 1	Time to Hospital 2
District 1	0.5	5	8
District 2	0.6	6	9
District 3	0.4	7	10
District 4	0.3	5	7
District 5	0.4	6	8
District 6	0.6	7	9
District 7	0.7	9	5
District 8	0.9	10	6
District 9	1.0	11	7
District 10	0.2	7	3
District 11	0.6	8	4
District 12	0.1	9	5

5.3 MORE GENERAL LOGISTICS MODELS

I t is probably fair to state that the majority of network models used in real applications are similar to the Midwest Electric transportation model from the previous section in the sense of being *logistics* models. That is, their objective is to ship goods from one set of locations to another set of locations at minimum cost, subject to various constraints. (We will consider *non-logistics* network models in the next section.) There are many variations of these logistics models. The simplest models include a single product that needs to be shipped according to one mode of transportation (trucks, for example) in a particular period of time. More complex models—and much larger ones—can include multiple products, multiple modes of transportation, and/or multiple time periods. However, they are all variations of the **minimum cost network flow model (MCNFM)** we will discuss in this section.

Minimum Cost Network Flow Models

Basically, the general MCNFM is like the transportation model except for two possible differences. First, arc capacities are often imposed on some or all of the arcs. These become simple upper bound constraints in the model. Second and more significant, there can be inflows *and* outflows associated with any node. Nodes are generally categorized as **net suppliers**, **net demanders**, or **transshipment points**. A net supplier is a location that starts with a certain supply (or possibly a capacity for supplying). A net demander is the opposite; it requires that a certain amount end up there. A transshipment point is a location where goods pass through. The best way to think of these categories is in terms of **net inflow** or **net outflow.** The net inflow for any node is defined as total inflow minus total outflow for that node. The net outflow is the negative of this—total outflow minus total inflow. Then a net supplier is a node with positive net outflow, a net demander is a node with positive net inflow, and a transshipment point is a node with net outflow (and net inflow) equal to 0. It is important to realize that inflows are sometimes allowed to net suppliers, but their net outflows must be positive. Similarly, outflows from net demanders are sometimes allowed, but their net inflows must be positive.

There are typically two types of constraints in MCNFMs (other than nonnegativity of flows). The first type represents the arc capacity constraints, simple upper bounds on the flows. The second type represents the flow balance constraints, one for each node. For a net supplier, this constraint is of the form **NetOutflow=OriginalSupply** (or possibly **NetOutflow<=Capacity**). For a net demander, it is of the form **NetInflow>= Demand** (or possibly **NetInflow=Demand**). Finally, for a transshipment point, it is of the form **NetInflow=0** (which is equivalent to **NetOutflow=0**, whichever you prefer). If we represent the network graphically, then it easy to "see" these constraints. We simply examine the flows on the arrows leading into and out of the various nodes. We illustrate the typical situation in the following example.

EXAMPLE 5.3

PRODUCING AND SHIPPING TOMATO PRODUCTS AT REDBRAND

The RedBrand Company produces tomato products at three plants. These products can be shipped directly to their two customers or they can first be shipped to the company's two warehouses and then to the customers. A network representation of RedBrand's problem appears in Figure 5.11. We see that nodes 1, 2, and 3 represent the plants (suppliers, denoted by S), nodes 4 and 5 represent the warehouses (transshipment points, denoted by T), and nodes 6 and 7 represent the customers (demanders, denoted by D). Note that we allow the possibility of some shipments among plants, among warehouses, and among customers. Also, note that some arcs have arrows on both ends. This means that flow is allowed in either direction.

FIGURE 5.11
Graphical Representation of RedBrand Logistics Model

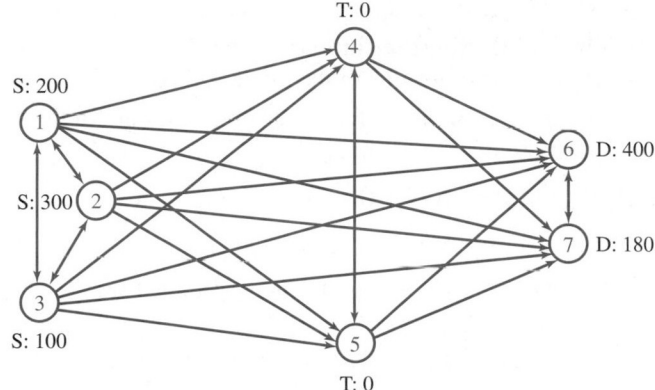

The cost of producing food at each plant is the same, so RedBrand is concerned with minimizing the total shipping cost incurred in meeting customer demands. The production capacity of each plant (in tons per year) and the demand of each customer are shown in Figure 5.11. The cost of shipping a ton of food (in thousands of dollars) between each pair of points is given in Table 5.15, where a dash indicates that Red-Brand cannot ship along that arc. We also assume that at most 200 tons of food can be shipped between any two nodes. RedBrand wants to determine a minimum-cost shipping schedule.

TABLE 5.15		**Shipping Costs for RedBrand Example**						
					To Node			
		1	2	3	4	5	6	7
	1	—	5.0	3.0	5.0	5.0	20.0	20.0
	2	9.0	—	9.0	1.0	1.0	8.0	15.0
	3	0.4	8.0	—	1.0	0.5	10.0	12.0
From Node	4	—	—	—	—	1.2	2.0	12.0
	5	—	—	—	0.8	—	2.0	12.0
	6	—	—	—	—	—	—	1.0
	7	—	—	—	—	—	7.0	—

Solution

We need to keep track of the following:

- amount shipped along each arc of the network
- total amount shipped into each node (the inflow)
- total amount shipped out of each node (the outflow)
- total shipping cost

DEVELOPING THE SPREADSHEET MODEL

To set up the spreadsheet model, proceed as follows. (See Figure 5.12 and the file REDBRAND1.XLS. Also, refer to the network in Figure 5.11.)

❶ Input data. Enter the unit shipping costs (in thousands of dollars) in the CostMatrix range, the common arc capacity in the ArcCapacity cell, the supply capacities in the Capacities range, and the demands in the Demands range. Note that we have blackened the cells in the CostMatrix range that do not correspond to arcs in the network. No costs are entered in these cells.

❷ Origin and destination indices. Enter the indices (1 to 7) for the origins and destinations of the various arcs in the range A18:B43.

❸ Shipping costs on arcs. To transfer the cost data in the CostMatrix range to the UnitCosts range, enter the formula

=INDEX(CostMatrix,A18,B18)

in cell C18 and copy it down column C.

❹ Flows on arcs. Enter *any* initial values for the flows in the range D18:D43. These flows are the changing cells.

❺ Arc capacities. To indicate a common arc capacity for all arcs, enter the formula

=ArcCapacity

in cell F18 and copy it down column F.

	A	B	C	D	E	F	G	H	I	J	K	L	M
1	RedBrand shipping model												
2											Range names used:		
3	Unit shipping costs										CostMatrix - D6:J12		
4				To							ArcCapacity - C14		
5			Node index	Plant 1	Plant 2	Plant 3	Whse 1	Whse 2	Cust 1	Cust 2	Origins - A18:A43		
6	From	Plant 1	1		$5.00	$3.00	$5.00	$5.00	$20.00	$20.00	Dests - B18:B43		
7		Plant 2	2	$9.00		$9.00	$1.00	$1.00	$8.00	$15.00	UnitCosts - C18:C43		
8		Plant 3	3	$0.40	$8.00		$1.00	$0.50	$10.00	$12.00	Flows - D18:D43		
9		Whse 1	4					$1.20	$2.00	$12.00	PlantNetOutflows - I19:I21		
10		Whse 2	5				$0.80		$2.00	$12.00	Capacities - K19:K21		
11		Cust 1	6							$1.00	WhseNetFlows - I25:I26		
12		Cust 2	7						$7.00		CustNetInflows - I30:I31		
13											Demands - K30:K31		
14	Common arc capacity		200								TotalCost - B45		
15													
16	Network formulation						Node balance constraints						
17	Origin	Destination	Unit Cost	Flow		Arc Capacity	Plant constraints						
18	1	2	5	0	<=	200	Node	Net outflow			Capacity		
19	1	3	3	180	<=	200	1	180	<=		200		
20	1	4	5	0	<=	200	2	300	<=		300		
21	1	5	5	0	<=	200	3	100	<=		100		
22	1	6	20	0	<=	200							
23	1	7	20	0	<=	200	Warehouse constraints						
24	2	1	9	0	<=	200	Node	Net outflow			Required		
25	2	3	9	0	<=	200	4	0	=		0		
26	2	4	1	120	<=	200	5	0	=		0		
27	2	5	1	0	<=	200							
28	2	6	8	180	<=	200	Customer constraints						
29	2	7	15	0	<=	200	Node	Net inflow			Demand		
30	3	1	0.4	0	<=	200	6	400	>=		400		
31	3	2	8	0	<=	200	7	180	>=		180		
32	3	4	1	80	<=	200							
33	3	5	0.5	200	<=	200							
34	3	6	10	0	<=	200							
35	3	7	12	0	<=	200							
36	4	5	1.2	0	<=	200							
37	4	6	2	200	<=	200							
38	4	7	12	0	<=	200							
39	5	4	0.8	0	<=	200							
40	5	6	2	200	<=	200							
41	5	7	12	0	<=	200							
42	6	7	1	180	<=	200							
43	7	6	7	0	<=	200							
44													
45	Total cost	$3,260											

FIGURE 5.12 Spreadsheet Model for RedBrand Example

⑥ Flow balance constraints. Nodes 1, 2, and 3 are net suppliers, nodes 4 and 5 are transshipment points, and nodes 6 and 7 are net demanders. Therefore, set up the left sides of the flow balance constraints appropriately for these three cases. Specifically, enter the net outflow for node 1 in cell I19 with the formula

=SUMIF(Origins,H19,Flows)-SUMIF(Dests,H19,Flows)

and copy it down to cell I21. Note how this formula subtracts flows into node 1 from flows out of node 1 to obtain net outflow for node 1. Next, copy this *same* formula to cells I25 and I26 for the warehouses. (Remember that for transshipment points, the left side of the constraint can be net outflow *or* net inflow. If net outflow is 0, then net inflow must also be 0.) Finally, enter the net inflow for node 6 in cell I30 with the formula

=SUMIF(Dests,H30,Flows)-SUMIF(Origins,H30,Flows)

and copy it to cell I31. This formula subtracts flows out of node 6 from flows into node 6 to obtain the net inflow for node 6.

⑦ Total shipping cost. Calculate the total shipping cost (in thousands of dollars) in the TotCost cell with the formula

=SUMPRODUCT(UnitCosts,Flows)

USING THE SOLVER

The Solver dialog box should be set up as in Figure 5.13. We want to minimize total shipping costs, subject to the three types of flow balance constraints and the arc capacity constraints.

FIGURE 5.13
Solver Dialog Box
for RedBrand Model

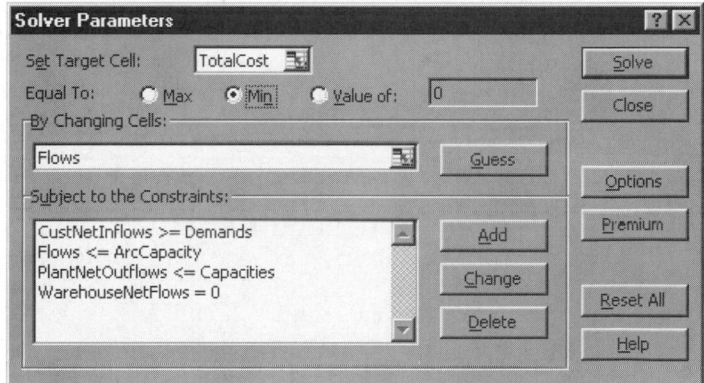

From the optimal solution in Figure 5.12, we see that RedBrand's customer demand can be satisfied with a shipping cost of $3,260,000. This solution appears graphically in Figure 5.14 (page 212). Note in particular that plant 1 produces 180 tons (under capacity) and ships it all to plant 3, not directly to warehouses or customers. Also, note that all shipments from the warehouses go directly to customer 1. Then customer 1 ships 180 tons to customer 2. We purposely chose (probably unrealistic) unit shipping costs to produce this type of behavior, just to show that it *can* happen. As you can see, the costs of shipping from plant 1 directly to warehouses or customers are relatively large compared to shipping directly to plant 3. Similarly, the costs of shipping from plants or warehouses directly to customer 2 are prohibitive. Therefore, we ship to customer 1 and let customer 1 forward some of its shipment to customer 2.

FIGURE 5.14
Optimal Flows for
RedBrand Example

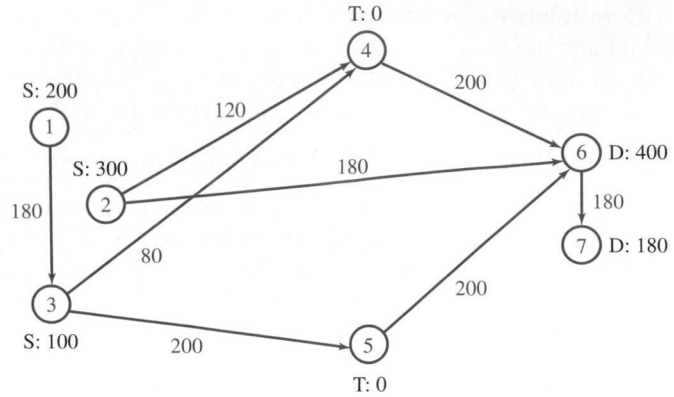

Sensitivity Analysis How much effect does the arc capacity have on the optimal solution? Currently, we see that three of the arcs with positive flow are at the arc capacity of 200. We can use SolverTable to see how sensitive this number and the total cost are to the arc capacity. In this case the single input cell is the ArcCapacity cell. We will vary it from 150 to 300 in increments of 25, and we will keep track of two outputs: total cost and the number of arcs at arc capacity. When we want to keep track of an output that does not already exist, we simply create it with an appropriate formula in a new cell before running SolverTable. This is shown in Figure 5.15. The formula in cell C47 is

=COUNTIF(Flows,ArcCapacity)

which counts the arcs with flow equal to arc capacity. The SolverTable output shows what we would expect. As the arc capacity decreases, more flows bump up against it, and the total cost increases. But even when the arc capacity is 300, two flows are constrained by it. In this sense, even this large an arc capacity costs RedBrand money.

FIGURE 5.15
Sensitivity to Arc
Capacity

	A	B	C	D	E	F	G
47	Number of routes at arc capacity		3				
48							
49	Sensitivity of total cost and number of routes at arc capacity to arc capacity						
50			$B$45	$C$47			
51		150	$4,120	6			
52		175	$3,643	6			
53		200	$3,260	3			
54		225	$2,998	3			
55		250	$2,735	3			
56		275	$2,473	3			
57		300	$2,320	2			

Variations of the Model There are many variations of the RedBrand shipping problem that can handled by a network formulation. We consider two possible variations. First, suppose that RedBrand ships *two* products along the given network. We assume that the unit shipping costs are the same for either product (although this assumption could easily be relaxed), but the arc capacity (which we now change to 300) represents the maximum flow of *both* products that can flow on any arc. In this sense, the two products are competing for arc capacity. Each plant has a separate production capacity for each product, and each customer has a separate demand for each product.

The spreadsheet model for this variation appears in Figure 5.16. (See the file REDBRAND2.XLS.) Very little needs to be changed from the original model—even the Solver dialog box stays the same. We need to (1) have two columns of changing

RedBrand shipping model with two products competing for arc capacity

Unit shipping costs (assumed the same for both products)

		Node index	Plant 1	Plant 2	Plant 3	Whse 1	Whse 2	Cust 1	Cust 2
						To			
From	Plant 1	1		$5.00	$3.00	$5.00	$5.00	$20.00	$20.00
	Plant 2	2	$9.00		$9.00	$1.00	$1.00	$8.00	$15.00
	Plant 3	3	$0.40	$8.00		$1.00	$0.50	$10.00	$12.00
	Whse 1	4					$1.20	$2.00	$12.00
	Whse 2	5				$0.80		$2.00	$12.00
	Cust 1	6							$1.00
	Cust 2	7						$7.00	

Common arc capacity 300

Range names used:
CostMatrix - C6:J12
ArcCapacity - C14
Origins - A18:A43
Dests - B18:B43
UnitCosts - C18:C43
Flows1 - D18:D43
Flows2 - E18:E43
TotalFlows - F18:F43
PlantNetOutflows - K19:L21
Capacities - N19:O21
WhseNetFlows - K25:L26
CustNetInflows - K30:L31
Demands - N30:O31
TotalCost - B45

Network formulation

Origin	Destination	Unit Cost	Flow1	Flow2	TotalFlow		Arc Capacity
1	2	5	0	0	0	<=	300
1	3	3	180	120	300	<=	300
1	4	5	0	20	20	<=	300
1	5	5	0	0	0	<=	300
1	6	20	0	0	0	<=	300
1	7	20	0	0	0	<=	300
2	1	9	0	0	0	<=	300
2	3	9	0	0	0	<=	300
2	4	1	100	0	100	<=	300
2	5	1	0	0	0	<=	300
2	6	8	200	100	300	<=	300
2	7	15	0	0	0	<=	300
3	1	0.4	0	0	0	<=	300
3	2	8	0	0	0	<=	300
3	4	1	180	0	180	<=	300
3	5	0.5	100	200	300	<=	300
3	6	10	0	0	0	<=	300
3	7	12	0	20	20	<=	300
4	5	1.2	0	0	0	<=	300
4	6	2	280	20	300	<=	300
4	7	12	0	0	0	<=	300
5	4	0.8	0	0	0	<=	300
5	6	2	100	200	300	<=	300
5	7	12	0	0	0	<=	300
6	7	1	180	120	300	<=	300
7	6	7	0	0	0	<=	300

Total cost $5,570

Node balance constraints

Plant constraints

Node	Net outflow1	Net outflow2		Capacity1	Capacity2
1	180	140	<=	200	200
2	300	100	<=	300	100
3	100	100	<=	100	100

Warehouse constraints

Node	Net outflow1	Net outflow2		Required1	Required2
4	0	0	=	0	0
5	0	0	=	0	0

Customer constraints

Node	Net inflow1	Net inflow2		Demand1	Demand2
6	400	200	>=	400	200
7	180	140	>=	180	140

FIGURE 5.16 RedBrand Model with Two Products

cells (columns D and E), (2) apply the previous logic to both products separately in the flow balance constraints, and (3) apply the arc capacities to the *total* flows in column F (which are the sums of flows in columns D and E).

A second variation of the model is appropriate for perishable goods. (See the file REDBRAND3.XLS.) We again assume that there is a single product, but that some percentage of the product that is shipped to warehouses perishes and cannot be sent on to customers. This means that the total inflow to a warehouse is *greater than* the total outflow from the warehouse. We model this behavior as shown in Figure 5.17 (page 214). The "shrinkage factor" in the ShrinkFactor cell, the percentage that does *not* spoil in the warehouses, becomes a new input. It is then incorporated into the warehouse flow balance constraints by entering the formula

=SUMIF(Origins,H25,Flows)-ShrinkFactor*SUMIF(Dests,H25,Flows)

in cell I25 and copying it to cell I26. This formula says that what goes out (the first term) is 90% of what goes in. The other 10% disappears. Of course, shrinkage results in a larger total cost—about 50% larger—than in the original RedBrand model. Interestingly, however, some units are still sent to both warehouses, and the entire capacity of all plants is now used. Finally, you can check that a feasible solution exists even for a shrinkage factor of 0% (where everything sent to warehouses disappears). The solution then is to send everything directly from plants to customers—at a steep cost.

	A	B	C	D	E	F	G	H	I	J	K	L	M
1	**RedBrand shipping model with shrinkage at warehouses**												
2											**Range names used:**		
3	**Unit shipping costs**										CostMatrix - C6:J12		
4				**To**							ArcCapacity - C14		
5			Node index	Plant 1	Plant 2	Plant 3	Whse 1	Whse 2	Cust 1	Cust 2	Origins - A18:A43		
6	**From**	Plant 1	1		$5.00	$3.00	$5.00	$5.00	$20.00	$20.00	Dests - B18:B43		
7		Plant 2	2	$9.00		$9.00	$1.00	$1.00	$8.00	$15.00	UnitCosts - C18:C43		
8		Plant 3	3	$0.40	$8.00		$1.00	$0.50	$10.00	$12.00	Flows - D18:D43		
9		Whse 1	4					$1.20	$2.00	$12.00	PlantNetOutflows - I19:I21		
10		Whse 2	5				$0.80		$2.00	$12.00	Capacities - K19:K21		
11		Cust 1	6							$1.00	WhseNetFlows - I25:I26		
12		Cust 2	7						$7.00		CustNetInflows - I30:I31		
13											Demands - K30:K31		
14	**Common arc capacity**		200		**Shrinkage factor**		90%				TotalCost - B45		
15											ShrinkFactor - G14		
16	**Network formulation**							**Node balance constraints**					
17	Origin	Destination	Unit Cost	Flow		Arc Capacity		Plant constraints					
18	1	2	5	0	<=	200		Node	Net outflow		Capacity		
19	1	3	3	200	<=	200		1	200	<=	200		
20	1	4	5	0	<=	200		2	300	<=	300		
21	1	5	5	0	<=	200		3	100	<=	100		
22	1	6	20	0	<=	200							
23	1	7	20	0	<=	200		Warehouse constraints					
24	2	1	9	0	<=	200		Node	Net outflow		Required		
25	2	3	9	0	<=	200		4	0	=	0		
26	2	4	1	100	<=	200		5	0	=	0		
27	2	5	1	0	<=	200							
28	2	6	8	200	<=	200		Customer constraints					
29	2	7	15	0	<=	200		Node	Net inflow		Demand		
30	3	1	0.4	0	<=	200		6	400	>=	400		
31	3	2	8	0	<=	200		7	180	>=	180		
32	3	4	1	0	<=	200							
33	3	5	0.5	100	<=	200							
34	3	6	10	200	<=	200							
35	3	7	12	0	<=	200							
36	4	5	1.2	0	<=	200							
37	4	6	2	90	<=	200							
38	4	7	12	0	<=	200							
39	5	4	0.8	0	<=	200							
40	5	6	2	90	<=	200							
41	5	7	12	0	<=	200							
42	6	7	1	180	<=	200							
43	7	6	7	0	<=	200							
44													
45	**Total cost**	$4,890											
46													

FIGURE 5.17 RedBrand Model with Shrinkage ■

MODELING ISSUES

1. Spreadsheet Solvers use the simplex method to solve network flow models. However, the simplex method can be simplified dramatically for these types of models. The simplified version of the simplex method, called the **network simplex method**, is much more efficient than the ordinary simplex method. Specialized computer codes have been written to implement the network simplex method, and all large network flow problems are solved by using the network simplex method. This is fortunate because real network models can be extremely large. See Winston (1994) for a discussion of this method.
2. If the given supplies and demands for the nodes are integers and all arc capacities are integers, then the network flow model will always have an optimal solution with all integer flows. Again, this is very fortunate for large problems—we get integer solutions "for free" without having to use an integer programming algorithm. ■

Production Distribution and Inventory at Agrico and Citgo

Agrico Chemical Company is a large producer of chemical fertilizers. Glover et al. (1979) developed a network flow model to help Agrico answer questions such as

- How many units of each fertilizer should be produced each month?
- How should products be shipped to distribution centers and customers?

The key to the Agrico model was to create a **dynamic network**. For each location in a dynamic network, there are nodes representing the location at different points in time. For example, there might be a node for plant 1 at times 1, 2, and 3. A "flow" from the plant 1–time 1 node to the plant 1–time 2 node, for example, corresponds to holding inventory. The Agrico model has saved the company an estimated $8 million annually in holding, production, and distribution costs.

A similar model developed by Klingman et al. (1987) helped Citgo Petroleum to optimize its refinery and distribution operations. This model has saved Citgo over $16 million annually. (This model was also discussed in Chapter 1.) ■

Maximum Flow Models

Many situations can be modeled by a network in which each arc has a capacity that limits the quantity of a product that can be shipped through that arc. In these situations the objective is typically to transport the maximum amount of flow from a starting point (called the **source**) to a terminal point (called the **sink**). Such problems represent a special case of the network flow model known as the **maximum flow model**. The following is a typical example of the maximum flow model.

EXAMPLE 5.4

DISTRIBUTING OIL THROUGH PIPELINES AT EXCRON OIL

Excron Oil Company has a pipeline distribution network as shown in Figure 5.18. Each node corresponds to a storage tank, and the numbers on the arcs represent flow capacities (per hour). Note that flows are allowed in both directions between some, but not all, of the tanks. Excron wants to determine the maximum flow that can be sent from tank 1 to tank 8 per hour. The company is also considering doubling the capacity of all arcs leading out of tank 1 and all arcs leading into tank 8, and it wants to know whether this will allow it to double the maximum flow per hour from tank 1 to tank 8.

FIGURE 5.18
Network for
Maximum Flow
Model

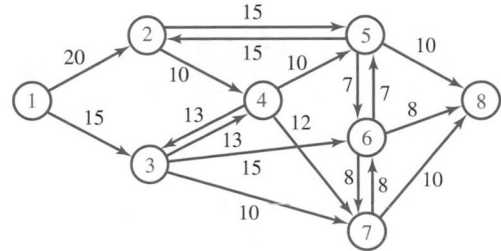

Solution

Parts of this model are much like the general MCNFM. We must include the typical flow balance constraints (inflow equals outflow, except for the source and sink nodes), and we need the usual arc capacity constraints. But the difficulty is modeling the maximum flow objective appropriately. One approach is to note that the total flow through the network, for any set of flows, is the larger of the total outflow from node 1 and the total inflow to node 8. However, this would require us to use the MAX function in Excel, which Solver does not handle well. An alternative method is to constrain the flows out of the source by the capacities on arcs leading out of the source, and then to maximize the sum of all flows into the sink. There are no costs in the model.

DEVELOPING THE SPREADSHEET MODEL

The completed model and corresponding Solver dialog box appear in Figures 5.19 and 5.20. (See the file MAXFLOW.XLS.) The model is very similar to the general MCNFM formulation and can be completed with the following steps.

❶ Enter arcs. Enter the information on all arcs in the network in the range A5:B22.

❷ Flows. Enter *any* values for the flows in the Flows range.

❸ Capacities. Enter the given arc capacities in the range E5:E22.

❹ Flows out of source and into sink. There are no flows into the source, so enter the total flow out of the source in cell H5 with the formula[4]

=SUMIF(Origins,G5,Flows)

Similarly, there are no flows out of the sink, so enter the total flow into the sink in cell H12 with the formula

=SUMIF(Dests,G12,Flows)

This value is the total flow through the network that we will attempt to maximize.

	A	B	C	D	E	F	G	H	I	J
1	Excron Oil maximum flow model									
2										
3	Network arcs						Flow balance constraints			
4	Origin	Destination	Flow		Capacity		Node	Net outflow		Required
5	1	2	13	<=	20		1	28		
6	1	3	15	<=	15		2	0	=	0
7	2	4	3	<=	10		3	0	=	0
8	2	5	10	<=	15		4	0	=	0
9	3	4	0	<=	13		5	0	=	0
10	3	6	15	<=	15		6	0	=	0
11	3	7	3	<=	10		7	0	=	0
12	4	3	3	<=	13		8	28		
13	4	5	0	<=	10					
14	4	7	0	<=	12		Range names used:			
15	5	2	0	<=	15		Origins - A5:A22			
16	5	6	0	<=	7		Dests - B5:B22			
17	5	8	10	<=	10		Flows - C5:C22			
18	6	5	0	<=	7		Capacities - E5:E22			
19	6	7	7	<=	8		NetOutflows - H6:H11			
20	6	8	8	<=	8		MaxFlow - H12			
21	7	6	0	<=	8					
22	7	8	10	<=	10					

FIGURE 5.19 Maximum Flow Model

[4]Actually, the formula in this cell is not necessary, but it is useful as a check. The total flow out of the source *must* equal the total flow into the sink, by flow balance.

FIGURE 5.20
Solver Dialog Box
for Maximum Flow
Model

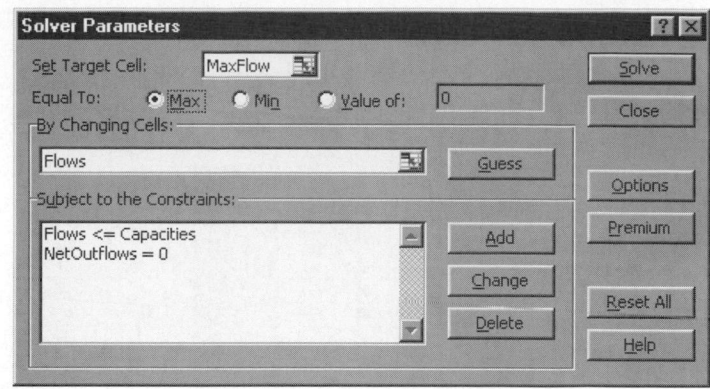

⑤ Net outflows at intermediate nodes. Because there is flow balance at each intermediate node, we could set each node's net outflow to 0 or its net inflow to 0. We do the former. Therefore, enter the formula

=SUMIF(Origins,G5,Flows)-SUMIF(Dests,G5,Flows)

in cell H6 to calculate the net outflow for node 2, and copy this down for nodes 3–7. Note that the range named NetOutflows corresponds to these intermediate nodes only.

USING THE SOLVER

The Solver setup is straightforward. We maximize the total flow into the sink (the MaxFlow cell), with the Flows range as the changing cells, subject to the constraints Flows<=Capacities and NetOutflows=0. We also check the Assume Linear Model and Assume Non-Negative boxes.

The optimal solution is represented graphically in Figure 5.21, where only the arcs with positive flows are shown. In a sense, the "intermediate" arcs are not constraining. This is because the total flow of 28 is the most we could hope to send into node 8, given that the capacities of the arcs leading into this node add to 28.

Sensitivity Analysis   What if we could expand the capacities of the arcs leading out of the source and into the sink? Here, we actually answer a slightly more general question than Excron asked by using SolverTable, as shown in Figure 5.22 (page 218). Instead of just doubling capacity, we allow the selected arcs' capacities—those in rows 5, 6, 17, 20, and 22—to expand by any factor entered in the ExpFactor cell. For example, the formula in cell E5 is

=ExpFactor*Model!E5

(In our file, the original model is in a sheet called Model, and the expansion model is in a separate sheet, so this formula retrieves original capacity data from the Model sheet.)

FIGURE 5.21
Optimal Flows for
Excron Problem

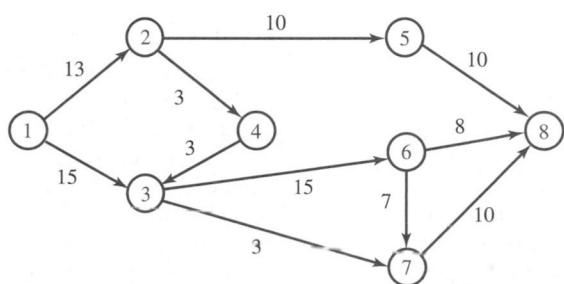

FIGURE 5.22
Effects of Capacity
Expansion for
Selected Arcs

	A	B	C	D	E	F	G	H	I	J
1	Excron Oil maximum flow model									
2										
3	Network arcs						Flow balance constraints			
4	Origin	Destination	Flow		Capacity		Node	Net outflow		Required
5	1	2	31	<=	40		1	56		
6	1	3	25	<=	30		2	0	=	0
7	2	4	16	<=	10		3	0	=	0
8	2	5	15	<=	15		4	0	=	0
9	3	4	0	<=	13		5	0	=	0
10	3	6	15	<=	15		6	0	=	0
11	3	7	10	<=	10		7	0	=	0
12	4	9	0	<=	13		8	56		
13	4	5	5	<=	10					
14	4	7	11	<=	12					
15	5	2	0	<=	15		Range names used:			
16	5	6	0	<=	7		Origins - A5:A22			
17	5	8	20	<=	20		Dests - B5:B22			
18	6	5	0	<=	7		Flows - C5:C22			
19	6	7	0	<=	8		Capacities - E5:E22			
20	6	8	16	<=	16		NetOutflows - H6:H11			
21	7	6	1	<=	8		MaxFlow - H12			
22	7	8	20	<=	20		ExpFactor - C24			
23										
24	Capacity expansion factor		2							
25										
26	Sensitivity of maximum flow to expansion factor									
27			$H$12							
28		1	28							
29		2	55							
30		3	62							
31		4	62							
32		5	62							

Now we run SolverTable with cell ExpFactor as the single input cell, allowing it to vary from 1 to 5 in increments of 1, and we keep track of the maximum flow. As we see, if capacity doubles in these arcs, the maximum flow also doubles. However, for larger expansion factors, *other* arc capacities prevent Excron from taking full advantage of the expansions. For example, if the arc capacities out of node 1 and into node 8 triple, the maximum flow does not triple—it increases only from 28 to 62. Also, any *additional* capacity expansion for these arcs has no effect whatsoever. ■

ADDITIONAL APPLICATIONS

Determining Manufacturing Throughput with the Maximum Flow Model

Maxwell and Wilson (1981) used the maximum flow model to determine the maximum number of parts per minute that a manufacturing system could produce. See Problem 82 for an example of this type of application. ■

PROBLEMS

Skill-Building Problems

14. Widgetco manufactures widgets at two factories, one in Memphis and one in Denver. The Memphis factory can produce up to 150 widgets per day, and the Denver factory can produce up to 200 widgets per day. Widgets are shipped by air to customers in Los Angeles and Boston. The customers in each city require 130 widgets per day. Because of the deregulation of air fares, Widgetco believes that it might be cheaper to first fly some widgets to New York or Chicago and then fly them to their final destinations. The costs of flying a widget are shown in Table 5.16.

  a. Determine how to minimize the total cost of shipping the required widgets to the customers.

  b. Suppose the capacities of both factories are reduced in increments of 10 widgets per day. Use SolverTable to see how much the common reduction can be before the total cost increases; before there is no feasible solution.

15. General Ford produces cars at L.A. and Detroit and has a warehouse in Atlanta. The company supplies cars to customers in Houston and Tampa. The costs of shipping a car between various points are listed in Table 5.17, where a dash means that a shipment is not allowed. L.A. can produce up to 1100 cars, and Detroit can produce up to 2900 cars. Houston must receive 2400 cars, and Tampa must receive 1500 cars.

  a. Determine how to minimize the cost of meeting demands at Houston and Tampa.

  b. Modify the answer to part **a** if shipments between L.A. and Detroit are not allowed.

  c. Modify the answer to part **a** if shipments between Houston and Tampa are allowed at a cost of $5 per car.

16. Sunco Oil produces oil at two wells. Well 1 can produce up to 150,000 barrels per day, and well 2 can produce up to 200,000 barrels per day. It is possible to ship oil directly from the wells to Sunco's customers in Los Angeles and New York. Alternatively, Sunco could transport oil to the ports of Mobile and Galveston and then ship it by tanker to New York or Los Angeles. Los Angeles requires 160,000 barrels per day, and New York requires 140,000 barrels per day. The costs of shipping 1000 barrels between various locations are shown in Table 5.18, where a dash indicates shipments that are not allowed. Determine

TABLE 5.16   Shipping Costs for Widgetco Problem

From	To					
	Memphis	Denver	N.Y.	Chicago	L.A.	Boston
Memphis	—	—	$8	$13	$25	$28
Denver		—	$15	$12	$26	$25
N.Y.	—	—	—	$6	$16	$17
Chicago	—	—	$6	—	$14	$16
L.A.	—	—	—	—	—	—
Boston	—	—	—	—	—	—

TABLE 5.17   Shipping Costs for General Ford Problem

From	To				
	L.A.	Detroit	Atlanta	Houston	Tampa
L.A.	—	$140	$100	$90	$225
Detroit	$145	—	$111	$110	$119
Atlanta	$105	$115	—	$113	$78
Houston	$89	$109	$121	—	—
Tampa	$210	$117	$82	—	—

TABLE 5.18   Shipping Costs for Sunco Problem

From	To					
	Well 1	Well 2	Mobile	Galveston	N.Y.	L.A.
Well 1	—	—	$10	$13	$25	$28
Well 2	—	—	$15	$12	$26	$25
Mobile	—	—	—	$6	$16	$17
Galveston	—	—	$6	—	$14	$16
N.Y.	—	—	—	—	—	$15
L.A.	—	—	—	—	$15	—

how to minimize the transport costs in meeting the oil demands of Los Angeles and New York.

17. Nash Auto has two plants, two warehouses, and three customers. The locations of these are as follows: The plants are in Detroit and Atlanta, the warehouses are in Denver and New York, and the customers are in Los Angeles, Chicago, and Philadelphia. Cars are produced at plants, then shipped to warehouses, and finally shipped to customers. Detroit can produce 150 cars per week, and Atlanta can produce 100 cars per week. Los Angeles requires 80 cars per week, Chicago requires 70, and Philadelphia requires 60. It costs $10,000 to produce a car at each plant. The costs of shipping a car between various cities are listed in Table 5.19. Assume that during a week, at most 50 cars can be shipped from a warehouse to any particular city. Determine how to meet Nash's weekly demands at minimum cost.

18. Each hour an average of 900 cars enter the network in Figure 5.23 at node 1 and seek to travel to node 6. The number above each arc in this figure is the maximum number of cars that can pass by any point on the arc during a one-hour period. The times it takes a car to traverse the various arcs are shown in Table 5.20. Determine how to minimize the total time required for all cars to travel from node 1 to node 6.

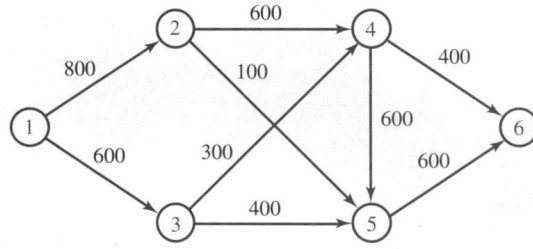

FIGURE 5.23 Traffic Problem

19. Fordco produces cars in Detroit and Dallas. The Detroit plant can produce up to 6500 cars, and the Dallas plant can produce up to 6000 cars. Producing a car costs $2000 in Detroit and $1800 in Dallas. Cars must be shipped to three cities. City 1 must receive 5000 cars, city 2 must receive 4000 cars, and city 3 must receive 3000 cars.

TABLE 5.20	Travel Times for Traffic Problem
Arc	Time (minutes)
(1, 2)	10
(1, 3)	50
(2, 5)	70
(2, 4)	30
(5, 6)	30
(4, 5)	30
(4, 6)	60
(3, 5)	60
(3, 4)	10

The costs of shipping a car from each plant to each city are given in Table 5.21. At most 2700 cars can be sent from a given plant to a given city. Determine how to minimize the cost of meeting all demands.

TABLE 5.21	Shipping Costs for Fordco Problem		
		To	
From	City 1	City 2	City 3
Detroit	$800	$600	$300
Dallas	$500	$200	$200

20. Each year Data Corporal produces up to 400 computers in Boston and up to 300 computers in Raleigh. Los Angeles customers must receive 400 computers, and 300 computers must be supplied to Austin customers. Producing a computer costs $800 in Boston and $900 in Raleigh. Computers are transported by plane and can be sent through Chicago. The costs of sending a computer between pairs of cities are shown in Table 5.22.
   a. Determine how to minimize the total (production plus distribution) cost of meeting Data Corporal's annual demand.
   b. How would you modify the model in part **a** if at most 200 units could be shipped through Chicago?

TABLE 5.19	Shipping Costs for Nash Auto Problem				
			To		
From	Denver	N.Y.	L.A.	Chicago	Philadelphia
Detroit	$1253	$637	—	—	—
Atlanta	$1398	$841	—	—	—
Denver	—	—	$1059	$996	$1691
N.Y.	—	—	$2786	$802	$100

TABLE 5.22 Shipping Costs for Data Corporal Problem

From	To		
	Chicago	**Austin**	**Los Angeles**
Boston	$80	$220	$280
Raleigh	$100	$140	$170
Chicago	—	$40	$50

21. Fly-by-Night Airlines must determine how many connecting flights daily can be arranged between Juneau, Alaska, and Dallas, Texas. Connecting flights must stop in Seattle and then stop in Los Angeles or Denver. Because of limited landing space, Fly-by-Night is limited to making the number of daily flights between pairs of cities shown in Table 5.23.

TABLE 5.23 Data for Fly-by-Night Problem

	Maximum daily flights
Juneau–Seattle	3
Seattle–L.A.	2
Seattle–Denver	3
L.A.–Dallas	1
Denver–Dallas	2

    a. Determine how to maximize the number of connecting flights daily from Juneau to Dallas.

    b. Suppose the maximum number of daily flights from Juneau to Seattle and from Los Angeles to Dallas could each be increased by the same amount. Use SolverTable to determine the effect of this increase on the total number of flights possible from Juneau to Dallas. Explain your findings in words.

22. Flying Lion Airlines needs to ship 20 tons of freight from New York to Los Angeles by tomorrow night. The number of tons that can be shipped on each of Flying Lion's flights is listed in Table 5.24. Can 20 tons of freight make it by tomorrow?

Skill-Extending Problems

23. In Problem 16, assume that before being shipped to Los Angeles or New York, all oil produced at the wells must be refined at either Galveston or Mobile. To refine 1000 barrels of oil costs $12 at Mobile and $10 at Galveston. Assuming that both Mobile and Galveston have infinite refinery capacity, determine how to minimize the daily cost of transporting and refining the oil requirements of Los Angeles and New York.

24. Rework the previous problem under the assumption that Galveston has a refinery capacity of 150,000

TABLE 5.24 Freight Capacities for Flying Lion Problem

	Capacity (in tons)
N.Y.–Pittsburgh	10
N.Y.–Indy	11
N.Y.–Chicago	3
N.Y.–Dallas	3
Pittsburgh–Indy	2
Pittsburgh–Minneapolis	8
Indy–Chicago	10
Indy–L.A.	2
Chicago–Minneapolis	4
Chicago–L.A.	8
Minneapolis–L.A.	7
Dallas–L.A.	13

barrels per day and Mobile has a refinery capacity of 180,000 barrels per day.

25. Oilco has oil fields in San Diego and Los Angeles. The San Diego field can produce up to 500,000 barrels per day, and the Los Angeles field can produce up to 400,000 barrels per day. Oil is sent from the fields to a refinery, either in Dallas or in Houston. (Assume that each refinery has unlimited capacity.) To refine 100,000 barrels costs $700 at Dallas and $900 at Houston. Refined oil is shipped to customers in Chicago and New York. Chicago customers require 400,000 barrels per day, and New York customers require 300,000 barrels per day. The costs of shipping 100,000 barrels of oil (refined or unrefined) between cities are shown in Table 5.25 (page 222).

    a. Determine how to minimize the total cost of meeting all demands.

    b. If each refinery had a capacity of 380,000 barrels per day, how would you modify the model in part **a**?

26. At present there are 500 long-distance calls that must be routed from New York to Los Angeles and 400 calls that must be routed from Philadelphia to L.A. On route to L.A. from Philly or New York, calls are sent through Indianapolis or Cleveland, then through Dallas or Denver, and finally to L.A.

TABLE 5.25	Shipping Costs for Oilco Problem			
			To	
From	Dallas	Houston	New York	Chicago
Los Angeles	$300	$110	—	—
San Diego	$420	$100	—	—
Dallas	—	—	$450	$550
Houston	—	—	$470	$530

The number of calls that can be routed between any pair of cities is shown in Table 5.26. The phone company wants to know how many of the $500 + 400 = 900$ calls originating in New York and Philadelphia can be routed to L.A. Set this up as a MCNFM; that is, specify the nodes, arcs, shipping costs, and arc capacities. Then solve it.

TABLE 5.26	Data for Phone Call Problem
Cities	Maximum calls
N.Y.–Indy	300
N.Y.–Clev.	200
Phil.–Indy	250
Phil.–Clev.	250
Indy–Denver	180
Indy–Dallas	220
Clev.–Denver	160
Clev.–Dallas	260
Denver–L.A.	500
Dallas–L.A.	400

27. Seven types of packages are to be delivered by five trucks. There are three packages of each type, and the capacities of the five trucks are 6, 4, 5, 4, and 3 packages, respectively. Determine whether the packages can be loaded so that no truck carries two packages of the same type.

28. Four workers are available to perform jobs 1, 2, 3, and 4. Unfortunately, three workers can do only certain jobs: worker 1, only job 1; worker 2, only jobs 1 and 2; worker 3, only job 2; worker 4, any job. Determine whether all jobs can be assigned to a suitable worker.

29. The Hatfields, Montagues, McCoys, and Capulets are going on their annual family picnic. Four cars are available to transport the families to the picnic.

The cars can carry the following numbers of people: car 1, four; car 2, three; car 3, three; and car 4, four. There are four people in each family, and no car can carry more than two people from any one family. Determine the maximum number of people that can be transported to the picnic.

30. Suppose the number of cars per hour given in Table 5.27 can travel between any two of the cities 1, 2, 3, and 4. Determine how many cars can be sent from city 1 at noon to city 4 at 3 P.M. (*Hint*: Have portions of the network represent noon–1 P.M., 1 P.M.–2 P.M., and 2 P.M.–3 P.M.)

TABLE 5.27	Data for Car Travel Problem			
			To	
From	1	2	3	4
1	—	200	150	250
2	200	—	220	230
3	150	220	—	180
4	250	230	180	—

31. During the next 4 months a construction firm must complete three projects. Project 1 must be completed no later than 3 months from now and requires 8 worker-months of labor. Project 2 must be completed no later than 4 months from now and requires 10 worker-months of labor. Project 3 must be completed no later than 2 months from now and requires 12 worker-months of labor. Each month, 8 workers are available. During a given month, no more than 6 workers can work on a single job. Determine whether all three projects can be completed on time. (*Hint*: If the maximum flow in the network is 30, all projects can be completed on time.)

5.4 NON-LOGISTICS NETWORK MODELS

lthough many real applications of network models have a logistics context, there are many non-logistics problems that can be formulated to *look like* network models. This is fortunate for several reasons. First, the ability to represent a problem graphically as a network, with nodes and arcs, helps users to visualize the model in a more intuitive way. Second, once we recognize a particular problem as being a network model, we can apply any of our knowledge about general network models to this problem. Finally—and this is probably the most important point for real applications—specialized network algorithms can be used to take advantage of the special network structure. This enables companies to solve very large models that might not be possible to solve otherwise. In this section we will look at several non-logistics problems that can be formulated as network models.

Assignment Models

Assignment models are used to assign, on a one-to-one basis, members of one set to members of another set in a least-cost manner. The typical assignment model discussed in most management science textbooks is the assignment of machines to jobs. For example, suppose there are 4 jobs and 5 machines. Each machine can be used on at most one job, and every job must be completed. Every pairing of a machine and a job has a given job completion time. The problem is to assign the machines to the jobs so that the total time to complete all jobs is minimized. To see how this is a network problem, recall the transportation problem of sending goods from suppliers to customers. Now think of the machines as the suppliers, the jobs as the customers, and the assignment times as the unit shipping costs. The capacities and demands are all equal to 1 because each machine can be used at most once and each job must be completed at least once (actually, exactly once). Finally, there is an arc from every machine to every job, and the flows on these arcs are all 0 or 1—a particular machine is either paired with a particular job (a flow of 1) or it isn't (a flow of 0). Therefore, we can formulate this assignment problem *exactly* like we formulated the Midwest Electric transportation problem in Example 5.1 by using the appropriate input values.

An example of this model appears in Figure 5.24 (page 224) with the corresponding Solver dialog box shown in Figure 5.25. (See the file ASSIGNMENT.XLS.) It is exactly like the Midwest Electric transportation model except that the "capacities" and "demands" are all 1, and "costs" are times. We can see the assignments by checking which changing cells contain 1. In this problem, the assignments are: machine 1 to job 2, machine 2 to job 4, machine 3 to job 3, and machine 4 to job 1. Machine 5 is not assigned to any job. The total job completion time is 15.

We examine a more realistic assignment problem in the following example.

FIGURE 5.24
Assignment of
Machines to Jobs

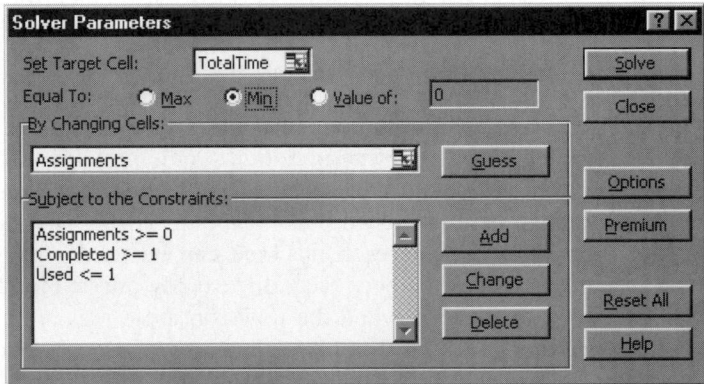

	A	B	C	D	E	F	G	H	I
1	**Assignment of jobs to machines**								
2									
3	**Times to perform jobs on various machines**								
4			**Job**						
5			1	2	3	4			
6	**Machine**	1	14	5	8	7			
7		2	2	12	6	5			
8		3	7	8	3	9			
9		4	2	4	6	10			
10		5	5	5	4	8			
11									
12	**Assignments**								
13			**Job**						
14			1	2	3	4	Used		Capacity
15	**Machine**	1	0	1	0	0	1	<=	1
16		2	0	0	0	1	1	<=	1
17		3	0	0	1	0	1	<=	1
18		4	1	0	0	0	1	<=	1
19		5	0	0	0	0	0	<=	1
20		Completed	1	1	1	1			
21			>=	>=	>=	>=			
22		Required	1	1	1	1			
23									
24	**Total time**	15							

Range names used:
Times: C6:F10
Assignments: C15:F19
Used: G15:G19
Completed: C20:F20
TotalTime: B24

FIGURE 5.25
Solver Dialog Box
for Assignment of
Machines to Jobs

Solver Parameters

Set Target Cell: TotalTime

Equal To: ○ Max ● Min ○ Value of: 0

By Changing Cells:
Assignments

Subject to the Constraints:
Assignments >= 0
Completed >= 1
Used <= 1

[Solve] [Close] [Guess] [Options] [Premium] [Add] [Change] [Delete] [Reset All] [Help]

EXAMPLE 5.5

ASSIGNING SCHOOL BUSES TO ROUTES AT SPRING VIEW

The city of Spring View is taking bids from six bus companies on the eight routes that must be driven in the surrounding school district. Each company enters a bid on how much it will charge to drive selected routes, although not all companies bid on all routes. The data appear in Table 5.28. (Blank cells indicates routes on which a company does not bid.) The city needs to select which companies to assign to which routes with the specifications that (1) if a company does not bid on a route, it cannot be assigned to that route, (2) exactly one company must be assigned to each route, and (3) a company can be assigned to at most two routes. The objective is to minimize the total cost of covering all routes.

Company	Route 1	Route 2	Route 3	Route 4	Route 5	Route 6	Route 7	Route 8
TABLE 5.28			Bids on Bus Routes					
1		8200	7800	5400		3900		
2	7800	8200		6300		3300	4900	
3		4800				4400	5600	3600
4			8000	5000	6800		6700	4200
5	7200	6400		3900	6400	2800		3000
6	7000	5800	7500	4500	5600		6000	4200

Solution

We formulate this model in the "network" way. You can imagine nodes for the bus companies on the left, nodes for the routes on the right, and all arrows going from left to right. All flows are 0 or 1—a company is either assigned to a route or it isn't. The constraint that a bus company can be assigned to at most two routes is handled by constraining the outflow from any company node to be at most 2. To ensure that each route is covered by one company, we constrain the inflow to each route node to be equal to 1.

The model and corresponding Solver dialog box appear in Figures 5.26 and 5.27 (page 226). (See the file BUSROUTES.XLS.) Because this model is so similar to the Midwest Electric transportation model (the alternative version in Figure 5.7), we will not repeat all of the details here. The key steps are as follows.

❶ Arcs lists. The list of arcs (company–route pairs) in rows 16–46 correspond to the nonblank cells only in the CostMatrix range. There is no point in including arcs that are infeasible.

❷ Costs and flows. The costs in the Costs range are found with the usual method. The formula in cell C16 is

=INDEX(CostMatrix,A16,B16)

which is then copied down column C. Then enter any values in the Flows range.

❸ Inflows and outflows. Because no arcs point *into* company nodes and no arcs point *out of* route nodes, we require only *outflows* for company nodes and *inflows* for route nodes. To calculate these, enter the formulas

=SUMIF(Origins,H16,Flows)

and

=SUMIF(Destinations,H24,Flows)

in cells I16 and I24, and copy them down their respective ranges.

❹ Total cost. Calculate the total cost to the city in the TotalCost cell with the formula

=SUMPRODUCT(Costs,Flows)

The optimal solution in Figure 5.26 indicates the following assignments: company 1 covers route 3, company 2 covers routes 6 and 7, company 3 covers route 2, company 5 covers routes 4 and 8, and company 6 covers routes 1 and 5. The total cost to the city of this assignment is $40,300. Note that company 4 is not assigned to any routes. After all, there is no constraint that every company must be assigned to at least one route, and company 4 is evidently underbid by at least one company for all routes.

	A	B	C	D	E	F	G	H	I	J	K	L	M
1	**Assignment of bus companies to routes**												
2													
3	**Bids from companies for routes**										Range names used:		
4	Company	Route 1	Route 2	Route 3	Route 4	Route 5	Route 6	Route 7	Route 8		CostMatrix - B5:I10		
5	1		8200	7800	5400		3900				MaxRoutes - D12		
6	2	7800	8200		6300		3300	4900			Origins - A16:A46		
7	3		4800				4400	5600	3600		Destinations - B16:B46		
8	4			8000	5000	6800		6700	4200		Costs - C16:C46		
9	5	7200	6400		3900	6400	2800		3000		Flows - D16:D46		
10	6	7000	5800	7500	4500	5600		6000	4200		Outflows - I16:I21		
11											Inflows - I24:I31		
12	Maximum routes assigned to any company			2							TotalCost - B48		
13													
14	**Network formulation**							**Flow balance constraints**					
15	Origin	Destination	Cost	Flow		Upper Bound		Company	Flow out		Max		
16	1	2	8200	0	<=	1		1	1	<=	2		
17	1	3	7800	1	<=	1		2	2	<=	2		
18	1	4	5400	0	<=	1		3	1	<=	2		
19	1	6	3900	0	<=	1		4	0	<=	2		
20	2	1	7800	0	<=	1		5	2	<=	2		
21	2	2	8200	0	<=	1		6	2	<=	2		
22	2	4	6300	0	<=	1							
23	2	6	3300	1	<=	1		Route	Flow in		Required		
24	2	7	4900	1	<=	1		1	1	=	1		
25	3	2	4800	1	<=	1		2	1	=	1		
26	3	6	4400	0	<=	1		3	1	=	1		
27	3	7	5600	0	<=	1		4	1	=	1		
28	3	8	3600	0	<=	1		5	1	=	1		
29	4	3	8000	0	<=	1		6	1	=	1		
30	4	4	5000	0	<=	1		7	1	=	1		
31	4	5	6800	0	<=	1		8	1	=	1		
32	4	7	6700	0	<=	1							
33	4	8	4200	0	<=	1							
34	5	1	7200	0	<=	1							
35	5	2	6400	0	<=	1							
36	5	4	3900	1	<=	1							
37	5	5	6400	0	<=	1							
38	5	6	2800	0	<=	1							
39	5	8	3000	1	<=	1							
40	6	1	7000	1	<=	1							
41	6	2	5800	0	<=	1							
42	6	3	7500	0	<=	1							
43	6	4	4500	0	<=	1							
44	6	5	5600	1	<=	1							
45	6	7	6000	0	<=	1							
46	6	8	4200	0	<=	1							
47													
48	**Total cost**	40300											

FIGURE 5.26 Bus Route Assignment Model

FIGURE 5.27
Solver Dialog Box
for Bus Route
Assignment Model

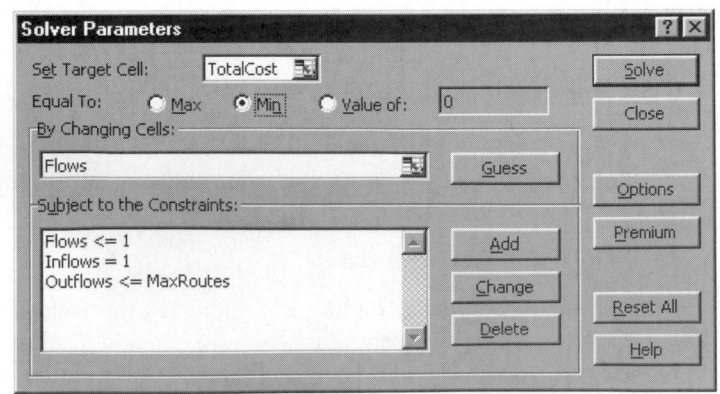

If we wanted to require that all companies be assigned to at least one route, we would simply put a *lower* bound of 1 on all of the outflows from the company nodes (in rows 16–21). Of course, this would increase the total cost to the city.

Sensitivity Analysis One interesting sensitivity analysis is to see what effect the maximum routes upper bound constraint has on the total cost. Presumably, if we allow more routes per bus company (assuming this is physically possible for the companies), the companies who tend to bid lowest will be assigned to the bulk of the routes, and the total cost will decrease. The analysis itself is straightforward, with no modifications of the model necessary. We specify the MaxRoutes cell as the single input cell, allow it to vary from 1 to 7, say, in increments of 1, and keep track of total cost. The resulting output appears in Figure 5.28. We see first that if each company can be assigned to only one route, there is no feasible solution. But this is clear—there are eight routes to cover and only six companies! For larger values of the MaxRoutes value, the total cost begins to decreases, but only until MaxRoutes reaches 3. From that point, the city achieves no added flexibility by allowing companies to travel more routes. Evidently, there is no single company or pair of companies who are consistently underbidding all others.

FIGURE 5.28
Sensitivity to the
Maximum Number
of Routes

	A	B	C	D	E	F	G	H
50	Sensitivity of total cost to maximum routes per company							
51		$B$48						
52	1	Not feasible						
53	2	40300						
54	3	39500						
55	4	39500						
56	5	39500						
57	6	39500						
58	7	39500						

The first problem is clearly infeasible because there are only 6 companies and there are 8 routes. There is a cost savings from being allowed to assign 3 (rather than 2) routes to a company, but there is no incentive to assign more than 3 routes to any company.

The following model is considerably more challenging, but we believe it is also much more interesting.[5] As with many problems that can be formulated as assignment models, the trick here is to recognize that it indeed involves appropriate assignments.

EXAMPLE 5.6

CREW SCHEDULING AT BRANEAST AIRLINES

Braneast Airlines must staff the daily flights between New York and Chicago shown in Table 5.29 (page 228).[6] Each of Braneast's crews lives in either New York or Chicago. Each day a crew must fly one New York–Chicago flight and one Chicago–New York flight with at least one hour of downtime between flights. For example, a Chicago-based crew could fly the 9–13 Chicago–New York flight and return on the 14–16 New York–Chicago flight. This would incur a downtime of one hour. Braneast wants to schedule crews so as to cover all flights and minimize the total downtime.

---

[5]This model can easily be omitted if desired.
[6]All times are represented as military time. For example, time 13 corresponds to 1 P.M.

TABLE 5.29	Flight Data for Braneast Problem					
Flight	Leave Chicago	Arrive N.Y.	Flight	Leave N.Y.	Arrive Chicago
1	6 A.M.	10 A.M.	1	7 A.M.	9 A.M.
2	9 A.M.	1 P.M.	2	8 A.M.	10 A.M.
3	Noon	4 P.M.	3	10 A.M.	Noon
4	3 P.M.	7 P.M.	4	Noon	2 P.M.
5	5 P.M.	9 P.M.	5	2 P.M.	4 P.M.
6	7 P.M.	11 P.M.	6	4 P.M.	6 P.M.
7	8 P.M.	Midnight	7	7 P.M.	8 P.M.

Solution

The trick is to set this up as an assignment model. Because there are seven flights in each direction, we need seven crews. (Actually, it is conceivable that with a particular set of flight times and the one-hour downtime constraint, seven crews might not provide *any* feasible solutions, but this is fortunately not the case for this particular problem.) Each of the seven crews will be based in either Chicago or New York. We do not know at this point how many of each there will be, but this information will be an output of the model. There are two sets of nodes and arcs, one for crews based in Chicago and one for crews based in New York. Consider the crews based in Chicago. Each such crew will be assigned to two flights, the first starting in Chicago, and the second starting in New York. Furthermore, such an assignment is possible only if the flight from New York leaves at least one hour after the flight from Chicago arrives in New York. With this in mind, we can imagine an origin node corresponding to the flight from Chicago, a destination node corresponding to the flight from New York, and an arc between them from origin to destination. If the flow on this node is 1, a Chicago-based crew is assigned to this pair of flights. Otherwise, if the flow on this node is 0, no crew is assigned to this pair of flights. Of course, similar statements can be made for crews based in New York.

DEVELOPING THE SPREADSHEET MODEL

Once you understand the conceptual idea, the implementation in Excel is fairly straightforward. The completed spreadsheet model appears in Figure 5.29. (See the file CREWSCHED.XLS.) It can be formed with the following steps.

1 **Enter inputs.** Enter the given flight information in the ranges B6:C12 and F6:G12. Because we plan to use this information with lookup functions later on, we have named the ranges A6:C12 and E6:G12 as C_LTable and NY_LTable. The labels in columns A and E serve only to identify the various flights.

2 **Find feasible assignments.** To fill in the Chicago-based crews section, find each early flight leaving from Chicago that can be paired with a later flight leaving from New York such that there is at least one hour of downtime in between. Then enter the flight codes of all such pairs of flights in columns A and B. (There are 8 such pairs, as listed in rows 17–24.) Then do the same for the pairs that could be handled by New York-based crews. (Because of the particular timing of flights, there are many more such pairs, 23 in all, as listed in rows 28–50.) Note that all of this information is entered *manually*—there are no formulas involved.

FIGURE 5.29
Airline Crew Scheduling Model

Crew scheduling model

Range names used:
- C_LTable - A6:C12
- NY_LTable - E6:G12
- Origins1 - A17:A24
- Dests1 - B17:B24
- Downtimes1 - C17:C24
- Flows1 - D17:D24
- Origins2 - A28:A50
- Dests2 - B28:B50
- Downtimes2 - C28:C50
- Flows2 - D28:D50
- TotFlows - I17:I30
- TotDowntime - B52

Flight information

Chicago-NY flights				NY-Chicago flights		
Flight	Departs	Arrives		Flight	Departs	Arrives
1C	6	10		1NY	7	9
2C	9	13		2NY	8	10
3C	12	16		3NY	10	12
4C	15	19		4NY	12	14
5C	17	21		5NY	14	16
6C	19	23		6NY	16	18
7C	20	24		7NY	19	20

Network formulation — Chicago-based crews

Flow balance constraints

Origin	Destination	Downtime	Flow		Node	FlowOut	FlowIn	Total flow		Required
1C	4NY	2	1		1C	1	0	1	=	1
1C	5NY	4	0		2C	1	0	1	=	1
1C	6NY	6	0		3C	0	1	1	=	1
1C	7NY	9	0		4C	0	1	1	=	1
2C	5NY	1	0		5C	0	1	1	=	1
2C	6NY	3	0		6C	0	1	1	=	1
2C	7NY	6	1		7C	0	1	1	=	1
3C	7NY	3	0		1NY	1	0	1	=	1
					2NY	1	0	1	=	1

NY-based crews

Origin	Destination	Downtime	Flow		Node	FlowOut	FlowIn	Total flow		Required
1NY	3C	3	0		3NY	1	0	1	=	1
1NY	4C	6	1		4NY	0	1	1	=	1
1NY	5C	8	0		5NY	1	0	1	=	1
1NY	6C	10	0		6NY	1	0	1	=	1
1NY	7C	11	0		7NY	0	1	1	=	1
2NY	3C	2	1							
2NY	4C	5	0							
2NY	5C	7	0							
2NY	6C	9	0							
2NY	7C	10	0							
3NY	4C	3	0							
3NY	5C	5	0							
3NY	6C	7	1							
3NY	7C	8	0							
4NY	4C	1	0							
4NY	5C	3	0							
4NY	6C	5	0							
4NY	7C	6	0							
5NY	5C	1	1							
5NY	6C	3	0							
5NY	7C	4	0							
6NY	6C	1	0							
6NY	7C	2	1							

Total downtime | 26

❸ **Downtimes for feasible assignments.** Calculate the downtime for each feasible pair of flights by using lookup functions to extract the information from the flight schedules. Specifically, enter the formula

=VLOOKUP(B17,NY_LTable,2)-VLOOKUP(A17,C_LTable,3)

in cell C17 and copy it down for other flight pairs starting in Chicago. This simply subtracts the beginning time of the second flight in the pair from the ending time of the first flight in the pair. (See why we use military time?) Similarly, enter the formula

=VLOOKUP(B28,C_LTable,2)-VLOOKUP(A28,NY_LTable,3)

in cell C28 and copy it down for other flight pairs starting in New York. (If you are used to the INDEX function by now, you might want to see what changes would be needed to use it rather than the VLOOKUP function. Ultimately, it's a matter of taste.)

④ Flows. Enter *any* flows in the Flows1 and Flows2 ranges in column D. Remember that these will eventually be set to 0's and 1's, indicating that an assignment is either made or it isn't.

⑤ Flow balance constraints. There is a node in the network for each flight and a flow balance constraint for each node—hence 14 flow balance constraints. However, things get a bit tricky because each flight could be either the first or second flight in a given flight pair. For example, consider flight 3C. The network representation involving this flight appears as in Figure 5.30. Flight 3C is the later flight for the top two arrows (corresponding to rows 28 and 33 of the model), and it is the earlier flight for the bottom arrow (corresponding to row 24 of the model). Now comes the key observation for this particular model. We require that flight 3C be flown exactly once, so exactly one of these arrows must have flow 1 and the others must have flow 0. Therefore, we *add* this node's total inflow to its total outflow and constrain this sum to be 1.[7] To implement this in the spreadsheet, enter the formulas

=SUMIF(Origins1,F17,Flows1)

and

=SUMIF(Dests2,F17,Flows2)

in cells G17 and H17, and copy them to the range G18:H23 to take care of the flights leaving from Chicago. Then enter the formulas

=SUMIF(Origins2,F24,Flows2)

and

=SUMIF(Dests1,F24,Flows1)

in cells G24 and H24, and copy them to the range G25:H30 to take care of the flights leaving from New York. Finally, add these inflows and outflows in column I (in the TotFlows range). As the spreadsheet model indicates (with equal signs and 1's in columns J and K), we will eventually constrain these sums to be 1.

FIGURE 5.30
Arcs for Flight 3C

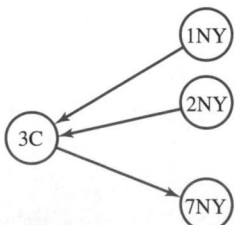

⑥ Total downtime. Calculate the total downtime in the TotDowntime cell with the formula

=SUMPRODUCT(Downtimes1,Flows1)
+SUMPRODUCT(Downtimes2,Flows2)

---

[7]Admittedly, this is not the usual flow balance constraint, but it works here. You might want to search for an alternative way of constructing the network.

USING SOLVER

The Solver dialog box should appear as in Figure 5.31. Note that the *only* constraints (other than nonnegativity of the changing cells) are that the total flow into and out of each node must be 1. This, plus the fact that network models with integer inputs automatically have integer solutions, implies that the flows on all arcs will be 0 or 1.

The optimal solution in Figure 5.29 indicates that there should be two Chicago-based crews and five New York-based crews. This is because there are two 1's in the Flows1 range and five 1's in the Flows2 range. These 1's indicate the crew assignments. For example, one Chicago-based crew flies the 1C and 4NY flights, and the other flies the 2C and 7NY flights. The total downtime for all seven crews is 26 hours.

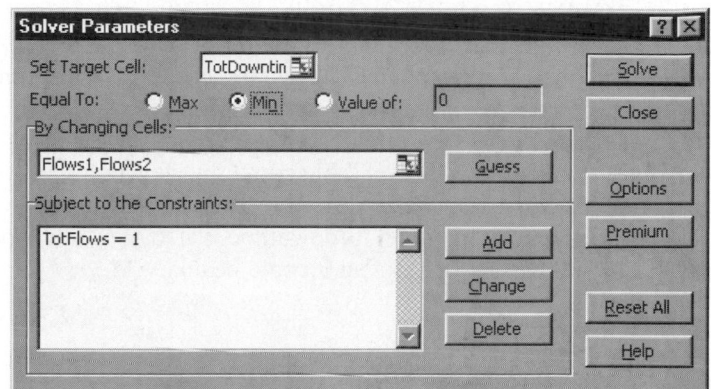

Sensitivity Analysis The only inputs to Braneast's model are the flight times, so we consider one possible sensitivity analysis involving these flight times. Suppose the 1C flight from Chicago is delayed by one or more hours. How will this affect the optimal solution? We need to vary the input section, as shown in Figure 5.32. The original flight times are entered in cells L6 and M6, a flight delay is entered in cell L9, and formulas are entered in cells B6 and C6. (The formula in B6 is **=L6+$L$9**, which is copied to C6.) After running SolverTable, allowing the delay to vary from 0 to 3 in increments of 1 and keeping track of the total downtime and the numbers of crews based in each city, we obtain the results in Figure 5.33 (page 232). Unfortunately, there is a subtle problem we forgot to take care of. (Before reading on, see if you can spot it.)

The problem is that when we delay flight 1C, one or more flight pairings that had at least one hour of downtime originally might no longer have this minimal required downtime. In fact, the Solver solution when the delay is 3 hours schedules a crew to the

	A	B	C	D	E	F	G	H	I	J	K	L	M
1	**Crew scheduling model**												
2									Range names used:				
3	**Flight information**								C_LTable - A6:C12				
4	Chicago-NY flights				NY-Chicago flights				NY_LTable - E6:G12			Original flight 1C times	
5	Flight	Departs	Arrives		Flight	Departs	Arrives		Origins1 - A17:A24			Departs	Arrives
6	1C	9	13		1NY	7	9		Dests1 - B17:B24			6	10
7	2C	9	13		2NY	8	10		Downtimes1 - C17:C24				
8	3C	12	16		3NY	10	12		Flows1 - D17:D24			Delay in flight 1C	
9	4C	15	19		4NY	12	14		Origins2 - A28:A50			3	
10	5C	17	21		5NY	14	16		Dests2 - B28:B50				
11	6C	19	23		6NY	16	18		Downtimes2 - C28:C50				
12	7C	20	24		7NY	19	20		Flows2 - D28:D50				
13									TotFlows - I17:I30				
14	**Network formulation**					**Flow balance constraints**			TotDowntime - B52				

FIGURE 5.32 Modified Input Section to Allow for a Delay

FIGURE 5.33
SolverTable Output
for Sensitivity to
Flight Delay

	A	B	C	D	E	F
52	Total downtime	23				
53						
54	Numbers of crews					
55	Chicago-based	2				
56	New York-based	5				
57						
58	Sensitivity of total downtime and number of crews to delay in flight 1C					
59			$B$52	$B$55	$B$56	
60		0	26	2	5	
61		1	25	2	5	
62		2	24	2	5	
63		3	23	2	5	

pairing 1C–4NY. But this is infeasible—the 1C flight gets into New York at time 13, and the 4NY flight leaves New York at time 12. So the SolverTable solution reported for delays of 3 (and 2) correspond to infeasible schedules. Unfortunately, there is no easy fix for running this sensitivity analysis. Recall that we *manually* entered the pairings (in columns A and B, rows 17–50 of Figure 5.29 that have downtime at least 1. To run this sensitivity analysis with SolverTable correctly, we would need to modify the original model so that Solver gets to choose from all *possible* pairings, with the constraint that a pairing can be chosen only if its downtime is at least 1. The model would grow larger and somewhat more complex, but it could be done. ■

ADDITIONAL APPLICATIONS

Assigning School Buses to Routes

Each year school bus drivers "bid" on the bus routes they are willing to drive. For example, driver 1 may submit a bid of $40,000 for transporting the students on route 8, and so on. After receiving all bids, the local school board must allocate the routes to the drivers. An assignment model can be used to minimize the cost of covering all routes. Our local school district (Monroe County of Indiana) actually uses such a model.

Saving on Airline Commuting

Consider the business commuter who must make multiple air trips between two cities such as Pittsburgh and Chicago. In today's deregulated world, the price of a round-trip ticket varies greatly. For example, if you leave on a Sunday and return on a Monday you pay much more than if you leave on a Saturday and return on a Monday. Hansen and Wendell (1982) realized that a business commuter who makes many air trips between two cities can use the assignment model to save a great deal on airfare. See Problem 73 for details. The trick is to buy several round-trip tickets and for each trip use ticket coupons from parts of two *different* round-trip tickets.

Workforce Assignment in the Military

Using a version of the assignment model, Klingman and Phillips (1984) assigned army personnel to jobs. Their problem involved 10,000 people and 10,000 jobs! Their actual model involved multiple objectives (see Chapter 9). Two objectives were involved: (1) maximize the number of jobs filled by a qualified person and (2) maximize the fit between people and jobs, where there is a rating given for the assignment of each person to each job. ■

Shortest Route Models

In many applications it is important to find the shortest path between two points in a network. This is a special case of the MCNFM. Suppose that we want to find the shortest path between node i and node j in a network. To find this shortest path we create a MCNFM in which the net supply for node i is equal to 1 and the net demand for node j is equal to 1. All other nodes are transshipment points. If there is an arc joining two nodes in the network, the "shipping cost" equals the length of the arc. The "flow" through each arc in the network (in the optimal solution) will be 0 or 1 to indicate that the shortest path either includes the arc or it doesn't. However, no arc capacities are required in the model. The fact that net supplies and net demands are never greater than 1 in magnitude ensures that the optimal flows will be 0 and 1. The value of the objective is then equal to the sum of the distances of the arcs involved in the path.

A Geographical Shortest Route Model

The following example illustrates the shortest path model in the context of a geographic network.

EXAMPLE 5.7

SHORTEST WALK ACROSS THE STATE

Maude Jenkins, a 90-year old woman, is planning to walk across the state, west to east, to gain support for a political cause she favors.[8] She wants to travel the shortest distance to get from city 1 to city 10, using the arcs (roads) shown in Figure 5.34. The numbers on the arcs are miles. Note that arcs with double-headed arrows indicate that travel is possible in both directions (and the distance is the same in both directions). What route should Maude take?

FIGURE 5.34
Network for Shortest Path Problem

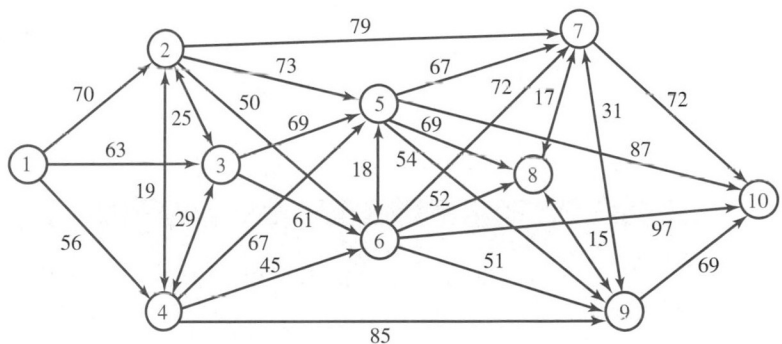

Solution

The network model is exactly like the general MCNFM. All we need to specify is that node 1 has a net supply of 1 (you can think of it as Maude herself), node 10 has a net demand of 1, and all other nodes are transshipment nodes. The completed model and associated Solver dialog box appear in Figures 5.35 and 5.36 (page 234).

---

[8]Far-fetched? This is based on a real 90-year-old woman who, at the time of this writing, is halfway across the *country*. We assume she finished!

FIGURE 5.35
Shortest Path Model

	A	B	C	D	E	F	G	H	I
1	**Shortest path model**								
2									
3	Network arcs					Flow balance constraints			
4	Origin	Dest	Distance	Flow		Node	Outflow		Required
5	1	2	70	0		1	1	=	1
6	1	3	63	0					
7	1	4	56	1		Node	NetOutflow		Required
8	2	3	25	0		2	0	=	0
9	2	4	19	0		3	0	=	0
10	2	5	73	0		4	0	=	0
11	2	6	50	0		5	0	=	0
12	2	7	79	0		6	0	=	0
13	3	2	25	0		7	0	=	0
14	3	4	29	0		8	0	=	0
15	3	5	69	0		9	0	=	0
16	3	6	61	0					
17	4	2	19	0		Node	Inflow		Required
18	4	3	29	0		10	1	=	1
19	4	5	67	0					
20	4	6	45	1					
21	4	9	85	0			Range names used:		
22	5	6	18	0			Origins - A5:A39		
23	5	7	67	0			Dests - B5:B39		
24	5	8	69	0			Dists - C5:C39		
25	5	9	54	0			Flows - D5:D39		
26	5	10	87	0			Outflow - G5		
27	6	5	18	0			NetOutflows - G8:G15		
28	6	7	72	0			Inflow - G18		
29	6	8	52	0			TotDist - B41		
30	6	9	51	0					
31	6	10	97	1					
32	7	8	17	0					
33	7	9	31	0					
34	7	10	72	0					
35	8	7	17	0					
36	8	9	15	0					
37	9	7	31	0					
38	9	8	15	0					
39	9	10	69	0					
40									
41	Total distance	198							

FIGURE 5.36
Solver Dialog Box
for Shortest Path
Model

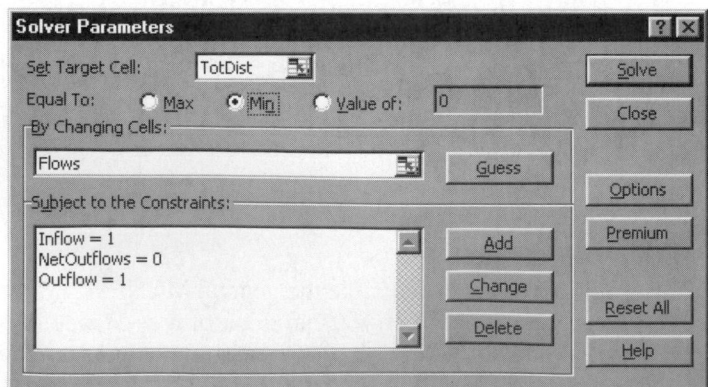

(See the file SHORTPATH.XLS.) Because this is so similar to the general MCNFM, we will omit most of the details. But note the following.

❶ There is an arc listed in columns A and B for each arc in the graphical network. If the arc goes in both directions, it is listed twice (2 to 4 and 4 to 2, for example) with an equal distance in both directions.

❷ We list the three types of nodes separately for clarity. Node 1 is a net supplier with a supply of 1. In fact, no arcs point into it, so we need only calculate its outflow with the formula

=SUMIF(Origins,F5,Flows)

in cell G5. Similarly, node 10 has only inflows, which we calculate in cell G18 with the formula

=SUMIF(Dests,F18,Flows)

The intermediate nodes are all transshipment nodes, so we calculate the *net* outflow for node 2 in cell G8 with the formula

=SUMIF(Origins,F8,Flows)-SUMIF(Dests,F8,Flows)

and copy it down for the rest of the intermediate nodes.

❸ The objective to minimize is total distance, calculated in the TotDist cell with the formula

=SUMPRODUCT(Dists,Flows)

Once Solver finds the optimal flows, which are 0's and 1's, it is easy to identify the shortest path—we just "follow the 1's." According to Figure 5.35, Maude first goes from node 1 to node 4 (see row 7), then she goes from node 4 to node 6 (see row 20), and finally she goes from node 6 to node 10 (see row 31). Using this route from 1 to 10, Maude must walk 198 miles, the sum of the distances on the three arcs she traverses. ■

An Equipment Replacement Model

Although shortest path problems often involve traveling through a network, this is not always the case. For example, when should you trade your car in for a new car? As a car gets older, the maintenance cost per year increases and it might become worthwhile to buy a new car. If your goal is to minimize the average annual cost of owning a car (ignoring discounting), then it is possible to set up a shortest path representation of this problem. Actually, the method we discuss can be used in any situation where equipment replacement is an issue. Of course, many people trade in a car because they like the "feel" of a new car. We will not model this aspect of the problem; we will consider only the financial aspects. The following is an example of how equipment replacement can be modeled as a shortest path problem.

EXAMPLE **5.8**

EQUIPMENT REPLACEMENT AT VANBUREN METALS

VanBuren Metals is a manufacturing company that uses many large machines to work on metals. These machines require frequent maintenance because of wear and tear, and VanBuren finds that it is sometimes advantageous, from a cost point of view, to replace machines rather than continue to maintain them. For one particular class of machine, the company has estimated the quarterly costs of maintenance, the salvage value of reselling an old machine, and the cost to purchase a new machine.[9] We assume that the maintenance cost and the salvage value depend on the *age* of the current machine (at the beginning of the quarter), as well as the quarter in which they occur, whereas the purchase cost depends only on the quarter in which it is purchased. Essentially, maintenance costs increase with age and salvage values decrease with age, but maintenance costs, salvage values, and purchase costs all increase through time because of inflation. VanBuren would like to devise a strategy for purchasing machines over the next 5 years. As a matter of policy, the company never sells a machine that is less than 1 year old, and it never keeps a machine that is more than 3 years old. Also, the machine in use at the beginning of the current quarter is brand new.

Solution

The company's first challenge is to estimate maintenance costs, salvage values, and purchase costs in *future* months. Although we could simply give these in a table and proceed directly to the optimization model, it is instructive to see how a company might actually estimate these monetary values from past data. Presumably, the company owns several of these machines (maybe hundreds), and it has lots of historical data on maintenance, resales, and purchases.

The file VANBUREN.XLS contains four sheets. The first three of these (Maint-Data, SalvData, and PurchData) contain historical data for the past 6 years on similar machines. (The fourth sheet, Model, contains the model.) The MaintData sheet has average maintenance costs from each of the past 24 quarters for machines of all ages from 0 to 11 quarters. The SalvData sheet has average salvage values from the past 24 quarters for resales of machines from ages 4 to 12. (As a reminder, a maintenance cost is based on the machine's age at the *beginning* of a quarter. A salvage value is based on the machine's age at the *end* of the quarter when it is sold.) The PurchData sheet has average purchase costs from the past 24 quarters. The company needs to estimate future costs from these historical data. To do so, it assumes that the data are driven by "reasonable" models with unknown parameters that need to be estimated.

Estimation Model One reasonable model for maintenance costs is that, in the absence of inflation, they increase by a fixed percentage each quarter. Then inflation tacks on a fixed percentage per quarter to these "base" values. Such a model is given by the equation

$$\text{Estimated Maintenance Cost} = (ae^{bA})e^{cQ} \qquad \text{(5.1)}$$

Here, A is the age of the machine, Q is the quarter (where $Q = 1$ corresponds to the first quarter observed, 6 years ago), and a, b, and c are constants to be estimated. We can interpret b as the approximate percentage increase in maintenance costs per extra quarter of age, and we can interpret c as the approximate inflation rate per quarter. To estimate these constants, we can use Solver.[10] (See Figure 5.37.) The idea is to calculate estimated maintenance costs in column D, given trial values of the constants in the range B5:B7, calculate the squared differences between observed and estimated values

---

[9]One issue in these types of models is the time period to be used. We will assume that VanBuren uses quarters. Therefore, the only times it considers purchasing new machines are beginnings of quarters.

[10]This is actually a preview of nonlinear optimization (covered in Chapter 7) and forecasting (covered in Chapter 16). If you like, you can skip the details for now and simply accept the results.

FIGURE 5.37
Estimation Model for
Maintenance Costs

	A	B	C	D	E	F	G
1	**Historical data on maintenance costs**						
2							
3	Assumed form of maintenance cost function: Cost = a*EXP(b*Age)*EXP(c*Quarter)						
4	Coefficients						
5	a	140.779					
6	b	0.190					
7	c	0.011					
8	MSE	421.0129					
9							
10	Quarter	Age	MaintCost	Estimated	SqrErr		
11	1	0	145	142.35	7.01		
12	1	1	170	172.08	4.32		
13	1	2	212	208.01	15.90		
14	1	3	254	251.45	6.51		
15	1	4	302	303.96	3.83		
16	1	5	377	367.43	91.60		
17	1	6	464	444.16	393.80		
18	1	7	543	536.90	37.16		
19	1	8	663	649.02	195.42		
291	24	4	390	392.52	6.34		
292	24	5	457	474.48	305.64		
293	24	6	553	573.56	422.88		
294	24	7	691	693.34	5.46		
295	24	8	810	838.12	790.62		
296	24	9	1043	1013.13	891.99		
297	24	10	1289	1224.70	4134.94		
298	24	11	1392	1480.44	7821.22		

in column E, average these squared errors in cell B8, and use Solver to minimize this "mean square error" (MSE). The steps are as follows.

❶ Constants. Enter *any* constants in cells B5 through B7 (although reasonable values will better ensure that Solver will converge to the correct values).

❷ Estimated costs. Use equation (5.1) to calculate estimated costs by entering the formula

=$B$5*EXP($B$6*B11)*EXP($B$7*A11)

in cell D11 and copying it down column D.

❸ Squared errors. It is typical in estimation problems of this type to minimize the average (or sum) of squared differences between observed and estimated values. Therefore, calculate the squared errors by entering the formula

=(C11-D11)^2

in cell E11 and copying it down column E.

❹ Mean square error. Calculate the average of the squared errors in cell B8 with the formula

=AVERAGE(E11:E298)

❺ Use Solver. The Solver setup is particularly easy. Just enter cell B8 as the cell to minimize, and B5:B7 as the changing cells. There are no constraints. Also, do *not* check the nonnegativity or linear boxes under Solver options. In particular, this is not a linear model because of the *squared* errors.

The solution shown in Figure 5.37 indicates a reasonably good fit. (You can scan the data to see how close the estimated costs are to the observed costs.) The values of

b and c indicate that maintenance costs increase about 19% per quarter and inflation tacks on about 1.1% per quarter. We can interpret a as the "base" maintenance cost for a brand new machine in quarter 0; it is about $140.

We can proceed similarly with salvage values and purchase costs. The salvage value model we propose is identical to the maintenance cost model except that there is a minus sign next to the constant b. This is because the salvage value of a machine *decreases* with age. The estimation model for salvage values appears in Figure 5.38. We see that the salvage values decrease by about 15% per extra quarter of age, and the relevant inflation rate is about 1.2% per quarter. The model for purchase costs is simpler because there is no Age variable. (We assume VanBuren purchases all brand new machines.) Therefore, the only thing that affects purchase costs is inflation. The purchase cost model appears in Figure 5.39. We see that purchase costs increase by only about 0.8% per quarter.

FIGURE 5.38
Estimation Model
for Salvage Values

	A	B	C	D	E	F	G
1	Historical data on salvage values						
2							
3	Assumed form of salvage values function: SalvVal = a*EXP(-b*Age)*EXP(c*Quarter)						
4	Coefficients						
5	a	2003.739					
6	b	0.150					
7	c	0.012					
8	MSE	286.96					
9							
10	Quarter	Age	SalvVal	Estimated	SqrErr		
11	1	4	1116	1113.08	8.53		
12	1	5	980	957.97	485.26		
13	1	6	803	824.48	461.28		
14	1	7	689	709.59	423.78		
15	1	8	617	610.70	39.63		
16	1	9	529	525.60	11.54		
221	24	7	980	943.51	1331.19		
222	24	8	781	812.04	963.18		
223	24	9	704	698.88	26.24		
224	24	10	624	601.49	506.77		
225	24	11	517	517.67	0.45		
226	24	12	437	445.53	72.81		

FIGURE 5.39
Estimation Model
for Purchase Costs

	A	B	C	D	E	F
1	Historical data on purchase costs					
2						
3	Assumed form of purchase cost function: PurchCost = a*EXP(c*Quarter)					
4	Coefficients					
5	a	3547.393				
6	c	0.008				
7	MSE	4462.5749				
8						
9	Quarter	PurchCost	Estimated	SqrErr		
10	1	3535	3577.44	1801.29		
11	2	3529	3607.74	6200.67		
12	3	3744	3638.30	11171.70		
13	4	3606	3669.12	3984.38		
14	5	3801	3700.20	10160.39		
15	6	3756	3731.54	598.11		
30	21	4270	4234.84	1236.57		
31	22	4326	4270.71	3057.41		
32	23	4232	4306.88	5607.19		
33	24	4391	4343.36	2269.32		

Optimization Model Now that we have models for estimating future costs, we can develop a *decision* model for when to replace machines. This is a shortest path model. There are two keys to understanding how it works: (1) the meaning of nodes and arcs, and (2) the calculation of costs on arcs. From there, the modeling details are *exactly* as in the previous example. The network is constructed as follows. There is a node for each future quarter, including the current quarter and the quarter exactly 5 years from now. (Remember that VanBuren wants to plan for 5 years ahead.) We label these nodes 25 through 45 to be consistent with the historical quarters labeled 1 through 24.

There is an arc from each node to each *later* node that is at least 4 quarters ahead but no more than 12 quarters ahead. (Again, recall that VanBuren never sells a machine less than 1 year old, and never keeps a machine more than 3 years.) Several of these arcs are shown in Figure 5.40. (Of course, many nodes and arcs are *not* shown in this figure.) Consider the arc from node 33 to node 41, for example. "Using" this arc on the shortest path (that is, putting a flow of 1 on it) means starting with a brand new machine in quarter 33, keeping it for 8 quarters, and selling it and purchasing a new machine at the beginning of quarter 41. An entire strategy for the 5-year period is a string of such arcs. For example, if the shortest path is 25–33–41–45, then VanBuren keeps the first machine for 8 quarters, purchases a second machine in quarter 33, keeps it for 8 quarters, purchases a third machine in quarter 41, keeps it for 4 quarters, and finally trades it in for a new machine in quarter 45.

FIGURE 5.40
Selected Nodes and
Arcs for Machine
Replacement
Network

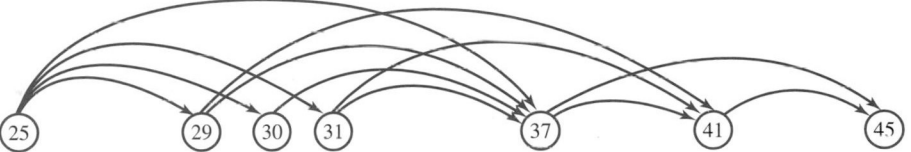

Given the meaning of the arcs, the calculation of arc costs is a matter of careful bookkeeping. Again, consider the arc from node 33 to node 41. The cost on this arc is the total maintenance cost for this machine during these 8 quarters, minus the salvage value of an 8-quarter old machine sold in quarter 41, plus the cost of a new machine purchased in quarter 41. The total maintenance cost for this machine is a bit tricky. It is the maintenance cost of a 0-quarter old machine in quarter 33, plus the maintenance cost of a 1-quarter old machine in quarter 34, plus the maintenance cost of a 2-quarter old machine in quarter 35, and so on. Of course, to calculate any of these costs, we use the cost models developed from the historical data.

Part of the spreadsheet model appears in Figure 5.41 (page 240). (Several columns have been hidden, and only the first few rows are shown.) This part of the model can be completed with the following steps.

❶ Cost model parameters. Copy the parameters of the cost functions in the cost model sheets to the range B5:D7. Note the descriptive range names we have used for these cells.

❷ Arcs. In the body of the figure, columns A and B indicate the arcs in the network. Enter these "origins" and "destinations" manually. This is admittedly tedious. Just make sure that the difference between them is at least 4 and no greater than 12, the origin is at least 25, and the destination is no more than 45.

❸ Differences. Calculate the differences between the values in columns B and A in column C. These differences indicate how many quarters the machine is kept for each arc.

	A	B	C	D	E	F	N	O	P	Q	R	S
1	**Machine replacement model - shortest path formulation**											
2												
3	Parameters of maintenance cost, salvage value, purchase cost functions											
4		MaintCost	SalvVal	PurchCost								
5	a	140.779	2003.739	3547.393								
6	b	0.190	0.150									
7	c	0.011	0.012	0.008								
8												
9	Network arcs			Maintenance costs in quarter:								
10	Origin	Dest	QtrsToKeep	1	2	3	11	12	SalvVal	PurchCost	TotalCost	Flow
11	25	29	4	186	227	278	0	0	1575	4530	3986	0
12	25	30	5	186	227	278	0	0	1372	4569	4642	0
13	25	31	6	186	227	278	0	0	1196	4608	5364	0
14	25	32	7	186	227	278	0	0	1042	4647	6177	1
15	25	33	8	186	227	278	0	0	908	4686	7108	0
16	25	34	9	186	227	278	0	0	791	4726	8191	0
17	25	35	10	186	227	278	0	0	689	4766	9465	0
18	25	36	11	186	227	278	1384	0	601	4806	10978	0
19	25	37	12	186	227	278	1384	1692	523	4847	12788	0
20	26	30	4	188	230	281	0	0	1594	4569	4016	0
21	26	31	5	188	230	281	0	0	1389	4608	4680	0
22	26	32	6	188	230	281	0	0	1210	4647	5410	0
23	26	33	7	188	230	281	0	0	1055	4686	6232	0
24	26	34	8	188	230	281	0	0	919	4726	7174	0
25	26	35	9	188	230	281	0	0	801	4766	8269	0
26	26	36	10	188	230	281	0	0	698	4806	9557	0
27	26	37	11	188	230	281	1399	0	608	4847	11087	0
28	26	38	12	188	230	281	1399	1711	530	4888	12917	0
29	27	31	4	190	232	284	0	0	1614	4608	4047	0
30	27	32	5	190	232	284	0	0	1406	4647	4718	0
31	27	33	6	190	232	284	0	0	1226	4686	5457	0
32	27	34	7	190	232	284	0	0	1068	4726	6288	0
33	27	35	8	190	232	284	0	0	931	4766	7240	0
34	27	36	9	190	232	284	0	0	811	4806	8347	0
35	27	37	10	190	232	284	0	0	707	4847	9650	0
36	27	38	11	190	232	284	1415	0	616	4888	11197	0

Range names used for cost parameters:
MCBase - B5
MCIncr - B6
MCInfl - B7
SVBase - C5
SVDecr - C6
SVInfl - C7
PCBase - D5
PCInfl - D7

Range names used for model:
Origins - A11:A118
Dests - B11:B118
Costs - R11:R118
Flows - S11:S118
Outflow - V11
NetOutflows - V14:V32
Inflow - V35
TotalCost - B120

FIGURE 5.41 Arc Information in Machine Replacement Model

❹ **Maintenance costs.** Calculate the quarterly maintenance costs in columns D through O. For example, for the arc from 25 to 29 in row 11, cell D11 contains the maintenance cost in the first quarter of this period, cell E11 contains the maintenance cost in the second quarter of this period, and so on. Fortunately, you can calculate all of these maintenance costs at once by entering the formula

**=IF(D$10<=$C11,MCBase*EXP(MCIncr*(D$10-1))
EXP(MCInfl($A11+D$10-1)),0)**

in cell D11 and copying it to the range D11:O118. The IF function is used to ensure that no maintenance costs for this machine are incurred unless it is still owned. The rest of this rather complex formula is the Excel implementation of equation (5.1).

❺ **Salvage values and purchase costs.** In a similar way, calculate the salvage values in column P by entering the formula

=SVBase*EXP(-SVDecr*$C11)*EXP(SVInfl*($B11))

in cell P11 and copying down column P. Then calculate the purchase costs in column Q by entering the formula

=PCBase*EXP(PCInfl*($B11))

in cell Q11 and copying down column Q.

6 **Total arc costs.** Calculate the total costs on the arcs as total maintenance cost minus salvage value plus purchase cost. To do this, enter the formula

=SUM(D11:O11)-P11+Q11

in cell R11, and copy it down column R.

7 **Flows.** Enter *any* flows on the arcs in column S.

From this point, the model is developed *exactly* as in the shortest path model of Example 5.7, with node 25 as the "origin" node and node 45 as the "destination" node. We create the flow balance constraints, calculate the total network cost, and use Solver exactly as before, so we won't repeat the details here. (See Figure 5.42.) Also, to find the shortest path, we follow the 1's in the Flows range. Although not all of the rows appear in Figure 5.41, you can check in the VANBUREN.XLS file that only three arcs have flows of 1: 25–32, 32–39, and 39–45. Therefore, VanBuren should keep the current machine for 7 quarters, resell it and buy a new machine in quarter 32, keep the second machine for 7 quarters, resell it and buy a new machine in quarter 39, keep it for 6 quarters, and finally resell it and buy a new machine in quarter 45. The total (net) cost of this strategy is $18,795.

FIGURE 5.42
Constraints and Objective for Machine Replacement Model

	U	V	W	X
9	Flow balance constraints			
10	Node	Outflow		Required
11	25	1	=	1
12				
13	Node	NetOutflow		Required
14	26	0	=	0
15	27	0	=	0
16	28	0	=	0
17	29	0	=	0
18	30	0	=	0
19	31	0	=	0
20	32	0	=	0
21	33	0	=	0
22	34	0	=	0
23	35	0	=	0
24	36	0	=	0
25	37	0	=	0
26	38	0	=	0
27	39	0	=	0
28	40	0	=	0
29	41	0	=	0
30	42	0	=	0
31	43	0	=	0
32	44	0	=	1
33				
34	Node	Inflow		Required
35	45	1	=	1
36				
37	Total cost	$18,795		

MODELING ISSUES

1. As the model now stands, VanBuren is *forced* to resell the current machine and purchase a new one at the end of the 5-year period. This is because the cost of every arc leading into the last node, node 45, includes a salvage value and a purchase cost. This feature of the model is not as bad as it might seem. *Every* path from node 25 to node 45 includes the purchase cost in quarter 45, so this cost has no effect

on which path is best. The effect of including the salvage value in arcs into node 45 is to penalize strategies that end with old machines after 5 years. Regardless of how we model the problem, we probably *ought* to penalize such strategies in some way. In addition, VanBuren will probably use a rolling planning horizon—that is, it will implement only short-term decisions from the model. Hopefully, the way we model the end of the 5-year horizon has little effect on these early decisions.

2. Continuing the previous point, suppose VanBuren implements a rolling planning horizon. Then at the beginning of quarter 26, it will solve a new 5-year problem, but it will start quarter 26 with a 1-quarter old machine. In general, how can we change the model to allow the machine in the first quarter to be one or more quarters old? This is somewhat trickier than it might appear. For example, suppose the first quarter is quarter 29, and the current machine is 4 quarters old. Then because of the company's policy, we must allow arcs out of node 29 to arcs 30 through 37. For example, the arc from 29 to 31 would imply selling the current machine when it is 6 quarters old—which is certainly allowable. But arcs out of nodes 30 and beyond should still have the same "at least 4, no more than 12" gap. For example, there would be arcs from node 30 to nodes 34 through 42. This is because being at node 30, say, means having a brand new machine. ■

ADDITIONAL APPLICATIONS

Replacing Vehicles at Phillips Petroleum Company

Waddell (1983) used the shortest path model to help Phillips Petroleum Company schedule replacement of individual highway tractors, cars, and trucks. The model allowed for the possibility of leasing vehicles, as well as purchasing them. Replacement of vehicles was allowed at 3-month intervals. The goal was to find a vehicle replacement policy that would minimize discounted costs over a planning horizon of 20 years. The following costs were included in the model:

- maintenance and operating costs such as fuel, oil, salaries of repair personnel, and so on
- leasing cost for leased vehicles
- purchase cost for purchased vehicles
- state license fees and road taxes
- cost of purchasing vehicle
- savings due to investment tax credits and investment depreciation

When the model was applied to cars and trucks, vehicles were grouped according to their age, odometer mileage, and function. It is estimated that the equipment replacement model saves Phillips $90,000 annually when applied to tractors alone. ■

An Airline Scheduling Model

We finish this section with a model that is realistic, complex, and not at all an obvious network model. However, once we see the network structure lurking in the background, the model simplifies tremendously. If you don't believe us, just try modeling the problem in any way *other* than as a network model.

EXAMPLE 5.9

SCHEDULING FLIGHTS AT TRICITIES AIRLINES

TriCities Airlines flies several daily commuter flights to and from the three cities New York, Washington, D.C., and Boston. The company has been flying a fixed daily schedule of flights, but it is now deciding whether to change this schedule. Each potential flight has an estimated net revenue that is based on the typical number of passengers for the flight. The company owns 4 airplanes, and it does not anticipate buying any more. There is a fixed cost per plane per day that flies any flights. However, a plane that is not used does not incur this fixed cost. We assume (although this could be relaxed) that there is no required delay time on the ground, so that if a flight arrives in Boston at time 10, it can leave on a new flight at time 10. (We will measure time in military time.) Also, any plane that arrives to a city after its last flight of the day has two options. It can sit overnight in that city, or, at some cost, it can be flown empty to another city overnight. The company's objective is to maximize its net profit per day, which equals net revenues from flights flown, minus fixed costs of flying planes, minus overnight costs of flying empty.

Solution

We first discuss how this problem can be modeled as a MCNFM—which is certainly not obvious. The trick is to have a node for each city/time combination. Because we allow flights on the half-hour, this means having nodes of the form Boston8, Boston8.5, and so on, up to WashDC20 (assuming, as we do, that the earliest flight leaves at time 8 and the latest flight arrives at time 20). There are three types of arcs. The most obvious type is a "flight" arc. For example, if there is a flight from Boston at time 12.5 that arrives at Washington, D.C., at time 14, then there is a flight arc from node Boston12.5 to node WashDC14. The flow on such an arc represents the number of planes that fly this flight. Because each flight can be flown at most once, we impose a capacity of 1 on all such flight arcs. The "cost" on a flight arc is the net revenue for flying the flight. (In this model it is more natural to use net revenues as the arc "costs," so that we will actually be finding the *maximum* "cost" network flow.)

The other arcs are less obvious. If a flight arrives into New York, say, at time 13, it might sit on the ground until time 14.5, at which time it leaves for another city. We model this with the "ground" arcs NY13–NY13.5, NY13.5–NY14, and NY14–NY14.5. In general, the flow on any ground arc represents the number of planes sitting on the ground in that city for that half-hour period. These ground arcs have no capacities and no costs.

Finally, the real trick involves relating one day to the next. Suppose one or more planes end up in New York at the end of the day, at time 20. They can either sit overnight in New York or they can be flown to another city, where they will be available at time 8 the next morning. To model this, we use "overnight" arcs. The flow on an overnight arc such as NY20–NY8 represents the number of planes that sit overnight in New York. It has no capacity and a cost equal to the fixed cost of operating a plane. In contrast, the flow on an overnight arc such as NY20–Boston8 represents the number of planes flown overnight from New York to Boston. It has no capacity and a cost equal to the fixed cost of operating a plane plus the cost of flying a plane empty overnight. Note the total flow on all overnight arcs equals the total number of planes being used—all planes being used must be *somewhere* overnight. In fact, we put a "side" constraint on this total—it must be less than or equal to the number of planes owned, 4.

A few of the nodes and arcs for this network are shown in Figure 5.43. The flight arcs are the diagonal arcs, the ground arcs all point one step to the right, and the overnight arcs go backward from right to left.

With this network, there is flow balance (inflow equals outflow) at *every* node. This might be called "conservation of planes." The same planes continue to circulate through the network day after day. Of course, if we wanted *different* schedules on different days of the week, we would have to change the model, and it would become considerably more complex.

FIGURE 5.43
Selected Nodes and Arcs for Flights Model

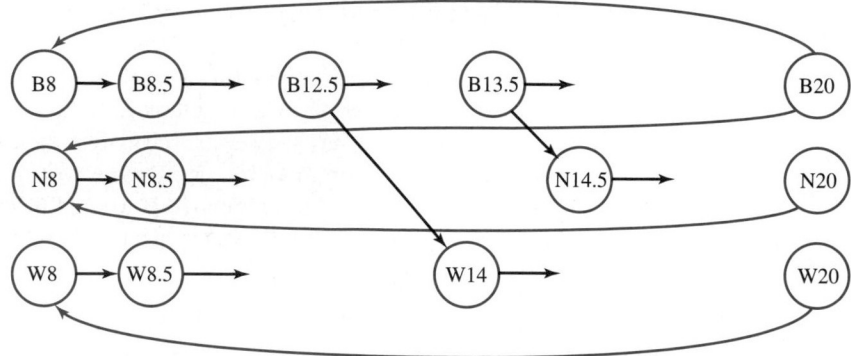

DEVELOPING THE SPREADSHEET MODEL

The finished model is quite large, so we will show it in pieces. (See the file FLIGHTS. XLS.) Figure 5.44 shows the *potential* flight schedule, plus several other inputs. Recall that TriCities wants to select the appropriate *subset* of these flights to fly, which could be all of them. (All monetary values are expressed in hundreds of dollars.) Note that the cost of flying a plane empty overnight is a constant. We could easily allow this cost to depend on the origin and destination of the flight.

The information on the three types of arcs appears in Figures 5.45, 5.46 (page 246), and 5.47 (page 246). The flight arcs correspond exactly to the available flights in Figure 5.44. Note that each flight arc has a capacity of 1. There are many ground arcs (note the hidden rows in Figure 5.46), each extending one half-hour into the day, and their costs are all 0. Finally, there are only nine ground arcs. Each has a fixed cost, and those that represent empty overnight flights also have an overnight cost. By the way, there are possible shortcuts for generating the origin and destination labels in these figures. For the flight arcs, you can enter the "text" formula

=B10&D10

in cell A37 and copy it to the range A37:B59. This "concatenates" the city names and times from the flight input table. Similarly, to generate the labels for the many ground arcs, you can generate the sequence of times, 8, 8.5, 9, and so on, in another section of the spreadsheet with the Edit/Fill/Series command, then use a text formula to concatenate each city name with these times. For example, if the series of times starts in cell AA1, you can enter the formula

="Boston"&AA1

in cell A63 and copy it down to get all Boston origin labels.

The rest is straightforward. As usual, we fill out a table of flow balance constraints, as shown in Figure 5.48 (page 246). (Note that many rows have been hidden.) There

Figure 5.44

	A	B	C	D	E	F	G	H
1	**Flight scheduling model**							
2								
3	**Input data**							
4	Planes owned	4						
5	Fixed cost per plane	15						
6	Overnight cost	5						
7								
8	**Flight information**							
9	Flight Number	Origin	Destination	Departs	Arrives	Net Revenue		
10	1357	Boston	NY	8	9	25		
11	8322	Boston	NY	9.5	10.5	30		
12	5903	Boston	WashDC	12.5	14	39		
13	1207	Boston	WashDC	13.5	15	24		
14	1671	Boston	NY	13.5	14.5	24		
15	5671	Boston	WashDC	16	17.5	35		
16	7133	Boston	NY	16.5	17.5	29		
17	4166	NY	Boston	9.5	11	28		
18	3842	NY	Boston	12	13.5	13		
19	1537	NY	WashDC	13	14.5	18		
20	9320	NY	Boston	14	16	22		
21	3042	NY	Boston	16.5	18	28		
22	3752	NY	Boston	18	19.5	34		
23	9677	NY	WashDC	18	20	39		
24	6212	NY	Boston	18.5	20	15		
25	6811	WashDC	NY	9	11	12		
26	9195	WashDC	NY	12.5	14	28		
27	8350	WashDC	NY	13	15	13		
28	9480	WashDC	Boston	13.5	15.5	18		
29	7555	WashDC	NY	14	15.5	33		
30	9041	WashDC	Boston	14	15.5	28		
31	7539	WashDC	Boston	14.5	16.5	19		
32	2710	WashDC	Boston	16	17.5	15		

Range names used:
PlanesOwned - B4
FCostPerPlane - B5
ONightCostPerFlight - B6
Origins1 - A37:A59
Dests1 - B37:B59
NetRevenues - C37:C59
Flows1 - D37:D59
Origins2 - A63:A134
Dests2 - B63:B134
Flows2 - D63:D134
Origins3 - A138:A146
Dests3 - B138:B146
FCosts - C138:C146
ONightCosts - D138:D146
Flows3 - E138:E146
NetOutflows - I37:I111
PlanesUsed - B150
TotNetRev - B153
TotFCost - B154
TotONightCost - B155
Profit - B156

FIGURE 5.44 Inputs for Flights Problem

FIGURE 5.45 Flight Arcs

Figure 5.45

	A	B	C	D	E	F
35	Flight arcs					
36	OriginCityTime	DestCityTime	Net revenue	Flow		Capacity
37	Boston8	NY9	25	1	<=	1
38	Boston9.5	NY10.5	30	1	<=	1
39	Boston12.5	WashDC14	39	1	<=	1
40	Boston13.5	WashDC15	24	0	<=	1
41	Boston13.5	NY14.5	24	1	<=	1
42	Boston16	WashDC17.5	35	1	<=	1
43	Boston16.5	NY17.5	29	1	<=	1
44	NY9.5	Boston11	28	1	<=	1
45	NY12	Boston13.5	13	1	<=	1
46	NY13	WashDC14.5	18	1	<=	1
47	NY14	Boston16	22	1	<=	1
48	NY16.5	Boston18	28	1	<=	1
49	NY18	Boston19.5	34	1	<=	1
50	NY18	WashDC20	39	1	<=	1
51	NY18.5	Boston20	15	0	<=	1
52	WashDC9	NY11	12	1	<=	1
53	WashDC12.5	NY14	28	1	<=	1
54	WashDC13	NY15	13	0	<=	1
55	WashDC13.5	Boston15.5	18	0	<=	1
56	WashDC14	NY15.5	33	1	<=	1
57	WashDC14	Boston15.5	28	0	<=	1
58	WashDC14.5	Boston16.5	19	1	<=	1
59	WashDC16	Boston17.5	15	0	<=	1

FIGURE 5.46
Ground Arcs

	A	B	C	D
61	Ground arcs			
62	OriginCityTime	DestCityTime	Cost	Flow
63	Boston8	Boston8.5	0	1
64	Boston8.5	Boston9	0	1
65	Boston9	Boston9.5	0	1
66	Boston9.5	Boston10	0	0
67	Boston10	Boston10.5	0	0
68	Boston10.5	Boston11	0	0
69	Boston11	Boston11.5	0	1
70	Boston11.5	Boston12	0	1
71	Boston12	Boston12.5	0	1
72	Boston12.5	Boston13	0	0
73	Boston13	Boston13.5	0	0
74	Boston13.5	Boston14	0	0
75	Boston14	Boston14.5	0	0
125	WashDC15	WashDC15.5	0	0
126	WashDC15.5	WashDC16	0	0
127	WashDC16	WashDC16.5	0	0
128	WashDC16.5	WashDC17	0	0
129	WashDC17	WashDC17.5	0	0
130	WashDC17.5	WashDC18	0	1
131	WashDC18	WashDC18.5	0	1
132	WashDC18.5	WashDC19	0	1
133	WashDC19	WashDC19.5	0	1
134	WashDC19.5	WashDC20	0	1

FIGURE 5.47
Overnight Arcs

	A	B	C	D	E
137	OriginCityTime	DestCityTime	FixedCost	OvernightCost	Flow
138	Boston20	Boston8	15	0	2
139	Boston20	NY8	15	5	0
140	Boston20	WashDC8	15	5	0
141	NY20	Boston8	15	5	0
142	NY20	NY8	15	0	0
143	NY20	WashDC8	15	5	0
144	WashDC20	Boston8	15	5	0
145	WashDC20	NY8	15	5	0
146	WashDC20	WashDC8	15	0	2

FIGURE 5.48
Flow Balance
Constraints for
Flights Model

	H	I	J	K
34	**Flow balance constraints**			
35				
36	Node	NetOutflow		Required
37	Boston8	0	=	0
38	Boston8.5	0	=	0
39	Boston9	0	=	0
40	Boston9.5	0	=	0
41	Boston10	0	=	0
42	Boston10.5	0	=	0
43	Boston11	0	=	0
44	Boston11.5	0	=	0
45	Boston12	0	=	0
46	Boston12.5	0	=	0
47	Boston13	0	=	0
48	Boston13.5	0	=	0
102	WashDC15.5	0	=	0
103	WashDC16	0	=	0
104	WashDC16.5	0	=	0
105	WashDC17	0	=	0
106	WashDC17.5	0	=	0
107	WashDC18	0	=	0
108	WashDC18.5	0	=	0
109	WashDC19	0	=	0
110	WashDC19.5	0	=	0
111	WashDC20	0	=	0

is a constraint for each node—that is, each city/time combination. The typical formula for net outflow in cell I37, which can be copied down column I, is

=SUMIF(Origins1,H37,Flows1)+SUMIF(Origins2,H37,Flows2)
+SUMIF(Origins3,H37,Flows3)-(SUMIF(Dests1,H37,Flows1)
+SUMIF(Dests2,H37,Flows2)+SUMIF(Dests3,H37,Flows3))

This looks complex, but it is simply the sum of outflows from the three types of arcs minus the sum of inflows from the three types of arcs. Because there must be flow balance at each node, we constrain each net outflow to be 0.

Figures 5.49 and 5.50 show the rest of the model and the Solver dialog box. To find the number of planes used, we sum the flows on all overnight arcs in cell B150 with the formula

=SUM(Flows3)

Then we calculate the various monetary values with the usual SUMPRODUCT functions. For example, the formula for total net revenue from flights is

=SUMPRODUCT(NetRevenues,Flows1)

Finally, we combine these into a profit objective in cell B156 with the formula

=TotNetRev-TotFCost-TotONightCost

The Solver dialog box follows easily—and is remarkably compact for such a large and complex model.

The optimal solution can be seen primarily from Figures 5.45 and 5.47. The former indicates that TriCities should fly only 17 of the potential 23 flights. The latter shows that no overnight flights should be flown. It also shows that all four planes are used. Two of these will sit overnight in Boston, and the other two will sit overnight in Washington, D.C. The daily profit from this solution is $39,600.

FIGURE 5.49
Rest of Flights
Model

	A	B	C	D
148	**Constraint on planes**			
149		Number used		Number owned
150		4	<=	4
151				
152	**Monetary values**			
153	Net revenues	456		
154	Fixed costs	60		
155	Overnight costs	0		
156	Profit	396		

FIGURE 5.50
Solver Dialog Box
for Flights Model

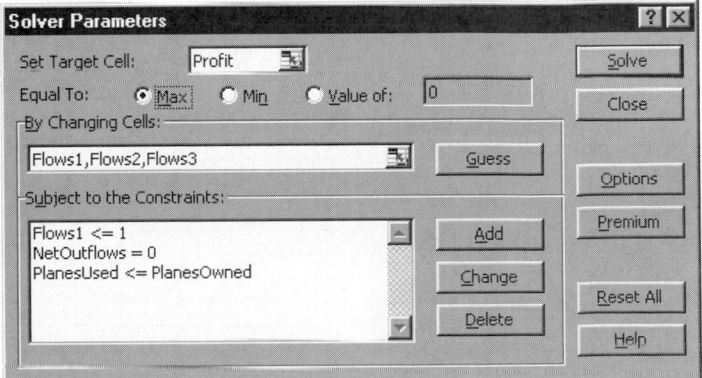

Sensitivity Analysis There are many interesting sensitivity analyses we might run. For example, what if TriCities had more planes? To answer this, we run SolverTable with the PlanesOwned cell as the single input cell, allowing it to vary from 4 to 8 in increments of 1, and we keep track of the monetary values, as well as the number of flights flown. (This latter output is calculated in cell B158 with the formula **=SUM(Flows1)**.) The results appear in Figure 5.51. As expected, profit and the number of flights flown both increase when the company owns more planes, but this analysis does not take the cost of *purchasing* more planes into account. TriCities would need to trade off the cost of new planes with this increased profit.

FIGURE 5.51
Sensitivity to Planes
Owned

	A	B	C	D	E	F	G
152	**Monetary values**						
153	Net revenues	551					
154	Fixed costs	105					
155	Overnight costs	10					
156	Profit	436					
157							
158	Flights flown	22					
159							
160	**Sensitivity of monetary values and flights flown to planes owned**						
161			$B$153	$B$154	$B$155	$B$156	$B$158
162		4	456	60	0	396	17
163		5	495	75	0	420	19
164		6	523	90	5	428	21
165		7	551	105	10	436	22
166		8	551	105	10	436	22

From Figure 5.51, we see that TriCities still does not fly all 23 potential flights, even with 8 planes. Could it? We can answer this question easily by changing the objective from maximizing profit to maximizing the number of flights flown (in cell B158) and rerunning Solver. If you do so, you will find that the maximum is 23. Therefore, TriCities *could* fly all 23 flights with 8 planes, but the cost structure makes it more profitable to fly only 22. The driving factor here is evidently the fixed cost per plane. When TriCities owns 8 planes, the optimal profit solution *uses* only 7 of these planes.

A final sensitivity analysis involves empty overnight flights. When TriCities owns 7 planes, Figure 5.51 indicates (see cell E165) that it flies two empty overnight flights. (These are both from Boston to Washington, D.C.) What would happen to this solution if, as a matter of company policy, empty overnight flights were not allowed? There are three ways we could modify the model to answer this question. First, we could impose a huge cost of overnight flights, effectively ruling them out. Second, we could impose capacities of 0 on the overnight flight arcs (in Figure 5.47). Third, we could simply eliminate these arcs. We used the first method, with the results shown in Figure 5.52. The solution changes fairly dramatically. Now TriCities uses only 5 of its 7 planes, it flies only 19 (instead of 22) flights, and its profit decreases from $43,600 to $42,000.

FIGURE 5.52
Model with
Overnight Flights
Disallowed

	A	B	C	D
148	**Constraint on planes**			
149		Number used		Number owned
150		5	<=	7
151				
152	**Monetary values**			
153	Net revenues	495		
154	Fixed costs	75		
155	Overnight costs	0		
156	Profit	420		
157				
158	Flights flown	19		

PROBLEMS

Skill-Building Problems

32. Five employees are available to perform four jobs. The time it takes each person to perform each job is given in Table 5.30. Determine the assignment of employees to jobs that minimizes the total time required to perform the four jobs. (A dash indicates that a person cannot do that particular job.)

| TABLE 5.30 | Times for Job Assignment Problem |

	Time (hours)			
	Job 1	Job 2	Job 3	Job 4
Person 1	22	18	30	18
Person 2	18	—	27	22
Person 3	26	20	28	28
Person 4	16	22	—	14
Person 5	21	—	25	28

33. Based on Machol (1970). Doc Councillman is putting together a relay team for the 400-meter relay. Each swimmer must swim 100 meters of breaststroke, backstroke, butterfly, or freestyle, and each swimmer can swim only one race. Doc believes that each swimmer will attain the times given in Table 5.31. To minimize the team's time for the race, which swimmers should swim which strokes?

| TABLE 5.31 | Times for Swimming Relay Problem |

	Time (seconds)			
	Free	Breast	Butterfly	Back
Gary Hall	54	54	51	53
Mark Spitz	51	57	52	52
Jim Montgomery	50	53	54	56
Chet Jastremski	56	54	55	53

34. A company is taking bids on four construction jobs. Three contractors have placed bids on the jobs. Their bids (in thousands of dollars) are given in Table 5.32. (A dash indicates that the contractor did not bid on the given job.) Contractor 1 can do only one job, but contractors 2 and 3 can each do up to two jobs. Determine the minimum cost assignment of contractors to jobs.

| TABLE 5.32 | Bids for Contractor Problem |

	Job 1	Job 2	Job 3	Job 4
Contractor 1	50	46	42	40
Contractor 2	51	48	44	—
Contractor 3	—	47	45	45

35. Suppose it costs $10,000 to purchase a new car. The annual operating cost and resale value of a used car are shown in Table 5.33. Assuming that you have a new car at present, determine a replacement policy that minimizes your net costs of owning and operating a car for the next 6 years.

| TABLE 5.33 | Data for Car Resale Problem |

Age of Car (years)	Resale Value	Operating Cost
1	$7000	$300
2	$6000	$500
3	$4000	$800
4	$3000	$1200
5	$2000	$1600
6	$1000	$2200

36. It costs $40 to buy a telephone from the department store. Assume that I can keep a telephone for at most 5 years and that the estimated maintenance cost each year of operation is as follows: year 1, $20; year 2, $30; year 3, $40; year 4, $60; year 5, $70. I have just purchased a new telephone. Assuming that a telephone has no salvage value, determine how to minimize the total cost of purchasing and operating a telephone for the next 6 years.

37. At the beginning of year 1, a new machine must be purchased. The cost of maintaining a machine, depending on its age, is given in Table 5.34. The

| TABLE 5.34 | Maintenance Costs for Machine Problem |

Age at Beginning of Year	Maintenance Cost for Next Year
0	$38,000
1	$50,000
2	$97,000
3	$182,000
4	$304,000

cost of purchasing a machine at the beginning of each year is given in Table 5.35. There is no trade-in value when a machine is replaced. The goal is to minimize the total (purchase plus maintenance) cost of having a machine for 5 years. Determine the years in which a new machine should be purchased.

TABLE 5.35   **Purchase Costs for Machine Problem**

	Purchase Cost
Year 1	$170,000
Year 2	$190,000
Year 3	$210,000
Year 4	$250,000
Year 5	$300,000

38. Eight students need to be assigned to four dorm rooms at Faber College. Based on "incompatibility measurements," the cost incurred for any pair of students rooming together is shown in Table 5.36. How should the students be assigned to the four rooms to minimize the total incompatibility cost?

TABLE 5.36   **Matrix of Incompatibilities**

Student	2	3	4	5	6	7	8
1	9	3	4	2	1	5	7
2		4	5	6	7	8	3
3			4	2	8	3	5
4				3	2	4	6
5					8	7	6
6						2	3
7							4

Skill-Extending Problems

39. The Chicago Board of Education is taking bids on the city's four school bus routes. Four companies have made the bids in Table 5.37.

TABLE 5.37   **Bids for Busing Problem**

	Route 1	Route 2	Route 3	Route 4
Company 1	$2500	$3000	$1500	—
Company 2	—	$4000	—	$4000
Company 3	$3000	—	$2000	—
Company 4	—	—	$4000	$5000

a. Suppose each bidder can be assigned only one route. How can Chicago minimize its cost of running the four bus routes?

b. Suppose that each company can be assigned two routes. How can Chicago minimize its cost of running the four bus routes?

40. Greydog Bus Company operates buses between Boston and Washington, D.C. A bus trip between these two cities takes 6 hours. Federal law requires that a driver have more than 4 hours between trips. A driver's workday consists of two trips: one from Boston to Washington and one from Washington to Boston. The departure times for the buses are listed in Table 5.38. Greydog's goal is to minimize the total downtime for all drivers. How should Greydog assign crews to trips? (*Note:* It is permissible for a driver's "day" to overlap midnight. For example, a Washington-based driver can be assigned to the Washington–Boston 3 P.M. trip and the Boston–Washington 6 A.M. trip.)

41. Based on Ravindran (1971). A library must build shelving to shelve 200 4-inch-high books, 100 8-inch-high books, and 80 12-inch-high books. Each book is 0.5 inch thick. The library has several ways to store the books. For example, an 8-inch-high shelf can be built to store all books of height less than or equal to 8 inches, and a 12-inch-high shelf can be built for the 12-inch books. Alternatively, a 12-inch-high shelf can be built to store all books. The library believes it costs $2300 to build a shelf and that a cost of $5 per square inch is incurred for book storage. (Assume that the area required to store a book is given by the height of the storage area multiplied by the book's thickness.) Determine how to shelve the books at minimum cost. (*Hint*: Create nodes 0, 4, 8, and 12, and make the cost associated with the arc joining nodes i and j equal to the total cost of shelving all books of height $> i$ and $\leq j$ on a single shelf.)

42. A company sells seven types of boxes, ranging in volume from 17 to 33 cubic feet. The demand and size for each box type are given in Table 5.39. The variable cost (in dollars) of producing each box type is equal to the volume of the box. A fixed cost of $1000 is incurred to produce any of a particular box type. If the company desires, demand for a box type can be satisfied by a box type of a larger size. Determine how to minimize the cost of meeting the demand for boxes.

TABLE 5.38 Departure Times

Trip from Boston	Departure Time	Trip from Washington	Departure Time
B1	6:00 A.M.	W1	5:30 A.M.
B2	7:30 A.M.	W2	9:00 A.M.
B3	11:30 A.M.	W3	3:00 P.M.
B4	7:00 P.M.	W4	6:30 P.M.
B5	12:30 A.M.	W5	Midnight

TABLE 5.39 Data for Box Problem

	Box						
	1	2	3	4	5	6	7
Size	33	30	26	24	19	18	17
Demand	400	300	500	700	200	400	200

5.5 PROJECT SCHEDULING MODELS

Network models can be used as an aid in the scheduling of large, complex projects that consist of many activities. If the duration of each activity is known with certainty, the **critical path model** (CPM) can be used to determine the length of time needed to complete a project. If the durations of the activities are not known with certainty, then **Monte Carlo simulation** (see Chapter 12) can be used to estimate the probability that a project will be completed by a given deadline.

CPM has been successfully used in many applications, including the following:

- scheduling construction projects such as office buildings, highways, and swimming pools
- scheduling the movement of a 400-bed hospital from Portland, Oregon, to a suburban location
- developing a countdown and "hold" procedure for space flights
- installing a new computer system
- designing and marketing a new product
- completing a corporate merger
- building a ship

To apply CPM, we need a list of the activities that make up the project. The project is considered complete when all of the activities have been completed. Each activity has a set of activities called its **predecessors** that must be completed before the activity begins. A project network is used to represent the precedence relationships among activities. In our discussion, the arcs in a network represent the activities, and the nodes are used to specify event times. The configuration of arcs and nodes is based on the precedence relationships. More specifically, it is best to think of a node as representing the time when all arcs—that is, activities—leading into the node are finished. For example, suppose that activity F can begin only when activities D and E are finished. Then we call activities D and E the predecessors of activity F, and we represent the relationship among them as in Figure 5.53 (page 252). The node in

FIGURE 5.53
Illustrating
Precedence
Relationships

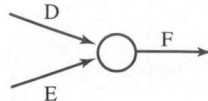

this network represents the time when both D and E are finished. Therefore, it also represents the time when F can start. This type of project network is called an **activity on arc** (AOA) network.[11]

In general, we draw the network so that arcs leading into any node are predecessors of arcs leading out of the node. This is typically straightforward, and it often requires a *single* arc for each activity. However, it is sometimes necessary to include multiple arcs for a given activity. As an example, consider the list of activities and their predecessors in Table 5.40. We need to indicate that D can start when B has finished, but that E can

TABLE 5.40   A Small Project

Activity	Predecessors
A	None
B	A
C	None
D	B
E	B, C

start only when both B and C are finished. This project can be represented as in Figure 5.54. Node 1 is the start of the project, node 2 is when activity A is finished, node 3 is when activity B is finished, node 4 is when both activities B and C are finished, and node 5 is when the project is finished. Traditionally, analysts have omitted the arc from node 2 to node 4 and have instead drawn a "dummy" arc (usually a dotted line) from node 3 to node 4. We believe the logic is easier to understand by drawing *two* activity B arcs, as in the figure.

FIGURE 5.54
Network Requiring
Two Activity B Arcs

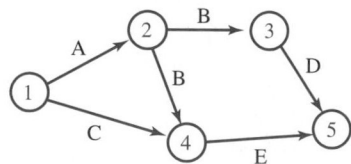

Given a list of activities and predecessors, an AOA representation of a project can be constructed by using the following rules:

1. A node (called the **start node** and usually labeled node 1) is included in the network to represent the start of the project. There is an arc leading out of it for all activities that have no predecessors.

2. A node (called the **finish node** and usually labeled n, where n is the number of nodes) is included in the network to represent the completion of the project. There

---

[11]There is an alternative graphical representation called activity on node (AON) that is favored by some analysts. Here nodes represent activities, and arcs are used to represent the precedence relationships. We believe the AOA representation is more common, so we have decided to use it.

is an arc leading into it for all activities that are not predecessors of any other activities.

3. All nodes between the start and finish nodes represent event times. If an activity's arc leads out of such a node, then all of this activity's predecessors should have arcs leading into the node.

4. It is common to write the activity times on the arcs. If an activity is represented by multiple arcs, such as activity B in Figure 5.54, then its activity time is written on each of these arcs.

5. Nodes should be numbered so that if there is an arc from node i to node j, then $i < j$. In words, arcs should point from lower-numbered nodes to higher-numbered nodes.

Drawing project networks can be confusing at first. There is not always a unique way to do it, and the number of nodes required is not always obvious. However, if you follow the above rules, particularly rule 3, you should soon catch on to the process.

Finding the Critical Path

There are two problems we typically analyze with CPM. The first, which we will discuss in this subsection, concerns the time to complete the project. The second, to be discussed in the next subsection, concerns ways of reducing the time to complete the project. In any project there are **critical** activities. These are activities that keep the project from being completed any sooner. More precisely, a critical activity is one such that if its activity time increases, the time to complete the project necessarily increases. The set of critical activities is called the **critical path** of the project. The critical path is important for practical reasons. It indicates the activities that we should attempt to speed up, because this will have a beneficial effect on the overall project time. In contrast, if an activity is *not* on the critical path, then speeding it up might not have any effect on the overall project time. The following example illustrates how we can find the critical path and the overall project time for a typical project.

EXAMPLE 5.10

BUILDING A NEW ROOM

Tom Lingley, an independent contractor, has agreed to build a new room on an existing house. He plans to begin work on Monday morning, June 1. The main question is when will he complete his work, given that he works only on weekdays. The owner of the house is particularly hopeful that the room will be ready in 15 or fewer working days—that is, by the end of Friday, June 19. The work proceeds in stages, labeled A through J, as summarized in Table 5.41 (page 254). Three of these activities, E, F, and G, will be done by separate independent subcontractors. Lingley wants to know how long the project will take, given the activity times (durations) in the table. He also wants to identify the critical activities.

Solution

The project network appears in Figure 5.55 (page 254). The activity time for each activity is shown on its arc. Note that, as in Figure 5.54, activity B requires two arcs to represent the precedence relationships correctly.

TABLE 5.41	Activity Time Data		
Description	Index	Predecessors	Duration (Days)
Prepare foundation	A	None	4
Put up frame	B	A	4
Order custom windows	C	None	11
Erect outside walls	D	B	3
Do electrical wiring	E	D	4
Do plumbing	F	D	3
Put in duct work	G	D	4
Hang dry wall	H	E, F, G	3
Install windows	I	B, C	1
Paint and clean up	J	H	2

FIGURE 5.55
Network Representation of Room Construction Project

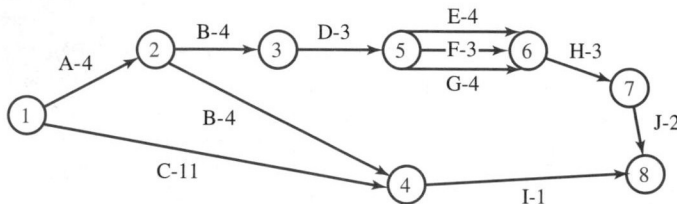

We suggest that you verify rule 3 from our general discussion—if an activity's arc leads out of a node, then all of this activity's predecessors should have arcs leading into the node.

The key to the solution is finding event times for each node in the network, where the event time for node i is the earliest time we could reach that point in the network. Denote the event time for node i by E_i. We begin by setting $E_1 = 0$. Node 1 is the start node, so its event time is 0—right away. Also, if node n is the finish node, then the earliest the entire project can be completed is at time E_n. Therefore, the total project time is E_8 for our example. In general, let i and j be any nodes joined by an arc with activity time t_{ij}. Then we must have

$$E_j \geq E_i + t_{ij} \qquad (5.2)$$

The reasoning is that the event at node j cannot occur until at least time t_{ij} after the event at node i. As an example, the event at node 4 (in the figure) cannot occur until both activities B and C are finished. Activity B can be finished at time $E_2 + 4$, and activity C can be finished at time $E_1 + 11$, so we must have $E_4 \geq E_2 + 4$ and $E_4 \geq E_1 + 11$.

Actually, we can do better than this. The event time E_j is equal to the *maximum* of the quantities $E_i + t_{ij}$, where the maximum is taken over all arcs that lead into node j. For example, E_4 is the larger of $E_2 + 4$ and $E_1 + 11$. We could use this relationship to iteratively find the event times. In fact, we will do this when we revisit this example in the context of simulation in Chapter 12. (See Problem 76 for a method of finding the critical path and its length that does *not* use linear programming.) For right now, however, we will not use maximums (primarily because we will need to use the Solver in the next subsection, and the Solver does not like maximums). Instead, we will exploit inequalities (5.2).

DEVELOPING THE SPREADSHEET MODEL

The completed spreadsheet model appears in Figure 5.56. It can be developed with the following steps.

❶ Enter data. The data for this model include the predecessors and activity times (durations) in the range C5:D14.

❷ Event times. We will eventually use the Solver to find the event times that satisfy inequalities (5.2). For now, enter any event times in the EventTimes range (and enter 0 in cell B18 for the start node). The EventTime range will be the changing cell range.

❸ Network information. Enter the information in the range D18:F28. This comes directly from the network in Figure 5.55.

❹ Inequalities. Now we implement inequalities (5.2) in the range G18:I28. We could enter the formulas one cell at a time, but it is more convenient to use VLOOKUP functions. To do so, enter the formula

=VLOOKUP(F18,LTable2,2)

in cell G18 and copy it down. Each of these values corresponds to E_j. Then enter the formula

=VLOOKUP(E18,LTable2,2)+VLOOKUP(D18,LTable1,3)

in cell I18 and copy it down. Each of these values corresponds to $E_i + t_{ij}$. As usual, make sure you understand exactly how these formulas work. Lookup functions can be intimidating, but they can save a lot of work. (Try entering the appropriate formulas *without* using lookup functions. We did so originally and kept making mistakes!)

❺ Project time. Enter the formula

=B25

in cell B30. This creates a link to the event time for the final node in cell B25—that is, to the time to complete the project.

	A	B	C	D	E	F	G	H	I	J	K	L	M
1	Room construction project												
2													
3	Data on activity network												
4	Activity	Index	Predecessors	Duration									
5	Prepare foundation	A	None	4									
6	Put up frame	B	A	4		Range names used:							
7	Order custom windows	C	None	11		LTable1 - B5:D14							
8	Erect outside walls	D	B	3		LTable2 - A18:B25							
9	Do electrical wiring	E	D	4		EventTimes - B18:B25							
10	Do plumbing	F	D	3		EndTimes - G18:G28							
11	Put in duct work	G	D	4		StTimesPlusDurs - I18:I28							
12	Hang dry wall	H	E,F,G	3		ProjTime - B30							
13	Install windows	I	B,C	1									
14	Paint and clean up	J	H	2									
15													
16	Node event times			Arcs (activities), corresponding nodes, and time constraints									
17		Node	Time	Activity	StartNode	EndNode	EndTime		StartTime + Duration				
18		1	0	A	1	2	4	>=	4	*			
19		2	4	B	2	3	8	>=	8	*			
20		3	8	B	2	4	19	>=	8				
21		4	19	C	1	4	19	>=	11				
22		5	11	D	3	5	11	>=	11	*			
23		6	15	E	5	6	15	>=	15	*			
24		7	18	F	5	6	15	>=	14				
25		8	20	G	5	6	15	>=	15				
26				H	6	7	18	>=	18	*			
27				I	4	8	20	>=	20				
28				J	7	8	20	>=	20	*			
29													
30	Project time	20											

Activities with asterisks next to them have positive shadow prices in the sensitivity report. They are on the critical path.

FIGURE 5.56 Room Construction Project Model

USING THE SOLVER

We want to choose the event times to minimize the project time and satisfy inequalities (5.2). Therefore, set up the Solver as shown in Figure 5.57.

When we click on Solve and see the dialog box indicating that the Solver has found the optimal solution, we now request a sensitivity report, which appears in Figure 5.58. We stated in Chapter 3 that these sensitivity reports can sometimes be misleading, but they provide useful information in this example. Specifically, consider the Shadow Price column of the sensitivity report. Each row of this table corresponds to one of the inequalities in the model—that is, to one of the activities in the project. In general, a shadow price indicates the change in the target cell if the right side of a constraint increases by 1. Because our constraints include activity times on their right sides (the t_{ij}'s), each shadow price indicates how much the total project time will increase if the corresponding activity time increases by 1. We see that some activity time increases have no effect on the project time (0 shadow prices), whereas others have a positive effect. This is how we find the critical path. It includes exactly those activities with *positive* shadow prices. We have indicated these with asterisks in Figure 5.56. The activities that are on the critical path are A, B, D, E, H, and J. If the activity time for any of these increases, the total project time will increase. However, the activity times for activities *not* on the critical path could increase, at least a little, with no effect on the total project time.

FIGURE 5.57
Solver Dialog Box for Project Model

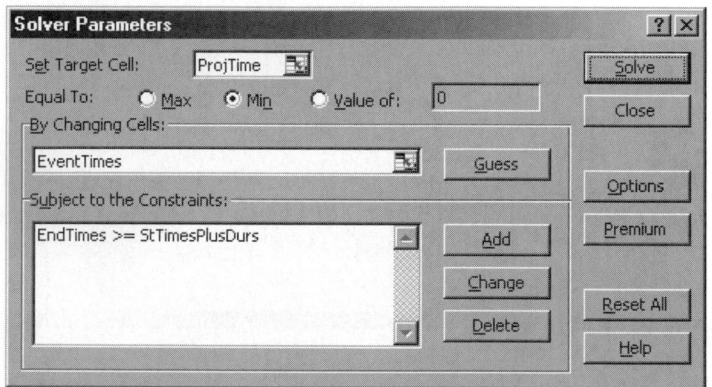

FIGURE 5.58
Sensitivity Report for Room Scheduling Model

	Cell	Name	Final Value	Shadow Price	Constraint R.H. Side	Allowable Increase	Allowable Decrease
17	Constraints						
20	$G$18	A EndTime	4	1	0	1E+30	4
21	$G$19	B EndTime	8	1	0	1E+30	8
22	$G$20	B EndTime	19	0	0	11	1E+30
23	$G$21	C EndTime	19	0	0	8	1E+30
24	$G$22	D EndTime	11	1	0	1E+30	8
25	$G$23	E EndTime	15	1	0	1E+30	0
26	$G$24	F EndTime	15	0	0	1	1E+30
27	$G$25	G EndTime	15	0	0	0	1E+30
28	$G$26	H EndTime	18	1	0	1E+30	8
29	$G$27	I EndTime	20	0	0	8	1E+30
30	$G$28	J EndTime	20	1	0	1E+30	8

Crashing the Activities

The objective in many project scheduling analyses is to find a minimum-cost method of readjusting activity times to meet a deadline. The term **crashing the activities** is often used to mean *reducing* the activity times. Of course, it typically costs money to crash activities—hiring extra workers, using extra equipment, using overtime, and so on—so the problem becomes one of crashing just the right activities in just the right amounts to meet a deadline at minimum cost. It is fairly easy to modify the previous model to incorporate a deadline and crashing. We illustrate the procedure in the following continuation of Example 5.10.

EXAMPLE 5.10 (CONTINUED)

BUILDING A NEW ROOM

Tom Lingley knows that if the room construction activities continue to take as long as listed in Table 5.41, the entire project will take 20 working days to complete. Unfortunately, he is under pressure to finish it in 15 working days. He estimates that each activity could be crashed by a certain amount at a certain cost. Specifically, he estimates the cost per day of activity time reduction and the maximum possible days of reduction for each activity in Table 5.42. For example, activity A's duration could be reduced from 4 days to 3 days at cost $150, or it could be reduced from 4 days to 2 days at cost $300. (It is even possible to have a fractional reduction, such as from 4 days to 2.5 days at cost $225.) How can Tom meet the 15-day deadline at minimal cost?

TABLE 5.42	Crashing Inputs	
Activity	Cost per Day	Max Reduction
A	150	2
B	160	2
C	80	4
D	80	1
E	160	2
F	150	1
G	130	2
H	100	1
I	70	0.5
J	100	1

Solution

The overall solution is very similar to the model without crashing, so we will discuss only the required changes.

MODIFYING THE MODEL

The modified model appears in Figure 5.59 (page 258). The following changes are required.

	A	B	C	D	E	F	G	H	I	J	K	L	M
1	Room construction project with crashing												
2													
3	Data on activity network						Crashing constraints						
4	Activity	Index	Predecessors	Duration	Cost/day		Reduction		Max reduction				
5	Prepare foundation	A	None	4	$150		2	<=	2		Range names used:		
6	Put up frame	B	A	4	$160		0	<=	2		LTable1 - B5:G14		
7	Order custom windows	C	None	11	$80		0	<=	4		UnitCosts - E5:E14		
8	Erect outside walls	D	B	3	$80		1	<=	1		Reductions - G5:G14		
9	Do electrical wiring	E	D	4	$160		0	<=	2		MaxReds - I5:I14		
10	Do plumbing	F	D	3	$150		0	<=	1		LTable2 - A18:B25		
11	Put in duct work	G	D	4	$130		0	<=	2		EventTimes - B19:B25		
12	Hang dry wall	H	E,F,G	3	$100		1	<=	1		EndTimes - G18:G28		
13	Install windows	I	B,C	1	$70		0	<=	0.5		StTimesPlusDurs - I18:I28		
14	Paint and clean up	J	H	2	$100		1	<=	1		ProjTime - B30		
15											Deadline - D30		
16	Node event times					Arcs (activities), corresponding nodes, and time constraints					TotalCost - B32		
17		Node	Time		Activity	StartNode	EndNode	EndTime		StartTime + Duration			
18		1	0		A	1	2	2	>=	2	*		
19		2	2		B	2	3	6	>=	6	*		
20		3	6		B	2	4	14	>=	6		Activities with asterisks next to	
21		4	14		C	1	4	14	>=	11		them have positive shadow	
22		5	8		D	3	5	8	>=	8	*	prices in the sensitivity report.	
23		6	12		E	5	6	12	>=	12	*	They are on the critical path.	
24		7	14		F	5	6	12	>=	11			
25		8	15		G	5	6	12	>=	12			
26					H	6	7	14	>=	14	*		
27					I	4	8	15	>=	15			
28					J	7	8	15	>=	15	*		
29													
30	Deadline constraint	15		<=	15								
31													
32	Total cost	$580											

FIGURE 5.59 Crashing Model

❶ **Reduction variables.** We need changing cells for the amounts of crashing. Enter any initial values for these in the Reductions range.

❷ **Inequalities.** The left sides of the inequalities in the range G18:I28 are the same as before, but on the right sides we need to account for the crashing. Do this by entering the formula

=VLOOKUP(E18,LTable2,2)+(VLOOKUP(D18,LTable1,3)-VLOOKUP(D18,LTable1,6))

in cell I18 and copying it down. Note how we expanded the LTable1 definition so that we could capture the activity time reductions with the last VLOOKUP function.

❸ **Deadline.** The project time cell, B30, is calculated as before. However, it is no longer the target cell; it is now the left side of the deadline constraint.

❹ **Total cost.** Calculate the total crashing cost in cell B32 with the formula

=SUMPRODUCT(Reductions,UnitCosts)

USING THE SOLVER

The Solver dialog box is straightforward, so we do not show it here. We want to minimize the total cost subject to inequalities (5.2), the deadline constraint, and the upper bounds on the reductions. The changing cell ranges are the Reductions and EventTimes ranges. We again ask for a sensitivity report so that we can identify the positive shadow prices and hence the critical path.

The solution in Figure 5.59 indicates that the critical path has not changed—it still consists of activities A, B, D, E, H, and J. However, by spending $580, Tom can reduce the activity times for activities A, D, H, and J enough to meet the 15-day deadline. Note the power of the Solver model. By including both the Reductions and EventTimes ranges as changing cells, the model simultaneously adjusts the reductions and then calculates the project time until the deadline is met at minimal cost.

Sensitivity Analysis This chapter is already long enough, so we will not pursue any sensitivity analysis. But a natural sensitivity analysis is to find a project cost/project time trade-off. To do so, we would use SolverTable, with the Deadline cell as the single input cell, and keep track of the total crashing cost. This trade-off information should be very useful in many real-world project analyses. ■

MODELING ISSUES

1. The crashing cost functions we have used are *linear* in the amount of reduction—each day of reduction (for a given activity) costs the same amount. This is probably unrealistic. Each extra day of reduction typically costs *more* than the previous day. However, if we can specify the nonlinear relationship between amount of reduction and cost (probably by estimating it from historical data), then Solver's nonlinear algorithms should be able to solve the problem with very little modification to the model. Alternatively, there might only be discrete crashing opportunities available. For example, there might be two types of equipment we could purchase to reduce some activity's duration, each involving a certain cost and leading to a certain reduction. This kind of discrete choice could be handled with binary (0–1) variables, the topic of the next chapter.

2. This introductory account of project scheduling barely scratches the surface. The topic can become very complex, and various versions of it are used routinely by many companies. Indeed, entire software packages such as Microsoft Project (and some courses) are devoted entirely to this topic. We will not pursue it any further here, but we will briefly discuss project scheduling with *uncertainty* in the activity times when we discuss simulation in Chapter 12. ■

PROBLEMS

Skill-Building Problems

43. A company has a project that consists of 11 activities, described in Table 5.43. Draw a project network and then use LP to find the critical path and the minimum number of days required to complete this project.

44. The promoters of a rock concert in Indianapolis must perform the tasks shown in Table 5.44 (page 260) before the concert can be held. (All durations are in days.)
    a. Draw the project network.
    b. Use LP to find the critical path and the minimum number of days needed to prepare for the concert.

45. Consider the (simplified) list of activities and predecessors that are involved in building a house, as listed in Table 5.45 (page 260).
    a. Draw a project network and use LP to find the critical path and the minimum number of days needed to build the house.

TABLE 5.43	Data for 11-Activity Project	
Activity	**Predecessors**	**Duration (Days)**
A	None	6
B	None	4
C	A	3
D	B	9
E	B	10
F	B	12
G	C, D	9
H	E	2
I	F	3
J	G, H	15
K	I	9

TABLE 5.44   Rock Concert Activities

	Description	Predecessors	Duration
Activity A	Find site	—	3.0
Activity B	Find engineers	A	2.0
Activity C	Hire opening act	A	6.0
Activity D	Set radio and TV ads	C	2.0
Activity E	Set up ticket agents	A	3.0
Activity F	Prepare electronics	B	3.0
Activity G	Print advertising	C	5.0
Activity H	Set up transportation	C	1.0
Activity I	Rehearsals	F, H	1.5
Activity J	Last-minute details	I	2.0

TABLE 5.45   House-Building Activities

	Description	Predecessors	Duration (days)
Activity A	Build foundation	—	5
Activity B	Build walls and ceilings	A	8
Activity C	Build roof	B	10
Activity D	Do electrical wiring	B	5
Activity E	Put in windows	B	4
Activity F	Put on siding	E	6
Activity G	Paint house	C, F	3

b. Suppose that by hiring additional workers, the duration of each activity can be reduced. The costs per day of reducing the duration of the activities are given in Table 5.46. Use LP to find the strategy that minimizes the cost of completing the project within 20 days.

46. Horizon Cable is about to expand its cable TV offerings in Smalltown by adding MTV and other exciting stations. The activities in Table 5.47 must be completed before the service expansion can be completed. Draw the project network and use LP to find the critical path and the minimum number of weeks needed to complete the project.

47. A company is planning to manufacture a product that consists of three parts (A, B, and C). The company anticipates that it will take 5 weeks to design the three parts and determine the way in which these parts must be assembled to make the final product. Then the company estimates that it will take 4 weeks to make part A, 5 weeks to make part B, and 3 weeks to make part C. The company

must test part A after it is completed, and this takes 2 weeks. The assembly line process will then proceed as follows: assemble parts A and B (2 weeks) and then attach part C (1 week). Then the final product must undergo 1 week of testing.
a. Draw the project network.
b. Use LP to find the critical path and the minimum amount of time needed to complete the project.

48. When an accounting firm audits a corporation, the first phase of the audit involves obtaining "knowledge of the business." This phase of the audit requires the activities listed in Table 5.48.
a. Draw the project network and use LP to determine the critical path and the minimum number of days needed to complete the first phase of the audit.
b. Assume that the first phase must be completed within 30 days. The duration of each activity can be reduced by incurring the costs shown in Table 5.49. Use LP to find the strategy that minimizes the cost of meeting this deadline.

TABLE 5.46	Reducing House-Building Activity Times	
Activity	**Cost per Day of Reducing Duration of Activity**	**Maximum Possible Reduction in Duration of Activity (days)**
Foundation	$30	2
Walls and ceiling	$15	3
Roof	$20	1
Electrical wiring	$40	2
Windows	$20	2
Siding	$30	3
Paint	$40	1

TABLE 5.47	Cable Company Activities		
	Description	**Predecessors**	**Duration (weeks)**
Activity A	Choose stations	—	2
Activity B	Get town council to approve expansion	A	4
Activity C	Order converters	B	3
Activity D	Install new dish	B	2
Activity E	Install converters	C, D	10
Activity F	Change billing system	B	4

TABLE 5.48	Audit Activities		
	Description	**Predecessors**	**Duration (days)**
Activity A	Determine terms of engagement	—	3
Activity B	Appraisal of auditability risk and materiality	A	6
Activity C	Identification of types of transactions and possible errors	A	14
Activity D	Systems description	C	8
Activity E	Verification of systems description	D	4
Activity F	Evaluation of internal controls	B, E	8
Activity G	Design of audit approach	F	9

TABLE 5.49	Reducing Audit Activity Times	
Activity	**Cost per Day of Reducing Duration of Activity**	**Maximum Possible Reduction in Duration of Activity (days)**
Activity A	$100	3
Activity B	$80	4
Activity C	$60	5
Activity D	$70	2
Activity E	$30	4
Activity F	$20	4
Activity G	$50	4

5.6 CONCLUSION

In this chapter we have discussed a number of management science problems that can be formulated as network models. Often these problems are of a logistics nature—shipping goods from one set of locations to another. However, we have also seen that problems that do not involve shipping or traveling along a physical network can sometimes be formulated as network models. Examples include the machine replacement problem and the flight scheduling models in Section 5.4.

There are at least two advantages to formulating a problem as a network model. First, streamlined versions of the simplex method exist for various forms of network models. These enable companies to solve extremely large problems that might not be solvable with ordinary LP solution algorithms. Second, the graphical representation of network models often makes them easier to visualize. Once a problem can be visualized graphically, then it might be simpler to formulate (on a spreadsheet or otherwise) and ultimately solve.

PROBLEMS

Skill-Building Problems

49. For this problem, refer to the Midwest Electric example (Example 5.1).
   a. The current unit shipping cost from plant 1 to city 1 is $8, and no units are shipped along this route. Use SolverTable to see how the total cost and the units shipped along the plant 1 to city 1 route depend on the unit cost for this route as it decreases in multiples of $0.50 from its current value. How low must this unit cost be before it is optimal to ship any units along this route?
   b. The current capacity at plant 1 is 35 units, and the optimal solution calls for plant 1 to be used at capacity. Use SolverTable to see how much Midwest Electric would be willing to pay for each extra 5 units of capacity up to 100 units (that is, up to 65 *extra* units).

50. Consider the assignment model of machines to jobs in Figure 5.24 (page 224). Use SolverTable to see how much we would need to decrease the time needed to do job 1 on machine 1 before it would be optimal to assign job 1 to machine 1.

51. Televco produces TV picture tubes at three plants. Plant 1 can produce up to 50 tubes per week; plant 2, up to 100 tubes per week; and plant 3, up to 50 tubes per week. Tubes are shipped to three customers. The profit earned per tube depends on the site where the tube was produced and on the customer who purchases the tube, as listed in Table 5.50. Customer 1 is willing to purchase up to 80 tubes per week; customer 2, up to 90; and

customer 3, up to 100. Find a shipping and production plan that will maximize Televco's profit.

52. Five workers are available to perform four jobs. The time it takes each worker to perform each job is given in Table 5.51. Determine how to assign workers to jobs so as to minimize the total time required to perform the four jobs.

TABLE 5.50 Profits for TV Problem

From	To Customer 1	Customer 2	Customer 3
Plant 1	$75	$60	$69
Plant 2	$79	$73	$68
Plant 3	$85	$76	$70

TABLE 5.51 Times for Job Assignment Problem

	Job 1	Job 2	Job 3	Job 4
Worker 1	10	15	10	15
Worker 2	12	8	20	16
Worker 3	12	9	12	18
Worker 4	6	12	15	18
Worker 5	16	12	8	12

53. A company must meet the following demands for a product: January, 30 units; February, 30 units; March, 20 units. Demand can be backlogged at a cost of $5 per unit per month. All demand must be met by the end of March. Thus, if one unit of January demand is met during March, a backlogging cost of 5(2) = $10 is incurred. Monthly production capacity and unit production cost during each month are given in Table 5.52. A holding cost of $20 per unit is assessed on the inventory at the end of each month. Determine how to minimize the total cost (including backlogging, holding, and production costs) of meeting demand.

TABLE 5.52	Data for Production Problem	
	Production Capacity	Unit Production Cost
January	35	$400
February	30	$420
March	35	$410

54. Appletree Cleaning has five maids. To complete cleaning my house, they must vacuum, clean the kitchen, clean the bathroom, and do general straightening up. The time (in minutes) it takes each maid to do each job is shown in Table 5.53. Each maid is assigned one job. Determine assignments that minimize the total number of maid-hours needed to clean my house.

55. Based on Evans (1984). Currently, State University can store 200 files on hard disk, 100 files in computer memory, and 300 files on tape. Users want to store 300 word-processing files, 100 packaged-program files, and 100 data files. Each month a typical word-processing file is accessed eight times; a typical packaged-program file, four

times; and a typical data file, two times. When a file is accessed, the time it takes for the file to be retrieved depends on the type of file and on the storage medium. (See Table 5.54.) The goal is to minimize the total time per month that users spend accessing their files. Determine where files should be stored.

TABLE 5.54	Retrieval Times for Computer Problem		
	Word Processing	Packaged Program	Data
Hard disk	5	4	4
Memory	2	1	1
Tape	10	8	6

56. The Gotham City Police have just received three calls for police. At present, five cars are available. The distance (in city blocks) of each car from each call is given in Table 5.55. Gotham City wants to minimize the total distance cars must travel to respond to the three police calls. Determine which cars should respond to which call.

TABLE 5.55	Distances for Gotham City Problem		
	Call 1	Call 2	Call 3
Car 1	10	11	18
Car 2	6	7	7
Car 3	7	8	5
Car 4	5	6	4
Car 5	9	4	7

TABLE 5.53	Cleaning Times for Appletree Problem			
	Vacuum	Clean Kitchen	Clean Bathroom	Straighten Up
Maid 1	60	50	20	10
Maid 2	90	80	70	30
Maid 3	80	50	90	40
Maid 4	70	70	80	30
Maid 5	50	50	60	40

57. There are three school districts in the town of Busville. The numbers of black and white students in each district are shown in Table 5.56. The Supreme Court requires the schools in Busville to be racially balanced. Thus, each school must have exactly 300 students, and each school must have the same number of black students. The distances between districts are also shown in Table 5.56. Determine how to minimize the total distance that students must be bused while still satisfying the Supreme Court's requirements. Assume that a student who remains in his or her own district does not need to be bused.

TABLE 5.56	Data for Busville Problem			
	Students		**Distance to**	
	Whites	**Blacks**	**District 2**	**District 3**
District 1	210	120	3 miles	5 miles
District 2	210	30	—	4 miles
District 3	180	150	4 miles	—

58. Delko is considering hiring people for four types of jobs. The company would like to hire the number of people in Table 5.57 for each type of job. Delko can hire four types of people. Each type is qualified to perform two types of jobs, as shown in Table 5.58. A total of 20 type 1, 30 type 2, 40 type 3, and 20 type 4 people have applied for jobs. Determine how Delko can maximize the number of employees assigned to suitable jobs, assuming that each person can be assigned to at most one job. (*Hint*: Set this up as a transportation model where the "supplies" are the applicants.)

TABLE 5.57	Number of People Required for Delko Problem			
	Job			
	1	**2**	**3**	**4**
Number of people	30	30	40	20

TABLE 5.58	Jobs Qualified for in Delko Problem			
	Person Type			
	1	**2**	**3**	**4**
Jobs qualified for	1, 2	2, 3	3, 4	1, 4

59. A truck must travel from New York to Los Angeles. As shown in Figure 5.60, several routes are available. The number associated with each arc is the number of gallons of fuel required by the truck to traverse the arc. Determine the route from New York to Los Angeles that uses the minimum amount of gas.

60. Telephone calls from New York to Los Angeles are transported as follows. The call is sent first to either Chicago or Memphis, then routed through either Denver or Dallas, and finally sent to Los Angeles. The number of phone lines joining each pair of cities is shown in Table 5.59. Determine the maximum number of calls that can be sent from New York to Los Angeles at any given time.

TABLE 5.59	Data for Telephone Problem
	Number of Telephone Lines
N.Y.–Chicago	500
N.Y.–Memphis	400
Chicago–Denver	300
Chicago–Dallas	250
Memphis–Denver	200
Memphis–Dallas	150
Denver–L.A.	400
Dallas–L.A.	350

61. Before a new product can be introduced at Jiffyco, the activities shown in Table 5.60 must be completed, where all times are in weeks.

a. Draw the project network and use LP to determine a critical path and the minimum number of weeks required before the new product can be introduced.

b. The duration of each activity can be reduced by up to 2 weeks at the following cost per week: A, $80; B, $60; C, $30; D, $60; E, $40; F, $30; G, $20. Determine how to minimize the cost of getting the product into the stores by Christmas, assuming that it is now 12 weeks until Christmas.

FIGURE 5.60
Network for Truck
Problem

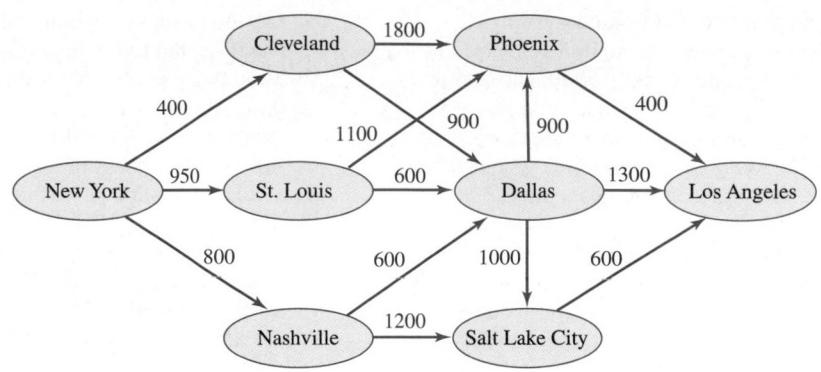

TABLE 5.60	Data for Jiffyco Problem		
	Description	**Predecessors**	**Duration (weeks)**
Activity A	Design product	—	6
Activity B	Survey the market	—	5
Activity C	Place orders for raw material	A	3
Activity D	Receive raw materials	C	2
Activity E	Build prototype of product	A, D	3
Activity F	Develop ad campaign	B	4
Activity G	Set up plant for mass production	E	4
Activity H	Deliver product to stores	G, F	2

62. During each of the next 2 months you can produce up to 50 units per month of a product at a cost of $12 per unit during month 1 and $15 per unit during month 2. The customer is willing to buy up to 60 units per month during each of the next 2 months. The customer will pay $20 per unit during month 1 and $16 per unit during month 2. It costs $1 per unit to hold a unit in inventory for a month. Determine how to maximize profit.

Skill-Extending Problems

63. In the RedBrand example (Example 5.3), suppose that the company could add up to 100 tons of capacity, in increments of 10 tons, to any *single* plant. Use SolverTable to determine the yearly savings in cost from having extra capacity at the various plants. Assume that the capacity will cost $28,000 per ton right now. Also, assume that the annual cost savings from having the extra capacity will extend over 10 years, and that the total 10-year savings will be discounted at an annual 10% interest rate. How much extra capacity should the company purchase, and which plant should be expanded?

(*Hint:* Use the PV function to find the present value of the total cost saving over the 10-year period. You can assume that the costs occur at the *ends* of the respective years.)

64. Based on Jacobs (1954). The Carter Caterer Company must have the following number of clean napkins available at the beginning of each of the next 4 days: day 1, 1500; day 2, 1200; day 3, 1800; day 4, 600. After being used, a napkin can be cleaned by one of two methods: fast service or slow service. Fast service costs 10 cents per napkin, and a napkin cleaned via fast service is available for use the day after it is last used. Slow service costs 6 cents per napkin, and these napkins can be reused 2 days after they are last used. New napkins can be purchased for a cost of 20 cents per napkin. Determine how to minimize the cost of meeting the demand for napkins during the next 4 days.

65. Kellwood, a company that produces a single product, has three plants and four customers. The three plants will produce 3000, 5000, and 5000 units, respectively, during the next time period. Kellwood has made a commitment to sell 4000 units to customer 1, 3000 units to customer 2, and at least 3000 units to customer 3. Both customers 3 and 4 also want to buy as many of the remaining units as possible. The profit associated with shipping a unit from each plant to each customer is given in Table 5.61. Determine how to maximize Kellwood's profit.

66. Sonico can produce up to 35 units per month. The demands of its primary customers must be met on time each month. If it wishes, Sonico can also sell units to secondary customers each month. A holding cost of $10 per unit is assessed against each month's ending inventory. The relevant data are shown in Table 5.62. Determine how Sonico can maximize its profit during the next 3 months.

67. During the next 3 months Shoemakers must meet (on time) the following demands for shoes: month 1, 1000 pairs; month 2, 1500 pairs; month 3, 1800 pairs. It takes 1 hour of labor to produce a pair of shoes. During each of the next 3 months, the following numbers of regular-time labor hours are available: month 1, 1000 hours; month 2, 1200 hours; month 3, 1200 hours. Each month the company can require workers to put in up to 400 hours of overtime. Workers are paid only for the hours they work, and a worker receives $4 per hour for regular-time work and $6 per hour for overtime work. At the end of each month, a holding cost of $1.50 per pair of shoes is incurred.

a. Use a MCNFM to minimize the total cost incurred in meeting the demands of the next 3 months.

b. How would you modify your answer if demand could be backlogged at a cost of $20 per pair per month? (*Note*: All demand must still be met by the end of month 3.)

TABLE 5.61 **Profits for Kellwood Problem**

From	Customer 1	Customer 2	Customer 3	Customer 4
Plant 1	$65	$63	$62	$64
Plant 2	$68	$67	$66	$62
Plant 3	$63	$60	$59	$60

To

TABLE 5.62 **Data for Sonico Problem**

	Production Cost/Unit	Primary Demand	Available for Secondary Demand	Sales Price/Unit
Month 1	$130	20	15	$160
Month 2	$120	15	20	$150
Month 3	$130	25	15	$170

68. Excelco produces a product at two plants: 1 and 2. The unit production cost and production capacity during each period are given in Table 5.63. The product is instantaneously shipped to the company's only customer according to the unit shipping costs given in Table 5.64. If a unit is produced and shipped during period 1, it can still be used to meet a period 2 demand, but a holding cost of $13 per unit in inventory is assessed. At the end of period 1, at most 600 units can be held in inventory. Demands are as follows: 900 in period 1, 1100 in period 2. Determine how to minimize the cost of meeting all demands on time.

69. Based on Mulvey (1982). State University has three professors who each teach four courses per year. Each year, four sections of marketing, finance, and production must be offered. At least one section of each class must be offered during each semester (fall and spring). The professors' time preferences and preferences for teaching various courses are listed in Table 5.65. The total satisfaction a professor earns teaching a class is the sum of the semester satisfaction and the course satisfaction. For example, professor 1 derives a satisfaction of $3 + 6 = 9$ from teaching marketing during the fall semester. Use a network flow model to assign professors to courses so as to maximize the total satisfaction of the three professors.

70. Based on Brown, Geoffrion, and Bradley (1981). During the next 2 months Machineco must meet (on time) the demands for three types of products, as listed in Table 5.66. Two machines are available to produce these products. Machine 1 can produce only products 1 and 2, and machine 2 can produce only products 2 and 3. Each machine can be used for up to 40 hours per month. Table 5.67 shows the time required to produce one unit of each product (independent of the type of machine), the cost of producing one unit of each product on each type of machine, and the cost of holding one unit of each product in inventory for 1 month. Determine how Machineco can minimize the total cost of meeting all demands on time.

TABLE 5.63	Production Costs and Capacities for Excelco Problem	
	Unit Production	
	Cost	**Capacity**
Plant 1 (Period 1)	$33	700
Plant 1 (Period 2)	$43	400
Plant 2 (Period 1)	$30	900
Plant 2 (Period 2)	$41	900

TABLE 5.64	Shipping Costs for Excelco Problem	
	Period 1	**Period 2**
Plant 1 to Customer	$51	$60
Plant 2 to Customer	$42	$71

TABLE 5.65	Preferences for University Problem		
	Prof. 1	**Prof. 2**	**Prof. 3**
Fall preference	3	5	4
Spring preference	4	3	4
Marketing	6	4	5
Finance	5	6	4
Production	4	5	6

TABLE 5.66	Demands for Machineco Problem		
	Product 1	**Product 2**	**Product 3**
Month 1	50 units	70 units	80 units
Month 2	60 units	90 units	120 units

TABLE 5.67	Other Data for Machineco Problem			
	Production	**Production Cost**		**Holding**
	Time (minutes)	**Machine 1**	**Machine 2**	**Cost**
Product 1	30	$40	—	$15
Product 2	20	$45	$60	$10
Product 3	15	—	$55	$5

71. I have put four valuable paintings up for sale. Four customers are bidding for the paintings. Customer 1 is willing to buy two paintings, but each other customer is willing to purchase at most one painting. The prices that each customer is willing to pay are given in Table 5.68. Determine how to maximize the total revenue received from the sale of the paintings.

72. Powerhouse produces capacitors at three locations: Los Angeles, Chicago, and New York. Capacitors are shipped from these locations to public utilities in five regions of the country: northeast (NE), northwest (NW), midwest (MW), southeast (SE), and southwest (SW). The cost of producing and shipping a capacitor from each plant to each region of the country is given in Table 5.69. Each plant has an annual production capacity of 100,000 capacitors. Each year, each region of the country must receive the following number of capacitors:

NE, 55,000; NW, 50,000; MW, 60,000; SE, 60,000; SW, 45,000. Powerhouse believes that shipping costs are too high, and it is therefore considering building one or two more production plants. Possible sites are Atlanta and Houston. The costs of producing a capacitor and shipping it to each region of the country are given in Table 5.70. It costs $3 million (in current dollars) to build a new plant, and operating each plant incurs a fixed cost (in addition to variable shipping and production costs) of $50,000 per year. A plant at Atlanta or Houston will have the capacity to produce 100,000 capacitors per year. Assume that future demand patterns and production costs will remain unchanged. If costs are discounted at a rate of 11.11% per year, how can Powerhouse minimize the net present value (NPV) of all costs associated with meeting current and future demands?

TABLE 5.68	Bids for Painting Problem			
	Painting 1	**Painting 2**	**Painting 3**	**Painting 4**
Customer 1	$8000	$11,000	—	—
Customer 2	$9000	$13,000	$12,000	$7000
Customer 3	$9000	—	$11,000	—
Customer 4	—	—	$12,000	$9000

TABLE 5.69	Costs at Current Locations for Powerhouse Problem				
			To		
From	**NE**	**NW**	**MW**	**SE**	**SW**
L.A.	$27.86	$4.00	$20.54	$21.52	$13.87
Chicago	$8.02	$20.54	$2.00	$6.74	$10.67
N.Y.	$2.00	$27.86	$8.02	$8.41	$15.20

TABLE 5.70	Costs at New Locations for Powerhouse Problem				
			To		
From	**NE**	**NW**	**MW**	**SE**	**SW**
Atlanta	$8.41	$21.52	$6.74	$3.00	$7.89
Houston	$15.20	$13.87	$10.67	$7.89	$3.00

73. Based on Hansen and Wendell (1982). During the month of July, Pittsburgh resident Bill Fly must make four round-trip flights between Pittsburgh and Chicago. The dates of the trips are shown in Table 5.71. Bill must purchase four round-trip tickets. Without a discounted fare, a round-trip ticket between Pittsburgh and Chicago costs $500. If Bill's stay in a city includes a weekend, he gets a 20% discount on the round-trip fare. If his stay in a city is at least 21 days, he receives a 35% discount, and if his stay is more than 10 days, he receives a 30% discount. However, at most one discount can be applied toward the purchase of any ticket. Determine how to minimize the total cost of purchasing the four round-trip tickets. (*Hint*: It might be beneficial to pair one half of one round-trip ticket number with half of another round-trip ticket.)

TABLE 5.71   **Flights for Bill Fly Problem**

Leave Pittsburgh	Leave Chicago
Monday, July 1	Friday, July 5
Tuesday, July 9	Thursday, July 11
Monday, July 15	Friday, July 19
Wednesday, July 24	Thursday, July 25

74. Three professors must be assigned to teach six sections of finance. Each professor must teach two sections of finance, and each has ranked the six time periods during which finance is taught, as shown in Table 5.72. A ranking of 10 means that the professor wants to teach at that time, and a ranking of 1 means that he or she does not want to teach at that time. Determine an assignment of professors to sections that maximizes the total satisfaction of the professors.

75. Based on Denardo et al. (1988). Three fires have just broken out in New York. Fires 1 and 2 each require two fire engines, and fire 3 requires three fire engines. The "cost" of responding to each fire depends on the time at which the fire engines arrive. Let t_{ij} be the time in minutes when the jth engine arrives at fire i (if it is dispatched to that location). Then the cost of responding to each fire is as follows: fire 1, $6t_{11} + 4t_{12}$; fire 2, $7t_{21} + 3t_{22}$; fire 3, $9t_{31} + 8t_{32} + 5t_{33}$. There are three fire companies that can respond to the three fires. Company 1 has three engines available, and companies 2 and 3 each have two engines available. The time (in minutes) it takes an engine to travel from each company to each fire is shown in Table 5.73.

  a. Determine how to minimize the cost associated with assigning the fire engines. (*Hint*: Seven demand points are necessary.)

  b. Would the formulation in part **a** still be valid if the cost of fire 1 were $4t_{11} + 6t_{12}$?

TABLE 5.73   **Travel Times for Fire Problem**

	Fire 1	Fire 2	Fire 3
Company 1	6	7	9
Company 2	5	8	11
Company 3	6	9	10

TABLE 5.72   **Preferences for Teaching Problem**

	9 A.M.	10 A.M.	11 A.M.	1 P.M.	2 P.M.	3 P.M.
Professor 1	8	7	6	5	7	6
Professor 2	9	9	8	8	4	4
Professor 3	7	6	5	6	9	5

76. We used a linear programming model in Section 5.5 to find the critical path and its length for a project consisting of several activities. This problem indicates a method for finding the same information without using linear programming. Use it to solve Tom Lingley's project in Example 5.5 (without crashing).

  a. We claimed that if E_j is the earliest time we can arrive at node j, then $E_j = \max(E_i + t_{ij})$ for all nodes j (other than the start node, which has $E_1 = 0$), where the maximum is over all arcs leading into node j. Use this relationship to iteratively calculate the E_j's in a spreadsheet. (*Hint*: Calculate them in the order E_1, E_2, E_3, and so on. This is the reason for requiring that arcs lead from lower-numbered nodes to higher-numbered nodes.)

  b. Without linear programming, we do not get the shadow prices we used to identify the critical activities. However, an alternative method is to increase the duration of any activity by a small amount (say, 0.01), use the procedure in part **a** to calculate the length of the project, and see if the project length has increased. If it has, then this activity must be on the critical path; otherwise, it must not be. Use this idea to identify the critical path for Lingley's project.

Modeling Problems

77. Solve the Sailco example (Example 5.2) for each of the following modifications. (Solve each part independently.)

  a. Suppose that demand can be backlogged at a cost of $30 per sailboat per month. (*Hint*: Now it is permissible to "ship" from, say, month 2 production to month 1 demand.)

  b. If demand for a sailboat is not met on time, the sale is lost and an opportunity cost of $450 is incurred.

  c. Sailboats can be held in inventory for a maximum of 2 months.

  d. At a cost of $440 per sailboat, Sailco can purchase up to 10 sailboats per month from a subcontractor.

78. A company produces several products at several different plants. The products are then shipped to two warehouses for storage and are finally shipped to one of many customers. How would you use a network flow model to help the company reduce its production and distribution costs? Pay particular attention to discussing the data you would need to implement a network flow model.

79. You want to start a campus business to match compatible male and female students for dating. How would you use the models in this chapter to help you run your business?

80. A company sells lengths of wood varying from 1 to 12 feet in length. It might not be desirable to stock lengths of each type of wood sold. For example, demand for an 8-foot board could be met by cutting a 9-foot board. Develop a network model to determine which lengths of wood should be stocked, given a typical demand pattern for various lengths.

81. You have been assigned to ensure that each high school in the Indianapolis area is racially balanced. Explain how you would use a network model to help attain this goal.

82. A drug must go through three stages of production before production is complete. Stage 1 must be completed at machine 1. Stage 2 can be completed at either machine 2 or machine 3. Stage 3 can be completed at either machine 4 or machine 5. Each stage of the production process results in a batch size of a certain number of units being processed in a given time period. For example, machine 2 might be able to process 300 units in a 2-hour time period. Show how a maximum flow model could be used to determine the maximum number of finished units of the drug that could be produced during an 8-hour period.

83. Consider a building that must be evacuated if a disaster occurs. How could you use a maximum flow model to determine the maximum number of people who could be evacuated in a 30-minute period?

84. Show how a maximum flow model with several sources and sinks could be converted into a maximum flow model with a *single* source and sink.

85. You own a plot large enough for a single tree. At various times you cut down the tree to obtain some wood to sell. As soon as the tree is cut down, you can plant another tree. Develop a shortest (or longest) path model that would help you determine how to maximize your revenue from selling wood during the next 100 years. Would this model still be applicable if your plot contained *many* trees?

Optimized Motor Carrier Selection at Westvaco

A typical paper mill might produce 1200 tons of paper per day to fill orders from 250 customers. One hundred truckload shipments per day would not be unusual for a mill served by 20 motor carriers. The carriers will generally accept shipments to any destination that they serve, subject to daily volume commitments and equipment availability. Each carrier has a different and somewhat complex rate structure. Given a pool of orders that must be shipped on a given day, the mill's problem is to assign truckloads to carriers to minimize its total shipping cost.

Westvaco Company Overview

Each year Westvaco sells over $2 billion worth of manufactured paper, paperboard, and specialty chemicals. Production occurs at five domestic paper mills and four chemical plants. In addition, Westvaco has many converting locations, which manufacture liquid packaging, envelopes, folding cartons, and corrugated boxes. Some of Westvaco's products include

- Fine papers, often used in printing applications (magazines and annual reports)
- Bleached paperboard, used in packaging (milk and juice cartons, freezer to oven entrees, and so forth)
- Kraft paper, used for corrugated boxes and decorative laminates (such as Formica)

- Chemicals, including activated carbon printing ink resins

Transportation Function

The corporate transportation function has a dual role at Westvaco. It supports the operating locations by negotiating freight rates and service commitments with rail, truck, and ocean carriers. In addition, it serves as an internal consulting group for reviewing operations in the field and making recommendations on streamlining tasks, making organizational changes to support changing customer requirements, and supporting the implementation of new technology.

Local traffic departments are responsible for day-to-day operations of mills and plants, including carrier assignments, dispatching, and switching lists for the railroads.

Production Overview

The production cycle is summarized in Figure 5.61.

Orders The majority of paper orders are for rolls, where customers request a specific grade and size of paper (diameter and width), amount (pounds, or linear or square feet), and delivery date. The orders typically range in width from 8 to 70 inches. With greater emphasis on just-in-time production by Westvaco's customers, delivery dates are sometimes specified in half-hour time windows. Orders

FIGURE 5.61
Production Cycle Overview

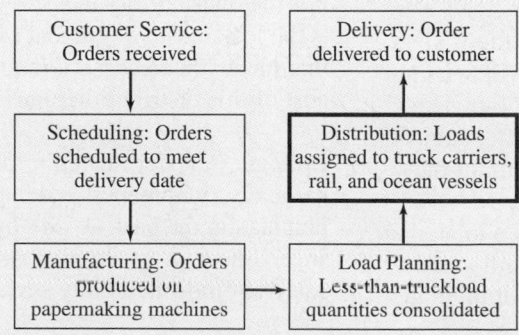

that arrive before or after the time window are not accepted.

Scheduling Once orders are received, they are scheduled on paper machines up to 200 inches wide. The paper business is heavily capital intensive: new machines can cost over $400 million each. Machines usually run 24 hours a day and scheduling is done to minimize waste while meeting shipping date requirements. After production of a "parent" roll, the orders are cut on a rewinder into the exact order size.

Load Planning Each morning a load planner must review the previous day's production to divide large orders and consolidate less-than-truckload (LTL) orders into truckload quantities. Special attention is necessary to ensure that delivery requirements are met for orders that are consolidated. Orders typically weigh between 1000 and 150,000 pounds. A truck can generally pull a trailer with 46,000 to 48,000 pounds of paper. Depending on the construction of the trailer, this is the maximum weight limit that can be loaded while remaining under federal weight limits. Some care must also be taken to remain within axle weight limits. The goal of the load planner is to maximize the weight on a trailer while determining a route that minimizes the total number of miles traveled per day, with no truck making more than four stops (three stops plus the final destination).

Distribution This case focuses on the distribution problem shown in the bold box in Figure 5.61. After loads are planned, they are turned over to a transportation planner to assign carriers to loads. The planner has a contract for each carrier that gives the rates to each destination served (state or zip code range). The rates include a mileage charge, a stop-off charge, and a minimum charge per truckload. The transportation planner also has a list of the trailers available for each carrier. The planner will select a carrier for a given shipment based on the knowledge of the best carriers for a given traffic lane, subject to availability. Some carriers have minimum daily volume commitments that must be met.

After the carrier is selected for a given load, the planner updates the information in the mill's mainframe computer and displays this information in the shipping area. The selected carrier's trailer is spotted and brought to the loading dock and loading commences. The shipment information is then phoned or faxed to the carrier.

A Sample Distribution Problem Table 5.74 contains a scaled-down version of a typical distribution problem faced by a transportation planner at Westvaco's paper mill in Wickliffe, Kentucky. The load planner has determined that 32 truckloads are needed to distribute last night's production. In the shipping area there are 33 drivers from 6 carriers waiting for their trucks to be loaded. One truck will not be needed today. The carrier PSST has 4 trucks in the shipping area, and Westvaco has a contractual obligation to use all 4 of these trucks today. (In practice, it would not be unusual for a transportation planner to assign 25 truckloads to 20 carriers in a single day.)

The mileage numbers in Table 5.74 represent the total number of miles for the trip from Wickliffe to the final destination, including any intermediate stops. The total charge is calculated as follows. Suppose that the Roseville, Minnesota, trip is assigned to carrier IRST. The cost to Westvaco would be $600(1.13) + 3(75) = \$903$. (If the cost calculated this way were less than IRST's minimum truckload charge of $400, the cost to Westvaco would be $400.) Stop-off charges apply only to intermediate stops and not the final destination. Four truckloads are needed to go to Atlanta, Georgia. These truckloads can be assigned to a single carrier, or they can be split among several carriers. If carrier MRST is assigned one of these truckloads, the cost is $612(0.87) = \$532$.

Question

For the distribution data shown in Table 5.74, what is the least-cost assignment of truckloads to carriers that meets the necessary requirements? What is the cost of this distribution plan?

Epilogue Carrier selection at Westvaco was done manually (with pencil and paper!) by transportation planners in the past. A side-by-side test of a spreadsheet linear programming solution versus manual selection indicated daily savings in the range of 3%

TABLE 5.74 Current Distribution Data for Westvaco Case Study

Destination	State	Trips	Stops	Miles	Carrier					
					ABCT	IRST	LAST	MRST	NEST	PSST
Atlanta	GA	4	0	612	*	0.88	1.15	0.87	0.95	1.05
Everett	MA	1	3	612	*	1.18	1.27	1.39	1.35	1.28
Ephrata	PA	3	0	190	*	3.42	1.73	1.71	1.82	2.00
Riverview	MI	5	0	383	0.79	1.01	1.25	0.96	0.95	1.11
Carson	CA	1	2	3063	*	0.80	0.87	*	1.00	*
Chamblee	GA	1	0	429	*	1.23	1.61	1.22	1.33	1.47
Roseville	MN	1	3	600	1.24	1.13	1.89	1.32	1.41	1.41
Hanover	PA	1	0	136	*	4.78	2.23	2.39	2.26	2.57
Sparks	NV	2	0	2439	*	1.45	*	1.20	*	*
Parsippany	NJ	1	1	355	*	1.62	1.36	1.39	1.03	1.76
Effingham	IL	5	0	570	0.87	0.87	1.25	0.87	0.90	1.31
Kearny	NJ	7	0	324	*	2.01	1.54	1.53	1.28	1.95
Minimum charge per truckload					350	400	350	300	350	300
Stop-off charge					50	75	50	35	50	50
Available pulls					4	8	7	7	3	4
Commitment					1	7	6	0	0	4

Note: Asterisks (*) indicate carrier does not travel to the destination; rates in dollars/mile.

to 6%, and so the project was approved. With annual trucking costs of about $15 million, the total savings with the new approach have been significant. In addition to this benefit, there have been a number of serendipitous side effects. The optimization technique removes the guesswork from carrier selection, especially on weekends, where revolving coverage added significant variability to the carrier selection process. The technique adds accountability to the transportation planner's position and, tied to a reason code for changing the carrier, offers a clear answer to management questions regarding carrier selection. Finally, the time savings have also been significant. The carrier assignment portion of the transportation planner's job can be done much faster than before.[12]

[12]*Acknowledgment*: This case was co-authored with Dave Rimple, who identified and implemented this project at Westvaco.

6

Linear Optimization Models with Integer Variables

KLM AIRCRAFT MAINTENANCE

A s we discussed in Chapter 4, many management science applications deal with workforce scheduling. These problems can be extremely complex and frequently require an integer programming approach to handle a variety of constraints. As an example, Dijkstra et al. (1994) report the use of integer programming in their article "Planning the Size and Organization of KLM's Aircraft Maintenance Personnel." KLM Royal Dutch Airlines, the major Dutch carrier since 1919, owns (as of 1993) about 90 aircraft of eight different types. To guarantee safety, KLM carries out high-quality aircraft maintenance, both on its own aircraft and on aircraft belonging to about 30 other carriers, according to fairly strict schedules. Maintenance standards require KLM engineers to perform routine maintenance between flights and major inspections after a certain number of flight hours. The company employs about 400 maintenance engineers, many of whom are highly skilled for their demanding jobs. Each of these highly skilled engineers is licensed to work on at most two types of aircraft (B737s and B747s, for example) and at most one particular skill (mechanical, electrical, or radio operations). For this reason the engineers operate in nearly identical teams of about 20 engineers each, so that each team has the capabilities required to service all aircraft.

The workload varies considerably across days of the week and within a given day. To respond to this workload in a timely manner, it is important for KLM to determine the composition of its maintenance teams and to schedule these teams optimally. KLM realized that its workforce scheduling problem was too complex for "manual" analysis and therefore employed a management science team.

The team built a decision support system (DSS) to help KLM solve its maintenance scheduling problem. The DSS includes a database module, an analysis module, and a graphical user interface. In simple terms, the database module gathers all of the necessary data about flight timetables, required maintenance, required skill levels, and other necessary information. It then feeds these data into the analysis module, which uses integer programming to either (1) minimize the size of the maintenance teams subject to meeting a specified service level or (2) maximize the service level subject to the composition of existing teams. Because both of these problems result in large and difficult integer programming models, good approximations have been developed to yield near-optimal results. The graphical user interface then allows the users to see the results of the analysis and ask a number of what-if questions.

The managers at KLM have been quite satisfied with the DSS. They consider it a valuable tool for analyzing both strategic and tactical problems, and they have advocated expanding its use into other departments of KLM such as the helicopter department. ■

6.1 INTRODUCTION

In this chapter we see how many complex problems can be modeled using 0–1 variables and other variables that are forced to assume integer values. A **0–1 variable** is a variable that must equal 0 or 1. Usually a 0–1 variable corresponds to an activity that either is or is not undertaken. If the 0–1 variable corresponding to the activity equals 0, then the activity is not undertaken; if it equals 1, the activity is undertaken. A 0–1 variable is often called a **binary variable**.

Optimization models in which some or all of the variables must be integers are known as **integer programming** (IP) models. We first saw an integer programming model in our discussion of scheduling postal workers in Example 4.1 of Chapter 4. In this chapter we illustrate many of the "tricks of the trade" that are needed to formulate IP models of complex situations. You should be aware that a spreadsheet Solver typically has a much harder time solving an IP problem than an LP problem. In fact, a spreadsheet Solver is sometimes unable to solve an IP problem, even if the IP problem has an optimal solution. The reason is that these problems are inherently difficult to solve, no matter what software package is used. However, as we will see in this chapter, our ability to *model* complex problems increases tremendously when we are able to use binary variables.

6.2 APPROACHES TO OPTIMIZATION WITH INTEGER VARIABLES

When the Solver solves a linear model without integer constraints, it uses a very efficient algorithm, the simplex method, to perform the optimization. As we saw briefly in Section 3.3, this method examines the "corner" points of the feasible region and returns the best corner point as the optimal solution. The simplex method is efficient because it typically needs to examine only a very small fraction of the hundreds, thousands, or even millions of possible corner points before determining the best corner point.

The main difference between LP and IP models is that LP models allow fractional values such as 0.137 and 5.3246 for the changing cells, whereas IP models allow only integer values for integer-constrained changing cells. This might make you think that IP models are easier to solve. After all, there are many fewer integer values in a given region than there are continuous values, so searching through the integers should be quicker. However, it turns out that IP models are *much* more difficult to solve than LP models, primarily because we cannot rely on the simplex method. Although several solution methods have been suggested by researchers—and new methods for specialized problems are still being developed—the solution procedure used by the Solver is called **branch and bound**, which is a special case of **implicit enumeration**. Although we will not go into the details of the algorithms, we will discuss briefly what Solver is doing. This way you can appreciate some of the difficulties with IP models, and you might also understand some of the messages you see in the status bar as the Solver performs its optimization.

Consider a model with 40 changing cells, all constrained to be binary. Because there are only two values for each binary variable, 0 and 1, there are at most 2^{40} feasible solutions. (Some of these might not be feasible because they do not satisfy other constraints.) Unfortunately, 2^{40} is an extremely large number, so it would take even a very fast computer a long time to check each one of them. Therefore, the naive method of **complete enumeration** of all possible solutions (look at each solution and select the best) is usually impractical. However, it might be practical to use *implicit* enumeration. This approach examines only a fraction of all 2^{40} potential solutions, hopefully a small fraction, and in doing so, it guarantees that solutions not examined have no chance of being optimal. To see how this works, suppose we find a feasible solution with a profit of $500. If we can somehow guarantee that each solution in a particular subset of solutions has profit *less* than $500, then we can ignore this entire subset because it cannot possibly contain the profit-maximizing solution.

This general idea is the essence of the branch and bound method used by the Solver in IP models. The "branching" part means that the algorithm systematically searches through the set of all feasible integer solutions, creating branches, or subsets, of solutions as it goes. For example, if x_1 is a binary variable, one branch might have $x_1 = 0$ and another branch might have $x_1 = 1$. Then if x_2 is another binary variable, two branches might be created off the $x_1 = 0$ branch—one with $x_2 = 0$ and one with $x_2 = 1$. By forming enough branches, we can eventually sweep out all possible integer solutions.

The key, however, is the "bounding" part of the algorithm. Suppose, for the sake of argument, that the objective is to maximize profit. Also, suppose that partway through the solution procedure, the *best* feasible integer solution so far has profit $500. This is called the **incumbent** solution—the best so far. Its profit represents a *lower bound* on the optimal profit. That is, we know the optimal solution has profit at least $500 because we *have* a solution with profit $500. This is the easy part of the bounding procedure. We just use the best profit found so far as a lower bound for the optimal profit.

The hard part is finding suitable *upper bounds*. Here is the idea. Suppose we are considering the branch where $x_1 = 0$ and $x_2 = 1$. If we could somehow show that *any* solution that has $x_1 = 0$ and $x_2 = 1$ can have a profit of at most $490 (or any number less than our incumbent $500), then we could ignore this entire branch. Therefore, we want to find an upper bound for each branch that (1) is easy to find in terms of computing time and (2) is as low as possible. Why do we want as low an upper bound as possible? Suppose the upper bound we find for the $x_1 = 0$ and $x_2 = 1$ branch is $515. Then because the incumbent is only $500, this branch might have some potential. That is, it might contain a solution with profit greater than the incumbent. Therefore, we have to pursue it, which costs computer time. The lower the upper bounds we can produce, the quicker we can "prune" branches, and the faster the algorithm will be.

The procedures used to find "good" upper bounds for branches are beyond the level of this book. Fortunately, the Solver takes care of the details. However, you should now understand some of the messages you will see in the status bar when you run the Solver on IP models. For example, try running the Solver on the cutting stock model in Example 6.7 with a tolerance of 0%. You will see plenty of these messages, where the incumbent objective value and the current subproblem (or branch) quickly flash by. For this particular cutting stock model, the Solver quickly finds an incumbent solution that is in fact optimal, but it must examine literally thousands of branches before it can *guarantee* that the incumbent is optimal. After a minute or two of computing, we had seen results for 10,000 branches, and there was no end in sight!

6.3 CAPITAL BUDGETING MODELS

Perhaps the simplest IP model is the following capital budgeting example. It perfectly illustrates the "go–no go" nature of many IP models.

EXAMPLE 6.1

SELECTING INVESTMENTS AT TATHAM

The Tatham Company is considering seven investments. The cash required for each investment and the net present value (NPV) each investment adds to the firm are given in Table 6.1. The cash available for investment is $15,000. Tatham wants to find the investment policy that maximizes its NPV. The crucial assumption here is that if Tatham wishes to take part in any of these investments, it must go "all the way." It cannot, for example, go halfway in investment 1 by investing $2500 and realizing an NPV of $8000. (If partial investments were allowed, we wouldn't need IP; we could use LP.)

Solution

The solution of this problem is quite straightforward. Tatham must keep track of

- investments chosen
- total cash required for the chosen investments
- total NPV from the chosen investments

TABLE 6.1	Data for Tatham Capital Budgeting Example	
	Cash Required	**NPV Added**
Investment 1	$5,000	$16,000
Investment 2	$2,500	$8,000
Investment 3	$3,500	$10,000
Investment 4	$6,000	$20,000
Investment 5	$7,000	$22,000
Investment 6	$4,500	$12,000
Investment 7	$3,000	$8,000

DEVELOPING THE SPREADSHEET MODEL

To keep track of which investments are chosen, we use a 0–1 variable for each investment. If a particular investment is chosen, the 0–1 variable for this investment will equal 1; if it is not chosen, the 0–1 variable will equal 0. To form the spreadsheet model, which is shown in Figure 6.1, proceed as follows. (See the file TATHAM1.XLS.)

① Inputs. Enter the NPV for each investment in the NPVs range, the cost required by each investment in the Costs range, and the amount of available cash in the Budget cell.

② 0–1 values for investments. Enter *any* trial 0–1 values for the investments in the Investments range. (Even fractional values such as 0.5 can be entered in these cells. The Solver constraints will eventually force them to be 0 or 1.)

③ NPV contributions. Calculate the NPV contributed by the investments in the TotNPV cell with the formula

=SUMPRODUCT(Investments,NPVs)

Note that this formula "picks up" the NPV *only* for those investments with 0–1 variables equal to 1.

④ Cash invested. Calculate the total cash invested in the TotCost cell with the formula

=SUMPRODUCT(Investments,Costs)

Again, this picks up only the costs of the investments with 0–1 variables equal to 1.

	A	B	C	D	E	F	G	H	I	J	K
1	Tatham capital budgeting model										
2											
3	Input data on potential investments										
4	Investment	1	2	3	4	5	6	7			
5	Investment cost	$5,000	$2,500	$3,500	$6,000	$7,000	$4,500	$3,000			
6	NPV	$16,000	$8,000	$10,000	$20,000	$22,000	$12,000	$8,000		Range names used:		
7	NPV per investment dollar	$3.200	$3.200	$2.857	$3.333	$3.143	$2.667	$2.667		Costs - B5:H5		
8										NPVs - B6:H6		
9	Investment levels	1	0	1	1	0	0	0		Investments - B9:H9		
10										TotCost - B13		
11	Budget constraint									Budget - D13		
12		Amt invested		Budget						TotNPV - B15		
13		$14,500	<=	$15,000								
14												
15	Total NPV	$46,000										

FIGURE 6.1 Capital Budgeting Model

USING THE SOLVER

The Solver dialog box appears in Figure 6.2. We want to maximize the total NPV, subject to staying within the budget. However, we also need to *constrain* the changing cells to be 0–1. With the Solver for Excel 97 or Excel 2000, this is simple, as shown in the dialog box in Figure 6.3. We add a constraint with Investments in the left box and choose the "bin" option in the middle box. The "binary" in the right box is added automatically. (In previous versions of the Solver, we need three separate constraints— one to make the variables integer, one to make them nonnegative, and one to make them less than or equal to 1.) Note that if *all* changing cells are binary, we do not need to check Solver's Assume Non-Negative option (because 0 and 1 are certainly nonnegative), but we should still check the Assume Linear Model option if it applies, as it does here.

FIGURE 6.2
Solver Dialog Box for Capital Budgeting Model

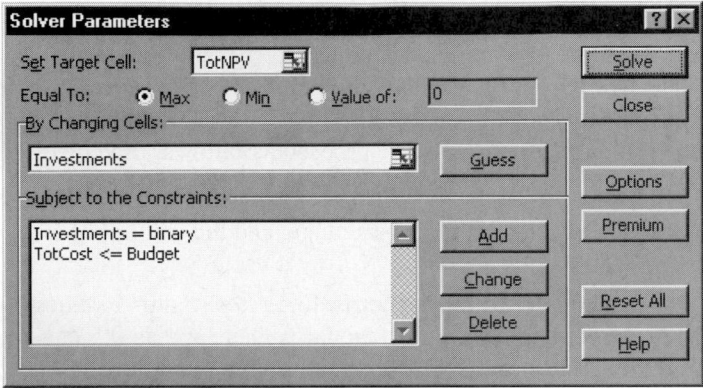

FIGURE 6.3
Specifying a Binary Constraint

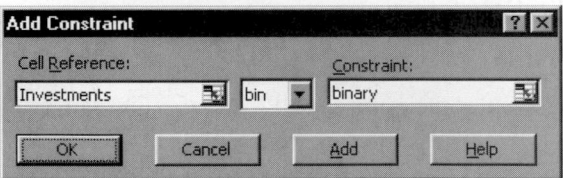

The optimal solution in Figure 6.1 indicates that Tatham can obtain a maximum NPV of $46,000 by selecting investments 1, 3, and 4. These three investments use up only $14,500 of the available budget, with $500 left over. However, this $500 is not enough—investing all the way is required, remember—to invest in any of the remaining investments.

If we rank Tatham's investments on the basis of NPV per dollar invested (see row 7 of Figure 6.1), the ranking from best to worst is 4, 1, 2, 5, 3, 6, 7. Using your economic intuition, you might expect the investments to be chosen in this order—until the budget runs out. However, the optimal solution does not do this. It selects investment 3 instead of investment 2 or 5. To understand why this is the case, suppose Tatham invests in the three highest-ranking investments: 4, 1, and 2. This uses up $13,500 of the budget, with $1500 left over and unusable. A better solution is to choose investments 4, 1, and 3, which uses the budget more efficiently. In general, the trick is to select a combination of investments that have "good" NPVs and use up all or almost all of the budget.

Sensitivity Analysis SolverTable can be used on models with binary variables exactly as we have used it in previous models. Here we see how the total NPV varies as the budget increases. We select the Budget cell as the single input cell, allow it to vary from $15,000 to $25,000 in increments of $1000, and keep track of the total NPV, the amount of the budget used, and the binary variables. The results appear in Figure 6.4. Clearly, Tatham can achieve a larger NPV with a larger budget, but as the numbers and the chart show, each extra $1000 of budget does *not* have the same effect on total NPV. The first few $1000 increases to the budget each add $4000 to total NPV. Then the jumps from $18,000 to $19,000 and from $19,000 to $20,000 add only $2000 to total NPV, but the jump from $20,000 to $21,000 again adds $4000 to total NPV. Note also how the selected investments vary wildly as the budget increases. This somewhat strange behavior is due to the all-or-nothing nature of the problem.

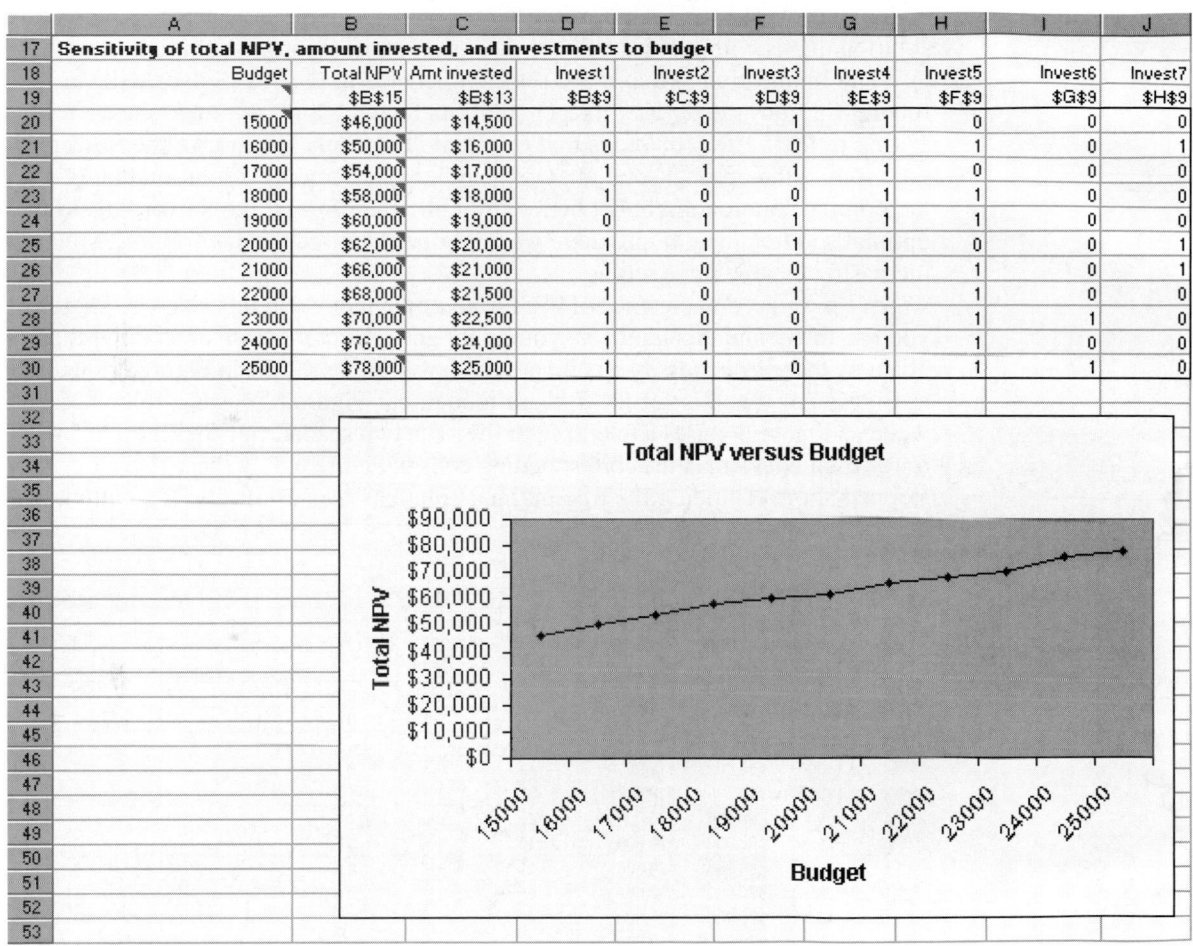

	A	B	C	D	E	F	G	H	I	J
17	Sensitivity of total NPV, amount invested, and investments to budget									
18	Budget	Total NPV	Amt invested	Invest1	Invest2	Invest3	Invest4	Invest5	Invest6	Invest7
19		$B$15	$B$13	$B$9	$C$9	$D$9	$E$9	$F$9	$G$9	$H$9
20	15000	$46,000	$14,500	1	0	1	1	0	0	0
21	16000	$50,000	$16,000	0	0	0	1	1	0	1
22	17000	$54,000	$17,000	1	1	1	1	0	0	0
23	18000	$58,000	$18,000	1	0	0	1	1	0	0
24	19000	$60,000	$19,000	0	1	1	1	1	0	0
25	20000	$62,000	$20,000	1	1	1	1	0	0	1
26	21000	$66,000	$21,000	1	0	0	1	1	0	1
27	22000	$68,000	$21,500	1	0	1	1	1	0	0
28	23000	$70,000	$22,500	1	0	0	1	1	1	0
29	24000	$76,000	$24,000	1	1	1	1	1	0	0
30	25000	$78,000	$25,000	1	1	0	1	1	1	0

FIGURE 6.4 Sensitivity to Budget

The Solver Tolerance Option

In the Solver Options dialog box there is a **Tolerance** option.[1] Excel's default tolerance is 5%. To explain the Tolerance option, we must first define the **LP relaxation** of an IP model. This is the same model as the IP model, except that all integer constraints

---

[1]If you are using Premium Solver, click on Options and then on Integer Options to find the Tolerance option.

are omitted. In particular, cells that are originally constrained to be 0 or 1 are allowed, under the LP relaxation, to have any fractional values between 0 and 1. For the capital budgeting example, the optimal solution to the LP relaxation has an optimal objective value of $48,714; it uses a fractional value for investment 5. This optimal objective value serves as an initial "best bound" (an *upper* bound) on the optimal integer solution. That is, the optimal objective value for this LP relaxation can only be better, never worse, than the optimal IP objective value.

A tolerance setting of 5% means that the Solver will stop as soon as it finds a feasible (integer) solution to the IP model that is within 5% of the "best bound." Initially, the optimal objective value of the LP relaxation serves as the best bound. As the Solver proceeds to find solutions that satisfy the integer constraints, it keeps updating the best bound. Thus, when the Solver stops, it is guaranteed to have an integer solution that is within at least 5% of the "true" optimal integer solution.

The implication is that if we set the tolerance to 0%, the Solver will (in theory) run until it finds the *optimal* integer solution. So why don't we always use a tolerance setting of 0%? The problem is that for many IP models, it can take the Solver a long time to find the optimal solution. On the other hand, finding a solution that is *close* to the optimal solution might not be too difficult. Therefore, if the Solver fails to find an optimal solution to an IP problem, we might be able to find a *near optimal* solution by increasing the tolerance setting.

We have used a tolerance of 0% for all of the models in this chapter. Therefore, if you use the default value of 5%, you *might* get a different (worse) solution than ours. To show that this is possible, compare the SolverTable results in Figure 6.5 with those in Figure 6.4. Each is for the Tatham model, but Figure 6.5 uses a tolerance of 5%, whereas Figure 6.4 uses a tolerance of 0%. The two shaded cells in Figure 6.5 indicate *lower* total NPVs than the corresponding cells in Figure 6.4. In these two cases, Solver stopped short of finding the true optimal solutions because it found solutions within the 5% tolerance.

FIGURE 6.5
Results with
Tolerance at 5%

	L	M	N	O	P	Q	R	S	T	U
17	Sensitivity of total NPV, amount invested, and investments to budget									
18	Budget	Total NPV	nt invested	Invest1	Invest2	Invest3	Invest4	Invest5	Invest6	Invest7
19		$B$15	$B$13	$B$9	$C$9	$D$9	$E$9	$F$9	$G$9	$H$9
20	15000	$46,000	$15,000	1	0	0	0	1	0	1
21	16000	$50,000	$16,000	0	0	0	1	1	0	1
22	17000	$54,000	$17,000	1	1	1	1	0	0	0
23	18000	$58,000	$18,000	1	0	0	1	1	0	0
24	19000	$60,000	$19,000	0	1	1	1	1	0	0
25	20000	$60,000	$20,000	1	0	1	0	1	1	0
26	21000	$66,000	$20,500	1	1	0	1	1	0	0
27	22000	$66,000	$20,500	1	1	0	1	1	0	0
28	23000	$70,000	$23,000	0	1	0	1	1	1	1
29	24000	$76,000	$24,000	1	1	1	1	1	0	0
30	25000	$78,000	$25,000	1	1	0	1	1	1	0

MODELING ISSUES

1. The following modifications of the Tatham example can be handled easily:
   - Suppose that at most two projects can be selected. In this case we add a constraint that the sum of the 0–1 variables for the investments is less than or equal to 2, that is, SUM(Investments)<=2. This constraint will be satisfied if 0, 1, or 2 investments are chosen, and it will be violated if 3 or more investments are chosen.

- Suppose that if investment 2 is selected, then investment 1 must also be selected. In this case we add a constraint saying that the 0–1 variable for investment 1 is greater than or equal to the 0–1 variable for investment 2, that is, B5>=C5. This constraint rules out the one possibility that is not allowed—namely, where investment 2 is selected but investment 1 is not.
- Suppose that either investment 1 or investment 3 (or both) *must* be selected. In this case we add a constraint that the sum of the 0–1 variables for investments 1 and 3 must be greater than or equal to 1, that is, B5+D5>=1. This rules out the possibility that both of these 0–1 variables are 0 so that neither investment is selected.

2. Capital budgeting models with multiple periods can also be handled. Figure 6.6 shows one possibility. (See the TATHAM2.XLS file.) The costs in rows 5 and 6 are *both* incurred if any given investment is selected. Now there are two budget constraints, one in each year, but otherwise the model is exactly as before. Note that some investments could have a cost of 0 in year 1 and a positive cost in year 2. This would effectively mean that these investments are undertaken in year 2 rather than year 1. Also, it would be easy to modify the model to incorporate costs in years 3, 4, and so on.

3. If Tatham could choose a *fractional* amount of an investment, then we could maximize its NPV by deleting the binary constraint. The optimal solution to the resulting LP model has a total NPV of $48,714. All of investments 1, 2, and 4, and 0.214 of investment 5 are chosen.[2] Note that there is no way to round the changing cell values from this LP solution to obtain the optimal IP solution. Sometimes the solution to an IP *without* the integer constraints bears little resemblance to the optimal IP solution.

4. Any IP involving 0–1 variables with only one constraint is called a **knapsack problem**. Think of the problem faced by a hiker going on an overnight hike. For example, imagine that the hiker's knapsack can hold only 14 pounds, and she must choose which of several available items to take on the hike. The benefit derived from each item is analogous to the NPV of each project, and the "weight" of each item is analogous to the cash required by each investment. The single constraint is analogous to the budget constraint, that is, only 14 pounds can fit in the knapsack.

	A	B	C	D	E	F	G	H	I	J	K
1	Tatham two-period capital budgeting model										
2											
3	Input data on potential investments										
4	Investment	1	2	3	4	5	6	7			
5	Year 1 cost	$5,000	$2,500	$3,500	$6,500	$7,000	$4,500	$3,000	Range names used:		
6	Year 2 cost	$2,000	$1,500	$2,000	$0	$500	$1,500	$0	NPVs - B7:H7		
7	NPV	$16,000	$8,000	$10,000	$20,000	$22,000	$12,000	$8,000	Investments - B9:H9		
8									TotCost - B13:B14		
9	Investment levels	1	1	0	1	0	0	0	Budget - D13:D14		
10									TotNPV - B16		
11	Budget constraints										
12		Amt invested		Budget							
13		$14,000	<=	$14,000							
14		$3,500	<=	$4,500							
15											
16	Total NPV	$44,000									

FIGURE 6.6 A Two-Period Capital Budgeting Model

[2]If you try this with the TATHAM1.XLS file, delete the binary constraint, but don't forget to constrain the Investments range to be nonnegative and less than or equal to 1.

In a knapsack problem the goal is to get the most value in the knapsack without overloading it. ∎

ADDITIONAL APPLICATIONS

Integer Programming at Monsanto

Monsanto [see Boykin (1985)] used an IP model to determine the settings of its chemical reactors that minimize the annual cost of meeting customer demands. The model is credited with saving Monsanto between $1 and $3 million annually. The model contained a 0–1 variable for each possible setting of each reactor. See Problem 62 for a scaled-down version of the Monsanto IP model.

Integer Programming in the Steel Industry

Fagersta AB, a Swedish steel company, used an integer programming model [see Westerberg et al. (1977)] to determine the best combination of steel ingots, scrap steel, and alloys to produce different kinds of steel. The model contained a 0–1 variable for each ingot that was available for purchase. The model is credited with reducing Fagersta AB's production costs by 6%. See Problem 61 for an example of the use of IP in the steel industry. ∎

PROBLEMS

Skill-Building Problems

1. Solve the following modifications of the Tatham example (Example 6.1).
   a. Suppose that at most two of projects 1–4 can be selected.
   b. Suppose that if investment 1 is selected, then investment 2 must also be selected.
   c. Suppose that at least one of investments 5–7 *must* be selected.
2. Suppose that in the Tatham example each investment requires $2000 during year 2 and only $5000 is available for investment during year 2.
   a. Assuming that available money uninvested at the

end of year 1 cannot be used during year 2, what combination of investments maximizes NPV?
   b. Suppose that any uninvested money at the end of year 1 is available for investment in year 2. How does your answer to part **a** change?
3. Coach Night is trying to choose the starting lineup for the basketball team. The team consists of seven players who have been rated on a scale of 1 (poor) to 3 (excellent) according to their ball-handling, shooting, rebounding, and defensive abilities. The positions that each player is allowed to play and the players' abilities are listed in Table 6.2. The five-player starting lineup must satisfy the following restrictions:

TABLE 6.2	Data for Basketball Problem				
	Position	Ball-Handling	Shooting	Rebounding	Defense
Player 1	G	3	3	1	3
Player 2	C	2	1	3	2
Player 3	G/F	2	3	2	2
Player 4	F/C	1	3	3	1
Player 5	G/F	1	3	1	2
Player 6	F/C	3	1	2	3
Player 7	G/F	3	2	2	1

- At least four members must be able to play guard (G), at least two members must be able to play forward (F), and at least one member must be able to play center (C).
- The average ball-handling, shooting, and rebounding level of the starting lineup must each be at least 1.8.
- Either player 2 or player 3 must start.

Given these constraints, Coach Night wants to maximize the total defensive ability of the starting team. Determine his starting team.

4. To graduate from Southeastern University with a major in operations research (OR), a student must complete at least two math courses, at least two OR courses, and at least two computer courses. Some courses can be used to fulfill more than one requirement: Calculus can fulfill the math requirement; Operations Research can fulfill the math and OR requirements; Data Structures can fulfill the computer and math requirements; Business Statistics can fulfill the math and OR requirements; Computer Simulation can fulfill the OR and computer requirements; Introduction to Computer Programming can fulfill the computer requirement; and Forecasting can fulfill the OR and math requirements. Some courses are prerequisites for others: Calculus is a prerequisite for Business Statistics; Introduction to Computer Programming is a prerequisite for Computer Simulation and for Data Structures; and Business Statistics is a prerequisite for Forecasting. Determine how to minimize the number of courses needed to satisfy the major requirements. (*Hint*: Since Calculus is a prerequisite for Business Statistics, for example, you will need a constraint that ensures that the changing cell for Calculus is greater than or equal to the changing cell for Business Statistics.)

5. Based on Bean et al. (1987). Boris Milkem's firm owns six assets. The expected selling price (in millions of dollars) for each asset is given in Table 6.3. For example, if asset 1 is sold in year 2, the firm receives $20 million. To maintain a regular cash flow,

TABLE 6.3 — Selling Prices for Milkem Problem

	Sold in		
	Year 1	**Year 2**	**Year 3**
Asset 1	15	20	24
Asset 2	16	18	21
Asset 3	22	30	36
Asset 4	10	20	30
Asset 5	17	19	22
Asset 6	19	25	29

Milkem must sell at least $20 million of assets during year 1, at least $30 million worth during year 2, and at least $35 million worth during year 3. Determine how Milkem can maximize his total revenue from assets sold during the next three years. In implementing this model, how might the idea of a rolling planning horizon be used?

6. The Cubs are trying to determine which of the following free-agent pitchers should be signed: Rick Sutcliffe (RS), Bruce Sutter (BS), Dennis Eckersley (DE), Steve Trout (ST), or Tim Stoddard (TS). The cost of signing each pitcher and the predicted number of victories each pitcher will add to the Cubs are shown in Table 6.4. Subject to the following restrictions, the Cubs want to sign the pitchers who will add the most victories to the team.
- At most $12 million can be spent.
- At most two right-handed pitchers can be signed.
- The Cubs cannot sign both BS and RS.

Determine who the Cubs should sign.

TABLE 6.4 — Data for Baseball Problem

Pitcher	Cost of Signing Pitcher (millions)	Victories Added to Cubs
RS (righty)	$6	6
BS (righty)	$4	5
DE (righty)	$3	3
ST (lefty)	$2	3
TS (righty)	$2	2

7. NASA must determine how many of three types of objects to bring on board the space shuttle. The weight and benefit of each of the items are given in Table 6.5. If the space shuttle can carry up to 26 pounds of items 1 through 3, which items should be taken on the space shuttle?

TABLE 6.5 — Data for NASA Problem

	Benefit	**Weight (pounds)**
Item 1	10	3
Item 2	15	4
Item 3	17	5

8. I am moving from New Jersey to Indiana and have rented a truck that can haul up to 1100 cubic feet of furniture. The volume and value of each item I am considering moving on the truck are given in Table 6.6 (page 286). Which items should I bring to Indiana?

TABLE 6.6	Data for Moving Problem	
	Value	Volume (cubic feet)
Bedroom set	$60	800
Dining room set	$48	600
Stereo	$14	300
Sofa	$31	400
TV set	$10	200

9. Four projects are available for investment. The projects require the cash flows and yield the net present values (in millions) shown in Table 6.7. If $6 million is available for investment at time 0, find the investment plan that maximizes NPV.

TABLE 6.7	Data for Project Selection Problem	
	Cash Outflow at Time 0	NPV
Project 1	$3	$5
Project 2	$5	$8
Project 3	$2	$3
Project 4	$4	$7

10. Consider the following puzzle. You are to select four three-letter "words" from the following list:

DBA DEG ADI FFD GHI BCD FDF BAI

For each word you earn a score equal to the position of the word's third letter in the alphabet. For example, DBA earns a score of 1, DEG earns a score of 7, and so on. Your goal is to choose the four words that maximize your total score, subject to the following constraint: The sum of the positions in the alphabet for the first letters of the four words chosen must be at least as large as the sum of the positions in the alphabet for the second letters of the words chosen. Use the Solver to solve this problem.

11. You are given a group of possible investment projects for your company's capital. For each project you are given the NPV the project would add to the firm, as well as the cash outflow required by each project during each year. Given the information in Table 6.8, determine the investments that maximize the firm's NPV. The firm has 30 million dollars available during each of the next five years. All numbers are in millions of dollars.

12. Based on Sonderman and Abrahamson (1985). In treating a brain tumor with radiation, physicians want the maximum amount of radiation possible to bombard the tissue containing the tumors. The constraint is, however, that there is a maximum amount of radiation that normal tissue can handle without suffering tissue damage. Physicians must therefore decide how to aim the radiation so as to maximize the radiation that hits the tumor tissue subject to the constraint of not damaging the normal tissue. As a simple example of this situation, suppose there are six types of radiation beams (beams differ in where they are aimed and their intensity) that can be aimed at a tumor. The region containing the tumor has been divided into six regions: three regions contain tumors and three contain normal tissue. The amount of radiation delivered to each region by each type of beam is shown in Table 6.9. If each region of normal tissue can handle at most 60 units of radiation, which beams should be used to maximize the total amount of radiation received by the tumors?

TABLE 6.8	Data for Capital Budgeting Problem					
	NPV	Year 1	Year 2	Year 3	Year 4	Year 5
Project 1	20	1	3	4	1	1
Project 2	25	3	4	2	1	2
Project 3	30	4	4	3	2	1
Project 4	35	6	5	3	2	3
Project 5	40	5	1	2	3	8
Project 6	42	4	5	2	5	5
Project 7	31	2	3	1	4	6
Project 8	33	0	0	3	6	7
Project 9	35	1	1	4	8	3
Project 10	37	3	2	4	1	6
Project 11	38	9	2	4	1	1
Project 12	39	8	7	1	1	1

TABLE 6.9   Data for Tumor Problem

Beam	Normal 1	Normal 2	Normal 3	Tumor 1	Tumor 2	Tumor 3
1	16	12	8	20	12	6
2	12	10	6	18	15	8
3	9	8	13	13	10	17
4	4	12	12	6	18	16
5	9	4	11	13	5	14
6	8	7	7	10	10	10

Skill-Extending Problems

13. Thailand inducts naval draftees at three drafting centers. Then the draftees must be sent to one of three naval bases for training. The cost of transporting a draftee from a drafting center to a base is given in Table 6.10. Each year 1000 men are inducted at center 1; 600 at center 2; and 700 at center 3. Base 1 can train 1000 men a year; base 2, 800 men; and base 3, 700 men. After the inductees are trained, they are sent to Thailand's main naval base. They may be transported on either a small ship or a large ship. Seven small and five large ships are available. It costs $5000 plus $2 per mile to use a small ship. A small ship can transport up to 200 men to the main base and can visit up to two bases on its way to the main base. It costs $10,000 plus $3 per mile to use a large ship. A large ship can visit up to three bases on its way to the main base and can transport up to 500 men. The possible "tours" for each type of ship are given in Table 6.11. (In this table, B stands for the main base.) Assume that draftees are assigned to training bases using the transportation model from Section 5.2. Determine how to minimize the total cost incurred in sending the men from the training bases to the main base.

TABLE 6.10   Transport Costs for Draftee Problem

From	To		
	Base 1	Base 2	Base 3
Center 1	$200	$200	$300
Center 2	$300	$400	$220
Center 3	$300	$400	$250

TABLE 6.11   Travel Data for Draftee Problem

	Locations Visited	Miles Traveled
Tour 1	B-1-B	370
Tour 2	B-1-2-B	515
Tour 3	B-2-3-B	665
Tour 4	B-2-B	460
Tour 5	B-3-B	600
Tour 6	B-1-3-B	640
Tour 7	B-1-2-3-B	720

TABLE 6.12   Data for Madonna Problem

	Type	Length (minutes)
Song 1	Ballad	4
Song 2	Hit	5
Song 3	Ballad	3
Song 4	Hit	2
Song 5	Ballad	4
Song 6	Hit	3
Song 7	Filler	5
Song 8	Ballad and Hit	4

14. You have been assigned to arrange the songs on the cassette version of Madonna's latest album. A cassette tape has two sides (1 and 2). The songs on each side of the cassette must total between 14 and 16 minutes in length. The length and type of each song are given in Table 6.12. The assignment of songs to the tape must satisfy the following conditions:

- Each side must have exactly two ballads.
- Side 1 must have at least three hit songs.
- Either song 5 or song 6 must be on side 1.

Determine whether there is an arrangement of songs satisfying these restrictions. (*Hint*: You do not need an objective function when using a spreadsheet Solver. In the Solver dialog box, just leave the Target Cell box empty.)

15. Cousin Bruzie of radio station WABC schedules radio commercials in 60-second blocks. This hour, the station has sold commercial time for commercials of 15, 16, 20, 25, 30, 35, 40, and 50 seconds. Determine the minimum number of

60-second blocks of commercials that must be scheduled to fit in all the current hour's commercials. (*Hint*: Certainly no more than eight blocks of time are needed.)

16. Based on Brown et al. (1987). A Sunco oil delivery truck contains five compartments, holding up to 2700, 2800, 1100, 1800, and 3400 gallons of fuel, respectively. The company must deliver three types of fuel (super, regular, and unleaded) to a customer. The demands, penalty per gallon short, and the maximum allowed shortage are given in Table 6.13. Each compartment of the truck can carry only one type of gasoline. Determine how to load the truck in a way that minimizes shortage costs.

17. Based on Bean et al. (1988). Simon's Mall has 10,000 square feet of space to rent and wants to determine the types of stores that should occupy the mall. The minimum number and maximum number of each type of store (along with the square footage of each type) are given in Table 6.14. The annual profit made by each type of store depends on how many stores of that type are in the mall. This dependence is given in Table 6.15 (where all profits are in units of $10,000). For example, if there are two department stores in the mall, each department store will earn $210,000 profit per year. Each store pays 5% of its annual profit as rent to Simon's. Determine how Simon can maximize its rental income from the mall.

18. WSP Publishing sells textbooks to college students. WSP has two sales representatives available to assign to the A–G state area. The number of college students (in thousands) in each state is given in Figure 6.7. Each sales rep must be assigned to two adjacent states. For example, a sales rep could be assigned to A and B, but not A and D. WSP's goal is

TABLE 6.15	Profits for Simon Mall Problem		
	Number of This Type in Mall		
Type of Store	**1**	**2**	**3**
Jewelry	9	8	7
Shoe	10	9	5
Department	27	21	20
Book	16	9	7
Clothing	17	13	10

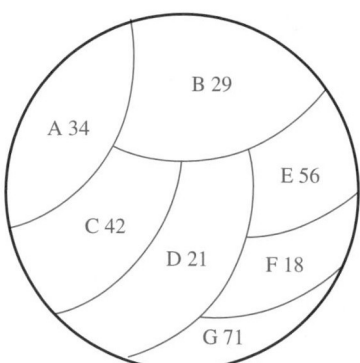

FIGURE 6.7 Map for WSP Problem

to maximize the total number of students in the states assigned to the sales reps. Determine where the sales reps should be assigned.

19. A power plant has three boilers. If a given boiler is operated, it can be used to produce a quantity of steam (in tons) between the minimum and maximum given in Table 6.16. The cost of producing a ton of steam on each boiler is also given. Steam from the

TABLE 6.13	Data for Sunco Problem		
Type of Gasoline	**Demand**	**Cost per Gallon Short**	**Maximum Shortage Allowed**
Super	2900	$10	500
Regular	4000	$8	500
Unleaded	4900	$6	500

TABLE 6.14	Store Data for Simon Mall Problem		
Store Type	**Square Footage**	**Minimum**	**Maximum**
Jewelry	500	1	3
Shoe	600	1	3
Department	1500	1	3
Book	700	0	3
Clothing	900	1	3

boilers is used to produce power on three turbines. If operated, each turbine can process an amount of steam (in tons) between the minimum and maximum given in Table 6.17. The cost of processing a ton of steam and the power produced by each turbine are also given. Determine how to minimize the cost of producing 8000 kwh of power.

20. Based on Salkin and Lin (1979). An Ohio company, Clevcinn, consists of three subsidiaries. Each has the respective average payroll, unemployment reserve fund, and estimated payroll given in Table 6.18. (All figures are in millions of dollars.) Any employer in the state of Ohio whose reserve to average payroll ratio is less than 1 must pay 20% of its estimated payroll in unemployment insurance premiums. Otherwise, if the ratio is at least 1, the employer pays 10%. Clevcinn can aggregate its subsidiaries and label them as separate employers. For example, if subsidiaries 2 and 3 are aggregated, they must pay 20% of their combined payroll in unemployment insurance premiums. Determine which subsidiaries should be aggregated.

21. Indiana University's Business School has two rooms that seat 50 students, one room that seats 100

students, and one room that seats 150 students. Classes are held five hours a day. At present, the four types of requests for rooms are listed in Table 6.19. The business school must decide how many requests of each type to assign to each type of room. Suppose that classes that cannot be assigned to a business school room are assigned to another campus building. Determine how to assign classes so as to minimize the number of hours students spend each week outside the business building.

TABLE 6.19	Room Requests for Indiana University Problem		
	Size Room Requested	Hours Requested	Number of Requests
Type 1	50 seats	2, 3, 4	3
Type 2	150 seats	1, 2, 3	1
Type 3	100 seats	5	1
Type 4	50 seats	1, 2	2

TABLE 6.16	Boiler Data for Power Plant Problem		
	Minimum Steam	Maximum Steam	Cost/Ton
Boiler 1	500	1000	$10
Boiler 2	300	900	$8
Boiler 3	400	800	$6

TABLE 6.17	Turbine Data for Power Plant Problem			
	Minimum Steam	Maximum Steam	Kwh per Ton of Steam	Processing Cost
Turbine 1	300	600	4	$2
Turbine 2	500	800	5	$3
Turbine 3	600	900	6	$4

TABLE 6.18	Data for Clevcinn Problem		
	Average Payroll	Reserve	Estimated Payroll
Subsidary 1	300	400	350
Subsidary 2	600	510	400
Subsidary 3	800	600	500

6.4 FIXED-COST MODELS

In many situations a fixed cost is incurred if an activity is undertaken at *any positive* level. This cost is independent of the level of the activity and is known as a **fixed cost** (or **fixed charge**). Here are three examples of fixed costs:

- The construction of a warehouse incurs a fixed cost that is the same whether the warehouse is built with a low or a high capacity level.

- A cash withdrawal from a bank incurs a fixed cost, independent of the size of the withdrawal, due to the time spent at the bank.

- A machine that is used to produce several products must be set up for the production of each product. Regardless of how many units of a product the company produces, it incurs the same fixed cost (lost production due to the setup time) for producing the product.

In these examples a fixed cost is incurred if an activity is undertaken at any positive level, whereas no fixed cost is incurred if the activity is not undertaken at all. Although it might not be obvious, this feature makes the problem inherently *nonlinear*, which means that a straightforward application of LP is not possible. However, the following example illustrates how a clever use of 0–1 variables can result in a *linear* model.

EXAMPLE 6.2

TEXTILE MANUFACTURING AT GREAT THREADS

The Great Threads Company is capable of manufacturing shirts, shorts, and pants. Each type of clothing requires that Great Threads have the appropriate type of machinery available. The machinery needed to manufacture each type of clothing must be rented at the following rates: shirt machinery, $1500 per week; shorts machinery, $1200 per week; pants machinery, $1600 per week. Each type of clothing requires the amounts of cloth and labor given in Table 6.20. This table also shows the unit variable cost and selling price for each type of clothing. There are 2000 hours and 2500 square yards of cloth available in a given week. The company wants to find a solution that maximizes its weekly profit.

TABLE 6.20	Data for Great Threads Example			
	Labor Hours	**Cloth (sq yd)**	**Sales Price**	**Unit Variable Cost**
Shirts	2.0	3.0	$35	$20
Shorts	1.0	2.5	$20	$10
Pants	6.0	4.0	$45	$25

Solution

We first note that the cost of producing x shirts during a week is 0 if $x = 0$, but it is $1500 + 20x$ if $x > 0$. This cost structure violates the proportionality assumption (discussed in Chapter 3) that is needed for a linear model. If proportionality were satisfied, then the cost of making, say, 10 shirts would be double the cost of making

5 shirts. However, because of the fixed cost, the total cost of making 5 shirts is $1600, and the cost of making 10 shirts is only $1700. This violation of proportionality requires us to resort to 0–1 variables to obtain a *linear* model.

To model the Great Threads problem, we need to keep track of the following:

■ number of shirts, shorts, and pants produced

■ 0–1 variable for each type of clothing that indicates whether *any* of that type of clothing is produced

■ resource usage of labor and cloth

■ total profit, which equals revenue from sales minus the cost of renting machines minus the variable cost of producing clothing

We must also ensure that if any of a given type of clothing is produced, then its 0–1 variable equals 1.

DEVELOPING THE SPREADSHEET MODEL

The spreadsheet model, shown in Figure 6.8, can now be formulated as follows. (See the file THREADS.XLS.)

❶ **Inputs.** Enter the given inputs in the shaded ranges.

❷ **0–1 values for shirts, shorts, and pants.** Enter *any* trial values for the 0–1 variables for shirts, shorts, and pants in the ProduceAny range. For example, if you enter a 1 in cell C16, you are implying that *some* shorts are produced.

❸ **Shirts, shorts, and pants produced.** Enter *any* trial values for the number of shirts, shorts, and pants produced in the Produced range. (At this point you could enter "illegal" values, such as 0 in cell B12 and a positive value in cell B14. However, Solver will eventually disallow such combinations where you avoid the fixed cost but produce the product anyway.)

FIGURE 6.8
Fixed-Cost Clothing Model

	A	B	C	D	E	F	G	H
1	**Great Threads fixed cost clothing model**							
2								
3	**Input data on products**	Shirts	Shorts	Pants		**Range names used:**		
4	Labor hours/unit	2	1	6		FixedCosts - B9:D9		
5	Cloth (sq. yd.)/unit	3	2.5	4		ProduceAny - B12:D12		
6						Production - B14:D14		
7	Selling price/unit	$35	$20	$45		Capacity - B16:D16		
8	Variable cost/unit	$20	$10	$25		Used - B19:B20		
9	Fixed cost for equipment	$1,500	$1,200	$1,600		Available - D19:D20		
10						TotRev - B23		
11	**Production plan**	Shirts	Shorts	Pants		TotVCost - B24		
12	Produce any? (1 if yes, 0 if no)	1	0	0		TotFCost - B25		
13						Profit - B26		
14	Units produced	833	0	0				
15		<=	<=	<=				
16	Capacity	833.33	0.00	0.00				
17								
18	**Constraints on resources**	Used		Available				
19	Labor hours	1666.67	<=	2000				
20	Cloth	2500.00	<=	2500				
21								
22	**Monetary values**							
23	Revenue	$29,167						
24	Variable cost	$16,667						
25	Fixed cost for equipment	$1,500						
26	Profit	$11,000						

4 **Labor and cloth used.** Calculate the total amount of labor hours used in cell B19 by entering the formula

=SUMPRODUCT(Production,B4:D4)

Then copy this to cell B20 to calculate the amount of cloth used.

5 **Effective capacities.** Now we come to the tricky part of the formulation. We need to ensure that if any of a given type of clothing is produced, then its 0–1 variable equals 1. This ensures that the model incurs the cost of renting a machine for this type of clothing. We could easily implement these constraints with IF statements. For example, to implement the constraint for shirts, we could enter the following formula in cell B12:

=IF(B14>0,1,0)

However, Excel's Solver is unable to deal with IF functions accurately. Therefore, we instead model the fixed cost constraints as follows:

$$\text{Shirts produced} \leq \text{(Maximum number of shirts that could} \qquad \textbf{(6.1)}$$
$$\text{be produced)} \times \text{(0–1 variable for shirts)}$$

Of course, there are similar inequalities for shorts and pants.

Here is the logic behind inequality (6.1). If the 0–1 variable for shirts is 0, then the right side of the inequality is 0, which means that the left side must be 0—no shirts can be produced. That is, if the 0–1 variable for shirts is 0, so that no fixed cost for shirts is incurred, then inequality (6.1) does not allow Great Threads to "cheat" and produce a positive number of shirts. On the other hand, if the 0–1 variable for shirts is 1, then the inequality is certainly true (and is essentially redundant). It simply says that the number of shirts produced must be no greater than the *maximum* number that could be produced. Inequality (6.1) rules out the one case we want it to rule out, namely, that Great Threads produces shirts but avoids the fixed cost. However, it will allow the 0–1 variable to be 1 (thus incurring the fixed cost) even if Great Threads plans to produce no shirts. Fortunately, this is not a problem. When the Solver maximizes the total profit, it will never obtain such a solution because the total profit could be increased by setting the 0–1 variable equal to 0 instead of 1.

To implement inequality (6.1), we need an upper limit on the number of shirts that could be produced. To obtain this, observe that the number of shirts that could be produced is limited by the smaller of

$$\frac{\text{Available labor hours}}{\text{Labor hours per shirt}}$$

and

$$\frac{\text{Available square yards of cloth}}{\text{Square yards of cloth per shirt}}$$

Therefore, the smaller of these can be used as the maximum needed in inequality (6.1). So in cell B16, calculate the "effective capacity" for shirts with the formula

=MIN($D$19/B4,$D$20/B5)*B12

Then copy this formula to the range C16:D16 for shorts and pants.[3]

---

[3]Why not set the maximum number of shirts that could be produced equal to a huge number like 1,000,000? The reason is that the Solver works most efficiently when the maximum is as "tight" (that is, as low) as possible.

6 **Revenues and costs.** Calculate the total sales revenue and the total variable cost by entering the formula

=SUMPRODUCT(Production,B7:D7)

in cell B23 and copying it to cell B24. Then calculate the total fixed cost in the TotFCost cell with the formula

=SUMPRODUCT(ProduceAny,FixedCosts)

Note that this formula picks up the fixed costs only for those products with 0–1 variables equal to 1. Finally, calculate the total profit in the Profit cell with the formula

$$=\text{TotRev-TotVCost-TotFCost}$$

USING THE SOLVER

The Solver dialog box appears in Figure 6.9. We maximize profit, subject to not using more hours or cloth than is available, and we ensure that production is no greater than effective capacity. The key is that this effective capacity is 0 if we decide not to produce any of a given product. Also, make sure to check the Assume Linear Model and Assume Non-Negative boxes under Solver options, and set the tolerance to 0%.

FIGURE 6.9
Solver Dialog
Box for Fixed-Cost
Model

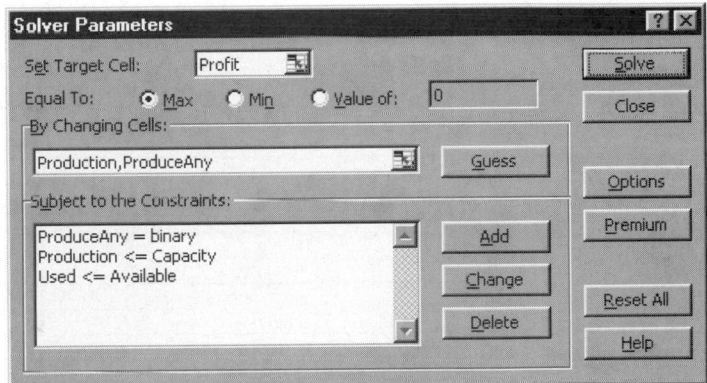

From the optimal solution in Figure 6.8, we see that Great Threads should produce about 833 shirts but no shorts or pants. The total profit is \$11,000. Note that the 0–1 variables for shorts and pants are both 0, which forces production of these products to be 0. However, the 0–1 variable for shirts, the product that is produced, is 1. This ensures that the fixed cost of producing shirts is included in the total cost.

It might be helpful to think of this solution as occurring in two stages. In the first stage the Solver determines which products to produce—in this case, shirts only. Then in the second stage, the Solver specifies how many shirts to produce. Because each shirt is profitable (once the fixed cost has been paid), Great Threads makes as many shirts as possible, which is 833 because of the cloth constraint. Of course, these two stages are interrelated, and the Solver considers both of them in its solution process.

The Great Threads management might not be very excited about being a shirts-only shop. Suppose the company wants to ensure that at least two types of clothing are produced at positive levels. One approach is to add another constraint, namely, that the sum of the 0–1 values in row 12 is greater than or equal to 2. You can check, however, that when this constraint is added and the Solver is rerun, the 0–1 variable for shorts becomes 1, but no shorts are produced! Shirts are relatively more profitable than shorts, so only shirts are produced. The new constraint forces Great Threads to rent an extra piece of machinery, but it doesn't force the company to use it. To force the company to produce some shorts, we would also need to add a constraint on the value in C14, such as C14>=100. Any of these additional constraints will cost Great Threads money, but if (as a matter of policy) the company wants to produce more than two types of clothing, this is the only option.

Sensitivity Analysis Because the optimal solution currently calls for only shirts to be produced, an interesting sensitivity analysis is to see how much "incentive" is required for other products to be produced. One way (but not the only way) to check this is to increase unit revenues from shorts and pants simultaneously in a two-way SolverTable. We did this, keeping track of the binary variables for all three products, with the results shown in Figure 6.10. For clarity, we have shaded the cells that contain 1's. These results are pretty much as expected. As the revenues from other products increase, the company eventually shifts from producing shirts to producing shorts and/or pants. (With these parameters, it *never* produces shirts and some other product.) The only possible surprise is in row 37. Here the unit revenue from shorts is still at its original value of $20. But when the unit revenue from pants increases to at least $60, Great Threads stops producing shirts and starts producing *both* shorts and pants. (See if you can explain why it doesn't switch *entirely* to pants.) On the other hand, when the unit revenue from pants stays at $60 or $65 and the unit revenue from shorts increases sufficiently, the company stops producing pants and switches entirely to shorts.

FIGURE 6.10
Sensitivity of Binary Variables to Unit Revenues of Shorts and Pants

	A	B	C	D	E	F	G	H
28	Sensitivity of binary variables to unit revenues from pants (top) and from shorts (side)							
29	$B$12	45	50	55	60	65		
30	20	1	1	1	0	0		
31	25	0	0	0	0	0		
32	30	0	0	0	0	0		
33	35	0	0	0	0	0		
34	40	0	0	0	0	0		
35								
36	$C$12	$45	50	55	60	65		
37	20	0	0	0	1	1		
38	25	1	1	1	1	1		
39	30	1	1	1	1	1		
40	35	1	1	1	1	1		
41	40	1	1	1	1	1		
42								
43	$D$12	45	50	55	60	65		
44	20	0	0	0	1	1		
45	25	0	0	0	1	1		
46	30	0	0	0	0	1		
47	35	0	0	0	0	0		
48	40	0	0	0	0	0		

ADDITIONAL APPLICATIONS

Locating Distribution Centers

When Dow Consumer Products (a manufacturer of food-care products) acquired the Texize home-care product lines of Morton Thiokol in 1985 to form DowBrands, Inc., the distribution channels of the two organizations remained, for the most part, separate.

Each had its own district and regional distribution centers for storing and then shipping products to the customer regions. This led to possible inefficiencies in a business where keeping logistics costs low is the key to survival. Robinson et al. (1993), acting as consultants for DowBrands, modeled the problem as a fixed-cost network problem—which distribution centers to keep open and which routes to use to satisfy which customers with which products. The study was highly successful and convinced DowBrands to close a significant number of distribution centers to reduce costs.

Locating Out-of-State Audit Offices

To increase the collection of state taxes from companies doing business in Texas, the state's auditors must often travel out of state. To reduce the cost associated with these trips, the state of Texas decided to locate auditors at several locations throughout the country. Fitzsimmons and Allen (1983) used a fixed-cost model to help the state of Texas locate out-of-state audit offices. See Problem 64 for a scaled-down version of this model.

Using Integer Programming to Immunize a Bond Portfolio

To minimize the interest-rate risk associated with an organization's assets and liabilities, it is important to match the *duration* of an organization's financial assets with the duration of its liabilities. This process is called **immunization**. In Problem 37 [based on Strong (1989)], we indicate how an IP model can be used to minimize the transaction costs associated with immunizing holdings against interest-rate risk. ■

PROBLEMS

Skill-Building Problems

22. Because of excessive pollution on the Momiss River, the state of Momiss is going to build some pollution control stations. Three sites (1, 2, and 3) are under consideration. Momiss is interested in controlling the pollution levels of two pollutants (1 and 2). The state legislature requires that at least 80,000 tons of pollutant 1 and at least 50,000 tons of pollutant 2 be removed from the river. The relevant data for this problem are shown in Table 6.21. (The last two columns indicate the number of tons of pollutants removed per ton treated.)
   a. Determine how to minimize the cost of meeting the state legislature's goals.

   b. Use SolverTable to analyze how a change in the requirement for pollutant 1 changes the optimal solution. Do the same for pollutant 2.

23. A manufacturer can sell product 1 at a profit of $2 per unit and product 2 at a profit of $5 per unit. Three units of raw material are needed to manufacture one unit of product 1, and six units of raw material are need to manufacture one unit of product 2. A total of 120 units of raw material are available. If any of product 1 is produced, a setup cost of $10 is incurred, and if any of product 2 is produced, a setup cost of $20 is incurred.
   a. Determine how to maximize the manufacturer's profit.

TABLE 6.21	Data for Momiss Pollution Problem			
	Cost of Building Station	Cost of Treating One Ton of Water	Amount Removed (tons)	
			Pollutant 1	Pollutant 2
Site 1	$100,000	$20	0.40	0.30
Site 2	$60,000	$30	0.25	0.20
Site 3	$40,000	$40	0.20	0.25

b. Use SolverTable to analyze how a change in the setup cost for product 1 affects the optimal solution. Do the same for the setup cost for product 2.

24. A company is considering opening warehouses in four cities: New York, Los Angeles, Chicago, and Atlanta. Each warehouse can ship 100 units per week. The weekly fixed cost of keeping each warehouse open is $400 for New York, $500 for Los Angeles, $300 for Chicago, and $150 for Atlanta. Region 1 of the country requires 80 units per week, region 2 requires 70 units per week, and region 3 requires 40 units per week. The costs (including production and shipping costs) of sending one unit from a plant to a region are shown in Table 6.22. The company wants to meet weekly demands at minimum cost, subject to the preceding information and the following restrictions:

- If the New York warehouse is opened, then the Los Angeles warehouse must be opened.
- At most two warehouses can be opened.
- Either the Atlanta or the Los Angeles warehouse must be opened.

TABLE 6.22	Costs for Warehouse Shipping Problem		
	To		
From	**Region 1**	**Region 2**	**Region 3**
New York	$20	$40	$50
Los Angeles	$48	$15	$26
Chicago	$26	$35	$18
Atlanta	$24	$50	$35

25. Glueco produces three types of glue on two different production lines. Each line can be utilized by up to seven workers at a time. Workers are paid $500 per week on production line 1 and $900 per week on production line 2. For a week of production it costs $1000 to set up production line 1 and $2000 to set up production line 2. During a week on a production line each worker produces the number of units of

TABLE 6.23	Production Data for Glueco Problem		
	Glue 1	**Glue 2**	**Glue 3**
Line 1	20	30	40
Line 2	50	35	45

glue shown in Table 6.23. Each week at least 120 units of glue 1, at least 150 units of glue 2, and at least 200 units of glue 3 must be produced. Determine how to minimize the total cost of meeting weekly demands.

26. Fruit Computer produces two types of computers: Pear computers and Apricot computers. The relevant data are given in Table 6.24. The equipment cost is a fixed cost; it is incurred if any of this type of computer is produced. A total of 3000 chips and 1200 hours of labor are available.
  a. Determine how Fruit can maximize its profit.
  b. Use SolverTable to analyze the effect on the optimal solution of a change in the selling price of Pear computers. Do the same for the selling price of Apricot computers.

27. Consider the Pigskin example (Example 3.3) from Chapter 3. Find Pigskin's optimal production policy if, in addition to the given production and holding costs, there is a fixed cost of $1000 during any month in which there is positive production. Assume now that maximum storage capacity is 200 footballs.

28. A product can be produced on four different machines. Each machine has a fixed setup cost, variable production cost per unit processed, and a production capacity, given in Table 6.25. A total of 2000 units of the product must be produced. Determine how to minimize the total cost.

29. Bookco Publishers is considering publishing five textbooks. The maximum number of copies of each textbook that can be sold, the variable cost of producing each textbook, the selling price of each textbook, and the fixed cost of a production run for each book are given in Table 6.26. For example, producing 2000 copies of book 1 brings in a revenue of $(2000)(50) = \$100,000$ but costs $80,000 + 25(2000) = \$130,000$.

TABLE 6.24	Data for Fruit Computer Problem			
	Labor (hours)	**Number of Chips**	**Equipment Cost**	**Selling Price**
Pear	1	2	$5000	$400
Apricot	2	5	$7000	$900

TABLE 6.25	Data for Machine Setup Problem		
	Fixed Cost	**Variable Cost**	**Capacity**
Machine 1	$1000	$20	900
Machine 2	$920	$24	1000
Machine 3	$800	$16	1200
Machine 4	$700	$28	1600

TABLE 6.26	Data for Bookco Problem			
	Maximum Demand	**Fixed Cost**	**Variable Cost**	**Selling Price**
Book 1	5000	$80,000	$25	$50
Book 2	4000	$50,000	$20	$40
Book 3	3000	$60,000	$15	$38
Book 4	4000	$30,000	$18	$32
Book 5	3000	$40,000	$22	$40

a. Determine how Bookco can maximize its profit if it can produce at most 10,000 books.

b. Use SolverTable to analyze the effect on the optimal solution of a change in the demand for book 1. Repeat for the demands for the other books.

30. Comquat owns four production plants at which personal computers are produced. Comquat can sell up to 20,000 computers per year at a price of $3500 per computer. For each plant, the production capacity, the production cost per computer, and the fixed cost of operating a plant for a year are given in Table 6.27. Determine how Comquat can maximize its yearly profit from computer production.

31. In the Sailco example (Example 5.2) from the previous chapter, suppose that a fixed cost of

$20,000 is incurred during each quarter that production takes place. Determine how Sailco can minimize the total cost of meeting the demands for the four quarters.

32. Eastinghouse sells air conditioners. The annual demand for air conditioners in each region of the country is as follows: East, 100,000; South, 150,000; Midwest, 110,000; West, 90,000. Eastinghouse is considering building its air conditioners in four different cities: New York, Atlanta, Chicago, and Los Angeles. The cost of producing an air conditioner in a city and shipping it to a region of the country is given in Table 6.28. Any factory can produce up to 150,000 air conditioners per year. The annual fixed cost of operating a factory

TABLE 6.27	Data for Comquat Computer Problem		
	Production Capacity	**Plant Fixed Cost**	**Cost per Computer**
Plant 1	10,000	$9 million	$1000
Plant 2	8,000	$5 million	$1700
Plant 3	9,000	$3 million	$2300
Plant 4	6,000	$1 million	$2900

TABLE 6.28	Production and Shipping Costs for Eastinghouse Problem			
	East	**South**	**Midwest**	**West**
New York	$206	$225	$230	$290
Atlanta	$225	$206	$221	$270
Chicago	$230	$221	$208	$262
Los Angeles	$290	$270	$262	$215

TABLE 6.29	Fixed Costs for Eastinghouse Problem
	Annual Fixed Cost
New York	$6.0 million
Atlanta	$5.5 million
Chicago	$5.8 million
Los Angeles	$6.2 million

in each city is given in Table 6.29. At least 50,000 units of the Midwest demand for air conditioners must come from New York and at least 50,000 units of the Midwest demand must come from Atlanta. Determine how Eastinghouse can minimize the annual cost of meeting demand for air conditioners.

33. During the next five periods the demands in Table 6.30 must be met on time. At the beginning of period 1, the inventory level is 0. Each period that production occurs a setup cost of $250 and a per-unit production cost of $2 are incurred. At the end of each period, a per-unit holding cost of $1 is incurred. Determine the cost-minimizing production schedule.

TABLE 6.30	Demands for Production-Inventory Problem
	Demand
Period 1	220
Period 2	280
Period 3	360
Period 4	140
Period 5	270

Skill-Extending Problems

34. Based on Efroymson and Ray (1966). Breadco Bakeries is a new bakery chain that sells bread to customers throughout the state of Indiana. Breadco is considering building bakeries in three locations: Evansville, Indianapolis, and South Bend. Each bakery can bake up to 900,000 loaves of bread each year. The cost of building a bakery at each site is $5 million in Evansville, $4 million in Indianapolis, and $4.5 million in South Bend. To simplify the problem, we assume that Breadco has only three customers. Their demands each year are 700,000 loaves (customer 1); 400,000 loaves (customer 2); and 300,000 loaves (customer 3). The total cost of baking and shipping a load of bread to a customer is given in Table 6.31. Assume that future shipping and production costs are discounted at a rate of 11.11% per year. Assume that once built, a bakery lasts forever. How would you minimize Breadco's total cost of meeting demand, present and future? (*Note*: Although your model is actually linear, the Excel Solver might report that "the conditions for Assume Linear Model are not satisfied" if you do not scale your changing cells and costs in "natural" units, as discussed in Chapter 3. For example, costs can be expressed in units of $1 million or $100,000, and annual shipments can be expressed in units of 100,000 loaves.)

35. A company sells seven types of boxes, ranging in volume from 17 to 33 cubic feet. The demand and size of each box are given in Table 6.32. The variable cost (in dollars) of producing each box is equal to the box's volume. A fixed cost of $1000 is incurred to produce any quantity of a particular box. If the company desires, demand for a box can be satisfied by a box of a larger size. Determine how to minimize the cost of meeting the demand for boxes.

TABLE 6.31	Costs for Breadco Problem		
	To		
From	**Customer 1**	**Customer 2**	**Customer 3**
Evansville	$0.16	$0.34	$0.26
Indianapolis	$0.40	$0.30	$0.35
South Bend	$0.45	$0.45	$0.23

TABLE 6.32	Data for Box Problem						
	Box						
	1	**2**	**3**	**4**	**5**	**6**	**7**
Size	33	30	26	24	19	18	17
Demand	400	300	500	700	200	400	200

36. A large drug company must determine how many sales representatives to assign to each of four sales districts. The cost of having n representatives in a district is $88{,}000 + 80{,}000n$ dollars per year. If a sales rep is based in a given district, the time it takes to complete a call on a doctor is that given in Table 6.33, where times are in hours. Each sales rep can work up to 160 hours per month. Each month a certain number of calls, given in Table 6.34, must be made in each district. A fractional number of representatives in a district is not permissible. Determine how many representatives should be assigned to each district.

TABLE 6.33	Times for Calls in Drug Rep Problem			
	Actual Sales Call District			
Rep's Base District	**1**	**2**	**3**	**4**
1	1	4	5	7
2	4	1	3	5
3	5	3	1	2
4	7	5	2	1

TABLE 6.34	Required Calls for Drug Rep Problem
	Number of Calls
District 1	50
District 2	80
District 3	100
District 4	60

37. Based on Strong (1989). In this problem you will use integer programming and the concept of bond duration to show how Wall Street firms can select an optimal bond portfolio. The duration of a bond (or any stream of payments) is defined as follows: Let $C(t)$ be the payment of the bond at time t ($t = 1, 2, \ldots, n$). Let r be the market interest rate. If the time-weighted average of the bond's payments is given by

$$\sum_{t=1}^{n} tC(t)/(1+r)^t$$

and the market price P of the bond is given by

$$P = \sum_{t=1}^{n} C(t)/(1+r)^t$$

then the duration D of the bond is given by

$$D = (1/P)\sum_{t=1}^{n} tC(t)/(1+r)^t$$

The duration of a bond measures the "average" time (in years) at which a randomly chosen \$1 of NPV is received. Suppose an insurance company needs to make payments of \$20,000 every 6 months for the next 10 years. If the market rate of interest is 10% per year, this stream of payments has an NPV of \$251,780 and a duration of 4.47 years. If we want to minimize the sensitivity of the bond portfolio to interest-rate risk (that is, *immunize* the bond portfolio) and still meet our payment obligations, then it has been shown that we should invest \$251,780 at the beginning of year 1 in a bond portfolio having a duration equal to the duration of the payment stream.

Suppose that the only cost of owning a bond portfolio is the transaction cost associated with the cost of purchasing the bonds. Let's suppose that six bonds are available. The payment streams for these six bonds are given in Table 6.35. The transaction

TABLE 6.35	Payment Streams for Bond Problem					
	Bond 1	**Bond 2**	**Bond 3**	**Bond 4**	**Bond 5**	**Bond 6**
Year 1	50	100	130	20	100	120
Year 2	60	90	130	20	100	100
Year 3	70	80	130	20	100	80
Year 4	80	70	130	20	100	140
Year 5	90	60	130	20	100	100
Year 6	100	50	130	80	100	90
Year 7	110	40	130	40	100	110
Year 8	120	30	130	150	100	130
Year 9	130	20	130	200	100	180
Year 10	1010	1040	1130	1200	1100	950

cost of purchasing any units of bond i equals $500 plus $5 per bond purchased. Thus, purchasing one unit of bond 1 costs $505 and purchasing ten units of bond 1 costs $550. Assume that a fractional number of bond i unit purchases is permissible, but in the interest of diversification, at most 100 units of any bond can be purchased. Treasury bonds can also be purchased (with no transaction cost). A treasury bond costs $980 and has a duration of 0.25 year (90 days). After computing the price and duration for each bond, determine the immunized bond portfolio that incurs the smallest total transaction cost. You may assume that the duration of a portfolio is a weighted average of the durations of the bonds included in the portfolio, where the weight associated with each bond is proportional to the money invested in that bond.

38. Based on Calloway et al. (1990). To satisfy telecommunication needs for the next 20 years, Telstar Corporation estimates that the number of circuits required between the United States and Germany, France, Switzerland, and the United Kingdom will be as given in Table 6.36. Two types of circuits can be created: cable and satellite. Two types of cable circuits (TA7 and TA8) are available. The fixed cost of building each type of cable and the circuit capacity of each type are given in Table 6.37. TA7 and TA8 cable go underseas from the United States to the English Channel. Thus, it costs an additional amount to extend these circuits to other European countries. The annual variable cost per circuit is given in Table 6.38. To create and use a satellite circuit, Telstar must launch a satellite, and each country using the satellite must have an earth station (or stations) to receive the signal. It costs $3 billion to launch a satellite. Each launched satellite can handle up to 140,000 circuits. All earth stations have a maximum capacity of 190 circuits and cost $6000 per year to operate. Determine how to supply the needed circuits and minimize total cost incurred during the next 20 years.

TABLE 6.36	Required Circuits for Telstar Problem
	Required Circuits
France	20,000
Germany	60,000
Switzerland	16,000
United Kingdom	60,000

TABLE 6.37	Building Costs and Capacities for Telstar Problem	
	Fixed Building Cost	Capacity
Cable TA7	$1.6 billion	8,500
Cable TA8	$2.3 billion	37,800

TABLE 6.38	Variable Costs for Telstar Problem
	Variable Cost per Circuit
France	$0
Germany	$310
Switzerland	$290
United Kingdom	$0

39. On Monday morning you have $3000 in cash on hand. For the next seven days the following cash requirements must be met: Monday, $5000; Tuesday, $6000; Wednesday, $9000; Thursday, $2000; Friday, $7000; Saturday, $2000; Sunday, $3000. At the beginning of each day you must decide how much money (if any) to withdraw from the bank. It costs $10 to make a withdrawal of any size. You believe that the opportunity cost of having $1 of cash on hand for a year is $0.20. Assume that opportunity costs are incurred on each day's ending balance. Determine how much money you should withdraw from the bank during each of the next seven days.

6.5 LOCKBOX MODELS

Companies (such as banks and credit card companies) that receive payments by mail must determine how many payment centers they should have for customers to mail payments to. Having too few payment centers results in a large amount of customer receipts being in the mail at any given time. This causes the company to lose a great deal of interest on its receipts. Having too many payment centers, however, results in large fixed costs. The problem of determining the number and location of payment centers that minimize the sum of fixed operating costs and lost interest costs is called a **lockbox problem**. The following is an example of a lockbox problem.

EXAMPLE   6.3

LOCATING LOCKBOXES AT JC NICKLES

JC Nickles receives credit card payments from four regions of the country (West, Midwest, East, and South). The average daily amounts of payments mailed from each region are as follows: West, $70,000; Midwest, $50,000; East, $60,000; South, $40,000. Nickles must decide where customers should mail their payments. An annual interest of 20% can be earned on cash received. Nickles is considering setting up payment centers (lockboxes) in four cities: Los Angeles, Chicago, New York, and Atlanta. The average number of days that elapse between the time a check is mailed and the check is credited to the Nickles account is given in Table 6.39. The annual cost of running a lockbox is $50,000. Each region must send all its money to a single city, and there is no limit on the amount of money a lockbox can handle. Nickles wants to determine the lockbox configuration that minimizes the sum of lost interest and lockbox costs.

TABLE 6.39	Times for Nickles Lockbox Example			
	L.A.	**Chicago**	**N.Y.**	**Atlanta**
West	2	6	8	8
Midwest	6	2	5	5
East	8	5	2	5
South	8	5	5	2

Solution

To solve this problem, we must keep track of the following:

- the location of the lockboxes
- the city to which each region sends its money
- the annual lost interest cost if a particular region sends its money to a particular city
- the total annual lost interest cost
- the total annual fixed cost

    We must also ensure that (1) each region sends its money *somewhere* and (2) Nickles pays for each lockbox it sets up.

DEVELOPING THE SPREADSHEET MODEL

The spreadsheet can be developed with the following steps. (See Figure 6.11 page 302) and the file NICKLES.XLS.)

❶   Inputs. Enter the given data in the shaded ranges.

❷   0–1 values for lockbox locations. We will use 0–1 variables to keep track of the cities where lockboxes are located. Enter *any* trial 0–1 values in the Locations range. For example, a 1 in cell D26 means that there is a lockbox in New York, whereas a 0 in cell E26 means that there is no lockbox in Atlanta.

❸   0–1 values for cities where regions send their money. In the Assignments range enter *any* 0–1 trial values to keep track of the city to which each region sends its money.

	A	B	C	D	E	F	G	H	I	J
1	**Nickles lockbox model**									
2										
3	**Financial data**									
4	Annual interest rate	20%						Range names used:		
5	Cost per lockbox	$50,000						InterestRate - B4		
6								UnitBoxCost - B5		
7	**Days in transit**							LostInterestValues -		
8		Lockbox location						B18:E21		
9	Check origin	Los Angeles	Chicago	New York	Atlanta		Payments per day	Locations - B26:E26		
10	West	2	6	8	8		$70,000	Assignments - B31:E34		
11	Midwest	6	2	5	5		$50,000	NAssignedTo - F31:F34		
12	East	8	5	2	5		$60,000	DupLocations - B36:E39		
13	South	8	5	5	2		$40,000	LostInterest - B42		
14								LockboxCost - B43		
15	**Annual lost interest for origin/location pair**							TotCost - B44		
16		Lockbox location								
17	Check origin	Los Angeles	Chicago	New York	Atlanta					
18	West	$28,000	$84,000	$112,000	$112,000					
19	Midwest	$60,000	$20,000	$50,000	$50,000					
20	East	$96,000	$60,000	$24,000	$60,000					
21	South	$64,000	$40,000	$40,000	$16,000					
22										
23	**Assignments and lockbox decisions**									
24	Locations of lockboxes (1 if located there, 0 if not)									
25		Los Angeles	Chicago	New York	Atlanta					
26		1	0	1	0					
27										
28	Assignments (1 if origin and lockbox location are paired, 0 if not)									
29		To lockbox location								
30	Sent from	Los Angeles	Chicago	New York	Atlanta	Sent?		Required		
31	West	1	0	0	0	1	=	1		
32	Midwest	0	0	1	0	1	=	1		
33	East	0	0	1	0	1	=	1		
34	South	0	0	1	0	1	=	1		
35			<=							
36		1	0	1	0					
37		1	0	1	0		4 duplications of Locations range			
38		1	0	1	0					
39		1	0	1	0					
40										
41	**Monetary summary**									
42	Lost interest	$142,000								
43	Lockbox cost	$100,000								
44	Total cost	$242,000								

FIGURE 6.11 Lockbox Model

For example, a 1 in cell B31 means that the West sends its money to Los Angeles, whereas a 0 in cell C32 means that the Midwest does *not* send its money to Chicago.

❹ **Number of cities each region sends money to.** Calculate the number of cities to which each region sends its money with row sums in the NAssignedTo range. That is, enter the formula

=SUM(B31:E31)

in cell F31 and copy it to the rest of the NAssignedTo range.

❺ **Total fixed cost.** Calculate the annual fixed cost in the LockBoxCost cell with the formula

=UnitBoxCost*SUM(Locations)

This is simply the fixed annual cost of a lockbox multiplied by the number of cities where lockboxes are located.

6 **Lost interest for each region–city combination.** To determine the amount of interest Nickles loses annually, we must determine how much revenue is lost if payments are sent from a particular region to a particular city. For example, how much annual interest is lost if customers from the West send their money to New York? On a given day, eight days' worth, or $560,000 (= 8[70,000]), of West payments would be in the mail and not earning interest. Because Nickles can earn 20% annually, each year West funds will result in $112,000 (= 0.20[560,000]) in lost interest. Calculate the annual lost interest costs for each region–city combination in the LostInterestValues range. Specifically, calculate the annual lost interest cost for sending money from the West to Los Angeles in cell B18 with the formula

=InterestRate*B10*$G10

Then copy this formula to the rest of the LostInterestValues range for the other region–city combinations.

7 **Total lost interest.** Calculate the total annual lost interest cost in the LostInterest cell with the formula

=SUMPRODUCT(LostInterestValues,Assignments)

Using 0–1 variables for the assignment of regions to cities ensures that this formula picks up only the lost interest costs that are due to actual assignments of regions to cities.

8 **Total cost.** Calculate the total annual cost in the TotCost cell with the formula

=LostInterest+LockboxCost

9 **Copy 0–1 variables.** We need to ensure that if a lockbox is used, Nickles pays for it. To do this, we add constraints of the following form for each possible combination of a region and city:

Assignment variable for region i, city j ≤ Fixed-cost variable for city j **(6.2)**

This constraint ensures that if region i sends its money to city j, then the fixed-cost variable for city j must equal 1, and Nickles pays for a lockbox at city j. If no region is assigned to city j, then the Solver can make the fixed-cost variable for city j equal to 0 or 1. However, because setting a fixed-cost variable to 0 is cheaper, this will be done whenever possible. We insert the 16 constraints of type (6.2) in the range B31:E39 by duplicating the Locations range [the right side of inequality (6.2)] in the DupLocations range. To do this, enter the formula

=B$26

in cell B36 and copy it to the rest of the DupLocations range. (*Note:* You might think you could specify inequality (6.2) as a constraint in the Solver dialog box by entering Assignments<=Locations. However, this will produce an error message. The problem is that the Assignments and Locations ranges are not the same size. This is why we created four duplicates of the Locations range.)

USING THE SOLVER

The completed Solver dialog box appears in Figure 6.12 (page 304). We minimize total cost, subject to the constraint that each region is assigned to exactly one lockbox location, the logical constraints in inequality (6.2), and binary constraints on both sets of changing cells. We also check the Assume Linear Model option and set the Solver tolerance to 0%.

FIGURE 6.12
Solver Dialog Box
for Lockbox Model

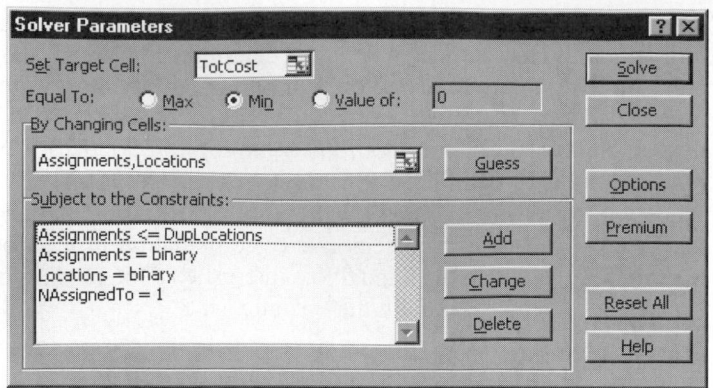

The optimal solution in Figure 6.11 indicates that Nickles needs lockboxes in Los Angeles and New York. The West sends its money to Los Angeles, and all other regions send their money to New York. An annual cost of $242,000 is incurred. Note that row 26 (and its four duplicates in rows 36–39) have 1's corresponding to Los Angeles and New York. These 1's pick up the fixed costs of locating lockboxes in Los Angeles and New York, and they allow the four regions to send their money to these two cities. The 1's in rows 31–34 indicate where the regions send their money. The logical fixed-cost constraints ensure that these rows can have 1's only in the columns where row 26 has 1's. That is, a region can send its money to a city only if a lockbox is located in that city.

Sensitivity Analysis An interesting sensitivity analysis is to see how the annual costs and location of lockboxes change as the annual interest rate varies. This is straightforward with SolverTable. We select the InterestRate cell as the single input cell, let it vary from, say, 5% to 35% in increments of 5%, and keep track of the relevant output cells. The SolverTable results appear in Figure 6.13. After some reflection, these results are not too surprising. As the interest rate increases, the potential cost of not having enough well-placed lockboxes increases. When the interest rate is 15% or less, Nickles needs only one lockbox, in Chicago. This is evidently the most "central" location for placing a *single* lockbox. However, when the interest rate is between 20% and 30%, Nickles needs two lockboxes, and it locates them in opposite sides on the country, in Los Angeles and New York. Finally, when the interest rate increases to 35%, a third lockbox is set up in Chicago.

	A	B	C	D	E	F	G	H
46	**Sensitivity of costs and lockbox locations to annual interest rate**							
47		$B$42	$B$43	$B$44	$B$26	$C$26	$D$26	$E$26
48	5%	$51,000	$50,000	$101,000	0	1	0	0
49	10%	$102,000	$50,000	$152,000	0	1	0	0
50	15%	$153,000	$50,000	$203,000	0	1	0	0
51	20%	$142,000	$100,000	$242,000	1	0	1	0
52	25%	$177,500	$100,000	$277,500	1	0	1	0
53	30%	$213,000	$100,000	$313,000	1	0	1	0
54	35%	$196,000	$150,000	$346,000	1	1	1	0

FIGURE 6.13 Sensitivity to Interest Rate ■

The **cash disbursement model** involves dispersing sites around the country to extend the time between the mailing of a check and the time the check clears. Shanker and Zoltners (1972) use a model similar to the lockbox model to solve this problem. See Problem 46 for an example of this model. ■

Skill-Building Problems

40. In the Nickles lockbox example (Example 6.3), use SolverTable to see the effect on the optimal number of lockboxes of increasing the cost per lockbox in increments of $10,000. How large must this cost be before there will be only two lockboxes? Only a single lockbox?

41. In the Nickles lockbox example (Example 6.3), at what level of daily payments received from the South would it be worthwhile to put a lockbox in Atlanta? Use SolverTable to determine this.

42. Ford has four automobile plants. Each is capable of producing the Taurus, Lincoln, or Escort, but it can produce only one of these cars. The fixed cost of operating each plant for a year and the variable cost of producing a car of each type at each plant are given in Table 6.40. Ford faces the following restrictions:

- Each plant can produce only one type of car.

- The total production of each type of car must be at a single plant. For example, if any Tauruses are made at plant 1, then all Tauruses must be made there.

  Each year Ford must produce 5 million of each type of car.
  a. Determine how to minimize the annual cost of producing these cars.
  b. Use SolverTable to see how a change in the demand for a type of car changes the optimal solution. Do this separately for each type of car.
  c. Use SolverTable to see how the optimal solution is affected by a change in the variable cost of producing a Lincoln.

43. At a machine tool plant, five jobs must be completed each day. The time it takes to do each job depends on the machine used to do the job. If a machine is used at all, there is a setup time required. The relevant times (in minutes) are given in Table 6.41.

TABLE 6.40   **Fixed and Variable Costs for Ford Problem**

	Fixed Cost	Variable Cost		
		Taurus	**Lincoln**	**Escort**
Plant 1	$70 billion	$12,000	$16,000	$9,000
Plant 2	$60 billion	$15,000	$18,000	$11,000
Plant 3	$40 billion	$17,000	$19,000	$12,000
Plant 4	$20 billion	$19,000	$22,000	$14,000

TABLE 6.41   **Times for Machine Tool Problem**

	Job 1	Job 2	Job 3	Job 4	Job 5	Setup Time
Machine 1	42	70	93	X	X	30
Machine 2	X	85	45	X	X	40
Machine 3	58	X	X	37	X	50
Machine 4	58	X	55	X	38	60
Machine 5	X	60	X	54	X	20

a. Determine how to minimize the sum of the setup and machine operation times needed to complete all jobs.

b. Use SolverTable to see how a change in the setup time for machine 4 changes the optimal solution.

c. Use SolverTable to see how a change in the required time for machine 1 to complete job 3 changes the optimal solution.

44. How would the Nickles lockbox formulation change if each city could handle at most $120,000 per day in payments?

Skill-Extending Problems

45. A 3×3 magic square is an arrangement of the digits 1 through 9 for which all three rows, three columns, and both diagonals of the square add up to the same number. For example,

1	4	9
2	6	5
3	7	8

is not a magic square. Use the Solver to find a 3×3 magic square. (*Hint*: You will have $9(9) = 81$ variables that you can put in a range consisting of 9 rows and 9 columns. The variable in row i and column j will equal 1 if digit i is assigned to position j in the square and will equal 0 otherwise.)

46. Based on Shanker and Zoltners (1972). Speaker's Clearinghouse must disburse sweepstakes checks to winners in four different regions of the country: Southeast (SE), Northeast (NE), Far West (FW), and Midwest (MW). The average daily amounts of the checks written to winners in each region of the country as follows: SE, $40,000; NE, $60,000; FW, $30,000; MW, $50,000. Speaker's must issue the checks the day they find that a customer has won. They can delay winners from quickly cashing their checks by giving a winner a check drawn on an out-of-the-way bank (this will cause the check to clear slowly). Four bank sites are under consideration: Frostbite Falls, Montana (FF), Redville, South Carolina (R), Painted Forest, Arizona (PF), and Beanville, Maine (B). The annual cost of maintaining an account at each bank is as follows: FF, $50,000; R, $40,000; PF, $30,000; B, $20,000. Each bank has a requirement that the average daily amount of checks written cannot exceed $90,000. The average number of days it takes a check to clear is given in Table 6.42. Assuming that money invested by Speaker's earns 15% per year, where should the company have bank accounts, and from which bank should a given customer's check be written?

47. You have nine circles. Three are red, three are green, and three are orange. You want to assign these circles to a 3×3 chessboard so that each row, column, and diagonal has one circle of each color. Use the Solver to accomplish this goal.

TABLE 6.42	Data for Clearinghouse Problem			
	FF	**R**	**PF**	**B**
SE	7	2	6	5
NE	8	4	5	3
FW	4	8	2	11
MW	5	4	7	5

6.6 PLANT AND WAREHOUSE LOCATION MODELS

Consider a company that must produce its goods at plants and store its goods at warehouses before shipping these goods to customers. Suppose that there is a fixed cost associated with the operation of each plant and warehouse. If the company is allowed to determine which warehouses and plants to open, then we have an IP problem called a **fixed-cost plant and warehouse location problem**. By solving such a problem, companies such as Hunt's Foods have saved millions of dollars in production and distribution costs. See Geoffrion and Graves (1976) for a documented application of a fixed-cost plant and warehouse location model that saved Hunt-Wesson over $1 million annually.

The following is a typical example of a fixed-cost plant and warehouse location problem. However, we note that real-world examples of this type of problem are often *much* larger, with many more potential plant and warehouse locations. They often require specialized solution algorithms, just as we remarked about general network problems in the previous chapter.

EXAMPLE 6.4

FACILITY LOCATION AND LOGISTICS PLANNING AT HUNTCO

Huntco produces tomato sauce at five different plants. The capacity (in tons) of each plant is given in Table 6.43. The tomato sauce is stored at one of three warehouses. The cost per ton of producing tomato sauce at each plant and shipping it to each warehouse is given in Table 6.44. Huntco has four customers. The cost of shipping a ton of sauce from each warehouse to each customer is given in Table 6.45. Each customer must receive the amount (in tons) of sauce given in Table 6.46. The annual fixed cost of operating each plant and warehouse is listed in Table 6.47 (page 308). Huntco's goal is to minimize the annual cost of meeting customer demands. The company wants to determine which plants and warehouses to open, as well as the optimal shipping plan.

TABLE 6.43   **Capacities for Huntco Example**

	Plant				
	1	2	3	4	5
Tons	300	200	300	200	400

TABLE 6.44   **Production and Shipping Costs for Huntco Example**

		To		
		Warehouse 1	Warehouse 2	Warehouse 3
	Plant 1	$800	$1000	$1200
	Plant 2	$700	$500	$700
From	Plant 3	$800	$600	$500
	Plant 4	$500	$600	$700
	Plant 5	$700	$600	$500

TABLE 6.45   **Shipping Costs to Customers for Huntco Example**

		To			
		Customer 1	Customer 2	Customer 3	Customer 4
	Warehouse 1	$40	$80	$90	$50
From	Warehouse 2	$70	$40	$60	$80
	Warehouse 3	$80	$30	$50	$60

TABLE 6.46   **Customer Requirements for Huntco Example**

	Customer			
	1	2	3	4
Requirement	200	300	150	250

TABLE 6.47	Fixed Costs for Huntco Example
	Fixed Annual Cost
Plant 1	$35,000
Plant 2	$45,000
Plant 3	$40,000
Plant 4	$42,000
Plant 5	$40,000
Warehouse 1	$40,000
Warehouse 2	$20,000
Warehouse 3	$60,000

Solution

To model Huntco's situation we need to keep track of the following:

- the shipments from plants to warehouses
- the shipments from warehouses to customers
- the fixed costs of operating plants and warehouses
- the shipping and production costs from plants to warehouses
- the shipping costs from warehouses to customers
- the total amount shipped out of each plant

We must also ensure that (1) Huntco pays the fixed costs for all plants and warehouses that it uses, (2) the amount shipped into each warehouse equals the amount received by each warehouse, and (3) each customer receives the specified demand.

DEVELOPING THE SPREADSHEET MODEL

The completed spreadsheet appears in Figure 6.14. (See the file HUNTCO.XLS.) It can be formed as follows.

1 **Inputs.** Enter the given data in the shaded ranges.

2 **Shipments.** Enter *any* trial values for the shipments from each plant to each warehouse in the Shipped1 range and *any* trial values for the shipments from each warehouse to each customer in the Shipped2 range.

3 **Binary fixed cost variables.** Enter *any* trial 0–1 values for the plant fixed-cost variables in the UsePlants range and the warehouse fixed-cost variables in the UseWhses range. The fixed-cost variable for a plant equals 1 if the plant is used and 0 if the plant is not used. Similarly, the fixed-cost variable for a warehouse equals 1 if the warehouse is used and 0 if the warehouse is not used.

4 **Amount shipped out of each plant.** Calculate the amounts shipped out of the plants as row sums in the ShippedOut1 range. Specifically, enter the formula

=SUM(B30:D30)

in cell E30 and copy it to the rest of the ShippedOut1 range.

5 **Upper limit on amount shipped out of each plant.** For each plant we need a constraint of the form

Total shipped out of plant $\leq$ Plant capacity $*$ Fixed-cost variable for plant   **(6.3)**

Huntco plant & warehouse location model

Range names used:
UnitCosts1 - B6:D10
FCosts1 - F6:F10
Capacities - H6:H10
UnitCosts2 - B15:E17
Fcosts2 - G15:G17
UsePlants - B21:B25
UseWhses - E21:E23
Shipped1 - B30:D34
ShippedOut1 - E30:E34
UpBounds1 - G30:G34
ShippedIn1 - B35:D35
ShippedOut2_Row - B37:D37
Shipped2 - B42:E44
ShippedOut2_Col - F42:F44
UpBound2 - H42:H44
ShippedIn2 - B45:E45
Demands - B47:E47
ShipCosts - B50:B51
FixedCosts - B52:B53
TotCost - B54

Plant to warehouse unit production, shipping costs, plant fixed costs, plant capacities

Plant	Warehouse 1	2	3		Fixed cost		Capacity
1	$800	$1,000	$1,200		$35,000		300
2	$700	$500	$700		$45,000		200
3	$800	$600	$500		$40,000		300
4	$500	$600	$700		$42,000		200
5	$700	$600	$500		$40,000		400

Warehouse to customer unit shipping costs, warehouse fixed costs

Warehouse	Customer 1	2	3	4	Fixed cost
1	$40	$80	$90	$50	$40,000
2	$70	$40	$60	$80	$20,000
3	$80	$30	$50	$60	$60,000

Plant use decisions / Warehouse use decisions

Plant	Use?	Warehouse	Use?
1	0	1	0
2	1	2	1
3	1	3	1
4	0		
5	1		

Plant to warehouse shipments (tons)

Plant	Warehouse 1	2	3	Shipped out		Capacity
1	0	0	0	0	<=	0
2	0	200	0	200	<=	200
3	0	0	300	300	<=	300
4	0	0	0	0	<=	0
5	0	0	400	400	<=	400
Shipped in	0	200	700			
	=	=	=			
Shipped out	0	200	700			

Warehouse to customer shipments (tons)

Warehouse	Customer 1	2	3	4	Shipped out		Upper bound
1	0	0	0	0	0	<=	0
2	200	0	0	0	200	<=	900
3	0	300	150	250	700	<=	900
Shipped in	200	300	150	250			
	>=	>=	>=	>=			
Demand	200	300	150	250			

Summary of costs

Plant to warehouse	$450,000
Warehouse to customer	$45,500
Fixed plant	$125,000
Fixed warehouse	$80,000
Total cost	$700,500

Note: Unless you set the Tolerance option in Solver to 0% (or some percentage smaller than the 5% default), you probably won't get quite this good a solution.

FIGURE 6.14 Plant and Warehouse Location Model

This inequality ensures that if Huntco uses the plant, then this plant's fixed-cost variable will equal 1 and the company will have to pay the plant's operating cost. In this case inequality (6.3) states that the total shipped out of the plant is less than or equal to the plant's capacity. We generate the right side of inequality (6.3) in the UpBounds1 range. Specifically, enter the formula

=B21*H6

in cell G30 and copy it to the rest of the UpBounds1 range. Note that if a plant is not used, the Solver is free to make this plant's fixed-cost variable 0, and no fixed cost for this plant will be incurred. Then inequality (6.3) will be satisfied trivially ($0 \leq 0$).

6 **Amount shipped into and out of each warehouse.** For each warehouse, we need "flow balance"—that is, we need the following constraint:

Total shipments into warehouse = Total shipments out of warehouse   **(6.4)**

To implement equation (6.4), first calculate the left side as column sums in the ShippedIn1 range. That is, enter the formula

=SUM(B30:B34)

in cell B35 and copy it to the rest of the ShippedIn1 range. For the right side of equality (6.4), first calculate total shipments out of warehouses as row sums in the ShippedOut2_Col *column* range. That is, enter the formula

=SUM(B42:E42)

in cell F42 and copy it to the rest of the ShippedOut2_Col range. Now put these totals in the ShippedOut2_Row *row* range by selecting this range, entering the formula

=TRANSPOSE(ShippedOut2_Col)

and pressing Ctrl-Shift-Enter. This allows us to compare a row with a row when we specify equation (6.4) in the Solver dialog box.

❼   **Upper limit on amount shipped out of each warehouse.** For each warehouse we need a constraint of the form

$$\text{Total shipped out of warehouse} \leq \text{UpperBound} * \text{Fixed-cost variable for warehouse}$$
$$\textbf{(6.5)}$$

Here, UpperBound is an upper bound on the most that could possibly be shipped out of any warehouse. Several possibilities for UpperBound could be used. We use the smaller of the total demand for all customers and the total capacity for all plants. If a warehouse's fixed-cost variable is 0, then inequality (6.5) ensures that this warehouse cannot be used, whereas if the fixed-cost variable is 1, then this inequality is satisfied automatically (and is essentially redundant). To operationalize inequality (6.5), note that we already have the left side in the ShippedOut2_Col range. To calculate the right side, enter the formula

=E21*MIN(SUM(Capacities),SUM(Demands))

in cell H42 and copy it to the rest of the UpBounds2 range.

❽   **Amount received by each customer.** Calculate the total amounts received by the customers as column sums in the ShippedIn2 range. That is, enter the formula

=SUM(B42:B44)

in cell B45 and copy it to the rest of the ShippedIn2 range.

❾   **Shipping costs.** Calculate the total costs of shipping from plants to warehouses and from warehouses to customers in cells B50 and B51 with the formulas

=SUMPRODUCT(UnitCosts1,Shipped1)

and

=SUMPRODUCT(UnitCosts2,Shipped2)

❿   **Fixed costs.** Calculate the annual fixed costs for operating plants and warehouses in cells B52 and B53 with the formulas

=SUMPRODUCT(FCosts1,UsePlants)

and

=SUMPRODUCT(FCosts2,UseWhses)

⓫   Total cost. Finally, calculate the total annual cost in the TotCost cell with the formula

=SUM(ShipCosts,FixedCosts)

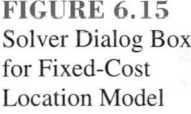

USING THE SOLVER

The completed Solver dialog box should appear as in Figure 6.15. We briefly explain this setup below.

❶   Objective. The objective to minimize is total annual cost.

❷   Changing cells. There are four sets of changing cells—two sets for amounts to ship and two sets of binary variables for which plants and warehouses to use.

❸   Plant upper bounds. The constraint ShippedOut1<=UpBounds1 operationalizes inequality (6.3).

❹   Warehouse upper bounds. The constraint ShippedOut2_Col<=UpBounds2 operationalizes inequality (6.5).

❺   Warehouse balance. The constraint ShippedIn1=ShippedOut2_Row operationalizes equation (6.4).

❻   Demand constraint. The constraint ShippedIn2>=Demands ensures that each customer receives the required amount.

The optimal solution in Figure 6.14 indicates that Huntco should use plants 2, 3, and 5 and warehouses 2 and 3. Of course, the optimal shipping plan, as specified in the Shipped1 and Shipped2 ranges, uses only these plants and warehouses. This solution incurs a total annual cost of $700,500. If you obtain an "optimal" solution with a total cost somewhat larger than this (probably around $719,000), check the Solver tolerance setting. If it is at its default level of 5%, the Solver might very well stop short of optimal. We obtained our solution by setting the tolerance to 0%.

FIGURE 6.15
Solver Dialog Box
for Fixed-Cost
Location Model

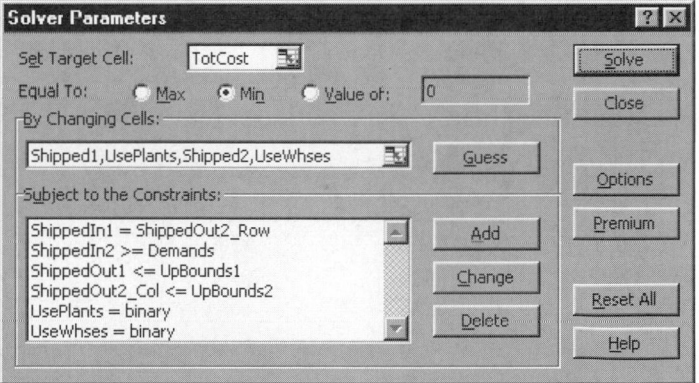

At this point, you might want to review the inputs for this problem and see whether the optimal solution appears reasonable from an economic point of view. For example, although plant 1 has a relatively small fixed cost, it has relatively large unit shipping costs. This is evidently the reason for not using plant 1. However, the situation is not so obvious for plant 4 or warehouse 1. We think you will agree that on logistics problems such as this—and this is not even a large problem—more than intuition is necessary!

We will not report any specific sensitivity analyses for this model, but many are possible. For example, we might check whether adding larger capacities at plants 1 and 4 would induce Huntco to open them. Or we might see what would happen if all of the fixed costs (or some subset of them) increased by some percentage. Or we might see what would happen if all customer demands increased by some percentage. SolverTable, after some slight model modifications, can easily analyze any of these situations. ■

PROBLEMS

Skill-Building Problems

48. In the Huntco example (Example 6.4), suppose that the company could stimulate demand by having its sales force concentrate on increasing the demand of a single customer. Use SolverTable appropriately to determine which customer the company should concentrate its efforts on. (You can assume that each customer pays the same price and that it is equally costly to stimulate the demand for each customer.)

49. Heinsco produces tomato sauce at five different plants. The plant capacities (in tons) are listed in

Table 6.48. The tomato sauce is stored at one of three warehouses. The cost per ton of producing tomato sauce at each plant and shipping it to each warehouse is given in Table 6.49. Heinsco has four customers. The cost of shipping a ton of sauce from each warehouse to each customer is given in Table 6.50. Each customer must be delivered the amount (in tons) of sauce given in Table 6.51. There is a fixed annual cost of operating each plant and warehouse, given in Table 6.52.

a. Determine the minimum-cost method for meeting customer demands.

b. Use SolverTable to see how a change in the capacity of plant 1 affects the total cost.

c. Use SolverTable to see how a change in the customer 2 demand affects the total cost.

50. Suppose in the previous problem that each customer's demand must be met from a *single* warehouse. Solve the previous problem with this restriction.

TABLE 6.48	Capacities for Heinsco Problem				
	Plant				
	1	**2**	**3**	**4**	**5**
Capacity	500	200	300	400	400

TABLE 6.49	Production and Shipping Costs for Heinsco Problem		
		To	
	Warehouse 1	**Warehouse 2**	**Warehouse 3**
From **Plant 1**	$600	$700	$500
Plant 2	$700	$500	$700
Plant 3	$800	$400	$900
Plant 4	$500	$600	$700
Plant 5	$700	$600	$500

TABLE 6.50	Shipping Costs to Customers for Heinsco Problem			
			To	
	Customer 1	**Customer 2**	**Customer 3**	**Customer 4**
From **Warehouse 1**	$60	$80	$40	$70
Warehouse 2	$70	$40	$60	$80
Warehouse 3	$50	$50	$50	$50

TABLE 6.51	Customer Requirements for Heinsco Problem			
	Customer			
	1	2	3	4
Requirement	400	300	250	350

TABLE 6.52	Fixed Costs for Heinsco Problem
	Fixed Annual Cost
Plant 1	$25,000
Plant 2	$35,000
Plant 3	$40,000
Plant 4	$50,000
Plant 5	$40,000
Warehouse 1	$30,000
Warehouse 2	$40,000
Warehouse 3	$30,000

6.7 SET-COVERING MODELS

In a set-covering model, each member of a given set (set 1) must be "covered" by an acceptable member of another set (set 2). The objective in a set-covering problem is to minimize the number of elements in set 2 that are needed to cover all of the elements in set 1. For example, set 1 might consist of all cities in a county and set 2 might consist of the cities in which a fire station is located. A member of set 2 "covers" a city in set 1 if the fire station is located, say, within 10 minutes of the city. The goal is to minimize the number of fire stations needed to cover all cities. Set-covering models have been applied to areas as diverse as airline crew scheduling, truck dispatching, political redistricting, and capital investment. The following is a typical example of a set-covering model.

EXAMPLE 6.5

HUB LOCATION AT WESTERN AIRLINES

Western Airlines has decided that it wants to design a "hub" system in the United States. Each hub is used for connecting flights to and from cities within 1000 miles of the hub. Western runs flights among the following cities: Atlanta, Boston, Chicago, Denver, Houston, Los Angeles, New Orleans, New York, Pittsburgh, Salt Lake City, San Francisco, and Seattle. The company wants to determine the smallest number of hubs it will need to cover all of these cities, where a city is "covered" if it is within 1000 miles of at least one hub. Table 6.53 (page 314) lists which cities are within 1000 miles of other cities.

Solution

The model must keep track of the following:

- the set of cities that each city covers (for example, San Francisco covers Los Angeles, Salt Lake City, San Francisco, and Seattle)
- cities that are selected as hubs

TABLE 6.53	Data for Western Set-Covering Example

	Cities Within 1000 Miles
Atlanta (AT)	AT, CH, HO, NO, NY, PI
Boston (BO)	BO, NY, PI
Chicago (CH)	AT, CH, NY, NO, PI
Denver (DE)	DE, SL
Houston (HO)	AT, HO, NO
Los Angeles (LA)	LA, SL, SF
New Orleans (NO)	AT, CH, HO, NO
New York (NY)	AT, BO, CH, NY, PI
Pittsburgh (PI)	AT, BO, CH, NY, PI
Salt Lake City (SL)	DE, LA, SL, SF, SE
San Francisco (SF)	LA, SL, SF, SE
Seattle (SE)	SL, SF, SE

- whether or not each city is covered by a hub
- the total number of cities chosen to be hubs

DEVELOPING THE SPREADSHEET MODEL

The spreadsheet model for Western appears in Figure 6.16. (See the file WESTERN1.XLS.) It can be developed as follows.

1 **Inputs.** Enter the information from Table 6.53 about which cities cover which other cities in the shaded range. A 1 in a cell indicates that the column city covers the

	A	B	C	D	E	F	G	H	I	J	K	L	M	N	O	P
1	Western Airlines Set Covering Problem															
2																
3							**Potential hub**									
4	Cities covered	AT	BO	CH	DE	HO	LA	NO	NY	PI	SL	SF	SE	# covered by		Required
5	AT	1	0	1	0	1	0	1	1	1	0	0	0	2	>=	1
6	BO	0	1	0	0	0	0	0	1	1	0	0	0	1	>=	1
7	CH	1	0	1	0	0	0	1	1	1	0	0	0	1	>=	1
8	DE	0	0	0	1	0	0	0	0	0	1	0	0	1	>=	1
9	HO	1	0	0	0	1	0	1	0	0	0	0	0	1	>=	1
10	LA	0	0	0	0	0	1	0	0	0	1	1	0	1	>=	1
11	NO	1	0	1	0	1	0	1	0	0	0	0	0	1	>=	1
12	NY	1	1	1	0	0	0	0	1	1	0	0	0	1	>=	1
13	PI	1	1	1	0	0	0	0	1	1	0	0	0	1	>=	1
14	SL	0	0	0	1	0	1	0	0	0	1	1	1	1	>=	1
15	SF	0	0	0	0	0	1	0	0	0	1	1	1	1	>=	1
16	SE	0	0	0	0	0	0	0	0	0	1	1	1	1	>=	1
17																
18	Used as hub?	0	0	0	0	1	0	0	1	0	1	0	0			
19																
20	Total hubs	3														
21							Range names:									
22							NCoveredBy: N5:N16									
23							TotHubs: B20									
24							Used: B18:M18									

FIGURE 6.16 Airline Hub Set-Covering Model

row city, whereas a 0 indicates that the column city does not cover the row city. For example, the three 1's in row 6 indicate that Boston, New York, and Pittsburgh are the only cities within 1000 miles of Boston. Also, enter 1's in the range P5:P16 to indicate that we need at least one hub within 1000 miles of each city.

② **Binary values for hub locations.** Enter *any* trial values of 0's or 1's in the Used range to indicate which cities are used as hubs. These are the changing cells.

③ **Cities covered by hubs.** We now determine the number of hubs that cover each city in the NCoveredBy range. Specifically, calculate the total number of hubs within 1000 miles of Atlanta in cell N5 with the formula

=SUMPRODUCT(B5:M5,Used)

Then copy this to the rest of the NCoveredBy range. Note that a value in this range can be 2 or greater. This indicates that the city in that row is within 1000 miles of more than one hub.

④ **Number of hubs.** Calculate the total number of hubs used in the TotHubs cell with the formula

=SUM(Used)

USING THE SOLVER

The Solver dialog box appears in Figure 6.17. We minimize the total number of hubs, subject to covering each city by at least one hub and ensuring that the changing cells are binary.

FIGURE 6.17
Solver Dialog Box for Set-Covering Model

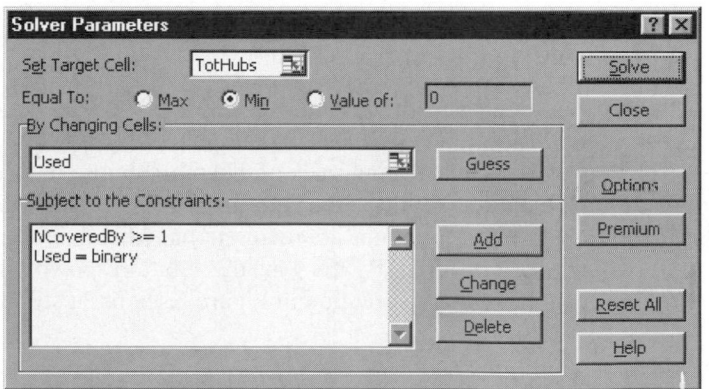

A graphical representation of the optimal solution appears in Figure 6.18 (page 316), where the double ovals indicate hub locations and the large circles indicate ranges covered by the hubs. (These large circles are not drawn to scale. In reality, they should be circles of radius 1000 miles centered at the hubs.) Three hubs—in Houston, New York, and Salt Lake City—are needed.[4] Would you have guessed this? The Houston hub covers Houston, Atlanta, and New Orleans. The New York hub covers Atlanta, Pittsburgh, Boston, New York, and Chicago. The Salt Lake City hub covers Denver, Los Angeles, Salt Lake City, San Francisco, and Seattle. Note that Atlanta is the only city covered by two of these hubs; it can be serviced by New York or Houston.

---

[4]There are multiple optimal solutions for this model, all requiring three hubs, so you might obtain a different solution from ours.

FIGURE 6.18
Graphical Solution to
Set-Covering Model

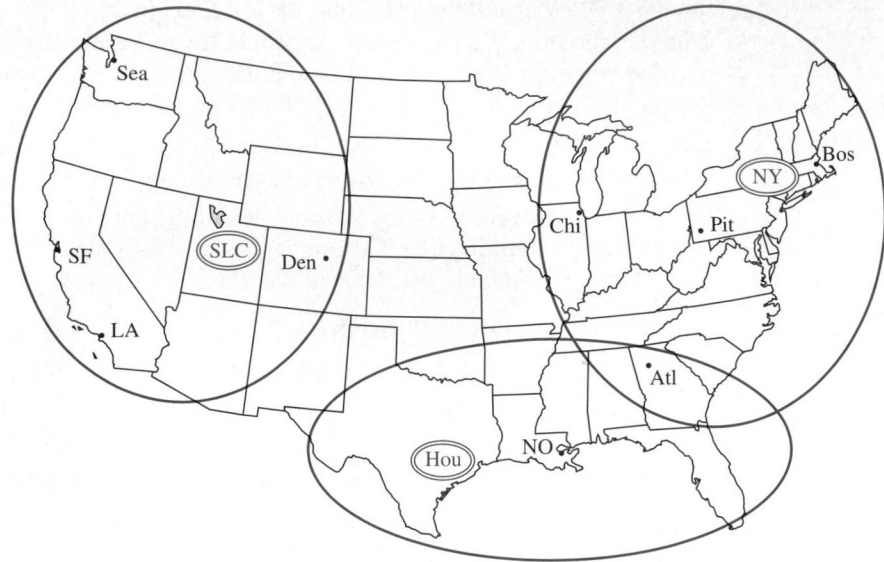

Sensitivity Analysis An interesting sensitivity analysis for Western's problem is to see how the solution is affected by the mile limit. Currently, a hub can service all cities within 1000 miles of it. What if the limit were 800 or 1200 miles, say? To answer this question, we first need to collect data on actual distances among all of the cities. Once we have a matrix of these distances, we can build the 0–1 matrix, as in the range B5:M16 in Figure 6.16, by using an IF function. The modified model appears in Figure 6.19. (See the file WESTERN2.XLS.) The typical formula in A22 is

=IF(A7<=MileLimit,1,0)

which is then copied to the rest of the A22:M33 range.[5] We then run SolverTable, selecting the MileLimit cell as the single input cell, letting it vary from 800 to 1200 in increments of 100, and keeping track of where the hubs are located and the number of hubs. The SolverTable results at the bottom show the effect of the mile limit. When it is lowered to 800 miles, four hubs are required, but when it is increased to 1100 or 1200, only two hubs are required. By the way, the solution shown for the 1000-mile limit is different from the previous solution in Figure 6.16, but it still requires three hubs.

---

[5]We have warned a couple of times about using IF functions in relationship to the Solver. However, the current use affects only the *inputs* to the problem, not quantities that depend on the changing cells. Therefore, it causes no problems.

Western Airlines Set Covering Problem

	A	B	C	D	E	F	G	H	I	J	K	L	M	N	O	P
3	Mile limit	1000														

Additional range name: MileLimit: B3

Distance matrix

		AT	BO	CH	DE	HO	LA	NO	NY	PI	SL	SF	SE
7	AT	0	1037	674	1398	789	2182	479	841	687	1878	2496	2618
8	BO	1037	0	1005	1949	1804	2979	1507	222	574	2343	3095	2976
9	CH	674	1005	0	1008	1067	2054	912	802	452	1390	2142	2013
10	DE	1398	1949	1008	0	1019	1059	1273	1771	1411	504	1235	1307
11	HO	789	1804	1067	1019	0	1538	356	1608	1313	1438	1912	2274
12	LA	2182	2979	2054	1059	1538	0	1883	2786	2426	715	379	1131
13	NO	479	1507	912	1273	356	1883	0	1311	1070	1738	2249	2574
14	NY	841	222	802	1771	1608	2786	1311	0	368	2182	2934	2815
15	PI	687	574	452	1411	1313	2426	1070	368	0	1826	2578	2465
16	SL	1878	2343	1390	504	1438	715	1738	2182	1826	0	752	836
17	SF	2496	3095	2142	1235	1912	379	2249	2934	2578	752	0	808
18	SE	2618	2976	2013	1307	2274	1131	2574	2815	2465	836	808	0

Potential hub

Cities covered	AT	BO	CH	DE	HO	LA	NO	NY	PI	SL	SF	SE	# covered by		Required
AT	1	0	1	0	1	0	1	1	1	0	0	0	1	>=	1
BO	0	1	0	0	0	0	0	1	1	0	0	0	1	>=	1
CH	1	0	1	0	0	0	1	1	1	0	0	0	1	>=	1
DE	0	0	0	1	0	0	0	0	0	1	0	0	1	>=	1
HO	1	0	0	0	1	0	1	0	0	0	0	0	1	>=	1
LA	0	0	0	0	0	1	0	0	0	1	1	0	1	>=	1
NO	1	0	1	0	1	0	1	0	0	0	0	0	1	>=	1
NY	1	1	1	0	0	0	0	1	1	0	0	0	1	>=	1
PI	1	1	1	0	0	0	0	1	1	0	0	0	1	>=	1
SL	0	0	0	1	0	1	0	0	0	1	1	1	1	>=	1
SF	0	0	0	0	0	1	0	0	0	1	1	1	1	>=	1
SE	0	0	0	0	0	0	0	0	0	1	1	1	1	>=	1

Used as hub?	0	1	0	0	0	0	1	0	0	1	0	0

Total hubs	3

Sensitivity of total hubs their locations to the mile limit

Locations of hubs

Mile limit	AT	BO	CH	DE	HO	LA	NO	NY	PI	SL	SF	SE	Total
	0	1	0	0	0	0	1	0	0	1	0	0	3
800	0	0	0	0	1	0	0	0	1	1	0	1	4
900	0	0	0	0	1	0	0	0	1	1	0	0	3
1000	0	1	0	0	0	0	1	0	0	1	0	0	3
1100	0	0	1	0	0	0	0	0	0	0	1	0	2
1200	0	0	1	0	0	0	0	0	0	0	0	1	2

FIGURE 6.19 Sensitivity to Mile Limit

ADDITIONAL APPLICATIONS

Station Staffing at Pan Am

Like many other airlines, Pan Am has used management science to determine optimal staffing levels for its support staff (for ticket counters, baggage loading and unloading, mechanical maintenance, and so on). Schindler and Semmel (1993) describe how Pan Am used a set-covering model to determine flexible shifts of full-time and part-time personnel in the United States, Latin and South America, and Europe. The model allowed the company to reduce its deployment of staff by up to 11% in work-hour requirements and suggested how existing staff could be used more efficiently.

Eaton et al. (1985) used a set-covering model to determine where emergency medical vehicles should be located in Austin, Texas. They determined the location of emergency medical facilities and vehicles that maximized (with a limited budget) the number of people receiving adequate emergency service. The Eaton model is estimated to have saved Austin over $10 million. See Problem 53 for a scaled-down version of this model. ■

PROBLEMS

Skill-Building Problems

51. Based on Walker (1974). The Smalltown Fire Department currently has seven conventional ladder companies and seven alarm boxes. The two closest ladder companies to each alarm box are listed in Table 6.54. The town council wants to maximize the number of conventional ladder companies that can be replaced with "tower" ladder companies. Unfortunately, political considerations dictate that a conventional company can be replaced only if, after replacement, at least one of the two closest companies to each alarm box is still a conventional company. Determine how to maximize the number of conventional companies that can be replaced by tower companies.

TABLE 6.54   Data for Fire Department Problem

	Two Closest Ladder Companies
Alarm Box 1	2, 3
Alarm Box 2	3, 4
Alarm Box 3	1, 5
Alarm Box 4	2, 6
Alarm Box 5	3, 6
Alarm Box 6	4, 7
Alarm Box 7	5, 7

52. At Blair General Hospital, six types of surgical operations are performed. The types of operations each surgeon is qualified to perform (indicated by an X) are listed in Table 6.55. Suppose that surgeons

1 and 2 dislike each other and cannot be on duty at the same time. Determine the minimum number of surgeons required so that the hospital can perform all types of surgery.

TABLE 6.55   Data for Hospital Problem

	Operation Number					
	1	2	3	4	5	6
Surgeon 1	X	X		X		
Surgeon 2			X		X	X
Surgeon 3			X		X	
Surgeon 4	X					
Surgeon 5		X				
Surgeon 6					X	X

Skill-Extending Problem

53. Based on Eaton et al. (1985). Gotham City has been divided into eight districts. The time (in minutes) it takes an ambulance to travel from one district to another is shown in Table 6.56. The population of each district (in thousands) is as follows: district 1, 40; district 2, 30; district 3, 35; district 4, 20; district 5, 15; district 6, 50; district 7, 45; district 8, 60. Suppose Gotham City has n ambulance locations. Determine the locations of ambulances that maximize the number of people who live within two minutes of an ambulance. Do this separately for $n = 1$; $n = 2$; $n = 3$; $n = 4$. (*Hint:* Set it up so that SolverTable can solve all four problems simultaneously.)

TABLE 6.56	Travel Distances for Gotham City Problem							

		To							
		1	**2**	**3**	**4**	**5**	**6**	**7**	**8**
	1	0	3	4	6	8	9	8	10
	2	3	0	5	4	8	6	12	9
	3	4	5	0	2	2	3	5	7
From	4	6	4	2	0	3	2	5	4
	5	8	8	2	3	0	2	2	4
	6	9	6	3	2	2	0	3	2
	7	8	12	5	5	2	3	0	2
	8	10	9	7	4	4	2	2	0

6.8   MODELS WITH EITHER–OR CONSTRAINTS

Consider a company that makes x units of a product, where x is a decision variable. It is possible that the company has only two options, due to economy-of-scale considerations. Either it produces no more than 100 units of the product, or it produces at least 1000 units of the product. This is a typical example of a problem with **either–or constraints**. The company's solution must satisfy either

$$x \leq 100 \quad \text{or} \quad x \geq 1000$$

In this section we analyze a problem with either–or constraints and see how a clever use of binary variables can transform it into a linear model.[6]

EXAMPLE   6.6

MANUFACTURING AT DORIAN AUTO

Dorian Auto is considering manufacturing three types of cars—compact, midsize, and large. The resources required and the profits yielded by each type of car are shown in Table 6.57. At present, 6000 tons of steel and 60,000 hours of labor are available. If any cars of a given type are produced, production of that type of car will be economically feasible only if at least 1000 cars of that type are produced. Dorian wants to find a production schedule that maximizes its profit.

TABLE 6.57	Data for Dorian Car Example		
	Compact	**Midsize**	**Large**
Steel required	1.5 tons	3 tons	5 tons
Labor required	30 hours	25 hours	40 hours
Profit	$2000	$3000	$4000

[6]In the first edition of this book, we presented a *general* method for handling either–or constraints and then implemented this general method in an example. However, the translation from general to specific confused even us! We believe the method used in Example 6.6, while slightly less general, is much easier to follow.

Solution

The model for this example must keep track of the following:

- the number of each car type produced
- the labor hours and steel used
- the profit earned

Also, we must ensure that Dorian produces either 0 or at least 1000 cars of each type—this is the either–or constraint.

DEVELOPING THE SPREADSHEET MODEL

The example can be modeled with the following steps. (See Figure 6.20 and the file DORIAN.XLS.)

❶ Inputs. Enter the input data in the shaded ranges.

❷ Number of cars produced. Enter *any* trial values for the number of cars of each type produced in the UnitsProduced range.

❸ Binary variables for minimum production. Enter *any* trial 0–1 values in the ProduceMin range. If a value in this range is 1, it means that Dorian must produce at least the minimum number of the corresponding car type. A value of 0 in this range means that Dorian must produce 0 of the corresponding car type.

❹ Lower limits on production. The either–or constraints are implemented with the binary variables in row 13 and the inequalities indicated in rows 15–19. To obtain the lower limits on production, enter the formula

=B7*B13

in cell B15 and copy it across row 15. This lower limit implies that if the binary variable in row 13 is 1, then Dorian must produce at least the minimum number of that

	A	B	C	D	E	F	G	H
1	**Dorian Auto production model with either-or constraints**							
2								
3	**Inputs**							
4	Type of car	Compact	Midsize	Large		**Range names used:**		
5	Steel (tons)/unit	1.5	3	5		UnitProfits - B9:D9		
6	Labor hours/unit	30	25	40		ProduceMin - B13:D13		
7	Minimum production (if any)	1000	1000	1000		MinProduction - B15:D15		
8						UnitsProduced - B17:D17		
9	Profit/unit	$2,000	$3,000	$4,000		Capacity - B19:D19		
10						ResourcesUsed - B22:B23		
11	**Production plan**					ResourcesAvail - D22:D23		
12	Type of car	Compact	Midsize	Large		SteelAvail - D22		
13	Produce at least minimum?	0	1	0		LaborAvail - D23		
14						Profit - B25		
15	Min production	0	1000	0				
16		<=	<=	<=				
17	Units produced	0	2000	0				
18		<=	<=	<=				
19	Capacity	0	2000	0				
20								
21	**Constraints on resources**	Used		Available				
22	Steel	6000	<=	6000				
23	Labor hours	50000	<=	60000				
24								
25	**Profit**	$6,000,000						

FIGURE 6.20 Dorian Auto Production Model

car type. However, if the binary variable is 0, then the lower bound in row 15 is 0 and is essentially redundant—it just says that production must be nonnegative.

⑤ Upper limits on production. To obtain upper limits on production, enter the formula

=B13*MIN(SteelAvail/B5,LaborAvail/B6)

in cell B19 and copy it across row 19. Note that the MIN term in this formula is the maximum number of compact cars Dorian could make if it devoted *all* of its resources to compact cars. (A similar upper limit was used in the Great Threads model in Example 6.2.) If the binary variable in row 13 is 1, this upper limit is essentially redundant—production could never be greater than this in any case. But if the binary variable is 0, then this upper limit is 0, which prevents Dorian from making any cars of this type. Summarizing the lower and upper limits, if the binary variable is 1, the production limits become

$$\text{Minimum production required} \leq \text{Production} \leq \text{Maximum production possible}$$

If the binary variable is 0, the limits become

$$0 \leq \text{Production} \leq 0$$

Exactly one of these cases must hold for each car type, so they successfully implement the either–or constraints. These lower and upper limits are the key to the model.

⑥ Steel and labor used. Calculate the tons of steel and number of labor hours used in the ResourcesUsed range by entering the formula

=SUMPRODUCT(B5:D5,UnitsProduced)

in cell B22 and copying it to cell B23.

⑦ Profit. Calculate the profit in the Profit cell with the formula

=SUMPRODUCT(UnitProfits,UnitsProduced)

USING THE SOLVER

The completed Solver dialog box should appear as in Figure 6.21. The objective is to maximize profit, the changing cells are the production quantities and the binary variables, and the constraints specify the production limits and resource availabilities.

The optimal solution in Figure 6.20 indicates, by the 0 values in row 13, that Dorian should not produce any compact or large cars. The value of 1 in cell C13,

FIGURE 6.21
Solver Dialog
Box for Dorian
Production Model

however, indicates that Dorian *must* produce at least the minimum number, 1000, of midsize cars. Actually, midsize cars are quite profitable, so Dorian produces as many as possible, 2000, before running into the steel availability constraint.

Sensitivity Analysis Dorian currently produces only one type of car. What type of incentive might cause the company to produce more than one car type? One possible answer is that the minimum production levels for each type, all currently 1000, are perhaps too high. We use SolverTable to see the effect of decreasing each of these minimum production levels by the same factor. The model must first be modified slightly, as shown in Figure 6.22. We record the original minimum production levels in the range F5:H5, and then we enter the formula

=DecrFactor*H5

in cell B7 and copy it across row 7. Next, we invoke SolverTable with the DecrFactor cell as the single input cell, varied from 0.2 to 1 in increments of 0.2, and we keep track of profit and all changing cell values. The SolverTable results indicate that when the minimum production levels are reduced to 200 or 400, Dorian produces both compact and midsize cars *above* the minimum level. When the minimum production level is 600, Dorian still produces both types, but it does not produce any more compacts than necessary. Finally, when the minimum production level is 800 or 1000, Dorian produces only midsize cars—as many as steel availability allows.

Does this sound correct? We checked it, and it *is* correct, but here is a test of your economic reasoning. As we stated, when the minimum production level is 600, Dorian

FIGURE 6.22 Sensitivity to Minimum Production Levels

Chapter 6 *Linear Optimization Models with Integer Variables*

produces compact and midsize cars, but it produces only the minimum number of compacts. This seems to imply that compacts extract less profit from the resources than midsize cars. But if this is the case, why doesn't Dorian produce the minimum number of compacts when the minimum production level is 200 or 400? For example, when it is 400, why doesn't Dorian produce 400 compacts and 1800 midsize cars (which just uses up the steel)? ■

PROBLEMS

Skill-Building Problems

54. State University must purchase 1100 computers from three vendors. Vendor 1 charges $500 per computer plus a total delivery charge of $5000. Vendor 2 charges $350 per computer plus a total delivery charge of $4000. Vendor 3 charges $250 per computer plus a total delivery charge of $6000. Vendor 1 will sell the university at most 500 computers, vendor 2, at most 900, and vendor 3, at most 400. The minimum order from a vendor is 200 computers. Determine how to minimize the cost of purchasing the needed computers.

55. Eastinghouse ships 12,000 capacitors per month to its customers. The capacitors can be produced at three different plants. The production capacity, fixed monthly cost of operation, and variable cost of producing a capacitor at each plant are given in

Table 6.58. The fixed cost for a plant is incurred only if the plant is used to make any capacitors. If a plant is used at all, at least 3000 capacitors per month must be produced at the plant. Determine how to minimize the company's monthly costs of meeting its customers' demands.

TABLE 6.58	Data for Eastinghouse Problem		
	Fixed Cost	Variable Cost	Production Capacity
Plant 1	$80,000	$20	6000
Plant 2	$40,000	$25	7000
Plant 3	$30,000	$30	6000

6.9 CUTTING STOCK MODELS

The final model we discuss in this chapter has found many real-world applications, especially in manufacturing. It is relevant in situations where a product is produced in a standard size, which must then be cut into one of several patterns to satisfy customer orders. In contrast to the other models in this chapter, this cutting stock model does not have *binary* variables, but it does have *integer* variables. As we will see, the model is relatively easy to formulate, but it can be very time-consuming for the Solver to solve. By this point, you might have forgotten our earlier warning that IP models are inherently more difficult to solve than general LP problems. The model in the following example will illustrate that this is definitely the case.

EXAMPLE 6.7

CUTTING PAPER ROLLS AT RHEEM PAPER

The Rheem Paper Company produces rolls of paper of various types for its customers. One type is produced in standard rolls that are 60 inches wide and (when unwound) 200 yards long. Customers for this type of paper order rolls that are all 200 yards long but can have any of the widths 12, 15, 20, 24, 30, or 40 inches. In a given week, Rheem waits for all orders and then decides how to cut its 60-inch rolls to satisfy the orders. For example, if there are 5 orders for 15-inch widths and 2 orders for 40-inch widths, Rheem could satisfy the order by producing 3 rolls, cutting each of the first two into a 40-inch and a 15-inch cut (with 5 inches left over) and cutting the third into 4 15-inch cuts (with one of these left over). Each week Rheem must decide how to cut its rolls in the most economical way to meet its orders. Specifically, it wants to produce as few rolls as possible.

Solution

Given the width of the rolls (60 inches) and the available widths (12, 15, 20, 24, 30, and 40), the first thing we must do in this model is "preprocess" the patterns that might be used. For example, one reasonable pattern is to cut a roll into 4 15-inch cuts. In fact, this is perfect—there is no waste. Another pattern is to cut a roll into a 12-inch, a 15-inch, and a 24-inch cut, with 9 inches left over and unusable. The only patterns we consider (called the "feasible" patterns) are the ones with no leftover paper that could be used for customer orders. For example, the pattern of a 12-inch cut and a 30-inch cut is not worth considering because we could still get another 12-inch (or 15-inch) cut from the remainder. There is no model for determining all of the feasible patterns. We simply go through all of the possibilities in a systematic way, as illustrated below. Once we have listed all possible patterns, the problem is then to decide how many rolls to cut into each pattern.

DEVELOPING THE SPREADSHEET MODEL

The spreadsheet model appears in Figure 6.23. (See the file CUTTING.XLS.) To develop it, proceed according to the following steps.

1 **Inputs.** Enter the roll width, the available widths, and the number of orders for each width in the shaded ranges. The orders we entered in the Required range (row 41) will change from week to week, but the same model can handle any values in this range.

2 **Patterns.** Enter the feasible patterns in columns B through G, starting in row 10. The numbers in each row indicate how many of each width is in the pattern. For example, the first pattern has 5 12-inch cuts with no waste. We calculate the waste in column H by entering the formula

=RollWidth-SUMPRODUCT(B$9:G$9,B10:G10)

and copying down. This waste column is useful as we try to list all feasible patterns. Specifically, the waste must be nonnegative, and it must be no greater than 12, the smallest available width. (If the waste were 12 or greater, we could get another usable cut from the pattern.) For this particular roll width and this particular set of available widths, there are 25 feasible patterns.

3 **Decision variables.** Enter *any* values into the NProduced range. These are the decision variables in this model. They indicate how many rolls we should cut into the various patterns.

4 **Widths obtained.** Calculate the number of each width obtained by entering the formula

=SUMPRODUCT(NProduced,B10:B34)

	A	B	C	D	E	F	G	H	I	J	K
1	**Cutting stock model**										
2									**Range names used:**		
3	Width of roll	60	inches						RollWidth - B3		
4									Nproduced - K10:K34		
5	Widths available	12	15	20	24	30	40		Obtained - B39:G39		
6									Required - B41:G41		
7	**Feasible ways of cutting up a roll**								RollsCut - B44		
8					Width						**Decisions**	
9	Pattern	12	15	20	24	30	40	Waste		Pattern	Rolls cut
10	1	5	0	0	0	0	0	0		1	0
11	2	3	1	0	0	0	0	9		2	0
12	3	3	0	1	0	0	0	4		3	0
13	4	3	0	0	1	0	0	0		4	12
14	5	2	2	0	0	0	0	6		5	0
15	6	2	1	1	0	0	0	1		6	0
16	7	2	0	0	0	1	0	6		7	1
17	8	1	3	0	0	0	0	3		8	0
18	9	1	1	0	1	0	0	9		9	0
19	10	1	1	0	0	1	0	3		10	0
20	11	1	0	2	0	0	0	8		11	0
21	12	1	0	1	1	0	0	4		12	0
22	13	1	0	0	2	0	0	0		13	10
23	14	1	0	0	0	0	1	8		14	2
24	15	0	2	1	0	0	0	10		15	0
25	16	0	2	0	1	0	0	6		16	0
26	17	0	2	0	0	1	0	0		17	9
27	18	0	1	2	0	0	0	5		18	0
28	19	0	1	1	1	0	0	1		19	0
29	20	0	1	0	0	0	1	5		20	1
30	21	0	0	3	0	0	0	0		21	6
31	22	0	0	1	0	1	0	10		22	0
32	23	0	0	1	0	0	1	0		23	4
33	24	0	0	0	1	1	0	6		24	0
34	25	0	0	0	0	2	0	0		25	2
35											
36	**Constraint on satisfying orders**										
37					Width						
38		12	15	20	24	30	40				
39	Obtained	50	19	22	32	14	7				
40		>=	>=	>=	>=	>=	>=				
41	Required	48	19	22	32	14	7				
42											
43	**Objective to minimize**										
44	Total rolls cut	47									

FIGURE 6.23 Cutting Stock Model

in cell B39 and copying it to the rest of the obtained range. For example, the value in cell B39 is the number of rolls of width 12 inches obtained from *all* of the possible patterns.

⑤ Rolls cut. Calculate the number of rolls cut in the RollsCut cell with the formula

=SUM(NProduced)

USING THE SOLVER

Fill out the Solver dialog box as indicated in Figure 6.24 (page 326). We want to minimize the number of rolls produced, subject to meeting customer orders. Also, the number cut according to each pattern must be integer (but not binary), and the Assume Linear Model and Assume Non-Negative options should be checked.

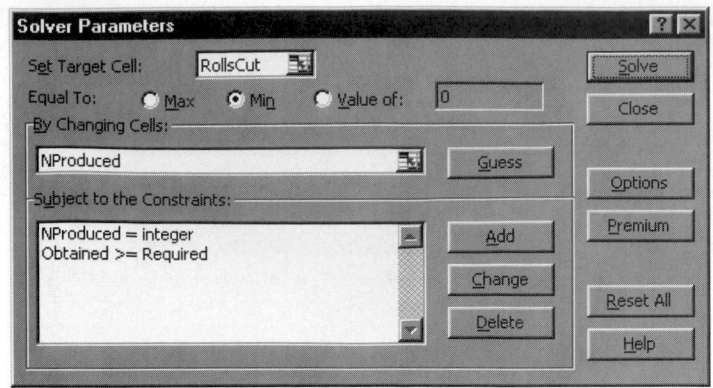

FIGURE 6.24
Solver Dialog Box for Cutting Stock Model

The solution indicates that Rheem can meet its customer orders this week with 47 rolls, cut as specified in rows 10 through 34. For example, 12 of the 47 rolls should be cut according to pattern 4, each with three 12-inch rolls and one 24-inch roll. Note that there are two sources of "waste" in this solution. First, there is the unusable waste from all leftover rolls with width less than 12 inches. For example, there is a 6-inch roll left over from the one roll cut into pattern 7. Second, there is some waste from the usable rolls that are not needed in this week's orders. Fortunately, it is minimal—only two 12-inch rolls left over. Actually, if Rheem solves this model on a weekly basis, the model could easily incorporate the inventory of usable leftover rolls from *previous* weeks.

Solver Tolerance Setting Until now, we have suggested setting the Solver tolerance to 0%. This guarantees *the* optimal solution. However, this example illustrates why the default tolerance setting is 5% (or at least not 0%). When we set the tolerance to 0% and clicked on Solve, the Solver quickly got to a solution that requires 47 rolls, but then it ran and ran and ran. (We got tired of waiting, so we pressed the Ctrl-Break key combination to stop it prematurely.) After some experimenting, we found that with the tolerance set at 2% or above, the solution was obtained almost instantaneously, but with the tolerance set at 1% or 0%, it ran seemingly forever. This behavior is not at all uncommon in IP models. The Solver often finds a very good or even optimal solution very quickly, but then it takes a long time to verify that it is optimal (or to find something slightly better). The moral is clear. If you set the tolerance to a low value and find that the Solver is taking forever without getting anywhere, press Ctrl-Break to get out. By that time, you probably already have a very good or even optimal solution. ∎

MODELING ISSUES

We did not perform any sensitivity analysis on this model because there is no obvious sensitivity analysis to perform. The only inputs are the roll width, the set of available widths, and the order amounts. Although it would make sense to perform sensitivity analysis on the order amounts, it would make more sense (in a realistic setting) to wait for next week's orders and simply solve the problem again. In contrast, the model is *not* set up to perform sensitivity analysis (with SolverTable) on the roll width or the set of available widths. If these change, the entire table of patterns must be recreated by hand. For example, if the roll width changed to 64 inches, patterns 2, 9, 11, 14, 15, and 22 would no longer be in the list (why not?), and several new patterns would enter the list (what are they?). ∎

Skill-Building Problem

56. Woodco sells 3-foot, 5-foot, and 9-foot pieces of lumber. Woodco's customers demand 25 3-foot boards, 20 5-foot boards, and 15 9-foot boards. Woodco meets its demands by cutting up 17-foot boards. How can it satisfy its customers' demands with the least amount of waste? Assume that all boards are the same width and thickness.

Skill-Extending Problem

57. The Mayfree Appliance Company requires sheet metal for its appliances. The company can purchase long coils of sheet metal in two different widths: 65 inches and 40 inches. The company must purchase the coils by linear foot of length: $1.20 per foot for a 64-inch coil and $1.00 per foot for a 40-inch coil. (This implies that a square foot, say, of the wider coil is less expensive.) Up to 4000 feet of the 65-inch coil is available, and up to 6000 feet of the 40-inch coil is available. There are manufacturing requirements for six different widths: 50, 45, 40, 35, 20, and 10 inches. Mayfree's requirements are expressed as lengths of the various widths. The company requires 1000 feet of 50-inch width, 2500 feet of 45-inch width, 3000 feet of 40-inch width, 2300 feet of 35-inch width, 1300 feet of 20-inch width, and 2000 feet of 10-inch width. Determine how much of each width coil Mayfree should purchase and how it should cut the coils into various widths to meet its requirements at minimal cost. (*Hint*: First, list all of the patterns that can be cut from a 65-inch coil, and do the same for a 40-inch coil. Then have a changing cell for each pattern that designates the number of linear feet to be cut in this pattern.)

6.10 CONCLUSION

Three important points emerge from this chapter. First, a wide variety of important problems can be modeled as IP problems. These can generally be identified as problems where at least some of the "activities" (such as producing at a particular plant, locating a lockbox at a particular city, making a particular investment, and so on) must either be done or not done; there is no in-between. Regular LP cannot be used for these problems; they must be modeled as IP problems.

The second point is that many important IP models are not simply LP models with integer constraints on the variables, such as a constraint that the number of refrigerators produced must be an integer. There are certainly IP examples of this type, where fractional values of the decision variables make no physical sense, but they can generally be solved by solving the associated LP problem and then rounding the solution to integer values. While there is no guarantee that the rounded solution will be optimal, it is often close to optimal. In contrast, most of the problems discussed in this chapter introduce binary decision variables that specify whether an activity is done or not. Using these 0–1 variables, the problem can then be modeled with linear constraints. However, if the resulting model is solved as an LP problem, *without* the integer constraints on the 0–1 variables, it is generally very difficult to round the fractional values of the 0–1 variables appropriately. Therefore, models with 0–1 variables require a different solution approach than LP problems.

Third, the solution approach required for IP problems, especially those with 0–1 variables, is inherently more difficult than the simplex method for LP problems. The relatively small examples in this chapter may have given the impression that a spreadsheet Solver can handle IP models just as easily as it handles LP models, but this is definitely not the case. If you continue to solve IP problems with a spreadsheet Solver, you will eventually run into a problem that the Solver is simply unable to solve, at least not in a reasonable amount of time. In fact, even with the most sophisticated IP computer codes on the most powerful computers, there are IP problems—from real applications—that continue to defy solution.

Skill-Building Problems

58. Based on Ellis and Corn (1984). The Transylvania Olympic Gymnastics Team consists of six people. Transylvania must choose three people to enter both the balance beam and floor exercises. They must also enter a total of four people in each event. The score that each individual gymnast can attain in each event is shown in Table 6.59. Determine how to maximize the total score attained by the Transylvania gymnasts.

TABLE 6.59	Data for Gymnastics Problem	
	Balance Beam	**Floor Exercise**
Gymnast 1	8.8	7.9
Gymnast 2	9.4	8.3
Gymnast 3	9.2	8.5
Gymnast 4	7.5	8.7
Gymnast 5	8.7	8.1
Gymnast 6	9.1	8.6

59. Based on Liggett (1973). A court decision has stated that the enrollment of each high school in Metropolis must be at least 20% black. The numbers of black and white high school students in each of the city's five school districts are shown in Table 6.60. The distance (in miles) that a student in each district must travel to each high school is shown in Table 6.61. School board policy requires that all students in a given district must attend the same school. Assuming that each school must have an enrollment of at least 150 students, determine how to minimize the total distance that Metropolis students must travel to high school.

TABLE 6.60	Students in Districts for School Problem	
	Whites	**Blacks**
District 1	80	30
District 2	70	5
District 3	90	10
District 4	50	40
District 5	60	30

60. Esperantia has coins with the following monetary values: $0.01, $0.05, $0.10, $0.20, $0.25, and $0.50. You work at the Two-Twelve Convenience Store and

TABLE 6.61	Distances for School Problem	
	High School 1	**High School 2**
District 1	1.0	2.0
District 2	0.5	1.7
District 3	0.8	0.8
District 4	1.3	0.4
District 5	1.5	0.6

must give a customer $0.91 in change. Determine how to minimize the number of coins needed to give the correct change.

61. Based on Westerberg, Bjorklund, and Hultman (1977). Newcor's steel mill has received an order for 25 tons of steel. The steel must be 5% carbon and 5% molybdenum by weight. The steel is manufactured by combining three types of metal: steel ingots, scrap steel, and alloys. Four individual steel ingots are available. At most, one of each can be purchased. The weight (in tons), cost per ton, and the carbon and molybdenum content of each ingot are given in Table 6.62. Three types of alloys can be purchased. The cost per ton and chemical makeup of each alloy are given in Table 6.63. Steel scrap can be purchased at a cost of $100 per ton. Steel scrap contains 3% carbon and 9% molybdenum. Determine how Newcor can minimize the cost of filling its order.

62. Based on Boykin (1985). Chemco annually produces 359 million pounds of the chemical maleic anhydride. A total of four reactors are available to produce maleic anhydride. Each reactor can be run on one of three settings. The cost (in thousands of dollars) and pounds produced (in millions) annually for each reactor and each setting are given in Table 6.64. A reactor can be run on only one setting for the entire year. Determine how Chemco can minimize the cost of meeting its annual demand for maleic anhydride.

63. Based on Zangwill (1992). Hallco runs a day shift and a night shift. Regardless of the number of units produced, the only production cost during a shift is a setup cost. It costs $8000 to run the day shift and $4500 to run the night shift. Demand for the next two days is as follows: day 1, 2000; night 1, 3000; day 2, 2000; night 2, 3000. It costs $1 per unit to hold a unit in inventory for a shift.

a. Determine a production schedule that minimizes the sum of setup and inventory costs. All demand must be met on time. (*Note*: Not all shifts have to be run.)

TABLE 6.62	Ingot Data for Newcor Problem			
	Weight	Cost per Ton	Carbon %	Molybdenum %
Ingot 1	5	$350	5	3
Ingot 2	3	$330	4	3
Ingot 3	4	$310	5	4
Ingot 4	6	$280	3	4

TABLE 6.63	Alloy Data for Newcor Problem		
	Cost per Ton	Carbon %	Molybdenum %
Alloy 1	$500	8	6
Alloy 2	$450	7	7
Alloy 3	$400	6	8

TABLE 6.64	Data for Chemco Problem		
	Setting	Cost	Pounds
Reactor 1	1	50	80
	2	80	140
	3	100	170
Reactor 2	1	65	100
	2	90	140
	3	120	215
Reactor 3	1	70	112
	2	90	153
	3	110	195
Reactor 4	1	40	65
	2	60	105
	3	70	130

TABLE 6.65	Costs for Auditing Problem			
	Northeast	Midwest	West	South
New York	$1100	$1400	$1900	$1400
Chicago	$1200	$1000	$1500	$1200
Los Angeles	$1900	$1700	$1100	$1400
Atlanta	$1300	$1300	$1500	$1050

York, Atlanta, and Los Angeles. The annual cost of basing auditors in any city is $100,000. The cost of sending an auditor from any of these cities to a given region of the country is given in Table 6.65. Determine how to minimize the annual cost of conducting out-of-state audits.

Skill-Extending Problems

65. Arthur Ross, Inc., must complete many corporate tax returns during the period February 15 to April 15. This year the company must begin and complete the five jobs shown in Table 6.66 (page 330) during this 8-week period. Arthur Ross employs four full-time accountants who normally work 40 hours per week. If necessary, however, they can work up to 20 hours of overtime per week for which they are paid $100 per hour. Determine how Arthur Ross can minimize the overtime cost incurred in completing all jobs by April 15.

66. Based on Muckstadt and Wilson (1968). PSI believes it will need the amounts of generating capacity (in millions of kwh) shown in Table 6.67 (page 330) during the next five years. The company has a choice of building (and then operating) power plants with the capacities (in millions of kwh) and costs (in millions of dollars) shown in Table 6.68. Determine how to minimize the total cost of

b. After listening to a seminar on the virtues of the Japanese theory of production, Hallco has cut its day shift setup cost to $1000 per shift and its night shift setup cost to $3500 per shift. Now determine a production schedule that minimizes the sum of setup and inventory costs. All demand must be met on time. Show that the decrease in setup costs has actually raised the average inventory level. Is this reasonable?

64. Based on Fitzsimmons and Allen (1983). The State of Texas frequently audits companies doing business in Texas. Since these companies often have headquarters located outside the state, auditors must be sent to out-of-state locations. Each year, auditors must make 500 trips to cities in the Northeast, 400 trips to cities in the Midwest, 300 trips to cities in the West, and 400 trips to cities in the South. Texas is considering basing auditors in Chicago, New

TABLE 6.66	Data for Ross Accounting Problem	
	Duration (weeks)	Accountant Hours per Week
Job 1	3	120
Job 2	4	160
Job 3	3	80
Job 4	2	80
Job 5	4	100

TABLE 6.67	Generating Capacities for PSI Problem
	Generating Capacity
Year 1	80
Year 2	100
Year 3	120
Year 4	140
Year 5	160

TABLE 6.68	Plant Data for PSI Problem		
	Generating Capacity	Construction Cost	Annual Operating Cost
Plant 1	70	$20	$1.5
Plant 2	50	$16	$0.8
Plant 3	60	$18	$1.3
Plant 4	40	$14	$0.6

meeting PSI's generating capacity requirements for the next five years.

67. Houseco Developers is considering erecting three office buildings. The time (in years) required to complete each of them and the number of workers required to be on the job at all times are shown in Table 6.69. Once a building is completed, it brings in the following amount of rent per year: building 1, $50,000; building 2, $30,000; building 3, $40,000. Houseco faces the following constraints:
   - During each year 60 workers are available.
   - At most one building can be started during any year.
   - Building 2 must be completed by the end of year 4.

   Determine the maximum total rent that can be earned by Houseco by the end of year 4.

68. Four trucks are available to deliver milk to five grocery stores. The capacity and daily operating cost of each truck are shown in Table 6.70. The demand of each grocery store can be supplied by only one

TABLE 6.69	Data for Houseco Problem	
	Project Duration	Workers Required
Building 1	2	30
Building 2	2	20
Building 3	3	20

TABLE 6.70	Data for Milk Delivery Problem	
	Capacity (gallons)	Daily Operating Cost
Truck 1	400	$45
Truck 2	500	$50
Truck 3	600	$55
Truck 4	1100	$60

truck, but a truck can deliver to more than one grocery. The daily demands of each grocery are as follows: grocery 1, 100 gallons; grocery 2, 200 gallons; grocery 3, 300 gallons; grocery 4, 500 gallons; grocery 5, 800 gallons. Determine how to minimize the daily cost of meeting the demands of the five groceries.

69. A county is going to build two hospitals. There are nine cities in which the hospitals can be built. The number of hospital visits per year made by people in each city and the x-y coordinates of each city are listed in Table 6.71. The county's goal is to minimize the total distance that patients must travel to hospitals. Where should it locate the hospitals? (*Hint*: You will need to determine the distance between each pair of cities. An easy way to do this is with lookup tables.)

TABLE 6.71	Data for Hospital Problem		
	x	y	Hospital Visits per Year
City 1	0	0	3000
City 2	10	3	4000
City 3	12	15	5000
City 4	14	13	6000
City 5	16	9	4000
City 6	18	6	3000
City 7	8	12	2000
City 8	6	10	4000
City 9	4	8	1200

70. It is currently the beginning of 1998. Gotham City is trying to sell municipal bonds to support improvements in recreational facilities and highways. The face values (in thousands of dollars) of the bonds and the due dates at which principal comes due are listed in Table 6.72. (The due dates are the *beginnings* of the years listed.) The Gold and Silver Company (GS) wants to underwrite Gotham City's bonds. A proposal to Gotham for underwriting this issue consists of the following:

- An interest rate, either 3%, 4%, 5%, 6%, or 7%, for each bond, where coupons are paid annually
- An up-front premium paid by GS to Gotham City

TABLE 6.72	Face Values and Due Dates of Bonds	
Bond	**Face Value**	**Due Date**
1	700	2000
2	450	2001
3	250	2002
4	600	2003
5	300	2004

GS has determined the set of fair prices (in thousands of dollars) for the bonds listed in Table 6.73. For example, if GS underwrites bond 2 maturing in 2001 at 5%, it would charge Gotham

City $444,000 for that bond. GS is constrained to use at most three different interest rates. GS wants to make a profit of at least $46,000, where its profit is equal to the sale price of the bonds minus the face value of the bonds minus the premium GS pays to Gotham City. To maximize the chance that GS will get Gotham City's business, GS wants to minimize the total cost of the bond issue to Gotham City, which is equal to the total interest on the bonds minus the premium paid by GS. For example, if the year 2000 bond (bond 1) is issued at a 4% rate, then Gotham City must pay two years of coupon interest: $2(0.04)(\$700,000) = \$56,000$. What assignment of interest rates to each bond and up front premiums ensure that GS will make the desired profit (assuming it gets the contract) and maximize the chance of GS getting Gotham City's business?

71. Based on Spencer et al. (1990). When you lease 800 phone numbers from AT&T for telemarketing, AT&T uses an optimization model to tell you where you should locate calling centers to minimize your operating costs over a 10-year horizon. To illustrate the model, suppose you are considering seven calling center locations: Boston, New York, Charlotte, Dallas, Chicago, Los Angeles, and Omaha. You know the average cost (in dollars) incurred if a telemarketing call is made from any these cities to any region of the country. You also know the hourly wage that you must pay workers in each city. This information is listed in Table 6.74.

TABLE 6.73	Fair Prices for Bonds				
Interest Rate	**Bond 1**	**Bond 2**	**Bond 3**	**Bond 4**	**Bond 5**
3%	695	427	233	504	248
4%	701	433	235	522	256
5%	715	444	247	548	268
6%	731	460	255	575	288
7%	750	478	269	605	307

TABLE 6.74	Calling Cost and Wage Information							
	Cost per call							
	New England	**Middle Atlantic**	**Southeast**	**Southwest**	**Great Lakes**	**Plains**	**Rocky Mountains**	**Pacific**	**Hourly Wage**
Boston	1.2	1.4	1.1	2.6	2.0	2.2	2.8	2.2	$14
New York	1.3	1.0	1.3	2.2	1.8	1.9	2.5	2.8	$16
Charlotte	1.5	1.4	0.9	1.9	2.1	2.3	2.6	3.3	$11
Dallas	2.0	1.8	1.2	1.0	1.7	2.2	1.8	2.7	$12
Chicago	2.1	1.9	2.3	1.5	0.9	1.3	1.2	2.2	$13
Los Angeles	2.5	2.1	1.9	1.2	1.7	1.5	1.4	1.0	$18
Omaha	2.2	2.1	2.0	1.3	1.4	0.6	0.9	1.5	$10

Assume that an average call requires 4 minutes of labor. You make calls 250 days per year, and the average number of calls made per day to each region of the country is listed in Table 6.75. The cost (in millions of dollars) of building a calling center in each possible location is listed in Table 6.76. Each calling center can make up to 5000 calls per day. Given this information, how can you minimize the discounted cost (at 10% per year) of running the telemarketing operation for 10 years? Assume all wage and calling costs are paid at the *ends* of the respective years.

Region	Daily Calls
New England	1000
Middle Atlantic	2000
Southeast	2000
Southwest	2000
Great Lakes	3000
Plains	1000
Rocky Mountains	2000
Pacific	4000

TABLE 6.76	Building Costs

City	Building Cost
Boston	2.7
New York	3.0
Charlotte	2.1
Dallas	2.1
Chicago	2.4
Los Angeles	3.6
Omaha	2.1

Modeling Problems

72. We have assumed that there is a fixed annual cost of running a lockbox operation that does not depend on the size of the operation. Can you improve on this assumption?

73. (This problem and the next three refer to the Huntco example in Section 6.6.) Huntco Foods produces hundreds of products. Modeling the shipment of each of these products would result in an IP that no computer could solve exactly. How might you deal with this problem?

74. Huntco Foods has thousands of customers. Modeling the shipment to each customer would

result in an IP that no computer could solve exactly. How might you deal with this problem?

75. Why do you think that Huntco insisted on each customer being serviced from a single distribution center?

76. Describe how you might estimate the fixed annual cost and variable shipping costs needed for the Huntco model. How would quantity discounts for large shipments influence your model?

77. Suppose that you want to divide a state containing 12 cities into five congressional districts. How might you use IP to assign cities to districts?

78. Based on Geoffrion and Graves (1976). Huntco Foods produces tomato sauce at its three plants in Los Angeles, New York, and St. Louis. The annual production capacity (in millions of pounds) of each plant is shown in Table 6.77. The variable cost of producing a pound of tomato sauce at any plant is $0.30 per pound.

TABLE 6.77	Production Capacities for Huntco Problem

Plant	Production Capacity
New York	9
Los Angeles	7
St. Louis	8

Tomato sauce can be stored at one of five potential warehouse sites. The potential warehouse sites are located in Philadelphia, Chicago, Atlanta, Indianapolis, and Kansas City. For it to be economical to use a warehouse, between 4.8 million and 10 million pounds of tomato sauce per year must be shipped through the warehouse. If a warehouse site is not used, it incurs no cost. To get some idea of the annual cost of operating a warehouse, Huntco has tabulated in the file HUNTDAT.XLS the annual cost of operating warehouses and the total amount of sauce shipped through the warehouse during a given year.

Huntco ships tomato sauce to six distributors. For administrative reasons, each distributor must receive all its sauce from a single warehouse. Each distributor receives two shipments per month of tomato sauce, and the annual amount of tomato sauce required by each distributor is shown in Table 6.78. You may assume that monthly demand for tomato sauce at each site is relatively constant.

The cost per pound of shipping tomato sauce depends on the distance the sauce is shipped. To relate the cost of shipping to the distance shipped, you may use the data in the file HUNTDAT.XLS,

TABLE 6.78 Annual Requirements for Huntco Problem

	Location	Annual Requirements (millions of pounds)
Distributor 1	Boston	2.0
Distributor 2	Memphis	2.5
Distributor 3	Detroit	4.0
Distributor 4	Denver	2.0
Distributor 5	Dallas	3.5
Distributor 6	San Francisco	5.0

which lists for the various shipments the weight of the shipment, the distance shipped, and the cost of the shipment.

The distance between each plant and potential warehouse site is shown in Table 6.79, and the distance between each warehouse and each distributor is shown in Table 6.80. (All distances are in miles.)

Determine how Huntco can minimize the annual total cost of getting tomato sauce from the plants to the customers.

79. The Wanderers Insurance Company has hired you to determine the number of sales divisions into which the country should be divided. Each division will need a president, vice president, and a divisional staff. The time needed to call on a client will depend on the distance of the salesperson from the client. Discuss how you would determine the optimal number of sales divisions and the allocation of the company's salesforce to the various divisions.

80. Ten different types of brownies are sold. You are thinking of developing a new brownie for sale. Brownies are rated on the basis of five qualities: price, chocolateness, chewiness, sweetness, and ease of preparation. You want to group the ten brownies on the market into three clusters. Each cluster should contain brownies that are relatively similar.
a. Why would this be useful to you?
b. How would you do it?

81. Telco, a national telemarketing firm, usually picks a number of sites around the country from which to make its calls. As a service, AD&D's telecommunication marketing department wants to help Telco choose the number and location of its sites. How can integer programming be used to approach this problem?

TABLE 6.79 Distances Between Plants and Warehouses

	Philadelphia	Chicago	Atlanta	Indianapolis	Kansas City
New York	100	802	841	713	1189
Los Angeles	2706	2054	2182	2073	1589
St. Louis	868	289	541	235	257

TABLE 6.80 Distances Between Warehouses and Distributors

	Boston	Memphis	Detroit	Denver	Dallas	San Francisco
Philadelphia	296	1000	576	1691	1452	2866
Chicago	963	530	266	996	917	2142
Atlanta	1037	371	699	1398	795	2496
Indianapolis	906	435	278	1058	865	2256
Kansas City	1391	451	743	600	489	1835

Giant Motor Company I

T his problem deals with strategic planning issues for a large company. The main issue is planning the company's production capacity for the coming year. At issue is the overall level of capacity and the type of capacity—for example, the degree of *flexibility* in the manufacturing system. The main tool used to aid the company's planning process in GMC I is a mixed integer programming (MIP) model. A *mixed* integer program has both integer and continuous variables. A continuation of this problem, GMC II (at the end of Chapter 10), deals with capacity planning in a multiperiod, multiscenario framework. In GMC II the MIP model is extended to handle the multiperiod stochastic nature of the problem.

Problem Statement

The Giant Motor Company (GMC) produces three lines of cars for the domestic (U.S.) market: Lyras, Libras, and Hydras. The Lyra is a relatively inexpensive subcompact car that appeals mainly to first-time car owners and to households using it as a second car for commuting. The Libra is a sporty compact car that is sleeker, faster, and roomier than the Lyra. Without any options, the Libra costs slightly more than the Lyra; additional options increase the price further. The Hydra is the luxury car of the GMC line. It is significantly more expensive than the Lyra and Libra, and it has the highest profit margin of the three cars.

Retooling Options for Capacity Expansion

Currently GMC has three manufacturing plants in the United States. Each plant is dedicated to producing a single line of cars. In its planning for the coming year, GMC is considering the retooling of its Lyra and/or Libra plants. Retooling either plant would represent a major expense for the company. The retooled plants would have significantly increased production capacities. Although having greater *fixed* costs, the retooled plants would be more efficient and have lower *marginal* production costs—that is, higher *marginal* profit contributions. In addition, the retooled plants would be *flexible*—they would have the capability of producing more than one line of cars.

The characteristics of the current plants and the retooled plants are given in Table 6.81. The retooled Lyra and Libra plants are prefaced by the word *new*. The fixed costs and capacities in Table 6.81 are given on an annual basis. A dash in the profit margin section indicates that the plant cannot manufacture that line of car. For example, the new Lyra plant would be capable of producing both Lyras and Libras but not Hydras. The new Libra plant would be capable of producing any of the three lines of cars. Note, however, that the new Libra plant has a slightly lower profit margin for producing Hydras than the Hydra plant. The flexible new Libra plant is capable of producing the luxury Hydra model but is not quite as efficient as the current Hydra plant that is dedicated to Hydra production.

The fixed costs are annual costs that are incurred by GMC independent of the number of cars that are produced by the plant. For the current plant configurations, the fixed costs include property taxes, insurance, payments on the loan that was taken out to construct the plant, and so on. If a plant is retooled, the fixed costs will include the previous fixed costs plus the additional cost of the renovation. The additional renovation cost will be an annual cost representing the cost of the renovation amortized over a long period.

Demand for GMC Cars

Short-term demand forecasts have been very reliable in the past and are expected to be reliable in the future. Longer-term forecasts are not so accurate; this complication will be considered in GMC II. The demand for GMC cars for the coming year is given in Table 6.82.

A quick comparison of plant capacities and demands in Tables 6.81 and 6.82 indicates that GMC is faced with insufficient capacity. Partially offsetting the lack of capacity is the phenomenon of **demand diversion**. If a potential car buyer walks into

TABLE 6.81	Plant Characteristics				
	Lyra	**Libra**	**Hydra**	**New Lyra**	**New Libra**
Capacity (in 1000s)	1000	800	900	1600	1800
Fixed cost (in $millions)	2000	2000	2600	3400	3700
	Profit Margin by Car Line (in $1000s)				
Lyra	2	—	—	2.5	2.3
Libra	—	3	—	3.0	3.5
Hydra	—	—	5	—	4.8

TABLE 6.82	Demand for GMC Cars
	Demand (in 1000s)
Lyra	1400
Libra	1100
Hydra	800

a GMC dealer showroom wanting to buy a Lyra but the dealer is out of stock, frequently the salesperson can convince the customer to purchase the better Libra car, which is in stock. Unsatisfied demand for the Lyra is said to be *diverted* to the Libra. Only rarely in this situation can the salesperson convince the customer to switch to the luxury Hydra model.

From past experience, GMC estimates that 30% of unsatisfied demand for Lyras is diverted to demand for Libras and 5% to demand for Hydras. Similarly, 10% of unsatisfied demand for Libras is diverted to demand for Hydras. For example, if the demand for Lyras is 1,400,000 cars, then the unsatisfied demand will be 400,000 if no capacity is added. Out of this unsatisfied demand, 120,000 ($= 400,000 \times 0.3$) will materialize as demand for Libras, and 20,000 ($= 400,000 \times 0.05$) will materialize as demand for Hydras. Similarly, if the demand for Libras is 1,220,000 cars (1,100,000 original demand plus 120,000 demand diverted from

Lyras), then the unsatisfied demand for Lyras would be 420,000 if no capacity is added. Out of this unsatisfied demand, 42,000 ($= 420,000 \times 0.1$) will materialize as demand for Hydras. All other unsatisfied demand is lost to competitors. The pattern of demand diversion is summarized in Table 6.83.

TABLE 6.83	Demand Diversion Matrix		
	Lyra	**Libra**	**Hydra**
Lyra	NA	0.3	0.05
Libra	0	NA	0.10
Hydra	0	0.0	NA

Question

GMC wants to decide whether to retool the Lyra and Libra plants. In addition, GMC wants to determine its production plan at each plant in the coming year. Based on the previous data, formulate a mixed integer programming model for solving GMC's production planning–capacity expansion problem for the coming year.[7]

[7]*Acknowledgment*: The idea for GMC I and II came from Eppen et al. (1989).

CHAPTER 7

Nonlinear
Optimization
Models

GASOLINE BLENDING AT TEXACO

Since the 1950s oil companies have been among the most dedicated users of management science methods, particularly mathematical programming models. They often run optimization models on a daily basis and consider them absolutely indispensable to their operations. DeWitt et al. (1989) describe one company's experiences in the article "OMEGA: An Improved Gasoline Blending System for Texaco." Texaco began using computerized blending models in many of its refineries in the 1960s. By the early 1980s, however, the company realized that these models were not being used routinely by all of its refineries, partly because the optimization routines themselves did not always work correctly. Therefore, a fresh analysis began and culminated in OMEGA, a decision support system that combines data acquisition with nonlinear optimization and presents the blending technicians at Texaco's refineries with graphical descriptions of the results. Texaco estimates (somewhat conservatively) that OMEGA has increased profits up to 30%, which translates to more than $30 million annually.

Generally, Texaco develops aggregated plans at a fairly broad level for medium-range decisions. For example, it creates a monthly operating plan for the entire downstream operation of a regional subdivision of the company. At this broad level of planning, the company makes enough simplifying assumptions to permit the use of linear programming for the blending portion of the model. However, for the short-term day-to-day scheduling of blending at the refineries, linear programming is unable to capture the complex chemical relationships between inputs and outputs. Therefore a nonlinear model is required.

The cause of the complexity of the problem is that Texaco uses various grades of crude oil, refines them into intermediate stocks with particular chemical properties, and finally blends these stocks into required blends of gasoline (such as the regular unleaded and super unleaded we buy at the gas station). Sometimes as many as 15 stocks are used to blend up to eight blends. The qualities of the blends are determined by the qualities of the stocks. Typical stock qualities include percentage of sulfur, octane indices, percentage of aromatics, lead content, and others. There are a number of equations that translate these stock qualities into blend qualities. Of particular importance are blend volatilities and octanes, both of which are related to input stock qualities by *nonlinear* equations. These nonlinear equations require Texaco to employ nonlinear programming. The resulting nonlinear models must take into account constraints on the availabilities of the stocks, the technical requirements on the various blends (such as the maximum percentage of lead allowed), and market considerations. The nonlinear optimizer within OMEGA has been able to perform the optimization quickly and accurately, with the performance results noted earlier.

An interesting aspect of the DeWitt article is its discussion of Texaco's experience with nonlinear optimizers. Until OMEGA, Texaco used a nonlinear optimization package that gave rather inconsistent results. Not only was it very slow, but it sometimes failed to provide *any* feasible solution to the problem, and it sometimes stopped at *different* solutions, depending on which initial solution was used. (Based on your experience with Excel's Solver in previous chapters, imagine how you would feel if you and your classmates all used the same spreadsheet model but all got different answers because of different initial trial values. You wouldn't have much faith in the Solver!) This was simply the state of the art at the time—nonlinear optimizers were far from perfect. Fortunately, advances have been made, and the nonlinear optimizer currently used by OMEGA does not suffer from these early problems. ■

7.1   INTRODUCTION

In many complex optimization problems the objective and/or the constraints are nonlinear functions of the decision variables. Such optimization problems are called **nonlinear programming** (NLP) problems. In this chapter we will discuss a variety of interesting problems with inherent nonlinearities, from product pricing to portfolio optimization to rating sports teams. This is a relatively long chapter because of the many examples, but as in previous chapters, we invite you to examine the models of most interest to you.

7.2 BASIC IDEAS OF NONLINEAR OPTIMIZATION

When we solve an LP problem with the Solver, we can guarantee that the solution obtained by the computer is an optimal solution. When we solve an NLP problem, however, it is sometimes possible that the Solver will obtain the wrong answer. For example, if we use the Solver to maximize the function in Figure 7.1, it might have difficulty. For the function graphed in this figure, points *A* and *C* are called **local maxima** because the function is larger at *A* and *C* than at nearby points. However, only point *A* actually maximizes the function; it is called the **global maximum**. The problem is that the Solver might get "stuck" near point *C*, concluding that *C* maximizes the function, and not find point *A*. Similarly, points *B* and *D* are **local minima** because the function has a lower value at *B* and *D* than at nearby points. However, only point *D* is a **global minimum**. If you ask the Solver to minimize this function, it might conclude—incorrectly—that point *B* is optimal.

FIGURE 7.1
Function with Local Maxima and Minima

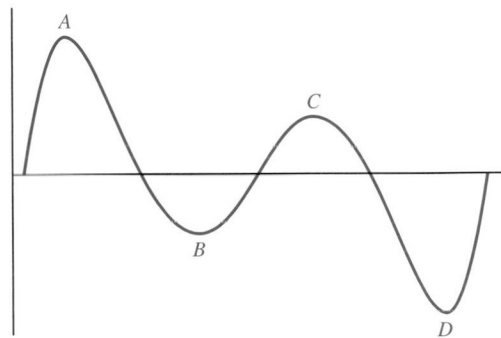

Convex and Concave Functions

Fortunately, there are certain types of NLPs that the Solver will solve correctly. To describe these NLPs, we need to define **convex** and **concave** functions. A function of one variable is *convex* in a region if its slope (rate of change) in that region is always nondecreasing. Equivalently, a function of one variable is convex if a line drawn connecting two points on the function never lies below the function.[1] See Figures 7.2 and 7.3 (page 340) for two examples of convex functions. In Figure 7.2 the function first decreases and then increases, but the slope is always increasing, first becoming less and less negative and then becoming more and more positive. In contrast, the function in Figure 7.3 is always decreasing, but again the slope is constantly increasing—it is becoming less and less negative.

The following are examples of convex functions:

$$y = cx^a, \quad \text{where } a \geq 1, c \geq 0, \text{ and } x \geq 0$$
$$y = ce^x, \quad \text{where } c \geq 0$$

Similarly, a function of one variable is *concave* in a region if its slope is always nonincreasing. Equivalently, a function of one variable is concave if a line drawn connecting two points on the function never lies above the function. See Figures 7.4

---

[1]For functions of several variables, the precise definition of convexity is more difficult to state. However, the geometric idea of convexity we give here will suffice for this book.

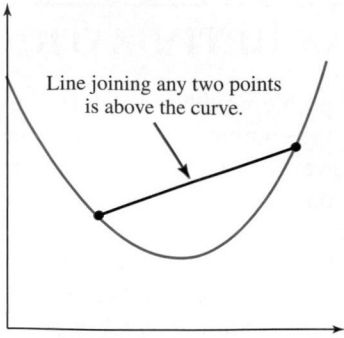

FIGURE 7.2
A Convex Function with a Global Minimum

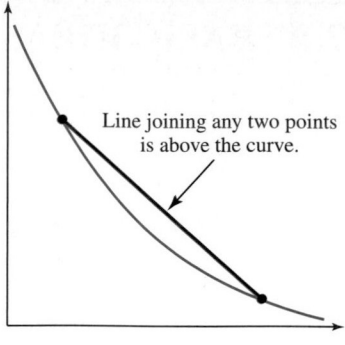

FIGURE 7.3
A Decreasing Convex Function

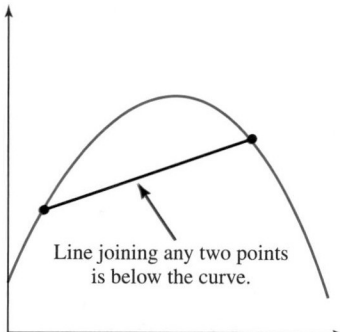

FIGURE 7.4
A Concave Function with a Global Maximum

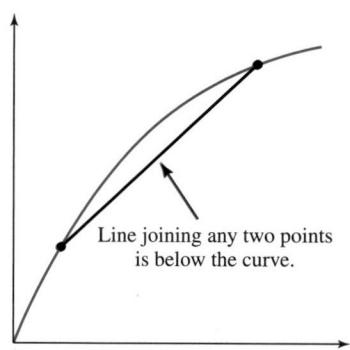

FIGURE 7.5
An Increasing Concave Function

and 7.5 for examples of concave functions. The first has a global maximum and the second is increasing, but the slopes of both are constantly decreasing.

The following are examples of concave functions:

$$y = c \ln x, \quad \text{where } c \geq 0 \text{ and } x > 0$$
$$y = cx^a, \quad \text{where } 0 < a \leq 1, c \geq 0, \text{ and } x \geq 0$$

A linear function ($y = ax + b$) is both convex and concave. This is because the slope of a linear function is constant.

Another, possibly more intuitive way to think about convex and concave functions is as follows. Imagine that you are walking up a hill. If you are on a stretch where the hill keeps getting steeper every step you take, you are on the convex part of the hill. If it keeps getting less steep, then you are on the concave part of the hill. Alternatively, if you are walking down a hill and it is getting less steep with every step you take, you are on the convex part of the hill; if it is getting more steep, you are on the concave part. In either case (walking uphill or downhill), if the steepness is not changing, you are on the linear part of the hill, which means it is both convex and concave.

It can be shown that the sum of convex functions is convex and the sum of concave functions is concave. Also, if you multiply any convex function by a positive constant, the result is still convex, and if you multiply any concave function by a positive constant, the result is still concave. However, if you multiply a convex function by a negative constant, the result is concave, and if you multiply a concave function by a negative constant, the result is convex.

Problems That Solvers Always Solve Correctly

As Figure 7.2 suggests, the Solver will perform well for a minimization problem if the objective function is convex. This is because convex functions cannot have any local minima that are not global minima. Similarly, Figure 7.4 suggests that the Solver will perform well for a maximization problem if the objective function is concave. These statements can be generalized to the situation where there are many decision variables and constraints. In fact, the following conditions imply that the Solver is guaranteed to find the global minimum or global maximum if it exists. (There are actually more general conditions than these, but the conditions stated here will suffice.)[2]

- **Conditions for Maximization Problems** The Solver is guaranteed to find the global maximum (if it exists) if
  1. the objective function is concave or the logarithm of the objective function is concave, and
  2. the constraints are linear
- **Conditions for Minimization Problems** The Solver is guaranteed to find the global minimum (if it exists) if
  1. the objective function is convex, and
  2. the constraints are linear

Therefore, if the constraints are linear, we need only check for the appropriate concavity or convexity of the objective function to assure that the Solver will find the optimal solution (as opposed to a local but nonglobal optimum).

When the Assumptions Do Not Hold

There are many problems for which the above conditions do not hold or cannot be verified. Because we are then not sure whether the Solver's solution is the optimal solution, the best strategy is to try several possible starting values for the changing cells, use the Solver with each of these, and take the best solution the Solver finds.

For example, consider the following NLP:

$$\max \ (x - 1)(x - 2)(x - 3)(x - 4)(x - 5) \tag{7.1}$$
$$\text{subject to } x \geq 1 \text{ and } x \leq 5$$

This is the function shown in Figure 7.1, where the graph extends from $x = 1$ to $x = 5$. Obviously, this function equals 0 when x equals 1, 2, 3, 4, or 5. (Just substitute any of these values for x in the function.) From the graph we see that the global maximum is between $x = 1$ and $x = 2$, but that there is a local maximum between $x = 3$ and $x = 4$. The spreadsheet in Figure 7.6 (page 342) shows the results of using the Solver to solve this problem. In columns A and B we show what happened when the starting value in the changing cell was $x = 1.5$. The Solver eventually found $x = 1.355567$ with a corresponding objective value of 3.631432. (The objective in cell B11 is the product of the five numbers above it, and the constraints are B5<=5 and B5>=1.) However, given the identical setup in columns D and E, but with a starting value of $x = 3.5$, the Solver found the local maximum $x = 3.543912$ and its corresponding objective

---

[2]The following discussion assumes that your spreadsheet contains no IF, MAX, MIN, or ABS statements that depend on changing cells. Current-generation spreadsheet Solvers are not equipped to deal with these functions, and errors often occur if they are present.

FIGURE 7.6
Function with Local
and Global Maxima

	A	B	C	D	E
1	**Function with Local and Global Maxima**				
2					
3	The function is: y = (x-1)(x-2)(x-3)(x-4)(x-5)				
4					
5	x	1.355567		x	3.54391
6	x-1	0.355567		x-1	2.54391
7	x-2	-0.64443		x-2	1.54391
8	x-3	-1.64443		x-3	0.54391
9	x-4	-2.64443		x-4	-0.45609
10	x-5	-3.64443		x-5	-1.45609
11	Product	3.631432		Product	1.4187

value of 1.418697. This second solution is not the correct solution to the problem in equation (7.1), but the Solver found it because of an "unlucky" starting value of x.

In general, if you try several starting combinations for the changing cells and the Solver obtains the same optimal solution in all cases, you can be fairly confident—but still not absolutely sure—that you have found the optimal solution to the NLP. On the other hand, if you try different starting values for the changing cells and obtain several different solutions, then the best you can do is keep the "best" solution you have found. That is, you should keep the solution with the lowest objective value (for a minimization problem) or the highest objective value (for a maximization problem).

In the next chapter we will discuss alternative solution methods that have recently been developed and incorporated into Excel add-in software. These alternative methods are particularly useful in problems that have several local optima and therefore do not satisfy the conditions we listed above. They also have the ability to handle spreadsheet modeling features, such as IF and MAX functions that the standard Solver cannot handle.

7.3 PRICING MODELS

Setting prices on products or services is becoming quite a science for many companies. A good example is pricing of hotel rooms and airline tickets. To many airline customers, ticket pricing appears to be madness on the part of the airlines (how can it cost less to fly thousands of miles to London than to fly a couple of hundred miles across the state?), but there is some method to the madness. In this section we will examine some pricing problems that can be modeled as NLPs. In Chapter 8 we will look at further examples of pricing models.

EXAMPLE 7.1

PRICING DECISIONS AT MADISON

The Madison Company manufactures and retails a certain product. The company wants to determine the price that maximizes its profit from this product. The unit cost of producing and marketing the product is $50. Madison will certainly charge at least $50 for the product to ensure that it makes *some* profit. However, there is a very competitive market for this product, so that Madison's demand will fall sharply as it increases its price. How should the company proceed?[3]

[3]This example and the next two are based on Dolan and Simon (1996).

Solution

If Madison charges P dollars per unit, then its profit will be $(P-50)D$, where D is the number of units demanded. The problem, however, is that D depends on P. As the price P increases, the demand D decreases. Therefore, the first step is to find how D varies with P—the demand function. In fact, this is the first step in almost any pricing problem. We will try two possibilities: a *linear* demand function of the form $D = a - bP$, and a *constant elasticity* demand function of the form $D = aP^b$. You might recall from microeconomics that the *elasticity* of demand is the percentage change in demand caused by a 1% increase in price. The larger the (magnitude of) elasticity is, the more demand reacts to price. The advantage of the constant elasticity demand function is that the elasticity remains constant over all points on the demand curve. For example, the elasticity of demand is the same when price is $60 as when price is $70. Actually, the exponent b is approximately equal to this constant elasticity. For example, if $b = -2.5$, then demand will decrease by about 2.5% if price increases by 1%. In contrast, the elasticity *changes* for different price levels if the demand function is linear. Nevertheless, both forms of demand functions are commonly used in economic models.

Regardless of the *form* of the demand function, the parameters of the function (a and b) need to be estimated before any price optimization can be performed. This can be done with Excel trend curves, as in Example 2.2 of Chapter 2. Suppose that Madison can estimate two points on the demand curve. (At least two are required. More than two could be used in the same way.) Specifically, suppose the company estimates demand to be 400 units when price equals $70 and 300 units when price equals $80. Then we create two X-Y charts of demand versus price from these two points and use the Chart/Add Trendline menu item with the option to list the equation of the trendline on the chart. For a linear demand curve, we select the Linear trendline, and for the constant elasticity demand curve, we select the Power trendline. The results appear in Figure 7.7. (When you do this, the constant for the power curve may appear as 4E+06. To get more significant digits, just click on the equation, then use the Format menu and the Number tab to format the number appropriately.)

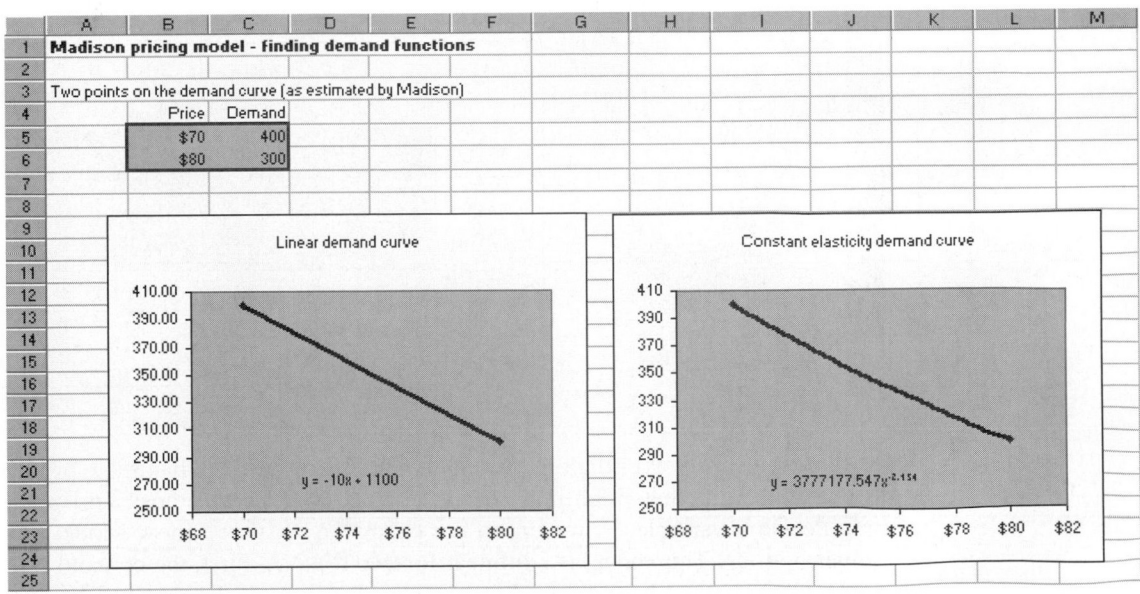

FIGURE 7.7 Determining Parameters of Demand Functions

DEVELOPING THE SPREADSHEET MODEL FOR PRICING

Once Madison has determined its demand function, the pricing decision is straightforward, as shown in Figure 7.8 for the constant elasticity model. (Again, the linear demand case is similar. The PRICING1.XLS file illustrates both cases.) The model requires the following steps.

1 Inputs. The inputs for this model are the unit cost and the parameters of the demand function found earlier. Enter them as shown.

2 Price. Enter any trial value for price. It will be the single changing cell.

3 Demand. Calculate the corresponding demand from the demand function by entering the formula

=Const*CEPrice^Elast

in the Demand cell.

4 Profit. Calculate the profit as net price times demand with the formula

=(CEPrice-UnitCost)*CEDemand

in the Profit cell.

FIGURE 7.8
Pricing Model with
Constant Elasticity
Demand

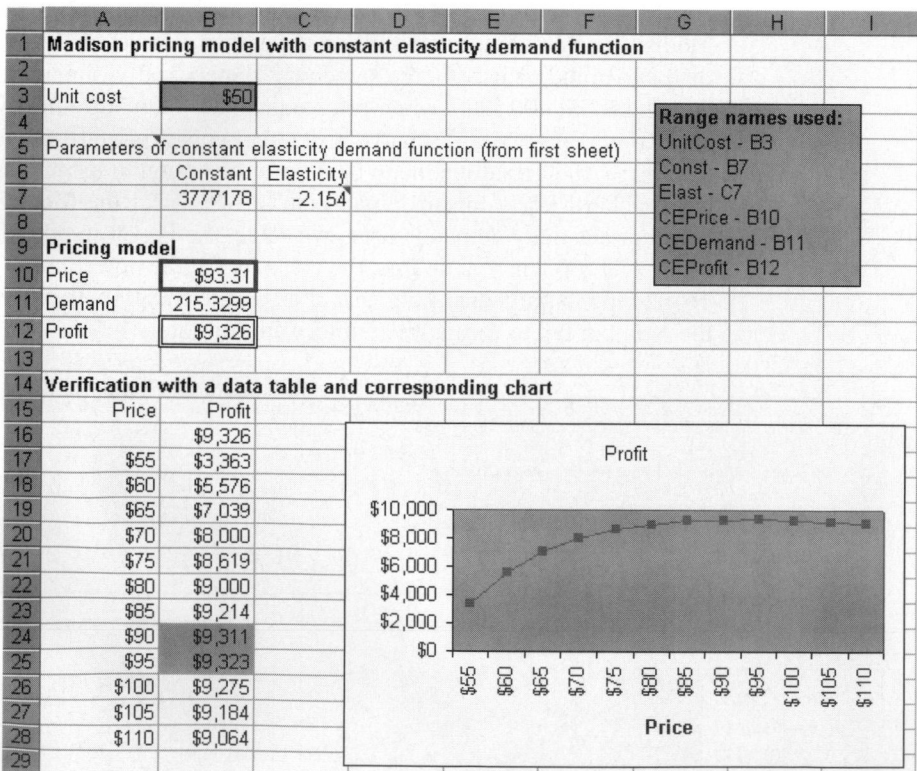

The relevant Solver dialog box appears in Figure 7.9. We maximize profit subject to the constraint that price must be at least as large as unit cost, and price is the only decision variable. However, do *not* check the Assume Linear Model box under Solver options. This model is nonlinear for two reasons. First, the demand function is nonlinear because Price is raised to a power. But even if the demand function were linear, profit would still be nonlinear. The reason is that it involves the *product* of price

FIGURE 7.9
Solver Dialog Box
for Pricing Model

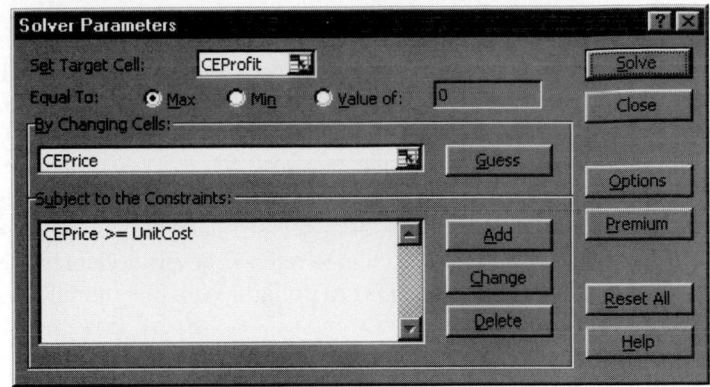

and demand, and demand is a function of price. This nonlinearity can be seen easily with the data table and corresponding chart in Figure 7.8. These show how profit varies with price—the relationship is clearly nonlinear. Profit increases to a maximum, then declines slowly. (By the way, this data table and chart are also useful for verifying that Solver indeed finds the profit-maximizing price.)

Sensitivity Analysis From an economic point of view, it should be interesting to see how the profit-maximizing price varies with the elasticity of the demand function. To do this, we use SolverTable with the elasticity in cell C7 as the single input cell, allowing it to vary from -2.4 to -1.8 in increments of 0.1. (Note that when the range of input values is negative, the one with the largest magnitude must be entered first in the SolverTable dialog box.) The results appear in Figure 7.10. When the demand is most elastic (at the top of the table), increases in price have a greater effect on demand. Therefore, the company cannot afford to set the price as high in this case.

FIGURE 7.10
Sensitivity to
Elasticity

	A	B	C	D
31	Sensitivity of optimal solution to elasticity			
32		Price	Demand	Profit
33		$B$10	$B$11	$B$12
34	-2.4	$85.71	86.66	$3,095
35	-2.3	$88.46	125.79	$4,838
36	-2.2	$91.67	182.10	$7,587
37	-2.1	$95.45	262.78	$11,945
38	-2.0	$100.00	377.72	$18,886
39	-1.9	$105.56	540.20	$30,011
40	-1.8	$112.50	767.53	$47,970

EXAMPLE 7.2

PRICING WITH EXCHANGE RATE CONSIDERATIONS AT MADISON

We continue Example 7.1, but we now assume that Madison manufactures its product in the United States and sells it in Germany. Given the prevailing exchange rate in dollars per Deutsche Mark (DM), Madison wants to determine the price in DM it should charge in Germany so that its profit in dollars is maximized. The company also wants to see how the optimal price and the optimal profit depend on exchange rate fluctuations.

Solution

The model appears in Figure 7.11. (See the file PRICING2.XLS.) It is very similar to the previous model, so we will highlight only the new features. The exchange rate in the ExRate cell indicates the number of dollars required to purchase one DM. For example, with an exchange rate of 0.63, it takes 63 cents to purchase one DM. Alternatively, $1/0.63 = 1.587$ DM are required to purchase one dollar. As this exchange rate decreases, we say that the dollar gets stronger; as it increases, the dollar gets weaker. Note that we *divide* by the exchange rate to convert dollars to DM, and we *multiply* by the exchange rate to convert DM to dollars. With this in mind, the model development is straightforward.

FIGURE 7.11
Pricing Model in a
Foreign Market

	A	B	C	D	E	F	G
1	Madison pricing problem in a German market						
2					Range names used:		
3	Unit cost ($)	50			UnitCost - B3		
4	Exchange rate ($/DM)	0.63			ExRate - B4		
5					UnitCostDM - B6		
6	Equivalent unit cost in DM	79.365			Const - B10		
7					Elast - C10		
8	Parameters of demand function in German market				Price - B13		
9		Constant	Elasticity		Demand - B14		
10		27556760	-2.4		Profit - B15		
11							
12	Pricing model (finding the right price in DM to maximize profit in $)						
13	Price (DM)	136.05					
14	Demand (in Germany)	208.60					
15	Profit ($)	7450.06					
16							
17	Sensitivity of price, demand, and profit to exchange rate						
18		$B13	$B14	$B15			
19	0.50	171.43	119.79	4278.29			
20	0.55	155.84	150.58	5377.90			
21	0.60	142.86	185.55	6626.82			
22	0.65	131.87	224.85	8030.35			
23	0.70	122.45	268.62	9593.51			
24	0.75	114.29	316.99	11321.12			
25	0.80	107.14	370.10	13217.78			
26	0.85	100.84	428.06	15287.90			
27	0.90	95.24	491.00	17535.75			

DEVELOPING THE SPREADSHEET MODEL

The following steps are required.

❶   Inputs. The inputs are the unit cost (in dollars), the exchange rate, and the parameters of the company's demand function for the German market. These latter values would need to be estimated exactly as we discussed in the previous example. We chose them arbitrarily for this example.

❷   Unit cost in DM. Although Madison's unit cost occurs in the United States and is expressed in dollars, it is convenient to express it in DM. Do this in the UnitCostDM cell with the formula

=UnitCost/ExRate

❸   Price, demand. As in the previous example, enter any price in the Price cell (now it is in DM), and calculate the demand from the demand function.

❹   Profit. The profit should be in dollars, so enter the formula

=(Price*ExRate-UnitCost)*Demand

in the Profit cell. Note that the unit cost is already in dollars, but the revenue from German sales needs to be converted to dollars.

USING THE SOLVER

The Solver dialog box is set up exactly as in Figure 7.9, except that the constraint on price is now Price>=UnitCostDM, so that DM are compared to DM. The optimal solution, with an exchange rate of 0.63, says that Madison should charge about 136 DM per unit in Germany. This will create demand for about 209 units, and the profit in dollars will be approximately $7450.

Sensitivity Analysis What happens when the dollar gets stronger or weaker? We use SolverTable with exchange rate as the single input, allowing it to vary from 0.50 to 0.90 in increments of 0.05, and we keep track of price, demand, and profit. As the results in Figure 7.11 indicate, as the dollar strengthens (the exchange rate decreases), Madison charges more in DM for the product, but it obtains a lower profit. The opposite is true when the dollar weakens. Are these results in line with your economic intuition? Note that when the dollar strengthens, DM are not worth as much to an American company. Therefore, when we convert the DM revenue to dollars in the profit cell, the profit tends to decrease. But in this case, why does the optimal price in DM *increase*? We'll say no more here—except that this should be a good question for class discussion! ∎

Many products create tie-ins to other products. For example, if you own a men's clothing store, you should realize that when a person buys a suit, he will probably also buy a shirt or a tie. Failure to realize this will cause you to price suits too high. The following example illustrates the idea.

EXAMPLE 7.3

PRICING SUITS AT THE MEN'S WAREHOUSE

Suits cost the Men's Warehouse $320. The current price of suits to customers is $350, which leads to annual sales of 300 suits. The elasticity of the demand for men's suits is estimated to be −2.5. Each purchase of a suit leads to an average of 2 shirts and 1.5 ties being sold. Each shirt contributes $25 to profit and each tie contributes $15 to profit. Determine a profit-maximizing price for suits.

Solution

As in the previous two examples, we first need to determine the demand function for suits. Although this could be a linear function or some other form, we will again assume a constant elasticity function of the form $D = aP^b$, where the exponent b is the elasticity. Then we can find the constant a from the current demand and price for suits: $300 = a350^{-2.5}$, so $a = 300/350^{-2.5}$. The solution from this point is practically the same as the solution to Example 7.1 except for the profit function. Each suit sold also generates demand for 2 shirts and 1.5 ties (on average), which contributes $2(25) + 1.5(15)$ extra dollars in profit. Therefore, it makes sense that the profit-maximizing price for suits will be *lower* than in the absence of shirts and ties—the company wants to generate more demand for suits so that it can reap the benefits from shirts and ties.

DEVELOPING THE SPREADSHEET MODEL

The spreadsheet solution appears in Figure 7.12. (See the file PRICING3.XLS.) We originally set up two models, one where shirts and ties are ignored and one where they are not, to see how the profit-maximizing price changes. However, a clever use of SolverTable allows us to treat both cases in one model. The details are as follows.

❶ Inputs. Enter all inputs in the shaded regions.

❷ Constant for demand function. Calculate the constant for the demand function in cell B9 with the formula

=CurrDemSuits/CurrPriceSuits^Elast

❸ Sensitivity factor. We will treat both cases, when shirts and ties are ignored and when they are not, by using SolverTable with a sensitivity factor as the input cell. When this factor is 0, the complementary products are ignored; when it is 1, they are taken into consideration. Enter 1 in the SensFactor cell for now. In general, this factor determines the average number of shirts and ties purchased with the purchase of a suit—we multiply this factor by the values in the UnitsPerSuit range. When this factor is 1, we get the values in the statement of the problem.

❹ Price, demand. Enter *any* price in the PriceSuits cell, and calculate the corresponding demand for suits in the DemandSuits cell with the formula

=Const*PriceSuits^Elast

❺ Profit. The total profit is the profit from suits alone, plus the extra profit from shirts and ties that are purchased along with suits. To calculate profit, enter the formula

=(PriceSuits-UnitCostSuits
  +SUMPRODUCT(SensFactor*UnitsPerSuit,UnitProfit))*DemandSuits

in the Profit cell.

❻ Solver setup. The Solver setup is the same as in Example 7.1. We maximize profit, with the price of suits as the only changing cell, and we constrain this price to be at least as large as the unit cost of suits.

FIGURE 7.12
Pricing Model with Complementary Products

	A	B	C	D	E	F	G	H	I
1	**Pricing complementary products**								
2									
3	Suits			Complementary products			**Range names**		
4	Current price	$350					**used:**		
5	Current demand	300			Ties	Shirts	CurrPriceSuits - B4		
6	Unit cost	$320		Units sold per suit	1.5	2	CurrDemSuits - B5		
7				Profit per unit	$15	$25	UnitCostSuits - B6		
8	Demand function			Sensitivity factor for units sold per suit			Const - B9		
9	Constant	6.88E+08				1	Elast - B10		
10	Elasticity	-2.5					UnitsPerSuit - E5:F5		
11							UnitProfit - E6:F6		
12	**Decision taking complementary products into account**						SensFactor - E9		
13	Price	$412.50					PriceSuits - B13		
14	Demand	198.9					DemandSuits - B14		
15	Profit	$32,826							
16									
17	**Sensitivity of price, demand, profit to sensitivity factor**								
18		Factor	Price	Demand	Profit				
19			$B$13	$B$14	$B$15				
20		0	$533.33	104.7	$22,328				
21		0.5	$472.92	141.4	$26,741				
22		1	$412.50	198.9	$32,826				
23		1.5	$352.08	295.6	$41,628				
24		2	$320.00	375.3	$54,423				

When sensitivity factor is 0, it is as if complementary products are ignored.

7 **SolverTable.** Run SolverTable with the SensFactor cell as the single input cell, varied, say, from 0 to 2 in increments of 0.5, and keep track of price, demand, and profit.

The SolverTable results show that when the company ignores shirts and ties (or, equivalently, suits do not generate any demand for shirts and ties), the optimal price is set high, at $533.33. However, as more ties and shirts are purchased by purchasers of suits, the optimal price of suits decreases fairly dramatically. As we would imagine, as more shirts and ties are purchased with suits, the company makes more profit—*if* it properly takes shirts and ties into account. For the situation in the problem statement, where the sensitivity factor should be set at 1, the optimal price is $412.50. How much profit does the company lose in this case if it ignores shirts and ties? You can answer this by entering $533.33 in the PriceSuits cell, keeping the sensitivity factor equal to 1. If you do so, you will find that profit decreases from $32,826 (cell D22) to $29,916, a drop of about 9%. ∎

Automobile and appliance dealers who profit from maintenance contracts would probably increase their profits significantly if they would factor the profits from the maintenance agreements into their determination of the prices of their major products. That is, we suspect that the prices of their major products are set too high—not from the customers' standpoint but the dealers'. Probably the ultimate "tie-in" reduction in price is the fact that many companies now give software away for free. They are hoping, of course, that the receiver of free software will later buy the "tie-in" product, which is the upgrade.

In many situations there are peak-load and off-peak-load demands for a product. In such a situation it is optimal for a producer to charge a larger price for peak-load service than for off-peak service. The following example illustrates this situation.

EXAMPLE 7.4

PEAK-LOAD PRICING AT FLORIDA POWER AND LIGHT

Florida Power and Light (FPL) faces demands during both peak-load and off-peak-load times. FPL must determine the price per kilowatt hour (kwh) to charge during both peak and off-peak periods. The daily demand for power during each period (in kwh) is related to price as follows:

$$D_p = 60 - 0.5P_p + 0.1P_o \tag{7.2}$$

$$D_o = 40 - P_o + 0.1P_p \tag{7.3}$$

Here, D_p and P_p are demand and price during peak times, whereas D_o and P_o are demand and price during off-peak times. Note that we are now using *linear* demand functions, not the constant elasticity demand functions from the previous two examples. (We do this for the sake of variety.) Also, note that because of the signs of the coefficients, an increase in the peak-load price decreases the demand for power during the peak period but increases the demand for power during the off-peak period. Similarly, an increase in the price for the off-peak period decreases the demand for the off-peak period but increases the demand for the peak period. In economic terms, this implies that peak-load power and off-peak power are **substitutes** for one another. It costs FPL

$10 per day to maintain 1 kwh of capacity. The company wants to determine a pricing strategy and capacity level that maximize its daily profit.

Solution

Due to the relationships between the demand and price variables, it is not at all obvious what FPL should do. The pricing decisions determine demand, and larger demand requires larger capacity, which costs money. In addition, revenue is price multiplied by demand, so it is not clear whether price should be low or high to increase revenue.

To solve this problem, we must keep track of the following:

- the peak and off-peak price
- the peak and off-peak demand
- the peak and off-peak revenue
- the capacity (in kwh)
- the cost of capacity
- the total profit

DEVELOPING THE SPREADSHEET MODEL

The spreadsheet model appears in Figure 7.13. (See the file PEAKLOAD.XLS.) It can be formed as follows.

1 **Inputs.** Enter the parameters of the demand functions and the cost of capacity in the shaded ranges.

2 **Prices and capacity level.** Enter *any* trial prices (per kwh) for peak and off-peak power in the Prices range, and enter *any* trial value for the capacity level in the Capacity cell. These are the three values FPL has control over, so they become the changing cells.

FIGURE 7.13
Peak-Load Pricing
Model

	A	B	C	D	E	F	G	H
1	**Florida Power & Light peak-load pricing model**							
2								
3	**Input data**							
4	Coefficients of demand functions							
5		Constant	Peak price	Off-peak price			Range names used:	
6	Peak-load demand	60	-0.5	0.1			PLConst - B6	
7	Off-peak demand	40	0.1	-1			PLCoeffs - C6:D6	
8							OPConst - B7	
9	Cost of capacity/kwh	$10					OPCoeffs - C7:D7	
10							UnitCost - B9	
11	**Decisions**						Prices - B13:C13	
12		Peak-load	Off-peak				Capacity - B15	
13	Prices	$70.31	$26.53				Demands - B19:C19	
14							Capacities - B21:C21	
15	Capacity	27.50					Revenue - B24	
16							Cost - B25	
17	**Constraints on demand**						Profit - B26	
18		Peak-load	Off-peak					
19	Demand	27.50	20.50					
20		<=	<=					
21	Capacity	27.50	27.50					
22								
23	**Monetary summary**							
24	Revenue	$2,477.30						
25	Cost of capacity	$275.00						
26	Profit	$2,202.30						

❸ Demands. Calculate the demand for the peak period by substituting into equation (7.2). That is, enter the formula

=PLConst+SUMPRODUCT(Prices,PLCoeffs)

in cell B19. Similarly, enter the formula

=OPConst+SUMPRODUCT(Prices,OPCoeffs)

in cell C19 for the off-peak demand.

❹ Copy capacity. To indicate the capacity constraints, enter the formula

=Capacity

in cells B21 and C21.

❺ Monetary values. Calculate the daily revenue, cost of capacity, and profit in the corresponding cells with the formulas

=SUMPRODUCT(Demands,Prices)
=Capacity*UnitCost

and

=Revenue-Cost

USING THE SOLVER

Fill in the Solver dialog box as shown in Figure 7.14. We maximize profit by setting appropriate prices and capacity, and we ensure that demand never exceeds capacity. (You might wonder why the "plural" Capacities range is specified in the constraint. Recall that we duplicated capacity in the range B21:C21, the Capacities range. We have two demands, so we need two capacities for the constraint, even though they both equal the single capacity value.)

FIGURE 7.14
Solver Dialog Box
for Peak-Load
Pricing Model

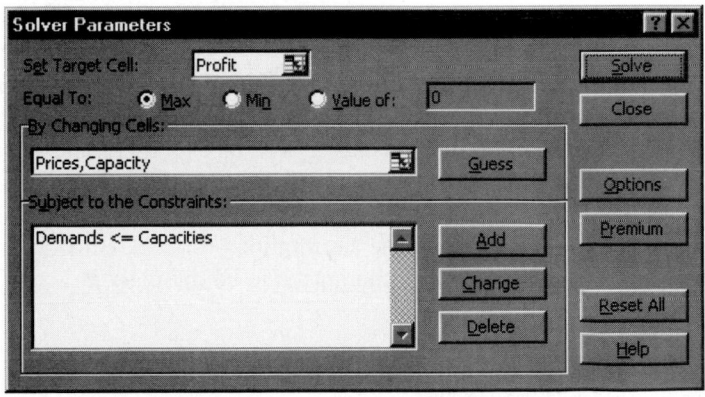

The Solver solution in Figure 7.13 indicates that FPL should charge $70.31 per kwh during the peak-load period and $26.53 during the off-peak-load period. These prices generate demands of 27.5 (peak) and 20.5 (off-peak), so that a capacity of 27.5 kwh is required. The cost of this capacity is $275. When this is subtracted from the revenue of $2477.30, the daily profit becomes $2202.30.

To gain some insight into this solution, consider what happens if FPL changes the peak-load price slightly from its optimal value of $70.31. If FPL decreases the price to $70, say, you can check that the peak-load demand increases to 27.65 and the off-peak demand decreases to 20.47. The net effect is that revenue increases slightly to $2478.78. However, the peak-load demand is now greater than capacity, so FPL must increase its capacity from 27.50 to 27.65. This costs an extra $1.50, which more than offsets the increase in revenue. A similar chain of effects occurs if FPL increases the peak price to $71. In this case, peak-load demand decreases, off-peak demand increases, and total revenue decreases. Although FPL can get by with lower capacity, the net effect is slightly less profit.

Sensitivity Analysis To gain even more insight, we use SolverTable to see the effects of changing the unit cost of capacity, which we allow to vary from $5 to $15 in increments of $1. The results appear in Figure 7.15. They indicate that as the cost of capacity increases, the peak-load price increases, the off-peak price stays constant, the amount of capacity decreases, and profit decreases. The latter two effects are probably intuitive, but we challenge you to explain the effects on price. In particular, why does the peak-load price *increase*, and why doesn't the off-peak price increase as well?

FIGURE 7.15
Sensitivity to Cost of
Capacity

	A	B	C	D	E
28	**Sensitivity of changing cells and profit to cost of capacity**				
29		Unit cost	Peak price	Off-peak price	Capacity	Profit
30			$B$13	$C$13	$B$15	$B$26
31		$5	$67.81	$26.53	28.75	$2,342.92
32		$6	$68.31	$26.53	28.50	$2,314.30
33		$7	$68.81	$26.53	28.25	$2,285.92
34		$8	$69.31	$26.53	28.00	$2,257.80
35		$9	$69.81	$26.53	27.75	$2,229.92
36		$10	$70.31	$26.53	27.50	$2,202.30
37		$11	$70.81	$26.53	27.25	$2,174.92
38		$12	$71.31	$26.53	27.00	$2,147.80
39		$13	$71.81	$26.53	26.75	$2,120.92
40		$14	$72.31	$26.53	26.50	$2,094.30
41		$15	$72.81	$26.53	26.25	$2,067.92

Is the Solver Solution Optimal? All of the constraints in this example are linear, so they certainly meet the assumptions for a maximization problem. Also, it can be shown that the objective (daily profit) is a concave function of peak price, off-peak price, and capacity level (although this is not obvious). Algebraically, this objective function is called **quadratic**, meaning that it is a sum of squared terms (such as P_p^2) and cross-product terms (such as $P_p P_o$). Not all quadratic functions are concave, but there is a test to check whether a given quadratic function is concave. We will not cover the details of this test, but we assure you that the quadratic function for this example passes the test. Therefore, the assumptions for a maximization problem are satisfied, and the Solver's solution is guaranteed to be optimal. ■

PROBLEMS

Skill-Building Problems

1. Suppose Ford currently sells 250,000 Ford Tauruses annually. The unit cost of a Taurus, including the delivery cost to a dealer, is $16,000. The current Taurus price is $20,000, and the current elasticity of demand for the Taurus is −1.5.
   a. Determine a profit-maximizing price for a Taurus.

   Do this when the demand function is of the constant elasticity type. Do it when the demand function is linear.
   b. Suppose Ford makes an average profit of $800 from servicing a Taurus purchased from a Ford dealer. (This is an average over the lifetime of the car.) How do your answers to part **a** change?

2. Suppose the current exchange rate is 100 yen per dollar. We currently sell 100 units of a product for 700 yen. The cost of producing and shipping the product to Japan is $5, and the current elasticity of demand is -3. Find the optimal price to charge for the product (in yen) for each of the following exchange rates: 60 yen/\$, 80 yen/\$, 100 yen/\$, 120 yen/\$, 140 yen/\$, and 160 yen/\$. Assume the demand function is linear.

3. Another way to derive a demand function is to break the market into segments and identify a low price, a medium price, and a high price. For each of these prices and market segments, we ask company experts to estimate product demand. Then we use Excel's trend curve fitting capabilities to fit a *quadratic* function that represents that segment's demand function. Finally, we add the segment demand curves to derive an aggregate demand curve. Try this procedure for pricing a candy bar. Assume the candy bar costs $0.55 to produce. The company plans to charge between $1.10 and $1.50 for this candy bar. Its marketing department estimates the demands shown in Table 7.1 (in thousands) in the three regions of the country where the candy bar will be sold. What is the profit-maximizing price, assuming that the *same* price will be charged in all three regions?

TABLE 7.1	Demand Estimates		
Price	Region 1 Demand	Region 2 Demand	Region 3 Demand
Low	$1.10	35	32	24
Medium	$1.30	34	27	17
High	$1.50	22	16	9

4. Widgetco produces widgets at plants 1 and 2. It costs $20x^{1/2}$ dollars to produce x units at plant 1 and $40x^{1/3}$ dollars to produce x units at plant 2. Each plant can produce up to 70 units. Each unit produced can be sold for $10. At most 120 widgets can be sold. Determine how Widgetco can maximize its profit.

5. If a monopolist produces q units, she can charge $100 - 4q$ dollars per unit. The fixed cost of production is $50 and the variable cost is $2 per unit.
   a. How can the monopolist maximize her profit?
   b. If the monopolist must pay a sales tax of $2 per unit, will she increase or decrease production (relative to the situation with no sales tax)?
   c. Continuing part b, use SolverTable to see how a change in the sales tax affects the optimal solution.
   d. Again continuing part b, use SolverTable to see how simultaneous changes in the fixed and variable costs of production affect the optimal output level. (Use a two-way table.)

6. It costs a company $12 to purchase an hour of labor and $15 to purchase an hour of capital. If L hours of labor and K units of capital are available, then $L^{2/3}K^{1/3}$ machines can be produced. Suppose the company has $10,000 to purchase labor and capital.
   a. What is the maximum number of machines it can produce?
   b. Use SolverTable to see how a change in the price of labor changes the optimal solution.
   c. Use SolverTable to see how a change in the price of capital changes the optimal solution.
   d. Use SolverTable to see how a change in the amount of money available changes the optimal solution.

7. In the previous problem what is the minimum-cost method of producing 100 machines? (Ignore the $10,000 budget constraint.)

8. A total of 160 hours of labor are available each week at $15 per hour. Additional labor can be purchased at $25 per hour. Capital can be purchased in unlimited quantities at a cost of $45 per unit. If K units of capital and L units of labor are available during a week, then $L^{1/2}K^{1/3}$ machines can be produced. Each machine sells for $270. How can the firm maximize its weekly profit?

9. A monopolist can purchase up to 17.25 ounces of a chemical for $10 per ounce. At a cost of $3 per ounce, the chemical can be processed into an ounce of product 1, or at a cost of $5 per ounce, the chemical can be processed into an ounce of product 2. If x_1 ounces of product 1 are produced, it sells for a price of $30 - x_1$ dollars per ounce. If x_2 ounces of product 2 are produced, it sells for a price of $50 - 2x_2$ dollars per ounce. Determine how the monopolist can maximize profit.

10. The cost per day of running a hospital is $200,000 + 0.002x^2$ dollars, where x is the number of patients served per day. What number of patients served per day minimizes the cost per patient of running the hospital?

11. A company can sell all it produces of a given output for $2 per unit. The output is produced by combining two inputs, 1 and 2. If q_1 units of input 1 and q_2 units of input 2 are used, the company can produce $q_1^{1/3} + q_2^{2/3}$ units of the output. If it costs $1 to purchase a unit of input 1 and $1.50 to purchase a unit of input 2, how can the company maximize its profit?

12. There are two firms producing widgets. It costs the first firm q_1^2 dollars to produce q_1 widgets and the second firm $0.5q_2^2$ dollars to produce q_2 widgets. If a total of q widgets are produced, consumers will pay $200 - q$ dollars for each widget. If the two manufacturers want to collude in an attempt to maximize the sum of their profits, how many widgets should each company produce? The model for this type of problem is called a **collusive duopoly model**.

13. A company manufactures two products. If it charges price p_i for product i, it can sell q_i units of product i, where $q_1 = 60 - 3p_1 + p_2$ and $q_2 = 80 - 2p_2 + p_1$. It costs \$25 to produce a unit of product 1 and \$72 to produce a unit of product 2. How many units of each product should the company produce, and what prices should it charge, to maximize its profit?

14. Based on Littlechild (1970). A power company faces demands during both peak and off-peak times. If a price of p_1 dollars per kilowatt-hour is charged during the peak time, customers will demand $60 - 0.5p_1$ kwh of power. If a price of p_2 dollars is charged during the off-peak time, customers will demand $40 - p_2$ kwh. The power company must have sufficient capacity to meet demand during both the peak and off-peak times. It costs \$10 per day to maintain each kilowatt-hour of capacity. Determine how the power company can maximize its daily revenues less operating costs.

15. Eli Daisy sells the drug Biscuitco in Germany. Currently Daisy charges 50 DM per unit of Biscuitco. The current demand is for 50,000 units of Biscuitco per month. The current exchange rate is 2 DM per dollar. This means that a DM is currently worth \$0.50. It costs Daisy \$12.00 to produce each unit of Biscuitco. Daisy's goal is to maximize its profit in U.S. dollars from Biscuitco. In computing its profit, the company converts the revenue received in DM to dollars using the current exchange rate. Assume the demand for Biscuitco follows a linear demand curve with elasticity currently equal to -3 (that is, a 1% increase in the price (in marks) of Biscuitco will reduce the demand in Germany for Biscuitco by 3%).
  a. What price should Daisy charge (in DM) for a unit of Biscuitco?
  b. Suppose the exchange rate changes to 4 DM per dollar. What effect does this have on the optimal price?

Skill-Extending Problems

16. Most economies have a goal of maximizing the average consumption per period. Assume that during each year, an economy saves the same (to be determined) percentage S of its production. During a year in which the beginning capital level is K, a quantity $K^{1/2}$ of capital is produced. If the economy saves a percentage S of its capital, then during the current year it consumes $(1 - S)K^{1/2}$ units of capital and, through savings, adds $SK^{1/2}$ units of capital. Also, during any year, 10% of all capital present at the beginning of the year depreciates or wears out.
  a. What annual savings percentage S maximizes the long-run average consumption level? Assume that year 50 represents the long run.
  b. Use SolverTable to see how the optimal value of

S depends on the annual depreciation rate.

17. Each morning during rush hour, 10,000 people want to travel from New Jersey to New York City. If a person takes the commuter train, the trip lasts 40 minutes. If x thousand people per morning drive to New York, it takes $20 + 5x$ minutes to make the trip. This problem illustrates a basic fact of life: If people make their decisions individually, they will cause more congestion than need actually occur!
  a. Show that if people make their decisions individually, an average of 4000 people will travel by road from New Jersey to New York. Here you should assume that people will divide up between the trains and roads in a way that makes the average travel time by road equal to the travel time by train. When this "equilibrium" occurs, nobody has an incentive to switch from the road to the train or vice versa.
  b. Show that the average travel time per person is minimized if 2000 people travel by road.

18. Based on Grossman and Hart (1983). A salesperson for Fuller Brush has three options: quit, put forth a low effort level, or put forth a high effort level. Suppose for simplicity that each salesperson will sell either \$0, \$5000, or \$50,000 worth of brushes. The probability of each sales amount depends on the effort level as described in Table 7.2. If a salesperson is paid w dollars, he or she earns a "benefit" of $w^{1/2}$ units. In addition, low effort costs the salesperson 0 benefit units, while high effort costs 50 benefit units. If a salesperson were to quit Fuller and work elsewhere, he or she could earn a benefit of 20 units. Fuller wants all salespeople to put forth a high effort level. The question is how to minimize the cost of encouraging them to do so. The company cannot observe the level of effort put forth by a salesperson, but it can observe the size of his or her sales. Thus, the wage paid to the salesperson is completely determined by the size of the sale. This means that Fuller must determine w_0, the wage paid for sales of \$0; w_{5000}, the wage paid for sales of \$5000; and $w_{50,000}$, the wage paid for sales of \$50,000. These wages must be set so that the salespeople value the expected benefit from high effort more than quitting and more than low effort. Determine how to minimize the expected cost of ensuring that all salespeople put forth high effort. (This problem is an example of **agency theory**.)

TABLE 7.2	**Probabilities for Sales Effort Problem**	
Size of Sale	**Low Effort**	**High Effort**
\$0	0.6	0.3
\$5,000	0.3	0.2
\$50,000	0.1	0.5

7.4 SALES FORCE ALLOCATION MODELS

How should a business allocate its sales force? Many companies have applied NLP to answer this question. For example, Syntex Labs [see Lodish et al. (1986)] increased the profitability of the company by over $1 million per year by using NLP to allocate its sales force among the company's seven main drugs. The following example presents a simplified sales force allocation model.

EXAMPLE 7.5

ASSIGNING SALESPEOPLE TO DRUGS AT PHARMADEX

Pharmadex sells four drugs. It costs Pharmadex $50,000 per year per salesperson. The annual revenue generated from each drug is a function of the number of salespeople assigned to the drug. This dependence is shown in Table 7.3, where S_i is the number of salespeople assigned to drug i, and revenue is expressed in thousands of dollars. If Pharmadex wants to maximize profit (revenue from sales minus salesperson costs), how many salespeople should it assign to each drug?

TABLE 7.3	**Revenue Functions for Pharmadex Example**
	Revenue
Drug 1	$200S_1^{0.5}$
Drug 2	$150S_2^{0.75}$
Drug 3	$180S_3^{0.6}$
Drug 4	$300S_4^{0.3}$

Solution

First, we note that as more salespeople are assigned to any particular drug, the marginal effect on revenue decreases—each additional salesperson generates less revenue than the previous salesperson. This is due to the fact that all exponents in Table 7.3 are less than 1. Therefore, it is not at all obvious how many salespeople Pharmadex should assign to each drug.

DEVELOPING THE SPREADSHEET MODEL

The spreadsheet model is straightforward, as shown in Figure 7.16 (page 356). (See the file PHARMADEX.XLS.) It requires the following steps.

1   Inputs. Revenue for each drug equals a constant times the number of salespeople assigned to the drug raised to a power. Enter these constants and powers in the range B9:E10, and enter the cost per salesperson in the UnitCost cell.

2   Number of salespeople assigned. Enter *any* trial values for the number of salespeople assigned to each drug in the Assigned range. Then use the SUM function to calculate the total number of salespeople in the TotAssigned cell.

	A	B	C	D	E	F	G	H
1	**Pharmadex salesforce allocation model**							
2								
3	**Assumptions:**							
4	Revenue for any drug is a constant times the number of salespeople raised to a power.					**Range names used:**		
5	All monetary values are expressed in $1000s.					UnitCost - B12		
6						Assigned - B16:E16		
7	**Coefficients of revenue functions (with revenues expressed in $1000s)**					TotAssigned - F16		
8	Drug	1	2	3	4	Revenues - B17:E17		
9	Constant	200	150	180	300	TotRevenue - F17		
10	Power	0.5	0.75	0.6	0.3	Profit - B19		
11								
12	Cost/salesperson	$50						
13								
14	**Salesforce allocations**							
15	Drug	1	2	3	4	Totals		
16	Number assigned	4	26	7	2	39		
17	Revenue	$400	$1,727	$579	$369	$3,075		
18								
19	**Profit**	$1,125						

FIGURE 7.16 Sales Force Allocation Model

❸ **Revenues.** Calculate the revenues earned in the Revenues range. Specifically, calculate the revenue earned by drug 1 in cell B17 with the formula

=B9*B16^B10

and copy it across to cell E17. Then calculate the total revenue in the TotRevenue with the SUM function.

❹ **Total profit.** Calculate the profit in the Profit cell with the formula

=TotRevenue-UnitCost*TotAssigned

USING THE SOLVER

The Solver dialog box (not shown) is particularly simple. We maximize profit, with the Assigned range as the changing cells and constrain this range to be integer. There are no other constraints. Because of the exponents in the revenue functions, the model is nonlinear, so the Assume Linear Model box should *not* be checked. From Figure 7.16, we see that Pharmadex can earn a profit of $1.125 million by assigning 4 salespeople to drug 1, 26 to drug 2, 7 to drug 3, and 2 to drug 4.

Sensitivity Analysis More salespeople mean more revenue—for any of the drugs. This is because any function of the form aS^b increases as S increases when a and b are positive, as they are here. There is no budget constraint in the model, so the only thing keeping the company from hiring an unlimited number of salespeople is the $50,000 cost per salesperson. How does the optimal solution change if this cost changes? We answer this with SolverTable, letting the unit cost vary from $30,000 to $70,000 in increments of $5000, and keeping track of profit and the assignments. The results appear in Figure 7.17. As you might expect, when the cost of a salesperson increases, fewer are hired, and the optimal profit decreases. Note that the number assigned to drug 2 is affected most by increases in the unit cost. With the largest exponent of the four revenue functions, drug 2 benefits most from extra salespeople, so many are assigned to it when salespeople are cheap. However, as they become more expensive, they become too expensive even for drug 2.

FIGURE 7.17
Sensitivity to Cost of
Salespeople

21	Sensitivity of profit and number assigned to the unit cost of a salesperson					
22	Unit cost	Profit	Assigned to 1	Assigned to 2	Assigned to 3	Assigned to 4
23		$B$19	$B$16	$C$16	$D$16	$E$16
24	30	$3,139	11	198	25	5
25	35	$2,236	8	107	17	4
26	40	$1,701	6	63	12	3
27	45	$1,358	5	39	9	3
28	50	$1,125	4	26	7	2
29	55	$959	3	18	5	2
30	60	$836	3	12	4	2
31	65	$740	2	9	4	2
32	70	$666	2	7	3	1

Is the Solver Solution Optimal? Because the only constraints for Pharmadex are the nonnegativity and integer constraints, we know the Solver will find the optimal solution if the objective is concave. Recall that for $S \geq 0$, the function aS^b is concave for $a > 0$ and $0 < b \leq 1$. Therefore, profit is the sum of concave functions minus a linear cost function; hence it is concave. Therefore, we know that the Solver solution is indeed optimal.

Modeling Tip The functions $\ln(x)$ and x^a (for $0 < a < 1$) are undefined when x is negative. If a Solver model uses either of these functions and contains the restriction that x is nonnegative, then in searching for an optimal solution, the Solver might try small negative values of x. This leads to the error message "Solver has encountered an error in target or constraint cell." If your model involves functions that are undefined when a variable x is negative, add a constraint (such as $x \geq 0.001$) to ensure that the Solver will never try negative values of x.

Estimating the Revenue Functions The parameters of the revenue functions in Table 7.3 allowed us to solve the optimization model, but how would a company obtain these parameters in the first place? We provide one possible method, drawing on the Syntex Labs case reported in Lodish et al. (1986). Managers at Syntex were asked, for each drug, to estimate the level of sales that would occur if the number of sales calls deviated from the current number by various percentages. To make it easier for managers to respond, the current sales level was "indexed" at 100. For example, managers might be asked for the sales response if the number of sales calls is cut to 50% of its current level. Then a response of 65, say, means that they believe the revenue from this drug will fall to 65% of its current level. From the managers' responses, we can estimate a revenue function of the form $R = aS^b$ (or any other form chosen).

A set of possible results appears in Figure 7.18 on page 358. (See the Estimation sheet in the PHARMADEX.XLS file.) The managers' responses appear in the range B5:C9. The values in column B of this range indicate the scenarios they were asked to evaluate—sales call levels as low as 1/10 of the current level, as high as 10 times the current level, and 50% above and 50% below the current level. Their responses in column C of this range indicate what they thought would happen to sales revenue, relative to the current level of revenue. For example, they thought that if sales calls increased by a factor of 10, revenue would increase only by a factor of 3. We then create an X-Y chart of these values and use the Chart/Trendline menu item in the usual way to obtain a power trendline with the equation superimposed. The constant and exponent from this equation are placed in cells F4 and F5.

However, the constant in cell F4 is not exactly the constant we would use in the salesforce optimization model. That is, it would not be one of the constants in Table 7.3.

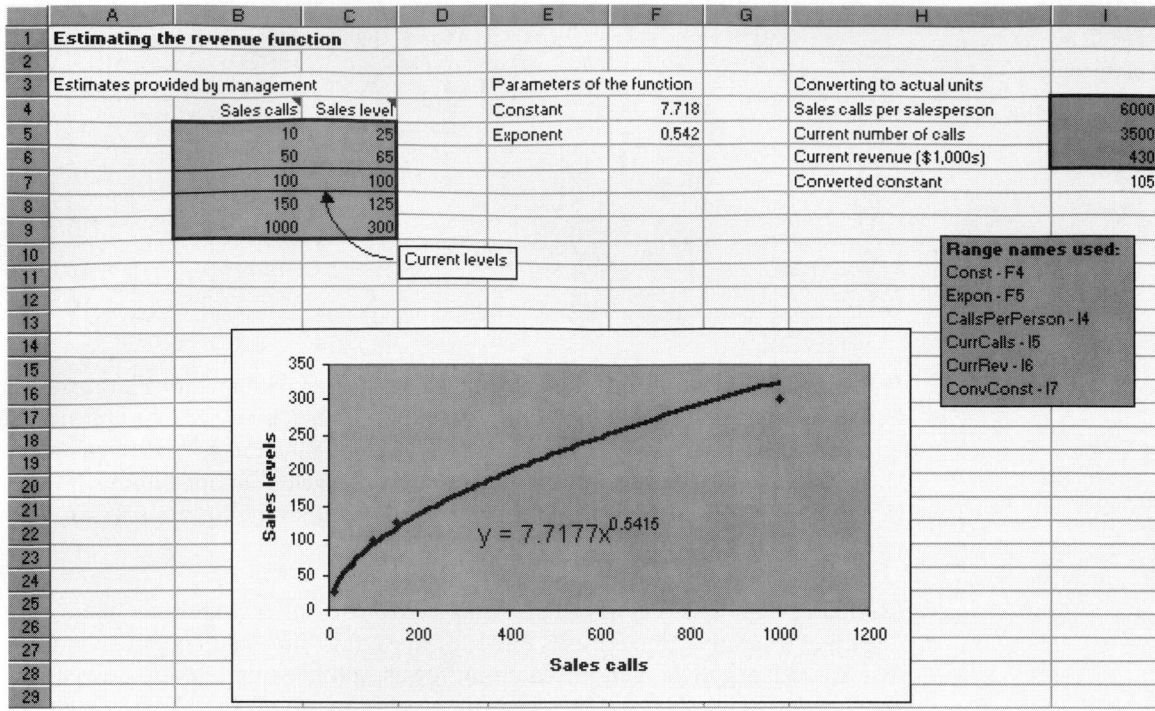

FIGURE 7.18 Estimating the Revenue Function

The equation we just estimated has R and C expressed relative to 100, whereas we want them in actual units. Also, we want S rather than C, where S is the number of salespeople, not the number of sales calls. We make the necessary conversion in column I of Figure 7.18. As inputs, we need the number of sales calls per salesperson, the current number of sales calls, and the current revenue, shown in the shaded cells. Then it can be shown algebraically that the relevant formula for the ConvConst cell is

=Const*(CurrRev/100)/(CurrCalls/100)*CallsPerPerson^Expon

The conclusion is that for this drug, we would use the equation $R = 105S^{0.542}$ to predict revenue R on the basis of S salespeople assigned to the drug. ∎

PROBLEMS

Skill-Building Problems

19. Q&H Company advertises during soap operas and football games. Each soap opera ad costs $50,000, and each football game ad costs $100,000. If S soap opera ads are purchased, they will be seen by $5S^{1/2}$ million men and $20S^{1/2}$ million women. If F football ads are purchased, they will be seen by $17F^{1/2}$ million men and $7F^{1/2}$ million women. The company wants at least 40 million men and at least 60 million women to see its ads.

    a. Determine how to minimize Q&H's cost of reaching the required number of viewers.

    b. How does this model violate the proportionality and additivity assumptions of LP?

    c. Suppose that the number of women (in millions) reached by F football ads and S soap opera ads is $7F^{1/2} + 20S^{1/2} - 0.2(FS)^{1/2}$. Why might this be a more realistic representation of the number of women viewers seeing Q&H's ads?

20. Beerco has $100,000 to spend on advertising in four markets. The sales revenue (in thousands of dollars) that can be created in each market by spending x_i thousand dollars in market i is given in Table 7.4.

    a. To maximize its sales revenue, how much money should Beerco spend in each market?

TABLE 7.4	Sales Revenue Functions for Beerco Problem
	Sales Revenue
Market 1	$10x_1^{0.4}$
Market 2	$8x_2^{0.5}$
Market 3	$12x_3^{0.3}$
Market 4	$6x_4^{0.6}$

b. Use SolverTable to see how a change in the advertising budget affects the optimal sales revenue.

21. It costs a company $6 per unit to produce a product. If the company charges price p dollars per unit and spends a dollars on advertising, it can sell $10,000p^{-2}a^{1/6}$ units of the product. Find the price and advertising level that maximize the company's profit.

22. A beer company has divided Bloomington into two territories. If the company spends x_1 dollars on promotion in territory 1, it can sell $60x_1^{1/2}$ cases of beer there, and if it spends x_2 dollars on promotion in territory 2, it can sell $40x_2^{1/2}$ cases of beer there. Each case of beer sold in territory 1 sells for $10 and incurs $5 in shipping and production costs. Each case of beer sold in territory 2 sells for $9 and incurs $4 in shipping and production costs. A total of $5000 is available for promotion.

a. How can the beer company maximize its profit?

b. If an extra dollar could be spent on promotion, by approximately how much would the company's profit increase? By how much would its revenue increase?

c. Use SolverTable to see how a change in the price of beer 1 affects the optimal solution. Do the same for a change in the price of beer 2.

23. A firm is planning to spend $10,000 on advertising. It costs $3000 per minute to advertise on television and $1000 per minute to advertise on radio. If the firm buys x minutes of television advertising and y minutes of radio advertising, its revenue in thousands of dollars is given by $-2x^2 - y^2 + xy + 8x + 3y$. How can the firm maximize its revenue?

24. Proctor and Ramble has given you $12 million to spend on advertising Huggys diapers during the next 12 months. At the beginning of January, Huggys has a 30% market share. During any month, 10% of the people who purchase Huggys defect to brand X, and a fraction $0.2a^{1/2}$ of customers who usually buy brand X switch to Huggys, where a is the amount spent on advertising in millions of dollars. For example, if you spend $4 million during a month, 40% of brand X's customers switch to Huggys. Your goal is to maximize Proctor and Ramble's average market share during the next 12 months, where the average is computed from each month's ending share. Determine an appropriate advertising policy. (*Hint*: Make sure you enter a nonzero trial value for each month's advertising expense or the Solver might give you an error message.)

7.5 FACILITY LOCATION MODELS

Suppose you need to find a location for a facility such as a warehouse, a tool crib in a factory, or a fire station. Your goal is to locate the facility so as to minimize the total distance that must be traveled to provide required services. Facility location problems such as these can usually be set up as NLP models. The following example is typical.

EXAMPLE 7.6

WAREHOUSE LOCATION AT LAFFERTY

The Lafferty Company wants to locate a warehouse from which it will ship products to four customers. The location (in the x-y plane) of the four customers and the number of shipments per year needed by each customer are given in Table 7.5. (All locations are in miles, relative to the point $x = 0$ and $y = 0$.) A single warehouse must be used to service all of the customers. Lafferty wants to determine the location of the warehouse that minimizes the total distance traveled from the warehouse to the customers.

TABLE 7.5	Data for Lafferty Example		
	x	y	Shipments per Year
Customer 1	5	10	200
Customer 2	10	5	150
Customer 3	0	12	200
Customer 4	12	0	300

Solution

For the spreadsheet model we need to keep track of the following:

- the x and y coordinates of the warehouse and each customer
- the distance between the warehouse and each customer
- the total annual distance traveled from the warehouse to customers

DEVELOPING THE SPREADSHEET MODEL

To develop the spreadsheet model, use the following steps. (See Figure 7.19 and the file LAFFERTY.XLS.)

① **Inputs.** Enter the given customer data in the shaded ranges.

② **Coordinates of warehouse.** Enter *any* trial values in Location range for the x- and y-coordinates of the warehouse.

③ **Distances from warehouse to customers.** Calculate the distances from the warehouse to the customers in the Distances range. To do so, recall that the (straight-line) distance between the two points (a, b) and (c, d) is

$$\sqrt{(c - a)^2 + (d - b)^2}$$

Therefore, enter the formula

=SQRT((B5-\$B\$11)^2+(C5-\$C\$11)^2)

in cell B14 and copy it to the rest of the Distances range.

④ **Total annual distance.** The total annual distance traveled from the warehouse to meet the demands of all customers is

$$\sum_{i=1}^{4} n_i d_i$$

where n_i is the number of trips per year for customer i and d_i is the distance from the warehouse to customer i. Therefore, calculate the total annual distance traveled from the customers to the warehouse in the TotDistance cell with the formula

=SUMPRODUCT(Shipments,Distances)

USING THE SOLVER

This model requires the "leanest" Solver setup so far. All we need to specify is that TotDistance should be minimized and the Location range contains the changing cells. There are no constraints, not even nonnegativity constraints. Also, because of the squares in the straight-line distance formula, this model is nonlinear, so the Assume Linear Model box should *not* be checked.

FIGURE 7.19
Facility Location
Model

	A	B	C	D	E	F
1	Lafferty facility location model					
2						
3	Customer data					
4		X-coordinate	Y-coordinate		Annual shipments	
5	Customer 1	5	10		200	
6	Customer 2	10	5		150	
7	Customer 3	0	12		200	
8	Customer 4	12	0		300	
9						
10	Warehouse location	X-coordinate	Y-coordinate			
11		9.314	5.029			
12						
13	Customer distances from warehouse					
14	Customer 1	6.582				
15	Customer 2	0.686		Range names used:		
16	Customer 3	11.634		Shipments - E5:E8		
17	Customer 4	5.701		Location - B11:C11		
18				Distances - B14:B17		
19	Total annual distance	5456.540		TotDistance - B19		
20						
21	Testing optimality					
22	Is this solution optimal? Test it yourself. Click on the left button to generate a "random" set of starting values for					
23	the changing cells. Then click on the right button to run Solver. Does it always take you to the same solution?					
24						
25						
26		Generate random values			Run Solver	
27						

The Solver solution in Figure 7.19 is represented graphically in Figure 7.20. The warehouse should be located at $x = 9.31$ and $y = 5.03$. Each year a total of 5456.54 miles will be traveled annually from the warehouse to the customers. This solution represents a compromise. On the one hand, Lafferty would like to position the facility near customer 4 because the largest number of trips are made to customer 4. However, because customer 4 is fairly far from the other customers, the warehouse is located in a more central position.

FIGURE 7.20
Graph of Solution to
Lafferty Example

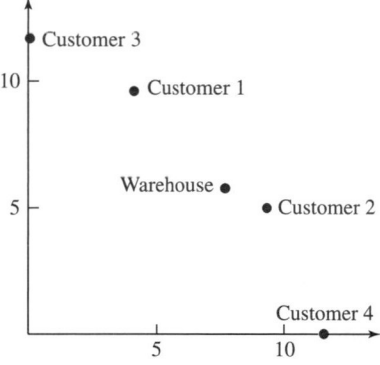

Sensitivity Analysis One possible sensitivity analysis is to see how the optimal location of the warehouse changes as the annual number of shipments to any particular customer increases. We do this for customer 4 in Figure 7.21 (page 362). We run SolverTable with the number of shipments to customer 4 (cell E8) as the single input cell, allowing it to vary from 300 to 700 in increments of 50, and we keep track of the total annual distance and the warehouse location coordinates. As expected, the total annual distance increases as the annual shipments to customer 4 increase. Also, the

FIGURE 7.21
Sensitivity Analysis
for Warehouse
Location

	A	B	C	D	E	F
28	Sensitivity of total distance and warehouse coordinates to shipments to customer 4					
29		$B$19	$B$11	$C$11		
30	300	5456.540	9.314	5.029		
31	350	5732.969	9.634	4.877		
32	400	6000.839	9.690	4.762		
33	450	6260.753	9.680	4.510		
34	500	6501.694	9.788	3.846		
35	550	6646.106	11.787	0.266		
36	600	6643.199	12.000	0.000		
37	650	6643.198	12.000	0.000		
38	700	6643.198	12.000	0.000		

warehouse gradually gets closer to customer 4. In fact, when the annual shipments to customer 4 are 600 or above, the optimal location for the warehouse is *at* customer 4.

Is the Solver Solution Optimal? The Lafferty model has no constraints. An NLP with no constraints is called an **unconstrained NLP**. Therefore, we know that the Solver will find an optimal solution if the objective is a convex function of the x- and y-coordinates of the warehouse. It can be shown (with some difficulty) that the annual distance traveled is indeed a convex function of the coordinates of the warehouse. Therefore, we know that the Solver solution is optimal. However, what if you do not know whether the objective is a convex function? Then the best strategy is to try different starting solutions in the Location range, run the Solver on each of them, and see whether they all take you to the same solution. In fact, we have made this easy for you in the LAFFERTY.XLS file. (Again see Figure 7.19.) We have written two short macros that are automated by clicking on buttons. Click on the left button to randomly generate a new starting location. Then click on the right button to run Solver. You should find that they always take you to the same solution.[4] ■

MODELING ISSUES

1. The straight-line distance function we used in the Lafferty example is relevant if the company is shipping by air. However, if it is shipping by road, we must take into account that most roads are built in a north–south or east–west direction. Then the relevant distance between points (a, b) and (c, d) is $|a - c| + |b - d|$, and this objective should be used in place of the square root objective. (See Problem 29.)

2. Besides assuming straight-line distance, we made two other assumptions in the Lafferty example: (1) exactly one warehouse will be built, and (2) this warehouse can be built *anywhere*. In real-world facility location problems, it might be necessary to modify these assumptions. First, it might be possible to build several warehouses. Second, the *possible* locations might be restricted to a certain subset of geographical locations. And third, the distances from all potential warehouse locations to customers might be given by a distance matrix, rather than calculated from some formula. In this situation, an IP model with binary variables would be more suitable. There would be a 0–1 variable for each potential warehouse location

---

[4]If you would like to write similar macros for other NLP models, it is fairly easy. With the LAFFERTY.XLS file open, press the Alt-F11 key combination to see the Visual Basic screen. The code for the macros is in the Module sheet for this file. Except for the line indicated and the range name of the changing cells, these macros can be used for other problems with no changes.

(either build there or don't) and a 0–1 variable for each warehouse–customer pair (either supply that customer from that warehouse or don't).

3. If our objective were to minimize the total distance traveled to meet customer demand, then it can be shown (see Problem 28) that the warehouse should be located at the "center of gravity" of all customer demands. For example, if one customer is located at (2, 3) and another at (4, 5), then the warehouse would need to be located at the "average" of these coordinates: (3, 4). ■

ADDITIONAL APPLICATIONS

Love and Yerex (1976) used a facility location model similar to Lafferty's to help Coastal Construction Company of Portsmouth, Virginia, locate two new production facilities. See Problem 29 for a scaled-down version of this type of application. ■

PROBLEMS

Skill-Building Problems

25. The area of a triangle with sides of length a, b, and c is

$$\sqrt{s(s-a)(s-b)(s-c)}$$

where s is half the perimeter of the triangle. Suppose that we have 600 feet of fence and we want to fence a triangular-shaped area. Determine how to maximize the fenced area.

26. Three cities are located at the vertices of an equilateral triangle. An airport is to be built at a location that minimizes the total (straight-line) distance from the airport to the three cities. Determine where to build the airport.

27. Based on Kolesar and Blum (1973). Suppose that a company must service customers lying in an area of A square miles with n warehouses. Kolesar and Blum showed that when the warehouse(s) are located properly, the average distance between a warehouse and a customer is $(A/n)^{1/2}$. Assume that it costs the company $60,000 per year to maintain a warehouse and $400,000 to build a warehouse. Also, assume that a $400,000 cost is equivalent to incurring a cost of $40,000 per year indefinitely. The company fills 160,000 orders per year, and the shipping cost per order is $1 per mile. If the company serves an area of 100 square miles, how many warehouses should it have?

28. A company has five factories. The x- and y-coordinates of the location of each factory are given in Table 7.6. The company wants to locate a warehouse at a point that minimizes the sum of the squared distances of the plants from the warehouse. Where should the warehouse be located?

TABLE 7.6	Locations for Factory Problem	
	x	y
Factory 1	6	−5
Factory 2	8	4
Factory 3	5	2
Factory 4	−5	4
Factory 5	−3	2

29. Based on Love and Yerex (1976). Steelco's main plant currently has a steel manufacturing area and shipping area located as shown in Figure 7.22 (where distances are in hundreds of feet). The company must determine where to locate a casting facility and an assembly and storage facility to minimize the daily cost of moving material through the plant.

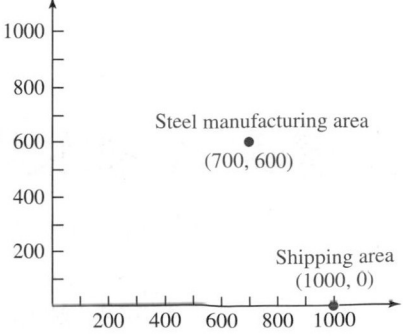

FIGURE 7.22 Existing Locations for Steelco Problem

The number of trips made each day and the cost per 100 feet of each trip are as shown in Table 7.7.

a. Assuming that all travel is in an east–west or north–south direction, determine where the casting and assembly/storage plants should be located to minimize daily transportation costs. (*Hint*: Use changing cells for the amount by which each area is east, west, north, and south of each facility.)

b. Assuming that all travel is in a straight line, determine where the casting and assembly/storage plants should be located.

30. Monroe County is trying to determine where to place the county fire station. The locations of the county's four major towns are as follows. Town 1 is at the point (10, 20); town 2 is at (60, 20); town 3 is at (40, 30); and town 4 is at (80, 60). (See Figure 7.23.) Town 1 averages 20 fires per year; town 2, 30 fires; town 3, 40 fires; and town 4, 25 fires. The county wants to build the fire station in a location that minimizes the average distance that a fire engine must travel to respond to a fire. Since most roads run in either an east–west or a north–south direction, we assume that the fire engine must do the same. For example, if the fire station is located at (30, 40) and

a fire occurs at town 4, the fire engine has to travel $|80 - 30| + |60 - 40| = 70$ miles to the fire.

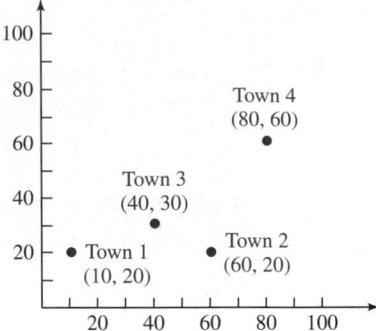

FIGURE 7.23 Existing Locations for Fire Station Problem

a. Determine where the fire station should be located.

b. Use SolverTable to see how the optimal location of the fire station changes as the number of fires at town 3 changes.

TABLE 7.7	Data for Steelco Problem		
		Daily Trips	**Cost/100 Feet**
From casting to assembly & storage		40	$0.10
From steel manufacturing to casting		8	$0.10
From steel manufacturing to assembly & storage		8	$0.10
From shipping to assembly & storage		2	$0.20

7.6 RATING SPORTS TEAMS

Sports fans always wonder which team is best in a given sport. Was Florida State, Notre Dame, or Nebraska number 1 during the 1993 NCAA football season? You might be surprised to learn that the Solver can be used to rate sports teams. We examine one method for doing this in the following example.

EXAMPLE 7.7

RATING NFL TEAMS

We wish to determine the rating of NFL teams for the 1998 season, based on all games played during the season (including the playoffs).

Solution

We examined the results of 249 NFL games from the 1998 season and entered the data into a spreadsheet, shown at the bottom of Figure 7.24 (see the file NFL98 RATINGS.XLS). (Some of these results are hidden in Figure 7.24 for reasons of space.) The teams are indexed 1–30, as shown at the top of the sheet. For example, team 1 is Arizona, team 2 is Atlanta, and so on. The first game entered (row 45) was team 16 (Minnesota) versus team 28 (Tampa Bay) at Minnesota. The margin of victory

	A	B	C	D	E	F
1	Rating NFL teams - sum of squared errors criterion					
2						
3	Home team advantage	3.48				
4					Range names used:	
5	Ratings of teams				HomeAd - B3	
6	Index	Team name	Rating		LTable - A7:C36	
7	1	Arizona Cardinals	79.47		Ratings - C7:C36	
8	2	Atlanta Falcons	95.14		AvgRating - B40	
9	3	Baltimore Ravens	79.67		Nominal - D40	
10	4	Buffalo Bills	89.41		Errors - F45:F293	
11	5	Carolina Panthers	83.24		SumSqErrors - B295	
12	6	Chicago Bears	81.33			
13	7	Cincinnati Bengals	74.12			
14	8	Dallas Cowboys	87.46			
15	9	Denver Broncos	96.08			
16	10	Detroit Lions	82.15			
17	11	Green Bay Packers	89.86			
18	12	Indianapolis Colts	79.08			
19	13	Jacksonville Jaguars	88.22			
20	14	Kansas City Chiefs	82.38			
21	15	Miami Dolphins	89.28			
22	16	Minnesota Vikings	99.07			
23	17	New England Patriots	87.79			
24	18	New Orleans Saints	84.71			
25	19	New York Giants	82.16			
26	20	New York Jets	95.12			
27	21	Oakland Raiders	79.78			
28	22	Philadelphia Eagles	72.68			
29	23	Pittsburgh Steelers	81.25			
30	24	St. Louis Rams	82.34			
31	25	San Diego Chargers	77.16			
32	26	San Francisco 49ers	95.07			
33	27	Seattle Seahawks	86.92			
34	28	Tampa Bay Buccaneers	86.27			
35	29	Tennessee Oilers	85.00			
36	30	Washington Redskins	77.82			
37						
38	Constraint on average rating (any nominal value could be used)					
39		Actual		Nominal		
40		85.0	=	85		
41						
42	Estimation model					
43		Results of games			Model predictions and errors	
44		Home team index	Visiting team index	Point spread	Predicted spread	Error
45		16	28	24	16.2776	7.7224
46		19	30	7	7.8232	-0.8232
47		3	23	-7	1.9023	-8.9023
292		18	2	-3	7.4137	-10.4137
293		9	20	13	4.4413	8.5587
294						
295	Sum of squared errors	28195.76				

FIGURE 7.24 NFL Ratings Model

for the home team is given in column D. We see that Minnesota won the game in row 45 by 24 points. A positive point spread in column D means that the home team won; a negative point spread indicates that the visiting team won. Our goal is to determine a set of ratings for the 30 NFL teams that most accurately predicts the outcomes of the games played.

Suppose that team i plays at home against team j. Then our prediction for the outcome of the game is that the point spread will be

$$\text{Predicted margin} = \text{Team } i \text{ rating} - \text{Team } j \text{ rating} + \text{Home advantage}$$

The home advantage is the number of points extra for the home team because of the psychological (or physical) advantage of playing on their home field. Football experts claim that this home field advantage in the NFL is about 3 points. However, we will estimate it, as well as the ratings. We define the prediction error to be

$$\text{Error} = \text{Actual point spread} - \text{Predicted point spread}$$

We wish to determine ratings that minimize the sum of squared prediction errors. To get a unique answer to the problem, we need to "normalize" the ratings—that is, fix the average rating to some nominal value. Because the well-known Sagarin ratings use a nominal value in the mid-80s, we will use a nominal value of 85. (*Any* nominal value could be used to produce exactly the same *relative* ratings.)

DEVELOPING THE SPREADSHEET MODEL

To produce the model in Figure 7.24, proceed as follows.

1 **Input game data.** If you want to find the ratings for any NFL season (or for the NBA, MLB, and so on), you will probably have to get the data off the Web. (We are fortunate to have an inside contact—the first author went to school with the famous Jeff Sagarin!)

2 **Changing cells.** Enter *any* value for the home field advantage and the 30 ratings in the HomeAd and Ratings ranges. Note that it would be possible to use a "given" value for the home field advantage, such as 3, but we will let the Solver choose the home field advantage that best describes the data.

3 **Average rating.** Enter the nominal rating in the Nominal cell, and average the ratings in the AvgRating cell with the formula

=AVERAGE(Ratings)

4 **Predictions.** We have entered the data on games played by referring to the team index numbers. This allows us to use lookup functions to predict the point spreads. To do this, enter the formula

=HomeAd+VLOOKUP(B45,LTable,3)-VLOOKUP(C45,LTable,3)

in cell E45 for the first game, and copy it down column E for the rest of the games.

5 **Errors.** We want to minimize the sum of squared errors. Therefore, enter the formula

=D45-E45

in cell F45, copy it down, and use Excel's SUMSQ function to sum the squares of the errors in the SumSqErrors cell:

=SUMSQ(Errors)

SOLVER

USING THE SOLVER

The completed Solver dialog box should appear as in Figure 7.25. This is another unconstrained model. We simply find the ratings and home field advantage that minimize the sum of squared prediction errors.

FIGURE 7.25
Solver Dialog Box for
NFL Ratings Model

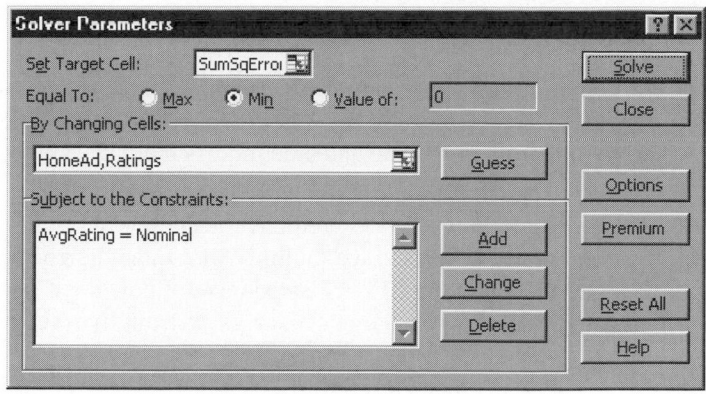

The solution in Figure 7.24 shows that a home field advantage of 3.48 provides the best fit. To give you a better picture of the ratings, we have sorted them from best to worst in Figure 7.26. You might recall that Denver won the Super Bowl, but that is not quite what the ratings predicted. (Of course, no mathematical model can accurately capture the effect of John Elway playing his final NFL game.) The actual values of the ratings are not as important as the *differences* between teams' ratings.

FIGURE 7.26
Sorted NFL Ratings

	G	H
5	**Sorted from best to worst**	
6	Team name	Rating
7	Minnesota Vikings	99.07
8	Denver Broncos	96.00
9	Atlanta Falcons	95.14
10	New York Jets	95.12
11	San Francisco 49ers	95.07
12	Green Bay Packers	89.86
13	Buffalo Bills	89.41
14	Miami Dolphins	89.28
15	Jacksonville Jaguars	88.22
16	New England Patriots	87.79
17	Dallas Cowboys	87.46
18	Seattle Seahawks	86.92
19	Tampa Bay Buccaneers	86.27
20	Tennessee Oilers	85.00
21	New Orleans Saints	84.71
22	Carolina Panthers	83.24
23	Kansas City Chiefs	82.38
24	St. Louis Rams	82.34
25	New York Giants	82.16
26	Detroit Lions	82.15
27	Chicago Bears	81.33
28	Pittsburgh Steelers	81.25
29	Oakland Raiders	79.78
30	Baltimore Ravens	79.67
31	Arizona Cardinals	79.47
32	Indianapolis Colts	79.08
33	Washington Redskins	77.82
34	San Diego Chargers	77.16
35	Cincinnati Bengals	74.12
36	Philadelphia Eagles	72.68

For example, we predict that if Atlanta played Arizona at Atlanta, Atlanta would win by $3.48 + (95.14 - 79.47) \approx 19$ points. Of course, there is a considerable amount of uncertainty in any game. We might *predict* Atlanta to win by 19 points, but the actual outcome could be much different. [5] ■

MODELING ISSUES

1. This model does not capture the effect of "intangibles" such as injuries to key players. If we were going to bet real money on NFL games, we might start with the ratings from the model and then modify them in a subjective fashion to capture any inside knowledge we might have.

2. We can improve the future predictive accuracy by giving more weight to more recent games. To do this, we multiply the squared error for a game k weeks ago by a factor such as $(0.95)^k$. As an example of how this "discounts" the importance of past games, this weighting gives a game from five weeks ago about 77% of the weight given to this week's game.

3. We can also use the Solver to find the set of ratings that minimize the sum of *absolute* prediction errors. When we did this with the 1998 data (see the SAE sheet of the NFL98RATINGS.XLS file), the ordering of teams change slightly, with the New York Jets coming out on top.

4. The average *absolute* error for the games in Figure 7.24 was 8.28 points per game. (This value does not appear in the figure.) If we used our ratings to forecast one more week of NFL games, we would probably see an average absolute error exceeding 8.28 points. This is because most forecasting models fail to perform as well on data they have not yet seen as on the data used to generate the forecasts. This phenomenon is called **overfitting**. ■

PROBLEMS

Skill-Building Problems

31. The file NFL96.XLS lists the scores of all NFL games played during the 1996 season. Use this data set to rank the NFL teams from best to worst.

32. The file NFL97.XLS lists the scores of all NFL games played during the 1997 season. Using all data except for the last game (which is the Super Bowl), rank the NFL teams from best to worst. Then make a forecast for this Super Bowl. (Note that the bookmakers favored Green Bay by 11 in this game, which Denver won, but you should find that our model is right on the money!)

33. In the Bloomington Girls Club Basketball League, the following games have been played: team A beat team B by 7 points, team C beat team A by 8 points, team B beat team C by 6 points, and team B beat team C by 9 points. Let A, B, and C represent "ratings" for the teams in the sense that if, say, team A plays team B, we predict that team A will win by $A - B$ points (or lose by $B - A$ points if $A - B$ is negative). (We assume that there is no home-court advantage.) Determine values of A, B, and C that best fit (in the least-squares sense) these results. To obtain a unique set of ratings, add the constraint that $A + B + C = 0$. This ensures that an "average" team will have a rating of 0.

34. The file BIG94.XLS contains the scores of the 1994 Big Ten Basketball season. Develop ratings for the 11 teams. Use a home team advantage of 5 points. Which was the best team? The worst team? If you are an Indiana fan, try it again after deleting Indiana's huge loss to Minnesota. See how much this "outlier" affects the results.

[5] In the previous edition of this book, the ratings were based on the 1991 season, and our beloved Indianapolis Colts were rated dead last. They showed some improvement in the 1998 season, but not much. Wait for the next edition!

7.7 ESTIMATING THE BETA OF A STOCK

For financial analysts it is important to be able to predict the return on a stock from the return on the market, that is, on a market index such as the S&P 500 index. Here, the **return** on an investment over a time period is the percentage change in its value over the time period. It is often hypothesized that

$$r_s = \alpha + \beta r_m + \varepsilon \tag{7.4}$$

where r_s is the return on a stock during a time period, r_m is the return on the market during the same time period, ε is a random "error" term, and α and β are constants that must be estimated. The true value of β in equation (7.4), which we will never know, but can only estimate, is called the **beta** of the stock. From equation (7.4) we see that an increase in the market return of 1% will increase the return on the stock by $\beta\%$ (on average). Therefore, β is a measure of the responsiveness of a stock's return to changes in the market return. The returns on stocks with large positive or negative β's are highly sensitive to the business cycle.

Sharpe's **capital asset pricing model** (CAPM) implies that stocks with large beta values are riskier and therefore must yield higher returns than those with small beta values. This implies that if you can estimate beta values more accurately than people on Wall Street, then you can better identify overvalued and undervalued stocks and make a lot of money!

How do people usually estimate the beta of a stock? Most often, they run a regression analysis with the monthly return on the stock as the "response" (or dependent) variable and the monthly return on the market as the "explanatory" (or independent) variable. Because we have not yet covered regression analysis (see Chapter 15), we will explore other methods for estimating betas in this section. Specifically, we discuss four methods that (in conjunction with the Solver) can be used to estimate α and β in equation (7.4). This requires a set of observations, where an observation gives both the market return and the return on the stock during a particular time period. (We will use monthly data.)

Let a and b denote potential estimates of the unknown parameters α and β. Then for month i we generate a prediction of the return on the stock with the equation

$$\widehat{r}_{si} = a + br_{mi} \tag{7.5}$$

Here, $\widehat{r}_{si}$ is the predicted stock return for period i, and r_{mi} is the actual market return for period i. The *error* for period i, labeled e_i, is defined as

$$e_i = r_{si} - \widehat{r}_{si} \tag{7.6}$$

That is, the error is the actual return of the stock minus the predicted return. If our predictions were perfect, then all of the errors in equation (7.6) would equal 0. However, this is generally impossible, so we will instead try to choose the estimates a and b to make the errors "close" to 0. We now discuss four possible criteria for choosing these estimates.

Criterion 1: Sum of Squared Errors (Least Squares)

Here we try to minimize the sum of the squared errors over all observations. The sum of the squared errors is a convex function of the estimates a and b, so the Solver is guaranteed to find the (unique) estimates of α and β that minimize the sum of squared errors. The main problem with the least squares criterion is that outliers [points for which the error in equation (7.6) is especially large] exert a disproportionate influence on the estimates of α and β.

Criterion 2: Weighted Sum of Squared Errors

Criterion 1 gives equal weight to older and more recent observations. It stands to reason that more recent observations might have more to say about the beta of a stock, at least for future predictions, than older observations. To incorporate this idea, we can give a smaller weight to the squared errors for older observations. While this method usually leads to more accurate predictions of the future than least squares, the least squares method has many desirable statistical properties that weighted least squares estimates do not possess.

Criterion 3: Sum of Absolute Errors (SAE)

Instead of minimizing the sum of the squared errors, we can minimize the sum of the absolute errors for all observations. This is often called the **sum of absolute errors (SAE)** approach. This method has the advantage of not being greatly affected by outliers. Unfortunately, little is known about the statistical properties of SAE estimates. Another drawback to SAE is that there can be more than one combination of a and b that minimizes SAE. However, SAE estimates have the advantage that they can be obtained with *linear* programming.

Criterion 4: Minimax

Here we try to minimize the *maximum* absolute error over all observations. This method might be appropriate for a highly risk-averse decision maker. (See Chapter 10.) This **minimax** criterion can also be implemented using LP.

The following example illustrates how the Solver can be used to obtain estimates of α and β for these four criteria.

EXAMPLE 7.8

ESTIMATING BETAS OF PROMINENT COMPANIES

We obtained five years of monthly closing price data for more than 30 company stocks, along with data for the S&P 500 market index over the same months. (We got these data from Yahoo!®'s finance Web page. Fortunately, the downloaded data are automatically adjusted for stock splits and dividends.) The data extend from July 1994 to June 1999. Do the betas for these stocks depend on the criterion used to estimate them? Are the estimates the same if we base them on only the most recent *three* years of data, rather than on all five years?

Solution

The data are in the file BETA.XLS. There is a separate sheet for each company, to hold its closing prices and calculated returns. A typical sheet, for American Express, appears in Figure 7.27. There is a similar sheet for the S&P 500 market index. We perform our calculations in a sheet named Model, as shown in Figure 7.28. For any selected company, we set up the sheet so that we can use any of the four criteria and either the 3-year period or the entire 5-year period simply by changing the target cell in the Solver dialog box. The following steps are required.

1. **Calculate returns.** The downloaded data from the Web are closing *prices*, not returns. To calculate the returns (in Figure 7.27), enter the formula

   =(B4-B5)/B5

FIGURE 7.27
Stock Price Data for
American Express

	A	B	C	D	E
1	Monthly closing prices and returns for American Express				
2					
3	Date	Close	Return		
4	Jun-99	130.125	0.07677		
5	May-99	120.848	-0.07365		
6	Apr-99	130.456	0.10988		
7	Mar-99	117.541	0.08724		
8	Feb-99	108.11	0.05468		
9	Jan-99	102.505	0.00593		
10	Dec-98	101.901	0.02436		
11	Nov-98	99.4775	0.13586		
12	Oct-98	87.5787	0.13847		
13	Sep-98	76.9266	-0.00481		
58	Dec-94	27.5869	0.00347		
59	Nov-94	27.4916	-0.04049		
60	Oct-94	28.6516	0.02405		
61	Sep-94	27.9788	0.08000		
62	Aug-94	25.9063	0.06132		
63	Jul-94	24.4095			
64					

in cell C4 and copy down through cell C62. (Note that there is no return for July 1994 because we do not have the closing price from June 1994.) Actually, you can calculate these returns simultaneously for *all* of the stocks, including the S&P 500 index. To do so, click on the tab of the leftmost sheet (S&P500), hold down the Shift key, and click on the tab of the rightmost sheet (IBM). This selects all of these sheets. Then enter the formula and copy down as instructed above.

	A	B	C	D	E	F	G	H	I	J	K
1	Estimation model for American Express: 5-year period, sum of squared errors estimation method										
2											
3	Parameters										
4	Alpha	0.0054									
5	Beta	1.3420									
6											
7	Weighting constant	0.995									
8											
9											
10		Date	Mkt return	Stock return	Predicted	Error	SqError	AbsError	Weight		
11		Jun-99	0.0544	0.07677	0.0785	-0.0017	0.00000	0.0017	1.0000		
12		May-99	-0.0250	-0.07365	-0.0281	-0.0455	0.00207	0.0455	0.9950		
13		Apr-99	0.0379	0.10988	0.0563	0.0536	0.00287	0.0536	0.9900		
14		Mar-99	0.0388	0.08724	0.0575	0.0298	0.00089	0.0298	0.9851		
15		Feb-99	-0.0323	0.05468	-0.0379	0.0926	0.00858	0.0926	0.9801		
16		Jan-99	0.0410	0.00593	0.0604	-0.0545	0.00297	0.0545	0.9752		
17		Dec-98	0.0564	0.02436	0.0810	-0.0567	0.00321	0.0567	0.9704		
18		Nov-98	0.0591	0.13586	0.0847	0.0511	0.00261	0.0511	0.9655		
19		Oct-98	0.0803	0.13847	0.1131	0.0253	0.00064	0.0253	0.9607		
20		Sep-98	0.0624	-0.00481	0.0891	-0.0939	0.00882	0.0939	0.9559		
21		Aug-98	-0.1458	-0.29332	-0.1903	-0.1030	0.01062	0.1030	0.9511		
22		Jul-98	-0.0116	-0.02967	-0.0102	-0.0195	0.00038	0.0195	0.9464		
68		Sep-94	-0.0269	0.08000	-0.0307	0.1107	0.01225	0.1107	0.7515		
69		Aug-94	0.0376	0.06132	0.0559	0.0055	0.00003	0.0055	0.7477		
70											
71	Possible objectives										
72			3-year	5-year							
73	SSE	0.10012	0.15525								
74	WSSE	0.09319	0.13713								
75	SAE	1.49874	2.44465								
76	MaxAE	0.10907	0.11068								

Range names used:
Alpha - B4
Beta - B5
AlphaBeta - B4:B5
Weight - B7
SqErr3 - F11:F45
SqErr5 - F11:F69
AbsErr3 - G11:G45
AbsErr5 - G11:G69
Weight3 - H11:H45
Weight5 - H11:H69
SSE3 - B73
SSE5 - C73
WSSE3 - B74
WSSE5 - C74
SAE3 - B75
SAE5 - C75
MaxAE - B76
MaxAE - C76

FIGURE 7.28 Beta Estimation Model

2. **Alpha, beta.** (From here on, all instructions relate to the Model sheet, shown in Figure 7.28.) Enter *any* values of alpha and beta in cells B4 and B5. These can be negative or positive.

3. **Links to returns.** Select cell B11, type =, and then point to cell C4 of the S&P500 sheet. This will enter the formula

   ='S&P500'!C4

   in the cell B11 and hence form a link to the first return in the S&P500 sheet. Create a similar link in cell C11 to the first return in the AXP (American Express) sheet. Then copy these down columns B and C.

4. **Predictions.** Predict the stock returns from equation (7.5) by entering the formula

   =Alpha+Beta*B11

   in cell D11 and copying down.

5. **Errors, squared errors, and absolute errors.** The "error" in any row is the actual stock return minus the predicted stock return. Therefore, enter the formulas

   =C11-D11
   =E11^2
   =ABS(E11)

   in cells E11, F11, and G11, and copy these down.

6. **Weights.** (This is for the weighted sum of squares criterion only.) Enter a desired weighting constant in cell B7. Then enter 1 in cell H11, enter the formula

   =Weight*H11

   in cell H12, and copy this formula down column H. This makes each weight a constant fraction of the previous weight.

7. **Objectives.** We set up eight possible objectives in the range B73:C76. Enter the formulas

   =SUM(SqErr3)
   =SUMPRODUCT(SqErr3,Weight3)
   =SUM(AbsErr3)
   =MAX(AbsErr3)

   in cells B73 through B76, and enter similar formulas, substituting 5 for 3, in cells C73 through C76.

USING THE SOLVER

The completed Solver dialog box should look similar to Figure 7.29, except that *any* of the eight possible objective cells can be used as the target cell. There are no constraints, not even nonnegativity constraints, and the Assume Linear Model box should *not* be checked.

The solution in Figure 7.28 indicates that American Express is fairly sensitive to the market, having a beta of well over 1 for the sum of squared errors criterion when all 5 years of data are used. If you change the objective, you will find that the beta for American Express is between 1.3 and 1.4 for all four criteria (using the weight 0.995 for weighted sum of squares) when all 5 years of data are used, and it increases slightly (as high as 1.46 for SAE) when only the most recent 3 years of data are used.

To run this analysis for any other stock, simply create the appropriate link to *its* returns in column C of the Model sheet and rerun the Solver. You will find that the

FIGURE 7.29
Solver Dialog Box
for Beta Estimation
Model

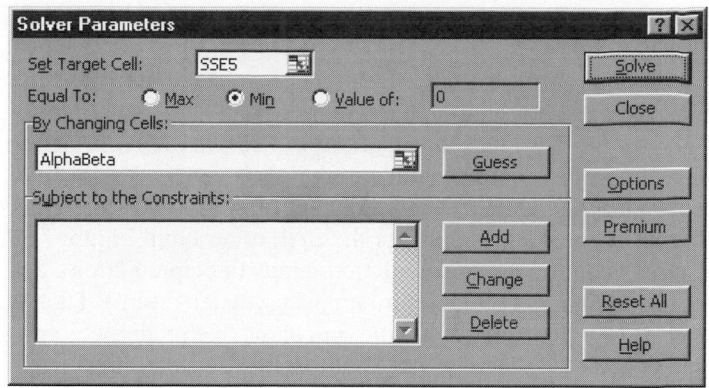

betas for different companies can vary widely. For example, the beta for Exxon is approximately 0.6 (using the SSE criterion with all 5 years of data), whereas it is between 0.9 and 1.1 for Coca Cola, McDonald's, and most of the other companies we selected.

Alternative Modeling Approaches You might have noticed that we ignored one of our own warnings in this example. Specifically, the SAE and minimax objectives we used depend on the ABS and MAX functions. Does the Solver provide the correct solution for these two criteria? We cannot answer with a definitive "yes," but it appears that the solutions are correct for the problems we solved. Basically, the Solver has difficulty with ABS and MAX functions when the objective or constraints are not sufficiently "smooth," and it appears that the objectives used here pass the smoothness test. However, we indicate in Figures 7.30 and 7.31 (page 374) alternative models for the SAE and minimax criteria. (See the files BETA3_ALT.XLS and BETA4_ALT.XLS.) The advantage of these alternative models is that they guarantee optimal Solver solutions. In fact, they are set up as *linear* models—so that the Assume Linear Model can be checked—and the Solver *always* solves linear models optimally. The drawback to

	A	B	C	D	E	F	G	H	I
1	Estimation model for American Express: 5-year period, sum of absolute errors estimation method								
2									
3	Parameters								
4	Alpha	0.0024							
5	Beta	1.3661							
6									
7		Date	Mkt return	Stock return	Predicted	OverPredict	UnderPredict	Over-Under		Error
8		Jun-99	0.0544	0.07677	0.0768	0.0000	0.00000	0.0000	=	0.0000
9		May-99	-0.0250	-0.07365	-0.0317	0.0000	0.04194	-0.0419	=	-0.0419
10		Apr-99	0.0379	0.10988	0.0542	0.0556	0.00000	0.0556	=	0.0556
11		Mar-99	0.0388	0.08724	0.0554	0.0318	0.00000	0.0318	=	0.0318
12		Feb-99	-0.0323	0.05468	-0.0417	0.0964	0.00000	0.0964	=	0.0964
13		Jan-99	0.0410	0.00593	0.0584	0.0000	0.05249	-0.0525	=	-0.0525
14		Dec-98	0.0564	0.02436	0.0794	0.0000	0.05505	-0.0550	=	-0.0550
15		Nov-98	0.0591	0.13586	0.0832	0.0527	0.00000	0.0527	=	0.0527
16		Oct-98	0.0803	0.13847	0.1121	0.0264	0.00000	0.0264	=	0.0264
17		Sep-98	0.0624	-0.00481	0.0876	0.0000	0.09244	-0.0924	=	-0.0924
64		Oct-94	0.0208	0.02405	0.0309	0.0000	0.00681	-0.0068	=	-0.0068
65		Sep-94	-0.0269	0.08000	-0.0343	0.1143	0.00000	0.1143	=	0.1143
66		Aug-94	0.0376	0.06132	0.0538	0.0076	0.00000	0.0076	=	0.0076
67										
68	SAE	2.4361								

FIGURE 7.30 Alternative Linear Model for SAE Criterion

these models is that they are somewhat more difficult to understand, relying as they do on modeling "tricks."

In both of these alternative models, we set up two new columns of changing cells for overprediction and underprediction which we constrain to be nonnegative. In the Solver solution, at least one of these will be 0 in each time period (we either overpredict or underpredict, but not both), so that their sum is the absolute prediction error. Then the trick is to calculate the prediction errors in two different ways. For example, we do this in columns G and I for the SAE criterion in Figure 7.30. Column G is column E minus column F (overprediction minus underprediction), and column I is column C minus column D (actual return minus predicted return). Then we constrain columns G and I to be equal, and we use the sum of the overpredictions and underpredictions—that is, the sum of absolute errors—as the objective to minimize. Note that this SAE model never uses the ABS function.

The alternative minimax model requires one further complication. We need to find the maximum absolute error without using the MAX function. Now the trick is to set up one more changing cell, in cell B7, as a trial value of the maximum absolute error. Then we constrain all overpredictions and underpredictions to be less than or equal to this trial value—this is indicated in columns E through I of Figure 7.31—and we set the objective in cell B70 equal to this trial value. When we minimize this objective, the constraints force the trial maximum error value to be just large enough so that it is no less than any of the overpredictions or underpredictions.

Like all spreadsheet modelers, we prefer straightforward models and hate to resort to tricks. However, until the Solver is capable of dealing accurately with functions such as MAX and ABS—which *will* undoubtedly occur in the near future—we must sometimes use clever "workarounds" to produce Solver-capable models.

	A	B	C	D	E	F	G	H	I	J	K	L
1	Estimation model for American Express: 5-year period, minimax estimation method											
2												
3	Parameters											
4	Alpha	0.0130										
5	Beta	1.3858										
6												
7	Trial max abs error	0.1043										
8												
9		Date	Mkt return	Stock return	Predicted	OverPredict		Max Error		UnderPredict	Over-Under		Error
10		Jun-99	0.0544	0.07677	0.0884	0.0000	<=	0.1043	>=	0.01166	-0.0117	=	-0.0117
11		May-99	-0.0250	-0.07365	-0.0216	0.0000	<=	0.1043	>=	0.05203	-0.0520	=	-0.0520
12		Apr-99	0.0379	0.10988	0.0656	0.0443	<=	0.1043	>=	0.00000	0.0443	=	0.0443
13		Mar-99	0.0388	0.08724	0.0667	0.0205	<=	0.1043	>=	0.00000	0.0205	=	0.0205
14		Feb-99	-0.0323	0.05468	-0.0318	0.0864	<=	0.1043	>=	0.00000	0.0864	=	0.0864
15		Jan-99	0.0410	0.00593	0.0698	0.0404	<=	0.1043	>=	0.10426	-0.0639	=	-0.0639
16		Dec-98	0.0564	0.02436	0.0911	0.0000	<=	0.1043	>=	0.06675	-0.0667	=	-0.0667
17		Nov-98	0.0591	0.13586	0.0949	0.0409	<=	0.1043	>=	0.00000	0.0409	=	0.0409
64		Dec-94	0.0123	0.00347	0.0300	0.0000	<=	0.1043	>=	0.02656	-0.0266	=	-0.0266
65		Nov-94	-0.0395	-0.04049	-0.0418	0.0013	<=	0.1043	>=	0.00000	0.0013	=	0.0013
66		Oct-94	0.0208	0.02405	0.0419	0.0000	<=	0.1043	>=	0.01781	-0.0178	=	-0.0178
67		Sep-94	-0.0269	0.08000	-0.0243	0.1043	<=	0.1043	>=	0.00000	0.1043	=	0.1043
68		Aug-94	0.0376	0.06132	0.0651	0.0000	<=	0.1043	>=	0.00377	-0.0038	=	-0.0038
69												
70	Max Abs Error	0.1043										

FIGURE 7.31 Alternative Linear Model for Minimax Criterion

Skill-Building Problems

35. Given the information in Table 7.8, use the four criteria discussed in this section to estimate the β (and α) for GM.

TABLE 7.8	Returns for GM Problem	
	Return on GM Stock	Return on S&P 500
1961	12%	21%
1962	2%	−3%
1963	38%	15%
1964	26%	20%
1965	18%	12%
1966	−10%	0%
1967	0%	10%
1968	9%	10%
1969	−2%	2%
1970	−1%	−15%

36. Widco has observed the daily production and daily variable production cost of widgets produced at its New York City plant. The data in Table 7.9 have been collected. Widco believes that daily production and daily variable costs are related as follows. For some numbers α and β,

Daily variable cost $= \alpha + \beta *$ Daily production
$+$ Error term

Use the four methods of this section to estimate α and β.

TABLE 7.9	Data for Widco Problem	
	Production	Variable Cost
Day 1	4000	$9,000
Day 2	6000	$12,000
Day 3	7000	$14,000
Day 4	1000	$5,000
Day 5	3000	$8,000

7.8 PORTFOLIO OPTIMIZATION

Given a set of investments, how do we find the portfolio that has the lowest risk and yields an acceptable expected return? This question was answered by Harry Markowitz in the 1950s. For his work on this and other investment topics, he received the Nobel Prize in economics in 1991. The ideas discussed in this section are the basis for most methods of **asset allocation** used by Wall Street firms. Asset allocation models are used, for example, to determine the percentage of assets to invest in stocks, gold, and Treasury bills. Before proceeding, however, we need to discuss some important formulas involving the expected value and variance of sums of random variables.

Weighted Sums of Random Variables

Let S_i be the (random) return earned during a year on a dollar invested in investment i. Thus if $S_i = 0.10$, a dollar invested at the beginning of the year grows to $1.10 at the end of the year, whereas if $S_i = -0.20$, a dollar invested at the beginning of the year decreases in value to $0.80. We assume that n investments are available. Let x_i be the fraction of our money invested in investment i. We assume that $x_1 + x_2 + \cdots + x_n = 1$, so that all of our money is invested. To rule out shorting a stock—that is, selling shares we don't own—we assume that $x_i \geq 0$. Then the annual return on our investments is given by the random variable R, where

$$R = x_1 S_1 + x_2 S_2 + \cdots + x_n S_n$$

Let μ_i be the expected value (also called the mean) of S_i, let σ_i^2 be the variance of S_i (so that σ_i is the standard deviation of S_i), and let ρ_{ij} be the correlation between S_i and S_j. To do any work with investments, you must understand how to use the following formulas, which relate the data for the individual investments to the expected return and the variance of return for a *portfolio* of investments.

$$\text{Expected value of } R = x_1\mu_1 + x_2\mu_2 + \cdots + x_n\mu_n \qquad (7.7)$$

$$\text{Variance of } R = x_1^2\sigma_1^2 + x_2^2\sigma_2^2 + \cdots + x_n^2\sigma_n^2 + \sum_{i \neq j} x_i x_j \rho_{ij}\sigma_i\sigma_j \qquad (7.8)$$

The latter summation in the variance formula is over all *pairs* of investments.

Because we never actually know the true expected values (μ_i's), variances (σ_i^2's), and correlations (ρ_{ij}'s), we must estimate them. If historical data are available, we can proceed as follows.

1. Estimate μ_i by $\overline{X}_i$, the sample average of returns on investment i over several previous years. You can use the Excel AVERAGE function to obtain $\overline{X}_i$.

2. Estimate σ_i^2 by s_i^2, the sample variance of returns on investment i over several previous years. You can use the Excel VAR function to obtain s_i^2.

3. Estimate σ_i by s_i, the sample standard deviation of returns on investment i. You can obtain s_i with the Excel STDEV function. (Alternatively, of course, you can obtain s_i as the square root of s_i^2.)

4. Estimate ρ_{ij} by r_{ij}, the sample correlation between past returns on investments i and j. You can find all of the r_{ij}'s by using Excel's CORREL function.

We now estimate the mean and variance of the return on a portfolio by replacing each parameter in equations (7.7) and (7.8) with its sample estimate. This yields

$$\text{Estimated expected value of } R = x_1\overline{X}_1 + x_2\overline{X}_2 + \cdots + x_n\overline{X}_n \qquad (7.9)$$

and

$$\text{Estimated variance of } R = x_1^2 s_1^2 + x_2^2 s_2^2 + \cdots + x_n^2 s_n^2 + \sum_{i \neq j} x_i x_j r_{ij} s_i s_j \qquad (7.10)$$

In keeping with common practice, we express the annual return on investments in decimal form. Thus a return of 0.10 on a stock means that the stock has increased in value by 10%.

Matrix Functions in Excel

Equation (7.10) for the variance of portfolio return looks fairly intimidating, particularly if there are many potential investments. Fortunately, we can take advantage of some built-in Excel matrix functions to expedite our work. In this subsection we illustrate how to use Excel's MMULT (matrix multiplication) and TRANSPOSE functions. Then in the next subsection we will put these to use in the portfolio selection model.

A **matrix** is a rectangular array of numbers. We say a matrix is an $i \times j$ matrix if it consists of i rows and j columns. For example,

$$\begin{bmatrix} 1 & 2 & 3 \\ 4 & 5 & 6 \end{bmatrix}$$

is a 2×3 matrix, and

$$\begin{bmatrix} 1 & 2 & 3 & 4 \end{bmatrix}$$

is a 1×4 matrix. If the matrix has only a single row, we call it a **row vector**. Similarly, if it has only a single column, we call it a **column vector**.

If matrix A has the same number of columns as matrix B has rows, then we can construct the matrix product of A and B, denoted AB. The i, j entry in AB is obtained by summing the products of the elements in row i of A with the corresponding elements in column j of B. If A is an $i \times r$ matrix and B is an $r \times j$ matrix, then AB is an $i \times j$ matrix.

For example, if

$$A = \begin{bmatrix} 1 & 2 & 3 \\ 2 & 4 & 5 \end{bmatrix}$$

and

$$B = \begin{bmatrix} 1 & 2 \\ 3 & 4 \\ 5 & 6 \end{bmatrix}$$

then AB is the following 2×2 matrix:

$$AB = \begin{bmatrix} 1(1) + 2(3) + 3(5) & 1(2) + 2(4) + 3(6) \\ 2(1) + 4(3) + 5(5) & 2(2) + 4(4) + 5(6) \end{bmatrix} = \begin{bmatrix} 22 & 28 \\ 39 & 50 \end{bmatrix}$$

The Excel MMULT function performs matrix multiplication in a single step. The spreadsheet in Figure 7.32 indicates how to multiply matrices of different sizes. (See the file MATRIXMULT.XLS.) For example, to multiply matrix 1 by matrix 2 (which is possible because matrix 1 has 3 columns and matrix 2 has 3 rows), we select the range B13:C14, type the formula

=MMULT(Mat1,Mat2)

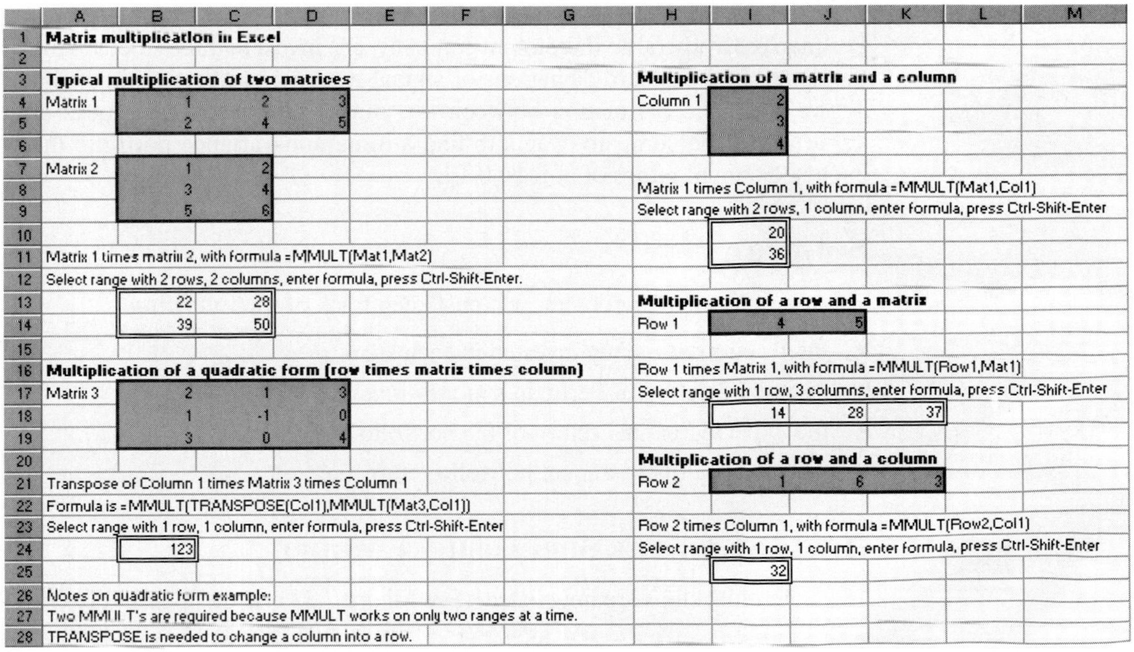

	A	B	C	D	E	F	G	H	I	J	K	L	M
1	**Matrix multiplication in Excel**												
2													
3	**Typical multiplication of two matrices**							**Multiplication of a matrix and a column**					
4	Matrix 1	1	2	3				Column 1	2				
5		2	4	5					3				
6									4				
7	Matrix 2	1	2										
8		3	4					Matrix 1 times Column 1, with formula =MMULT(Mat1,Col1)					
9		5	6					Select range with 2 rows, 1 column, enter formula, press Ctrl-Shift-Enter					
10									20				
11	Matrix 1 times matrix 2, with formula =MMULT(Mat1,Mat2)								36				
12	Select range with 2 rows, 2 columns, enter formula, press Ctrl-Shift-Enter.												
13		22	28					**Multiplication of a row and a matrix**					
14		39	50					Row 1	4	5			
15													
16	**Multiplication of a quadratic form (row times matrix times column)**							Row 1 times Matrix 1, with formula =MMULT(Row1,Mat1)					
17	Matrix 3	2	1	3				Select range with 1 row, 3 columns, enter formula, press Ctrl-Shift-Enter					
18		1	-1	0					14	28	37		
19		3	0	4									
20								**Multiplication of a row and a column**					
21	Transpose of Column 1 times Matrix 3 times Column 1							Row 2	1	6	3		
22	Formula is =MMULT(TRANSPOSE(Col1),MMULT(Mat3,Col1))												
23	Select range with 1 row, 1 column, enter formula, press Ctrl-Shift-Enter							Row 2 times Column 1, with formula =MMULT(Row2,Col1)					
24		123						Select range with 1 row, 1 column, enter formula, press Ctrl-Shift-Enter					
25									32				
26	Notes on quadratic form example:												
27	Two MMULT's are required because MMULT works on only two ranges at a time.												
28	TRANSPOSE is needed to change a column into a row.												

FIGURE 7.32 Examples of Matrix Multiplication in Excel

and press Ctrl-Shift-Enter (all three keys at once).[6] Note that we selected a range with 2 rows because matrix 1 has 2 rows, and we selected a range with 2 columns because matrix 2 has 2 columns.

The matrix multiplication in cell B24 indicates (1) how we can multiply three matrices together by using MMULT twice, and (2) how we can use the TRANSPOSE function to convert a column vector to a row vector (or vice versa), if appropriate. Here, we want to multiply Col1 by the product of Mat3 and Col1. However, Col1 is 3×1, and Mat3 is 3×3, so Col1 times Mat3 doesn't work. Instead, we must transpose Col1 to make it 1×3. Then the result of multiplying all three together is a 1×1 matrix (a number). We calculate it by selecting cell B24, typing the formula

=MMULT(TRANSPOSE(Col1),MMULT(Mat3,Col1))

and pressing Ctrl-Shift-Enter. We use MMULT twice because it can multiply only *two* matrices at a time.

The Basic Portfolio Selection Model

Most investors have two objectives in forming portfolios—to obtain a large expected return and to obtain a small variance (to minimize risk). The most common way of handling this two-objective problem is to specify a minimal expected return that we require and then minimize the variance subject to the constraint on expected return. The following example illustrates how we can use the Solver to do this.

EXAMPLE 7.9

PORTFOLIO OPTIMIZATION AT PERLMAN & BROTHERS

Perlman & Brothers, an investment company, can invest in three stocks. From past data, the means and standard deviations of annual returns have been estimated as shown in Table 7.10. The correlation between the annual returns on the stocks are listed in Table 7.11. The company wants to find a minimum-variance portfolio that yields an expected annual return of at least 0.12.

Solution

To model Perlman's problem, we must keep track of the following:

- the fraction of money invested in each stock
- the total fraction of Perlman's money invested
- the expected annual return of the portfolio
- the variance of the annual portfolio return

DEVELOPING THE SPREADSHEET MODEL

The individual steps are now listed. (See Figure 7.33 and the file PORTFOLIO1.XLS.)

---

[6]When you enter a matrix formula by pressing Ctrl-Shift-Enter, Excel surrounds the formula with curly brackets. These remind you that this is a matrix formula. However, you should *not* type the curly brackets.

TABLE 7.10	Estimated Means and Standard Deviations for Perlman Example	
	Mean	**Standard Deviation**
Stock 1	0.14	0.20
Stock 2	0.11	0.15
Stock 3	0.10	0.08

TABLE 7.11	Estimated Correlations for Perlman Example
Combination	**Correlation**
Stocks 1 and 2	0.6
Stocks 1 and 3	0.4
Stocks 2 and 3	0.7

❶ **Inputs.** Enter the inputs in the shaded ranges. These include the historical estimates of means, standard deviations, and correlations, as well as the required annual return.

❷ **Fractions invested.** Enter *any* trial values in the Invested range for the fractions of Perlman's money placed in the three investments. Then sum these with the SUM function in the TotInvested cell.

❸ **Expected annual return.** Use equation (7.3) to compute the expected annual return in the ExpReturn cell with the formula

=SUMPRODUCT(MeanReturns,Invested)

	A	B	C	D	E	F	G	H	I	J
1	Portfolio selection model									
2										
3	Stock input data									
4		Stock 1	Stock 2	Stock 3						
5	Mean return	0.14	0.11	0.1						
6	StDev of return	0.2	0.15	0.08						
7										
8	Correlations	Stock 1	Stock 2	Stock 3			Covariances	Stock 1	Stock 2	Stock 3
9	Stock 1	1	0.6	0.4			Stock 1	0.04	0.018	0.0064
10	Stock 2	0.6	1	0.7			Stock 2	0.018	0.0225	0.0084
11	Stock 3	0.4	0.7	1			Stock 3	0.0064	0.0084	0.0064
12										
13	Investment decisions									
14		Stock 1	Stock 2	Stock 3	Total		Required			
15	Fractions to invest	0.5	0	0.5	1	=	1			
16										
17	Constraint on expected portfolio return									
18		Actual		Required						
19		0.12	>=	0.12						
20										
21	Portfolio variance	0.0148								
22	Portfolio stdev	0.1217								
23										
24										
25										

Range names used:
MeanReturns - B5:D5
LTable - B4:D6
CovarMat - H9:J11
Invested - B15:D15
TotInvested - E15
ExpReturn - B19
ReqdReturn - D19
PortVar - B21

FIGURE 7.33 Basic Portfolio Model

4 **Portfolio variance.** This is the hard part. The most common way financial analysts express portfolio variance is with the matrix formula

$$\text{Portfolio variance} = \text{Invested} * \text{CovarMat} * \text{Transpose(Invested)} \qquad (7.11)$$

where Invested is a row vector of the fractions invested, and CovarMat is a matrix of covariances for the particular investments. [This formula is equivalent to equation (7.10).] We already have the Invested range, but we need to calculate a matrix of covariances. To do this, we need two facts: (1) the covariance between a return and itself is the *variance* of that return, and (2) the covariance between returns i and j is $\sigma_i \sigma_j \rho_{ij}$, the product of the standard deviations and the correlation. Actually, this expression covers both cases $\sigma_i \sigma_j \rho_{ij}$, because when $i = j$, $\sigma_i \sigma_j = \sigma_i^2$ and $\rho_{ij} = 1$.

To calculate the covariances in the CovarMat range, first enter the labels in the ranges G9:G11 and H8:J8, then enter the lookup formula

=HLOOKUP($G9,LTable,3)*B9*HLOOKUP(H$8,LTable,3)

in cell H9, and copy it to the rest of the CovarMat range. (This formula is a bit tricky, so take a close look at it. The term B9 captures the relevant correlation. The two HLOOKUP terms capture the appropriate standard deviations.)

Finally, use equation (7.11) to calculate the portfolio variance in the PortVar cell with the formula

=MMULT(Invested,MMULT(CovarMat,TRANSPOSE(Invested)))

5 **Portfolio standard deviation.** Most financial analysts talk in terms of portfolio *variance*. However, it is more intuitive to talk about portfolio *standard deviation*, which is calculated in cell B22 with the formula

=SQRT(PortVar)

Actually, we could use either cell B21 or B22 as the objective to minimize. Minimizing the square root of a function is equivalent to minimizing the function itself.

USING THE SOLVER

The completed Solver dialog box should appear as in Figure 7.34. The constraints specify that the expected return must be at least as large as the minimum required, and all of the company's money must be invested. We constrain the changing cells to be

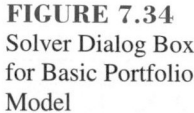

FIGURE 7.34
Solver Dialog Box
for Basic Portfolio
Model

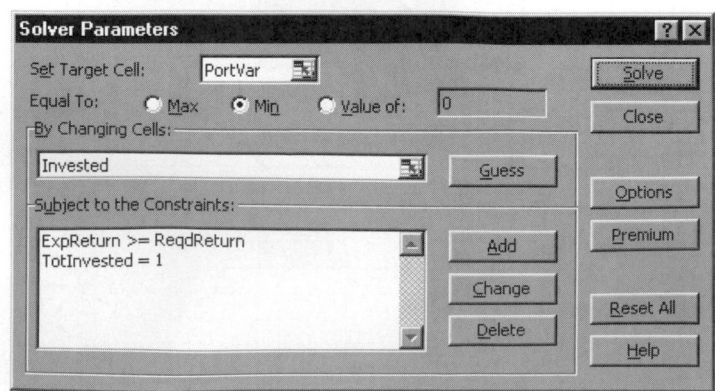

nonnegative, but because of the squared terms in the variance formula, we do *not* check the Assume Linear Model box.

The solution in Figure 7.33 indicates that the company should put half of its money in each of stocks 1 and 3, and it should not invest in stock 2 at all. This might be somewhat surprising, given that the ranking of riskiness of the stocks is 1, 2, 3, with stock 1 most risky but also having the highest expected return. However, the correlations play a definite role in portfolio selection, so we can usually not guess the optimal portfolio on the basis of the means and standard deviations of stock returns alone. We can interpret the portfolio standard deviation of 0.1217 in a probabilistic sense. Specifically, if we believe that stock returns are approximately *normally* distributed, then the probability is about 0.68 that the actual portfolio return will be within one standard deviation of the expected return, and the probability is about 0.95 that the actual portfolio return will be within two standard deviations of the expected return.

Is the Solver Solution Optimal? The constraints for this model are linear, and it can be shown that the portfolio variance is a convex function of the investment fractions. Therefore, we know that the Solver solution is optimal.

Sensitivity Analysis This model begs for a sensitivity analysis on the minimum required return. As the company requires larger returns (on average), it must assume a larger risk. We see how this occurs in Figure 7.35. We use SolverTable with the ReqdReturn cell as the single input cell, allowing it to vary from 0.10 to 0.14 in increments of 0.005. Note that values outside this range are of little interest. Stock 3 has the minimum expected return, 0.10, and stock 1 has the highest expected return, 0.14.

FIGURE 7.35
The Efficient Frontier

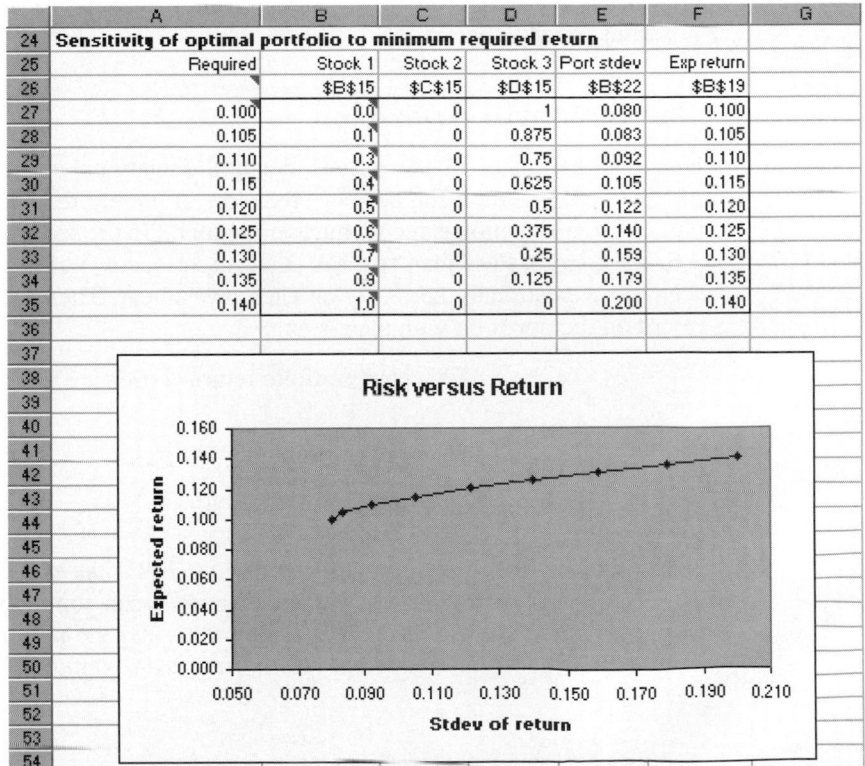

	A	B	C	D	E	F	G
24	Sensitivity of optimal portfolio to minimum required return						
25	Required	Stock 1	Stock 2	Stock 3	Port stdev	Exp return	
26		$B$15	$C$15	$D$15	$B$22	$B$19	
27	0.100	0.0	0	1	0.080	0.100	
28	0.105	0.1	0	0.875	0.083	0.105	
29	0.110	0.3	0	0.75	0.092	0.110	
30	0.115	0.4	0	0.625	0.105	0.115	
31	0.120	0.5	0	0.5	0.122	0.120	
32	0.125	0.6	0	0.375	0.140	0.125	
33	0.130	0.7	0	0.25	0.159	0.130	
34	0.135	0.8	0	0.125	0.179	0.135	
35	0.140	1.0	0	0	0.200	0.140	

Therefore, any portfolio will achieve at least 0.10, and no portfolio can achieve more than 0.14. The table indicates that the company puts more and more into risky stock 1 as the required return increases (and stock 2 is never used). The accompanying X-Y chart (with the option to "connect the dots") shows the risk–return trade-off. As the company takes on more risk, as measured by portfolio standard deviation, the expected return increases but at a decreasing rate. The curve in this chart is called the **efficient frontier**. Points on the efficient frontier can be achieved by appropriate portfolios. Points below the efficient frontier can be achieved, but they are not as good as points on the efficient frontier because they have a lower expected return for a given level of risk. In contrast, points above the efficient frontier are unachievable—the company cannot achieve this high an expected return for a given level of risk. ■

MODELING ISSUES

1. Typical real-world portfolio selection problems involve a large number of potential investments, certainly many more than three. This admittedly requires a lot more input data, particularly for the correlation matrix, but the basic model does not change at all. In particular, the formula for portfolio variance is exactly the same. This shows the power of using Excel's matrix functions.

2. If Perlman is allowed to short a stock, we simply allow the fraction invested in that stock to be negative. To implement this, we eliminate the nonnegativity constraints on the changing cells.

3. An alternative objective might be to minimize the probability that the portfolio loses money. (See Problem 43.) ■

The Scenario Approach

Historical estimates of the means, standard deviations, and correlations needed for portfolio optimization can be poor predictors of the future. An alternative approach to portfolio optimization is the **scenario approach**.[7] In the scenario approach we identify a few scenarios (less than ten, say) that might occur during the next year. For each scenario we estimate the return on each investment. Then we estimate the expected return on the portfolio with the formula

$$\text{Expected portfolio return} = ER = \sum_i r_i p_i \qquad (7.12)$$

and the variance of the portfolio with the formula

$$\text{Variance of portfolio return} = \sum_i (r_i - ER)^2 p_i \qquad (7.13)$$

Here r_i is the portfolio return under scenario i, ER is the expected portfolio return, p_i is the probability that scenario i will occur, and each summation is over all possible scenarios. Then we use the Solver as before to find the minimum variance portfolio that yields an acceptable expected return. Here is an example of the scenario approach.

[7]This section is based on Schrage (1996).

PORTFOLIO OPTIMIZATION AT SECURITY ANALYSIS

During the next year the Security Analysis Company (SAC) has identified seven equally likely scenarios. For each of three stocks, the annual return earned under each scenario is given in Table 7.12. SAC wants to find the minimum variance portfolio that yields an expected annual return of at least 0.13.

TABLE 7.12	Returns for the SAC Example		
	Stock 1	Stock 2	Stock 3
Scenario 1	−0.071	0.144	0.169
Scenario 2	0.056	0.107	−0.035
Scenario 3	0.038	0.321	0.133
Scenario 4	0.089	0.305	0.732
Scenario 5	0.090	0.195	0.021
Scenario 6	0.083	0.390	0.131
Scenario 7	0.035	−0.072	0.006

Solution

To model SAC's scenario example, we need to keep track of the following:

- the fraction of the portfolio invested in each stock
- the fraction of the money invested
- the return of the portfolio under each scenario
- the expected annual return of the portfolio
- the variance of the annual return on the portfolio

DEVELOPING THE SPREADSHEET MODEL

The problem can be modeled as follows. (See Figure 7.36 (page 384) and the file PORTFOLIO2.XLS.)

❶   **Inputs.** Enter the inputs in the shaded ranges. This includes the probabilities of the various scenarios, which are all 1/7.

❷   **Fractions invested.** Enter *any* trial values in the Invested range for the fractions invested in the various stocks and sum them in the TotInvested cell.

❸   **Portfolio returns.** Given the investment fractions, we can now calculate the portfolio return (*actual*, not expected) in the PortReturns range for each scenario. To do so, enter the formula

=SUMPRODUCT(B6:D6,Invested)

in cell B20 for scenario 1, and copy it to the rest of the PortReturns range for the other scenarios.

FIGURE 7.36
Scenario Model for
Portfolio Selection

	A	B	C	D	E	F	G	H
1	**Scenario model of portfolio selection**							
2								
3	**Scenario input data**							
4		Returns						
5	Scenario	Stock 1	Stock 2	Stock 3		Probability		
6	1	-0.071	0.144	0.169		0.143		
7	2	0.056	0.107	-0.035		0.143		
8	3	0.038	0.321	0.133		0.143		
9	4	0.089	0.305	0.732		0.143		
10	5	0.09	0.195	0.021		0.143		
11	6	0.083	0.39	0.131		0.143		
12	7	0.035	-0.072	0.006		0.143		
13								
14	**Investment decisions**							
15		Stock 1	Stock 2	Stock 3	Total		Required	
16	Fractions to invest	0.445	0.538	0.017	1	=	1	
17								
18	**Portfolio returns and squared deviations from mean**							
19	Scenario	Return	Sq Dev					
20	1	0.049	0.00660					
21	2	0.082	0.00232			**Range names used:**		
22	3	0.192	0.00383			Probs - F6:F12		
23	4	0.216	0.00744			Invested - B16:D16		
24	5	0.145	0.00023			TotInvested - E16		
25	6	0.249	0.01415			PortReturns - B20:B26		
26	7	-0.023	0.02343			SqDevs - C20:C26		
27						ExpReturn - B30		
28	**Constraint on expected portfolio return**					ReqdReturn - D30		
29		Actual		Required		PortVar - B32		
30		0.130	>=	0.13				
31								
32	Portfolio variance	0.008285						
33	Portfolio stdev	0.0910						

❹ **Expected annual return.** We now have a probability distribution of portfolio returns. The possible returns are listed in the PortReturns range, and the associated probabilities are listed in the Probs range. In this step and the next, we calculate the expected value and the variance of this probability distribution. In case you don't recall the relevant formulas from probability, we give them here. If a probability distribution has possible values v_1 through v_n, with associated probabilities p_1 through p_n, then its expected value is

$$\text{Expected value} = \sum_{i=1}^{n} v_i p_i \tag{7.14}$$

and its variance is

$$\text{Variance} = \sum_{i=1}^{n} (v_i - EV)^2 p_i \tag{7.15}$$

(where EV is the expected value). Therefore, use equation (7.14) to calculate the expected portfolio return in the ExpReturn cell with the formula

=SUMPRODUCT(PortReturns,Probs)

❺ **Portfolio variance.** To calculate the variance of portfolio return from equation (7.15), we need the squared deviations from the expected value. So first calculate these in the SqDevs range by entering the formula

=(B20-ExpReturn)^2

in cell C20 and copying it down. Then calculate the portfolio variance in the PortVar cell with the formula

=SUMPRODUCT(SqDevs,Probs)

USING THE SOLVER

We set up the Solver dialog box *exactly* as in the previous example. (See Figure 7.34.) The Solver solution in Figure 7.36 indicates that SAC obtains a minimum portfolio variance of 0.008285 or, equivalently, a standard deviation of 0.091. SAC's optimal portfolio is to invest 44.5% of its money in stock 1, 53.8% in stock 2, and 1.7% in stock 3. It is again possible to show that the portfolio variance is a convex function of the investment fractions, so we can be sure that this solution is indeed optimal. ■

MODELING ISSUES

1. If we assume that portfolio returns are normally distributed, then we are 68% certain that the annual return on the portfolio will be between 0.039 ($= 0.13 - 0.091$) and 0.221 ($= 0.13 + 0.091$), and we are 95% certain that it will be between -0.052 ($= 0.13 - 0.182$) and 0.312 ($= 0.13 + 0.182$).

2. In portfolio problems, minimizing **downside risk** of return might be a more reasonable objective than minimizing portfolio variance. Given a target return rate, the downside risk of a portfolio is the expected amount by which the return on the portfolio falls short of the target return. For example, suppose there are three equally likely scenarios, the target return is 0.13, and the portfolio returns under scenarios 1, 2, and 3 are 0.12, 0.14, and 0.11. Then we can determine the expected downside risk with this equation:

$$\text{Downside risk} = (1/3)(0.01) + (1/3)(0) + (1/3)(0.02) = 0.01 \quad ■$$

ADDITIONAL APPLICATIONS

Using the Scenario Approach at GM

Eppen et al. (1989) used the scenario approach to help General Motors analyze its plant capacities. In the resulting integer programming model, GM was able to adjust the capacity of plants and the types of products each plant could make. For example, plant 1 could be changed from a plant with a production capacity of 500,000 compacts per year into a plant with a production capacity of 200,000 compacts and 250,000 large cars per year. GM management identified five possible scenarios for each year (high inflation, recession, and so on) and forecasted demand for each product for each scenario. Given the choice of plant configurations at the beginning of each year, the model calculated the profit for each scenario. Then the integer programming model calculated the capacities and configurations for each plant to minimize the downside risk associated with the company's profit for the next five years. The model was instrumental in convincing top GM management that the company had a great deal of excess capacity. (See Problem 46 for an example of this type of model.)

Asset and Liability Management at Pacific Financial

Mulvey (1994) describes how he used a scenario approach at Pacific Financial Asset Management Company to allocate financial assets. The problem was to balance the risk and rewards of investment decisions in concert with the movements of the projected liabilities. Mulvey's approach extended the asset-only Markowitz model described in Examples 7.9 and 7.10 to handle liabilities. The objective of the integrated asset-liability system was to preserve the firm's wealth, measured as assets minus the present value of liabilities. Although this approach requires greater information, Mulvey claims that "its recommendations are more closely tailored to the investor's circumstances." ■

Models with Transaction Costs

In reality, there is a charge for buying and selling stocks. How can we incorporate these **transaction costs** into the portfolio optimization model? To illustrate, we reconsider the Perlman's portfolio optimization model in Example 7.9.

EXAMPLE 7.11

PORTFOLIO OPTIMIZATION WITH TRANSACTION COSTS AT PERLMAN & BROTHERS

Suppose that for every $1 traded in stock 1 or 2, Perlman must pay $0.01, and for every dollar traded in stock 3, it must pay $0.005. Suppose the company begins with 10% of its money invested in stock 1, 40% in stock 2, and 50% in stock 3. Perlman's goal is to obtain a portfolio of minimum variance that yields an expected annual return of at least 0.12.[8]

Solution

Suppose that Perlman initially has $1 invested total in these three stocks. (There is no loss in generality with this assumption. If the company had *any* number of dollars invested, we would track each of them exactly as we track this "typical" dollar.) Then it initially has $0.10 invested in stock 1, $0.40 in stock 2, and $0.50 in stock 3. It must now decide how to adjust its holdings in these stocks. If, for example, it increases its holdings in stock 1 to $0.30, there is a transaction cost of $0.01(20) = $0.002. The transactions are governed by the following balance equation:

$$\text{Final amount invested} + \text{Transaction costs} = \text{Initial amount invested} = \$1.00 \quad \textbf{(7.16)}$$

The company's goal is to minimize the variance of the annual expected return on the final portfolio, subject to equation (7.16) and the constraint that the expected value of its stocks a year from now must be at least $1.12.

Before discussing the details of the spreadsheet model, we note that this problem is more difficult to model than the problem without transaction costs. The main reason is that if $1 is currently invested and the company then makes some changes in its investments, the amount it will have invested after the changes is somewhat *less* than

---

[8]This section is also based on Schrage (1996).

$1, due to the transaction costs. Strictly speaking, then, when the company requires the expected value of its stocks a year from now to be at least $1.12, it is requiring a return of slightly *greater* than 0.12. Do you see why?

DEVELOPING THE SPREADSHEET MODEL

The completed spreadsheet model appears in Figure 7.37. (See the file PORTFO-LIO3.XLS.) Much of this model is identical to the previous model (see Figure 7.33), so we will discuss only the differences.

1 New inputs. Enter the unit transaction costs and the current holdings in rows 15 and 18.

2 Buy, sell amounts. The changing cells now indicate how much to buy and sell of the stocks, measured in fractions of a dollar. For example, the 0.554 in cell B22 indicates that Perlman buys $0.554 worth of stock 1, and the 0.5 in cell D23 indicates that the company sells all $0.50 of its holdings in stock 3. Enter *any* values in these cells.

3 Transaction costs. Calculate the transaction costs in the TransCosts range by entering the formula

=B15*SUM(B22:B23)

	A	B	C	D	E	F	G	H	I	J
1	**Portfolio selection model with transaction costs**									
2										
3	**Input data**									
4		Stock 1	Stock 2	Stock 3						
5	Mean return	0.14	0.11	0.1						
6	StDev of return	0.2	0.15	0.08						
7										
8	Correlations	Stock 1	Stock 2	Stock 3			Covariances	Stock 1	Stock 2	Stock 3
9	Stock 1	1	0.6	0.4			Stock 1	0.04	0.018	0.0064
10	Stock 2	0.6	1	0.7			Stock 2	0.018	0.0225	0.0084
11	Stock 3	0.4	0.7	1			Stock 3	0.0064	0.0084	0.0064
12										
13	Transactions costs (cost per dollar bought or sold)									
14		Stock 1	Stock 2	Stock 3						
15		0.01	0.01	0.005			**Range names used:**			
16							MeanReturns - B5:D5			
17	Current fractions owned	Stock 1	Stock 2	Stock 3			LTable - B4:D6			
18		0.1	0.4	0.5			CovarMat - H9:J11			
19							Transactions - B22:D23			
20	**Investment decisions**						TransCosts - B27:D27			
21		Stock 1	Stock 2	Stock 3			FinalOwned - B28:D28			
22	Amount bought	0.5540	0	0			FinalTotal - B32			
23	Amount sold	0	0.062658	0.5000			ExpReturn - D36			
24							ReqdReturn - D36			
25	**Accounting for all transactions**						PortVar - B38			
26		Stock 1	Stock 2	Stock 3						
27	Transactions costs	0.00554	0.000627	0.0025						
28	Final fractions owned	0.653992	0.337342	0						
29										
30	**Constraint that each dollar must be accounted for**									
31		Total		Required						
32		1	=	1						
33										
34	**Constraint on expected cash one year from now**									
35		Actual		Required						
36		1.12	>=	1.12						
37										
38	**Portfolio variance**	0.02761								
39	Portfolio stdev	0.1662								

Note next to cell D28: **Note:** Constrain this row to be nonnegative if short selling is not allowed.

FIGURE 7.37 Portfolio Model with Transaction Costs

in cell B27 and copying it across. We sum the buy and sell amounts, because the same transaction cost rate is incurred for buying or selling.

4 **Final holdings.** The final dollar holding for any stock is the initial amount held, plus any buy, minus any sell. Therefore, enter the formula

=B18+B22-B23

in cell B28 and copy it across.

5 **Total money.** The key to the model is that the company started with $1 of wealth, and it must all be accounted for, either in final holdings of stocks or in transaction costs. Therefore, enter the formula

=SUM(TransCosts,FinalOwned)

in the FinalTotal cell. We will eventually constrain this value to be 1.

6 **Expected return.** Row 36 requires that the expected value of the portfolio a year from now be at least $1.12. So see how much it will be worth, note that the final holding in stock 1, for example, will grow by an expected factor of 1.14 in a year. Therefore, calculate the mean worth of the stock in one year in the ExpReturn cell with the formula

=SUMPRODUCT(1+MeanReturns,FinalOwned)

7 **Portfolio variance.** Calculate the portfolio variance in the PortVar cell with the formula

=MMULT(FinalOwned,MMULT(CovarMat,TRANSPOSE(FinalOwned)))

It uses the same logic as in Example 7.9, but now it is based on the values in the FinalOwned range.

USING THE SOLVER

The completed Solver dialog box should appear as in Figure 7.38. We constrain the final amounts owned to be nonnegative to prevent selling short, and we add the FinalTotal to be 1 for proper accounting.

The Solver solution in Figure 7.37 indicates that Perlman should increase its holdings of stock 1 to $0.654, decrease its holdings of stock 2 to $0.337, and eliminate its holdings of stock 3. The variance of the annual return on the final portfolio is 0.0276, and the standard deviation is 0.166. As in Example 7.9, it can be shown that the portfolio variance is a convex function of the final holdings (which are linear functions of the decision variables); thus we can be sure that this is indeed the optimal solution.

FIGURE 7.38
Solver Dialog Box
for Transaction Costs
Model

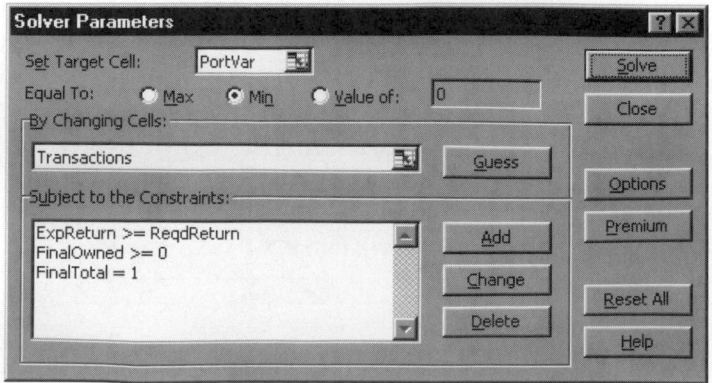

MODELING ISSUES

This analysis was performed for a typical dollar of investment. For an initial amount of *many* dollars, we simply treat each dollar the same way, as prescribed by the Solver solution. This is shown graphically in Figure 7.39 for a total investment amount of $10,000. Note that the final value of the holdings is slightly less than $10,000. The difference (aside from roundoff) represents the transactions costs.

FIGURE 7.39
Optimal Solution with $10,000 Total Investment

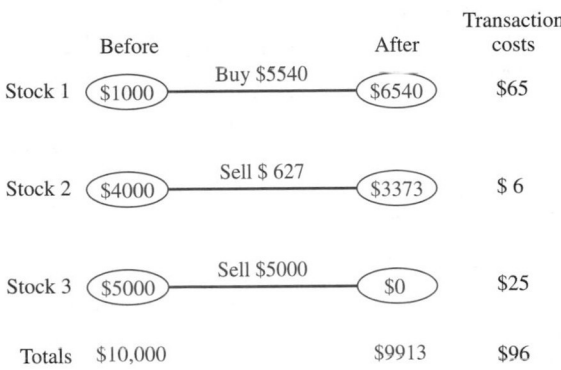

PROBLEMS

Skill-Building Problems

37. The annual returns on three different types of assets (T-bonds, stocks, and gold) during the years 1968–1988 are listed in Table 7.13. (See the file INV68.XLS.) For example, $1 invested in T-bonds at the beginning of 1978 grew to $1.07 by the end of 1978. You have $1000 to invest in these three investments. Your goal is to minimize the variance of the annual dollar return of your portfolio subject to the constraint that the expected return on the portfolio for a one-year period is at least 0.10.

| TABLE 7.13 | Data for Security Problem |

	Stocks	Gold	T-Bonds		Stocks	Gold	T-Bonds
1968	0.11	0.11	0.05	1979	0.19	0.59	0.10
1969	−0.09	0.08	0.07	1980	0.33	0.99	0.11
1970	0.04	−0.14	0.07	1981	−0.05	−0.25	0.15
1971	0.14	0.14	0.04	1982	0.22	0.04	0.11
1972	0.19	0.44	0.04	1983	0.23	−0.11	0.09
1973	−0.15	0.66	0.07	1984	0.06	−0.15	0.10
1974	−0.27	0.64	0.08	1985	0.32	−0.12	0.08
1975	0.37	0.00	0.06	1986	0.19	0.16	0.06
1976	0.24	−0.22	0.05	1987	0.05	0.22	0.05
1977	−0.07	0.18	0.05	1988	0.17	−0.02	0.06
1978	0.07	0.31	0.07				

a. Determine how much money you should invest in each investment.

b. Find an interval such that you are 95% sure that the change in the value of your assets during the next year will be within this interval (assuming normally distributed returns).

c. Find an interval such that you are 95% sure that the percentage annual return on your portfolio will be within this interval (assuming normally distributed returns).

38. Continuing the previous problem, suppose that at present you have $10,000 invested, with 30% of your investment in stocks, 50% in T-bonds, and 20% in gold. Assume that transactions incur costs. Every $100 of stocks traded costs you $1, every $100 of your gold portfolio traded costs you $2, and every $100 of your T-bonds portfolio traded costs you $5. Find the minimum-variance portfolio that yields an expected holdings one year from now of at least $11,000.

39. Consider three investments. You are given the following means, standard deviations, and correlations for the annual return on these three investments. The means are 0.12, 0.15, and 0.20. The standard deviations are 0.20, 0.30, and 0.40. The correlation between stocks 1 and 2 is 0.65, between stocks 1 and 3 is 0.75, and between stocks 2 and 3 is 0.41. You have $10,000 to invest and can invest no more than half of your money in any single stock. Determine the minimum-variance portfolio that yields an expected annual return of at least 0.14.

40. Assume there are four equally likely states of the world possible next year. The annual returns on gold, stocks, and T-bills for these scenarios are shown in Table 7.14. Determine the minimum-variance portfolio that has an expected return of at least 0.08.

TABLE 7.14 Data for Four-Scenario Problem

	Gold	Stocks	T-bills
Scenario 1	0.20	0.03	0.12
Scenario 2	0.12	0.05	0.10
Scenario 3	0.06	0.10	0.08
Scenario 4	0.01	0.15	0.06

41. There are five possible scenarios for the economy next year. The probability of each scenario, as well as the annual percentage return on stocks, bonds, and gold, are listed in Table 7.15.

a. Find the minimum-variance portfolio that yields an expected return of at least 0.09.

b. Find the portfolio that yields an expected return of at least 0.09 and minimizes the downside risk.

TABLE 7.15 Data for Five-Scenario Problem

	Probability	Stocks	Bonds	Gold
Depression	0.05	−0.05	0.01	0.30
Recession	0.20	0.00	0.02	0.16
Zero growth	0.30	0.10	0.06	0.10
Moderate growth	0.20	0.15	0.08	0.04
High growth	0.25	0.20	0.04	−0.02

Skill-Extending Problems

42. Using the notation from this section, show algebraically that the portfolio variance in equation (7.10) can be written in matrix form as the product

$$[x_1s_1 \ x_2s_2 \ \cdots \ x_ns_n] \ C \ [x_1s_1 \ x_2s_2 \ \cdots \ x_ns_n]^T$$

43. Reconsider the Perlman & Brothers portfolio example (Example 7.9). Suppose that your goal is to find (among all portfolios that invest all of your money in stocks 1, 2, and 3) the portfolio that minimizes the probability that you will lose money during the next year. Use the Solver to solve this problem. (*Hint:* You will need to assume that the returns on any portfolio follow a normal distribution. Then the Excel function NORMSDIST(x) will return the area under a standard normal curve to the left of a given number x. For example, NORMSDIST(1) returns 0.84, and NORMSDIST(−1) returns 0.16.)

44. The file STOCK83.XLS contains the percentage return on the market for the years 1984–1991 as well as the closing stock price for Ford, Lilly, Kellogg, Merck, and Hewlett-Packard for the same years. Use the approach outlined in Example 7.9 to determine the minimum-variance portfolio (of the stocks listed) that yields an expected return of at least 0.22.

45. If interest rates rise, GM will make less profit because fewer consumers will purchase cars. In this problem we will explore how the scenario approach to portfolio optimization could be used to aid GM in modifying its risk profile. Suppose that during the next year GM believes that five different interest rate scenarios can occur. The annual profit from GM's operations (in billions) and the probability of each scenario are listed in Table 7.16. To hedge against decreases in profits caused by increased interest rates, GM can pursue the following three derivative strategies:

- **Strategy 1:** Go long (or short) on T-bill futures contracts. Each futures contract costs $1000.

TABLE 7.16	Interest Rate Scenarios for GM Problem		
Interest Rate	Probability		Profit
5%	0.10		$6
7%	0.30		$4
8%	0.35		$2
10%	0.15		$1
11%	0.10		$0

For each interest rate, the percentage profit associated with a long position is listed in Table 7.17. (For a short position, take the negatives of the profits listed.)

TABLE 7.17	Profits from T-bill Futures
Interest Rate	Percent Profit on Long Futures Position
5%	24%
7%	1%
8%	−8%
10%	−24%
11%	−34%

- **Strategy 2:** Purchase put option 1 (on a long-term bond) at a cost of $1 per option. For each interest rate the percentage profit associated with put option 1 is that shown in Table 7.18.

TABLE 7.18	Profits from Put Option 1
Interest Rate	Percent Profit on Put Option 1
5%	−100%
7%	−100%
8%	−100%
10%	200%
11%	400%

- **Strategy 3:** Purchase put option 2 (on a long-term bond) at a cost of $5 per option. For each interest rate the percentage profit associated with put option 2 is that shown in Table 7.19.
a. Compute the mean and variance of GM's annual profit from operations.
b. GM wants to minimize the variance of its annual profit, subject to the constraint that its expected

TABLE 7.19	Profits for Put Option 2
Interest Rate	Percent Profit on Put Option 2
5%	−100%
7%	−100%
8%	12%
10%	48%
11%	92%

annual profit is at least $2.65 billion. Determine how GM can use the three derivatives to achieve this goal. (*Note*: You should scale profits to be in billions of dollars and purchases of the three derivatives to be in millions of units. Otherwise, the Solver might have difficulty obtaining the correct solution.)

c. Given a target, the **downside variance** of a random variable is the expected value of the square of the amount by which the target is unsatisfied on the low side. For example, suppose the target for a random variable is 2, and the value of the random variable is 0 or 3 with probability 0.5 each. Then the downside variance is

$$\text{Downside variance} = 0.5(2)^2 + 0.5(0)^2 = 2$$

Determine how GM can use the three derivatives to minimize the downside variance associated with a target of $3.2 billion annual profit, subject to the constraint that GM's expected annual profit is at least $2.65 billion.

46. You have been assigned to adjust the capacity of GM's three automobile production plants. The company believes that one of three demand scenarios (high, medium, or low) will persist indefinitely. Information about these three scenarios is listed in Table 7.20 (page 392). For each of GM's three plants there are three options: keep the current configuration, expand the plant, or close the plant. If a plant's configuration is changed, a changeover cost is incurred. There is an annual fixed cost of operating each plant in any configuration. The variable cost of producing a car at a plant also depends on the plant's configuration. The information about plant changes is listed in Table 7.21. Suppose that GM's goal is to maximize its expected discounted profit over an infinite horizon. Assume that a stream of annual profits can be converted to a discounted profit by multiplying the annual profit by 10. Determine a plant configuration and production schedule for each scenario that will achieve GM's goal.

TABLE 7.20	Demand Scenarios for GM Problem		
	Annual Demand	Price per Car	Probability
High demand	3.0 million	$15,000	0.25
Medium demand	2.4 million	$13,000	0.60
Low demand	1.6 million	$12,000	0.15

TABLE 7.21	Plant Change Data for GM Problem			
	Changeover Cost ($ billions)	Fixed Cost ($ billions)	Variable Cost per Car	Annual Capacity (millions)
Plant 1 expanded	3.0	1.5	$6000	1.0
Plant 1 current	0.0	1.0	$8000	0.6
Plant 1 closed	1.0	0.0	—	0.0
Plant 2 expanded	4.0	1.8	$5000	1.2
Plant 2 current	0.0	0.8	$7500	0.8
Plant 2 closed	1.5	0.0	—	0.0
Plant 3 expanded	3.0	2.0	$4000	1.3
Plant 3 current	0.0	1.5	$6000	0.7
Plant 3 closed	1.2	0.0	—	0.0

7.9   CONCLUSION

Although a large number of real-world problems can be approximated well by linear models, there are also many problems that are inherently nonlinear. We have analyzed a number of these in this chapter, including the important class of portfolio selection models where the risk (measured by portfolio variance) is a nonlinear function of the decision variables. We have purposely neglected much of the mathematics behind nonlinear optimization because of its technical difficulty. However, it is important to realize that nonlinear models present many more hazards for spreadsheet Solvers (or any other optimization software) than linear models. Unless we can verify that the assumptions for a minimization or maximization problem are satisfied—and this can be very difficult to do—there is no guarantee that the Solver will converge to the optimal solution (or even converge at all). The examples in this chapter were purposely kept small and "nice" so that the Solver could handle them and produce optimal solutions. Larger and more complex nonlinear models are not always so accommodating and frequently require solution methods beyond the scope of this book.

PROBLEMS

Skill-Building Problems

47. Refer back to the Franklin Company project scheduling example (Example 5.10 in Chapter 5) and let A be the number of days the duration of A is reduced, B be the number of days the duration of B is reduced, and so on. The costs of crashing the various activities are shown in Table 7.22. Each activity can be "crashed" to a duration of 0 days, if desired. Determine how to minimize the cost of finishing the project in 25 days or less.

TABLE 7.22	Costs in Activity Crashing Problem
	Cost to Crash
Activity A	$5A^2$
Activity B	$20B^2$
Activity C	$2C^2$
Activity D	$20D^2$
Activity E	$10E^2$
Activity F	$15F^2$

48. Suppose that a cylindrical soda can must have a volume of 26 cubic inches. If the soda company wants to minimize the surface area of the soda can, what should the ratio of the height to the radius of the can be? (*Hint:* The volume of a right circular cylinder is $\pi r^2 h$, and the surface area of a right circular cylinder is $2\pi r^2 + 2\pi rh$, where r is the radius and h is the height. Also, the value of π can be obtained in Excel with the function PI().)

49. I have $1000 to invest in three stocks. Let S_i be the random variable representing the annual return on $1 invested in stock i. For example, if $S_i = 0.12$, then $1 invested in stock i at the beginning of a year is worth $1.12 at the end of the year. The means are: $E(S_1) = 0.14$, $E(S_2) = 0.11$, $E(S_3) = 0.10$. The variances are: $Var\ S_1 = 0.20$, $Var\ S_2 = 0.08$, $Var\ S_3 = 0.18$. The correlations are: $r_{12} = 0.8$, $r_{13} = 0.7$, and $r_{23} = 0.9$. Determine the minimum-variance portfolio that attains an expected annual return of at least 0.12.

50. Fruit Computer Company produces Pear and Apricot computers. If the company charges price p_1 for Pear computers and p_2 for Apricot computers, it can sell q_1 Pear and q_2 Apricot computers, where $q_1 = 4000 - 10p_1 + p_2$ and $q_2 = 2000 - 9p_2 + 0.8p_1$. Manufacturing a Pear computer requires two hours of labor and three computer chips. An Apricot computer uses three hours of labor and one computer chip. At present, 5000 hours of labor and 4500 chips are available.
    a. Determine how to maximize Fruit's revenue.
    b. What is the most that Fruit would be willing to pay for another hour of labor?
    c. What is the most that Fruit would be willing to pay for another computer chip?

51. Oilco must determine how many barrels of oil to extract during each of the next two years. If Oilco extracts x_1 million barrels during year 1, each barrel can be sold for $30 - x_1$ dollars. If Oilco extracts x_2 million barrels during year 2, each barrel can be sold for $35 - x_2$ dollars. The cost of extracting x_1 million barrels during year 1 is x_1^2 million dollars, and the cost of extracting x_2 million barrels during year 2 is $2x_2^2$ million dollars. A total of 20 million barrels of oil are available, and at most $250 million can be spent on extraction. Determine how Oilco can maximize its profit (revenues less costs) for the next two years.

52. Five of a store's major customers are located as shown in Figure 7.40. Determine where the store should be located to minimize the sum of the squares of the (straight-line) distances that the customers will have to travel to the store.

FIGURE 7.40 Customers for Store Location Problem

53. A company uses a raw material to produce two types of products. When processed, each unit of raw material yields two units of product 1 and one unit of product 2. If x_1 units of product 1 are produced, each unit can be sold for $49 - x_1$ dollars, and if x_2 units of product 2 are produced, each unit can be sold for $30 - 2x_2$ dollars. It costs $5 to purchase and process each unit of raw material. Determine how the company can maximize its profit.

54. If a company charges price p dollars per unit for a product and spends a dollars on advertising, it can sell $10,000 + 5a^{1/2} - 100p$ units of the product. If the product costs $10 per unit to produce, how can the company maximize its profit?

55. With L labor hours and M machine hours, a company can produce $L^{1/3}M^{2/3}$ computer disk drives. Each disk drive sells for $150. If labor can be purchased at $50 per hour and machine hours can be purchased at $100 per hour, determine how the company can maximize its profit.

56. Suppose that we are hiring a weather forecaster to predict the probability that next summer will be rainy or sunny. The following suggests a method that can be used to ensure that the forecaster is accurate. Suppose that the actual probability of next summer being rainy is 0.6. (For simplicity, we assume that the summer can only be rainy or sunny.) If the forecaster announces a probability p that the summer will be rainy, he receives a payment of $1 - (1 - p)^2$ if the summer is rainy and a payment of $1 - p^2$ if the summer is sunny. Show that the forecaster will maximize his expected profit by announcing that the probability of a rainy summer is 0.6.

57. Consider the points (0, 0), (1, 1), and (2, 3). Determine the circle of smallest radius enclosing these three points. (*Note:* To "determine" a circle, you must specify its center and its radius.)

58. The cost of producing x units of a product during a month is $x^{1/2}$ dollars. Show that the minimum-cost method of producing 40 units during the next two months is to produce all 40 units during a single month.

59. A company uses raw material to produce two products. For $15 dollars, a unit of raw material can be purchased and processed into four units of product 1 and two units of product 2. If x_1 units of product 1 are produced, they can be sold at $25 - x_1$ dollars per unit. If x_2 units of product 2 are produced, they can be sold at $14 - x_2$ dollars per unit. (Negative prices are not permitted.) The company can choose the number of units of raw material that are purchased and processed. How can the company maximize its profit?

Skill-Extending Problems

60. Reconsider the Chandler Oil blending problem (Example 4.4 in Chapter 4) with the following modification. Suppose that Chandler can add a chemical called Superquality (SQ) to improve the quality level of gasoline and heating oil. If it adds an amount x of SQ to each barrel of gasoline, the quality level improves by $x^{1/2}$ over what it would have been. If the company adds an amount x of SQ to each barrel of heating oil, its quality level improves by $0.6x^{0.6}$ over what it would have been. The amount of SQ added to heating oil cannot exceed (by weight) 5% of the oils used to make heating oil. Similarly, the amount of SQ added to gasoline cannot exceed (by weight) 5% of the oils used to make gasoline. SQ can be purchased at a cost of $20 per barrel. Determine how Chandler Oil can maximize its profit.

Modeling Problems

61. For the product mix example (Example 3.1 in Chapter 3), discuss where you think the assumptions of a linear model are most likely to break down. How might an NLP formulation look in this situation?

62. For the Chandler Oil blending example (Example 4.4 in Chapter 4), discuss where you think the assumptions of a linear model are most likely to break down. How might an NLP formulation look in this situation?

63. For the SureStep aggregate planning example (Example 4.2 in Chapter 4), is it likely that the cost per worker of changing the size of the workforce during a month would be constant (as we assumed)? How could an NLP formulation account for a situation in which the cost per worker of changing the size of the workforce is not constant?

64. (This problem and the next problem refer to the sports ratings model in Section 7.6.) If you were going to give more recent games more weight, how might you determine whether the weight given to a game from k weeks ago should be, say, $(0.95)^k$ or $(0.9)^k$?

65. If you were going to use the approach from Section 7.6 to forecast future sports contests, what

problems might you encounter early in the season? How might you resolve these problems?

66. Kellpost Cereal Company sells four products: (1) Special L (a low-calorie, high-nutrition cereal); (2) Corn Bran (another low-calorie, high-nutrition cereal); (3) Admiral Smacks (a sugary cereal pitched at the children's market); and (4) Honey Pops (another sweet cereal pitched at the children's market). Kellpost has sufficient production capacity to produce a total of 10,000 boxes of cereal per month. For each of the last 16 months, Kellpost has kept track of the price and sales of each product. (These data are listed in the file CEREAL.XLS.) Market executives believe that Special L and Corn Bran may be substitutes for each other, as may be Admiral Smacks and Honey Pops. For example, this means that an increase in the price of Special L may raise the sales of Corn Bran. The variable cost of bringing a box of each cereal to market is as follows: Special L, $2.00; Corn Bran, $2.20; Admiral Smacks, $2.30; Honey Pops, $2.40.
   a. Use the given information to determine the price for each cereal that will enable Kellpost to maximize profits.
   b. Now suppose that Kellpost can increase its monthly production capacity. The cost (per year) of doing this is $20,000 per thousand boxes of added monthly capacity. Can you determine an optimal capacity level?

67. UE is going to invest $400 million dollars to acquire companies in the auto and/or electronics industry. How would you apply portfolio optimization to determine which companies should be purchased?

68. Your family owns a large farm that can grow wheat, corn, cotton, alfalfa, barley, pears, and apples. Each product requires a certain amount of labor each month and a certain number of hours of machine time. You have just studied portfolio optimization and want to help your family run its farm. What would you do?

69. A power company is trying to determine how much generating capacity to add for the next ten years. If more capacity must be added later, the per unit cost of adding capacity will drastically increase. Demand for the next ten years is, of course, uncertain. How would you structure this problem to determine the amount of capacity that should be added today?

70. Your company is about to market a new golf club. You have convened a focus group of 100 golfers and asked them to compare your club to the clubs produced by your competitors. You have found, for example, that 30 customers in the focus group would purchase your club if you charged $20, 28 customers would purchase your club if you charged $25, and so on. How would you use this information to determine the price at which your club should be sold?

GMS Stock Hedging

K ate Torelli, a security analyst for Lion-Fund, has identified a gold mining stock (ticker symbol GMS) as a particularly attractive investment. Torelli believes that the company has invested wisely in new mining equipment. Furthermore, the company has recently purchased mining rights on land that has high potential for successful gold extraction. Torelli notes that gold has underperformed the stock market in the last decade and believes that the time is ripe for a large increase in gold prices. In addition, she reasons that conditions in the global monetary system make it likely that investors may once again turn to gold as a safe haven in which to park assets. Finally, supply and demand conditions have improved to the point where there could be significant upward pressure on gold prices.

GMS is a highly leveraged company, so it is quite a risky investment by itself. Torelli is mindful of a passage from the annual report of a competitor, Baupost, which has an extraordinarily successful investment record: "Baupost has managed a decade of consistently profitable results despite, and perhaps in some respect due to, consistent emphasis on the avoidance of downside risk. We have frequently carried both high cash balances and costly market hedges. Our results are particularly satisfying when considered in the light of this sustained risk aversion." She would therefore like to *hedge* the stock purchase—that is, reduce the risk of an investment in GMS stock.

Currently GMS is trading at $100 per share. Torelli has constructed seven scenarios for the price of GMS stock one month from now. These scenarios and corresponding probabilities are shown in Table 7.23.

To hedge an investment in GMS stock, Torelli can invest in other securities whose prices tend to move in the direction opposite to that of GMS stock. In particular, she is considering over-the-counter put options on GMS stock as potential hedging instruments. The value of a put option increases as the price of the underlying stock decreases.[9] For example, consider a put option with a strike price of $100 and a time to expiration of one month. This means that the owner of the put has the right to sell GMS stock at $100 per share one month in the future. Suppose that the price of GMS falls to $80 at that time. Then the holder of the put option can exercise the option and receive $20 (= 100 − 80). If the price of GMS falls to $70, the option would be worth $30 (= 100 − 70). However, if the price of GMS rises to $100 or more, the option expires worthless.

[9]For a brief introduction to options see, for example, Cox and Rubinstein (1985), pp. 1–8, or Jarrow and Turnbull (1996), pp. 14–18.

TABLE 7.23	Scenarios and Probabilities for GMS Stock in One Month						
	Scenario 1	Scenario 2	Scenario 3	Scenario 4	Scenario 5	Scenario 6	Scenario 7
Probability	0.05	0.10	0.20	0.30	0.20	0.10	0.05
GMS stock price	150	130	110	100	90	80	70

TABLE 7.24	Put Option Prices (Today) for GMS Case Study		
	Put Option A	Put Option B	Put Option C
Strike price	90	100	110
Option price	$2.20	$6.40	$12.50

Torelli called an options trader at a large investment bank for quotes. The prices for three (European-style) put options are shown in Table 7.24. Torelli wishes to invest $10 million in GMS stock and put options.

Questions

1. Based on Torelli's scenarios, what is the expected return of GMS stock? What is the standard deviation of the return of GMS stock?

2. After a cursory examination of the put option prices, Torelli suspects that a good strategy is to buy one put option A for each share of GMS stock purchased. What are the mean and standard deviation of return for this strategy?

3. Assuming that Torelli's goal is to minimize the standard deviation of the portfolio return, what is the optimal portfolio that invests all $10 million? (For simplicity, assume that fractional numbers of stock shares and put options can be purchased. Assume that the amounts invested in each security must be nonnegative. However, the number of options purchased need *not* equal the number of shares of stock purchased.) What are the expected return and standard deviation of return of this portfolio? How many shares of GMS stock and how many of each put option does this portfolio correspond to?

4. Suppose that short selling is permitted—that is, the nonnegativity restrictions on the portfolio weights are removed. Now what portfolio minimizes the standard deviation of return?

Hint: A good way to attack this problem is to create a table of security returns, as indicated in Table 7.25. Only a few of the table entries are shown. To correctly compute the standard deviation of portfolio return, you will need to incorporate the scenario probabilities. If r_i is the portfolio return in scenario i, and p_i is the probability of scenario i, then the standard deviation of portfolio return is

$$\sqrt{\sum_{i=1}^{7} p_i (r_i - \mu)^2}$$

where $\mu = \sum_{i=1}^{7} p_i r_i$ is the expected portfolio return.

TABLE 7.25	Table of Security Returns			
	GMS Stock	**Put Option A**	**Put Option B**	**Put Option C**
Scenario 1			−100%	
2	30%			
⋮				
7				220%

Durham Asset Management

Durham Asset Management (DAM) is a small firm with 50 employees that manages the pension funds of small to medium-sized companies. Durham was founded in 1975 and has grown considerably throughout the years. Initially, DAM managed the pension funds of three small companies whose asset values totaled $30 million. By 1991 DAM's funds under management were valued at $2 billion.

James Franklin is a senior vice president at DAM, in charge of managing the equity portion of one of its largest pension funds. Franklin meets on a quarterly basis with company officials who supervise his decisions and oversee his performance. His work is measured on several levels, including both subjective and objective criteria. The subjective criteria include estimates of the quality of research reports. The objective criteria include the actual performance of Franklin's portfolio relative to a customized index of companies in DAM's investment universe. Franklin attempts to "beat" the index not by trying to time market moves, but by investing more heavily in those companies he expects to outperform the customized index and less heavily in those companies he expects to underperform the index.

Franklin has several research analysts who are charged with following the performance of several companies within specific industries. The research analysts prepare reports that analyze the past performance of the companies and prepare projections of future performance. The projections include assessments of the "most likely" or average performance anticipated over the next month.

Franklin analyzes their findings and often asks for additional information or suggests modifications to the analyses. After a period of careful review, the final forecasts for the next month are assembled and summarized. Each month the analysts' forecasts are compared to the actual results. Annual bonuses for the analysts are based in part on the comparison of these numbers.

It is now late December 1991, and the projections for January 1992 are indicated in Table 7.26.

TABLE 7.26	Projections for January 1992 for DAM Case Study
Company	**Forecasted Mean Return**
Aluminum Co. of America (ALCOA)	0.6%
Reynolds Metals	0.9%
Alcan Aluminum, Ltd.	0.8%
Walmart Store, Inc.	1.5%
Sears, Roebuck & Co.	0.8%
Kmart Corporation	1.3%
International Business Machines (IBM)	0.4%
Digital Equipment Corporation (DEC)	1.1%
Hewlett Packard Co. (HP)	0.7%
General Motors Corp. (GM)	1.2%
Ford Motor Co. (FORD)	0.9%
Chrysler Corp.	1.3%
Boeing Co.	0.3%
McDonnell Douglas Corp.	0.2%
United Technologies Corp.	0.7%

The projections have been made for 15 U.S. companies divided into five industry groups. The five industry groups are metals, retail, computer, automotive, and aviation.

Franklin would like to use the portfolio optimization approach to see what portfolios it would recommend. He has data containing end-of-month prices for the last two years for each of the companies. The data are contained in the spreadsheet DAM.XLS. Also included in the spreadsheet is information about dividends and stock splits. Using these data, James constructs a history of 24 monthly returns for each of the 15 companies.

The past data provide useful information about the volatility (standard deviation) of stock returns. They also give useful information about the degree of association (correlation) of returns between pairs of stocks. However, average returns from the past do not tend to be good predictors of future average returns. Rather than using the raw historical data directly, Franklin creates 24 future return scenarios by adjusting the 24 historical returns. The adjustments are made so that the means of the future scenario returns are consistent with the forecasts from Table 7.26. The adjustments are also made so that the volatilities and correlations of the future scenario returns are the same as in the historical data.

The exact procedure that Franklin uses for developing future scenario returns is described next. Let r_{ij}^0 denote the historical return of security j in month i (for $j = 1, \ldots, 15$ and $i = 1, \ldots, 24$). Suppose that the average historical return of security j is μ_j^0. For security j, denote the forecasted mean return in Table 7.26 by μ_j. (For example, $\mu_1 = 0.6\%$ and $\mu_2 = 0.9\%$, where the index 1 refers to ALCOA and 2 refers to Reynolds Metals.) Franklin creates the future scenario return r_{ij} for security j in scenario i using the following equation:

$$r_{ij} = r_{ij}^0 + \mu_j - \mu_j^0 \qquad \textbf{(7.17)}$$

Franklin assumes that any of the scenarios defined by equation (7.17) can occur with equal probability. DAM's policy is never to invest more than 30% of the funds in any one industry group. Franklin measures the risk of a portfolio by its standard deviation of return. He then solves a portfolio optimization model for various minimum levels of mean return to see which portfolios are recommended. After analyzing the trade-off between risk and return, Franklin makes a judgment as to which portfolio to hold for the coming month.

Questions

1. Use the information in the file DAM.XLS to create a history of 24 monthly returns for the 15 companies. Compute the historical average return of each stock. In particular, what was the historical return of ALCOA from 12/29/89 to 1/31/90? What was the historical return of Boeing from 5/31/90 to 6/29/90? Explain how you account for dividends and stock splits in computing monthly returns.

2. Develop 24 future scenario returns using equation (7.17). What is the explanation underlying it? In particular, what is the return of ALCOA if scenario 1 occurs? What is the return of Reynolds Metals if scenario 3 occurs?

3. Compute and graph the mean–standard deviation efficient frontier. Compute at least six points on the efficient frontier (including the minimum standard deviation and maximum expected return points). Create a table of results showing the following for each of your points on the efficient frontier: (1) the optimal portfolio weights, (2) mean portfolio return, and (3) standard deviation. (Briefly explain the equations and optimization model used in the spreadsheet.)[10]

[10]*Acknowledgment*: Thanks to Ziv Katalan and Aliza Schachter for assistance in developing this case.

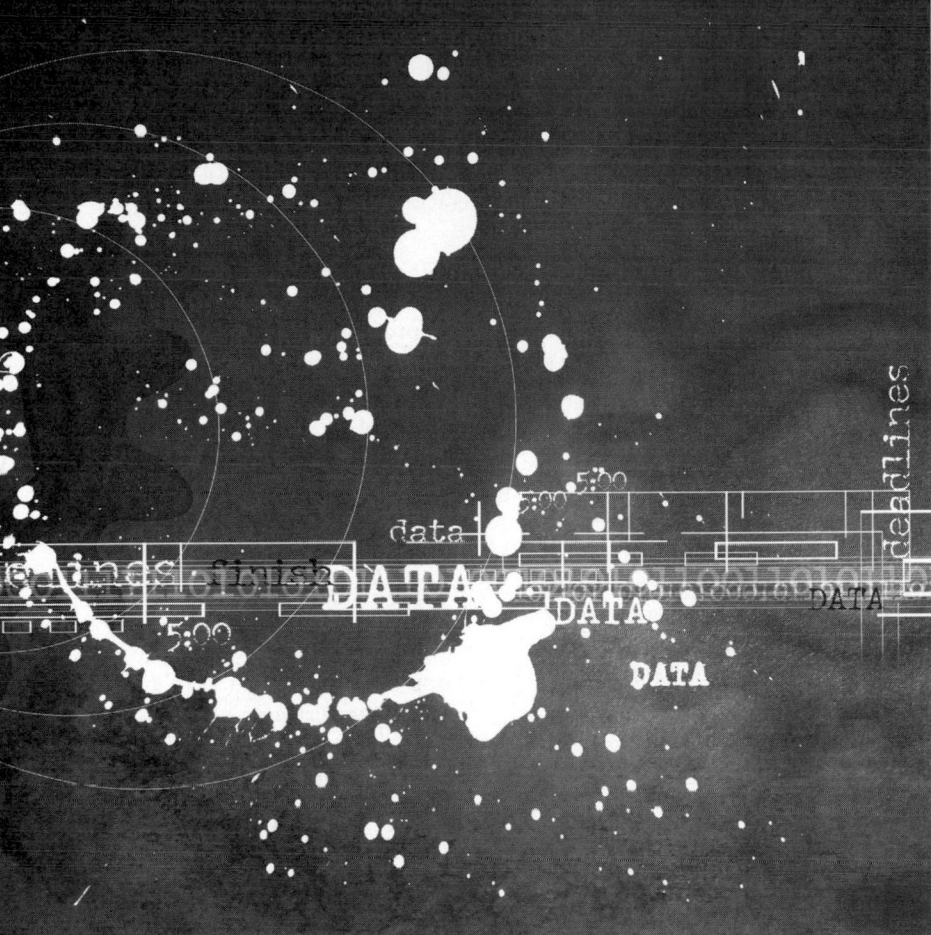

CHAPTER 8

Evolutionary Solver: An Alternative Optimization Procedure

DEVELOPING AN OPERATING-PLAN MODEL AT SANTA FE RAILWAY

Like many other companies, Santa Fe Railway faces increasing demands for customer service, cost pressures, and changing market conditions. This is particularly true in its intermodal business area, in which traffic moves on some combination of ship or truck and train. The company has averaged almost 8% growth per year in intermodal traffic handled during the period from 1989 to 1996. This increased growth and changing patterns of customer traffic has created difficult problems for Santa Fe, as described in Gorman (1998). The company needs to utilize its trains and rail lines efficiently from a cost standpoint, but it must also provide its customers with high-quality service. In addition, it must be flexible to change its operating plan quickly in response to changing customer traffic patterns.

Historically, Santa Fe's service design was rather myopic. Its service designers tried their best to make incremental refinements to current operations, but their thinking was based too much on historical procedures and could not adapt sufficiently to changing customer needs. They eventually decided to create an operating-plan model capable of building an operating plan for the intermodal business unit from scratch, one that could best adapt to the current and expected traffic patterns and would not be constrained by traditional patterns or historical schedules. As inputs, this model requires customer service requirements, engineering capabilities, and physical plant constraints. As outputs, it provides a weekly train timetable, traffic-to-train assignments, yard and railway line schedules, and equipment and locomotive flows. It simultaneously allocates physical rail network resources to trains and allocates scarce train space to traffic flows in a way that minimizes operating costs while meeting customer requirements.

The operating-plan problem can be decomposed into two problems: the train timetable problem and the traffic assignment problem. The former prescribes which trains will travel on which lines at which times. Given this information, the latter problem prescribes which customer loads are assigned to which trains. Each problem is huge, and much ingenuity was required to model and solve these problems. For the timetable problem, the original model represented each hour of the week for every possible train as a binary decision variable, where 1 indicates a train and 0 indicates no train. This model was impossibly large, so the service design team reduced its size by specifying a menu of allowable train routes (about 200) from which the model could choose. Even this reduced problem was much too large for "traditional" integer programming algorithms to solve, so the analysts did what is becoming more common in large optimization models: they turned to newer, emerging types of algorithms. In particular, they tried the genetic "survival of the fittest" algorithms we will discuss in this chapter, where they mixed schedules from a given population of schedules to carry over the best characteristics of these schedules on to the next "generation" of schedules. Unfortunately, genetic algorithms by themselves were painfully slow at producing useful populations of train schedules for this large problem. Therefore, they tried combining genetic algorithms with another type of algorithm, call tabu search, to speed up the process. (Tabu search is also a fairly new idea. It uses information from previous iterations to search in a promising direction. However, a "tabu list" prohibits the algorithm from undoing recent changes to the schedule or revisiting recent solutions.) This method of combining algorithms worked and enabled Santa Fe to solve the timetable problem reasonably quickly. The company was then able to solve the traffic assignment problem by a clever priority-based, shortest-path heuristic.

Santa Fe Intermodal has used its operating-plan model to study many major changes in rail operations: to predict train volumes based on long-term forecasts, to quantify the impact of containerization of intermodal business on train operations, and to develop a cost basis in contract negotiations for large amounts of incremental business. The model has shown the potential to improve global service by 4% while reducing costs by 6% over the previous operating plan. As R. Mark Schmidt, an analyst at Santa Fe, states, "Obviously, as with any major deviation from traditional processes, the acceptance of the operating-plan model has been a gradual one. Recent successes of the model are building confidences and as a result, the model is being interwoven into the intermodal service design process at Santa Fe." ∎

8.1 INTRODUCTION

In Chapters 3–7 we used the Excel Solver to solve many interesting and important problems. Unfortunately, there are many optimization problems for which the Solver is ill suited to find optimal solutions. However, **genetic algorithms** often perform well on optimization problems where the Solver performs poorly. The purpose of this chapter is to illustrate some interesting models that cannot be solved by the standard Solver, at least not easily or without tricks, but can be solved with genetic algorithms in a reasonably straightforward manner. In short, this chapter will greatly increase the types of optimization models we can solve.

Fortunately, the developer of the Excel Solver, Frontline Systems (www.frontsys. com), has recently developed a "Premium" Solver that uses genetic algorithms to find good solutions to many optimization problems that cannot be solved with the standard Excel Solver. The Premium Solver, included in the CD-ROM that accompanies this book (but not included in Microsoft Office), contains three separate "solvers":

- The Standard Simplex LP Solver that is used to solve linear models. This includes models where some or all of the changing cells are restricted to be binary and/or integer.

- The Standard GRG Nonlinear Solver that is used to solve nonlinear models when the target cell and constraints are "smooth" functions of the changing cells.

- The Evolutionary Solver that uses genetic algorithms to find good (close to optimal) solutions to more difficult problems, including those where the target cell and/or constraints are nonsmooth functions of the changing cells.

The first two of these implement essentially the same versions of the algorithms we have been using in the previous chapters to solve linear, integer, and nonlinear problems. Therefore, for the problems we have been solving, there is no real advantage to switching to the Premium Solver; the standard Excel Solver works fine. However, you might recall that the standard Solver cannot always handle models with IF, MAX, MIN, and several other Excel functions. The problem is that such models often contain nonsmooth functions in the target cell and/or the constraint cells. To use the standard Excel Solver on these models (if it is possible at all), we have to resort to various tricks to get them in smooth form. Fortunately, this is *not* necessary with the Evolutionary Solver, as we will illustrate in this chapter. It uses a type of algorithm, called a **genetic algorithm**, that is much more flexible.

Before discussing genetic algorithms and the Evolutionary Solver, we discuss the strengths and weaknesses of the standard Excel Solver.[1]

Consider an optimization model where the target cell is a linear function of the changing cells, the left and right sides of all constraints are linear functions of the changing cells, and all changing cells are allowed to contain fractional values—that is, there are no integer constraints. For such models, called linear models, the Solver is guaranteed to find an optimal solution (if an optimal solution exists). We have discussed many linear models in Chapters 3–5. The Solver is an excellent tool to use for any optimization problem that can be set up as a linear model, provided that the model does not exceed the Solver's size constraints—up to 200 changing cells and 100 constraints. Most larger linear models are difficult to handle in a spreadsheet format. These larger

---

[1]From here on in this chapter, when we refer to "the Solver" or the "standard Solver," we are referring to the Solver that ships with Excel. To refer to the Premium or Evolutionary Solver, we will include the Premium or Evolutionary names.

models are often solved using a modeling language such as LINGO, GAMS, or AMPL. With a modeling language, a user can generate, say, 10,000 supply constraints for a transportation model with one line of computer code. This makes it easy to compactly represent and solve large models. (We should also mention that Frontline Systems has developed a "large-scale" Solver capable of solving very large spreadsheet models. It is available as a commercial product.)

In Chapter 6 we considered linear models where some or all of the changing cells are constrained to be integers. In theory, the Solver should be able to find optimal solutions to these problems, but in practice it can take hours, days, or even weeks to find optimal solutions to integer-constrained models. This is not necessarily a weakness of the Solver—integer-constrained models are inherently difficult for *any* Solver—but algorithms other than the branch and bound algorithm used by the Solver work better for some integer models.

In the previous chapter, we discussed nonlinear models and saw that the standard Solver's nonlinear algorithm is capable of solving many of these. However, nonlinear models present two problems. First, as we learned in Section 7.2, the Solver can get "stuck" at a local maximum or a local minimum to a problem and never find the overall (or global) maximum or minimum to the problem. The function shown in Figure 7.6 illustrates this situation. In this example the Solver will fail to find the global optimal solution for certain starting solutions.

Second, we have emphasized that if a spreadsheet model uses IF, ABS, MAX, or MIN functions that depend on any of the model's changing cells, then the model is typically "nonsmooth," and the Solver might have difficulty finding an optimal solution. We illustrate one possibility in Figure 8.1 that could be caused by an IF function. The context here might be ordering a product with a quantity discount, so that the order quantity is on the horizontal axis and the total cost (ordering cost plus inventory holding cost) is on the vertical axis. The IF function specifies that if the order quantity is less than *A*, then one function specifies the total cost. If the order quantity is between *A* and *B*, another function specifies the total cost. Finally, if the order quantity is greater than *B*, a third function specifies the total cost. The resulting graph is not only nonlinear,

FIGURE 8.1
A Cost Function with Discontinuities

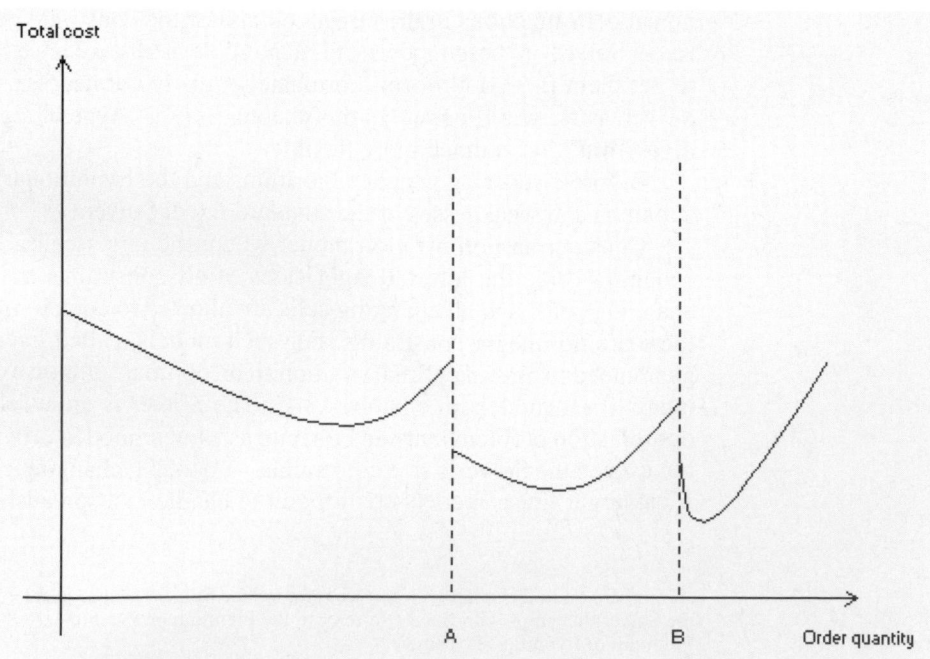

but it has **discontinuities** at A and B, where the total cost jumps from one value to another. The overall cost-minimizing order quantity is to the right of B, and if you select an initial solution to the right of B, the standard nonlinear Solver will probably locate the correct optimal solution. However, if you start at a point to the left of B, the standard Solver will almost certainly not be able to locate the correct solution.

The point of this discussion is that there are many models that the standard Solver can handle with no difficulty, but there are also models where the Solver is not well suited to finding optimal solutions. We now discuss a completely different solution method that is sometimes more successful at solving these "difficult" problems.

8.2 INTRODUCTION TO GENETIC ALGORITHMS

I n the early 1970s, John Holland of the University of Michigan realized that many features of natural evolution (such as survival of the fittest and mutation) could be used to help solve difficult optimization problems.[2] Because his methods were based on behavior observed in nature, Holland coined the name "genetic algorithm" to describe his algorithm. Simply stated, a genetic algorithm provides a method of intelligently searching an optimization model's feasible region for an optimal solution. Biological terminology is used to describe the algorithm. The target cell is called a **fitness function**, and a specification of values for all changing cells is called a **chromosome**. For most problems, a genetic algorithm codes changing cells in binary notation. For example, 1001 represents

$$1(2^3) + 0(2^2) + 0(2^1) + 1(2^0) = 8 + 1 = 9$$

Here is a rough outline of how a genetic algorithm (GA) might work. Suppose a company must decide how many units of each of two products to order. Because of quantity discounts, the function that represents total cost has discontinuities of the type observed in Figure 8.1. Actually, the total cost is even more complex than in Figure 8.1, because there are two products, not just one. However, the only requirement of the algorithm is that total cost $TC(Q_1, Q_2)$ can be calculated for any combination of the order quantities Q_1 and Q_2. Suppose Q_1 and Q_2 must each be between 0 and 500. (In this discussion we assume the model has no constraints other than lower and upper bounds on each changing cell. Later we discuss how a GA can handle other types of constraints.) Then the GA will use the following steps.

1. **Generate a population.** The GA randomly samples values of the changing cells between the lower and upper bounds to generate a set of (usually at least 50) chromosomes. The initial set of chromosomes is called the **population**. For example, two members of the population might be

   - Chromosome 1: $Q_1 = 100$ and $Q_2 = 400$ (or in binary, $Q_1 = 001100100$ and $Q_2 = 110010000$)
   - Chromosome 2: $Q_1 = 300$ and $Q_2 = 200$ (or in binary, $Q_1 = 100101100$ and $Q_2 = 011001000$)

   The initial population is constructed by randomly choosing points from the problem's feasible region. (Note that 9 binary digits are sufficient to represent any order quantity from 0 to 500.)

[2]Goldberg (1989), Davis (1991), and Holland (1975) are good references on genetic algorithms.

2. **Create a new generation.** Create a new generation of chromosomes in the hope of finding improvement. In the new generation, chromosomes with a smaller fitness function (in a minimization problem) have a greater chance of surviving to the next generation. Suppose in our example that chromosome 1 has a fitness value (total cost) of $2560 and chromosome 2 has a fitness value of $3240. Clearly, chromosome 1 should have a larger chance of surviving to the next generation. **Crossover** and **mutation** are also used to generate chromosomes for the next generation.

   a. Crossover (fairly common) "splices" together two chromosomes at a prespecified point. For example, if chromosomes 1 and 2 are combined by crossover and the crossover point is between the fourth and fifth digits (from the right), the resulting chromosomes (in binary) are

   - New chromosome 1: $Q_1 = 100100100$ and $Q_2 = 011000000$ (or $Q_1 = 292$ and $Q_2 = 192$)
   - New chromosome 2: $Q_1 = 001101100$ and $Q_2 = 110011000$ (or $Q_1 = 108$ and $Q_2 = 408$)

   Note that the two original Q_1's are used to create the two new Q_1's, and similarly for the Q_2's. For example, Q_1 for the new chromosome 1 splices together the left digits 10010 from Q_1 of the original chromosome 2 and the right digits 0100 from Q_1 of the original chromosome 1.

   b. Mutation (very rare) randomly selects a digit and changes it from 0 to 1 or vice versa. For example, if we mutate the left digit of Q_1 in chromosome 2, the new Q_1 in chromosome 2 becomes $Q_1 = 101101100$ (or $Q_1 = 364$). As this example indicates, mutation can provide a dramatic effect, taking us to a completely different location in the feasible region. Therefore, an occasional mutation is useful for getting the algorithm "unstuck."

3. **Stopping condition.** At each generation the best value of the fitness function in the generation is recorded, and the algorithm repeats step 2. If no improvement in the best fitness value is observed after many consecutive generations, then the GA terminates.

To handle a constraint such as $Q_1 + Q_2 \leq 700$, the GA adds (in a minimization problem), say, $M(Q_1 + Q_2 - 700)$ to the fitness function, where M is a suitably large number such as 1,000,000. Now any chromosome that violates the constraint will have a high value of the fitness function because the "penalty" $M(Q_1 + Q_2 - 700)$ will greatly increase the value of the new fitness function. This causes the GA to stay away from chromosomes that violate the constraint.

Strengths and Weaknesses of GAs

If you let a GA run long enough, it is *guaranteed* to find the solution to any optimization problem. The problem is that the sun could explode before the GA finds the optimal solution! In general, we never know how long we should run a GA. For the problems discussed in this chapter, an optimal solution was always found within 180 minutes (usually within 5 minutes or less, although timing will depend on the problem and some experimentation is invariably necessary). Therefore, we usually tell the Evolutionary Solver to run for 10,000 seconds and report the best solution found. Unfortunately, we will not know if the best solution we have found is optimal, but it is usually a "good" solution—that is, it is usually very close to being optimal.

As a rule, GAs do very well in problems with few constraints (excluding bounds on changing cells). In addition, the complexity of the target cell does not bother a GA.

For example, a GA can easily handle MIN, MAX IF, and ABS functions in spreadsheet models. This is the key advantage of GAs. On the other hand, GAs do not usually perform as well on problems having many constraints. For example, the standard Solver had no difficulty with the multiple-constraint linear models in Chapters 3–5, but GAs would not do nearly as well on them.

8.3 INTRODUCTION TO THE EVOLUTIONARY SOLVER

Genetic algorithms have been available for several years and have been implemented in several software packages. However, they have been available as Excel add-ins only recently. In this chapter we will use the Evolutionary Solver developed by Frontline Systems and available as part of the Premium Solver included on the CD-ROM in this book.[3] To get started with the Evolutionary Solver, we revisit the Great Threads example, Example 6.2, from Chapter 6.

EXAMPLE	8.1

TEXTILE MANUFACTURING AT GREAT THREADS

Recall that the Great Threads Company is capable of manufacturing shirts, shorts, and pants. Each type of clothing requires that Great Threads have the appropriate type of machinery available. The machinery needed to manufacture each type of clothing must be rented at the following rates: shirt machinery, $1500 per week; shorts machinery, $1200 per week; pants machinery, $1600 per week. Each type of clothing requires the amounts of cloth and labor given in Table 8.1. This table also shows the unit variable cost and selling price for each type of clothing. There are 2000 hours and 2500 square yards of cloth available in a given week. The company wants to find a solution that maximizes its weekly profit.

TABLE 8.1 Data for Great Threads Example

	Labor Hours	Cloth (sq. yd.)	Sales Price	Unit Variable Cost
Shirts	2.0	3.0	$35	$20
Shorts	1.0	2.5	$20	$10
Pants	6.0	4.0	$45	$25

Solution

In the solution to Example 6.2, we used 0–1 changing cells to indicate whether *any* of each product is produced and should therefore incur the corresponding fixed cost. Now, however, we will not use these 0–1 changing cells. We will instead model the fixed costs with simple IF functions. If the number of shirts produced is positive, for

---

[3]As we discussed in the appendix to Chapter 3, this is the only place in this book where the Premium Solver is required. For all other optimization models in this book, the standard Solver that ships with Excel is sufficient. However, the standard Solver does *not* include the Evolutionary Solver. Therefore, to solve the models in this chapter, you must install the Premium Solver.

example, then the fixed cost for the shirt machinery will be incurred; otherwise, it will not be incurred. This IF function simplifies the model. It unfortunately causes the standard Solver problems, but the Evolutionary Solver has no difficulty with it.

DEVELOPING THE SPREADSHEET MODEL

The completed model appears in Figure 8.2. (See the file GREATTHREADS.XLS.) Although the model is similar to that in Example 6.2, we repeat the key steps for convenience.

❶ **Changing cells.** Enter any values in the UnitsProduced range. This is the *only* range of changing cells for this model.

❷ **Upper limits on production**. When using the Evolutionary Solver, it is a good idea to put lower and upper limits on all changing cells. For this model, the lower limits are 0. To obtain upper limits in row 14, we calculate how much of each product could be produced if *all* resources were devoted to it. (This is the same logic we used in Example 6.2.) Enter the formula

=MIN($D$17/B4,$D$18/B5)

in cell B14 and copy it across row 14.

❸ **Resource availability.** Calculate the labor hours and cloth used in the Used range in the usual way with SUMPRODUCT functions.

❹ **Revenues, variable costs.** Calculate the revenues and variable costs by entering the formula

=B7*B$12

in cell B22 and copying it to the range B22:D23.

❺ **Fixed costs.** Calculate the fixed costs incurred by entering the formula

=IF(B12>0,B9,0)

	A	B	C	D	E	F	G	H
1	**Great Threads fixed cost clothing model**							
2								
3	**Input data on products**	Shirts	Shorts	Pants		**Range names used:**		
4	Labor hours/unit	2	1	6		UnitsProduced - B12:D12		
5	Cloth (sq. yd.)/unit	3	2.5	4		Capacities - B14:D14		
6						Used - B17:B18		
7	Selling price/unit	$35	$40	$65		Available - D17:D18		
8	Variable cost/unit	$20	$10	$25		Revenues - B22:D22		
9	Fixed cost for equipment	$1,500	$1,200	$1,600		VarCosts - B23:D23		
10						FixedCosts - B24:D24		
11	**Production plan**	Shirts	Shorts	Pants		Profit - B25		
12	Units produced	0	1000	0				
13		<=	<=	<=				
14	Capacity	833	1000	333				
15								
16	**Constraints on resources**	Used		Available				
17	Labor hours	1000.00	<=	2000				
18	Cloth	2500.00	<=	2500				
19								
20	**Monetary values**							
21		Shirts	Shorts	Pants				
22	Revenue	$0	$40,000	$0				
23	Variable cost	$0	$10,000	$0				
24	Fixed cost for equipment	$0	$1,200	$0				
25	Profit	$28,800						

FIGURE 8.2 Great Threads Model

in cell B24 and copying it to the FixedCosts range. This simple formula makes the model much more straightforward than the model with binary variables in Example 6.2. Fortunately, the Evolutionary Solver can handle it!

6 **Profit.** Calculate the profit in the Profit cell with the formula

=SUM(Revenues)-SUM(VarCosts)-SUM(FixedCosts)

USING THE EVOLUTIONARY SOLVER

The Evolutionary Solver uses genetic algorithms to obtain "good" solutions. It begins with a population containing, say, 150 sets of values—chromosomes—for the changing cells. For example, one chromosome might be (100, 500, 300). (This would be coded in binary form by the algorithm.) This chromosome represents producing 100 shirts, 500 shorts, and 300 pants. Chromosomes that yield large profits have more chance of surviving to the next generation of chromosomes. Chromosomes that yield low profits have little chance of surviving to the next generation. Occasionally, the Evolutionary Solver will drastically change—mutate—the value of a changing cell. Usually we stop the Evolutionary Solver after a specified time period (say 30 minutes) or when there has been no improvement in the target cell value after a given time. Here are some important remarks about the Evolutionary Solver.

- The Evolutionary Solver will usually find a good solution, but there is no guarantee that it will find the *best* solution.

- The Evolutionary Solver is not very efficient at handling constraints. The best way to handle constraints is to heavily penalize a violation of a constraint. The penalty is then included in the target cell. We will not use penalties in this example, but we will illustrate them in a later example.

- A good starting solution—the values you place in the changing cells—usually helps the Evolutionary Solver in its search for an optimal solution.

- The Evolutionary Solver places more of a burden on you to specify certain parameters of the algorithm. These parameters are specified in Options dialog boxes, as we will illustrate in the following example. Unfortunately, these parameters are not very intuitive to most users, and some experimentation may be necessary to find the "best" settings of these parameters for any given model. However, if you use the default settings or the settings we suggest, you should not experience problems.

- Much of the solution process is driven by random numbers that direct the search. Therefore, two people can get different solutions to the same problem. In fact, running the Solver a second time can yield a different solution!

- Once the Evolutionary Solver has found a good solution, you can use the GRG Nonlinear Solver (the nonlinear algorithm that is included with the Premium Solver software) to try to find a slightly better solution. If there is no improvement, you can probably infer that the solution found by the Evolutionary Solver is close to optimal.

In general, use the following steps to implement the Evolutionary Solver.

1 **Specify the target cell, changing cells, and constraints.** This is done in the usual way. The only difference is that you should put lower and upper bounds on all changing cells—in addition to any other constraints that might be in the model. At this point, the Solver dialog box should appear as in Figure 8.3 (page 408). As we discussed in the appendix to Chapter 3, the Premium button is a "toggle." When it reads Premium, this means you are using the standard Solver that ships with Excel. When you click on it, its caption changes to Standard, which means that you are using the Premium

FIGURE 8.3
Filling Out the
Solver Dialog Box

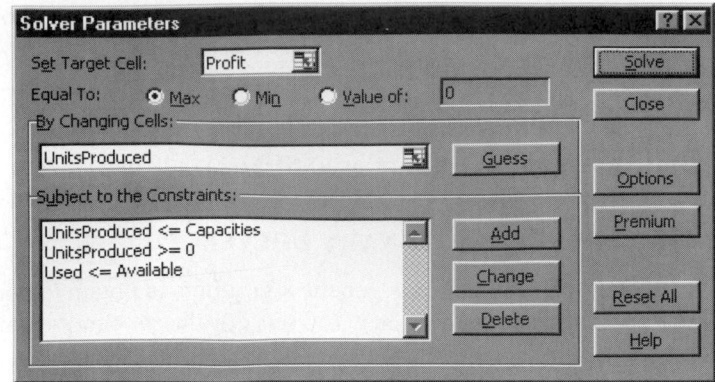

Solver. (This might sound backward, but just remember that the caption on the button indicates which Solver you will *switch to* if you click on the button.)

2 **Select the Evolutionary Solver.** Click on the Premium button, and then click on the dropdown list of available algorithms to select the Evolutionary Solver. (See Figure 8.4.) This is the option we will use throughout this chapter, but you can also experiment with the GRG Nonlinear option, especially after the Evolutionary Solver finds a "good" solution.

3 **Solver Options.** Click on the Options button to show the Solver Options dialog box in Figure 8.5. We suggest that you set the Max Time box to some fairly large value such as 10,000 seconds. The Iterations setting is not important for Evolutionary Solver, and you can leave Precision and Convergence as very small numbers. A population size of 150 is adequate for most problems, although you can keep the default population size of 100. In the problems we have tried, a mutation rate of 0.25 has worked rather well, although you might want to experiment with other values. We strongly suggest that you check the Required Bounds on Variables box. This forces you to put lower and upper limits on all changing cells.

4 **Limit Options.** Click on the Limit Options button to bring up the dialog box in Figure 8.6. If Max Time in the previous step is set to a large number, then setting the Max Subproblems and Max Feasible Sols boxes to a large number ensures that the algorithm will run a long time before prompting you whether to continue. Setting the Tolerance to 0.0005 and the Max Time Without Improvement to 30 ensures that the algorithm will stop if the Target Cell value has improved less than 0.05% during the last 30 seconds. You can experiment with these settings. For example, it might be necessary in some problems to increase the Max Time Without Improvement setting.

FIGURE 8.4
Selecting the
Evolutionary Solver

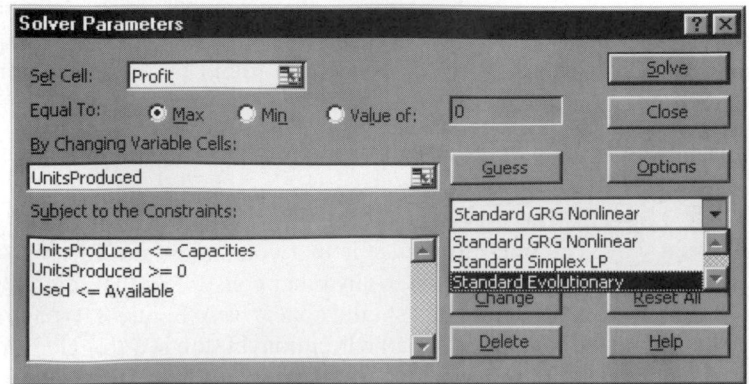

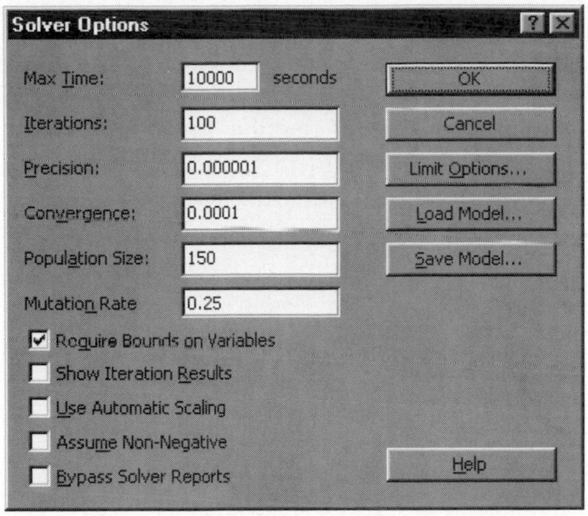

FIGURE 8.5
Solver Options
Dialog Box

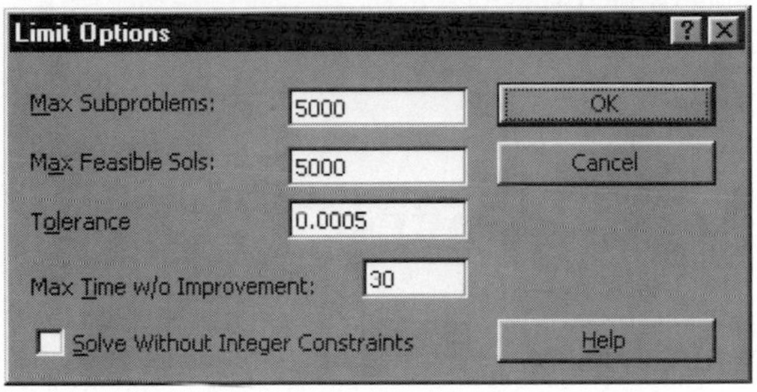

Solver Options

Max Time:	10000	seconds	OK
Iterations:	100		Cancel
Precision:	0.000001		Limit Options...
Convergence:	0.0001		Load Model...
Population Size:	150		Save Model...
Mutation Rate:	0.25		

☑ Require Bounds on Variables
☐ Show Iteration Results
☐ Use Automatic Scaling
☐ Assume Non-Negative
☐ Bypass Solver Reports   Help

FIGURE 8.6
Limit Options
Dialog Box

Limit Options

Max Subproblems:	5000	OK
Max Feasible Sols:	5000	Cancel
Tolerance:	0.0005	
Max Time w/o Improvement:	30	

☐ Solve Without Integer Constraints   Help

This would allow the algorithm more time to search for a better solution from the current best solution.

5   Solve. From the Limit Options dialog box, back your way out to the beginning Solver dialog box and click on Solve. You can watch the progress of the solution process in the status bar of your screen. In particular, watch the "Incumbent." It is the current best value of the target cell. Typically, this value increases (for a maximization problem) rapidly at first, then very slowly. If you get the sense that it is going nowhere after a minute or two (and you are tired of waiting), you can press the Esc key to stop the process. From there you can either let the process continue once again or accept the best solution to this point. Don't be surprised if the solution process takes *much* longer than you have experienced for Solver models in previous chapters. Genetic algorithms are not guaranteed to be fast, but they make up for it by being more flexible.

For this particular model, the Evolutionary Solver gets to the solution in Figure 8.2 almost instantaneously. Then it runs for 30 seconds (the time we specified in the Limit Options dialog box) without being able to find a better solution, at which time it quits. Note that this solution, which says that Great Threads should produce only shorts for a profit of $28,800, is exactly the same as the integer-constrained solution we obtained for this model in Chapter 6. Therefore, we *know* that this solution is optimal. However, if we had not solved this model by another method, we could not be absolutely certain that the Evolutionary Solver obtained the optimal solution. ■

Limits on Changing Cells: Required?

In the Evolutionary Solver Options dialog box in Figure 8.5, we checked the Required Bounds on Variables box, which forces us to include constraints with lower and upper bounds on the changing cells. Is it possible to leave this box unchecked and ignore bounds on the changing cells? Evidently, the answer is "yes," but it is not a good idea—the genetic algorithm will not work as well. Therefore, we suggest that you always check this box and always include bounds on the changing cells in your list of constraints.

8.4 NONLINEAR PRICING MODELS

We examined several pricing models in the previous chapter. Here we will examine one more such model, where customers of a certain product place less and less value on each succeeding item of the product. We will see that if the company selling the product sets a constant price per item, it will earn considerably less profit than if it uses a more imaginative pricing scheme, called a **two-part tariff**. In this pricing scheme, each customer pays a fixed amount each time she buys *any* amount of the product. In addition, she pays a variable amount per item purchased.

EXAMPLE 8.2

PRICING MENTHOS CANDY

Suppose we sell Menthos candy. Most people value the first pack of Menthos they purchase more than the second pack. They also value the second pack more than the third pack, and so on. How can we take advantage of this when pricing Menthos? If we charge a single price for each pack of Menthos, then few people are going to buy more than one or two packs. Alternatively, however, we can try the two-part tariff approach. Here we charge an "entry fee" to anyone who buys Menthos, plus a reduced price per pack purchased. For example, if a reasonable *single* price per pack is $1.10, then a reasonable two-part tariff might be an entry fee of $1.50 and a price of $0.50 per pack. This will give some customers an incentive to purchase many packs of Menthos. Because the total cost of purchasing *n* packs of Menthos is no longer a linear function of *n*—it is now "piecewise linear"—we refer to the two-part tariff as a nonlinear pricing strategy.

As usual with pricing models, the key input is customer sensitivity to price. Rather than having a single demand function, however, we now assume that each customer has his or her unique sensitivity to price. To keep the example fairly small, we will assume that four typical customers from the four market segments for the product have been asked what they would pay for each successive pack of Menthos, with the results listed in Figure 8.7. For example, customer 1 is willing to pay $1.24 for the first pack of Menthos, $1.03 for the second pack, and only $0.35 for the tenth pack. These four customers are considered representative of the market. If it costs $0.40 to produce a pack of Menthos, determine a profit-maximizing single price and a profit-maximizing two-part tariff. Assume that the four market segments have 10,000, 5000, 7500, and 15,000 customers, respectively, and that the customers within a market segment all respond identically to price.

FIGURE 8.7
Price Sensitivity of
Four Representative
Customers

	A	B	C	D	E
3	**Price sensitivity of 4 selected customers**				
4		Price willing to pay (or marginal value of packs)			
5	Pack #	Customer 1	Customer 2	Customer 3	Customer 4
6	1	1.24	0.92	1.27	1.49
7	2	1.03	0.85	1.11	1.24
8	3	0.89	0.69	0.96	1.10
9	4	0.80	0.58	0.85	0.97
10	5	0.77	0.50	0.73	0.81
11	6	0.66	0.43	0.63	0.71
12	7	0.59	0.36	0.51	0.63
13	8	0.51	0.32	0.45	0.53
14	9	0.42	0.26	0.39	0.42
15	10	0.35	0.22	0.32	0.35

Solution

We first set up the single-price model. Then, with very little modification, we formulate the two-part tariff model.

DEVELOPING THE SINGLE-PRICE MODEL

The single-price model appears in Figure 8.8 (page 412). (See the MENTHOS1.XLS file.) It can be formed with the following steps.

1 **Inputs.** Enter the inputs in the shaded ranges. Note that the large shaded range is just the price sensitivity table from Figure 8.7.

2 **Price.** The *only* decision variable in this model is the single price charged for every pack of Menthos sold. Enter any value in this Price cell.

3 **Total value table.** The values in the shaded price sensitivity range are *marginal* values, the most each customer would pay for the next pack of Menthos. In the range H6:K15 calculate the *total* value of n packs to each customer (for n from 1 to 10). First, enter the formula

=B6

in cell H6 and copy it across row 6. Then enter the formula

=H6+B7

in cell H7 and copy it to the range H7:K15.

4 **Total cost column.** Using the single-price scheme, each customer must pay np for n packs if the price is p. Calculate these amounts in the range E19:E28 by entering the formula

=UnitPrice*D19

Pricing Menthos - single price model

Price sensitivity of four types of customers

Price willing to pay (or marginal value of packs)

Pack #	Customer 1	Customer 2	Customer 3	Customer 4
1	1.24	0.92	1.27	1.49
2	1.03	0.85	1.11	1.24
3	0.89	0.69	0.96	1.10
4	0.80	0.58	0.85	0.97
5	0.77	0.50	0.73	0.81
6	0.66	0.43	0.63	0.71
7	0.59	0.36	0.51	0.63
8	0.51	0.32	0.45	0.53
9	0.42	0.26	0.39	0.42
10	0.35	0.22	0.32	0.35

Total value of purchases

Total value from this many packs

# of packs	Customer 1	Customer 2	Customer 3	Customer 4
1	1.24	0.92	1.27	1.49
2	2.27	1.77	2.38	2.73
3	3.16	2.46	3.34	3.83
4	3.96	3.04	4.19	4.80
5	4.73	3.54	4.92	5.61
6	5.39	3.97	5.55	6.32
7	5.98	4.33	6.06	6.95
8	6.49	4.65	6.51	7.48
9	6.91	4.91	6.90	7.90
10	7.26	5.13	7.22	8.25

Unit cost	$0.40

Total cost of packs

# of packs	Cost
1	0.80
2	1.60
3	2.40
4	3.20
5	4.00
6	4.80
7	5.60
8	6.40
9	7.20
10	8.00

Unit price	$0.80

Surplus (value minus cost) from purchasing

# of packs	Customer 1	Customer 2	Customer 3	Customer 4
1	0.44	0.12	0.47	0.69
2	0.67	0.17	0.78	1.13
3	0.76	0.06	0.94	1.43
4	0.76	-0.16	0.99	1.60
5	0.73	-0.46	0.92	1.61
6	0.59	-0.83	0.75	1.52
7	0.38	-1.27	0.46	1.35
8	0.09	-1.75	0.11	1.08
9	-0.29	-2.29	-0.30	0.70
10	-0.74	-2.87	-0.78	0.25

Customer behavior

	Customer 1	Customer 2	Customer 3	Customer 4
Max surplus	0.76	0.17	0.99	1.61
# purchased	4	2	4	5
Market size (1000s)	10	5	7.5	15

Total purchased (1000s)	155
Profit ($1000s)	62.000

Range names used:
UnitCost - B17
UnitPrice - B19
NPurch - B33:E33
MktSize - B34:E34
TotPurch - B36
Profit - B37

FIGURE 8.8 Single-Price Model

in cell E19 and copying down.

❺ **Surplus table.** This is the key to the model. We define the "surplus" for any customer from buying n packs as the total value of n packs minus the total cost of n packs, and we assume that the customer will buy the number of packs with the largest surplus. This makes sense economically. If a customer places more value on n packs than it costs to buy n packs, then presumably the customer will consider purchasing n packs. But a customer will not purchase n packs if they cost more than the customer values them. To calculate these surpluses, enter the formula

=H6-$E19

in cell H19 and copy it to the range H19:K28.

❻ **Maximum surplus.** Calculate the maximum surplus for each customer by entering the formula

=MAX(H19:H28)

in cell B32 and copying it across row 32.

❼ **Packs purchased.** For each customer we need to find the number of packs that corresponds to the maximum surplus. This can be done easily with Excel's MATCH function. Specifically, enter the formula

=IF(B32<0,0,MATCH(B32,H19:H28,0))

in cell B33 and copy it across row 33. This formula says that if the maximum surplus is negative, the customer will not purchase any packs at all. Otherwise, it matches the maximum surplus to the entries in the range H19:H28 and returns the index of the cell where the match occurs. In this example, the match for customer 1 occurs in the 4th cell of the range H19:H28, so that the MATCH function returns 4. Note that the last argument of the MATCH function is 0 if we want an *exact* match, as we do here. Then calculate the total number of packs purchased by *all* customers with the formula

=SUMPRODUCT(MktSize,NPurch)

in the TotPurch cell.

8 **Profit.** Calculate the profit in the Profit cell with the formula

=(UnitPrice-UnitCost)*TotPurch

USING THE EVOLUTIONARY SOLVER

First, note that the standard Solver will have trouble with this model because of the IF and MATCH functions. However, these present no difficulties to the Evolutionary Solver. We set it up as shown in Figure 8.9, using the same values for the various options as in the previous example. Note that we use an upper limit of $1.50 for the unit price. This suffices because the most any customer will pay for *any* pack of Menthos is $1.49.

FIGURE 8.9
Solver Dialog Box for Single-Price Model

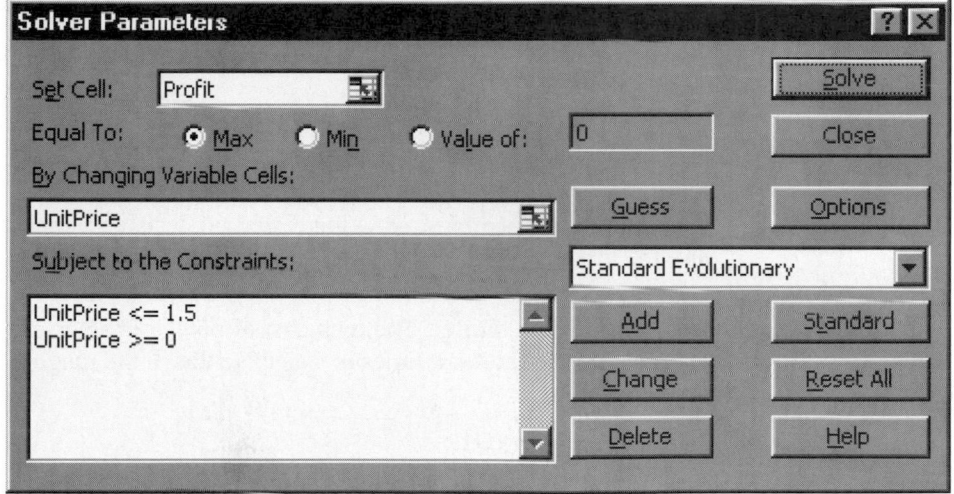

Again, the Solver converges to the solution in Figure 8.8 quickly and then tries for a long time—unsuccessfully—to find a better solution. We can be fairly certain that this solution is optimal, but this is not guaranteed. The single price of $0.80 produces a profit of $62,000. It strikes the best balance for these four market segments. A lower price would needlessly sacrifice revenue, whereas a higher price would cause at least one market segment to buy fewer packs.

DEVELOPING THE TWO-PART TARIFF MODEL

The two-part tariff model is so similar that we made a copy of the MENTHOS1.XLS file and then made the following modifications. (See Figure 8.10 (page 414) and the MENTHOS2.XLS file.) The steps that are the same as before are omitted.

Pack #	Price willing to pay (or marginal value of packs)				# of packs	Total value from this many packs			
	Customer 1	Customer 2	Customer 3	Customer 4		Customer 1	Customer 2	Customer 3	Customer 4
1	1.24	0.92	1.27	1.49	1	1.24	0.92	1.27	1.49
2	1.03	0.85	1.11	1.24	2	2.27	1.77	2.38	2.73
3	0.89	0.69	0.96	1.10	3	3.16	2.46	3.34	3.83
4	0.80	0.58	0.85	0.97	4	3.96	3.04	4.19	4.80
5	0.77	0.50	0.73	0.81	5	4.73	3.54	4.92	5.61
6	0.66	0.43	0.63	0.71	6	5.39	3.97	5.55	6.32
7	0.59	0.36	0.51	0.63	7	5.98	4.33	6.06	6.95
8	0.51	0.32	0.45	0.53	8	6.49	4.65	6.51	7.48
9	0.42	0.26	0.39	0.42	9	6.91	4.91	6.90	7.90
10	0.35	0.22	0.32	0.35	10	7.26	5.13	7.22	8.25

Price sensitivity of four typical customers   **Total value of purchases**

Total cost of packs   **Surplus (value minus cost) from purchasing**

Unit cost	$0.40	# of packs	Cost	# of packs	Customer 1	Customer 2	Customer 3	Customer 4
Price parameters		1	3.77	1	-2.53	-2.85	-2.50	-2.28
Fixed part	$3.37	2	4.16	2	-1.89	-2.39	-1.78	-1.43
Variable part	$0.39	3	4.55	3	-1.39	-2.09	-1.21	-0.72
		4	4.94	4	-0.98	-1.90	-0.75	-0.14
		5	5.33	5	-0.60	-1.79	-0.41	0.28
		6	5.73	6	-0.34	-1.76	-0.18	0.59
		7	6.12	7	-0.14	-1.79	-0.06	0.83
		8	6.51	8	-0.02	-1.86	0.00	0.97
		9	6.90	9	0.01	-1.99	0.00	1.00
		10	7.29	10	-0.03	-2.16	-0.07	0.96

Customer behavior

	Customer 1	Customer 2	Customer 3	Customer 4
Max surplus	0.01	-1.76	0.00	1.00
# purchased	9	0	8	9
Amount paid	6.902	0	6.510	6.902
Market size (1000s)	10	5	7.5	15

Total purchased (1000s)	285
Profit ($1000s)	107.376

Range names used:
UnitCost - B17
Fixed - B20
Variable - B21
NPurch - B33:E33
Revenues - B34:E34
MktSize - B35:E35
TotPurch - B37
Profit - B38

FIGURE 8.10 Two-Part Tariff Model

❶ **Decision variables.** Now there are two decision variables—the fixed entry fee and the variable cost per pack. Enter any values for these in the Fixed and Variable cells.

❷ **Total cost column.** The total cost of purchasing n packs is now the fixed entry fee plus the variable cost times n. Calculate this in the range E19:E28 by entering the formula

=Fixed+Variable*D19

in cell E19 and copying it to the rest of the range.

❸ **Revenues.** Calculate the amount paid by the customers in row 34 by entering the formula

=IF(B33>0,Fixed+Variable*B33,0)

in cell B34 and copying it across. Note that the entry fee is evidently too high for customer 2, so she does not purchase any packs, and there is no corresponding revenue.

❹ **Profit.** Calculate the profit in the Profit cell with the formula

=SUMPRODUCT(Revenues,MktSize)-UnitCost*TotPurch

The Evolutionary Solver setup is almost the same as before. However, we now select both the Fixed and Variable cells as changing cells, and we put upper limits on each of them. (We used $10 as an upper limit on Fixed and $1.50 for Variable, reasoning that these would almost certainly be large enough.) The solution in Figure 8.10 was found after a few seconds. It indicates that the company should charge all customers $3.37 plus $0.39 for each pack purchased. This pricing scheme is too high for the second market segment, which doesn't buy any packs, but it entices segments 1, 3, and 4 to purchase many more packs than they purchased with the single price of $0.80. (Check the price sensitivity columns for these segments. Can you see why they are willing to purchase so many packs with this particular two-part tariff?) More important, it yields a profit of $107,376, about 73% more than the profit from the single-price policy. The moral is clear—clever pricing schemes can make companies significantly larger profits than the simple pricing schemes we are accustomed to. ∎

Other Forms of Nonlinear Pricing

There are many other forms of nonlinear pricing, such as:

- Sell only single-item packs or packs with 6 items.
- Charge one price for the first n packs and another price for the rest.

With the Evolutionary Solver it is easy to experiment with these types of nonlinear pricing schemes and determine the profit earned by each of them. For example, if we allow Menthos to be sold only in a 1-pack or a 6-pack, you can show that we can earn a profit of $9.94 by charging $5.38 for a 6-pack and virtually any price for a 1-pack. Then we will sell three customers a 6-pack and make $17.14 − $7.20 = $9.94. Similarly, the best form of the "charge one price for first n packs and another price for remaining packs" scheme (where n is also a decision variable) is to sell up to 4 packs at $1.18 and $0.42 for each additional pack. See the book by Dolan (1996) for further discussion and applications of pricing models.

PROBLEMS

Skill-Building Problems

3. In Example 8.2, determine the optimal pricing policy if Menthos are sold in only a one-pack or a six-pack.

4. In Example 8.2, determine the best pricing policy if quantity discounts with a single-price breakpoint are used.

5. Based on Schrage (1997). Table 8.2 lists the size of the four main markets for Excel, Word, and the bundle of Excel and Word. It also shows how much members of each group are willing to pay for each

product combination. How can Microsoft maximize the revenue earned from these products? You should consider the following options:
- No bundling, where Word and Excel are sold separately
- Pure bundling, where purchasers can buy only Word and Excel together
- Mixed bundling, where purchasers can buy Word or Excel separately, or they can buy them as a bundle

TABLE 8.2	Data for Bundling Problem			
Market	**Size**	**Excel Only**	**Word Only**	**Bundled**
Business	70,000	450	110	530
Legal	50,000	75	430	480
Education	60,000	290	250	410
Home	45,000	220	380	390

8.5 COMBINATORIAL MODELS

Consider the following situations.

- Xerox must determine where to place maintenance facilities. The more maintenance facilities selected, the more copiers that will be sold due to better availability of maintenance. How can the company locate maintenance facilities to maximize total profit?
- A gasoline company is loading three different products on a tanker truck with five compartments. Each compartment can handle at most one product. How should the company load the truck to come as close as possible to meeting its delivery requirements?
- Fox has 30 different ads of different lengths that must be assigned to ten different 2-minute commercial breaks. How should the company assign ads to maximize its total ad revenue?
- John Deere must schedule its production of lawn mowers over the next 4 weeks. It wants to meet its forecasted demands, it wants to keep production hours fairly constant from week to week, and it wants to avoid model changeovers as much as possible. How should the company schedule its production?

Each of these problems is a **combinatorial** optimization problem that requires us to choose the best of many different combinations available. While combinatorial optimization problems can often be handled as linear Solver models with 0–1 changing cells, the formulation of the constraints needed to keep the model linear is often difficult. (We saw examples of the tricks required in the examples in Chapter 6.) However, with the Evolutionary Solver we need not worry about whether the constraints or the target cell are linear. The SUMIF and COUNTIF functions often prove useful in such problems. The two examples in this section illustrate typical combinatorial optimization problems.

Loading Products on a Truck

The following example will possibly appear simple when you first read it. It is not! The number of possible solutions is enormous, and it can take a Solver, even the Evolutionary Solver, quite a long time to find an optimal (or nearly optimal) solution.

EXAMPLE 8.3

LOADING A GAS STORAGE TRUCK

A gas truck contains five compartments with the capacities listed in Table 8.3. Three products must be shipped on the truck, and there can be at most one product per compartment. The demand for each product, the shortage cost per gallon, and the maximum allowable shortage for each product are listed in Table 8.4. How can we load the truck to minimize the shortage costs?

TABLE 8.3	Truck Capacities
Compartment	**Capacity (Gallons)**
1	2700
2	2800
3	1100
4	1800
5	3400

TABLE 8.4	Demand and Shortage Data		
Product	**Demand**	**Max Shortage Allowed**	**Cost per Gallon Short**
1	2900	900	$10
2	4000	900	$8
3	4900	900	$6

Solution

The objective in this problem is to minimize the total shortage cost. The decision variables indicate the type of product stored in each compartment and the amount of that product to load in the compartment. The constraints must ensure that we do not overfill any compartment and that we do not exceed the maximum allowable shortage.

DEVELOPING THE SPREADSHEET MODEL

The completed model appears in Figure 8.11 (page 418). (See the file GASSTORAGE.XLS.) It can be developed as follows.

❶ **Inputs.** Enter the inputs from Tables 8.3 and 8.4 into the shaded ranges.

❷ **Decision variables.** Enter any integer values (from 1 to 3) in the ProductsStored range and any values (integer or noninteger) in the AmtsStored range. These two ranges represent the changing cells.

❸ **Amounts stored total.** We need to know how many gallons of each product are stored on the truck. To calculate these from the information in the changing cells, we use the SUMIF function. Specifically, enter the formula

=SUMIF(ProductsStored,A21,AmtsStored)

in cell B21. This formula sums the values in the AmtsStored range for all rows where the product index, 1, in cell A21 matches the index in the ProductsStored range. Therefore, it calculates the total amount of product 1 stored on the truck. Copy this formula down for the other two products.

❹ **Shortages.** To calculate the shortages, enter the formula

=IF(B21<C21,C21-B21,0)

in cell D21 and copy it down. Note that we have dealt with shortages in previous chapters, but they always required some tricks to keep the models linear. Now we use straightforward IF functions, which present no difficult for the Evolutionary Solver.

FIGURE 8.11
Gas Truck Storage
Model

	A	B	C	D	E	F	G	H
1	Storing gas products in compartments							
2								
3	Unit shortage costs and penalty cost for violating shortage constraints							
4	Product	Cost/gallon						
5	1	$10.00				Range names used:		
6	2	$8.00				UnitCosts - B5:B7		
7	3	$6.00				UnitPenalty - B9		
8						ProductsStored - B13:B17		
9	Shortage penalty	$100				AmtsStored - C13:C17		
10						Capacities - E13:E17		
11	Storing decisions					Shortages - D21:D23		
12	Compartment	Product	Amount		Capacity	Violations - F21:F23		
13	1	2	2700.0	<=	2700	TotalCost - B28		
14	2	1	2800.0	<=	2800			
15	3	2	1100.0	<=	1100			
16	4	3	1786.8	<=	1800			
17	5	3	3158.0	<=	3400			
18								
19	Shortages							
20	Product	AmtStored	Demand	Shortage	MaxShortage	ShortageViolation		
21	1	2800.0	2900	100.0	900	0.0		
22	2	3800.0	4000	200.0	900	0.0		
23	3	4944.9	4900	0.0	900	0.0		
24								
25	Costs and penalties							
26	Shortage cost	$2,600.00						
27	Penalty cost	$0.00						
28	Total cost	$2,600.00						

❺   Shortage violations. We could *constrain* the shortages to be less than the maximum allowable shortages, but because the Evolutionary Solver works best with as few constraints as possible, we try another approach. (We use this approach in the following example as well.) We calculate the amount by which each maximum storage constraint is violated (if at all) and then add these violations, multiplied by a suitably large "penalty," to the cost objective. Because we will eventually minimize total cost, the Solver will try to stay away from solutions where this penalty is positive. Therefore, it will favor solutions where the maximum storage constraints are satisfied. To implement this strategy, calculate the maximum storage violations in column F by entering the formula

=IF(D21>E21,D21-E21,0)

in cell F21 and copying it down. The solution shown in Figure 8.11 does not have any violations, but the values in column F would be positive if any shortages in column D were greater than 900.

❻   Costs. Calculate the total shortage cost in cell B26 with the formula

=SUMPRODUCT(UnitCosts,Shortages)

Then calculate the penalty cost from maximum shortage violations in B27 with the formula

=UnitPenalty*SUM(Violations)

Note that we have chosen a penalty of $100 per unit shortage above the maximum allowed. Any large dollar value would suffice here. Finally, calculate the total cost in the TotCost cell by summing the values in cells B26 and B27.

USING THE EVOLUTIONARY SOLVER

The Solver setup for this model is straightforward, as shown in Figure 8.12. Unlike some previous models, there are now natural lower and upper limits for the changing cells. The ProductsStored range must be between 1 and 3 (and they must be integers) because there are only three products. The AmtsStored range must be between 0 and the given capacities of the compartments.

The solution in Figure 8.11 shows that product 1 should be stored in compartment 2, product 2 should be stored in compartments 1 and 3, and product 3 should be stored in compartments 4 and 5, the only compartments that end up with excess capacity. The demands for products 1 and 2 are not quite met, and the total shortage cost is $2600, but the shortages are well below the maximum shortages allowed. Therefore, there is no penalty cost for violating the maximum shortage constraints.

FIGURE 8.12
Solver Dialog Box
for Gas Storage
Model

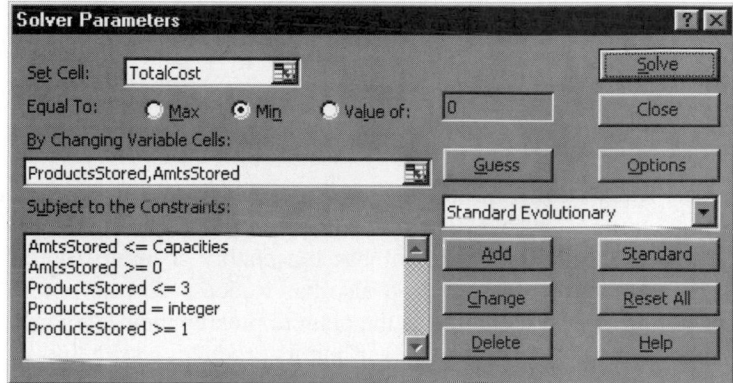

Sensitivity Analysis with SolverTable There is nothing that prevents us from using SolverTable on an Evolutionary Solver model—except possibly time. We fill in the SolverTable dialog box exactly as before. The only difference is that the Evolutionary Solver can take a lot of time to solve *one* problem, let alone a whole series of problems. Also, to provide some assurance that it will not stop prematurely at a suboptimal solution for at least one of the problems, we might have to experiment with the Evolutionary Solver settings in the Options dialog boxes, and it is not always obvious what the appropriate settings are.

We tried a sensitivity analysis on the capacity of compartment 3 for this example, allowing it to vary from 300 to 1100 in multiples of 200, and we obtained the results in Figure 8.13. We believe these results are optimal, but we are still not absolutely certain. (The equal objective values for capacities of 700 and 900 are somewhat suspicious.) Actually, we ran this same SolverTable several times, with different Solver option settings and different starting solutions, and we usually obtained *worse* results than in Figure 8.13 on at least one problem. This is not the fault of SolverTable or even

	A	B	C	D	E	F	G	H	I	J	K	L
30	Sensitivity of solution to capacity of compartment 3											
31												
32		$B$13	$C$13	$B$14	$C$14	$B$15	$C$15	$B$16	$C$16	$B$17	$C$17	$B$28
33	300	3	2700.0	1	2800.0	2	300.0	3	1800.0	2	3392.5	$5,860.33
34	500	3	2700.0	1	2800.0	2	500.0	3	1800.0	2	3400.0	$4,200.00
35	700	3	2700.0	1	2800.0	2	669.5	3	1800.0	2	3400.0	$3,400.00
36	900	3	2700.0	1	2800.0	2	669.5	3	1800.0	2	3400.0	$3,400.00
37	1100	2	2700.0	1	2800.0	2	1100.0	3	1800.0	3	3399.1	$2,600.00

FIGURE 8.13 SolverTable Results for Gas Storage Model

the fault of the Evolutionary Solver. This storage problem, like many combinatorial problems, is quite difficult, and unless we allow the Solver to run for a very long time, it can easily get stuck at a suboptimal solution fairly far from the optimal solution. For this reason, we will not mention SolverTable again in this chapter, but there is nothing to prevent you from trying it. You will just need to be patient! ∎

Finding a Good Production Schedule

Determining a monthly production schedule at a manufacturing facility such as a John Deere manufacturing plant is quite difficult. Many conflicting objectives must be balanced. The following example illustrates how these competing objectives can be modeled.[4]

EXAMPLE   8.4

SCHEDULING PRODUCTION OF LAWN MOWERS AT EASYRIDE

EasyRide, a lawn mower manufacturer, needs to set its weekly production schedule for the next 4 weeks. The company produces seven models of lawn mowers. At the beginning of each month, it has reasonably accurate forecasts for the demand of each model for the month. It also has forecasts for the portion of this demand from customers who will drive to the plant to pick up their lawn mowers. The company has four competing objectives regarding its production schedule.

- It wants to avoid costly model changeovers during each week as much as possible.

- It assumes that the "pickup" customers, those who drive to the plant to pick up their mowers, might arrive during week 1. Therefore, it wants to come as close as possible to producing the mowers demanded by these customers during week 1.

- The plant has three machining centers that the models go through. The company wants to keep weekly production hours as constant as possible across weeks at each of these centers.

- It wants to come as close as possible to producing as many mowers of each model as its monthly forecasts require.

Solution

It is typically not possible to satisfy all of EasyRide's objectives. Therefore, we will think of them as "targets." If any solution falls short of the target, we will penalize it—the farther from the target, the larger the penalty. This is an especially useful technique when using the Evolutionary Solver, which thrives on messy objective functions but does less well with a lot of constraints. Therefore, instead of using constraints, we will penalize deviations from targets, and we will use the total of penalties as the objective to minimize.

The data for the problem appear in Figure 8.14. (See the file LAWNMOWER.XLS.) Rows 5 and 6 indicate the forecasts of customer pickups and monthly totals, and rows

---

[4]This example is based on a model actually developed by John Deere, as described to the authors by John Deere managers.

	A	B	C	D	E	F	G	H	I	J	K	L
1	Lawnmower production model											
2												
3	Forecasts of demand											
4		Model 1	Model 2	Model 3	Model 4	Model 5	Model 6	Model 7				
5	Pickups	30	20	15	30	23	12	12				
6	Total	110	90	100	115	80	60	80				
7												
8	Hours per mower required in the machine centers									Range names used:		
9		Model 1	Model 2	Model 3	Model 4	Model 5	Model 6	Model 7		ProdLevels - B22:H25		
10	Center 1	3	2	2	2	2	4	2		Models - I22:I25		
11	Center 2	1	2	1	3	3	3	4		FCastDevs - B27:H27		
12	Center 3	2	3	0	4	3	3	2		Shortages - B28:H28		
13										HrDevs - H37:K39		
14	Unit penalty "costs"									TotPenalty - B46		
15	Model changeover	200										
16	Satisfy pickups	50										
17	Smooth production	1										
18	Meet forecasts	10										

FIGURE 8.14 Inputs for Lawn Mower Production Model

10–12 indicate the number of hours required at each machine center to produce a mower of each model. The unit penalty costs in rows 15–18 are not really "givens." They must be estimated by EasyRide to reflect trade-offs among the competing objectives. They imply the following.

- A changeover penalty of 200 is incurred for each model produced at any *positive* level during a week. For example, if 3 models are produced the first week, 4 the second, 3 the third, and 5 the fourth, the total changeover penalty is $(3 + 4 + 3 + 5)(200) = 3000$.

- A pickup shortage penalty of 50 is incurred for each unit of pickup demand not satisfied during week 1. For example, if 20 units of model 1 are produced during week 1, the pickup penalty for this model is $(10)(50) = 500$ because 20 is 10 short of the required 30.

- A smoothing production penalty of 1 is incurred during each week at each machine center per hour of deviation from the required weekly average at that center. Here, the "required" weekly average is based on the production levels needed to meet monthly forecasts. We will see how this is implemented shortly.

- A meeting monthly forecasts penalty of 10 is incurred per unit of each model produced above *or* below the monthly forecast. For example, if the total monthly production of model 1 is 105 or 115 (a deviation of 5 below or 5 above the monthly forecast), the penalty in either case is $(5)(10) = 50$.

Again, these unit penalties are not "givens," and they must be chosen carefully by EasyRide, perhaps on the basis of a sensitivity analysis. Clearly, if one unit penalty is too large, its corresponding objective will tend to dominate the solution. In the same way, if a unit penalty is too small, its corresponding objective will practically be ignored. We have tried to choose unit penalties that produce a reasonable solution, but you might want to experiment with others.

DEVELOPING THE SPREADSHEET MODEL

The completed model appears in Figure 8.15 (page 422). It can be developed with the following steps.

1 **Production schedule.** The decision variables are the weekly production levels of each model. Enter *any* values for these in the ProdLevels range. (Refer to Figure 8.14 for range names used.)

	Model 1	Model 2	Model 3	Model 4	Model 5	Model 6	Model 7	Models
20 Weekly production levels								
22 Week 1	30	37	17	30	29	12	12	7
23 Week 2	0	53	83	42	0	0	0	3
24 Week 3	80	0	0	0	51	0	46	3
25 Week 4	0	0	0	43	0	49	22	3
26 Mowers produced	110	90	100	115	80	61	80	
27 Deviations from forecasts	0	0	0	0	0	1	0	
28 Shortages for pickups	0	0	0	0	0	0	0	

30 Average hours need per week to meet monthly forecasts

31 Center 1	375
32 Center 2	368.75
33 Center 3	382.5

35 Hours used each week in each center

	Week 1	Week 2	Week 3	Week 4
37 Center 1	388	356	434	326
38 Center 2	382	315	417	364
39 Center 3	438	327	405	363

Deviations from hourly targets

	Week 1	Week 2	Week 3	Week 4
37 Center 1	13	19	59	49
38 Center 2	13.25	53.75	48.25	4.75
39 Center 3	55.5	55.5	22.5	19.5

41 Penalty costs

42 Model changeover	3200
43 Satisfy pickups	0
44 Smooth production	413
45 Meet forecasts	10
46 Total penalty	3623

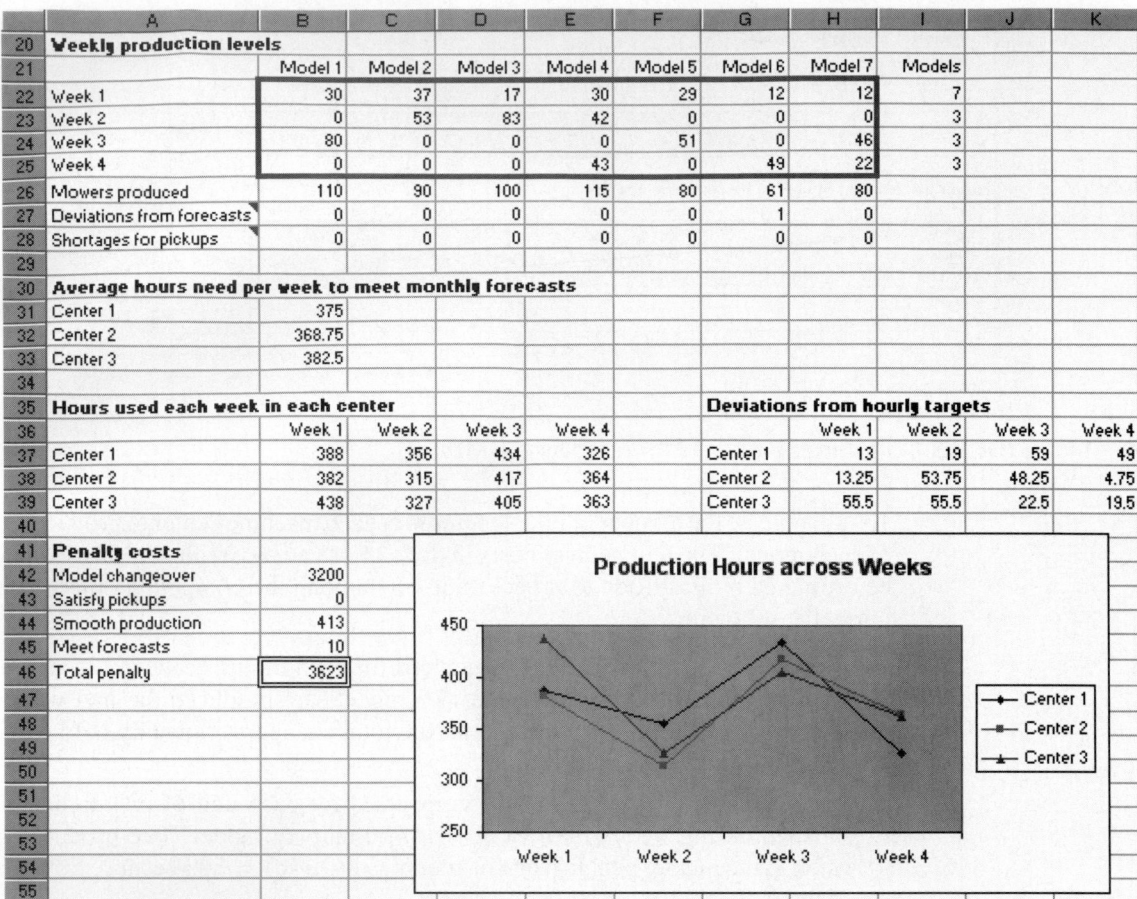

FIGURE 8.15 Model for Lawn Mower Production

2 **Models produced.** For the model changeover objective, we need to know how many different models are produced each week. Therefore, enter the formula

=COUNTIF(B22:H22,">0")

in cell I22 and copy it down.

3 **Deviations from forecasts.** For the objective of meeting forecasts, we need to calculate the total monthy production levels for each model and see how much they deviate from the monthly forecasts. To do this, enter the formulas

=SUM(B22:B25)

and

=ABS(B6-B26)

in cells B26 and B27 for model 1, and copy these across for the other models.

4 **Pickup shortages.** Here we need to see how much week 1 production of each model is short (if any) of the pickup demand. To do this, enter the formula

=IF(B22<B5,B5-B22,0)

in cell B28 and copy it across.

⑤ Hourly smoothing. This is the trickiest objective. We want to keep production hours at each machine center as constant as possible across weeks. Although there are undoubtedly other ways to implement this, we suggest the following approach. First, calculate the weekly average hours required at each machine center *if* we produce exactly enough in the month to meet monthly forecasts. Enter the formula

=SUMPRODUCT($B$6:$H$6,B10:H10)/4

in cell B31 for center 1 and copy it down for the other two centers. (Note that we divide by 4 to obtain a weekly average.) These weekly averages are our targets. Next, calculate the *actual* hours used at each center each week in the range B37:E39. Unfortunately, there is no way to enter a *single* formula and then copy it to the rest of the range. However, you can try the following. Enter the formula

=SUMPRODUCT($B$22:$H$22,$B10:$H10)

in cell B37 and copy it down to cell B39. Then copy the range B37:B39 to the range C37:E39. The resulting formulas for weeks 2–4 in columns C–E will not be quite correct, but they can be modified easily. Specifically, change the 22's in the column C formulas to 23's, change them to 24's in column D, and change them to 25's in column E. The point is that when copying is not possible, it might still be easier to copy a formula and then modify it rather than to enter new formulas from scratch. Finally, calculate the deviations from targets in the HrDevs range (H37:K39) by entering the formula

=ABS(B37-$B31)

in cell H37 and copying it to the rest of the range. (Here, copying *is* possible.)

⑥ Penalties. Calculate the various penalties in the range B42:B45. To do so, enter the formulas

=B15*SUM(Models)
=B16*SUM(Shortages)
=B17*SUM(HrDevs)

and

=B18*SUM(FCastDevs)

in cells B42 through B45. Then calculate the total penalty as their sum in the TotPenalty cell (B46).

USING THE EVOLUTIONARY SOLVER

The Solver setup for this model appears in Figure 8.16 (page 424). The objective is to minimize the total of penalties, the changing cells are the production levels, and there are no constraints other than lower and upper bounds and integer constraints on the production levels. As for the upper bounds, we chose 150 fairly arbitrarily. The largest monthly forecast for any model is 115, but it is possible that we might want production to exceed this forecast. Therefore, we build in some "padding" with the upper limit of 150.

After some experimenting, you will find that this is a difficult problem even for the Evolutionary Solver. Depending on the starting solution, it can take over an hour of computing time to find as good a solution as the one in Figure 8.15.[5] Therefore,

---

[5]We call this an "overnight problem." We start the Solver just before going to bed and let it run overnight!

FIGURE 8.16
Solver Setup for
Lawn Mower
Production Model

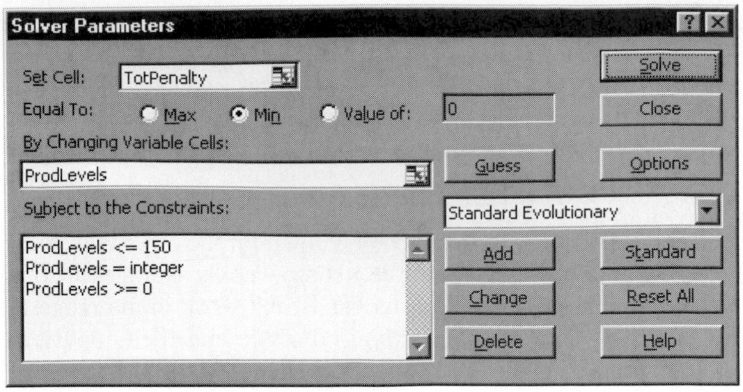

Solver Parameters

Set Cell: TotPenalty

Equal To: ○ Max ● Min ○ Value of: 0

By Changing Variable Cells:

ProdLevels

Subject to the Constraints:

ProdLevels <= 150
ProdLevels = integer
ProdLevels >= 0

Standard Evolutionary

Solve | Close | Guess | Options | Add | Standard | Change | Reset All | Delete | Help

make sure to enter large values in the Solver Options and Limit Options dialog boxes for Max Time, Iterations, Max Subproblems, Max Feasible Solns, and Max Time w/o Improvement. Otherwise, the Solver might quit prematurely at a solution far from optimal. Another possible strategy is to drop the integer constraint by checking the box in Figure 8.17. This will find a "good" non-integer solution relatively quickly. Then you can run the Solver again, starting from this non-integer solution, with the box unchecked to find a good integer solution.

The solution in Figure 8.15 represents the best compromise we could find. It produces all seven models during week 1 to keep the pickup shortages low. In fact, it has no pickup shortages. After that, it produces only three separate models each week to keep the changeover penalties low. Except for model 6, it produces exactly to the monthly forecasts, and the deviation for model 6 is only one unit above the forecast. Finally, all of this is done in a way to keep the production hours as constant as possible across weeks. Even so, the chart in Figure 8.15, based on the data in the range B37:E39, shows that the production hours still vary to some extent across weeks at each machine center. Of course, if you change the unit penalties to reflect different priorities on the objectives and then rerun the Solver, you could get a much different solution. For example, if EasyRide decides that pickup shortages are not such an important concern, it could reduce the unit shortage penalty from 50 to, say, 25 or even 5. Then the production schedule might shift so that all seven models are *not* produced in week 1.

FIGURE 8.17
Option to Ignore
Integer Constraints

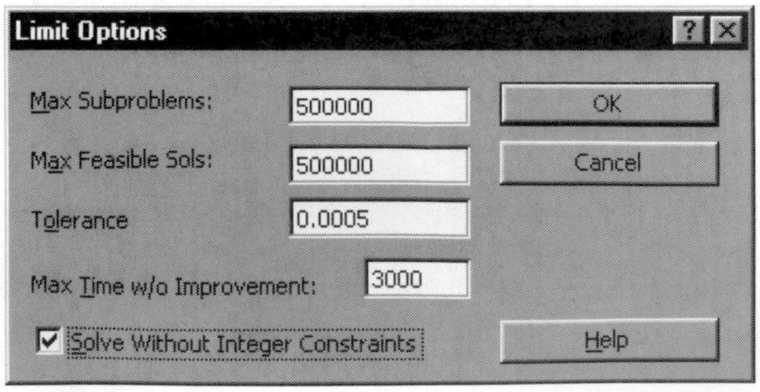

Limit Options

Max Subproblems: 500000

Max Feasible Sols: 500000

Tolerance 0.0005

Max Time w/o Improvement: 3000

☑ Solve Without Integer Constraints

OK | Cancel | Help

Skill-Building Problems

6. Xerox is trying to determine how many maintenance centers are needed in the mid-Atlantic states. Xerox earns $500 profit (excluding the cost of running maintenance centers) on each copier sale. The sales of copiers in each major market (Boston, New York, Philadelphia, Washington, Providence, and Atlantic City) depend on the proximity of the nearest maintenance facility. If there is a maintenance facility within 100 miles of a city, sales will be high; if there is a maintenance facility within 150 miles of a city, sales will be medium; otherwise, sales will be low. The predicted annual sales (that is, the meaning of low, medium, and high) are listed in Table 8.5.

TABLE 8.5	Predicted Sales		
City	Low Sales	Medium Sales	High Sales
Boston	500	600	700
New York	750	800	1000
Philadelphia	700	800	900
Washington	450	650	800
Providence	200	300	400
Atlantic City	300	350	450

It costs $200,000 per year to place a maintenance representative in a city. It is possible to locate a representative in any city except for Atlantic City and Providence. The distances between the cities are listed in Table 8.6. Where should maintenance representatives be located?

Skill-Extending Problems

7. You are the Democratic campaign manager for the state of Indiana. There are 15 cities in the state of Indiana. The numbers of Democrats and Republican voters in these cities (in thousands) are listed in Table 8.7. The Democrats control the state legislature, so they can redistrict as they wish. There will be eight congressional districts. Each city must be assigned in its entirety to a single district. Each district must contain between 150,000 and 250,000 voters. Use the Evolutionary Solver to assign voters to districts in a way that maximizes the number of districts that will vote Democratic. (*Hint*: You might find it convenient to use the SUMIF function. This function was used frequently in Chapter 5.)

TABLE 8.7	District Data	
City	Republican	Democrat
1	80	34
2	43	61
3	40	44
4	20	24
5	40	114
6	40	64
7	70	34
8	50	44
9	70	54
10	70	64
11	80	45
12	40	50
13	50	60
14	60	65
15	50	70

TABLE 8.6	Distances Between Cities			
	Boston	New York	Philadelphia	Washington
Boston	0	222	310	441
New York	222	0	89	241
Philadelphia	310	89	0	146
Washington	441	241	146	0
Providence	47	186	255	376
Atlantic City	350	123	82	178

8.6 FITTING AN S-SHAPED CURVE

Recall from Section 7.4 that we fit a power curve of the form $R = aS^b$, where S is sales force effort and R is revenue from sales of a product. This power curve has the property of diminishing returns—each extra unit of S contributes less and less to R. However, marketing researchers have found that the response to sales force effort is better described by a function of the following form:

$$R = a + \frac{(b-a)S^c}{d + S^c} \tag{8.1}$$

for suitable constants $a, b, c,$ and d. While the power curve always exhibits diminishing returns, this function can exhibit diminishing returns or look like an S-shaped curve, as in Figure 8.18. An S-curve starts out flat, gets steep, and then flattens out. This would be the correct form of the sales revenue function if sales effort needs to exceed some critical value to generate significant sales. The following example illustrates how we can use the Evolutionary Solver to estimate this type of curve.[6]

FIGURE 8.18
An S-Shaped Sales
Response Curve

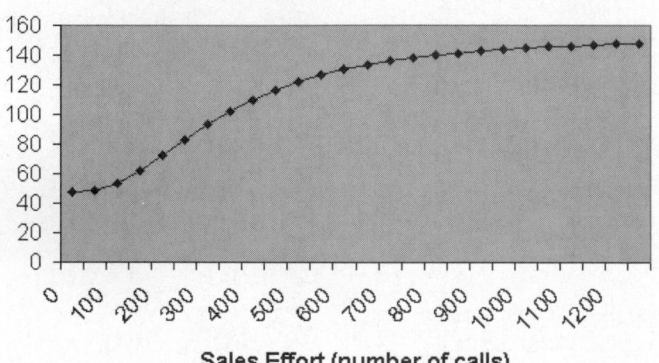

Sales Revenue versus Sales Effort

Sales Effort (number of calls)

[6]The model in this section has "smooth" functions, and it can be solved successfully with the nonlinear algorithm in the standard Solver *if* the initial solution is not too far from the optimal solution. However, the Evolutionary Solver is more likely to find the optimal solution, regardless of the initial solution.

EXAMPLE 8.5

ESTIMATING A SALES RESPONSE FUNCTION AT LYNTEX LABS

Lyntex Labs wants to estimate its sales response function that relates the revenue from sales of a certain drug to the number of sales calls made. Company experts estimate the revenue that would be obtained in the following five scenarios:

- No sales effort is assigned to the drug.
- Sales effort assigned to drug is cut in half.

- Sales force effort stays at the current level.
- Sales force effort is increased by 50%.
- Sales force effort "saturates" the market.

The resulting estimates appear in Table 8.8. Note that the current sales effort is 350,000 sales calls. Also, all sales revenue estimates are expressed relative to an "index" of 100, where 100 represents the current level of sales revenue. For example, the experts estimate that if sales effort is cut in half, sales revenue from the drug will decrease to 68% of the current level. Lyntex assumes that its sales revenue function is of the form in equation (8.1). It wants to find the constants a, b, c, and d that provide the best fit to the estimates in Table 8.8.

TABLE 8.8	Estimated Sales Revenues
Sales Calls (1000s)	**Sales Revenue**
0	47
175	68
350	100
525	126
3500	152

Solution

The model development is basically the same as for Example 7.5 of the previous chapter. (See Figure 8.19 and the file LYNTEX.XLS.) It can be accomplished with the following steps.

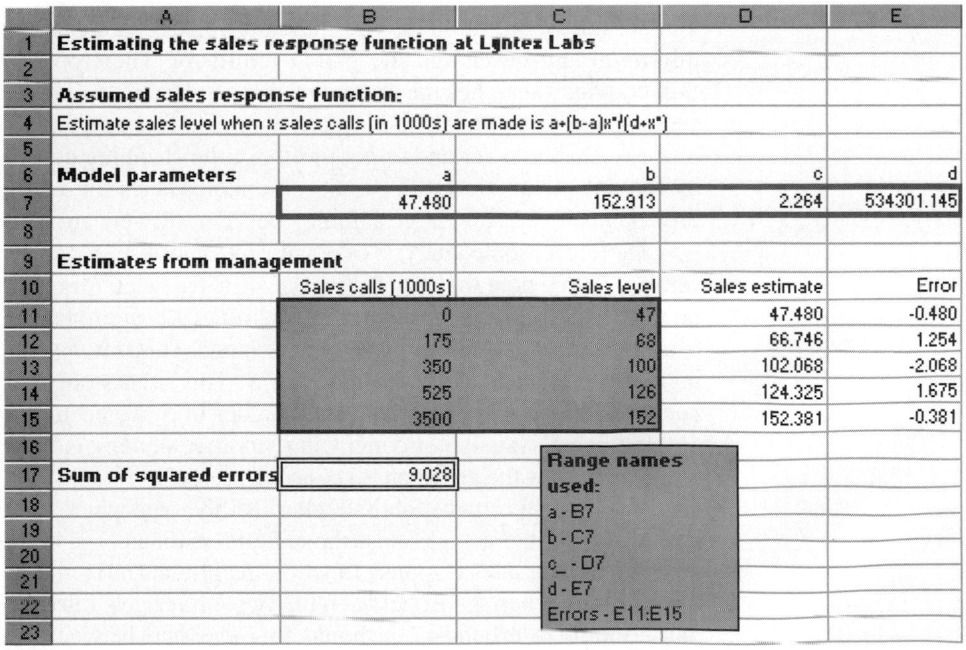

	A	B	C	D	E
1	Estimating the sales response function at Lyntex Labs				
2					
3	Assumed sales response function:				
4	Estimate sales level when x sales calls (in 1000s) are made is a+(b-a)x^c/(d+x^c)				
5					
6	Model parameters	a	b	c	d
7		47.480	152.913	2.264	534301.145
8					
9	Estimates from management				
10		Sales calls (1000s)	Sales level	Sales estimate	Error
11		0	47	47.480	-0.480
12		175	68	66.746	1.254
13		350	100	102.068	-2.068
14		525	126	124.325	1.675
15		3500	152	152.381	-0.381
16					
17	Sum of squared errors	9.028	Range names used:		
18			a - B7		
19			b - C7		
20			c_ - D7		
21			d - E7		
22			Errors - E11:E15		
23					

FIGURE 8.19 Sales Response Function Estimation

DEVELOPING THE SPREADSHEET MODEL

❶ **Inputs.** Enter the data in the shaded region from Table 8.8.

❷ **Decision variables.** The only decision variables are the constants a, b, c, and d of the sales response function. Enter any values for these. Note that we tried to give the corresponding cells range names of a, b, c, and d. However, Excel doesn't allow the range name c. (It also doesn't allow the range name r.) Instead, it changes this name to c_.

❸ **Predicted sales revenues.** In column D calculate the sales revenues levels (remember that these are relative to 100) predicted from equation (8.1). To do so, enter the formula

=a+(b-a)*B11^c_/(d+B11^c_)

in cell D11 and copy it down to cell D15.

❹ **Prediction errors.** For a good fit, we want the predictions in column D to match the experts' estimates in column C as closely as possible. We will minimize the sum of squared differences between the two columns. Therefore, first calculate the errors in column E by entering the formula

=C11-D11

in cell E11 and copying down. Then calculate the sum of squared errors in the SSE cell with the formula

=SUMSQ(Errors)

USING THE EVOLUTIONARY SOLVER

There are no IF, ABS, MAX, or MIN functions in this model, so we might try the standard Excel Solver (with the Assume Linear Model box unchecked), just as we did throughout the previous chapter. However, there might be *local* minima in this model that are not *global* minima. The standard Solver could easily get stuck at such a local minimum and never find the global minimum. Therefore, we use the Evolutionary Solver, which searches the entire feasible region and is much less likely to get stuck at such a local minimum. The only problem is to find a "decent" starting solution and to find reasonable lower and upper limits for the changing cells. It is difficult to tell, just by looking at equation (8.1), what reasonable values for a, b, c, and d might be. Must they be positive? How large can they be? The answers are certainly not obvious.

Therefore, some analysis of equation (8.1) is useful before we dive into the Solver settings. First, note that when $S = 0$, estimated sales R equals a. Therefore, a should be positive. Second, the fraction in equation (8.1) approaches $b - a$ as S get large, so b is the limiting value of R as S gets large. Third, we want S^c to increase when S increases, so that R will increase with S. This occurs only if c is positive. Finally, to keep the denominator positive for all values of S, we need d to be positive.

If this analysis is not convincing, another strategy is to graph equation (8.1) and then *watch* how the graph changes as we manually change a, b, c, and d. We do this in Figure 8.20. This chart is an X-Y chart (of the type where the dots are connected with lines). It plots the actual sales (the experts' estimates) in column C and the predicted values from the sales response function in column D. By changing the constants in row 4 and seeing when the fit between the two curves gets fairly good, we can quickly see that a should be around 47, b should be somewhere between 150 and 160, the exponent c should be somewhere 1.5 and 5, and the constant d should be a large positive number.

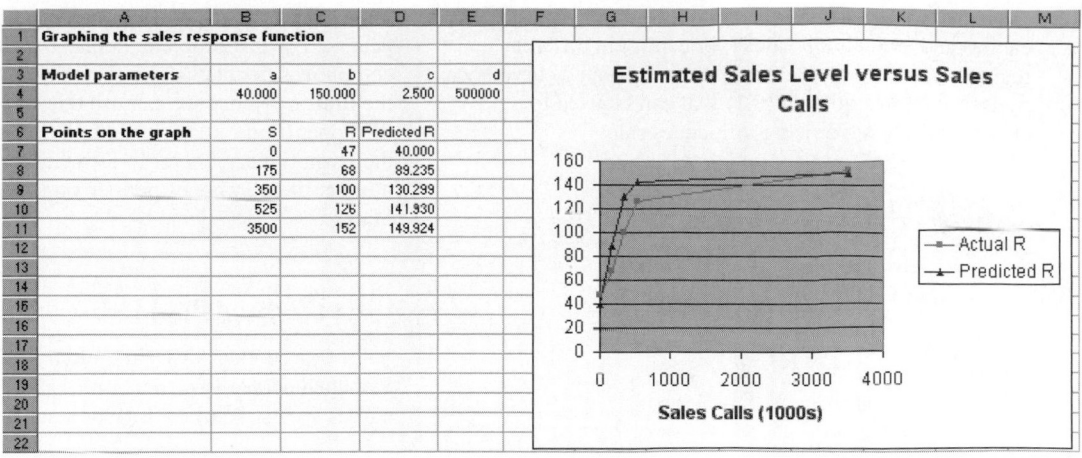

FIGURE 8.20 Graph of Sales Response Function

These are fairly liberal ranges, but all we are trying to obtain at this point are reasonable lower and upper limits for the Solver dialog box.

Using this (somewhat inexact) information, we fill in the Solver dialog box as shown in Figure 8.21. (The bounds on c_ and d that do not appear in this figure are c_>=1.5, d<=1000000, and d>=500.)

The best solution found by the Evolutionary Solver appears in Figure 8.19. Of course, there is nothing very intuitive about these particular values of a, b, c, and d. However, if you substitute them into row 4 of Figure 8.20, you will see that they provide a very good fit. In other words, the sales response function with these parameters should provide very useful predictions of sales levels.

FIGURE 8.21
Solver Dialog Box
for Sales Response
Estimation

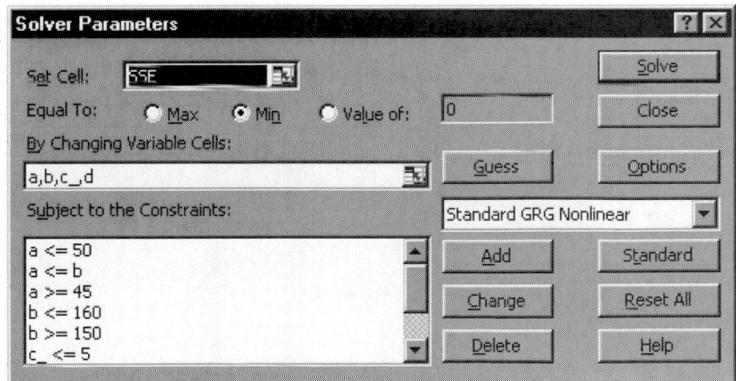

PROBLEMS

Skill-Building Problems

8. You are given the following information concerning how a change in sales force effort impacts sales:
  - A 50% cut in sales force effort reduces sales to 48% of its current value.
  - Zero sales force effort reduces sales to 15% of its current value.
  - A 50% increase in sales force effort increases sales by 20%.
  - A saturation of sales effort (a 10-fold increase) increases sales by 35%.

Fit an S-shaped curve as described by equation (8.1) to these data.

9. Table 8.9 contains data on annual advertising (per capita) and annual unit sales (per capita) in different regions of the country. Determine an S-shaped curve as described by equation (8.1) that can be used to determine how advertising influences sales.

TABLE 8.9	Advertising Data	
Region	Advertising per Capita ($)	Sales Units per Capita
1	0	5
2	2	7
3	4	13
4	6	22
5	8	25
6	10	27
7	12	31
8	14	33

10. The adoption level of a new product often can be modeled as an S-shaped curve called the Pearl (or logistic) curve. The equation of this curve is as follows:

$$Y = \frac{L}{1 + ae^{-bt}}$$

where Y is the adoption level, L is an (unknown) upper limit on adoptions, and a and b are parameters to be estimated. Table 8.10 lists information on

TABLE 8.10	Cell Phone Data	
Year	Population (thousands)	Cell Phones (thousands)
1	249,907	5,283
2	252,618	7,557
3	255,391	11,033
4	258,132	16,009
5	260,682	24,134
6	263,168	33,786
7	265,557	44,043
8	266,733	55,312

U.S. cell phones since 1990 (which corresponds to year 1). For this problem, define Y as the number of cell phones per capita. As t increases, Y approaches the limit L. Hence we can use this curve to estimate the upper limit on U.S. cell phones per person. Use the Evolutionary Solver to estimate the eventual number of cell phones per person in the United States.

Skill-Extending Problems

11. Sales of a product over time often follow an S-shaped curve. Two functions that yield S-shaped curves are the Pearl (or logistic) curve

$$Y = \frac{L}{1 + ae^{-bt}}$$

and the Gompertz curve

$$Y = Le^{-be^{-kt}}$$

Here, Y is annual sales, t is time (in years), L is the upper limit on sales, and a, b, and k are parameters to be estimated. (Actually, L must also be estimated.) Table 8.11 contains data for sales of answering machines in the United States. Use the Evolutionary Solver to fit a Pearl and a Gompertz curve to these data. Let $t = 0$ correspond to 1983. Which curve provides the better fit? (*Hint*: You need to use reasonable bounds for the parameters for each curve. For example, $L \geq 14.5$ is reasonable.)

TABLE 8.11	Answering Machine Data
Year	Sales
1983	2.2
1984	3.0
1985	4.2
1986	6.5
1987	8.8
1988	11.1
1989	12.5
1990	13.8
1991	14.5

8.7 PORTFOLIO OPTIMIZATION

I n the previous chapter we discussed one approach to portfolio optimization. There the objective was to minimize the portfolio variance subject to keeping the mean portfolio return above some required level. This resulted in a nonlinear model (because of the squares and product terms in the portfolio variance formula), but this nonlinear objective was sufficiently "smooth" to permit using the standard Solver. Now we will look at another possible objective. This objective is *not* smooth, so the Evolutionary Solver should be used.

EXAMPLE 8.6

BEATING THE S&P INDEX AT E. T. BARNEY

E. T. Barney, an investment company, wants to form a portfolio consisting of a number of well-known stocks. The objective is to find the appropriate portfolio that, based on historical data, has the largest probability of beating the S&P 500 market index. How should it proceed?[7]

Solution

The file BEATSP500.XLS contains monthly returns for a 5-year period for 31 large companies. See the shaded area in Figure 8.22. (Note that there are many hidden rows and columns in this figure.) We decided to base the optimization on the earliest 3 years of data. Then we can see how the portfolio based on these data performs on the most recent 2 years of data. You can create the model with the following steps.

	A	B	C	D	E	F	G	H	I	AF	AG	AH	AI
1	Maximizing the probability of beating the S&P 500												
2													
3	Weights on stocks for portfolio												
4		AXP	EK	CAT	WMT	XON	KO	JNJ	GM	IBM			
5		0.026429	0.030051	0.024391	0.025039	0.026944	0.044893	0.034787	0.029459	0.03281			
6													
7	Constraint on weights					Percent of months beating S&P 500							
8		Sum		Required		Old	82.86%						
9		1.000193	=	1		Recent	45.83%						
10													
11	Historical data on returns												
12	Date	AXP	EK	CAT	WMT	XON	KO	JNJ	GM	IBM	Port Return	S&P500	Beat S&P?
13	Jun-99	0.07677	0.00185	0.09339	0.13330	-0.03443	-0.09270	0.05803	-0.04348	0.11422	0.05026	0.05444	No
14	May-99	-0.07365	-0.08961	-0.14757	-0.07337	-0.03837	0.00643	-0.04720	-0.05782	0.11031	-0.03217	-0.02497	No
15	Apr-99	0.10988	0.17025	0.40821	-0.00203	0.17715	0.10896	0.04278	0.02371	0.18018	0.08891	0.03794	Yes
16	Mar-99	0.08724	-0.03494	0.00823	0.07151	0.06009	-0.03669	0.09517	0.05375	0.04418	0.04242	0.03879	Yes
17	Feb-99	0.05468	0.01893	0.05195	0.00145	-0.05249	-0.02201	0.00594	-0.07513	-0.07367	0.00845	-0.03228	Yes
18	Jan-99	0.00593	-0.09201	-0.05234	0.05602	-0.03932	-0.02519	0.01490	0.25415	-0.00610	0.02396	0.04101	No
19	Dec-98	0.02436	-0.00861	-0.06953	0.08244	-0.02500	-0.04371	0.03231	0.02415	0.11658	0.00680	0.05638	No
20	Nov-98	0.13586	-0.05738	0.10014	0.09050	0.04712	0.03913	-0.00011	0.11414	0.11195	0.08195	0.05913	Yes
21	Oct-98	0.13847	0.00813	0.01620	0.26430	0.01416	0.17245	0.04153	0.15148	0.15564	0.09507	0.08029	Yes
22	Sep-98	-0.00481	-0.01600	0.05952	-0.07300	0.07927	-0.11298	0.13406	-0.05591	0.14095	0.04267	0.06240	No
70	Sep-94	0.08000	0.04020	-0.06176	-0.05076	-0.03361	0.06155	0.03242	-0.06716	0.01643	-0.01509	-0.02688	Yes
71	Aug-94	0.06132	0.03682	0.06459	-0.01331	0.00000	0.03662	0.07299	-0.01797	0.10707	0.04423	0.03760	Yes

Range names used:
Weights - B5:AF5
SumWts - B9
PctOld - G8
BeatOld - AI37:AI71
BeatRecent - AI13:AI36

FIGURE 8.22 Portfolio Optimization Model

[7]We have not seen this particular objective discussed in finance books or articles, but it is clear from discussions with investors that the goal of "beating the market" is important. For an excellent discussion of investment models in general, we refer to the book by Luenberger (1997).

DEVELOPING THE SPREADSHEET MODEL

❶ **Enter weights.** As in the previous chapter, the portfolio is based on the fractions of each dollar invested in the various stocks. We call these the weights. Enter *any* values for the weights in the Weights range. We will eventually constrain these weights to be between 0 and 1. Then calculate the sum of the weights in the SumWts cell with the SUM function.

❷ **Portfolio returns.** For the historical period, the period of the data, calculate the portfolio returns by weighting the actual returns by the weights. To do this, enter the formula

=SUMPRODUCT(Weights,B13:AF13)

in cell AG13 and copy it down.

❸ **Beats S&P 500?** The returns from the S&P 500 market index appear in column AH. (These are given. As with the stock returns, they can be found on the Web.) For each month, see whether the portfolio beats the S&P 500 by entering the formula

=IF(AG13>AH13,"Yes","No")

in cell AI13 and copying down.

❹ **Objective.** Calculate the fraction of months during the earliest 3 years where the portfolio beats the S&P 500. Do this in the PctOld cell with the formula

=COUNTIF(BeatOld,"Yes")/COUNTA(BeatOld)

This is the objective we will attempt to maximize. Note that it contains IF functions (actually, COUNTIF). This is the feature that necessitates the Evolutionary Solver. For comparison, calculate the similar fraction for the most recent 2 years in the PctRecent cell with the formula

=COUNTIF(BeatRecent,"Yes")/COUNTA(BeatRecent)

❺ **Evolutionary Solver setup.** The Solver setup appears in Figure 8.23. We constrain the sum of the weights to be 1 so that all of our money is invested. We constrain the weights to be within 0 and 1 so that the investment in each stock is a positive fraction of the total investment. (If we allowed negative weights, this would correspond to short selling.)

There are several things to note about the optimal solution found in Figure 8.22. First, the sum of the weights is not exactly 1. This is due to roundoff. The Solver tries to find a solution that satisfies the constraints exactly, but equality constraints are not

FIGURE 8.23
Solver Dialog Box
for Portfolio
Optimization Model

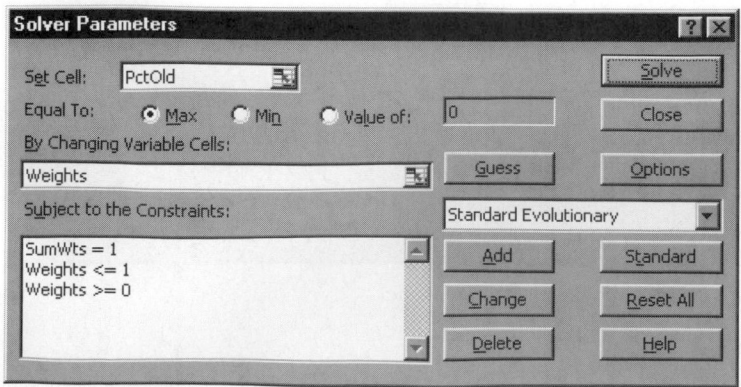

always met exactly. (At this point, we could get a more exact solution by running the GRG nonlinear Solver.) Second, this portfolio uses a fairly uniform set of weights. The largest fraction, about 8.2%, goes to United Technologies (UTX), whereas the smallest, about 0.2%, goes to Union Carbide (UK). Most of the other fractions are in the 2%–4% range. Perhaps this uniformity occurs because all of these companies are S&P 500 companies. Finally, this solution represents the portfolio that beats the S&P 500 most frequently *in the optimization period*—that is, the earliest 3 years. Whenever we base an optimization on a historical period, there is no guarantee that this solution will work as well in the *future*. We illustrate this by seeing how well the portfolio does in the 2 most recent years where we have data. Clearly, it does not do as well. The portfolio beats the S&P 500 about 83% of the time during the earliest 3 years, but only about 46% of the time during the most recent 2 years. Any time we use historical data to forecast what might happen in the future, we are making the implicit assumption that historical patterns will repeat themselves. As many forecasters have discovered to their dismay, this assumption is not always correct. ■

Is this method of portfolio optimization any better or worse than the variance-minimizing method discussed in the previous chapter? The answer probably depends on the investor's attitude toward risk. There is no guarantee that the probability-maximizing model in this chapter will achieve any particular return, although if it beats the market index consistently, it seems that it should provide a decent return. Also, there is no guarantee that this portfolio will provide an acceptable risk—measured by a small variance. Nevertheless, this model might have an intuitive appeal to many investors. If you can beat the S&P 500 consistently, you must be doing a good job!

PROBLEMS

Skill-Building Problems

12. From Yahoo.com under Business and Finance, download the monthly returns on any four stocks for years 1990–1996 and determine the portfolio that maximizes the chance of beating the S&P for those years.

13. Continuing the previous problem, determine the portfolio that minimizes the chance that you will lose money during any month, subject to the constraint that your expected monthly return is at least 1%.

8.8 CLUSTER ANALYSIS

Marketers often want to group objects into clusters of similar objects. For example, identifying similar customers could help a company identify market segments. Identifying a cluster of similar products could help a company identify its main competitors. Here are two actual examples of how America is divided into clusters.[8]

- Claritas divides each block of the United States into one of 62 clusters. These include Blue Blood Estates, New Homesteaders, Middle America, God's Country, and so on. For example, Blue Blood Estates consists primarily of America's richest

---

[8]The book by Johnson and Wichern (1998) has an excellent, although somewhat mathematically advanced, discussion of cluster analysis and the topic of the next section, discriminant analysis.

suburbs. (One in ten residents of Blue Blood Estates is a millionaire.) This is valuable information for marketers. For example, Blue Blood Estates residents consume imported beer at a rate nearly three times the national average.

■ SRI clusters families based on their financial status and demographics. For example, the cluster "Bank Traditionalists" consists of upper-middle-class families of larger than average size having school-age children. This cluster is a natural prospecting ground for life insurance salespeople.

The following example illustrates how we can use the Evolutionary Solver to cluster cities.

EXAMPLE 8.7

CLUSTERING LARGE CITIES IN THE UNITED STATES

The file CLUSTERS.XLS contains demographic data on 49 of the largest cities in the United States. Some of the data appear in the shaded region of Figure 8.24. For example, Atlanta is 67% African American, 2% Hispanic, and 1% Asian. It has a median age of 31, a 5% unemployment rate, and a per capita income of $22,000. We would like to group these 49 cities into four clusters of cities that are demographically similar. (We could then experiment with the number of clusters. For this discussion we will fix the number at four.) The basic idea is to choose a city to "anchor" or "center" each cluster. We then assign each city to the "nearest" cluster center, where "nearest" is defined in terms of the six demographic variables. The objective is then to minimize the sum of the squared distances from each city to its cluster anchor.

Solution

The first problem is that if we use raw units, percentage African American and Hispanic will drive everything because these values are more spread out than the other demographic attributes. We can see this by calculating means and standard deviations of the characteristics with the AVERAGE and STDEV functions. (See Figure 8.25, which also includes correlations between the attributes.) To remedy this problem we "standardize" each demographic attribute by subtracting the attribute's mean and dividing the difference by the attribute's standard deviation. For example, the average city has 24.347% African Americans with a standard deviation of 18.11%. Thus on a

	A	B	C	D	E	F	G	H	I	J	K	L	M	N
13	City data								Standardized					
14	Index	City	PctAfrAmer	PctHispanic	PctAsian	MedianAge	UnempRate	PCIncome	PctAfrAmer	PctHispanic	PctAsian	MedianAge	UnempRate	PCIncome
15	1	Albuquerque	3	35	2	32	5	18	-1.179	1.239	-0.363	0.061	-0.751	-0.875
16	2	Atlanta	67	2	1	31	5	22	2.355	-0.764	-0.452	-0.440	-0.751	0.324
17	3	Austin	12	23	3	29	3	19	-0.682	0.510	-0.273	-1.442	-1.495	-0.575
18	4	Baltimore	59	1	1	33	11	22	1.913	-0.825	-0.452	0.562	1.480	0.324
19	5	Boston	26	11	5	30	5	24	0.091	-0.218	-0.093	-0.941	-0.751	0.924
20	6	Charlotte	32	1	2	32	3	20	0.423	-0.825	-0.363	0.061	-1.495	-0.275
21	7	Chicago	39	20	4	31	9	24	0.809	0.328	-0.183	-0.440	0.736	0.924
22	8	Cincinnati	38	1	1	31	8	21	0.754	-0.825	-0.452	-0.440	0.364	0.024
23	9	Cleveland	47	5	1	32	13	22	1.251	-0.582	-0.452	0.061	2.224	0.324
24	10	Columbus	23	1	2	29	3	13	-0.074	-0.825	-0.363	-1.442	-1.495	-2.375
25	11	Dallas	30	21	2	30	9	22	0.312	0.389	-0.363	-0.941	0.736	0.324
26	12	Denver	13	23	2	34	7	23	-0.627	0.510	-0.363	1.063	-0.008	0.624
27	13	Detroit	76	3	1	31	9	21	2.852	-0.704	-0.452	-0.440	0.736	0.024
28	14	El Paso	3	69	1	29	11	13	-1.179	3.303	-0.452	-1.442	1.480	-2.375
29	15	Fort Worth	22	20	2	30	9	20	-0.130	0.328	-0.363	-0.941	0.736	-0.275
30	16	Fresno	9	30	13	28	13	16	-0.847	0.935	0.624	-1.942	2.224	-1.475

FIGURE 8.24 Demographic Data for Selected Cities

FIGURE 8.25
Summary Data for
Demographic
Attributes

	A	B	C	D	E	F	G	H
1	Summary measures for selected variables							
2			PctAfrAmer	PctHispanic	PctAsian	MedianAge	UnempRate	PCIncome
3		Mean	24.347	14.592	6.041	31.878	7.020	20.918
4		Standard deviation	18.110	16.472	11.145	1.996	2.689	3.334
5								
6	Table of correlations							
7			PctAfrAmer	PctHispanic	PctAsian	MedianAge	UnempRate	PCIncome
8		PctAfrAmer	1.000					
9		PctHispanic	-0.404	1.000				
10		PctAsian	-0.317	0.000	1.000			
11		MedianAge	0.010	-0.221	0.373	1.000		
12		UnempRate	0.308	0.341	-0.001	-0.007	1.000	
13		PCIncome	0.126	-0.298	0.374	0.480	0.014	1.000

standardized basis, Atlanta is larger by $(67 - 24.347)/18.11 = 2.355$ standard deviations on the percentage African American attribute than a typical city. By working with standardized values for each attribute, we ensure that the analysis will be unit-free. To create the standardized values shown in Figure 8.24, enter the formula

=(C15-AVERAGE(C$15:C$63))/STDEV(C$15:C$63)

in cell I15 and copy it across to column N and down to row 63.

DEVELOPING THE SPREADSHEET MODEL

Now that we have standardized values for all of the attributes, we can develop the spreadsheet model as follows. It is shown in two parts in Figures 8.26 and 8.27.

	A	B	C	D	E	F	G	H	I	J	K	L
1	Clustering cities											
2												
3	Cluster centers and standardized values									Range names used:		
4		Column offset:	9	10	11	12	13	14		CenterNames - A6:A9		
5	City	Index	PctAfrAmer	PctHispanic	PctAsian	MedianAge	UnempRate	PCIncome		Centers - B6:B9		
6	Los Angeles	24	-0.571	1.542	0.355	-0.440	1.480	0.024		SumSqDists - B11		
7	Omaha	34	0.627	-0.704	-0.452	0.061	-0.751	-0.275		LTable - A15:N63		
8	Memphis	25	1.693	-0.825	-0.452	0.061	0.736	-0.275		MinSqDists - T15:T63		
9	San Francisco	43	-0.737	-0.036	2.060	2.065	0.380	3.024				
10												
11	SumSqDists	165.348										

FIGURE 8.26 Decision Variables and Target Cell

	I	J	K	L	M	N	O	P	Q	R	S	T	U	V
13	Standardized							Squared distances to centers					Assigned to	
14	PctAfrAmer	PctHispanic	PctAsian	MedianAge	UnempRate	PCIncome		To 1	To 2	To 3	To 4	Minimum	Index	Center
15	-1.179	1.239	-0.363	0.061	-0.751	-0.875		7.017	4.447	15.086	27.044	4.447	2	Omaha
16	2.355	-0.764	-0.452	-0.440	-0.751	0.324		19.609	9.505	3.267	30.102	3.267	3	Memphis
17	-0.682	0.510	-0.273	-1.442	-1.495	-0.575		11.689	4.411	14.782	32.238	4.411	2	Omaha
18	1.913	-0.825	-0.452	0.562	1.480	0.324		13.526	12.057	1.213	26.962	1.213	3	Memphis
19	0.091	-0.218	-0.093	-0.941	-0.751	0.924		9.780	3.323	7.718	18.937	3.323	2	Omaha
20	0.423	-0.825	-0.363	0.061	-1.495	-0.275		16.303	1.677	6.601	23.980	1.677	2	Omaha
21	0.809	0.328	-0.183	-0.440	0.736	0.924		5.032	7.102	3.874	19.481	3.874	3	Memphis
22	0.754	-0.825	-0.452	-0.440	0.364	0.024		9.259	3.506	1.360	24.979	1.360	3	Memphis
23	1.251	-0.582	-0.452	0.061	2.224	0.324		9.381	12.753	2.827	28.641	2.827	3	Memphis
24	-0.074	-0.825	-0.363	-1.442	-1.495	-2.375		21.982	7.547	14.776	49.615	7.547	2	Omaha
25	0.312	0.389	-0.363	-0.941	0.736	0.324		3.521	5.660	4.751	24.715	3.521	1	Los Angeles
26	-0.627	0.510	-0.363	1.063	-0.008	0.624		6.415	3.849	9.537	13.078	3.849	2	Omaha
27	2.852	-0.704	-0.452	-0.440	0.736	0.024		17.971	14.656	1.700	36.153	1.700	3	Memphis
28	-1.179	3.303	-0.452	-1.442	1.480	-2.375		10.881	28.005	32.506	62.553	10.881	1	Los Angeles
29	-0.130	0.328	-0.363	-0.941	0.736	-0.275		3.079	4.537	5.663	27.534	3.079	1	Los Angeles
30	-0.847	0.935	0.624	-1.942	2.224	-1.475		5.578	18.203	18.378	46.094	5.578	1	Los Angeles
31	-1.289	-0.502	5.829	2.566	-0.751	0.924		49.812	47.617	58.327	19.602	19.602	4	San Francisco

FIGURE 8.27 Other Calculations for Cluster Analysis

① **Lookup table.** One key to the model is to have an index (1 to 49) for the cities so that we can refer to them by index and then look up their characteristics with a VLOOKUP function. Therefore, name the range A15:N63 as LTable.

② **Decision variables.** The only changing cells appear in the Centers range of Figure 8.26. They are the indices of the four cities chosen as cluster centers. Enter any four integers from 1 to 49 in these cells.

③ **Corresponding cities and standardized attributes.** We find the names and standardized attributes of the cluster centers with VLOOKUP functions. First, enter the function

=VLOOKUP(B6,LTable,2)

in cell A6 and copy it to the range A6:A9. Then enter the formula

=VLOOKUP($B6,LTable,C$4)

in C6 and copy it to the range C6:H9. Note, for example, that the standardized PctAfrAmer is the 9th column of the lookup table. This explains the "column off-set" entries in row 4.

④ **Squared distances to centers.** The next step is to see how "far" each city is from each of the cluster centers. Let z_i be standardized attribute i for a typical city, and let c_i be standardized attribute i for a typical cluster center. We measure the distance from this city to this cluster center with the usual "Euclidean" distance formula:

$$\text{Distance} = \sqrt{\sum_i (z_i - c_i)^2}$$

where the sum is over all six attributes. We can work just as well with *squared* distances, so we will ignore the square root sign in this formula.[9] These squared distances appear in columns P through S of Figure 8.27. For example, the value in cell P15 is the squared distance from Albuquerque to the first cluster center (Los Angeles), the value in Q15 is the squared distance from Albuquerque to the second cluster center (Omaha), and so on. These calculations can be performed in several equivalent ways. Probably the quickest way is to enter the formula

=SUMXMY2($I15:$N15,$C$6:$H$6)

in cell P15 and copy it to the range P15:S63. The function SUMXMY2 calculates the differences between the elements of the two range arguments and then sums the squares of these differences—exactly what we want. The copied versions in columns Q, R, and S will then have to be modified slightly. The 6's in the second range argument need to be changed to 7's in column Q, to 8's in column R, and 9's in column S.

⑤ **Assignments to cluster centers.** Each city will be assigned to the cluster center that has the smallest squared distance. Therefore, find the minimum squared distances in column T by entering the formula

=MIN(P15:S15)

in cell T15 and copying it down. Then identify the cluster index (1 through 4) and city name of the cluster center that yields the minimum. We can use the MATCH function to obtain the cluster index. Enter the formula

=MATCH(T15,P15:S15,0)

---

[9]Minimizing squared distances gives us the same solution as minimizing distances.

in cell U15 and copy it down. For example, the 4.447 minimum squared distance for Albuquerque corresponds to the second squared distance, so Albuquerque is assigned to the second cluster center. Finally, to get the *name* of the second cluster center, we can use the INDEX function. Enter the formula

=INDEX(CenterNames,U15,1)

in cell V15 and copy it down. Recall (from its use in Chapter 5) that this handy function has the form **=INDEX(*range,rowindex,columnindex*).** In this example, it returns the name in the second row and first (only) column of the CenterNames range (in Figure 8.26).

❻ Sum of squared distances. The objective is to minimize the sum of squared distances from all cities to the cluster centers to which they are assigned. Calculate this objective in the SumSqDists cell (in Figure 8.26) with the formula

=SUM(MinSqDists)

USING THE EVOLUTIONARY SOLVER

The Solver dialog box should be set up as shown in Figure 8.28. Because the changing cells represent *indices* of cluster centers, they must be integer-constrained, and suitable lower and upper limits are 1 and 49 (the number of cities). Make sure you set the Evolutionary Solver options as we described in Example 8.1. This problem is considerably harder to solve, and we want to allow the Solver plenty of time to search through a lot of potential solutions.

FIGURE 8.28
Solver Dialog Box for Cluster Model

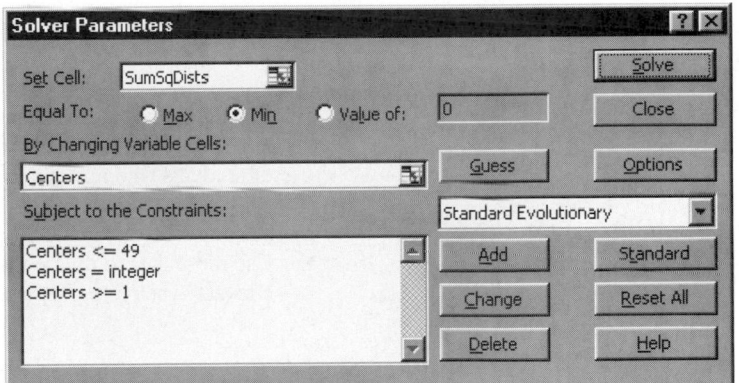

The solution in Figure 8.26, which uses Los Angeles, Omaha, Memphis, and San Francisco, is the best we found. You might find a slightly different solution, depending on your Solver settings and how long you let Solver run, but you should obtain a similar value in the target cell. If you look closely at the cities assigned to each cluster center, this solution begins to make intuitive sense. (See Figure 8.29, page 438.) The San Francisco cluster consists of rich, older, highly Asian cities. The Memphis cluster consists of highly African American cities with high unemployment rates. The Omaha cluster consists of average income cities with few minorities. The Los Angeles cluster consists of highly Hispanic cities with high unemployment rates.

Why four clusters? We could easily try three clusters (delete the fourth anchor) or five clusters (add another anchor). Note that when we *add* a cluster, the sum of squared distances will certainly decrease. In fact, we could obtain an objective value of 0 by using 49 clusters, one for each city, but this would hardly provide much information!

FIGURE 8.29
Clusters in Solver
Solution

	W	X	Y	Z	AA
14	Center:	Los Angeles	Memphis	Omaha	San Francisco
15		Dallas	Atlanta	Albuquerque	Honolulu
16		El Paso	Baltimore	Austin	San Francisco
17		Fort Worth	Chicago	Boston	Seattle
18		Fresno	Cincinnati	Charlotte	
19		Houston	Cleveland	Columbus	
20		Long Beach	Detroit	Denver	
21		Los Angeles	Memphis	Indianapolis	
22		Miami	New Orleans	Jacksonville	
23		NY	Oakland	Kansas City	
24		San Antonio	Philadelphia	Las Vegas	
25		San Diego	St. Louis	Milwaukee	
26		San Jose		Minneapolis	
27				Nashville	
28				Oklahoma City	
29				Omaha	
30				Phoenix	
31				Pittsburgh	
32				Portland	
33				Sacramento	
34				Toledo	
35				Tucson	
36				Tulsa	
37				Virginia Beach	

Therefore, to choose the "optimal" number of clusters, we would stop adding clusters when the sum of squared distances failed to decrease by a substantial amount. ∎

PROBLEMS

Skill-Building Problem

14. The file P8_14.XLS contains the following information about the top 25 MBA programs (according to the 1997 Business Week Guide): percentage of applicants accepted, percentage of accepted applicants who enroll, mean GMAT score of enrollees, mean undergraduate GPA of enrollees, annual cost of school (for state schools, this is the cost for out-of-state students), percentage of students who are minorities, percentage of students who are non-U.S. residents, and mean starting salary of graduates (in thousands of dollars). Use these data to divide the top 25 schools into four clusters. Then interpret your clusters.

8.9 DISCRIMINANT ANALYSIS

Discriminant analysis is a statistical tool used by analysts in marketing and other fields of business. It is somewhat similar to cluster analysis, but it is also quite different. In cluster analysis there are no predefined clusters. We look at the information on the different members of the population (cities, for example) to see which members should be clustered together because of similar characteristics. We do not even know the *number* of clusters to use. In discriminant analysis, however, the "clusters" (usually called groups) are predefined. For example, there might be two groups: users of a particular product and nonusers. We collect data on a sample (often called a **training sample**) of users and nonusers—their income, their ages, and other possibly relevant data—and we use these data to classify the customers as users or nonusers. The analysis is successful if we can correctly classify a large percentage of the customers in the training sample. Of course, we already know which group each customer in the training sample is in. Therefore, the real purpose is to see whether we can correctly classify a large percentage of customers outside of the training sample on the basis of their income, age, and so on.

Several situations where discriminant analysis has been used include the following:

- Based on gender, age, income, and residential location, can we classify a consumer as a user or nonuser of a new breakfast cereal?
- Based on income, type of residence, credit card debts, and other information, can we classify a consumer as a good or bad credit risk?
- Based on financial ratios, can we classify a company as a likely or unlikely candidate for bankruptcy?

In general, discriminant analysis can be used to classify members of two or more groups. We will focus only on two-group discriminant analysis. In this case we form a weighted combination of the data for each member, called a **discriminant score**, and classify the member into group 1 or group 2 depending on which side of a "cutoff" score the member's discriminant score falls. The problem is to find the appropriate weights for the discriminant scores and the appropriate cutoff score that maximize the percentage of correct classifications in the training sample. The following example illustrates the procedure.

EXAMPLE 8.8

CLASSIFYING SUBSCRIBERS AND NONSUBSCRIBERS TO THE WALL STREET JOURNAL

The file DISCRIM.XLS contains the annual income and size of investment portfolio (both in thousands of dollars) for 84 people. It also indicates whether each of these people subscribes or does not subscribe to the *Wall Street Journal*. Using income and size of investment portfolio, determine a classification rule that maximizes the number of people correctly classified as subscribers or nonsubscribers.

Solution

The model is actually simpler than for cluster analysis. Using appropriate weights, we create a discriminant score for each of the 84 customers. Then based on a cutoff score, we classify each customer as a subscriber or nonsubscriber, and we tally the number of correct classifications.

DEVELOPING THE SPREADSHEET MODEL

The model appears (with several hidden rows) in Figure 8.30 (page 440). It can be formed as follows.

❶ **Customer data.** Enter the customer data in the shaded range. This includes the data on the variables used for classification (income and investment amount), as well as an indication of which group each customer is in. These 84 customers represent the training sample, so we know which group (subscriber or nonsubscriber) each of them is in.

FIGURE 8.30
Discriminant
Analysis Model

	A	B	C	D	E	F	G
1	**Discriminant analysis**						
2							
3	**Weights for discriminant function**						
4		Income	InvestAmt				
5		-0.033	0.897				
6							
7	**Cutoff value for classification**						
8		37.362					
9							
10	**Customer data**						
11	Person	Income	InvestAmt	WSJSubscriber	Score	Classified as	Correct?
12	1	66.4	26.9	No	21.9	No	Yes
13	2	68.0	7.1	No	4.1	No	Yes
14	3	54.9	21.5	No	17.5	No	Yes
15	4	50.6	19.3	No	15.6	No	Yes
16	5	54.1	16.7	No	13.2	No	Yes
17	6	78.2	31.9	No	26.0	No	Yes
18	7	66.2	23.8	No	19.2	No	Yes
19	8	43.9	12.4	No	9.7	No	Yes
20	9	41.9	5.0	No	3.1	No	Yes
21	10	61.1	25.2	No	20.6	No	Yes
89	78	90.4	57.3	Yes	48.4	Yes	Yes
90	79	90.2	62.9	Yes	53.4	Yes	Yes
91	80	85.1	59.8	Yes	50.8	Yes	Yes
92	81	74.1	36.7	Yes	30.5	No	No
93	82	78.5	46.0	Yes	38.7	Yes	Yes
94	83	75.2	51.1	Yes	43.4	Yes	Yes
95	84	100.7	58.8	Yes	49.4	Yes	Yes
96							
97	**Classification matrix (actual along side, predicted along top)**						
98		Yes	No				
99	Yes	23	4				
100	No	2	55				
101							
102	**Percent correct classifications**						
103		92.86%					

Range names used:
Weights - B5:C5
Cutoff - B8
NoGroup - F12:F68
YesGroup - F69:F95
PctCorrect - B103

❷ Decision variables. The decision variables are the weights used to form discriminant scores and the cutoff value for classification. Enter any values for these in the Weights and Cutoff ranges.

❸ Discriminant scores. Each discriminant score is a weighted combination of the person's income and investment amount. To calculate these in column E, enter the formula

=SUMPRODUCT(Weights,B12:C12)

in cell E12 and copy it down.

❹ Classifications. We will classify a person as a nonsubscriber if the person's discriminant score is *below* the cutoff value and as a subscriber otherwise. Therefore, enter the formula

=IF(E12<Cutoff,"No","Yes")

in cell F12 and copy it down.

❺ Correct? Check whether each classification is correct by entering the formula

=IF(D12=F12,"Yes","No")

in cell G12 and copying it down.

❻ Tallies. It is customary to tally the classifications in a classification matrix. Do this in the range B99:C100 by entering the formulas

=COUNTIF(YesGroup,"Yes")

and

=COUNTA(YesGroup)-B99

in cells B99 and C99. Note that the YesGroup range contains the classifications for all *subscribers*. Then enter similar formulas in cells B100 and C100. These are based on the NoGroup range. Finally, calculate the objective, the percentage of all 84 people classified correctly, in the PctCorrect cell with the formula

=SUM(B99,C100)/SUM(B99:C100)

(Read this formula carefully. The first SUM contains a comma; the second contains a colon.)

USING THE EVOLUTIONARY SOLVER

First, note that the Evolutionary Solver is required because of the IF (and COUNTIF and COUNTA) functions used to make and tally the classifications. The completed Solver dialog box appears in Figure 8.31. It is straightforward except for the lower and upper limits on the changing cells. There are no natural weights or cutoff values to use. However, we can always constrain the weights to be between -1 and 1. (The reasoning is that if we solve the problem with weights equal to, say, -15 and 15, we can divide them *and* the resulting cutoff score by 15 and obtain exactly the same classifications.) To obtain lower and upper limits on the cutoff value, we first calculated the maximum sum of income and investment amount for any customer, which is slightly less than 160. This means that the largest discriminant score, using weights of 1, is no larger than 160, and the smallest discriminant score, using weights of -1, is no less than -160. Therefore, there is no need to consider cutoff values below -160 or above 160.

The solution shown in Figure 8.30 is certainly not unique. There are many other sets of weights and cutoff values that obtain a 92.86% correct classification rate, and you will probably obtain a different solution from ours. Note that only 6 of the 84 people are misclassified—4 subscribers are classified as nonsubscribers and 2 nonsubscribers are classified as subscribers. Also, we see from the weights that the classification is based primarily on the investment amount, with very little weight placed on income. Because of the *positive* weight on the investment amount, people with large investment amounts are classified as subscribers. Therefore, a subscriber such as person 81 is misclassified because his investment amount is abnormally small relative to other subscribers. On the other hand, a nonsubscriber is misclassified if his investment amount is abnormally large relative to other nonsubscribers.

FIGURE 8.31
Solver Dialog Box for Discriminant Analysis

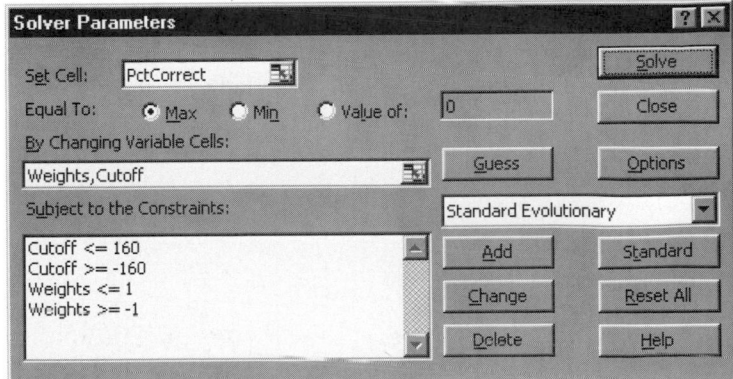

In a real application, we would use this analysis for people other than the 84 in the training sample. That is, we would calculate a discriminant score for each such person and classify each as a nonsubscriber if her discriminant score is less than the cutoff value. However, the percentage correctly classified would typically be less—maybe even considerably less—than the 92.86% rate we obtained in the training sample. ■

PROBLEMS

Skill-Building Problems

15. For the data in the file P8_15.XLS, develop a classification rule to classify students as likely admits, likely rejects, or borderline.

16. For data in the file P8_16.XLS, develop a rule to predict whether a person is likely to purchase our lasagna product. What variables appear to be the most useful?

17. The file P8_17.XLS contains information on the following items about 24 companies: EBITASS (earnings before income and taxes, divided by total assets), ROTC (return on total capital), and Group (1 for most admired companies and 2 for least admired companies). Use these data to develop a rule that can be used to classify a company as a most admired or least admired company. Which variable appears to be most important for this classification?

18. The file P8_18.XLS contains the following information for a random sample of 24 U.S. families: income (in thousands of dollars), lawn size (in thousands of square feet), and Group (1 for Rider Mower owners and 0 for others). Use these data to develop a rule for predicting whether a family is a Rider Mower owner. Which variable appears to be most important for this classification?

8.10 CONCLUSION

This chapter contains cutting-edge material. The standard Solver has been available for several years to solve many linear, integer, and nonlinear problems. However, it has not been able to solve the types of problems we have discussed in this chapter, except possibly by employing tricks or by using a lucky initial solution. With the Evolutionary Solver now available for the first time to a large audience, we are able to solve a much wider variety of problems, and the formulations are usually straightforward—they do not require tricks. The Evolutionary Solver is typically much slower than the standard Solver, especially for linear models with many constraints, because it uses a totally different search procedure. Because of this, we do not recommend that you try the Evolutionary Solver unless your model contains functions such as IF, COUNT, SUMIF, MIN, MAX, and ABS that the standard Solver cannot usually handle. But if your model is formulated more naturally by using such functions, or if you can think of no other way of formulating it, then the Evolutionary Solver should be very useful.

PROBLEMS

Skill-Building Problems

19. Fourteen jobs must be assigned to one of three identical machines. Our goal is to minimize the total time needed to complete all 14 jobs. The machine capacities and times needed for the jobs are given in Table 8.12. For example, job 8 requires 3 units of capacity on a machine for 2 hours. At any given time, a machine has 5 units of capacity. How should you assign the jobs to machines to ensure the earliest possible completion of all jobs?

TABLE 8.12	Job and Machine Data	
Job	Time	Capacity
1	2	2
2	1	3
3	1	3
4	3	2
5	4	1
6	3	1
7	3	4
8	2	3
9	1	4
10	2	2
11	1	2
12	2	2
13	2	1
14	3	1

20. Nine jobs need to be completed within 8 weeks. The number of weeks required to complete each job is given in Table 8.13. For example, job 2 requires 3 weeks. Each week, 160 hours of regular time labor

TABLE 8.13	Data on Jobs	
Job	Weeks	Due Date
1	4	7
2	3	6
3	5	5
4	4	4
5	4	5
6	2	4
7	3	4
8	2	4
9	5	5

are available. Up to 40 hours of overtime labor can be purchased each week at a cost of $10 per hour. Additional overtime hours cost $20 per hour.

a. Determine how to minimize the overtime cost incurred in completing the jobs within 8 weeks.

b. Table 8.13 also lists the due date for each job. For example, job 2 should be completed within 6 weeks. A penalty of $500 is incurred for each day a job is late. Determine how to minimize the sum of overtime and due date penalties.

21. The costs of producing product A, product B, or products A and B bundled together are $50, $90, and $140, respectively. Table 8.14 lists the sizes of the three market segments for these products and how much each of the segments is willing to pay for A alone, B alone, or the bundle. Under the assumption that a market segment will buy the product combination that yields the maximum nonnegative "surplus" (value minus cost) and a segment will buy no product if no product has a nonnegative surplus, determine an optimal set of product prices. Should the company offer all products for sale?

TABLE 8.14	Segment Information			
Segment	Size	A Alone	B Alone	Bundle
1	30	$100	$100	$195
2	100	$50	$96	$145
3	80	$80	$85	$195

22. Eight students need to be assigned to four dorm rooms (two students to a room) at Faber College. Based on incompatibility measures, the "cost" incurred if two students room together is shown in Table 8.15. How would you assign these students to rooms?

TABLE 8.15	Incompatibility Measures						
Student	2	3	4	5	6	7	8
1	9	3	4	2	1	5	7
2		4	5	6	7	8	3
3			4	2	8	3	5
4				3	2	4	6
5					8	7	6
6						2	3
7							4

23. Cook County needs to build two hospitals. There are nine cities where the hospitals can be built. The number of hospital visits made annually by the inhabitants of each city and the x and y coordinates of each city are listed in Table 8.16. To minimize the total distance that patients must travel to hospitals, where should the hospitals be located? Solve the problem when people can travel in straight lines ("as the crow flies") between cities. Then solve it when people must travel along a horizontal/vertical grid of roads. (*Hint:* Use lookup functions to generate the distances between each pair of cities.)

TABLE 8.16		Hospital Information	
City	x	y	Visits
1	0	0	3000
2	10	3	4000
3	12	15	5000
4	14	13	6000
5	16	9	4000
6	18	6	3000
7	8	12	2000
8	6	10	4000
9	4	8	1200

24. The file P8_24.XLS contains quarterly revenue for Nike for the years 1991–1998. It also contains quarterly "indicator" variables Q1, Q2, and Q3. Here Q1 is 1 for the first quarter of a fiscal year (July–September) and 0 otherwise. Q2 and Q3 are defined similarly for the second and third quarters of the fiscal year (October–December and January–March). The "Quarter #" variable is simply the chronological number of the quarter, 1–32. We would like to build a quantitative model to explain the variation in quarterly revenue. A reasonable model is as follows:

$$\text{Predicted Sales} = ab^{Quarter\#}c^{Q_1}d^{Q_2}e^{Q_3}$$

where a, b, c, d, and e are parameters to estimate.
  a. Find the values of a, b, c, d, and e that best fit this model.
  b. What does your model say about the trend and seasonal aspects of Nike sales? (*Hint:* The trend effect is captured by the term involving Quarter #. Seasonal effects may be interpreted relative to the quarter, Q4, that we have omitted from the analysis.)

25. Music radio WABC has commercials of the following lengths (in seconds): 15, 15, 20, 25, 30, 35, 40, 57. The commercials must be assigned to 60-second breaks. What is the fewest number of breaks that are needed to air all of the commercials?

26. A Wall Street firm is trying to package nine mortgages for sale. The sizes of the mortgages (in thousands of dollars) are listed in Table 8.17. To be sold, each package must consist of at least $1,000,000 in mortgages. What is the largest number of packages that can be created?

TABLE 8.17	Mortgage Data
Mortgage	Amount
1	910
2	870
3	810
4	64
5	550
6	250
7	120
8	95
9	55

27. During the next 12 months, the amounts of electric power (in thousands of kwh) listed in Table 8.18 are needed. This power can be supplied using four generators. The generating capacity (in thousands of kwh), the operating cost, the startup cost, and the shutdown cost (all costs in thousands of dollars) are

TABLE 8.18	Power Demands
Month	Demand
1	9
2	149
3	146
4	59
5	108
6	77
7	119
8	28
9	40
10	83
11	88
12	94

listed in Table 8.19. At the beginning of month 1, generators 1 and 2 are in operation. At the end of each month, we can either shut down an operating generator or start up a shutdown generator. How can

TABLE 8.19	Other Power Data			
	Generator 1	Generator 2	Generator 3	Generator 4
Capacity	60	50	40	30
Operating cost	6	5	4	3
Startup cost	3	3	3	2
Shutdown cost	2	2	2	1

we minimize the cost of meeting demand for power during the next 12 months?

28. Bus 99 serves towns 1–10. We assume that town k is $|k - j|$ miles from town j. The numbers of people in the towns who want to take the bus each hour are listed in Table 8.20. Bus 99 will make two stops and anyone who wants to take the bus will walk to the closest bus stop.

   a. If our goal is to minimize the total distance people walk, where should we stop the bus?

   b. If the bus made three stops, how much would the total walking distance be reduced?

TABLE 8.20	Bus Data
Town	Customers
1	13
2	98
3	48
4	63
5	3
6	79
7	17
8	21
9	12
10	68

29. Ten data sets must be assigned for storage to one of three disk drives. Each disk drive can store 885 megabytes. The sizes of the data sets (in megabytes) are listed in the file P8_29.XLS. When many people access a disk drive, there is a significant reduction in the speed at which the data are retrieved. To reduce the number of people accessing a disk drive, we strive to make the data sets on each disk drive as different as possible. To achieve this goal, we have assigned "penalties" for assigning similar data sets to the same disk drive. These penalties are also listed in the P8_29.XLS file. For example, if data sets 9 and 10 are assigned to the same drive, a penalty of 221 is incurred, whereas if disks 8 and 10 are assigned to the same drive, a penalty of only 35

is incurred. You can think of the penalty as the number of times two data sets are accessed at the same time. Assign the data sets to disk drives to minimize total penalties.

Skill-Extending Problems

30. Suppose you are the ad manager for Fox NFL football. Thirty bids for ads on today's game between the Packers and the Colts have been submitted. Information on these ads is given in the file P8_30.XLS. For example, ad 1 is 23 seconds in length and will bring in $53,000 in revenues. During the game, 14 1-minute slots are available for ads. Determine how Fox can maximize the revenue earned from game ads.

31. Assume that a consumer's purchase decision on an electric razor is based on four attributes, each of which can be set at one of three levels (1, 2, or 3). Using conjoint analysis (a type of analysis used in marketing research), our analysts have divided the market into five segments (labeled as customers 1, 2, 3, 4, and 5) and have determined the "part-worth" that each customer gives to each level of each attribute. These are listed in the file P8_31.XLS. Conjoint analysis usually assumes the customer buys the product yielding the highest total part-worth. Currently there is a single product in the market that sets all four attributes equal to 1. You are going to sell two types of electric razors. Design a product line that maximizes the number of market segments that will buy your product. For example, if you design a product that is level 2 of each attribute, then customer 1 will not buy the product because he values the current product at $1 + 4 + 4 + 4 = 13$ and values your product at $1 + 1 + 1 + 2 = 5$. Assume that in the case of a tie, the consumer does not purchase your product.

32. An important problem in manufacturing is the assembly line balancing problem. When setting up a manufacturing line, activities must be assigned to workstations. The maximum time spent at a workstation is called the cycle time. Minimizing the cycle time translates to maximizing the number of items that can be produced each hour. Here is a typical assembly line balancing problem that can be

solved with the Evolutionary Solver. Manufacture of a product consists of 10 activities (A–J) that require the times (in seconds) in Table 8.21 to complete. Certain activities must be completed before others. These precedence relations are given in Table 8.22. For example, activity A cannot be performed on a higher numbered workstation than activity B. Use the Evolutionary Solver to determine an assignment of activities to workstations that minimizes the total cycle time.

TABLE 8.21   **Activity Times**

Activity	Time
A	45
B	11
C	9
D	50
E	15
F	12
G	12
H	12
I	12
J	8
K	9

TABLE 8.22   **Precedence Relationships**

Before	After
A	B
B	C
C	F
C	G
F	J
G	J
J	K
D	E
E	H
E	I
H	J
I	J

33. A common approach to clustering is called **multidimensional scaling** (MDS). To apply MDS, we rank each pair of objects we want to cluster from least similar (higher number) to most similar (lower number). For example, in the file P8_33.XLS, we compared the similarity of 10 banks and found banks 5 and 10 to be most similar and banks 9 and 10 to be least similar. We now assign a location in the x-y plane to each bank. Our goal is to ensure that when we rank the distances between pair of banks, the ordering of these distances matches (as closely as possible) the similarity rankings of the banks.
   a. Constrain each bank to have an x and y coordinate between -1 and $+1$ and determine the "location" of each bank. (*Hint*: Use Excel's RANK function to rank the distances from smallest to largest.)
   b. How does this method lead to a natural clustering of banks?
   c. How could you determine whether you need more than two dimensions to adequately locate the banks?

Modeling Problems

34. The discussion at the beginning of Section 8.8 mentions Claritas. If you were in the direct-mail business, how would you use the information sold by Claritas to improve your profitability?
35. How would you use cluster analysis to help test market a consumer goods product?

Assigning MBA Students to Teams

The MBA program at State University has approximately 260 incoming students each Fall semester. These students are divided into cohorts of approximately 65 students each, and the students in each cohort sit through exactly the same set of Fall courses together. Much of the work in these courses is done in teams. To ensure that the teams are comparable, the MBA Office tries to divide the students in each cohort into 14 teams so that each team has the following qualities:

- It should have four or five members.
- It should have at least one member with a CPA.
- It should have at least one member with quantitative expertise.

- It should have at least one female.
- It should have at least one minority student.
- It should have at least one international student.

The file MBATEAMS.XLS indicates the characteristics of the students in a particular cohort of this year's incoming class. Your job is to use the Evolutionary Solver to see if you can create teams that have all of the desired properties. It is not clear whether this will be possible—for example, there might not be enough minority students to go around—so you should create "penalties" for failing to meet the various goals, where the penalties can be different for different goals.

## CHAPTER 9

Multi-Objective Decision Making

PUBLIC SECTOR TAX PLANNING

The government is a prime candidate for performing decision making that involves multiple (conflicting) objectives. Most governmental decisions have political ramifications, with each constituency benefiting along some dimensions but losing along others. A real example of such governmental decision making is discussed by Chrisman et al. (1989) in their paper "A Multiobjective Linear Programming Methodology for Public Sector Tax Planning." During the 1980s, the city of Peoria, Illinois, experienced a deterioration of its industrial base. As a result, its population and property values declined, which meant a decrease in property taxes. Because Peoria had always relied heavily on property taxes, it became more difficult for it to generate sufficient revenue for existing public services.

In response, the city funded a management science study to determine new ways to generate revenue that would be politically acceptable. Several forms of sales tax were suggested, such as a sales tax on everything but food, drugs, and durable goods, a sales tax on food and drugs, a sales tax on durable goods, and a sales tax on gasoline. Politically, the city had several objectives. It certainly needed to maintain its current level of tax revenue, but it also wanted to put less tax burden on low-income families, it wanted to reduce the property tax rate, and it wanted to keep businesses from moving out of Peoria. This suggested a multiple-objective linear programming (MOLP) approach. Specifically, the study identified four objectives: (1) reduce the property tax rate, (2) minimize the tax burden on low-income households, (3) minimize the flight of businesses and shoppers to the suburbs to escape higher sales taxes, and (4) minimize the gasoline tax rate.

Using these four objectives, the model then formulated a number of constraints, including (1) maintain the current level of tax revenues (at least), (2) ensure that the property tax rate does not increase, (3) ensure that the general sales tax rate excluding food, drugs, and durable goods is between 1% and 3%, and others. (Actually, as the city manager studied the model's output and saw results he didn't agree with, he suggested more constraints in order to produce different types of solutions. Remember that this took place in a *political* context!) The decision variables were the various tax rates, including the property tax rate and the proposed sales tax rates.

Unlike examples in previous chapters where there was a single objective, an MOLP model produces *many* solutions. The solutions worth examining are called **efficient solutions**, in the sense that any change in an efficient solution that makes one objective better automatically makes another objective worse. This means that the set of efficient solutions is the only set decision makers need to choose from, and they can make the choice by using their own preference function. This is indeed what happened in the Peoria study. After the city manager studied the set of efficient solutions, he was finally able to select a solution that he deemed best—it satisfied the constraints, it did well across the various objectives, and it was politically acceptable. Because of the political context, it might be hard to argue that the accepted solution was really "optimal," but the MOLP approach did what it was supposed to do. It allowed the city to make a decision based on rational criteria, it illustrated the trade-offs between the objectives associated with planning the tax structure, and it decreased the property tax rate from 2.76% to 1.64% while maintaining the level of tax revenue. (See Problem 41 for an illustration of this problem.) ■

9.1 INTRODUCTION

In many of your classes, you have probably discussed how to make good decisions. Usually, you assume that the correct decision optimizes a *single* objective, such as profit maximization or cost minimization. In most situations you encounter in business and life, however, there is more than one relevant objective. For example, when you graduate you will (we hope) receive several job offers. Which should you accept? Before deciding which job offer to accept, you might consider how each job "scores" on several objectives, such as salary, interest in work, quality of life in the city you will live in, and nearness to family. In this situation it is difficult to combine your four objectives into a single objective. Similarly, in determining an optimal investment portfolio, you want to maximize expected return but you also want to minimize risk. How do you reconcile these conflicting objectives? In this chapter we will discuss three tools, **goal programming**, **trade-off curves**, and the **Analytic Hierarchy Process (AHP)**, that decision makers can use to solve multiple-objective problems. Fortunately, all three of these tools can be implemented fairly easily on a spreadsheet.

9.2 GOAL PROGRAMMING

In many situations a company wants to achieve several objectives. Given limited resources, it may prove impossible to meet all objectives simultaneously. If the company can prioritize its objectives, then **goal programming** can often be used to choose good decisions. The following media selection problem is typical of the situations in which goal programming is useful.

EXAMPLE 9.1

DETERMINING AN ADVERTISING SCHEDULE AT LEON BURNIT

The Leon Burnit Ad Agency is trying to determine a TV advertising schedule for a client. The client has three goals (listed here in descending order of importance). It wants its ads to be seen by

- Goal 1: at least 65 million high-income men (HIM)
- Goal 2: at least 72 million high-income women (HIW)
- Goal 3: at least 70 million low-income people (LIP)

Burnit can purchase several types of TV ads: ads shown on live sports shows, on game shows, on news shows, on sitcoms, on dramas, and on soap operas. At most $700,000 total can be spent on ads. The advertising costs and potential audiences (in millions of viewers) of a 1-minute ad of each type are shown in Table 9.1. As a matter of policy, the client requires that at least two ads be placed on sports shows, on news shows, and on dramas. Also, it requires that no more than ten ads be placed on any single type of show. Burnit wants to find the advertising plan that best meets its client's goals.

TABLE 9.1   Data for Advertising Example

Ad Type	HIM	LIP	HIW	Cost
Sports show	7	4	8	$120,000
Game show	3	5	6	$40,000
News	6	5	3	$50,000
Sitcom	4	5	7	$40,000
Drama	6	8	6	$60,000
Soap opera	3	4	5	$40,000

Solution

First, we build a spreadsheet model to see whether all of the goals can be met simultaneously. In this spreadsheet model we must keep track of the following:

- the number of sports and soap opera ads placed
- the cost of the ads
- the number of exposures to each group (HIM, HIW, and LIP)
- the deviation from the exposure goal of each group

DEVELOPING THE SPREADSHEET MODEL

The spreadsheet model can be formed as follows. (See Figure 9.1 and the Model sheet of the file BURNIT1.XLS.)

❶ Inputs. Enter all inputs in the shaded ranges.

❷ Numbers of ads. Enter *any* trial values for the numbers of ads in the Ads range.

❸ Total cost. Calculate the total amount spent on ads in the TotCost cell with the formula

=SUMPRODUCT(UnitCosts,Ads)

❹ Exposures obtained. Calculate the number of people (in millions) in each group that the ads reach in the Obtained range. Specifically, enter the formula

=SUMPRODUCT(B7:G7,Ads)

in cell B26 for the HIM group, and copy this to the rest of the Obtained range for the other two groups.

USING THE SOLVER

The completed Solver dialog box appears in Figure 9.2. At this point there is no objective to maximize or minimize. We are simply looking for *any* solution that meets all of the constraints. When we click on Solve, we get the message that there is no feasible solution. It is impossible to meet all of the client's goals and stay within this budget. To see how large the budget must be, we ran SolverTable with the Budget cell

	A	B	C	D	E	F	G
1	Advertising model - possible to meet all goals?						
2							
3	Note: All monetary values are in $1000s, and all exposures to ads are in millions of exposures.						
4							
5	Exposures to various groups per unit of advertising						
6		Sports ad	Game show ad	News show ad	Sitcom ad	Drama ad	Soap opera ad
7	High-income men	7	3	6	4	6	3
8	High-income women	4	5	5	5	8	4
9	Low-income people	8	6	3	7	6	5
10							
11	Cost/unit	120	40	50	40	60	40
12							
13	Advertising plan						
14		Sports ad	Game show ad	News show ad	Sitcom ad	Drama ad	Soap opera ad
15	Minimum ads required	2	0	2	0	2	0
16		<=	<=	<=	<=	<=	<=
17	Number purchased	2.000	0.000	2.000	4.000	3.333	0.000
18		<=	<=	<=	<=	<=	<=
19	Maximum ads allowed	10	10	10	10	10	10
20							
21	Budget constraint	Total cost			Budget		Range names used:
22		$700	<=		$700		UnitCosts - B11:G11
23							MinAds - B15:G15
24	Goals for numbers of exposures						Ads - B17:G17
25		Exposures			Goal		MaxAds - B19:G19
26	High-income men	62.000	>=		75		TotCost - B22
27	High-income women	64.667	>=		72		Budget - D22
28	Low-income people	70.000	>=		70		Exposures - B26:B28
29							Goals - D26:D28

FIGURE 9.1 Feasibility of Meeting All Goals

FIGURE 9.2
Solver Dialog
Box for Finding
a Feasible Solution

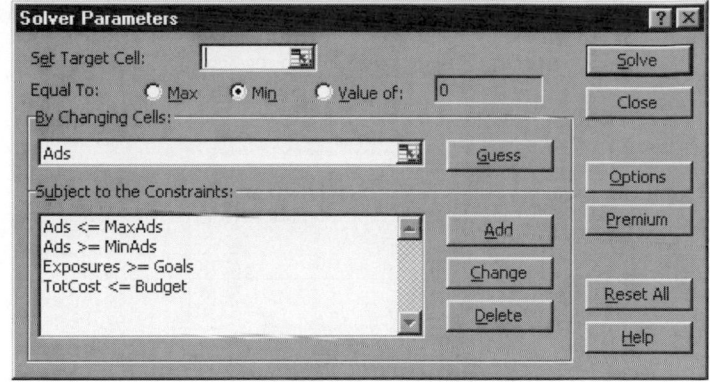

FIGURE 9.3
Checking How Large
the Budget Must Be

as the single input cell, varied from 700 to 850, and *any* cell as the output cell. The results appear in Figure 9.3. They show that unless the budget is greater than $775,000, it is impossible to meet all of the client's goals.

	A	B	C	D
30	Sensitivity to budget (to see how large it must be to meet all goals)			
31		$B$26		
32	700	Not feasible		
33	725	Not feasible		
34	750	Not feasible		
35	775	Not feasible		
36	800	75.000		
37	825	75.000		
38	850	75.000		

Now that we know that a $700,000 budget is not sufficient to meet all of the client's goals, we use goal programming to see how close Burnit can come to these goals. First, we introduce some terminology. The upper and lower limits on the ads of each type and the budget constraints are considered **hard** constraints in this model. This means that they cannot be violated under any circumstances. The goals on exposures, on the other hand, are considered **soft** constraints. The client certainly wants to satisfy these goals, but it is willing to come up somewhat short—in fact, it must because of the limited budget. In goal programming models the soft constraints are prioritized. We first try to satisfy the goals with the highest priority (in this case, HIM exposures). If there is still any room to maneuver, we then try to satisfy the goals with the next highest priority (HIW exposures). If there is *still* room to maneuver, we move on to the goals with the third highest priority, and so on.

DEVELOPING THE GOAL PROGRAMMING MODEL

In general, goal programming requires several consecutive Solver runs, one for each priority level. However, it is possible to set up the model so that we can make these consecutive runs with only minor modifications from one run to the next. We illustrate the procedure in Figure 9.4 on page 454. (See the Goals sheet of the file BURNIT1.XLS.) To develop this model, first make a copy of the original Model sheet shown in Figure 9.1. Then modify it using the following steps.

❶ **New changing cells.** The exposure constraints are no longer shown as "hard" constraints. Instead, we introduce changing cells in the DevUnder and DevOver ranges (Dev is short for "deviations") to indicate how much under or over each goal we are.

	A	B	C	D	E	F	G
24	**Goals for numbers of exposures**						
25		Exposures	Amt under goal	Amt over goal	Balance		Goal
26	High-income men	65.000	0	0	65.000	=	65
27	High-income women	60.250	11.75	0	72.000	=	72
28	Low-income people	58.750	11.25	0	70.000	=	70
29							
30	**Deviations from goals (amounts below goals, or 0 if currently meeting goal)**						
31		Deviation		Already obtained			
32	High-income men	0.000	<=	65.000			
33	High-income women	11.750	<=	72.000			
34	Low-income people	11.250	<=	70.000			
35							
36		Extra range names used:					
37		DevUnder - C26:C28					
38		DevOver - D26:D28					
39		Balances - E26:E28					
40		Goals - G26:G28					
41		DevUnder1 - B32:B34					
42		Obtained - D32:D34					
43		Dev1 - B32					
44		Dev2 - B33					
45		Dev3 - B34					
46							

Note beside rows 32–34: Initially, enter large values in these cells (such as the original goals). Then, as high priority goals are met or partially met, enter the actual deviations obtained here (one at a time).

FIGURE 9.4 Minimizing Deviation for Highest Priority Goal

Enter any values in these ranges. (We entered 0's.) Note that in the Solver solution, at least one of these two types of deviations will always be 0 for each goal—we will either be below the goal or above the goal, but not both.

❷ **Balance equations.** To tie these new changing cells to the rest of the model, we create "balances" in column E that must logically equal the goals in column G. To do this, enter the formula

=B26+C26-D26

in cell E26 and copy it down. The logical balance equation for each group specifies that the actual number of exposures, plus the number under the goal, minus the number over the goal, *must* equal the goal.

❸ **Constraints on deviations under.** The client is concerned only with too *few* exposures, not with too many. Therefore, we set up constraints on the "under" deviations in rows 32–34. On the left side, in column B, enter links to the DevUnder range by entering the formula

=C26

in cell B32 and copying down. (We have named this range DevUnder1 because it is basically a copy of the DevUnder range.)

❹ **Highest priority goal.** The first Solver run will try to achieve the highest priority goal (HIM exposures). To do so, we minimize the Dev1 cell. Do this as shown in Figure 9.4. Then set up the Solver dialog box as shown in Figure 9.5. (Also, check the Assume Linear Model and Assume Non-Negative boxes.) The constraints include the hard constraints, the balance constraint, and the DevUnder1<=Obtained constraint. Note that we have entered the goals themselves in the Obtained range. Therefore, the DevUnder1<=Obtained constraint at this point is essentially redundant—the "under" deviations cannot possibly be greater than the goals themselves. (Do you see why?) We include it because it will become important in later Solver runs, which will then require only minimal modifications. The solution from this Solver run is the one shown

FIGURE 9.5
Solver Dialog Box
for Highest Priority
Goal

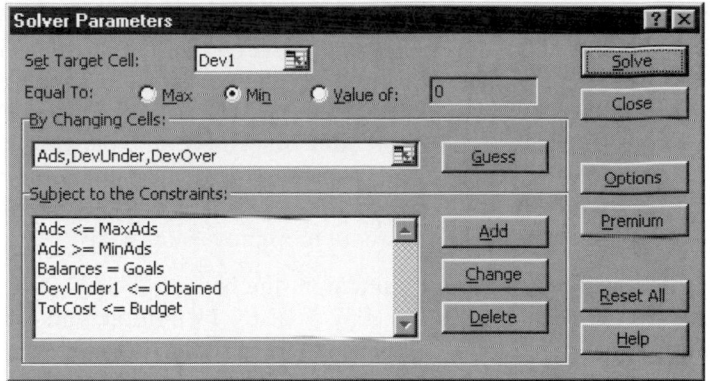

in Figure 9.4. It shows that Burnit can satisfy the HIM goal completely. However, the other two goals are not satisfied because their "under" deviations are positive.

❺ **Second highest priority goal.** Now we come to the key aspect of goal programming. Once a high priority goal is satisfied as fully as possible, we move on to the next highest priority goal. However, we do not want to lose what we already gained with the high priority goal. Therefore, we constrain its "under" deviation to be no greater than what we have already achieved. In this case we achieved a deviation of 0 in step 4, so enter 0 in cell D32 for the upper limit of the HIM "under" deviation. Then run the Solver again, changing only one thing in the Solver dialog box—make the Dev2 cell the target cell. Effectively, we are constraining the "under" deviation for the HIM group to remain at 0, and we are then minimizing the "under" deviation for the HIW group. The solution from this second Solver run appears in Figure 9.6. As we promised, the HIM goal has not suffered at all, but we are now a little closer to the HIW goal than before. It was under by 11.75 before, and now it is under by only 11. The lowest priority goal (for the LIP group) essentially "comes along for the ride" in this step. It could either improve or get worse. It happened to get worse, moving from under by 11.25 to under by 18.

	A	B	C	D	E	F	G
24	**Goals for numbers of exposures**						
25		Exposures	Amt under goal	Amt over goal	Balance		Goal
26	High-income men	65.000	0	0	65.000	=	65
27	High-income women	61.000	11	0	72.000	=	72
28	Low-income people	52.000	18	0	70.000	=	70
29							
30	**Deviations from goals (amounts below goals, or 0 if currently meeting goal)**						
31		Deviation			Already obtained		
32	High-income men	0.000	<=		0.000		
33	High-income women	11.000	<=		11.000		
34	Low-income people	18.000	<=		70.000		
35							
36				Extra range names used:			
37				DevUnder - C26:C28			
38				DevOver - D26:D28			
39				Balances - E26:E28			
40				Goals - G26:G28			
41				DevUnder1 - B32:B34			
42				Obtained - D32:D34			
43				Dev1 - B32			
44				Dev2 - B33			
45				Dev3 - B34			
46							

Initially, enter large values in these cells (such as the original goals). Then, as high priority goals are met or partially met, enter the actual deviations obtained here (one at a time).

FIGURE 9.6 Minimizing Deviation for Second Priority Goal

6 **Lowest priority goal.** You can probably guess the last step by now. We minimize the Dev3 cell, the deviation for the LIP group, while ensuring that the two higher priority goals are achieved as fully as in steps 4 and 5. As the model is set up, only two changes are necessary—enter 11 in cell D33 and change the Solver target cell to the Dev3 cell. When you run Solver this time, however, you will find that there is no room left to maneuver. The solution remains exactly the same as in Figure 9.6. This occurs frequently in goal programming models. After satisfying the first goal or two as fully as possible, there is often no room to improve later goals.

To summarize Burnit's situation, the budget of $700,000 allows it to satisfy the client's HIM goal, miss the HIW goal by 11 million, and miss the LIP goal by 18 million. Given the priorities on these three goals, this is the best possible solution.

Sensitivity Analysis Sensitivity analysis should be a part of goal programming just as it is for previous models we have discussed. However, there is no quick way to do it (at least none we have thought of). SolverTable works on only a *single* objective, whereas goal programming requires a sequence of objectives. Therefore, if we wanted to see how the solution to Burnit's model changes with different budgets, say, we would need to go through the above steps several times and keep track of the results manually. This is certainly possible, but it is tedious.

Effect of changing priorities With three goals, there are six possible orderings of the goals. The goal programming solutions corresponding to these orderings are listed in Figure 9.7. Row 4 corresponds to the ordering we used in the example. Clearly, the solution can change if the priorities of the goals change. For example, when we give the HIW goal the highest priority (rows 6, 7), *none* of the goals are achieved completely. (Problem 1 asks you to verify the details.)

	A	B	C	D	E	F	G	H	I	J	K	L
1	Results from changing priorities											
2												
3	Priority 1	Priority 2	Priority 3	Dev1	Dev2	Dev3	Sports ad	Game show ad	News show ad	Sitcom ad	Drama ad	Soap opera ad
4	HIM	HIW	LIP	0	11	18	2	0	5	0	3.5	0
5	HIM	LIP	HIW	0	11.75	11.25	2	0	5	2.25	2	0
6	HIW	HIM	LIP	3	6	12	2	0	2	0	6	0
7	HIW	LIP	HIM	3	6	12	2	0	2	0	6	0
8	LIP	HIM	HIW	1.956	9.304	0	2	0	3.043	4.696	2	0
9	LIP	HIW	HIM	3	7.333	0	2	0	2	4	3.333	0

FIGURE 9.7 Effect of Changing Priorities ■

MODELING ISSUES

1. The results for the Burnit model are based on allowing the numbers of ads to have noninteger values. However, they could easily be constrained to integer values, and the solution method would remain exactly the same.

2. Each priority level in the Burnit model contains exactly one goal. It is easy to generalize to the case where a given priority level can have multiple goals, each modeled with a certain deviation from a target. When we run the Solver for this priority level, we would use a weighted average of these deviations as the objective to minimize.

3. All of the deviations in the objectives of the Burnit model are "under" deviations. However, it is certainly possible to include "over" deviations as objectives. For

example, if the budget constraint were treated as a soft constraint, we would try to minimize its "over" deviation to stay as little over the budget as possible. It is even possible for *both* the "under" and "over" deviations of some goal to be included as objectives. This would occur in a situation where we want to come as close as possible to some target value—neither under nor over.

4. The use of changing cells for the "under" and "over" deviations might not be intuitive. However, it serves two purposes. First, it provides exactly the information we need for the objectives in goal programming. Second, it keeps the model linear. We tried using an IF function instead (without the under and over cells) to capture the "under" deviations. It looked great, but even when we unchecked the Assume Linear Model box, the Solver obtained the wrong answer! ■

ADDITIONAL APPLICATIONS

Goal programming has been applied to many situations where multiple objectives are present. Here are some examples.

- Optimally blending sausage. The conflicting objectives are cost, protein content, and fat content. See Problem 6 and Steuer (1984).
- Admitting students to a college. The conflicting objectives involve class size, diversity, in-state versus out-of-state mix, and academic quality of the class. See Problem 10 and Lee and Moore (1974).
- Assigning different types of employees (partners, junior associates, and so on) to different jobs at a CPA firm. The conflicting objectives are monthly billings and the number of workers of each type that the company can hire. See Problem 7 and Welling (1977).
- Determining the projects that a manufacturing firm should implement. The conflicting objectives include return on investment, cost, technological risk, and productivity improvement.
- Determining the type of recreation facilities that a city should build. The conflicting objectives include limitations on land use and maintenance cost, as well as desired usage of each facility. See Problem 13 and Taylor and Keown (1984).
- Determining the optimal product mix. The conflicting objectives include profit, maintaining a desired cash balance, and maintaining a desired value of the firm's current ratio. See Problem 42 and Sartoris and Spruill (1974).
- Determining the optimal set of ingot molds to use for steel production. Bethlehem Steel did this. Their primary goal was to minimize the number of molds used for steel production. Their secondary goal was to minimize the weight of the steel that needed to be produced to fill the company's orders. See Vasko et al. (1955) and Problem 18. ■

PROBLEMS

Skill-Building Problems

1. For each set of priorities of goals, solve the Leon Burnit problem and verify that the values in Figure 9.7 are correct.

2. Gotham City must determine how to allocate ambulances during the next year. It costs $5000 per year to run an ambulance. Each ambulance must be assigned to one of two districts. Let x_i be the number of ambulances assigned to district i, $i = 1, 2$. The

average time (in minutes) it takes for an ambulance to respond to a call from district 1 is $40 - 3x_1$; for district 2 the time is $50 - 4x_2$. Gotham City has three goals (listed in order of priority):

■ Goal 1: At most $100,000 per year should be spent on ambulance service.
■ Goal 2: Average response time in district 1 should be at most five minutes.
■ Goal 3: Average response time in district 2 should be at most five minutes.

a. Use preemptive goal programming to determine how many ambulances to assign to each district.
b. How would your answer change if goal 2 had the highest priority, then goal 3, and then goal 1?

3. Fruit Computer Company is ready to make its annual purchase of computer chips. Fruit can purchase chips (in lots of 100) from three suppliers. Each chip's quality is rated as excellent, good, or mediocre. During the coming year Fruit needs 5000 excellent chips, 3000 good chips, and 1000 mediocre chips. The characteristics of the chips purchased from each supplier are shown in Table 9.2. Each year, Fruit has budgeted $28,000 to spend on chips. If Fruit does not obtain enough chips of a given quality, it can special-order additional chips at $10 per excellent chip, $6 per good chip, and $4 per mediocre chip. Fruit assesses a penalty of $1 for each dollar it goes over the annual budget (in payments to suppliers). Determine how Fruit can minimize the penalty associated with meeting the annual chip requirements. Also use preemptive goal programming to determine a purchasing strategy. Let the budget constraint have the highest priority, followed in order by the restrictions on excellent, good, and mediocre chips.

4. Hiland Appliance must determine how many color TVs and VCRs to stock. It costs Hiland $300 to purchase a color TV and $200 to purchase a VCR. A color TV requires three square yards of storage space, and a VCR requires one square yard. The sale of a color TV earns Hiland a profit of $150, and each VCR sale earns a profit of $100. Hiland has set the following goals (listed in order of importance):

■ Goal 1: A maximum of $20,000 can be spent on purchasing color TVs and VCRs.
■ Goal 2: Highland should earn at least $11,000 profit from the sale of color TVs and VCRs.

■ Goal 3: Color TVs and VCRs should not use up more than 200 square yards of storage space.

Use a preemptive goal programming model to determine how many color TVs and VCRs Hiland should order. How would the preemptive goal formulation be modified if Hiland's second goal were to have a profit of *exactly* $11,000?

5. Stockco produces two products. Relevant information for each product is shown in Table 9.3. Stockco has a goal of $48 in profits and incurs a $1 penalty for each dollar it falls short of this goal. A total of 32 hours of labor are available. A $2 penalty is incurred for each hour of overtime (labor over 32 hours) used, and a $1 penalty is incurred for each hour of available labor that is unused. Marketing considerations require that at least seven units of product 1 be produced and at least ten units of product 2 be produced. For each unit (of either product) by which production falls short of demand, a penalty of $5 is assessed.

TABLE 9.3	Data for Stockco Problem	
	Product 1	**Product 2**
Labor hours required	4	2
Contribution to profit	$4	$2

a. Determine how to minimize the total penalty incurred by Stockco.
b. Suppose the company sets (in order of importance) the following goals:
   ■ Goal 1: Avoid underutilization of labor.
   ■ Goal 2: Meet demand for product 1.
   ■ Goal 3: Meet demand for product 2.
   ■ Goal 4: Do not use any overtime.
   Use preemptive goal programming to determine an optimal production schedule.

6. Based on Steuer (1984). Deancorp produces sausage by blending beef head, pork chuck, mutton, and water. The cost per pound, fat per pound, and protein per pound for these ingredients are listed in Table 9.4. Deancorp needs to produce 100 pounds of sausage and has set the following goals, listed in order of priority:
   ■ Goal 1: Sausage should consist of at least 15% protein.

TABLE 9.2	Data for Fruit Computer Problem			
	Number of Chips per Lot of 100			
	Excellent	**Good**	**Mediocre**	**Price per 100**
Supplier 1	60	20	20	$400
Supplier 2	50	35	15	$300
Supplier 3	40	20	40	$250

- Goal 2: Sausage should consist of at most 8% fat.
- Goal 3: Cost per pound of sausage should not exceed $0.08.

Use preemptive goal programming model to determine the composition of sausage.

TABLE 9.4	Data for Deancorp Sausage Problem			
	Beef Head	Pork Chuck	Mutton	Water
Fat (per lb)	0.05	0.24	0.11	0
Protein (per lb)	0.20	0.26	0.08	0
Cost (in cents)	12	9	8	0

7. Based on Welling (1977). The Touche Young accounting firm must complete three jobs during the next month. Job 1 will require 500 hours of work, job 2 will require 300 hours, and job 3 will require 100 hours. At present the firm consists of five partners, five senior employees, and five junior employees, each of whom can work up to 40 hours per month. The dollar amount (per hour) that the company can bill depends on the type of accountant assigned to each job, as shown in Table 9.5. (The "X" indicates that a junior employee does not have enough experience to work on job 1.) All jobs must be completed. Touche Young has also set the following goals, listed in order of priority:
- Goal 1: Monthly billings should exceed $74,000.
- Goal 2: At most one partner should be hired.
- Goal 3: At most three senior employees should be hired.
- Goal 4: At most one junior employee should be hired.

Use preemptive goal programming to help Touche solve its problem.

TABLE 9.5	Data for Touche Young Accounting Problem		
	Job 1	Job 2	Job 3
Partner	160	120	110
Senior employee	120	90	70
Junior employee	X	50	40

8. There are four teachers in the Faber College Business School. Each semester, 200 students take each of the following courses: Marketing, Finance, Production, and Statistics. The "effectiveness" of each teacher in teaching each course is given in Table 9.6. Each teacher can teach a total of 200 students during the semester. The dean has set a goal of obtaining an average teaching effectiveness level of at least 6 in each course. Deviations from this goal in any course are considered equally important. Determine the semester's teaching assignments.

TABLE 9.6	Data for Teaching Problem			
	Marketing	Finance	Production	Statistics
Teacher 1	7	5	8	2
Teacher 2	7	8	9	4
Teacher 3	3	5	7	9
Teacher 4	5	5	6	7

9. There are 17 neighborhoods in the city of Bloomington. The number of high school students in each neighborhood and the time required to drive from each neighborhood to each of the city's two high schools (North and South) are listed in Table 9.7. The Bloomington Board of Education needs to determine how to assign students to high schools. All students in a given neighborhood must be assigned to the same high school. The Board has set (in order of priority, from highest to lowest) the following goals:
- Ensure that the difference in enrollment at the two high schools differs by at most 50.
- Ensure that average student travel time is at most 13 minutes.
- Ensure that at most 4% of the students must travel at least 25 minutes to school.

TABLE 9.7	Data for Bloomington High School Problem		
Neighborhood	Number of Students	Minutes to South	Minutes to North
1	200	8	30
2	200	8	35
3	180	4	27
4	100	6	25
5	150	4	22
6	220	10	26
7	150	11	32
8	180	13	34
9	150	12	28
10	210	15	32
11	220	16	19
12	230	20	18
13	120	12	24
14	210	19	16
15	180	18	15
16	190	32	4
17	160	28	3

a. Determine an optimal assignment of students to high schools.

b. If the difference between enrollment at the two high schools could differ by at most 100 (a change in goal 1), how would your answer change?

Skill-Extending Problems

10. Based on Lee and Moore (1974). Faber College is admitting students for the class of 2001. Data on its applicants are shown in Table 9.8. It has set four goals for this class, listed in order of priority:

- Goal 1: The entering class should include at least 5000 students.
- Goal 2: The entering class should have an average SAT score of at least 640.
- Goal 3: The entering class should consist of at least 25% out-of-state students.
- Goal 4: At least 2000 members of the entering class should not be business majors.

Use preemptive goal programming to determine how many applicants of each type to admit. Assume that all applicants who are admitted will decide to attend Faber.

TABLE 9.8	Data on Faber's Applicants		
	SAT Score	**Business Majors**	**Non-Business Majors**
In-state	700	1500	400
In-state	600	1300	700
In-state	500	500	500
Out-of-state	700	350	50
Out-of-state	600	400	400
Out-of-state	500	400	600

11. During the next four quarters, Wivco faces the following demands for globots: quarter 1, 13; quarter 2, 14; quarter 3, 12; quarter 4, 15. Globots can be produced by regular-time labor or by overtime labor. Production capacity (number of globots) and production costs during the next four quarters are shown in Table 9.9. Wivco has set the following goals in order of importance:

- Goal 1: Each quarter's demand should be met on time.
- Goal 2: Inventory at the end of each quarter should not exceed three units.
- Goal 3: Total production cost should be no greater than $250.

Use a preemptive goal programming model to determine Wivco's production schedule for the next four quarters. Assume that at the beginning of the first quarter, one globot is in inventory.

12. Lucy's Music Store at present employs five full-time employees and three part-time employees. The normal workload is 40 hours per week for full-time employees and 20 hours per week for part-time employees. Each full-time employee is paid $6 per hour for work up to 40 hours per week and can sell five recordings per hour. A full-time employee who works overtime is paid $10 per hour. Each part-time employee is paid $3 per hour and can sell three recordings per hour. It costs Lucy $6 to buy a recording, and each recording sells for $9. Lucy has weekly fixed expenses of $500. She has established the following weekly goals, in order of priority:

- Goal 1: Sell at least 1600 recordings per week.
- Goal 2: Earn a profit of at least $2200 per week.
- Goal 3: Full-time employees should work at most 100 hours of overtime.
- Goal 4: To promote a sense of job security, the number of hours by which each full-time employee fails to work 40 hours should be minimized.

Use a preemptive goal programming model to determine how many hours per week each employee should work.

13. Based on Taylor and Keown (1984). Gotham City is trying to determine the type and location of recreational facilities to build during the next decade. Four types of facilities are under consideration: golf courses, swimming pools, gymnasiums, and tennis courts. Six sites are under consideration. If a golf course is built, it must be built at either site 1 or site 6. Other facilities can be built at sites 2–5. The amounts of available land (in thousands of square feet) at sites 2–5 are given in Table 9.10. The cost of building each facility (in thousands of dollars), the annual maintenance cost

TABLE 9.9	Data for Wivco Production Problem			
	Regular Time		**Overtime**	
	Capacity	**Cost per Unit**	**Capacity**	**Cost per Unit**
Quarter 1	9	$4	5	$6
Quarter 2	10	$4	5	$7
Quarter 3	11	$5	5	$8
Quarter 4	12	$6	5	$9

TABLE 9.10	Available Land for Gotham Problem			
	Site			
	2	**3**	**4**	**5**
Available land	70	80	95	120

(in thousands of dollars) for each facility, and the land (in thousands of square feet) required for each facility are given in Table 9.11. The number of user days (in thousands) for each type of facility, shown in Table 9.12, depends on where it is built.

TABLE 9.11	Costs and Land Requirements for Gotham Problem		
	Construction Cost	**Maintenance Cost**	**Land Required**
Golf	$340	$80	Not relevant
Swimming	$300	$36	29
Gymnasium	$840	$50	38
Tennis courts	$85	$17	45

TABLE 9.12	User Days for Gotham Problem					
	Site					
	1	**2**	**3**	**4**	**5**	**6**
Golf	31	X	X	X	X	27
Swimming	X	25	21	32	32	X
Gymnasium	X	37	29	28	38	X
Tennis courts	X	20	23	22	20	X

a. Consider the following set of priorities:
- Priority 1: The amount of land used at each site should be no greater than the amount of land available.
- Priority 2: Construction costs should not exceed $1.2 million.
- Priority 3: User days should exceed 200,000.

- Priority 4: Annual maintenance costs should not exceed $200,000.

For this set of priorities, use preemptive goal programming to determine the type and location of recreation facilities in Gotham City.

b. Consider the following set of priorities:
- Priority 1: The amount of land used at each site should be no greater than the amount of land available.
- Priority 2: User days should exceed 200,000.
- Priority 3: Construction costs should not exceed $1.2 million.
- Priority 4: Annual maintenance costs should not exceed $200,000.

For this set of priorities, use preemptive goal programming to determine the type and location of recreation facilities in Gotham City.

14. A small aerospace company is considering eight projects:
- Project 1: Develop an automated test facility.
- Project 2: Bar code all inventory and machinery.
- Project 3: Introduce a CAD/CAM system.
- Project 4: Buy a new lathe and deburring system.
- Project 5: Institute an FMS (Flexible Manufacturing System).
- Project 6: Install a LAN (Local Area Network).
- Project 7: Develop an AIS (Artificial Intelligence Simulation).
- Project 8: Set up a TQM (Total Quality Management) program.

Each project has been rated on five attributes: return on investment (ROI), cost, productivity improvement, workforce requirements, and degree of technological risk. These ratings are given in Table 9.13. The company has set the following five goals (listed in order of priority):
- Goal 1: Achieve an ROI of at least $3250.
- Goal 2: Limit cost to $1300.
- Goal 3: Achieve a productivity improvement of at least 6.
- Goal 4: Limit workforce use to 108.
- Goal 5: Limit technological risk to a total of 4.

Use preemptive goal programming to determine which projects should be undertaken.

TABLE 9.13	Ratings for Aerospace Problem							
	Project							
	1	**2**	**3**	**4**	**5**	**6**	**7**	**8**
Return on investment (ROI)	$2070	$456	$670	$350	$495	$380	$1500	$480
Cost	$900	$240	$335	$700	$410	$190	$500	$160
Productivity improvement	3	2	2	0	1	0	3	2
Workforce requirements	18	18	27	36	42	6	48	24
Degree of technological risk	3	2	4	1	1	0	2	3

15. A new president has just been elected and has set the following economic goals (listed from highest to lowest priority):

- Goal 1: Balance the budget (this means revenues are at least as large as costs).
- Goal 2: Cut spending by at most $150 billion.
- Goal 3: Raise at most $550 billion in taxes from the upper class.
- Goal 4: Raise at most $350 billion in taxes from the lower class.

Currently the government spends $1 trillion per year. Revenue can be raised in two ways: through a gas tax and through an income tax. You must determine: G, the per-gallon tax rate (in cents); T_1, the tax rate charged on the first $30,000 of income; T_2, the tax rate charged on any income earned over $30,000; and C, the cut in spending (in billions). If the government chooses G, T_1, and T_2, then we assume that the revenue given in Table 9.14 (in billions of dollars) is raised. Of course, the tax rate on income over $30,000 must be at least as large as the tax rate on the first $30,000 of income. Use preemptive goal programming to help the president meet his goals.

TABLE 9.14	Data for Government Economy Problem	
	Low Income	**High Income**
Gas tax	G	$0.5G$
Tax on income up to $30,000	$20T_1$	$5T_1$
Tax on income over $30,000	0	$15T_2$

16. The HAL computer must determine which of eight research and development (R&D) projects to undertake. For each project, four quantities are of interest: (1) the net present value (NPV, in millions of dollars) of the project; (2) the annual growth rate in sales generated by the project; (3) the probability that the project will succeed; and (4) the cost (in millions of dollars) of the project. The relevant information is given in Table 9.15. HAL has set the following four goals:

- Goal 1: The total NPV of all chosen projects should be at least $200 million.
- Goal 2: The average probability of success for all projects chosen should be at least 0.75.
- Goal 3: The average growth rate of all projects chosen should be at least 15%.
- Goal 4: The total cost of all chosen projects should be at most $1 billion.

For the following sets of priorities, use preemptive (integer) goal programming to determine the projects that should be selected.

a. Goal 2, Goal 4, Goal 1, Goal 3.
b. Goal 1, Goal 3, Goal 4, Goal 2.

17. Based on Klingman and Phillips (1984). The Marines need to fill three types of jobs in two cities (Los Angeles and Chicago). The numbers of jobs of each type that must be filled in each city are shown in Table 9.16. The Marines available to fill these jobs have been classified into six groups according to the types of jobs each person is capable of doing, the type of job each person prefers, and the city in

TABLE 9.16	Marine Jobs to Be Filled	
	Job Type	**Jobs to Fill**
Los Angeles	1	1000
Los Angeles	2	2000
Los Angeles	3	1500
Chicago	1	2000
Chicago	2	1000
Chicago	3	1000

TABLE 9.15	Data for R&D Problem			
	NPV (millions)	**Annual Growth Rate**	**Probability of Success**	**Cost (millions)**
Project 1	$40	20%	0.75	$220
Project 2	$30	16%	0.70	$140
Project 3	$60	12%	0.75	$280
Project 4	$45	8%	0.90	$240
Project 5	$55	18%	0.65	$300
Project 6	$40	18%	0.60	$200
Project 7	$40	18%	0.60	$200
Project 8	$90	19%	0.65	$440

which each person prefers to live. The data for each of these six groups are shown in Table 9.17. The Marines have the following three goals, listed from highest priority to lowest priority:
- Ensure that all jobs are filled by qualified workers.
- Ensure that at least 8000 employees are assigned to the jobs they prefer.
- Ensure that at least 8000 employees are assigned to their preferred cities.

Determine how the Marines should assign their workers. (*Note*: You may allow fractional assignments of workers.)

18. Based on Vasko et al. (1955). Bethlehem Steel can fill orders using five different types of steel molds. Up to three different molds of each type can be purchased. Each individual mold can be used to fill up to 100 orders per year. Six different types of orders must be filled during the coming year. The waste (in tons) incurred if a type of mold is used to fill an order is shown in Table 9.18 (where an "x" indicates that a type of mold cannot be used to fill an order). The number of each order type that must be filled during the coming year is shown in Table 9.19. Bethlehem Steel has the following two goals, listed in order of priority.
- Since molds are very expensive, Bethlehem wants to use at most five molds.
- Bethlehem wants to have at most 600 tons of total waste.

Use preemptive goal programming to determine how Bethlehem should fill the coming year's orders.

TABLE 9.18   **Waste in Bethlehem Problem**

	Order Type					
	1	2	3	4	5	6
Mold 1	1	2	3	4	5	6
Mold 2	x	1	2	3	4	5
Mold 3	x	x	1	2	3	4
Mold 4	x	x	x	1	2	3
Mold 5	x	x	x	x	1	2

TABLE 9.19   **Number of Orders for Bethlehem Problem**

	Number of Orders
Order 1	80
Order 2	60
Order 3	40
Order 4	100
Order 5	120
Order 6	140

TABLE 9.17   **Group Data for Marine Problem**

	Number of People	Jobs They Can Do	Preferred Job	Preferred City
Group 1	1500	1, 2	1	Los Angeles
Group 2	1500	2, 3	2	Los Angeles
Group 3	1500	1, 3	1	Chicago
Group 4	1500	1, 3	3	Chicago
Group 5	1500	2, 3	3	Los Angeles
Group 6	1500	3	3	Chicago

9.3   PARETO OPTIMALITY AND TRADE-OFF CURVES

In a multiple-objective problem with no uncertainty, we often search for Pareto optimal solutions. We will assume that the decision maker has exactly two objectives and that the set of feasible points under consideration must satisfy a prescribed set of constraints.

First, we need to define some terms. A solution (call it A) to a multiple-objective problem is called **Pareto optimal** if no other feasible solution is at least as good as A with respect to every objective and strictly better than A with respect to at least one objective. A related concept is **domination**. We say a feasible solution B **dominates** a feasible solution A to a multiple-objective problem if B is at least as good as A with respect to every objective and is strictly better than A with respect to at least one objective. From this definition, it follows that Pareto optimal solutions are feasible solutions that are not dominated.

If we graph the "score" of all Pareto optimal solutions in the x–y plane with the x-axis score being the score on objective 1 and the y-axis score being the score on objective 2, the graph is called a **trade-off curve**. It is also called the **efficient frontier**. To illustrate, suppose that the set of feasible solutions for a multiple-objective problem is the shaded region bounded by the curve AB and the first quadrant in Figure 9.8. If we want to maximize both objectives 1 and 2, then the curve AB is the set of Pareto optimal points.

FIGURE 9.8
Trade-off Curve for
Maximizing Two
Objectives

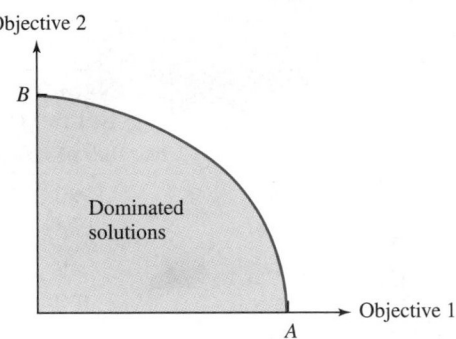

As another illustration, suppose the set of feasible solutions for a multiple-objective problem is all shaded points in the first quadrant bounded from below by the curve AB in Figure 9.9. If our goal is to maximize objective 1 and minimize objective 2, then the curve AB is the set of Pareto optimal points.

FIGURE 9.9
Trade-off Curve for
Maximizing
Objective 1,
Minimizing
Objective 2

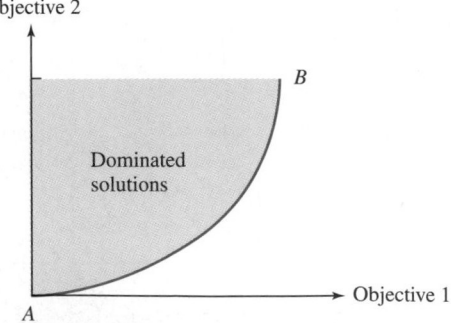

To find a trade-off curve, proceed according to the following steps.

Steps for Finding a Trade-off Curve

1. Choose an objective, say objective 1, and determine its best attainable value V_1. For the solution attaining V_1, find the value of objective 2 and label it V_2. Then (V_1, V_2) is a point on the trade-off curve.

2. For values V of objective 2 that are better than V_2, solve the optimization problem in step 1 with the additional constraint that the value of objective 2 is at least as good as V. Varying V (over values of V preferred to V_2) yields other points on the trade-off curve.

3. In step 1 we obtained one "endpoint" of the trade-off curve. If we determine the best value of objective 2 that can be attained, we obtain the other endpoint of the trade-off curve.

We will illustrate the concept of Pareto optimality (and how to determine Pareto optimal solutions) with the following example.

EXAMPLE 9.2

MAXIMIZING PROFIT AND MINIMIZING POLLUTION AT CHEMCON

Chemcon plans to produce eight products. The profit per unit, the labor and raw material used per unit produced, and the pollution emitted per unit produced are given in Table 9.20. This table also includes lower and upper limits on production that Chemcon has imposed. Currently 1300 labor hours and 1000 units of raw material are available. Chemcon's two objectives are to maximize profit and minimize pollution produced. Chemcon wants to graph the trade-off curve for this problem.

TABLE 9.20   **Data for Chemcon Example**

Product	1	2	3	4	5	6	7	8
Labor hrs/unit	5	5	1	4	3.5	4	2	3.5
Raw material/unit	3	4.5	5	5	4.5	2	3.5	3
Pollution/unit	25	29	35	26	17	25	28	6
Profit/unit	53	69	73	69	51	49	71	40
Min production	0	30	0	10	20	50	30	0
Max production	190	110	140	140	190	190	110	150

Solution

The model itself is a straightforward version of the product mix model from Chapter 3. We want the product mix that stays within the lower and upper production limits, uses no more labor or raw material than are available, keeps pollution low, and keeps profit high. None of the formulas in the spreadsheet model (see Figure 9.10 on page 466 and the file CHEMCON.XLS) presents anything new, so we will focus instead on the solution procedure.

Referring to the general three-step procedure for finding the trade-off curve, we let profit be objective 1 and pollution be objective 2. To obtain one endpoint of the curve (step 1), we maximize profit and *ignore* pollution. That is, we maximize the Profit cell and delete the constraint indicated in row 26 from the Solver dialog box. You can check that the solution has profit $20,089 and pollution level 8980. (This is *not* the solution shown in the figure.) At the other end of the spectrum (step 3), we can minimize the pollution in cell B26 and ignore any constraint on profit. You can check that this solution has pollution level 3560 and profit $8360. In other words, profit can get as high as $20,089 by ignoring pollution or as low as $8360 by focusing entirely on pollution, and pollution can get as low as 3560 by ignoring profit or as high as 8980 by focusing entirely on profit. These establish the extremes. Now we search for points in between (step 2).

Fortunately, SolverTable is just what we need. According to step 2, we need to constrain pollution to various degrees and see how large profit can be. This is indicated in Figure 9.10, where the objective is to maximize profit with an upper limit on pollution.

	A	B	C	D	E	F	G	H	I	J	K	L
1	Chemcon profit versus pollution model											
2												
3	Input data											
4	Product	1	2	3	4	5	6	7	8			
5	Labor hours/unit	5	5	1	4	3.5	4	2	3.5			
6	Raw material/unit	3	4.5	5	5	4.5	2	3.5	3			
7												
8	Pollution/unit	25	29	35	26	17	25	28	6			
9	Profit/unit	$53	$69	$73	$69	$51	$49	$71	$40			
10												
11	Production plan											
12	Product	1	2	3	4	5	6	7	8			
13	Min production	0	30	0	10	20	50	30	0			
14		<=	<=	<=	<=	<=	<=	<=	<=			
15	Units produced	0.0	30.0	0.0	10.0	21.1	50.0	48.6	150.0			
16		<=	<=	<=	<=	<=	<=	<=	<=			
17	Max production	190	110	140	140	190	190	110	150			
18												
19	Constraints on resources											
20		Used		Available								
21	Labor hours	1086.0	<=	1300								
22	Raw material	1000.0	<=	1000								
23												
24	Constraint on pollution											
25		Actual		Upper bound								
26		5000.0	<=	5000								
27												
28	Objective to maximize											
29	Profit	$15,738										

Range names used:
UnitPollutions - B8:I8
UnitProfits - B9:I9
MinProduction - B13:I13
UnitsProduced - B15:I15
MaxProduction - B17:I17
Used - B21:B22
Available - D21:D22
Pollution - B26
UpBound - D26
Profit - B29

FIGURE 9.10 Chemcon Model

(We would get the same effect by minimizing pollution and putting a *lower* limit on profit.) The only upper limits on pollution we need to consider are those between the extremes, 3560 and 8980. Therefore, we use SolverTable with the setup shown in Figure 9.11. Note that we have used the option to enter non-equally-spaced inputs: 3560, 4000, 4500, and so on, ending with 8980. Alternatively, equally-spaced inputs could be used. All we require is a representative set of values between the extremes. The results appear in Figure 9.12.

FIGURE 9.11
SolverTable Dialog Box

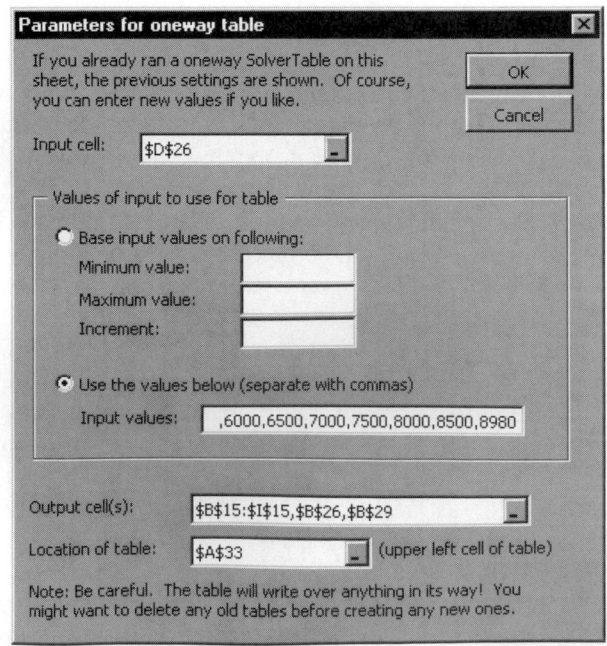

Parameters for oneway table

If you already ran a oneway SolverTable on this sheet, the previous settings are shown. Of course, you can enter new values if you like.

Input cell: $D$26

Values of input to use for table

○ Base input values on following:
Minimum value:
Maximum value:
Increment:

● Use the values below (separate with commas)
Input values: ,6000,6500,7000,7500,8000,8500,8980

Output cell(s): $B$15:$I$15,$B$26,$B$29
Location of table: $A$33   (upper left cell of table)

Note: Be careful. The table will write over anything in its way! You might want to delete any old tables before creating any new ones.

OK
Cancel

	A	B	C	D	E	F	G	H	I	J	K
31	**Sensitivity of units produced, pollution, and profit to upper bound on pollution**										
32	Upper bound	Product1	Product2	Product3	Product4	Product5	Product6	Product7	Product8	Pollution	Profit
33		$B$15	$C$15	$D$15	$E$15	$F$15	$G$15	$H$15	$I$15	$B$26	$B$29
34	3560	0.0	30.0	0.0	10.0	20.0	50.0	30.0	0.0	3560.0	$8,360
35	4000	0.0	30.0	0.0	10.0	20.0	50.0	30.0	73.3	4000.0	$11,293
36	4500	0.0	30.0	0.0	10.0	22.4	50.0	30.0	150.0	4500.0	$14,480
37	5000	0.0	30.0	0.0	10.0	21.1	50.0	48.6	150.0	5000.0	$15,738
38	5500	0.0	30.0	0.0	10.0	20.0	50.0	72.9	123.3	5500.0	$16,336
39	6000	0.0	30.0	0.0	10.0	20.0	50.0	96.7	95.6	6000.0	$16,916
40	6500	0.0	30.0	0.0	10.0	20.0	60.5	110.0	73.0	6500.0	$17,474
41	7000	0.0	30.0	0.0	10.0	20.0	84.3	110.0	57.1	7000.0	$18,006
42	7500	0.0	30.0	0.0	10.0	20.0	108.1	110.0	41.3	7500.0	$18,537
43	8000	0.0	30.0	0.0	10.0	20.0	131.9	110.0	25.4	8000.0	$19,069
44	8500	0.0	30.0	0.0	10.0	20.0	155.7	110.0	9.5	8500.0	$19,601
45	8980	0.0	30.0	0.0	10.0	20.0	190.0	98.6	0.0	8980.0	$20,089

FIGURE 9.12 SolverTable Results

These results show that as we allow more pollution, profit increases. Also, the product mix shifts considerably. Product 8, a low polluter with a low profit margin, eventually leaves the mix when pollution is allowed to increase, which makes sense. It is less clear why the level of product 6 increases so dramatically. It is only a moderate polluter and has a moderate profit margin, so the key is evidently that it requires low levels of labor and raw materials. The trade-off curve itself is created as an X-Y chart (with the points connected) directly from columns J and K of the table. It appears in Figure 9.13. This chart indicates that profit indeed increases as Chemcon allows more pollution, but at a decreasing rate. For example, when pollution is allowed to increase from 4000 to 4500, Chemcon can make an extra $3187 in profit. However, when pollution is allowed to increase from 8000 to 8500, the extra profit is only $532. All points below the curve are dominated—for a given level of pollution, the company can achieve a larger profit—and all points above the curve are unattainable.

FIGURE 9.13
Trade-off Curve for
Profit Versus
Pollution

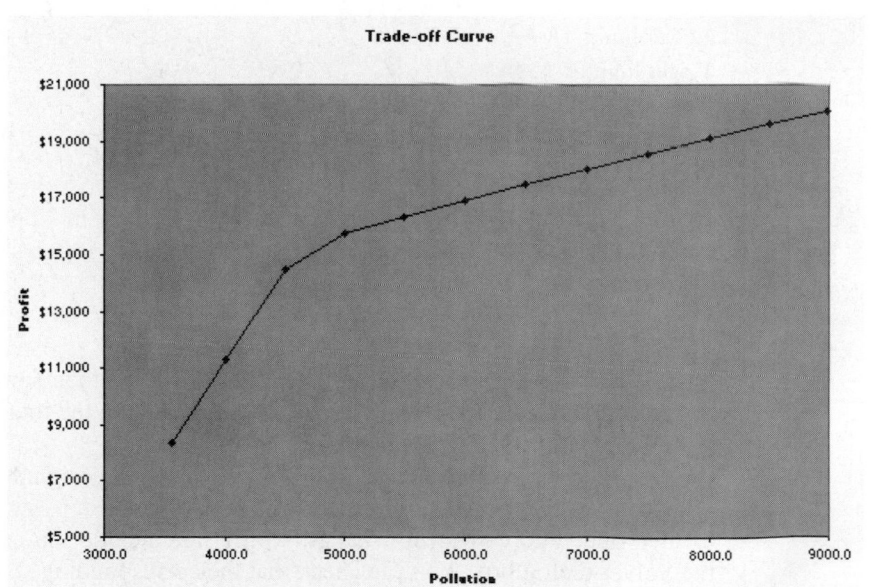

Trade-off curves are not confined to linear models. The following example illustrates a trade-off curve in a situation where the objective is a nonlinear function of the changing cells.

EXAMPLE　9.3

TRADE-OFFS BETWEEN EXPOSURES TO MEN AND WOMEN AT LEON BURNIT

This example is a modification of the Burnit advertising example in Example 9.1. Now we assume that Burnit's client is concerned only with *two* groups of people, men and women. Also, the number of exposures to these groups is now a nonlinear square root function of the number of ads placed of any particular type. This implies a marginal decreasing effect of ads—each extra ad of a particular type reaches fewer extra people than the previous ad of this type. The data for this problem appear in Tables 9.21 and 9.22. The first of these specifies the proportionality constants for the square root exposure functions. For example, if 5 ads are placed in sports shows, this will achieve $15\sqrt{5} = 33.541$ million exposures to men, but only $5\sqrt{5} = 11.180$ million exposures to women. Evidently, what works well for men does not work so well for women, and vice versa. Given a budget of $1.5 million, find the trade-off curve for exposures to men versus exposures to women.

TABLE 9.21 **Proportionality Constants for Square Root Exposure Functions**

	Sports Show	Game Show	News Show	Sitcom	Drama	Soap Opera
Men	15	3	7	7	8	1
Women	5	5	6	10	9	4

TABLE 9.22 **Data on Ads for Burnit Example**

	Sports Show	Game Show	News Show	Sitcom	Drama	Soap Opera
Cost/ad ($1000s)	120	40	50	40	60	20
Lower limit	2	0	2	0	2	0
Upper limit	10	5	10	5	10	5

Solution

Again, the model itself is straightforward, as shown in Figure 9.14. (See the file BURNIT2.XLS.) We calculate the exposures achieved in rows 22 and 23 by entering the formula

=B8*SQRT(B$17)

in cell B22 and copying it to the range B22:G23. We then sum these in the TotExp-ToWomen and TotExpToMen ranges, and we calculate the total cost in the usual way with the SUMPRODUCT function.

For the three-step trade-off curve procedure, we designate exposures to men as objective 1 and exposures to women as objective 2. For step 1, we maximize exposures to men and ignore women. That is, we do *not* include the constraint in row 30 in the Solver dialog box. You can check that the corresponding solution achieves 89.515 million exposures to men and 79.392 million exposures to women. Reversing the roles of men and women (step 3), you can check that if we maximize exposures to women and ignore men, we achieve 89.220 million exposures to women and only 84.899 million exposures to men.

FIGURE 9.14 Advertising Model

Spreadsheet contents:

	A	B	C	D	E	F	G
1	Burnit nonlinear advertising model						
3	Assumption: The number of exposures (in millions) to each group is proportional to the square root						
4	of the number of ads of a particular type shown.						
6	Proportionality constants for exposure functions						
7		Sports ad	Game show ad	News show ad	Sitcom ad	Drama ad	Soap opera ads
8	Exposures to men	15	3	7	7	8	1
9	Exposures to women	5	5	6	10	9	4
11	Cost/ad ($1,000s)	120	40	50	40	60	20
13	Advertising plan						
14		Sports ad	Game show ad	News show ad	Sitcom ad	Drama ad	Soap opera ad
15	Minimum ads required	2	0	2	0	2	0
16		<=	<=	<=	<=	<=	<=
17	Number purchased	3.540	2.748	6.225	5.000	6.579	2.966
18		<=	<=	<=	<=	<=	<=
19	Maximum ads allowed	10	5	10	5	10	5
21	Exposures obtained	Sports ad	Game show ad	News show ad	Sitcom ad	Drama ad	Soap opera ad
22	Men	28.221	4.973	17.465	15.652	20.520	1.722
23	Women	9.407	8.289	14.970	22.361	23.085	6.889
25	Budget constraint	Total cost		Budget			
26		1500.000	<=	1500			
28	Constraint on minimal exposures to women						
29		Actual		Lower bound			
30		85.000	>=	85			
32	Objective to maximize						
33	Exposures to men	88.554					

Range names used:
UnitCosts - B11:G11
MinAds - B15:G15
Ads - B17:G17
MaxAds - B19:G19
ExpToMen - B22:G22
ExpToWomen - B23:G23
TotCost - B26
Budget - D26
TotExpToWomen - B30
LowBound - D30
TotExpToMen - B33

All other points on the trade-off curve are between these two extremes, and they can again be found easily with SolverTable. We now set up the Solver to maximize exposures to men, and we include the lower limit constraint on exposures to women in the Solver dialog box. (Do you see why it is a *lower* limit constraint in this example, whereas it was an upper limit constraint in the previous example? There we wanted to make pollution low. Here we want to make exposures to women high.) The lower limit cell (D30) becomes the single input cell for SolverTable, and we allow it to vary from (slightly greater than) 79.392 to (slightly less than) 89.220 with suitable values in between. The results appear in table form in Figure 9.15 and in graphical form in Figure 9.16 (page 470).

As we go down the table (or to the right in the chart), we require more exposures to women, which has an increasingly negative effect on exposures to men. Not surprisingly, the corresponding solutions place more ads in the shows watched predominantly

	A	B	C	D	E	F	G	H	I
35	Sensitivity of ads purchased, exposures to women, and exposures to men to lower bound on exposures to women								
36		Sports ad	Game show ad	News show ad	Sitcom ad	Drama ad	Soap opera ad	To women	To men
37		$B$17	$C$17	$D$17	$E$17	$F$17	$G$17	$B$30	$B$33
38	79.393	4.833	1.744	6.072	5.000	5.508	0.776	79.393	89.515
39	80	4.715	1.835	6.100	5.000	5.620	0.928	80.000	89.506
40	81	4.503	1.994	6.143	5.000	5.807	1.215	81.000	89.449
41	82	4.280	2.163	6.178	5.000	5.997	1.555	82.000	89.336
42	83	4.048	2.347	6.204	5.000	6.186	1.954	83.000	89.156
43	84	3.801	2.538	6.220	5.000	6.383	2.421	84.000	88.900
44	85	3.540	2.745	6.228	5.000	6.578	2.969	85.000	88.554
45	86	3.262	2.976	6.217	5.000	6.777	3.604	86.000	88.096
46	87	2.964	3.225	6.189	5.000	6.979	4.357	87.000	87.500
47	88	2.600	3.580	6.173	5.000	7.269	5.000	88.000	86.713
48	89	2.057	4.276	6.207	5.000	7.863	5.000	89.000	85.478
49	89.219	2.000	5.000	5.387	5.000	8.177	5.000	89.219	84.934

FIGURE 9.15 SolverTable Results for Advertising Model

FIGURE 9.16
Trade-off Curve for
Advertising Example

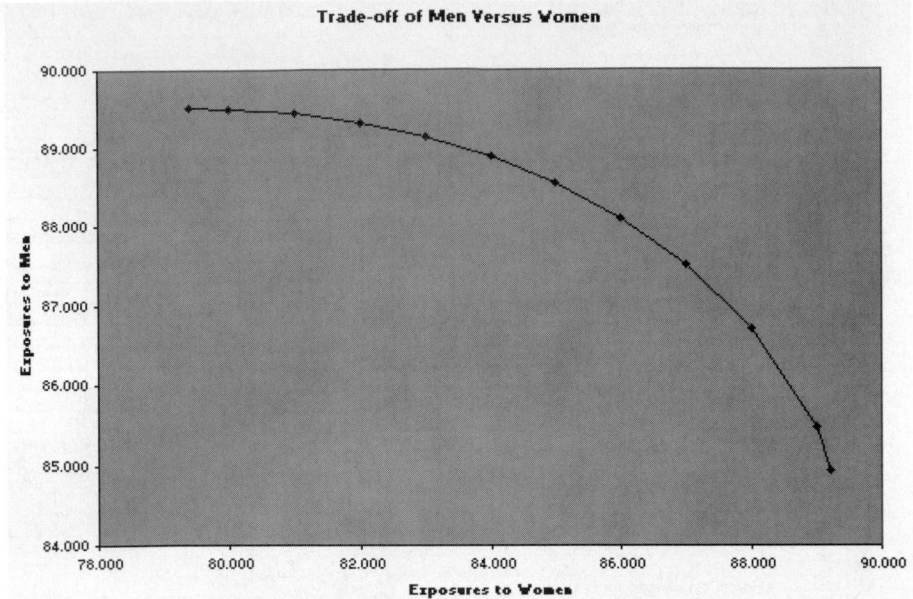

by women (game shows, dramas, and soaps) and fewer ads in sports and news shows. The upper limit of 5 placed on sitcom ads prevents us from seeing how the number of sitcom ads would change if it were not constrained. It would probably change fairly dramatically, given that these ads are relatively cheap and they tend to reach more women than men.

Technical note We ran into two problems that you might experience. First, depending on the starting solution, it is possible that one of the changing cells can become slightly negative (due to numerical roundoff), in which case the SQRT function is undefined and you get an error message. To remedy this, add a constraint like Ads>=0.0001. Second, when we ran SolverTable, it indicated "no feasible solution" to the problem in row 49 of Figure 9.15, although we know there is a feasible solution. This can sometimes occur with nonlinear models, depending on the starting solution used. SolverTable uses the solution from the previous problem as the starting solution for the next problem. This seems reasonable, but it *can* produce this error. If it does, try running the Solver on this particular problem again with your own initial solution (such as all 0's). This is what we did to get the values in row 49. ■

MODELING ISSUES

1. A trade-off curve is useful because it gives the ultimate decision maker many solutions to choose from, none of which is dominated by any others. However, it does *not* specify a "best" solution. The decision maker still has to make the difficult decision of which solution from the trade-off curve to implement. This can be done subjectively or with the help of a **multiattribute utility function**. However, it is difficult to estimate these types of functions, so their use in real-world applications has been limited.

2. We can generalize to a situation where there are more than two objectives by constructing trade-off curves between each *pair* of objectives. ■

Skill-Building Problems

19. Widgetco produces two types of widgets. Each widget is made of steel and aluminum and is assembled with skilled labor. The resources used and the per-unit profit contribution (ignoring cost of overtime labor purchased) for each type of widget are given in Table 9.23. At present, 200 pounds of steel, 300 pounds of aluminum, and 300 hours of labor are available. Extra overtime labor can be purchased for $10 per hour. Construct a trade-off curve between the objectives of maximizing profit and minimizing overtime labor.

TABLE 9.23	Data for Widgetco Problem	
	Type 1	**Type 2**
Steel	6 lb	12 lb
Aluminum	8 lb	20 lb
Skilled labor	11 hr	24 hr
Profit contribution	$500	$1100

20. Plantco produces three products. Three workers work for Plantco, and the company must determine which product(s) each worker should produce. The number of units each worker would produce if he or she spent the whole day producing each type of product is given in Table 9.24. The company is also interested in maximizing the happiness of its workers. The amount of happiness "earned" by a worker who spends the entire day producing a given product is given in Table 9.25. Construct a trade-off curve between the objectives of maximizing total units produced daily and total worker happiness.

TABLE 9.24	Worker Productivity for Plantco Problem		
	Product 1	**Product 2**	**Product 3**
Worker 1	20	12	10
Worker 2	12	15	9
Worker 3	6	5	10

TABLE 9.25	Happiness Values for Plantco Problem		
	Product 1	**Product 2**	**Product 3**
Worker 1	6	8	10
Worker 2	6	5	9
Worker 3	9	10	8

21. If a company spends a on advertising (measured in thousands of dollars) and charges a price of p dollars per unit, then it can sell $1000 - 100p + 20a^{1/2}$ units of the product. The cost per unit of producing the product is $6. Construct a trade-off curve between the objectives of maximizing profit and maximizing the number of units sold.

22. GMCO produces three types of cars: compact, medium, and large. The variable cost per car and production capacity (per year) for each type of car are given in Table 9.26. The annual demand for each type of car depends on the prices of the three types of cars, given in Table 9.27. In this latter table, P_C is the price charged for a compact car (in thousands of dollars). The variables P_M and P_L are defined similarly for medium and large cars. Suppose that each compact gets 30 mpg, each medium car gets 25 mpg, and each large car gets 18 mpg. GMCO wants to keep the planet pollution free, so in addition to maximizing profit, it wants to maximize the average miles per gallon attained by the cars it sells. Construct a trade-off curve between these two objectives.

TABLE 9.26	Variable Costs and Production Capacities for GMCO Problem	
	Cost	**Production Capacity**
Compact	$10,000	2000
Medium	$14,000	1500
Large	$18,000	1000

TABLE 9.27	Demand Functions for GMCO Problem
	Demand
Compact	$2500 - 100P_C + 3P_M$
Medium	$1800 - 30P_M + 2P_C + P_L$
Large	$1300 - 20P_L + P_M$

23. In Section 5.5 of Chapter 5, we discussed crashing the length of the Franklin Company project. For this example construct a trade-off curve between the cost of crashing the project and duration of the project.

24. Referring to the Perlman & Brothers example from Chapter 7 (see Example 7.9), construct a trade-off curve between the chosen portfolio's expected return and variance (with variance on the horizontal axis). In finance terminology this trade-off curve is called the **efficient frontier**.

9.4 THE ANALYTIC HIERARCHY PROCESS

When multiple objectives are important to a decision maker, it is often difficult to choose between alternatives. For example, if you are choosing a job, one job might offer the highest starting salary but rate poorly on other objectives such as quality of life in the city where the job is located and the nearness of the job to your family. Another job offer might rate highly on these latter objectives but have a relatively low starting salary. In this case it might be difficult for you to choose between job offers. Thomas Saaty's **Analytic Hierarchy Process (AHP)** provides a powerful tool that can be used to make decisions in situations where multiple objectives are present. We present an example to illustrate such a case.[1] (*Note*: We will use matrix notation and matrix multiplication in this section. You may need to review the discussion of matrices in Section 7.9.)

EXAMPLE 9.4

USING AHP TO SELECT A JOB

Jane is about to graduate from college and is trying to determine which job to accept. She plans to choose among the offers by determining how well each job offer meets the following four objectives:

- Objective 1: High starting salary
- Objective 2: Quality of life in city where job is located
- Objective 3: Interest of work
- Objective 4: Nearness of job to family

Solution

To illustrate how AHP works, suppose that Jane is facing three job offers and must determine which offer to accept. In this example there are four objectives, as listed above. For each objective, AHP generates a weight (by a method to be described shortly). By convention, the weights are always chosen so that they sum to 1. Suppose that Jane's weights are $w_1 = 0.5115$, $w_2 = 0.0986$, $w_3 = 0.2433$, and $w_4 = 0.1466$. These weights indicate that a high starting salary is the most important objective, followed by interest of work, nearness to family, and quality of life.

Next suppose that Jane determines (again by a method that will be described shortly) how well each job "scores" on each objective. For example, suppose these scores are those listed in Table 9.28. We see from this table that job 1 best meets the

TABLE 9.28 Job Scores on Objectives in AHP Example

	Salary	Quality of Life	Interest of Work	Nearness to Family
Job 1	0.5714	0.1593	0.0882	0.0824
Job 2	0.2857	0.2519	0.6687	0.3151
Job 3	0.1429	0.5889	0.2431	0.6025

[1]The leading software package for implementing AHP is Expert Choice, developed by Expert™ Choice Inc.

objective of a high starting salary, but scores worst on all other objectives. Note that the scores of the jobs on each objective are "normalized," which means that for each objective, the sum of the scores of the jobs on that objective is 1.

Given the weights for the objectives and the scores shown in Table 9.28, Jane can now determine which job offer to accept. Specifically, for each job we calculate an overall score that is a weighted sum of the scores for that job, using the w's as weights. For example, the overall score for job 1 weights the scores in the first row of Table 9.28:

$$\begin{aligned} \text{Job 1 score} &= 0.5115(0.5714) + 0.0986(0.1593) \\ &\quad + 0.2433(0.0882) + 0.1466(0.0824) \\ &= 0.3415 \end{aligned}$$

Similarly, the overall scores for jobs 2 and 3 are obtained by weighting the scores in the second and third rows of Table 9.28:

$$\begin{aligned} \text{Job 2 score} &= 0.5115(0.2857) + 0.0986(0.2519) \\ &\quad + 0.2433(0.6687) + 0.1466(0.3151) \\ &= 0.3799 \\ \text{Job 3 score} &= 0.5115(0.1429) + 0.0986(0.5889) \\ &\quad + 0.2433(0.2431) + 0.1466(0.6025) \\ &= 0.2786 \end{aligned}$$

Because the overall score for job 2 is the largest, AHP suggests that Jane should accept this job.

Pairwise Comparison Matrices To obtain the weights for the various objectives, we begin by forming a matrix A, known as the pairwise comparison matrix. The entry in row i and column j of A, labeled a_{ij}, indicates how much more (or less) important objective i is than objective j. "Importance" is measured on an integer-valued scale from 1 to 9, with each number having the interpretation shown in Table 9.29. The phrases in this table, such as "strongly more important than," are suggestive only. They simply indicate discrete points on a continuous scale that can be used to compare the relative importance of any two objectives.

TABLE 9.29	Interpretation of Values in Pairwise Comparison Matrix
Value of a_{ij}	**Interpretation**
1	Objectives i and j are equally important.
3	Objective i is slightly more important than j.
5	Objective i is strongly more important than j.
7	Objective i is very strongly more important than j.
9	Objective i is absolutely more important than j.

For example, if $a_{13} = 3$, then objective 1 is slightly more important than objective 3. If $a_{ij} = 4$, a value not in the table, then objective i is somewhere between slightly and strongly more important than objective j. If objective i is *less* important than objective j, we use the reciprocal of the appropriate index. For example, if objective i is slightly less important than objective j, then $a_{ij} = 1/3$. Finally, for all objectives i, we use the convention that $a_{ii} = 1$.

For consistency, it is necessary to set $a_{ji} = 1/a_{ij}$. For example, if $a_{13} = 3$, then it is necessary to have $a_{31} = 1/3$. This simply states that if objective 1 is slightly more important than objective 3, then objective 3 is slightly less important than job 1. It is usually easier to determine all a_{ij}'s that are greater than 1 and then use the relationship $a_{ji} = 1/a_{ij}$ to determine the remaining entries in the pairwise comparison matrix.

To illustrate, suppose that Jane has identified the following pairwise comparison matrix for her four objectives:

$$A = \begin{bmatrix} 1 & 5 & 2 & 4 \\ 1/5 & 1 & 1/2 & 1/2 \\ 1/2 & 2 & 1 & 2 \\ 1/4 & 2 & 1/2 & 1 \end{bmatrix}$$

The rows and columns of A each correspond to Jane's four objectives: salary, quality of life, interest of work, and nearness to family. Considering the first row, for example, she believes that salary is more important, in various degrees, than quality of life, interest of work, and nearness to family.

The entries in this matrix have built-in pairwise consistency because we require $a_{ij} = 1/a_{ji}$ for each i and j. However, they might not be consistent when three (or more) alternatives are considered simultaneously. For example, Jane claims that salary is strongly more important than quality of life ($a_{12} = 5$) and that salary is very slightly more important than interesting work ($a_{13} = 2$). But she also says that interesting work is very slightly more important than quality of life ($a_{32} = 2$). The question is whether these ratings are all consistent with one another. They are not, at least not exactly. It can be shown that some of Jane's pairwise comparisons are slightly inconsistent. When a person is asked to make this many pairwise comparisons, slight inconsistencies are common and fortunately do not cause serious difficulties. An index that can be used to measure the consistency of Jane's preferences will be discussed later in this section.

Determining the Weights Although the ideas behind AHP are fairly intuitive, the mathematical reasoning required to derive the weights for the objectives is quite advanced. Therefore, we simply describe how it is done.

Starting with the pairwise comparison matrix A, we find the weights for Jane's four objectives using the following two steps.

1. For each of the columns of A, divide each entry in the column by the sum of the entries in the column. This yields a new matrix (call it A_{norm}, for "normalized") in which the sum of the entries in each column is 1.

    For Jane's pairwise comparison matrix, this step yields

$$A_{norm} = \begin{bmatrix} 0.5128 & 0.5000 & 0.5000 & 0.5333 \\ 0.1026 & 0.1000 & 0.1250 & 0.0667 \\ 0.2564 & 0.2000 & 0.2500 & 0.2667 \\ 0.1282 & 0.2000 & 0.1250 & 0.1333 \end{bmatrix}$$

2. Estimate w_i, the weight for objective i, as the average of the entries in row i of A_{norm}.

    For Jane's matrix this yields

$$w_1 = \frac{0.5128 + 0.5000 + 0.5000 + 0.5333}{4} = 0.5115$$

$$w_2 = \frac{0.1026 + 0.1000 + 0.1250 + 0.0667}{4} = 0.0986$$

$$w_3 = \frac{0.2564 + 0.2000 + 0.2500 + 0.2667}{4} = 0.2433$$

$$w_4 = \frac{0.1282 + 0.2000 + 0.1250 + 0.1333}{4} = 0.1466$$

Intuitively, why does w_1 approximate the weight for objective 1 (salary)? Here is the reasoning. The proportion of weight that salary is given in pairwise comparisons of each objective to salary is 0.5128. Similarly, 0.50 represents the proportion of total weight that salary is given in pairwise comparisons of each objective to quality of life. Therefore, we see that each of the four numbers averaged to obtain w_1 represents a measure of the total weight attached to salary. Averaging these numbers should give a good estimate of the proportion of the total weight given to salary.

Determining the Score of Each Decision Alternative on Each Objective Now that we have determined the weights, we need to determine how well each job scores on each objective. To determine these scores, we use the same scale described in Table 9.29 to construct a pairwise comparison matrix for each objective. Consider the salary objective, for example. Suppose that Jane assesses the following pairwise comparison matrix. We denote this matrix as A_1 because it reflects her comparisons of the three jobs with respect to the first objective, salary.

$$A_1 = \begin{bmatrix} 1 & 2 & 4 \\ 1/2 & 1 & 2 \\ 1/4 & 1/2 & 1 \end{bmatrix}$$

The rows and columns of this matrix correspond to the three jobs. For example, the first row means that Jane believes job 1 is superior to job 2 (and even more superior to job 3) in terms of salary. To find the relative scores of the three jobs on salary, we now apply the *same* two-step procedure as above to the salary pairwise comparison matrix A_1. That is, we first divide each column entry by the column sum to obtain

$$A_{1,\text{norm}} = \begin{bmatrix} 0.5714 & 0.5714 & 0.5714 \\ 0.2857 & 0.2857 & 0.2857 \\ 0.1429 & 0.1429 & 0.1429 \end{bmatrix}$$

Then we average the numbers in each row to obtain the vector of scores for the three jobs on salary, denoted by S_1:

$$S_1 = \begin{bmatrix} 0.5714 \\ 0.2857 \\ 0.1429 \end{bmatrix}$$

That is, the scores for jobs 1, 2, and 3 on salary are 0.5714, 0.2857, and 0.1429. In terms of salary, job 1 is clearly the favorite.

Next, we repeat these calculations for Jane's other objectives. Each of these objectives requires a pairwise comparison matrix, which we will denote as A_2, A_3, and A_4. Suppose that Jane's pairwise comparison matrix for quality of life is

$$A_2 = \begin{bmatrix} 1 & 1/2 & 1/3 \\ 2 & 1 & 1/3 \\ 3 & 3 & 1 \end{bmatrix}$$

Then the corresponding normalized matrix is

$$A_{2,\text{norm}} = \begin{bmatrix} 0.1667 & 0.1111 & 0.2000 \\ 0.3333 & 0.2222 & 0.2000 \\ 0.5000 & 0.6667 & 0.6000 \end{bmatrix}$$

and by averaging, we obtain

$$S_2 = \begin{bmatrix} 0.1593 \\ 0.2519 \\ 0.5889 \end{bmatrix}$$

Here, job 3 is the clear favorite. However, this might not have much impact because Jane puts relatively little weight on quality of life.

For interest of work, suppose the pairwise comparison matrix is

$$A_3 = \begin{bmatrix} 1 & 1/7 & 1/3 \\ 7 & 1 & 3 \\ 3 & 1/3 & 1 \end{bmatrix}$$

Then the same types of calculations show that the scores for jobs 1, 2, and 3 on interest of work are

$$S_3 = \begin{bmatrix} 0.0882 \\ 0.6687 \\ 0.2431 \end{bmatrix}$$

Finally, suppose the pairwise comparison matrix for nearness to family is

$$A_4 = \begin{bmatrix} 1 & 1/4 & 1/7 \\ 4 & 1 & 1/2 \\ 7 & 2 & 1 \end{bmatrix}$$

In this case the scores for jobs 1, 2, and 3 on nearness to family are

$$S_4 = \begin{bmatrix} 0.0824 \\ 0.3151 \\ 0.6025 \end{bmatrix}$$

Determining the Best Alternative Let's summarize what we have determined so far. Jane first assesses a pairwise comparison matrix A that measures the relative importance of each of her objectives to one another. From this matrix we obtain a vector of weights that summarizes the relative importance of the objectives. Next, Jane assesses a pairwise comparison matrix A_i for each objective i. This matrix measures how well each job compares to other jobs with regard to this objective. For each matrix A_i we obtain a vector of scores S_i that summarizes how the jobs compare in terms of achieving objective i.

The final step is to combine the scores in the S_i vectors with the weights in the w vector. Actually, we have already done this. Note that the columns of Table 9.28 are the S_i vectors we just obtained. If we form a matrix S of these score vectors and multiply this matrix by w, we obtain a vector of overall scores for each job, as shown below:

$$Sw = \begin{bmatrix} 0.5714 & 0.1593 & 0.0882 & 0.0824 \\ 0.2857 & 0.2519 & 0.6687 & 0.3151 \\ 0.1429 & 0.5889 & 0.2431 & 0.6025 \end{bmatrix} \times \begin{bmatrix} 0.5115 \\ 0.0986 \\ 0.2433 \\ 0.1466 \end{bmatrix} = \begin{bmatrix} 0.3415 \\ 0.3799 \\ 0.2786 \end{bmatrix}$$

These are the same overall scores that we obtained earlier. As before, the largest of these overall scores is for job 2, so AHP suggests that Jane should accept this job. Job 1 follows closely behind, with job 3 somewhat farther behind.

Checking for Consistency As mentioned earlier, any pairwise comparison matrix can suffer from inconsistencies. We now describe a procedure to check for inconsistencies.

We illustrate this on the A matrix and its associated vector of weights w. The same procedure can be used on any of the A_i matrices and their associated "weights" vector S_i.

1. Compute Aw. For the example, we obtain

$$Aw = \begin{bmatrix} 1 & 5 & 2 & 4 \\ 1/5 & 1 & 1/2 & 1/2 \\ 1/2 & 2 & 1 & 2 \\ 1/4 & 2 & 1/2 & 1 \end{bmatrix} \times \begin{bmatrix} 0.5115 \\ 0.0986 \\ 0.2433 \\ 0.1466 \end{bmatrix} = \begin{bmatrix} 2.0774 \\ 0.3958 \\ 0.9894 \\ 0.5933 \end{bmatrix}$$

2. Find the ratio of each element of Aw to the corresponding weight in w and average these ratios. For the example, this calculation is

$$\frac{\frac{2.0774}{0.5115} + \frac{0.3958}{0.0986} + \frac{0.9894}{0.2433} + \frac{0.5933}{0.1466}}{4} = 4.0477$$

3. Compute the consistency index (labeled CI) as

$$CI = \frac{(\text{Step 2 result}) - n}{n - 1}$$

where n is the number of objectives. For the example this is $CI = \frac{4.0477 - 4}{4 - 1} = 0.0159$.

4. Compare CI to the random index (labeled RI) in Table 9.30 for the appropriate value of n.

TABLE 9.30	Random Indices for Consistency Check for AHP Example							
n	2	3	4	5	6	7	8	9	10
RI	0	0.58	0.90	1.12	1.24	1.32	1.41	1.45	1.51

To be a perfectly consistent decision maker, each ratio in step 2 should equal n. This implies that a perfectly consistent decision maker has $CI = 0$. The values of RI in Table 9.30 give the average value of CI if the entries in A were chosen at random (subject to the constraints that a_{ii}'s must equal 1, and $a_{ij} = 1/a_{ji}$). If the ratio of CI to RI is sufficiently small, then the decision maker's comparisons are probably consistent enough to be useful. Saaty suggests that if $CI/RI < 0.10$, then the degree of consistency is satisfactory, whereas if $CI/RI > 0.10$, serious inconsistencies exist and AHP may not yield meaningful results. In Jane's example, $CI/RI = 0.0159/0.90 = 0.0177$, which is much less than 0.10. Therefore, Jane's pairwise comparison matrix A does not exhibit any serious inconsistencies. (You can check that the same is true of her other pairwise comparison matrices A_1 through A_4.)

DEVELOPING THE SPREADSHEET MODEL

We now show how to implement AHP on a spreadsheet. (See Figure 9.17 on page 478 and the file JOBSAHP.XLS.)

❶ **Inputs.** Enter the pairwise comparison matrices in the shaded ranges. (Note that you can enter fractions such as 1/7 in cell C24, and have them appear as fractions, by formatting the cells with the Fraction option.)

❷ **Normalized matrix.** Calculate the normalized matrix for the first pairwise comparison matrix in the range G5:J8. This can be done quickly as follows. Starting with

	A	B	C	D	E	F	G	H	I	J	K	L	M
1	Job selection using analytical hierarchy process												
2													
3	Pairwise comparisons among objectives						Normalized matrix					Weights	
4		Salary	Life quality	Work interest	Near family								
5	Salary	1	5	2	4		0.5128	0.5000	0.5000	0.5333		0.5115	
6	Life quality	1/5	1	1/2	1/2		0.1026	0.1000	0.1250	0.0667		0.0986	
7	Work interest	1/2	2	1	2		0.2564	0.2000	0.2500	0.2667		0.2433	
8	Near family	1/4	2	1/2	1		0.1282	0.2000	0.1250	0.1333		0.1466	
9													
10	Pairwise comparisons among jobs on salary						Normalized matrix					Scores	
11		Job 1	Job 2	Job 3									
12	Job 1	1	2	4			0.5714	0.5714	0.5714			0.5714	
13	Job 2	1/2	1	2			0.2857	0.2857	0.2857			0.2857	
14	Job 3	1/4	1/2	1			0.1429	0.1429	0.1429			0.1429	
15													
16	Pairwise comparisons among jobs on quality of life						Normalized matrix					Scores	
17		Job 1	Job 2	Job 3									
18	Job 1	1	1/2	1/3			0.1667	0.1111	0.2000			0.1593	
19	Job 2	2	1	1/3			0.3333	0.2222	0.2000			0.2519	
20	Job 3	3	3	1			0.5000	0.6667	0.6000			0.5889	
21													
22	Pairwise comparisons among jobs on interest of work						Normalized matrix					Scores	
23		Job 1	Job 2	Job 3									
24	Job 1	1	1/7	1/3			0.0909	0.0968	0.0769			0.0882	
25	Job 2	7	1	3			0.6364	0.6774	0.6923			0.6687	
26	Job 3	3	1/3	1			0.2727	0.2258	0.2308			0.2431	
27													
28	Pairwise comparisons among jobs on nearness to family						Normalized matrix					Scores	
29		Job 1	Job 2	Job 3									
30	Job 1	1	1/4	1/7			0.0833	0.0769	0.0870			0.0824	
31	Job 2	4	1	1/2			0.3333	0.3077	0.3043			0.3151	
32	Job 3	7	2	1			0.5833	0.6154	0.6087			0.6025	
33													
34	Determining best job												
35	Matrix of scores						Weighted scores					Range names used:	
36		Salary	Life quality	Work interest	Near family							Scores - B37:E39	
37	Job 1	0.5714	0.159	0.088	0.082		0.3415					Weights - L5:L8	
38	Job 2	0.2857	0.252	0.669	0.315		0.3799 ←	job 2 has the highest score					
39	Job 3	0.1429	0.589	0.243	0.602		0.2786						

FIGURE 9.17 AHP Job Selection Model

the cursor in cell G5, drag the cursor so that the range G5:J8 is highlighted. Then type the formula

=B5/SUM(B$5:B$8)

and press Control-Enter (both keys at once). You have just learned a quicker way than copying and pasting!

❸ **Weights of objectives.** In the range L5:L8, calculate the weights for each objective. Again, do this the quick way. Starting with the cursor in cell L5, highlight the range L5:L8. Then type the formula

=AVERAGE(G5:J5)

and press Control-Enter.

❹ **Scores for jobs on objectives.** Repeat the same calculations in steps 2 and 3 for the other pairwise comparison matrices to obtain the normalized matrices in columns G through I and scores vectors in column L.

❺ **Overall job scores.** In the Scores range form a matrix of job scores on the various objectives. To get the score vector in the range L12:L14 into the Scores range, for example, highlight the Scores range, type the formula

=L12

and press Control-Enter. Do likewise for the other three scores vectors in column L.

Then to obtain the overall job scores (from the formula Sw), highlight the range G37:G39, type the formula

=MMULT(Scores,Weights)

and press Control-Shift-Enter. (Remember that Control-Shift-Enter is used to enter a matrix function. In contrast, Control-Enter is equivalent to copying a formula to a highlighted range.)

Again we see that job 2 is the most preferred of the three jobs.

Calculating the Consistency Index We now show how to compute the consistency index CI for each of the pairwise comparison matrices. (See Figure 9.18, which is also part of the file JOBSAHP.XLS. Note that we have hidden columns G through K to save space. These contain the normalized matrices from step 2 above.) The following steps are relevant for the first pairwise comparison matrix. The others are done in analogous fashion.

❶ Product of comparison matrix and vector of weights (or scores). Calculate the product of the first pairwise comparison matrix and the weights vector in the range N5:N8 by highlighting this range, typing

=MMULT(B5:E8,L5:L8)

and pressing Control-Shift-Enter.

	A	B	C	D	E	F	L	M	N	O
1	Job selection using analytical hierarchy process								Checking consistency	
2										
3	Pairwise comparisons among objectives						Weights		Product	Ratios
4		Salary	Life quality	Work interest	Near family					
5	Salary	1	5	2	4		0.5115		2.0774	4.0611
6	Life quality	1/5	1	1/2	1/2		0.0986		0.3958	4.0161
7	Work interest	1/2	2	1	2		0.2433		0.9894	4.0672
8	Near family	1/4	2	1/2	1		0.1466		0.5933	4.0459
9									CI	0.0159
10	Pairwise comparisons among jobs on salary						Scores		CI/RI	0.0176
11		Job 1	Job 2	Job 3						
12	Job 1	1	2	4			0.5714		1.7143	3
13	Job 2	1/2	1	2			0.2857		0.8571	3
14	Job 3	1/4	1/2	1			0.1429		0.4286	3
15									CI	0
16	Pairwise comparisons among jobs on quality of life						Scores		CI/RI	0.0000
17		Job 1	Job 2	Job 3						
18	Job 1	1	1/2	1/3			0.1593		0.4815	3.0233
19	Job 2	2	1	1/3			0.2519		0.7667	3.0441
20	Job 3	3	3	1			0.5889		1.8222	3.0943
21									CI	0.0270
22	Pairwise comparisons among jobs on interest of work						Scores		CI/RI	0.0465
23		Job 1	Job 2	Job 3						
24	Job 1	1	1/7	1/3			0.0882		0.2648	3.0018
25	Job 2	7	1	3			0.6687		2.0154	3.0139
26	Job 3	3	1/3	1			0.2431		0.7306	3.0054
27									CI	0.0035
28	Pairwise comparisons among jobs on nearness to family						Scores		CI/RI	0.0061
29		Job 1	Job 2	Job 3						
30	Job 1	1	1/4	1/7			0.0824		0.2473	3.0005
31	Job 2	4	1	1/2			0.3151		0.9460	3.0019
32	Job 3	7	2	1			0.6025		1.8096	3.0035
33									CI	0.0010
34									CI/RI	0.0017

FIGURE 9.18 Checking for Consistency

❷ Ratios. In cell O5 calculate the ratio of the two cells to its left with the formula

=N5/L5

and copy this to the range O6:O8.

❸ Consistency index. Calculate the consistency index CI in cell O9 with the formula

=(AVERAGE(O5:O8)–4)/3

Then in cell O10 calculate the ratio of CI to RI (for $n = 4$) with the formula

=O9/0.90

(The 0.90 comes from Table 9.30. For the other four pairwise comparison matrices in Figure 9.18, we use $n = 3$ and $RI = 0.58$.)

As Figure 9.18 illustrates, all of the pairwise comparison matrices are quite consistent—the CI/RI ratio for each is well less than 0.10. ∎

MODELING ISSUES

1. In Jane's job selection example, suppose that quality of life depends on two "subobjectives": recreational and educational facilities. Then we need a pairwise comparison matrix to calculate the proportion of the quality of life score that is determined by recreational facilities and the proportion that is determined by educational facilities. Next, we need to determine how each job scores (separately) on recreational facilities and educational facilities. Then we can again determine a "quality of life score" for each job and proceed with AHP as before. Using this idea, AHP can handle a *hierarchy* of objectives and subobjectives—hence the term "hierarchy" in the name of the procedure. (See Problem 31.)

2. Although the JOBSAHP.XLS file can be used as a "template" for other AHP problems, it is clear by now that typical users would not want to go to all of this trouble to create a spreadsheet model, certainly not from scratch. If you intend to make any real decisions with AHP, you will want to acquire special-purpose software such as Expert Choice. To give you some feeling for this software, we have included a VBA application of AHP in the companion book *VBA for Modelers* (which can be purchased separately). ∎

ADDITIONAL APPLICATIONS

Automated Manufacturing Decisions Using AHP

Weber (1993) reports the successful use of AHP in deciding which of several technologies to purchase for automated manufacturing. As he discusses, these decisions can have several types of impacts: quantitative financial (such as purchase cost), quantitative nonfinancial (such as throughput, cycle time, and scrap, which are difficult to translate directly into dollars), and qualitative (such as product quality and manufacturing flexibility, which are also difficult to translate into dollars). When the decision maker is trying to rate the different technologies along nonmonetary criteria, then he or she should use the method discussed in this section. (For example, how much more do you prefer technology 1 to technology 2 in the area of product quality?) However, he advises that when quantitative financial data are available (for example, technology 1 costs twice as much as technology 2), then this "objective" information should be used in the AHP preference matrices. Weber developed a software package called AutoMan to implement the AHP method. This software has been purchased by over 800 decision makers since its first release in 1989.

Other Applications of AHP

We close by noting that AHP has been used by decision makers in many areas, including accounting, finance, marketing, energy resource planning, microcomputer selection, sociology, architecture, and political science. See Zahedi (1986), Golden et al. (1989), and Saaty (1988) for a discussion of applications of AHP. ■

PROBLEMS

Skill-Building Problems

25. Each professor's annual salary increase is determined by his or her performance in three areas: teaching, research, and service to the university. The administration has assessed the pairwise comparison matrix for these objectives as shown in Table 9.31. The administration has compared two professors with regard to their teaching, research, and service over the past year. The pairwise comparison matrices are shown in Table 9.32.

TABLE 9.31 Pairwise Comparisons of Objectives in Salary Problem

	Teaching	Research	Service
Teaching	1	1/3	5
Research	3	1	7
Service	1/5	1/7	1

a. Which professor should receive a bigger raise?
b. Does AHP indicate how large a raise each professor should be given?
c. Check the pairwise comparison matrix for consistency.

TABLE 9.32 Pairwise Comparisons of Professors in Salary Problem

Teaching

	Professor 1	Professor 2
Professor 1	1	4
Professor 2	1/4	1

Research

	Professor 1	Professor 2
Professor 1	1	1/3
Professor 2	3	1

Service

	Professor 1	Professor 2
Professor 1	1	6
Professor 2	1/6	1

26. Your company is about to purchase a new personal computer. Three objectives are important in determining which computer you should purchase: cost, user-friendliness, and software availability. The pairwise comparison matrix for these objectives is shown in Table 9.33. Three computers are being

TABLE 9.33 Pairwise Comparisons of Objectives in Computer Purchasing Problem

	Cost	User-friendliness	Software Availability
Cost	1	1/4	1/5
User-friendliness	4	1	1/2
Software availability	5	2	1

considered for purchase. The performance of each computer with regard to each objective is indicated by the pairwise comparison matrices in Table 9.34.

a. Which computer should you purchase?

b. Check the pairwise comparison matrices for consistency.

27. You are ready to select your mate for life and have determined that physical attractiveness, intelligence, and personality are key factors in selecting a satisfactory mate. Your pairwise comparison matrix for these objectives is shown in Table 9.35. Three people (Chris, Jamie, and Pat) are begging to be your mate. (This problem attempts to be gender-neutral!) Your view of these people's attractiveness, intelligence, and personality is given in the pairwise comparison matrices in Table 9.36.

a. Who should you choose as your lifetime mate?

b. Evaluate all pairwise comparison matrices for consistency.

28. In determining where to invest your money, two objectives, expected rate of return and degree of risk, are considered to be equally important. Two investments (1 and 2) have the pairwise comparison matrices shown in Table 9.37.

a. How would you rank these investments?

b. Now suppose another investment (investment 3) is available. The pairwise comparison

matrices for these investments are shown in Table 9.38. (Observe that the entries in the comparison matrices for investments 1 and 2 have not changed.) How would you now rank the investments? Contrast your ranking of investments 1 and 2 with your answer from part a.

TABLE 9.36	Pairwise Comparisons of People in Mating Problem		
Attractiveness	Chris	Jamie	Pat
Chris	1	5	3
Jamie	1/5	1	1/2
Pat	1/3	2	1
Intelligence	Chris	Jamie	Pat
Chris	1	1/6	1/4
Jamie	6	1	2
Pat	4	1/2	1
Personality	Chris	Jamie	Pat
Chris	1	4	1/4
Jamie	1/4	1	1/9
Pat	4	9	1

TABLE 9.34	Pairwise Comparisons of Computers in Computer Purchasing Problem		
Cost	Computer 1	Computer 2	Computer 3
Computer 1	1	3	5
Computer 2	1/3	1	2
Computer 3	1/5	1/2	1
User-friendliness	Computer 1	Computer 2	Computer 3
Computer 1	1	1/3	1/2
Computer 2	3	1	5
Computer 3	2	1/5	1
Software Availability	Computer 1	Computer 2	Computer 3
Computer 1	1	1/2	1/7
Computer 2	2	1	1/5
Computer 3	7	5	1

TABLE 9.35	Pairwise Comparisons of Objectives in Mating Problem		
	Attractiveness	Intelligence	Personality
Attractiveness	1	3	5
Intelligence	1/3	1	3
Personality	1/5	1/3	1

TABLE 9.37   Pairwise Comparisons in Investment Problem

Expected Return	Investment 1	Investment 2
Investment 1	1	1/2
Investment 2	2	1

Degree of Risk	Investment 1	Investment 2
Investment 1	1	3
Investment 2	1/3	1

TABLE 9.38   Expanded Pairwise Comparisons in Investment Problem

Expected Return	Investment 1	Investment 2	Investment 3
Investment 1	1	1/2	4
Investment 2	2	1	8
Investment 3	1/4	1/8	1

Degree of Risk	Investment 1	Investment 2	Investment 3
Investment 1	1	3	1/2
Investment 2	1/3	1	1/6
Investment 3	2	6	1

29. You are trying to determine which MBA program to attend. You have been accepted at two schools: Indiana and Northwestern. You have chosen three attributes to use in helping you make your decision: cost, starting salary for graduates, and ambience of school (can we party there?). Your pairwise comparison matrix for these attributes is shown in Table 9.39. For each attribute, the pairwise comparison matrix for Indiana and Northwestern is shown in Table 9.40. Which MBA program should you attend?

TABLE 9.39   Pairwise Comparisons of Attributes in School Problem

	Cost	Salary	Ambience
Cost	1	1/4	2
Salary	4	1	7
Ambience	1/2	1/7	1

30. You are trying to determine which of two secretarial candidates (John or Sharon) to hire. The three objectives that are important to your decision are personality, typing ability, and intelligence. You have assessed the pairwise comparison matrix for the three objectives in Table 9.41. The score of each employee on each objective is shown in

TABLE 9.40   Pairwise Comparisons of Indiana and Northwestern

Cost	Indiana	Northwestern
Indiana	1	6
Northwestern	1/6	1

Salary	Indiana	Northwestern
Indiana	1	1/6
Northwestern	6	1

Ambience	Indiana	Northwestern
Indiana	1	4
Northwestern	1/4	1

TABLE 9.41   Pairwise Comparisons of Objectives in Secretary Problem

	Personality	Typing Ability	Intelligence
Personality	1	1/4	1/3
Typing ability	4	1	1/2
Intelligence	3	2	1

Table 9.42 (page 484). If you follow the AHP method, which employee should you hire?

TABLE 9.42	Candidate Scores in Secretary Problem		
	Personality	Typing Ability	Intelligence
John	0.4	0.6	0.2
Sharon	0.6	0.4	0.8

Skill-Extending Problems

31. A consumer is trying to determine which type of frozen dinner to eat. She considers three attributes to be important: taste, nutritional value, and price. Nutritional value is considered to be determined by cholesterol and sodium level. Three types of dinners are under consideration. The pairwise comparison matrix for the three attributes is shown in Table 9.43. Among the three frozen dinners, the pairwise comparison matrix for each attribute is shown in Table 9.44. To determine how each dinner rates on nutrition, you will need the pairwise comparison matrix for cholesterol and sodium in Table 9.45.

TABLE 9.43	Pairwise Comparisons of Attributes for Food Problem		
	Taste	Nutrition	Price
Taste	1	3	1/2
Nutrition	1/3	1	1/5
Price	2	5	1

TABLE 9.44	Pairwise Comparisons of Dinners in Food Problem		
Taste	**Dinner 1**	**Dinner 2**	**Dinner 3**
Dinner 1	1	5	3
Dinner 2	1/5	1	1/2
Dinner 3	1/3	2	1
Sodium	**Dinner 1**	**Dinner 2**	**Dinner 3**
Dinner 1	1	1/7	1/3
Dinner 2	7	1	2
Dinner 3	3	1/2	1
Cholesterol	**Dinner 1**	**Dinner 2**	**Dinner 3**
Dinner 1	1	1/8	1/4
Dinner 2	8	1	2
Dinner 3	4	1/2	1
Price	**Dinner 1**	**Dinner 2**	**Dinner 3**
Dinner 1	1	4	1/2
Dinner 2	1/4	1	1/6
Dinner 3	2	6	1

TABLE 9.45	Pairwise Comparison of Sodium and Cholesterol in Food Problem	
	Cholesterol	Sodium
Cholesterol	1	5
Sodium	1/5	1

Which frozen dinner would the consumer prefer? (*Hint*: The nutrition score for a dinner equals the score of the dinner on sodium multiplied by the weight for sodium plus the score for the dinner on cholesterol multiplied by the weight for cholesterol.)

32. Based on Lin et al. (1984). You have been hired by Arthur Ross to determine which of the following accounts receivable methods should be used in an audit of the Keating Five and Dime Store: analytic review (method 1), confirmations (method 2), or test of subsequent collections (method 3). The three criteria used to distinguish among the methods are reliability, cost, and validity. The pairwise comparison matrix for the three criteria is shown in Table 9.46. The pairwise comparison matrices of the three accounting methods for the three criteria are shown in Table 9.47. Use AHP to determine which auditing procedure should be used. Also check the first pairwise comparison matrix for consistency.

TABLE 9.46	Pairwise Comparisons of Criteria in Accounting Problem		
	Reliability	**Cost**	**Validity**
Reliability	1	5	7
Cost	1/5	1	2
Validity	1/7	1/2	1

TABLE 9.47	Pairwise Comparisons of Methods in Accounting Problem		
Reliability	**Method 1**	**Method 2**	**Method 3**
Method 1	1	1/6	1/2
Method 2	6	1	4
Method 3	2	1/4	1
Cost	**Method 1**	**Method 2**	**Method 3**
Method 1	1	5	3
Method 2	1/5	1	1/2
Method 3	1/3	2	1
Validity	**Method 1**	**Method 2**	**Method 3**
Method 1	1	3	2
Method 2	1/3	1	1/2
Method 3	1/2	2	1

9.5 CONCLUSION

Whenever we face a problem with multiple competing objectives, as is the case in many real-world problems, we are forced to make trade-offs between these objectives. This is usually a very difficult task, and not all management scientists agree on the best way to proceed. When the objectives are very different in nature, no method can disguise the inherent complexity of comparing "apples to oranges." Although one method, finding Pareto optimal solutions and drawing the resulting trade-off curve, locates solutions that are not dominated by any others, we still face the problem of choosing one of the (many) Pareto optimal solutions to implement. The other two methods we have discussed in this chapter, goal programming and AHP, make trade-offs and ultimately locate an "optimal" solution. These methods are not without their critics, but when they are used carefully, they have the potential to help solve some difficult and important real-world problems.

PROBLEMS

Skill-Building Problems

33. The Pine Valley Board of Education must hire teachers for the coming school year. The types of teachers and the salaries that must be paid are given in Table 9.48. For example, 20 teachers who are qualified to teach history and science have applied for jobs, and each of these teachers must be paid an annual salary of $21,000. Each teacher who is hired teaches the two subjects he or she is qualified to teach. Pine Valley needs to hire 35 teachers qualified to teach history, 30 teachers qualified to teach science, 40 teachers qualified to teach math, and 32 teachers qualified to teach English. The board has $1.4 million to spend on teachers' salaries. A penalty cost of $1 is incurred for each dollar the board goes over budget. For each teacher by which Pine Valley's goals are unmet, the following costs are incurred (because of the lower quality of education): science, $30,000; math, $28,000; history, $26,000; and English, $24,000. Determine how the board can minimize its total cost due to unmet goals.

TABLE 9.48 Data for Pine Valley Problem

Teacher Can Teach	Number Applying	Annual Salary
History and science	20	$21,000
History and math	15	$22,000
English and science	12	$23,000
English and math	14	$24,000
English and history	13	$25,000
Science and math	12	$26,000

34. Stockco fills orders for three products for a local warehouse. Stockco must determine how many of each product should be ordered at the beginning of the current month. This month, 400 units of product 1, 500 units of product 2, and 300 units of product 3 will be demanded. The cost and space taken up by one unit of each product are shown in Table 9.49. If Stockco runs out of stock before the end of the month, the stockout costs shown in Table 9.49 are incurred. Stockco has $17,000 to spend on ordering products and has 3700 square feet of warehouse space. A $1 penalty is assessed for each dollar spent over the budget limit, and a $10 cost is assessed for every square foot of warehouse space needed.

TABLE 9.49 Data for Stockco Problem

	Space (sq ft)	Cost	Stockout Cost
Product 1	6	$20	$16
Product 2	5	$18	$10
Product 3	4	$16	$8

a. Determine Stockco's optimal ordering policy.
b. Suppose that Stockco has set the following goals, listed in order of priority:
- Goal 1: Spend at most $17,000.
- Goal 2: Use at most 3700 square feet of warehouse space.
- Goal 3: Meet demand for product 1.
- Goal 4: Meet demand for product 2.
- Goal 5: Meet demand for product 3.
  Develop a preemptive goal programming model for Stockco.

35. BeatTrop Foods is trying to choose one of three companies to merge with. Seven factors are important in this decision:
- Factor 1: Contribution to profitability
- Factor 2: Growth potential
- Factor 3: Labor environment
- Factor 4: R&D ability of company
- Factor 5: Organizational fit
- Factor 6: Relative size
- Factor 7: Industry commonality

The pairwise comparison matrix for these factors is as follows:

$$\begin{bmatrix} 1 & 3 & 7 & 5 & 1 & 7 & 1 \\ 1/3 & 1 & 9 & 1 & 1 & 5 & 1 \\ 1/7 & 1/9 & 1 & 1/7 & 1/5 & 1/2 & 1/4 \\ 1/5 & 1 & 7 & 1 & 1/4 & 7 & 1/3 \\ 1 & 1 & 5 & 4 & 1 & 5 & 3 \\ 1/7 & 1/5 & 2 & 1/7 & 1/5 & 1 & 1/6 \\ 1 & 1 & 4 & 3 & 1/3 & 6 & 1 \end{bmatrix}$$

The three contenders for merger have the following pairwise comparison matrices for each factor:

$$\text{Factor 1: } \begin{bmatrix} 1 & 9 & 3 \\ 1/9 & 1 & 1/5 \\ 1/3 & 5 & 1 \end{bmatrix}$$

$$\text{Factor 2: } \begin{bmatrix} 1 & 7 & 4 \\ 1/7 & 1 & 1/3 \\ 1/4 & 3 & 1 \end{bmatrix}$$

$$\text{Factor 3: } \begin{bmatrix} 1 & 1/5 & 1/3 \\ 5 & 1 & 2 \\ 3 & 1/2 & 1 \end{bmatrix}$$

$$\text{Factor 4: } \begin{bmatrix} 1 & 6 & 3 \\ 1/6 & 1 & 1/2 \\ 1/3 & 2 & 1 \end{bmatrix}$$

$$\text{Factor 5: } \begin{bmatrix} 1 & 1/9 & 1/5 \\ 9 & 1 & 4 \\ 5 & 1/4 & 1 \end{bmatrix}$$

$$\text{Factor 6: } \begin{bmatrix} 1 & 1/7 & 1/4 \\ 7 & 1 & 3 \\ 4 & 1/3 & 1 \end{bmatrix}$$

$$\text{Factor 7: } \begin{bmatrix} 1 & 1/7 & 1/3 \\ 7 & 1 & 3 \\ 3 & 1/3 & 1 \end{bmatrix}$$

Use AHP to determine the company that BeatTrop should merge with.

36. Productco produces three products. Each product requires labor, lumber, and paint. The resource requirements, unit price, and variable cost (exclusive of raw materials) for each product are given in Table 9.50. At present, 900 labor hours, 1550 gallons of paint, and 1600 board feet of lumber are available. Additional labor can be purchased at $6 per hour. Additional paint can be purchased at $2 per gallon. Additional lumber can be purchased at $3 per board foot. For the following two sets of priorities, use preemptive goal programming to determine an optimal production schedule. For set 1:
- Priority 1: Obtain profit of at least $10,500.
- Priority 2: Purchase no additional labor.
- Priority 3: Purchase no additional paint.
- Priority 4: Purchase no additional lumber.
  For set 2:
- Priority 1: Purchase no additional labor.
- Priority 2: Obtain profit of at least $10,500.
- Priority 3: Purchase no additional paint.
- Priority 4: Purchase no additional lumber.

TABLE 9.50   **Data for Productco Problem**

	Labor	Lumber	Paint	Price	Variable Cost
Product 1	1.5	2	3	$26	$10
Product 2	3.0	3	2	$28	$6
Product 3	2.0	4	2	$31	$7

Skill-Extending Problems

37. Jobs at Indiana University are rated on three factors:
- Factor 1: Complexity of duties
- Factor 2: Education required
- Factor 3: Mental and/or visual demands

For each job at IU, the requirement for each factor has been rated on a scale of 1–4, with a 4 in factor 1 representing high complexity of duty, a 4 in factor 2 representing high educational requirement, and a 4 in factor 3 representing high mental and/or visual demands. IU wants to determine a formula for grading each job. To do this, it will assign a point value to the score for each factor that a job requires. For example, suppose that level 2 of factor 1 yields a point total of 10, level 3 of factor 2 yields a point total of 20, and level 3 of factor 3 yields a point total of 30. Then a job with these requirements has a point total of $10 + 20 + 30 = 60$. A job's hourly salary equals half its point total. IU has two goals (listed in order of priority) in setting up the points given to each level of each job factor.
- Goal 1: When increasing the level of a factor by 1, the points should increase by at least 10. For example, level 2 of factor 1 should earn at least 10 more points than level 1 of factor 1. Goal 1 is to minimize the sum of deviations from this requirement.

- Goal 2: For the benchmark jobs referred to in Table 9.51, the actual point total for each job should come as close as possible to the point total listed in the table. Goal 2 is to minimize the sum of the absolute deviations of the point totals from the desired scores.

TABLE 9.51   **Data for IU Benchmark Jobs**

	Factor 1 Level	Factor 2 Level	Factor 3 Level	Desired Score
Job 1	4	4	4	105
Job 2	3	3	2	93
Job 3	2	2	2	75
Job 4	1	1	2	68

Use preemptive goal programming to find appropriate point totals. What salary should a job with skill levels of 3 for each factor be paid?

38. A hospital outpatient clinic performs four types of operations. The profit per operation, as well as the minutes of X-ray time and laboratory time used, are given in Table 9.52. The clinic has 500 private rooms and 500 intensive care rooms. Type 1 and type 2 operations require a patient to stay in an intensive care room for one day, whereas type 3 and type 4 operations require a patient to stay in a private room for one day. Each day the hospital is required to perform at least 100 operations of each type. The hospital has set the following goals (listed in order of priority):
- Goal 1: Earn a daily profit of at least $100,000.
- Goal 2: Use at most 50 hours daily of X-ray time.
- Goal 3: Use at most 40 hours daily of laboratory time.

TABLE 9.52   **Data for Hospital Problem**

	Type of Operation			
	1	2	3	4
Profit	$200	$150	$100	$80
X-ray time (minutes)	6	5	4	3
Lab time (minutes)	5	4	3	2

Use preemptive goal programming to determine the types of operations that should be performed.

39. You are trying to determine which city to live in. New York and Chicago are under consideration. Four objectives will determine your decision: housing cost, cultural opportunities, quality of schools and universities, and crime level. The weight for each objective is in Table 9.53. For each objective

(except for quality of schools and universities), New York and Chicago scores are given in Table 9.54. Suppose that the score for each city on the quality of schools and universities depends on two things: a score on public school quality and a score on university quality. The pairwise comparison matrix for public school and university quality is shown in Table 9.55. To see how each city scores on public school quality and university quality, use the pairwise comparison matrices in Table 9.56. You should be able to derive a score for each city on the quality of schools and universities objective. Then use AHP to determine where you should live.

TABLE 9.53   **Weights for Objectives in City Problem**

Objective	Weight
Housing cost	0.50
Culture	0.10
Education	0.20
Crime	0.20

TABLE 9.54   **Scores for Cities in City Problem**

	New York	Chicago
Housing cost	0.30	0.70
Culture	0.70	0.30
Crime	0.40	0.60

TABLE 9.55   **Pairwise Comparison of Education Objectives in City Problem**

	Public School Quality	University Quality
Public school quality	1	4
University quality	1/4	1

TABLE 9.56   **Pairwise Comparison of Cities for Education in City Problem**

Public School Quality	New York	Chicago
New York	1	4
Chicago	1/4	1

University Quality	New York	Chicago
New York	1	1/3
Chicago	3	1

40. At Lummins Engine Corporation, production employees work ten hours per day, four days per week. Each day of the week, at least the following number of employees must be working: Monday–Friday, seven employees; Saturday and Sunday, three employees. Lummins has set the following goals, listed in order of priority:

- Goal 1: Meet employee requirements with 11 workers.
- Goal 2: The average number of weekend days off per employee should be at least 1.5 days.
- Goal 3: The average number of consecutive days off an employee gets during the week should exceed 2.8 days.

  Use preemptive goal programming to determine how to schedule Lummins employees.

41. You are the mayor of Gotham City and you must determine a tax policy for the city. Five types of taxes are used to raise money:

- Property taxes. Let p be the property tax rate.
- A sales tax on all items except food, drugs, and durable goods. Let s be the sales tax rate.
- A sales tax on durable goods. Let d be the durable goods sales tax rate.
- A gasoline sales tax. Let g be the gasoline sales tax rate.
- A sales tax on food and drugs. Let f be the sales tax on food and drugs.

  The city consists of three groups of people: low income (LI), middle income (MI), and high income (HI). The amount of revenue (in millions of dollars) raised from each group by setting a particular tax at a 1% level is given in Table 9.57. For example, a 3% tax on durable good sales will raise 360 million dollars from low-income people. Your tax policy must satisfy the following restrictions:

- Restriction 1: The tax burden on MI people cannot exceed $2.8 billion.
- Restriction 2: The tax burden on HI people cannot exceed $2.4 billion.
- Restriction 3: The total revenue raised must exceed the current level of $6.5 billion.
- Restriction 4: s must be between 1% and 3%.

TABLE 9.57   **Data for Gotham City Tax Problem**

	p	s	d	g	f
LI	900	300	120	30	90
MI	1200	400	100	20	60
HI	1000	250	60	10	40

Given these restrictions, the city council has set the following three goals (listed in order of priority):

- Goal 1: Limit the tax burden on LI people to $2 billion.
- Goal 2: Keep the property tax rate under 3%.
- Goal 3: If their tax burden becomes too high, 20% of the LI people, 20% of the MI people, and 40% of the HI people may consider moving to the suburbs. Suppose that this will happen if their total tax burden exceeds $1.5 billion. To discourage this exodus, goal 3 is to keep the total tax burden on these people below $1.5 billion.

  Use preemptive goal programming to determine an optimal tax policy.

42. Based on Sartoris and Spruill (1974). Wivco produces two products, which it sells on both a cash and credit basis. Revenues from credit sales will not have been received but are included in determining profit earned during the current 6-month period. Sales during the next 6 months can be made either from units produced during the next 6 months or from beginning inventory. Relevant information about products 1 and 2 is as follows.

- During the next 6 months, at most 150 units of product 1 can be sold on a cash basis, and at most 100 units of product 1 can be sold on a credit basis. It costs $35 to produce each unit of product 1, and each sells for $40. A credit sale of a unit of product 1 yields $0.50 less profit than a cash sale (because of delays in receiving payment). Two hours of production time are needed to produce each unit of product 1. At the beginning of the 6-month period, 60 units of product 1 are in inventory.
- During the next 6 months, at most 175 units of product 2 can be sold on a cash basis, and at most 250 units of product 2 can be sold on a credit basis. It costs $45 to produce each unit of product 2, and each sells for $52.50. A credit sale of a unit of product 2 yields $1.00 less profit than a cash sale. Four hours of production time are needed to produce each unit of product 2. At the beginning of the 6-month period, 30 units of product 2 are in inventory.
- During the next 6 months, Wivco has 1000 hours for production available. At the end of the next 6 months, Wivco incurs a 10% holding cost on the value of ending inventory (measured relative to production cost). An opportunity cost of 5% is also assessed against any cash on hand at the end of the 6-month period.

a. Formulate and solve an LP that yields Wivco's maximum profit during the next 6 months. What is Wivco's ending inventory position? Assuming an initial cash balance of $0, what is Wivco's ending cash balance?

b. Since an ending inventory and cash position of $0 is undesirable (for ongoing operations), Wivco is considering other options. At the beginning of the 6-month period, Wivco can obtain a loan (secured by ending inventory) that incurs an interest cost equal to 5% of the value of the loan. The maximum value of the loan is 75% of the value of the ending inventory. The loan will be repaid one year from now. Wivco has the following goals (listed in order of priority):

- Goal 1: Make the ending cash balance of Wivco come as close as possible to $75.
- Goal 2: Make profit come as close as possible to the profit level obtained in part **a**.
- Goal 3: At any time, Wivco's current ratio is defined to be

$$\text{Current ratio} = \frac{\text{Wivco's assets}}{\text{Wivco's liabilities}}$$

Assuming initially that current liabilities equal $150, 6 months from now Wivco's current ratio will equal

$$\text{Current ratio} = \frac{CB + AR + EI}{150 + \text{Size of loan}}$$

where CB is the ending cash balance, AR is the value of accounts receivable, and EI is the value of the ending inventory. Six months from now, Wivco wants the current ratio to be as close as possible to 2.

Use preemptive goal programming to determine Wivco's production and financial strategy.

Modeling Problems

43. How might you use preemptive goal programming to help Congress balance the budget?

44. A company is considering buying up to five other businesses. Given knowledge of the company's view of the trade-off between risk and return, how could trade-off curves be used to determine the companies that should be purchased?

45. How would you use AHP to determine the greatest sports record of all time? (Many believe it is Joe Dimaggio's 56-game hitting streak.)

46. You are planning to renovate a hospital. How would you use AHP to help determine what improvements to include in the renovation?

47. You are planning to overhaul a hospital computer system. How would you use AHP to determine the type of computer system to install?

48. You have been commissioned to assign 100 remedial education teachers to the 40 schools in the St. Louis School System. What are some objectives you might consider in assigning the teachers to schools?

49. You have been hired as a consultant to help design a new airport in northern Indiana that will supplant O'Hare as Chicago's major airport. Discuss the objectives you consider important in designing and locating the airport.

50. In the Indiana MBA program we need to divide a class of 60 students into ten six-person teams. In the interest of diversity we have the following goals (listed in descending order of importance):

- at least one woman per team
- at least one member of a minority per team
- at least one student with a financial or accounting background per team
- at least one engineer per team

Explain how you could use the material in this chapter to develop a model to assign students to teams.

Play Time Toy Company

Play Time Toy faces a highly seasonal pattern of sales. In the past, Play Time has used a *seasonal* production schedule, where the amount produced each month matches the sales for that month. Under this production plan, inventory is maintained at a constant level. The production manager, Thomas Lindop, is proposing a switch to a *level*, or constant, production schedule. This schedule would result in significant savings in production costs but would have higher storage and handling costs, fluctuating levels of inventories, and would also have implications for financing. Jonathan King, president of Play Time Toy, has been reviewing pro forma income statements, cash budgets, and balance sheets for the coming year under the two production scenarios. Table 9.58 shows the pro forma analysis under seasonal production, and Table 9.59 shows the pro forma analysis under level production.

TABLE 9.58 **Seasonal Production**

| Annual net profit | 237 | Play Time Toy Company | | | | | | | | | | | |

| | Actual | Projected for 1991 | | | | | | | | | | | | |
	Dec 1990	Jan	Feb	Mar	Apr	May	June	July	Aug	Sept	Oct	Nov	Dec	Total
Production (sales value)	850	108	126	145	125	125	125	145	1,458	1,655	1,925	2,057	1,006	9000
Inventory (sales value)	813	813	813	813	813	813	813	813	813	813	813	813	813	

INCOME STATEMENT		Jan	Feb	Mar	Apr	May	June	July	Aug	Sept	Oct	Nov	Dec	Total
Net sales		108	126	145	125	125	125	145	1,458	1,655	1,925	2,057	1,006	9,000
Cost of goods sold														
Materials & regular wages		70	82	94	81	81	81	94	950	1,079	1,254	1,340	656	5,865
Overtime wages		0	0	0	0	0	0	0	61	91	131	151	0	435
Gross profit		38	44	51	44	44	44	51	447	486	539	565	350	2,700
Operating expenses		188	188	188	188	188	188	188	188	188	188	188	188	2,256
Inventory cost		0	0	0	0	0	0	0	0	0	0	0	0	0
Profit before int & taxes		(150)	(144)	(137)	(144)	(144)	(144)	(137)	259	298	351	377	162	444
Net interest payments		10	2	1	1	2	2	2	3	7	18	19	19	86
Profit before taxes		(160)	(146)	(138)	(146)	(146)	(147)	(140)	256	290	333	359	144	358
Taxes		(55)	(50)	(47)	(50)	(50)	(50)	(48)	87	99	113	122	49	122
Net profit		(106)	(97)	(91)	(96)	(97)	(97)	(92)	169	192	220	237	95	237

| | Actual | Projected for 1991 | | | | | | | | | | | |
BALANCE SHEET	Dec 1990	Jan	Feb	Mar	Apr	May	June	July	Aug	Sept	Oct	Nov	Dec
Cash	175	782	1,365	1,116	934	808	604	450	175	175	175	175	175
Accts receivable	2,628	958	234	271	270	250	250	270	1,603	3,113	3,580	3,982	3,063
Inventory	530	530	530	530	530	530	530	530	530	530	530	530	530
Net P/E	1,070	1,070	1,070	1,070	1,070	1,070	1,070	1,070	1,070	1,070	1,070	1,070	1,070
Total Assets	4,403	3,340	3,199	2,987	2,804	2,658	2,454	2,320	3,378	4,888	5,355	5,757	4,838
Accts payable	255	32	38	44	38	38	38	44	437	497	578	617	302
Notes payable	680	0	0	0	0	0	0	0	408	1,600	1,653	1,656	966
Accrued taxes	80	25	(24)	(151)	(232)	(282)	(363)	(411)	(324)	(256)	(143)	(21)	(4)
Long term debt	450	450	450	450	450	450	425	425	425	425	425	425	400
Equity	2,938	2,832	2,736	2,644	2,548	2,452	2,355	2,263	2,431	2,623	2,843	3,080	3,175
Total liab & equity	4,403	3,340	3,199	2,987	2,804	2,658	2,454	2,320	3,378	4,888	5,355	5,757	4,838

TABLE 9.59 **Level Production**

Annual net profit   373   Play Time Toy Company

	Actual Dec 1990	Projected for 1991 Jan	Feb	Mar	Apr	May	June	July	Aug	Sept	Oct	Nov	Dec	Total
Production (sales value)	850	750	750	750	750	750	750	750	750	750	750	750	750	9000
Inventory (sales value)	813	1455	2079	2684	3309	3934	4559	5164	4456	3551	2376	1069	813	

INCOME STATEMENT		Jan	Feb	Mar	Apr	May	June	July	Aug	Sept	Oct	Nov	Dec	Total
Net sales		108	126	145	125	125	125	145	1,458	1,655	1,925	2,057	1,006	9,000
Cost of goods sold														
Materials & regular wages		70	82	94	81	81	81	94	950	1,079	1,254	1,340	656	5,865
Overtime wages		0	0	0	0	0	0	0	0	0	0	0	0	0
Gross profit		38	44	51	44	44	44	51	508	576	671	717	350	3,135
Operating expenses		188	188	188	188	188	188	188	188	188	188	188	188	2,256
Inventory cost		0	2	6	10	13	17	20	16	11	4	0	0	100
Profit before int & taxes		(150)	(147)	(143)	(154)	(158)	(161)	(158)	304	377	478	529	162	779
Net interest payments		10	3	2	5	10	15	21	26	32	37	31	22	214
Profit before taxes		(160)	(149)	(146)	(159)	(168)	(177)	(179)	277	346	441	498	141	565
Taxes		(55)	(51)	(50)	(54)	(57)	(60)	(61)	94	118	150	169	48	192
Net profit		(106)	(99)	(96)	(105)	(111)	(117)	(118)	183	228	291	329	93	373

BALANCE SHEET	Actual Dec 1990	Projected for 1991 Jan	Feb	Mar	Apr	May	June	July	Aug	Sept	Oct	Nov	Dec
Cash	175	556	724	175	175	175	175	175	175	175	175	175	175
Accts receivable	2,628	958	234	271	270	250	250	270	1,603	3,113	3,580	3,982	3,063
Inventory	530	948	1,355	1,749	2,157	2,564	2,971	3,365	2,904	2,314	1,549	697	530
Net P/E	1,070	1,070	1,070	1,070	1,070	1,070	1,070	1,070	1,070	1,070	1,070	1,070	1,070
Total Assets	4,403	3,533	3,383	3,265	3,672	4,059	4,466	4,880	5,752	6,672	6,374	5,924	4,838
Accts payable	255	225	225	225	225	225	225	225	225	225	225	225	225
Notes payable	680	0	0	108	704	1,259	1,900	2,493	3,087	3,693	2,953	2,005	836
Accrued taxes	80	25	(25)	(155)	(240)	(297)	(389)	(450)	(355)	(269)	(119)	50	66
Long term debt	450	450	450	450	450	450	425	425	425	425	425	425	400
Equity	2,938	2,832	2,734	2,637	2,533	2,422	2,305	2,187	2,370	2,599	2,890	3,218	3,311
Total liab & equity	4,403	3,533	3,383	3,265	3,672	4,059	4,466	4,880	5,752	6,672	6,374	5,924	4,838

Greg Cole, chief financial officer of Play Time, prepared the two tables. He explained that the pro forma analyses in Tables 9.58 and 9.59 take fully into account the 11% interest payments on the unsecured loan from Bay Trust Company and the 3% interest received from its cash account. An interest charge of 11%/12 on the balance of the loan at the end of a month must be paid the next month. Similarly, an interest payment of 3%/12 on the cash balance at the end of a month is received in the next month.

The inventory available at the end of December 1990 is $530,000 (measured in terms of cost to produce). Mr. Cole assumed that this inventory represents a sales value of $530,000/0.651667 = $813,300.

The inventory and overtime costs in Tables 9.58 and 9.59 are based on the cost information developed by Mr. Lindop. This information is summarized in Table 9.60.

Mr. Cole further explained how the cost information was used in the pro forma analyses. For example, in Table 9.58, the production in August is $1,458,000. The overtime cost in August is therefore calculated to be $61,000 (= 0.15 × (1,458,000 − 1,049,000)). Play Time uses LIFO (last-in, first-out) accounting, so overtime costs are always charged in

TABLE 9.60	Play Time Cost Information

- **Gross margin.** The cost of goods sold (excluding overtime costs) is 65.1667% of sales under any production schedule. Materials costs are 30% of sales. All other nonmaterials costs, including regular wages but excluding overtime wages, are 35.1667% of sales.

- **Overtime cost.** Running at capacity but without using any overtime, the plant can produce $1,049,000 of monthly sales. Units produced in excess of this capacity in a month incur an additional overtime cost of 15% of sales. (The monthly production capacity of the plant running on full overtime is $2,400,000 of sales. Since November has the maximum level of projected sales at $2,057,000, the capacity on full overtime should never pose a problem.)

- **Inventory cost.** The plant has a limited capacity to store finished goods. It can store $1,663,000 worth of sales at the plant. Additional units must be moved and stored in rented warehouse space. The cost of storage, handling, and insurance of finished goods over this capacity is 7% of the sales value of the goods per year, or 7%/12 per month.

the month that they occur.[2] The annual overtime cost for the seasonal production plan is $435,000. In Table 9.59, under level production, finished goods worth $5,164,000 are in inventory at the end of July. The inventory cost for the month is $20,000 ($= 0.07/12 \times (5,164,000 - 1,663,000)$). The annual inventory cost for the level production plan is $100,000.

Mr. Lindop felt that a minimum of $813,300 of inventory (measured in terms of sales value, or $530,000 measured in terms of cost to produce) must be kept on hand at the end of each month. This

inventory level represents a reasonable safety stock, required since orders do not occur uniformly during a month.

Mr. King was impressed at the possible increase in profit from $237,000 under the seasonal production plan to $373,000 under level production. While studying the pro forma projections, Mr. King realized that some combination of the two production plans might be even better. He asked Mr. Lindop to try to find a production plan with a higher profit than the seasonal and level plans.

Mr. Lindop proceeded to develop a spreadsheet-based linear programming model to maximize annual net profit.

Questions

Note: Mr. Lindop's model is contained in the file PLAYTIME.XLS. The spreadsheet is ready to be optimized, but it has not been optimized yet.

1. Run the optimization model in the file PLAYTIME.XLS. What is the optimal production plan? What is the optimal annual net profit? How does this optimal production plan compare to the seasonal and level production plans?

2. Suppose that Play Time's bankers will not extend any credit over $1.9 million—in other words, the loan balance in any month cannot exceed $1.9 million. Modify the spreadsheet model to take into account this restriction. What is the optimal production plan in this case? What is the optimal annual net profit?

3. Annual profit is a measure of reward for Play Time Toy. The maximum loan balance is a measure of risk for the bank. Construct a trade-off curve between optimal annual profit and the maximum loan balance.

[2]This assumes that overtime production is used only to satisfy current demand and not to build up inventory.

10

Decision Making Under Uncertainty

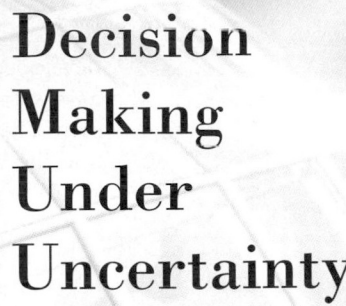

DECISION AND RISK ANALYSIS AT DU PONT

F ormal decision analysis in the face of uncertainty frequently occurs at the most strategic levels of a company's planning process and typically involves teams of high-level managers from all areas of the company. This is certainly the case with Du Pont, as reported by two internal decision analysis experts, Krumm and Rolle (1992), in their article "Management and Application of Decision and Risk Analysis in Du Pont." Du Pont's formal use of decision analysis began in the 1960s, but because of a lack of computing power and distrust of the method by senior-level management, it never really got a foothold. However, by the mid-1980s things had changed considerably. The company was involved in a faster-moving, more uncertain environment, more people throughout the company were empowered to make decisions, and these decisions had to be made more quickly. In addition, the computing power had arrived to make large-scale quantitative analysis feasible. Since that time, Du Pont has embraced formal decision-making analysis in all its businesses, and the trend is almost certain to continue.

The article describes a typical example of decision analysis within the company. One of Du Pont's businesses, Business Z (so-called for reasons of confidentiality), was stagnating. It was not set up to respond quickly to changing customer demands, and its financial position was declining due to lower prices and market share. A decision board and a project team were empowered to turn things around. The project team developed a detailed timetable to accomplish three basic steps: frame the problem, assess uncertainties and perform the analysis, and implement the recommended decision. The first step involved setting up a "strategy table" to list the possible strategies and the factors that would affect or be affected by them. The three basic strategies were (1) a base-case strategy (continue operating as is), (2) a product differentiation strategy (develop new products), and (3) a cost leadership strategy (shut down the plant and streamline the product line).

In the second step, the team asked a variety of experts throughout the company for their assessments of the likelihood of key uncertain events. In the analysis step they then used all of the information gained to determine the strategy with the largest expected net present value. Two important aspects of this analysis step were the extensive use of sensitivity analysis (many what-if questions) and the emergence of new "hybrid" strategies that dominated the strategies that had been considered to that point. In particular, the team finally decided on a product differentiation strategy that also decreased costs by shutting down some facilities in each plant.

By the time of the third step, implementation, the decision board needed little convincing. Since all of the key people had been given the opportunity to provide input to the process, everyone was convinced that the right strategy had been selected. All that was left was to put the plan in motion and monitor its results. The results were impressive. Business Z made a complete turnaround, and its net present value increased by close to $200 million. Besides this tangible benefit, there were definite intangible benefits from the overall process. As Du Pont's vice president for finance said, "The D&RA [decision and risk analysis] process improved communication within the business team as well as between the team and corporate management, resulting in rapid approval and execution. As a decision maker, I highly value such a clear and logical approach to making choices under uncertainty and will continue to use D&RA whenever possible." ■

10.1 INTRODUCTION

In this chapter we will provide a formal framework for analyzing decision problems that involve uncertainty. We will discuss the most frequently used criteria for choosing among alternative decisions, how probabilities are used in the decision-making process, how decisions made at an early stage affect decisions made at a later stage, how a decision maker can quantify the value of information, and how attitudes toward risk can affect the analysis. Throughout, we will employ a powerful graphical tool—decision trees—to guide the analysis. A decision tree enables the decision maker to view all important aspects of the problem at once: the decision alternatives, the uncertain outcomes and their probabilities, the economic consequences, and the chronological order of events. We will show how to implement decision trees in Excel by taking advantage of a very powerful and flexible add-in from Palisade called PrecisionTree.

Many examples of decision making under uncertainty exist in the business world. Here are several examples.

- Companies routinely place bids for contracts to complete a certain project within a fixed time frame. Often these are sealed bids, where each of several companies presents in a sealed envelope a bid for completing the project; then the envelopes are opened, and the low bidder is awarded the bid amount to complete the project. Any particular company in the bidding competition must deal with the possible uncertainty of its *actual* cost of completing the project (should it win the bid), as well as the uncertainty involved in what the other companies will bid. The trade-off is between bidding low in order to win the bid and bidding high in order to make a profit.

- Whenever a company contemplates introducing a new product into the market, there are a number of uncertainties that affect the decision, probably the most important being the customers' reaction to this product. If the product generates high customer demand, then the company will make a large profit. But if demand is low (and, after all, the vast majority of new products do poorly), then the company might not even recoup its development costs. Because the level of customer demand is critical, the company might try to gauge this level by test marketing the product in one region of the country. If this test market is a success, the company can then be more optimistic that a full-scale national marketing of the product will also be successful. But if the test market is a failure, the company can cut its losses by abandoning the product.

- Borison (1995) describes an application of formal decision analysis by Oglethorpe Power Corporation (OPC), a Georgia-based electricity supplier. The basic decision OPC faced was whether to build a new transmission line to supply large amounts of electricity to parts of Florida and, if they decided to build it, how to finance this project. OPC had to deal with several sources of uncertainty: the cost of building new facilities, the demand for power in Florida, and various market conditions, such as the spot price of electricity.

- Ulvila (1987) describes the decision analysis performed by the U.S. Postal Service regarding the purchase of automation equipment. One of the investment decisions was which type of OCR (optical character recognition) equipment the Postal Service should purchase (or convert) for reading single- and/or multiple-line addresses on packages. An important factor in this decision was the level of use by businesses of the "zip+4" (nine-digit zip codes). Zip+4 usage had been recommended for some time but was used only sporadically. The Postal Service was uncertain about the future level of business zip+4 usage. If businesses used the nine-digit codes heavily in the future, then a certain type of (expensive) OCR equipment would be most economical. If business use of zip+4 did not increase, then purchasing this equipment would be a waste of money. The decision was an extremely important one, given the expense of the proposed equipment and the fact that the Postal Service would have to live with whatever equipment it purchased for a number of years.

- Utility companies must make many decisions that have significant environmental and economic consequences. [Balson et al. (1992) provide a good discussion of such consequences.] For these companies it is not necessarily enough to conform to federal or state environmental regulations. Recent court decisions have found companies liable—for huge settlements—when accidents occurred, even though the companies followed all existing regulations. Therefore, when utility companies decide, say, whether to replace equipment or mitigate the effects of environmental pollution, they must take into account the possible environmental consequences (such as injuries to people) as well as economic consequences (such as lawsuits). An aspect of these situations that makes decision analysis particularly difficult is that the potential "disasters" are often extremely improbable; hence, their likelihoods are very difficult to assess accurately.

10.2 ELEMENTS OF A DECISION ANALYSIS

Although decision making under uncertainty occurs in a wide variety of contexts, all problems have three elements in common: (1) the set of decisions (or strategies) available to the decision maker, (2) the set of possible outcomes and the probabilities of these outcomes, and (3) a value model that prescribes results, usually monetary values, for the various combinations of decisions and outcomes. Once these elements are known, the decision maker can find an "optimal" decision, depending on the optimality criterion chosen. Rather than discussing these elements in the abstract, we introduce them in the context of the following extended example.

EXAMPLE   10.1

BIDDING FOR A GOVERNMENT CONTRACT AT SCITOOLS

SciTools Incorporated, a company that specializes in scientific instruments, has been invited to make a bid on a government contract. The contract calls for a specific number of these instruments to be delivered during the coming year. The bids must be sealed (so that no company knows what the others are bidding), and the low bid wins the contract. SciTools estimates that it will cost $5000 to prepare a bid and $95,000 to supply the instruments if it wins the contract. On the basis of past contracts of this type, SciTools believes that the possible low bids from the competition, if there is any competition, and the associated probabilities are those shown in Table 10.1. In addition, SciTools believes there is a 30% chance that there will be *no* competing bids.

TABLE 10.1 **Data for Bidding Example**

Low Bid	Probability
Less than $115,000	0.2
Between $115,000 and $120,000	0.4
Between $120,000 and $125,000	0.3
Greater than $125,000	0.1

Solution

Let's discuss the three elements of SciTools' problem. First, SciTools has two basic strategies: submit a bid or do not submit a bid. If SciTools submits a bid, then it must decide how much to bid. Based on SciTools' cost to prepare the bid and its cost to supply the instruments, there is obviously no point in bidding less than $100,000— SciTools wouldn't make a profit even if it won the bid. Although any bid amount over

$100,000 might be considered, the data in Table 10.1 might persuade SciTools to limit its choices to $115,000, $120,000, and $125,000.[1]

The next element of the problem involves the uncertain outcomes and their probabilities. We have assumed that SciTools knows exactly how much it will cost to prepare a bid and how much it will cost to supply the instruments if it wins the bid. (In reality, these are probably estimates of the actual costs.) Therefore, the only source of uncertainty is the behavior of the competitors—will they bid, and if so, how much? From SciTools' standpoint, this is difficult information to obtain. The behavior of the competitors depends on (1) how many competitors are likely to bid and (2) how the competitors assess *their* costs of supplying the instruments. However, we will assume that SciTools has been involved in similar bidding contests in the past and can, therefore, predict competitor behavior from past competitor behavior. The result of such prediction is the assessed probability distribution in Table 10.1 and the 30% estimate of the probability of no competing bids.

The last element of the problem is the value model that transforms decisions and outcomes into monetary values for SciTools. The value model is straightforward in this example, but it can become quite complex in other applications, especially when the time value of money is involved and some quantities (such as the costs of environmental pollution) are difficult to quantify. If SciTools decides right now not to bid, then its monetary value is $0—no gain, no loss. If it makes a bid and is underbid by a competitor, then it loses $5000, the cost of preparing the bid. If it bids B dollars and wins the contract, then it makes a profit of $B - $100,000$, that is, B dollars for winning the bid, less $5000 for preparing the bid, less $95,000 for supplying the instruments. For example, if it bids $115,000 and the lowest competing bid, if any, is greater than $115,000, then SciTools makes a profit of $15,000.

It is often convenient to list the monetary outcomes in a **payoff table**, as shown in Table 10.2. For each possible decision and each possible outcome, the payoff table lists the monetary value to SciTools, where a positive value represents a profit and a negative value represents a loss. At the bottom of the table, we list the probabilities of the various outcomes. For example, the probability that the competitors' low bid is less than $115,000 is 0.7 (the probability of at least one competing bid) multiplied by 0.2 (the probability that the lowest competing bid is less than $115,000, given that there is at least one competing bid).

It is sometimes possible to simplify payoff tables to better understand the essence of the problem. In the present example, if SciTools bids, then the only necessary information about the competitors' bid is whether it is lower or higher than SciTools'

TABLE 10.2	Payoff Table for SciTools Bidding Example				
		Competitors' Low Bid ($1000s)			
		No Bid	<115	>115, <120	>120, <125	>125
SciTools'	No Bid	0	0	0	0	0
Bid	115	15	−5	15	15	15
($1000s)	120	20	−5	−5	20	20
	125	25	−5	−5	−5	25
	Probability	0.3	0.7(0.2)	0.7(0.4)	0.7(0.3)	0.7(0.1)

[1]The problem with a bid such as $117,000 is that the data in Table 10.1 make it impossible to calculate the probability of SciTools winning the contract if it bids this amount. Other than this, however, there is nothing that rules out such an "in-between" bid.

bid. That is, SciTools cares only whether it wins the contract or not. Therefore, an alternative way of presenting the payoff table is shown in Table 10.3.

The third and fourth columns of this table indicate the payoffs to SciTools, depending on whether it wins or loses the bid. The rightmost column shows the probability that SciTools wins the bid for each possible decision. For example, if SciTools bids $120,000, then it wins the bid if there are no competing bids (probability 0.3) or if there are competing bids but the lowest of these is greater than $120,000 (probability $0.7(0.3 + 0.1)$). In this case the total probability that SciTools wins the bid is $0.3 + 0.28 = 0.58$.

TABLE 10.3	Alternative Payoff Table for SciTools Bidding Example		
		Monetary value		**Probability That SciTools Wins**
		SciTools Wins	**SciTools Loses**	
SciTools'	**No bid**	NA	0	0.00
Bid	**115**	15	−5	0.86
($1000s)	**120**	20	−5	0.58
	125	25	−5	0.37

Risk Profiles From Table 10.3 we can obtain **risk profiles** for each of SciTools' decisions. A risk profile simply lists all possible monetary values and their corresponding probabilities. For example, if SciTools bids $120,000, there are two monetary values possible, a profit of $20,000 or a loss of $5000, and their probabilities are 0.58 and 0.42, respectively. On the other hand, if SciTools decides not to bid, there is a sure monetary value of $0—no profit, no loss.

A risk profile can also be illustrated graphically as a bar chart. There is a bar above each possible monetary value with height proportional to the probability of that value. For example, the risk profile for a $120,000 bid decision is a bar chart with two bars, one above −$5000 with height 0.42 and one above $20,000 with height 0.58. The risk profile for the "no bid" decision is even simpler. It has a single bar above $0 with height 1. We have not shown these bar charts for this example because they are so simple, but in more complex examples they can provide very useful information.

Expected Monetary Value (EMV) From the information we have discussed so far, it is not at all obvious which decision SciTools should make. The "no bid" decision is certainly safe, but it is certain to make zero profit. If SciTools decides to bid, the probability that it will lose $5000 is smallest with the $115,000 bid, but this bid has the smallest potential profit. Of course, if SciTools knew what the competitors were going to do, its decision would be easy. However, this uncertainty is the defining aspect of the problems in this chapter. The decision must be made *before* the uncertainty is resolved.

The most common way to make the choice is to calculate the **expected monetary value (EMV)** of each alternative and then choose the alternative with the largest EMV. The EMV is a weighted average of the possible monetary values, weighted by their probabilities. Formally, if v_i is the monetary value corresponding to outcome i and p_i is its probability, then EMV is defined as

$$\text{EMV} = \sum v_i p_i$$

In words, EMV is the mean of the probability distribution of possible monetary outcomes.

TABLE 10.4	EMVs for SciTools Bidding Example	
Alternative	**EMV Calculation**	**EMV**
No bid	0(1)	$0
Bid $115,000	15,000(0.86) + (−5000)(0.14)	$12,200
Bid $120,000	20,000(0.58) + (−5000)(0.42)	$9,500
Bid $125,000	25,000(0.37) + (−5000)(0.63)	$6,100

The EMVs for SciTools' problem are listed in Table 10.4. They indicate that if SciTools uses the EMV criterion for making its decision, it should bid $115,000, as this yields the largest EMV.

It is very important to understand what an EMV implies and what it does not imply. If SciTools bids $115,000, then its EMV is $12,200. However, SciTools will certainly *not* earn a profit of $12,200. It will earn $15,000 or it will lose $5000. So what does the EMV of $12,200 really mean? It means that if SciTools could enter many "gambles" like this, where on each gamble it would win $15,000 with probability 0.86 or lose $5000 with probability 0.14, then *on average* it would win $12,200 per gamble. In other words, the EMV can be interpreted as a long-term average.

It might seem peculiar, then, to base a one-time decision on EMV, which represents a long-term average. There are two ways to explain this apparent inconsistency. First, most companies make frequent decisions under uncertainty. Although each decision might have its own unique characteristics, it seems reasonable that if the company plans to make many such decisions, it should be willing to "play the averages," as it does when it uses EMV as the decision criterion. Second, even if this is the only such decision the company is *ever* going to make, decision theorists have proven that under certain conditions, maximizing EMV is a rational basis for making this decision. These "certain conditions" relate to the decision maker's attitude toward risk. As we will discuss later in this chapter, if the decision maker is risk averse and the possible monetary payoffs or losses are large relative to her wealth, then EMV is *not* the appropriate decision criterion to use. However, the EMV criterion has proved useful in the vast majority of decision-making applications, so we will use it throughout most of this chapter.

Decision Trees By now, we have gone through most of the steps of solving SciTools' problem. We have listed the decision alternatives, the uncertain outcomes and their probabilities, and the profits and losses from all combinations of decisions and outcomes. We have then calculated the EMV for each alternative and have chosen the alternative with the largest EMV. All of this can be done efficiently using a graphical tool called a **decision tree**. The decision tree that corresponds to SciTools' problem appears in Figure 10.1 (page 500). (This figure is actually part of an Excel spreadsheet and was created with the PrecisionTree add-in. We will explain how it was created shortly.)

Decision Tree Conventions To understand Figure 10.1, we need to know the following conventions that have been established for decision trees.

1. Decision trees are composed of **nodes** (circles, squares, and triangles) and **branches** (lines).

2. The nodes represent points in time. A **decision node** (a square) is a time when the decision maker makes a decision. A **probability node** (a circle) is a time when the result of an uncertain event becomes known. An **end node** (a triangle) indicates

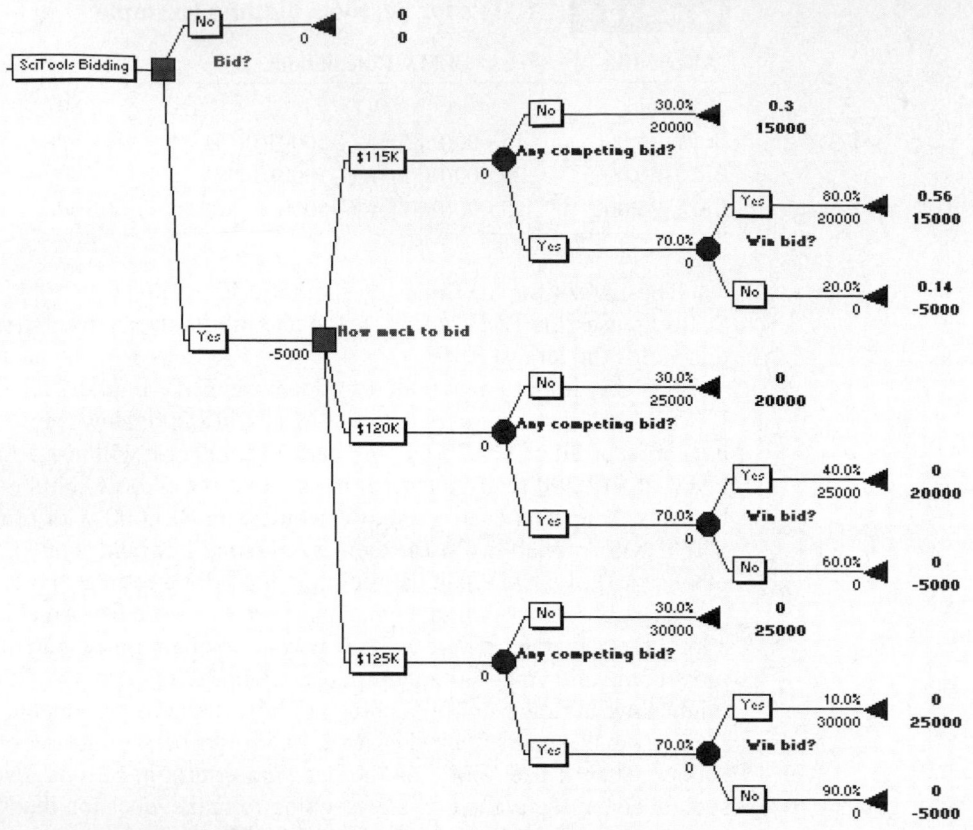

FIGURE 10.1 Decision Tree for SciTools Bidding Example

that the problem is completed—all decisions have been made, all uncertainty has been resolved, and all payoffs/costs have been incurred.

3. Time proceeds *from left to right*. This means that any branches leading into a node (from the left) have already occurred. Any branches leading out of a node (to the right) have not yet occurred.

4. Branches leading out of a decision node represent the possible decisions; the decision maker can choose the preferred branch. Branches leading out of probability nodes represent the possible outcomes of uncertain events; the decision maker has no control over which of these will occur.

5. Probabilities are listed on probability branches. These probabilities are *conditional* on the events that have already been observed (those to the left). Furthermore, the probabilities on branches leading out of any particular probability node must sum to 1.

6. Individual monetary values are shown on the branches where they occur, and cumulative monetary values are shown to the right of the end nodes. (Actually, PrecisionTree shows two values to the right of each end node. The top one is the probability of getting to that end node, and the bottom one is the associated monetary value.)

The decision tree in Figure 10.1 illustrates these conventions for a **single-stage** decision problem, the simplest type of decision problem. In a single-stage problem all decisions are made *first*, and then all uncertainty is resolved. Later in this chapter we will see **multistage** decision problems, where decisions and outcomes alternate. That is, a decision maker makes a decision, then some uncertainty is resolved, then the decision maker makes a second decision, then some further uncertainty is resolved, and so on. Because these multistage decisions problems are inherently more complex, we will focus initially on single-stage problems.

Once a decision tree has been drawn and labeled with probabilities and monetary values, it can be solved easily. The solution for the decision tree in Figure 10.1 is shown in Figure 10.2. Among other things, it shows that the decision to bid $115,000 is optimal (follow the decision branches with "True" above them), with a corresponding EMV of $12,200 (the value under "Bid?" at the left of the tree). This is consistent with what we saw earlier for this example.

Folding Back Procedure The solution procedure used to develop Figure 10.2 is called **folding back** on the tree. Starting at the right of the tree and working back to the left, the procedure consists of two types of calculations.

1. At each probability node, we calculate the EMV (sum of monetary values times probabilities) and write it below the name of the node. For example, consider the node (top right) after SciTools' decision to bid $115,000 and after it learns that

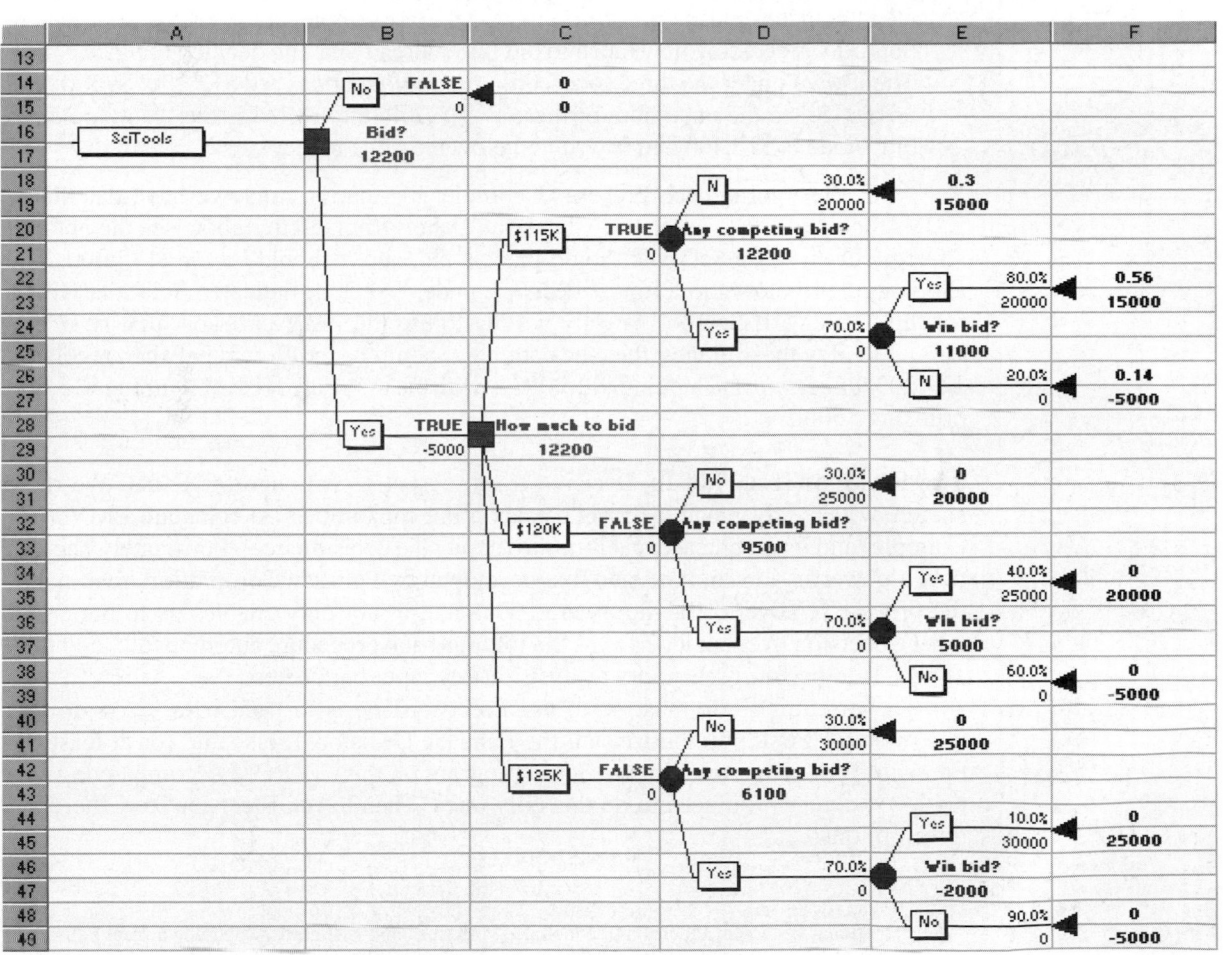

FIGURE 10.2 Result of Folding Back to Obtain Optimal Decision

there will be a competing bid. From that point, SciTools will either win $15,000 with probability 0.8 or lose $5000 with probability 0.2. The corresponding EMV is

$$0.8(15,000) + 0.2(-5000) = 11,000$$

and this value is entered below the node name "Win bid?".

Now, back up a step and consider the preceding probability node (the one to the left of the "Win bid?" node). At this point, SciTools has bid $115,000 and is about to discover whether there will be a competing bid. If there is none, with probability 0.3, then SciTools will win $15,000. But if there is a competing bid, with probability 0.7, the EMV from that point on is the $11,000 we just calculated. Essentially, this $11,000 summarizes the consequences of being at the "Win bid?" node, and SciTools acts the same as if it were going to receive $11,000 *for certain*. Therefore, the EMV for the "Any competing bid?" node is

$$0.3(15,000) + 0.7(11,000) = 12,200$$

This EMV is written below the node name.

2. Decision nodes are much easier. At each decision node we find the maximum of the EMVs and write it below the node name. PrecisionTree indicates the winner by placing "True" on the decision branch with the maximum EMV and "False" on all other branches emanating from this node. For example, consider the node where SciTools is deciding how much to bid (after already having decided to place a bid). The EMVs under the three succeeding *probability* nodes are $12,200, $9500, and $6100. Since the maximum of these is $12,200, the EMV for the "How much to bid" node is $12,200 and is written below the node name.

After the folding-back process is completed—that is, after we have calculated EMVs for all nodes—we can trace the "True" labels from left to right to see the optimal strategy. In this case SciTools should place a bid, and it should be for $115,000. The EMV written below the leftmost decision node, $12,200, indicates SciTools' EMV for this strategy. If SciTools is truly willing to use the EMV criterion, that is, if it is willing to play the averages, then the company should be indifferent between receiving $12,200 *for certain* and bidding $115,000—with the associated risk of winning $15,000 or losing $5000.

The PrecisionTree Add-In Decision trees present a challenge for Excel. We must somehow take advantage of Excel's calculating capabilities (to calculate EMVs, for example) and its graphical capabilities (to depict the decision tree). Fortunately, there is now a powerful add-in, PrecisionTree developed by Palisade Corporation, that makes the process relatively straightforward.[2] This add-in not only enables us to build and label a decision tree, but it performs the folding-back procedure automatically and then allows us to perform sensitivity analysis on key input parameters.

The first thing you must do to use PrecisionTree is to "add it in." You do this in two steps. First, you must install the Palisade Decision Tools suite (or at least the PrecisionTree program) with the Setup program on the CD-ROM accompanying this book. Of course, you need to do this only once. Then to run PrecisionTree, there are three options:

---

[2]The educational version of PrecisionTree included with this book is slightly scaled down from Palisade's commercial version of PrecisionTree. The difference you are most likely to notice is that the educational version permits only 50 nodes—of all types combined—in a decision tree.

- If Excel is not currently running, you can launch Excel *and* PrecisionTree by clicking on the Windows Start button and selecting the PrecisionTree item from the Palisade Decision Tools group of the Programs group.
- If Excel is currently running, the procedure in the previous bullet will launch PrecisionTree on top of Excel.
- If Excel is already running and the Decision Tools toolbar in Figure 10.3 is showing, you can start PrecisionTree by clicking on its icon (the third from the left).

FIGURE 10.3
Palisade Decision
Tools Toolbar

You will know that PrecisionTree is ready for use when you see its toolbar (shown in Figure 10.4) and a PrecisionTree menu to the left of the Help menu. By the way, if you want to unload PrecisionTree *without* closing Excel, use the PrecisionTree/Help/About menu item and click on Unload. It's a bit unconventional, but it works.

Using PrecisionTree PrecisionTree is quite easy to use—at least its most basic items are—but it can be confusing at first. We will lead you through the steps for the SciTools example. (The file SCITOOLS.XLS shows the results of this procedure, but you should work through the steps on your own, starting with a blank spreadsheet.)

1. **Inputs.** Enter the inputs shown in columns A and B of Figure 10.5.
2. **New tree.** Click on the new tree button (the far left button) on the PrecisionTree toolbar, and then click on any cell (say, cell A14) below the input section to start a new tree. Click on the name box of this new tree (it probably says "tree #1") to open a dialog box. Type in a descriptive name for the tree, such as SciTools Bidding, and click on OK. You should now see the beginnings of a tree, as shown in Figure 10.6 (page 504).
3. **Decision nodes and branches.** From here on, keep the finished tree in Figure 10.2 in mind. This is the finished product we eventually want. To obtain decision nodes

FIGURE 10.4
PrecisionTree
Toolbar

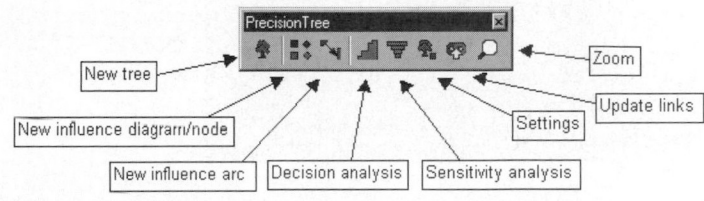

FIGURE 10.5
Inputs for SciTools
Bidding Example

	A	B	C
1	**SciTools Bidding Example**		
2			
3	**Inputs**		
4	Cost to prepare a bid	$5,000	
5	Cost to supply instruments	$95,000	
6			**Range names**
7	Probability of no competing bid	0.3	BidCost: B4
8	Comp bid distribution (if they		PrNoBid: B7
9	<$115K	0.2	ProdCost: B5
10	$115K to $120K	0.4	
11	$120K to $125K	0.3	
12	>$125K	0.1	

FIGURE 10.6
Beginnings of a New
Tree

11	$120K to $125K	0.3
12	>$125K	0.1
13		
14	SciTools Bidding	1
15		0
16		

and branches, click on the (only) triangle end node to open the dialog box in Figure 10.7. Click on the green square to indicate that this is a decision node, and fill in the dialog box as shown. We're calling this decision "Bid?" and specifying that there are two possible decisions. The tree expands as shown in Figure 10.8. The boxes that say "branch" show the default labels for these branches. Click on either of them to open another dialog box where you can provide a more descriptive name for the branch. Do this to label the two branches "No" and "Yes." Also, you can enter the immediate payoff/cost for either branch right below it. Since there is a $5000 cost of bidding, enter the formula

=-BidCost

right below the "Yes" branch in cell B19. (It is negative to reflect a *cost*.) The tree should now appear as in Figure 10.9.

4. **More decision branches.** The top branch is completed; if SciTools does not bid, there is nothing left to do. So click on the bottom end node, following SciTools' decision to bid, and proceed as in the previous step to add and label the decision

FIGURE 10.7
Dialog Box for
Adding a New
Decision Node and
Branches

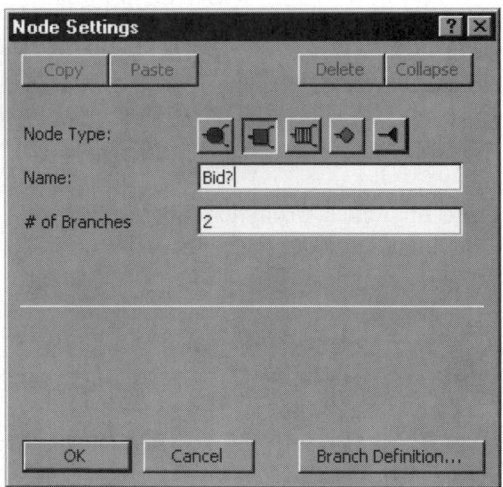

FIGURE 10.8
Tree with Initial
Decision Node and
Branches

14			branch	TRUE	1
15				0	0
16	SciTools Bidding			Bid?	
17				0	
18			branch	FALSE	0
19				0	0
20					

FIGURE 10.9
Decision Tree with
Decision Branches
Labeled

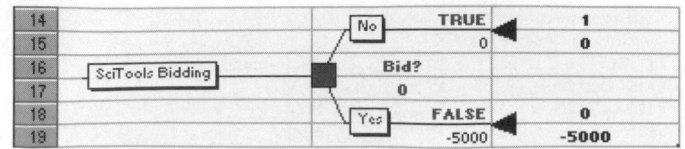

14			No	TRUE	1
15				0	0
16	SciTools Bidding			Bid?	
17				0	
18			Yes	FALSE	0
19				-5000	-5000

node and three decision branches for the amount to bid. (Refer to Figure 10.2.) The tree to this point should appear as in Figure 10.10. Note that there are no monetary values below these decision branches because no *immediate* payoffs or costs are associated with the bid amount decision.

5. **Probability nodes and branches.** We now need a probability node and branches from the rightmost end nodes to capture whether the competition bids. Click on the top one of these end nodes to bring up the same dialog box as in Figure 10.7. Now, however, click on the red circle box to indicate that this is a probability node. Label it "Any competing bid?", specify two branches, and click on OK. Then label the two branches "No" and "Yes." Next, repeat this procedure to form another probability node (with two branches) following the "Yes" branch, call it "Win bid?", and label its branches as shown in Figure 10.11.

6. **Copying probability nodes and branches.** You could now repeat the same procedure from the previous step to build probability nodes and branches following the other bid amount decisions, but because they're structurally equivalent, you can save a lot of work by using PrecisionTree's copy and paste feature. Click on the leftmost probability node to open a dialog box and click on Copy. Then click on either end node to bring up the same dialog box and click on Paste. Do this again with the other end node. Decision trees can get very "bushy," but this copy and paste feature can make them much less tedious to construct.

FIGURE 10.10
Tree with All Decision Nodes and Branches

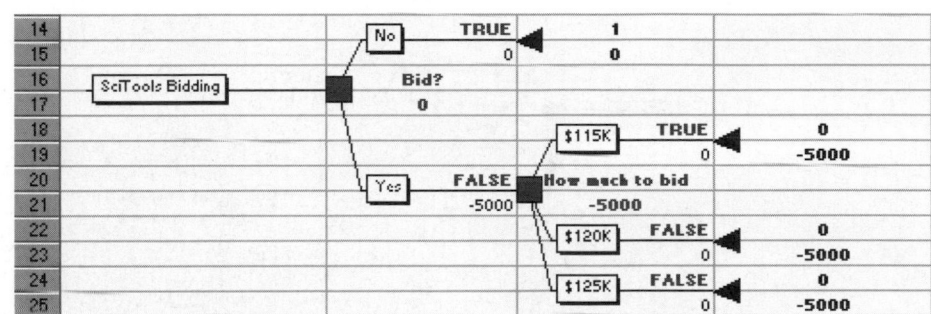

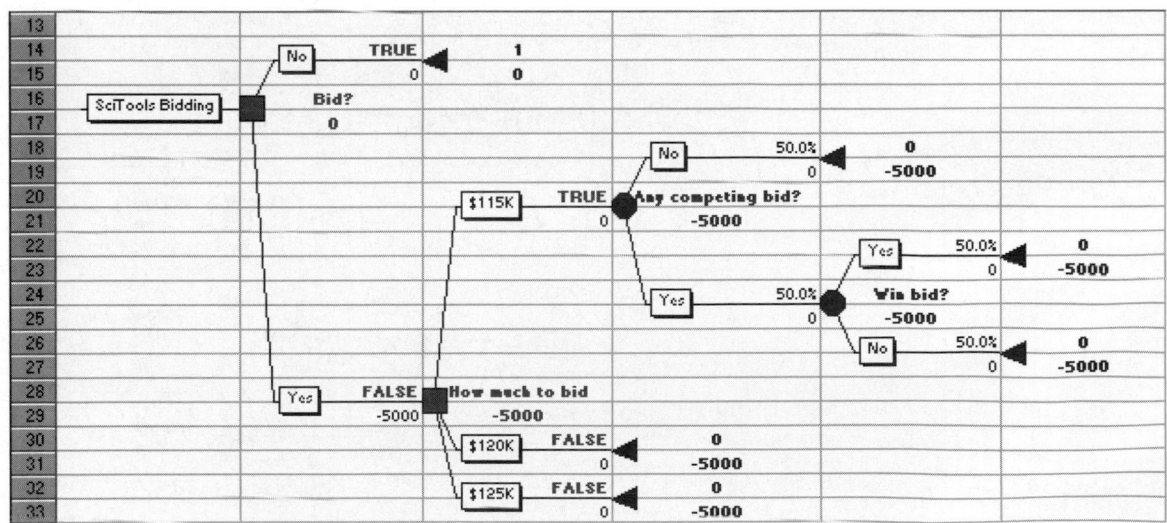

FIGURE 10.11 Decision Tree with One Set of Probability Nodes and Branches

7. **Labeling probability branches.** You should now have the decision tree shown in Figure 10.12. It is structurally the same as the completed tree in Figure 10.2, but the probabilities and monetary values on the probability branches are not correct. Note that each probability branch has a value above and below the branch. The value above is the probability (the default values make the branches equally likely), and the value below is the monetary value (the default values are 0). We can enter any values or formulas in these cells, exactly as we do in typical Excel worksheets. As usual, it is a good practice to refer to input cells in these formulas whenever possible. We'll get you started with the probability branches following the decision to bid $115,000. First, enter the probability of no competing bid in cell D18 with the formula

=PrNoBid

and enter its complement in cell D24 with the formula

=1-D18

Next, enter the probability that SciTools wins the bid in cell E22 with the formula

=SUM(B10:B12)

and enter its complement in cell E26 with the formula

=1-E22

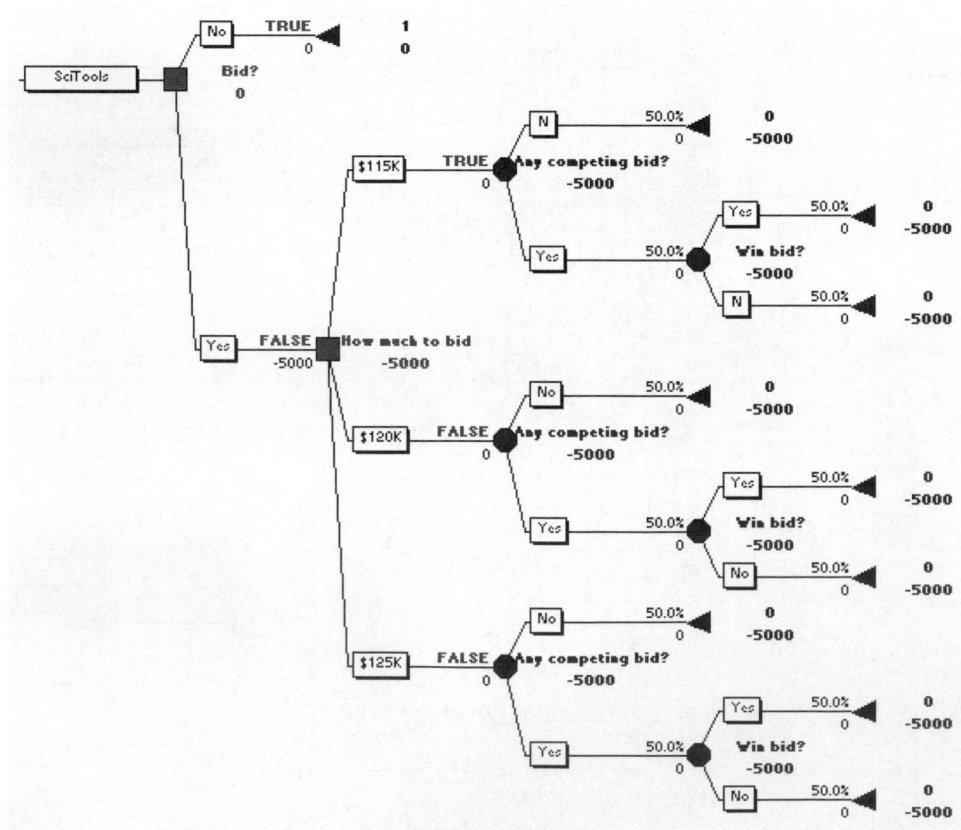

FIGURE 10.12 Structure of Completed Tree

(Remember that SciTools wins the bid only if the competitor bids higher, and in this part of the tree, SciTools is bidding $115,000.) For the monetary values, enter the formula

=115000-ProdCost

in the two cells, D19 and E23, where SciTools wins the contract. Note that we already subtracted the cost of the bid (cell B29), so we shouldn't do so again. This would be double-counting, and it should always be avoided in decision problems.

8. **Enter the other formulas on probability branches.** Using the previous step and Figure 10.2 as a guide, enter formulas for the probabilities and monetary values on the other probability branches, that is, those following the decision to bid $120,000 or $125,000.

We're finished! The completed tree in Figure 10.2 shows the best strategy and its associated EMV, as we discussed earlier. Note that we never have to perform the folding-back procedure manually. PrecisionTree does it for us. In fact, the tree is completed as soon as we finish entering the relevant inputs. In addition, if we change any of the inputs, the tree reacts automatically. For example, try changing the bid cost in cell B4 from $5000 to some large value such as $20,000. You'll see that the tree calculations update automatically, and the best decision is then *not* to bid, with an associated EMV of $0.

Risk Profile of Optimal Strategy Once the decision tree is completed, PrecisionTree has several tools we can use to gain more information about the decision analysis. First, we can see a risk profile and other information about the *optimal* decision. To do so, click on the fourth button from the left on the PrecisionTree toolbar (it looks like a staircase) and fill in the resulting dialog box as shown in Figure 10.13. (You can experiment with other options.) The Policy Suggestion option allows us to see only that part of the tree that corresponds to the best decision, as shown in Figure 10.14 (page 508).

The Risk Profile option allows us to see a graphical risk profile of the optimal decision. (If we checked the Statistics Report box, we would also see this information numerically.) As the risk profile in Figure 10.15 (page 508) shows, there are only two possible monetary outcomes if SciTools bids $115,000. It either wins $15,000 or loses $5000, and the former is much more likely. (The associated probabilities are 0.86 and 0.14.) This graphical information is even more useful when there are a larger number of possible monetary outcomes. We can see what they are and how likely they are.

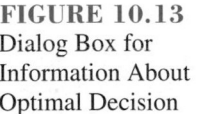

FIGURE 10.13
Dialog Box for Information About Optimal Decision

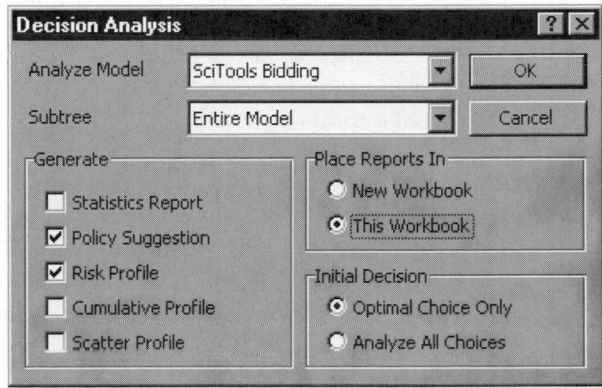

FIGURE 10.14
Subtree for Optimal
Decision

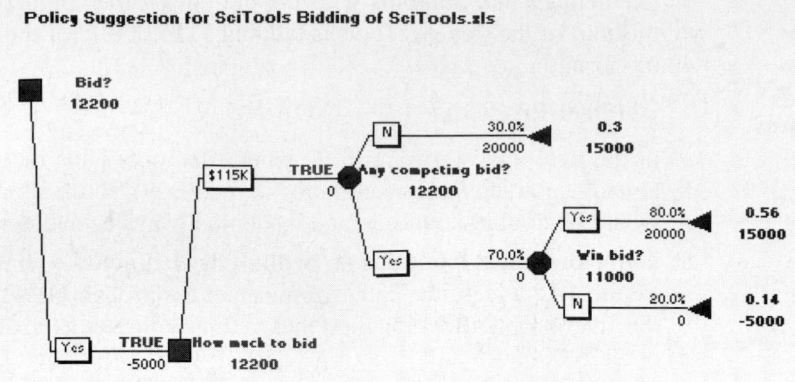

FIGURE 10.15
Risk Profile of
Optimal Decision

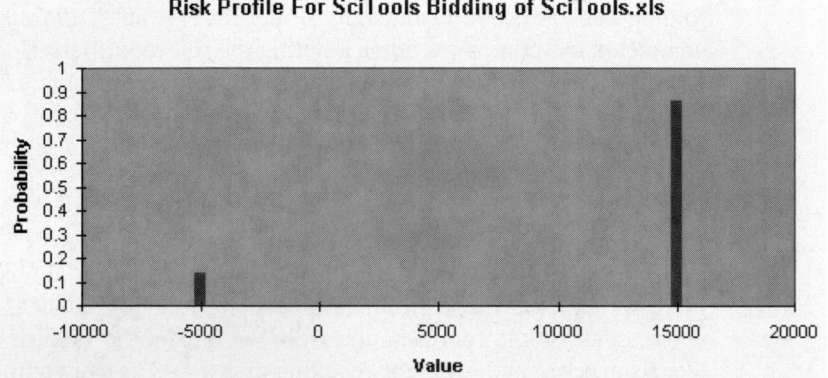

Sensitivity Analysis We have already stressed the importance of a follow-up sensitivity analysis for any decision problem, and PrecisionTree makes this relatively easy to perform. First, we can enter any values into the input cells and watch how the tree changes. But we can get more systematic information by clicking on PrecisionTree's sensitivity button, the fifth from the left on the toolbar (it looks like a tornado). This brings up the dialog box in Figure 10.16. It requires an EMV cell (and an optional descriptive name) to analyze at the top and one or more input cells in the middle. The specifications for these input cells are actually entered at the bottom of the dialog box.

The cell to analyze (at the top) is usually the EMV cell at the far left of the decision tree—this is the cell shown in the figure—but it can be any EMV cell. For example, if we *assume* SciTools will prepare a bid and we want to see how sensitive the EMV from that point on is to inputs, we could select cell C29 (refer to Figure 10.2) to analyze. Next, for any input cell such as the production cost cell (B5), we enter a minimum value, a maximum value, a base value (probably the original value in the model), and a step size. For example, to specify these for the production cost, we clicked on the Suggest Values button. This default setting varies the production cost by as much as 10% from the original value in either direction in a series of 10 steps. We can also enter our own desired values. We did so for the probability of no competing bids, varying its value from 0 to 0.6 in a sequence of 12 steps.

When we click on Run Analysis, PrecisionTree varies each of the specified inputs (one at a time if we select the One Way option) and presents the results in several ways in a *new* Excel file with Sensitivity, Tornado, and Spider Graph sheets. The Sensitivity sheet includes several charts, a typical one of which appears in Figure 10.17. This shows how the EMV varies with the production cost for *both* of the original decisions

FIGURE 10.16
Sensitivity Analysis
Dialog Box

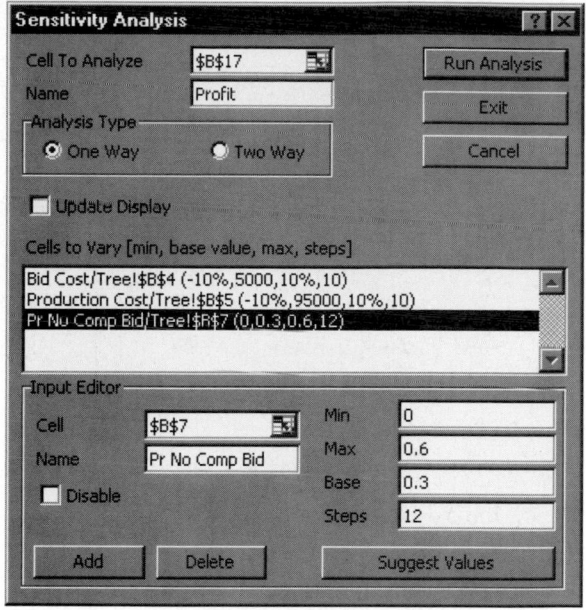

FIGURE 10.17
EMV versus
Production Cost for
Each of Two
Decisions

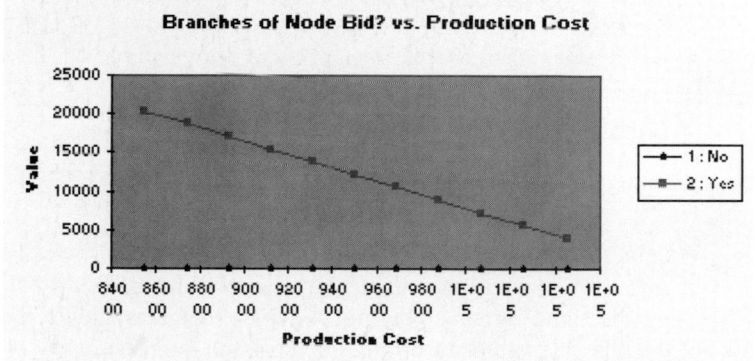

(bid or don't bid). This type of graph is useful for seeing whether the optimal decision *changes* over the range of the input variable. It does so only if the two lines cross. In this particular graph it is clear that the "Bid" decision dominates the "No bid" decision over the production cost range we selected.

The Tornado sheet shows how sensitive the EMV of the *optimal* decision is to each of the selected inputs over the ranges selected. (See Figure 10.18 (page 510).) The length of each bar shows the percentage change in the EMV in either direction, so the longer the bar, the more sensitive this EMV is to the particular input. The bars are always arranged from longest on top to shortest on the bottom—hence the name *tornado* chart. Here we see that production cost has the largest effect on EMV, and bid cost has the smallest effect.

Finally, the Spider Chart sheet contains the chart in Figure 10.19. It shows how much the optimal EMV varies in magnitude for various percentage changes in the input variables. The steeper the slope of the line, the more the EMV is affected by a particular input. We again see that the production cost has a relatively large effect, whereas the other two inputs have relatively small effects.

Each time we click on the sensitivity button, we can run a different sensitivity analysis. An interesting option is to run a two-way analysis (by clicking on the Two

FIGURE 10.18
Tornado Chart for
SciTools Example

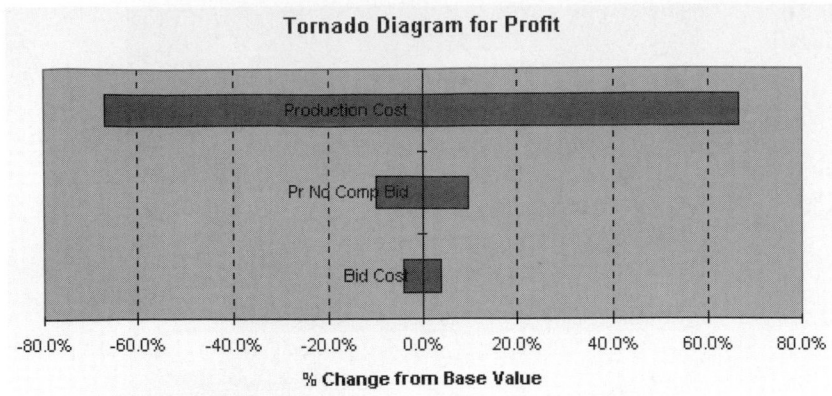

FIGURE 10.19
Spider Chart for
SciTools Example

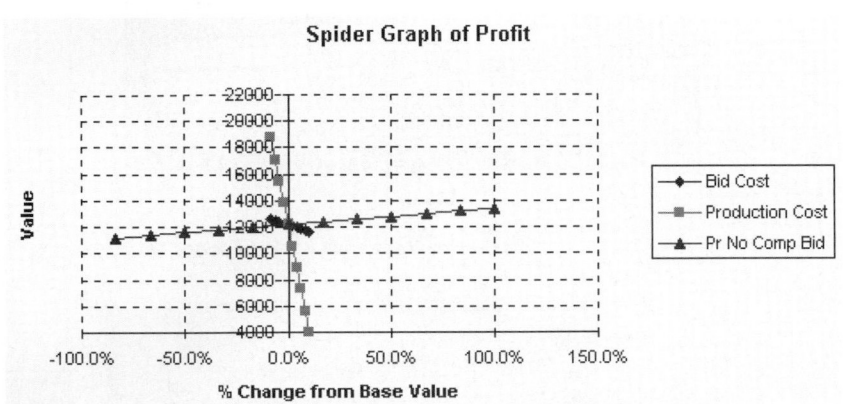

Way button in Figure 10.16). Then we see how the selected EMV varies as each *pair* of inputs vary simultaneously. We analyzed the EMV in cell C29 with this option, using the same inputs as before. A typical result is shown in Figure 10.20. For each of the possible values of production cost and the probability of no competitor bid, this chart indicates which bid amount is optimal. (By choosing cell C29, we are assuming SciTools will bid; the question is only how much.) As we see, the optimal bid amount remains $115,000 unless the production cost *and* the probability of no competing bid are both large. Then it becomes optimal to bid $125,000. This makes sense intuitively. As the chance of no competing bid increases and a larger production cost must be recovered, it seems reasonable that SciTools should increase its bid.

FIGURE 10.20
Two-Way Sensitivity
Analysis

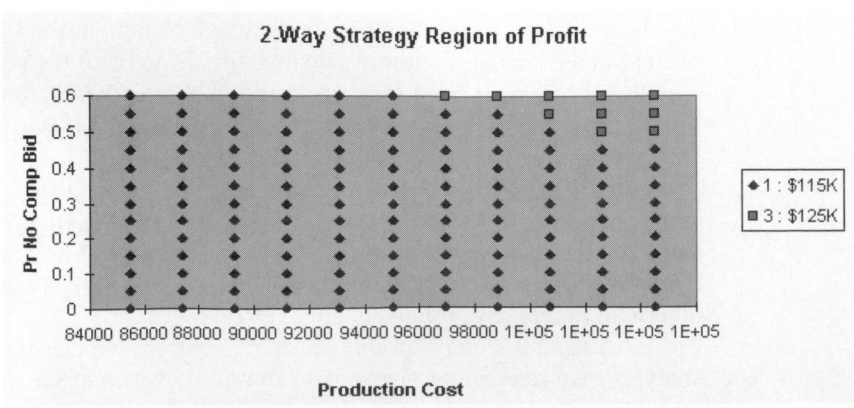

We reiterate that a sensitivity analysis is always an important aspect in real decision analyses. If we had to construct decision trees by hand—with paper and pencil—a sensitivity analysis would be virtually out of the question. We would have to recompute everything each time through. Therefore, one of the most valuable features of the PrecisionTree add-in is that it enables us to perform sensitivity analyses in a matter of seconds. ■

PROBLEMS

Skill-Building Problems

1. The SweetTooth Candy Company knows it will need 10 tons of sugar 6 months from now to implement its production plans. Jean Dobson, SweetTooth's purchasing manager, has essentially two options for acquiring the needed sugar. She can either buy the sugar at the going market price when she needs it, 6 months from now, or she can buy a futures contract now. The contract guarantees delivery of the sugar in 6 months but the cost of purchasing it will be based on today's market price. Assume that possible sugar futures contracts available for purchase are for 5 tons or 10 tons only. No futures contracts can be purchased or sold in the intervening months. Thus, SweetTooth's possible decisions are: (1) purchase a futures contract for 10 tons of sugar now, (2) purchase a futures contract for 5 tons of sugar now and purchase 5 tons of sugar in 6 months, or (3) purchase all 10 tons of needed sugar in 6 months. The price of sugar bought now for delivery in 6 months is $0.0851 per pound. The transaction costs for 5-ton and 10-ton futures contracts are $65 and $110, respectively. Finally, Ms. Dobson has assessed the probability distribution for the possible prices of sugar 6 months from now (in dollars per pound). Table 10.5 contains these possible prices and their corresponding probabilities.

   a. Given that SweetTooth wants to acquire the needed sugar in the least-cost way, formulate a payoff table that specifies the cost (in dollars) associated with each possible decision and possible sugar price in the future.

   b. Use the PrecisionTree add-in to identify the strategy that minimizes SweetTooth's expected cost of meeting its sugar demand. Also, perform sensitivity analysis on the optimal decision and

summarize your findings. In response to which model inputs is the expected cost value more sensitive?

   c. Generate a risk profile for SweetTooth's optimal decision.

2. Carlisle Tire and Rubber, Inc. is considering expanding production to meet potential increases in the demand for one of its tire products. Carlisle's alternatives are to construct a new plant, expand the existing plant, or do nothing in the short run. The market for this particular tire product may expand, remain stable, or contract. Carlisle's marketing department estimates the probabilities of these market outcomes as 0.25, 0.35, and 0.40, respectively. Table 10.6 contains Carlisle's estimated payoff (in dollars) table.

   a. Use the PrecisionTree add-in to identify the strategy that maximizes this tire manufacturer's expected profit. Also, perform sensitivity analysis on the optimal decision and summarize your findings. In response to which model inputs is the expected profit value most sensitive?

TABLE 10.5 **Distribution of Possible Sugar Prices**

Possible Sugar Prices in 6 Months ($/pound)	Probability
0.078	0.05
0.083	0.25
0.087	0.35
0.091	0.20
0.096	0.15

TABLE 10.6 **Payoff Table for Carlisle's Decision Problem**

Decision/Market Outcome	Market Expands	Market Stable	Market Contracts
Construct a new plant	400,000	−100,000	−200,000
Expand existing plant	250,000	−50,000	−75,000
Do nothing	50,000	0	−30,000

b. Generate a risk profile for Carlisle's optimal decision.

3. A local energy provider offers a landowner $180,000 for the exploration rights to natural gas on a certain site and the option for future development. This option, if exercised, is worth an additional $1,800,000 to the landowner, but this will occur only if natural gas is discovered during the exploration phase. The landowner, believing that the energy company's interest in the site is a good indication that gas is present, is tempted to develop the field herself. To do so, she must contract with local experts in natural gas exploration and development. The initial cost for such a contract is $300,000, which is lost forever if no gas is found on the site. If gas is discovered, however, the landowner expects to earn a net profit of $6,000,000. Finally, the landowner estimates the probability of finding gas on this site to be 60%.

   a. Formulate a payoff table that specifies the landowner's payoff (in dollars) associated with each possible decision and each outcome with respect to finding natural gas on the site.

   b. Use the PrecisionTree add-in to identify the strategy that maximizes the landowner's expected net earnings from this opportunity. Also, perform sensitivity analysis on the optimal decision and summarize your findings. In response to which model inputs is the expected profit value most sensitive?

   c. Generate a risk profile for landowner's optimal decision.

4. Techware Incorporated is considering the introduction of two new software products to the market. In particular, the company has four options regarding these two proposed products: introduce neither product, introduce product 1 only, introduce product 2 only, or introduce both products. Research and development costs for products 1 and 2 are $180,000 and $150,000, respectively. Note that the first option entails no costs because research and development efforts have not yet begun. The success of these software products depends on the trend of the national economy in the coming year and on the consumers' reaction to these products. The company's revenues earned by introducing product 1 only, product 2 only, or both products in various states of the national economy are given in Table 10.7. The probabilities of observing a strong, fair, and weak trend in the national economy in the coming year are 0.30, 0.50, and 0.20, respectively.

   a. Formulate a payoff table that specifies Techware's net revenue (in dollars) for each possible decision and each outcome with respect to the trend in the national economy.

   b. Use the PrecisionTree add-in to identify the strategy that maximizes Techware's expected net revenue from the given marketing opportunities. Also, perform sensitivity analysis on the optimal decision and summarize your findings. In response to which model inputs is the expected net revenue value most sensitive?

   c. Generate a risk profile for Techware's optimal decision.

5. Consider an investor with $10,000 available to invest. He has the following options regarding the allocation of his available funds: (1) he can invest in a risk-free savings account with a guaranteed 3% annual rate of return; (2) he can invest in a fairly safe stock, where the possible annual rates of return are 6%, 8%, or 10%; or (3) he can invest in a more risky stock where the possible annual rates of return are 1%, 9%, or 17%. Note that the investor can place all of his available funds in any one of these options, or he can split his $10,000 into two $5000 investments in any two of these options. The joint probability distribution of the possible return rates for the two stocks is given in Table 10.8.

   a. Formulate a payoff table that specifies this investor's return (in dollars) in one year for each possible decision and each outcome with respect to the two stock returns.

   b. Use the PrecisionTree add-in to identify the strategy that maximizes the investor's expected earnings in one year from the given investment opportunities. Also, perform sensitivity analysis on the optimal decision and summarize your findings. In response to which model inputs is the expected earnings value most sensitive?

   c. Generate a risk profile for this investor's optimal decision.

6. A buyer for a large department store chain must place orders with an athletic shoe manufacturer 6 months prior to the time the shoes will be sold in the department stores. In particular, the buyer must

TABLE 10.7 Revenue Table for Techware's Decision Problem

Decision/Trend in National Economy	Strong	Fair	Weak
Introduce neither product	$0	$0	$0
Introduce product 1 only	$500,000	$260,000	$120,000
Introduce product 2 only	$420,000	$230,000	$110,000
Introduce both products	$820,000	$390,000	$200,000

TABLE 10.8	**Joint Probability Distribution of Safe and Risky Stock Return Rates**		
Safe Stock Return Rates (S)/ Risky Stock Return Rates (R)	**$R = 1\%$**	**$R = 9\%$**	**$R = 17\%$**
$S = 6\%$	0.10	0.05	0.10
$S = 8\%$	0.25	0.05	0.20
$S = 10\%$	0.10	0.05	0.10

decide on November 1 how many pairs of the manufacturer's newest model of tennis shoes to order for sale during the upcoming summer season. Assume that each pair of this new brand of tennis shoes costs the department store chain $45 per pair. Furthermore, assume that each pair of these shoes can then be sold to the chain's customers for $70 per pair. Any pairs of these shoes remaining unsold at the end of the summer season will be sold in a closeout sale next fall for $35 each. The probability distribution of consumer demand for these tennis shoes (in hundreds of pairs) during the upcoming summer season has been assessed by market research specialists and is provided in Table 10.9. Finally, assume that the department store chain must purchase these tennis shoes from the manufacturer in lots of 100 pairs.

TABLE 10.9	**Distribution of Consumer Demand for Tennis Shoes**
Consumer Demand	**Probability**
1	0.025
2	0.050
3	0.075
4	0.100
5	0.150
6	0.200
7	0.175
8	0.100
9	0.075
10	0.050

a. Formulate a payoff table that specifies the contribution to profit (in dollars) from the sale of the tennis shoes by this department store chain for each possible purchase decision (in hundreds of pairs) and each outcome with respect to consumer demand.

b. Use the PrecisionTree add-in to identify the strategy that maximizes the department store chain's expected profit earned by purchasing and subsequently selling pairs of the new tennis shoes. Also, perform sensitivity analysis on the optimal decision and summarize your findings. In response to which model inputs is the expected earnings value most sensitive?

c. Generate a risk profile for the buyer's optimal decision.

Skill-Extending Problems

7. In designing a new space vehicle, NASA needs to decide whether to provide 0, 1, or 2 backup systems for a critical component of the vehicle. The first backup system, if included, comes into use only if the original system fails. The second backup system, if included, comes into use only if the original system and the first backup system both fail. NASA engineers claim that each system, independently of the others, has a 1% chance of failing if called into use. Each backup system costs $70,000 to produce and install within the vehicle. Once the vehicle is in flight, the mission will be scrubbed only if the original system and all backups fail. The cost of a scrubbed mission, in addition to production costs, is assessed to be $8,000,000.

a. Use the PrecisionTree add-in to identify the strategy that minimizes NASA's expected total cost. Also, perform sensitivity analysis on the optimal decision and summarize your findings. In response to which model inputs is the expected earnings value most sensitive?

b. Generate a risk profile for NASA's optimal decision.

8. Mr. Maloy has just bought a new $30,000 sport utility vehicle. As a reasonably safe driver, he believes that there is only about a 5% chance of being in an accident in the forthcoming year. If he is involved in an accident, the damage to his new vehicle depends on the severity of the accident. The probability distribution for the range of possible accidents and the corresponding damage amounts (in dollars) are given in Table 10.10 (page 514). Mr. Maloy is trying to decide whether he is willing to pay $170 each year for collision insurance with a $300 deductible. Note that with this type of insurance, he pays the *first* $300 in damages if he causes an accident and the insurance company pays the remainder.

TABLE 10.10	Distribution of Accident Types and Corresponding Damage Amounts	
Type of Accident	Conditional Probability	Damage to Vehicle
Minor	0.60	$200
Moderate	0.20	$1,000
Serious	0.10	$4,000
Catastrophic	0.10	$30,000

TABLE 10.11	Distribution of Defective Components in a Lot
Proportion of Defective Components	Probability
0.05	0.50
0.10	0.25
0.25	0.15
0.50	0.10

a. Formulate a payoff table that specifies the cost (in dollars) associated with each possible decision and type of accident.

b. Use the PrecisionTree add-in to identify the strategy that minimizes Mr. Maloy's annual expected total cost. Also, perform sensitivity analysis on the optimal decision and summarize your findings. In response to which model inputs is the expected earnings value most sensitive?

c. Generate a risk profile for Mr. Maloy's optimal decision.

9. The purchasing agent for a microcomputer manufacturer is currently negotiating a purchase agreement for a particular electronic component with a given supplier. This component is produced in lots of 1000, and the cost of purchasing a lot is $30,000. Unfortunately, past experience indicates that this supplier has occasionally shipped defective components to its customers. Specifically, the proportion of defective components supplied by this supplier is described by the probability distribution given in Table 10.11. While the microcomputer manufacturer can repair a defective component at a cost of $20

each, the purchasing agent is intrigued to learn that this supplier will now assume the cost of replacing defective components in excess of the first 100 faulty items found in a given lot. This guarantee may be purchased by the microcomputer manufacturer prior to the receipt of a given lot at a cost of $1000 per lot. The purchasing agent is interested in determining whether it is worthwhile for her company to purchase the supplier's guarantee policy.

a. Formulate a payoff table that specifies the microcomputer manufacturer's total cost (in dollars) of purchasing and repairing (if necessary) a complete lot of components for each possible decision and each outcome with respect to the proportion of defective items.

b. Use the PrecisionTree add-in to identify the strategy that minimizes the expected total cost of achieving a complete lot of satisfactory microcomputer components. Also, perform sensitivity analysis on the optimal decision and summarize your findings. In response to which model inputs is the expected earnings value most sensitive?

c. Generate a risk profile for the purchasing agent's optimal decision.

10.3 MORE SINGLE-STAGE EXAMPLES

All applications of decision making under uncertainty follow the procedures discussed so far. We first identify the possible decision alternatives, assess relevant probabilities, and calculate monetary values. Then we use a decision tree (or influence diagram) to identify the alternative with the largest EMV and follow this up with a thorough sensitivity analysis. We can also examine the risk profiles for the various alternatives. This is particularly useful if criteria other than EMV maximization are considered, as we will discuss in Section 7.8. In this section we will illustrate the process with several single-stage examples, where the decision maker makes one decision and then learns which of several uncertain outcomes occurs. In the next section we will examine multistage examples, where two or more sequential decisions must be made.

The following example illustrates a decision problem most of us face on an annual basis, although most of us probably do not go to the trouble of analyzing it formally.

EXAMPLE   10.2

SELECTING HEALTH CARE PLANS AT STATE UNIVERSITY

Each year employees at State University are asked to decide on one of three health care plans. The terms of these are as follows:[3]

Plan 1: The monthly cost is $24. There is a $500 deductible. The participant pays all expenses until payments for the year equal $500. After that, 90% of remaining expenses are paid by the insurer.

Plan 2: This is the same as plan 1, except that the monthly cost is $1 and the deductible amount is $1000.

Plan 3: The monthly cost is $20. There is no deductible. The employee pays 30% of all medical expenses. The rest is paid by the insurer.

Which of these three plans should an employee choose?

Solution

Clearly, the solution will vary from one employee to another, depending on the assessed probability distribution of medical expenses. To illustrate, however, we will consider an employee who assesses the distribution of yearly medical expenses shown in Table 10.12. These expenses include hospital visits, surgery, office visits, and prescriptions, all of which are covered under the terms of the plans. As in the previous example, this distribution is only an approximation of the real distribution, which would contain a continuum of expenses. However, it is probably adequate for making a decision among the three plans.

TABLE 10.12	Distribution of Medical Expenses for Insurance Example
Total Medical Expense	**Probability**
$200	0.30
$600	0.50
$1000	0.15
$5000	0.03
$15,000	0.02

The next step is to determine the employee's cost for each plan and each outcome. For example, suppose that the employee chooses plan 1 and incurs $600 in expenses. Then the total cost is the cost of the insurance plus the full amount of the first $500 in expenses plus 10% of the last $100 in expenses, that is,

$$24(12) + 500 + 0.1(100) = \$798$$

However, if this employee's medical expenses are only $200, then the cost is

$$24(12) + 200 = \$488$$

[3] We assume that these terms apply only to the employee; that is, these are not family plans.

The costs for the other plans and other outcomes can be calculated in a similar manner. We list all of the costs in Table 10.13.

The choice is certainly not clear from this table. The plan with the lowest premium, plan 2, looks good if the year's medical expenses are low. This is also true for the no-deductible plan, plan 3, although its cost is quite large in case of a disaster. For moderate medical expenses, plan 1 is obviously inferior, but it is the best for guarding against a disaster. These trade-offs could be illustrated by risk profiles, which you might want to examine. Instead, we turn directly to the decision tree.

TABLE 10.13	Employee Cost Table for Insurance Example		
Medical Expense	**Plan 1**	**Plan 2**	**Plan 3**
$200	$488	$212	$300
$600	$798	$612	$420
$1000	$838	$1012	$540
$5000	$1238	$1412	$1740
$15,000	$2238	$2412	$4740

USING PRECISIONTREE

The decision tree can be formed with the following steps.

1 **Inputs.** Enter the inputs for the three plans and the probabilities from Table 10.12 in the top left portion of the spreadsheet (down to row 15). (See Figure 10.21 and the file MEDICAL.XLS.)

2 **Cost table.** For later use in the decision tree, calculate the costs to the employee (not counting insurance premiums) in the range B19:D23. To do this, enter the formula

=IF($A19<=B$6,$A19,B$6+B$7*($A19-B$6))

FIGURE 10.21
Inputs and Cost Table for Medical Example

	A	B	C	D
1	**Medical insurance problem**			
2				
3	Inputs for plans			
4		Plan1	Plan2	Plan3
5	Monthly cost	$24	$1	$20
6	Deductible	$500	$1,000	$0
7	Copay Pct	10%	10%	30%
8				
9	Distribution of medical expenses			
10		Expense	Prob	
11		$200	0.3	
12		$600	0.5	
13		$1,000	0.15	
14		$5,000	0.03	
15		$15,000	0.02	
16				
17	Out of pocket cost table (plan along top, expense along side), not including premiums			
18		Plan1	Plan2	Plan3
19	$200	$200	$200	$60
20	$600	$510	$600	$180
21	$1,000	$550	$1,000	$300
22	$5,000	$950	$1,400	$1,500
23	$15,000	$1,950	$2,400	$4,500

in cell B19 and copy this to the range B19:D23. This IF function says that if the medical expense is less than the deductible, the employee pays it all. Otherwise, the employee pays the deductible amount plus a percentage of the remainder.

3 **Decision tree.** Use PrecisionTree to create the decision tree shown in Figure 10.22. Here are some tips. First, create the decision node and decision branches, and enter formulas for their values as 12 times the relevant monthly premiums. Then create a single probability node and its branches, label the branches, and enter formulas for the probabilities with *absolute* references. For example, enter the formula

=$C$11

for the probability of the top branch. Next, copy the probability node to the end nodes below it. (Do you see the effect of the absolute references?) Finally, link the values for all of the probability branches to the cells in the cost table. (We know of no quick way to do this. We entered 15 separate formulas, one for each branch. However, it is much easier to create a cost table and link branch formulas to it than to create the branch formulas directly from input values.)

4 **Minimize costs.** If we quit here, we would mistakenly choose the *worst* of the three plans. This is because PrecisionTree *maximizes* EMV by default, and in this problem we want to *minimize* the EMV of the costs. However, this is simple to change. Click on the name box at the far left in the decision tree. This brings up a dialog box (not shown here) where we can select the Minimize option.

FIGURE 10.22
Decision Tree for
Medical Insurance
Example

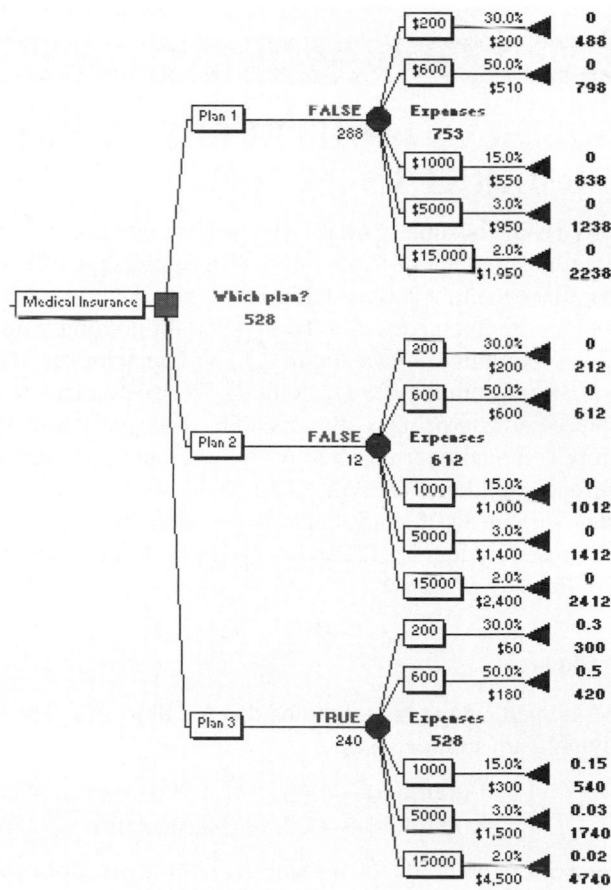

As we see from Figure 10.22, the optimal plan is plan 3. Its EMV—an expected *cost*—is $528. The EMVs for plans 1 and 2 are $753 and $612. Evidently, this employee's chances of large medical expenses where plan 3 is at its worst are not large enough to outweigh plan 3's no-deductible benefit. However, we might want to experiment with various inputs, either the properties of the plans or the employee's medical expense distribution, to see whether plan 3 continues to be the preferred plan. For example, if the probabilities in Table 10.12 change to 0.30, 0.40, 0.15, 0.10, and 0.05, so that large expenses are much more probable, the EMVs for the three plans become $827, $722, and $750. Now plan 2 is preferred, although the difference in EMV between plans 2 and 3 is quite small.

We can use this insurance example to illustrate one *nonmonetary* aspect of decision problems that is difficult to incorporate into a decision tree. At the university where we teach, there is another insurance plan in addition to the types in the example. Its premiums are low, and there are *no* copayments—the insurer pays all medical expenses. This plan is clearly the cheapest of all plans offered, but it is not chosen by many employees. Why? The plan is through an HMO, where all employees must go to a specified set of physicians; otherwise, the plan does not pay their expenses. Evidently, many employees believe that the "cost" of having to go to physicians they would not choose otherwise outweighs the dollar savings from the plan. ■

The following example illustrates one method for using a *continuous* probability distribution in a decision tree model.

EXAMPLE 10.3

PURCHASING LIGHTBULBS AT FRESHWAY SUPERMARKETS

FreshWay, a chain of supermarkets, requires 24,000 fluorescent lightbulbs for its stores. There are two suppliers of these lightbulbs. Supplies A offers them at $4.00 per bulb and will replace the first 900 defective bulbs with guaranteed good ones for $3.00 each. It will replace all defectives after the first 900 for nothing. Supplier B is similar. It will charge $4.15 per bulb, replace the first 1200 defectives for $1.00 each, and replace all defectives after the first 1200 for nothing. FreshWay plans to sell these lightbulbs for $4.40 apiece and charge its customers nothing for replacement of defectives. The only uncertainty is the number of defective bulbs from either supplier. Based on historical data from each supplier, FreshWay believes that the percentage of defectives is normally distributed with mean 4% and standard deviation 1% from supplier A, and mean 4.2% and standard deviation 1.2% from supplier B. Which supplier should be chosen to maximize FreshWay's EMV?

Solution

Let p be the percentage of lightbulbs that are defective. Then the profit to FreshWay from buying from supplier A is

$$\text{Profit} = \begin{cases} 24{,}000(4.40 - 4.00) - (24{,}000p)(3.00) & \text{if } p \leq 900/24{,}000 \\ 24{,}000(4.40 - 4.00) - (900)(3.00) & \text{if } p > 900/24{,}000 \end{cases}$$

A similar expression holds for supplier B. The only random quantity in this expression is p, which is normally distributed. The question is how we can model the *continuous* distribution of p in a *discrete* decision tree—that is, a tree with a discrete number of probability branches. The method usually used is to approximate the continuous normal distribution by a discrete distribution with a relatively small number, say 5, of equally likely values.

The idea is to divide the normal distribution into an equal number of equal probability regions and take the midpoint (in a probability sense) of each region as a value for the decision tree. For example, if we use five points, then each region has probability 0.2. The probability halfway between 0 and 0.2 is 0.1, so the first point on the tree is the 10th percentile of the normal distribution. Similarly, the next point is the 30th percentile, the next is the 50th, the next is the 70th, and the last is the 90th.

Figure 10.23 illustrates the calculations. (See the file LIGHTBULB.XLS.) Through row 13 we enter the given inputs for the problem. Then in rows 17–26 we enter the information we'll use in the decision tree regarding the percentage defective for each supplier. This information is based on the five-point approximation to the normal distribution. For example, the 10th percentile of the normal distribution for supplier A is found in cell C17 with the formula

=NORMINV(B17,\$B\$12,\$C\$12)

and this is copied down to cell C21. Then the cost to FreshWay from defectives, assuming the value in C17 is the percentage of defectives, is calculated in cell D17 with the formula

=\$C\$7*IF(C17<=\$D\$7/Quantity,Quantity*C17,\$D\$7)

and it is copied down to cell D21. Similar formulas are used for supplier B.

FIGURE 10.23
Inputs and Calculations for Lightbulb Example

	A	B	C	D
1	FreshWay lightbulb purchasing example			
2			Range names	
3	Quantity	24000	Quantity: B3	
4	Selling price	$4.40	SellingPrice: B4	
5				
6		UnitCost	ReplaceCost	Charge for first:
7	Supplier A	$4.00	$3.00	900
8	Supplier B	$4.15	$1.00	1200
9				
10	Distribution of percent defective: normal			
11		Mean	Stdev	
12	Supplier A	4.0%	1.0%	
13	Supplier B	4.2%	1.2%	
14				
15	Percentages to use on decision tree			
16		Midpoint probability	Percentile	FreshWay's cost
17	Supplier A	0.1	2.72%	$1,957.28
18		0.3	3.48%	$2,502.43
19		0.5	4.00%	$2,700.00
20		0.7	4.52%	$2,700.00
21		0.9	5.28%	$2,700.00
22	Supplier B	0.1	2.66%	$638.91
23		0.3	3.57%	$856.97
24		0.5	4.20%	$1,008.00
25		0.7	4.83%	$1,159.03
26		0.9	5.74%	$1,200.00

USING PRECISIONTREE

It is now straightforward to construct the decision tree shown in Figure 10.24 (page 520). We enter the revenue from selling the bulbs and the cost of purchasing them in cells B33 and B47. For example, the formula in cell B33 is

=Quantity*(SellingPrice-B7)

FIGURE 10.24
Decision Tree for
Lightbulb Example

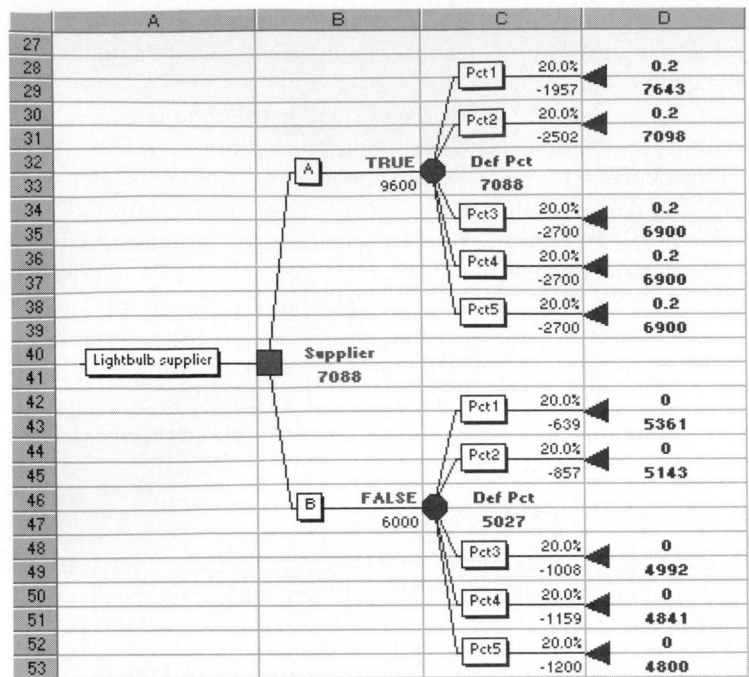

Then we link the monetary values below the probability branches to the relevant cells in the D17:D26 range.

The EMVs for suppliers A and B are $7088 and $5027, so supplier A is the clear choice. Evidently, the higher price charged by supplier B and its slightly higher mean percentage of defects outweigh its better deal on replacing defectives. Of course, if supplier B really wants to get FreshWay's business, it could attempt to sweeten its deal in a number of ways. Sensitivity analysis is useful to see how the EMV for supplier B (in cell C47) is affected by the various input parameters. We tried this, varying the inputs in cells B8, C8, D8, and B13 by PrecisionTree's default values (10% in either direction) and keeping track of the change in the EMV for supplier B. The tornado chart in Figure 10.25 makes it very clear that the most important input is the unit purchase cost. The effects of the other three inputs are practically negligible in comparison. If supplier B wants FreshWay's business, it will have to lower its unit purchase cost.

FIGURE 10.25
Tornado Chart to
Analyze the EMV
for Supplier B

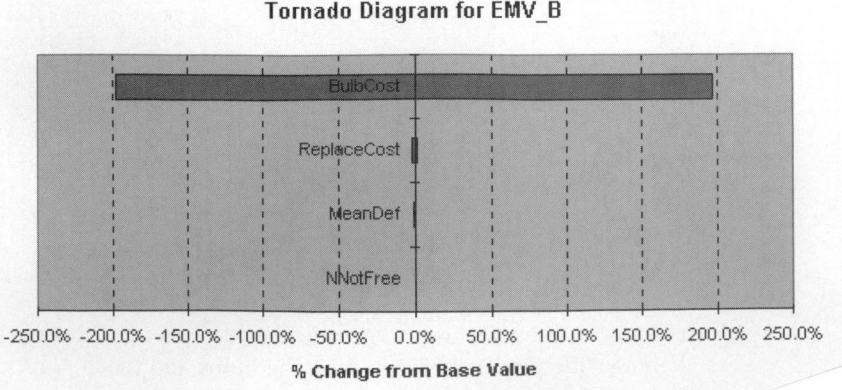

MODELING ISSUES

The discrete approximation used in Example 10.3 can be used in *any* decision tree with continuous probability distributions, regardless of whether they are normal. We first need to decide how many values to have in the discrete approximation. The usual choices are 5 or 3. (Surprisingly, a three-point approximation does an adequate job in many situations.) Then we need to use the "inverse" function—in the previous example it was the NORMINV function—to find the values to use in the decision tree. The appropriate inverse function is available in Excel for a number of widely used continuous distributions. ∎

Skill-Building Problems

10. Each day the manager of a local bookstore must decide how many copies of the community newspaper to order for sale in her shop. She must pay the newspaper's publisher $0.40 for each copy and sells the newspapers to local residents for $0.50 each. Newspapers that are unsold at the end of day are considered worthless. The probability distribution of the number of copies of the newspaper purchased daily at her shop is provided in Table 10.14. Employ a decision tree to find the bookstore manager's profit-maximizing daily order quantity.

TABLE 10.14 **Distribution of Daily Local Newspaper Demand**

Daily Demand for Local Newspaper	Probability
10	0.10
11	0.15
12	0.30
13	0.20
14	0.15
15	0.10

11. Two construction companies are bidding against one another for the right to construct a new community center building in Lewisburg, Pennsylvania. The first construction company, Fine Line Homes, believes that its competitor, Buffalo Valley Construction, will place a bid for this project according to the distribution shown in Table 10.15. Furthermore, Fine Line Homes estimates that it will cost $160,000 for its own company to construct this building. Given its fine reputation and long-standing service

TABLE 10.15 **Distribution of Possible Competing Bids for Construction Project**

Buffalo Valley Construction's Bid	Probability
$160,000	0.40
$165,000	0.30
$170,000	0.20
$175,000	0.10

within the local community, Fine Line Homes believes that it will likely be awarded the project in the event that it and Buffalo Valley Construction submit exactly the same bids. Employ a decision tree to identify Fine Line Homes' profit-maximizing bid for the new community center building.

12. Suppose that you have sued your employer for damages suffered when you recently slipped and fell on an icy surface that should have been treated by your company's physical plant department. Specifically, your injury resulting from this accident was sufficiently serious that you, in consultation with your attorney, decided to sue your company for $500,000. Your company's insurance provider has offered to settle this suit with you out of court. If you decide to reject the settlement and go to court, your attorney is confident that you will win the case but is uncertain about the amount the court will award you in damages. He has provided his assessment of the probability distribution of the court's award to you in Table 10.16 (page 522). Let S be the insurance provider's proposed out-of-court settlement (in dollars). For which values of S will you decide to accept the settlement? For which values of S will you choose to take your chances in court? Of course, you are seeking to maximize the expected payoff from this litigation.

TABLE 10.16	Distribution of Possible Court Award Amounts

Amount of Court Award	Probability
$0	0.025
$50,000	0.075
$100,000	0.100
$200,000	0.125
$300,000	0.175
$400,000	0.200
$500,000	0.300

13. Suppose that one of your colleagues has $2000 available to invest. Assume that all of this money must be placed in one of three investments: a particular money market fund, a stock, or gold. Each dollar your colleague invests in the money market fund earns a virtually guaranteed 12% annual return. Each dollar he invests in the stock earns an annual return characterized by the probability distribution provided in Table 10.17. Finally, each dollar he invests in gold earns an annual return characterized by the probability distribution given in Table 10.18.

   a. If your colleague must place all of his available funds in a single investment, which investment should he choose to maximize his expected earnings over the next year?

TABLE 10.17	Distribution of Annual Returns for Given Stock

Annual Returns for Given Stock	Probability
0%	0.10
6%	0.20
12%	0.40
18%	0.20
24%	0.10

TABLE 10.18	Distribution of Annual Returns for Gold

Annual Returns for Gold	Probability
−36%	0.10
−12%	0.20
12%	0.40
36%	0.20
60%	0.10

b. Suppose now that your colleague can place all of his available funds in one of these three investments as before, or he can invest $1000 in one alternative and $1000 in another. Assuming that he seeks to maximize his expected total earnings in one year, how should he allocate his $2000?

Skill-Extending Problems

14. A home appliance company is interested in marketing an innovative new product. The company must decide whether to manufacture this product essentially on its own or employ a subcontractor to manufacture it. Table 10.19 contains the estimated probability distribution of the cost of manufacturing 1 unit of this new product (in dollars) under the alternative that the home appliance company produces the item on its own. Table 10.20 contains the estimated probability distribution of the cost of purchasing 1 unit of this new product (in dollars) under the alternative that the home appliance company commissions a subcontractor to produce the item.

   a. Assuming that the home appliance company seeks to minimize the expected unit cost of manufacturing or buying the new product, should the company make the new product or buy it from a subcontractor?

   b. Perform sensitivity analysis on the optimal expected cost. Under what conditions, if any,

TABLE 10.19	Distribution of Unit Production Cost under "Make" Alternative

Cost Per Unit	Probability
$50	0.20
$53	0.25
$55	0.30
$57	0.20
$59	0.05

TABLE 10.20	Distribution of Unit Production Cost under "Buy" Alternative

Cost Per Unit	Probability
$50	0.10
$53	0.20
$55	0.40
$57	0.20
$59	0.10

would the home appliance company select an alternative different from the one you identified in part **a**?

15. A grapefruit farmer in central Florida is trying to decide whether to take protective action to limit damage to his crop in the event that the overnight temperature falls to a level well below freezing. He is concerned that if the temperature falls sufficiently low and he fails to make an effort to protect his grapefruit trees, he runs the risk of losing his entire crop, which is worth approximately $75,000. Based on the latest forecast issued by the National Weather Service, the farmer estimates that there is a 60% chance that he will lose his entire crop if it is left unprotected. Alternatively, the farmer can insulate his fruit by spraying water on all of the trees in his orchards. This action, which would likely cost the farmer C dollars, would prevent total devastation but might not completely protect the grapefruit trees from incurring some damage as a result of the unusually cold overnight temperatures. Table 10.21 contains the assessed distribution of possible damages (in dollars) to the insulated fruit in light of the cold weather forecast. Of course, this farmer seeks to minimize the expected total cost of coping with the threatening weather.

TABLE 10.21	Distribution of Damages to Insulated Grapefruit Crop
Damage to Grapefruit Crop	**Probability**
$0	0.30
$5000	0.15
$10,000	0.10
$15,000	0.15
$20,000	0.30

a. Find the maximum value of C below which the farmer will choose to insulate his crop in hopes of limiting damage as result of the unusually cold weather.

b. Set C equal to the value identified in part **a**. Perform sensitivity analysis to determine under what conditions, if any, the farmer might be better off not spraying his grapefruit trees and taking his chances in spite of the threat to his crop.

16. Consider again the department store buyer's decision problem described in Problem 6. Assume now that consumer demand for the new tennis shoes model (in hundreds of pairs) during the upcoming summer season is *normally* distributed with mean 6 and standard deviation 1.5.

a. Formulate a payoff table that specifies the contribution to profit (in dollars) from the sale of the tennis shoes by this department store chain for each possible purchase decision (in hundreds of pairs) and each outcome with respect to consumer demand. Use an appropriate discrete approximation of the given normal demand distribution.

b. Construct a decision tree to identify the buyer's course of action that maximizes the expected profit (in dollars) earned by the department store chain from the purchase and subsequent sale of tennis shoes in the coming year.

17. Consider again the purchasing agent's decision problem described in Problem 9. Assume now that the proportion of defective components supplied by this supplier is well described by the *triangular* distribution with parameters 0, 0, and 1. (This is called the **right triangular** distribution with range 1.)

a. Formulate a payoff table that specifies the microcomputer manufacturer's total cost (in dollars) of purchasing and repairing (if necessary) a complete lot of components for each possible decision and each outcome with respect to the proportion of defective items. Use an appropriate discrete approximation of the given triangular distribution for the proportion of defective items.

b. Construct a decision tree to identify the purchasing agent's course of action that minimizes the expected total cost (in dollars) of achieving a complete lot of satisfactory components.

18. A retired partner from Goldman Sachs has 1 million dollars available to invest in particular stocks or bonds. Each investment's annual rate of return depends on the state of the economy in the forthcoming year. Table 10.22 (page 524) contains the distribution of returns for these stocks and bonds as a function of the economy's state in the coming year. This investor wants to allocate her $1 million to maximize her expected total return 1 year from now.

a. If $X = Y = 15\%$, find the optimal investment strategy for this investor.

b. For which values of X (where $10\% < X < 20\%$) and Y (where $12.5\% < Y < 17.5\%$), if any, will this investor prefer to place all of her available funds in the given stocks to maximize her expected total return one year from now?

c. For which values of X (where $10\% < X < 20\%$) and Y (where $12.5\% < Y < 17.5\%$), if any, will this investor prefer to place all of her available funds in the given bonds to maximize her expected total return one year from now?

TABLE 10.22	Distribution of Annual Returns for Given Stocks and Bonds		
State of the Economy	Probability	Annual Returns for Given Stocks	Annual Returns for Given Bonds
Very strong	0.20	25%	20%
Moderately strong	0.40	20%	17.5%
Fair	0.25	$X\%$	$Y\%$
Moderately weak	0.10	10%	12.5%
Very weak	0.05	5%	10%

10.4 MULTISTAGE DECISION PROBLEMS

So far, all of the examples have required a single decision. We now examine a problem where the decision maker must make at least two decisions that are separated in time, such as when a company must decide whether to buy information that will help it make a second decision. The following example illustrates the typical situation.

EXAMPLE 10.4

MARKETING A NEW PRODUCT AT ACME

The Acme Company is trying to decide whether to market a new product. As in many new-product situations, there is considerable uncertainty about whether the new product will eventually "catch on." Acme believes that it might be prudent to introduce the product in a regional test market before introducing it nationally. Therefore, the company's first decision is whether to conduct the test market. Acme estimates that the fixed cost of the test market is $3 million. If it decides to conduct the test market, it must then wait for the results. Based on the results of the test market, it can then decide whether to market the product nationally, in which case it will incur a fixed cost of $90 million. On the other hand, if the original decision is *not* to run a test market, then the final decision—whether to market the product nationally—can be made without further delay. Acme's unit margin, the difference between its selling price and its unit variable cost, is $18 (in the test market and in the national market).

Acme classifies the results in either the test market or the national market as great, fair, or awful. Each of these is accompanied by a forecast of total units sold. These sales volumes (in 1000s of units) are 200, 100, and 30 for the test market and 6000, 3000, and 900 for the national market. Based on previous test markets for similar products, Acme estimates that probabilities of the three test market outcomes are 0.3, 0.6, and 0.1. Then, based on historical data from previous products that were test marketed and eventually marketed nationally, it assesses the probabilities of the national market outcomes given each possible test market outcome. If the test market is great, the probabilities for the national market outcomes are 0.8, 0.15, and 0.05. If the test market is fair, these probabilities are 0.3, 0.5, and 0.2. If the test market is awful, they are 0.05, 0.25, and 0.7. (Note how the probabilities of the national market outcomes tend to mirror the test market outcomes.)

The company wants to use a decision tree approach to find the best strategy.

Solution

We begin by discussing the three basic elements of this decision problem: the possible strategies, the possible outcomes and their probabilities, and the value model. The possible strategies are clear. Acme must first decide whether to conduct a test market. Then it must decide whether to introduce the product nationally. However, it is important to realize that if Acme decides to conduct a test market, it can base the national market decision on the results of the test market. In this case its final strategy will be a **contingency plan**, where it conducts the test market, then introduces the product nationally if it receives sufficiently positive test market results and abandons the product if it receives sufficiently negative test market results. The optimal strategies from many multistage decision problems involve similar contingency plans.

Regarding the uncertain outcomes and their probabilities, we note that the given probabilities—probabilities of test market outcomes and *conditional* probabilities of national market outcomes given test market outcomes—are exactly the ones we need in the decision tree. This is because the test market outcome is known *before* the national market outcome will occur. However, suppose Acme decides not to run a test market and then decides to market nationally. Then what are the probabilities of the national market outcomes?

It is important to realize that we cannot simply assess three *new* probabilities for this situation. These probabilities are *implied* by the given probabilities. This follows from the rules of conditional probability. If we let T_1, T_2, and T_3 be the test market outcomes, and N be any of the national market outcomes, then by the addition rule for probability and the conditional probability formula,

$$P(N) = P(N \text{ and } T_1) + P(N \text{ and } T_2) + P(N \text{ and } T_3) \qquad \textbf{(10.1)}$$

$$= P(N|T_1)P(T_1) + P(N|T_2)P(T_2) + P(N|T_3)P(T_3) \qquad \textbf{(10.2)}$$

(This is sometimes called the **law of total probability**.) For example, if N_1 represents a great national market, then from equation (10.1),

$$P(N_1) = (0.8)(0.3) + (0.3)(0.6) + (0.05)(0.1) = 0.425$$

Similarly, we find that $P(N_2) = 0.37$ and $P(N_3) = 0.205$. These are the probabilities we need to use for the probability branches when no test market is used.

Finally, the monetary values in the tree are straightforward. There are fixed costs of test marketing or marketing nationally, and these are incurred as soon as these "go ahead" decisions are made. From that point, we observe the sales volumes and multiply them by the unit margin to obtain the profits.

USING PRECISIONTREE

The inputs for the decision tree appear in Figure 10.26 (page 526). (See file ACME. XLS.) The only calculated values in this part of the spreadsheet are in row 28, which follow from equation (10.1). Specifically, the formula in cell B28 is

=SUMPRODUCT(B22:B24,$B$16:$B$18)

which we copy across row 28. The tree is then straightforward to build and label, as shown in Figure 10.27 (page 527). Note how the fixed costs of test marketing and marketing nationally appear on the decision branches where they occur, so that only the selling profits need to be placed on the probability branches. Also, the probabilities on the various probability branches are exactly those listed in Figure 10.26.

The interpretation of this tree is fairly straightforward if we realize that each value just below each node name is an EMV. For example, the 807 in cell B43 is the EMV for

FIGURE 10.26
Inputs for Acme
Marketing Example

	A	B	C	D
1	**Acme marketing example**			
2				
3	Fixed costs ($1000s)		**Range names:**	
4	Test mkt	$3,000	NatlMktCost: B5	
5	National mkt	$90,000	TestMktCost: B4	
6			UnitMargin: B18	
7	Unit margin	$18		
8				
9	Possible quantities sold (1000s)			
10		Test mkt	Natl mkt	
11	Great	200	6000	
12	Fair	100	3000	
13	Awful	30	900	
14				
15	Probabilities of test outcomes			
16	Great	0.30		
17	Fair	0.60		
18	Awful	0.10		
19				
20	Probabilities of natl mkt outcomes, given test mkt outcomes			
21		Natl great	Natl fair	Natl awful
22	Test great	0.80	0.15	0.05
23	Test fair	0.30	0.50	0.20
24	Test awful	0.05	0.25	0.70
25				
26	Probabilities of natl mkt outcomes without test mkt (calculated from above inputs)			
27		Natl great	Natl fair	Natl awful
28		0.425	0.370	0.205

the entire decision problem. It means that Acme's best EMV is $807,000. As another example, the 5910 in cell D47 means that if Acme ever gets to that point—the test market has been conducted and it has been great—the EMV for ACME is $5,910,000. Each of these EMVs has been calculated by the folding-back procedure we discussed earlier, starting from the right and working back toward the left. PrecisionTree takes EMVs at probability nodes and maximums at decision nodes.

We can also see Acme's optimal strategy by following the "TRUE" branches from left to right. Acme should first run a test market. If the test market results are great, then the product should be marketed nationally. However, if the test market results are only fair or awful, the product should be abandoned. In these cases the prospects from a national market look bleak, so Acme should cut its losses. (And there *are* losses. In these latter two cases, Acme has spent $3,000,000 on the test market and has recouped only $1,800,000 or $540,000 on test market sales.)

The risk profile from the optimal strategy appears in Figure 10.28 (page 528). It is based on the data in Figure 10.29 (page 528). (These were obtained by clicking on PrecisionTree's "staircase" button and selecting the Statistics and Risk Profile options.) We see that there is a small chance of two possible large losses (approximately $73 million and $35 million), there is a 70% chance of a moderate loss of about $1 or $2 million, and there is a 24% chance of an $18.6 million profit. Of course, the net effect is an EMV of $807,000.

You might argue that the large potential losses and the slightly higher than 70% chance of *some* loss should persuade Acme to abandon the product right away—without a test market. However, this is what "playing the averages" with EMV is all about. Since the EMV of this optimal strategy is greater than 0, the EMV of abandoning the product right away, Acme should go ahead with this optimal strategy if the company is indeed an EMV maximizer. In Section 10.8 we will see how this reasoning can change if Acme is a risk-averse decision maker—as it might be with multimillion dollar losses looming in the future!

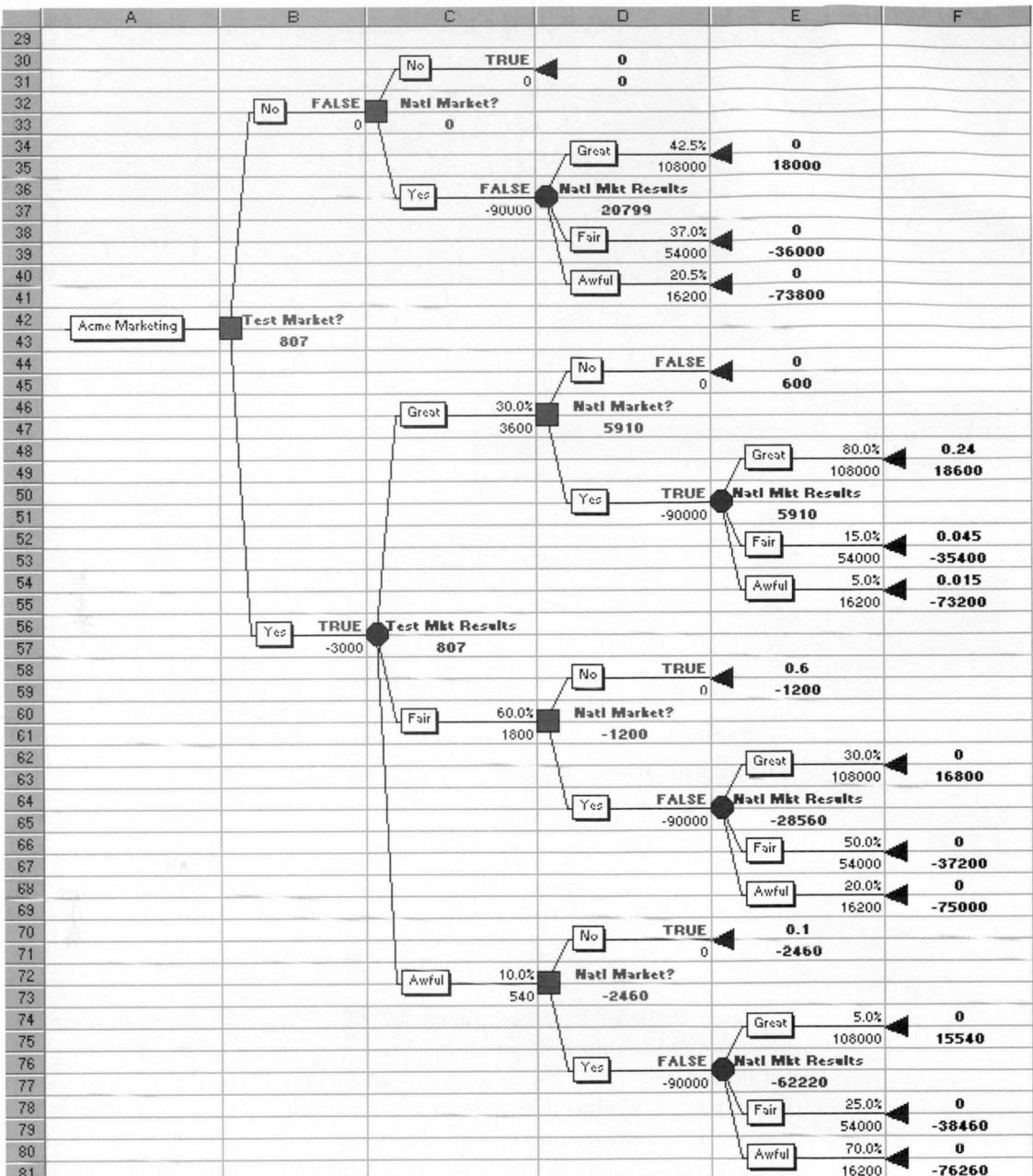

FIGURE 10.27 Decision Tree for Acme Marketing Example

Expected Value of Sample Information The role of the test market in the Acme marketing example is to provide information in the form of more accurate probabilities of national market results. Information usually costs something, as it does in Acme's problem. Currently, the fixed cost of the test market is $3 million, which is evidently not too much to pay because Acme's best strategy is to conduct the test market. However, we might ask how much this test market is worth. This is easy to answer. From the decision tree in Figure 10.27, we see that the EMV from test marketing is $807,000 better than the decision *not* to test market (and then abandon the product). Therefore, if the fixed cost of test marketing were any more than $807,000 above its current value,

FIGURE 10.28
Risk Profile of
Optimal Strategy

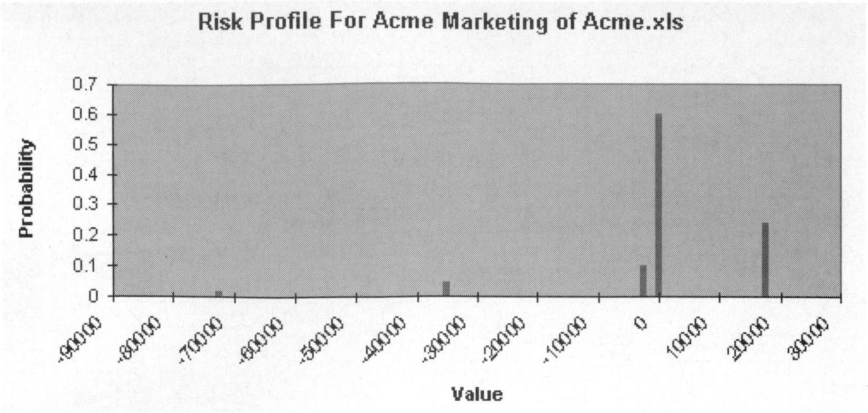

FIGURE 10.29
Distribution of
Profit/Loss from the
Optimal Strategy

	A	B	C
16	PROFILE:		
17	#	X	P
18	1	-73200	0.015
19	2	-35400	0.045
20	3	-2460	0.1
21	4	-1200	0.6
22	5	18600	0.24

Acme would be better not to run a test market. Equivalently, the most Acme would be willing to pay for the test market (as a fixed cost) is $3.807 million.

This value is called the **expected value of sample information**, or **EVSI**. In general, we can write the following expression for EVSI:

$$\text{EVSI} = \text{EMV with } \textit{free} \text{ information} - \text{EMV without information}$$

In Acme's problem, the EMV with free information is $3.807 million (just don't charge for the test market fixed cost), and the EMV without any test market information is $0 (because Acme abandons the product when there is no test market available). Therefore,

$$\text{EVSI} = \$3.807 - \$0 = \$3.807 \text{ million}$$

Expected Value of Perfect Information The reason for the term *sample* is that the information does not remove all uncertainty about the future. That is, even after the test market results are in, there is still uncertainty about the national market results. Therefore, we might go one step further and ask how much *perfect* information is worth. We can imagine perfect information as an envelope that contains the true final outcome (of the national market). That is, either "the national market will be great," "the national market will be fair," or "the national market will be awful" is written inside the envelope. Admittedly, no such envelope exists, but if it did, how much would Acme be willing to pay for it?

We can answer this question with the simple decision tree in Figure 10.30. Now the probability node on the left corresponds to opening the envelope. Its probabilities are the same as before (when there is no test market available). Note the reasoning here. Acme doesn't know what the contents of the envelope will be, so we need a probability node. However, once the envelope is opened, the true national market outcome will be revealed. At that point Acme's decision is fairly obvious. If it learns that a national market will be great, it knows the product will be profitable and will market it. Otherwise, if it learns that the national market will be fair or poor, it knows

FIGURE 10.30
EVPI for Acme
Marketing Example

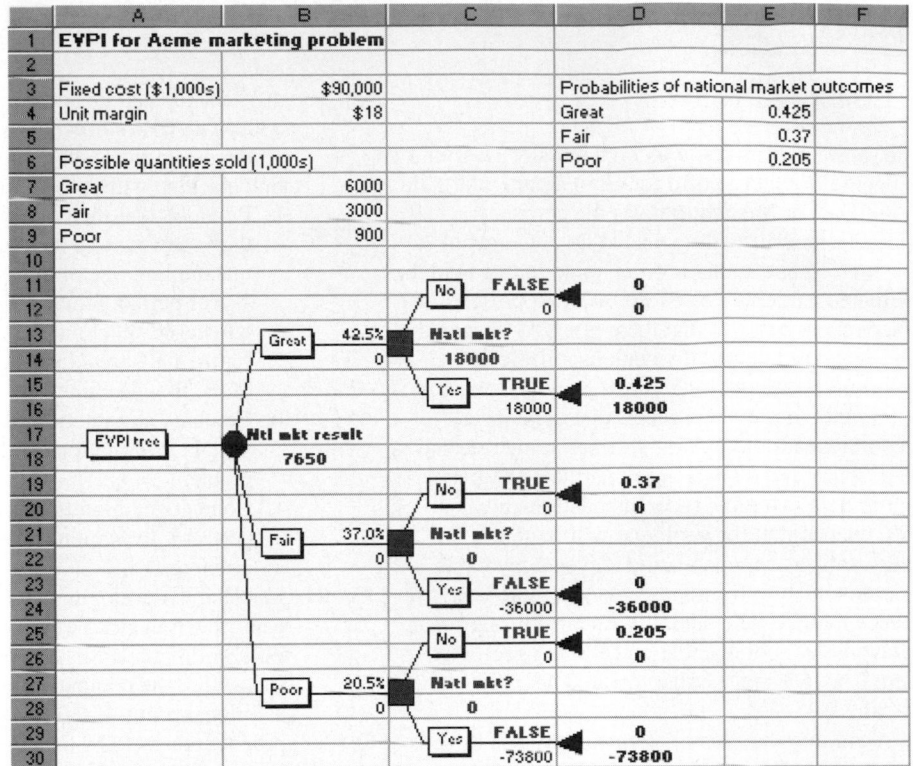

that there will be a loss from marketing nationally, so it will abandon the product. Folding back in the usual way produces an EMV of $7.65 million.

Now compare this $7.65 million with the EMV in the top part of Figure 10.27 that results from no test market, namely, $0. The difference, $7.65 million, is called the **expected value of perfect information**, or **EVPI**. It represents the maximum amount the company would pay for perfect information about the final outcome (of the national market). In general, the expression for EVPI is

EVPI = EMV with *free* perfect information − EMV with no information

In Acme's case this expression becomes

EVPI = $7.65 − $0 = $7.65 million

The EVPI may appear to be an irrelevant concept since perfect information is almost never available—at *any* price. However, it is often useful because it represents an *upper bound* on the EVSI for any potential sample information. That is, no sample information can ever be worth more than the EVPI. For example, if Acme is contemplating an expensive test market with an anticipated fixed cost of more than $8 million, then there is really no point in pursuing it any further. The information gained from this test market, no matter how reliable it is, cannot possibly justify its cost because its cost is greater than the EVPI. ■

Skill-Building Problems

19. The senior executives of an oil company are trying to decide whether to drill for oil in a particular field in the Gulf of Mexico. It costs the company $300,000 to drill in the selected field. Company executives believe that if oil is found in this field its estimated value will be $1,800,000. At present, this oil company believes that there is a 50% chance that the selected field actually contains oil. Before drilling, the company can hire a geologist at a cost of $30,000 to prepare a report that contains a recommendation regarding drilling in the selected field. There is a 55% chance that the geologist will issue a favorable recommendation and a 45% chance that the geologist will issue an unfavorable recommendation. Given a favorable recommendation from the geologist, there is a 75% chance that the field actually contains oil. Given an unfavorable recommendation from the geologist, there is a 15% chance that the field actually contains oil.

   a. Assuming that this oil company wishes to maximize its expected net earnings, determine its optimal strategy through the use of a decision tree.

   b. Compute and interpret the expected value of sample information (EVSI) in this decision problem.

   c. Compute and interpret the expected value of perfect information (EVPI) in this decision problem.

20. A local certified public accountant must decide which of two copying machines to purchase for her expanding business. The cost of purchasing the first machine is $4500, and the cost of maintaining the first machine each year is uncertain. The CPA's office manager believes that the annual maintenance cost for the first machine will be $0, $150, or $300 with probabilities 0.35, 0.35, and 0.30, respectively. The cost of purchasing the second machine is $3000, and the cost of maintaining the second machine through a guaranteed maintenance agreement is $225 per year.

     Before the purchase decision is made, the CPA can hire an experienced copying machine repairperson to evaluate the quality of the first machine. Such an evaluation would cost the CPA $60. If the repairperson believes that the first machine is satisfactory, there is a 65% chance that its annual maintenance cost will be $0 and a 35% chance that its annual maintenance cost will be $150. If, however, the repairperson believes that the first machine is unsatisfactory, there is a 60% chance that its annual maintenance cost will be $150 and a 40% chance that its annual maintenance cost will be $300. The CPA's office manager believes that the repairperson will issue a satisfactory report on the first machine with probability 0.50.

   a. Provided that the CPA wishes to minimize the expected total cost of purchasing and maintaining one of these two machines for a 1-year period, which machine should she purchase? When, if ever, would it be worthwhile for the CPA to obtain the repairperson's review of the first machine?

   b. Compute and interpret the expected value of sample information (EVSI) in this decision problem.

   c. Compute and interpret the expected value of perfect information (EVPI) in this decision problem.

21. FineHair is developing a new product to promote hair growth in cases of male pattern baldness. If FineHair markets the new product and it is successful, the company will earn $500,000 in additional profit. If the marketing of this new product proves to be unsuccessful, the company will lose $350,000 in development and marketing costs. In the past, similar products have been successful 60% of the time. At a cost of $50,000, the effectiveness of the new restoration product can be thoroughly tested. If the results of such testing are favorable, there is an 80% chance that the marketing efforts of this new product will be successful. If the results of such testing are not favorable, there is a mere 30% chance that the marketing efforts of this new product will be successful. FineHair currently believes that the probability of receiving favorable test results is 0.60.

   a. Identify the strategy that maximizes FineHair's expected net earnings in this situation.

   b. Compute and interpret the expected value of sample information (EVSI) in this decision problem.

   c. Compute and interpret the expected value of perfect information (EVPI) in this decision problem.

22. Hank is considering placing a bet on the upcoming showdown between the Penn State and Michigan football teams in State College. The winner of this contest will represent the Big Ten Conference in the Rose Bowl on New Year's Day. Without any additional information, Hank believes that each team has an equal chance of winning this big game. If he wins the bet, he will win $500; if he loses the bet, he will lose $550. Before placing his bet, he may decide to pay his friend Al, who happens to be a football sportswriter for the *Philadelphia Enquirer*, $50 for Al's expert prediction on the game. Assume that Al predicts that Penn State will win similar games 55% of the time, and that Michigan will win similar games 45% of the time. Furthermore, Hank knows that when Al predicts that Penn State will win, there is a 70% chance that Penn State will indeed win the football game. Finally, when Al predicts that Michigan will win, there is a 20% chance that Penn State will proceed to win the upcoming game.

a. In order to maximize his expected profit from this betting opportunity, how should Hank proceed in this situation?

b. Compute and interpret the expected value of sample information (EVSI) in this decision problem.

c. Compute and interpret the expected value of perfect information (EVPI) in this decision problem.

23. A product manager at Clean & Brite seeks to determine whether her company should market a new brand of toothpaste. If this new product succeeds in the marketplace, C&B estimates that it could earn $1,800,000 in future profits from the sale of the new toothpaste. If this new product fails, however, the company expects that it could lose approximately $750,000. If C&B chooses not to market this new brand, the product manager believes that there would be little, if any, impact on the profits earned through sales of C&B's other products. The manager has estimated that the new toothpaste brand will succeed with probability 0.55. Before making her decision regarding this toothpaste product, the manager can spend $75,000 on a market research study. Such a study of consumer preferences will yield either a positive recommendation with probability 0.50 or a negative

recommendation with probability 0.50. Given a positive recommendation to market the new product, the new brand will eventually succeed in the marketplace with probability 0.75. Given a negative recommendation regarding the marketing of the new product, the new brand will eventually succeed in the marketplace with probability 0.25.

a. In order to maximize expected profit in this case, what course of action should the C&B product manager take?

b. Compute and interpret the expected value of sample information (EVSI) in this decision problem.

c. Compute and interpret the expected value of perfect information (EVPI) in this decision problem.

Skill-Extending Problems

24. A publishing company is trying to decide whether to publish a new business law textbook. Based on a careful reading of the latest draft of the manuscript, the publisher's senior editor in the business textbook division assesses the distribution of possible payoffs earned by publishing this new book. Table 10.23 contains this probability distribution. Before making a final decision regarding the publication of the book, the editor can learn more about the text's potential for success by thoroughly surveying business law instructors teaching at universities across the country. Historical frequencies based on similar surveys administered in the past are provided in Table 10.24.

a. Find the strategy that maximizes the publisher's expected payoff (in dollars).

TABLE 10.23	Distribution of Payoffs for New Business Law Textbook	
Textbook Performance	Probability	Estimated Payoff (if published)
Very strong	0.20	$100,000
Moderately strong	0.20	$50,000
Fair	0.20	$0
Poor	0.40	−$50,000

TABLE 10.24	Historical Frequencies of Combinations of Past Survey Results and Actual Outcomes			
Survey Indication/ Actual Performance	Very Strong	Moderately Strong	Fair	Poor
Very strong	13	12	2	3
Moderately strong	10	20	6	4
Fair	5	12	15	8
Poor	1	3	9	22

b. What is the most (in dollars) that the publisher should be willing to pay to conduct a new survey of business law instructors?

c. If the actual cost of conducting the given survey is less than the amount identified in part **a**, what should the publisher do?

d. Assuming that a survey could be constructed that provides "perfect information" to the publisher, how much should the company be willing to pay to acquire and implement such a survey?

25. Sharp Outfits is trying to decide whether to ship some customer orders now via UPS or wait until after the threat of another UPS strike is over. If Sharp Outfits decides to ship the requested merchandise now and the UPS strike takes place, the company will incur $60,000 in delay and shipping costs. If Sharp Outfits decides to ship the customer orders via UPS and no strike occurs, the company will incur $4000 in shipping costs. If Sharp Outfits decides to postpone shipping its customer orders via UPS, the company will incur $10,000 in delay costs regardless of whether or not UPS goes on strike. Let p represent the probability that UPS will go on strike and impact Sharp Outfits's shipments.

a. For which values of p, if any, does Sharp Outfits minimize its expected total cost by choosing to postpone shipping its customer orders via UPS?

b. Suppose now that, at a cost of $1000, Sharp Outfits can purchase information regarding the likelihood of a UPS strike in the near future. Based on similar strike threats in the past, the probability that this information indicates the occurrence of a UPS strike is 27.5%. If the purchased information indicates the occurrence of a UPS strike, the chance of a strike actually occurring is 0.105/0.275. If the purchased information does not indicate the occurrence of a UPS strike, the chance of a strike actually occurring is 0.680/0.725. Provided that $p = 0.15$, what strategy should Sharp Outfits pursue to minimize its expected total cost?

c. Continuing part **b**, compute and interpret the expected value of sample information (EVSI) when $p = 0.15$.

d. Continuing part **b**, compute and interpret the expected value of perfect information (EVPI) when $p = 0.15$.

10.5 BAYES' RULE

I n multistage decision problems we typically have alternating sets of decision nodes and probability nodes. The decision maker makes a decision, some uncertain outcomes are observed, the decision maker makes another decision, more uncertain outcomes are observed, and so on. In the resulting decision tree, all probability branches at the *right* of the tree are conditional on outcomes that have occurred earlier, to their left. Therefore, the probabilities on these branches are of the form $P(A|B)$, where B is an event that occurs *before* event A in time. However, it is sometimes more natural to assess conditional probabilities in the opposite order, that is, $P(B|A)$. Whenever this is the case, we require **Bayes' rule** to obtain the probabilities we need on the tree. Essentially, Bayes' rule is a mechanism for updating probabilities as new information becomes available. We illustrate the mechanics of Bayes' rule in the following example. [See Feinstein (1990) for a real application of this example.]

EXAMPLE 10.5

DRUG TESTING COLLEGE ATHLETES

If an athlete is tested for a certain type of drug usage (steroids, say), then the test result will be either positive or negative. However, these tests are never perfect. Some athletes who are drug free test positive, and some who are drug users test negative. The former are called false positives; the latter are called false negatives. We will assume that 5%

of all athletes use drugs, 3% of all tests on drug-free athletes yield false positives, and 7% of all tests on drug users yield false negatives. The question then is what we can conclude from a positive or negative test result.

Solution

Let D and ND denote that a randomly chosen athlete is or is not a drug user, and let $T+$ and $T-$ indicate a positive or negative test result. We are given the following probabilities. First, since 5% of all athletes are drug users, we know that $P(D) = 0.05$ and $P(ND) = 0.95$. These are called **prior** probabilities because they represent the chance that an athlete is or is not a drug user *prior* to the results of a drug test. Second, from the information on drug test accuracy, we know the conditional probabilities $P(T+|ND) = 0.03$ and $P(T-|D) = 0.07$. But a drug-free athlete tests either positive or negative, and the same is true for a drug user. Therefore, we also have the probabilities $P(T-|ND) = 0.97$ and $P(T+|D) = 0.93$. These four conditional probabilities of test results given drug user status are often called the **likelihoods** of the test results.

Given these priors and likelihoods, we want **posterior** probabilities such as $P(D|T+)$, the probability that an athlete who tested positive is a drug user, or $P(ND|T-)$, the probability that an athlete who tested negative is drug free. They are called posterior probabilities because they are assessed *after* the drug test results. This is where Bayes' rule enters. We will develop Bayes' rule in some generality and then apply it to the present example.

Let A be any "information" event, such as the result of a drug test, and let $B_1, B_2, \ldots, B_n$ be any mutually exclusive and exhaustive set of events. That is, exactly one of the B_i's must occur. To apply Bayes' rule, we assume that the prior probabilities $P(B_1), P(B_2), \ldots, P(B_n)$ are given, as are the likelihoods $P(A|B_i)$ for each i. Then we want the posterior probabilities $P(B_i|A)$ for each i. Bayes' rule shows how to find these. For any i, we have

$$P(B_i|A) = \frac{P(A|B_i)P(B_i)}{P(A|B_1)P(B_1) + \cdots + P(A|B_n)P(B_n)}$$ **Bayes' rule**

This formula says that a typical posterior probability is a ratio. The numerator is a likelihood times a prior, and the denominator is the sum of likelihoods times priors.

Before illustrating Bayes' rule numerically, we make two other observations about the terms in Bayes' rule. First, we can use the multiplication rule of probability to write any product of a likelihood and a prior as

$$P(A|B_i)P(B_i) = P(A \text{ and } B_i)$$

The probability on the right, that *both* A and B_i occur, is called a **joint** probability. Second, we can use the definition of conditional probability directly to write

$$P(B_i|A) = \frac{P(A \text{ and } B_i)}{P(A)}$$

Therefore, the probability in the denominator of Bayes' rule is really just the probability of A:

$$P(A) = P(A|B_1)P(B_1) + \cdots + P(A|B_n)P(B_n)$$

As we will see shortly, this natural by-product of Bayes' rule will come in very handy in decision trees.

It is fairly easy to implement Bayes' rule in a spreadsheet, as illustrated in Figure 10.31 for the drug example. Here A corresponds to either test result, and B_1 and B_2 correspond to D and ND. (See the file DRUGBAYES.XLS.[4]) In words, we want to see how the chances of D and ND change after seeing the results of the drug test.

The given priors and likelihoods are listed in the ranges B5:C5 and B9:C10. We then calculate the products of likelihoods and priors in the range B15:C16. The formula in cell B15 is

=B$5*B9

and this is copied to the rest of the B15:C16 range. Their row sums are calculated in the range D15:D16. These represent the unconditional probabilities of the two possible results. They are also (as we saw above) the denominators of Bayes' rule. Finally, we calculate the posterior probabilities in the range B21:C22. The formula in cell B21 is

=B15/$D15

and this is copied to the rest of the B21:C22 range. The various 1's in the margins of Figure 10.31 are row sums or column sums that must equal 1. We show them only as checks of our logic.

FIGURE 10.31
Bayes' Rule for
Drug-Testing
Example

	A	B	C	D
1	Illustration of Bayes' rule using drug example			
2				
3	Prior probabilities of drug user status			
4		User	Non-user	
5		0.05	0.95	1
6				
7	Likelihoods of test results, given drug user status			
8		User	Non-user	
9	Test positive	0.93	0.03	
10	Test negative	0.07	0.97	
11		1	1	
12				
13	Joint probabilities of drug user status and test results			
14		User	Non-user	Unconditional
15	Test positive	0.0465	0.0285	0.075
16	Test negative	0.0035	0.9215	0.925
17				1
18				
19	Posterior probabilities of drug user status			
20		User	Non-user	
21	Test positive	0.620	0.380	1
22	Test negative	0.004	0.996	1

Note that a negative test result leaves little doubt that the athlete is drug free. The posterior probability that the athlete is drug free, given a negative test result, is 0.996. However, there is still a lot of doubt about an athlete who tests positive. The posterior probability that the athlete uses drugs, given a positive test result, is only 0.620. This asymmetry occurs because of the prior probabilities. We are fairly certain that a randomly selected athlete is drug free because only 5% of all athletes use drugs. It takes a lot of evidence to convince us otherwise. This initial bias, plus the fact that the test produces a few false positives, means that athletes with positive test results still have a decent chance (probability 0.380) of being drug free. Is this a valid argument

[4]The Bayes2 sheet in this file illustrates how Bayes' rule can be used when there are more than two possible test results and/or drug user categories.

for not requiring drug testing of athletes? We explore this question in the following continuation of the drug-testing example. It all depends on the "costs." (It might also depend on whether there is a second type of test that could help confirm the findings of the first test. However, we won't consider such a test.) ∎

EXAMPLE 10.5 (CONTINUED)

DRUG TESTING COLLEGE ATHLETES

The administrators at State University are trying to decide whether to institute mandatory drug testing for the athletes. They have the same information about priors and likelihoods as in the previous example, but now they want to use a decision tree approach to see whether the benefits outweigh the costs.[5]

Solution

We have already discussed the uncertain outcomes and their probabilities. Now we need to discuss the decision alternatives and the monetary values—the other two elements of a decision analysis. We will assume that there are only two alternatives: perform drug testing on all athletes or don't perform any drug testing. In the former case we assume that if an athlete tests positive, this athlete is barred from sports.

The "monetary" values are more difficult to assess. They include

- the benefit B from correctly identifying a drug user and barring him or her from sports
- the cost C_1 of the test itself for a single athlete (materials and labor)
- the cost C_2 of falsely accusing a nonuser (and barring him or her from sports)
- the cost C_3 of not identifying a drug user (either by not testing at all or by obtaining a false negative)
- the cost C_4 of violating a nonuser's privacy by performing the test

It is clear that only C_1 is a direct monetary cost that is easy to measure. However, the other "costs" and the benefit B are real, and they must be compared on some scale to enable administrators to make a rational decision. We will do so by comparing everything to the cost C_1, to which we will assign value 1. (This does not mean that the cost of testing an athlete is necessarily $1; it just means that we will express all other costs as multiples of C_1.) Clearly, there is a lot of subjectivity involved in making these comparisons, so sensitivity analysis on the final decision tree is a must.

Before developing this decision tree, it is useful to form a benefit–cost table for both alternatives and all possible outcomes. Because we will eventually maximize expected net *benefit*, all benefits in this table have a positive sign and all costs have a negative sign. These net benefits appear in Table 10.25 (page 536). The first two columns are relevant if no tests are performed; the last four are relevant when testing is performed. For example, if a positive test is obtained for a nonuser, there are three

---

[5]Again, see Feinstein (1990) for an enlightening discussion of this drug-testing problem at a real university.

TABLE 10.25　Net Benefit for Drug-Testing Example

Don't Test		Perform Test			
D	ND	D and $T+$	ND and $T+$	D and $T-$	ND and $T-$
$-C_3$	0	$B - C_1$	$-(C_1 + C_2 + C_4)$	$-(C_1 + C_3)$	$-(C_1 + C_4)$

costs: the cost of the test (C_1), the cost of falsely accusing the athlete (C_2), and the cost of violating the nonuser's privacy (C_4). The other entries are obtained similarly.

The solution with PrecisionTree shown in Figure 10.32 is now fairly straightforward. (See the file DRUG.XLS.) We first enter all of the benefits and costs in an input section. These, together with the Bayes' rule calculations from before, appear at the top of the spreadsheet. Then we use PrecisionTree in the usual way to build the tree and enter the links to the values and probabilities.

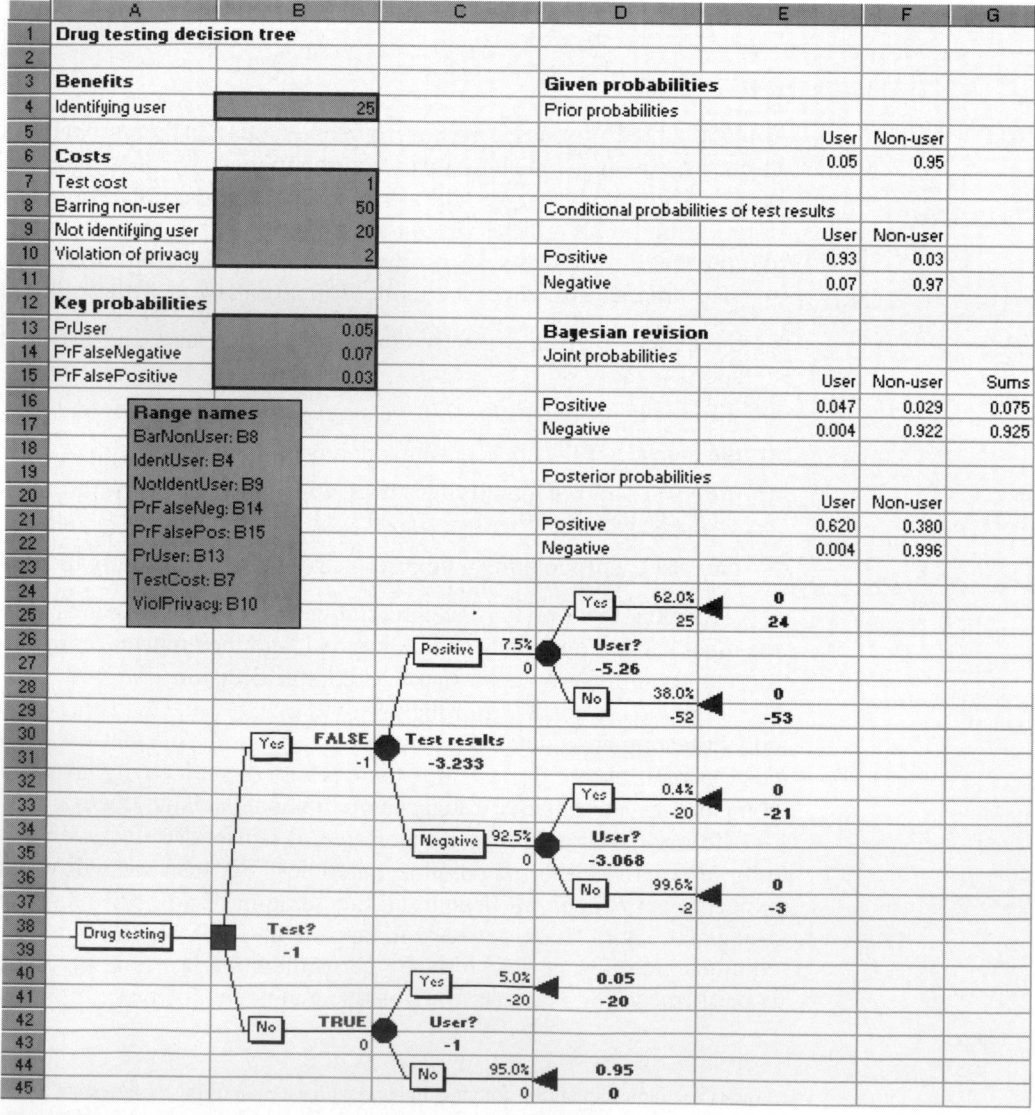

FIGURE 10.32 Decision Tree for Drug-Testing Example

Before we interpret this solution, we discuss the timing (from left to right). If drug testing is performed, the result of the drug test is observed first (a probability node). Each test result leads to an action (bar from sports or don't), and then the eventual benefit or cost depends on whether the athlete uses drugs (again a probability node). You might argue that the university never knows for certain whether the athlete uses drugs, but we must include this information in the tree to get the benefits and costs correct. If no drug testing is performed, then there is no intermediate test result node or branches.

Now to the interpretation. First, we discuss the benefits and costs shown in Figure 10.32. These were chosen fairly arbitrarily, but with some hope of reflecting reality. They say that the largest cost is falsely accusing (and barring) a nonuser. This is 50 times as large as the cost of the test. The benefit of identifying a drug user is only half this large, and the cost of not identifying a user is 40% as large as barring a nonuser. The violation of privacy of a nonuser is twice as large as the cost of the test. Based on these values, the decision tree implies that drug testing should *not* be performed. The EMVs for testing and for not testing are both negative, indicating that the costs outweigh the benefits for each, but the EMV for not testing is slightly *less* negative.[6]

What would it take to change this decision? We'll start with the assumption, probably accepted by most people in our society, that the cost of falsely accusing a nonuser (C_2) ought to be the largest of the benefits or costs in the range B4:B10. In fact, because of possible legal costs, we might argue that C_2 should be *more* than 50 times the cost of the test. But if we increase C_2, the scales are tipped even farther in the direction of not testing. On the other hand, if the benefit B from identifying a user and/or the cost C_3 for not identifying a user increase, then testing might be the preferred alternative. We tried this, keeping C_2 constant at 50. When B and C_3 both had value 45, no testing was still optimal, but when they both increased to 50—the same magnitude as C_2—then testing won out by a small margin. However, it would be difficult to argue that B and C_3 should be of the same magnitude as C_2.

Other than the benefits and costs, the only other thing we might vary is the accuracy of the test, measured by the error probabilities in cells B14 and B15. Presumably, if the test makes fewer false positives and false negatives, testing might be a more attractive alternative. We tried this, keeping the benefits and costs the same as those shown in Figure 10.32 but changing the error probabilities. Even when each error probability was decreased to 0.01, however, the no-testing alternative was still optimal—by a fairly wide margin.

In summary, based on a number of reasonable assumptions and parameter settings, this example has shown that it is difficult to make a case for mandatory drug testing. ∎

---

[6]The university in the Feinstein (1990) study came to the same conclusion.

Skill-Building Problems

26. Consider a population of 2000 individuals, 800 of whom are women. Assume that 300 of the women in this population earn at least $60,000 per year, and 200 of the men earn at least $60,000 per year.

  a. What is the probability that a randomly selected individual from this population earns less than $60,000 per year?

  b. If a randomly selected individual is observed to earn less than $60,000 per year, what is the probability that this person is a man?

  c. If a randomly selected individual is observed to earn at least $60,000 per year, what is the probability that this person is a woman?

27. Yearly automobile inspections are required for residents of the state of Pennsylvania. Suppose that 18% of all inspected cars in Pennsylvania have problems that need to be corrected. Unfortunately, Pennsylvania state inspections fail to detect these problems 12% of the time. Consider a car that is inspected and is found to be free of problems. What is the probability that there is indeed something wrong that the inspection has failed to uncover?

28. Consider again the landowner's decision problem described in Problem 3. Suppose now that, at a cost of $90,000, the landowner can request that a soundings test be performed on the site where natural gas is believed to be present. The company that conducts the soundings concedes that 30% of the time the test will indicate that no gas is present when it actually is. When natural gas is not present in a particular site, the soundings test is accurate 90% of the time.

  a. Given that the landowner pays for the soundings test and the test indicates that gas is present, what is the landowner's revised estimate of the probability of finding gas on this site?

  b. Given that the landowner pays for the soundings test and the test indicates that gas is not present, what is the landowner's revised estimate of the probability of not finding gas on this site?

  c. Should the landowner request the given soundings test at a cost of $90,000? Explain why or why not. If not, when (if ever) would the landowner choose to obtain the soundings test?

29. The chief executive officer of a firm in a highly competitive industry believes that one of her key employees is providing confidential information to the competition. She is 90% certain that this informer is the vice-president of finance, whose contacts have been extremely valuable in obtaining financing for the company. If she decides to fire this vice-president and he is the informer, she estimates

that the company will gain $500,000. If she decides to fire this vice-president but he is not the informer, the company will lose his expertise and still have an informer within the staff; the CEO estimates that this outcome would cost her company about $2.5 million. If she decides not to fire this vice-president, she estimates that the firm will lose $1.5 million whether or not he actually is the informer (since in either case the informer is still with the company).

Before deciding whether to fire the vice-president for finance, the CEO could order lie detector tests. To avoid possible lawsuits, the lie detector tests would have to be administered to all company employees, at a total cost of $150,000. Another problem she must consider is that the available lie detector tests are not perfectly reliable. In particular, if a person is lying, the test will reveal that the person is lying 95% of the time. Moreover, if a person is not lying, the test will indicate that the person is not lying 85% of the time.

  a. In order to minimize the expected total cost of managing this difficult situation, what strategy should the CEO adopt?

  b. Should the CEO order the lie detector tests for all of her employees? Explain why or why not.

  c. Determine the maximum amount of money that the CEO should be willing to pay to administer lie detector tests.

30. A customer has approached a bank for a $10,000 one-year loan at a 12% interest rate. If the bank does not approve this loan application, the $10,000 will be invested in bonds that earn a 6% annual return. Without additional information, the bank believes that there is a 4% chance that this customer will default on the loan, assuming that the loan is approved. If the customer defaults on the loan, the bank will lose $10,000.

At a cost of $100, the bank can thoroughly investigate the customer's credit record and supply a favorable or unfavorable recommendation. Past experience indicates that in cases where the customer did not default on the approved loan, the probability of receiving a favorable recommendation on the basis of the credit investigation was 77/96. Furthermore, in cases where the customer defaulted on the approved loan, the probability of receiving a favorable recommendation on the basis of the credit investigation was 1/4.

  a. What course of action should the bank take to maximize its expected profit?

  b. Compute and interpret the expected value of sample information (EVSI) in this decision problem.

c. Compute and interpret the expected value of perfect information (EVPI) in this decision problem.

31. A company is considering whether to market a new product. Assume, for simplicity, that if this product is marketed, there are only two possible outcomes: success or failure. The company assesses that the probabilities of these two outcomes are p and $1 - p$, respectively. If the product is marketed and it proves to be a failure, the company will lose $450,000. If the product is marketed and it proves to be a success, the company will gain $750,000. Choosing not to market the product results in no gain or loss for the company.

The company is also considering whether to survey prospective buyers of this new product. The results of the consumer survey can be classified as favorable, neutral, or unfavorable. In similar cases where proposed products proved to be market successes, the likelihoods that the survey results were favorable, neutral, and unfavorable were 0.6, 0.3, and 0.1, respectively. In similar cases where proposed products proved to be market failures, the likelihoods that the survey results were favorable, neutral, and unfavorable were 0.1, 0.2, and 0.7, respectively. The total cost of administering this survey is C dollars.

a. Let $p = 0.4$. For which values of C, if any, would this company choose to conduct the consumer survey?

b. Let $p = 0.4$. What is the largest amount that this company would be willing to pay for perfect information about the potential success or failure of the new product?

c. Let $p = 0.5$ and $C = \$15,000$. Find the strategy that maximizes the company's expected earnings in this situation. Does the optimal strategy involve conducting the consumer survey? Explain why or why not.

32. The U.S. government is attempting to determine whether immigrants should be tested for a contagious disease. Let's assume that the decision will be made on a financial basis. Furthermore, assume that each immigrant who is allowed to enter the United States and has the disease costs the country $100,000. Also, each immigrant who is allowed to enter the United States and does not have the disease will contribute $10,000 to the national economy. Finally, assume that x percent of all potential immigrants have the disease. The U.S. government can choose to admit all immigrants, admit no immigrants, or test immigrants for the disease before determining whether they should be admitted. It costs T dollars to test a person for the disease; the test result is either positive or negative. A person who does not have the disease *always* tests negative. However, 20% of all people who *do* have

the disease test negative. The government's goal is to maximize the expected net financial benefits per potential immigrant.

a. Let $x = 10$ (i.e., 10%). What is the largest value of T at which the U.S. government will choose to test potential immigrants for the disease?

b. How does your answer to the question in part **a** change when x increases to 15?

c. Let $x = 10$ and $T = \$100$. Find the government's optimal strategy in this case.

d. Let $x = 10$ and $T = \$100$. Compute and interpret the expected value of perfect information (EVPI) in this decision problem.

Skill-Extending Problems

33. A city in Ohio is considering replacing its fleet of gasoline-powered automobiles with electric cars. The manufacturer of the electric cars claims that this municipality will experience significant cost savings over the life of the fleet if it chooses to pursue the conversion. If the manufacturer is correct, the city will save about $1.5 million dollars. If the new technology employed within the electric cars is faulty, as some critics suggest, the conversion to electric cars will cost the city $675,000. A third possibility is that less serious problems will arise and the city will break even with the conversion. A consultant hired by the city estimates that the probabilities of these three outcomes are 0.30, 0.30, and 0.40, respectively.

The city has an opportunity to implement a pilot program that would indicate the potential cost or savings resulting from a switch to electric cars. The pilot program involves renting a small number of electric cars for 3 months and running them under typical conditions. This program would cost the city $75,000. The city's consultant believes that the results of the pilot program would be significant but not conclusive; she submits Table 10.26 (page 540), a compilation of probabilities based on the experience of other cities, to support her contention. For example, the first row of her table indicates that given that a conversion to electric cars actually results in a savings of $1.5 million, the conditional probabilities that the pilot program will indicate that the city saves money, loses money, and breaks even are 0.6, 0.1, and 0.3, respectively.

a. What actions should this city take to maximize the expected savings?

b. Should the city implement the pilot program at a cost of $75,000?

c. Compute and interpret the expected value of sample information (EVSI) in this decision problem.

TABLE 10.26	Likelihoods of Pilot Program Outcomes Given Actual Conversion Outcomes		
Actual Outcome of Conversion/ Pilot Program Indication	**Savings**	**Loss**	**Break Even**
Savings	0.6	0.1	0.3
Loss	0.1	0.4	0.5
Break Even	0.4	0.2	0.4

34. A manufacturer must decide whether to extend credit to a retailer who would like to open an account with the firm. Past experience with new accounts indicates that 45% are high-risk customers, 35% are moderate-risk customers, and 20% are low-risk customers. If credit is extended, the manufacturer can expect to lose $60,000 with a high-risk customer, make $50,000 with a moderate-risk customer, and make $100,000 with a low-risk customer. If the manufacturer decides not to extend credit to a customer, the manufacturer neither makes nor loses any money.

Prior to making a credit extension decision, the manufacturer can obtain a credit rating report on the retailer at a cost of $2000. The credit agency concedes that its rating procedure is not completely reliable. In particular, the credit rating procedure will rate a low-risk customer as a moderate-risk customer with probability 0.10 and as a high-risk customer with probability 0.05. Furthermore, the given rating procedure will rate a moderate-risk customer as a low-risk customer with probability 0.06 and as a high-risk customer with probability 0.07. Finally, the rating procedure will rate a high-risk customer as a low-risk customer with probability 0.01 and as a moderate-risk customer with probability 0.05.

a. Find the strategy that maximizes the manufacturer's expected net earnings.

b. Should the manufacturer routinely obtain credit rating reports on those retailers who seek credit approval? Why or why not?

c. Compute and interpret the expected value of sample information (EVSI) in this decision problem.

35. A television network earns an average of $1.6 million each season from a hit program and loses an average of $400,000 each season on a program that turns out to be a flop. Of all programs picked up by this network in recent years, 25% turn out to be hits and 75% turn out to be flops. At a cost of C dollars, a market research firm will analyze a pilot episode of a prospective program and issue a report predicting whether the given program will end up being a hit. If the program is actually going to be a hit, there is a 90% chance that the market researchers will predict the program to be a hit. If the program is actually going to be a flop, there is a 20% chance that the market researchers will predict the program to be a hit.

a. Assuming that $C = \$160,000$, identify the strategy that maximizes this television network's expected profit in responding to a newly proposed television program.

b. What is the maximum value of C that this television network should be willing to incur in choosing to hire the market research firm?

c. Compute and interpret the expected value of perfect information (EVPI) in this decision problem.

10.6 INCORPORATING ATTITUDES TOWARD RISK

Rational decision makers are sometimes willing to violate the EMV maximization criterion when large amounts of money are at stake. These decision makers are willing to sacrifice some EMV to reduce risk. Are you ever willing to do so personally? Consider the following scenarios.

1. You have a chance to enter a lottery where you will win $100,000 with probability 0.1 or win nothing with probability 0.9. Alternatively, you can receive $5000 for certain. How many of you—truthfully—would take the certain $5000, even though the EMV of the lottery is $10,000? Or change the $100,000 to $1,000,000 and the $5000 to $50,000 and ask yourself whether you'd prefer the sure $50,000!

2. You can either buy collision insurance on your expensive new car or not buy it, where the insurance costs a certain premium and carries some deductible provision. If you decide to pay the premium, then you are essentially paying a certain amount to avoid a gamble—the possibility of wrecking your car and not having it insured. You can be sure that the premium is greater than the expected cost of damage; otherwise, the insurance company would not stay in business. Therefore, from an EMV standpoint you should not purchase the insurance. But how many of you drive without this type of insurance?

These examples, the second of which is certainly realistic, illustrate situations where rational people do not behave as EMV maximizers. Then how do they act? This question has been studied extensively by many researchers, both mathematically and behaviorally. Although the answer is still not agreed upon universally, most researchers believe that if certain basic behavioral assumptions hold, people are **expected utility** maximizers—that is, they choose the alternative with the largest expected utility. Although we will not go deeply into the subject of expected utility maximization, the discussion in this section will acquaint you with the main ideas.

Utility Functions

We begin by discussing an individual's **utility function**. This is a mathematical function that transforms monetary values—payoffs and costs—into **utility values**. Essentially, an individual's utility function specifies the individual's preferences for various monetary payoffs and costs and, in doing so, it automatically encodes the individual's attitudes toward risk. Most individuals are **risk averse**, which means intuitively that they are willing to sacrifice some EMV to avoid risky gambles. In terms of the utility function, this means that every extra dollar of payoff is worth slightly less to the individual than the previous dollar, and every extra dollar of cost is considered slightly more costly (in terms of utility) than the previous dollar. The resulting utility functions are shaped as shown in Figure 10.33. Mathematically, these functions are said to be **increasing** and **concave**. The increasing part means that they go uphill—everyone prefers more money to less money. The concave part means that they increase at a decreasing rate. This is the risk-averse behavior.

There are two problems involved in implementing utility maximization in a real decision analysis. The first is obtaining an individual's (or company's) utility function; we will discuss this below. The second is using the resulting utility function to find the best decision. This second step is actually quite straightforward. We simply substitute

FIGURE 10.33
Risk-Averse Utility
Function

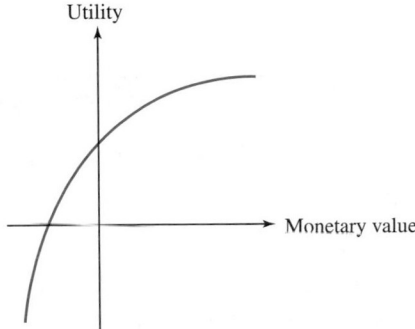

utility values for monetary values in the decision tree and then fold back as usual. That is, we calculate expected *utilities* at probability branches and take maximums (of expected utilities) at decision branches. We will look at a numerical example later in this section. So the real work involves finding an individual's (or company's) utility function in the first place.

Assessing a Utility Function

We will outline a method that can be used to estimate a person's utility function. There are two things we must understand about this method. First, it asks the person to make a series of trade-offs. Because each of us has different attitudes toward risk, we will not all make the trade-offs in the same way. Therefore, each of us will obtain our own utility function. Second, even a particular person's utility function is not unique. If $U(x)$ represents a person's utility function, then it turns out that $aU(x) + b$ also describes that person's utility function, for any constants a and b with $a > 0$. They are equivalent in the sense that they lead to exactly the same decisions.

We take advantage of this nonuniqueness by specifying two points on the utility function. Specifically, we begin by asking the person for two monetary values that represent the worst possible loss and the best possible gain imaginable. Let's say these values are $-A$ and B. Then we *arbitrarily* assign utility values 0 and 1 to these two monetary values, that is, $U(-A) = 0$ and $U(B) = 1$. Don't worry about the absolute magnitudes, 0 and 1, we've assigned—we could assign any other values, such as 14 and 320. The important thing is to use these as "anchors" and then obtain other utility values in terms of them.

The procedure is as follows. Given any two known utility values, say, $U(x)$ and $U(y)$, where x and y are monetary values, we present the person with a choice between the following two options:

- Option 1: Obtain a certain payoff of z.
- Option 2: Obtain a payoff of either x or y, depending on the flip of a fair coin.

Then we ask the person to select the monetary value z in option 1 so that he or she is *indifferent* between the two options. If the person is indifferent, then the expected utilities from the two options must be equal. We will call the resulting value of z the **indifference value**. This leads to the equation for $U(z)$:

$$U(z) = 0.5U(x) + 0.5U(y) \qquad \textbf{(10.3)}$$

In words, we have generated a new utility value from two known utility values. This process continues until we have enough utility values to approximate a utility curve. (Note that if any of x, y, and z are negative, then "payoff" really means "cost.") We will illustrate this procedure with the following example.

EXAMPLE   10.6

ASSESSING THE UTILITY FUNCTION FOR A SMALL BUSINESS

John Jacobs owns his own business. Because he is about to make an important decision where large losses or large gains are at stake, he wants to use the expected utility criterion to make his decision. He knows that he must first assess his own utility function, so he hires a decision analysis expert, Susan Schilling, to help him out. How might the session between John and Susan proceed?

Solution

Susan first asks John for the largest loss and largest gain he can imagine. He answers with the values $200,000 and $300,000, so she assigns utility values $U(-200,000) = 0$ and $U(300,000) = 1$ as anchors for the utility function. Now she presents John with the choice between two options:

- Option 1: Obtain a payoff of z (really a loss if z is negative).
- Option 2: Obtain a loss of $200,000 or a payoff of $300,000, depending on the flip of a fair coin.

Susan reminds John that the EMV of option 2 is $50,000 (halfway between $-$200,000 and $300,000). He realizes this, but because he is quite risk averse, he would far rather have $50,000 for certain than take the gamble in option 2. Therefore, the indifference value of z must be less than $50,000. Susan then poses several values of z to John. Would he rather have $10,000 for sure or take option 2? He says he'd rather take the $10,000. Would he rather *pay* $5000 for sure or take the gamble in option 2? (This is like an insurance premium.) He says he'd rather take option 2. By this time, we know the indifference value of z must be less than $10,000 and greater than $-$5000. With a few more questions of this type, John finally decides on $z = 5000 as his indifference value. He is indifferent between obtaining $5000 for sure and taking the gamble in option 2. We can substitute these values into equation (10.3):

$$U(5000) = 0.5U(-200,000) + 0.5U(300,000) = 0.5(0) + 0.5(1) = 0.5$$

Note that John is giving up $45,000 in EMV because of his risk aversion. The EMV of the gamble in option 2 is $50,000, and he is willing to accept a *sure* $5000 in its place.

The process would then continue. For example, since she now knows $U(5000)$ and $U(300,000)$, Susan could ask John to choose between these options:

- Option 1: Obtain a payoff of z.
- Option 2: Obtain a payoff of $5000 or a payoff of $300,000, depending on the flip of a fair coin.

If John decides that his indifference value is now $z = $130,000$, then with equation (10.3) we know that

$$U(130,000) = 0.5U(5000) + 0.5U(300,000) = 0.5(0.5) + 0.5(1) = 0.75$$

Note that John is now giving up $22,500 in EMV because the EMV of the gamble in option 2 is $152,500. By continuing in this manner, Susan can help John assess enough utility values to approximate a continuous utility curve. ■

As this example illustrates, utility assessment is tedious. Even in the best of circumstances, when a trained consultant attempts to assess the utility function of a single person, the process requires the person to make a series of choices between hypothetical alternatives involving uncertain outcomes. Unless the person has some training in probability, these choices can be difficult to understand, let alone make, and it is unlikely that the person will answer *consistently* as the questioning proceeds. The process is even more difficult when a company's utility function is being assessed. Because company executives involved typically have different attitudes toward risk, it is difficult for these people to reach a consensus on a common utility function.

Exponential Utility

For these reasons there are classes of "ready-made" utility functions that have been developed. One important class is called **exponential utility** and has been used in many financial investment analyses. An exponential utility function has only one adjustable numerical parameter, and there are straightforward ways to discover the most appropriate value of this parameter for a particular individual or company. So the advantage of using an exponential utility function is that it is relatively easy to assess. The drawback is that exponential utility functions do not capture all types of attitudes toward risk. Nevertheless, their ease of use has made them popular.

An exponential utility function has the following form:

$$U(x) = 1 - e^{-x/R} \tag{10.4}$$

Here x is a monetary value (a payoff if positive, a cost if negative), $U(x)$ is the utility of this value, and $R > 0$ is an adjustable parameter called the **risk tolerance**. Basically, the risk tolerance measures how much risk the decision maker will tolerate. The larger the value of R, the less risk averse the decision maker is. That is, a person with a large value of R is more willing to take risks than a person with a small value of R.

To assess a person's (or company's) exponential utility function, we need only to assess the value of R. There are a couple of tips for doing this. First, it has been shown that the risk tolerance is approximately equal to that dollar amount R such that the decision maker is indifferent between the following two options:

- Option 1: Obtain no payoff at all.
- Option 2: Obtain a payoff of R dollars or a loss of $R/2$ dollars, depending on the flip of a fair coin.

For example, if you are indifferent between a bet where you win $1000 or lose $500, with probability 0.5 each, and not betting at all, then your R is approximately $1000. From this criterion it certainly makes intuitive sense that a wealthier person (or company) ought to have a larger value of R. This has been found in practice.

A second tip for finding R is based on empirical evidence found by Ronald Howard, a prominent decision analyst. Through his consulting experience with several large companies, he discovered tentative relationships between risk tolerance and several financial variables—net sales, net income, and equity. [See Howard (1992).] Specifically, he found that R was approximately 6.4% of net sales, 124% of net income, and 15.7% of equity for the companies he studied. For example, according to this prescription, a company with net sales of $30 million should have a risk tolerance of approximately $1.92 million. Howard admits that these percentages are only guidelines. However, they do indicate that larger and more profitable companies tend to have larger values of R, which means that they are more willing to take risks involving given dollar amounts.

We illustrate the use of the expected utility criterion, and exponential utility in particular, with the following example.

EXAMPLE 10.7

DECIDING WHETHER TO ENTER RISKY VENTURES AT VENTURE LIMITED

Venture Limited is a company with net sales of $30 million. The company currently must decide whether to enter one of two risky ventures or do nothing. The possible outcomes of the less risky venture are a $0.5 million loss, a $0.1 million gain, and a $1 million gain. The probabilities of these outcomes are 0.25, 0.50, and 0.25. The possible outcomes of the more risky venture are a $1 million loss, a $1 million gain, and a $3 million gain. The probabilities of these outcomes are 0.35, 0.60, and 0.05. If Venture Limited can enter at most one of the two risky ventures, what should it do?

Solution

We will assume that Venture Limited has an exponential utility function. Also, based on Howard's guidelines, we will assume that the company's risk tolerance is 6.4% of its net sales, or $1.92 million. (We'll do a sensitivity analysis on this parameter later on.) We can substitute into equation (10.4) to find the utility of any monetary outcome. For example, the gain from doing nothing is $0, and its utility is

$$U(0) = 1 - e^{-0/1.92} = 1 - 1 = 0$$

As another example, the utility of a $1 million loss is

$$U(-1) = 1 - e^{-(-1)/1.92} = 1 - 1.683 = -0.683$$

These are the values we use (instead of monetary values) in the decision tree.

USING PRECISIONTREE

Fortunately, PrecisionTree takes care of all the details. After we build a decision tree and label it (with monetary values) in the usual way, we click on the name of the tree (the box on the far left of the tree) to open the dialog box in Figure 10.34. We then fill in the utility function information as shown in the upper right section of the dialog box. This says to use an exponential utility function with risk tolerance 1.92. It also indicates that we want expected utilities (as opposed to EMVs) to appear in the decision tree.

FIGURE 10.34
Dialog Box for Specifying the Exponential Utility Criterion

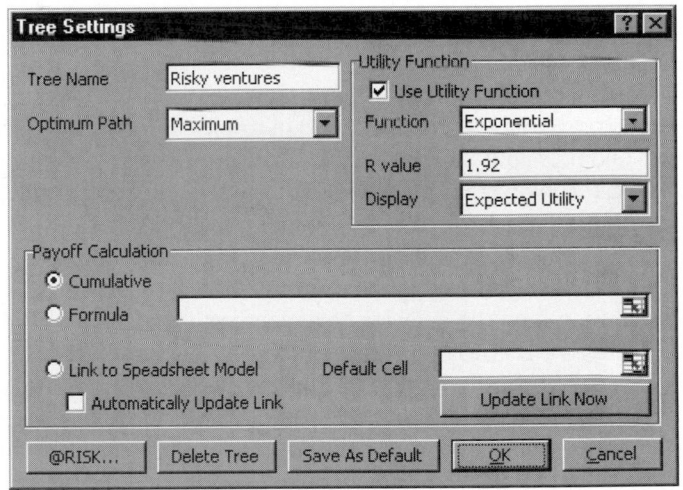

The completed tree for this example appears in Figure 10.35 (page 546). (See the file VENTURE.XLS.) We build it in exactly the same way as usual and link probabilities and monetary values to its branches in the usual way. For example, there is a link in cell C22 to the monetary value in cell A10. However, the expected values shown in the tree (those shown in color on your screen) are expected *utilities*, and the optimal decision is the one with the largest expected utility. In this case the expected utilities for doing nothing, investing in the less risky venture, and investing in the more

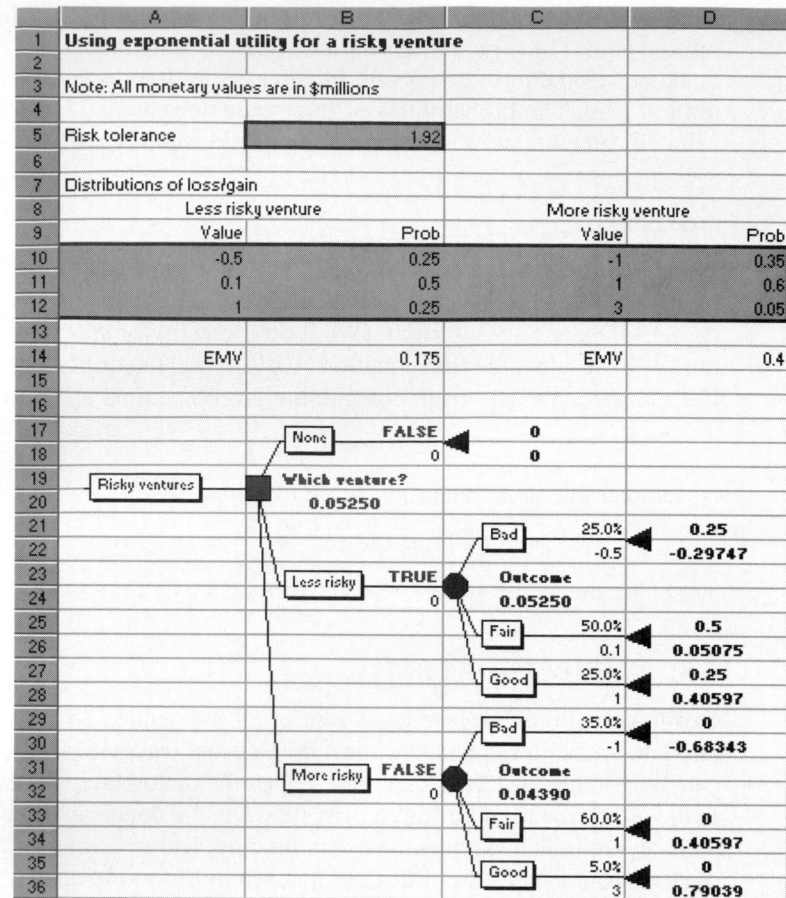

FIGURE 10.35
Decision Tree for Risky Venture Example

risky venture are 0, 0.0525, and 0.0439. Therefore, the optimal decision is to invest in the less risky venture.

Note that the EMVs of the three decisions are $0, $0.175 million, and $0.4 million. The latter two of these are calculated in row 14 as the usual "sumproduct" of monetary values and probabilities. So from an EMV point of view, the more risky venture is definitely best. However, Venture Limited is sufficiently risk averse, and the monetary values are sufficiently large, that the company is willing to sacrifice EMV to reduce its risk.

How sensitive is the optimal decision to the key parameter, the risk tolerance? We can answer this by changing the risk tolerance (through the dialog box in Figure 10.34) and watching how the decision tree changes.[7] You can check that when the company becomes *more* risk tolerant, the more risky venture eventually becomes optimal. In fact, this occurs when the risk tolerance increases to approximately $2.075 million. In the other direction, when the company becomes *less* risk tolerant, the "do nothing" decision eventually becomes optimal. This occurs when the risk tolerance decreases to approximately $0.715 million. So the "optimal" decision depends heavily on the attitudes toward risk of Venture Limited's top management.

Certainty Equivalents Now suppose that Venture Limited has only two options. It can either enter the less risky venture or receive a *certain* dollar amount x and avoid

---

[7]We show the risk tolerance in cell B5, but the values in the decision tree are not linked to that cell. We need to go through the dialog box to change the risk tolerance.

the gamble altogether. We want to find the dollar amount x such that the company is indifferent between these two options. If it enters the risky venture, its expected utility is 0.0525, calculated above. If it receives x dollars for certain, its (expected) utility is

$$U(x) = 1 - e^{-x/1.92}$$

To find the value x where it is indifferent between the two options, we set $1 - e^{-x/1.92}$ equal to 0.0525, or $e^{-x/1.92} = 0.9475$, and solve for x. Taking natural logarithms of both sides and multiplying by -1.92, we obtain

$$x = -1.92 \ln(0.9475) \approx \$0.104 \text{ million}$$

This value is called the **certainty equivalent** of the risky venture. The company is indifferent between entering the less risky venture and receiving $0.104 million to avoid it. Although the EMV of the less risky venture is $0.175 million, the company acts as if it is equivalent to a sure $0.104 million. In this sense, the company is willing to give up the difference in EMV, $71,000, to avoid a gamble.

By a similar calculation, the certainty equivalent of the more risky venture is approximately $0.086 million. That is, the company acts as if this more risky venture is equivalent to a sure $0.086 million, when in fact its EMV is a hefty $0.4 million! So in this case it is willing to give up the difference in EMV, $314,000, to avoid this particular gamble. Again, the reason is that the company dislikes risk. We can see these certainty equivalents in PrecisionTree by adjusting the Display box in Figure 10.34 to show Certainty Equivalent. The tree then looks as in Figure 10.36. The certainty equivalents we just discussed appear in cells C24 and C32.

FIGURE 10.36
Decision Tree with
Certainty Equivalents

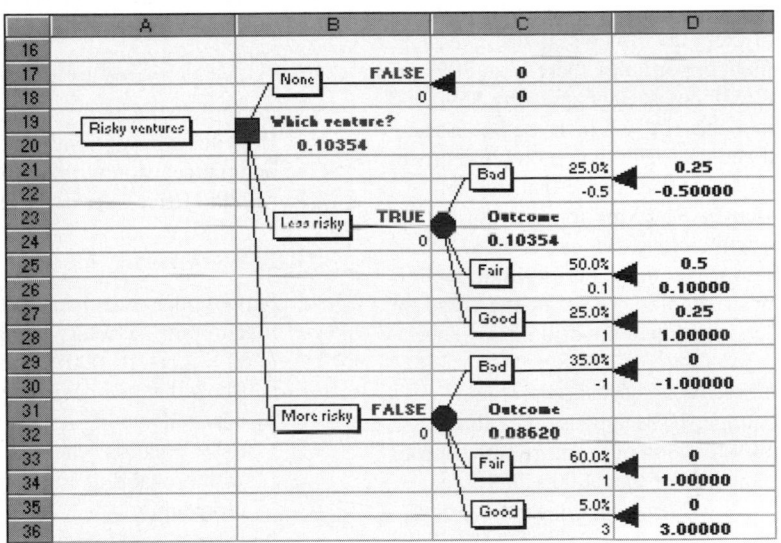

Is Expected Utility Maximization Used?

The above discussion indicates that utility maximization is a fairly involved task. The bottom line, then, is whether the difficulty is worth the trouble. Theoretically, expected utility maximization might be interesting to researchers, but is it really used? The answer appears to be: not very often. For example, one recent article on the practice of decision making [see Kirkwood (1992)] quotes Ronald Howard—the same person we quoted earlier—as having found risk aversion to be of practical concern in only

5% to 10% of business decision analyses. This same article quotes the president of a Fortune 500 company as saying, "Most of the decisions we analyze are for a few million dollars. It is adequate to use expected value (EMV) for these."

With these comments in mind, it is clear that knowledge of expected utility maximization is an important requirement for anyone intending to specialize in the field. In some of the greatest success stories, expected utility maximization was indeed implemented. For nonspecialists, however, a passing knowledge of the concepts is sufficient.

PROBLEMS

Skill-Building Problems

36. Suppose that a decision maker's utility as a function of his wealth, x, is given by $U(x) = \ln x$ (the natural logarithm of x).
   a. Is this decision maker risk averse? Explain why or why not.
   b. The decision maker now has $10,000 and two possible decisions. For decision 1, he loses $500 for certain. For decision 2, he loses $0 with probability 0.9 and loses $5000 with probability 0.1. Which decision maximizes the expected utility of his net wealth?

37. An investor has $10,000 in assets and can choose between two different investments. If she invests in the first investment opportunity, there is an 80% chance that she will increase her assets by $590,000 and a 20% chance that she will increase her assets by $190,000. If she invests in the second investment opportunity, there is a 50% chance that she will increase her assets by $1.19 million and a 50% chance that she will increase her assets by $1000. This investor has an exponential utility function for final assets with a risk tolerance parameter equal to $600,000. Which investment opportunity will she prefer?

38. Consider again FreshWay's decision problem described in Example 10.3. Suppose now that FreshWay's utility function of profit π, earned from the acquisition and sale of the 24,000 fluorescent lightbulbs, is $U(\pi) = \ln(\pi)$. Find the course of action that maximizes FreshWay's expected utility. How does this optimal decision compare to the optimal decision with an EMV criterion? Explain any difference in the two decisions.

39. Consider again the landowner's decision problem described in Problem 3. Suppose now that the landowner's utility function of financial gain x is $U(x) = x^2$. Find the course of action that maximizes the landowner's expected utility. How does this optimal decision compare to the optimal decision with an EMV criterion? Explain any difference in the two decisions.

40. Consider again Techware's decision problem described in Problem 4. Suppose now that Techware's utility function of net revenue r (measured in dollars), earned from the given marketing opportunities, is $U(r) = 1 - e^{-r/350,000}$.
   a. Find the course of action that maximizes Techware's expected utility. How does this optimal decision compare to the optimal decision with an EMV criterion? Explain any difference in the two optimal decisions.
   b. Repeat part **a** when Techware's utility function is $U(r) = 1 - e^{-r/50,000}$.

41. Consider again the bank's customer loan decision problem in Problem 30. Suppose now that the bank's utility function of profit π (in dollars) is $U(\pi) = 1 - e^{-\pi/10,000}$. Find the strategy that maximizes the bank's expected utility in this case. How does this optimal strategy compare to the optimal decision with an EMV criterion? Explain any difference in two optimal strategies.

Skill-Extending Problems

42. Suppose that a decision maker has a utility function for monetary gains x given by $U(x) = (x + 10,000)^{0.5}$.
   a. Show that this decision maker is indifferent between gaining nothing (i.e., $0) and entering a risky situation where she gains $80,000 with probability 1/3 and loses $10,000 with probability 2/3.
   b. If there is a 10% chance that one of the decision maker's family heirlooms, valued at $5000, will be stolen during the next year, what is the most that she would be willing to pay each year for an insurance policy that completely covers the potential loss of her cherished item?

43. A decision maker is going to invest $2000 for a period of 6 months. Two potential investments are available to him: U.S. Treasury bills and gold. If this decision maker invests the $2000 in T-bills, he is sure to end the 6-month period with $2592. If this decision maker invests in gold, there is a 75% chance that he will end the 6-month period with

$800 and a 25% chance that he will end up with $20,000. The decision maker's utility function of ending up with x dollars is $U(x) = \sqrt{x}$.

a. Should this decision maker invest in gold or T-bills?

b. Suppose the decision maker invests a proportion y of his $2000 in T-bills and the remaining fraction $(1 - y)$ of his available funds in gold. In this case his gain or loss from either investment is reduced proportionally. For example, if he invests half of his money in gold, he will either lose $600 with probability 0.75 or gain $9000 with probability 0.25. Given the same utility function $U(x) = \sqrt{x}$, find the investor's optimal choice of y.

10.7 CONCLUSION

In this chapter we have discussed methods that can be used in decision-making problems in which future uncertainty is a key element. Perhaps the most important skill we can gain from this chapter is the ability to approach decision problems that include uncertainty in a systematic manner. This systematic approach requires the decision maker to list all possible decisions or strategies, list all possible uncertain outcomes, assess the probabilities of these outcomes (possibly with the aid of Bayes' rule), calculate all necessary monetary values, and finally do the calculations necessary to obtain the best decision. If large dollar amounts are at stake, it might also be necessary to perform a utility analysis, where the decision maker's feelings toward risk are taken into account. Once the basic analysis has been completed, using "best guesses" for the various parameters of the problem, a sensitivity analysis should be conducted to see whether the best decision continues to be best within a range of problem parameters.

PROBLEMS

Skill-Building Problems

44. Ford is going to produce a new vehicle, the Pioneer, and wants to determine the amount of annual capacity it should build. Ford's goal is to maximize the profit from this vehicle over the next 10 years. Each vehicle will sell for $13,000 and incur a variable production cost of $10,000. Building 1 unit of annual capacity will cost $3000. Each unit of capacity will also cost $1000 per year to maintain, even if the capacity is unused. Demand for the Pioneer is unknown but marketing estimates the distribution of annual demand to be as shown in Table 10.27. Assume that unit sales during a year is the minimum of capacity and annual demand.

a. Explain why a capacity of 1,300,000 is not a good choice.

b. Which capacity level should Ford choose?

45. You are CEO of the venture capital firm D&D. Billy comes to you with an investment proposition. You estimate that your distribution of cash flows from this investment is as shown in Table 10.28.

TABLE 10.27	Distribution of Annual Demand
Annual Demand	**Probability**
400,000	0.25
900,000	0.50
1,300,000	0.25

TABLE 10.28	Distribution of Cash Flow
Cash Flow	**Probability**
−1,000,000	0.35
500,000	0.60
3,000,000	0.05

a. If you are trying to maximize the expected value of the firm's cash flows, should you take the project?

b. Suppose you assess your firm to be risk averse, with an exponential utility function. You also use the rule of thumb that the firm's risk tolerance is about 6.4% of its annual revenues, which are $30 million. Determine whether D&D should enter the venture.

46. Pizza King (PK) and Noble Greek (NG) are competitive pizza chains. Pizza King believes there is a 25% chance that NG will charge $6 per pizza, a 50% chance NG will charge $8 per pizza, and a 25% chance that NG will charge $10 per pizza. If PK charges price p_1 and NG charges price p_2, PK will sell $100 + 25(p_2 - p_1)$ pizzas. It costs PK $4 to make a pizza. PK is considering charging $5, $6, $7, $8, or $9 per pizza. In order to maximize its expected profit, what price should PK charge for a pizza?

47. Sodaco is considering producing a new product: Chocovan soda. Sodaco estimates that the annual demand for Chocovan, D (in thousands of cases), has the following probability distribution: $P(D = 30) = 0.30$, $P(D = 50) = 0.40$, $P(D = 80) = 0.30$. Each case of Chocovan sells for $5 and incurs a variable cost of $3. It costs $800,000 to build a plant to produce Chocovan. Assume that if $1 is received every year (forever), this is equivalent to receiving $10 at the present time. If Sodaco decides to build the plant and produce Chocovan, find the expected net present value of its profit.

48. Many decision problems have the following simple structure. A decision maker has two possible decisions, 1 and 2. If decision 1 is made, a *sure* cost of c is incurred. If decision 2 is made, there are two possible outcomes, with costs c_1 and c_2 and probabilities p and $1 - p$. We assume that $c_1 < c < c_2$. The idea is that decision 1, the riskless decision, has a "moderate" cost, whereas decision 2, the risky decision, has a "low" cost c_1 or a "high" cost c_2.
  a. Find the decision maker's cost table, that is, the cost for each possible decision and each possible outcome.
  b. Calculate the expected cost from the risky decision.
  c. List as many scenarios as you can think of that have this structure. (Here's an example to get you started. Think of insurance, where you pay a sure premium to avoid a large possible loss.)

49. During the summer, Olympic swimmer Adam Johnson swims every day. On sunny summer days he goes to an outdoor pool, where he may swim for no charge. On rainy days he must go to a domed pool. At the beginning of the summer, he has the option of purchasing a $15 season pass to the domed pool, which allows him use for the entire summer. If he doesn't buy the season pass, he must pay $1 each time he goes there. Past meteorological records

indicate that there is a 60% chance that the summer will be sunny (in which case there is an average of 6 rainy days during the summer) and a 40% chance the summer will be rainy (an average of 30 rainy days during the summer).

Before the summer begins, Adam has the option of purchasing a long-range weather forecast for $1. The forecast predicts a sunny summer 80% of the time and a rainy summer 20% of the time. If the forecast predicts a sunny summer, there is a 70% chance that the summer will actually be sunny. If the forecast predicts a rainy summer, there is an 80% chance that the summer will actually be rainy. Assuming that Adam's goal is to minimize his total expected cost for the summer, what should he do? Also find the EVSI and the EVPI.

50. Erica is going to fly to London on August 5, and return home on August 20. It is now July 1. On July 1, she may buy a one-way ticket (for $350) or a round-trip ticket (for $660). She may also wait until August to buy a ticket. On August 1, a one-way ticket will cost $370, and a round-trip ticket will cost $730. It is possible that between July 1 and August 1, her sister (who works for the airline) will be able to obtain a free one-way ticket for Erica. The probability that her sister will obtain the free ticket is 0.30. If Erica has bought a round-trip ticket on July 1 and her sister has obtained a free ticket, she may return "half" of her round trip to the airline. In this case, her total cost will be $330 plus a $50 penalty. Use a decision tree approach to determine how to minimize Erica's expected cost of obtaining round-trip transportation to London.

51. A nuclear power company is deciding whether to build a nuclear power plant at Diablo Canyon or at Roy Rogers City. The cost of building the power plant is $10 million at Diablo and $20 million at Roy Rogers City. If the company builds at Diablo, however, and an earthquake occurs at Diablo during the next 5 years, construction will be terminated and the company will lose $10 million (and will still have to build a power plant at Roy Rogers City). Without further expert information the company believes there is a 20% chance that an earthquake will occur at Diablo during the next 5 years. For $1 million, a geologist can be hired to analyze the fault structure at Diablo Canyon. She will predict either that an earthquake will occur or that an earthquake will not occur. The geologist's past record indicates that she will predict an earthquake on 95% of the occasions for which an earthquake will occur and no earthquake on 90% of the occasions for which an earthquake will not occur. Should the power company hire the geologist? Also find the EVSI and the EVPI.

52. Joan's utility function for her asset position x (for x between 0 and \$160,000) is given by $U(x) = \sqrt{x}/400$.
   a. Is Joan risk averse? Explain.
   b. Currently, Joan's assets consist of \$10,000 in cash and a \$90,000 home. During a given year, there is a 0.001 probability that Joan's home will be destroyed by fire or other causes. How much should Joan be willing to pay for insurance that covers her home completely from this type of destruction?

53. My current annual income is \$40,000. I believe that I owe \$8000 in taxes. For \$500, I can hire a CPA to review my tax return. There is a 20% chance she will save me \$4000 in taxes and an 80% chance she won't save me anything. If x is my disposable income for the current year, my utility function is given by $U(x) = \sqrt{x}/200$.
   a. Am I risk averse or risk seeking?
   b. Should I hire the accountant?

Skill-Extending Problems

54. City officials in Ft. Lauderdale, Florida, are trying to decide whether to evacuate coastal residents in anticipation of a major hurricane that may make landfall near their city within the next 48 hours. Based on previous studies, it is estimated that it will cost approximately 1 million dollars to evacuate the residents living along the coast of this major metropolitan area. However, if city officials choose not to evacuate their residents and the storm strikes Fort Lauderdale, there would likely be some deaths as a result of the hurricane's storm surge along the coast. While city officials are reluctant to place an economic value on the loss of human life resulting from such a storm, they realize that it may ultimately be necessary to do so to make a sound judgment in this situation. Prior to making the evacuation decision, city officials consult hurricane experts at the National Hurricane Center in Coral Gables regarding the accuracy of past predictions. They learn that in similar past cases, hurricanes that were *predicted* to make landfall near a particular coastal location actually did so 60% of the time. Moreover, they learn that in past similar cases hurricanes that were predicted *not* to make landfall near a particular coastal location actually did so

20% of the time. Finally, in response to similar threats in the past, weather forecasters have issued predictions of a major hurricane making landfall near a particular coastal location 40% of the time.
   a. Let L be the economic valuation of the loss of human life resulting from a coastal strike by the hurricane. Employ a decision tree to help these city officials make a decision that minimizes the expected cost of responding to the threat of the impending storm as a function of L. To proceed, you might begin by choosing an initial value of L and then perform sensitivity analysis on the optimal decision by varying this model parameter. Summarize your findings.
   b. For which values of L will these city officials *always* choose to evacuate the coastal residents, regardless of the Hurricane Center's prediction?

55. A homeowner wants to decide whether he should install an electronic heat pump in his home. Given that the cost of installing a new heat pump is fairly large, the homeowner would like to do so only if he can count on being able to recover the initial expense over *five* consecutive years of cold winter weather. Upon reviewing historical data on the operation of heat pumps in various kinds of winter weather, he computes the expected annual costs of heating his home during the winter months with and without a heat pump in operation. These cost figures are shown in Table 10.29. The probabilities of experiencing a mild, normal, colder than normal, and severe winter are $0.2(1-x)$, $0.5(1-x)$, $0.3(1-x)$, and x, respectively.
   a. Given that $x = 0.1$, what is the most that the homeowner is willing to pay for the heat pump?
   b. If the heat pump costs \$500, how large must x be before the homeowner decides it is economically worthwhile to install the heat pump?
   c. Given that $x = 0.1$, compute and interpret the expected value of perfect information (EVPI) when the heat pump costs \$500.
   d. Repeat part **c** when $x = 0.15$.

56. Consider a company that manufactures computer memory chips in lots of ten chips. From past experience, the company knows that 80% of all lots contain 10% defective chips, and 20% of all lots contain 50% defective chips. If an *acceptable* (that is, 10% defective) batch of chips is sent on to the next stage of production, processing costs of

TABLE 10.29	Expected Winter Heating Costs for Homeowner's Decision Problem			
Decision Alternatives	**Mild**	**Normal**	**Colder than Normal**	**Severe**
Purchase pump	\$420	\$590	\$720	\$900
Don't purchase pump	\$358	\$503	\$612	\$765

$10,000 are incurred. If an *unacceptable* (that is, 50% defective) batch is sent on to the next stage of production, processing costs of $40,000 are incurred. This company also has the option of reworking a batch of chips at a cost of $10,000. A reworked batch is guaranteed to be acceptable. Alternatively, at a cost of $1000, the company can test one memory chip from each batch in an attempt to determine whether the given batch is unacceptable. If a randomly selected chip is found to be defective, the batch from which the chip came is acceptable with probability 8/18. If a randomly selected chip is found *not* to be defective, the batch from which the chip came is acceptable with probability 72/82.

a. Determine how this company can minimize the expected total cost per batch of computer memory chips.

b. Compute and interpret the expected value of sample information (EVSI) in this decision problem.

c. Compute and interpret the expected value of perfect information (EVPI) in this decision problem.

d. Suppose now that this manufacturer's utility function of cost c per batch is $U(c) = -c^{0.5}$. Find the strategy that maximizes the manufacturer's expected utility. How does this optimal strategy compare to the optimal decision with an EMV criterion? Explain any difference in two optimal strategies.

57. Patty is trying to determine whether to take management science or statistics. If she takes management science, she believes there is a 10% chance she will receive an A, a 40% chance she will receive a B, and a 50% chance she will receive C. If Patty takes statistics, she has a 70% chance of receiving a B, a 25% chance of a C, and a 5% chance of a D. Patty is indifferent between the following two options:

■ Option 1: Receiving a B for certain
■ Option 2: A 70% chance at an A and a 30% chance at a D

Patty is also indifferent between the following two options:

■ Option 3: Receiving a C for certain
■ Option 4: A 25% chance at an A and a 75% chance at a D

In order to maximize the expected utility associated with her final grade, which course should Patty take?

58. Many men over 50 take the PSA blood test. The purpose of the PSA test is to detect prostate cancer early. Dr. Rene Labrie of Quebec conducted a study to determine whether the PSA test can actually prevent cancer deaths. In 1989, Dr. Labrie randomly divided all male registered voters between 45 and 80 in Quebec City into two groups. Two-thirds of the men were asked to be tested for prostate cancer and one-third were not asked. Eventually, 8137 men were screened for prostate cancer (PSA plus digital rectal exam) in 1989; 38,056 men were not screened. By 1997 only 5 of the screened men had died of prostate cancer while 137 of the men who were not screened had died of prostate cancer. (*Source*: *New York Times* May 19,1998)

a. Discuss why this study seems to indicate that screening for prostate cancer saves lives.

b. Despite the results of this study, many doctors are not convinced that early screening for prostate cancer saves lives. Can you see why they doubt the conclusions of the study?

59. You have just been chosen to appear on "Hoosier Millionaire"! The rules are as follows: There are four hidden cards. One says "STOP" and the other three have dollar amounts of $150,000, $200,000, and $1,000,000. You get to choose a card. If the card says "STOP," you win no money. At any time you may quit and keep the largest amount of money that has appeared on any card you have chosen, or you may continue. If you continue and choose the STOP card, however, you win no money. As an example, you might first choose the $150,000 card, then the $200,000 card, and then choose to quit and receive $200,000.

a. If your goal is to maximize your expected payoff, what strategy should you follow?

b. Suppose your utility function for an increase in cash satisfies $U(0) = 0$, $U(\$40,000) = 0.25$, $U(\$120,000) = 0.50$, $U(\$400,000) = 0.75$ and $U(\$1,000,000) = 1$. Are you risk averse? Explain.

c. After drawing a curve through the points in part **b**, determine a strategy that maximizes your expected utility. (Alternatively, you might want to assess and use your *actual* utility function.)

60. You are trying to determine how much money to put in your Tax Saver Benefit (TSB) plan. At the beginning of the calendar year, a TSB allows you to put money into an account. The money in the account can be used to pay for medical expenses incurred during the year. Once the TSB is exhausted, you must pay the medical expenses out of pocket. The benefit of the TSB is that money placed in the TSB is not subject to federal taxes. The catch is that any money left in the TSB at the end of the year is lost to you. Suppose the federal tax rate is 40% and your current annual salary is $50,000. You believe that it is equally likely that your medical expenses during the current year will be $3000, $4000, $5000, $6000, or $7000.

a. If you are risk neutral and want to maximize your expected disposable income, how much should you put in your TSB?

b. Suppose you assess a utility function for disposable income given by $U(x) = 0.000443x^{0.713595}$. (Who said they all have to have nice round numbers?) Are you risk averse? How much should you put in the TSB?

61. Peter is thinking of purchasing an advertising company from Amanda. At present, only Amanda (not Peter) knows the current value of the company. Peter knows, however, that there is an equal chance that the company is worth 10, 20, 30, 40, 50, 60, 70, 80, 90, or 100 million dollars. Amanda will accept an offer from Peter only if Peter bids at least the value of the company. For example, if Amanda knows the company is worth $20 million, she will accept any bid of $20 million or higher. As soon as Peter purchases the company, his reputation as a skilled businessman immediately increases the actual value of the company by 80%.

a. Suppose Peter is risk neutral and is considering bidding 10, 20, 30, 40, 50, 60, 70, 80, 90, or 100 million dollars. What should he bid?

b. Suppose Peter's utility function for financial gains or losses (in millions of dollars) is given by $U(x) = ((x + 82)/144)^{1.7}$. Determine whether Peter is risk averse or risk seeking and determine Peter's optimal decision.

62. Sarah Chang is the owner of a small electronics company. In 6 months a proposal is due for an electronic timing system for the 1998 Olympic Games. For several years, Chang's company has been developing a new microprocessor, a critical component in a timing system that would be superior to any product currently on the market. However, progress in research and development has been slow, and Chang is unsure about whether her staff can produce the microprocessor in time. If they succeed in developing the microprocessor (probability p_1), there is an excellent chance (probability p_2) that Chang's company will win the $1 million Olympic contract. If they do not, there is a small chance (probability p_3) that she will still be able to win the same contract with an alternative, inferior timing system that has already been developed.

If she continues the project, Chang must invest $200,000 in research and development. In addition, making a proposal (which she will decide whether to do after seeing whether the R&D is successful or not) requires developing a prototype timing system at an additional cost of $50,000. Finally, if Chang wins the contract, the finished product will cost an additional $150,000 to produce.

a. Develop a decision tree that can be used to solve Chang's problem. You can assume in this part that she is using EMV (of her net profit) as a decision criterion. Build the tree so that she can enter any values for p_1, p_2, and p_3 (in input

cells) and automatically see her optimal EMV and optimal strategy from the tree.

b. If $p_2 = 0.8$ and $p_3 = 0.1$, what value of p_1 makes Chang indifferent between abandoning the project and going ahead with it?

c. How much would Chang be willing to pay the Olympic organization (now) to guarantee her the contract in the case where her company is successful in developing the contract? (This guarantee is in force only if she is successful in developing the product.) Assume $p_1 = 0.4$, $p_2 = 0.8$, and $p_3 = 0.1$.

d. Suppose now that this a "big" project for Chang. Therefore, she decides to use expected utility as her criterion, with an exponential utility function. Using some trial and error, see which risk tolerance changes her initial decision from "go ahead" to "abandon" when $p_1 = 0.4$, $p_2 = 0.8$, and $p_3 = 0.1$.

63. Suppose an investor has the opportunity to buy the following contract, a stock call option, on March 1. The contract allows him to buy 100 shares of ABC stock at the end of March, April, or May at a guaranteed price of $50 per share. He can "exercise" this option at most once. For example, if he purchases the stock at the end of March, he can't purchase more in April or May at the guaranteed price. The current price of the stock is $50. Each month, we assume the stock price either goes up by a dollar (with probability 0.6) or down by a dollar (with probability 0.4). If the investor buys the contract, he is hoping that the stock price will go up. The reasoning is that if he buys the contract, the price goes up to $51, and he buys the stock (that is, he exercises his option) for $50, he can turn around and sell the stock for $51 and make a profit of $1 per share. On the other hand, if the stock price goes down, he doesn't have to exercise his option; he can just throw the contract away.

a. Use a decision tree to find the investor's optimal strategy (that is, when he should exercise the option), *assuming* he purchases the contract.

b. How much should he be willing to pay for such a contract?

64. The Ventron Engineering Company has just been awarded a $2 million development contract by the U.S. Army Aviation Systems Command to develop a blade spar for its Heavy Lift Helicopter program. The blade spar is a metal tube that runs the length of and provides strength to the helicopter blade. Due to the unusual length and size of the Heavy Lift Helicopter blade, Ventron is unable to produce a single-piece blade spar of the required dimensions, using existing extrusion equipment and material.

The engineering department has prepared two alternatives for developing the blade spar:

(1) sectioning or (2) an improved extrusion process. Ventron must decide which process to use. (Backing out of the contract at any point is not an option.) The risk report has been prepared by the engineering department. The information from it is explained below.

The sectioning option involves joining several shorter lengths of extruded metal into a blade spar of sufficient length. This work will require extensive testing and rework over a 12-month period at a total cost of $1.8 million. While this process will definitely produce an adequate blade spar, it merely represents an extension of existing technology.

To improve the extrusion process, on the other hand, it will be necessary to perform two steps: (1) improve the material used, at a cost of $300,000, and (2) modify the extrusion press, at a cost of $960,000. The first step will require 6 months of work, and if this first step is successful, the second step will require another 6 months of work. If both steps are successful, the blade spar will be available at that time, that is, a year from now. The engineers estimate that the probabilities of succeeding in steps 1 and 2 are 0.9 and 0.75, respectively. However, if either step is unsuccessful (which will be known only in 6 months for step 1 and in a year for step 2), Ventron will have no alternative but to switch to the sectioning process—and incur the sectioning cost on top of any costs already incurred.

Development of the blade spar must be completed within 18 months to avoid holding up the rest of the contract. If necessary, the sectioning work can be done on an accelerated basis in a 6-month period, but the cost of sectioning will then increase from $1.8 million to $2.4 million.

Frankly, the Director of Engineering, Dr. Smith, wants to try developing the improved extrusion process. This is not only cheaper (if successful) for the current project, but its expected side benefits for future projects could be sizable. Although these side benefits are difficult to gauge, Dr. Smith's best guess is an additional $2 million. (Of course, these side benefits are obtained only if both steps of the modified extrusion process are completed successfully.)

a. Develop a decision tree to maximize Ventron's EMV. This includes the revenue from this project, the side benefits (if applicable) from an improved extrusion process, and relevant costs. You don't need to worry about the time value of money; that is, no discounting or NPVs are required. Summarize your findings in words in the spreadsheet.

b. What value of side benefits would make Ventron indifferent between the two alternatives?

c. How much would Ventron be willing to pay, right now, for perfect information about both

steps of the improved extrusion process? (This information would tell Ventron, right now, the ultimate success/failure outcomes of both steps.)

65. Ligature, Inc. is a company that does contract work for publishing companies. It specializes in writing textbooks for secondary schools. Because states such as Texas and California typically adopt only about four to eight textbooks for any given subject and grade level (from which individual schools can choose), the potential for large profits is great.

Ligature is currently negotiating a contract with Brockway and Coates (B&C), a large publishing company, to write a social studies series for grades 9–12. Actually, the development of the books is already well under way, and the only details not yet worked out concern the fee B&C will pay Ligature. Ligature has always operated on a fixed fee basis. Under this arrangement, B&C would pay Ligature its costs, in this case $4.15 million, plus 25%. Ligature would receive this payment in 6 months, at the beginning of year 1. Although this is still an option, the companies have also been discussing a royalty arrangement as an alternative.

Under the royalty plan, B&C would still pay Ligature its $4.15 million costs at the beginning of year 1, but Ligature would then receive yearly royalty payments at the ends of years 1 through 5. These payments would depend on (1) total sales over the five years, (2) the timing of sales, and (3) the negotiated royalty rate, that is, Ligature's percentage of each sales dollar. As for timing, both parties agree that 10% of total sales will be in year 1, 20% will be in each of the next 2 years, 30% will be in year 4, and 20% will be in year 5. They also estimate that the probability distribution of total sales is discrete, with possible values $25 million, $30 million, $50 million, and $70 million, and corresponding probabilities 0.10, 0.45, 0.30, and 0.15.

To guard its interests, B&C has imposed the following restriction to any royalty agreement. It places a cap on the amount Ligature can earn through the royalty scheme. Specifically, the royalties, discounted back to the beginning of year 1 at a 10% discount rate, cannot exceed 33% of Ligature's $4.15 million costs. Obviously, this limits B&C's downside exposure, regardless of the negotiated royalty rate or how well the books sell.

Ligature is interested in maximizing the NPV of its profit from this project (discounted back to the beginning of year 1), using a 10% discount rate. The following steps lead you through the required calculations to "solve" the problem. No decision tree is required for this problem.

a. The file P10_65.XLS supplies the inputs in an input section (blue border), and it has a calculation section (red border). First, calculate the upper part of the calculation section. To do so, enter any trial value for total sales in cell G8 and do the necessary calculations to eventually find (in cell G17) the NPV to Ligature from the royalty agreement. At this point, you can use any royalty rate in the RoyRate cell (C28).

b. Using the calculations from part **a**, complete the data table in the middle part of the calculation section. It should show the NPV to Ligature for any potential value of total sales. Then use these NPVs to calculate the expected NPV to Ligature in the ExpNPV cell (G27).

c. Suppose the current "offer on the table" is a 3% royalty rate. In the bottom part of the calculation section, use IF comparisons to see which arrangement, fixed fee or royalty, each party would favor.

d. Continuing part **c** (with the 3% offer on the table), what do you think the two parties will eventually agree upon? That is, will they stick with the 3% royalty rate, move to a different royalty rate, or settle on the fixed fee arrangement? Answer below cell B36.

66. The American chess master Jonathan Meller is playing the Soviet expert Yuri Gasparov in a two-game exhibition match. Each win earns a player one point, and each draw earns a half point. The player who has the most points after two games wins the match. If the players are tied after two games, they play until one wins a game; then the first player to win a game wins the match. During each game, Meller has two possible strategies: to play a daring strategy or to play a conservative strategy. His probabilities of winning, losing, and drawing when he follows each strategy are shown in Table 10.30. To maximize his probability of winning the match, what should the American do?

TABLE 10.30 **Probabilities for Chess Problem**

Strategy	Win	Loss	Draw
Daring	0.45	0.55	0.00
Conservative	0.00	0.10	0.90

67. Based on Balson et al. (1992). An electric utility company is trying to decide whether to replace its PCB transformer in a generating station with a new and safer transformer. To evaluate this decision, the utility needs information about the likelihood of an incident, such as a fire, the cost of such an incident, and the cost of replacing the unit. Suppose that the total cost of replacement as a present value is $75,000. If the transformer is replaced, there is virtually no chance of a fire. However, if the current transformer is retained, the probability of a fire is

assessed to be 0.0025. If a fire occurs, then the cleanup cost could be high ($80 million) or low ($20 million). The probability of a high cleanup cost, given that a fire occurs, is assessed at 0.2.

a. If the company uses EMV as its decision criterion, should it replace the transformer?

b. Perform a sensitivity analysis on the key parameters of the problem that are difficult to assess, namely, the probability of a fire, the probability of a high cleanup cost, and the high and low cleanup costs. Does the optimal decision from part **a** remain optimal for a "wide" range of these parameters?

c. Do you believe EMV is the correct criterion to use in this type of problem involving environmental accidents?

68. Based on Mellichamp et al. (1993). Construction equipment managers typically have many large pools of engines, transmissions, and other equipment units to maintain. One approach to this maintenance is to use oil analysis, where the oil from any of these is subjected periodically to an inspection. These inspections can sometimes signal an impending failure (for example, too much iron in the oil), and preventive maintenance is then performed (at a relatively low cost), eliminating the risk of failure (failure would result in a relatively high cost). However, oil analysis costs money, and it is not perfect. That is, it can indicate that a unit is defective when in fact it is not about to fail, and it can indicate that a unit is nondefective when in fact it is about to fail. As a possible substitute for oil analysis, the company could simply change the oil periodically, thereby reducing the probability of a failure.

Suppose the company has four alternatives: (1) do nothing, (2) use oil analysis only, (3) replace oil only, or (4) replace oil and do oil analysis. For option (1) the probability of a failure is p_1, and the cost of a failure is C_1. For option (2), the probability of a failure remains at p_1. If the unit is about to fail, the oil analysis will indicate this with probability $1 - \alpha$; if the unit is not about to fail, the oil analysis will indicate this with probability $1 - \beta$. (Therefore, α and β are the error probabilities of the oil analysis.) The oil analysis itself costs C_2, and if it indicates that a failure is about to occur, the oil will be changed, at cost C_3, and preventive maintenance will be performed. The cost of maintenance to restore a unit that is about to fail is C_4, whereas the cost of maintenance for a unit that is not about to fail is C_5. The only difference between options (3) and (4) is that the probability of a failure decreases to p_2 after changing the oil. The values of these parameters for a particular class of units (engines in light trucks, say) appear in Table 10.31 (page 556).

TABLE 10.31 **Parameters for Oil Analysis Problem**

Parameter	Value
p_1	0.10
p_2	0.04
α	0.30
β	0.20
C_1	$1200.00
C_2	$20.00
C_3	$14.80
C_4	$500.00
C_5	$250.00

TABLE 10.32 **Probabilities for Water Pollution Problem**

Event	Probability
Significant market	0.6 ± 0.15
Technically feasible	0.6 ± 0.15
Board sanctions plant expenditures	0.8 ± 0.2
Commercial success	0.8 ± 0.2

a. For these parameters, develop a decision tree to find the company's best decision and the corresponding expected cost.

b. If the company has 500 units, what should it do? What is the expected cost for the entire fleet?

c. Suppose that the company has different types of units. For example, the cost of an oil change might be higher for some, or the cost of a failure might be higher or lower. Run a sensitivity analysis on any of the parameters you believe might be "key" parameters and see whether the optimal decision changes in ways you would anticipate.

69. Based on Hess (1993). A company that is heavily involved in R&D projects believes it might have the potential to develop a very lucrative commercial product that would (if successful) reduce pulp mill water pollution. At the current stage, however, everything is quite uncertain, and the company is trying to decide whether to go ahead with its R&D or abandon the product. The following are the primary risks:

■ Would market tests confirm that there is a significant market for the product?

■ Could the company develop a new process for making this product—that is, is it technically feasible?

■ Even if there is a significant market and the process is technically feasible, would the company's board sanction the new plant capital necessary to produce the product on a commercial scale?

■ Assuming the answers to the above questions are all yes and the plant is built, would the venture turn out to be successful?

We assume that each of these questions has a yes or no answer. The probabilities of yes answers are shown in Table 10.32. The plus-or-minus value

indicates the company's uncertainty about the true probabilities.

The primary economic factors are the following:

■ the research expenses to identify a new production process for the product

■ the marketing development cost to determine whether there is a significant market

■ the process development costs, including presanction engineering

■ the commercial development costs, both before and after the board's sanction

■ the venture value (net present value) if successful

The estimates of these values are shown in Table 10.33. Again, the plus-or-minus values indicate the company's considerable uncertainty about the values. All values are in millions of dollars.

The timing of events is as follows:

■ Decide whether to abandon product now. (This is really the only nontrivial decision the company will make.) If not, then:

■ Spend on research and marketing development. If marketing development indicates an insignificant market for the product *or* research indicates that the process is technically infeasible, cut expenses and quit. Otherwise:

■ Spend on process and commercial development. If company board then declines to sanction money for plant, cut expenses and quit. Otherwise:

■ Spend on further commercial development. By this time, the company has made all of its decisions. If the venture turns out to be a commercial success, then it gains the venture value for a success (less expenses so far). Otherwise, the company has lost the money spent so far, but that is all.

Analyze the company's problem. Obviously, with the high degree of uncertainty, sensitivity analysis is the key. Note that there are many uncertainties about the input parameters in Tables 10.32 and 10.33. In fact, there are far too many to allow you to try every combination. Therefore, just try a few combinations that you believe might be the most important.

TABLE 10.33	Monetary Estimates for Water Pollution Problem
Expense or Gain	**Net Present Value**
Research expense	$0.8 \pm 25\%$
Market development expense	$0.2 \pm 25\%$
Process development expense (presanction)	$3.0 \pm 25\%$
Commercial development expense (presanction)	$0.5 \pm 25\%$
Commercial development expense (postsanction)	$1.0 \pm 25\%$
Value if successful	$25.0 \pm 50\%$

GMC Motor Company II

This case is a continuation of GMC I (from Chapter 6). Management at GMC is generally pleased with the modeling effort that has been done for capacity planning in the coming year. However, some managers have asked about the effect demand forecasts for the second year out could have on the recommended *strategy*.

Although demand forecasts for the coming year are considered to be quite reliable, forecasts two or more years in the future have been less accurate. Accordingly, analysts at GMC formulate several demand scenarios in the future, and assign probabilities to each scenario. The situation for the coming two years is summarized in Table 10.34.

Three demand scenarios are possible in the second year. Scenario A corresponds to a robust economic expansion and increasing market share for GMC cars. Scenario B represents little change from the first year, although there is a relative shift away from the smaller Lyra to the larger Libra and Hydra models. Scenario C represents an economic recession and decreased demand for all car lines. In scenario C, the decrease in demand for Libras and Hydras is larger than for the economical Lyras. Analysts give scenario A a slightly higher probability of occurring than scenarios B and C.

Management at GMC wants to consider all possible configurations of capacity in the next two years. As before, the Lyra and/or Libra plants can be retooled, *but retooling can be done in either the first or second year*. Because of the enormous costs of changing a plant configuration, a plant that is retooled in the first year cannot be returned to its original configuration in the second year. The costs and characteristics of the original and retooled plants are the same in either year. For convenience, these are repeated in Table 10.35.

In addition to selecting the plant configurations for each year, GMC needs to determine the production plan at each plant in each year. The sequence of events and decisions is as follows. At the beginning of a year, GMC must decide on the plant configurations. Demand occurs during the year, and based on the observed demand, GMC plans its production accordingly. For example, in the second year, GMC must decide on its plant configurations *before* the demand scenario is revealed, but can determine its production plan *after* the demand scenario is revealed. This sequence of events is consistent with the relative time periods involved. Reconfiguring a plant is a major undertaking that must be planned in advance, so this decision must be made before the demand scenario is revealed. Production during a year can be altered to best meet the demand as it develops during the year. For modeling purposes, the production decision can be made after the demand scenario is revealed. Also, no inventory is carried from one year to the next.

The demand diversion matrix is assumed to be constant for both years. For convenience, it is repeated in Table 10.36.

Questions

GMC wants to decide whether to retool the Lyra and Libra plants in each of the coming two years. In addition, GMC wants to determine its production plan at each plant for each year. Based on the previous data, formulate a mixed integer programming model for solving GMC's production planning–capacity expansion problem for the coming two years. Assume that GMC's objective is to maximize total average profit for the two years. For simplicity, assume that no discounting of profits is done for the second year.

In the past, GMC had solved problems separately for each scenario. The three optimal solutions were compared and then a final decision was made. What are the three optimal solutions corresponding to each scenario? (For example, assuming that scenario A occurs with probability 1.0, what is the optimal solution? Then repeat for scenarios B and C.) How do the three separate optimal solutions compare to the overall optimal solution found before?[8]

[8]*Acknowledgment*: The idea for GMC I and II came from Eppen et al. (1989).

TABLE 10.34 Demand Forecasts and Probabilities for GMC Case Study

Model	First Year	Second Year		
		Scenario A	Scenario B	Scenario C
Lyra	1400	1700	1300	1300
Libra	1100	1500	1200	800
Hydra	800	1100	850	600
Probability	1	0.4	0.3	0.3

TABLE 10.35 Plant Characteristics for GMC Case Study

	Lyra	Libra	Hydra	New Lyra	New Libra
Capacity (in 1000s)	1000	800	900	1600	1800
Fixed cost (in $millions)	2000	2000	2600	3400	3700
Profit Margin by Car Line (in 1000s)					
Lyra	2	–	–	2.5	2.3
Libra	–	3	–	3	3.5
Hydra	–	–	5	–	4.8

TABLE 10.36 Demand Diversion Matrix for GMC Case Study

	Lyra	Libra	Hydra
Lyra	–	0.3	0.05
Libra	0	–	0.10
Hydra	0	0.0	–

Jogger Shoe Company

The Jogger Shoe Company is trying to decide whether to make a change in its most popular brand of running shoes. The new style would cost the same to produce, and it would be priced the same, but it would incorporate a new kind of lacing system that (according to its marketing research people) would make it more popular. There is a fixed cost of $300,000 of changing over to the new style. The unit contribution to before-tax profit for either style is $8. The tax rate is 35%. Also, because the fixed cost can be depreciated and will therefore affect the after-tax cash flow, we need a depreciation method. We assume it is straight-line depreciation.

The current demand for these shoes is 190,000 pairs annually. The company assumes this demand will continue for the next 3 years if the current style is retained. However, there is uncertainty about demand for the new style, if it is introduced. The company models this uncertainty by assuming a normal distribution in year 1, with mean 220,000 and standard deviation 20,000. The company also assumes that this demand, whatever it is, will remain constant for the next 3 years. However, if demand in year 1 for the new style is sufficiently low, the company can always switch back to the current style and realize an annual demand of 190,000. The company wants a strategy that will maximize the expected net present value (NPV) of total cash flow for the next 3 years, where a 15% interest rate is used for the purpose of calculating NPV.

Westhouser Paper Company

The Westhouser Paper Company in the state of Washington currently has an option to purchase a piece of land with good timber forest on it. It is now May 1, and the current price of the land is $2.2 million. Westhouser does not actually need the timber from this land until the beginning of July, but its top executives fear that another company might buy the land between now and the beginning of July. They assess that there is 1 chance out of 20 that a competitor will buy the land during May. If this does not occur, they assess that there is 1 chance out of 10 that the competitor will buy the land during June. If Westhouser does not take advantage of its current option, it can attempt to buy the land at the beginning of June or the beginning of July, provided that it is still available.

Westhouser's incentive for delaying the purchase is that its financial experts believe there is a good chance that the price of the land will fall significantly in one or both of the next two months. They assess the possible price decreases and their probabilities in Tables 10.37 and 10.38. Table 10.37 shows

TABLE 10.37	Distribution of Price Decrease in May
Price Decrease	**Probability**
$0	0.5
$60,000	0.3
$120,000	0.2

the probabilities of the possible price decreases during May. Table 10.38 shows the *conditional* probabilities of the possible price decreases in June, *given* the price decrease in May. For example, if the price decrease in May is $60,000, then the possible price decreases in June are $0, $30,000, and $60,000 with respective probabilities 0.6, 0.2, and 0.2.

If Westhouser purchases the land, it believes that it can gross $3 million. (This does not count the cost of purchasing the land.) But if it does not purchase the land, it believes that it can make $650,000 from alternative investments. What should the company do?

TABLE 10.38	Distribution of Price Decrease in June				
		Price Decrease in May			
$0		**$60,000**		**$120,000**	
June Decrease	**Probability**	**June Decrease**	**Probability**	**June Decrease**	**Probability**
$0	0.3	$0	0.6	$0	0.7
$60,000	0.6	$30,000	0.2	$20,000	0.2
$120,000	0.1	$60,000	0.2	$40,000	0.1

## CHAPTER 11

Introduction to Simulation Modeling

CALL PROCESSING SIMULATION AT AT&T

Simulation is a versatile tool that allows companies to ask many what-if questions about changes in their systems without actually changing the systems themselves. As reported in the article "AT&T's Call Processing Simulator (CAPS) Operational Design for Inbound Call Centers" by Brigandi et al. (1994), AT&T has used a simulation model called CAPS to help its corporate customers design and operate their call centers. These call centers are the locations into which customers phone, usually using 800 numbers, for customer service, telephone shopping, and other services. The system that is used to handle these calls—the way calls are routed to agents, the number of lines open, the prerecorded messages given to customers, the way customer queues are handled, and so on—can be extremely complex and difficult to understand, let alone optimize. Therefore, AT&T developed the CAPS simulation tool to simulate a variety of operating policies for its corporate customers. AT&T reports that it has used this tool to regain more than $1 billion from a customer base of approximately 2000 corporate customers per year. The CAPS tool has improved the customers' call center operations dramatically and has helped sell these customers on further AT&T services.

As an example, a major airline's reservation system was supported by 19 separate call centers located near domestic and international airports. In 1992, the airline decided to consolidate its reservations centers. AT&T helped the airline by running a series of CAPS studies to determine the characteristics of efficient, load-balanced call centers that would accomplish the airline's goals. The airline was particularly interested in reducing its 10% blocked-call rate while using its resources more efficiently. The result of the CAPS studies was a $25 million savings in the airline's reservations call-center operations costs and an ability to handle approximately 3000 more reservation sales calls per day. At the same time, AT&T strengthened its position as the 800-number service communications carrier of choice with the airline. Its annual billed network services for the airline increased by 5% on a base of $49 million. ■

11.1 INTRODUCTION

A simulation model is a computer model that imitates a real-life situation. It is like other mathematical models, but it explicitly incorporates uncertainty in one or more input quantities. When we run a simulation, we allow these random quantities to take on various values, and we keep track of any resulting output quantities of interest. In this way, we are able to see how the outputs vary as a function of the varying inputs.

The fundamental advantage of a simulation model is that it shows us an entire distribution of results, not simply a single bottom-line result. As an example, suppose an automobile manufacturer is planning to develop and market a new model car. The company is ultimately interested in the net present value (NPV) of the profits from this car over the next 10 years. However, there are many uncertainties surrounding this car, including the yearly customer demands for it and the cost of developing it. We could develop a spreadsheet model for the 10-year NPV, using our *best guesses* for these various uncertain quantities. We could then report the NPV based on these best guesses, with the implicit understanding that this best-guess NPV is going to occur. However, this would provide a very incomplete analysis. It is much better to treat the uncertainty explicitly with a simulation model. This involves entering probability distributions for the uncertain quantities and seeing how the NPV varies as the uncertain quantities vary. Each different set of values for the uncertain quantities can be considered a scenario. Simulation allows us to generate many scenarios, each leading to a particular NPV. In the end, we see a whole distribution of NPVs, not a single best guess. We can see what the NPV will be on average, and we can also see worst-case and best-case results.

Simulation models are also extremely useful for determining how sensitive a system is to changes in operating conditions. For example, we might simulate the operations of a supermarket. Once the simulation model has been developed, we can then run it (with suitable modifications) to ask a number of what-if questions. For example, if the supermarket experiences a 20% increase in business, what will happen to the average time customers must wait for service?

A great benefit of computer simulation is that it enables us to answer these types of what-if questions without actually changing (or building) a physical system. For example, the supermarket might want to experiment with the number of open registers to see the effect on customer waiting times. The only way it can *physically* experiment with more registers than it currently owns is to purchase more equipment. Then if it determines that this equipment is not a good investment—customer waiting times do not decrease appreciably—the company is stuck with expensive equipment it doesn't need. Computer simulation is a much less expensive alternative. It provides the company with an electronic replica of what would happen *if* the new equipment were purchased. Then, if the simulation indicates that the new equipment is worth the cost, the company can be confident that purchasing it is the right decision. Otherwise, it can abandon the idea of the new equipment *before* the equipment has been purchased.

Simulation modeling in a spreadsheet is quite similar to the other modeling applications in this book. We begin with input quantities and then relate these with appropriate spreadsheet formulas to produce outputs of interest. The main difference is that simulation uses *random* numbers to drive the whole process. These are generated with special functions that return different random numbers each time they are entered. Each time the spreadsheet recalculates, all of the random numbers change. This gives us the ability to model the logical process once and then use the recalculation feature repeatedly to generate many different scenarios. By collecting the data from these scenarios, we see which outputs are most likely and we see the best-case and worst-case scenarios.

In this chapter we will illustrate spreadsheet models that can be developed with the basic Excel package. Because simulation is becoming such an important tool for analyzing real problems, add-ins to Excel are being developed to streamline the process of analyzing simulation models. Therefore, we will also introduce @Risk, one of the most popular simulation add-ins. This add-in not only augments the simulation capabilities of Excel, but it also enables users to develop models more quickly and easily.

The purpose of this chapter is to introduce basic simulation concepts, show how simulation models can be developed in Excel, and demonstrate the capabilities of the @Risk add-in. We will do all of this in the context of a relatively simple "newsvendor" ordering model. Then, armed with the necessary simulation tools, we will explore a number of interesting and useful simulation models in the next chapter.[1]

11.2   REAL APPLICATIONS OF SIMULATION

There are many published applications of simulation. These cover a wide variety of topics, as we discuss briefly in this section.

Burger King developed a simulation model for its restaurants [see Swart and Donno (1981)]. This model was used to justify business decisions such as the following:

- Should a restaurant open a second drive-through window?

- How much would customer waiting time increase if a new sandwich were added to the menu?

Many companies (Cummins Engine, Merck, Procter & Gamble, Kodak, and United Airlines, to name a few) have used simulation to determine which of several possible

---

[1] For those instructors who used the previous version of this book, note that the organization of the simulation chapters is now quite different than before. There is no longer one chapter for models without @Risk and another for models with @Risk. Because @Risk is on the CD-ROM that accompanies this book, we use it throughout both simulation chapters.

investment projects they should choose. This is often referred to as **risk analysis** [see Hertz (1964)].

As an example, consider a situation where a company must choose a single investment. If the future cash flows for each investment project are known with certainty, then most companies advocate choosing the investment with the largest net present value (NPV). However, if future cash flows are not known with certainty, then it is not clear how to choose between competing projects. Using simulation, we can obtain a histogram of the NPV for a project. Then we can answer such questions as:

- Which project is the riskiest?
- What is the probability that an investment will yield at least a 20% return?
- What is the probability that the NPV of an investment will be less than −$1 billion, that is, a loss of more than $1 billion?

When several investments are compared using simulation, it may become apparent that some are riskier than others. Therefore, contrary to what many finance textbooks advise, the investment with the largest *expected* NPV may not be the best investment; it may be too risky! In the next chapter, we will develop a simulation model for a single investment opportunity to gauge its potential for large profits as well as large losses.

To illustrate the use of simulation in corporate finance, we refer to Norton (1994). This article describes a simulation model (called a **Monte Carlo model**) that was used by Merck, the world's largest drug company, to determine whether Merck should pay $6.6 billion to acquire Medco, a mail-order drug company. The model contained inputs concerning the following:

- possible scenarios for the future of the U.S. health-care system, such as a single-payer system, universal coverage, and so forth
- possible future changes in the mix of generic and brand-name drugs
- probability distributions of profit margins for each product
- assumptions about competitors' reactions to a merger with Medco

The Merck model contained thousands of equations. A simulation was performed to see how the merger would perform under various possible scenarios. As Merck's CFO, Judy Lewent, says, "Monte Carlo techniques are a very, very powerful tool to get a more intelligent look at a range of outcomes. It's almost never useful in this kind of environment to build a single bullet forecast." Merck's model indicated that the merger with Medco would benefit Merck regardless of the type of health insurance plan (if any) the federal government enacted.

Other applications of simulation include the following:

1. Companies must constantly make inventory-ordering decisions in the face of unknown demand. In special cases, analytic (nonsimulation) models can be used to help make decisions. However, when the problems become more complex, simulation often provides the only feasible solution method. The example carried through this chapter concerns an ordering decision with uncertain demand.

2. Firms must often bid against competitors to win a contract. If a firm's bid is too low, it will probably win the contract, but it will make very little profit on the contract. On the other hand, if the firm bids too high, it will probably not win the contract at all. The firm must decide how much to bid, although the competitors' bids are uncertain. In the next chapter, we will develop a simulation model that can help a firm choose the bid amount that maximizes its expected profit.

3. One of the most important challenges manufacturing firms face is achieving a high level of quality in their products. They must meet the increasingly tight specifications set by their customers. Perhaps the most visible advocate of quality, Edwards Deming, stated that many companies spend too much time "tampering" with their manufacturing processes instead of making the fundamental changes that are required to achieve lasting quality. In the next chapter, we will build a simulation model of Deming's famous funnel experiment. It clearly shows how tampering with a stable process can have a disastrous effect on quality.

4. Large corporate projects can frequently be divided into smaller activities. (A prime example is the Apollo space mission.) To create the project's schedule, the company must estimate the length of time required to finish the project. It might also wish to expedite activities most critical to finishing the project to speed up the schedule. We discussed a version of this problem in Chapter 5, where all of the activity times were assumed to be known with certainty. It is much more realistic to assume that these times can only be estimated with probability distributions. In this case simulation is required. We will examine this topic in the next chapter.

5. Investors face a bewildering array of securities to choose from. Some of these, such as stocks and bonds, are reasonably straightforward (although still risky). Others, particularly derivatives (such as futures and stock options), can be extremely complex. Simulation is the perfect tool for analyzing these investment instruments. In the next chapter, we will illustrate a fairly simple case of an investor trading in the stock market.

11.3 GENERATING UNIFORMLY DISTRIBUTED RANDOM NUMBERS

All spreadsheet packages are capable of generating random numbers between 0 and 1. These are the "building blocks" of all computer simulations. In Excel, we generate a random number between 0 and 1 by entering the formula

=RAND()

in any cell. (The pair of parentheses to the right of RAND indicates that this is an Excel function with no arguments. These parentheses *must* be included.) In addition to being between 0 and 1, the numbers created by this function have two properties that make them behave like we would expect "random" numbers to behave:

1. Each time the RAND function is used, all numbers between 0 and 1 have the same chance of occurring. This means, for example, that approximately 10% of the numbers generated by the RAND function will be between 0.0 and 0.1; 10% of the numbers will be between 0.65 and 0.75; 60% of the numbers will be between 0.20 and 0.80; and so on. This property is often expressed by saying that the random numbers are **uniformly distributed** between 0 and 1.

2. Different random numbers generated by the computer are probabilistically independent. This implies, for instance, that if we generate a random number in cell A5, its value tells us nothing about the values of any other random numbers generated in the spreadsheet. Therefore, if one call of the RAND function yields a large random number (say, 0.98) in cell A5, then there is still a 50% chance that a number generated by RAND in cell A6 (or any other cell) will yield a value less than 0.50.

To illustrate the RAND function, we generated 500 random numbers by entering this function in cell A4 and copying it to the range A5:A504. Figure 11.1 displays the output. (See the file RANDNUM.XLS.) When you try this on your PC, you will undoubtedly obtain different random numbers. This will happen throughout the chapter and is a characteristic of simulation. No two answers are ever exactly alike. Now try the following. Press the "recalculate" (F9) key. All of the random numbers change. In fact, each time you press the F9 key or do anything to your spreadsheet to effect a recalculation, all of the cells containing the RAND function change.

A histogram of the 500 random numbers for our illustration appears in Figure 11.2. (This histogram was generated by the histogram tool in the StatPro add-in. Also, if you try this on your PC, the shape of your histogram will not be identical to the one shown in Figure 11.2 because it will probably be based on *different* random numbers.) From property 1, we would expect equal numbers of observations in the 10 categories. Although the heights of the bars are *not* exactly equal, the differences are due to chance—not to a faulty random number generator.

FIGURE 11.1
Five Hundred
Random Numbers

	A	B	C	D	E
1	**500 random numbers found with RAND() function**				
2	Note: These are formatted to show only 4 decimal places.				
3					
4	Random				
5	0.2547				
6	0.0350				
7	0.4220				
8	0.3278				
9	0.1576				
10	0.7592				
11	0.0175				
12	0.6219				
13	0.6178				
498	0.2900				
499	0.2355				
500	0.3786				
501	0.7235				
502	0.4897				
503	0.0947				
504	0.1558				

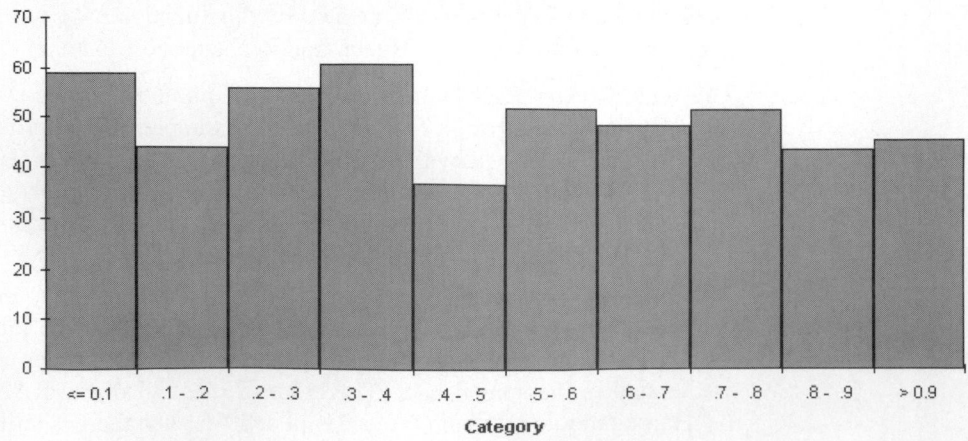

FIGURE 11.2 Histogram of the 500 Random Numbers

Although we will not pursue the details, you should realize that the "random" numbers generated by the RAND function (or by any other package's random number generator) are not really random. They are often called **pseudo-random numbers**. Each successive random number follows the previous random number by a somewhat complex arithmetic operation. For someone who knows the details of this arithmetic operation, it is possible to predict ahead of time exactly which random numbers will be generated by the RAND function. This is quite different from using a "true" random mechanism, such as spinning a wheel, to get the next random number—a mechanism that would be impractical on a computer. Indeed, mathematicians and computer analysts have studied many ways to produce random numbers that have the two properties just mentioned, and they have developed many competing random number generators, one of which is the RAND function implemented in Excel. Some of these are "better" than others (in terms of satisfying the desired properties more exactly), but we believe the generator implemented in Excel is appropriate for our purposes. (The same can be said for the random number generator used in @Risk.)

Freezing Random Numbers   The automatic recalculation of random numbers can be useful sometimes and annoying other times. There are situations where we want the random numbers to stay fixed—that is, we want to "freeze" them at their current values. The following three-step method will do this.

1. **Select the range.** Select the range that you want to freeze, such as A5:A504 in Figure 11.1.

2. **Copy.** Use the Copy command to copy this range.

3. **Paste Special with Values.** With the range still selected, select Paste Special from the Edit menu and choose the Values option. This procedure pastes a copy of the range onto itself, except that the entries are now *numbers*, not *formulas*. Therefore, whenever the spreadsheet recalculates, these numbers will not change.

PROBLEMS

Skill-Building Problems

1. Use the RAND function and the Copy command to generate a set of 100 random numbers.
   a. What fraction of the random numbers are smaller than 0.5?
   b. What fraction of the time is a random number less than 0.5 followed by a random number greater than 0.5?
   c. What fraction of the random numbers are larger than 0.8?
   d. Freeze these random numbers. However, instead of pasting them over the original random numbers, paste them onto a new range. Then press the F9 recalculate key. The original random numbers should change, but the pasted copy should remain the same.

2. We all hate to bring change to a store. By using random numbers, we could eliminate the need for change and give the store and the customer a fair deal. This problem indicates how it could be done.
   a. Suppose that you buy something for $0.20. How could you use random numbers (built into the cash register system) to decide whether you should pay $1.00 or nothing? This would eliminate the need for change!
   b. If you bought something for $9.60, how would you use random numbers to eliminate the need for change?
   c. In the long run, why is this method fair to both the store and the customers? Would you personally (as a customer) be willing to abide by such a system?

11.4 SIMULATION WITH BUILT-IN EXCEL TOOLS

I n this section we will show how spreadsheet simulation models can be developed and analyzed with Excel's built-in tools—no add-ins. To illustrate the procedure, we will simulate a simple "newsvendor" problem. This problem occurs when a company (such as a newsvendor) must make a one-time purchase of a product (such as a newspaper) to meet customer demands for a certain period of time. If the company orders too few newspapers, it will lose potential profit by not having enough on hand to satisfy its customers. If it orders too many, it will have worthless newspapers left over at the end of the day. The following example illustrates this basic problem in a slightly different context.

EXAMPLE   11.1

ORDERING CALENDARS AT WALTON BOOKSTORE

In August, Walton Bookstore must decide how many of next year's nature calendars to order. Each calendar costs the bookstore $7.50 and is sold for $10. After February 1, all unsold calendars will be returned to the publisher for a refund of $2.50 per calendar. Walton believes that the number of calendars it can sell by February 1 follows the probability distribution shown in Table 11.1. Walton wants to develop a simulation model to help it decide how many calendars to order.

TABLE 11.1	Probability Distribution of Demand for Walton Example
Calendars Demanded	**Probability**
100	0.30
150	0.20
200	0.30
250	0.15
300	0.05

Solution

We first discuss the probability distribution in Table 11.1. It is a **discrete** distribution with only five possible values: 100, 150, 200, 250, and 300. In reality, it is clear that other values of demand are possible. For example, there could be demand for exactly 187 calendars. In spite of its apparent lack of realism, we use this discrete distribution for two reasons. First, its simplicity is a nice feature to get us started with simulation modeling. Second, discrete distributions are often used in real business simulation models. Even though the discrete distribution is only an *approximation* to reality, it can still give us important insights into the actual problem. As for the probabilities listed in Table 11.1, they are typically drawn from historical data or (if historical data are lacking) educated guesses. In this case, the manager of Walton Bookstore has presumably looked at demands for calendars in previous years, and he has used any information he has about the market for next year's calendars to estimate, for example, that the probability of a demand for 200 calendars is 0.30. The five probabilities in this table *must* sum to 1. Beyond this requirement, we want them to be as reasonable and consistent with reality as possible.

DEVELOPING THE SIMULATION MODEL

Now we discuss the ordering model. For a *fixed* order quantity, we will show how Excel can be used to simulate 1000 replications (or any other number of replications). Each replication is an independent replay of the events that occur. To illustrate, suppose we want to simulate profit if Walton orders 200 calendars. Figure 11.3 illustrates the results obtained by simulating 1000 independent replications for this order quantity.[2] (See the file WALTON1.XLS.) To do this, use the following steps.

1 **Inputs.** Enter the cost data in the range B4:B6, the probability distribution of demand in the range E5:F9, and the proposed order quantity, 200, in cell B9. Pay particular attention to the way the probability distribution is entered. Columns E and F contain the demand values and the individual probabilities from Table 11.1. It is

	A	B	C	D	E	F	G	H	I
1	**Simulation of Walton's bookstore**								
2									
3	**Cost data**			**Demand distribution**					
4	Unit cost	$7.50			Cum Prob	Demand	Probability		
5	Unit price	$10.00			0.00	100	0.30	**Range names**	
6	Unit refund	$2.50			0.30	150	0.20	**used:**	
7					0.50	200	0.30	UnitCost - B4	
8	**Decision variable**				0.80	250	0.15	UnitPrice - B5	
9	Order quantity	200			0.95	300	0.05	UnitRefund - B6	
10								Lookup - D5:E9	
11	**Summary measures for simulation below**							OrderQuan - B9	
12	Average profit	$197.38						AvgProfit - B12	
13	Stdev of profit	$321.82		95% confidence interval for expected profit				StdevProfit - B13	
14	Minimum profit	-$250.00		Lower limit	$177.43			Profits - G19:G1018	
15	Maximum profit	$500.00		Upper limit	$217.32				
16									
17	**Simulation**								
18	Replication	Random #	Demand	Revenue	Cost	Refund	Profit		
19	1	0.5279	200	$2,000	$1,500	$0	$500		
20	2	0.9117	250	$2,000	$1,500	$0	$500		
21	3	0.5765	200	$2,000	$1,500	$0	$500		
22	4	0.0251	100	$1,000	$1,500	$250	-$250		
23	5	0.1877	100	$1,000	$1,500	$250	-$250		
24	6	0.3948	150	$1,500	$1,500	$125	$125		
25	7	0.2403	100	$1,000	$1,500	$250	-$250		
26	8	0.1169	100	$1,000	$1,500	$250	-$250		
27	9	0.6386	200	$2,000	$1,500	$0	$500		
28	10	0.6780	200	$2,000	$1,500	$0	$500		
1012	994	0.8798	250	$2,000	$1,500	$0	$500		
1013	995	0.5215	200	$2,000	$1,500	$0	$500		
1014	996	0.3815	150	$1,500	$1,500	$125	$125		
1015	997	0.1507	100	$1,000	$1,500	$250	-$250		
1016	998	0.3880	150	$1,500	$1,500	$125	$125		
1017	999	0.3753	150	$1,500	$1,500	$125	$125		
1018	1000	0.4464	150	$1,500	$1,500	$125	$125		

FIGURE 11.3 Walton Bookstore Simulation Model

[2]Note that there are a number of hidden rows in Figure 11.3. This will be the case for several of the spreadsheet figures in this chapter.

also convenient (see step 3 for the reasoning) to have the cumulative probabilities in column D. To obtain these, first enter the value 0 in cell D5. Then enter the formula

=F5+D5

in cell D6 and copy it to the range D7:D9.

2 **Generate random numbers.** Enter a random number in cell B19 with the formula

=RAND()

and copy this to the range B20:B1018. Then freeze the random numbers in this range as described earlier, that is, with the Copy and Paste Special/Values commands. (*Important note*: From here on, the values in your spreadsheet will differ from those shown here because of different random numbers.)

3 **Generate demands.** The key to the simulation is the generation of the customer demands in the range C19:C1018 from the random numbers in column B and the probability distribution of demand. Here is how it works. We divide the interval from 0 to 1 into five segments: from 0.0 to 0.3 (length 0.3), from 0.3 to 0.5 (length 0.2), from 0.5 to 0.8 (length 0.3), from 0.8 to 0.95 (length 0.15), and from 0.95 to 1.0 (length 0.05). Note that these lengths are the probabilities of the various demands. Then we associate a demand with each random number depending on which interval the random number falls in. For example, the random number in cell A19, 0.5279, falls in the third interval, so we associate the third possible demand value, 200, with this random number.

There are two ways to implement this procedure. The first is to use a nested IF statement in cell C19 (and copy it down column C). However, this is quite complex even for a demand distribution with only five values, and it becomes unmanageable for a demand distribution with many possible values. A simpler way is to use a VLOOKUP function. To do this, we create a "lookup table" in the range D5:E9 (range-named Lookup). This table has the cumulative probabilities in column D and the possible demand values in column E. In fact, the whole purpose of the cumulative probabilities in column D is to allow us to use the VLOOKUP command. To generate the simulated demands, enter the formula

=VLOOKUP(B19,Lookup,2)

in cell C19 and copy it to the range C20:C1018. For each random number in column B, this function compares the random number to the values in D5:D9 and returns the appropriate demand from E5:E9.

This step is the key to the simulation, so make sure you understand exactly what it entails. The rest is "bookkeeping," as we illustrate in the following steps. First, however, we note that the random numbers in column B are not really necessary. They could be included in the VLOOKUP function directly, as in

=VLOOKUP(RAND(),Lookup,2)

4 **Revenue.** Once the demand is known, the number of calendars sold is the smaller of the demand and the order quantity. For example, if 150 calendars are demanded, 150 will be sold. But if 250 are demanded, only 200 can be sold (because Walton orders only 200). Therefore, to calculate the revenue in cell D19, enter the formula

=UnitPrice*MIN(C19,OrderQuan)

5 **Ordering cost.** The cost of ordering the calendars does not depend on the demand; it is the unit cost multiplied by the number ordered. Calculate this cost in cell E19 with the formula

=UnitCost*OrderQuan

6 **Refund.** If the order quantity is greater than the demand, there is a refund of $2.50 for each calendar left over; otherwise, there is no refund. Therefore, enter the total refund in cell F19 with the formula

=UnitRefund*MAX(OrderQuan-C19,0)

For example, if demand is 150, then 50 calendars are left over, and this MAX is 50, the larger of 50 and 0. However, if demand is 250, then no calendars are left over, and this MAX is 0, the larger of −50 and 0. (This calculation could also be accomplished with an IF function instead of a MAX function.)

7 **Profit.** Calculate the profit in cell G19 with the formula

=D19-E19+F19

8 **Copy to other rows.** Do the same bookkeeping for the other 999 replications by copying the range D19:G19 to the range D20:G1018.

9 **Summary measures.** Each profit value in column G corresponds to one randomly generated demand. We usually want to see how these vary from one replication to another. First, calculate the average and standard deviation of the 1000 profits in cells B12 and B13 with the formulas

=AVERAGE(Profits)

and

=STDEV(Profits)

Similarly, calculate the smallest and largest of the 1000 profits in cells B14 and B15 with the MIN and MAX functions.

10 **Confidence interval for expected profit.** Calculate a 95% confidence interval for the expected profit in cells E13 and E14 with the formulas

=AvgProfit-1.96*StdevProfit/SQRT(1000)

and

=AvgProfit+1.96*StdevProfit/SQRT(1000)

At this point, it is a good idea to stand back and see what we have accomplished. First, in the body of the simulation, rows 19–1018, we randomly generated 1000 possible demands and the corresponding profits. Because there are only five possible demand values (100, 150, 200, 250, and 300), there are only five possible profit values: −$250, $125, $500, $500, and $500. Also, note that for the order quantity 200, the profit is $500 regardless of whether demand is 200, 250, or 300. A tally of the profit values in these rows (including the hidden rows) indicates that there are 290 rows with profit equal to −$250 (demand 100), 227 rows with profit equal to $125 (demand 150), and 483 rows with profit equal to $500 (demand 200, 250, or 300). The average of these 1000 profits is $197.38, and their standard deviation is $321.82. (Again, remember that your answers will probably differ from these because your random numbers will differ from those shown in Figure 11.3.)

Probability Distribution of Profit Typically, we want a computer simulation to yield one or more output variables, such as profit, for our analysis. These output variables depend on random inputs, such as demand. Our goal is to estimate the probability distributions of the outputs. In the Walton simulation we estimate the probability distribution of profit to be:

$$P(\text{Profit} = -\$250) = 290/1000 = 0.29$$

$$P(\text{Profit} = \$125) = 227/1000 = 0.227$$

$$P(\text{Profit} = \$500) = 483/1000 = 0.483$$

We also estimate the mean of this distribution to be \$197.38 and its standard deviation to be \$321.82.

It is important to realize that if the entire simulation were run again with *different* random numbers (such as the ones you might have generated on your PC), the answers would be slightly different. This is the primary reason for the confidence interval in cells E13 and E14. This interval expresses our uncertainty about the *mean* of the profit distribution. Our best guess for this mean is the average of the 1000 profits that we happened to observe. However, because the corresponding confidence interval is somewhat wide, from \$177.43 to \$217.32, we are not at all sure of the *true* mean of the profit distribution. If we ran this simulation again with different random numbers, the average profit might be quite different from the average profit we observed, \$197.38. (The other summary statistics would probably also be different.)

Notes About Confidence Intervals It is common in computer simulations to estimate the mean of some distribution by the average of the simulated observations, just as we estimated the mean of the profit distribution by the average of 1000 profits. The usual practice is then to accompany this estimate with a **confidence interval**, which indicates the accuracy of the estimate.[3] You might recall from statistics that to obtain a confidence interval for the mean, you start with the estimated mean and then add and subtract a multiple of the **standard error** of the estimated mean. If we denote the estimated mean (that is, the average) by $\overline{X}$, we have

Confidence interval for the mean $= \overline{X} \pm (\text{Multiple} \times \text{Standard Error of } \overline{X})$

The standard error of $\overline{X}$ is the standard deviation of the observations divided by the square root of n, the number of observations:

$$\text{Standard error of } \overline{X} = \frac{\text{Standard deviation of observations}}{\sqrt{n}} = \frac{s}{\sqrt{n}}$$

Here, s is the symbol for the standard deviation of the observations. We obtain it with the STDEV function in Excel.

The "multiple" in the confidence interval formula depends on the confidence level and the number of observations. If the confidence level is 95%, for example, then the multiple is usually very close to 2, so a good guideline is to go out two standard errors on either side of the average to obtain an approximate 95% confidence interval for the mean:

$$\overline{X} \pm 2 \frac{s}{\sqrt{n}}$$

To be more precise, if n is reasonably large, which is almost always the case in simulations, the central limit theorem from statistics implies that the correct multiple is the number from the standard normal distribution that cuts off probability 0.025 in each tail. This is a famous number in statistics: 1.96. Because 1.96 is very close to 2, it is acceptable for all practical purposes to use 2 instead of 1.96 when forming the confidence interval.

---

[3] For later reference, we note that @Risk does *not* report confidence intervals. However, it provides the ingredients—sample means and sample standard deviations—necessary to calculate confidence intervals.

Analysts often plan a simulation so that the confidence interval for the mean of some important output will be sufficiently narrow. The reasoning is that narrow confidence intervals imply more precision about the estimated mean of the output variable. If the confidence level is fixed at some value such as 95%, then the only way to narrow the confidence interval is to simulate more replications. Assuming that the confidence level is 95%, the following value of n is required to ensure that the resulting confidence interval will have length approximately equal to some prespecified value L:

$$n = \frac{16 \times (\text{Estimated Stdev})^2}{L^2}$$

To use this formula, we must have an estimate of the standard deviation of the output variable.

For example, in the Walton simulation we saw that with $n = 1000$, the resulting 95% confidence interval for the mean profit has length $\$217.32 - \$177.43 = \$39.89$. Suppose that we want to reduce this length to $25—that is, we want $L = \$25$. We do not know the exact standard deviation of the profit distribution, but we can estimate it from the simulation as $321.82. Therefore, to obtain the required confidence interval length L, we need to simulate n replications, where

$$n = \frac{16 \times 321.82^2}{25^2} \approx 2652$$

(When this formula produces a non-integer, it is common to round upward.) The claim, then, is that if we rerun the simulation with 2652 replications rather than 1000 replications, the length of the 95% confidence interval for the mean profit will be close to $25.

Finding the Best Order Quantity We are not yet finished with the Walton example. So far, we have run the simulation for only a single order quantity, 200. Walton's ultimate goal is to find the *best* order quantity—that is, the order quantity that maximizes the mean profit. We can do this with a data table. Specifically, we can use a data table to rerun the simulation for other order quantities. We show this data table in Figure 11.4. (This is still part of the WALTON1.XLS file.)

FIGURE 11.4
Data Table for
Walton Bookstore
Simulation

	A	B	C	D	E
1020	Data table for average profit versus order quantity				
1021	Order quantity	AvgProfit			
1022		$197.38			
1023	100	$250.00			
1024	125	$258.13			
1025	150	$266.25			
1026	175	$231.81			
1027	200	$197.38			
1028	225	$112.31			
1029	250	$27.25			
1030	275	($88.38)			
1031	300	($204.00)			

To form this table, enter the trial order quantities shown in the range A1023:A1031, enter the formula **=AvgProfit** in cell B1022 and select the data table range, A1022: B1031. Then use the Data/Table command, specifying that the column input cell is B9 (see Figure 11.3). Finally, construct a bar chart of the average profits in the data table, as in Figure 11.5 (page 576).

Note that an order quantity of 150 appears to maximize the average profit. Its average profit of $266.25 is slightly higher than the average profits from nearby order

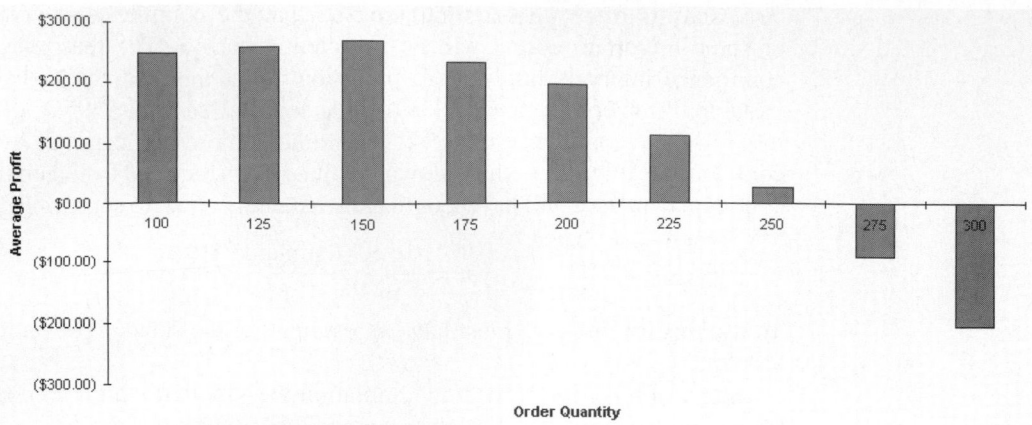

FIGURE 11.5 Average Profit versus Order Quantity

quantities and much higher than the profit gained from an order of 200 or more calendars. However, again keep in mind that this is a simulation, so that all of these average profits depend on the particular random numbers we generated. If we reran the simulation with different random numbers, it is conceivable that some other order quantity could be best.

To Freeze or Not To Freeze In developing this simulation model, we suggested that you freeze the random numbers in column B. If you neglect this step, every time you press the F9 key or make any change to your spreadsheet model, a new set of simulated answers (including those in the data table) will appear. Depending on the speed of your computer, this recalculation can take a few seconds, even for a relatively small simulation. For larger simulations, the recalculation time can be quite large, which is one of the primary reasons you might want to freeze your random numbers right away. However, the drawback is that once the random numbers are frozen, you are stuck with that particular set of random numbers. In most of the rest of this chapter, we will *not* freeze the random numbers. This way we will be able to generate many different scenarios simply by pressing the F9 key.

Using a Data Table to Repeat Simulations The Walton simulation is a particularly simple "one-line" simulation model. We are able to capture all of the logic—generating a demand and calculating the corresponding profit—in a single row. Then to replicate the simulation, we can simply copy this row down as far as we like. Many simulation models are significantly more complex and require more than one row to capture the logic. Nevertheless, they still result in one or more output quantities (such as profit) that we want to replicate. We now illustrate another method that is more general (still using the Walton example). It uses a *data table* to generate the replications. Refer to Figure 11.6 and the file WALTON2.XLS.

Through row 19, this model is exactly like the previous model. That is, we use the given data at the top of the spreadsheet to construct a typical "prototype" of the simulation in row 19.[4] However, we no longer copy this row down—and we do *not* freeze the cell with the random number, A19. Instead, we form a data table in the range A23:B1023 to replicate the basic simulation 1000 times. In column A we list

---

[4]Actually, we use our earlier suggestion. We eliminate an explicit random number cell and enter the formula **=VLOOKUP(RAND(),Lookup,2)** for demand in cell A19.

	A	B	C	D	E	F	G	H	I
1	Simulation of Walton's bookstore								
2									
3	Cost data			Demand distribution					
4	Unit cost	$7.50		CumProb	Demand	Probability		Range names used:	
5	Unit price	$10.00		0.00	100	0.30		UnitCost - B4	
6	Unit refund	$2.50		0.30	150	0.20		UnitPrice - B5	
7				0.50	200	0.30		UnitRefund - B6	
8	Decision variable			0.80	250	0.15		Lookup - D5:E9	
9	Order quantity	200		0.95	300	0.05		OrderQuan - B9	
10								AvgProfit - B12	
11	Summary measures from simulation below							StdevProfit - B13	
12	Average	$198.13		95% confidence interval for expected profit				Demand - A19	
13	StDev	$328.15		Lower limit	$177.79			Profit - E19	
14	Minimum	-$250.00		Upper limit	$218.46			Profits - B24:B1023	
15	Maximum	$500.00							
16									
17	Simulation								
18	Demand	Revenue	Cost	Refund	Profit				
19	250	$2,000	$1,500	$0	$500				
20									
21	Data table for replications, each shows profit from that replication								
22	Replication	Profit							
23		$500							
24	1	$125							
25	2	$500							
26	3	$125							
27	4	$500							
28	5	$500							
29	6	-$250							
30	7	$500							
31	8	$500							
32	9	-$250							
33	10	-$250							
1018	995	$500							
1019	996	-$250							
1020	997	-$250							
1021	998	-$250							
1022	999	$500							
1023	1000	$500							

FIGURE 11.6 Using a Data Table to Simulate Replications

the replication numbers, 1–1000. The formula for the data table in cell B23 is **=Profit**. This forms a link to the profit from the prototype row for use in the data table. Then we select the Data/Table menu item and enter *any blank cell* (such as C23) as the column input cell. (No row input cell is necessary, so its box should be left empty.) This tricks Excel into repeating the row 19 calculations 1000 times, each time with a new random number, and reporting the profits in column B of the data table. (If we wanted to see other simulated quantities, such as revenue, for each replication, we could add extra output columns to the data table.)

To understand this procedure, you must understand exactly how data tables work. When we create a data table, Excel takes each value in the left column of the data table (here column A), substitutes it into the cell we designate as the column input cell, recalculates the spreadsheet, and returns the "bottom line" value (or values) we have requested in the top row of the data table (such as profit). It might seem silly to substitute each replication number from column A into a blank cell such as cell C23, but this part is really irrelevant. The important part is the *recalculation*. Each recalculation leads to a new random demand and the corresponding profit, and these profits are the quantities we want. Of course, this means that we should *not* freeze the quantity in cell A19 before forming the data table. The whole point of the data table is to use a different random number for each replication, and this will occur only if the random number in row 19 is left unfrozen.

Excel Tip Here is a useful Excel tip for speeding up recalculation. Use the Tools/Option command, click on the Calculation tab, click on the Automatic Except Tables option, and click on OK. Now when you change anything in your spreadsheet, everything will recalculate in the normal way *except* data tables. Data tables will not recalculate until you intentionally press the F9 key. Data tables can require lots of computing time, so this option can come in very handy. However, be aware that if you set this option and then form a data table, you will have to press F9 to make the data table recalculate the *first* time. Otherwise, you will see the same output value the whole way down the data table.

Using a Two-Way Data Table We can carry this method one step further to see how the profit depends on the order quantity. Here we use a two-way data table with the replication number along the side and possible order quantities along the top. See Figure 11.7 and the file WALTON3.XLS. Now the data table range is A23:F1023, and the driving formula, entered in cell A23, is again **=Profit**. The column input cell should

	A	B	C	D	E	F	G	H	I
1	Simulation of Walton's bookstore								
2									
3	Cost data			Demand distribution					
4	Unit cost	$7.50		CumProb	Demand	Probability		Range names used:	
5	Unit price	$10.00		0.00	100	0.30		UnitCost - B4	
6	Unit refund	$2.50		0.30	150	0.20		UnitPrice - B5	
7				0.50	200	0.30		UnitRefund - B6	
8	Decision variable			0.80	250	0.15		Lookup - D5:E9	
9	Order quantity	200		0.95	300	0.05		OrderQuan - B9	
10								Demand - A19	
11	Summary measures of simulated profits for each order quantity							Profit - E19	
12				Order quantity					
13		100	150	200	250	300			
14	Average profit	$250.00	$285.00	$170.00	$100.00	-$360.00			
15	Stdev profit	$0.00	$161.78	$318.20	$435.22	$496.57			
16									
17	Simulation								
18	Demand	Revenue	Cost	Refund	Profit				
19	100	$1,000	$1,500	$250	-$250				
20									
21	Data table showing profit for replications with various order quantities								
22	Replication			Order quantity					
23	($250.00)	100	150	200	250	300			
24	1	$250	$0	-$250	$250	-$750			
25	2	$250	$375	$500	$250	-$375			
26	3	$250	$375	-$250	$250	-$750			
27	4	$250	$375	$500	-$500	$0			
28	5	$250	$0	$500	$625	-$750			
29	6	$250	$375	$500	$625	-$750			
30	7	$250	$375	-$250	$625	-$750			
31	8	$250	$0	$500	$250	-$750			
32	9	$250	$375	$500	-$500	$375			
1017	994	$250	$0	$500	-$500	-$750			
1018	995	$250	$0	$500	-$500	$0			
1019	996	$250	$375	$500	-$500	-$750			
1020	997	$250	$375	-$250	-$125	$0			
1021	998	$250	$0	-$250	-$500	-$375			
1022	999	$250	$0	$500	$250	-$375			
1023	1000	$250	$0	$500	-$500	$375			

FIGURE 11.7 Using a Two-Way Data Table for the Simulation Model

again be *any blank cell*, and the row input cell should be B9 (the order quantity). Each cell in the body of the data table shows a simulated profit for a particular replication and a particular order quantity, and each is based on a *different* random number.

By averaging the numbers in each column of the data table (see row 14), we again see that 150 appears to be the best order quantity. It is also helpful to construct a bar chart of these averages, similar to the one shown in Figure 11.5. Now, however, assuming you have not frozen anything, the data table and the corresponding chart will change each time you press the F9 key. To see whether 150 is always the best order quantity, you can press the F9 key and see whether the bar above 150 continues to be the highest. ∎

By now you should appreciate the usefulness of data tables in spreadsheet simulations. They allow us to take a "prototype" simulation and replicate its key results as often as we like. This method makes summary statistics (over the entire group of replications) and corresponding charts fairly easy to obtain. Nevertheless, it can be a lot of work to create the data tables and charts. We will see shortly how the @Risk add-in does a lot of this work for us.

PROBLEMS

Skill-Building Problems

3. In August 1997, a car dealer is trying to determine how many 1998 cars to order. Each car ordered in August 1997 costs $10,000. The demand for the dealer's 1998 models has the probability distribution shown in Table 11.2. Each car sells for $15,000. If demand for 1998 cars exceeds the number of cars ordered in August, the dealer must reorder at a cost of $12,000 per car. Excess cars can be disposed of at $9000 per car. Use simulation to determine how many cars to order in August. For your optimal order quantity, find a 95% confidence interval for the expected profit.

TABLE 11.2	Demand Distribution for Car Problem

Cars Demanded	Probability
20	0.30
25	0.15
30	0.15
35	0.20
40	0.20

4. In the Walton Bookstore example, suppose that Walton receives no money for the first 50 excess calendars returned but receives $2.50 for every calendar after the first 50 returned. Does this change the optimal order quantity?

5. A sweatshirt supplier is trying to decide how many sweatshirts to print for the upcoming NCAA basketball championships. The final four teams have emerged from the quarterfinal round, and there is now a week left until the semifinals, which are then followed in a couple of days by the finals. Each sweatshirt costs $10 to produce and sells for $25. However, in 3 weeks, any leftover sweatshirts will be put on sale for half price, $12.50. The supplier assumes that the demand for his sweatshirts during the next three weeks (when interest is at its highest) has the distribution shown in Table 11.3. The residual demand, after the sweatshirts have been put on sale, has the distribution shown in Table 11.4 (page 580). The supplier, being a profit maximizer, realizes that every sweatshirt sold, even at the sale price, yields a profit. However, he also realizes that any sweatshirts produced but not sold (even at the sale price) must be thrown away, resulting in a $10 loss per sweatshirt.

TABLE 11.3	Demand Distribution at Regular Price

Demand (1000s)	Probability
7	0.05
8	0.10
9	0.25
10	0.30
11	0.20
12	0.10

TABLE 11.4	Demand Distribution at Reduced Price	
Demand (1000s)	**Probability**	
2	0.20	
3	0.30	
4	0.20	
5	0.15	
6	0.10	
7	0.05	

Analyze the supplier's problem with a simulation model.

Skill-Extending Problem

6. In the Walton Bookstore example with a discrete demand distribution, explain why an order quantity other than one of the possible demands cannot maximize the expected profit. (*Hint*: Consider an order of 190 calendars. If this maximizes expected profit, then it must yield a higher expected profit than an order of 150 or 100. But then an order of 200 calendars must also yield a larger expected profit than 190 calendars. Why?)

11.5 GENERATING RANDOM NUMBERS FROM OTHER PROBABILITY DISTRIBUTIONS

We have seen that the RAND function is capable of generating numbers that are uniformly distributed between 0 and 1. However, in many situations we want the random numbers to have a probability distribution other than this uniform distribution. For example, we might want to use a discrete distribution—several possible values and associated probabilities—as we did in the Walton example. In this case, assuming that we have only Excel's built-in capabilities, we must find a way to transform the uniform random numbers into the discrete distribution we require. We saw how to do this in the example, using a VLOOKUP function on the cumulative probabilities. Once you know this "trick," you can use it to generate random numbers from *any* discrete distribution.

In general, however, there are many probability distributions we might want to use in simulation models. These include some well-known distributions, such as the normal distribution, and some that are less well known. We then face two issues: Which distributions should we use, and how do we generate random values from them?

Regarding the first question, we typically choose the distribution on the basis of historical data and/or its shape and general characteristics. For example, suppose we want to simulate random checkout times at a supermarket. We could gather data on many actual checkout times, create a histogram of these, and try to match this histogram to one of several theoretical probability distributions. In fact, this is exactly what the software package BestFit from Palisade does. (BestFit is now incorporated into @Risk, as we will discuss shortly.) We feed it data, and it suggests the best-fitting probability distribution(s)—which we could then use in a simulation model. If there are no relevant historical data, we might choose the probability distribution on general considerations. For example, we might choose the normal distribution because of its symmetry and bell shape.

Once we choose a probability distribution, whether it be the normal or some other distribution, we need a way to generate random values from this distribution. There are two basic ways to do this:

1. Use Excel's built-in functions to transform uniform random numbers (from the RAND function) appropriately.

2. Use the functions supplied with a simulation add-in such as @Risk.

As an example, suppose we want to generate a normally distributed random value with mean 100 and standard deviation 10. We can do this in Excel with the formula

=NORMINV(RAND(),100,10)

Excel's built-in NORMINV function takes three arguments: a probability, a mean, and a standard deviation. It returns the value that has the specified probability to the left of it under the given normal curve. If the specified probability is a *random* number between 0 and 1, then this formula returns a random normally distributed value. This is probably not obvious, but it works correctly. (You can check it as follows. Enter this formula into a cell, copy it to about 1000 other cells, and then create a histogram of the resulting numbers. You should see that the histogram is bell-shaped and is centered approximately around 100.)

The problem with using built-in Excel functions is that we have to know the appropriate transformations. (Would you have guessed the NORMINV function?) In addition, there are some common probability distributions, such as the **triangular** distribution in Figure 11.8, for which there are no simple transformations available—that is, there is no simple way to generate random numbers from this triangular distribution by using only built-in Excel functions. This is unfortunate because the triangular distribution is a favorite of many simulation modelers. It is easy to describe: (1) its triangular shape is determined a minimum possible value a, a most likely value c, and a maximum possible value b, and (2) it can be symmetric or skewed in either direction by selecting appropriate values of a, b, and c. We certainly want to be able to simulate from a triangular distribution in simulation models.

In short, if we rely only on built-in Excel functions, we are quite limited in the probability distributions we can use for simulation models. Fortunately, this is not the case if we use a simulation add-in such as @Risk. It offers a large number of easy-to-remember functions that can be used to simulate from various probability distributions. We will discuss these in more detail in the rest of this chapter and in the next chapter, but we mention a few of them here. (Note that all of @Risk's functions begin with RISK, as in RISKDISCRETE.)

- If you want to simulate from a discrete distribution, where the possible values are in a range named Values and the probabilities are in a range named Probs, use the formula

  =RISKDISCRETE(Values,Probs)

  That's all there is to it. No cumulative probabilities are necessary, and no VLOOKUP is necessary.

- If you want to simulate from a normal distribution, where the mean and standard deviation of this distribution are in cells range-named Mean and Stdev, use the formula

  =RISKNORMAL(Mean,Stdev)

  No NORMINV function is necessary.

FIGURE 11.8
Triangular
Distribution

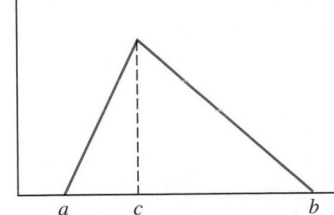

- If you want to simulate from a triangular distribution, where the minimum, most likely, and maximum possible values are in cells range-named Min, ML, and Max, use the formula

  =RISKTRIANG(Min,ML,Max)

The only drawback to using these functions is that you must have @Risk added in—it must be loaded in memory. If it is not loaded and you enter one of these functions in a cell, Excel will not recognize it, and it will give you an error message.

We hope by this time that we have stimulated your interest in @Risk. We have claimed that it can save you a lot of work and it offers you a large collection of probability distributions to use. In the next section, we discuss this powerful simulation add-in in some detail.

PROBLEM

Skill-Building Problem

7. We suggested a way to generate normally distributed random numbers with Excel's built-in functions. Check whether this method really does what it is supposed to do. Enter the label Normal in cell A1, enter the formula

=NORMINV(RAND(),100,10)

in cell A2, and copy this formula down to cell A501 to generate 500 random numbers. Then create a histogram (we suggest using StatPro) of these random numbers. Also, summarize them with the AVERAGE and STDEV functions. Are the average and standard deviation approximately what they should be? Does the histogram have approximately the anticipated shape?

11.6 INTRODUCTION TO @RISK

Spreadsheet simulation modeling has become extremely popular in recent years, both in the academic and corporate communities.[5] Much of the reason for this popularity is due to simulation add-ins such as @Risk. There are two primary advantages to using such an add-in. First, an add-in gives us easy access to many probability distributions we might want to use in our simulation models. We already mentioned how the RISKDISCRETE, RISKNORMAL, and RISKTRIANG functions, among others, are easy to use and remember. Second, an add-in allows us to perform simulations much more easily than is possible with Excel alone. For example, to replicate a simulation in Excel, we typically need to build a data table. Then we have to calculate summary statistics, such as averages, standard deviations, and percentiles, with built-in Excel functions. If we want graphs to enhance the analysis, we have to create them. In short, we have to perform a number of time-consuming steps for each simulation. Simulation add-ins such as @Risk perform much of this work for us automatically.

Although we will concentrate on @Risk in this book, it is not the only available simulation add-in for Excel. A worthy competitor is Crystal Ball,® developed by Decisioneering (www.decisioneering.com). Crystal Ball has much of the same functionality

---

[5]The authors of this book are very aware of this trend. We have been involved in teaching @Risk modeling to managers of several companies, including GM and Eli Lilly, that eventually want *all* of their managers to understand spreadsheet simulation modeling.

as @Risk. In addition, because of the relative ease of developing "home-grown" applications in Excel with Excel's built-in macro language Visual Basic for Applications, individuals are developing their own simulation add-ins for Excel. However, we have a natural bias for @Risk—we have been permitted by its developer, the Palisade Corporation (www.palisade.com), to include it in the CD-ROM that accompanies this book. If it were not included, you would have to purchase it from Palisade at a fairly steep price. Indeed, neither @Risk, Crystal Ball, nor any other simulation add-in is included with Microsoft Office—you must purchase them separately.

Here is an overview of some of @Risk's features. We will explain all of these in more detail later in this section.

1. @Risk contains a number of functions such as RISKNORMAL and RISKDISCRETE that make it easy to generate observations from the most important probability distributions. We discussed these briefly in the previous section.

2. @Risk has a "gallery" of input probability distributions to choose from.[6] This gallery lets you see the shapes of various distributions (normal and triangular, for example), and it lets you adjust the parameters of these distributions in an intuitive way so that you can pick the most appropriate one for your model. Palisade has also developed a separate software package, BestFit, to help you identify probability distributions that provide good fits to historical data. Fortunately, the BestFit functionality is now built into @Risk.

3. You can specify any cell or range of cells in the simulation model as **output cells**. When you run the simulation, @Risk automatically keeps statistics (averages, standard deviations, percentiles, and others) on the values generated in these output cells across the replications. It can also create graphs such as histograms based on these values.

4. @Risk has a special function, the RISKSIMTABLE function, that allows you to run the same simulation several times, using a different value of some key input each time. For example, suppose that you would like to simulate an inventory ordering policy (as in the Walton Bookstore example). Your ultimate purpose is to compare simulation outputs across a number of possible order quantities such as 100, 150, 200, 250, and 300. If you use an appropriate formula involving the RISKSIMTABLE function, the entire simulation will be performed for each of these order quantities separately. Then you can compare their outputs when attempting to choose the "best" order quantity.

In the remainder of this section we will illustrate some of @Risk's functionality by revisiting the Walton Bookstore example. Then in the next chapter, we will use @Risk to help develop a number of interesting simulation models. Throughout our discussion, you should keep one very important idea in mind. The development of a simulation model is basically a two-step procedure. The first step is to build the model itself. This step requires you to build in all of the logic that transforms inputs (including @Risk functions such as RISKDISCRETE) into outputs (such as profit). This is where most of the work and thinking go, exactly as in models from previous chapters, and @Risk cannot do this for you. It is *your* job to enter the formulas that link inputs to outputs appropriately. However, once this logic has been incorporated, @Risk takes over in the second step. It automatically replicates your model, with different random numbers on each replication, and it reports any summary measures that you request in tabular or graphical form. Therefore, @Risk can greatly decrease the amount of "busy work" you need to do, but it is not a magic bullet!

---

[6]This is a new feature in @Risk 4.0. It is very much like one of Crystal Ball's most popular features.

EXAMPLE 11.2

USING @RISK AT WALTON BOOKSTORE

Recall that Walton Bookstore buys calendars for $7.50, sells them at the regular price of $10, and gets a refund of $2.50 for all calendars that cannot be sold. The company does not know exactly how many calendars its customers will demand, but it does have historical data on demands for similar calendars in previous years. (See the Data sheet of the WALTON4.XLS file.) Walton wants to use these historical data to determine a reasonable probability distribution for next year's demand for calendars. Then it wants to use this probability distribution, together with @Risk, to simulate the profit for any particular order quantity. It eventually wants to find the "best" order quantity.

Solution

We will use this example to illustrate many (but certainly not all) of @Risk's features. We first see how it helps us to choose an appropriate "input" distribution for demand. Then we will use it to build a simulation model for a specific order quantity and generate outputs from this model. Finally, we will see how the RISKSIMTABLE function enables us to simultaneously generate outputs from several order quantities so that we can choose a "best" order quantity.

Loading @Risk To follow this discussion, you need to have Excel open with @Risk added in. The first step, if you have not already done it, is to install the Palisade Decision Tools suite with the Setup program on the CD-ROM that accompanies this book. Then you can load @Risk by clicking on the Windows Start button, selecting the Programs group, selecting the Palisade Decision Tools group, and finally selecting @Risk 4.0 for Excel. If Excel is already open, this will load @Risk inside Excel. If Excel is not yet open, this will launch Excel and @Risk simultaneously. (When you are asked whether you want to load the macros, click on Yes.) Once @Risk is loaded, you will see two new toolbars, the Decision Tools toolbar in Figure 11.9, and the @Risk toolbar in Figure 11.10.[7,8] You will also have a new @Risk menu added to the usual Excel menu bar.

FIGURE 11.9
Decision Tools
Toolbar

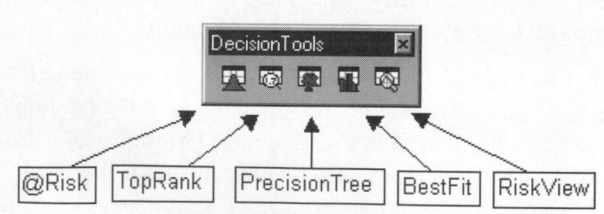

Fitting a Probability Distribution Some of the historical demand data appear in Figure 11.11. As the text box indicates, Walton believes the probability distribution of

---

[7]We have had occasional problems with @Risk "locking up." This is probably not the fault of @Risk; it is probably a case of having too many programs in memory at once. Therefore, we recommend that you close other applications before loading @Risk.

[8]The Decision Tools toolbar simply lets you open other programs in the suite, such as the PrecisionTree add-in used in Chapter 10. Your toolbar might also include buttons for Evolver and RiskOptimizer, two other packages Palisade produces. However, these programs are not included with the suite on our CD-ROM.

FIGURE 11.10
@Risk Toolbar

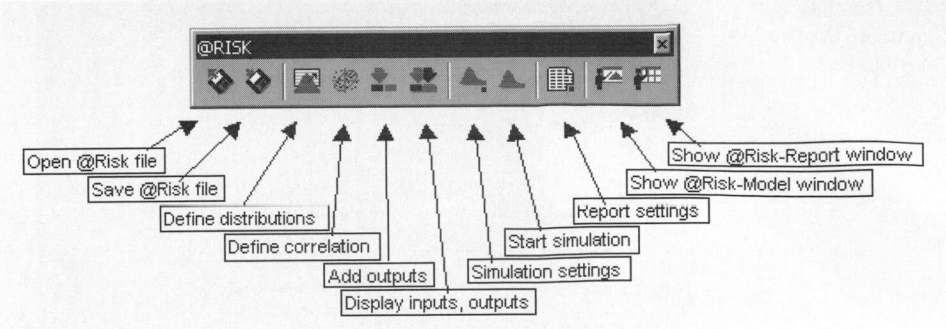

FIGURE 11.11
Historical Demand
Data

	A	B	C	D	E	F	G	H
1	**Historical demand data**							
2	Each value in column A is the demand for a similar calendar in some previous							
3	year. Walton believes the probability distribution of demand for this year's calendar							
4	should be similar to the histogram for these historical demands.							
5								
6	**Demand**							
7	285							
8	144							
9	250							
10	194							
11	216							
12	199							
13	267							
14	240							
15	160							
16	203							
17	201							
115	137							
116	161							
117	106							
118	265							
119	103							
120	291							
121	117							

demand for next year's calendars should closely match the histogram for the historical data. To see which probability distributions match the histogram well, we can use @Risk's fitting ability, using the following steps.

1. **Model window.** Click on the Show @Risk-Model Window toolbar button. @Risk has two windows that get you (seemingly) outside of Excel: the Model and Results windows. The former helps in setting up the model; the latter shows results from running a simulation. For now, we require the Model window.

2. **Insert a Fit Tab.** Once the Model window is showing, select the Insert/Fit Tab menu item. This brings up a one-column "spreadsheet" on the left.

3. **Copy and paste data.** We want to copy the historical data to this mini-spreadsheet. To do so, go back to the Excel window (click on the Excel icon at the bottom of the screen), copy the historical data, go back to the @Risk Model window, and paste the data—copy and paste work in the usual way.

4. **Select candidate distributions.** @Risk has many probability distributions from which to select. To see the candidates, select the Fitting/Specify Distributions to Fit menu item. This brings up the dialog box in Figure 11.12 (page 586). You can check as many of the candidates as you like. Some are undoubtedly unfamiliar to

FIGURE 11.12
Candidate Probability
Distributions

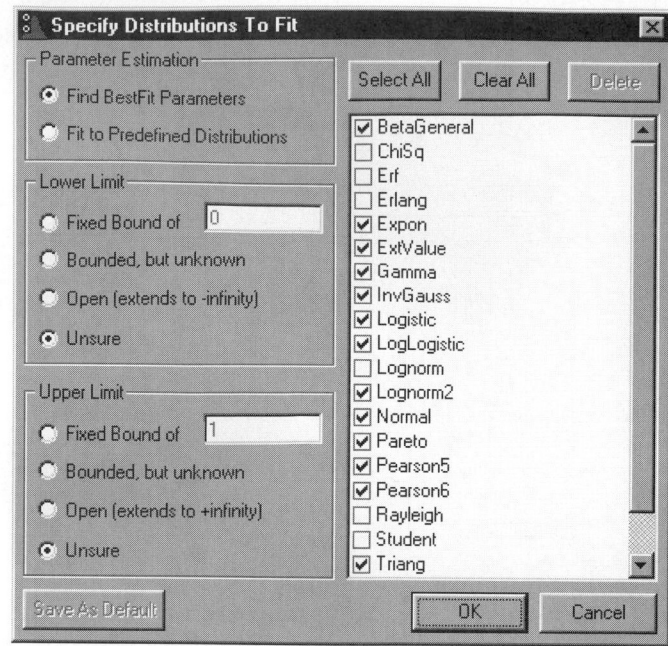

you, so you might want to stick with familiar distributions such as the normal and triangular. However, we clicked on OK to accept the defaults shown in the figure.

5. **Do the fitting.** Select the Fitting/Run Fit Now menu item to see which of the candidate distributions most closely match the historical data. @Risk evaluates the fits in several different ways (using technical measures we will not discuss in detail), and it also allows you to check the fits visually. After it runs, you will see a screen as in Figure 11.13. This screen shows one of the candidate distributions (we selected to display the normal distribution) superimposed on the histogram of the data. In this example, it shows that the best-fitting *normal* distribution has mean 168.130 and standard deviation 57.619. By clicking on any name in the list of distributions (where Normal is currently highlighted), you can see the fit from any of the other candidate distributions. @Risk actually ranks these distributions from best fit (the top one) to worst fit (the bottom one) according to one of three measures. These measures are listed in the Test Value row of the GOF (goodness-of-fit) table on the right—the lower the test value, the better the fit. For these data, the normal distribution is actually in the middle of the pack, with the BetaGeneral distribution edging out the others for best fit.[9] Nevertheless, as the chart shows, the normal distribution fits the historical data quite well, and we will use it for the simulation model. If nothing else, it is familiar.

6. **Examine the selected distribution.** From a managerial standpoint, you might want to examine the probability distribution selected in the previous step in some detail. To do so, select the Insert/Distribution Window menu item (still from the @Risk Model window) and fill it out as shown in Figure 11.14. Specifically, select Fit Results in the Source box, select By Name in the Choose box, and click on Normal. @Risk provides a very user-friendly interface for examining the resulting

---

[9]This is somewhat surprising since we simulated the historical data from the normal distribution in the first place. It just shows that several probability distributions can match a given data set equally well for all practical purposes.

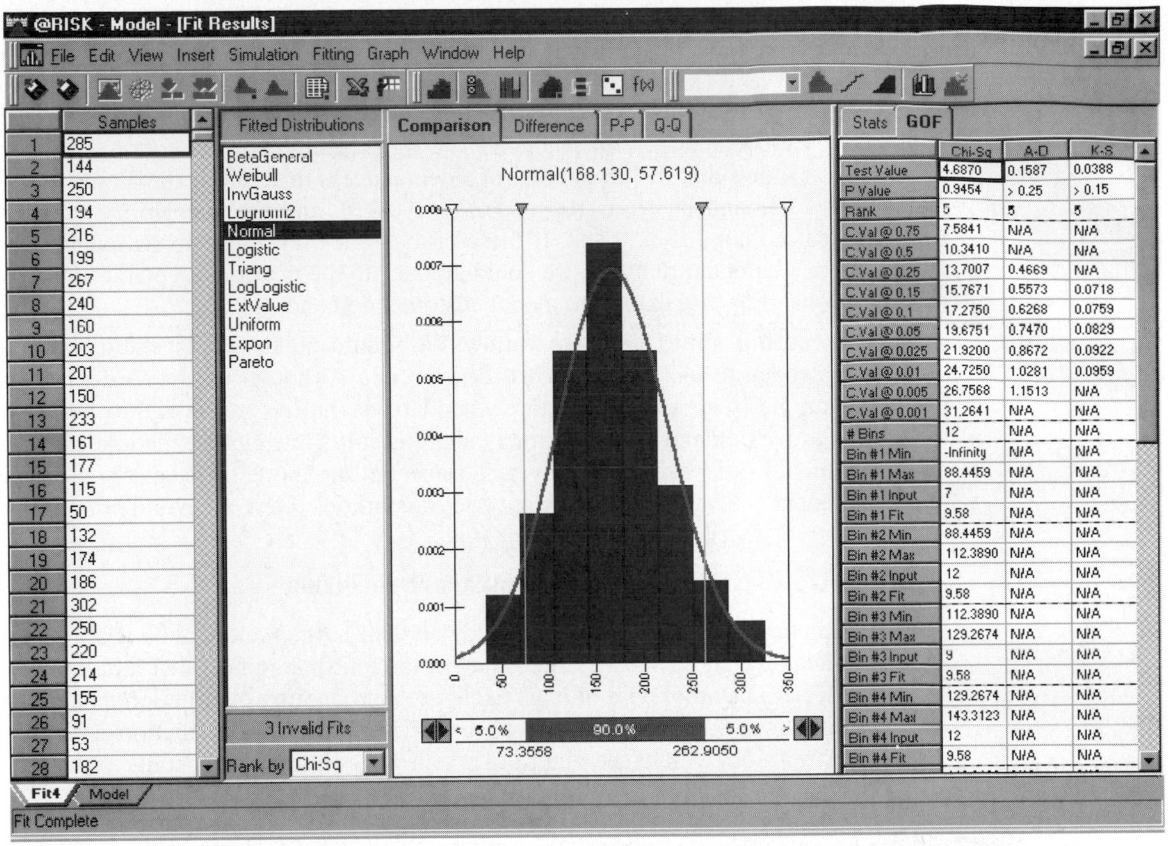

FIGURE 11.13 Fit to Historical Data Histogram

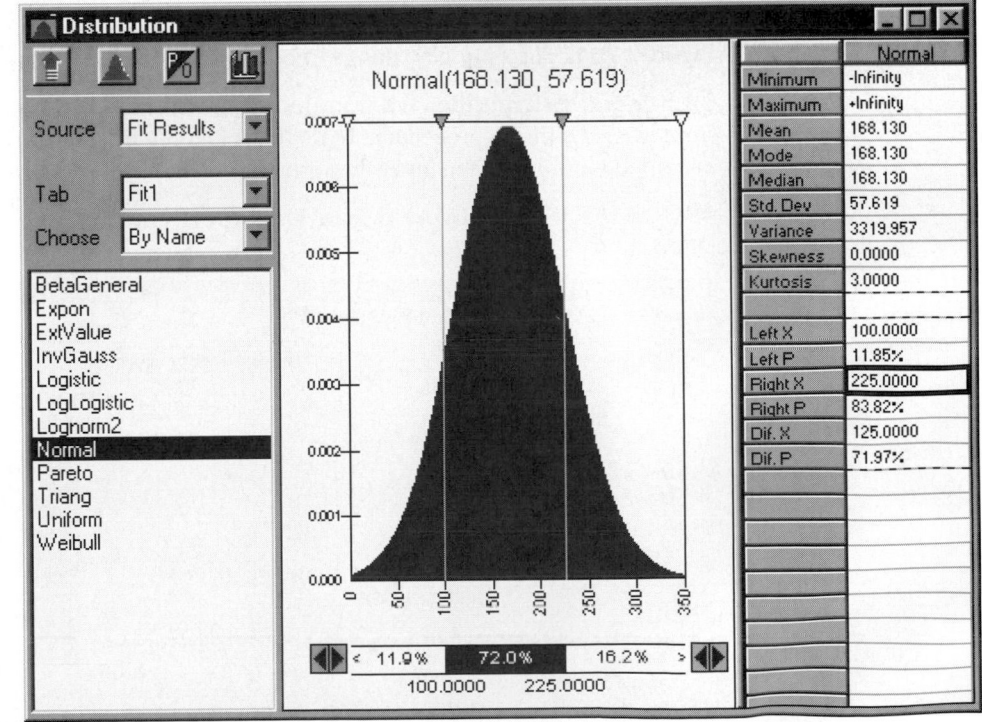

FIGURE 11.14
Examining the
Selected Probability
Distribution

normal distribution. It has two "sliders" (the two middle triangles above the curve) that you can drag in either direction to see probabilities of various areas under the curve. Also, you can enter "X values" or "P values" directly into the boxes in the right column to obtain equivalent information. For example, we entered 100 for Left X and 225 for Right X. The right column (or the bottom of the graph) then shows that the probability of a demand less than 100 is 0.119, the probability of a demand between 100 and 225 is 0.720, and the probability of a demand greater than 225 is 0.162. If these probabilities do not seem reasonable for next year's calendar demand, we could go back to the previous step and select another probability distribution to model customer demand.

7. **A caution about negative values.** We should point out that there is a potential drawback to using this normal distribution. Although the mean demand in this example is approximately three standard deviations to the right of 0, so that a negative demand is very unlikely, there is still some chance that one can occur— which would not make physical sense in our model. To ensure that negative demands do *not* occur, there are two possibilities. First, we could use a **truncated** normal distribution of the form

=RISKTNORMAL(MeanDem,StdevDem,0,1000)

This function disallows values below the third argument or above the fourth argument. (We chose such a large value for the fourth argument that it has no practical effect.) The other possibility is to choose a probability distribution that, by its very definition, does not allow negative values. One such distribution is the Weibull distribution, which (see Figure 11.13) provides one of the best fits to the historical data anyway.

DEVELOPING THE SIMULATION MODEL

Now that we have chosen a probability distribution for demand, the spreadsheet model for profit is essentially the same as we developed earlier *without* @Risk. It appears in Figure 11.15. The only new things to be aware of are the following.

❶ **Input distribution.** We want to use the normal distribution for demand found from @Risk's fitting procedure. To do this, enter the fitted mean and standard deviation in cells E4 and E5. Then enter the formula

=ROUND(RISKNORMAL(MeanDem,StdevDem),0)

FIGURE 11.15
Simulation Model with a Fixed Order Quantity

	A	B	C	D	E	F	G	H
1	Simulation of Walton's Bookstore using @RISK							
2								
3	Cost data			Demand distribution: normal				
4	Unit cost	$7.50		Mean	168.1			
5	Unit price	$10.00		Stdev	57.6	From running @Risk's		
6	Unit refund	$2.50				fitting procedure		
7								
8	Decision variable					Range names used:		
9	Order quantity	200				UnitCost - B4		
10						UnitPrice - B5		
11	Simulated quantities					UnitRefund - B6		
12	Demand	Revenue	Cost	Refund	Profit	MeanDem - E4		
13	130	$1,300	$1,500	$175	-$25	StdevDem - E5		
14						OrderQuan - B9		
15	Summary measures of profit, using @Risk statistical functions					Demand - A13		
16	Minimum	-$1,307.50				Profit - E13		
17	Maximum	$500.00						
18	Mean	$164.11						
19	Stdev	$335.05						

in cell A13 for the random demand. This uses the RISKNORMAL function to generate a normally distributed demand with the fitted mean and standard deviation. Because demands should be integers, we use Excel's ROUND function, with second argument 0, to round this value to 0 decimals.

❷ **Output cell.** When we run the simulation, we want @Risk to keep track of profit. In @Risk's terminology, we need to designate the Profit cell, E13, as an **output cell**. There are two ways to designate a cell as an output cell. One way is to highlight it and then click on the Add Output Cell button on the @Risk toolbar. (See Figure 11.10.) An equivalent way is to add **RISKOUTPUT()+** to the cell's formula. Either way, the formula in cell E13 changes from

=B13+D13-C13

to

=RISKOUTPUT()+B13+D13-C13

The plus sign following RISKOUTPUT() does *not* indicate addition. It is simply @Risk's way of saying: Keep track of the value in this cell (for reporting reasons) as the simulation progresses. Any number of cells can be designated in this way as output cells. They are typically the "bottom line" values of primary interest.

❸ **Inputs and outputs.** @Risk keeps a list of all input cells (cells with @Risk random functions) and output cells. If you want to check the list at any time, click on the Display Inputs, Outputs button on the @Risk toolbar. (See Figure 11.10.) It provides an Explorer-like list, as in Figure 11.16.

FIGURE 11.16
List of Inputs and Outputs

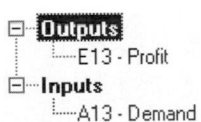

❹ **Summary functions.** @Risk provides several functions for summarizing output values. We illustrate these in the range B16:B19. They contain the formulas

=RISKMIN(Profit)
=RISKMAX(Profit)
=RISKMEAN(Profit)

and

=RISKSTDDEV(Profit)

The values in these cells are not of any use until we run the simulation. However, once the simulation runs, these formulas capture summary statistics of profit. For example, the RISKMEAN function calculates the average of the profits generated during the simulation. Although these same summary statistics also appear in @Risk output reports, it is sometimes handy to have them in the same worksheet as the model. (To see more about these functions, click on Excel's "function wizard" button, the f_x button, and consult the @Risk Statistics group.)

RUNNING THE SIMULATION

Now that we have developed the model for Walton, the rest is straightforward. The procedure is always the same. We specify the simulation settings and the report settings and then run the simulation.

❶   Simulation settings. We must first tell @Risk how we want the simulation to be run. To do so, click on the Simulation Settings button on the @Risk toolbar. Click on the Iterations tab and fill out the dialog box as in Figure 11.17. This says that we want to replicate the simulation 1000 times, each with a new random demand. (@Risk uses the term "iteration" instead of "replication." We actually prefer the latter, but we will use both terms interchangeably.) Then click on the Sampling tab and fill out the dialog box as in Figure 11.18. For technical reasons, it is *always* best to use Latin Hypercube sampling—it is more efficient. We also recommend checking the Monte Carlo button in the Standard Recalc group. Although this has no effect on the ultimate results, it means that you will see *random* numbers in the spreadsheet—that is, values that change when you press the F9 key. Otherwise, if you select the default Expected Value button, the values in the spreadsheet will not appear to be random—they will not change when you press the F9 key. We find this disconcerting.

❷   Report settings. @Risk has many options for displaying the outputs from a simulation. The outputs can be placed in an @Risk Results window or on new sheets of your Excel workbook (or both). They can also be shown in more or less detail. Click on the Report Settings button on the @Risk toolbar (see Figure 11.19) to select some of these options. In this dialog box, we have requested a summary of the simulation and detailed statistics, and we have asked that they be shown both in the @Risk Results window and on new sheets in the current Excel workbook.

FIGURE 11.17
Setting the Number of Iterations (Replications)

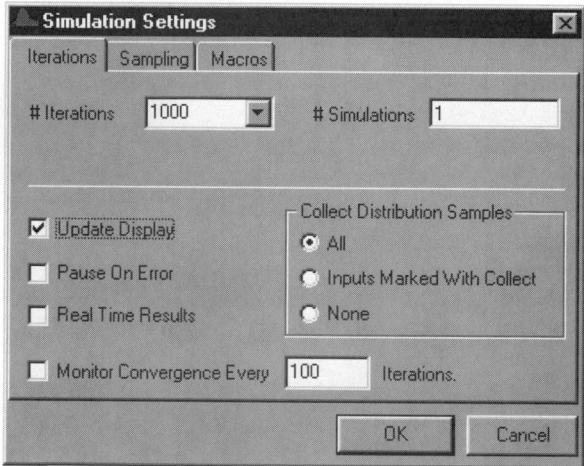

FIGURE 11.18
Other Simulation Settings

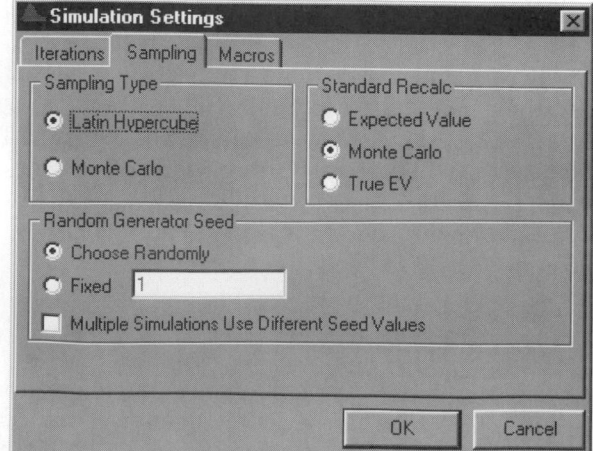

FIGURE 11.19
@Risk Results
Settings Dialog Box

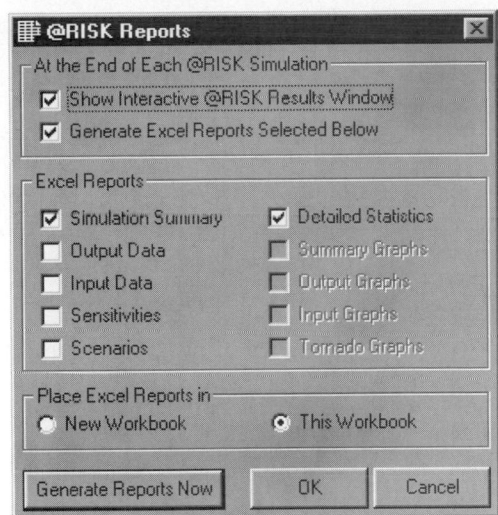

@RISK Reports

At the End of Each @RISK Simulation
- ☑ Show Interactive @RISK Results Window
- ☑ Generate Excel Reports Selected Below

Excel Reports
- ☑ Simulation Summary
- ☐ Output Data
- ☐ Input Data
- ☐ Sensitivities
- ☐ Scenarios
- ☑ Detailed Statistics
- ☐ Summary Graphs
- ☐ Output Graphs
- ☐ Input Graphs
- ☐ Tornado Graphs

Place Excel Reports in
- ○ New Workbook
- ● This Workbook

[Generate Reports Now] [OK] [Cancel]

❸ **Run the simulation.** We are finally ready to run the simulation! To do so, simply click on the Start Simulation button on the @Risk toolbar. (We think of this as the "red piano" button.) At this point, @Risk repeatedly generates a random number for each random input cell, recalculates the worksheet, keeps track of all output cell values. You can watch the progress at the bottom left of the screen.

Analyzing the Output @Risk generates a large number of output measures. We discuss the most important of these now.

1. **Summary Report.** Assuming that the top box in Figure 11.19 is checked (which we recommend), we are immediately transferred to the @Risk Results window. This window contains the summary results in Figure 11.20. The top line summarizes the 1000 profits generated during the simulation. The smallest of these was −$1307.50, the largest was $500, they averaged $164.11, 5% of them were below −$475, and 95% of them were below $500. (Actually, there were many iterations with a profit of $500, so the 95th percentile shown is the *same* as the maximum profit.) Note that the summary measures reported here match those from the RISKMIN, RISKMAX, and RISKMEAN functions in Figure 11.15. @Risk summarizes not only the output cells (profit for this example), but also the random input cells (demand). As we feared, at least one generated demand was *negative*. However, the occurrence of one or two negative demands out of 1000 probably has little effect on the overall results.

2. **Detailed Statistics.** W can also request more detailed statistics within the @Risk Results window with the Insert/Detailed Statistics menu item. (There is also a toolbar button for doing this.) Some of these detailed statistics appear in Figure 11.21.

@RISK - Results - [Summary Statistics]

File Edit View Insert Simulation Results Window Help

	Cell	Name	Minimum	Mean	Maximum	x1=	p1=	x2=	p2=	x2-x1=	p2-p1=
Outputs	E13	Profit	-1307.5	164.105	500	-475	5%	500	95%	975	90%
E13- Profit											
Inputs	A13	[Input] Demand	-40.50664	164.3073	338.6504	69.62578	5%	254.5937	95%	184.9679	90%
A13- Demand											

FIGURE 11.20 @Risk Summary Report

FIGURE 11.21
Detailed Statistics
Window

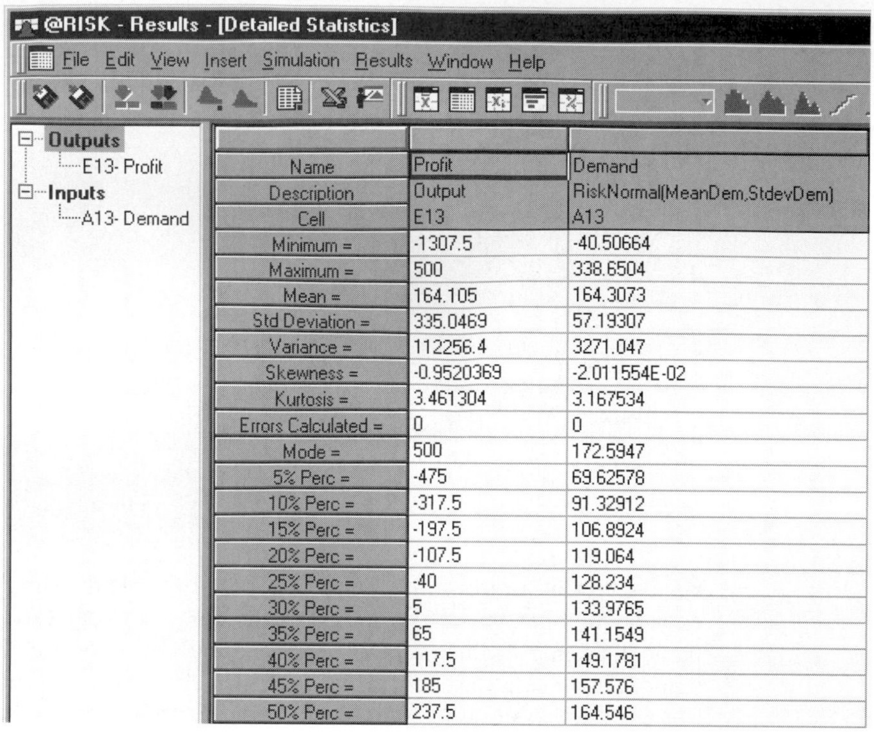

Name	Profit	Demand
Description	Output	RiskNormal(MeanDem,StdevDem)
Cell	E13	A13
Minimum =	-1307.5	-40.50664
Maximum =	500	338.6504
Mean =	164.105	164.3073
Std Deviation =	335.0469	57.19307
Variance =	112256.4	3271.047
Skewness =	-0.9520369	-2.011554E-02
Kurtosis =	3.461304	3.167534
Errors Calculated =	0	0
Mode =	500	172.5947
5% Perc =	-475	69.62578
10% Perc =	-317.5	91.32912
15% Perc =	-197.5	106.8924
20% Perc =	-107.5	119.064
25% Perc =	-40	128.234
30% Perc =	5	133.9765
35% Perc =	65	141.1549
40% Perc =	117.5	149.1781
45% Perc =	185	157.576
50% Perc =	237.5	164.546

Also, the Outputs tree shows: **Outputs** — E13- Profit; **Inputs** — A13- Demand.

All of the information from Figure 11.20 is here, plus some. (Other percentiles and a few other measures extend below this figure.) For example, the 25th percentile indicates that 25% of the 1000 profits generated were below −$40. Also, because the 30th percentile for profit is positive, we estimate that the probability of breaking even, with an order quantity of 200, is somewhere between 0.25 and 0.30.

3. **Target values.** By scrolling to the bottom of the detailed statistics list (see Figure 11.22), you can enter any target value or target percentage. If you enter a target value, @Risk calculates the corresponding percentage, and vice versa. Here we entered a target profit of $0, and @Risk calculated the corresponding percentage as 27.4%. This means that 27.4% of the 1000 profits were $0 or negative. @Risk provides room for up to 10 target value/percentage pairs.

4. **Simulation data.** The results to this point *summarize* the simulation. It is also possible to see the full results—the data, demands and profits, from all 1000

FIGURE 11.22
Target Values and
Percentiles

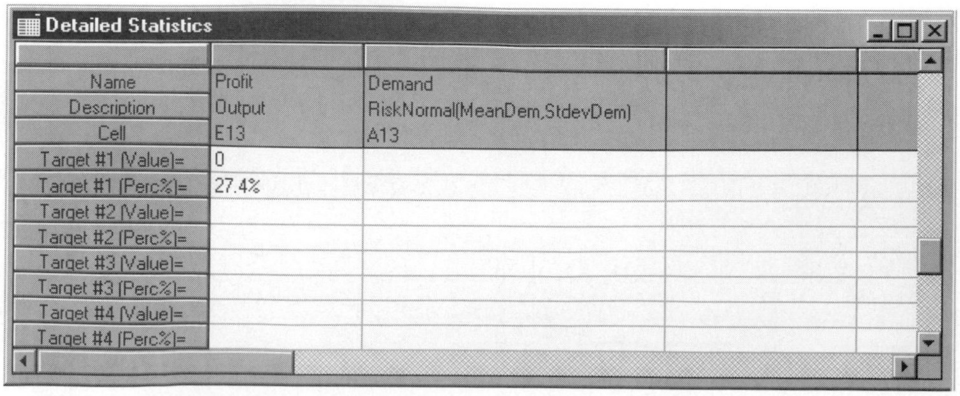

Name	Profit	Demand		
Description	Output	RiskNormal(MeanDem,StdevDem)		
Cell	E13	A13		
Target #1 (Value)=	0			
Target #1 (Perc%)=	27.4%			
Target #2 (Value)=				
Target #2 (Perc%)=				
Target #3 (Value)=				
Target #3 (Perc%)=				
Target #4 (Value)=				
Target #4 (Perc%)=				

replications. To do this, select the Insert/Data menu item. A portion of the data for this simulation appears in Figure 11.23.

5. **Charts.** To see the results graphically, click on the Profit item in the left pane (the Explorer-like list) of the Results window and then select the Insert/Graph/Histogram menu item. This creates a histogram of the 1000 profits from the simulation, as shown in Figure 11.24. The same interface is available that we saw earlier—namely, we can move the "sliders" at the top of the chart to the left or right to see various probabilities. For example, we see in the figure that 5.2% of the simulated profits are below −$475. Also, we see that the distribution of profit is very skewed to the left when the order quantity is 200. Normally distributed inputs do not always lead to normally distributed outputs! Why does this skewness occur? If demand is greater than 200, the order quantity level, then 200 calendars will be sold and profit will be $500, regardless of the *exact* demand. Therefore, there is a reasonably good chance (almost 30%) that profit will be exactly $500. On the other side, where demand is less than 200, profit gradually decreases as demand decreases. This leads to the skewness.

6. **Outputs in Excel.** Often we will want the simulation outputs, including charts, in an Excel workbook. The easiest way to get the numerical information in Figures 11.20 and 11.21 into an Excel workbook is to fill out the Report Settings dialog box as we did in Figure 11.19. Then separate sheets are created to hold the reports.

FIGURE 11.23
Simulation Data
Window

	Name	Profit	Demand	
	Description	Output	RiskNormal(MeanDem,StdevDem)	
	Iteration# / Cell	E13	A13	
1		50	140.30432	
2		95	145.73213	
3		-160	111.57539	
4		87.50000	145.15906	
5		-295	94.40015	
6		-430	75.91013	
7		-865	17.51978	
8		500	244.57419	

FIGURE 11.24
Histogram of
Simulated Profits

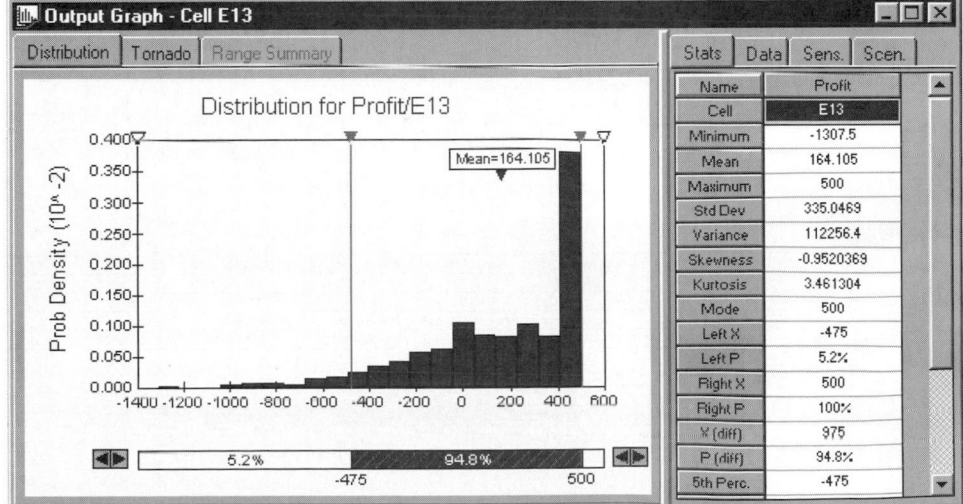

For example, the basic summary report appears as in Figure 11.25. To transfer an @Risk chart to an Excel workbook, click on the right button on the @Risk Results toolbar (it shows a histogram with an Excel logo above the chart). This creates the chart in a *new* Excel workbook, which we can then copy to the original workbook if we like.

This has been a quick tour through @Risk's report capabilities. We urge you to experiment with the user-friendly interface. For example, we illustrated histograms only. @Risk allows you to create other types of charts as well, such as cumulative ascending or cumulative descending charts, and these charts can be formatted in many ways. Another feature in the Results window is the ability to store various results in separate tabbed "sheets," similar to the sheets in an Excel workbook. These allow you to organize your work, which could be especially useful for complex simulation projects. The many possibilities can be intimidating at first, but all of the features are quite easy and intuitive once you give them a try.

Using RISKSIMTABLE Walton's ultimate goal is to choose an order quantity that provides a large average profit (and little risk, if possible). We could rerun the simulation model several times, each time with a different order quantity in the OrderQuan cell, and compare the results. However, this has two drawbacks. First, it takes a lot of time and work. The second drawback is more subtle. Each time we run the simulation, we get a *different* set of random demands. Therefore, one of the order quantities could win the contest just by luck. For a fairer comparison, it would be better to test each order quantity on the *same* set of random demands.

The RISKSIMTABLE function in @Risk enables us to obtain a fair comparison quickly and easily. We illustrate it in Figure 11.26. (See the file WALTON5.XLS.) There are two modifications to the previous model. The first is that we have listed order quantities we want to test in a range named OrderQuanList. Second, instead of entering a *number* in cell B9, we enter the formula

=RISKSIMTABLE(OrderQuanList)

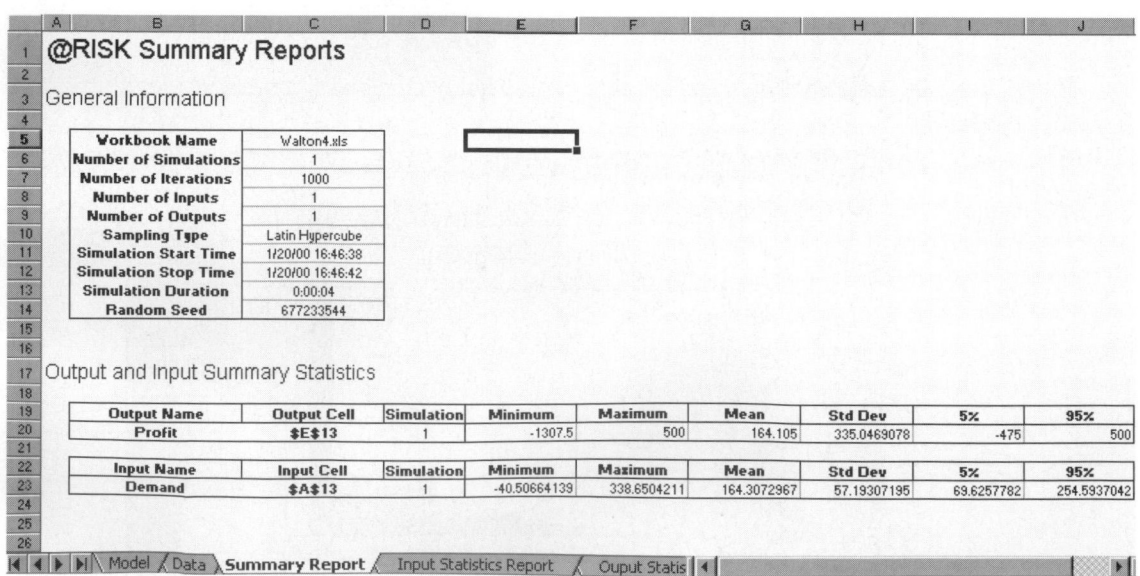

FIGURE 11.25 Summary Report in an Excel Worksheet

FIGURE 11.26
Model with a
RISKSIMTABLE
Function

	A	B	C	D	E	F	G	H
1	Simulation of Walton's Bookstore using @RISK							
2								
3	Cost data			Demand distribution: normal				
4	Unit cost	$7.50		Mean	168.1			
5	Unit price	$10.00		Stdev	57.6	From running @Risk's		
6	Unit refund	$2.50				fitting procedure		
7								
8	Decision variable			Possible order quantities				
9	Order quantity	100		100	150	200	250	300
10								
11	Simulated quantities					Range names used:		
12	Demand	Revenue	Cost	Refund	Profit	UnitCost - B4		
13	96	$960.00	$750.00	$10.00	$220.00	UnitPrice - B5		
14						UnitRefund - B6		
15						MeanDem - E4		
16						StdevDem - E5		
17						OrderQuan - B9		
18						OrderQuanList - D9:H9		
19						Demand - A13		
20						Profit - E13		
21								

Note that the list does not need to be entered in the spreadsheet (although we believe this is a good idea). We could instead enter the formula

=RISKSIMTABLE({100, 150, 200, 250, 300})

where the list of numbers must be enclosed in curly brackets. In either case, the worksheet displays the first member of the list, 100, and the corresponding calculations for this first order quantity. However, the model is now set up to run the simulation for *all* order quantities in the list.

To do this, click on the Simulation Settings button on the @Risk toolbar and fill out the Iterations dialog box as shown in Figure 11.27. Specifically, enter 1000 for the number of iterations and 5 for the number of simulations. @Risk will then run five simulations of 1000 iterations each, one simulation for each order quantity in the list, and it will use the *same* 1000 random demands for each simulation.

FIGURE 11.27
Simulation Settings
for Multiple
Simulations

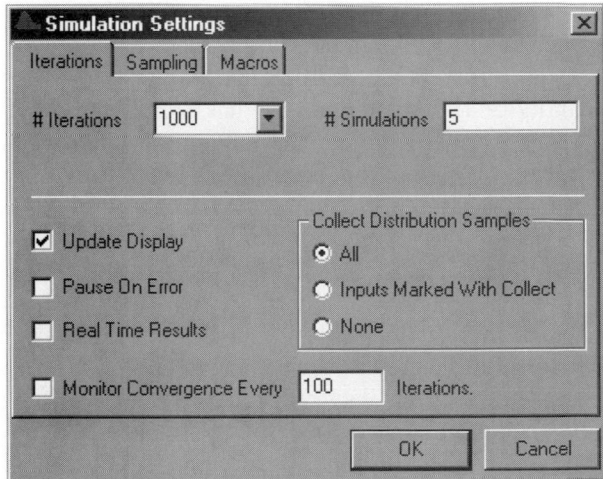

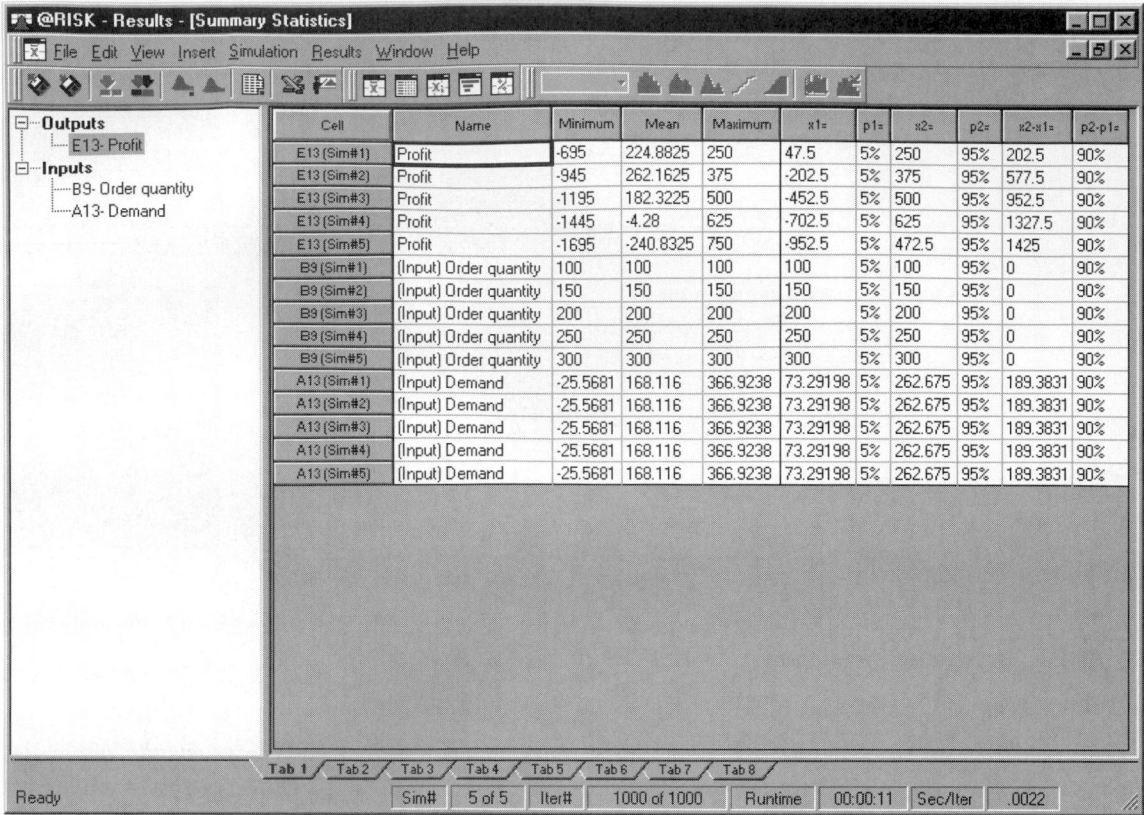

FIGURE 11.28 Summary Statistics from Five Simulations

After running the simulations, the Report window shows the results for all five simulations. For example, the basic summary report appears as in Figure 11.28. (A list of detailed statistics for all simulations is also available.) The first five lines show summary statistics of profit for the five order quantities in the list. It is clear that order quantities of 250 or 300 (simulations #4 and #5) are terrible—they average *negative* profits—and an order quantity of 150 (simulation #2) leads to the largest *average* profit. However, the decision is still not completely clear. Note that an order quantity of 200 (simulation #3) has more downside risk but more upside potential, whereas an order quantity of 100 (simulation #1) has exactly the opposite characteristics. Although we do not show them here, the same information can be seen graphically. A separate histogram of profit from each simulation is easy to obtain. Indeed, much of the appeal of @Risk (and of simulation modeling in general) is that we can see all of these characteristics—averages, minimums, maximums, percentiles, charts—and use them to make informed decisions. ∎

We conclude this section with one final modification of the Walton Bookstore example. To this point, there has been a single random quantity, demand. Often there are several random quantities, each reflecting some uncertainty, and we want to include each of these in the simulation model. The following example illustrates how this can be done, and it also illustrates a very useful feature of @Risk, its sensitivity analysis.

EXAMPLE 11.3

ADDITIONAL UNCERTAINTY AT WALTON BOOKSTORE

As in the previous Walton Bookstore example, Walton needs to place an order for next year's calendar. We continue to assume that the calendars will sell for $10 and customer demand for the calendars at this price is normally distributed with mean 168.1 and standard deviation 57.6. However, there are now two other sources of uncertainty. First, the maximum number of calendars Walton's supplier can supply is uncertain and is modeled with a triangular distribution. Its parameters are 125 (minimum), 250 (maximum), and 200 (most likely). Once Walton places an order, the supplier will charge $7.50 per calendar *if* he can supply the entire Walton order. Otherwise, he will charge only $7.25 per calendar. Second, unsold calendars can no longer be returned to the supplier for a refund. Instead, Walton will put them on sale for $5 apiece after February 1. At that price, Walton believes the demand for leftover calendars is normally distributed with mean 50 and standard deviation 10. Any calendars *still* left over, say, after March 1, will be thrown away. Walton plans to order 200 calendars and wants to use simulation to analyze the resulting profit.

Solution

As before, we first need to develop the model. Then we can run the simulation with @Risk and examine the results.

DEVELOPING THE SIMULATION MODEL

The completed model appears in Figure 11.29. (See the file WALTON6.XLS.) The model itself requires a bit more logic than the previous Walton model. It can be developed with the following steps.

❶ Random inputs. There are three random inputs in this model: the most the supplier can supply Walton, the customer demand when the selling price is $10, and the customer demand for sale-price calendars. Generate these in cells A16, D16, and G16 (using the ROUND function to obtain integers) with the formulas

=ROUND(RiskTriang(E9,E10,E11),0)

	A	B	C	D	E	F	G	H	I
1	Simulation of Walton's Bookstore using @RISK								
2							Range names used:		
3	Cost data			Demand distribution: normal			UnitCost1 - B4		
4	Unit cost if supply >= order	$7.50			Regular price	Sale price	UnitCost2 - B5		
5	Unit cost if supply < order	$7.25		Mean	168.1	50.0	UnitPrice1 - B6		
6	Regular price	$10.00		Stdev	57.6	10.0	UnitPrice2 - B7		
7	Sale price	$5.00					OrderQuan - B10		
8				Supply distribution: triangular			MaxSupply - A16		
9	Decision variable			Minimum	125		Supply - B16		
10	Order quantity	200		Most likely	200		Demand1 - D16		
11				Maximum	250		Leftover - E16		
12							Demand2 - G16		
13	Simulated quantities						Profit - G16		
14					At regular price		At sale price		
15	Maximum supply	Actual supply	Cost	Demand	Revenue	Left over	Demand	Revenue	Profit
16	190	190	$1,378	142	$1,420	48	51	$240	$283

FIGURE 11.29 Simulation Model with Several Random Inputs

=ROUND(RiskNormal(E5,E6),0)

and

=ROUND(RiskNormal(F5,F6),0)

Note that we generate the random *potential* demand for calendars at the sale price even though there might not be any calendars left to put on sale.

❷ Actual supply. The number of calendars supplied to Walton is the smaller of the number ordered and the maximum the supplier is able to supply. Calculate this value in cell B16 with the formula

=MIN(MaxSupply,OrderQuan)

❸ Order cost. Walton gets the reduced price, $7.25, if the supplier cannot supply the entire order. Otherwise, Walton must pay $7.50 per calendar. Therefore, calculate the total order cost in cell C16 with the formula

=IF(MaxSupply>=OrderQuan,UnitCost1,UnitCost2)*Supply

❹ Other quantities. The rest of the model is straightforward. Calculate the revenue from regular-price sales in cell E16 with the formula

=UnitPrice1*MIN(Supply,Demand1)

Calculate the number left over after regular-price sales in cell F16 with the formula

=MAX(Supply-Demand1,0)

Calculate the revenue from sale-price sales in cell H16 with the formula

=UnitPrice2*MIN(Leftover,Demand2)

Finally, calculate profit and designate it as an output cell for @Risk in cell I16 with the formula

=RISKOUTPUT()+E16+H16-C16

We could also designate other cells (the revenue cells, for example) as output cells, but we have chosen to have a single output cell, Profit.

USING @RISK

As always, the next steps are to specify the simulation settings (we chose 1000 iterations and 1 simulation), specify the report settings (we used the same as in the previous example), and run the simulation. When there are several random input cells, @Risk generates a value from each of them *independently* and calculates the corresponding profit on each iteration. (It is also possible to correlate the inputs, as we will demonstrate in the next section.) Selected results appear in Figures 11.30 and 11.31. They indicate an average profit of $255.66, a 5th percentile of −$410.50, a 95th percentile of $514.25, and a distribution of profits that is again skewed to the left.

Sensitivity Analysis We now demonstrate a feature of @Risk that is particularly useful when there are several random input cells. This feature lets us see which of these inputs is most related to, or *correlated* with, an output cell. To perform this analysis, select the Insert/Graph/Tornado Graph menu item from the @Risk Results window. In the resulting dialog box, select Profit as the output variable, and click on the Correlation Sensitivity button. This produces the results in Figure 11.32. (The "regression" option produces similar results, but we believe the correlation option is

Cell	Name	Minimum	Mean	Maximum	x1=	p1=	x2=	p2=	x2-x1=	p2-p1=
I16	Profit	-1460	255.6617	547.25	-410.5	5%	514.25	95%	924.75	90%
A16	(Input) Maximum supply	125.5471	192.6882	248.9847	146.747	5%	234.5776	95%	87.8306	90%
D16	(Input) Demand	-23.27701	165.5648	317.5606	73.30844	5%	257.8153	95%	184.5068	90%
G16	(Input) Demand	18.59517	50.00206	84.08738	32.78491	5%	66.8224	95%	34.03749	90%

FIGURE 11.30 @Risk Summary Report

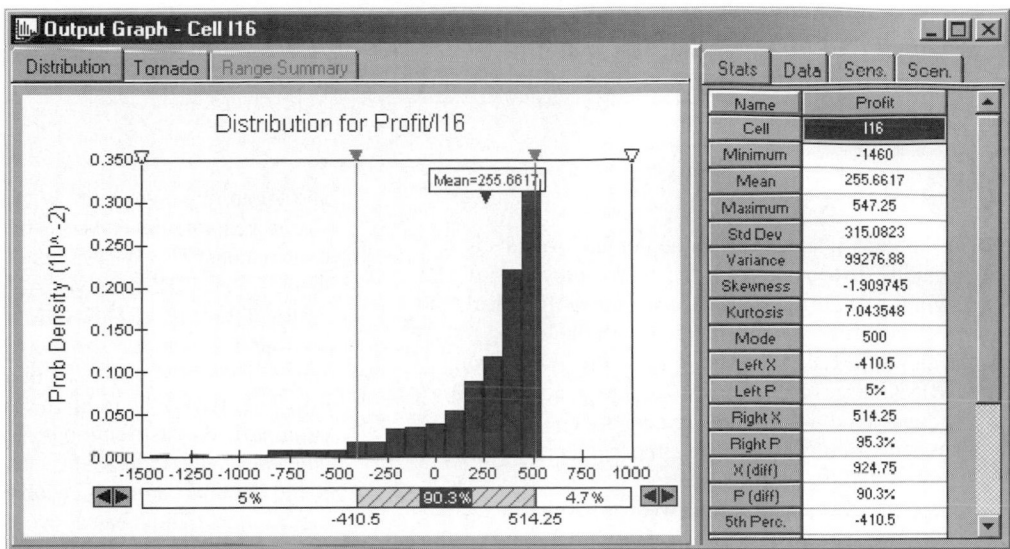

FIGURE 11.31 Histogram of Simulated Profits

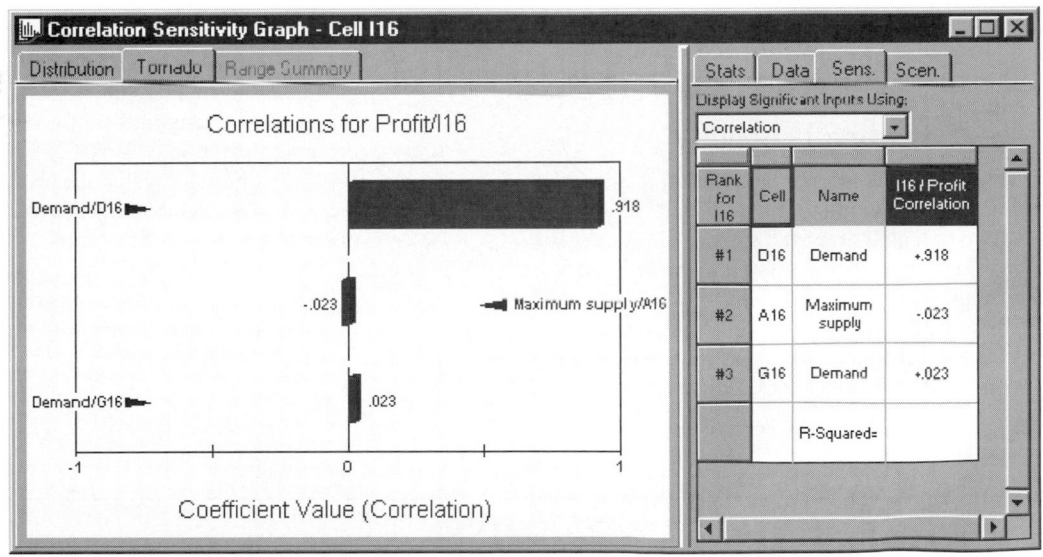

FIGURE 11.32 Tornado Graph for Sensitivity Analysis

easier to understand.) This figure shows graphically and numerically how each of the random inputs correlates with profit—the higher the (magnitude of the) correlation, the stronger the relationship between that input and profit. In this sense, we see that the regular-price demand has by far the strongest effect on profit. The other two inputs, maximum supply and sale-price demand, are not nearly as important because they are nearly unrelated to profit. Identifying important input variables can be important for real applications. If a random input is highly correlated with an important output, then it might be worth the time and cost to learn more about this input and possibly reduce the amount of uncertainty involving it. ■

PROBLEMS

Skill-Building Problems

8. In Problem 3, suppose that the demand for cars is normally distributed with mean 100 and standard deviation 15. Use @RISK to determine the "best" order quantity—that is, the one with the largest mean profit. Using the statistics and/or graphs from @RISK, discuss whether this order quantity would be considered best by the car dealer. (The point is that a decision maker can use more than just *mean* profit in making a decision.)

9. Use @RISK to analyze the sweatshirt situation in Problem 5. Do this for the discrete distributions given in the problem. Then do it for normal distributions. For the normal case, assume that the regular demand is normally distributed with mean 9800 and standard deviation 1300 and that the demand at the reduced price is normally distributed with mean 4800 and standard deviation 1300.

Skill-Extending Problem

10. Although the normal distribution is a reasonable input distribution in many situations, it does have two potential drawbacks: (1) it allows negative values, even though they may be extremely improbable, and (2) it is a symmetric distribution. Many situations are modeled better with a distribution that allows only positive values and is skewed to the right. Two of these are the gamma

and lognormal distributions, and @RISK enables you to generate observations from each of these distributions. The @RISK function for the gamma distribution is RISKGAMMA, and it takes two arguments, as in **=RISKGAMMA(3,10).** The first argument, which must be positive, determines the shape. The smaller it is, the more skewed the distribution is to the right; the larger it is, the more symmetric the distribution is. The second argument determines the scale, in the sense that the product of it and the first argument equals the mean of the distribution. (The mean above is 30.) Also, the product of the second argument and the square root of the first argument is the standard deviation of the distribution. (Above, it is $\sqrt{3}(10) = 17.32$.) The @RISK function for the lognormal distribution is RISKLOGNORM. It has two arguments, as in **=RISKLOGNORM(40,10).** These arguments are the mean and standard deviation of the distribution.

Rework Example 11.2 for the following demand distributions. Do the simulated outputs have any different qualitative properties with these skewed distributions than with the normal distribution used in the example?

a. Gamma distribution with parameters 2 and 85
b. Gamma distribution with parameters 5 and 35
c. Lognormal distribution with mean 170 and standard deviation 60

11.7 CORRELATION IN @RISK

U ntil now, all of the random numbers we have generated with @RISK functions have been probabilistically independent. This means, for example, that if one value is much larger than its mean, the next value is completely unaffected. It is no more likely to be abnormally large or small than if the first value had been average or less than average. Sometimes we do not want this independence.

Instead, we want the random numbers to be correlated in some way. If they are positively correlated, then large numbers tend to go with large numbers, and small with small. If they are negatively correlated, large tend to go with small and small with large. As an example, we might expect daily stock price changes for two companies in the same industry to be positively correlated. If Exxon's price increases, we might expect Amoco's price to increase as well. @RISK allows us to build in this correlated behavior with the RISKCORRMAT function, as we illustrate in the following example.

EXAMPLE 11.4

MCDONALD'S CORRELATED REVENUES AT LOCAL STORES

Midtown is a medium-sized city with five McDonald's restaurants. Each year, each of these restaurants experiences a random percentage growth in revenue, where this growth rate is normally distributed with mean 10% and standard deviation 5%. The growth rates for the different restaurants are influenced by some of the same factors: the general economy, the strength of the local economy, and the success of national advertising campaigns by McDonald's, for example. Therefore, they are *not* probabilistically independent. Rather, they are positively correlated, with estimates of the correlations listed in Table 11.5. For example, the correlation between the growth rates of restaurants 1 and 2 is 0.7. These rather large correlations mean that if one restaurant experiences a large growth rate, they all tend to do so, whereas if one does poorly, they all tend to do poorly. The revenues for 1999 for these five restaurants, in millions, were $1.987, $2.325, $2.231, $1.681, and $2.013. Use simulation to estimate the total revenue from these stores in the year 2000.

TABLE 11.5	Correlation Matrix for Growth Rates				
	Rest. 1	Rest. 2	Rest. 3	Rest. 4	Rest. 5
Rest. 1	1	0.7	0.6	0.8	0.6
Rest. 2	0.7	1	0.8	0.8	0.8
Rest. 3	0.6	0.8	1	0.5	0.7
Rest. 4	0.8	0.8	0.5	1	0.6
Rest. 5	0.6	0.8	0.7	0.6	1

Solution

The simulation model is very straightforward, except for the correlated growth rates.

DEVELOPING THE SIMULATION MODEL

The model appears in Figure 11.33 on page 602. (See the file MCDONALDS1.XLS.) It can be developed as follows.

1 Inputs. Enter the inputs in the shaded ranges. These include the 1999 revenues and the parameters of the growth rate distributions, including the correlation matrix.

	A	B	C	D	E	F	G	H	I	J
1	Tracking profits from McDonalds stores in Midtown									
2										
3	Inputs									
4	Revenues in 1999						All monetary values are in $millions.			
5		Restaurant 1	Restaurant 2	Restaurant 3	Restaurant 4	Restaurant 5				
6		1.987	2.325	2.231	1.681	2.013				
7							Range names used:			
8	Growth rate for each store -- normally distributed						MeanGrowth - B9			
9	Mean	10%					StdevGrowth - B10			
10	Stdev	5%					CMat - B14:F18			
11										
12	Correlation matrix for growth rates across stores in any year									
13		Restaurant 1	Restaurant 2	Restaurant 3	Restaurant 4	Restaurant 5				
14	Restaurant 1	1	0.7	0.6	0.8	0.6				
15	Restaurant 2	0.7	1	0.8	0.8	0.8				
16	Restaurant 3	0.6	0.8	1	0.5	0.7				
17	Restaurant 4	0.8	0.8	0.5	1	0.6				
18	Restaurant 5	0.6	0.8	0.7	0.6	1				
19										
20	Simulated revenues for 2000									
21	Restaurant	1	2	3	4	5	Total			
22		2.0844	2.6248	2.4168	2.0367	2.2185	11.381			

FIGURE 11.33 Simulation Model with Correlations

❷ **Revenues.** To generate a random year 2000 revenue, we multiply the 1999 revenue by 1 plus the growth rate. To do this, enter the formula

=B6*(1+RISKNORMAL(MeanGrowth,StdevGrowth, RISKCORRMAT(CMat,B$21)))

in cell B22 and copy it across to cell F22. Then sum these revenues for all restaurants in cell G22. Note that normally distributed growth rates require the usual RISKNORMAL function, but this function now takes an extra argument to account for the correlations. In general, this argument is of the form RISKCORRMAT(*Matrix, Index*). The *Matrix* argument is a reference to the correlation matrix, and *Index* is an integer from 1 to the number of correlated variables (5 in this example). The *Index* argument is 1 for the formula in B22, it is 2 for the formula in C22, and so on. This *Index* indicates which of the rows (or columns) of the correlation matrix to associate with any particular value.

USING @RISK

We set up and run @Risk exactly as before. For this example, we set the number of iterations to 1000 and the number of simulations to 1. After running @Risk, we obtain the histogram of total revenue for 2000 in Figure 11.34. The mean, $11.262, is almost exactly what we would expect. The total 1999 revenue, as you can check, was $10.237, and we expect a 10% growth rate at each restaurant, which should increase revenue to $10.237(1.10) = $11.261. But what about the variability?

We answer this question by comparing these results, with correlated growth rates, to the results from a model with uncorrelated growth rates. To do this, we simply change the off-diagonal values in the CMat range to 0 and rerun the simulation. (The diagonal values in a correlation matrix should *always* be 1—a variable is always perfectly correlated with itself.) The results with independence are summarized by the histogram in Figure 11.35. The mean is the same as before, but the standard deviation has decreased by about 50%. If you step back and think about it, this should not come as a surprise. It is the same principle that investors use when they diversify. They do not build a portfolio with stocks that all move together—unless they like risk. In the

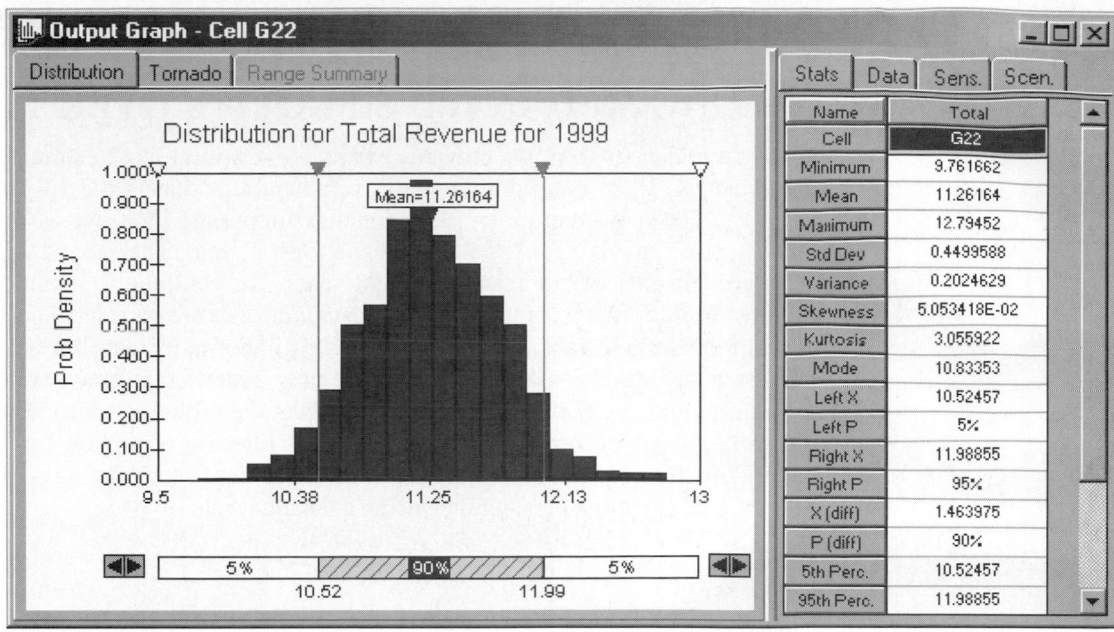

FIGURE 11.34 Histogram of Total Revenue with Correlated Growth Rates

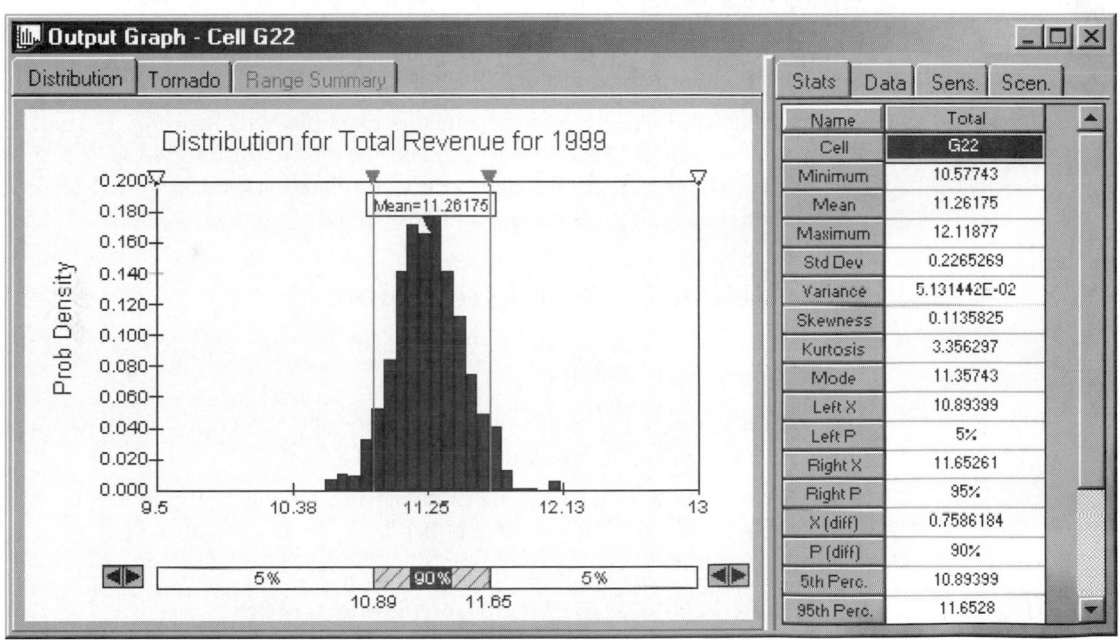

FIGURE 11.35 Histogram with Uncorrelated Growth Rates

same way, if you invested in all five of these McDonald's restaurants, the high positive correlations would make your investment a risky one. Of course, if they all do well, you could make a lot of money. But if any restaurant does poorly, then they are all likely to do poorly, and you could lose a lot of money! ∎

We extend this McDonald's example to a multiyear example. This allows us to illustrate two of @Risk's very useful features: its summary chart for showing random behavior over time, and its ability to handle correlations over time in a realistic way.

EXAMPLE 11.5

TRACKING MCDONALD'S PROFITS OVER TIME

Using the same data as from the previous example, we would like to simulate the net present value (NPV) of the profit from all five restaurants during the 10-year period from 2000 to 2009. We require two additional assumptions. First, we assume that a restaurant's profit in any year is 5% of revenue for that year. The second assumption concerns growth rates across restaurants and years. We continue to assume that the growth rates for different restaurants *in any particular year* are correlated according to the correlation matrix in Table 11.5. (Also, they are still normally distributed with mean 10% and standard deviation 5%.) However, we now assume that growth rates across years are probabilistically independent. For example, the growth rates for restaurant 1 in 2000 and 2001 are uncorrelated, as are the growth rates for restaurant 1 in 2000 and restaurant 2 in 2001. Use these assumptions to analyze the stream of yearly profits and the NPV of profits from all restaurants, using a discount rate of 10%.

Solution

For the 10-year period, we require 50 random growth rates, 10 for each restaurant. We could correlate these correctly by building an appropriate 50×50 correlation matrix and letting the *Index* argument of the RISKCORRMAT function vary from 1 to 50. This would be tedious. Fortunately, Palisade built a new feature into the latest version of @Risk that allows us to model this common correlation structure (correlation within years, independence across years) fairly easily. They added a third argument to the RISKCORRMAT function, which in this example will be *year*. For each year, the *Index* argument will vary from 1 to 5, and we will require only one 5×5 correlation matrix, as before. Essentially, each year's correlated values are based on this common correlation matrix, but different years' growth rates are independent.

DEVELOPING THE SIMULATION MODEL

The simulation model appears in Figure 11.36. (See the file MCDONALDS2.XLS.) It can be developed as follows.

❶ Inputs. Enter the inputs in the shaded range. The only two new inputs are the profit percentage and the discount rate.

❷ Revenues. It is possible to calculate the revenues efficiently if we index the restaurants from 1 to 5 in row 24 and list the years in column A. After entering these, enter the formula

=B7*(1+RISKNORMAL(MeanGrowth,StdevGrowth, RISKCORRMAT(CMat,B$24,$A25)))

for restaurant 1 and year 2000 in cell B25 and copy it across to cell F25. For the other years, enter the formula

=B25*(1+RISKNORMAL(MeanGrowth,StdevGrowth, RISKCORRMAT(CMat,B$24,$A26)))

in cell B26 and copy it to the range B26:F34. Note that the second argument in RISKCORRMAT is the restaurant index, which achieves correlations within a given year. The third argument is the year. It instructs @Risk to generate *independent* sets of five correlated variables across the different years.

	A	B	C	D	E	F	G	H	I	J	K	L
1	Tracking profits from McDonalds stores in Midtown											
2												
3	Inputs											
4	Profit (as % of revenue)	5%										
5	Last year's (1999) revenues											
6			Store 1	Store 2	Store 3	Store 4	Store 5					
7			1.987	2.325	2.231	1.681	2.013					
8												
9	Discount rate	10%										
10												
11	Growth rate (for each store, each year) -- normally distributed											
12	Mean	10%										
13	Stdev	5%										
14												
15	Correlation matrix for growth rates across stores in any year											
16			Store 1	Store 2	Store 3	Store 4	Store 5					
17	Store 1		1	0.7	0.6	0.8	0.6					
18	Store 2		0.7	1	0.8	0.8	0.8					
19	Store 3		0.6	0.8	1	0.5	0.7					
20	Store 4		0.8	0.8	0.5	1	0.6					
21	Store 5		0.6	0.8	0.7	0.6	1					
22												
23	Simulated revenues and total profits											
24	Year\Store		1	2	3	4	5	Total Profit				
25		2000	2.1857	2.5575	2.4541	1.8491	2.2143	0.563				
26		2001	2.4043	2.8133	2.6995	2.0340	2.4357	0.619				
27		2002	2.6447	3.0946	2.9695	2.2374	2.6793	0.681				
28		2003	2.9092	3.4040	3.2664	2.4612	2.9472	0.749				
29		2004	3.2001	3.7444	3.5930	2.7073	3.2420	0.824				
30		2005	3.5201	4.1189	3.9524	2.9780	3.5662	0.907				
31		2006	3.8721	4.5308	4.3476	3.2758	3.9228	0.997				
32		2007	4.2593	4.9838	4.7823	3.6034	4.3150	1.097				
33		2008	4.6852	5.4822	5.2606	3.9637	4.7465	1.207				
34		2009	5.1538	6.0305	5.7866	4.3601	5.2212	1.328				
35												
36	NPV of total profit	5.119										

Assumptions

1. All monetary values are in $millions.
2. Growth rates for different stores in any year are correlated according to the correlation matrix in the CMat range. Growth rates in different years are assumed to be probabilistically independent.

Range names used:
ProfitPct - B4
DiscRate - B9
MeanGrowth - B12
StdevGrowth - B13
CMat - B17:F21
Profits - G25:G34

FIGURE 11.36 10-Year Simulation Model for McDonald's

3 **Profits.** Calculate the yearly profits by entering the formula

=ProfitPct*SUM(B25:F25)

in cell G25 and copying it down. We would like to designate this whole Profits range as an @Risk output range. To do so, highlight it and click on the Add Outputs button on the @Risk toolbar. You will be asked to give this output range a name. We suggest Profits, although any name will do. (This name is for internal @Risk purposes. It is *not* the same as an Excel range name.) After doing this, you will notice that the formulas in the Profits range change slightly. For example, the formula in cell G27 becomes

=RISKOUTPUT(,"Profits",3)+ProfitPct*SUM(B27:F27)

This indicates that cell G27 is the third cell in the Profits output range. (If you remember this syntax, you can type this formula directly into the cell. We find it easier to click on the Add Outputs button.)

4 **NPV.** Calculate the NPV of profits in cell B36 and designate it as an additional @Risk output cell with the formula

=RISKOUTPUT()+NPV(DiscRate,Profits)

USING @RISK

We again set the number of iterations to 1000 and the number of simulations to 1. After running @Risk, we obtain outputs for the NPV cell and the Profits range. The

best ways to summarize the NPV output are the usual ones. For example, a histogram of NPV appears in Figure 11.37. It indicates a mean NPV of about $5.12 million and considerable variation. As in the previous single-year example, this variation is about twice as large as if the growth rates were uncorrelated, as shown in Figure 11.38. (To obtain this histogram, set all off-diagonal correlations in the CMat range to 0 and rerun @Risk.)

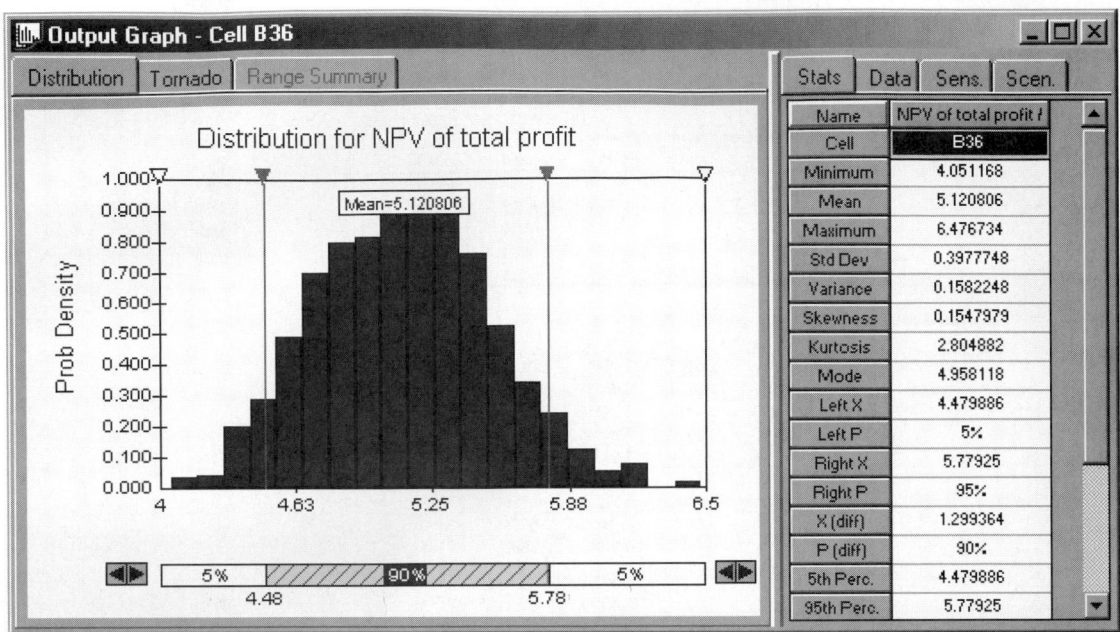

FIGURE 11.37 Histogram of NPV with Correlated Growth Rates

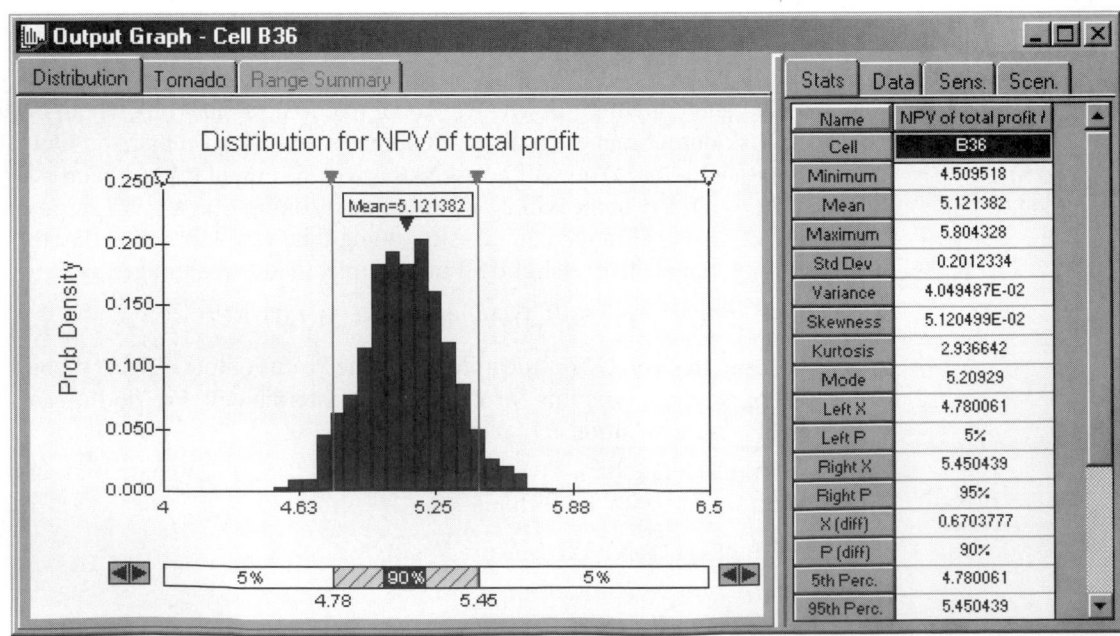

FIGURE 11.38 Histogram of NPV with Uncorrelated Growth Rates

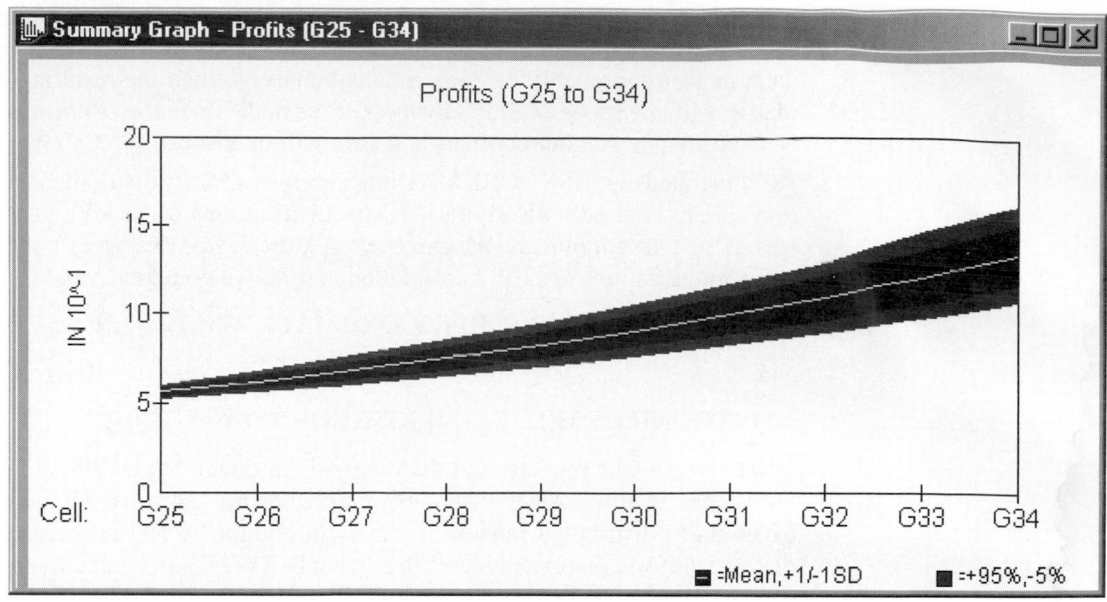

FIGURE 11.39 Summary Chart of Profits

Summary Charts If we designate a whole range, such as Profits, as an @Risk output range, we can still examine each individual cell of this range. For example, we could obtain a histogram of profit in 2004. The real advantage to designating an output *range* is that we can obtain an @Risk summary chart for the whole range, as shown in Figure 11.39. (The easiest way to create this chart is to right-click on the Profits item in the Explorer-type list in the @Risk Results window and then select Summary Chart.) This type of chart is perfect for time series variables. It allows us to see the trend and variability through time. The middle line in this chart tracks mean values. The inner band extends to one standard deviation on each side of the mean, and the outer band extends to the 5th and 95th percentiles. The situation shown here is typical. As we project farther into the future, the amount of variability (uncertainty) increases. However, the upward exponential growth is clear. It is a result of the expected 10% growth per year. ∎

MODELING ISSUES

1. Correlations must be between −1 and +1, but when choosing a correlation matrix, there are two other rules you need to be aware of. First, a correlation matrix must be symmetric. For example, the correlation between restaurant 1 and restaurant 2 must equal the correlation between restaurant 2 and restaurant 1. In Figure 11.33, this means, for example, that the values in cells B15 and C14 must be equal. We can force this by entering a *value* in cell C14 and the *formula* **=C14** in cell B15. Then we need only enter values above the diagonal.

   The second rule is more difficult to state. Certain "patterns" of correlations are not allowed because no set of data could ever give rise to them. For example, we tried changing the 0.7 correlation in cells C14 and B15 to −0.7 and rerunning the simulation. @Risk responded with an error message stating that this is an invalid correlation matrix. Evidently, it is impossible for restaurants 1 and 2 to have a large *negative* correlation and to be highly positively correlated with all other restaurants. If we estimate the correlation matrix from historical growth rate data, as would probably be done in a real analysis, then the resulting correlation matrix will always be "valid." However, if we make up our own correlations, there is some chance that our correlation matrix will be invalid.

2. We illustrated the RISKCORRMAT function for *normally* distributed values. However, it can be used with any of @Risk's distributions by tacking on RISKCORRMAT as a last argument. We can even mix them. For example, assuming CMat is the range name for a 2×2 correlation matrix, we could enter the formulas

=RISKTRIANG(10,12,18,RISKCORRMAT(CMat,1))

and

=RISKDUNIFORM({1, 2, 3, 4},RISKCORRMAT(CMat,2))

into cells A4 and B4, say, and then copy them down. What @Risk does behind the scenes in this case is essentially the following. It generates a sequence of triangularly distributed random numbers in column A and another sequence of discrete uniform random numbers in column B. Then it sorts them in some complex way until their correlation is approximately as specified in the correlation matrix. ■

PROBLEMS

Skill-Building Problem

11. Bottleco produces six-packs of soda cans. Each can is supposed to contain at least 12 ounces of soda. If the total weight in a six-pack is under 72 ounces, Bottleco is fined $100 and receives no sales revenue for the six-pack. Each six-pack sells for $3.00. It costs Bottleco $0.02 per ounce of soda put in the cans. Bottleco can control the mean fill rate of its soda-filling machines. The amount put in each can by a machine is normally distributed with standard deviation 0.10 ounce.

   a. Assume that the weight of each can in a six-pack has a 0.8 correlation with the weight of the other cans in the six-pack. What mean fill quantity (within 0.05 ounce) maximizes expected profit per six-pack?

   b. If the weights of the cans in the six-pack are probabilistically independent, what mean fill quantity (within 0.05 ounce) will maximize expected profit per six-pack?

   c. How can you explain the difference in the answers to parts **a** and **b**?

Skill-Extending Problem

12. The Business School at State University currently has three parking lots, each containing 155 spaces. Two hundred faculty have been assigned to each lot. On a peak day, an average of 70% of all lot 1 parking sticker holders show up, an average of 72% of all lot 2 parking sticker holders show up, and an average of 74% of all lot 3 parking sticker holders show up.

   a. Given the current situation, estimate the probability that on a peak day, at least one faculty member with a sticker will be unable to find a spot. Assume that the number who show up at each lot is independent of the number who show up at the other two lots. (*Hint*: Use the RISKBINOMIAL function.)

   b. Now suppose the numbers of people who show up at the three lots are correlated (correlation 0.9). Does your solution work as well? Why or why not?

11.8 CONCLUSION

Simulation has traditionally not received the attention it deserves in management science courses. The primary reason for this has been the lack of easy-to-use simulation software. Now with Excel's built-in simulation capabilities, plus powerful and affordable add-ins such as @Risk and Crystal Ball, simulation is receiving its rightful emphasis. The world is full of uncertainty, which is what makes simulation so valuable. Simulation models provide important insights that are missing in models that do not incorporate uncertainty explicitly. In addition, simulation models are relatively easy to understand and develop. Therefore, we suspect that simulation models (along with optimization models) will soon be the primary emphasis of many management science courses—if they are not already. In this chapter we have illustrated the basic ideas of simulation, how to perform simulation with Excel built-in tools, and how @Risk greatly enhances Excel's basic capabilities. In the next chapter we will build on what we have learned here by developing and analyzing simulation models in a variety of business areas.

PROBLEMS

Skill-Building Problems

13. Six months before its annual convention, the American Medical Association must determine how many rooms to reserve. At this time, the AMA can reserve rooms at a cost of $50 per room. The AMA believes the number of doctors attending the convention will be normally distributed with a mean of 5000 and a standard deviation of 1000. If the number of people attending the convention exceeds the number of rooms reserved, extra rooms must be reserved at a cost of $80 per room.
   a. Use simulation with @Risk to determine the number of rooms that should be reserved to minimize the expected cost to the AMA.
   b. Rework part **a** for the case where the number attending has a triangular distribution with minimum value 2000, maximum value 7000, and most likely value 5000. Does this change the substantive results from part **a**?

14. You have made it to the final round of "Let's Make a Deal." You know that there is $1 million prize behind either door 1, door 2, or door 3. It is equally likely that the prize is behind any of the three doors. The two doors without a prize have nothing behind them. You randomly choose door 2. Before you see whether the prize is behind door 2, host Monty Hall opens a door that has no prize behind it. To be specific, suppose that before door 2 is opened, Monty reveals that there is no prize behind door 3. You now have the opportunity to switch and choose door 1. Should you switch? Use a spreadsheet to simulate this situation 1000 times. For each

replication use an @RISK function to generate the door behind which the prize sits. Then use another @RISK function to generate the door that Monty will open. Assume that Monty plays as follows: Monty knows where the prize is and will open an empty door, but he cannot open door 2. If the prize is really behind door 2, Monty is equally likely to open door 1 or door 3. If the prize is really behind door 1, Monty must open door 3. If the prize is really behind door 3, Monty must open door 1.

15. A new edition of our management science textbook will be published 1 year from now. Our publisher currently has 2000 copies on hand and is deciding whether to do another printing before the new edition comes out. The publisher estimates that demand for the book during the next year is governed by the probability distribution in the file P11_15.XLS. A production run incurs a fixed cost of $62,000 plus a variable cost of $10 per book printed. Books are sold for $30 per book. Any demand that cannot be met incurs a penalty cost of $2 per book, due to loss of goodwill. Half of any leftover books can be sold to Barnes and Noble for $3 per book. My publisher is interested in maximizing expected profit. The following print run sizes are under consideration: 0 (no production run), 1000, 2000, 4000, 6000, and 8000. What decision would you recommend? Use simulation with at least 100 replications. For your optimal decision, our publisher can be 90% certain that the actual profit associated with remaining sales of the current edition will be between what two values?

16. It is equally likely that annual unit sales for Widgetco's widgets will be low or high. If sales are low (60,000), the company can sell the product for $10 per unit. If sales are high (100,000), a competitor will enter and Widgetco can sell the product for only $8 per unit. The variable cost per unit has a 25% chance of being $6, a 50% chance of being $7.50, and a 25% chance of being $9. Annual fixed costs are $30,000.

   a. Use simulation, with at least 400 replications, to estimate Widgetco's expected annual profit.

   b. Construct a 95% confidence interval for Widgetco's annual expected profit.

   c. Now suppose that annual unit sales, variable cost, and unit price are equal to their respective expected values—that is, there is no uncertainty. Determine Widgetco's annual profit for this scenario.

   d. Can you conclude from the results in parts **a** and **c** that the expected profit from a simulation is equal to the profit from the scenario where each input assumes its expected value? Explain.

17. W. L. Brown, a direct marketer of women's clothing, needs to determine how many telephone operators to schedule during each part of the day. W. L. Brown estimates that the number of phone calls received each hour of a typical 8-hour shift can be described by the probability distribution in the file P11_17.XLS. Each operator can handle 15 calls per hour and costs the company $20 per hour. Each phone call that is not handled is assumed to cost the company $6 in lost profit. Considering the options of employing 6, 8, 10, 11, 13, 14, or 20 operators, use simulation to determine the number of operators that minimizes the expected hourly cost (labor costs plus lost profits).

18. Assume that all of your job applicants must take a test, and that the scores on this test are normally distributed. The "selection ratio" is the cutoff point you use in your hiring process. For example, a selection ratio of 20% means that you will accept applicants for jobs who rank in the top 20% of all applicants. If you choose a selection ratio of 20%, the average test score of those selected will be 1.40 standard deviations above average. Use simulation to verify this fact, proceeding as follows.

   a. Show that if you want to accept only the top 20% of all applicants, you should accept applicants whose test scores are at least 0.84 standard deviation above average. (No simulation is required here. Just use the appropriate Excel normal function.)

   b. Now generate 400 test scores from a normal distribution with mean 0 and standard deviation 1. The average test score of those selected is the average of the scores that are at least 0.84. To determine this, use Excel's DAVERAGE function. To do so, put a heading Score in cell A3, generate the 400 test scores in the range A4:A403, and name the range A3:A403 Data. In cells C3 and C4, enter the *labels* Score and >0.84. (The range C3:C4 is called the *criterion* range.) Then calculate the average of all applicants who will be hired by entering the formula =DAVERAGE(Data,"Score",C3:C4) in any cell. This average should be close to the theoretical average, 1.40. [This formula works as follows. Excel finds all observations in the Data range that satisfy the criterion described in the range C3:C4 (Score>0.84). Then it averages the values in the Score column (the second argument of DAVERAGE) corresponding to these entries. Look in online help for more about Excel's database functions.]

   c. What information would you need to determine an "optimal" selection ratio? How could you determine an optimal selection ratio?

19. Lemington's is trying to determine how many Jean Hudson dresses to order for the spring season. Demand for the dresses is assumed to follow a normal distribution with mean 400 and standard deviation 100. The contract between Jean Hudson and Lemington's works as follows. At the beginning of the season, Lemington's reserves x units of capacity. Lemington's must take delivery for at least $0.8x$ dresses and can, if desired, take delivery on up to x dresses. Each dress sells for $160 and Jean charges $50 per dress. If Lemington's does not take delivery on all x dresses, it owes Jean a $5 penalty for each unit of reserved capacity that was unused. For example, if Lemington's orders 450 dresses and demand is for 400 dresses, then Lemington's will receive 400 dresses and owe Jean 400($50) + 50($5). How many units of capacity should Lemington's reserve to maximize its expected profit?

20. Dilbert's Department Store is trying to determine how many Hanson T-shirts to order. Currently the shirts are sold for $21.00, but at later dates the shirts will be offered at a 10% discount, then 20% discount, then 40% discount, then 50% discount, and finally 60% discount. Demand at the full price of $21.00 is believed to be normally distributed with mean 1800 and standard deviation 360. Demand at various discounts is assumed to be a multiple of full price demand. These multiples, for discounts of 10%, 20%, 40%, 50%, and 60% are, respectively, 0.4, 0.7, 1.1, 2, and 50. For example, if full-price demand were 2500, then at a 10% discount, customers would be willing to buy 1000 T-shirts. The unit cost of purchasing T-shirts depends on the number of T-shirts ordered, as shown in Table 11.6. Use simulation to see how many T-shirts Dilbert's should order. Model the problem so that Dilbert's

TABLE 11.6	Cost Data for Dilbert's
Order Quantity	**Unit Cost**
0–1499	$15.00
1500–3499	$14.25
3500–5999	$13.54
6000+	$12.86

first orders some quantity of T-shirts, then discounts deeper and deeper, as necessary, to sell all of the shirts.

21. Suppose we own 100 shares of each four stocks. The annual return on each stock is assumed to follow a normal distribution, with the mean and standard deviation for each stock, as well as the correlations between stocks, listed in the file P11_21.XLS. The current stock prices are also listed in this file. During each of the next 5 years, each stock pays 5% of its year-ending price in dividends.
   a. Develop a simulation model to find the total dividends we will receive during the next 5 years. (*Hint:* Recall that stock returns are percentage *changes* in stock prices. Simulate returns for future years by using a combination of the RISKNORMAL and RISKCORRMAT functions, the latter with *three* arguments. The assumption is that returns across stocks for a given year are correlated, but returns across years are uncorrelated.)
   b. We are 95% sure that the total dividends during the next 5 years will be between what two values?
   c. Redo parts **a** and **b** under the assumption that the returns of the four stocks are uncorrelated. Explain why your answer here is much narrower than your part **b** answer.

Skill-Extending Problems

22. It is surprising (but true) that if 23 people are in the same room, there is about a 50% chance that at least two people will have the same birthday. Suppose you want to estimate the probability that if 30 people are in the same room, at least two of them will have the same birthday. You can proceed as follows.
   a. Generate the "birthdays" of 30 different people. Ignoring the possibility of a leap year, each person has a 1/365 chance of having a given birthday (call the days of the year 1, 2, . . . , 365). You can use a formula involving the INT and RAND functions to generate birthdays.
   b. Once you have generated 30 people's birthdays, how can you tell whether at least two people have the same birthday? The key here is to use Excel's RANK function. (You can learn how to

use this function with Excel's Function Wizard.) This function returns the rank of a number relative to a given group of numbers. In the case of a tie, two numbers are given the same rank. For example, if the set of numbers is 4, 3, 2, 5, the RANK function will return 2, 3, 4, 1. If the set of numbers is 4, 3, 2, 4, the RANK function will return 1, 3, 4, 1.
   c. After using the RANK function, you should be able to determine whether at least two of your 30 people have the same birthday.

23. United Electric sells refrigerators for $400 with a 1-year warranty. The warranty works as follows. If any part of the refrigerator fails during the first year after purchase, UE replaces the refrigerator for an average cost of $100. As soon as a replacement is made, another 1-year warranty period begins for the customer. If a refrigerator fails outside the warranty period, we assume that the customer immediately purchases another UE refrigerator. Suppose that the amount of time a refrigerator lasts follows a normal distribution with a mean of 1.8 years and a standard deviation of 0.3 year.
   a. Estimate the average profit per year UE earns from a customer.
   b. How could the approach of this problem be used to determine the optimal warranty period?

24. A TSB (Tax Saver Benefit) plan allows you to put money into an account at the beginning of the calendar year that can be used for medical expenses. This amount is not subject to federal tax—hence the phrase TSB. As you pay medical expenses during the year, you are reimbursed by the administrator of the TSB until the TSB account is exhausted. From that point on, you must pay your medical expenses out of your own pocket. On the other hand, if you put more money into your TSB than the medical expenses you incur, this extra money is lost to you. Your annual salary is $50,000 and your federal income tax rate is 30%.
   a. Assume that your medical expenses in a year are normally distributed with mean $2000 and standard deviation $500. Build an @RISK model in which the output is the amount of money left to you after paying taxes, putting money in a TSB, and paying any extra medical expenses. Experiment with the amount of money put in the TSB, using a RISKSIMTABLE function.
   b. Rework part **a**, but this time assume a gamma distribution for your annual medical expenses. Use $\alpha = 16$ and $\beta = 125$ as the two parameters of this distribution. These imply the same mean and standard deviation as in part **a**, but the distribution of medical expenses is now skewed to the right, which is probably more realistic. Using simulation, see whether you should now

put more or less money in a TSB than in the symmetric case in part **a**.

25. At the beginning of each week, a machine is in one of four conditions: 1 = excellent; 2 = good; 3 = average; 4 = bad. The weekly revenue earned by a machine in state 1, 2, 3, or 4 is $100, $90, $50, or $10, respectively. After observing the condition of the machine at the beginning of the week, the company has the option, for a cost of $200, of instantaneously replacing the machine with an excellent machine. The quality of the machine deteriorates over time, as shown in Table 11.7. Four maintenance policies are under consideration:

- Policy 1: Never replace a machine.
- Policy 2: Immediately replace a bad machine.
- Policy 3: Immediately replace a bad or average machine.
- Policy 4: Immediately replace a bad, average, or good machine.

   Simulate each of these policies for 50 weeks (using 250 iterations each) to determine the policy that maximizes expected weekly profit. Assume that the machine at the beginning of week 1 is excellent.

26. Simulation can be used to illustrate a number of results from statistics that are difficult to understand with nonsimulation arguments. One is the famous central limit theorem, which says that if you sample enough values from *any* population distribution and then average these values, the resulting average will be approximately normally distributed. Confirm this by using @RISK with the following population distributions (run a separate simulation for each): (a) discrete with possible values 1 and 2 and probabilities 0.2 and 0.8; (b) exponential with mean 1 (use the RISKEXPON function with the single argument 1); (c) triangular with minimum, most likely, and maximum values equal to 1, 9, and 10. (Note that each of these distributions is very nonnormal.) Run each simulation with 10 values in each average, and run 1000 iterations to simulate 1000 averages. Create a histogram of the averages to see that it is indeed bell-shaped. Then repeat, using 30 values in each average. Are the histograms based on 10 values qualitatively different from those based on 30?

27. In statistics we often use observed data to test a hypothesis about a population or populations. The basic method is that we use the observed data to calculate a test statistic (a single number). If the magnitude of this test statistic is sufficiently large, we reject the "null" hypothesis in favor of the "research" hypothesis. As an example, consider a researcher who believes teenage girls sleep longer than teenage boys on average. She collects observations on $n = 40$ randomly selected girls and $n = 40$ randomly selected boys. (We assume that each observation is the average sleep time over several nights for a given person.) The averages are $\overline{X}_1 = 7.9$ hours for the girls and $\overline{X}_2 = 7.6$ hours for the boys. The standard deviation of the 40 observations for girls is $s_1 = 0.5$ hour; for the boys it is $s_2 = 0.7$ hour. The researcher, consulting her statistics textbook, then calculates the test statistic

$$\frac{\overline{X}_1 - \overline{X}_2}{\sqrt{s_1^2/40 + s_2^2/40}} = \frac{7.9 - 7.6}{\sqrt{0.25/40 + 0.49/40}} = 2.206$$

Based on the fact that 2.206 is "large," she claims that her research hypothesis is confirmed—girls *do* sleep longer than boys.

   You are skeptical of this claim, so you check it out by running a simulation. In your simulation you assume that girls and boys have the *same* mean and standard deviation of sleep times in the entire population, say, 7.7 and 0.6. You also assume that the distribution of sleep times is normal. Then you repeatedly simulate 40 girl and 40 boy observations from this distribution and calculate the above test statistic. The question is whether the observed test statistic, 2.206, is "extreme." If it is larger than most or all of the test statistics you simulate, then the researcher is justified in her claim; otherwise, this large a statistic could have happened just by chance, even if the girls and boys have identical population means. Use @RISK to see which is the case.

28. The file P11_28.XLS contains monthly points on the interest rate yield curve for the years 1985–1992. For example, a 3-month bond in January 1985 had a yield of 7.76%, whereas a 30-year bond had a yield of 11.45%. We would like to use simulation to

TABLE 11.7   Description of Machine Deterioration

Present Machine State	Probability That Machine Begins Next Week As			
	Excellent	Good	Average	Bad
Excellent	0.7	0.3		
Good		0.7	0.3	
Average			0.6	0.4
Bad				1.0 (until replaced)

project the yields for the next 60 months—that is, for 1993–1997—starting from December 1992.

  a. Develop a simulation model to do this, assuming normally distributed *changes* in the yields for any given bond maturity and correlations between the various maturities. (*Hints*: For each maturity, calculate the monthly differences. Then use Excel's AVERAGE, STDEV, and CORREL functions to estimate means, standard deviations, and correlations for the differences. Finally, use a combination of RISKNORMAL and RISKCORRMAT, the latter with *three* arguments, to generate 60 new months of yields, where each will add a simulated change to a previous value.)

  b. Does your simulation produce any *negative* yields? If so, how might you remedy this problem with a more realistic model?

Modeling Problems

29. Big Hit Video needs to determine how many copies of a new video to purchase. Assume that the company's goal is to purchase a number of copies that will maximize its expected profit from the video during the next year. Describe how you would use simulation to solve this problem. To simplify matters, assume that each time a tape is rented, it is rented for one day.

30. Many people who are involved in a small auto accident do not file a claim because they are afraid their insurance premiums will be raised. Suppose that City Farm Insurance has three rates. If you file a claim, you are moved to the next higher rate. How might you use simulation to determine whether a particular claim should be filed?

31. A building contains 1000 lightbulbs. Each bulb lasts at most 5 months. The company maintaining the building is trying to decide whether it is worthwhile to practice a "group replacement" policy. Under a group replacement policy, all bulbs are replaced every T months (where T is to be determined). Also, bulbs are replaced when they burn out. Assume that it costs $0.05 to replace each bulb during a group replacement and $0.20 to replace each burned-out bulb if it is replaced individually. How would you use simulation to determine whether a group replacement policy is worthwhile?

Ski Jacket Production

E gress, Inc. is a small company that designs, produces, and sells ski jackets and other coats. The creative design team has labored for weeks over its new design for the coming winter season. It is now time to decide how many ski jackets to produce in this production run. Because of the lead times involved, no other production runs will be possible during the season.

Predicting ski jacket sales months in advance of the selling season can be quite tricky. Egress has been in operation for only three years, and its ski jacket designs were quite successful in two of those years. Based on realized sales from the last three years, current economic conditions, and professional judgment, twelve Egress employees have independently estimated demand for their new design for the upcoming season. Their estimates are shown in Table 11.8.

TABLE 11.8   Estimated Demands

14,000	16,000
13,000	8,000
14,000	5,000
14,000	11,000
15,500	8,000
10,500	15,000

To assist in the decision on the number of units for the production run, management has gathered the data in Table 11.9. Note that S is the price Egress charges retailers. Any ski jackets that do not sell during the season can be sold by Egress to discounters

TABLE 11.9   Monetary Values

Variable production cost per unit (C):	$80
Selling price per unit (S):	$100
Salvage value per unit (V):	$30
Fixed production cost (F):	$100,000

for V per jacket. The fixed cost of plant and equipment is F. This cost is incurred irrespective of the size of the production run.

Questions

1. Egress management believes that a normal distribution is a reasonable model for the unknown demand in the coming year. What mean and standard deviation should Egress use for the demand distribution?

2. Use a spreadsheet model to simulate 1000 possible outcomes for demand in the coming year. Based on these scenarios, what is the expected profit if Egress produces $Q = 7800$ ski jackets? What is the expected profit if Egress produces $Q = 12,000$ ski jackets? What is the standard deviation of profit in these two cases?

3. Based on the same 1000 scenarios, how many ski jackets should Egress produce to maximize expected profit? Call this quantity Q^*.

4. Should Q^* equal mean demand or not? Explain.

5. Create a histogram of profit at the production level Q^*. Create a histogram of profit when the production level Q equals mean demand. What is the probability of a loss greater than $100,000 in each case?

Ebony Bath Soap

Management of Ebony, a leading manufacturer of bath soap, is trying to control its inventory costs. The weekly cost of holding one unit of soap in inventory is $30 (one unit is 1000 cases of soap). The marketing department estimates that weekly demand averages 120 units, with a standard deviation of 15 units, and is reasonably well modeled by a normal distribution. If demand exceeds the amount of soap on hand, those sales are *lost*—that is, there is no backlogging of demand. The production department can produce at one of three levels: 110, 120, or 130 units per week. The cost of changing production from one week to the next is $3000.

Management would like to evaluate the following production policy. If the current inventory is less than $L = 30$ units, then produce 130 units in the next week. If the current inventory is greater than $U = 80$ units, then produce 110 units in the next week. Otherwise, continue at the previous week's production level.

Ebony currently has 60 units of inventory on hand. Last week's production level was 120.

Questions

1. Create a spreadsheet to simulate 52 weeks of operation at Ebony. Graph the inventory of soap over time. What is the total cost (inventory cost plus production change cost) for the 52 weeks?

2. Use a simulation of 500 iterations to estimate the average 52-week cost with values of U ranging from 30 to 80 in increments of 10. Keep $L = 30$ for every trial.

3. Calculate the sample mean and standard deviation of the 52-week cost under each policy. Using those results, construct 95% confidence intervals for the average 52-week cost for each value of U. Graph the average 52-week cost versus U. What is the best value of U for $L = 30$?

4. What other production policies might be useful to investigate?

CHAPTER **12**

Simulation
Models

AUTOMATING OPERATIONS AT THE UNITED
STATES POSTAL SERVICE

One of the key benefits of simulation methodology is that it allows a company to see how important outputs respond to various scenarios. Each scenario, which is determined by certain inputs and operating policies, can be simulated, and statistics can be collected. By running enough scenarios, the company obtains useful information about which inputs and policies tend to produce the best outputs. This methodology was used in the 1980s by the United States Postal Service (USPS), as described in the article "Management Science in Automating Postal Operations: Facility and Equipment Planning in the United States Postal Service" by Cebry et al. (1992). At the time, the USPS was faced with increasing competitive pressure from a variety of competitors, including other advertising media, alternative retail and delivery companies, and electronic mail. Automation technology was identified as the only way to handle an increase in mail volume, to maintain cost competitiveness, and to provide adequate service.

The process of getting mail from the sender to the receiver is an extremely complex one. Mail enters the process as a mixed product—many types of mail addressed in various ways to many geographical regions—and it must be sorted in several stages before it can eventually reach the proper destination. The USPS recognized the need for automated equipment to speed up this process and to save on labor costs. In fact, by the early 1980s it had purchased OCR (optical character recognition) machines that could identify the destination (at least on some mail) and attach a bar code corresponding to the ZIP code to the mail. It had also purchased bar code sensing machines that could read these bar codes and automatically help sort the mail. Part of the cost effectiveness of these new machines relied on heavy use by businesses of the new nine-digit ZIP codes. Unfortunately, businesses were somewhat slow to use the nine-digit codes.

At about this time, the USPS realized that it needed to use management science methods to utilize its existing automation equipment most effectively and to plan appropriately for the future. It hired a consulting company, Kenan Systems Corporation, to help compare automation alternatives. The result was META, a simulation model that quantifies the impacts of changes in mail processing and delivery operations. The META model is very complex, but it can be described briefly as follows.

Mail of various types and of various volumes enters the system and progresses through a number of "links." Each of the links is one step in the overall sorting process that gets the mail from its origin to its final destination. The META model takes as its inputs various mail streams (types of mail with similar characteristics) and routes these streams through the links of the sorting process according to user-specified rules. For example, a rule might specify which mail streams receive highest priority on certain automation equipment at each link. Each set of mail streams and each set of rules corresponds to a single scenario in the simulation model. Given a typical scenario, the model simulates the throughput of the system, the number of errors made, the amount of labor required, and the total cost. These outputs are then compared to identify the best policies for the USPS to implement.

The META model, first developed in 1985, has proved to be extremely useful and versatile. Using this simulation tool, the USPS formulated a corporate automation plan (CAP), which was first released in 1989. By the time CAP was to be fully implemented in 1995, the postal service expected it to save 100,000 work years annually, which translates to over $4 billion. Just as important, by using the model as part of an ongoing planning process, the USPS ensured that it would implement future technologies in a timely and cost-effective manner. ■

12.1   INTRODUCTION

In the previous chapter we introduced most of the important concepts for developing and analyzing spreadsheet simulation models. We also discussed many of the available features in the powerful simulation add-in, @Risk, that is included in the CD-ROM that accompanies this book. Now we apply the tools to a wide variety of situations that can be analyzed by simulation. For convenience, we group the applications into four general areas: (1) operations models, (2) financial models, (3) marketing models, and (4) games of chance. The only overriding theme in this chapter is that simulation can be applied to obtain important insights in all of these areas. You should not feel constrained to cover all of the models in this chapter or to cover them in the order they are presented. Rather, you can cover just the ones of most interest to you, and in practically any order.

12.2 OPERATIONS MODELS

Whether we are discussing the operations of a manufacturing or a service company, there is likely to be uncertainty that can be modeled by simulation. In this section we look at examples of bidding for a government contract (uncertainty in the bids by competitors), Deming's famous funnel experiment in quality control (inherent randomness in the process), drug production (uncertainty in the yield), component redundancy (uncertainty in the number that will fail in their mission), and project scheduling (uncertainty in the duration of activities).[1]

Bidding Models

In situations where a company must bid against competitors, simulation can often be used to determine the company's optimal bid. Usually the company does not know what its competitors will bid, but it might have an idea about the *range* of the bids its competitors will choose. In this section we will show how to use simulation to determine a bid that maximizes the company's expected profit.

EXAMPLE 12.1

BIDDING FOR A GOVERNMENT CONTRACT

The Miller Construction Company is trying to decide whether to make a bid on a construction project. Miller believes it will cost the company $10,000 to complete the project (if it wins the contract), and it will cost $350 to prepare a bid. Four potential competitors are going to bid against Miller. The lowest bid will win the contract (and the winner will then be given the winning bid amount to complete the project). Based on past history, Miller believes that each competitor's bid will be a multiple of its (Miller's) cost to complete the project, where this multiple has a triangular distribution with minimum, most likely, and maximum values 0.9, 1.3, and 2.5. These four competitors' bids are also assumed to be independent of one another. If Miller decides to prepare a bid, then it has decided that its bid amount will be a multiple of $500 in the range from $10,500 to $15,000. The company wants to use simulation to determine which strategy to use to maximize its expected profit.

Solution

The logic is straightforward. We first simulate the competitors' bids. Then for any bid Miller makes, we see whether Miller wins the contract, and if so, what its profit is.

---

[1]Additional simulation models in the operations area will be examined in the next two chapters. In Chapter 13 we will develop a simulation model of a dynamic ordering policy when customer demand is uncertain, and in Chapter 14 we will develop queueing simulations when customer arrival times and service times are uncertain.

DEVELOPING THE SIMULATION MODEL

The spreadsheet model appears in Figure 12.1. (See the file BIDDING.XLS.) It can be developed with the following steps. (Note that this model does not check the possibility of Miller not bidding at all. But this case is easy. If Miller opts not to bid, its profit is a certain $0.)

❶ **Inputs.** Enter the inputs in the shaded cells. These include Miller's costs, Miller's possible bids, and the parameters of the triangular distribution for the competing bids.

❷ **Miller's bid.** We can test all of Miller's possible bids simultaneously with the RISKSIMTABLE function. Do this in cell B15 with the formula

=RISKSIMTABLE(PossibleBids)

❸ **Competitors' bids.** Generate random bids for the four competitors in the Comp-Bids range by entering the formula

=RISKTRIANG($B$9,$B$10,$B$11)*ProjectCost

in cell B19 and copying across. Of course, Miller will not see these other bids until it has submitted its own bid.

❹ **Win contract?** See whether Miller wins the bid by entering the formula

=RISKOUTPUT()+IF(MillerBid<MIN(CompBids),1,0)

in cell B23. Here, 1 means that Miller wins the bid, and 0 means a competitor wins the bid. Note that we are designating this cell as an output cells for @Risk.

❺ **Miller's profit.** If Miller submits a bid, the bid cost is lost for sure. Beyond that, the profit to Miller is the bid amount minus the cost of completing the project if the bid is won. Otherwise, Miller makes nothing. So enter the formula

=RISKOUTPUT()+IF(B23=1,MillerBid-ProjectCost,0)-BidCost

in cell C23. We also designate this as an output cell.

	A	B	C	D	E	F	G	H	I	J	K
1	**Bidding Problem**										
2											
3	**Inputs**							Range names used:			
4	Our cost to prepare a bid	$350						BidCost: B4			
5	Our cost to complete project	$10,000						ProjectCost: B5			
6								PossibleBids - B13:K13			
7	**Assumption on each competitor's bid**							MillerBid - B15			
8	Each competitor bids a multiple of our bid, where the multiple is triangularly distributed with parameters:							CompBids: B19:E19			
9	Min	0.9									
10	Most likely	1.3									
11	Max	2.5									
12											
13	**Miller's possible bids**	$10,500	$11,000	$11,500	$12,000	$12,500	$13,000	$13,500	$14,000	$14,500	$15,000
14											
15	**Miller's bid**	$10,500									
16											
17	**Simulated competitor bids**										
18	Competitor	1	2	3	4						
19	Competitor's bid	$15,667	$15,667	$15,667	$15,667						
20											
21	**Simulation model for Miller**										
22		Wins bid?	Profit								
23		1	$150								

FIGURE 12.1 Bidding Simulation Model

@RISK

USING @RISK

We set the number of iterations to 1000 and the number of simulations to 10 (because there are 10 bid amounts Miller wants to test). The summary results appear in Figure 12.2. For each simulation—that is, each bid amount—there are two outputs: 1 or 0 to indicate whether Miller wins the contract and Miller's profit. A little thought should convince you that each of these can have only two possible values for any bid amount. For example, if Miller bids $12,000, it will either win or lose the contract, and its profit will be either $1650 or −$350. This is reflected in the histogram of profit for this bid amount in Figure 12.3, where there are only two bars. The two possible values of the outputs appear in the Minimum and Maximum columns of Figure 12.2.

FIGURE 12.2
Summary Results
from @Risk

Summary Statistics

Cell	Name	Minimum	Mean	Maximum
B23 (Sim#1)	Wins bid?	0	0.866	1
B23 (Sim#2)	Wins bid?	0	0.77	1
B23 (Sim#3)	Wins bid?	0	0.665	1
B23 (Sim#4)	Wins bid?	0	0.545	1
B23 (Sim#5)	Wins bid?	0	0.415	1
B23 (Sim#6)	Wins bid?	0	0.307	1
B23 (Sim#7)	Wins bid?	0	0.212	1
B23 (Sim#8)	Wins bid?	0	0.15	1
B23 (Sim#9)	Wins bid?	0	0.095	1
B23 (Sim#10)	Wins bid?	0	0.064	1
C23 (Sim#1)	Profit	-350	83	150
C23 (Sim#2)	Profit	-350	420	650
C23 (Sim#3)	Profit	-350	647.5	1150
C23 (Sim#4)	Profit	-350	740	1650
C23 (Sim#5)	Profit	-350	687.5	2150
C23 (Sim#6)	Profit	-350	571	2650
C23 (Sim#7)	Profit	-350	392	3150
C23 (Sim#8)	Profit	-350	250	3650
C23 (Sim#9)	Profit	-350	77.5	4150
C23 (Sim#10)	Profit	-350	-30	4650

FIGURE 12.3
Histogram of Profit
for a $12,000 Bid

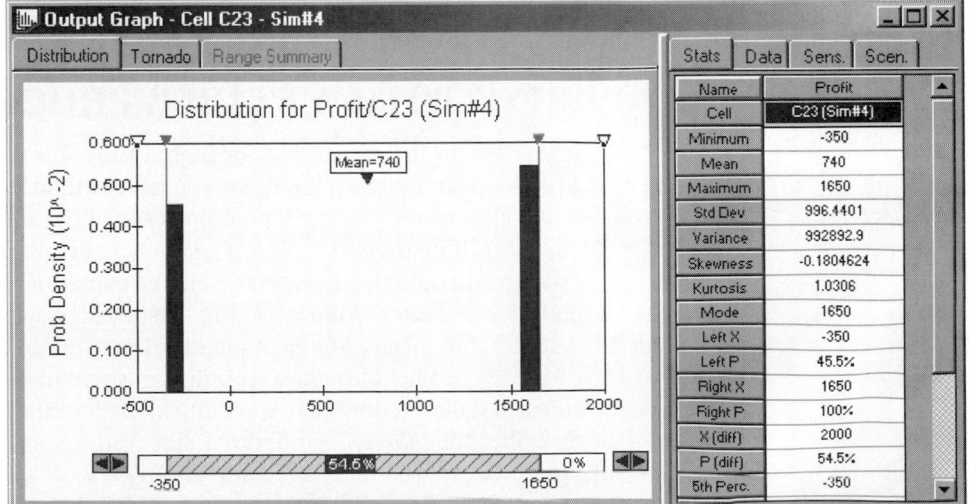

The Mean column, on the other hand, indicates the *average* of these values over the 1000 iterations. For example, the mean of 0.545 for the "Wins Bid?" output for simulation #4 indicates that Miller wins the contract on 54.5% of the iterations when bidding $12,000. The mean profit of $740 for this bid amount is simply a weighted average of the two possible profits, $1650 and −$350. Specifically, you can check that it is

$$0.545(1650) + 0.455(-350) = 740$$

The other means in the output can be interpreted similarly.

What should Miller bid? First, it is clear that Miller *should* bid. Not bidding means no profit, whereas all of the possible bids except for the last one lead to a positive expected profit with at most a $350 loss. If Miller is an EMV maximizer, as we discussed in Chapter 10, then the $12,000 bid should be chosen because it has the highest mean profit. However, if Miller is risk averse, a smaller bid amount might be attractive. As the bid amounts increase, the upside potential is greater, but the chance of not winning the bid and losing $350 increases. ■

Deming's Funnel Experiment

Edwards Deming was an American statistician whose views on quality management revolutionized the way companies do business across the world. Deming has been given much of the credit for Japan's spectacular post–World War II economic recovery. He traveled around the United States giving a famous 4-day seminar on quality management. After attending his seminar, many U.S. companies (including Xerox, GM, and Ford) reorganized their businesses to reflect Deming's management philosophy as embraced in his famous 14 points. For example, GM's Saturn plant is run almost completely in accordance with Deming's 14 points. We strongly recommend Deming's book *Out of the Crisis* (1986). It's terrific!

An important component of Deming's seminar was his famous funnel experiment. The funnel experiment is designed to show how businesses often greatly overadjust "stable" processes. We illustrate how it works in the following example.

EXAMPLE   12.2

TAMPERING WITH A STABLE PROCESS

Suppose that you are in the business of drilling a tiny hole in the exact center of a square piece of wood. In the past, the holes you have drilled were, on average, in the center of the wood, and the x- and y-coordinates each had a standard deviation of 0.1 inch. Also, the drilling process has been *stable*—that is, the holes average being in the center of the square, and the deviations from the center of the square (measured in both the x- and y-coordinates) follow a normal distribution with mean 0 and standard deviation 0.1 inch. This means, for example, that the x-coordinate is within 0.1 inch of the center for 68% of the holes, the x-coordinate is within 0.2 inch of the center for 95% of the holes, and the x-coordinate is within 0.3 inch of the center for 99.7% of the holes. This describes the *inherent* variability in the drilling process. Without changing the hole-drilling process, you must live with this amount of variation.

Now suppose that you drill a hole and its x- and y-coordinates are $x = 0.1$ and $y = 0$ [where the center of the square has coordinates $(0, 0)$]. A natural reaction is to reduce the x-setting of the drill by 0.1 to correct for the fact that the x-coordinate was too high. Then if the next hole has coordinates $x = -0.2$ and $y = 0.1$, you might try to increase the x-coordinate by 0.2 and decrease the y-coordinate by 0.1. Deming's funnel experiment shows that this method of continually readjusting a stable process—he calls it "tampering"—will actually *increase* the variability of the coordinates of the position where the hole is drilled. In other words, tampering will generally make a process worse!

To illustrate the effects of tampering, Deming placed a funnel above a target on the floor and dropped small balls through the funnel in an attempt to hit the target. As he demonstrated, many balls did *not* hit the target. His goal, therefore, was to make the balls fall as close to the target as possible. Deming proposed four rules for adjusting the positioning of the funnel.

Rule 1. Never move the funnel.

Rule 2. After each ball is dropped, move the funnel—*relative to its previous position*—to compensate for any error. To illustrate, suppose the target has coordinates $(0, 0)$ and the funnel begins directly over the target. If the ball lands at $(0.5, 0.1)$ on the first drop, we compensate by repositioning the funnel at $(0 - 0.5, 0 - 0.1) = (-0.5, -1)$. If the second drop has coordinates $(1, -2)$, we then reposition the funnel at $(-0.5 - 1, -0.1 - (-2)) = (-1.5, 1.9)$.

Rule 3. Move the funnel—*relative to its original position at* $(0, 0)$—to compensate for any error. For example, if the ball lands at $(0.5, 0.1)$ on the first drop, we compensate by repositioning the funnel at $(0 - 0.5, 0 - 0.1) = (-0.5, -1)$. If the second drop has coordinates $(1, -2)$, we then reposition the funnel at $(0 - 1, 0 - (-2)) = (-1, 2)$.

Rule 4. Always reposition the funnel directly over the last drop. Therefore, if the first ball lands at $(0.5, 1)$, we position the funnel at $(0.5, 1)$. If the second drop has coordinates $(1, 2)$, we position the funnel at $(1, 2)$. This rule might be followed, for example, by an automobile manufacturer's painting department. With each new batch of paint, they attempt to match the color of the previous batch—regardless of whether the previous color was "correct."

Do you believe any of these latter three rules will outperform rule 1, the "leave it alone" rule? Is so, read on—you might surprised.

Solution

To see how these rules work, we assume that the x-coordinate on each drop is normally distributed with mean equal to the x-coordinate of the funnel position and standard deviation of 1. A similar statement holds for the y-coordinate. Also, we assume that the x- and y-coordinates are selected independently of one another. These assumptions describe the inherent variability in the process of dropping the balls.

To see how the rules work, let F_0, X_0, and F_1 be, respectively, the x-coordinates of the funnel position on the previous drop, the outcome of the previous drop, and the repositioned funnel position for the next drop. Then rule 1 never repositions, so that $F_1 = F_0$. Rule 2 repositions relative to the previous funnel position, so that $F_1 = F_0 - X_0$. Rule 3 repositions relative to the original position (at 0), so that $F_1 = 0 - X_0 = -X_0$. Finally, rule 4 repositions at the previous drop, so that $F_1 = X_0$. Similar equations hold for the y-coordinate.

For the simulation model, we simulate 50 consecutive drops of the ball from each of the four rules. Our single output measure is the (straight-line) distance of the final drop from the target. A rule is presumably a good one if the mean distance is small and the standard deviation of this distance is also small.

DEVELOPING THE SIMULATION MODEL

Given the repositioning equations for the rules, the simulation model is straightforward. In fact, we can use a RISKSIMTABLE function to test all four rules simultaneously. The completed model appears in Figure 12.4. (See the file FUNNEL.XLS.) It can be developed with the following steps.

❶ Rule. Enter the formula

=RISKSIMTABLE({1, 2, 3, 4})

in cell B3 to indicate that we want to simulate all four rules. Note that if individual values are listed in RISKSIMTABLE, they must be enclosed in curly brackets. No curly brackets should be used if the list is referenced by a range.

❷ Position funnel. Enter 0 in cells B7 and C7 to indicate that the original funnel position is above the target at (0,0). Then implement the positioning equations by entering the formula

=IF(Rule=1,B7,IF(Rule=2,B7-D7,IF(Rule=3,-D7,D7)))

in cell B8 and copying it to the range B8:C56. Note how this formula references the location of the previous drop. The IF function captures the logic for all four rules.

❸ Simulate drops. Simulate the positions of the drops by entering the formula

=RISKNORMAL(B7,1)

in cell D7 and copying it to the range D7:E56. This says that the ball's drop position is normally distributed with mean equal to the funnel's position and standard deviation 1.

❹ Distance. Calculate the final distance from the target in cell C58 with the formula

=RISKOUTPUT()+SQRT(SUMSQ(D56:E56))

Here we have used the SUMSQ function to get the sum of squares for the distance formula. We have also indicated that this is an output cell for @Risk.

	A	B	C	D	E	F	G	H	I	J
1	**Deming's funnel experiment**									
2				Range name used:						
3	Rule to use		1	Rule - B3						
4										
5			Funnel positioned at:		Drop lands at:		Explanation of rules:			
6		Drop	Xpos	Ypos	Xdrop	Ydrop	Rule 1: Never move the funnel			
7		1	0	0	2.29	-0.74	Rule 2: Move the funnel, relative to its previous position, to compensate for the previous error.			
8		2	0.00	0.00	-1.41	-2.18	Rule 3: Move the funnel, relative to its original position, to compensate for the previous error.			
9		3	0.00	0.00	-0.04	-0.82	Rule 4: Reposition the funnel over the previous drop.			
10		4	0.00	0.00	1.77	2.23				
11		5	0.00	0.00	1.24	0.55				
12		6	0.00	0.00	-0.50	-0.15				
52		46	0.00	0.00	-0.16	-1.75				
53		47	0.00	0.00	1.73	-0.11				
54		48	0.00	0.00	0.39	0.96				
55		49	0.00	0.00	-0.59	-2.02				
56		50	0.00	0.00	-0.77	1.70				
57										
58	Distance of final drop from target		1.865							

FIGURE 12.4 Funnel Experiment Simulation Model

USING @RISK

We set the number of iterations to 1000 and the number of simulations to 4 (because of simulating the four rules simultaneously). Selected summary measures for the final distance from the target for all four rules appear in Figure 12.5. We also show histograms of this distance for rules 1, 2, and 3 in Figures 12.6, 12.7, and 12.8 (page 626). (The histogram for rule 4 is practically identical to the one for rule 3.)

These results prove Deming's point about tampering. Rule 2 might not appear to be too much worse than rule 1, but its mean distance and standard deviation of distances are both about 40% higher than for rule 1. Rules 3 and 4 are disastrous. Their mean

FIGURE 12.5
Summary Results from @Risk for All Rules

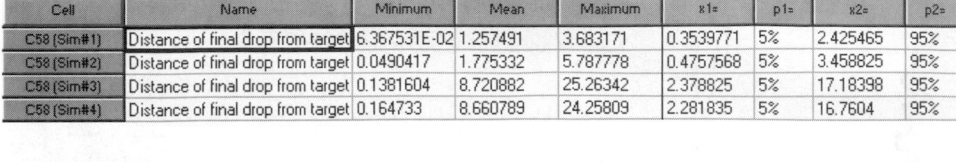

Cell	Name	Minimum	Mean	Maximum	x1=	p1=	x2=	p2=
C58 (Sim#1)	Distance of final drop from target	6.367531E-02	1.257491	3.683171	0.3539771	5%	2.425465	95%
C58 (Sim#2)	Distance of final drop from target	0.0490417	1.775332	5.787778	0.4757568	5%	3.458825	95%
C58 (Sim#3)	Distance of final drop from target	0.1381604	8.720882	25.26342	2.378825	5%	17.18398	95%
C58 (Sim#4)	Distance of final drop from target	0.164733	8.660789	24.25809	2.281835	5%	16.7604	95%

FIGURE 12.6
Histogram of Distance from Target for Rule 1

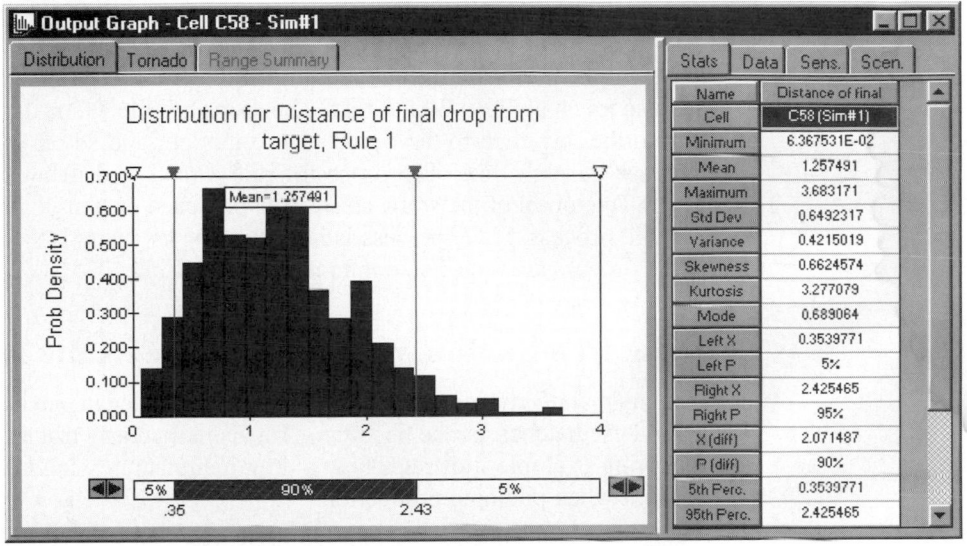

FIGURE 12.7
Histogram of Distance from Target for Rule 2

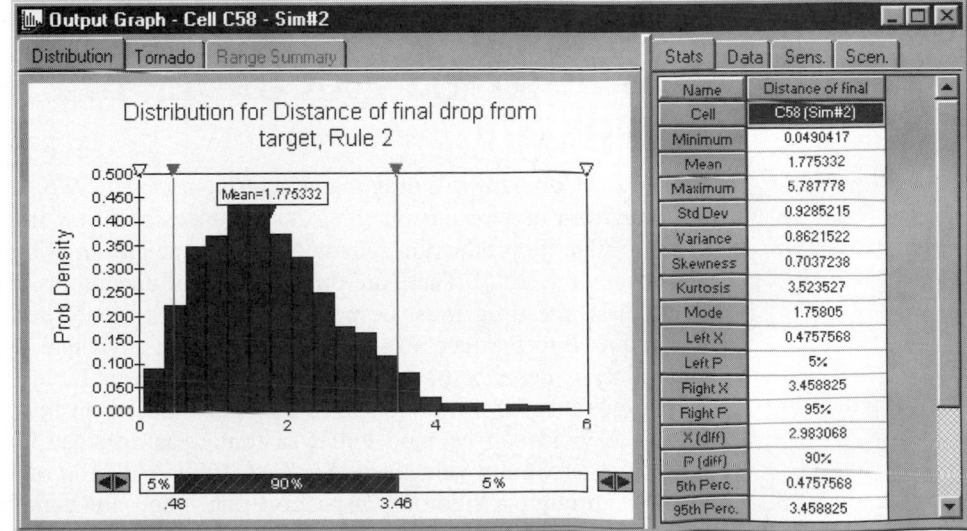

FIGURE 12.8
Histogram of
Distance from Target
for Rule 3

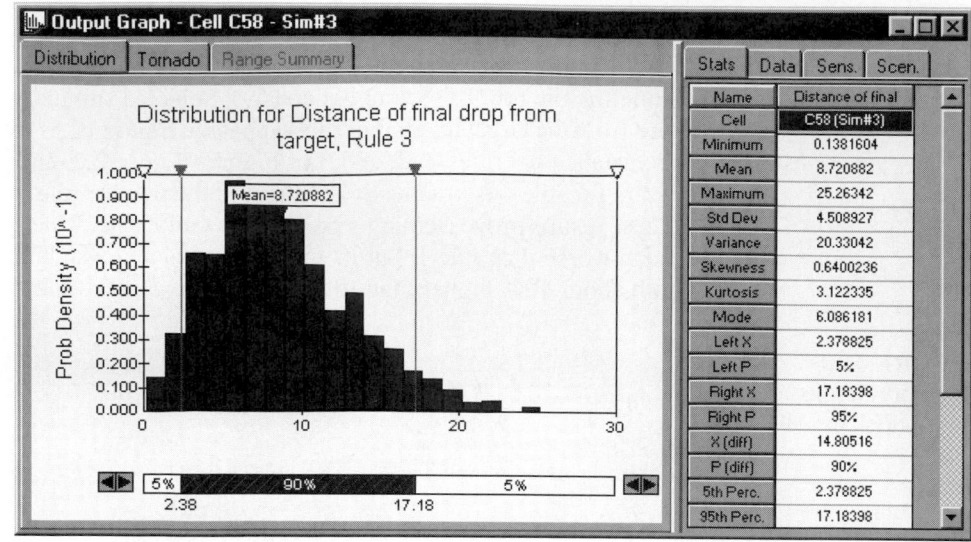

Output Graph - Cell C58 - Sim#3

Distribution for Distance of final drop from target, Rule 3

Mean=8.720882

Name	Distance of final
Cell	C58 (Sim#3)
Minimum	0.1381604
Mean	8.720882
Maximum	25.26342
Std Dev	4.508927
Variance	20.33042
Skewness	0.6400236
Kurtosis	3.122335
Mode	6.086181
Left X	2.378825
Left P	5%
Right X	17.18398
Right P	95%
X (diff)	14.80516
P (diff)	90%
5th Perc.	2.378825
95th Perc.	17.18398

distances are more than seven times higher than for rule 1, and their standard deviations are also much higher. (Why is this? The drops for rule 3 tend to swing back and forth— first to the left, then to the right, then to the left, and so on—and the swings tend to increase through time. The drops for rule 4 tend to drift away from the target over time.) The moral of the story, as Deming preached, is that you should not tamper with a stable process. If the process is not behaving as desired, then *fundamental* changes to the process are required, not a lot of tinkering. ■

Drug Production Models with Uncertain Yield

In many manufacturing settings, products are produced in batches, and the usable *yields* from these batches can be uncertain. This is particularly true in the drug industry. The following example illustrates how a drug manufacturer can take this uncertainty into account when planning production.

EXAMPLE 12.3

TRYING TO MEET AN ORDER DUE DATE AT WOZAC

The Wozac Company is a drug manufacturing company. Wozac has recently accepted an order from its best customer for 8000 ounces of a new miracle drug, and Wozac wants to plan its production schedule to meet the customer's promised delivery date of December 1, 2000. There are three sources of uncertainty that make planning difficult. First, the drug must be produced in batches, and there is uncertainty in the time required to produce a batch, which could be anywhere from 5 to 11 days. This uncertainty is described by the discrete distribution in Table 12.1. Second, the yield (usable quantity) from any batch is uncertain. Based on historical data, Wozac believes the yield can be modeled by a triangular distribution with minimum, most likely, and maximum values equal to 600, 1000, and 1100 ounces. Third, all batches must go through a rigorous inspection once they are completed. The probability that a typical batch passes inspection is only 0.8. With probability 0.2, the batch

TABLE 12.1	Distribution of Days to Complete a Batch

Days	Probability
5	0.05
6	0.10
7	0.20
8	0.30
9	0.20
10	0.10
11	0.05

fails inspection, and *none* of it can be used to help fill the order. Wozac wants to use simulation to help decide how many days prior to the due date it should begin production.

Solution

The idea is to simulate successive batches—their days to complete, their yields, and whether they pass inspection—and keep a running total of the usable ounces obtained so far. We then use IF functions to see whether the order is complete or another batch is required. We simulate only as many as batches as are required to meet the order, and we keep track of the days required to produce all of these batches. In this way we can "back up" to see when production must begin to meet the due date.

DEVELOPING THE SIMULATION MODEL

The completed model appears in Figure 12.9 (page 628). It can be developed as follows.

1 **Inputs.** Enter all of the inputs in the shaded cells.

2 **Batch indexes.** We do not know ahead of time how many batches will be required to fill the order. We want to have enough rows in the simulation to cover the worst case that is likely to occur. After some experimentation we found that 25 batches are almost surely enough. Therefore, enter the batch indexes 1–25 in column A of the simulation section. (If 25 were not enough, we could always add more rows.) The idea, then, is to fill the entire range B29:F53 with formulas. However, we will use IF functions in these formulas so that if enough has already been produced to fill the order, blanks are inserted in the remaining cells.

3 **Days for batches.** Simulate the days required for batches in column B. First, enter the formula

=RISKDISCRETE(Days,Probs)

in cell B29. Then enter the general formula

=IF(OR(F29="Yes",F29=""),"",RISKDISCRETE(Days,Probs))

in cell B30 and copy it down to cell B53. Note how the IF function enters a blank in this cell if either of two conditions is true: the order was just completed in the previous batch or it has been completed for some time. Similar logic will appear in later formulas.

4 **Batch yields.** Simulate the batch yields in column C. First, enter the formula

=RISKTRIANG(B23,C23,D23)

	A	B	C	D	E	F	G	H	I	J	K
1	Planning production of a drug										
2											
3	**Assumptions:**										
4	The drug is produced in similar-sized batches, although the yield in each batch is random. Also, the number of days to										
5	produce a batch is random. Each batch is inspected, and if it doesn't pass inspection, none of that batch can be used.										
6											
7	Input section										
8	Amount required (ounces)	8000				Range names used:					
9	Promised delivery date	12/1/00				AmtReqd - B8					
10						DueDate - B9					
11	Distribution of days needed to produce a batch (discrete)					Days - B13:B19					
12			Days	Probability		Probs - C13:C19					
13			5	0.05		PrPass - B25					
14			6	0.10		DaysReqd - I29					
15			7	0.20							
16			8	0.30							
17			9	0.20							
18			10	0.10							
19			11	0.05							
20											
21	Distribution of yield (ounces) from each batch (triangular)										
22			Min	Most likely	Max						
23			600	1000	1100						
24											
25	Probability of passing inspection	0.8									
26											
27	Simulation model							Summary measures			
28		Batch	Days	Yield	Pass?	CumYield	Enough?	Batches required	11		
29		1	8	935.2	Yes	935.2	Not yet	Days to complete	87		
30		2	10	1041.1	Yes	1976.3	Not yet	Day to start	9/5/00		
31		3	8	943.8	Yes	2920.1	Not yet				
32		4	7	809.2	Yes	3729.3	Not yet	@Risk summary outputs			
33		5	11	934.7	Yes	4664.0	Not yet	Max batches reqd	20		
34		6	9	648.4	Yes	5312.3	Not yet				
35		7	8	793.9	Yes	6106.3	Not yet	Avg days reqd	94	8/29/00	
36		8	6	938.8	Yes	7045.1	Not yet	Min days reqd	54	10/8/00	
37		9	5	945.2	Yes	7990.2	Not yet	Max days reqd	167	6/17/00	
38		10	9	896.4	No	7990.2	Not yet	5th perc days reqd	73	9/19/00	
39		11	6	1011.6	Yes	9001.8	Yes	95th perc days reqd	121	8/2/00	
40		12									
41		13						Probability of meeting due date for several starting dates			
42		14						7/15/00	0.990		
43		15						8/1/00	0.954		
44		16						8/15/00	0.850		
45		17						9/1/00	0.511		
46		18						9/15/00	0.125		
47		19									
48		20									
49		21									
50		22									
51		23									
52		24									
53		25									

FIGURE 12.9 Drug Production Simulation Model

in cell C29. Then enter the general formula

=IF(OR(F29="Yes",F29=""),"",RISKTRIANG($B$23,$C$23,$D$23))

in cell C30 and copy it down to cell C53.

❺ **Pass inspection?** Check whether each batch passes inspection with the formulas

=IF(RAND()<PrPass,"Yes","No")

and

=IF(OR(F29="Yes",F29=""),"",IF(RAND()<PrPass,"Yes","No"))

in cells D29 and D30, and copy the latter down to cell D53. Note that we could use @Risk's RISKUNIFORM(0,1) function instead of RAND(), but there is no advantage to doing so.

6 **Order filled?** We keep track of the cumulative usable production and whether the order has been filled in columns E and F. First, enter the formulas

=IF(D29="Yes",C29,0)

and

=IF(E29>=AmtReqd,"Yes","Not yet")

in cells E29 and F29 for batch 1. Then enter the general formulas

=IF(OR(F29="Yes",F29=""),"",IF(D30="Yes",C30+E29,E29))

and

=IF(OR(F29="Yes",F29=""),"",IF(E30>=AmtReqd,"Yes","Not yet"))

in cells E30 and F30, and copy them down to row 53. Note that the entry in column F is "Not enough" if the order is not yet complete. In the row that completes the order, it changes to "Yes," and then it is blank in succeeding rows.

7 **Summary measures.** Calculate the batches and days required in cells I28 and I29 with the formulas

=RISKOUTPUT()+COUNT(B29:B53)

and

=RISKOUTPUT()+SUM(B29:B53)

These are the two cells we will use as output cells for @Risk. Also, calculate the day the order should be started to just meet the due date in cell I30 with the formula

=DueDate-I29

This formula uses date subtraction to find an elapsed time. Of course, it assumes that production occurs every day of the week, which we will assume.)

This completes the simulation model development. The other entries in columns H–J will be explained shortly.

USING @RISK

We set the number of iterations to 1000 and the number of simulations to 1. After running @Risk, we obtain the histograms of the number of batches required and the number of days required in Figures 12.10 and 12.11 (page 630).

How should Wozac use this information? The key questions are how many batches will be required and when to start production. We have entered several of @Risk's statistical functions directly in the spreadsheet to help answer these questions. (Recall that these @Risk statistical functions provide useful information only *after* @Risk has been run.) For the first question, we use the formula

=RISKMAX(I28)

in cell I33. (Refer to Figure 12.9.) It shows that the worst case from the 1000 iterations, in terms of batches required, is 20 batches. (If this maximum were 25, we would add more rows to the simulation model and run @Risk again!)

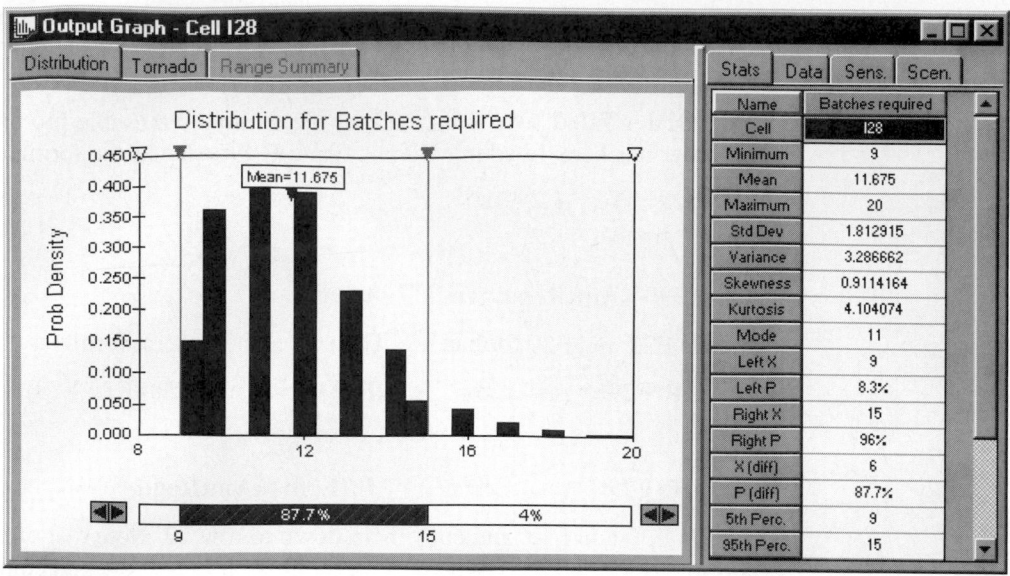

FIGURE 12.10 Histogram of Batches Required

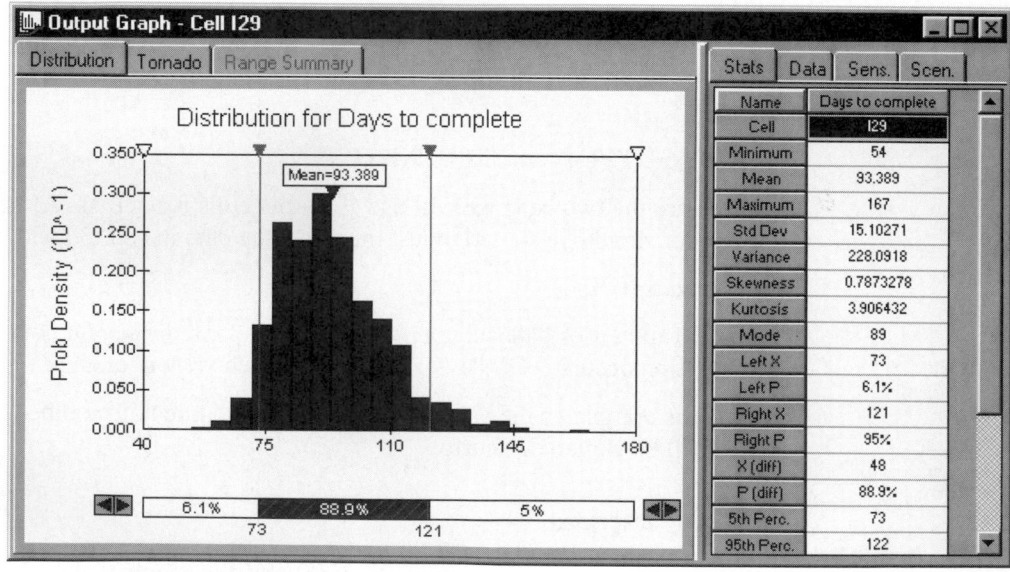

FIGURE 12.11 Histogram of Days to Complete Order

We can answer the second question in two ways. First, we can calculate summary measures for days required and then back up from the due date. We do this in the range I35:J39. The formulas in column I are

=INT(RISKMEAN(DaysReqd))
=RISKMIN(DaysReqd)
=RISKMAX(DaysReqd)
=RISKPERCENTILE(DaysReqd,0.05)

and

=RISKPERCENTILE(DaysReqd,0.95)

(The first uses the INT function to produce an integer.) We then subtract each of these from the due date to obtain the potential starting dates in column J. Wozac should realize the pros and cons of these starting dates. For example, if it wants to be 95% sure of meeting the due date, it should start production on August 2. If it instead starts on September 19, there is only a 5% chance of meeting the due date.

Alternatively, we can use @Risk's RISKTARGET function to find the probability of meeting the due date for *any* starting date, such as those in the range H42:H46. We enter the formula

=RISKTARGET(DaysReqd,DueDate-H42)

in cell I42 and copy it down. This function returns the fraction of iterations where the (random) value in the first argument is less than or equal to the (fixed) value in the second argument. For example, we see that 85% of the iterations have a value of DaysReqd less than or equal to 108, the number of days between August 15 and the due date.

What is our recommendation to Wozac? We suggest going with the 95th percentile—begin production on August 2. Then there is only a 5% chance of failing to meet the due date. ∎

Component Redundancy Models

To extend the useful lifetimes of various devices, redundancy is often built in. For example, in space modules there is massive redundancy. If the primary unit fails, a backup takes over. If the backup fails, there might be a second backup to take over, and so on. In this section we will simulate the time to failure of one such system. In doing so, we will discuss the effect on simulation results of different input probability distributions. Although it is tempting to use one of the well-known distributions, particularly the normal distribution, for most simulations, you should be aware that there are quite a few candidate distributions available and that the simulated results can vary depending on which candidate you choose. We will compare four available distributions in the following example.

EXAMPLE 12.4

COMPONENT REDUNDANCY AT FAILSAFE

The FailSafe Company operates a machine that consists of 3 identical modules **in series**. This means that the machine works as long as *all* of the modules work. Each of the modules depends on a specific component. If this component fails, the module fails—and the machine fails. To extend the time until machine failure, redundancy is built in at the component level. Specifically, 15 identical components are placed **in parallel** in each module. This means that a module works as long as *at least one* component in that module is working. Each component lasts a random time before failure, where these times are probabilistically independent and each has mean 100 hours and standard deviation 20 hours. FailSafe wants to use simulation to find the distribution of the time until machine failure.

Solution

Let C_{ij} be the time until failure for component j in module i. Also, let M_i be the time until failure for module i, and let T be the time until machine failure. Then from the system configuration, we have

$$M_i = \max(C_{i1}, C_{i2}, \ldots, C_{i,15})$$

and

$$T = \min(M_1, M_2, M_3)$$

In words, a module lasts as long as the *best* of its components, and the machine lasts as long as the *worst* of its modules. Therefore, all we need to do is generate the random component times, the C_{ij}'s, and use Excel's MAX and MIN functions to find the time until machine failure, T.

Choosing a Probability Distribution We are told that times until component failures have mean 100 and standard deviation 20 (probably estimated from historical component failure data), but which *distribution* of component failure times should we use? Should it be symmetric and bell-shaped, or should it be skewed in one direction or the other? We will test four possible distributions: normal, lognormal, gamma, and Weibull. The normal is the symmetric bell-shaped distribution. The other three are less well known, but they are frequently used to model times until failure. They all have the attractive property that they generate positive values only. (We know that times to failure cannot be negative). Also, all three are skewed to a certain extent.

To see the possibilities, we open @Risk's Model window and select the Insert/Distribution Window menu item. This allows us to choose from many distributions, including the four we are recommending here, and to adjust their parameters. Note that each of these distributions is specified by two parameters.[2] For the normal and lognormal, the parameters are the mean and standard deviation directly. For the gamma and Weibull, the parameters are called alpha and beta. These parameters control the exact location and shape of the distributions, but they are *not* the mean and standard deviation. If we want them to have mean 100 and standard deviation 20, we have to manipulate alpha and beta appropriately. (This can be done by trial and error in the @Risk Model window, or it can be done by consulting @Risk's online help or a book on probability.)

The lognormal, gamma, and Weibull distributions with mean 100 and standard deviation 20 appear in Figures 12.12, 12.13, and 12.14 (page 634). They all look similar to each other and to the normal distribution (not shown), and only the Weibull indicates some "obvious" skewness. If we were fitting distributions to historical failure time data, these might all provide very good fits. The question, then, is whether it matters which we use in the simulation. Will they all give approximately the same results? We will see shortly.

DEVELOPING THE SIMULATION MODEL

The simulation model appears in Figure 12.15 (page 635). It can be developed as follows. (See the REDUNDANCY.XLS file.)

---

[2]The latter three can also be shifted to the right or even the left of 0. However, we will not change this shift parameter.

FIGURE 12.12
Lognormal
Distribution

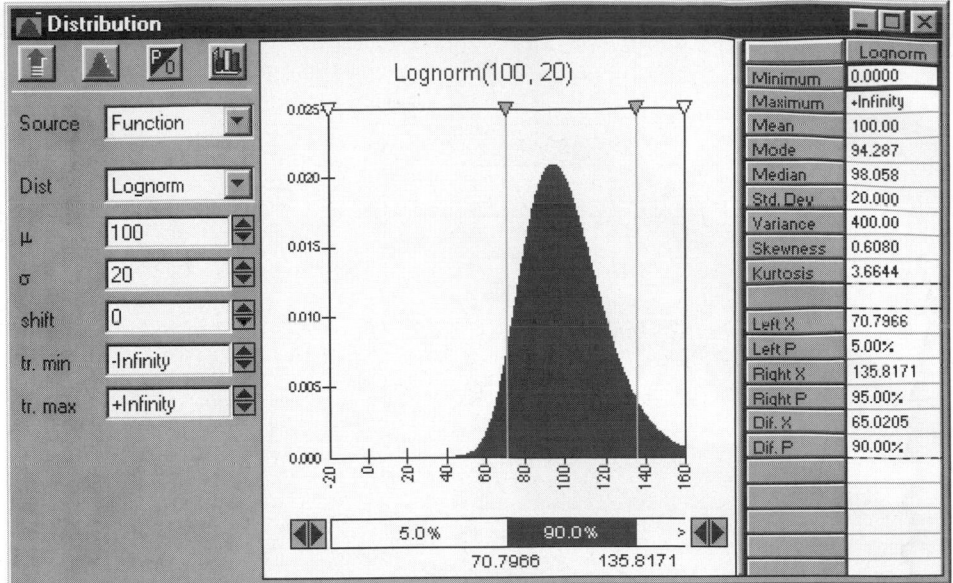

FIGURE 12.13
Gamma Distribution

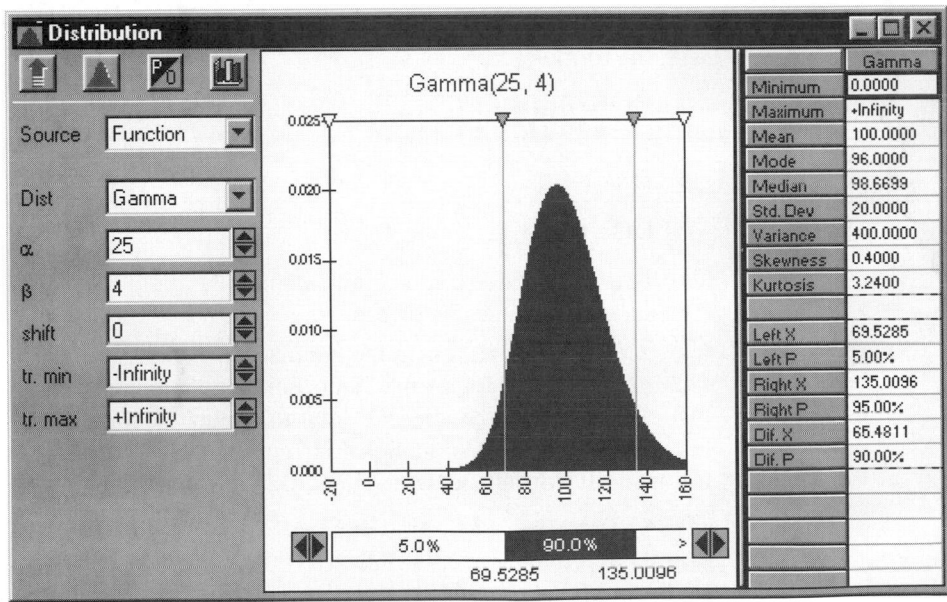

❶ Machine configuration. We stated that there are 3 modules in series, each consisting of 15 components. Enter these values in cells B4 and B5. We actually develop a slightly more general model, where the machine can consist of up to 10 modules in series, each of which can have up 20 modules in parallel.

❷ Parameters of probability distributions. Enter the parameters of the four candidate probability distributions in the shaded range. These are the parameters from the @Risk Model window that yield means of 100 and standard deviations of 20.

❸ Distribution to use. We can actually test all four distributions simultaneously by using a RISKSIMTABLE function. Do this by entering the formula

=RISKSIMTABLE({1, 2, 3, 4})

FIGURE 12.14
Weibull Distribution

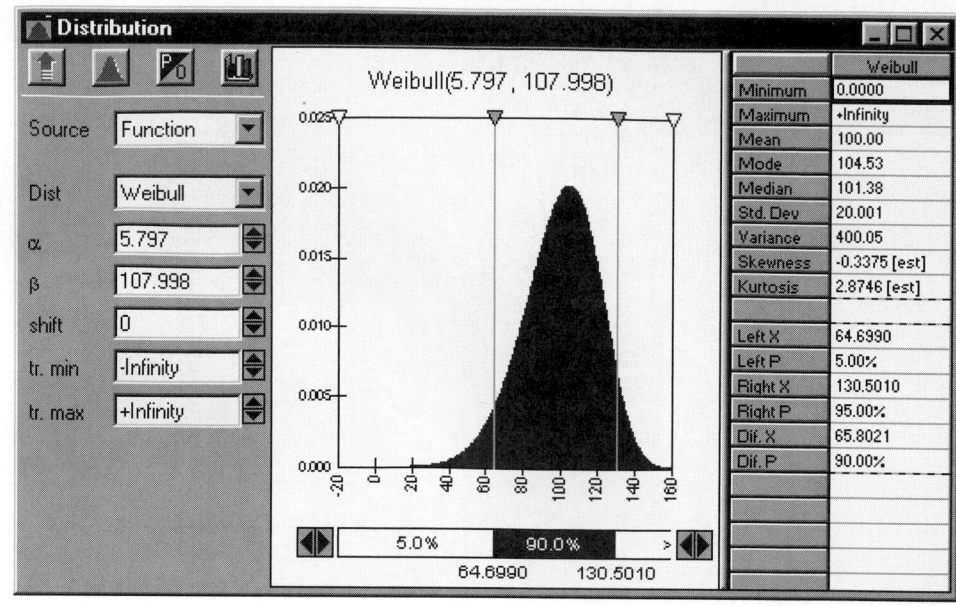

in cell B16. Then get the name and parameters of this distribution in cells B17 to B19 with the formulas

=HLOOKUP(Dist,LTable,2)
=HLOOKUP(Dist,LTable,3)

and

=HLOOKUP(Dist,LTable,4)

The latter two of these cells, range-named Par1 and Par2, will supply the parameters for the random values in the next step.

4   **Component times.** In the simulation section we enter 1–10 along the top and 1–20 along the side for the maximum number of modules and components, respectively, that our model can handle. We want to generate enough component lifetimes in this table for the numbers of modules and components in cells B4 and B5. Do this with the following IF formula, entered in cell B24 and copied to the range B24:K43:

=IF(AND($A24<=NComps,B$23<=NMods),IF(Dist=1,RISKNORMAL
(Par1,Par2),IF(Dist=2,RISKLOGNORM(Par1,Par2),
IF(Dist=3,RISKGAMMA(Par1,Par2),RISKWEIBULL(Par1,Par2)))),"")

Although this looks intimidating, it is really straightforward. The AND condition checks whether the component and module indices are less than or equal to the values in the NComps and NMods cells. If they aren't, a blank is entered. Otherwise, the appropriate @Risk function is called with the parameters in the Par1 and Par2 cells.

5   **Module times.** Calculate the times until module failures in row 45 by entering the formula

=IF(B23<=NMods,MAX(B24:B43),"")

in cell B45 and copying it across to column K. Note that the MAX (or MIN) of a range that includes blanks ignores the blanks.

	A	B	C	D	E	F	G	H	I	J	K
1	**Component redundancy model**										
2											
3	**Configuration**										
4	Modules in series	3	<-- up to 10								
5	Components per module	15	<-- up to 20								
6											
7	**Possible component lifetime distributions**										
8	Distribution	1	2	3	4		**Range names used:**				
9	Name	Normal	Lognormal	Gamma	Weibull		NMods - B4				
10	Parameter 1	100	100	25	5.797		NComps - B5				
11	Parameter 2	20	20	4	107.998		LTable - B8:E11				
12	Mean	100	100	100	100		Dist - B16				
13	Stdev	20	20	20	20		Par1 - B18				
14							Par2 - B19				
15	**Distribution to use**						ModLives - B45:K45				
16	Index	1					SysLife - B47				
17	Name	Normal									
18	Parameter 1	100									
19	Parameter 2	20									
20											
21	**Simulation of component lifetimes**										
22		Modules									
23	Components	1	2	3	4	5	6	7	8	9	10
24	1	121.924	74.355	125.400							
25	2	104.111	62.348	93.388							
26	3	108.288	65.973	94.212							
27	4	110.237	77.703	116.948							
28	5	88.076	122.071	48.740							
29	6	61.323	97.024	111.532							
30	7	98.066	118.781	96.356							
31	8	71.557	115.828	127.678							
32	9	102.010	99.955	78.890							
33	10	121.338	106.118	125.067							
34	11	72.674	100.911	112.056							
35	12	138.787	109.070	90.299							
36	13	91.021	100.069	88.845							
37	14	112.295	82.718	76.155							
38	15	76.673	116.707	79.441							
39	16										
40	17										
41	18										
42	19										
43	20										
44											
45	**Module lifetimes**	138.787	122.071	127.678							
46											
47	**System lifetime**	122.071									

FIGURE 12.15 Component Redundancy Simulation Model

❻ Machine time. Calculate the time until machine failure in cell B47 with the formula

=RISKOUTPUT()+MIN(ModLives)

This is the only cell we designate as an @Risk output cell.

USING @RISK

We set the number of iterations to 1000 and the number of simulations to 4 (one for each distribution). After running @Risk, we form the histograms of time (in hours) until machine failure, one for each distribution, in Figures 12.16–12.19 (pp. 636–637).

FIGURE 12.16
Distribution of
System Lifetime for
Normal Distribution

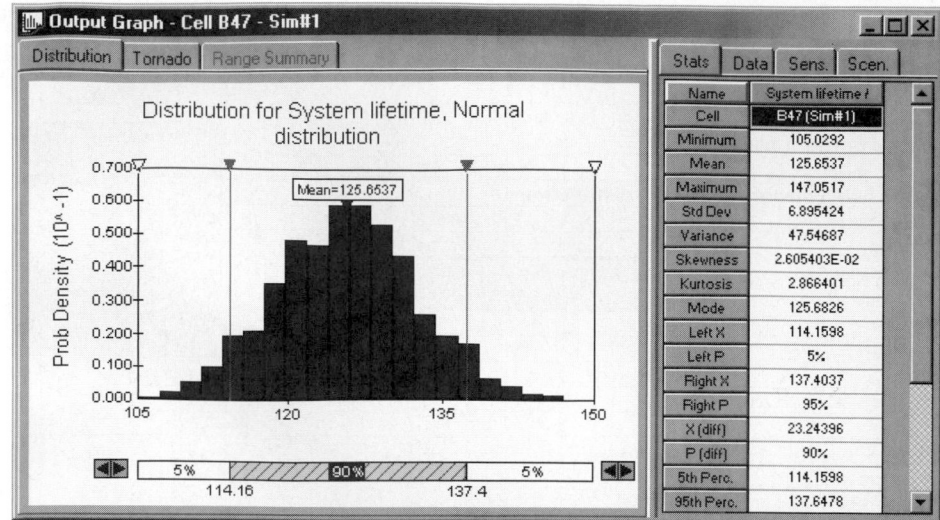

FIGURE 12.17
Distribution of
System Lifetime for
Lognormal
Distribution

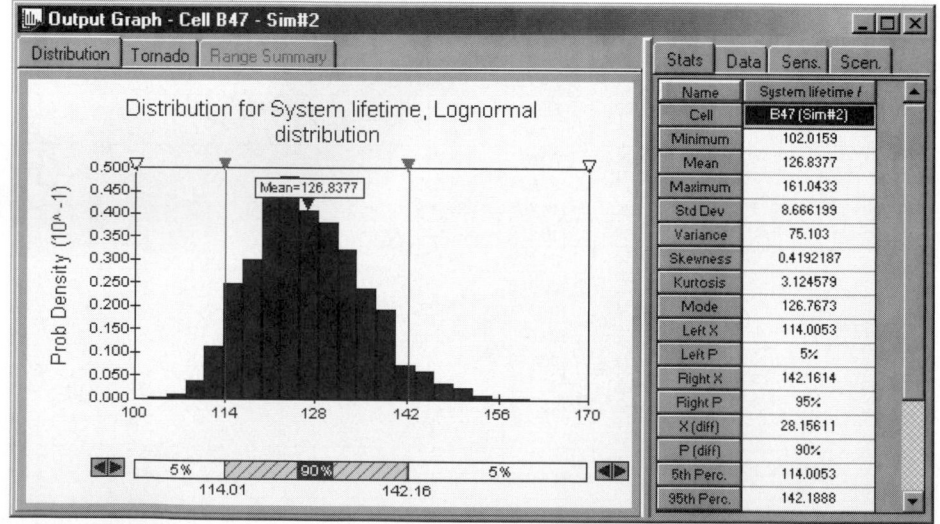

FIGURE 12.18
Distribution of
System Lifetime for
Gamma Distribution

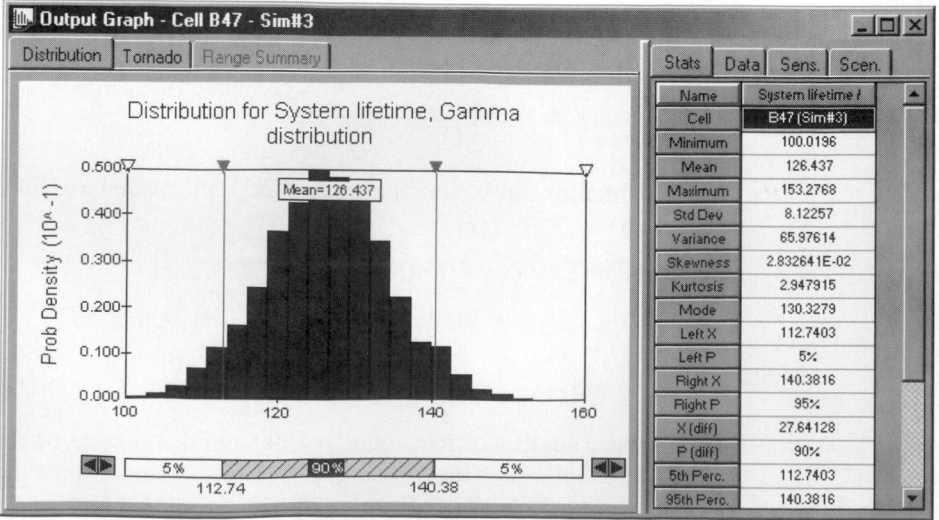

FIGURE 12.19
Distribution of
System Lifetime for
Weibull Distribution

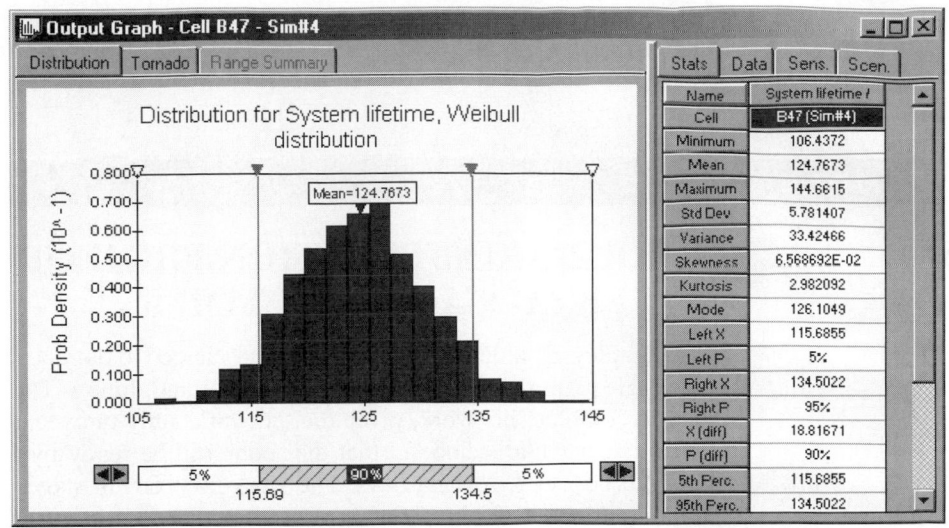

Does the input distribution affect the distribution of machine lifetime? At first glance, the answer appears to be "No." The four distributions have similar shapes and their means and standard deviations are similar. However, means and standard deviations might not be as relevant in a real situation as worst-case (or nearly worst-case) results. Therefore, it might be better to compare maximums or 95th percentiles. Admittedly, even these do not vary greatly (for example, the 95th percentile varies from about 134 hours with the Weibull distribution to about 142 hours with the lognormal distribution), but there *are* differences.

We conclude from this example that the input distribution(s) can make a difference in the results, particularly when best-case or worst-case results are of primary interest. Therefore, it pays to spend some time in real simulation applications fitting distributions to any relevant historical data that exist. Fortunately, as we saw in the previous chapter, @Risk's fitting capabilities make this fairly easy. ■

Project Scheduling Models

In Chapter 5 we used linear programming to determine the length of time needed to complete a project. We also learned how to identify critical activities, where an activity is critical if increasing its activity time by a small amount increases the length of time needed to complete the project by the same amount. Our discussion in Chapter 5 required the assumption that all activity times are known with certainty. In reality, these times are usually uncertain. Of course, this implies that the length of time needed to complete the project is also uncertain. It also implies that for each activity, there is a *probability* (not necessarily equal to 0 or 1) that the activity is critical.

To illustrate, suppose that activities A and B can begin immediately. Activity C can then begin as soon as activities A and B are both completed, and the project is completed as soon as activity C is completed. Activity C is clearly on the critical path, but what about A and B? Let's say that the *expected* activity times of A and B are 10 and 12. If we use these expected times and ignore any uncertainty about the actual times—that is, if we proceed as we did in Chapter 5—then activity B is definitely a critical activity. However, suppose there is some positive probability that A can have duration 12 and B can have duration 11. Under this scenario, A is a critical activity. Therefore, we cannot say in advance which of the activities, A or B, will be critical. However, by using simulation we can see how *likely* it is that each of these activities is critical. We can also see how long the entire project is likely to take. We illustrate with the following example. It is the same example as in Chapter 5 (without crashing). We repeat the "story" here for convenience.

EXAMPLE   12.5

A ROOM CONSTRUCTION PROJECT WITH UNCERTAIN ACTIVITY TIMES

Tom Lingley, an independent contractor, has agreed to build a new room on an existing house. He plans to begin work on Monday morning, June 1. The main question is when will he complete his work, given that he works only on weekdays. The owner of the house is particularly hopeful that the room will be ready by Saturday, June 27, that is, in 20 or fewer working days. The work proceeds in stages, labeled A through J, as summarized in Table 12.2. Three of these activities, E, F, and G, will be done by separate independent subcontractors. The *expected* durations of the activities (in days) are shown in the table. (These are the same activity times that were used in Example 5.5 of Chapter 5.) However, these are only best guesses. Lingley knows that the *actual* activity times can vary because of unexpected delays, worker illnesses, and so on. He would like to use computer simulation to see (1) how long the project is likely to take, (2) how likely it is that the project will be completed by the deadline, and (3) which activities are likely to be critical.

TABLE 12.2   **Activity Time Data**

Description	Index	Predecessors	Expected Duration
Prepare foundation	A	None	4
Put up frame	B	A	4
Order custom windows	C	None	11
Erect outside walls	D	B	3
Do electrical wiring	E	D	4
Do plumbing	F	D	3
Put in duct work	G	D	4
Hang dry wall	H	E, F, G	3
Install windows	I	B, C	1
Paint and clean up	J	H	2

Solution

We first need to choose distributions for the uncertain activity times. Then, given any randomly generated activity times, we will illustrate a method for calculating the length of the project and identifying the activities on the critical path.

The Pert Distribution As always, there are several reasonable candidate probability distributions we could use for the random activity times. Here we illustrate a distribution that has become popular in project scheduling, called the Pert distribution.[3] As shown

---

[3] It is named after the acronym PERT (Program Review and Evaluation Technique) that is synonymous with project scheduling in an uncertain environment.

in Figure 12.20, it is a "rounded" version of the triangular distribution that is specified by three parameters: a minimum value, a most likely value, and a maximum value. The distribution in the figure uses the values 7, 10, and 19 for these three values, which implies a mean of 11. We will use this distribution for activity C. Similarly, for the other activities, we choose parameters for the Pert distribution that lead to the means in Table 12.2. In reality, it would be done the other way around. The contractor would estimate the minimum, most likely, and maximum parameters for the various activities, and the means would follow from these. (We wanted to keep the means the same as the activity times from Chapter 5 as a basis for comparison.)

FIGURE 12.20
Pert Distribution

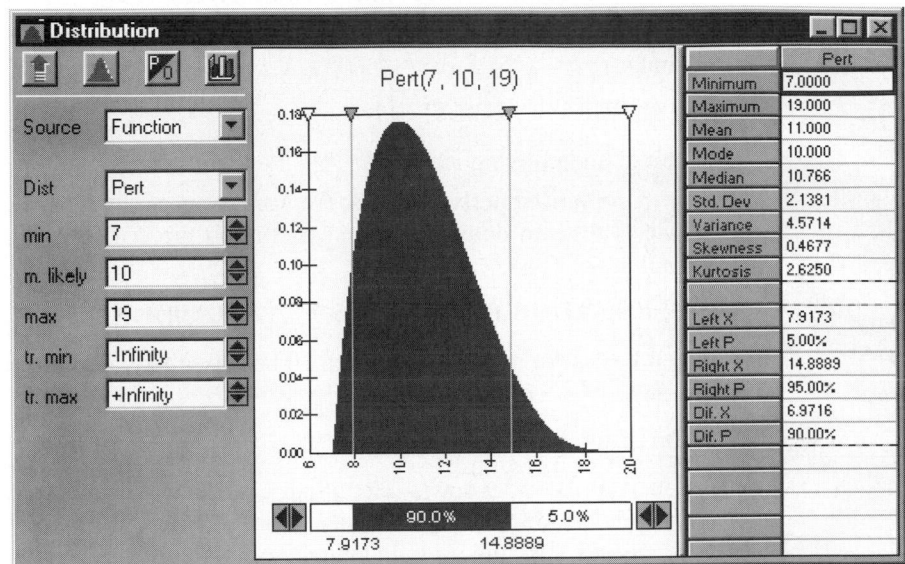

DEVELOPING THE SIMULATION MODEL

The key to the model is representing the project network in activity-on-arc form, as in Figure 12.21, and then finding E_j for each j, where E_j is the earliest time we can get to node j. We stated in Chapter 5 that when the nodes are numbered so that all arcs go from lower-numbered nodes to higher-numbered nodes, we can calculate the E_j's iteratively, starting with $E_1 = 0$, with the equation

$$E_j = \max(E_i + t_{ij}) \tag{12.1}$$

Here, the maximum is taken over all arcs leading into node j, and t_{ij} is the activity time on such an arc. Then E_n is the time to complete the project, where n is the index of the finish node. This will make it very easy to calculate the project length.

We also need a method for identifying the critical activities for any given activity times. By definition, an activity is critical if a small increase in its activity time causes the project time to increase. Therefore, we will keep track of two sets of activity times

FIGURE 12.21
Project Network for
Room-Building
Project

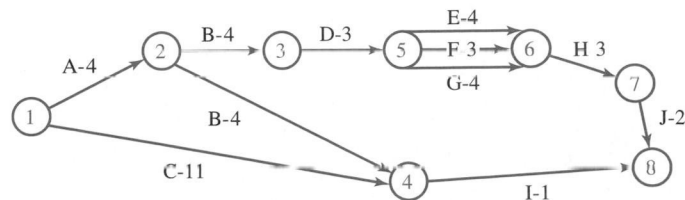

and associated project times. The first uses the simulated activity times. The second adds a small amount, such as 0.001 day, to a "selected" activity's time. By using the RISKSIMTABLE function with a list as long as the number of activities, we can make each activity the "selected" activity in this method. The spreadsheet model appears in Figure 12.22, and the details are as follows. (See the PROJECTSIM.XLS file.)

❶ Inputs. Enter the parameters of the Pert activity time distributions in the shaded cells and the implied means next to them. As discussed above, we actually chose the minimum, most likely, and maximum values while in @Risk's Model window to achieve the means in Table 12.2. Note that some of these distributions are symmetric about the most likely value, whereas others are skewed.

❷ Activity times. Generate random activity times in column I by entering the formula

=RISKPERT(E5,F5,G5)

in cell I5 and copying it down.

❸ Augmented activity times. We want to successively add a small amount to each activity's time to determine whether it is on the critical path. To do this, enter the formula

=RISKSIMTABLE({1, 2, 3, 4, 5, 6, 7, 8, 9, 10})

in cell B16. (We use a list of length 10 because there are 10 activities.) Then enter the formula

=I5+IF(Index=C5,0.001,0)

in cell J5 and copy it down. (Here, Index is the range name of cell B16.) For example, if we are checking whether activity D (the 4th activity) is critical, the Index cell will be 4, and we will run a simulation where activity D's time is augmented by 0.001 and the other activity times are unchanged.

	A	B	C	D	E	F	G	H	I	J
1	**Room construction project**									
2										
3	**Data on activity network**					Parameters of PERT distributions				
4	Activity	Code	Numeric index	Predecessors	Min	Most likely	Max	Implied mean	Duration	Duration+
5	Prepare foundation	A	1	None	1.5	3.5	8.5	4	3.749	3.750
6	Put up frame	B	2	A	3	4	5	4	3.633	3.633
7	Order custom windows	C	3	None	7	10	19	11	8.844	8.844
8	Erect outside walls	D	4	B	2	2.5	6	3	2.283	2.283
9	Do electrical wiring	E	5	D	3	3.5	7	4	3.586	3.586
10	Do plumbing	F	6	D	2	2.5	6	3	2.753	2.753
11	Put in duct work	G	7	D	2	4	6	4	3.238	3.238
12	Hang dry wall	H	8	E,F,G	2.5	3	3.5	3	3.061	3.061
13	Install windows	I	9	B,C	0.5	1	1.5	1	1.155	1.155
14	Paint and clean up	J	10	H	1.5	2	2.5	2	1.887	1.887
15										
16	**Index of activity to increase**	1								
17										
18	**Event times**									
19		Node	Event time	Event time+						
20		1	0	0						
21		2	3.749	3.750						
22		3	7.382	7.383						
23		4	8.844	8.844						
24		5	9.665	9.666						
25		6	13.251	13.252						
26		7	16.313	16.314						
27		8	18.200	18.201						
28										
29	**Increase in project time?**	1								

FIGURE 12.22 Project Scheduling Simulation Model

4   Event times. We want to use equation (12.1) to calculate the node event times in the range B20:B27. There is no quick way to enter the required formulas. (We see no way of using copy and paste.) We need to use the project network as a guide for each node. Begin by entering 0 in cell B20. Then enter the appropriate formulas in the other cells. For example, the formulas in cells B22, B23, and B27 are

=B21+I6
=MAX(B20+I7,B21+I6)

and

=RISKOUTPUT()+MAX(B23+I13,B26+I14)

To understand these, note that node 3 has only one arc leading into it, and this arc originates at node 2. No MAX is required for this node's equation. In contrast, node 4 has two arcs leading into it, from nodes 1 and 2, so a MAX is required. Similarly, node 8 requires a MAX because it has two arcs leading into it. Also, it is the finish node, so we designate its event time cell as an @Risk output cell—it contains the time to complete the project.

5   Augmented event times. Copy the formulas in the range B20:B27 to the range C20:C27 to calculate the event times when the selected activity's time is augmented by 0.001.

6   Project time increases? To check whether the selected activity's increased activity time increases the project time, enter the formula

=RISKOUTPUT()+IF(C27>B27,1,0)

If this calculates to 1, then the selected activity is critical for these particular activity times. Otherwise, it is not. Note that this cell is also designated as an @Risk output cell.

USING @RISK

We set the number of iterations to 1000 and the number of simulations to 10 (one for each activity that we want to check for being critical). After running @Risk, we request the histogram of project times in Figure 12.23 (page 642). Recall from the example in Chapter 5 that when the activity times are not considered random, the project time is 20 days. Now it varies from a low of 16.09 days to a high of 25.20 days, with an average of 20.38 days.[4] Although the 5th and 95th percentiles appear in the figure, it might be more interesting (and depressing) to Tom Lingley to see the probabilities of various project times being exceeded. For example, we entered 20 in the Left X box next to the histogram. The Left P value implies there is about a 59% chance that the project will not be completed within 20 days. Similarly, the values in the Right X and Right P boxes imply that the chance of the project lasting longer than 23 days is slightly greater than 5%. This is certainly not good news for Lingley, and he might have to resort to the crashing we discussed in Chapter 5.

The summary measures for the B29 output cell appear in Figure 12.24 (page 642). Each "simulation" in this output represents one selected activity being increased slightly. The Mean column indicates the fraction of iterations where the project time increases as a result of the selected activity's time increase. Hence, it represents the

---

[4]It can be shown mathematically that the expected project time is *always* greater than when the expected activity times are used to calculate the project time, as we did in Chapter 5. In other words, an assumption of certainty always leads to an underestimation of the true expected project time.

FIGURE 12.23
Histogram of Project
Completion Time

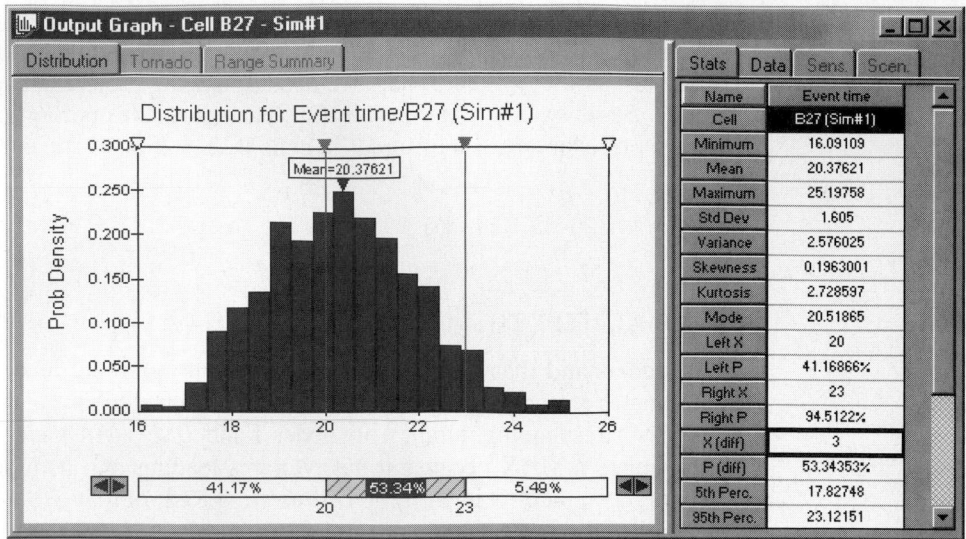

FIGURE 12.24
Probabilities of
Activities Being
Critical

probability that this activity is critical. For example, the first activity (A) is always critical, the third activity (C) is never critical, and the fifth activity (E) is critical about 44% of the time. More specifically, we see that the critical path always includes activities A, B, D, H, J, and one of the three "parallel" activities E, F, and G. ■

PROBLEMS

Skill-Building Problems

1. If the number of competitors in the Miller bidding example were to double, how would the optimal bid change?

2. Again referring to the Miller bidding example, if the average bid for each competitor stayed the same, but their bids exhibited less variability, would the optimal bid increase or decrease? To study this question assume that each competitor's bid, expressed as a multiple of Miller's cost to complete the project, follows each of the following distributions.

a. Triangular with parameters 1.0, 1.3, and 2.4
b. Triangular with parameters 1.2, 1.3, and 2.2
c. Check (in @Risk's Model window) that the distributions in parts **a** and **b** have the same mean as the original triangular distribution in the example, but smaller standard deviations. What is the common mean? Why is it not the same as the most likely value, 1.3?

3. Rerun Deming's funnel experiment simulation, but now keep track of the x-coordinate of the 50th drop for each rule. Summarize your findings.

4. A car company paints all its cars yellow. In the company vault there is a sample of the original yellow used to paint this year's cars. Suppose that each time a new batch of yellow paint is mixed up, the company matches the new batch to the most recent batch—not the original. Which of the four funnel rules does this illustrate? What would you expect to occur?

5. Suppose missile tests indicate that on average, a missile misses a target by 50 feet. Suppose a missile is fired, and it lands 80 feet east of the target. Then the army adjusts the control mechanism on the missile to a setting 80 feet west of the current setting. Which of the rules from Deming's funnel experiment is being followed here? Is the army's strategy a good one?

6. In Example 12.4 we simulated the time until failure of the machine. Suppose that the machine has a mission to accomplish. To accomplish this mission, it must survive at least 125 hours. The component times are assumed to be gamma distributed with $\alpha = 25$ and $\beta = 4$, as in the example. The company wants to know how many components to include in parallel (in each of the three modules) so that there is a 95% probability that the machine will fulfill its mission. Use @RISK to determine the number of components to include. (You can extend the model to more than 20 components per module if necessary.)

7. Consider a device that requires two batteries to function. If either of these batteries dies, the device will not work. Currently there are two brand new batteries in the device, and there are three extra brand new batteries. Each battery, once it is placed in the device, lasts a random amount of time that is lognormally distributed with mean 20 hours and standard deviation 5 hours. When any of the batteries in the device dies, it is immediately replaced by an extra (if an extra is still available). Use @RISK to simulate the time the device can last with the batteries currently available.

8. For the room-building project in Example 12.5, find a 95% confidence interval for the mean total project time, based on 500 iterations. Then rerun the simulation with 2000 iterations and find the new 95% confidence interval for the mean total project time. How do the two confidence intervals compare?

9. The city of Bloomington is about to build a new water treatment plant. Once the plant is designed (D), we can select the site (S), the building contractor (C), and the operating personnel (P). Once the site is selected, we can erect the building (B). We can order the water treatment machine (W) and prepare the operations manual (M) only after the contractor is selected. We can begin training (T) the operators when both the operations manual and operating personnel selection are completed. When the treatment plant and the building are finished, we can install the treatment machine (I). Once the treatment machine is installed and operators are trained, we can obtain an operating license (L). The estimated mean and standard deviation of the time (in months) needed to complete each activity are given in Table 12.3. Use simulation to estimate the probability that the project will be completed in (a) under 50 days and (b) more than 55 days. Also estimate the probabilities that B, I, and T are critical activities.

TABLE 12.3	Activity Time Information for Water Treatment Problem	
	Mean	**Standard Deviation**
Activity D	6	1.5
Activity S	2	3.0
Activity C	4	1.0
Activity P	3	1.0
Activity B	24	6.0
Activity W	14	4.0
Activity M	3	0.4
Activity T	4	1.0
Activity I	6	1.0
Activity L	3	6.0

10. To complete an addition to the Business Building, the activities in Table 12.4 need to be completed (all times are in months). The project is completed once Room 111 has been destroyed and the main structure has been built.

TABLE 12.4	Information on Activities for Business Building Problem		
	Predecessors	**Mean Time**	**Standard Deviation**
Activity A: Hire workers	—	4	0.6
Activity B: Dig big hole	A	9	2.5
Activity C: Pour foundation	B	5	1.0
Activity D: Destroy room	A	7	2.0
Activity E: Build main structure	C	10	1.5

a. Estimate the probability that it will take at least 3 years to complete the addition.

b. For each activity, estimate the probability that it will be a critical activity.

11. To build Indiana University's new law building, the activities in Table 12.5 must be completed (all times are in months).

a. Estimate the probability that the project will take less than 30 months to complete.

b. Estimate the probability that the project will take more than 3 years to complete.

c. For each of the activities A, B, C, and G, estimate the probability that it is a critical activity.

Skill-Extending Problems

12. Consider the following variation of the model in Example 12.4. Suppose that there are m modules in series and that module i consists of n_i components in parallel. The components in module i are identical in that they have a common lognormal distribution with mean μ_i and standard deviation σ_i. However, these parameters can depend on i, that is, they can vary from one module to another. Use @RISK to simulate the time to machine failure when $m = 3$, $n_1 = 5$, $n_2 = 8$, and $n_3 = 3$. Use the parameters $\mu_1 = 100$, $\mu_2 = 90$, $\mu_3 = 120$, $\sigma_1 = 20$, $\sigma_2 = 25$, and $\sigma_3 = 30$. As part of your simulation, find the fraction of the iterations in which machine failure is caused by failure of module 1; by failure of module 2; by failure of module 3.

13. Referring to the previous problem, suppose your job is to build as reliable a machine as possible with a given budget. You again have $m = 3$ modules, and you already own exactly one component for each module. For c_i dollars apiece, you can purchase as many extra components for module i as you like, but you have only C dollars to spend. Run several simulations, using the same distributions as in the previous problem, to see how you should best spend your money. Assume that $c_1 = \$100$, $c_2 = \$80$, $c_3 = \$140$, and $C = \$500$.

14. Rework the previous problem, but instead of basing your decision on the time until machine failure (which you want to maximize), base it on the probability that the machine will last at least 125 hours. That is, for any configuration of components, your only interest is in the fraction of iterations in which the machine lasts at least 125 hours. Will you allocate your budget in the same way with this objective?

TABLE 12.5 **Information on Activities for Law Building Problem**

	Predecessors	Mean Time	Standard Deviation
Activity A: Obtain funding	—	6	0.6
Activity B: Design building	A	8	1.3
Activity C: Prepare site	A	2	0.2
Activity D: Lay foundation	B, C	2	0.3
Activity E: Erect walls and roof	D	3	1.0
Activity F: Finish exterior	E	3	0.6
Activity G: Finish interior	D	7	1.5
Activity H: Landscape grounds	F, G	5	1.2

12.3 FINANCIAL MODELS

The opportunities for using simulation in financial applications are numerous. Future cash flows, future stock prices, and future interest rates are some of the many uncertain variables financial analysts must deal with. In every direction they turn, they see uncertainty. In this section we will analyze a few typical financial applications that can benefit from simulation modeling.

Financial Planning Models

Many companies, such as GM, Eli Lilly, Procter & Gamble, and Pfizer, use simulation in their capital budgeting and financial planning processes. Simulation can be used to model the uncertainty associated with future cash flows. In particular, simulation can be used to answer questions such as the following:

- What are the mean and variance of a project's net present value (NPV)?
- What is the probability that a project will have a negative NPV?
- What are the mean and variance of a company's profit during the next fiscal year?
- What is the probability that a company will have to borrow more than $2 million during the next year?

The following example illustrates how simulation can be used to evaluate an investment opportunity.

EXAMPLE   12.6

DEVELOPING A NEW CAR AT GF AUTO

General Ford (GF) Auto Corporation is developing a new type of compact car. This car is assumed to generate sales for the next 10 years. GF has gathered information about the following quantities through focus groups with the marketing and engineering departments.

- **Fixed cost of developing car.** This cost is assumed to be normally distributed with mean and standard deviation $2.3 billion and $0.5 billion. The fixed cost is incurred at the beginning of year 1, before any sales are recorded.

- **Variable production cost.** This cost, which includes all variable production costs required to build a single car, is assumed to be normally distributed during year 1 with mean and standard deviation $7800 and $600. Each year after year 1, the variable production cost is the previous year's variable production cost multiplied by an inflation factor. Each year this inflation factor is assumed to be normally distributed with mean 1.05 (a 5% increase) and standard deviation 0.015. All production costs are assumed to occur at the ends of the respective years.

- **Selling price.** The price in year 1 is already set at $11,800. After year 1 the price will increase by the same inflation factor that drives production costs. Like production costs, revenues from sales are assumed to occur at the ends of the respective years.

- **Demand.** The demand for the car in year 1 is assumed to be normally distributed with mean 100,000 and standard deviation 10,000. After year 1 the demand in a given year is assumed to be normally distributed with mean equal to the *actual* demand in the previous year and standard deviation 10,000. For example, if the observed demand in year 3 is 105,000, then the demand distribution in year 4 has mean 105,000. An implication of this assumption is that demands in successive years are *not* probabilistically independent. For example, if the demand in one year is large, the mean demand for the next year is also large, so that the actual demand for the next year will tend to be large.

- **Production.** In any particular year GF plans to base its production policy on the probability distribution of demand for that year—*before* the actual demand for that year is observed. In particular, if the expected demand in year t is μ and the standard deviation of demand is σ, then GF's policy is to produce $\mu + k\sigma$ cars, where k is a multiple that GF will have to select. For example, if it chooses $k = 1$, then its production quantity in any year will be one standard deviation above the expected demand. From the properties of the normal distribution, using $k = 1$ implies that the chances are approximately 5 out of 6 of meeting all demand for the year. (This is because a normal random variable has approximate probability 5/6 of being no more than one standard deviation *above* the mean.) If demand in any year is greater than production, the excess demand is lost. However, if production in any year is greater than demand, GF will sell the excess cars at an end-of-year discount of 30%.

- **Interest rate.** GF plans to use a 10% interest rate to discount future cash flows. This means, for example, that a cash flow of $1 at the beginning of year 1 is equivalent to a cash flow of $1.10 at the end of year 1.

    Given these assumptions, GF wants to develop a simulation model that will evaluate its NPV for this new car over the 10-year time horizon.

Solution

This model is like most financial multiyear spreadsheet models. The completed model looks complex, but most of the work is for the first year or two. From that point, we simply copy to the other years to complete the model.

DEVELOPING THE SIMULATION MODEL

The simulation model for GF appears in Figure 12.25. (See the file GFAUTO.XLS.) It can be formed as follows.

	A	B	C	D	E	F	G	H	I	J	K
1	GF new car simulation										
2				All cash flows are assumed to occur at the ends of the respective years except for the fixed costs, which occur at the beginning of year 1.							
3	Input section								Range names used:		
4	Fixed costs			Demand in year 1					FCMean - B6		
5	Normal distribution ($ billions)			Normal distribution (1000s of cars)					FCStdev - B7		
6	Mean	2.3		Mean	100				VC1Mean - B11		
7	Stdev	0.5		Stdev	10				VC1Stdev - B12		
8									InflMean - B16		
9	Variable production cost per car in year 1			Demand in other years					InflStdev - B17		
10	Normal distribution ($1000s)			Normal distribution (1000s of cars)					Price1 - B29		
11	Mean	7.8		Mean	demand from previous year				IntRate - B22		
12	Stdev	0.6		Stdev	10				Dem1Mean - E6		
13									Dem1Stdev - E7		
14	Inflation factor			Production policy					DemStdev - E12		
15	Normal distribution			Production each year is the mean demand plus a multiple of the st dev of					ProdFactor - E20		
16	Mean	1.05		demand (for that year). If demand is greater than supply, excess demand is lost.					Discount - E23		
17	Stdev	0.015		If the supply is greater than demand, the excess are sold at a discount.					Costs - B33:K33		
18									Revenues - B34:K34		
19	Selling price in year 1			Multiple (k) of st dev used for setting production quantity							
20	No uncertainty ($1000s)	11.8			0.8						
21											
22	Interest rate	10%		Year-end discount for leftover cars at the end of the year							
23					30%						
24											
25	Simulation section										
26	Year	1	2	3	4	5	6	7	8	9	10
27	Inflation factor	N/A	1.050	1.050	1.050	1.050	1.050	1.050	1.050	1.050	1.050
28	Production (1000s)	108	108.000	108.000	108.000	108.000	108.000	108.000	108.000	108.000	108.000
29	Demand (1000s)	100.000	100.000	100.000	100.000	100.000	100.000	100.000	100.000	100.000	100.000
30	Var prod cost ($1000s)	7.800	8.190	8.600	9.029	9.481	9.955	10.453	10.975	11.524	12.100
31	Selling price ($1000s)	11.8	12.390	13.010	13.660	14.343	15.060	15.813	16.604	17.434	18.306
32											
33	Production cost ($ millions)	842.400	884.520	928.746	975.183	1023.942	1075.140	1128.897	1185.341	1244.608	1306.839
34	Sales revenue ($ millions)	1246.08	1308.384	1373.803	1442.493	1514.618	1590.349	1669.866	1753.360	1841.028	1933.079
35											
36	Fixed cost ($ millions)	$2,300									
37											
38	NPV ($ millions)										
39	Production costs	$6,267.30									
40	Revenue	$9,270.60									
41											
42	Total NPV ($ millions)	$703.30									

FIGURE 12.25 GF Auto Simulation Model

❶ Inputs. Enter the various inputs in the shaded cells.

❷ Production multiplier. The only real decision GF has to make is the multiplier k for its production level. To experiment with several values of this multiplier, enter the formula

=RISKSIMTABLE({0.8, 1, 1.2})

in cell E20. Other (or more) values could be tried here.

❸ Variable cost inflation factors. Rows 26–42 contain a single 10-year simulation. The approach is to enter appropriate formulas in columns B and C for years 1 and 2, then copy the year 2 formulas to the columns for the other years, and finally calculate the values in rows 36, 39, 40, and 42. Begin by entering the variable production cost inflation factor relating year 2 to year 1 in cell C27 with the formula

=RISKNORMAL(InflMean,InflStdev)

and copy this across to the rest of row 27.

❹ Production quantities. The production quantity in year 1 is based on the expected demand and the standard deviation of demand in year 1, so enter the formula

=Dem1Mean+ProdFactor*Dem1Stdev

in cell B28. For other years, the expected demand is the previous year's actual demand, and this is used to calculate the production quantity. Therefore, for year 2 enter the formula

=B29+ProdFactor*DemStdev

in cell C28 and copy it across to the rest of row 28.

❺ Demands. Generate the demand in year 1 in cell B29 with the formula

=RISKNORMAL(Dem1Mean,Dem1Stdev)

As in the previous step, the expected demand in year 2 is the actual demand from year 1, so generate the demand for year 2 in cell C29 with the formula

=RISKNORMAL(B29,DemStdev)

and copy this to the rest of row 29 to generate demands for the other years.

❻ Variable production costs. Generate the variable production cost for year 1 in cell B30 with the formula

=RISKNORMAL(VC1Mean,VC1Stdev)

Then use the inflation factor in row 27 to generate the variable production cost for year 2 in cell C30 with the formula

=B30*C27

and copy this across to the rest of row 30.

❼ Selling prices. Enter the (nonrandom) selling price for year 1 in cell B31 with the formula

=Price1

Then generate the price for year 2 in cell C31 with the formula

=B31*C27

and copy this across to the rest of row 31.

⑧ Production costs. The production cost for any year is the production quantity multiplied by the variable production cost, so enter the formula

=B28*B30

in cell B33 and copy it to the rest of row 33. (Note that because the production quantity is in thousands of cars and variable production cost is in thousands of dollars, the resulting product will automatically be in *millions* of dollars.)

⑨ Revenues. The revenue in any year is calculated in one of two possible ways. If demand is greater than the production quantity, revenue is the selling price multiplied by the production quantity. Otherwise, if demand is less than the production quantity, revenue is the selling price multiplied by the demand, plus the discounted sales price multiplied by the number of cars left over. Therefore, calculate the revenue for year 1 in cell B34 with the formula

=IF(B28<B29,B31*B28,B31*(B29+(1-Discount)*(B28-B29)))

and copy this to the rest of row 34.

⑩ Fixed cost. Generate the fixed cost of developing the car in cell B36 with the formula

=RISKNORMAL(FCMean,FCStdev)*1000

Note that the factor of 1000 converts billions of dollars to millions.

⑪ NPVs. Calculate the NPV of all production costs (in millions of dollars) in cell B39 with the formula

=NPV(IntRate,Costs)

Similarly, enter the formula

=NPV(IntRate,Revenues)

in cell B40 for revenues. Note that the NPV function takes two arguments: the interest rate used for discounting and a stream of cash flows, beginning with the flow at the *end* of year 1.

⑫ Total NPV. Calculate the total NPV in cell B42 with the formula

=RISKOUTPUT()+B40-B36-B39

(This is the only cell we designate as an @Risk output cell.) The fixed costs occur at the *beginning* of year 1, so they are not discounted when calculating total NPV.

USING @RISK

We set the number of iterations to 1000 and the number of simulations to 3 (one for each trial value of the multiplier k). After running @Risk, we obtain the summary measures for total NPV in Figure 12.26. We see that the multiplier k definitely makes a difference. The value $k = 1.2$ is better in all respects than $k = 0.8$ or $k = 1.0$. It has a higher mean, more upside potential (higher maximum and 95th percentile), and slightly less downside risk (less negative minimum and 5th percentile). Based on these results, GF might want to experiment with even larger values of k. Higher values of k mean larger production quantities. This will result in more end-of-year discounted sales, but it is evidently better than lost sales from insufficient supply.

The corresponding histogram for $k = 1.2$ appears in Figure 12.27. Its wide spread indicates the large amount of uncertainty about the 10-year NPV for this car. GF could make a lot of money, or it could lose a lot. We entered two representative values in

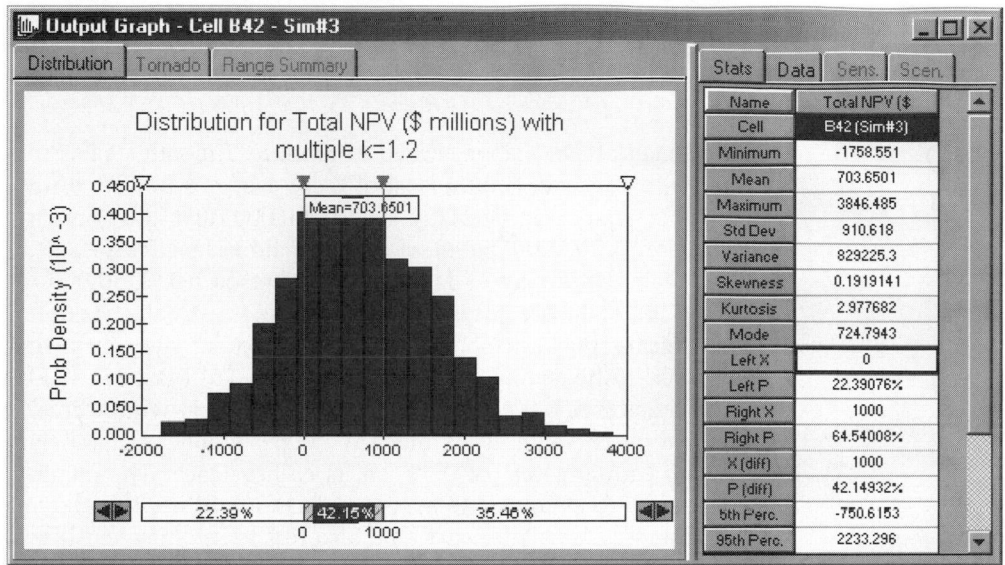

Cell	Name	Minimum	Mean	Maximum	x1=	p1=	x2=	p2=
B42 (Sim#1)	Total NPV ($ millions)	-1773.31	673.077	3741.24	-758.8632	5%	2174.746	95%
B42 (Sim#2)	Total NPV ($ millions)	-1765.93	689.6397	3793.863	-758.7481	5%	2206.259	95%
B42 (Sim#3)	Total NPV ($ millions)	-1758.551	703.6501	3846.485	-750.6153	5%	2233.296	95%

FIGURE 12.26 Summary Measures for Total NPV

FIGURE 12.27 Histogram of Total NPV

the Left X and Right X boxes. They show that the probability of a *negative* NPV is slightly greater than 0.22 and the probability of NPV being less than $1 billion is about 0.65. We certainly would not discourage the company from proceeding with this car, because there is a lot of potential for profit, but it should also be aware of the potential for loss. ∎

Cash Balance Models

All companies track their cash balance through time. As specific payments come due, companies may need to take out short-term loans in order to keep a minimal cash balance. The following example illustrates one such application.

EXAMPLE 12.7

MAINTAINING A MINIMAL CASH BALANCE AT ENTSON

The Entson Company believes that its monthly sales during the period from November 2000 to July 2001 are normally distributed with the means and standard deviations given in Table 12.6 (page 650). Each month Entson incurs fixed costs of $250,000. In March taxes of $150,000 and in June taxes of $50,000 must be paid. Dividends of

TABLE 12.6	Monthly Sales (in Thousands of Dollars) for Entson								
	Nov.	**Dec.**	**Jan.**	**Feb.**	**Mar.**	**Apr.**	**May**	**Jun.**	**Jul.**
Mean	1500	1600	1800	1500	1900	2600	2400	1900	1300
St Dev	70	75	80	80	100	125	120	90	70

$50,000 must also be paid in June. Entson estimates that its receipts in a given month are a weighted sum of sales from the current month, the previous month, and two months ago with weights 0.2, 0.6, and 0.2. In symbols, if R_t and S_t represent receipts and sales in month t, then

$$R_t = 0.2S_{t-2} + 0.6S_{t-1} + 0.2S_t \qquad (12.2)$$

The materials and labor needed to produce a month's sales must be purchased one month in advance, and the cost of these averages to 80% of the product's sales. For example, if sales in February are $1,500,000, then the February materials and labor costs are $1,200,000, but these must be paid in January.

At the beginning of January 2001, Entson has $250,000 in cash. The company would like to ensure that each month's ending cash balance never dips below $250,000. This means that Entson might have to take out short-term (one-month) loans. For example, if the ending cash balance at the end of March is $200,000, Entson will take out a loan for $50,000, which it will then pay back (with interest) one month later. The interest rate on a short-term loan is 1% per month. At the beginning of each month, Entson earns interest of 0.5% on its cash balance. The company would like to use simulation to estimate the maximum loan it will need to take out to meet its desired minimum cash balance. It would also like to see how sensitive the results are to the sales data, shown in Table 12.6. In particular, considering the data in this table as a "base case," it would like to run a simulation in which the means are 20% below the values in the table and another simulation in which the means are 20% above those in the table.

Solution

There is a considerable amount of bookkeeping in this simulation, so it is a good idea to list the events in chronological order that occur each month.

- Entson observes its beginning cash balance.
- Entson receives interest on its beginning cash balance.
- Receipts arrive and expenses are paid (including payback of the previous month's loan, if any, with interest).
- If necessary, Entson takes out a short-term loan.
- The final cash balance is observed, which becomes next month's beginning cash balance.

DEVELOPING THE SIMULATION MODEL

The completed simulation model appears in Figure 12.28. (See the file CASH-BAL.XLS.) It requires the following steps.

1 **Inputs.** Enter the inputs in the shaded cells. Note that we are going to simulate loans only for the period from January 2001 to June 2001. However, we need sales figures in November and December from the previous year to generate receipts for

	A	B	C	D	E	F	G	H	I	J	K	L	M
1	Entson cash balance simulation												
2						All monetary values are in $1000s.							
3	Input section												
4	Distribution of monthly sales (normal)												
5		Nov	Dec	Jan	Feb	Mar	Apr	May	Jun	Jul	Range names used:		
6	Mean	1500	1600	1800	1500	1900	2800	2400	1900	1300	RecFactors - B14:D14		
7	St Dev	70	75	80	80	100	125	120	90	70	CostPct - B17		
8											InitCash - B19		
9	Monthly fixed cost			250	250	250	250	250	250		MinCashBal - B20		
10	Tax, dividend expenses			0	0	150	0	0	100		IntRateLoan - B23		
11											IntRateCash - B24		
12	Receipts in any month are of form: A*(sales from 2 months ago)+B*(previous month's sales)+C*(current month's sales), where:										BaseLev - B26		
13		A	B	C							BaseLevList - D26:F26		
14		0.2	0.6	0.2							Loans - D44:I44		
15											IntPayments - E41:J41		
16	Cost of materials and labor for next month, spent this month, is a percentage of product's sales from next month, where the percentage is:												
17		80%											
18													
19	Initial cash in Jan	250											
20	Min cash balance	250											
21													
22	Monthly interest rates												
23	Loan interest rate	1.0%											
24	Interest rate on cash	0.5%											
25				Base levels to investigate									
26	Base level of sales	80%		80%	100%	120%							
27													
28	Simulation section												
29		Nov	Dec	Jan	Feb	Mar	Apr	May	Jun	Jul			
30	Actual sales	1200.000	1280.000	1440.000	1200.000	1520.000	2080.000	1920.000	1520.000	1040.000			
31													
32	Cash, receipts												
33	Beginning cash balance			250.000	337.250	250.000	250.000	250.000	250.000				
34	Interest on cash balance			1.250	1.686	1.250	1.250	1.250	1.250				
35	Receipts			1296	1360	1312	1568	1936	1872				
36	Costs												
37	Fixed costs			250	250	250	250	250	250				
38	Tax, dividend expenses			0	0	150	0	0	100				
39	Material, labor expenses			960.000	1216.000	1664.000	1536.000	1216.000	832.000				
40	Loan payback (principal)			0.000	17.064	767.814	984.564	513.314	0.000				
41	Loan payback (interest)			0.000	0.171	7.678	9.846	5.133	0.000				
42													
43	Cash balance before loan			337.250	232.936	-517.814	-734.564	-263.314	427.936				
44	Loan amount (if any)			0.000	17.064	767.814	984.564	513.314	0.000				
45	Final cash balance			337.250	250.000	250.000	250.000	250.000	427.936				
46													
47	Maximum loan	984.564											
48	Total intest on loans	22.828											

FIGURE 12.28 Cash Balance Simulation Model

January and February. Also, we need July 2001 sales to generate the material and labor costs paid in June 2001.

❷ **Scenarios.** Enter the formula

=RISKSIMTABLE(BaseLevList)

in cell B26. This allows us to run three simulations simultaneously. The middle value in the list, 1, corresponds to the base case. The other two values, 0.8 and 1.2, correspond to the scenarios in which mean sales are 20% below and 20% above the base case.

❸ **Actual sales.** Generate the sales in row 30 by entering the formula

=RISKNORMAL(B6*BaseLev,B7)

in cell B30 and copying across.

❹ **Beginning cash balance.** For January 2001 enter the cash balance with the formula

=InitCash

in cell D33. Then for the other months enter the formula

=D45

in cell E33 and copy it across row 33.

❺ Incomes. Entson's incomes (interest on cash balance and receipts) are calculated in rows 34 and 35. To calculate these, enter the formulas

=IntRateCash*D33

and

=SUMPRODUCT(RecFactors,B30:D30)

in cells D34 and D35 and copy them across rows 34 and 35. This latter formula, which is based on equation (12.2), multiplies the fixed weights in row 14 by the relevant sales and adds these products to calculate receipts.

❻ Expenses. Entson's expenses (fixed costs, taxes and dividends, material and labor costs, and payback of the previous month's loan) are calculated in rows 37–41. Calculate these by entering the formulas

=D9
=D10
=CostPct*E30
=D44

and

=D44*IntRateLoan

in cells D37, D38, D39, E40, and E41 and copying these across rows 37–41. (For the loan payback, we are assuming that no loan payback is due in January.)

❼ Cash balance before loan. Calculate the cash balance before the loan (if any) by entering the formula

=SUM(D33:D35)-SUM(D37:D40)

in cell D43 and copying it across row 43.

❽ Amount of loan. If the value in row 43 is below the minimum cash balance ($250,000), Entson must borrow enough to bring the cash balance up to this minimum. Otherwise, no loan is necessary. Therefore, enter the formula

=MAX(MinCashBal-D43,0)

in cell D44 and copy it across row 44.

❾ Final cash balance. Calculate the final cash balance by entering the formula

=D43+D44

in cell D45 and copying it across row 45.

❿ Maximum loan, total interest. We will keep track of two outputs, the maximum loan required and the total interest paid on all loans. Calculate the maximum loan from January to June in cell B47 with the formula

=RISKOUTPUT()+MAX(Loans)

Then calculate the total interest paid on all loans in cell B48 with the formula

=RISKOUTPUT()+SUM(IntPayments)

USING @RISK

We set the number of iterations to 1000 and the number of simulations to 3 (one for each value in the BaseLevList range). After running @Risk, we obtain the results in Figures 12.29 and 12.30. The summary values in Figure 12.29 indicate that for the base case (simulation #2) the maximum loan varied considerably, from a low of $463,255 to a high of $1,446,719. The average was $945,007. They also show that when sales are *below* the base case (simulation #1), the maximum loan tends to be larger. The opposite is true when sales are above the base case (simulation #3). This makes sense. Sales generate cash, so that when sales are low, less cash is generated and higher loans are required. We also see that Entson is spending about $20,000 on average in interest on the loans (in the base case), although the actual amounts vary considerably from one iteration to another.

We can also gain insights by creating a summary chart of the series of loans. (See the preceding chapter for a discussion of @Risk's summary chart feature.) To obtain this chart, we must first identify the Loans range as an output range. To do so, highlight this range and click on the Add Output cells button on the @Risk toolbar (from within Excel). You will be asked to name this output range. We used the name Loans. You will then see that the formulas in row 44 change. For example, the formula in cell D44 becomes

=RISKOUTPUT(,"Loans",1)+MAX(MinCashBal-D43,0)

The first part of this formula simply tells @Risk that this is the first cell of an output range named Loans.

FIGURE 12.29
Summary Measures for All Simulations

Cell	Name	Minimum	Mean	Maximum	x1=	p1=	x2=	p2=
B47 (Sim#1)	Maximum loan	496.2768	985.5227	1487.102	725.0826	5%	1260.107	95%
B47 (Sim#2)	Maximum loan	463.2547	945.0069	1446.719	684.0605	5%	1219.736	95%
B47 (Sim#3)	Maximum loan	430.2325	904.3671	1406.299	644.8983	5%	1179.047	95%
B48 (Sim#1)	Total intest on	10.02795	23.35689	40.00323	15.86434	5%	31.35686	95%
B48 (Sim#2)	Total intest on	7.077289	19.87827	34.07298	12.93145	5%	27.20266	95%
B48 (Sim#3)	Total intest on	5.827201	17.06782	29.93618	11.15806	5%	23.70617	95%

FIGURE 12.30
Histogram of Maximum Loan for Base-Case Simulation

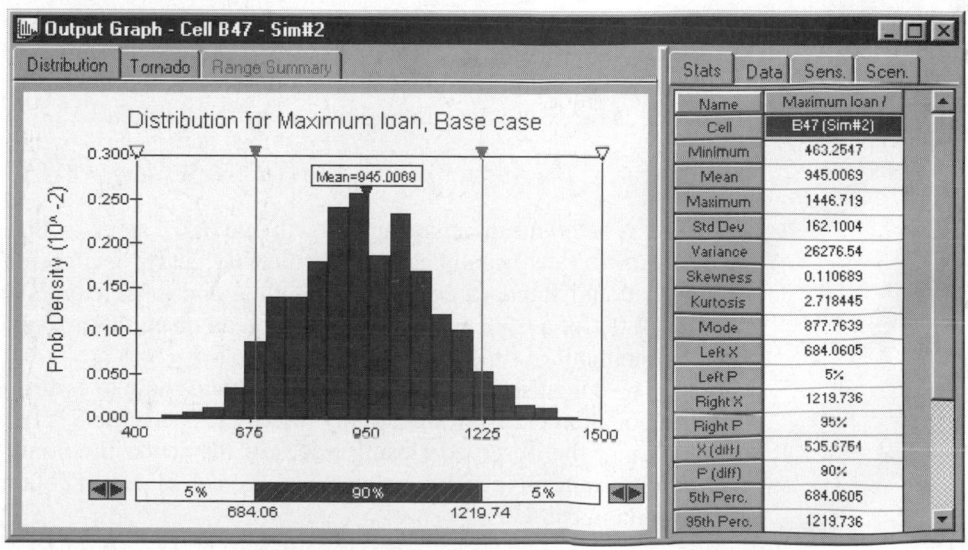

After running the simulation, we can then request a summary chart for this output range. (The easiest way to do so is to right-click on the Loans output in the Explorer-type list and select a summary chart.) The summary chart for the Loans range appears in Figure 12.31. This chart clearly shows how the loans vary through time. The middle line is the expected loan amount. The inner bands extend to one standard deviation on each side of the mean, and the outer bands extend to the 5th and 95th percentiles. We see that the largest loans will be required in March and April.

FIGURE 12.31
Summary Chart of
Loans Through Time

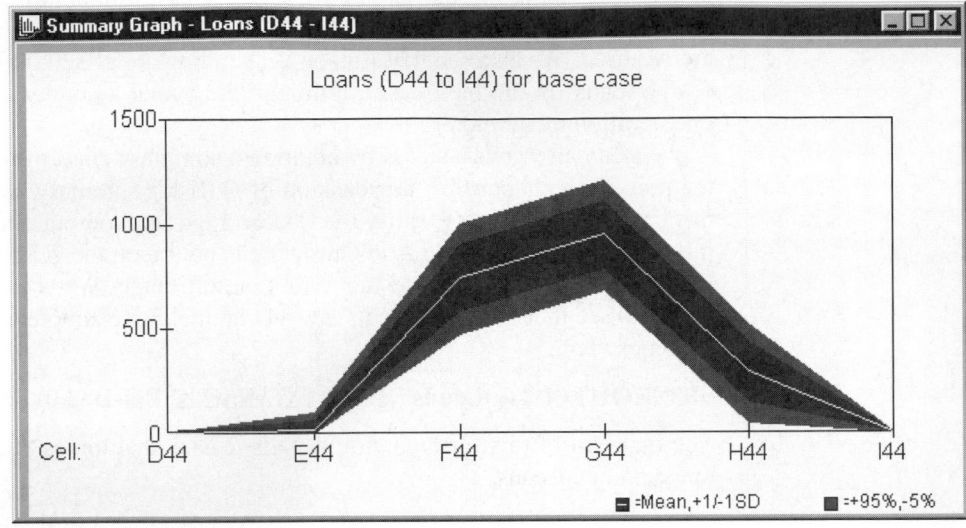

Simulating Stock Prices and Options

In this section we illustrate how @RISK can be used to simulate stock prices. Then we will show how to analyze derivative securities such as call options with simulation.

Modeling the Price of a Stock

An enormous amount of research has been devoted to discovering the way stock prices change. Although there is not complete agreement on the best model of stock price changes, one popular model states that price changes follow a lognormal distribution. Essentially, this means that the logarithm of a stock's price at any time is a normally distributed random variable. To be more specific, the stock price p_t at any time t in the future is related to the current price p_0 by the formula

$$p_t = p_0 \exp\left[(\mu - 0.5\sigma^2)t + \sigma Z \sqrt{t}\right] \tag{12.3}$$

Here, μ is the mean percentage growth rate of the stock, σ is the standard deviation of the growth rate, usually called the **volatility**, and Z is a normal random variable with mean 0 and standard deviation 1. Both μ and σ are expressed as decimals, such as $\mu = 0.06$ for a 6% mean growth rate, and all quantities are measured with respect to a common unit of time, such as a year.

The spreadsheet in Figure 12.32 illustrates how to estimate the parameters μ and σ in equation (12.3) from monthly returns. (See the file STOCKRETURNS.XLS.) We first enter the observed closing prices of the stock in column B. The corresponding monthly returns (percentage changes) are calculated in column C. For example, the formula in cell C6 is

=(B6–B5)/B5

FIGURE 12.32
Calculating Mean and
Standard Deviation of
Stock Returns

	A	B	C	D	E	F
1	Estimating mean and standard deviation of stock returns					
2						
3	Historical data					
4	Month	Closing	Return	1+Return	Ln(1+Return)	
5	0	$25.00				
6	1	$24.70	-0.01200	0.98800	-0.01207	
7	2	$23.70	-0.04049	0.95951	-0.04133	
8	3	$22.90	-0.03376	0.96624	-0.03434	
9	4	$22.81	-0.00393	0.99607	-0.00394	
10	5	$22.89	0.00351	1.00351	0.00350	
11	6	$22.56	-0.01442	0.98558	-0.01452	
12	7	$23.94	0.06117	1.06117	0.05937	
13	8	$24.37	0.01796	1.01796	0.01780	
14	9	$24.99	0.02544	1.02544	0.02512	
15	10	$26.09	0.04402	1.04402	0.04308	
16	11	$26.14	0.00192	1.00192	0.00191	
17	12	$26.90	0.02907	1.02907	0.02866	
18						
19	Monthly values			Mean	0.61%	
20				StDev	2.88%	
21						
22	Annual values			Mean	7.33%	
23				StDev	9.99%	

The return of -0.012 corresponds to a decrease of 1.2%. We then add 1 to each return in column C to obtain column D, and we take the natural logarithms of the numbers in column D to obtain column E. For example, the formula in cell E6 is

=LN(D6)

The average of the numbers in column E, calculated in cell E19 with the AVERAGE function, represents the mean monthly growth rate. Similarly, the standard deviation calculated in cell E20 represents the standard deviation of the monthly growth rate. (It can be calculated with the STDEV or the STDEVP function with slightly different results; we used the latter.) To obtain the mean yearly growth rate in cell E22, we multiply the mean monthly growth rate by 12. To obtain the standard deviation of the yearly growth rate in cell E23, we multiply the monthly standard deviation by $\sqrt{12}$. Thus, our estimate of the mean yearly growth rate of the stock price is 7.33%. The standard deviation of the growth rate is 9.99%.

Now that we know how analysts find the mean and standard deviation of a stock's growth rate, we use equation (12.3) and simulation to value certain derivative securities.[5]

Valuing a European Call Option

A **European option** on a stock gives the owner of the option the right to buy (if the option is a **call** option) or sell (if the option is a **put** option) one share of a stock on a particular date for a particular price. The price at which an option holder can buy or sell the stock is called the **exercise price** (or **strike price**) of the option. The date by which the option must be used (or "exercised") is called the **exercise date**.

For example, suppose that a stock is currently selling for $50 and you purchase a call option with an exercise price of $56 and a 3-month exercise date. What will you earn from this option? If T represents the exercise date and p_T represents the price of the stock at time T, you will earn $0 if $p_T \leq 56$, and you will earn $(p_T - 56)$ dollars if $p_T > 56$. Here is the reasoning. If $p_T \leq 56$, you have the option, if you want to use

---

[5]Derivative securities get their name because their value is *derived* from the value of an underlying security such as a stock. There are a wide variety of derivative securities available in the market. We will discuss some of the simplest ones.

it, of buying a share of stock for *more* than it is worth. This would be an irrational thing to do, so you would let your option expire—without ever using it. In this case, we say that you are "out of the money." On the other hand, if $p_T > 56$, you could buy a share at the option price of \$56, sell it for the current price of p_T, and make a profit of $p_T - 56$ dollars. In this case we say that you are "in the money."

We have omitted one thing, however. You must pay for the option in the first place. The question is, what is a fair price for such an option? Because option trading is a multibillion-dollar business, this is an important question! Black and Scholes (1973) were the first to derive a formula for pricing options. Shortly after that, Cox et al. (1979) derived a different but equivalent method for pricing options. We will use their method, which is based on the following extremely important result.

Option Pricing Result The price of an option on a non-dividend-paying stock must be the expected discounted value of the cash flows from an option on a stock having the same standard deviation as the stock on which the option is written and growing at the risk-free rate of interest. Here, discounting is done continuously at the risk-free rate. (If the stock pays dividends, the risk-free rate should be replaced by the difference between the risk-free rate and the dividend rate in what follows.)

One surprising implication of this result is that the price of the option does *not* depend on the growth rate of the stock itself, only on the risk-free rate and the standard deviation of the growth rate of the stock.

In the following example we will use @RISK to estimate the price of a European option.

EXAMPLE **12.8**

PRICING A EUROPEAN CALL OPTION

A share of AnTech stock currently sells for \$42. A European call option with an expiration date of 6 months and an exercise price of \$40 is available. The stock has an annual standard deviation of 20%. The stock price has tended to increase at a rate of 15% per year. The risk-free rate is 10% per year. What is a fair price for this option?

Solution

According to the result of Cox et al., we need to know the mean of the cash flow from this option, discounted to time 0, assuming that the stock price increases at the risk-free rate. Therefore, we will simulate many 6-month periods, each time finding the discounted cash flow of the option. The average of these discounted cash flows represents an estimate of the true mean—that is, it estimates the fair price of the option.

DEVELOPING THE SIMULATION MODEL

The spreadsheet model is quite simple, as shown in Figure 12.33. (See the file AN-TECH1.XLS.) It can be formed as follows.

❶ **Inputs.** Enter the inputs in the shaded cells. Note that the exercise date is expressed in years. Also, note that we enter the mean growth rate of the stock in cell B6. However, as we noted above, this value is not required in the model.

❷ **Simulated stock price at exercise date.** Using equation (12.3) with μ equal to the *risk-free* rate, simulate the stock price in 6 months by entering the formula

FIGURE 12.33
Determining the
Price of a Call
Option

	A	B	C	D	E
1	**Pricing a European call option with simulation**				
2					
3	**Input section**			Range names used:	
4	Current stock price	$42		CurrPrice - B4	
5	Exercise price	$40		ExerPrice - B5	
6	Mean annual return	15%		Volatility - B7	
7	StDev of annual return	20%		RFRate - B8	
8	Risk-free rate	10%		Duration - B9	
9	Option duration (years)	0.5		FutPrice - B12	
10				OptCFlow - B13	
11	**Simulation section**			DiscVal - B14	
12	Stock price in 6 months (growing at risk-free rate)	$44.13			
13	Option cash flow at termination	$4.13			
14	Discounted value of option	$3.93			
15					
16	**Value of option (average of discounted value)**	$4.76	<-- based on 10,000 iterations		
17					
18	Standard deviation of discounted value	$4.96			
19	95% confidence interval for the fair price	$4.66	to	$5.06	

=CurrPrice*EXP((RFRate-0.5*Volatility^2)*Duration+Volatility*RISKNORMAL(0,1)*SQRT(Duration))

in cell B12.

❸ Cash flow from option. Calculate the cash flow from the option by entering the formula

=MAX(FutPrice-ExerPrice,0)

in cell B13. This says that if the future price in cell B12 is greater than the exercise price in cell B5, we make the difference; otherwise, we never exercise the option and make nothing.

❹ Discount the cash flow. Discount the cash flow in cell B14 with the formula

=RISKOUTPUT()+EXP(-Duration*RFRate)*OptCFlow

This represents the net present value of the cash flow (if any) realized at the exercise date. Because the price of the option will be the average of this discounted value, it must be designated as an @Risk output cell.

❺ Average of output cell. We might as well take advantage of @Risk's RISKMEAN function to get the eventual price of the option on the spreadsheet itself. To do this, enter the formula

=RISKMEAN(DiscVal)

in cell B16.

USING @RISK

Because this is a small simulation model and we want an accurate average in cell B16, we can afford to run a lot of iterations. Therefore, we set the number of iterations to 10,000 and the number of simulations to 1. After running @Risk, the value $4.76 appears in cell B16. According to the result of Cox et al., this average is an estimate of the fair price for the option. It turns out (from the Black–Scholes formula) that $4.76 is the correct price for this option—the simulation got it exactly right! We recognize, however, that the simulated mean might not be exactly equal to the true mean. Therefore, we calculate a 95% confidence interval for the true mean in row 19. To do this, we first enter the formula

=RISKSTDDEV(DiscVal)

in cell B18. This standard deviation indicates the variability of the discounted cash flow across the 10,000 iterations. Then we go out 1.96 standard errors on each side of the mean to form the confidence interval in row 19, where the standard error is the standard deviation in cell B18 divided by the square root of 10,000. Based on the simulation, we cannot be absolutely sure of the option price, but we are 95% confident that it is between $4.66 and $5.06.[6] ∎

We now extend the previous example by simulating a portfolio that includes a company's stock and a call option on that stock.

EXAMPLE 12.9

RETURN ON A PORTFOLIO WITH A STOCK AND AN OPTION ON THE STOCK

Suppose the investor buys one share of AnTech stock at the current price and an option on this stock for $4.76, the fair price we calculated. Use simulation to find the return on the investor's portfolio as of the exercise date.

Solution

By this time, we know that the price of the option is $4.76. The purpose of the current simulation is totally different. It is to simulate the behavior of a portfolio. Therefore, we should now let the stock price grow at *its* mean rate, not the risk-free rate, to generate the stock price in 6 months. The rest is basically bookkeeping.

DEVELOPING THE SIMULATION MODEL

The spreadsheet model appears in Figure 12.34. (See the file ANTECH2.XLS.) It can be developed as follows.

❶ Inputs. Enter the values in the shaded range. These are the same as before, but they now include the known price of the call option.

❷ Future stock price. Generate the random stock price in 6 months in cell B13 with the formula

=CurrPrice*EXP((MeanReturn-0.5*Volatility^2)*Duration+Volatility*RISKNORMAL(0,1)*SQRT(Duration))

This again uses equation (12.3), but it uses the stock's mean growth rate, not the risk-free rate, for μ.

❸ Option cash flow. Calculate the cash flow from the option exactly as before by entering the formula

=MAX(FutPrice-ExerPrice,0)

in cell B14.

---

[6]Despite this rather wide confidence interval, we have found that simulation with @Risk finds option prices remarkably accurately. This appears to be due to the fact that we are using Latin hypercube sampling, not the more common Monte Carlo sampling, in the simulation.

FIGURE 12.34
Simulating a
Portfolio Return
Containing a Call
Option

	A	B	C	D	E
1	Return on a portfolio with stock and a call option on the stock				
2					
3	Input section				
4	Current stock price	$42		Range names used:	
5	Exercise price	$40		CurrPrice - B4	
6	Mean annual return	15%		ExerPrice - B5	
7	StDev of annual return	20%		MeanReturn - B6	
8	Risk-free rate	10%		Volatility - B7	
9	Option duration (years)	0.5		RFRate - B8	
10	Price of option (from Black-Scholes)	$4.76		Duration - B9	
11				OptPrice - B10	
12	Simulation section			FutPrice - B13	
13	Stock price in 6 months (growing at stock's rate)	$48.704		OptCFlow - B14	
14	Option cash flow at termination	$8.704		EndPortVal - B16	
15				PortCost - B17	
16	Ending value of portfolio	$57.408		PortReturn - B18	
17	Initial cost	$46.760			
18	Return from portfolio	22.771%			
19					
20	Summary measures from @Risk (based on 10,000 iterations)				
21	Mean return	9.439%			
22	Stdev of return	25.546%			
23	Min return	-45.848%			
24	Max return	155.365%			
25	5th percentile of return	-24.048%			
26	95th percentile of return	56.362%			
27	Probability of a positive return	0.591			

④ Portfolio value. In 6 months the portfolio will be worth the price of the stock plus the cash flow from the option. Calculate this in cell B16 with the formula

=SUM(FutPrice,OptCFlow)

Then in cells B17 and B18, calculate the amount we paid for the portfolio and its return (the percentage change) with the formulas

=CurrPrice+OptPrice

and

=RISKOUTPUT()+(EndPortVal-PortCost)/PortCost

Note that the portfolio return is the only cell designated as an @Risk output cell.

⑤ @Risk summary statistics. We again show the basic summary results from @Risk on the spreadsheet by using its RISKMEAN, RISKSTDDEV, RISKMIN, RISKMAX, RISKPERCENTILE, and RISKTARGET functions. For example, the formulas in cells B25 and B27 are

=RISKPERCENTILE(PortReturn,0.05)

and

=1-RISKTARGET(PortReturn,0)

USING @RISK

After running @Risk for 10,000 iterations, we obtain the values in the range B21:B27 of Figure 12.34. (Of course, this same information appears in the @Risk Results window.) The mean return from this portfolio is about 9.4%, but there is considerable variability. There is a 5% chance that it will lose about 24%, and there is a 5% chance that it will gain about 56%. The probability that it will provide a *positive* return is about 0.59.

If you have any intuition for financial portfolios, you have probably noticed that this investor is "putting all her eggs in one basket." If the stock price increases, she gains by owning the share of stock and she also gains from holding the option (since she is more likely to be "in the money"). However, if the price of the stock decreases, she loses money on her share of stock and her option is worthless. A safer strategy is to **hedge** her bets. She can purchase one share of the stock and purchase a *put* option on the stock. Recall that a put option allows her to sell a share of stock for the exercise price at the exercise date. With a put option, the investor hopes the stock price will decrease because she can then sell a share at the exercise price and immediately buy it back at the decreased stock price, thus earning a profit. Therefore, a portfolio consisting of a share of stock and a put option on the stock covers the investor in both directions. It has less upside potential, but it decreases the downside risk. ■

Valuing a More Exotic Call Option

The European call option is rather simple. There are a variety of other derivative securities currently available. In fact, their variety and complexity are what make them attractive—and dangerous for the unsuspecting investor. Here we will examine one variation of the basic call option. It is called an **Asian** option. Its payoff depends, not on the price at expiration of the underlying stock, but on the *average* price of the stock over the lifetime of the option. That is, if the exercise price of the option is p_e and the average price of the stock over the lifetime of the option is p_{avg}, then the payoff at the expiration date from the option is the larger of $p_{avg} - p_e$ and 0.

To price an Asian option (or any number of other exotic options), we again need to find the expected discounted value of the cash flow from the option, assuming that the stock grows at the risk-free rate. The following example illustrates how to approximate this expected value with simulation.

EXAMPLE   **12.10**

PRICING AN ASIAN OPTION

Consider a stock currently priced at $100 per share. Its mean annual return is 15% and the standard deviation of its annual return is 30%. What is the value of an Asian option that expires in 52 weeks (1 year) with an exercise price of $100? Assume that the risk-free rate is 9%.

Solution

To value this option, we will base p_{avg} on the average of the weekly (simulated) stock prices, assuming that the stock price grows at the risk-free rate. This requires us to generate weekly stock prices from equation (12.3). The key is to interpret p_0 and p_t correctly in equation (12.3). To generate any week's price from the previous week's price, we identify p_0 with the previous week's price and p_t with the current week's price. The appropriate value of t is 1/52 (measured as a fraction of a year).

DEVELOPING THE SIMULATION MODEL

The spreadsheet model appears in Figure 12.35. (See the file ASIAN.XLS.) It can be formed as follows.

	A	B	C	D	E	F	G	H
1	Pricing an Asian call option with simulation							
2								
3	Input section			Weekly prices (growing at risk-free rate)				
4	Current stock price	$100		Week	Simulated price			
5	Exercise price	$110		0	$100.00			
6	Mean annual return	15%		1	$98.65	Range names used:		
7	StDev of annual return	30%		2	$100.09	CurrPrice - B4		
8	Risk-free rate	9.0%		3	$90.06	ExerPrice - B5		
9	Option duration (years)	1.0		4	$96.50	Volatility - B7		
10				5	$94.70	RFRate - B8		
11	Simulation section			6	$102.55	Duration - B9		
12	Average of weekly prices	$94.697		7	$100.93	AvgWkPrice - B12		
13	Option cash flow at termination	$0.000		8	$100.90	OptCFlow - B13		
14	Discounted value of option	$0.000		9	$107.00	DiscVal - B14		
15				10	$98.23	WeeklyPrices - E5:E57		
16	Value of option (average of discounted value)	$4.75		11	$102.18			
17				12	$108.80			
18				13	$108.26			
55				50	$96.16			
56				51	$101.04			
57				52	$102.04			

FIGURE 12.35 Determining the Price of an Asian Option

❶ Inputs. Enter the inputs in the shaded range. As in the valuation of the European call option, we enter the mean growth rate of the stock in cell B6 even though it is not used in the simulation.

❷ Weekly prices. Enter the initial price (week 0) in cell E5 with the formula

=CurrPrice

Then to generate each weekly price from the previous one, enter the formula

=E5*EXP((RFRate-0.5*Volatility^2)*(1/52)+Volatility*RISKNORMAL(0,1)*SQRT(1/52))

in cell E6 and copy it to the range E7:E57. Note that the unit of time is always 1/52 of a year.

❸ Discounted value of option. Enter the formulas

=AVERAGE(WeeklyPrices)
=MAX(AvgWkPrice-ExerPrice,0)

and

=RISKOUTPUT()+EXP(-Duration*RFRate)*OptCFlow

in cells B12, B13, and B14. These are exactly as in the European call option example, except that the payoff in cell B13 is based on the *average* in cell B12, not on the ending price of the stock. Again, the discounted value cell is the @Risk output cell, because the price of the option will be estimated by the average value in this cell.

❹ Average of output cell. We again show the main @Risk summary measure in the spreadsheet itself. Enter the formula

=RISKMEAN(DiscVal)

in cell B16. (We could also create a confidence interval for this mean, as in the Antech example.)

USING @RISK

After running @Risk for 5000 iterations, the value in cell B16 is $4.75. This is our estimate for the price of this Asian option. (The actual market price of this particular option turns out to be $4.68, very close to our estimate.) ∎

We all want to invest our money wisely for retirement. How should we do it? The stock market is currently doing very well, but it has not always done so, and there are always rumors that the current bull market could turn bearish. Would it be better to invest in bonds or fixed income securities such as T-bills? We will investigate this question in the following example. Actually, we are taking the advice from an article in the January 11, 1999, issue of *Fortune Magazine*, that advocated using simulation to evaluate various investment strategies for retirement.

EXAMPLE 12.11

INVESTING FOR RETIREMENT

Attorney Sally Evans has just begun her career. At age 25, she has 40 years until retirement, but she realizes that now is the time to start investing. She plans to invest $1000 at the beginning of each of the next 40 years. Each year, she plans to put fixed percentages—the same each year—of this $1000 into stocks, bonds, and T-bills. However, she is not sure which percentages (we will call them investment weights) to use. She does have historical annual returns from stocks, bonds, and T-bills from 1946 to 1994. These are listed in the file RETIREMENT.XLS. This file also includes inflation factors for these years. For example, for 1993 the annual returns for stocks, bonds, and T-bills were 9.99%, 18.24%, and 2.90%, and the inflation rate was 2.75%. Sally would like to use simulation to help decide what investment weights to use, with the objective of achieving a large investment value, in *today's* dollars, at the end of 40 years.

Solution

The most difficult modeling aspect is settling on a way to use historical returns and inflation factors to generate *future* values of these quantities. We will use a "scenario" approach. We think of each historical year as a possible scenario, where the scenario specifies the returns and inflation factor for that year. Then for any future year, we randomly choose one of these scenarios, using a RISKDISCRETE function. It seems intuitive that more recent scenarios ought to have a larger chance of being chosen. To implement this idea, we give a weight (not to be confused with the investment weights) to each scenario, starting with weight 1 for 1994. Then the weight for any year is a "damping factor" multiplied by the weight from the next year. For example, the weight for 1986 is the damping factor multiplied by the weight for 1987. To change these weights to probabilities, we simply divide each weight by the sum of all the weights. The damping factor we will illustrate is 0.98. Others could be used instead, and we are frankly not sure which will produce the most realistic results. (This is an important question for financial research!)

The other difficult part of the solution is knowing which investment weights to try. This is really an optimization problem—find three weights that add to 1 and produce the largest mean final cash. Palisade has another software package, RiskOptimizer, that solves this type of optimization–simulation problem. However, we will simply try several sets of weights, where some percentage is put into stocks and the remainder is split evenly between bonds and T-bills, and see which does best. You can try other sets if you like.

DEVELOPING THE SIMULATION MODEL

The historical data and simulation model appear in Figures 12.36 and 12.37. (Again, see the RETIREMENT.XLS file.) It can be developed as follows.

FIGURE 12.36
Historical Data, Inputs, and Probabilities

	A	B	C	D	E	F	G
1	**Planning for retirement**						
2							
3	**Inputs**						
4	Damping factor	0.98				**Range names used:**	
5	Yearly investment	$1,000				Damper - B4	
6	Planning horizon	40	years			Invest - B5	
7						Horizon - B6	
8	**Alternative sets of weights to test**					LTable1 - A10:D12	
9		Index	Bills	Bonds	Stocks	Index - A17	
10		1	0.10	0.10	0.80	Weights - B17:D17	
11		2	0.20	0.20	0.60	Years - A21:A69	
12		3	0.30	0.30	0.40	Probs - G21:G69	
13						LTable2 - A21:E69	
14	**Weights used**		Column offset for lookup1			LTable3 - I20:Q59	
15			2	3	4		
16		Index	Bills	Bonds	Stocks		
17		1	0.10	0.10	0.80		
18							
19	**Historical data and probabilities**						
20		Year	Bills	Bonds	Stocks	Inflation	ProbWts	Probability
21		1946	0.0035	-0.0010	-0.0807	0.1817	0.3792	0.0121
22		1947	0.0050	-0.0263	0.0571	0.0901	0.3869	0.0123
23		1948	0.0081	0.0340	0.0550	0.0271	0.3948	0.0126
24		1949	0.0110	0.0645	0.1879	-0.0180	0.4029	0.0128
25		1950	0.0120	0.0006	0.3171	0.0579	0.4111	0.0131
26		1951	0.0149	-0.0394	0.2402	0.0587	0.4195	0.0134
64		1989	0.0837	0.1811	0.3149	0.0465	0.9039	0.0288
65		1990	0.0781	0.0618	-0.0317	0.0611	0.9224	0.0294
66		1991	0.0560	0.1930	0.3055	0.0306	0.9412	0.0300
67		1992	0.0351	0.0805	0.0767	0.0290	0.9604	0.0306
68		1993	0.0290	0.1824	0.0999	0.0275	0.9800	0.0312
69		1994	0.0390	-0.0777	0.0131	0.0267	1.0000	0.0318
70						Sums -->	31.4199	1.0000

FIGURE 12.37
Simulation Model

	I	J	K	L	M	N	O	P	Q
12	**Summary measures from simulation below**								
13	Final cash (future dollars)		317456						
14	Deflator		0.1338						
15	Final cash (today's dollars)		42484						
16									
17				Column offset for lookup2					
18	**Simulation model**			2	3	4	5		
19		Year	Beginning cash	Scenario	Bills	Bonds	Stocks	Inflation	Ending cash	Deflator
20		1	1000	1990	1.0781	1.0618	0.9683	1.0611	989	0.942
21		2	1989	1949	1.0110	1.0645	1.1879	0.9820	2303	0.960
22		3	3303	1956	1.0246	0.9441	1.0656	1.0286	3466	0.933
23		4	4466	1979	1.1038	0.9878	1.1844	1.1331	5165	0.823
24		5	6165	1967	1.0421	0.9081	1.2398	1.0304	7317	0.799
25		6	8317	1991	1.0560	1.1930	1.3055	1.0306	10557	0.775
54		35	254815	1981	1.1471	1.0185	0.9509	1.0894	249026	0.185
55		36	250026	1946	1.0035	0.9990	0.9193	1.1817	233947	0.156
56		37	234947	1977	1.0512	0.9933	0.9282	1.0677	222497	0.147
57		38	223497	1964	1.0354	1.0351	1.1648	1.0119	254538	0.145
58		39	255530	1000	1.0521	0.9974	1.1106	1.0472	279413	0.138
59		40	280413	1971	1.0439	1.1323	1.1431	1.0336	317456	0.134

❶ Inputs. Enter the data in the shaded regions. These include the historical returns and inflation factors (shown as decimals), the alternative sets of investment weights we plan to test, and other inputs. Note that we develop the model so that any time horizon, up to 40 years, can be accommodated by entering the appropriate value in cell B6.

❷ Weights. The investment weights we will use for the model are in row 17. (For example, the first set puts 80% in stocks and 10% in each of bonds and T-bills.) We do this with a RISKSIMTABLE and VLOOKUP combination in the usual way. Specifically, enter the formulas

=RISKSIMTABLE(A10:A12)

and

=VLOOKUP(Index,LTable1,B15)

in cells A17 and B17, and copy the latter to the range C17:D17.

❸ Probabilities. Enter value 1 in cell F69. Then enter the formula

=Damper*F69

in cell F68 and copy it *up* to cell F21. Sum these values with the SUM function in cell F70. Then to convert them to probabilities (numbers that add to 1), enter the formula

=F21/$F$70

in cell G21 and copy it down to cell G69. Note how the probabilities for more recent years are considerably larger. When we randomly select scenarios, the recent years will have a larger chance of being chosen.

❹ Scenarios. Moving to the model in Figure 12.37, we want to simulate 40 scenarios in columns K–O, one for each year of Sally's investing. To do this, enter the formulas

=RISKDISCRETE(Years,Probs)

and

=1+VLOOKUP($K20,LTable2,L$18)

in cells K20 and L20, and then copy this latter formula to the range M20:O20. Make sure you understand how the RISKDISCRETE and VLOOKUP functions combine to capture the data from a randomly selected historical year. This is the key to the simulation.

❺ Beginning, ending cash. The bookkeeping part is straightforward. Begin by entering the formula

=Invest

in cell J20 for the initial investment. Then enter the formulas

=J20*SUMPRODUCT(Weights,L20:N20)

and

=Invest+P20

in cells P20 and J21 for ending cash in the first year and beginning cash in the second year. The former shows how the beginning cash grows in a given year. The latter implies that Sally reinvests her previous money, plus she invests a new $1000. Copy these formulas down columns J and P.

6 **Deflators.** We eventually want to deflate future dollars to today's dollars. The proper way to do this is to calculate deflators (or deflation factors). Do this by entering the formula

=1/O20

in cell Q20. Then enter the formula

=Q20/O21

in cell Q21 and copy it down.

7 **Summary measures.** For any time horizon specified in cell B6, we can pick off the information we need with a third VLOOKUP. Do this by entering the formulas

=VLOOKUP(Horizon,LTable3,8)
=VLOOKUP(Horizon,LTable3,9)

and

=RISKOUTPUT()+K13*K14

in cells K13–K15. This last quantity is the output we will examine with @Risk.

USING @RISK

We set the number of iterations to 1000 and the number of simulations to 3 (one for each set of investment weights we want to test). Summary results appear in Figure 12.38. The first simulation, which invests the most heavily in stocks, is easily the winner. Its mean final cash, slightly above $127,000 in today's dollars, is much greater than the means for the other two sets of weights. It also has a *much* larger upside potential (its 95th percentile is over $325,000), and even its downside is roughly equivalent to the others (its 5th percentile is the best, and its minimum is slightly worse than the minimum for simulation 2).

Cell	Name	Minimum	Mean	Maximum	x1=	p1=	x2=	p2=
K15 (Sim#1)	Final cash (today's dollars)	13128.41	127135.4	844089.1	29371.24	5%	325235.4	95%
K15 (Sim#2)	Final cash (today's dollars)	14182.9	86215.84	475834.8	27097.04	5%	187043.8	95%
K15 (Sim#3)	Final cash (today's dollars)	13017.54	58782.02	261800.4	23805.56	5%	111477	95%

Summary Statistics

FIGURE 12.38 Summary Results from @Risk

Nevertheless, the histogram for simulation 1 (put 80% in stocks), shown in Figure 12.39 (page 666), indicates the tremendous amount of variability—and skewness—in the distribution of final cash. A useful concept we might introduce here is **value at risk (VAR)**. It is defined as the 5th percentile of a distribution and is often the value investors worry about. Perhaps Sally should rerun the simulation with different investment weights, with an eye on the weights that maximize her VAR. Right now it is $29,371—not too good considering that she invested $40,000 total. She might not like the prospect of a 5% chance of ending up with no more than this!

We also encourage you to try running this simulation with other investment weights, both for the 40-year horizon and for shorter time horizons such as 10 or 15 years. Even though the stock strategy appears to be best for a long horizon, it might not fare as well for a shorter horizon.

FIGURE 12.39
Histogram of Final
Cash with 80% in
Stocks

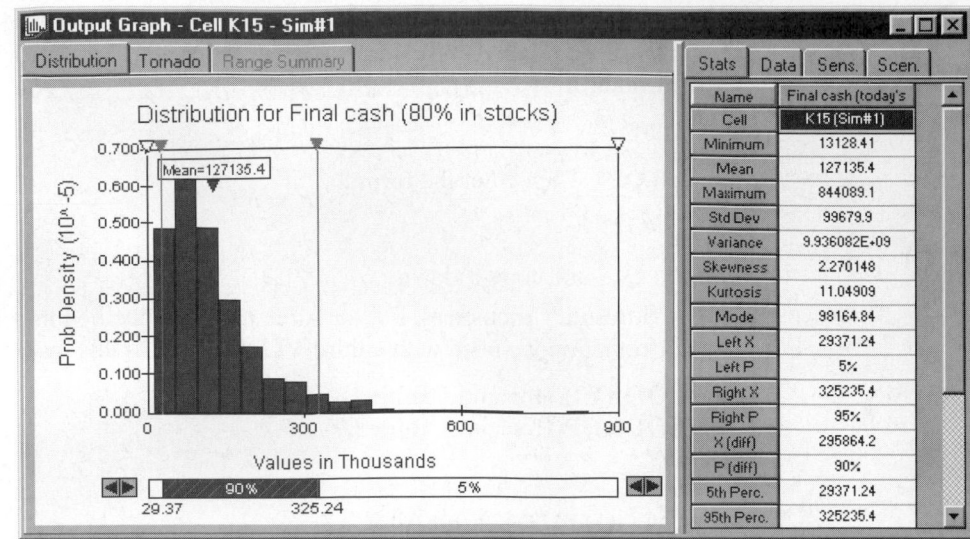

PROBLEMS

Skill-Building Problems

15. Based on Kelly (1956). You currently have $100. Each week you can invest any amount of money you currently have in a risky investment. With probability 0.4 the amount you invest is tripled (e.g., if you invest $100, you increase your asset position by $300), and with probability 0.6 the amount you invest is lost. Consider the following investment strategies:

a. Each week invest 10% of your money.
b. Each week invest 30% of your money.
c. Each week invest 50% of your money.

Use @Risk to simulate 100 weeks of each strategy 500 times. Which strategy appears to be best? (In general, if you can multiply your investment by M with probability p and lose your investment with probability q, you should invest a fraction $\frac{p(M-1)-q}{M-1}$ of your money each week. This strategy maximizes the expected growth rate of your fortune and is known as the **Kelly criterion**.)

16. Based on Marcus (1990). The Balboa mutual fund has beaten the Standard and Poor's 500 during 11 of the last 13 years. People use this as an argument that you can "beat the market." Here is another way to look at it that shows that Balboa's beating the market 11 out of 13 times is not unusual. Consider 50 mutual funds, each of which has a 50% chance of beating the market during a given year. Use simulation to estimate the probability that over a 13-year period the "best" of the 50 mutual funds will beat the market for at least 11 out of 13 years. This probability turns out to exceed 40%, which means that the best mutual fund's beating the market 11 out of 13 years is not an unusual occurrence!

17. Recall from the GF example that the company's ordering policy is determined by the factor k, the number of standard deviations above the mean for the production quantity. We found the $k = 1.2$ was the best of the values we tried. Rerun the simulation using other values of k. Which value of k would you recommend that GF use?

18. Amanda has 30 years to save for her retirement. At the beginning of each year, she puts $5000 into her retirement account. At any point in time, all of Amanda's retirement funds are tied up in the stock market. Suppose the annual return on stocks follows a normal distribution with mean 12% and standard deviation 25%. What is the probability that at the end of 30 years, Amanda will have reached her goal of having $1,000,000 for retirement? Assume that if Amanda reaches her goal *before* 30 years, she will stop investing. (*Hint*: Each year you should keep track of Amanda's beginning cash position—for year 1, this is $5000—and Amanda's ending cash position. Of course, Amanda's ending cash position for a given year is a function of her beginning cash position and the return on stocks for that year. To estimate the probability that Amanda will meet her goal, use an IF statement that returns 1 if she meets her goal and 0 otherwise.)

19. You have been asked to simulate the cash inflows to a toy company for the next year. Monthly sales are independent random variables. Mean sales for the months January–March and October–December are $80,000, and mean sales for the months April–September are $120,000. The standard deviation for each month's sales is 20% of the month's mean sales. We model the method used to collect monthly sales as follows:

- During each month a certain fraction of new sales will be collected. All new sales not collected become one month overdue.
- During each month a certain fraction of one-month overdue sales is collected. The remainder becomes two months overdue.
- During each month a certain fraction of two-month overdue sales is collected. The remainder are written off as bad debts.

You are given the information in the file P12_19.XLS from some past months. Using this information, build a simulation model that generates the total cash inflow for each month. Develop a simple forecasting model and build the error of your forecasting model into the simulation. Assuming that there are $120,000 of one-month-old sales outstanding and $140,000 of two-month-old sales outstanding during January, you are 95% sure that total cash inflow for the year will be between what two values?

20. The current price of HAL computer stock is $280. Its closing price during each of the next twelve months is given in Table 12.7. Use these data to estimate the annual mean and standard deviation of the return on HAL stock.

TABLE 12.7

	Closing Price
Month 1	$290.00
Month 2	$300.00
Month 3	$282.00
Month 4	$286.50
Month 5	$291.40
Month 6	$308.00
Month 7	$298.32
Month 8	$304.50
Month 9	$308.23
Month 10	$310.40
Month 11	$308.21
Month 12	$309.34

21. A stock currently sells for $100. The risk-free rate is 12% per year, and the stock's annual volatility is 20%. By considering exercise prices of $90, $100, and $110, show how the value of a call option depends on the option's exercise price. Assume the exercise date of the option is 1 year from now.

22. Referring to the retirement example (Example 12.11), rerun the model for a planning horizon of 10 years; 15 years; 25 years. For each, try to find the set of investment weights that maximize the VAR (the 5th percentile) of final cash in today's dollars. Does it appear that a portfolio heavy in stocks is better for long horizons but not for shorter horizons?

Skill-Extending Problems

23. Mary Higgins is a freelance writer with enough spare time on her hands to play the stock market fairly seriously. Each morning she observes the change in stock price of a particular stock and decides whether to buy or sell, and if so, how many shares to buy or sell. We will assume that on day 1, she has $100,000 cash to invest and that she spends part of this to buy her first 500 shares of the stock at the current price of $50 per share. From that point on, she follows a fairly simple "buy low, sell high" strategy. Specifically, if the price has increased three days in a row, she sells 25% of her shares of the stock. If the price has increased two days in a row (but not three), she sells 10% of her shares. In the other direction, if the price has decreased three days in a row, she buys 25% more shares, whereas if the price has decreased only two days in a row, she buys 10% more shares. We will assume a fairly simple model of stock price changes, as described in Table 12.8. Each day the price can change by as much as $2 in either direction, and the probabilities depend on the previous price change—decrease, increase, or no change. Build a simulation model of this strategy for a period of 75 trading days. (You can assume that the stock price on each of the previous two days was $49.) Decide on interesting @Risk output cells, and then run @Risk for 500 iterations and report your findings.

TABLE 12.8 Price Change Distributions for Investment Problem

	Probabilities Following		
Price Change	Decrease	Increase	No Change
−$2	0.20	0.10	0.15
−$1	0.25	0.15	0.20
$0	0.30	0.30	0.30
+$1	0.15	0.25	0.20
+$2	0.10	0.20	0.15

24. Dord Motors is considering whether to introduce a new model called the Racer. The profitability of the Racer will depend on the following factors:

- The fixed cost of developing the Racer is equally likely to be $3 or $5 billion.
- Year 1 sales are normally distributed with mean 200,000 and standard deviation 50,000. Year 2 sales are normally distributed with mean equal to actual year 1 sales and standard deviation 50,000. Year 3 sales are normally distributed with mean equal to actual year 2 sales and standard deviation 50,000.
- The selling price in year 1 is $13,000. The year 2 selling price will be

$$1.05[\text{year 1 price} + \$30(\% \text{ diff1})]$$

where % diff1 is the percentage by which actual year 1 sales differ from expected year 1 sales. The 1.05 factor accounts for inflation. For example, if the year 1 sales figure is 180,000, which is 10% below the expected year 1 sales, then the year 2 price will be

$$1.05[13,000 + 30(-10)] = \$13,335$$

Similarly, the year 3 price will be

$$1.05[\text{year 2 price} + \$30(\% \text{ diff2})]$$

where % diff2 is the percentage by which actual year 2 sales differ from expected year 2 sales.
- The variable cost is equally likely to be $5000, $6000, $7000, or $8000 during year 1 and is assumed to increase by 5% each year.

Your goal is to estimate the NPV of the new car during its first 3 years. Assume that cash flows are discounted at 10%. Simulate 1000 trials and estimate the mean and standard deviation of the NPV for the first 3 years of sales. Also, determine a 95% confidence interval for the mean NPV of the Racer during its first 3 years of operation.

25. Use @Risk to solve the previous problem, but now assume that the fixed cost of developing the Racer is triangularly distributed with minimum, most likely, and maximum values $3, $4, and $5 billion. Also, assume that the variable cost per car in year 1 is triangularly distributed with minimum, most likely, and maximum values $5000, $7000, and $8000.

26. Truckco produces the OffRoad truck. The company wants to gain information about the discounted profits earned during the next 3 years. During a given year, the total number of trucks sold in the United States is

$$500,000 + 50,000G - 40,000I$$

where G is the percentage increase in GDP during the year and I is the percentage increase in the consumer price index (CPI) during the year.

During the next 3 years, Value Line has made the predictions listed in Table 12.9. In the past, 95% of Value Line's G predictions have been accurate within 6%, and 95% of Value Line's I predictions have been accurate within 5%. We assume that the actual G and I values are normally distributed each year.

TABLE 12.9	Predictions for Truckco Problem		
	Year		
	1	**2**	**3**
GNP	3%	5%	4%
INF	4%	7%	3%

At the beginning of each year, a number of competitors might enter the trucking business. The probability distribution of the number of competitors that will enter the trucking business is that given in Table 12.10. Before competitors join the industry at the beginning of year 1, there are two competitors. During a year that begins with n competitors (after competitors have entered the business, but before any have left), OffRoad will have a market share given by $0.5(0.9)^n$. At the end of each year, there is a 20% chance that any competitor will leave the industry.

TABLE 12.10	Distribution of Number of New Competitors for Truckco Problem
Number of New Competitors	**Probability**
0	0.50
1	0.30
2	0.10
3	0.10

The selling price of the truck and the production cost per truck are given in Table 12.11. Simulate 1000 replications of Truckco's profit for the next 3 years. Estimate the mean and standard deviation of the discounted 3-year profits, using a discount rate of 10%. You can use Excel's NPV function here. Do the same if there is a 50% chance during each year that any competitor will leave the industry.

27. Based on Altman (1986). The Weaver Company, a textile firm, wants to simulate its cash budget for the year 2001. We make the following assumptions. (All

TABLE 12.11	Prices and Costs for Truckco Problem		
	Year 1	Year 2	Year 3
Sales price	$15,000	$16,000	$17,000
Variable cost	$12,000	$13,000	$14,000

cash amounts are in thousands of dollars except where noted for the long-term loan.)

- Each month the monthly "base" sales follow a normal distribution with a mean of $70,000 and a standard deviation of $15,000. Then the *actual* sales in any month is the monthly base sales multiplied by a seasonal index for the month. The seasonal indices are listed in Table 12.12.

TABLE 12.12	Seasonal Indices for Weaver Problem		
	Index		Index
Jan	0.85	Jul	1.03
Feb	0.87	Aug	1.06
Mar	0.90	Sep	1.06
Apr	0.91	Oct	1.10
May	0.94	Nov	1.12
Jun	1.02	Dec	1.13

- Cash sales for a month are 10% of monthly sales.
- Monthly collections for January and February are each $50,000. For other months, monthly collections are 90% of sales from 2 months ago.
- Monthly total cash receipts equal cash sales plus monthly collections.
- Together, labor and material costs are a certain fraction (called the cost factor) of monthly sales. This cost factor (the same for each month of the year) is normally distributed with mean 0.7 and standard deviation 0.03.
- Monthly cash disbursements include the following:
  - Monthly labor costs equal the cost factor multiplied by 20% of monthly sales.
  - Monthly material costs are $33,000 for January. In any other month they equal the cost factor multiplied by 80% of the previous month's sales.
  - Monthly operating expenses are 19% of monthly base sales.
  - The quarterly interest payment in January is $2780. In April, July, and October, it is composed of the interest on the average loan balance for last 3 months, paid at the

short-term rate of interest for 3 months, plus 3 months of interest on the $96 million dollar long-term loan, paid at 8.5% annually. The short-term interest rate for the year is normal with mean 14% and standard deviation 1%.
  - Taxes are paid in January, April, July, and October. Each payment is $4000.
  - Dividends of $2000 are paid in February, May, August, and November.
  - Capital expenditures are $4500 in March, $4600 in June, $4800 in September, and $4900 in December.
- At the beginning of January, there is a cash balance of −$7015. The desired ending cash balance for a given month (after adjusting the loan balance) is 18.8% of monthly sales.
- Cash evolves as follows:
  - Beginning cash for month t equals the desired ending cash for month $t − 1$.
  - End-of-month cash for month t equals the beginning cash for month t plus the net cash flow for month t.
  - For all but January, the ending loan balance for month t equals the ending loan balance for month $t − 1$ plus the desired cash for month t minus the end-of-month cash for month t.
  - For January, the ending loan balance equals the ending January desired cash balance minus the January end-of-month cash.

Simulate Weaver's yearly cash budget 1000 times. Find the mean and standard deviation of the firm's total net cash flow for 2001 as well as the mean and standard deviation of the firm's monthly average loan balance for 2001. What is the probability that the firm's 2001 net cash flow will be negative? What is the probability that the firm's ending loan balance will be negative? Note that the monthly net cash flow equals the monthly cash receipts minus the monthly cash disbursements.

28. You are considering a 10-year investment project. At present, the expected cash flow each year is $1000. Suppose, however, that each year's cash flow is normally distributed with mean equal to *last* year's actual cash flow and standard deviation $100. For example, suppose that the actual cash flow in year 1 is $1200. Then year 2 cash flow is normal with mean $1200 and standard deviation $100. Also, at the end of year 1, your best guess is that each later year's expected cash flow will be $1200.
    a. Estimate the mean and standard deviation of the NPV of this project. Assume that cash flows are discounted at a rate of 10% per year.
    b. Now assume that the project has an abandonment option. At the end of each year you can abandon the project for the value given in Table 12.13. For example, suppose that year 1 cash flow is $400. Then at the end of year 1, you expect cash flow

TABLE 12.13	Abandonment Values for Investment Problem			
	Value		**Value**	
Year 1	$6200	Year 6	$3300	
Year 2	$5700	Year 7	$2570	
Year 3	$5180	Year 8	$1780	
Year 4	$4580	Year 9	$920	
Year 5	$3980	Year 10	$0	

for each remaining year to be $400. This has an NPV of less than $6200, so you should abandon the project and collect $6200 at the end of year 1. Estimate the mean and standard deviation of the project with the abandonment option. How much would you pay for the abandonment option? (*Hints*: You can abandon a project at most once. Thus in year 5, for example, you abandon only if the sum of future expected NPVs is less than the year 5 abandonment value *and* the project has not yet been abandoned. Also, once you abandon the project, the actual cash flows for future years will be 0. So the future cash flows after abandonment should disappear.)

29. Toys For U is developing a new Madonna doll. The company has made the following assumptions:
    - It is equally likely that the doll will sell for 2, 4, 6, 8, or 10 years.
    - At the beginning of year 1, the potential market for the doll is 1 million. The potential market grows by an average of 5% per year. Toys For U is 95% sure that the growth in the potential market during any year will be between 3% and 7%. It uses a normal distribution to model this.
    - The company believes its share of the potential market during year 1 will be at worst 20%, most likely 40%, and at best 50%. It uses a triangular distribution to model this.
    - The variable cost of producing a doll during year 1 is equally likely to be $4 or $6.
    - Each year the selling price and variable cost of producing the doll will increase by 5%. The current selling price is $10.
    - The fixed cost of developing the doll (which is incurred right away, at time 0) is equally likely to be $4, $8, or $12 million.
    - Right now there is one competitor in the market. During each year that begins with four or fewer competitors, there is a 20% chance that a new competitor will enter the market.
    - We determine year t sales (for $t > 1$) as follows. Suppose that at the end of year $t - 1$, n competitors are present. Then we assume that during year t, a fraction $0.9 - 0.1n$ of the company's loyal customers (last year's

purchasers) will buy a doll during the next year, and a fraction $0.2 - 0.04n$ of customers currently in the market who did not purchase a doll last year will purchase a doll from the company this year. We can now generate a prediction for year t sales. Of course, this prediction will not be exactly correct. We assume that it is sure to be accurate within 15%, however. (There are different ways to model this. You can choose any method that is reasonable.)
    - Cash flows are discounted at 10% per year.
    a. Use @RISK to estimate the expected NPV of this project. Also, find a 95% confidence interval for this expected value.
    b. Use the percentiles in @RISK's output to find an interval such that you are 95% certain that the company's *actual* NPV will be within this interval.
    c. Explain the difference between the two intervals in parts **a** and **b**.

30. Estimates of Toyco's mean monthly sales for the months October 2000–March 2002 are as shown in Table 12.14. Your goal is to model Toyco's 2001 cash budget given the following assumptions:

TABLE 12.14			
	2000	**2001**	**2002**
January		$70,000	$130,000
February		$80,000	$130,000
March		$80,000	$140,000
April		$90,000	
May		$100,000	
June		$100,000	
July		$90,000	
August		$100,000	
September		$110,000	
October	$40,000	$120,000	
November	$50,000	$120,000	
December	$60,000	$130,000	

- At the beginning of each month Toyco wants to have a cash balance of at least $20,000, and it will borrow sufficient funds to achieve this goal.
- All sales are for credit—70% of all payments are collected in the first month after sale, 20% in the second month after sale, and 10% are collected in the third month after sale.
- Inventory at the beginning of each month should equal forecasted sales for the next 3 months.
- Merchandise purchased for sale incurs a cost equal to 75% of sales. On purchases made each

month, 70% is paid in the first month after purchase and 30% is paid in the second month after purchase.

- Selling and administrative expenses incurred during a month equal $8500 + 0.09(Sales). These expenses are paid at a rate of 70% during the current month and 30% in the month following.
- The beginning cash balance in January 2001 is the required amount, $20,000.
- There is no outstanding loan in to pay back in January 2001.
- If money must be borrowed, it is borrowed month-to-month at an interest rate of 0.7%. Borrowing takes place in multiples of $1000. To model this, use the CEILING function. For example, the formula =**CEILING(2500,1000)** evaluates to 3000. (Note that you will need an IF statement because CEILING(-500, 1000) is not defined.)
- In February 2001, capital expenditures of $20,000 are incurred. In July and October of 2001, capital expenditures of $30,000 are incurred.
- Existing fixed assets are depreciated at $100 per month. Additional capital expenses are depreciated on a straight-line basis at a rate of 1% per month, beginning in the month after the capital expense is incurred.
- The sales for each month have a standard deviation of 15,000 about the forecasted sales.

a. Use your model to predict average profit for 2001. How high is profit likely to go? How low?
b. To be sure of having enough money to borrow, how big a line of credit would you need for 2000?
c. Suppose you could ensure that all accounts receivable could be collected in the month after the sale and that beginning inventory for each month could be trimmed to 80% of the next 3 months' forecasted sales. How would this new scenario change your answers to parts **a** and **b**?

31. If you own a stock, buying a put option on the stock will greatly reduce your risk. This is the idea behind **portfolio insurance**. To illustrate, consider a stock (Trumpco) that currently sells for $56 and has an annual volatility of 30%. Assume the risk-free rate is 8% and you estimate that the stock's annual growth rate is 12%.
a. Suppose you own one share of Trumpco. Use simulation to estimate the probability distribution of the percentage return earned on this stock during a 1-year period.
b. Now suppose you also buy a put option (for $2.38) on Trumpco. The option has an exercise price of $50 and an exercise date 1 year from now. Use simulation to estimate the probability distribution of the percentage return on your

portfolio over a 1-year period. Can you see why this strategy is called a portfolio insurance strategy?
c. Use simulation to show that the put option should, indeed, sell for $2.38.

32. For the data in the previous problem, the following is an example of a **butterfly spread**: sell two calls with an exercise price of $50; buy one call with an exercise price of $40 and one call with an exercise price of $60. Simulate the cash flows from this portfolio.

33. Cryco stock currently sells for $69. The annual growth rate of the stock is 15%, and the stock's annual volatility is 35%. The risk-free rate is currently 5%. You have bought a 6-month European put option on this stock with an exercise price of $70.
a. Use @Risk to value this option.
b. Use @Risk to analyze the distribution of percentage returns (for a 6-month horizon) for the following portfolios:
- Portfolio 1: Own one share of Cryco.
- Portfolio 2: Own one share of Cryco and buy the put described in part **a**.
  Which portfolio has the larger expected return? Explain why portfolio 2 is known as portfolio insurance.

34. A **knockout call option** loses all value at the instant the price of the stock drops below a given "knockout level." Determine a fair price for a knockout call option when the current stock price is $20, the exercise price is $21, the knockout price is $19.50, the mean annual growth rate of the stock is 12%, the annual volatility is 40%, the risk-free rate is 10%, and the exercise date is 1 month from now (where we assume there are 21 trading days in the month and 250 in a year).

35. Suppose an investor has the opportunity to buy the following contract (a stock call option) on March 1. The contract allows him to buy 100 shares of ABC stock at the end of March, April, or May at a guaranteed price of $50 per share. He can exercise this option at most once. For example, if he purchases the stock at the end of March, he cannot purchase more in April or May at the guaranteed price. If the investor buys the contract, he is hoping that the stock price will go up. The reasoning is that if he buys the contract, the price goes up to $51, and he buys the stock (that is, he exercises his option) for $50, he can then sell the stock for $51 and make a profit of $1 per share. Of course, if the stock price goes down, he doesn't have to exercise his option; he can just throw the contract away.

Assume that the stock price change each month is normally distributed with mean 0 and standard deviation 2. The investor uses the following strategy. At the end of March, he exercises the option only if the stock price is above $51.50. At the end of April, he exercises the option (assuming he hasn't exercised it yet) only if the price is above $50.75. At the end of May, he exercises the option (assuming he hasn't exercised it yet) only if the price is above $50.00. (This isn't necessarily his best strategy, but it's a reasonable one.) Simulate 250 replications of this strategy and answer the following.

a. Estimate the probability that he will exercise his option.
b. Estimate his net profit with this strategy. (This doesn't include the price of the contract.)
c. Estimate the probability that he will net over $300.
d. Estimate the worth of this contract to him.

12.4 MARKETING MODELS

There are certainly plenty of opportunities for marketing departments to use simulation. They face uncertainty in the brand-switching behavior of customers, the entry of new brands into the market, customer preferences for different attributes of products, the effects of advertising on sales, and others. We will examine some interesting marketing applications of simulation in this section.

Models of Customer Loyalty

What is a loyal customer worth to a company? This is an extremely important question for companies. (It is an important part of customer relationship management, or CRM, currently one of the hottest topics in marketing.) Companies know that if customers become dissatisfied with the company's product, they are likely to switch and never return. The loss in profit can be large, particularly since long-standing customers tend to be more profitable in any year than new customers. The following example uses a reasonable model of customer loyalty and simulation to estimate the worth of a customer to a company. It is based on the excellent discussion of customer loyalty in Reichheld (1996).

EXAMPLE 12.12

THE LONG-TERM VALUE OF A CUSTOMER AT DOITQUICK

DoItQuick is a software company that sells programs to individuals for keeping track of home finances, home inventory, and other common tasks. The company has done extensive research into its costs and revenues, and it has discovered that new customers are much less profitable on an annual basis than long-standing customers. There are several reasons for this. Long-standing customers tend to require less in overhead costs (mail advertising, help over the phone, price discounts), they tend to order more merchandise annually, and they help DoItQuick make money by referring new customers to the company's products. The company estimates (from historical customer behavior) that a customer who has been loyal for n years—that is, has bought from the company for n consecutive years—contributes a *normally* distributed random amount of profit in the nth year that has mean and standard deviation as listed in Figure 12.40. For example, a customer in her first year contributes a mean *loss* of $40, with a corresponding standard deviation of $6. In contrast, a customer in his fifth year contributes a mean *gain* of $85,

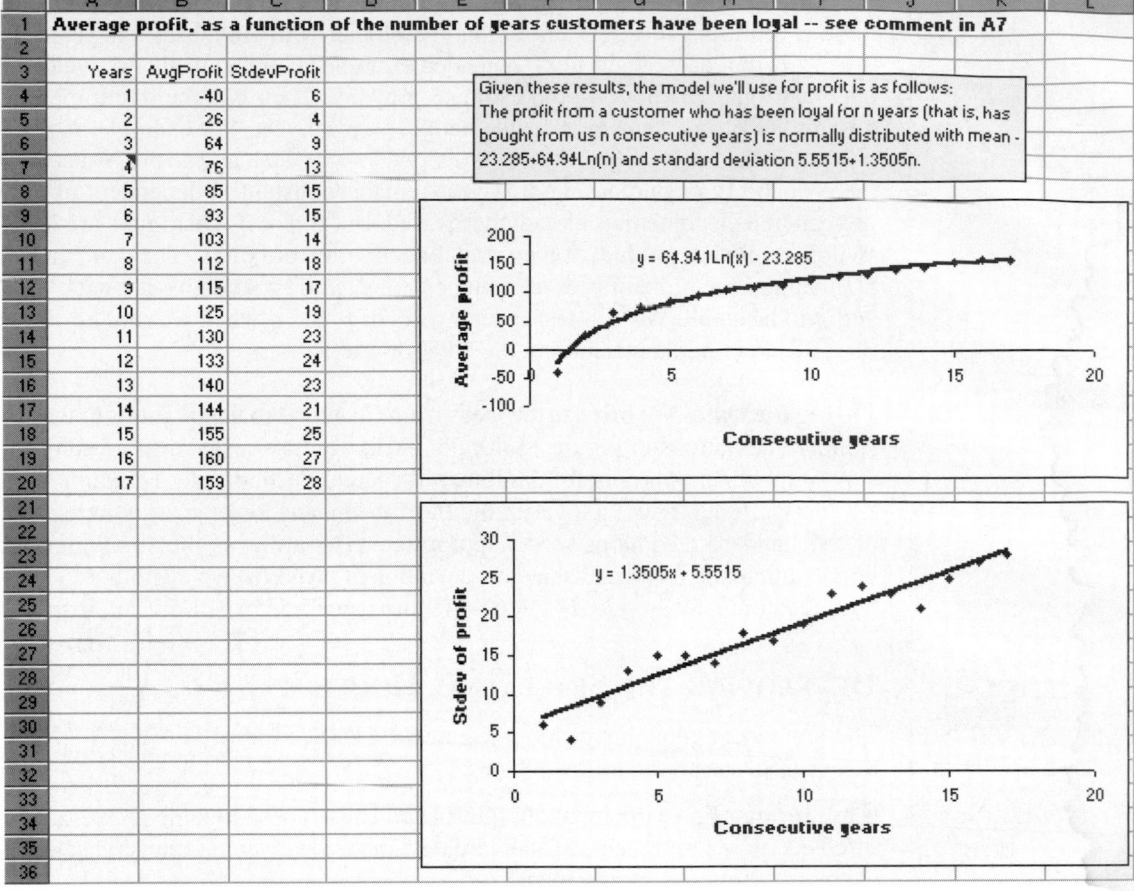

FIGURE 12.40 Profit as a Function of Years as Customer

with a corresponding standard deviation of $15. DoItQuick is interested is seeing how much profit a typical customer is worth over his or her years with the company.

This depends on the probability of retention. To model retention, let $r(n)$ be the probability that a customer who has purchased for n consecutive years does *not* purchase the next year. If this occurs, we assume that the customer switches loyalty and never purchases from DoItQuick again. A consultant has suggested to DoItQuick that a reasonable model of customer retention is to let $r(1) = 1 - p$ for some p between 0 and 1, and to use the equation

$$r(n) = qr(n-1) \tag{12.4}$$

for $n > 2$, where q is a positive constant.

What does this model mean, and how can it and the data in Figure 12.40 be used to simulate the net present value (NPV) of profit over a 20-year period from a typical customer who has made his or her first purchase from DoItQuick this year? Assume an interest rate of 10% for discounting.

Solution

The solution is broken into several parts. First, we will explain the consultant's retention model. Then we will fit curves to the profit data in Figure 12.40. Finally, we will develop the simulation model and run it with @Risk.

Explaining the Retention Model The consultant's retention model makes sense. First, p represents the probability that a customer who purchases this year for the first time will purchase again next year. For example, if 90% of all first-year customers purchase again, then we would estimate p by 0.9. Then q is the fraction by which the probability of *not* remaining loyal changes year by year. For example, if $p = 0.9$ and $q = 0.95$, then $r(1) = 0.1, r(2) = 0.095, r(3) = 0.0903$, and so on. Note that if $q = 1$, the probability of purchasing next year remains constant, independent of the number of years the customer has already purchased. But if $q < 1$, customers are less likely to switch to another product as they stay longer with DoItQuick. The company wants the $r(n)$ values, the probabilities of losing customers, to be small, so it wants p to be large and q to be small. We will test several pairs of p and q when we run the simulation to see how these parameters affect the NPV of profit.

Fitting the Data We first use the ideas from Chapter 2 to fit equations to the means and standard deviations in Figure 12.40. For each, we draw a scatterplot versus year, then superimpose an appropriate trendline with Excel's Chart/Add Trendline menu item. As shown in the figure, a logarithmic fit of the means looks good, whereas a linear fit of the standard deviations seems appropriate. Therefore, in the simulation model we will estimate the mean and standard deviation of profit from a customer in her nth year with the company as $-23.285 + 64.941 \ln(n)$ and $5.5515 + 1.3505n$, respectively.

DEVELOPING THE SIMULATION MODEL

The simulation model appears in Figure 12.41. (See the file LOYALTY.XLS.) It can be developed with the following steps.

❶ Inputs. Enter the inputs in the shaded cells. These include the parameter of the fitted equations for mean and standard deviation, the discount rate, and selected values of the retention parameters p and q.

❷ Simulation index. We will use RISKSIMTABLE to run the simulation 12 times, once for each combination of p and q. To set up the model to do this, enter the formula

=RISKSIMTABLE(SimIndexes)

in cell B11. Then obtain the corresponding values of p and q in cells B13 and B15 with the formulas

=VLOOKUP(SimIndex,LookupTable,2)

and

=VLOOKUP(SimIndex,LookupTable,3)

❸ Profits. We want to simulate the profits from a customer for as long as the customer remains loyal to the company. To do so, first calculate the appropriate means and standard deviations in columns B and C of the simulation section with the formulas

=InterceptMean+SlopeMean*LN(A21)

and

=InterceptStdev+SlopeStdev*A21

in cells B21 and C21, and copy them down for all 20 years. Then generate the actual profits from this customer in column D as long as the customer remains loyal. Start by generating the first-year profit in cell D21 with the formula

=RISKNORMAL(B21,C21)

	A	B	C	D	E	F	G	H	I	J	K	L
1	**Customer loyalty model**											
2												
3	**Assumptions**									**Pairs of p and q to test**		
4	The mean profit this year for a customer who is purchasing for the nth consecutive year is a+b*Ln(n), where									Index	p	q
5	a	-23.285								1	0.8	0.95
6	b	64.94								2	0.8	0.975
7	The stdev of profit this year for a customer who is purchasing for the nth consecutive year is c+dn, where									3	0.8	1
8	c	5.5515								4	0.85	0.95
9	d	1.3505								5	0.85	0.975
10										6	0.85	1
11	Simulation index	1								7	0.9	0.95
12	A customer who is buying for the first year has probability p of buying at least one more year, where									8	0.9	0.975
13	p	0.8								9	0.9	1
14	A customer who has bought for n>=2 consecutive years will *not* buy next year with probability r(n), where r(n)=q*r(n-1)									10	0.95	0.95
15	q	0.95								11	0.95	0.975
16										12	0.95	1
17	Discount rate	10%										
18												
19	**Simulation of the profits from a customer who buys this year for the first time**											
20	Year	Mean	Stdev	Profit	PrQuitting	Quits?						
21	1	-23.285	6.902	-23.285	0.200	No						
22	2	21.728	8.253	21.728	0.190	No						
23	3	48.059	9.603	48.059	0.181	No						
24	4	66.741	10.954	66.741	0.171	No						
25	5	81.232	12.304	81.232	0.163	No						
26	6	93.072	13.655	93.072	0.155	Yes						
27	7	103.082	15.005									
28	8	111.754	16.356									
29	9	119.403	17.706									
30	10	126.245	19.057									
31	11	132.434	20.407									
32	12	138.085	21.758									
33	13	143.283	23.108									
34	14	148.095	24.459									
35	15	152.576	25.809									
36	16	156.767	27.160									
37	17	160.704	28.510									
38	18	164.416	29.861									
39	19	167.927	31.211									
40	20	171.258	32.562									
41												
42	**Summary measures from simulation**											
43	NPV	$181.46										
44	Years as customer	6										

If q is 1, the probability of retention stays constant (at value p) every year. Otherwise, if q is less than 1, the probability of retention increases every year.

Range names used:
InterceptMean - B5
SlopeMean - B6
InterceptStdev - B8
SlopeStdev - B9
SimIndexes - K5:K16
SimIndex - B11
PrKeepBuying1 - B13
RetFactor - B15
DiscRate - B17
Profits - D21:D40

FIGURE 12.41 Customer Loyalty Simulation Model

Then for succeeding years, enter the formula

=IF(OR(F21="Yes",D21=""),"",RISKNORMAL(B22,C22))

in cell D22 and copy it down. The OR condition checks whether the customer has discontinued buying from DoItQuick. If so, a blank is entered. Otherwise, a normally distributed profit is generated.

❹ **Probabilities of quitting.** Calculate the probabilities of quitting (never buying from DoItQuick again) in column E from the retention model. To do so, enter the formula

=1-PrKeepBuying1

in cell E21. Then for succeeding years, enter the formula

=IF(OR(F21="Yes",D21=""),"",RetFactor*E21)

in cell E22 and copy it down. Note that the range names PrKeepBuying1 and RetFactor correspond to p and q.

⑤ Quits? We keep track of the customer's status in column F. First, enter the formula

=IF(RAND()<E21,"Yes","No")

in cell F21. Then enter the formula

=IF(OR(F21="Yes",D21=""),"",IF(RAND()<=E22,"Yes","No"))

in cell F22 and copy it down. As indicated in Figure 12.41, this logic will produce several values of "No," followed by a single "Yes" and then blanks. For example, if the "Yes" comes in the year 4 row, the customer will buy for 4 years and then quit.

⑥ Output cells. We will keep track of the NPV of profit and the number of years remaining loyal for this customer as @Risk outputs. Calculate these in cells B43 and B44 with the formulas

=RISKOUTPUT()+NPV(DiscRate,Profits)

and

=RISKOUTPUT()+COUNT(Profits)

Note that the COUNT function counts nonblank cells only.

USING @RISK

We set the number of iterations to 1000 and the number of simulations to 12 (one for each combination of p and q). Selected summary results appear in Figure 12.42. For a change, we copied and pasted the @Risk results to the spreadsheet so that we could easily see how they vary with p and q. The bar charts of the means clearly show how large values of p and small values of q are best for the company. For example, if q is

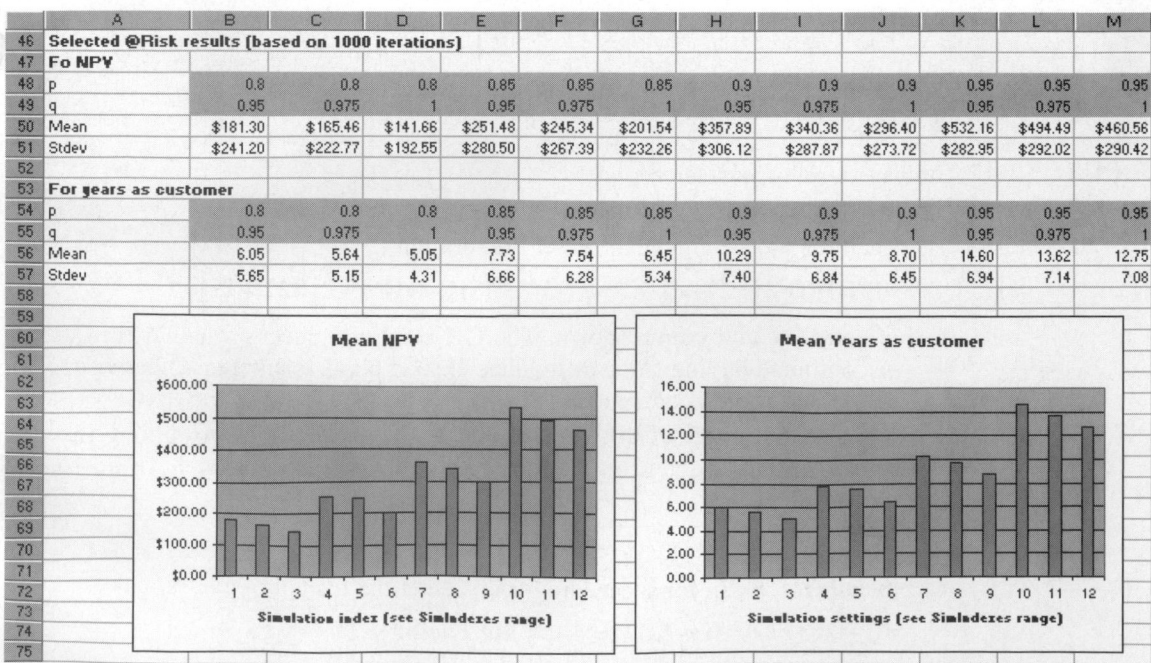

	A	B	C	D	E	F	G	H	I	J	K	L	M
46	Selected @Risk results (based on 1000 iterations)												
47	Fo NPV												
48	p	0.8	0.8	0.8	0.85	0.85	0.85	0.9	0.9	0.9	0.95	0.95	0.95
49	q	0.95	0.975	1	0.95	0.975	1	0.95	0.975	1	0.95	0.975	1
50	Mean	$181.30	$165.46	$141.66	$251.48	$245.34	$201.54	$357.89	$340.36	$296.40	$532.16	$494.49	$460.56
51	Stdev	$241.20	$222.77	$192.55	$280.50	$267.39	$232.26	$306.12	$287.87	$273.72	$282.95	$292.02	$290.42
52													
53	For years as customer												
54	p	0.8	0.8	0.8	0.85	0.85	0.85	0.9	0.9	0.9	0.95	0.95	0.95
55	q	0.95	0.975	1	0.95	0.975	1	0.95	0.975	1	0.95	0.975	1
56	Mean	6.05	5.64	5.05	7.73	7.54	6.45	10.29	9.75	8.70	14.60	13.62	12.75
57	Stdev	5.65	5.15	4.31	6.66	6.28	5.34	7.40	6.84	6.45	6.94	7.14	7.08

FIGURE 12.42 Selected Summary Results from @Risk

fixed at value 0.95, the mean NPV of profit from this typical customer is $181.30, then $251.48, then $357.89, and finally $532.16 as p increases from 0.8 to 0.85 to 0.9 to 0.95. The message should be clear. By increasing the probability of keeping customers loyal, the company can make a big improvement in its bottom line. ∎

Consumer Preference Models with Correlated Values

Toward the end of the previous chapter, we discussed @Risk's ability to simulate correlated values. Now we will put this feature to use, in a natural way, in a marketing context.[7]

EXAMPLE 12.13

ESTIMATING MARKET SHARE FOR NEW BRANDS AT BISQUAKE

There are currently two brands of brownies on the market. The Bisquake Company plans to enter the brownie market with one of two new brands. Each of the existing brands and potential new brands is characterized by three attributes: sweetness (measured on a 1 to 10 scale), chewiness (measured on a 1 to 10 scale), and price per box. These attributes are listed in Table 12.15. Each customer is assumed to choose one of these brands over the others on the basis of a weighted combination of the three attributes. Specifically, each customer is assumed to calculate a score for each brand as

$$\text{Score} = w_s * \text{Sweetness} + w_c * \text{Chewiness} + w_p * \text{Price}$$

where the w's are weights. (We would expect w_s and w_c to be positive because most customers prefer more of these attributes to less, but we would expect w_p to be negative because customers prefer lower prices.) The customer then purchases the brand with the largest score.

TABLE 12.15	Attributes of Brands in Brownie Example		
	Sweetness	**Chewiness**	**Price**
Existing brand 1	8	6	$3.00
Existing brand 2	10	7	$3.80
Potential new brand 1	8	6	$2.00
Potential new brand 2	10	9	$4.50

Each customer's weights are different, depending on how important sweetness, chewiness, and price are to the customer. However, we might expect these weights to be correlated. For example, we might expect the sweetness and chewiness weights to be positively correlated. If a customer attaches a lot of importance to sweetness, he might also attach a lot of weight to chewiness. We will assume the population of customers have normally distributed weights with the means and standard deviations shown in Table 12.16 (page 678). We will also assume that the correlations between these weights are those given in Table 12.17 (page 678). Note that the correlation

---

[7]This example is based on the work of Hauser and Gaskin (1984).

TABLE 12.16	Means and Standard Deviations of Weights for Brownie Example	
	Mean	Standard Deviation
Sweetness	5.0	1.0
Chewiness	4.0	0.6
Price	−9.0	2.0

TABLE 12.17	Correlations Between Weights in Brownie Example		
	Sweetness	Chewiness	Price
Sweetness	1.00	0.80	0.70
Chewiness	0.80	1.00	0.60
Price	0.70	0.65	1.00

between a variable and itself is always 1. The other correlations, which are all positive, imply that if a customer puts a large weight on one attribute, he will tend to put a large weight on the other two attributes.

Bisquake wants to use simulation to determine the new brand (from the two possibilities) that is likely to obtain the larger market share.

Solution

A single iteration of the simulation will simulate the behavior of a single customer. That is, it will generate this customer's weights, find this customer's scores for each of the brands, and see whether this customer prefers new brand 1 or new brand 2 to the existing brands. By performing many iterations, we can simulate the behavior of many customers and approximate the fraction of the entire customer population who prefer either of the new brands to the existing brands.

DEVELOPING THE SIMULATION MODEL

The simulation model appears in Figure 12.43. (See the file BROWNIE.XLS.) It can be formed as follows.

1 **Inputs.** Enter the inputs in the shaded ranges. These include the given means, standard deviations, and correlations for customers' scores on the attributes. They also include the *actual* attributes of the two existing and two new brands.

2 **Simulated weights.** @Risk's method of generating correlated random numbers might not be very intuitive, but it is quite easy once you see how it works. We want the weights in the SimWeights range to be normally distributed with the means and standard deviations in the range B6:D7, but we also want them to be correlated. To accomplish this, generate the first weight (for sweetness) in cell B24 with the formula

=RISKNORMAL(B6,B7,RISKCORRMAT(CorrMatrix,B23))

Then copy this to the range C24:D24 to generate the weights for the other two attributes. As we discussed in the previous chapter, the third argument of RISKNORMAL is RISKCORRMAT, which itself has the arguments CorrMatrix and B23. This formula instructs @Risk to generate a normal random number but to correlate it with other potential random numbers, using the correlations in the first column of the CorrMatrix

FIGURE 12.43
Simulation Model
with Correlated
Values

	A	B	C	D	E	F	G
1	**New product decision with correlated preferences**						
2							
3	**Input section**						
4	Normal distribution of customers' weights for attributes						
5		Sweetness	Chewiness	Price		Range names used:	
6	Mean	5	4	-9		CorrMatrix - B11:D13	
7	StDev	1	0.6	2		SimWeights - B23:D23	
8						ExBrScores - B26:B27	
9	Correlations between customers' weights for attributes						
10		Sweetness	Chewiness	Price			
11	Sweetness	1	0.8	0.7			
12	Chewiness	0.8	1	0.65			
13	Price	0.7	0.65	1			
14							
15	Attributes of existing brands and possible new brands						
16		Sweetness	Chewiness	Price			
17	Existing brand 1	8	6	$3.00			
18	Existing brand 2	10	7	$3.80			
19	New brand 1	8	6	$2.00			
20	New brand 2	10	9	$4.50			
21							
22	**Simulation section**						
23	Attribute index	1	2	3			
24	Generated weights	3.03	2.62	-8.67			
25							
26	Scores for brands						
27	Existing brand 1	13.94					
28	Existing brand 2	15.68					
29	New brand 1	22.61					
30	New brand 2	14.86					
31							
32	Will either new brand be chosen? (1 if yes, 0 if no)						
33	New brand 1	1					
34	New brand 2	0					
35							
36	**Percentage of time new brands will be chosen (summary measures from @Risk)**						
37	New brand 1	64.7%					
38	New brand 2	76.6%					

range. It uses the *first* column because the second argument of RISKCORRMAT, cell B23, has value 1. For chewiness, this second argument is 2, and for price it is 3. This second argument essentially designates the *position* in the correlation matrix for a particular random value.

❸ Scores for brands. Calculate this customer's scores for the four brands in the range B27:B30 by entering the formula

=SUMPRODUCT(SimWeights,B17:D17)

in cell B27 and copying it to the range B28:B30. This formula weights the attributes of each brand with the customer's weights.

❹ Is either new brand chosen? One of the new brands will be chosen if its score is larger than the *larger* score of the two existing brands. Therefore, enter the formula

=RISKOUTPUT()+IF(B29>MAX(ExBrScores),1,0)

in cell B33 to check whether new brand 1 is preferred to the existing brands. Then copy it to cell B34 to do the same for new brand 2.

❺ Summarize output cells. The @Risk output cells, B33 and B34, contain 1 or 0 depending on whether either new brand is preferred to existing brands. We want to determine the fraction of time these will be 1. To do so, we can run the simulation for many iterations and calculate the *means* of the output cells. This is because the average of a sequence of 0's and 1's is the fraction that are 1's. (Make sure you understand why.) We can calculate these fractions directly in the spreadsheet by entering the formula

=RISKMEAN(B33)

in cell B37 and copying it to cell B38.

USING @RISK

We set the number of iterations to 1000 and the number of simulations to 1. After running @Risk, we see from cells B37 and B38 that new brand 1 is preferred to existing brands in 64.7% of the iterations, and new brand 2 is preferred to existing brands in 76.6% of the iterations. Based on this information, new brand 2 appears to be the more promising brand for BisQuake to market.

We might ask how dependent these results are on the correlations we chose in the correlation matrix. Note that the correlations are all positive. This means that if a customer puts a lot of weight on sweetness, she also tends to put a lot of weight on chewiness. The positive correlation between sweetness (or chewiness) and price is less intuitive. It says that large weights on sweetness tend to go with "large" weights on price. But because price weights are negative (everyone prefers lower prices to higher prices), a "large" weight on price means a less negative weight for price—for example, -5 is "larger" than -8. So the positive correlation between sweetness and price really means that if a customer puts a lot of weight on sweetness, he cares less about price.

For the sake of argument, suppose you think that the weights a customer assigns to the three attributes are probabilistically independent. Then we should change the correlations in all cells of the correlation matrix (except for the 1's down the diagonal) to 0 and rerun the simulation. When we did this, the values in cells B37 and B38 changed to 69.8% and 82.2%. This is not a dramatic change, but it does show that correlations can make a difference. ∎

Market Share Models

We conclude this marketing section with a rather complex model of market share behavior. This model is based on the type of competition faced by two dominant brands in an industry, such as Coca Cola and Pepsi. These companies continually attempt to take market share from one another. However, there are also smaller companies that enter and exit the market. These smaller companies can sometimes take market share from the giants, and vice versa. The following example illustrates one possible model of such behavior. Even though it is already fairly complex, it could be made much more complex by including marketing initiatives (advertising and price cuts, for example) by any of the competitors.

EXAMPLE 12.14

ESTIMATING DYNAMIC MARKET SHARES WITH TWO DOMINANT BRANDS

Sweetness and IceT are the two dominant companies in the bottled iced tea market. They each currently possess 49% of the iced tea market, with three smaller companies splitting the remaining 2%. At the beginning of any year, a random number of new small companies enter the iced tea market. The actual number of new entries is assumed to be Poisson distributed with mean 1.[8] After the new entries enter the market, there is a random shift in market share among all competitors. Essentially, all competitors lose a random percentage of their market share to other competitors. We will assume that each of these percentages is triangularly distributed with the parameters given in Table 12.18. For example, the percentage of Sweetness's market share lost to IceT has a triangular distribution with minimum value 1%, most likely value 5%, and maximum value 10%. Similarly, the percentage of market share Sweetness will lose to *each* of the small companies has parameters 0.5%, 1%, and 3%. Therefore, the more small companies there are in the market, the more of its market share Sweetness will tend to lose to them.

At the end of each year, each of the small companies has a 50% chance of exiting the iced tea market. We assume that each small company that exits loses its market share to Sweetness or IceT (not to remaining small companies). The percentage of this market share that goes to Sweetness is triangularly distributed with parameters 40%, 50%, and 60%. The remainder goes to IceT.

The dominant companies, Sweetness and IceT, want to use simulation to see how their market share is likely to change over the next 10 years.

TABLE 12.18	Parameters of Lost Market Share Percentages		
	Minimum	Most Likely	Maximum
From Sweetness			
To IceT	1.0%	5%	10%
To each small company	0.5%	1%	3%
From IceT			
To Sweetness	1.0%	5%	10%
To each small company	0.5%	1%	3%
From Small Companies			
To Sweetness	5.0%	10%	15%
To IceT	5.0%	10%	15%

Solution

The spreadsheet model is somewhat tedious to develop, but the ideas are straightforward. At the beginning of any year, we observe the market shares of Sweetness, IceT, and the small companies (combined). Next, we simulate the number of new entrants. Then we simulate the shifts in market share during the year. Next, we simulate the number of small companies that exit at the end of the year, and we simulate their market shares that go to Sweetness and IceT. Finally, we tally the total market share at the end of the year for all competitors.

DEVELOPING THE SIMULATION MODEL

The completed spreadsheet model appears in Figures 12.44 (page 682) and 12.45 (page 683). (See the file ICETEA.XLS.) It can be formed with the following steps.

[8]The Poisson distribution is a frequently used *discrete* distribution, particularly for the number of "events" that occur during some time period. This distribution is completely characterized by a single parameter—its mean. Its standard deviation is equal to the square root of the mean. Its possible values are all nonnegative integers.

FIGURE 12.44
Input Data for
Market Share Model

	A	B	C	D	E	F	G
1	**Iced tea market share simulation**						
2							
3	**Input section**						
4	Current market shares of dominant companies						
5	Sweetness	0.49		**Range name used:**			
6	IceT	0.49		MeanEntries - B16			
7							
8	Current data on small companies						
9	Number	3					
10	Combined market share	0.02					
11							
12	Probability any small company will exit industry in any year						
13		0.5					
14							
15	Mean number of new entries in any year (Poisson distributed)						
16		1					
17							
18	Percentage of market share of each exiter that goes to Sweetness - the rest go to IceT (triangularly distributed)						
19		Minimum	Most likely	Maximum			
20		0.4	0.5	0.6			
21							
22	Percentage of companies' market shares lost to each other and to small companies						
23	Sweetness	Minimum	Most likely	Maximum			
24	to IceT	0.01	0.05	0.1			
25	to each small company	0.005	0.01	0.03			
26	IceT						
27	to Sweetness	0.01	0.05	0.1			
28	to each small company	0.005	0.01	0.03			
29	Small companies						
30	to Sweetness	0.05	0.1	0.15			
31	to IceT	0.05	0.1	0.15			

❶ Inputs. Enter the inputs shown in the shaded ranges of Figure 12.44.

❷ Beginning market shares. For year 1 the beginning market shares are inputs. For example, find the beginning market share for Sweetness in cell B35 with the formula

=B5

For every other year, the beginning market shares are the ending market shares from the previous year. For example, find the beginning market share for Sweetness in year 2 by entering the formula

=B66

in cell C35. Then copy this to the range C35:K37 for all competitors over the remaining years.

❸ Entries to the market. In year 1, find the number of small companies before entries, the number of new entries, and the number of small companies after entries by entering the formulas

=B9
=RISKPOISSON(MeanEntries)

and

=SUM(B40:B41)

in cells B40, B41, and B42. Note that the RISKPOISSON function, which takes a single argument, generates the number of new entries in a single year. For year 2, the number of small companies before entries is the remaining number from year 1. Therefore, enter the formula

=B58

	A	B	C	D	E	F	G	H	I	J	K
33	**Simulation section**										
34	Beginning market shares	Year 1	Year 2	Year 3	Year 4	Year 5	Year 6	Year 7	Year 8	Year 9	Year 10
35	Sweetness	0.490	0.458	0.495	0.516	0.524	0.494	0.497	0.489	0.497	0.474
36	IceT	0.490	0.484	0.483	0.484	0.476	0.474	0.450	0.446	0.463	0.477
37	Small companies (combined)	0.020	0.058	0.023	0.000	0.000	0.032	0.052	0.065	0.040	0.049
38											
39	Small companies before and after new entries										
40	Number of smalls before entries	3	5	1	0	0	3	2	2	1	1
41	Number entering at beginning	2	1	1	0	3	0	0	0	0	1
42	Total number of smalls	5	6	2	0	3	3	2	2	1	2
43											
44	Market shares lost during year										
45	Sweetness										
46	to IceT	0.038	0.015	0.020	0.018	0.039	0.026	0.028	0.019	0.042	0.024
47	to smalls (combined)	0.016	0.039	0.019	0.000	0.018	0.026	0.013	0.014	0.008	0.018
48	IceT										
49	to Sweetness	0.019	0.026	0.035	0.026	0.028	0.041	0.029	0.012	0.023	0.035
50	to smalls (combined)	0.026	0.052	0.010	0.000	0.014	0.026	0.009	0.014	0.008	0.025
51	Small companies										
52	to Sweetness	0.002	0.005	0.003	0.000	0.000	0.003	0.005	0.009	0.003	0.005
53	to IceT	0.001	0.008	0.002	0.000	0.000	0.003	0.005	0.004	0.004	0.003
54											
55	Information on exiters										
56	Market share of smalls before exits	0.058	0.136	0.047	0.000	0.032	0.078	0.065	0.079	0.049	0.084
57	Number of smalls exiting at end	0	5	2	0	0	1	0	1	0	2
58	Number of smalls remaining	5	1	0	0	3	2	2	1	1	0
59	Combined market share of exiters	0.000	0.114	0.047	0.000	0.000	0.026	0.000	0.040	0.000	0.084
60											
61	Market shares gained from exiters										
62	to Sweetness	0.000	0.061	0.022	0.000	0.000	0.012	0.000	0.020	0.000	0.043
63	to IceT	0.000	0.053	0.024	0.000	0.000	0.014	0.000	0.020	0.000	0.041
64											
65	Market shares at end										
66	Sweetness	0.458	0.495	0.516	0.524	0.494	0.497	0.489	0.497	0.474	0.514
67	IceT	0.484	0.483	0.484	0.476	0.474	0.450	0.446	0.463	0.477	0.486
68	Small companies (combined)	0.058	0.023	0.000	0.000	0.032	0.052	0.065	0.040	0.049	0.000

FIGURE 12.45 Market Share Simulation Model

in cell C40. Then copy the formulas in cells C40, B41, and B42 across these rows.

❹ **Market shares lost during the year.** Generate the percentage of its market share Sweetness loses to IceT and to the small companies (combined) in year 1 by entering the formulas

=RISKTRIANG($B$24,$C$24,$D$24)*B35

and

=RISKTRIANG($B$25,$C$25,$D$25)*B35*B42

in cells B46 and B47 and then copy these across rows 46 and 47. Note that the latter of these multiplies the random percentage of market share lost by the number of small companies currently in the market. Next, enter similar formulas in rows 49, 50, 52, and 53 for market share lost by IceT and the small companies. For example, the formula in cell B53 is

=RISKTRIANG($B$31,$C$31,$D$31)*B37

❺ **Exiters.** Rows 56–59 contain information about small companies before and after exiting. To calculate this information, enter the formulas

=SUM(B37,B47,B50)-SUM(B52:B53)
=IF(B42>0,RISKBINOMIAL(B42,$B$13),0)
=B42-B57

and

=IF(B42>0,(B57/B42)*B56,0)

in cells B56, B57, B58, and B59. Then copy these across rows 56–59. The formula in B56 tallies the market shares lost and gained for the small companies before exiting takes place. The formula in cell B57 uses the RISKBINOMIAL function to generate the number of small companies that exit. This function takes two arguments: the number of small companies and the probability that any company exits. Because it is not defined if the number of small companies is 0, we need the IF function. The formula in B59 finds the amount of market share possessed by the exiting companies under the assumption that all small companies have an equal market share. Again, it uses an IF function to take care of the case where there are no remaining small companies—never divide by 0!

6 **Market share gained by exiters.** The assumption of the model is that the market share of the exiters in row 63 is split randomly between Sweetness and IceT. To generate the split, enter the formula

=RISKTRIANG($B$20,$C$20,$D$20)*B59

and

=B59-B62

in cells B62 and B63. Then copy these across rows 62 and 63.

7 **Year-end market shares.** Calculate the year-end market shares of Sweetness, IceT, and the small companies (combined) by entering the formulas

=SUM(B35,B49,B52,B62)-SUM(B46:B47)
=SUM(B36,B46,B53,B63)-SUM(B49:B50)

and

=B56-B59

in cells B66, B67, and B68. Then copy these across rows 66–68. If you like, you can check that the year-end market shares sum to 100% for each year, as they should.

8 **@Risk outputs.** We have not yet designated any cells as @Risk output cells. There are at least two possibilities. If we are interested in only the *final* market shares after 10 years, we should designate cells K66, K67, and K68 as output cells. Alternatively, if we want to see how market shares move through time, we can specify whole ranges as output ranges. (This is the alternative we used.) For example, if we highlight the range B66:K66, click on the Add Outputs button of the @Risk toolbar, and name this output range Sweetness (or some such suggestive name), then this whole range becomes an output range that @Risk keeps track of. When you do this, the formulas change slightly. For example, the formula in cell B66 becomes

=RISKOUTPUT(,"Sweetness",1)+SUM(B35,B49,B52,B62)-SUM(B46:B47)

to indicate that this is the *first* cell in the Sweetness output range.

USING @RISK

We set the number of iterations to 1000 and the number of simulations to 1. After running @Risk, we obtain histograms of market share after 10 years as in Figures 12.46 and 12.47. (The histogram for Sweetness, not shown, is similar to the one for IceT.) We see that the final IceT market share is essentially symmetric around

FIGURE 12.46
Final Market Share
for IceT

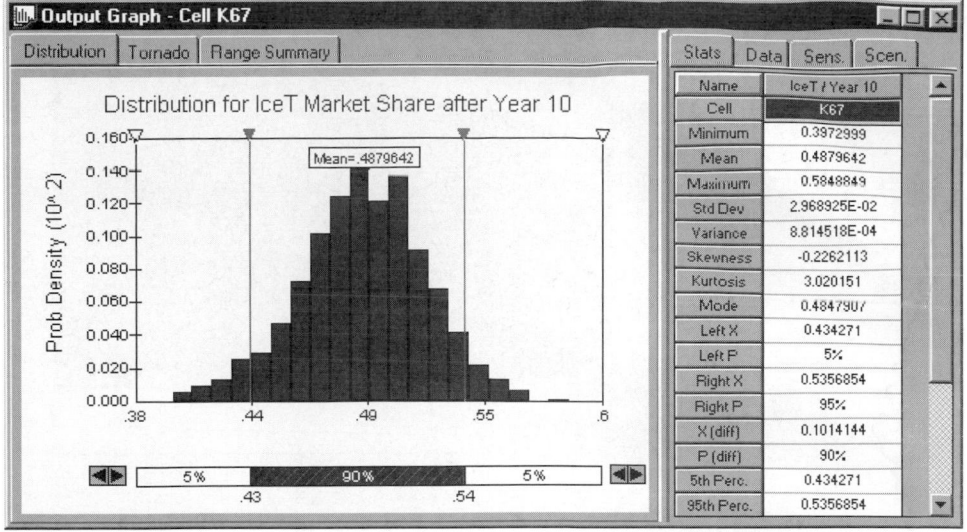

FIGURE 12.47
Final Market Share
for Small Companies

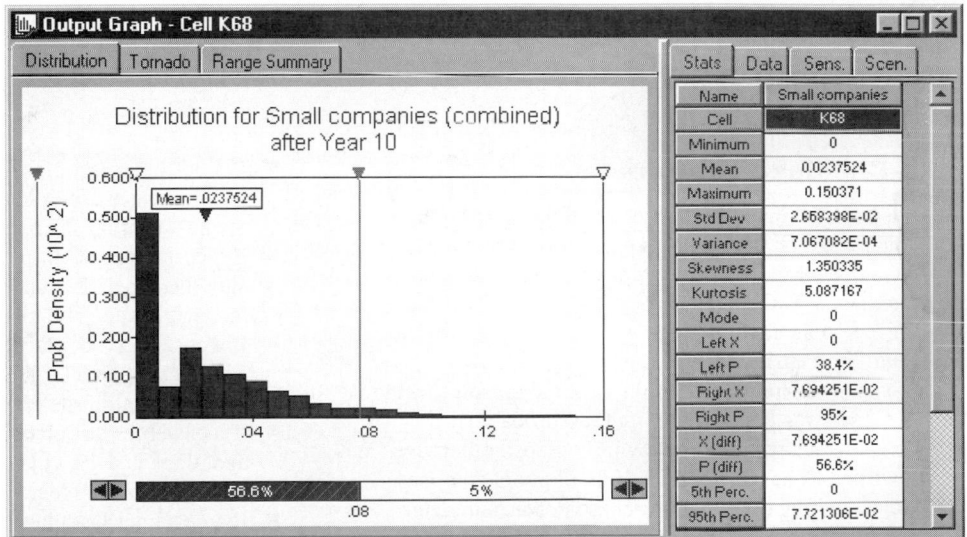

its original value of 49%, although there is considerable variability. In contrast, the final market share for the small companies (combined) has a good chance of being 0, although there is a small probability that it could be considerably larger—up to 8%, say.

Assuming that we designate whole rows as output ranges, such as row 66 for Sweetness, we can obtain a summary chart of the company's market share through time, as in Figure 12.48 (page 686). (See the preceding chapter for details on @Risk's summary chart feature.) This chart shows that the mean market share for Sweetness remains approximately constant through time. However, as we stand at the beginning of year 1 and try to predict the future, there is more uncertainty the farther out we look. This is a general rule. It is almost always harder to make long-range forecasts than short-range forecasts!

FIGURE 12.48
Summary Chart for
Sweetness Market
Share

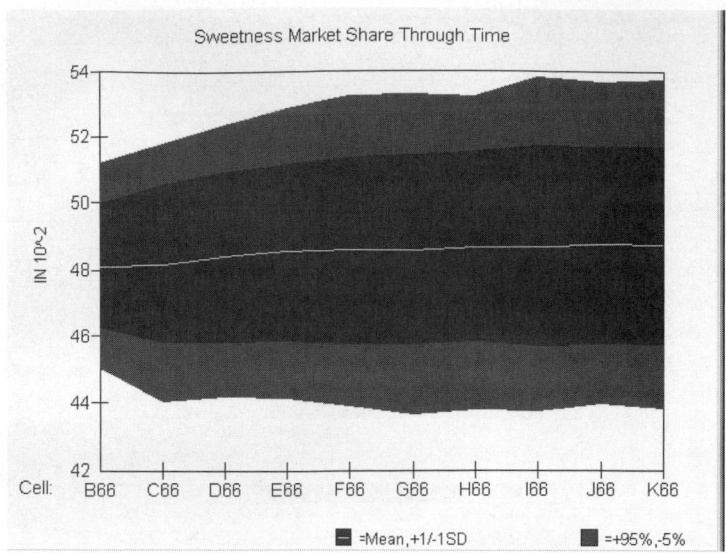

Sweetness Market Share Through Time

IN 10^2

Cell: B66 C66 D66 E66 F66 G66 H66 I66 J66 K66

━ =Mean,+1/-1SD   ■ =+95%,-5%

Skill-Building Problems

36. Suppose that Coke and Pepsi are fighting for the cola market. Each week each person in the market buys one case of Coke or Pepsi. If the person's last purchase was Coke, there is a 0.90 probability that this person's next purchase will be Coke; otherwise, it will be Pepsi. (We are considering only two brands in the market.) Similarly, if the person's last purchase was Pepsi, there is a 0.80 probability that this person's next purchase will be Pepsi; otherwise, it will be Coke. Currently half of all people purchase Coke, and the other half purchase Pepsi. Simulate one year of sales in the cola market and estimate each company's average weekly market share. Do this by assuming that the total market size is fixed at 100 customers. (*Hint*: Use the RISKBINOMIAL function.)

37. Seas Beginning sells clothing by mail order. An important question is when to strike a customer from their mailing list. At present, they strike a customer from their mailing list if a customer fails to order from six consecutive catalogs. They want to know whether striking a customer from their list after a customer fails to order from four consecutive catalogs will result in a higher profit per customer. The following data are available:

- If a customer placed an order the last time she received a catalog, then there is a 20% chance she will order from the next catalog.

- If a customer last placed an order one catalog ago, there is a 16% chance she will order from the next catalog she receives.

- If a customer last placed an order two catalogs ago, there is a 12% chance she will order from the next catalog she receives.

- If a customer last placed an order three catalogs ago, there is an 8% chance she will order from the next catalog she receives.

- If a customer last placed an order four catalogs ago, there is a 4% chance she will order from the next catalog she receives.

- If a customer last placed an order five catalogs ago, there is a 2% chance she will order from the next catalog she receives.

  It costs $1 to send a catalog, and the average profit per order is $15. Assume a customer has just placed an order. To maximize expected profit per customer, would Seas Beginning make more money canceling such a customer after six non-orders or four non-orders?

38. Based on Babich (1992). Suppose that each week every family in the United States buys a gallon of orange juice from company A, B, or C. Let p_A denote the probability that a gallon produced by company A is of unsatisfactory quality, and define p_B and p_C similarly for companies B and C. If the last gallon of juice purchased by a family is satisfactory, then the next week they will purchase a gallon of juice from the same company. If the last gallon of juice purchased by a family is not satisfactory, then the family will purchase a gallon from a competitor. Consider a week in which A families have purchased juice A, B families have purchased juice B, and C families have purchased juice C. Assume that families that switch brands during a period are allocated to the remaining brands in a manner that is proportional to the current market shares of the other brands. Thus, if a customer switches from brand A, there is probability $B/(B + C)$ that he will switch to brand B and probability $C/(B + C)$ that he will switch to brand C. Suppose that 1,000,000 gallons of orange juice are purchased each week.

a. After a year, what will the market share for each firm be? Assume $p_A = 0.10$, $p_B = 0.15$, and $p_C = 0.20$. (*Hint*: You will need to use the RISKBINOMIAL function to see how many people switch from A and then use the RISKBINOMIAL function again to see how many switch from A to B and from A to C.)

b. Suppose a 1% increase in market share is worth $10,000 per week to company A. Company A believes that for a cost of $1 million per year it can cut the percentage of unsatisfactory juice cartons in half. Is this worthwhile? (Use the same values of p_A, p_B, and p_C as in part **a**.)

Skill-Extending Problems

39. Suppose that GLC earns a $4000 profit each time a person buys a car. We want to determine how the expected profit earned from a customer depends on the quality of GLC's cars. We assume a typical customer will purchase 10 cars during her lifetime. She will purchase a car now (year 1) and then purchase a car every 5 years—during year 6, year 11, and so on. For simplicity, we assume that Hundo is GLC's only competitor. We also assume that if the consumer is satisfied with the car she purchases, she will buy her next car from the same company, but if she is not satisfied, she will buy her next car from the other company. Hundo produces cars that satisfy 80% of its customers. Currently, GLC produces cars that also satisfy 80% of its customers. Consider a customer whose first car is a GLC car. If profits are discounted at 10% annually, use simulation to estimate the value of this customer to GLC. Also estimate the value of a customer to GLC if it can raise its customer satisfaction rating to 85%; to 90%; to 95%.

40. The Mutron Company is thinking of marketing a new drug used to make pigs healthier. At the beginning of the current year, there are 1,000,000 pigs that might use the product. Each pig will use Mutron's drug or a competitor's drug once a year.

The number of pigs is forecasted to grow by an average of 5% per year. However, this growth rate is not a sure thing. Mutron assumes that each year's growth rate is an independent draw from a normal distribution, with probability 0.95 that the growth rate will be between 3% and 7%. Assuming it enters the market, Mutron is not sure what its share of the market will be during year 1, so it models this with a triangular distribution. Its worst-case share is 20%, its most likely share is 40%, and its best-case share is 70%. In the absence of any *new* competitors entering this market (in addition to itself), Mutron believes its market share will remain the same in succeeding years. However, there are three potential entrants (in addition to Mutron). At the beginning of each year, each entrant that has not already entered the market has a 40% chance of entering the market. The year after a competitor enters, Mutron's market share will drop by 20% for each *new* competitor who entered. For example, if two competitors enter the market in year 1, Mutron's market share in year 2 will be reduced by 40% from what it would have been with no entrants. Note that if all three entrants have entered, there will be no more entrants. Each unit of the drug sells for $2.20 and incurs a variable cost of $0.40. Profits are discounted by 10% annually.

a. Assuming that Mutron enters the market, use simulation to find a 95% confidence interval for its expected net present value (NPV) for the next 10 years from the drug.

b. Again assuming that Mutron enters the market, it can be 95% certain that its *actual* NPV from the drug is between what two values?

41. You are unemployed and 21 years old and searching for a job. Until you accept a job offer, the following situation occurs. At the beginning of each year, you receive a job offer. The annual salary associated with the job offer is equally likely to be any number between $20,000 and $100,000. You must immediately choose whether to accept the job offer. If you accept an offer with salary x, you receive x per year while you work (we assume you retire at age 70), including the current year. Assume that cash flows are discounted so that a cash flow received 1 year from now has a present value of 0.9. You have adopted the following policy. You will accept the first job offer that exceeds w dollars.

a. Use simulation to determine the value of w (within $10,000) that maximizes the expected NPV of earnings you will receive the rest of your working life?

b. Repeat part **a**, assuming now that you get a 3% raise in salary every year after the first year you accept the job.

12.5 SIMULATING GAMES OF CHANCE

We realize that this is a book about "business" applications. However, it is instructive (and fun) to see how simulation can be used to analyze games of chance, including sports contests. Indeed, many analysts refer to "Monte Carlo" simulation, and you can guess where that name comes from—the gambling casinos of Monte Carlo.

Simulating the Game of Craps

Most games of chance are great candidates for simulation since they are, by their very nature, driven by randomness. In this section we will examine one such game that is extremely popular in the gambling casinos: the game of craps. In its most basic form, the game of craps is played as follows. A player rolls two dice and calculates the sum of the two sides turned up. If this sum is 7 or 11, the player wins right away. If the sum is 2, 3, or 12, the player loses right away. Otherwise, if this sum is any other number (4, 5, 6, 8, 9, or 10), that number becomes the player's "point." Then the dice are thrown repeatedly until the sum is the original point or 7. In case the point occurs before a 7, the player wins. But if a 7 occurs before the point, the player loses. The following example uses simulation to determine the properties of this game.

EXAMPLE 12.15

ESTIMATING THE PROBABILITY OF WINNING AT CRAPS

Joe Gamble loves to play craps at the casinos. He suspects that his chances of winning are less than 50-50, but he figures that he can at least play for quite a while before losing all of his cash. Assuming that he starts with $50 and each bet is worth $5, he wants to know whether he can play 100 games without going broke.

Solution

We will solve this problem in two parts. First, we will simulate a single game. By running this simulation for many iterations, we will find the probability that Joe wins a single game. If his intuition is correct (and surely it must be, or the casino could not stay in business), this probability will be less than 0.5. As a by-product, we will also see how many tosses of the dice are needed to determine the outcome of a single game. Then we will run a second simulation, using the probability from the first simulation, to determine whether Joe can play 100 games without going broke.

DEVELOPING THE SIMULATION MODEL

The first simulation model is for a single game, which we will iterate repeatedly. (See Figure 12.49 and the file CRAPS1.XLS.) There is a subtle problem here—we do not know how many tosses of the dice are necessary to determine the outcome of a single game. Theoretically, the game could continue forever, with the player waiting for his point or a 7. However, it is extremely unlikely that more than, say, 40 tosses will be necessary in a single game. (This can be shown by a probability argument, but we will

FIGURE 12.49
Simulation of Craps
Game

	A	B	C	D	E	F	G
1	**Craps Simulation**						
2							
3	**Simulated tosses**						
4	Toss	Die 1	Die 2	Sum	Win on this toss?	Lose on this toss?	Continue?
5	1	1	4	5	0	0	Yes
6	2	3	6	9	0	0	Yes
7	3	4	2	6	0	0	Yes
8	4	3	3	6	0	0	Yes
9	5	1	3	4	0	0	Yes
10	6	3	5	8	0	0	Yes
11	7	4	1	5	1	0	No
12	8	1	4	5			
13	9	6	1	7			
14	10	3	5	8			
15	11	5	6	11			
16	12	2	5	7			
17	13	1	1	2			
18	14	1	2	3			
19	15	6	1	7			
40	36	4	5	9			
41	37	2	1	3			
42	38	5	5	10			
43	39	6	5	11			
44	40	6	6	12			
45							
46	**Summary results from simulation**						
47	Win? (1 if yes, 0 if no)	1					
48	Number of tosses	7					

not present it here.) Therefore, we will simulate 40 tosses and use only those that are necessary to determine the outcome of a single game. The steps required to simulate a single game are as follows.

1 **Simulate tosses.** Simulate the results of 40 tosses in the range B5:D44 by entering the formula

=RISKDUNIFORM({1, 2, 3, 4, 5, 6})

in cells B5 and C5 and the formula

=SUM(B5:C5)

in cell D5. Then copy these to the range B6:D44. The @RISK function RISKDUNIFORM takes a list of numbers and randomly selects one of the numbers from this list, where each number has equal probability (in this case 1/6). DUNIFORM stands for discrete uniform.

2 **First toss outcome.** Determine the outcome of the first toss with the formulas

=IF(OR(D5=7,D5=11),1,0)
=IF(OR(D5=2,D5=3,D5=12),1,0)

and

=IF(AND(E5=0,F5=0),"Yes","No")

in cells G5, H5, and I5. Note that we use the OR condition to check whether Joe wins right away (in which case a 1 is recorded in cell G5). Similarly, the OR condition in cell H5 checks whether he loses right away. In cell I5, we use the AND condition to check whether both cells G5 and H5 are 0, in which case the game continues. Otherwise, the game is over.

③ Outcomes of other tosses. Assuming the game continues beyond the first toss, Joe's point is the value in cell D5. Then we are waiting for a toss to have the value in cell D5 or 7, whichever occurs first. To implement this logic, enter the formulas

=IF(OR(G5="No",G5=""),"",IF(D6=$D$5,1,0))
=IF(OR(G5="No",G5=""),"",IF(D6=7,1,0))

and

=IF(OR(G5="No",G5=""),"",IF(AND(E6=0,F6=0),"Yes","No"))

in cells G6, H6, and I6. Then copy these to the range G7:I44. The OR condition in each formula checks whether the game just ended on the previous toss or has been over for some time, in which case blanks are entered. Otherwise, the first two formulas check whether Joe wins or loses on this toss. If both of these return 0, the third formula returns "Yes" (and the game has just ended). Otherwise, it returns "No" (and the game continues).

④ Game outcomes. We keep track of two aspects of the game in @Risk output cells: whether Joe wins or loses and how many tosses are required. To find these, enter the formulas

=RISKOUTPUT()+SUM(E5:E34)

and

=RISKOUTPUT()+COUNT(E5:E34)

in cells B47 and B48. Note that both functions, SUM and COUNT, ignore blank cells.

USING @RISK

We set the number of iterations to 10,000 and the number of simulations to 1. After running @Risk, we obtain the summary results in Figures 12.50 and 12.51 (among others). Perhaps the most important result is the mean value in the first row of the summary table. This is the average of the sequence of 1's (wins) and 0's (losses) in cell B47. Hence, it is the fraction of times Joe won. This value is quite accurate. It can be shown with a probability argument that the probability of winning in craps is 0.493. From the outputs on the number of plays, we see that one game lasted 29 tosses, but that most games are over after a few tosses.

FIGURE 12.50
Summary Results
from @Risk

Cell	Name	Minimum	Mean	Maximum	x1=	p1=	x2=	p2=
B47	Win? (1 if yes, 0 if no)	0	0.4933	1	0	5%	1	95%
B48	Number of tosses / Di	1	3.3965	29	1	5%	10	95%

The purpose of the second simulation is to see whether Joe can play 100 games before going broke. In case he does go broke, we keep track of the number of games he was able to play.

DEVELOPING THE SIMULATION MODEL

A portion of the simulation model appears in Figure 12.52. (It shows an example where Joe went broke on the 24th play. The rows for plays 26–100 are not shown in the figure. See the file CRAPS2.XLS for the full model.) The following steps are required.

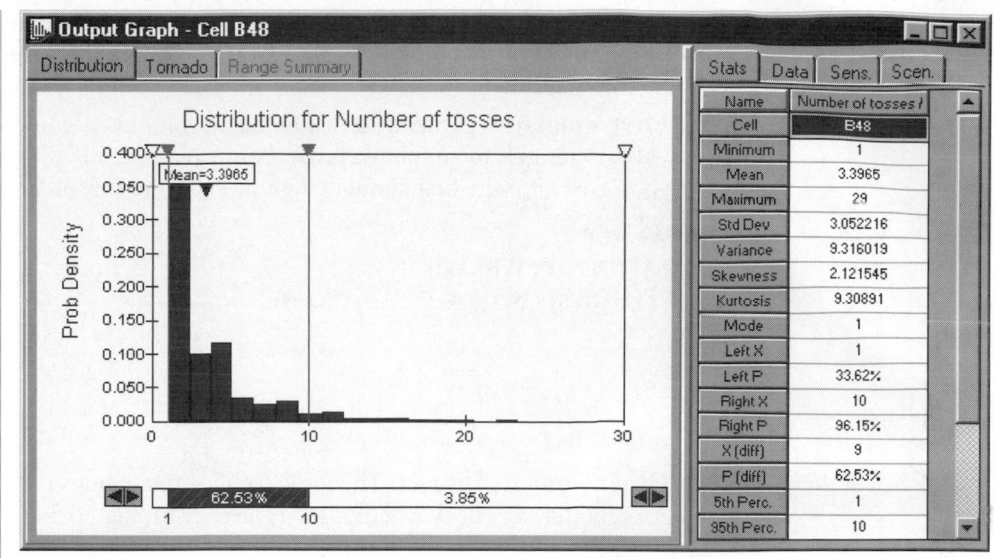

FIGURE 12.51 Histogram of Number of Tosses in a Game

	A	B	C	D	E	F	G	H
1	**Simulating craps to see whether Joe goes broke**							
2								
3	**Input section**							
4	Probability of winning	0.493		Range names used:				
5	Initial wealth	$50		PrWin - B4				
6	Bet on each game	$5		InitWealth - B5				
7	Maximum games	100		BetSize - B6				
8								
9	**Simulation of games**						**Summary results from simulation**	
10	Game	Wealth before	Won?	Wealth after	Broke yet?		Went broke? (1 if yes, 0 if no)	1
11	1	$50	0	$45	No		Number of plays	24
12	2	$45	1	$50	No			
13	3	$50	1	$55	No			
14	4	$55	1	$60	No			
15	5	$60	0	$55	No			
16	6	$55	0	$50	No			
17	7	$50	0	$45	No			
18	8	$45	1	$50	No			
19	9	$50	1	$55	No			
20	10	$55	0	$50	No			
21	11	$50	0	$45	No			
22	12	$45	0	$40	No			
23	13	$40	1	$45	No			
24	14	$45	1	$50	No			
25	15	$50	0	$45	No			
26	16	$45	0	$40	No			
27	17	$40	0	$35	No			
28	18	$35	0	$30	No			
29	19	$30	0	$25	No			
30	20	$25	0	$20	No			
31	21	$20	0	$15	No			
32	22	$15	0	$10	No			
33	23	$10	0	$5	No			
34	24	$5	0	$0	Yes			
35	25							

FIGURE 12.52 Simulation Model of Joe's Plays

1 **Inputs.** Enter the inputs in the shaded range. Note that we have used the theoretical probability, 0.493, of winning on a particular game, not the simulated value from the previous simulation.

2 **First simulated game.** The results of the simulated games appear in the range B11:B110. Although Joe might go broke before playing all 100 games, we simulate all 100 just in case. For the first simulated game enter the formulas

=InitWealth
=IF(RAND()<PrWin,1,0)
=IF(C11=1,B11+BetSize,B11-BetSize)

and

=IF(D11=0,"Yes","No")

in cells B11–E11.

3 **Other simulated games.** The logic for the other games is the same as for the first game, except that we check whether Joe is already broke. To do this, enter the formulas

=IF(OR(E11="Yes",E11=""),"",D11)
=IF(OR(E11="Yes",E11=""),"",IF(RAND()<PrWin,1,0))
=IF(OR(E11="Yes",E11=""),"",IF(C12=1,B12+BetSize,B12-BetSize))

and

=IF(OR(E11="Yes",E11=""),"",IF(D12=0,"Yes","No"))

in cells B12–E12 and copy these down to row 110. As in the previous model, blanks will be entered after Joe goes broke—if this ever happens.

4 **Output cells.** Joe goes broke only if the label in cell D110 is "Yes" or blank. Also, the number of games he plays is the number of nonblank values in column C. Therefore, enter the formulas

=RISKOUTPUT()+IF(OR(E110="Yes",E110=""),1,0)

and

=RISKOUTPUT()+COUNT(C11:C110)

in cells H10 and H11 to calculate these outputs.

USING @RISK

We set the number of iterations to 1000 and the number of simulations to 1. After running @Risk, we obtain the outputs in Figures 12.53 and 12.54. As in the previous model, the mean in the first row of the summary table indicates the fraction of time Joe goes broke—about 41% of the time. The histogram indicates that he gets to play 100 games most of the time, but that there are a few times when he goes broke early. In fact, there was at least one iteration out of 1000 where he went broke after only 10 plays. This could occur in only one way: he lost 10 games in a row! On the more optimistic side, the 5th percentile shows that Joe will be able to play more than 24 games about 95% of the time.

FIGURE 12.53
Summary Measures from @Risk

Cell	Name	Minimum	Mean	Maximum	x1=	p1=	x2=	p2=
H10	Went broke? (1 if yes, 0 if no)	0	0.413	1	0	5%	1	95%
H11	Number of plays	10	80.944	100	24	5%	100	95%

Summary Statistics

FIGURE 12.54
Histogram of
Number of Plays

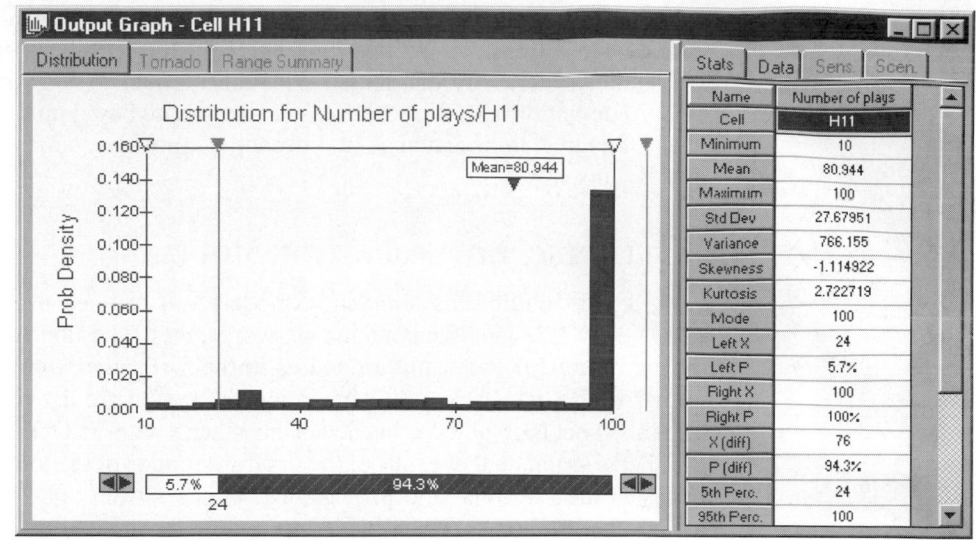

Simulating the NCAA Basketball Tournament

Each year the suspense reaches new levels as "March madness" approaches, the time of the NCAA Basketball Tournament. Which of the 64 teams in the tournament will reach the "Sweet Sixteen," which will go on to the prestigious "Final Four," and which team will be crowned champion? The excitement at Indiana University is particularly high, given the presence of Bobby Knight (coach) and Jeff Sagarin (sports rater), so it has become a yearly tradition at Indiana (at least for the authors) to simulate the NCAA Tournament right after the 64-team field has been announced. We share that simulation in the following example.

EXAMPLE 12.16

MARCH MADNESS IN 1999

As of press time for this book, the most recent NCAA Basketball Tournament was the 1999 tournament. You might recall that Duke was an overwhelming favorite to win—but it didn't win. (The University of Connecticut beat Duke in the finals.) Of course, on the Sunday evening when the 64-team field was announced, we did not know which team would win. All we knew were the pairings (which teams would play which other teams) and the team ratings, based on Sagarin's nationally syndicated rating system. How could we use this information to simulate the entire tournament? How accurate were the simulation's predictions? How could you repeat this simulation for future tournaments?

Solution

We need to make one probabilistic assumption. From that point, it is a matter of "playing out" the games and doing the required bookkeeping. To understand the one probabilistic assumption, suppose team A plays team B and Sagarin's ratings for these teams are 85 and 78, for example. Then Sagarin predicts that the actual point differential in the game (team A's score minus team B's score) will be the difference between the ratings, 7. We take this one step further. We assume the *actual* point differential is normally distributed with mean equal to Sagarin's prediction, 7, and standard deviation 10. (Why 10? This is an estimate based on the analysis of historical data.) Of course, if the actual point differential is positive, team A wins. If it is negative, team B wins.

DEVELOPING THE SIMULATION MODEL

We will only outline the simulation model. You can see the full details in the file NCAA_99.XLS. This file contains six worksheets. The first lists the teams and their Sagarin ratings. If two teams are paired in the first round, they are placed next to one another in the list. (Also, all teams in a given region are listed together.) Information from this sheet is obtained as needed in later sheets with VLOOKUP functions. The next four sheets simulate the results of the first four rounds of the tournament. The last sheet simulates the semifinal and final games. Winners from one round are automatically carried over to the next round with appropriate formulas. Because the model requires several sheets, we cannot use @Risk, at least not the academic version that comes with this book. (This version requires that the model be within a 100-row, 40-column range on a *single* sheet.) Therefore, we go back to the methods discussed at the beginning of Chapter 11. This requires two changes from the @Risk way of doing things. First, we must use a combination of the NORMINV and RAND functions to generate normally distributed random numbers. Second, we need to use a data table to replicate the simulation—that is, replay the entire tournament many times. This data table appears on the same sheet as the final game.

Selected portions of the simulation model and results appear in Figures 12.55, 12.56, and 12.57 (page 696). We now describe the essential features of the model.

❶ Teams and ratings. We first enter the teams and their ratings, as shown in Figure 12.55. The teams shown here were in the East region. Duke played Florida A&M in the first round, Charleston played Tulsa, and so on.

❷ Simulate rounds. Jumping ahead to the third-round simulation in Figure 12.56, we capture the winners from the previous sheet (named Round 2) and then simulate the games in round 3. For example, the formulas in the range B5:G5 are

FIGURE 12.55
Tournament Teams and Their Sagarin Ratings

	A	B	C	D	E	F	G	H	I
1	Simulation of NCAA tournament, using Sagarin ratings								
2									
3	Final Sagarin ratings of teams								
4	Index	Team	Rating						
5	1	Duke	105.90						
6	2	Florida A&M	58.90						
7	3	Charleston	82.40						
8	4	Tulsa	82.20						
9	5	Wisconsin	89.40						
10	6	SW Missouri	82.70						
11	7	Tennessee	86.60						
12	8	Delaware	77.80						
13	9	Temple	86.60						
14	10	Kent State	82.30						
15	11	Cincinnati	91.20						
16	12	George Mason	76.70						
17	13	Texas	81.70						
18	14	Purdue	84.80						
19	15	Miami Fla	90.00						
20	16	Lafayette	73.60						

Assumption: The actual point spread for each game is normally distributed with mean equal to difference between Sagarin ratings, standard deviation 10.

Range name on this sheet:
LTable - B5:C68

FIGURE 12.56
Simulation of Round
Three

	A	B	C	D	E	F	G
1	Results of Round 3						
2							
3	East						
4	Game	Indexes	Teams	Predicted	Simulated	Index of winner	Winner
5	1	1	Duke	23.2	39.06	1	Duke
6		6	SW Missouri				
7	2	9	Temple	-3.4	-13.31	15	Miami Fla
8		15	Miami Fla				
9							
10	Midwest						
11	Game	Indexes	Teams	Predicted	Simulated	Index of winner	Winner
12	1	17	Michigan State	13.5	11.63	17	Michigan State
13		24	Oklahoma				
14	2	27	Kentucky	9.2	11.80	27	Kentucky
15		29	Washington				
16							
17	West						
18	Game	Indexes	Teams	Predicted	Simulated	Index of winner	Winner
19	1	33	Connecticut	10.3	0.55	33	Connecticut
20		37	Iowa				
21	2	41	Florida	-5.4	-15.94	47	Stanford
22		47	Stanford				
23							
24	South						
25	Game	Indexes	Teams	Predicted	Simulated	Index of winner	Winner
26	1	49	Auburn	6.2	-0.98	55	Ohio State
27		55	Ohio State				
28	2	59	St John's	-4.4	-8.06	63	Maryland
29		63	Maryland				

='Round 2'!F5
=VLOOKUP(B5,LTable,2)
=VLOOKUP(B5,LTable,3)-VLOOKUP(B6,LTable,3)
=NORMINV(RAND(),D5,10)
=IF(E5>0,B5,B6)

and

=VLOOKUP(F5,LTable,2)

Column B gets the indices of the second round winners from column F of the Round 2 sheet. Columns C and D get the names and differences between ratings from the original data in Figure 12.55. Column E simulates the point differentials in the games. Columns F and G record the indices and names of the winners.

3   **Replications.** After using the logic in the previous step to play out all of the rounds, we finally get the (simulated) tournament champion in cell G12 of Figure 12.57. Then we create a link to this cell in cell J4 and create a data table in the range I4:J104 (remember, with any blank cell as the column input cell) to replicate the tournament and record the winner 100 times.

4   **Tally the winners.** A nice final touch is to list all 64 teams in column L and then tally the number of replications where each team won the tournament with a COUNTIF function. Specifically, the formula in M4 is

=COUNTIF(Winners,"="&L4)

which can then be copied down column M.

    The results in Figure 12.57 show what a strong favorite Duke was. Duke won the tournament in 62 of the 100 replications![9] The closest competitors were Auburn, the

---

[9]This is actually a low estimate. When we recalculated the data table several times, Duke sometimes won more than 75 times.

Semifinals / Finals simulation

Game	Indexes	Teams	Predicted	Simulated	Index of winner	Winner
Semifinals						
1	1	Duke	13.1	23.36	1	Duke
	27	Kentucky				
2	33	Connecticut	1	1.43	33	Connecticut
	49	Auburn				
Finals						
1	1	Duke	9.3	10.47	1	Duke
	33	Connecticut				

Range name on this sheet:
Winners - J5:J104

100 replications of tournament | **Tournament wins**

Replication	Winner	Team	Wins
	Duke	Duke	59
1	Cinncinati	Florida A&M	0
2	Duke	Charleston	0
3	Duke	Tulsa	0
4	Duke	Wisconsin	0
5	Duke	SW Missouri	0
6	Duke	Tennessee	0
7	Cinncinati	Delaware	0
8	Kentucky	Temple	0
9	Michigan State	Kent State	0
10	Duke	Cinncinati	3
11	Connecticut	George Mason	0
12	Duke	Texas	0
13	Auburn	Purdue	0
14	Duke	Miami Fla	0
15	Connecticut	Lafayette	0
16	Duke	Michigan State	5
17	Duke	St Mary'S	0
18	Duke	Villanova	0
19	Cinncinati	Mississippi	0
20	Duke	UNC Charlotte	0

FIGURE 12.57 Simulation of the Final Four and Replications of the Simulation

University of Connecticut, and Michigan State, with 9, 8, and 7 wins, respectively. The majority of the 64 teams never won at all. As with any simulation, the results of this simulation depend on random numbers and are never definitive, but the model was certainly good at picking the best two teams in 1999.

To use this same file in future years, all you need to change are the data in Figure 12.55—the 64 teams in the tournament and their final Sagarin ratings from the regular season. The rest of the sheets will recalculate automatically. To get new random numbers—and a new set of replications in the data table—just press the F9 key. Check our Web site (www.indiana.edu/~mgtsci) after the tournament pairings have been announced. We plan to put an updated version of this file there each year. ■

PROBLEMS

Skill-Building Problems

42. The game of Chuck-a-Luck is played as follows: You pick a number between 1 and 6 and toss three dice. If your number does not appear, you lose $1. If your number appears x times, you win $$x$. On the average, how much money will you win or lose on each play of the game? Use simulation to find out.

43. A *martingale* betting strategy works as follows. We begin with a certain amount of money and repeatedly play a game in which we have a 40% chance of winning any bet. In the first game, we bet $1. From then on, every time we win a bet, we bet $1 the next time. Each time we lose, we double our bet. Currently we have $63. Assume we have unlimited credit, so that we can bet more money than we have. Use simulation to find a 95% confidence interval for the expected profit we will have earned after playing the game 50 times.

Skill-Extending Problems

44. Based on Morrison and Wheat (1984). When the team is behind late in the game, a hockey coach usually waits until there is one minute left before pulling the goalie. Actually coaches should pull their goalies much sooner. Suppose that if both teams are at full strength, each team scores an average of 0.05 goal per minute. Also, suppose that if you pull your goalie you score an average of 0.08 goal per minute while your opponent scores an average of 0.12 goal per minute. Suppose you are one goal behind with 5 minutes left in the game. Consider the following two strategies:

- Pull your goalie if you are behind at any point in the last 5 minutes of the game; put him back in if you tie the score.
- Pull your goalie if you are behind at any point in the last minute of the game; put him back in if you tie the score.

Which strategy maximizes your chance of winning or tying the game? Simulate the game using 10-second increments of time. Use the @RISKBINOMIAL function to determine whether a team scores a goal in a given 10-second segment. This is reasonable because the probability of scoring two or more goals in a 10-second period is near 0.

45. You are playing Pete Sampras in tennis, and you have a 42% chance of winning each point. (You are *good*!)

    a. Use simulation to estimate the probability you will win a particular game. Note that the first player to score at least 4 points and have at least 2 more points than his or her opponent wins the game.

    b. Use simulation to determine your probability of winning a set. Assume that the first player to win 6 games wins the set if he or she is at least 2 games ahead; otherwise, the first player to win 7 games wins the set.

    c. Use simulation to determine your probability of winning a match. Assume that the first player to win 3 sets wins the match.

12.6 USING TOPRANK WITH @RISK FOR POWERFUL MODELING

In this section we will illustrate how another Palisade Decision Tools add-in, TopRank, can be used together with @Risk as a very powerful modeling combination. As we have seen, @Risk introduces uncertainty explicitly into a spreadsheet model. It does so by allowing several inputs to have probability distributions. Then it simulates random values from these. However, if there are many inputs in a model, it is often a good idea to see which of them have large effects on a key output variable. Those that have a relatively minor effect can be treated as nonrandom, with "best guesses" used as their values. We can then focus on the more important input variables and model them, with probability distributions, in an appropriate manner.

TopRank is a what-if tool that allows us to see which of many inputs have large effects on an output variable. We first develop a spreadsheet model in the usual way, using best-guess values for all inputs. We then use TopRank to vary each of the inputs through a designated range, while holding the other inputs constant. TopRank reports the corresponding variation of any output we select. We can then see, usually through one of several charts, which inputs are most critical. At this point we could either conclude the analysis or switch to @Risk and model the key inputs with appropriate probability distributions.

This latter strategy is basically what Palisade had in mind when it bundled TopRank and @Risk together. In fact, the Decision Tools toolbar shown in Figure 12.58 allows us to toggle between @Risk and TopRank by clicking on the appropriate button. If TopRank is open and we click on the @Risk button, @Risk takes the place of TopRank. If @Risk is open and we click on the TopRank button, then TopRank takes the place of @Risk.

The following example, which will illustrate how TopRank and @Risk can work in tandem, is an extremely important one. Simulation in the business world is often used to analyze potential products. The profitability of a new product is highly uncertain

FIGURE 12.58
Decision Tools Suite Toolbar

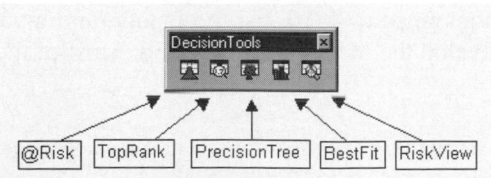

because it depends on many uncertain quantities. Many companies the authors have worked with (including General Motors and Eli Lilly) begin the analysis of every new product by determining the uncertain quantities that might affect the profitability of the product. This analysis is often the deciding factor in whether the product is developed and marketed.

EXAMPLE **12.17**

NEW PRODUCT DEVELOPMENT AT SIMTEX

SimTex, a pharmaceutical company, is in the early stages of developing a new drug called Biathnon. As with most new drugs, the future of Biathnon is highly uncertain. For example, its introduction into the market could be delayed, pending tests by the Food and Drug Administration (FDA). Also, its market could be diminished by a potential rival product from SimTex's competition. SimTex has identified the following key inputs that will affect Biathnon's future profitability:

- number of years after product is developed until it is produced (due to potential FDA delays)
- number of years the product sells
- initial cost incurred in developing the product
- salvage value obtained from equipment after production of the product has been discontinued
- fixed production cost incurred during years in which the product is manufactured
- unit cost of producing the product
- unit price for the product
- initial demand for the product during first year it is sold
- annual percentage growth in demand for the product
- percentage of demand for the product that is lost to the competition
- discount rate used to discount cash flows from the product

These are the inputs to a profitability model for Biathnon. A natural question is how changes in the inputs affect the key output—the NPV of Biathnon over its lifetime. How can SimTex use TopRank and @Risk to analyze this NPV?

Solution

The first step is to develop a profitability model for Biathnon's NPV as a function of the various inputs. For this first step, we use "best guess" values for the inputs.

DEVELOPING THE BASIC MODEL

This model appears in Figure 12.59. (See the file SIMTEX1.XLS.[10]) We spell out the particular assumptions in rows 4–10, list the inputs (and give them range names) in rows 13–23, and develop the model in rows 27–38. Most of the details are as follows.

---

[10]We split this example into three separate files—one for the base model, one for the TopRank model, and one for the @Risk model.

	A	B	C	D	E	F	G	H	AE	AF
1	Model of new product by SimTex									
2										
3	Assumptions									
4	Development costs occur at the end of year 0									
5	It takes some years (specified in cell B13) until production begins									
6	Initial demand, fixed costs, variable costs, and revenues begin in this year									
7	The product is produced for the lifetime specified in cell B14									
8	At the end of the product lifetime, the salvage value is obtained									
9	All revenues, costs occur at the ends of the respective years									
10	The NPV is discounted back to the beginning of year 1									
11										
12	Inputs									
13	Years delayed	2								
14	Lifetime of product (years)	12								
15	Development cost	$120,000								
16	Salvage value	$20,000								
17	Annual fixed cost	$6,000								
18	Unit cost	$2								
19	Unit price	$5								
20	Initial demand	20000								
21	Annual demand growth	10%								
22	Sales lost to competition	20%								
23	Discount rate	10%								
24										
25	Financial model (shown for any number of years the product *might* live)									
26										
27	Year	0	1	2	3	4	5	6	29	30
28	Development cost	$120,000								
29	Is product being produced?	No	No	No	Yes	Yes	Yes	Yes	No	No
30	Fixed cost		$0	$0	$6,000	$6,000	$6,000	$6,000	$0	$0
31	Total demand		0	0	20000	22000	24200	26620	0	0
32	SimTex's demand		0	0	16000	17600	19360	21296	0	0
33	Variable cost		$0	$0	$32,000	$35,200	$38,720	$42,592	$0	$0
34	Revenue		$0	$0	$80,000	$88,000	$96,800	$106,480	$0	$0
35	Salvage value		$0	$0	$0	$0	$0	$0	$0	$0
36	Net profit	-$120,000	$0	$0	$42,000	$46,800	$52,080	$57,888	$0	$0
37										
38	NPV of profit	$284,237								

Range names:
Delay: B13
Life: B14
DevCost: B15
SalvVal: B16
FixCost: B17
UnitCost: B18
UnitPrice: B19
InitDem: B20
DemGrowth: B21
PctDemLost: B22
DiscRate: B23

FIGURE 12.59 Basic SimTex Model

❶ **Timing.** The key to this model is the timing in row 29—whether Biathnon is being produced in any year. To allow for general (even noninteger) values in the Delay and Life input cells, enter the formula

=IF(AND(B27>ROUND(Delay,0),B27<=ROUND(Delay+Life),0),"Yes","No")

in cell B29 and copy it across row 29. For example, with the inputs used in this "base-case" model, Biathnon is produced only in years 3–14, so these are the only years (from year 1 on) that contribute to NPV.

❷ **Financials and other formulas.** The formulas in the other cells are then straightforward. For year 1 (column C) the formulas in rows 30–36 are

=IF(C29="Yes",FixCost,0)
=IF(AND(B29="No",C29="Yes"),InitDem,IF(C29="Yes",B31*(1+DemGrowth),0))
=IF(C31=0,0,C31*(1-PctDemLost))
=IF(C32=0,0,C32*UnitCost)
=IF(C32=0,0,C32*UnitPrice)
=IF(AND(C29="Yes",D29="No"),SalvVal,0)

and

=-C28-C30-C33+C34+C35

The second of these formulas (in cell C31) might require some explanation. The first IF checks whether production occurs this year but not the previous year. If so, this must be the first year of production, so that the demand is the initial demand. Otherwise, the second IF checks whether production is still occurring. If so, then demand is the previous year's demand plus the growth percentage. Similarly, the formula for salvage value in cell C35 checks whether production occurs this year but not next year. If so, then this must be the year when the salvage value is obtained.

❸ NPV. Calculate the NPV (discounted to the beginning of year 0) in cell B38 with the formula

=NPV(DiscRate,C36:AF36)+B36

Note that the fixed cost in cell B36 is *not* discounted.

Now that the model has been developed, we could use trial and error (or data tables) to see how the NPV reacts to changes in the inputs. However, TopRank does this easily. Actually, it can be used in a number of ways. We will describe only one of them, although it appears to us to be the most useful.

USING TOPRANK

To use TopRank, we leave the model alone but change the input section.[11] Instead of entering *constants* in the input cells, we enter TopRank's RISKVARY function. This function has the syntax

$$=RISKVARY(base,minimum,maximum,rangetype,steps,distribution)$$

where:

- *base* is the base case (best guess) for the input
- *minimum* is the smallest possible value for the input
- *maximum* is the largest possible value for the input
- *rangetype* is 0, 1, or 2 and determines the way *minimum* and *maximum* should be entered (even though 0 is the default value, we will use *rangetype* 2—see the TopRank manual for more details)
- *steps* is the number of values from *minimum* to *maximum* to use for this input
- *distribution* is an optional argument that we will omit

We set up the input section for TopRank as shown in Figure 12.60. (See the file SIMTEX2.XLS.) All entries in columns C–E are *constants* (not formulas). For example, for the development cost in row 15, the base case is $120,000, but we want to examine development costs from 90% to 150% of this base case—that is, from $108,000 to $180,000. We then enter the formula

=RISKVARY(D13,C13*D13,E13*D13,2,8)

in cell B13 and copy it down to cell B23. This formula tells TopRank to vary this input from its minimum to its maximum in 8 steps. (The next-to-last argument, 2, implies that the second and third arguments are the actual minimum and maximum.)

---

[11]This discussion assumes TopRank is open within Excel. It can be opened exactly like @Risk, from the Start button of Windows.

FIGURE 12.60
Inputs for SimTex
Model

	A	B	C	D	E
12	**Inputs**	Actual	Low	Base	High
13	Years delayed	2	50%	2	300%
14	Lifetime of product (years)	12	50%	12	200%
15	Development cost	$120,000	90%	$120,000	150%
16	Salvage value	$20,000	0%	$20,000	150%
17	Annual fixed cost	$6,000	80%	$6,000	125%
18	Unit cost	2	50%	$2	150%
19	Unit price	5	60%	$5	125%
20	Initial demand	20000	30%	20000	120%
21	Annual demand growth	10%	50%	10%	120%
22	Sales lost to competition	20%	0%	20%	200%
23	Discount rate	10%	60%	10%	200%

To use TopRank, we proceed in three steps, very much like in @Risk: (1) use the Change Settings button (see the TopRank toolbar in Figure 12.61) to make various settings; (2) use the Add Output Cells button to select one or more output cells; and (3) use the Run What-if Analysis button to perform the calculations.

For step (1), we suggest changing only one of the default settings. After clicking on the Change Settings button, click on the Input ID tab, and then *uncheck* the Automatically Insert AutoVary Functions box. (Otherwise, TopRank will give you a lot of results you probably don't want.) For step (2), highlight the NPV cell (B38) and click on the Add Output Cells button. Finally, run the analysis in step (3) by clicking on the Run What-if Analysis button. TopRank then varies each input cell from its minimum to its maximum, using the number of steps you specified and keeping the *other* inputs at their base levels, and keeps track of all of the NPVs. Like @Risk, it also takes you into its own window.

FIGURE 12.61
TopRank Toolbar

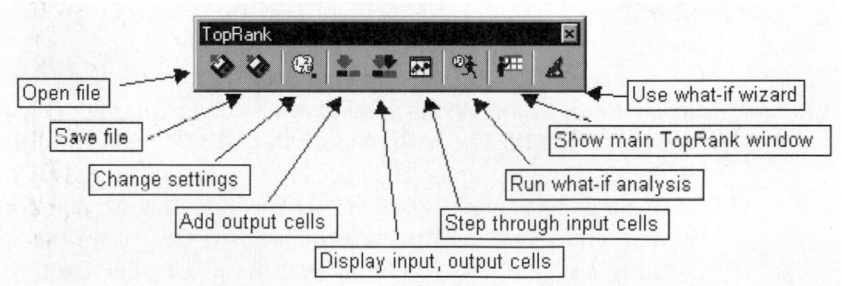

Perhaps the best way to understand the TopRank results is through a tornado chart. To create a tornado chart, click on the Graph button in the TopRank window. You have a choice of three chart types: tornado, spider, and sensitivity. Choose the tornado type to obtain the chart in Figure 12.62 (page 702).[12]

Each bar in the chart indicates the variation in NPV as an individual input varies from its minimum to its maximum. For example, NPV decreases by about 70% and increases by about 147% (from its base-case value) when product lifetime varies from its minimum (6 years) to its maximum (24 years). Because the longer bars are always on the top and the shortest are always on the bottom, the inputs at the top of the chart

[12]In Office 97 or 2000, you can paste a TopRank graph into your worksheet. First, use TopRank's File/Save As menu item to save the graph as a bitmap (.bmp) file. Then get back into Excel, select the Insert/Picture/From File menu item, and select the .bmp file you saved. The downside to this procedure is that bitmap files are *very* large in terms of memory requirements.

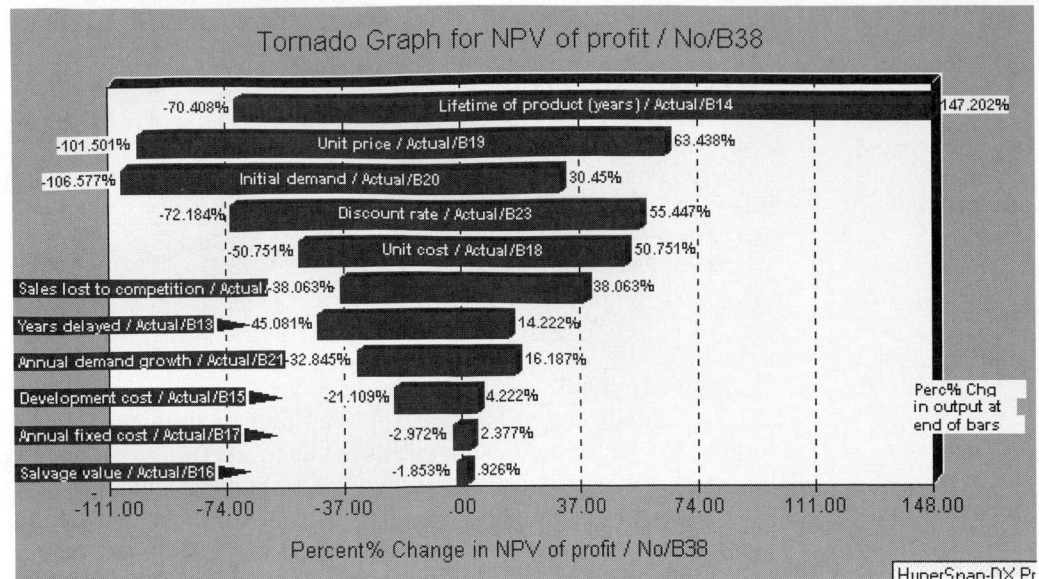

FIGURE 12.62 TopRank Tornado Chart

are always the most important ones. In this case, the five most important inputs are product lifetime, unit price, initial demand, discount rate, and unit production cost.

Clearly, if SimTex is going to simulate the product's NPV, it should spend most of its time accurately assessing the probability distributions of these five key inputs. In contrast, the tornado chart indicates that annual fixed cost and salvage value have virtually no effect on NPV. Therefore, little effort should be spent trying to estimate their values accurately—the base-case values will suffice.

Before proceeding to a simulation, we mention the two other chart types available in TopRank: spider charts and sensitivity charts. A spider chart for the SimTex model appears in Figure 12.63. To produce this chart, click on the TopRank Graph button and select the Spider option. Then because the default spider chart shows *all* of the inputs and is quite cluttered, right-click on the chart, choose the Format/Variables to Graph option, and select the five most important inputs from the tornado chart. This chart is fairly straightforward. For each of the five inputs, there is a curve that shows the

FIGURE 12.63
TopRank Spider
Chart

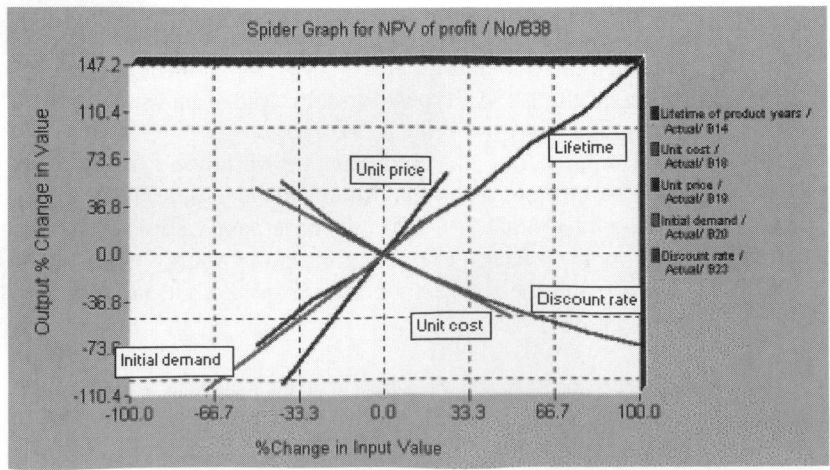

percentage change in NPV as a function of the percentage change in the input (over the range we specified for the input).

From this spider chart we learn, not surprisingly, that changes in unit price, unit cost, and initial demand result in *linear* changes in NPV. Also, a 1% increase in unit price results in a *larger* percentage increase in NPV than does a 1% percentage increase in initial demand. (Can you see why?) As the discount rate increases, NPV decreases, but the rate of decrease slows; after a while increases in the discount rate cannot decrease NPV much further. Increases in product lifetime appear to increase product NPV in a complex, nonlinear fashion.

The final TopRank chart type, a sensitivity chart, is similar to a spider chart, except that it shows one input only. Also, it shows *actual* values rather than percentage changes. To get a sensitivity chart for any input/output combination, click on the desired input and output in the TopRank Results window, and then click on the Graph button and select the Sensitivity option. For example, a graph of NPV versus product lifetime appears in Figure 12.64.

Running an @RISK Simulation The sensitivity analysis with TopRank has indicated that the five key drivers of NPV are product lifetime, unit price, unit cost, initial product demand, and discount rate. We now run an @Risk simulation of this model to estimate the distribution of NPV earned from Biathnon. We keep all inputs other than the five key inputs fixed at their base values, and we use @Risk functions for the key inputs. Actually, we will use random functions for product lifetime, unit price, unit cost, and initial demand, and we will vary discount rate systematically with a RISKSIMTABLE function.[13]

Which probability distributions should we use to model the product lifetime, unit price, unit cost, and initial demand inputs? There are several ways to proceed in

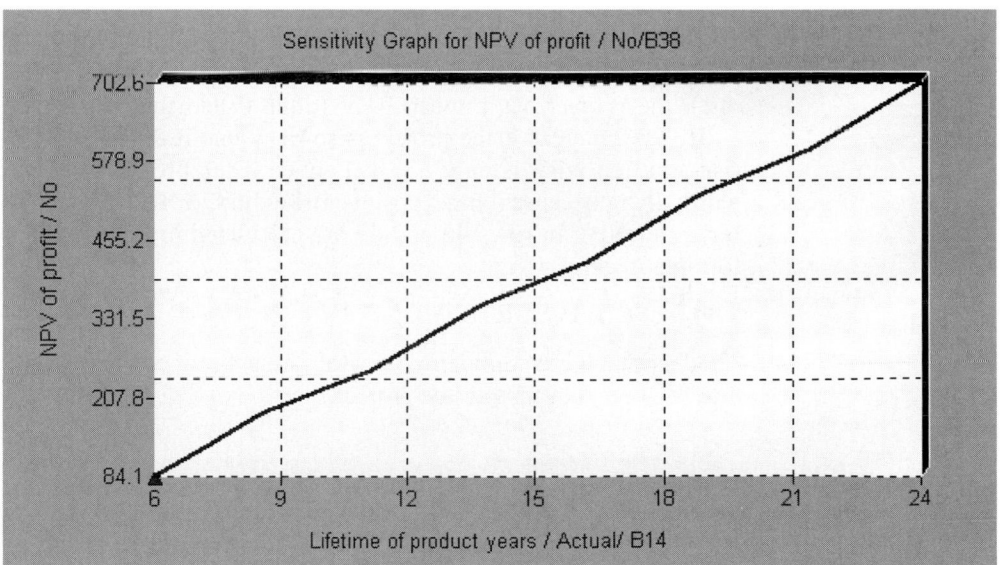

FIGURE 12.64 TopRank Sensitivity Chart

general. First, if we have a lot of historical data on any input, we could use the fitting capabilities of @Risk to fit a distribution to the historical data. It is unlikely that SimTex has relevant historical data that would pertain to this *new* product, so we will not pursue this approach. Second, we could use @Risk's Model window to examine *shapes* of potential candidate distributions. Finally, we could choose a *simple* distribution that management understands and then assess its parameters.

We chose the latter approach, using the triangular distribution for each of the random inputs. The use of a triangular random variable is common at many companies such as General Motors and Eli Lilly. The triangular distribution is often used because, unlike the normal distribution, it makes no assumption that the distribution of the uncertain quantity is symmetric about the mean or most likely value. In fact, the use of the triangular distribution at GM to model uncertain quantities in the analysis of new products grew directly out of deterministic tornado chart analysis.

To assess a triangular distribution for any input, all we need are minimum, most likely, and maximum values for the input. We use the same values of these that we used in the TopRank analysis. They are shown in columns E–G of Figure 12.65. Then we enter the usual @Risk formulas in random input cells. For example, the formula in cell B14 is

=RISKTRIANG(E14,F14,G14)

Next, we model various discount rates in cell B23 with a RISKSIMTABLE function in the usual way, using the discount rates in the range E23:H23. This allows us to try a discount rate appropriate for a less risky project (6%), a project of average risk (10%), and a project of higher risk (15% or 20%). Finally, we designate the NPV as the single @Risk output cell.

We now run @Risk in the usual way, using 500 iterations and 4 simulations (one for each discount rate). Selected results appear in Figure 12.66. (See the file SIM-TEX3.XLS.) For a change, we copied information from the @Risk Results window, pasted it into Excel, and made suitable modifications. We see that if the project is assessed to be less risky than the company's typical project (justifying a 6% discount rate), the project has a mean NPV (often called the risk-adjusted project NPV) of $405,390, whereas if the project is so risky that it deserves a 20% discount rate, the risk-adjusted NPV is only $37,421. Even if the project is extremely risky, it is still worth doing because it has a positive risk-adjusted NPV. The 95% confidence intervals for mean NPV in rows 46 and 47 are calculated in the usual way. For example, the formula in cell B46 is

=B42-1.96*B43/SQRT(500)

The fact that these confidence intervals are entirely positive is another good reason for SimTex to go ahead with the project.

FIGURE 12.65
Parameters for
Triangular
Distributions and
Discount Rates

	A	B	C	D	E	F	G	H
12	**Inputs**	Actual			Parameters for triangular distributions			
13	Years delayed	2	non-random		Minimum	Most likely	Maximum	
14	Lifetime of product (years)	14.76	triangular		6	12	24	
15	Development cost	$120,000	non-random					
16	Salvage value	$20,000	non-random					
17	Annual fixed cost	$6,000	non-random					
18	Unit cost	$2.20	triangular		$1.00	$2.00	$3.00	
19	Unit price	$5.13	triangular		$3.00	$5.00	$6.25	
20	Initial demand	17947.0	triangular		6000	20000	24000	
21	Annual demand growth	10%	non-random					
22	Sales lost to competition	20%	non-random		Risksimtable values for discount rate			
23	Discount rate	6%	use risksimtable		6%	10%	15%	20%

FIGURE 12.66
Selected @Risk
Results

	A	B	C	D	E
40	**Selected results from @Risk (500 iterations)**				
41	Discount rate	6%	10%	15%	20%
42	Mean =	$405,390	$233,432	$109,165	$37,421
43	Std Deviation =	$286,205	$174,434	$104,168	$68,328
44					
45	95% confidence intervals for mean NPV				
46	Lower limit	$380,303	$218,142	$100,034	$31,432
47	Upper limit	$430,477	$248,721	$118,296	$43,410

12.7 CONCLUSION

We claimed in the previous chapter that spreadsheet simulation, especially together with an add-in like @Risk, is a very powerful tool. After seeing the examples in this chapter, you should now realize how powerful, and flexible, simulation can be. Unlike Solver optimization models, where there are advantages to model simplifications such as linearity, virtually anything goes in simulation models. All we need to be able to do is relate outputs to inputs with appropriate formulas, where any of these inputs can reflect uncertainty with probability distributions. The results of the simulation then show how bad things can get, how good they can get, and what we might expect on average. It is no wonder that companies like GM, Eli Lilly, and many others are placing an increasing reliance on simulation models to analyze their corporate operations.

PROBLEMS

Skill-Building Problems

46. You now have $3. You will toss a fair coin four times. Before each toss you can bet any amount of your money (including none) on the outcome of the toss. If heads comes up, you win the amount you bet. If tails comes up, you lose the amount you bet. Your goal is to reach $6. It turns out that you can maximize your chance of reaching $6 by betting either the money you have on hand or $6 minus the money you have on hand, whichever is smaller. Use simulation to estimate the probability that you will reach your goal.

47. You now have $1000, all of which is invested in a sports team. Each year there is a 60% chance that the value of the team will increase by 60% and a 40% chance that the value of the team will decrease by 60%. Estimate the mean and median value of your investment after 100 years. Explain the large difference between the estimated mean and median.

48. Suppose you have invested 25% of your portfolio in four different stocks. The mean and standard deviation of the annual return on each stock are as shown in Table 12.19. The correlations between the annual returns on the four stocks are shown in Table 12.20.

TABLE 12.19

	Mean	Standard Deviation
Stock 1	15%	20%
Stock 2	10%	12%
Stock 3	25%	40%
Stock 4	16%	20%

TABLE 12.20

	Stock 1	Stock 2	Stock 3	Stock 4
Stock 1	1.00	0.80	0.70	0.60
Stock 2	0.80	1.00	0.75	0.55
Stock 3	0.70	0.75	1.00	0.65
Stock 4	0.60	0.55	0.65	1.00

a. What is the probability that your portfolio's annual return will exceed 20%?

b. What is the probability that your portfolio will lose money during the course of a year?

49. Suppose that the current prices of the four stocks in the previous problem are $14, $16, $18, and $20. I have just bought an option involving these four stocks. If the price of stock 1 in 6 months is $17 or more, the option enables me to buy, if I desire, one share of each stock for $20 at that time. Otherwise, the option is worthless. For example, if the stock prices in 6 months are $18, $19, $21, and $22, then I would exercise my option to buy stocks 3 and 4 and receive $(21 - 20) + (22 - 20) = \$3$ in profit. How much is this option worth if the risk-free rate is 8%?

50. A ticket from Indianapolis to Orlando on Deleast Airlines sells for $150. The plane can hold 100 people. It costs Deleast $8000 to fly an empty plane. Each person on the plane incurs variable costs of $30 (for food and fuel). If the flight is overbooked, anyone who cannot get a seat receives $300 in compensation. On average, 95% of all people who have a reservation show up for the flight. To maximize expected profit, how many reservations for the flight should Deleast book? (*Hint*: The function RISKBINOMIAL can be used to simulate the number who show up. It takes two arguments: the number of reservations booked and the probability that any ticketed person shows up.)

51. In the machine redundancy example, Example 12.4, we assumed that all components in parallel have *independent* times to failure. This might not be realistic. For example, the reason for component failures might be stress from an external force that operates on all components simultaneously. This would induce positive correlation between the component failures times: if one fails early, others are likely to fail early as well. Assume that the times until component failure are lognormally distributed with mean 100 hours and standard deviation 20 hours, as in the example. However, suppose the correlation between any two component failure times is 0.5. Simulate the time until machine failure when there are three components in parallel in each of three modules (where the modules are in series, as in the example).
    a. Assume that all nine failure times are correlated.
    b. Repeat part a, but now assume the failure times for components within a given module are correlated, but the failure times for components in different modules are uncorrelated.
    (*Hint*: Remember the third argument of RISKCORRMAT we discussed in the previous chapter.)

52. Consider a drill press containing three drill bits. The current policy (called **individual replacement**) is to replace a drill bit when it fails. The firm is considering changing to a **block replacement** policy in which all three drill bits are replaced whenever a single drill bit fails. Each time the drill press is shut down, the cost is $100. A drill bit costs $50, and the variable cost of replacing a drill bit is $10. Assume that the time to replace a drill bit is

negligible. Also, assume that the time until failure for a drill bit follows an exponential distribution with a mean of 100 hours. This can be modeled in @RISK with the formula **=RISKEXPON(100).** Determine which replacement policy (block or individual replacement) should be implemented.

53. Freezco sells refrigerators. Any refrigerator that fails before it is 3 years old must be replaced. Of all refrigerators, 3% fail during their first year of operation; 5% of all 1-year-old refrigerators fail during their second year of operation; and 7% of all 2-year-old refrigerators fail during their third year of operation.
    a. Estimate the fraction of all refrigerators that will have to be replaced.
    b. It costs $500 to replace a refrigerator, and Freezco sells 10,000 refrigerators per year. If the warranty period were reduced to 2 years, how much per year in replacement costs would be saved?

54. The annual demand for Wozac, a prescription drug manufactured and marketed by the NuFeel Company, is normally distributed with mean 50,000 and standard deviation 12,000. We assume that demand during each of the next 10 years is an independent random draw from this distribution. NuFeel needs to determine how large a Wozac plant to build to maximize its expected profit over the next 10 years. If the company builds a plant that can produce x units of Wozac per year, it will cost $16 for each of these x units. NuFeel will produce only the amount demanded each year, and each unit of Wozac produced will sell for $3.70. Each unit of Wozac produced incurs a variable production cost of $0.20. It costs $0.40 per year to operate a unit of capacity.
    a. Among the capacity levels of 30,000, 35,000, 40,000, 45,000, 50,000, 55,000, and 60,000 units per year, which level maximizes expected profit? Use simulation to answer this question.
    b. Using the capacity from your answer to part a, NuFeel can be 95% certain that expected profit for the 10-year period will be between what two values?
    c. Using the capacity from your answer to part a, NuFeel can be 95% certain that *actual* profit for the 10-year period will be between what two values?

55. We are trying to determine the proper capacity level for a new electric car. A unit of capacity gives us the potential to produce one car per year. It costs $10,000 to build a unit of capacity and the cost is charged equally over the next 5 years. It also costs $400 per year to maintain a unit of capacity (whether or not it is used). Each car sells for $14,000 and incurs a variable production cost of $10,000. The annual demand for the electric car

during each of the next 5 years is believed to be normally distributed with mean 500,000 and standard deviation 100,000. The demands during different years are assumed to be independent. Profits are discounted at a 10% annual interest rate. We are working with a 5-year planning horizon. Capacity levels of 300,000, 400,000, 500,000, 600,000 and 700,000 are under consideration.

   a. Assuming we are risk neutral, use simulation to find the optimal capacity level.

   b. Using the answer to part **a,** we can be 95% certain that the expected discounted 5-year profit is between what two values?

   c. Using the answer to part **a,** there is a 5% chance that the *actual* discounted profit will exceed what value?

   d. Using the answer to part **a,** there is a 5% chance that the *actual* discounted profit will be less than what value?

   e. If we are risk averse, how might the optimal capacity level change?

56. Consider an oil company that bids for the rights to drill in offshore areas. The value of the right to drill in a given offshore area is highly uncertain, as are the bids of the competitors. This problem will demonstrate the "winner's curse." The winner's curse states that the optimal bidding strategy entails bidding a substantial amount below your assumed value of the product for which you are bidding. The idea is that if you do not bid under your assumed value, your uncertainty about the actual value of the product will often lead you to win bids for products on which you (after paying your high bid) lose money. Suppose Royal Conch Oil (RCO) is trying to determine a profit-maximizing bid for the right to drill on an offshore oil site. The actual value of the right to drill is unknown, but it is equally likely to be any value between $10 million and $110 million. Seven competitors will bid against RCO. Each bidder's (including RCO's) estimate of the value of the drilling rights is equally likely to assume any number between 50% and 150% of the actual value. Based on past history, RCO believes that each competitor is equally likely to bid between 40% and 60% of its value estimate. Given this information, what fraction (within 0.05) of RCO's estimated value should it bid to maximize its expected profit? (Note: Use the RISKUNIFORM function to model the actual value of the field and the competitors' bids.)

Skill-Extending Problems

57. We begin year 1 with $500. At the beginning of each year, we put half of our money under our mattress and invest the other half in Whitewater stock. During each year, there is a 50% chance that the Whitewater stock will double, and there is a 50% chance that we will lose half of our investment. To illustrate, if the stock doubles during the first year, we will have $375 under the mattress and $375 invested in Whitewater during year 2. We want to estimate our annual return over a 50-year period. If we end with F dollars, then our annual return is $(F/500)^{1/50} - 1$. For example, if we end with $10,000, our annual return is $20^{1/50} - 1 = 0.062$, or 6.2%. Run 100 replications of an appropriate simulation. Based on the results, we can be 95% certain that our annual return will be between what two values?

58. Suppose you buy an electronic device that you operate continuously. The device costs you $100 and carries a 1-year warranty. The warranty states that if the device fails during its first year of use, you get a new device for no cost, and this new device carries exactly the same warranty. However, if it fails after the first year of use, the warranty is of no value. You need this device for the next 6 years. Therefore, any time the device fails outside its warranty period, you must pay $100 for another device of the same kind. (We assume the price does not increase during the 6-year period.) The time until failure for a device is gamma distributed with parameters $\alpha = 2$ and $\beta = 0.5$. (This implies a mean of 1 year.) Use @RISK to simulate the 6-year period. Include as outputs (1) your total cost, (2) the number of failures during the warranty period, and (3) the number of devices owned during the 6-year period.

59. Rework the previous problem for a case in which the 1-year warranty requires you to pay for the new device even if failure occurs during the warranty period. Specifically, if the device fails at time t, measured relative to the time it went into use, you must pay $100t$ for a new device. For example, if the device goes into use at the beginning of April and fails 9 months later, at the beginning of January, you must pay $75. The reasoning is that you got 9/12 of the warranty period for use, so you should pay that fraction of the total cost for the next device. As before, however, if the device fails outside the warranty period, you must pay the full $100 cost for a new device.

60. Based on Hoppensteadt and Peskin (1992). The following model (the Reed–Frost model) is often used to model the spread of an infectious disease. Suppose that at the beginning of period 1, the population consists of 5 diseased people (called infectives) and 95 healthy people (called susceptibles). During any period there is a 0.05 probability that a given infective person will encounter a particular susceptible. If an infective encounters a susceptible, there is a 0.5 probability that the susceptible will contract the disease. An infective lives an average of 10 periods with the

disease. To model this, we assume that there is a 0.10 probability that an infective dies during any given period. Use @RISK to model the evolution of the population over 100 periods. Use your results to answer the following questions. (*Hint:* During any period there is a probability $0.05(0.50) = 0.025$ that an infective will infect a particular susceptible. Thus the probability that a particular susceptible is not infected during a period is $(1 - 0.025)^n$, where n is the number of infectives present at the end of the previous period.)

a. What is the probability that the population will die out?

b. What is the probability that the disease will die out?

c. On the average, what percentage of the population becomes infected by the end of period 100?

d. Suppose that people use infection "protection" during encounters. The use of protection reduces the probability that a susceptible will contract the disease during a single encounter with an infective from 0.50 to 0.10. Now answer parts **a–c** under the assumption that everyone uses protection.

61. Chemcon has taken over the production of Nasacure from a rival drug company. Chemcon must build a plant to produce Nasacure by the beginning of 2001. Once the plant is built, the plant's capacity cannot be changed. Each unit sold brings in $10 in revenue. The fixed cost (in dollars) of producing a plant that can produce x units per year of the drug is given by

$$\text{Fixed cost} = 5{,}000{,}000 + 10x$$

This cost is assumed to be incurred at the end of 2001. In fact, we assume that all cost and sales cash flows are incurred at the ends of the respective years. If a plant of capacity x is built, the variable cost of producing a unit of Nasacure is given by

$$\text{Variable cost per unit} =$$
$$6 - 0.1(x - 1{,}000{,}000)/100{,}000$$

For example, a plant capacity of 1,100,000 units has a variable cost of $5.90. Each year a plant operating cost of $1 per unit of capacity is also incurred.

Based on a forecasting sales model from the previous 10 years, Chemcon forecasts that demand in year t, D_t, is related to the demand in the previous year, D_{t-1}, by the equation

$$D_t = 67{,}430 + 0.985 D_{t-1} + e_t$$

where e_t is a random term that is normally distributed with mean 0 and standard deviation 29,320. The demand in 2000 was 1,011,000 units. If demand for a year exceeds production capacity, all demand in excess of plant capacity is lost. Chemcon

wants to determine a capacity level that will maximize expected discounted profits (using an interest rate of 10%) for the time period 2001–2010.

62. The Tinkan Company produces 1-pound cans for the Canadian salmon industry. Each year the salmon spawn during a 24-hour period and must be canned immediately. Tinkan has the following agreement with the salmon industry. The company can deliver as many cans as it chooses. Then the salmon are caught. For each can by which Tinkan falls short of the salmon industry's needs, the company pays the industry a $2 penalty. Cans cost Tinkan $1 to produce and are purchased for $2 per can. If any cans are left over, they are returned to Tinkan and the company reimburses the industry $2 for each extra can. These extra cans are put in storage for next year. Each year a can is held in storage, a carrying cost equal to 20% of the can's production cost is incurred. It is well known that the number of salmon harvested during a year is strongly related to the number of salmon harvested the previous year. In fact, using past data, Tinkan estimates that the harvest size in year t, H_t (measured in the number of cans required), is related to the harvest size in the previous year, H_{t-1}, by the equation

$$H_t = H_{t-1} e_t$$

where e_t is normally distributed with mean 1.02 and standard deviation 0.10.

Tinkan plans to use the following production strategy. For some value of x, it will produce enough cans at the beginning of year t to bring its inventory up to $x + \widehat{H}_t$, where $\widehat{H}_t$ is the predicted harvest size in year t. Then it will deliver these cans to the salmon industry. For example, if it uses $x = 100{,}000$, the predicted harvest size is 500,000 cans, and 80,000 cans are already in inventory, then Tinkan will produce and deliver 520,000 cans. Given that the harvest size for the previous year was 550,000 cans, use simulation to help Tinkan develop a production strategy that will maximize its expected profit over the next 20 years.

Modeling Problems

63. Two companies, A and B, share practically all of the market share for a product with a large national market. (Coca Cola and Pepsi represent an example.) They compete vigorously with tactics such as advertising blitzes and coupons for reduced prices. Of course, they also try to outguess what the other is going to do. For this problem, we take the point of view of company A, which must decide what marketing strategies to take each week. These might be proactive or reactive. A proactive tactic might be to offer 20%-off coupons during a week, regardless of what company B is doing (or has been doing). A reactive tactic might be to offer 20%-off coupons during a week after company B does so. We assume that company A can react to company B's actions only after the current week. For example, if company B does something in week 20, company A will not learn about this until week 20, so it won't be able to react until week 21 (or later).

Each week the total market share is divided up by companies A and B. For example, their shares might be 45% and 55%. Using these values for illustration, some of A's 45% might move to B the next week, and some of B's 55% might move to A the next week. The sizes of these movements are random, but they will depend on actions A and B take during the week. (They might even depend on actions taken in previous weeks. Consider the possible delayed effect of advertising, for example.) You can assume that the net change in company A's market share is normally distributed with mean and standard deviation that depend on current (and possibly previous) actions. You can make this dependence as simple or as complex as you like.

The revenues and costs are as follows:

- Each percentage point in market share is worth a certain amount per week in net profit. This is composed of revenue (per percentage point) minus costs (per percentage point).
- An advertising blitz costs a certain amount per week. (For simplicity, we assume that each company advertises regularly at some "normal"

level. The cost of this is included in the cost per week mentioned above. However, an advertising "blitz" represents something special, and it might be expensive!)
- Instead of, or in addition to, an advertising blitz, either company can issue coupons (at essentially no cost) for a certain percentage off the regular selling price. Then the revenue per percentage point of market share decreases by this coupon percentage.

Remember that we are taking company A's point of view. It can decide each week whether to conduct an advertising blitz, issue coupons, do both, or do neither. These decisions can be based on company B's actions in previous weeks, or company A can ignore company B's decisions. In any case, company B's actions can be generated randomly. To simplify the problem, assume that four fixed probabilities determine company B's actions each week: the probabilities of (1) an advertising blitz, (2) issuing coupons, (3) doing both, or (4) doing neither. (In reality, these probabilities shouldn't be fixed. They ought to depend on the previous actions of both companies, but this would make the simulation model extremely complex.)

Your job is to develop a strategy for company A that produces a large average weekly profit over the next 2 years, that is, 104 weeks. You can assume any market shares for the two companies at the beginning of week 1. How might you proceed?

A College Fund Investment Decision

Your next-door neighbor, Scott Jansen, has a 12-year-old daughter, and he wants to pay the tuition for her first year of college 6 years from now. The tuition for the first year will be $17,500. Scott has gone through his budget and finds that he can invest $200 per month for the next 6 years. Scott has opened accounts at two mutual funds. The first fund follows an investment strategy designed to match the return of the S&P 500. The second fund invests in short-term Treasury bills. Both funds have very low fees.

Scott has decided to follow a strategy in which he contributes a fixed fraction of the $200 to each fund. An adviser from the first fund suggested that each month he invest 80% of the $200 in the S&P 500 fund and the other 20% in the T-bill fund. The adviser explained that the S&P 500 has averaged much larger returns than the T-bill fund. Even though stock returns are risky investments in the short run, the risk would be fairly minimal over the longer 6-year period. An adviser from the second fund recommended just the opposite: invest 20% in the S&P 500 fund and 80% in T-bills, he said. Treasury bills are backed by the United States government. If you follow this allocation, he said, your average return will be lower, but at least you will have enough to reach your $17,500 target in 6 years.

Not knowing which adviser to believe, Scott has come to you for help.

Questions

1. The spreadsheet COLLEGE.XLS contains 261 monthly returns of the S&P 500 and Treasury bills from January 1970 through September 1991. Suppose that in each of the next 72 months (6 years), it is equally likely that any of the historical returns will occur. Develop a spreadsheet model to simulate the two suggested investment strategies over the 6-year period. Plot the value of each strategy over time for a single iteration of the simulation. What is the total value of each strategy after 6 years? Do either of the strategies reach the target?

2. Simulate 1000 iterations of the two strategies over the 6-year period. Create a histogram of the final fund values. Based on your simulation results, which of the two strategies would you recommend? Why?

3. Suppose that Scott needs to have $19,500 to pay for the first year's tuition. Based on the same simulation results, which of the two strategies would you recommend now? Why?

4. What other real-world factors might be important to consider in designing the simulation and making a recommendation?

Bond Investment Strategy

An investor is considering the purchase of zero-coupon U.S. Treasury bonds. A 30-year zero-coupon bond yielding 8% can be purchased today for $9.94. At the end of 30 years, the owner of the bond will receive $100. The yield of the bond is related to its price by the following equation:

$$P = \frac{100}{(1+y)^t} \qquad (12.5)$$

where P is the price of the bond, y is the yield of the bond, and t is the maturity of the bond measured in years. Evaluating equation (12.5) for $t = 30$ and $y = 0.08$ gives $P = 9.94$.

The investor is planning to purchase a bond today and sell it one year from now. The investor is interested in evaluating the *return* on the investment in the bond. Suppose, for example, that the yield of the bond one year from now is 8.5%. Then the price of the bond one year later will be $9.39 ($= 100/(1 + 0.085)^{29}$). The time remaining to maturity is $t = 29$, since one year has passed. The return for the year is -5.54% [$= (9.39 - 9.94)/9.94$].

In addition to the 30-year-maturity zero-coupon bond, the investor is considering the purchase of zero-coupon bonds with maturities of 2, 5, 10, or 20 years. All of the bonds are currently yielding 8.0%.

(Bond investors describe this as a *flat yield curve*.) The investor cannot predict the future yields of the bonds with certainty. However, the investor believes that the yield of each bond one year from now can be modeled by a normal distribution with a mean of 8% and a standard deviation of 1%.

Questions

1. Suppose that the yields of the five zero-coupon bonds are all 8.5% one year from today. What are the returns of each bond over the period?

2. Using a simulation with 1000 iterations, estimate the expected return of each bond over the year. Estimate the standard deviations of the returns. Construct 95% confidence intervals for the expected returns.

3. Comment on the following statement: "The expected yield of the 30-year bond one year from today is 8%. At that yield, its price would be $10.73. The return for the year would be 8% [$= (10.73 - 9.94)/9.94$]. Hence, the average return for the bond should be 8% as well. A simulation isn't really necessary. Any difference between 8% and the answer in Question 2 must be due to simulation error."

Financials at Carco[14]

You are the chief financial officer (CFO) for Carco, a small car rental company. You are trying to get some idea of what Carco's financial and income statements will look like during the current year (year 0) and the next 5 years. The following relationships hold:

- Current assets for each year are a "current assets factor" multiplied by the year's sales, where the current assets factors for different years are independent normal random variables with mean 0.15 and standard deviation 0.02.

- Each year, fixed assets at cost equals depreciation plus net fixed assets.

- Accumulated depreciation in year 0 equals $330. For year t ($t \geq 1$), the depreciation equals the accumulated depreciation in year $t - 1$ plus 10% of the fixed assets at cost for year $t - 1$.

- Net fixed assets for year t equals a "net fixed assets factor" multiplied by year t sales, where the net fixed assets factors for different years are independent normal random variables with mean 0.77 and standard deviation 0.04.

- Total assets each year equals net fixed assets plus current assets.

- Current liabilities each year equals a "current liabilities factor" multiplied by the year's sales, where the current liabilities factor for different years are independent normal random variables with mean 0.08 and standard deviation 0.01.

- Long-term debt for year 0 is $280.

- For $t \geq 1$, the long-term debt for year t is the year t debt-equity ratio multiplied by the sum of year t retained earnings and the year t stock. Carco wants to have the following debt-equity ratios in years 1 through 5: 0.48, 0.46, 0.44, 0.42, and 0.40.

- Stock in year 0 is $450. For $t \geq 1$, year t stock equals the sum of year $t - 1$ stock and year t new stock.

[14]This case is based on Benninga (1989).

- Year 0 retained earnings equals $110. For $t \geq 1$, year t retained earnings is the sum of year $t - 1$ retained earnings and year t retention.

- Each year, total liabilities is the sum of current liabilities, long-term debt, stock, and retained earnings.

- The amount of new stock issued each year must be enough to make total assets equal to total liabilities.

- The interest rate on current debt is 10.5%, and the interest rate on new debt is 9.5%. During each of the next 5 years, 20% of the current $280 in long-term debt must be paid off. Then the *total* amount of new debt during year t is the year t long-term debt minus the amount of initial debt still remaining.

- The new debt for year t equals the *total* new debt for year t minus the *total* new debt for year $t - 1$.

- Year 0 sales equals $1000, and for $t \geq 1$, year t sales equals a "sales factor" multiplied by year $t - 1$ sales, where the sales factors for different years are independent normal random variables with mean 1.1 and standard deviation 0.05. (This does *not* mean that sales during successive years are independent!)

- Year t expense equals an "expense factor" multiplied by year t sales, where the expense factors for different years are independent normal random variables, with mean 0.80 and standard deviation 0.06.

- To calculate yearly interest payments, remember that interest is 10.5% on old debt and 9.5% on new debt.

- Depreciation for year 0 is $0, and for $t \geq 1$, year t depreciation is 10% of the year $t - 1$ fixed assets at cost.

- The before-tax profit each year is the sales minus the sum of expenses, interest payments, and depreciation.

- The tax rate is 47%.

- Dividends each year are 70% of after-tax profits.

- Retention each year is 30% of after-tax profits.

Set up a spreadsheet to model the current year (year 0) and next 5 years of Carco's financial future. Now simulate the firm's future 500 times. Use your output to answer the following questions. (*Note*: Your spreadsheet is allowed to contain circular references. There are many of these. For example, stock purchased each year depends on long-term debt, and long-term debt depends on stock. To resolve the circular references, use the Tools/Options menu item, click on the Calculations tab, check the Iterations box, and enter 20 as the Maximum Number of Iterations. This ensures that the spreadsheet will recalculate itself 20 times, which in turn ensures that the values in the spreadsheet will converge to the correct values.

Questions

1. There is only a 5% chance that total new debt will exceed what value?

2. On the average, total interest payments for the next 5 years will equal what value?

3. What is the probability that profit will be negative during year 5?

13

Inventory
Models

CONTROL OF INVENTORY AND SERVICE AT HEWLETT-PACKARD

All inventory models have the common characteristic that they attempt to find the right balance between having enough inventory on hand to meet customer demand but not so much as to incur excess costs. However, there are many variations of the basic inventory model. One of these is described by Lee et al. (1993) in their article "Hewlett-Packard Gains Control of Inventory and Service through Design for Localization." The article discusses HP's Deskjet-Plus Printer Division and its problem of manufacturing and distributing these printers. The printers are manufactured in Vancouver and are then shipped by sea to three distribution centers (DCs), one in North America, one in the Far East, and one in Europe. These DCs then supply the printers to the customers in their regions. The problem is to determine the quantity and location for printer inventory. In particular, should the printers be stored in Vancouver or at the DCs?

This problem is complicated by a "localization" issue. Different regions require slightly different specifications on their printers. For example, the type of power supply module (with the correct voltage and plugs) and the appropriate manual vary from region to region. In the past, HP had "localized" the printers at the manufacturing plant in Vancouver. It bundled the various packages together in the factory—some for Asian markets, some for European markets, and so on—and then sent the appropriate bundles to the DCs as demand forecasts dictated. However, this policy was not very effective from a cost or a customer service standpoint. The policy forced HP to carry too much inventory at its factory, and (largely because of the long shipping times) it did not allow HP to respond quickly enough to changes in forecasts of demands.

The company decided to try a "DC-localization" policy instead, at least for its Far East and European DCs. Under this policy, the Vancouver factory shipped only the "generic" printers to the DCs and allowed the DCs to carry the bulk of the printer inventory. These DCs also carried an ample supply of localization materials, such as appropriate power supply modules and manuals. An important key in being able to implement this policy was that the printers had to be redesigned slightly so that the staff at the DCs could simply attach the localization materials to the printers at the last minute. (Without these design changes, the DCs would have lacked the technical skills to assemble the parts!) The rationale for this DC-localization policy was fairly obvious. The DCs could carry just enough printer inventory to meet customer demand on time and could react quickly to changes in the demand forecasts. The Vancouver plant wouldn't have to carry a wide range of inventory just to be able to respond to every possible contingency. In addition, there were other less obvious benefits. For example, the unbundled printers were less bulky and hence less costly to transport.

Although this change in policy sounded good, HP developed a mathematical inventory model (of the type we will discuss in this chapter) to verify that it would save costs. The model predicted that a smaller *total* printer inventory would be carried under the new policy, although there would be more inventory in localization materials at the DCs. Nevertheless, since the value of a printer is much greater than the value of a power supply module or a manual, the total dollar value of inventory would be reduced by about 18%—a very significant figure considering the millions of dollars involved. In addition, the models were run with a *fixed* level of customer service. In other words, HP could satisfy its customers just as well with 18% less money tied up in inventory. (Alternatively, this implied that HP could *increase* the level of customer service by carrying the same amount of inventory as before.) The company not only went ahead with this new policy, but it adapted it to other new products in Vancouver and other parts of Hewlett-Packard. ■

13.1 INTRODUCTION

Inventory management is one of the most important decisions faced by many companies. These companies include not only retailers that stock products for sale to customers like yourself, but also companies that supply other companies. They all face two competing pressures. The first is the pressure to have enough inventory on hand. The most obvious reason for this is that they do not want to run out of products that customers demand. Another prominent reason, however, is the cost of ordering, as we will discuss throughout this chapter. If there is a fixed cost incurred each time the company orders from its supplier, where this cost does not depend on the order size, then there is an incentive for the company to place large orders to minimize its annual ordering costs.

The second pressure related to inventory management is the pressure to carry as little inventory as possible. The most obvious reasons for this are the cost of storing items and the interest costs involved in tying up money in inventory. If the company has to pay cash for items that end up sitting on the shelf for long periods of time, it is losing potential interest on this money that could be invested elsewhere. Storage space is sometimes an issue as well. Some companies simply do not have the space to store as much inventory as they might like.

These two competing pressures are at the heart of most inventory models. Companies want to order enough, but they do not want to order too much. The balance is typically not easy to find, so we need models to determine the best ordering (or production) policy. An inventory problem can usually be broken up into two parts: (1) *how much* to order on each ordering opportunity and (2) *when* to order. When we assume that customer demand is known, the resulting models are called **deterministic** models. If customer demand is known and the order quantity has been determined, it is then relatively easy to specify when the orders should be placed. A more realistic situation occurs when customer demand is uncertain. In this case, the decision on when to place orders becomes more difficult. We want to place them early enough so that the chance of running out before the orders arrive is fairly small. These more difficult problems require **probabilistic** inventory models.

13.2 CATEGORIES OF INVENTORY MODELS

Researchers have analyzed many inventory models, both deterministic and probabilistic. We will discuss only the most basic of these models, which have been used extensively in real applications. We begin by discussing several important issues and introducing some terminology.

Deterministic Versus Probabilistic Models

We have already mentioned the distinction between deterministic and probabilistic inventory models. In deterministic models we assume that all inputs to the problem, particularly customer demand, are known when the decisions are being made. In reality, a company must always forecast future demands with some type of forecasting model. The outputs of this forecasting model might include a mean demand and a standard deviation of demand. In deterministic models, however, we use only the mean and discard any information about the uncertainty, such as the standard deviation. This makes the resulting models simpler, but usually less realistic. Probabilistic models use this information about uncertainty explicitly. They are typically more difficult to analyze, but they are likely to produce better decisions, especially when the level of uncertainty is high.

External Versus Internal Demand

A second factor in inventory modeling is whether demand for the product is generated *externally* or *internally*. **External demand** (or **independent demand**) occurs when the company that sells the product cannot directly control the extent or the timing of customer demand. For example, a retailer who orders products from a supplier and then waits to see how many customers will request these products faces external demand. Ordering decisions are influenced by, but do not affect, customer demand.

In contrast, **internal demand** (or **dependent demand**) occurs in most assembly and manufacturing processes. Consider, for example, a company that manufactures refrigerators. There is external demand for the finished product, but there is internal demand for the parts that go into the finished product. Once the company forecasts how many refrigerators its customers will require, say, in the next month, it must then determine an appropriate production schedule to produce these. This production schedule will necessitate having inventories of the refrigerator's component parts and subassemblies on hand at the right time. In short, the production schedule determines, in large part, the inventory required for all of the individual parts and subassemblies. The coordination of all of these—ensuring that everything is on hand when it is needed—is a complex problem that we will not discuss in this book. We will analyze external demand only.

Ordering Versus Production

A third factor in inventory modeling is whether the company orders the products from a supplier or produces them internally. If the products are ordered, then there is typically an order **lead time**, the time elapsed from when the order is placed until it arrives. In ordering models there is also usually a fixed cost (also called a **setup** or **ordering** cost) each time an order is placed, where this cost is independent of the order quantity. In contrast, if products are produced internally, then it takes time to produce a batch of items. This time is determined by a production rate, such as 10 units per hour, and possibly by a setup time, the fixed time necessary to set up any machinery to produce a specific type of product. As in ordering models, there might also be a setup cost each time a batch is produced, where this cost is independent of the batch size.

Continuous Versus Periodic Review

A fourth factor in inventory modeling is whether inventory is reviewed continuously or periodically. In a **continuous review** model, the inventory is monitored continually and orders can be placed at any time. Typically, there is a **reorder point**—a specific inventory level—such that when the inventory on hand reaches this reorder point, an order is placed immediately. This could happen Wednesday afternoon, Friday morning, or any other time. In contrast, in **periodic review** models there is some standard time, such as every Monday morning, when the inventory is reviewed and an ordering decision is made. Except possibly for emergency orders, these are the only times when orders are placed. Continuous review models can certainly be implemented, given today's computerized access to inventory levels in real time, and these models can result in lower annual costs than periodic review models. However, when a company stocks many products (hundreds or even thousands), it might be more convenient to order these, say, only on Monday mornings.

Single-Product Versus Multiple-Product Models

A final factor in inventory modeling concerns the number of products involved. Models that consider only a single product are conceptually and mathematically simpler, so we will initially analyze single-product models. However, most companies have many different products that must be considered simultaneously. If the company orders these items from a supplier, then it may be wise to synchronize the orders in some way to minimize ordering costs. We will look at one such model of synchronization in Section 13.4.

13.3 TYPES OF COSTS IN INVENTORY MODELS

We now briefly discuss the types of costs typically involved in inventory modeling.

Ordering (or Setup) Cost

We have already mentioned the **ordering** (or **setup**) cost. This is the fixed cost incurred every time an order is placed or a batch is produced. Its key property is that it is independent of the amount ordered or produced. This ordering cost includes the cost of paperwork and billing each time an order is placed and could include other costs as well, such as paying a truck driver to deliver the order to the company's warehouse. If the product is produced rather than ordered, this cost might include the cost to set up equipment.

Unit Purchasing (or Production) Cost

The **unit purchasing** (or **production**) cost is the cost for each additional unit purchased or produced. For example, to order 100 units the company might have to pay a setup cost of $500 plus $3 per unit, for a total of $800. Here, $3 is the unit purchasing cost. If the company produces the product, then the unit production cost might include the cost of raw materials and the labor cost for each unit produced. Sometimes the unit purchasing cost is not constant, but changes according to some quantity discount schedule. We will consider a quantity discount model in Section 13.4.

Holding (or Carrying) Cost

The **holding** (or **carrying**) cost is the cost that motivates the company to keep less inventory on hand. This cost generally has two components, the **financial holding** cost and the **nonfinancial holding** cost. The nonfinancial holding cost is usually the cost of storing the product. For example, this might be the cost of renting warehouse space. The financial holding cost is the opportunity cost of having money tied up in inventory when that money could instead be earning interest in other investments. Actually, there may be other holding costs, such as spoilage, insurance, and overhead, that vary according to the amount and type of inventory on hand.

Shortage (or Penalty) Cost

We also need to measure the cost of running out of inventory. This **shortage** (or **penalty**) cost is often the most difficult cost to measure. For one thing, it depends on how the company handles shortages. At one extreme, there are **lost sales** models, where any demands that occur when inventory is zero are simply lost. These customers take their business elsewhere. At the other extreme, there are **complete backlogging** models, where demands that occur when inventory is zero are satisfied as soon as a new order arrives.[1] Both of these models—or any in between, the **partial backlogging** models—have negative effects for the company. There is lost business, loss of goodwill, and possibly emergency shipments with higher costs. The problem, however, is that it can be difficult to put a dollar value on the "cost" of running out of inventory. An alternative is to specify a **service level**, such as meeting at least 95% of the demand on time.

---

[1]We also say the excess demand is **backordered**. Both terms, backlog and backorder, mean that these orders are kept on the books and are satisfied when additional shipments arrive.

Revenue

Finally, there is the **selling price** of the product and the resulting revenue to the company. In many situations the revenue is a fixed amount that is not affected by any ordering decisions. This occurs when the selling price is constant and the company intends to satisfy all demand eventually. In such cases we can add the total revenue to the relevant costs, but it will not affect any decisions. On the other hand, there are times, such as in lost sales models, when the selling price affects the ordering decision. Here the shortage cost depends on how much revenue is lost by not having enough inventory on hand, and this clearly depends on the selling price.

13.4 ECONOMIC ORDER QUANTITY (EOQ) MODELS

We now examine a class of models called **economic order quantity** (EOQ) models. These are the most basic of all the inventory planning models. Developed originally in 1915 by F. W. Harris of Westinghouse Corporation, they are also among the earliest management science models. Despite their simplicity, they have been applied by numerous companies, and they continue to play a prominent role in inventory management.

We begin by studying the most basic EOQ model. Then we will examine several interesting variations of this basic model. All of these models make the following assumptions:

- A company orders a single product from a supplier and sells this product to its customers.
- Orders can be placed at any time (continuous review).
- There is a constant, known demand rate for the product, usually expressed in units per year (annual demand).
- There is a constant, known lead time for delivery of the product from the supplier.
- There is a fixed ordering cost each time the product is ordered, independent of the size of the order.
- The price the company charges for the product is fixed.
- The annual holding cost is proportional to the average amount of inventory on hand.

The constant demand rate means, for example, that if the yearly demand is 52,000 units, then each week's demand is approximately 1000 units—there are no peaks or valleys during the year. The known lead time means that if the company places an order on Monday and the lead time is 3 days, then the order will arrive, with certainty, on Thursday. We will discuss the holding cost in more detail shortly.

The Basic EOQ Model

The most basic EOQ model adds the following two assumptions.

- No stockouts are allowed—that is, the company must never allow itself to run out of inventory.
- The unit cost of purchasing the product from the supplier is constant. In particular, there are no quantity discounts available.

We analyze this basic EOQ model in the following example.

EXAMPLE 13.1

ORDERING CAMERAS AT MACHEY'S

Machey's Department Store sells 1200 cameras per year, and the demand pattern throughout the year is very steady. The store orders its cameras from a regional warehouse, and it usually takes a week for the cameras to arrive after an order has been placed. Each time an order is placed, an ordering cost of $35 is incurred. The store pays $100 for each camera and sells them for $130 apiece. There is no physical storage cost, but the store's annual cost of capital is estimated at 10% per year—that is, it can earn 10% on any excess cash it invests. The store wants to determine how often it should order cameras, when it should place orders, and how many cameras it should order in each order.

Solution

We first discuss some basic quantities and relationships. Let $D = 1200$ be the annual demand. Because it occurs steadily through the year, Machey's will place an order for Q cameras every time it is about to run out. Therefore, the only decision variable is Q, the order quantity. Once we know Q, the number of orders per year is given by

$$\text{Number of orders per year} = D/Q \qquad (13.1)$$

Equivalently, the time between orders (measured as a fraction of a year) is Q/D. For example, if $Q = 300$, Machey's will place $D/Q = 4$ orders per year, and the time between orders will be $Q/D = 0.25$ year (3 months). The timing of orders is straightforward. Because the lead time is 1 week and the demand in a week is $D/52 \approx 23$, Machey's should place an order when its inventory drops to 23 cameras.[2] This way, the order will arrive just as inventory runs out. A graph of the company's inventory through time appears in Figure 13.1. The key aspect in this figure is that the inventory level jumps up to Q whenever an order arrives and decreases linearly (due to demand) until the next order arrives.

The problem is to find an order quantity Q that maximizes Machey's annual profit. There are several components of the annual profit. First, each time Machey's places an order, it incurs a fixed ordering cost, labeled K. For this example, $K = \$35$. Because

FIGURE 13.1
Inventory Level for Basic EOQ Model

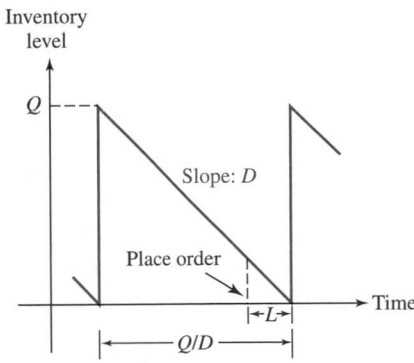

---

[2]Unfortunately, this reasoning is not quite correct when the order quantity Q is smaller than the demand during the lead time, DL. However, this case is rather unusual, and we will not discuss it here.

there are D/Q orders placed per year, the annual ordering cost is

$$\text{Annual ordering cost} = KD/Q \qquad (13.2)$$

On top of this, Machey's pays a variable cost, labeled c, for each camera it purchases. Here, $c = \$100$. Because the annual demand is $D = 1200$ and all demand must be met, the annual variable cost is $cD = \$120,000$. Note that this cost does *not* depend on Q. Similarly, the company's revenue from each camera, labeled r, is $r = \$130$, so its annual revenue is rD. This is also unaffected by the order quantity Q.

Now we consider the annual holding cost. There is no cost for physically storing the cameras, but Machey's loses money from potential investments by having excess cash tied up in inventory. If we let i be Machey's annual cost of capital, where $i = 0.10$ (10%), then it can be shown from a net present value (NPV) argument that the relevant annual holding cost is i multiplied by the average monetary value of inventory, where this average is over the entire year. Because the inventory decreases linearly from Q to 0 between orders, the average level of the inventory at a typical point in time is $(Q + 0)/2 = Q/2$, which implies that the average monetary value of inventory is $cQ/2$. Therefore, the annual holding cost from money tied up in inventory is

$$\text{Annual financial holding cost} = icQ/2 \qquad (13.3)$$

(In general, if there were also a storage cost of s dollars per unit held in storage per year, then the total annual holding cost would be $(s + ic)Q/2$.)

We can now develop a spreadsheet to optimize Machey's annual profit.

DEVELOPING THE SPREADSHEET MODEL

The spreadsheet model appears in Figure 13.2. (See the file EOQ1.XLS.) In the interest of space, we will not list the individual steps for developing this model. All of the formulas are based directly on the discussion above. For example, the annual holding cost, determined by equation (13.3), is calculated in cell B18 with the formula

=IntRate*UnitPurchCost*OrderQuan/2

Note that the only changing cell is the OrderQuan cell. It drives all of the quantities below it except for the annual purchase cost and the annual revenue, which do not depend on the order quantity. (They could actually be omitted from the model, although Machey's would then not be able to see its overall profit.) Also, note that we have included the lead time in the spreadsheet model, although it is never used in any formulas. Its only role is to determine *when* to order. We already saw that Machey's should place its order when its inventory drops to 23 cameras.

USING THE SOLVER

The Solver setup (not shown) is particularly simple. We maximize annual profit with a single changing cell, the order quantity cell. There are *no* constraints other than nonnegativity of the order quantity. (If you like, you can also constrain the order quantity to be an integer. However, this is not really necessary. For all practical purposes, it suffices to round the Solver solution to the nearest integer.) Also, the Assume Linear Model should *not* be checked. The reason is that the decision variable Q appears in the denominator of equation (13.2) for the annual ordering cost. This makes the model nonlinear.

The Solver solution specifies that Machey's should order 91 or 92 cameras each time it orders. This will result in about 13 orders per year, or about one order every 28 days. Note that the annual ordering cost and the annual financial holding cost for this optimal solution are equal. This is no coincidence. It always occurs in the basic EOQ model. Because the annual purchasing cost and revenue do not depend on the order

FIGURE 13.2
Basic EOQ Model

	A	B	C	D	E	F
1	**Machey's EOQ model**					
2						
3	**Inputs**					
4	Fixed ordering cost	$35				
5	Annual interest rate	10%		**Range names used:**		
6	Unit purchasing cost	$100		FixedCost - B4		
7	Selling price per unit	$130		IntRate - B5		
8	Annual demand	1200		UnitPurchCost - B6		
9	Lead time in years	1/52		UnitPrice - B7		
10				AnnDemand - B8		
11	**Ordering model**			LeadTime - B9		
12	Order quantity Q	91.65		OrderQuan - B12		
13	Orders per year	13.09		OrdersPerYear - B13		
14	Time between orders (days)	27.88		AnnProfit - B21		
15						
16	**Monetary values**					
17	Annual fixed ordering cost	$458		affected by order quantity		
18	Annual holding cost	$458				
19	Annual purchasing cost	$120,000		unaffected by order quantity		
20	Annual revenue	$156,000				
21	Annual profit	$35,083				
22						
23	**Alternative EOQ formula**	91.65				

quantity, the problem is essentially a trade-off between too many orders (high fixed ordering costs) and too much inventory (high holding costs). It can be shown with calculus that the Solver always chooses the order quantity that makes these two costs equal.

EOQ formula A feature of some nonlinear models, including this EOQ model, is that they have no constraints and can be solved with calculus—without the need for a spreadsheet Solver. Although we will not pursue the details, the calculus solution, shown in cell B23 of Figure 13.2, is that the optimal order quantity satisfies

$$Q = \sqrt{2KD/(s + ic)} \tag{13.4}$$

(where s, the storage cost, is 0 for this example). The advantage of this well-known "square-root formula" is that it gives us immediate insight into the effects of changes in inputs. For example, the effect of quadrupling the annual demand is to double the optimal order quantity. The disadvantage of this formula is that it holds only under the assumptions we have described. If a company wants to modify the EOQ model to meet any special circumstances, it would do better to develop a flexible spreadsheet model and then use the Solver instead of relying on a formula it does not fully understand. ∎

EOQ Models with Quantity Discounts

The next example illustrates one of many possible variations of the basic EOQ model. In this variation the company placing the order can obtain quantity discounts from its supplier.

EXAMPLE 13.2

ORDERING FLOPPY DISKS WITH QUANTITY DISCOUNTS AT AJ TAYLOR

The accounting firm of AJ Taylor buys boxes of floppy disks (ten disks to a box) from a large mail-order distributor. The firm uses approximately 5000 boxes per year at a fairly constant rate. The distributor offers the following quantity discount. If fewer than 500 boxes are ordered, the cost per box is $10. If at least 500 but fewer than 800 boxes are ordered, the cost per box is $9.50. If at least 800 boxes are ordered, the cost per box is $9.25. The fixed cost of placing an order is $25. The company's cost of capital is 12% per year, and there is no storage cost. The firm wants to find the optimal order quantity and the corresponding total annual cost.

Solution

A clever use of a lookup table and the SolverTable add-in makes it easy to modify the basic EOQ model to solve this problem. The idea is to solve *three* separate basic EOQ models, one for each region of the purchase cost function. For example, in the second region the unit purchase cost is specified as $9.50. We can force the order quantity to be within this region by adding constraints that it must be between 500 and 799. After solving the three models, we simply take the lowest of the three optimal costs.

DEVELOPING THE SPREADSHEET MODEL

The completed model appears in Figure 13.3. (See the file EOQ2.XLS.) The accompanying Solver dialog box appears in Figure 13.4. Again, we will not spell out all of the details, but only the key points.

❶ **Purchase cost function.** Enter the parameters of the purchase cost function in the LTable range. We have used the range name LTable because we will use this information in a lookup function later on. Note that we have entered a maximum order of 2000 in column D. Any large value will suffice here.

❷ **Specify a region.** We set up the model for a particular region of the purchase cost function. In general, enter any value (1, 2, or 3) in cell B14. (We show results for region 3.) Then use the HLOOKUP function to obtain the required information in cells B15–B17. Specifically, enter the formula

=HLOOKUP(B14,LTable,2)

in cell B15, and enter similar formulas in cells B16 and B17, except with third arguments 3 and 4, respectively.

❸ **Basic EOQ.** Given the unit purchase cost in cell B15, formulate the rest of the EOQ model exactly like we did in the previous example. (This time, however, note that there is no revenue. Everything is in terms of costs, so that we are minimizing.)

USING THE SOLVER

We set up the Solver to minimize the total annual cost and specify the order quantity cell as the single changing cell. We also include the constraints OrderQuan>=LoLim and OrderQuan<=UpLim in the Solver dialog box. This will force the order quantity to be inside the region for which the unit purchase cost is relevant. We then run SolverTable with cell B14 as the single input, varied from 1 to 3 in increments of 1, and keep track of the order quantity and the total annual cost. This is the key. When SolverTable varies the region in cell B14, it automatically varies the unit purchase cost and the lower and upper limits on the order quantity. So we get three Solver solutions for the price of one!

The SolverTable results indicate the minimum annual costs for the three regions. If the company is forced to order in the second region, at a unit cost of $10, its minimal cost is $50,548 and this is achieved by ordering about 456 units. If the company is forced to order in the second region, at a unit cost of $9.50, its minimal cost is $48,035 and this is achieved by ordering 500 units, the minimum order quantity in this region.

FIGURE 13.3
EOQ Model with
Quantity Discounts

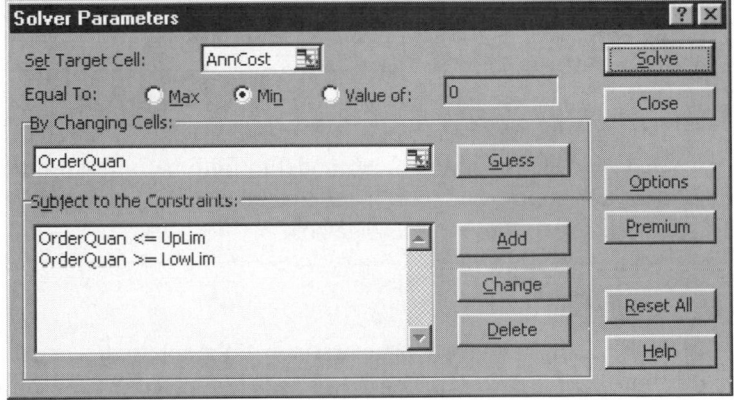

	A	B	C	D	E	F	G
1	AJ Taylor's EOQ model with quantity discounts						
2							
3	**Inputs**					Range names used:	
4	Fixed ordering cost	$25				FixedCost - B4	
5	Annual interest rate	12%				IntRate - B5	
6	Annual demand	5000				AnnDemand - B6	
7						LTable - B9:D12	
8	**Purchase cost function**					UnitPurchCost - B15	
9	Region	1	2	3		LoLim - B16	
10	Unit purchase cost	$10.00	$9.50	$9.25		UpLim - B17	
11	Min quantity	0	500	800		OrderQuan - B20	
12	Max quantity	499	799	2000		OrdersPerYear - B21	
13						AnnCost - B28	
14	**Region analyzed**	3					
15	Unit purchase cost	$9.25					
16	Min quantity	800					
17	Max quantity	2000					
18							
19	**Ordering model**			Using SolverTable to solve in all regions			
20	Order quantity Q	800.00		Region	Order quantity	Cost	
21	Orders per year	6.25			$B$20	$B$28	
22	Time between orders (days)	58.40		1	456.44	$50,548	
23				2	500.00	$48,035	
24	**Monetary values**			3	800.00	$46,850	
25	Annual fixed ordering cost	$156					
26	Annual holding cost	$444					
27	Annual purchasing cost	$46,250					
28	Total annual cost	$46,850					

FIGURE 13.4
Solver Dialog Box
for Quantity
Discount Model

Finally, if the company is forced to order in the third region, at a unit cost of $9.25, its minimal cost is $46,850 and this is achieved by ordering 800 units, again the minimum order quantity in this region. Therefore, Taylor should use the smallest of these three costs—that is, it should order 800 units for a total annual cost of $46,850. ∎

EOQ Models with Shortages Allowed

In the basic EOQ model we assume that the company decides, as a matter of policy, not to allow any shortages. Because the demand rate and the lead time are known, the ordering can be done so that an order arrives just as the inventory level reaches zero. This means that it is possible to *prevent* shortages from occurring. However, it might be in the company's best interests to allow a few shortages if the "penalty" for a shortage is not too large. As discussed in Section 13.2, this opens up a wide range of possible models.

First, are shortages backlogged or are these demands simply lost? And what about the penalty cost for a shortage? Does the penalty relate only to the number of units short per year or also to the amount of time shortages last? After all, a customer might be twice as unhappy if she has to wait two days instead of one day for her demand to be satisfied. Whichever type of shortage cost we assume, the practical difficulty is then assessing a specific dollar value for this cost. For example, what is the cost of having a customer wait at all? What is the cost of having a customer wait three days?

We will illustrate a **complete backlog** model, where the penalty cost is charged per unit short per amount of time short. In this case the annual penalty cost is a constant p multiplied by the product of the average number of units backlogged and the average amount of time a customer has to wait for a backlogged unit. The constant p is the penalty cost charged for each customer who has to wait one unit of time for one backlogged item. The following example is typical.

EXAMPLE 13.3

ORDERING AUDIO CDS AT GMB WITH SHORTAGES ALLOWED

GMB is a mail-order distributor of audio CDs that sells approximately 50,000 CDs per year. Each CD is packaged in a jewel case that GMB buys from a supplier. The fixed cost of placing an order for jewel cases is $100. GMB pays $0.50 for each jewel case, and its cost of capital is 10%. The cost of storing a jewel case for one year is $0.50. GMB believes it can afford to run out of jewel cases from time to time, reasoning that this will simply make the time between customer orders and customer deliveries a bit longer. It knows that there is some cost of doing this—impatient customers might take their business elsewhere—but it is not sure what dollar amount p to attach to this cost. It decides to use a trial value of $p = \$52$, reasoning that this value implies a $1 penalty for each extra week a customer has to wait because of a backlogged jewel case. GMB wants to develop a spreadsheet model to find the optimal order quantity, the optimal amount to backlog, and the optimal annual cost. It also wants to see how sensitive these quantities are to the unit shortage cost p.

Solution

As in the basic EOQ model, the first step of the solution is to develop the components of the total annual cost. The key is again a saw-toothed graph, shown in Figure 13.5. Now there are two decision variables: Q, the order quantity, and b, the maximum amount

FIGURE 13.5
EOQ Model with Shortages Allowed

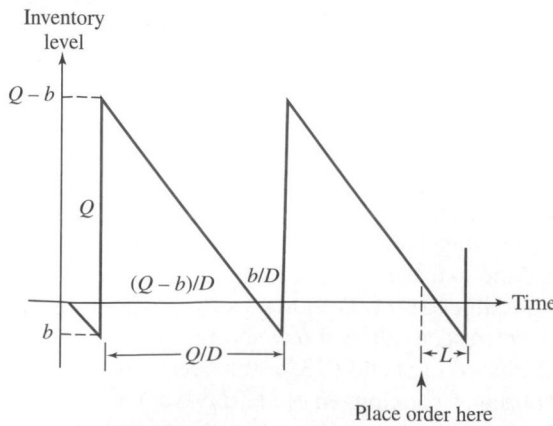

backlogged. Each cycle has length Q/D, the time to deplete Q units at demand rate D. But now a cycle has two parts. During time $(Q - b)/D$ (the time required to deplete the first $Q - b$ units), there is positive inventory and demands are being met on time. During the last section of each cycle, of length b/D (the time it would take to delete b units), the inventory is negative, which means that shortages exist. The order for Q units is placed so that it arrives precisely when the inventory level reaches $-b$. When this order arrives, b units are used immediately to satisfy backlogged demand and the other $Q - b$ units go into on-hand inventory. Therefore, right after any order arrives, there are $Q - b$ units in inventory. Note that if there is an order lead time of L, then the order is placed when the inventory level is DL units above its lowest point, $-b$. This is exactly analogous to the basic EOQ model, since DL is the amount of demand during the lead time.[3]

The total cost function, a function of both Q and b, is now fairly straightforward. The annual setup cost is KD/Q, the same as before, because there are D/Q orders per year. The annual purchase cost is cD because all demand is eventually satisfied. (In this section we assume a constant unit purchasing cost; no quantity discounts are available.) The annual financial holding cost is again the interest rate times half of the purchase cost of an order, $icQ/2$.

To find the annual storage cost, refer to Figure 13.5. The storage cost per cycle is the unit storage cost s multiplied by the average inventory when inventory is positive, $(Q - b)/2$, multiplied by the amount of time during a cycle when inventory is positive, $(Q - b)/D$. To obtain the annual storage cost, we multiply the cost per cycle by the number of cycles per year, D/Q, to obtain

$$\text{Annual storage cost} = s[(Q - b)/2][(Q - b)/D](D/Q) = s(Q - b)^2/(2Q) \quad \textbf{(13.5)}$$

Again referring to Figure 13.5, the average shortage cost per cycle is p multiplied by the average amount short when the inventory level is negative, $b/2$, multiplied by the amount of time during a cycle when inventory is negative, b/D. Multiplying the shortage cost per cycle by the number of cycles per year, D/Q, gives

$$\text{Annual shortage cost} = p(b/2)(b/D)(D/Q) = pb^2/(2Q) \quad \textbf{(13.6)}$$

DEVELOPING THE SPREADSHEET MODEL

We can now develop the spreadsheet model for GMB, which appears in Figure 13.6. (See the file EOQ3.XLS.) We again omit most of the details, since all formulas are based directly on the cost equations we have just developed. For example, the formula in cell B21 for the annual shortage cost is

=ShortCost*MaxBacklog^2/(2*OrderQuan)

This follows directly from equation (13.6).

USING THE SOLVER

The Solver setup is also straightforward. We minimize the total annual cost, with the OrderQuan and MaxBacklog cells as the changing cells and the Assume Non-Negative option checked. (We also constrained the changing cells to be integers, but this is not really necessary—we could always round noninteger solutions to integers with little effect on costs.)

The solution indicates that GMB should order 4283 units each time it orders, and it should plan its ordering so that there is a backlog of 41 units when an order arrives.

---

[3]As before, this must be modified slightly if $DL > Q$

FIGURE 13.6
Optimal Solution
with Shortages
Allowed

	A	B	C	D	E
1	GMB's EOQ model with shortages allowed				
2					
3	Inputs			Range names used:	
4	Fixed ordering cost	$100		FixedCost - B4	
5	Storage cost per unit per year	$0.50		StorCost - B5	
6	Annual interest rate	10%		IntRate - B6	
7	Unit purchasing cost	$0.50		UnitPurchCost - B7	
8	Shortage cost per unit per year	$52		ShortCost - B8	
9	Annual demand	50000		AnnDemand - B9	
10				OrderQuan - B12	
11	Ordering model			MaxBacklog - B13	
12	Order quantity Q	4283		AnnOrders - B15	
13	Maximum backlog b	41		AnnCost - B23	
14	Time between orders	0.086			
15	Orders per year	11.7			
16					
17	Monetary values				
18	Annual setup cost	$1,167			
19	Annual financial holding cost	$107			
20	Annual storage cost	$1,050			
21	Annual shortage cost	$10			
22	Annual purchasing cost	$25,000			
23	Total annual cost	$27,335			
24					
25	Sensitivity of Q, b, and total annual cost to p				
26		$B$12	$B$13	$B$23	
27	10	4360	208	$27,294	
28	30	4296	70	$27,328	
29	50	4283	42	$27,335	
30	70	4278	30	$27,338	
31	90	4275	24	$27,339	
32	110	4273	19	$27,340	

For example, if the order lead time is 1 week (1/52 year), then because the demand during lead time is $DL = 50,000/52 \approx 962$, GMB should place an order when the inventory level reaches $962 - 41 = 921$. That way, the backlog will be 41 units by the time the order arrives. The optimal policy indicates that almost 12 orders will be placed per year, or about 1 per month. The total annual cost is $27,335. However, only $2335 of this is affected by the ordering policy. The other $25,000 is the total purchase cost, which is incurred regardless of the timing or quantity of orders.

To see the effect of the unit shortage cost p on the optimal solution, we ran SolverTable with the ShortCost cell as the single input cell, varied from $10 to $110 in increments of $20, and recorded the order quantity, the maximum backlog, and the annual cost as outputs. These results appear in Figure 13.6 from row 26 down. The entries in this table show that Q, b, and the total annual cost are fairly insensitive to p, except that b becomes quite large when p is very small. (This makes sense. Why should GMB worry about making customers wait if it believes the penalty for making them wait is very low?) This information should make GMB more comfortable, knowing that its estimate of p is not that crucial. ■

Reducing the Setup Cost

There has been a lot of talk in the past few years about striving for zero inventory. The argument is that the less inventory a company carries, the more efficiently it is operating its business.[4] The question is whether this argument can be justified from

[4]See the article by Zangwill (1992) for a discussion of the merits of keeping inventory low.

an economic point of view, at least in the context of the EOQ models we have been discussing. We have seen that the main reason for carrying more inventory is the fixed setup cost K. If K is large, it is economical to order in larger quantities, which means that the average inventory level is large. So if this is true, what incentive is there for a company to strive for zero inventory?

One possible answer to this question is to reconsider whether the setup cost is really *fixed*. Is a company automatically stuck with some value of K, or is it possible to reduce this value of K and thereby justify smaller order quantities and smaller inventory levels? This is an interesting modeling question. How can we mathematically model the cost of reducing K?

One researcher, Evan Porteus, has proposed a model where a company can make a one-time investment to reduce the value of K. [See Porteus (1985).] Specifically, if the company's current setup cost is K_0, he assumes that by investing $f(K)$ dollars, the company can reduce the setup cost from K_0 to K, where $K < K_0$. Having a smaller value of K will certainly imply a lower total annual cost, but this reduction must be weighed against the one-time investment required to reduce the setup cost. Also, the optimal *amount* of setup cost reduction must be determined. Therefore, K becomes a decision variable along with the order quantity Q in the basic EOQ model. (We do not allow quantity discounts or shortages in this section.)

There are two modeling problems here. The first is to choose a reasonable form for the function $f(K)$. The second is to find a way to turn a one-time investment cost, $f(K)$, into an equivalent *annual* cost, so that the cost of reducing the setup cost is comparable to the annual operating costs we have been discussing. For the first problem, Porteus assumes that the investment required to reduce the setup cost from K_0 to K is of the form

$$f(K) = a_0 + a_1 \ln(K)$$

for some constants a_0 and a_1. (Here, ln is the natural logarithm.) This form is not as strange as it might look. It implies that each 10% decrease in K costs a *fixed* dollar amount. (The 10% figure is chosen for convenience; the same argument can be used for any other percentage.) Specifically, it can be shown that the cost of reducing K by 10% is $a_1 \ln(0.9) = -0.1054a_1$ dollars, regardless of whether the reduction is from \$300 to \$270, \$30 to \$27, \$3 to \$2.70, or any other 10% change. This constant cost per 10% decrease is a reasonable property for $f(K)$ to have.

We can fully specify the $f(K)$ function—that is, find a_0 and a_1—if we are given two inputs: the initial setup cost K_0 and the cost of a 10% reduction in K. To illustrate, suppose that the initial setup cost is $K_0 = \$500$ and it takes a one-time investment of \$1000 to reduce this by 10%. Then we set $-0.1054a_1 = 1000$ to obtain $a_1 = -9491$. Also, because it costs zero dollars to stay at level K_0, we have $f(K_0) = 0$, which implies that

$$0 = a_0 + a_1 \ln(K_0) = a_0 - 9491 \ln(500) = a_0 - 58{,}984$$

or $a_0 = 58{,}984$.

Now we tackle the second problem. The investment cost $f(K)$ is a one-time investment. However, it is equivalent to an annual investment in perpetuity of $if(K)$ dollars, where i is the annual interest rate. This follows from a net present value argument that we will not present here. In words, if the company were to pay $if(K)$ dollars at the beginning of each year forever, this would be equivalent in net present value terms to a one-time payment of $f(K)$ dollars. Putting all of this together, the total annual cost to the company is $if(K)$ plus the annual operating cost from any of our previous models. In addition to any previous decision variables such as Q, we now need to choose K, subject to the constraint $K \le K_0$. We illustrate the procedure in the following example.

EXAMPLE 13.4

REDUCING THE SETUP COST AT COMPSERVE

The CompServe Company stocks expensive laser printers. The annual demand for this product is 300 units. The cost from CompServe's supplier is $1000 per printer, the cost of capital is 10%, and the storage cost per printer per year is $30. CompServe currently incurs a setup cost of $800 per order, but it believes that by streamlining its ordering and delivery operations, it can reduce this value and thereby achieve smaller inventory levels. Specifically, it estimates that each 10% reduction in setup cost will require a $1500 investment. However, preliminary analysis shows that it is physically impossible to reduce the setup cost below $50, regardless of the amount invested. Should the company invest in setup cost reductions, and if so, how will this affect its ordering policy?

Solution

We must first find the parameters a_0 and a_1 of the investment cost function $f(K)$ by using the information on the original setup cost, $800, and the cost per 10% setup cost reduction, $1500. Then we can express all annual costs in terms of the decision variables K and Q and use the Solver to optimize. The details are explained below.

DEVELOPING THE SPREADSHEET MODEL

The spreadsheet solution shown in Figure 13.7 is very similar to the solution for the basic EOQ model. (See the file EOQ4.XLS.) We list some key steps below.

❶ Parameters of setup cost reduction function. Calculate the parameters a_0 and a_1 of the setup cost reduction function in the Intercept and Slope cells using the procedure outlined above. Specifically, calculate a_1 with the formula

=TenPctCost/LN(0.9)

Then calculate a_0 with the formula

=-Slope*LN(InitSetupCost)

This formula ensures that the cost of making *no* setup cost reduction is 0.

❷ Cost of reducing setup cost. Enter the one-time investment in setup cost reduction in cell B23 with the formula

=Intercept+Slope*LN(SetupCost)

Then enter the equivalent annual cost in cell B24 with the formula

=IntRate*OneTimeCost

USING THE SOLVER

The rest of the model is exactly like the basic EOQ model. To set up the Solver, we identify annual cost as the objective to minimize, with the SetupCost and OrderQuan cells as the changing cells. We constrain SetupCost to be less than or equal to InitSetupCost and greater than or equal to MinSetupCost, and we select the Assume Non-Negative option. We also constrain the order quantity to be an integer.

As Figure 13.7 indicates, CompServe should first invest $28,991 to reduce the setup cost from $800 to $104.40. Then its optimal order quantity is 22 printers, and the total annual cost, including the investment in setup cost reduction, is $305,753. Of

FIGURE 13.7
Solution to Setup
Cost Reduction
Example

	A	B	C	D	E	F
1	**CompServe's EOQ model with possible setup cost reduction**					
2						
3	**Inputs**					
4	Initial setup cost	$800		**Range names used:**		
5	Minimal setup cost achievable	$50		InitSetupCost - B4		
6	Storage cost per unit per year	$30		MinSetupCost - B5		
7	Annual interest rate	10%		StorCost - B6		
8	Unit purchasing cost	$1,000		IntRate - B7		
9	Annual demand	300		UnitPurchCost - B8		
10	Cost of 10% reduction in setup cost	$1,500		AnnDemand - B9		
11				TenPctCost - B10		
12	**Parameters of setup cost reduction function**			Intercept - B13		
13	Intercept (a0)	95168		Slope - B14		
14	Slope (a1)	-14237		SetupCost - B17		
15				OrderQuan - B18		
16	**Analysis using the Solver**			AnnOrders - B20		
17	Setup cost K after reduction	$104.40		AnnCost - B28		
18	Order quantity Q	22				
19	Time between orders	0.073				
20	Orders per year	13.64				
21						
22	**Monetary values**					
23	One-time investment to reduce setup cost	$28,991				
24	Equivalent annual cost to reduce setup cost	$2,899				
25	Annual setup cost	$1,424				
26	Annual holding cost	$1,430				
27	Annual purchasing cost	$300,000				
28	Total annual cost	$305,753				

course, only $5753 of this is affected by the decision variables. The other $300,000 is the unavoidable annual purchase cost.

Has setup cost reduction worked? If this example is solved with the basic EOQ model, using the original $800 as the setup cost, you can check that the optimal order quantity is 61 units and the annual cost (not counting the $300,000 purchase cost) is approximately $7900. When setup cost reduction is allowed, the company reduces its setup cost from $800 to slightly over $100, and the ordering quantity drops sharply to 22 units. Instead of ordering about five times a year (300/61), it now orders almost 14 times a year (300/22). Also, the annual cost decreases by over $2000. Since the company's initial investment of almost $29,000 is equivalent to about $2900 per year, the savings in annual ordering and holding costs is about $4900. In addition, there may be other intangible benefits from holding less inventory, as Zangwill (1992) and many other authors have noted. ■

Synchronizing Orders for Several Products

Until now, we have assumed that a company orders a single product only. If it orders several products, it could calculate the EOQ for each product and order them according to separate schedules. However, there might be economies, particularly reduced setup costs, from synchronizing the orders so that several products are ordered simultaneously. This should be particularly attractive for products that come from the same supplier. Then, for example, the same truck might be able to deliver orders for several products, thereby reducing the setup cost involved with the delivery. We will develop a model in this section that takes advantage of synchronization, and we will compare it to the "individual EOQs" policy that uses no synchronization and treats the separate products independently. Although this model can be developed for any number of products, we will keep things relatively simple by assuming that there are only *two* products. We illustrate the approach in the following example.

EXAMPLE   13.5

SYNCHRONIZED ORDERING AT SLEEPEASE

Sleepease, a retailer of bedding supplies, orders king-size and queen-size mattresses from a regional supplier. There is a fairly constant demand for each of these products. The annual demand for queens is 2200; for kings it is 250. The unit purchasing costs for queen-size and king-size mattresses are $100 and $120, and the company's cost to store either of these for one year is $15. Sleepease's ordering cost is based primarily on the fixed cost of delivering a batch of mattresses. This ordering cost is $500 if either queens or kings are ordered separately, but the ordering cost is only $650 if both are ordered together. Sleepease's cost of capital is 13%. The company wants to know whether synchronizing orders is better than not synchronizing them, and if so, it wants to find the best synchronized ordering policy.

Solution

The only real cost benefit from synchronization is reduced setup costs. Let $K_1 = \$500$ be the setup cost for ordering queens when this is the only product ordered. Define $K_2 = \$500$ similarly for kings. When both products are ordered simultaneously, we denote the setup cost for the order by $K_{12} = \$650$. The important point is that K_{12} is considerably less than $K_1 + K_2$. This reflects the economy of scale achieved when both products are ordered together rather than individually. All other parameters (s, c, D, and i) are defined as before, except that each product has its own values of s, c, and D.

To model this problem, consider the graph in Figure 13.8. This depicts a synchronization policy where queens are ordered three times as often as kings. In general, let t_1 and t_2, respectively, be the time between orders of queens and kings, and let T be the cycle time, defined as the larger of t_1 and t_2. (In the graph, $t_2 > t_1$, so $T = t_2$.) Also, let n_1 and n_2, respectively, be the number of times queens and kings are ordered during a cycle. (In the graph, $n_1 = 3$ and $n_2 = 1$.) Then under a synchronization model, n_1 and n_2 are both positive integers, and at least one of them equals 1. (Actually, they could both be 1, in which case queens and kings are always ordered together.)

For the optimization model it is convenient to let T, n_1, and n_2 be the decision variables—that is, the changing cells in the spreadsheet. We can easily recover the order quantities Q_1 and Q_2 from these values as follows. First, we know that t_1, the time between orders of queens, is T/n_1. Similarly, $t_2 = T/n_2$. Then given t_1 and t_2,

FIGURE 13.8
EOQ with
Synchronization

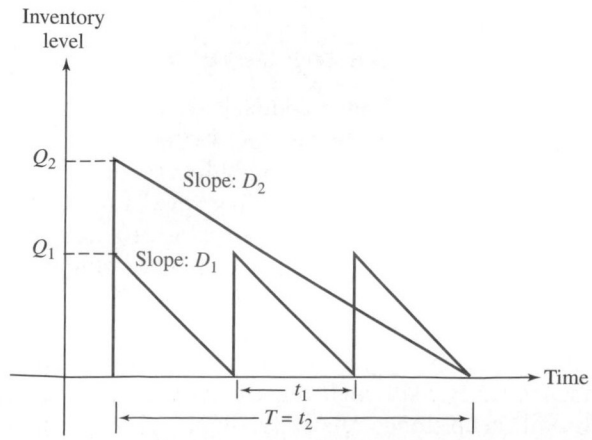

the order quantities Q_1 and Q_2 must be $Q_1 = D_1 t_1$ and $Q_2 = D_2 t_2$ (because we want each Q to decrease to 0 in time t at rate D).

To develop the total annual cost, the purchasing and holding costs are exactly as before (for each product). Therefore, we concentrate on the setup cost. During an ordering cycle of length T, both products are ordered together exactly once, for a setup cost of K_{12}. Then product j (for $j = 1$ or $j = 2$) is ordered $n_j - 1$ times by itself, for a setup cost of $K_j(n_j - 1)$. (For at least one of the two products, this latter term is 0. For example, it is 0 for product 2 in Figure 13.8.) The number of cycles per year is $1/T$, so the total annual setup cost is

$$\text{Annual setup cost} = [K_{12} + (n_1 - 1)K_1 + (n_2 - 1)K_2]/T \qquad (13.7)$$

We are now ready to develop the spreadsheet model.

DEVELOPING THE SPREADSHEET MODEL

The spreadsheet model appears in Figure 13.9. (See the file EOQ5.XLS.) The top part of the spreadsheet shows the analysis for the synchronized ordering policy. It can be formed as follows.

1 **Inputs.** Enter the inputs in rows 4, 5, 8, and 9. Note that (as usual) the combined holding costs in the HoldCosts range are storage costs plus the interest rate multiplied by the purchasing costs.

FIGURE 13.9
Solution to
Synchronized
Ordering Example

	A	B	C	D	E	F	G	H	I
1	Synchronized Ordering of Two Products								
2									
3	**Inputs**								
4	Interest rate	13%							
5	Joint setup cost	$650					Range names used:		
6							IntRate - B4		
7	Product	Setup cost (individual)	Storage cost	Purchasing cost	Combined holding cost	Annual demand	JtSetupCost - B5 IndSetupCosts - B8:B9 PurchCosts - D8:D9		
8	Queens	$500	$15	$100	$28	2200	HoldCosts E8:E9		
9	Kings	$500	$15	$120	$31	250	AnnDemands - F8:F9		
10							NOrders - B14:B15		
11	**Optimal synchronized policy**						CycTime - B17		
12							AnnCost - B23		
13	Product	Number of orders per cycle	Time between orders	Orders per year	Order quantity				
14	Queens	2	0.122	8.2	269				
15	Kings	1	0.245	4.1	61				
16									
17	Cycle time (years)	0.245							
18									
19	Costs affected by ordering policy								
20	Annual setup cost	$4,702							
21	Annual holding cost	$4,702							
22	Annual purchasing cost	$250,000							
23	Total annual cost	$259,404							
24									
25	**Optimal policy with no synchronization (using individual EOQs)**								
26									
27	Product	EOQ	Time between orders	Orders per year	Annual setup costs	Annual holding costs			
28	Queens	280	0.127	7.8	$3,924	$3,924			
29	Kings	90	0.362	2.8	$1,383	$1,383			
30					$5,307	$5,307			
31	Annual purchasing cost	$250,000							
32	Total annual cost	$260,614							

② **Orders per cycle and cycle time.** Enter *any* trial values in the NOrders and CycTime ranges. The values in the NOrders range correspond to n_1 and n_2; the value in the CycTime range corresponds to T.

③ **Timing of orders.** Calculate the times between orders, t_1 and t_2, in the range C14:C15 by entering the formula

=CycTime/B14

in cell C14 and copying it down. Then calculate the orders per year in the range D14:D15 as the reciprocals of the values in C14:C15.

④ **Order quantities.** Calculate the order quantity for queens in cell E14 with the formula

=F8*C14

and copy this to cell E15 for the kings. Again, this expresses the order quantity as the annual demand multiplied by the time between orders.

⑤ **Annual setup cost.** Calculate the annual setup cost in cell B20 with the formula

=(JtSetupCost+SUMPRODUCT(NOrders-1,IndSetupCosts))/CycTime

This follows directly from equation (13.7). (Note how the term NOrders-1 is used inside the SUMPRODUCT function. It takes the values in the NOrders range, subtracts 1 from each of them, and multiplies these by the values in the IndSetupCosts range.)

⑥ **Other costs.** Calculate the other costs exactly as in previous EOQ models, except that now the holding and purchasing costs must be summed over the two products, queens and kings.

Using the Solver

We can now use the Solver to find the optimal synchronized policy. We minimize the annual cost, using the NOrders and CycTime ranges as the changing cells. The constraints are that CycTime should be nonnegative and the NOrders values should be integers and greater than or equal to 1 (to ensure that Sleepease will order each product a positive integer number of times per cycle).

We see that there are about 4 cycles every year. Queens are ordered twice every cycle, and kings are ordered only once. The total annual cost (not counting the purchasing cost) from this synchronized ordering policy is $9404. For comparison, the bottom part of the spreadsheet in Figure 13.9 shows the unsynchronized policy from using individual EOQs. Now queens and kings are both ordered slightly less frequently than before, but because the orders are not synchronized, there are more ordering times per year. By comparing setup and holding costs, we see that this unsynchronized policy costs about 11% more than the best synchronized policy ($10,614 versus $9404). In addition, there might be an important noneconomic advantage of synchronizing orders—the ordering process is simply easier to manage.

Would you have guessed that queens would be ordered more frequently than kings? The reason is that the number of orders per year for either product is D/Q. From the EOQ square-root formula, we know that the optimal number of orders per year is proportional to the square root of D. Now, kings and queens have very similar setup costs K (if ordered separately) and holding costs h. Therefore, their relative ordering frequencies are determined by their demand rates, and queens have a much larger demand rate. Thus, it makes sense to order queens more frequently. (The analysis would not be this straightforward if kings and queens had different values for all three parameters K, D, and h.) ■

More Than Two Products

Virtually the same spreadsheet could be used for more than two products, provided that we make a simplifying assumption. This assumption is that a setup cost reduction is available only when the company places an order for all of the products simultaneously. Unfortunately, it is probably more realistic to assume that there is a setup cost reduction when *any* subset of products is ordered simultaneously. To illustrate, suppose that there are four products, product 1 is ordered once per cycle, products 2 and 3 are ordered twice per cycle, and product 4 is ordered four times per cycle. (See Figure 13.10.) When all four products are ordered together at the beginning of a cycle, there is definitely a setup cost reduction, but there is probably also some setup cost reduction when products 2, 3, and 4 are ordered together in the middle of a cycle. If we allow this possibility, however, and then try to optimize over all possible synchronizations, the problem becomes difficult to model in a spreadsheet. Therefore, we will not pursue this multiple-product model any further here.

FIGURE 13.10
Another Way to Synchronize

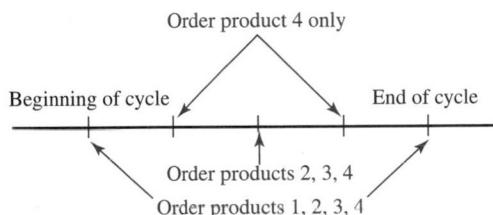

PROBLEMS

Skill-Building Problems

1. Each month, a gas station sells 4000 gallons of gasoline. Each time the parent company refills the station's tanks, it charges the station $50 plus $0.70 per gallon. The annual cost of holding a gallon of gasoline is $0.30.
   a. How large should the station's orders be?
   b. How many orders per year will the station place?
   c. How long will it be between orders?
   d. Would the EOQ assumptions be satisfied in this situation? Why or why not?
   e. If the lead time is 2 weeks, what is the reorder point? If the lead time is 10 weeks, what is the reorder point?

2. A bakery that orders cartons of bread mix has used an EOQ model to determine that an order quantity of 90 cartons per order is economically optimal. The bakery needs 150 cartons per month to meet demand. It takes L days for the bakery's supplier to deliver an order. When should the bakery place its orders when $L = 2$, when $L = 5$, and when $L = 10$? (Assume that the bakery and its supplier both work 7-day weeks and that there are 30 days per month.)

3. Consider the basic EOQ model. We want to know the sensitivity of (1) the optimal order quantity, (2) the sum of the annual order cost and the annual holding cost (not including the annual purchase cost cD), and (3) the time between orders to various parameters of the problem.
   a. How do (1), (2), and (3) change if the setup cost K decreases by 10%?
   b. How do (1), (2), and (3) change if the annual demand doubles?
   c. How do (1), (2), and (3) change if the cost of capital increases by 10%? (For this part, assume that the storage cost s is zero.)
   d. How do (1), (2), and (3) change if the changes in parts **a**, **b**, and **c** all occur simultaneously?

4. Based on Baumol (1952). Money in your savings account earns interest at a 10% annual rate. Each time you go to the bank, you waste 15 minutes in line, and your time is worth $10 per hour. During each year you need to withdraw $10,000 to pay your bills.
   a. How often should you go to the bank?
   b. Each time you go to the bank, how much money should you withdraw?
   c. If your need for cash increases, will you go to the bank more often or less often?
   d. If the interest rate increases, will you go to the bank more often or less often?

e. If the bank adds more tellers, will you go to the bank more often or less often?

5. The efficiency of an inventory system is often measured by the **turnover ratio**. The turnover ratio (TR) is defined by

$$TR = \frac{\text{Cost of goods sold per year}}{\text{Average value of on-hand inventory}}$$

a. Does a high turnover ratio indicate an efficient inventory system?

b. If the EOQ model is being used, determine TR in terms of K, D, h, and Q.

c. Suppose that D increases. Show that TR will also increase. Does this make intuitive sense?

6. A consulting firm is trying to determine how to minimize the annual costs associated with purchasing computer paper. Each time an order is placed an ordering cost of $20 is incurred. The price per box of computer paper depends on Q, the number of boxes ordered, as shown in Table 13.1. The annual holding cost is 20% of the dollar value of inventory. During each month, the consulting firm uses 80 boxes of computer paper. Determine the optimal order quantity and the number of orders placed each year.

TABLE 13.1	Data for Computer Paper Problem
Number of Boxes Ordered	**Price per Box**
$Q < 300$	$10.00
$300 \leq Q < 500$	$9.80
$Q \geq 500$	$9.70

7. Each year Shopalot Stores sells 10,000 cases of soda. The company is trying to determine how many cases to order each time it orders. It costs $5 to process each order, and the cost of carrying a case of soda in inventory for 1 year is 20% of the purchase price. The soda supplier offers Shopalot the schedule of quantity discounts shown in Table 13.2, where Q is the number of cases ordered per order. Each time an order is placed, how many cases of soda should the company order?

TABLE 13.2	Data for Shopalot Problem
Number of Cases Ordered	**Price per Case**
$Q < 200$	$4.40
$200 \leq Q < 400$	$4.20
$Q \geq 400$	$4.00

8. The Gilette Company buys a product using the price schedule given in Table 13.3. The company estimates the unit holding cost at 10% of the purchase price and the ordering cost at $40 per order. Gilette's annual demand is 460 units.

a. Determine how often the company should order.

b. Determine the optimal order quantity.

c. At what price should the company order?

TABLE 13.3	Data for Gilette Problem
Order Quantity	**Price per Unit**
0–99 units	$20.00
100–199	$19.50
200–499	$19.00
500 or more	$18.75

9. The manager of a hardware store decides to use the EOQ with shortages model to determine her ordering policy for tape measures. Using economic considerations, she determines that she should use an order quantity of $Q = 30$ and have a maximum shortage of $b = 3$. The lead time for her supplier to deliver an order is L working days, where there are 6 working days in a week. (Essentially, you can ignore Sundays.) The weekly demand is for 20 tape measures. What reorder point should the manager use if $L = 3$; if $L = 5$; if $L = 10$? (*Hint*: Now the manager should plan her orders so that the inventory level is $-b$ when an order arrives.)

10. A luxury car dealer must pay $20,000 for each car purchased. The annual holding cost is estimated to be 25% of the dollar value of inventory. The dealer sells an average of 500 cars per year. He is willing to backlog some demand but estimates that if he is short one car for one year he will lose $20,000 worth of future profits. Each time the dealer places an order for cars, the ordering cost is $10,000. Determine the luxury car dealer's optimal ordering policy. What is the maximum shortage that will occur? Assume it costs $5000 to store a car for a year (this is in addition to the holding cost above).

11. Reconsider Example 13.1. Each time Machey's orders cameras, it incurs a $35 ordering cost. Assume that Machey's could make an investment to decrease this ordering cost. Suppose that any 10% decrease costs a fixed amount C dollars. Using $i = 0.10$ and the Solver, experiment with different values of C to see how Machey's optimal order quantity is affected. Assume the minimum possible ordering cost is $10.

12. The particular logarithmic function proposed in Section 13.4 is just one possibility for the cost of a setup reduction. In the previous problem, suppose instead that Machey's has only three possibilities. It can either leave the setup cost as it is, it can spend C_1 dollars to reduce the setup cost to $25, or it can spend C_2 dollars to reduce it to $15. Analyze these possibilities for various values of C_1 and C_2 to see which is optimal in terms of total annual cost.

13. Chicago Mercy Hospital needs to order drugs that are used to treat heart attack victims. Annually 500 units of drug 1 and 800 units of drug 2 are used. The unit purchasing cost for drug 1 is $150 per unit, and the unit cost of purchasing drug 2 is $300. It costs $20 to store a unit of each drug for a year. When only drug 1 is ordered, an order for drug 1 costs $400. When only drug 2 is ordered, an order for drug 2 costs $600. If both drugs are ordered at the same time, the cost of placing an order is $800. Chicago Mercy's annual cost of capital is 18%. Determine a cost-minimizing ordering policy.

14. Software EG, a retail company, orders two kinds of software from TeleHard Software. Annually, Software EG sells 800 units of product 1 and 400 units of product 2. The unit purchasing cost is $30 per unit of product 1 and $25 per unit of product 2. It costs $5 to store a unit of either product for a year. The cost of placing an order for either product separately or both products together is $100. Software EG's annual cost of capital is 14%. Determine a cost-minimizing ordering policy.

Skill-Extending Problems

15. Based on Ignall and Kolesar (1972). Father Dominic's Pizza Parlor receives 30 calls per hour for delivery of pizza. It costs Father Dominic's $10 to send out a truck to deliver pizzas. It is estimated that each minute a customer spends waiting for a pizza costs the pizza parlor $0.20 in lost future business.
   a. How often should Father Dominic's send out a truck?
   b. What would the answer be if a truck could carry only five pizzas?

16. Suppose that instead of ordering the amount Q specified by the EOQ formula, we use the order quantity $0.8Q$. Show that the sum of the annual ordering cost and the annual holding cost increases by 2.5%.

17. In terms of K, D, and h, what is the average length of time that an item spends in inventory before being used to meet demand? Explain how this result can be used to characterize a fast-moving or slow-moving item.

18. A drugstore sells 30 bottles of antibiotics per week. Each time it orders antibiotics, there is a fixed ordering cost of $10 and a cost of $10 per bottle. Assume that the store's cost of capital is 10% and there is no storage cost, and suppose that antibiotics

spoil and cannot be sold if they spend more than 1 week in inventory. When the drugstore places an order, how many bottles of antibiotics should it order?

19. During each year, CSL Computer Company needs to train 27 service representatives. It costs $12,000 to run a training program, regardless of the number of students being trained. Service reps earn a monthly salary of $1500, so CSL does not want to train them before they are needed. Each training session takes 1 month.
   a. State the assumptions needed for the EOQ model to be applicable.
   b. How many service reps should be in each training group?
   c. How many training programs should CSL undertake each year?
   d. How many trained service reps will be available when each training program begins?

20. A hospital orders its thermometers from a hospital supply firm. The cost per thermometer depends on the order quantity Q, as shown in Table 13.4. The annual holding cost is 25% of the purchasing cost. Let Q_{80} be the optimal EOQ order quantity if the cost per thermometer is $0.80, and let Q_{79} be defined similarly if the cost per thermometer is $0.79.
   a. Explain why Q_{79} will be larger than Q_{80}.
   b. Explain why the optimal order quantity must be Q_{79}, Q_{80}, or 100.
   c. If $Q_{80} > 100$, explain why the optimal order quantity must be Q_{79}.
   d. If $Q_{80} < 100$ and $Q_{79} < 100$, explain why the optimal order quantity must be Q_{80} or 100.
   e. If $Q_{80} < 100$ and $Q_{79} > 100$, explain why the optimal order quantity must be Q_{79}.

TABLE 13.4	Data for Hospital Problem
Order Quantity	Price per Thermometer
$Q < 100$	$0.80
$Q \geq 100$	$0.79

21. In the previous problem, suppose that the cost per order is $1 and the monthly demand is 50 thermometers. What is the optimal order quantity? What is the smallest discount the supplier could offer that would still be accepted by the hospital?

22. Suppose that instead of measuring shortage in terms of cost per shortage per year, a cost of P dollars is incurred for each unit the firm is short. This cost does not depend on the length of time before the backlogged demand is satisfied. Determine a new expression for the annual shortage cost as a

function of Q and b, and solve GMB's problem (Example 13.3) with this way of costing shortages for reasonable values of P. (What values of P do you think are reasonable?)

23. The penalty cost p used in the shortage model might be very difficult to estimate. Instead, a company might use a service level constraint, such as, "95% of all demand must be met from on-hand inventory." Solve Problem 10 with this constraint instead of the $20,000 penalty cost. Now the problem is to minimize the total annual ordering and holding costs subject to meeting the service level constraint.

13.5 PROBABILISTIC INVENTORY MODELS

In most situations, companies that make ordering and production decisions face uncertainty about the future. Probably the most common and important element of uncertainty is customer demand, but there can be others. For example, there can be uncertainty in the amount of lead time between placement and receipt of an order. A company that faces this uncertainty has three basic options. First, it can use best guesses for uncertain quantities and proceed according to one of the deterministic models we developed in the previous section. Second, it can develop a probabilistic analytical (nonsimulation) model to deal with the uncertainty. The advantage to such a model is that we can calculate "bottom line" results, such as expected cost, and then use the Solver to optimize. The disadvantage is that these analytical models can become mathematically complex. The third possibility is to develop a simulation model. The advantage of a simulation model is that it is relatively easy to develop, regardless of the complexity of the problem. The disadvantage is that it can be difficult, or at least time-consuming, to find *optimal* ordering policies from a simulation.[5]

In this section we will analyze the same EOQ model as in the previous section, but with one important difference. Now the demand during any period of time is random and only its probability distribution is known. This is more realistic, but it greatly complicates the analysis. We will assume that the company uses an (R, Q) ordering policy, a type of ordering policy used by many companies. It is a continuous review policy that is determined by two numbers, R and Q. The reorder point R is the "reorder" point. When the company's inventory level drops to R, this automatically triggers the placement of an order. The order quantity Q specifies how much to order each time an order is placed.

When a company chooses R, it must take into account the effects of running out of inventory. If the company believes shortages are very expensive or undesirable, it should choose a relatively large value of R. This leads to a relatively large value of **safety stock**, the expected amount of inventory left over—the cushion—by the time the next order arrives. On the other hand, if shortages are not considered too expensive or undesirable, the company can afford to use a lower value of R, with a smaller resulting level of safety stock. In this section we will show how to determine an appropriate balance between leftovers and shortages.

We also must determine the appropriate order quantity Q. It turns out that the choices of R and Q can be made almost independently. The choice of R depends largely on how we measure shortage costs (or customer service), whereas the choice of Q depends mostly on the same cost factors we considered in the deterministic EOQ models. Specifically, the company wants to order enough to avoid frequent setup costs but as little as possible to avoid excessive holding costs. We will develop a Solver model that can be used to determine Q and R simultaneously, as illustrated in the following example.

---

[5]Fortunately, this is less true now than it used to be. Palisade, for example, has developed a software package called RiskOptimizer that uses a genetic algorithm to optimize a specified output in a simulation model. We refer to Winston (1999) for a discussion of simulation models that utilize RiskOptimizer.

EXAMPLE 13.6

ORDERING CAMERAS WITH UNCERTAIN DEMAND AT MACHEY'S

In Example 13.1 we considered Machey's department store, which sells, on average, 1200 cameras per year. The store pays a setup cost of $35 per order, and the holding cost is $10 per camera per year. It takes 1 week for an order to arrive once it is placed. In that example the optimal order quantity Q was found to be 92 cameras. Now we assume that the annual demand is normally distributed with mean 1200 and standard deviation 70. Machey's wants to know when to order and how many cameras to order at each ordering opportunity.

Solution

Suppose the company places an order for Q cameras every time its inventory level drops to R. Our goal is to find "good" values of Q and R. There are two aspects of this model that are critical to its solution: demand during lead time and the "cost" of running out of inventory.

Demand During Lead Time and Safety Stock The most critical probabilistic quantity is the amount of demand during an order lead time. To illustrate, suppose that Machey's uses $R = 30$ as the reorder point. This means that an order is placed as soon as the inventory level drops to 30 cameras. This order will arrive 1 week later. If the demand during this lead time is 25 cameras, say, then no shortage will occur, and there will be 5 cameras on hand when the order arrives. However, if the demand during this period is 35 cameras, then there will be a shortage of 5 cameras by the time the order arrives. Therefore, the demand during lead time, in conjunction with the choice of R, determines the extent of shortages. Before we can continue, we need to analyze this quantity in some detail.

Let D_{AD} be the annual demand, and let D_{LD} be the demand during an order lead time of length L. (For clarity, we use subscripts AD for annual demand and LD for lead time demand.) From the statement of the problem, D_{AD} is normally distributed with mean $\mu_{AD} = 1200$ and standard deviation $\sigma_{AD} = 70$. By making appropriate probability assumptions, it can be shown that D_{LT} is also normally distributed, and its mean and standard deviation are $\mu_{LD} = L\mu_{AD}$ and $\sigma_{LD} = \sqrt{L}\sigma_{AD}$. Because the lead time is 1 week ($L = 1/52$), Machey's expected demand during lead time is $\mu_{LD} = (1/52)(1200) \approx 23$ cameras, and the standard deviation of demand during lead time is $\sigma_{LD} = \sqrt{1/52}(70) \approx 9.7$ cameras.

Given these values, you might think that Machey's should set its reorder point R equal to 23, the mean demand during lead time. But then there would be a 50–50 chance of stocking out before the order arrives (because the probability that a normal random variable is greater than its mean is 0.5). What if the company instead sets R equal to 1 standard deviation above the mean—that is, $R = 23 + 9.7 \approx 33$? Then the probability of a stockout is $P(D_{LD} > 33)$. This can be found with the NORMDIST function in Excel. The syntax for this function is NORMDIST(x,μ,σ,1). It returns the probability of a normal random variable with mean μ and standard deviation σ being to the left of a specified value x. Therefore, we find $P(D_{LD} > 33)$, the probability of a stockout, with the formula **=1–NORMDIST(33,23,9.7,1)**, which is approximately 0.15. (See Figure 13.11 on page 598.)

FIGURE 13.11
Probability Under a
Normal Distribution

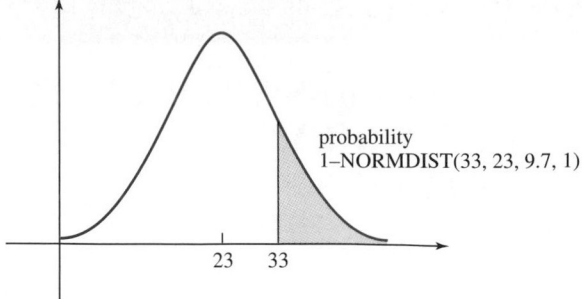

probability
1−NORMDIST(33, 23, 9.7, 1)

In general, suppose that Machey's decides to set R equal to k standard deviations above the mean, where k is a multiplier that must be determined. That is, it uses the reorder level

$$R = \mu_{LD} + k\sigma_{LD} = \mu_{LD} + \text{safety stock} \tag{13.8}$$

In effect, the multiplier k becomes the decision variable. Usually k is positive (and we will require it to be positive in this section). The term $k\sigma_{LD}$ then becomes the safety stock. To summarize the reasoning, Machey's expects an amount μ_{LD} to be demanded during the 1-week lead time. However, because shortages are undesirable, it orders when the inventory level is $k\sigma_{LD}$ above μ_{LD}. Therefore, it expects the inventory level to be $k\sigma_{LD}$, a positive value, when the order arrives. This value is its cushion against larger than expected demand—hence the term "safety stock." But although the company plans for this safety stock to exist, there is no guarantee that it will exist. As we saw in the previous probability calculation with $k = 1$, there is about a 15% chance that the safety stock of 10 units will be depleted before the order arrives and a stockout will occur. We want to choose k and the order quantity Q in an optimal manner.

Finding the Expected Costs We now develop an expression for Machey's expected total annual cost as a function of the order quantity Q and k. In the following discussion we will refer to an **order cycle**. Such a cycle begins each time an order arrives and ends just before the *next* order arrives. (See Figure 13.12.)

FIGURE 13.12
Depiction of an
Order Cycle

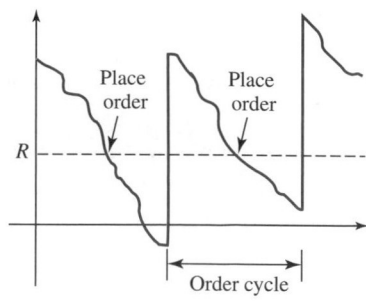

We first consider the annual setup and holding costs. If an order quantity Q is used, then it takes an expected amount of time Q/μ_{AD} to deplete this inventory. (Remember that μ_{AD} is the expected annual demand. It plays the same role as D in the deterministic EOQ models.) Therefore, there are an expected μ_{AD}/Q order cycles per year, so that the expected annual setup cost is $K\mu_{AD}/Q$. For the holding cost, consider any order cycle. The lowest inventory level during a cycle is expected to be $k\sigma_{LD}$, the safety stock. The highest inventory level occurs when the order arrives and the expected inventory jumps up to $Q + k\sigma_{LD}$. Therefore, the expected average inventory level during a typical cycle is $[k\sigma_{LD} + (Q + k\sigma_{LD})]/2$, and we multiply this by the unit holding cost h to obtain the expected annual holding cost. Simplifying the algebra slightly leads to the following expressions for expected annual setup and holding costs:

$$\text{Expected annual setup cost} = K\mu_{AD}/Q \tag{13.9}$$

$$\text{Expected annual holding cost} = h(Q/2 + k\sigma_{LD}) \tag{13.10}$$

where (for Machey's) $K = \$35$, $h = \$10$, $\mu_{AD} = 1200$, $\sigma_{LD} = 9.7$, and Q and k need to be determined.

Two Ways to "Cost" Shortages We now consider two alternative models of "costing" shortages. It is important to realize that neither of these models is clearly superior to the other. It is up to Machey's to decide which model is more in line with the company's goals. Model 1 assumes that there is a shortage cost of p per unit short. In this model, a cycle with a shortage of 5 units is 5 times as costly as a cycle with a shortage of only 1 unit. For example, suppose Machey's uses model 1 with $p = \$10$. If the *average* number of shortages during each of its order cycles is 2 and there are 13 order cycles during the year, then its annual shortage cost is $260.

Model 2 gets around the difficult problem of assessing *dollar* shortage costs by instead specifying a "service level." Specifically, it requires that the fraction of demand that can be met from on-hand inventory must be at least s, where s is a number between 0 and 1. For example, if Machey's uses model 2 with $s = 0.98$, then it will choose its ordering policy so that at least 98% of all customer demand can be met from on-hand inventory.

Before we can solve Machey's problem on a spreadsheet, we must develop formulas for the shortage cost (or service level) for these two shortage-costing models.

Expected Shortage Cost for Model 1 In model 1 Machey's assesses a shortage cost of p per unit short during any order cycle. Therefore, to evaluate the expected annual shortage cost, we must find the expected number of shortages per order cycle. Let $E(B)$ be the expected number of units short during a typical order cycle. Then the expected shortage cost during this cycle is $pE(B)$, and the expected annual shortage cost is the expected shortage cost per cycle multiplied by the expected number of cycles per year, μ_{AD}/Q. This leads to the following expected total annual cost:

$$\text{Model 1 expected annual shortage cost} = pE(B)\mu_{AD}/Q \tag{13.11}$$

The problem is to find an expression for $E(B)$. It can be shown that this expected value is related to a well-known quantity called the **normal loss function**. Fortunately, this can be calculated with built-in Excel functions. The formula for $E(B)$ is[6]

$$E(B) = [n(k) - kP(Z > k)]\sigma_{LD} \tag{13.12}$$

Here, $n(k)$ is the standard normal density function evaluated at k, and Z is a standard normal random variable. (Recall that *standard* normal implies mean 0 and standard deviation 1.) We now show how to implement model 1 for the camera example.

---

[6]This is one of the few times in this book where you will have to take our word for it. The derivation of this formula is well beyond the level of this book.

DEVELOPING THE SPREADSHEET FOR MODEL 1

We now assume that Machey's decides to use model 1, with $p = \$10$ as the unit shortage cost. The spreadsheet solution appears in Figure 13.13. (See the file CAMERA1.XLS.) It can be developed as follows.

❶ Inputs. Enter the inputs in the shaded range.

❷ Lead time demand. Calculate the mean and standard deviation of lead time demand in cells B12 and B13 with the formulas

=LT*MeanAD

and

=SQRT(LT)*StdevAD

❸ Decision variables. Enter any values in cells B16 and B17 for the order quantity Q and the multiplier k. These will be the changing cells.

❹ Safety stock and reorder point. The decision variables determine the safety stock and the reorder point. Calculate them in cells B18 and B19 with the formulas

=k*StdevLD

and

=MeanLD+SS

❺ Expected backorders. Use equation (13.12) to calculate the expected number of backorders per order cycle, $E(B)$, in cell B20 with the formula

=(NORMDIST(k,0,1,0)-k*(1-NORMSDIST(k)))*StdevLD

Note that this formula uses two related functions, NORMDIST and NORMSDIST. The first of these takes four arguments: a value, the mean, the standard deviation, and 0 or 1. When the fourth argument is 1 (the usual case), the function returns a cumulative

FIGURE 13.13
Optimal Solution for Model 1

	A	B	C	D	E	F
1	**Optimal (R,Q) ordering policy for model 1**					
2						
3	**Inputs**					
4	Setup cost per order	$35				
5	Holding cost per unit per year	$10				
6	Expected annual demand	1200				
7	Stdev of annual demand	70		**Range names used:**		
8	Lead time in years	0.0192		SetupCost - B4		
9	Shortage cost per unit short	$10		HoldCost - B5		
10				MeanAD - B6		
11	**Lead time demand**			StdevAD - B7		
12	Mean	23.077		LT - B8		
13	Stdev	9.707		ShortCost - B9		
14				MeanLD - B12		
15	**Ordering policy**			StdevLD - B13		
16	Order quantity	96.2		OrderQuan - B16		
17	Factor k for safety stock calculation	1.40		k - B17		
18	Safety stock	13.6		SS - B18		
19	Reorder point	36.7		MeanShort - B20		
20	Expected shortage per cycle	0.35		TotCost - B25		
21						
22	Annual setup cost	$437				
23	Annual holding cost	$617				
24	Annual shortage cost	$44				
25	Total annual cost	$1,098				

(left-hand tail) probability, but when this argument is 0, it returns the value of the density function. Here it is used, with a fourth argument equal to 0, to evaluate the standard normal density at value k. The second function, the NORMSDIST function, takes only one argument, a value. (The "S" in NORMSDIST stands for *standard* normal.) It returns the probability to the left of this value under the standard normal curve. To obtain the probability to the right of the value k, we subtract the NORMSDIST probability from 1. (See Figure 13.14.)

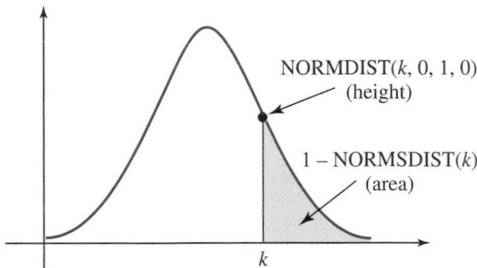

FIGURE 13.14
NORMDIST and
NORMSDIST
Functions

NORMDIST(k, 0, 1, 0)
(height)

$1 -$ NORMSDIST(k)
(area)

k

❻ **Expected annual costs.** Use equations (13.9)–(13.11) to calculate the expected annual setup, holding, and shortage costs in cells B22–B24 with the formulas

=SetupCost*MeanAD/OrderQuan
=HoldCost*(SS+OrderQuan/2)

and

=ShortCost*MeanShort*MeanAD/OrderQuan

Then calculate the expected total annual cost in cell B25 by summing the costs in cells B22–B24.

USING THE SOLVER

We set up the Solver to minimize the expected total annual cost. The only constraints are nonnegativity constraints on the changing cells, B16 and B17. As usual, we do *not* check the Assume Linear Model box. This model is nonlinear in both Q and k.

The interpretation of the Solver solution in Figure 13.13 is that Machey's should wait until the inventory level drops to approximately 37 cameras and then place an order for 96 cameras. The actual number of backorders during an order lead time is a discrete random variable with possible values 0, 1, 2, and so on. However, the *expected* number of backorders, a weighted average of these possible values, is $E(B) = 0.35$, so that the expected shortage cost during any order cycle is $pE(B) = \$3.50$. Multiplying this by the expected number of cycles per year (1200/96.2) gives the expected annual shortage cost of approximately \$44.

Service Level Constraint for Model 2 Model 2 uses a service level constraint instead of a dollar shortage cost. To model this constraint, we need an expression for the fraction of demand met directly from existing inventory. Note that Q items are ordered each cycle, and the expected shortage per cycle is $E(B)$, which we evaluated for model 1. Therefore, the expected fraction of demand met on time is $1 - E(B)/Q$, and the model 2 service level constraint becomes:

$$1 - E(B)/Q \geq s \qquad \text{(13.13)}$$

DEVELOPING THE SPREADSHEET FOR MODEL 2

The spreadsheet for model 2 appears in Figure 13.15. (See the file CAMERA2.XLS.) It assumes a service level where at least 98% ($s = 0.98$) of customer demands must be satisfied with existing inventory. This model is very similar to the one shown in Figure 13.13, so we list only the changes.

❶ Required service level. There is no unit shortage cost input. Instead, enter the required service level in cell D22.

❷ Actual service level. Use the left side of inequality (13.13) to calculate the expected fraction of demand met with existing inventory in cell B22 with the formula

=1-MeanShort/OrderQuan

❸ Expected total annual cost. The total cost now includes only the setup and holding costs (which are the same as before).

USING THE SOLVER

We again minimize the expected total annual cost, but we now add the service level constraint in row 22. There is no longer a shortage *cost* to penalize shortages. Instead, the company requires that 98% of all demand be met from existing inventory.

Compared to the solution for model 1, the solution in Figure 13.15 has a slightly larger order quantity Q and a significantly lower multiplier k. Therefore, this model specifies that Machey's should order a bit more on each order, and it should hold less safety stock—that is, it should let its inventory drop lower before ordering. Why are the solutions from the two models different? One way to understand the difference is to substitute the optimal values of Q and k from model 1 into the spreadsheet for model 2. If you do this, you will find that Q and k from model 1 lead to a service level (in cell B22) of 0.996 in model 2. This large service level, much larger than the 0.98 required,

FIGURE 13.15
Optimal Solution
for Model 2

	A	B	C	D	E	F
1	Optimal (R,Q) ordering policy for model 2					
2						
3	**Inputs**			Range names used:		
4	Setup cost per order	$35		SetupCost - B4		
5	Holding cost per unit per year	$10		HoldCost - B5		
6	Expected annual demand	1200		MeanAD - B6		
7	Stdev of annual demand	70		StdevAD - B7		
8	Lead time in years	0.0192		LT - B8		
9				MeanLD - B11		
10	**Lead time demand**			StdevLD - B12		
11	Mean	23.077		OrderQuan - B15		
12	Stdev	9.707		k - B16		
13				SS - B17		
14	**Ordering policy**			MeanShort - B19		
15	Order quantity	98.1		ActLev - B22		
16	Factor k for safety stock calculation	0.49		ReqdLev - D22		
17	Safety stock	4.7		TotCost - B26		
18	Reorder point	27.8				
19	Expected shortage per cycle	1.96				
20						
21	**Service level constraint**	Actual		Required		
22		0.980	>=	0.98		
23						
24	Annual setup cost	$428				
25	Annual holding cost	$538				
26	Total annual cost	$966				

can be attained only with increased safety stock. Evidently, the unit penalty cost of $10 in model 1 is *equivalent* to a required service level of 0.996 in model 2. Alternatively, if we want a service level of 0.98 in model 2, then the equivalent model 1 unit penalty cost must be considerably less than $10.

This is an important concept. Machey's might favor model 2 because a service level constraint is easier to estimate than a unit shortage cost. However, any particular service level in model 2 is really equivalent to an appropriate unit shortage cost in model 1. To find the equivalent unit shortage cost p for any required service level s, we could proceed as follows. First, we would add a formula in the model 1 spreadsheet to capture the expected fraction of demand met with existing inventory [the left side of inequality (13.13)]. Then we would run the Solver repeatedly on model 1, each time with a different value of p, until the service level is (approximately) equal to s. We actually tried this, with the results in Table 13.5. This shows, for example, that a required service level of 98% is evidently not very stringent. It is equivalent to a unit shortage cost of only $2.60.

TABLE 13.5	Equivalent Shortage Costs and Service Levels for Camera Example

p_2	Service Level
$10	99.6%
$8	99.5%
$6	99.3%
$4.50	99.0%
$2.60	98.0%

Random Lead Times Throughout this section, we have assumed that the lead time for orders is a known quantity. It is not difficult to modify the analysis for the case where the lead time L is random. This is important, because it is not at all uncommon in real applications for ordering lead times to be uncertain—suppliers might not be able to deliver according to a precise schedule.

When L is random, we need to estimate its mean and standard deviation (from historical lead time data), which we denote by μ_L and σ_L. Given these values, the expected demand during lead time becomes

$$\mu_{LD} = \mu_L \mu_{AD}$$

and the standard deviation of demand during lead time becomes

$$\sigma_{LD} = \sqrt{\mu_L \sigma_{AD}^2 + \mu_{AD}^2 \sigma_L^2}$$

For example, suppose as before that $\mu_{AD} = 1200$ and $\sigma_{AD} = 70$. However, instead of L being fixed at 1/52, it is uncertain with mean $\mu_L = 1/52$ and $\sigma_L = 1/104$, so that the standard deviation of the lead time is half a week. Then μ_{LD} is still 23.077 units [$= (1/52)(1200)$], but the standard deviation of demand during lead time is

$$\sigma_{LD} = \sqrt{(1/52)70^2 + 1200^2(1/104)^2} = 15.079$$

This is considerably larger than $\sigma_{LD} = 9.7$ when L was known with certainty. Intuitively, we can see that the extra uncertainty about the lead time adds to the uncertainty about the demand during lead time.

Once we use these formulas to obtain μ_{LD} and σ_{LD}, we can find the optimal (R, Q) exactly as in the nonrandom lead time case. For example, we reran the Solver for model 2 using $\sigma_{LD} = 15.079$ in cell B12. (Nothing else needs to be changed.) The order quantity increased slightly from 98.1 to 100.8, the safety stock increased from 4.7 to 11.1, the reorder point increased from 27.8 to 34.2, and expected total annual cost increased from $966 to $1032. In short, when the lead time is uncertain, a company needs to order earlier, which means larger safety stock and higher inventory holding costs. ■

PROBLEMS

Skill-Building Problems

24. Suppose the annual demand for Soni CD players at an appliance store is normally distributed with mean 150 and standard deviation 45. When the store orders these CD players from its supplier, it takes an amount of time L for the order to arrive, where L is measured as a fraction of a year. In each of the following, find the mean μ_{LD} and the standard deviation σ_{LD} of the demand during lead time.
   a. Assume that L is known to be 3/52, that is, 3 weeks.
   b. Assume that L is uncertain, with mean 3/52 and standard deviation 1/52.
25. In the previous problem assume that it costs $300 to place an order. The holding cost per CD player held in inventory per year is $15. The cost each time a customer orders a CD player that is not in stock is estimated at $40. (All demand is backlogged.)
   a. Find the optimal ordering policy for parts **a** and **b** of the previous problem (when lead time is known for certain and when it is not).
   b. How much more is the expected annual holding cost when L is random than when it is known with certainty? Why is this cost greater in the random case?
26. How do your answers to part **a** of the previous problem change if, instead of incurring a $40 penalty cost for each shortage, the store has a service level requirement of meeting 95% of all customer demands on time? In each case (L known with certainty and L random) what penalty cost p is this service level requirement equivalent to?
27. A hospital orders its blood from a regional blood bank. Each year, the hospital uses an average of 1040 pints of type O blood. Each order placed with the regional blood bank incurs a cost of $20. The lead time for each order is 5 days. It costs the hospital $20 to hold one pint of blood in inventory for a year. The stockout cost per pint is estimated to be $50. Annual demand for type O blood is normally distributed with standard deviation 43.26 pints.
   a. Determine the optimal order quantity, reorder point, and safety stock level. Assume that 365

days equal 1 year and that all demand is backlogged.
   b. What service level requirement (from model 2) is equivalent to this $50 stockout cost?
28. A firm experiences demand with a mean of 100 units per day. Lead time demand is normally distributed with mean 1000 units and standard deviation 200 units. It costs $6 to hold one unit for 1 year. If the firm wants to meet 90% of all demand on time, what will be the annual cost of holding safety stock? (Assume that each order costs $50.)
29. In Example 13.6, we discussed the equivalence between the model with shortage costs and the model with a service level constraint. Another way to see this equivalence is with SolverTable. Starting with the CAMERA1.XLS file, add a formula somewhere in the spreadsheet to calculate the expected fraction of demand met with existing inventory, $1 - E(B)/Q$. Then use SolverTable, with the unit shortage cost as the single input varied from $0.50 to $15 in increments of $0.50. As outputs, keep track of the order quantity, the safety stock, the reorder point, the fraction of demand met with existing inventory, and the expected annual setup, holding, and shortage costs. Discuss whether these go in the direction you would expect. Also, discuss how these results relate the two models, one with shortage costs and the other with a service level constraint. (What is equivalent to what?)

Skill-Extending Problems

30. The first model we developed in this section assumes that the total shortage cost is proportional to the amount of demand that cannot be met from on-hand inventory. Similarly, the second model assumes that the service level constraint is in terms of the fraction of all customer demand that can be met with on-hand inventory. Consider the following variations of these models. The first, labeled model 3, assumes that a shortage cost is incurred on every order cycle that experiences a stockout. This cost is independent of the *size* of the stockout. The second model, labeled model 4, prescribes a service level constraint—namely, the fraction of order cycles that must experience no stockouts.

a. In each of these new models, we need to be able to calculate the probability of a stockout during an order cycle. This is the probability that the demand during lead time is greater than the safety stock. Assuming that demand during lead time is still normally distributed, how can this probability be calculated? (*Hint*: Use the NORMDIST function.)

b. Given your method in part **a**, solve the following problem. Furnco sells secretarial chairs. Annual demand is normally distributed with mean 1040 chairs and standard deviation 130 chairs. Furnco orders its chairs from its flagship store. It costs $100 to place an order, and the lead time is 2 weeks. Furnco estimates that each order cycle in which there is a stockout causes a loss of $250 in future goodwill. Furnco pays $60 for each chair and sells it for $100. The annual cost of holding a chair in inventory is 30% of its purchase cost. Assuming that all demand is backlogged, what are the optimal reorder point and the safety stock level?

c. Continuing part **b**, what model 4 service level constraint is this $250 stockout cost equivalent to?

31. (This problem uses the new models for costing shortages discussed in the previous problem.) Referring to Problem 24 and using the ordering and holding costs from Problem 25, assume now that the store's service level requirement obligates it to meet customer demand on 95% of all order cycles. What (R, Q) policy should it use? Then find the model penalty cost per ordering cycle with a stockout that gives an equivalent (R, Q) policy. Answer these questions for the case where L is known with certainty and where it is random.

32. Explain the following statement: Faster-moving items require larger safety stocks than slower-moving items. (*Hint*: If Q/μ_{AD} is large, does this imply that an item is fast moving or slow moving?)

13.6   ORDERING SIMULATION MODELS

Analytical models such as the one in the previous section are useful and often provide important insights. Unfortunately, they can quickly lead to dead ends. As problems become more complex, the required mathematical models become too difficult for most managers to comprehend. In fact, mathematical models do not even exist for many realistic problems. Therefore, it is useful to turn to simulation, where virtually "anything goes." Simulation allows us to combine assumptions about uncertain quantities and ordering policies, and then play out the events as they occur through time. We already illustrated a "one-period" ordering simulation model in Chapter 11 when we discussed Walton Bookstore's calendars. The following example illustrates a somewhat more ambitious ordering simulation.

EXAMPLE   13.7

SIMULATING ORDERING POLICIES AT HOME REPAIR

Home Repair is a large hardware retail store that often has to place orders for hammers. The setup cost for placing an order is $500, independent of the size of the order. The unit cost per hammer is $20. Home Repair estimates that the cost of holding a hammer in inventory for 1 week is $3. The company defines its **inventory position** at the beginning of any week as the number of hammers in inventory plus any that have already been ordered but have not yet arrived. The company's ordering policy is an (s, S) policy, a common periodic review policy used by many companies. This policy, defined by two numbers s and S, where $s < S$, specifies that if the inventory position at the beginning of the week is at level x, where x is less than or equal to s, exactly enough hammers will be ordered to bring the inventory position up to S—that is, Home

Repair will order $S - x$ hammers. Otherwise, if the inventory position is greater than s, no order will be placed that week. If an order is placed, it will arrive after a lead time of 1, 2, or 3 weeks with probabilities 0.7, 0.2, and 0.1.

The weekly demand for hammers is uncertain, but it can be described by a normal distribution with mean 300 and standard deviation 75. The company's policy is to satisfy all demand in the week it occurs. If weekly demand cannot be satisfied completely from on-hand inventory, then an emergency order will be placed at the end of the week for the shortage. This order will arrive virtually instantaneously, but at a steep cost of $35 per hammer.

It is currently the beginning of week 1, and the current inventory of hammers, including any that might just have arrived, is 600. There are no other orders on the way. Home Repair wants to simulate several (s, S) policies to see which does best in terms of total costs over the next 52 weeks.

Solution

We will use @Risk to simulate a 52-week period and keep track of the total costs for this period for each of several (s, S) policies. There is no way to optimize over all possible (s, S) policies (except by using a package such as Palisade's RiskOptimizer), but it is possible to test a number of "representative" policies and choose the best of these.

DEVELOPING THE SIMULATION MODEL

The simulation model is shown in Figures 13.16 and 13.17. (See the file ORDERSIM.-XLS.) It is mostly a matter of careful bookkeeping, as we describe in the following steps.

❶ Inputs. Enter the inputs in the shaded ranges in Figure 13.16. These include the various costs, the parameters of the demand distribution, the current inventory situation, and possible combinations of s and S to test. (You can try other, or more, pairs if you like.) Note that the values in cells B30 and B31 are 0 because we have assumed that no orders are currently on the way. However, we develop the model so that it could respond to nonzero values in these cells. They would correspond to orders placed before week 1 but not due in until after week 1.

❷ Ordering policy. As usual, we set up the model with a RISKSIMTABLE function so that we can test all of the selected ordering policies simultaneously. To do this, enter the formula

=RISKSIMTABLE(E29:E36)

in cell B34. Then enter the formulas

=VLOOKUP(B34,PolicyTable,2)

and

=VLOOKUP(B34,PolicyTable,3)

in cells B34 and B35 to capture the values of s and S that will be used in the simulation.

❸ Beginning inventory. Moving to the simulation model in Figure 13.17, our strategy is the same as in most multiperiod models. We fill in the logic for the first few weeks and then copy down. We begin with column B, which contains the beginning on-hand inventory, right after any order has arrived. For week 1, this is the initial 600 hammers, so enter the formula

=InitInv

in cell B44. For later weeks we have to sum the final inventory from the previous week

Evaluating an ordering policy

Assumptions:
A company uses an ordering policy determined by two integers: s (reorder point) and S (order up to quantity). At the beginning of each week, right after any shipments have arrived, its inventory position is examined. This includes onhand inventory plus any that has been ordered but has not yet arrived. If the inventory position is greater than s, no ordering is done. But if it is less than or equal to s, an order is placed to bring the inventory position up to S, and this order arrives after a random lead time of one to three weeks. All demand is satisfied on time -- one way or the other. Either it is satisfied from onhand inventory, or if demand in any week is greater than onhand inventory, the demand is met by an emergency shipment (at a high cost).

Range names used:
FCost - B13
VCost - B14
HCost - B15
ECost - B16
LeadTimes - B20:B22
Probs - C20:C22
MeanDem - B25
StdevDem - B26
InitInv - B29
Due2 - B30
Due3 - B31
ReorderPt - B35
OrderUpToQ - B36
PolicyTable - E29:G36

Costs

Fixed order cost	$500
Variable order cost	$20
Inventory holding cost	$3
Emergency shipment cost	$35

Distribution of order lead time

Number of weeks	Probability
1	0.7
2	0.2
3	0.1

Distribution of demand in a week - Normal (rounded to nearest integer)

Mean	300
Stdev	75

Other inputs / **Ordering policies to try**

Other inputs		Policy	s	S
Initial inventory	600	1	200	500
Due in week 2	0	2	350	500
Due in week 3	0	3	350	750
		4	500	750
Order parameters		5	400	1000
Policy index	1	6	600	1000
Reorder point R	200	7	500	1250
Order up to quantity Q	500	8	700	1250

FIGURE 13.16 Inputs for Simulation Model

Summary measures from 52-week simulation below

	Fixed order	Var order	Holding	Emergency	Total
Cost totals	$10,500	$179,920	$22,977	$229,215	$442,612

Simulation	Inventory and order quantities, and lead time information								Costs			
Week	Begin onhand	Due in	Inv position	Amt ordered	Week order arrives	Demand	End onhand	Emerg orders	Fixed order	Variable order	Holding	Emergency
1	600	0	600	0	NA	261	339	0	$0	$0	$1,409	$0
2	339	0	339	0	NA	393	0	54	$0	$0	$509	$1,890
3	0	0	0	500	5	324	0	324	$500	$10,000	$0	$11,340
4	0	500	500	0	NA	330	0	330	$0	$0	$0	$11,550
5	500	0	500	0	NA	415	85	0	$0	$0	$878	$0
6	85	0	85	415	7	381	0	296	$500	$8,300	$128	$10,360
7	415	0	415	0	NA	334	81	0	$0	$0	$744	$0
8	81	0	81	419	9	332	0	251	$500	$8,380	$122	$8,785
9	419	0	419	0	NA	373	46	0	$0	$0	$698	$0
10	46	0	46	454	11	282	0	236	$500	$9,080	$69	$8,260
11	454	0	454	0	NA	225	229	0	$0	$0	$1,025	$0
12	229	0	229	0	NA	144	85	0	$0	$0	$471	$0
13	85	0	85	415	14	246	0	161	$500	$8,300	$128	$5,635
48	0	0	0	500	50	225	0	225	$500	$10,000	$0	$7,875
49	0	500	500	0	NA	287	0	287	$0	$0	$0	$10,045
50	500	0	500	0	NA	227	273	0	$0	$0	$1,160	$0
51	273	0	273	0	NA	231	42	0	$0	$0	$473	$0
52	42	0	42	458	53	316	0	274	$500	$9,160	$63	$9,590

FIGURE 13.17 Simulation of 52-Week Period

and the amount due in, if any, from previous orders. To do this, enter the formulas

=H44+Due2+SUMIF($F$44:F44,A45,$E$44:E44)
=I45+Due3+SUMIF($F$44:F45,A46,$E$44:E45)

and

=H46+SUMIF($F$44:F46,A47,$E$44:E46)

in cells B45–B47. This last formula is general, so copy it down to the other weeks. Note the usefulness of the SUMIF function. It sums all previous orders from column E that are due in at the beginning of the current week listed in column A. For example, in week 4 it looks for any due dates in the range F44:F46 that equal 4 and sums the corresponding order quantities.

4   **Due in.** In column C we record the amounts already ordered but not yet in, so that we can calculate the inventory position in column D. Do this by entering the formulas

=Due2+Due3
=Due3+SUMIF($F$44:F44,">"&A45,$E$44:E44)

and

=SUMIF($F$44:F45,">"&A46,$E$44:E45)

in cells C44–C46, and copy this latter formula down. The SUMIF function is used essentially as in the previous step, but now we want conditions (the middle argument) such as ">1". To do this in Excel, we must put the greater than sign in quotes, followed by an ampersand (&), and then a cell reference.

5   **Inventory position.** The inventory position is the amount on hand plus the amount due in, so enter the formula

=B44+C44

in cell D44 and copy it down.

6   **Order.** Following the logic of the (s, S) ordering policy, calculate the order quantity in cell E44 with the formula

=IF(D44<=ReorderPt,OrderUpToQ-D44,0)

and copy it down. Then to see when this order arrives (if there is an order), enter the formula

=IF(E44>0,A44+RISKDISCRETE(LeadTimes,Probs),"NA")

in cell F44 and copy it down.

7   **Demand.** Generate random demands in column G (rounded to the nearest integer) by entering the formula

=ROUND(RISKNORMAL(MeanDem,StdevDem),0)

in cell G44 and copying it down.

8   **End inventory and emergency orders.** If customer demand is less than on-hand inventory, then ending inventory is the difference; otherwise it is 0. Therefore, enter the formula

=MAX(B44-G44,0)

in cell H44 and copy it down. Similarly, there are emergency orders only if customer demand is greater than on-hand inventory, so enter the formula

=MAX(G44-B44,0)

in cell I44 and copy it down.

9   **Weekly costs.** The weekly costs are straightforward. Calculate them for week 1 in cells J44–M44 with the formulas

=IF(E44>0,FCost,0)
=VCost*E44

=HCost*(B44+H44)/2

and

=ECost*I44

and then copy these down. Note that we are basing the holding cost in any week on the *average* of the beginning and ending inventories for that week. It would be no more difficult to base it on the ending inventory only.

⑩   Summary measures. Calculate the total costs of the various types in row 40 and designate them as @Risk output cells. For example, the formula in cell B40 is

=RISKOUTPUT()+SUM(J44:J95)

It is important to look carefully at the completed model before running @Risk. Press the F9 key a few times, to get new random numbers, and check whether all of the logic, particularly in columns B and C, is working the way it should. It is easy to make errors, especially in the timing of order arrivals, in a model as complex as this one, and there is no sense in running @Risk on a model that contains logical errors!

USING @RISK

We use @Risk exactly as in Chapters 11 and 12. We set the number of iterations to 500 (each simulates a 52-week period) and the number of simulations to 8 (one for each combination of s and S we want to test). After running @Risk and copying selected outputs back to Excel, we obtained the results in Figure 13.18. The two shaded cells correspond to the smallest *average* 52-week total costs among all pairs of s and S. Home Repair might prefer the policy with $s = 500$ and $S = 750$ (at least among these particular policies). It has the smallest average total cost, it has the smallest 5th percentile, it is essentially tied for the smallest median (50th percentile), and its 95th percentile is close to the smallest. Even with this ordering policy, however, there is still considerable variability—from about $364,000 for the best of the 500 iterations to about $454,000 for the worst.

	A	B	C	D	E	F	G	H	I	J	K	L
97	Selected @Risk results for total cost (based on 500 iterations)											
98	Reorder point s	200	350	350	500	400	600	500	700			
99	Order up to quantity S	500	500	750	750	1000	1000	1250	1250			
100	Minimum	$390,598	$377,910	$374,522	$364,364	$359,364	$363,637	$378,733	$391,083			
101	Maximum	$495,198	$488,932	$462,790	$454,839	$473,991	$456,879	$464,049	$456,974			
102	Mean	$442,405	$430,299	$420,503	$408,894	$417,876	$409,231	$421,320	$421,697			
103	Stdev	$17,196	$17,797	$17,314	$15,979	$16,741	$14,437	$14,824	$12,361			
104	5th perc	$414,097	$401,932	$390,075	$382,018	$392,422	$385,615	$397,081	$402,864			
105	10th perc	$420,372	$407,581	$396,751	$388,064	$396,943	$391,815	$402,327	$406,346			
106	15th perc	$424,053	$411,506	$402,232	$392,326	$400,478	$395,366	$405,919	$409,082			
107	20th perc	$427,718	$415,143	$405,883	$395,550	$404,000	$397,394	$408,717	$410,654			
108	25th perc	$431,502	$417,676	$408,814	$398,820	$406,427	$399,721	$411,111	$411,994			
109	30th perc	$434,118	$419,181	$411,750	$400,883	$408,867	$401,917	$413,680	$414,016			
110	35th perc	$436,345	$423,092	$414,596	$402,956	$410,777	$403,437	$415,415	$416,490			
111	40th perc	$437,774	$425,201	$416,045	$404,483	$413,456	$405,313	$418,015	$417,865			
112	45th perc	$440,079	$426,855	$418,458	$406,425	$415,049	$406,469	$419,899	$419,492			
113	50th perc	$442,648	$430,672	$421,127	$408,413	$416,691	$408,359	$421,593	$421,416			
114	55th perc	$444,602	$432,997	$423,504	$410,355	$419,392	$410,041	$423,078	$422,642			
115	60th perc	$447,394	$435,118	$425,625	$412,356	$421,892	$411,798	$424,920	$424,553			
116	65th perc	$449,681	$437,195	$427,197	$413,923	$424,126	$414,169	$427,053	$426,162			
117	70th perc	$452,116	$439,832	$429,566	$416,529	$426,112	$416,324	$429,065	$427,905			
118	75th perc	$454,231	$442,588	$432,269	$418,725	$428,423	$418,016	$431,237	$429,514			
119	80th perc	$456,665	$445,396	$434,995	$421,542	$431,713	$420,738	$433,381	$431,941			
120	85th perc	$458,557	$449,195	$438,168	$426,483	$435,274	$423,453	$436,509	$435,395			
121	90th perc	$463,014	$453,289	$442,617	$430,339	$439,008	$428,976	$440,490	$437,704			
122	95th perc	$470,192	$459,458	$450,013	$426,448	$446,570	$434,493	$444,858	$443,423			
123												

Model

FIGURE 13.18 Selected Results from @Risk

We do not want to suggest that this simulation model is particularly "easy." The random lead times require some tricky logic. However, an analytical (nonsimulation) model of a situation as complex as Home Repair's would be totally out of the question for all but the most mathematically clever analysts. Simulation brings such complex models within the grasp of nonmathematicians. In addition, the modeling process itself often yields insights, such as why one ordering policy is better than another, that would not be apparent otherwise.

PROBLEMS

Skill-Building Problems

33. A department store is trying to decide how many JP Desksquirt II printers to order. Since JP is about to come out with a new model in a few months, the store will order only a limited number of model IIs. The cost per printer is $200, and each printer is sold for $230. If any model IIs are still in stock when the next model comes out, they will be sold for $150 apiece. If a customer wants a model II and there are none left, the store will special order the printer at an extra cost (to the store) of $25. These printers are not in great demand. The store estimates that the number of model IIs that will be demanded during the next few months (before the next model comes out) is equally likely to be any value from 10 to 20, inclusive. Develop a simulation model that can help the store determine the "best" number of printers to order, assuming that only one order will ever be placed.

34. Every 4 years, Blockbuster Publishers revises its textbooks. It has been 3 years since the best-selling book *The Joy of Excel* has been revised. At present, 2000 copies of the book are in stock, and Blockbuster must determine how many copies of the book to print for the next year. The sales department believes that sales during the next year are governed by a triangular distribution with parameters 4000, 6000, and 9000. Each copy of *Joy* sold during the next year brings the publisher a revenue of $35. Any copies left at the end of the next year cannot be sold at full price but can be sold for $5 to Bonds Ennoble and Gitano's bookstores. The cost of a printing of the book is $50,000 plus $15 per book printed.
   a. Use simulation to help the publisher decide how many copies of *Joy* to print.
   b. Does your answer change if 4000 copies are currently in stock?

35. Lowland Appliance replenishes its stock of color TVs three times a year. Each order takes 1/9 of a year to arrive. Annual demand for the color TVs follows a normal distribution with a mean of 990 and a standard deviation of 40. Assume that the cost

of holding a TV in inventory for a year is $100. Assume that Lowland begins with 500 TVs in inventory, the cost of a shortage is $150, and the cost of placing an order is $500.
   a. Suppose that whenever inventory is reviewed and the inventory level is I, an order for $480 - I$ TVs is placed. Use simulation to estimate the average annual cost of such a policy. Such a policy is called an **order-up** policy.
   b. Use simulation to estimate the average annual cost for order-up policies when Lowland orders up to 200, 400, 600, and 800 TVs.

36. Computco sells personal computers. The demand for its computers during a month follows a normal distribution, with a mean of 400 and standard deviation of 100. Each time an order is placed, costs of $600 per order and $1500 per computer are incurred. Computers are sold for $2800, and if Computco does not have a computer in stock, the customer will buy a computer from a competitor. At the end of each month a holding cost of $10 per computer is incurred. Orders are placed at the end of each month, and they arrive at the beginning of the next month. Four ordering policies are under consideration:
   ■ Policy 1: Place an order for 900 computers whenever the end-of-month inventory is 50 or less.
   ■ Policy 2: Place an order for 600 computers whenever the end-of-month inventory is 200 or less.
   ■ Policy 3: Place an order for 1000 computers whenever end-of-month inventory is 400 or less.
   ■ Policy 4: Place an order for 1200 computers whenever end-of-month inventory is 500 or less.
   Using simulation, run 500 iterations of an appropriate model to determine which ordering policy maximizes expected profit for a 2-year period. To get a more accurate idea of expected profit, you can credit Computco with a salvage value of $1500 for each computer left at the end of the last month. Assume that 400 computers are in inventory at the beginning of the first month.

Skill-Extending Problems

37. In the Walton Bookstore examples from Chapter 11, we assumed that there is a single product. Suppose instead that there are two competing products sold by a company. Sales of either product tend to take away sales from the other product. That is, the demands for the two products are negatively correlated. The company first places an order for each product. Then during a period of time, there is demand D_1 for product 1 and demand D_2 for product 2. These demands are normally distributed with means 1000 and 1200 and standard deviations 250 and 350. The correlation between D_1 and D_2 is ρ, where ρ is a negative number between -1 and 0. The unit cost of each product is $7.50, the unit price for each product is $10, and the unit refund for any unit of either product not sold is $2.50. The company must decide how many units of each product to order. Use @RISK to help the company by experimenting with different order quantities. Try this for $\rho = -0.3$, $\rho = -0.5$, and $\rho = -0.7$. What recommendation can you give about the "best" order quantities as the demands become more highly correlated (in a negative direction)?

38. Work the previous problem when the demands are *positively* correlated, as they might be with products like peanut butter and jelly. Now use $\rho = 0.3$, $\rho = 0.5$, and $\rho = 0.7$ in your simulations.

39. A highly perishable drug spoils after 3 days. A hospital estimates that it is equally likely to need between 1 and 9 units of the drug daily. Each time an order for the drug is placed, a fixed cost of $200 is incurred as well as a purchase cost of $50 per unit. Orders are placed at the end of each day and arrive at the beginning of the following day. It costs no money to hold the drug in inventory, but a cost of $100 is incurred each time the hospital needs a unit of the drug and does not have any available. The following three policies are under consideration:

- If we end the day with fewer than 5 units, order enough to bring next day's beginning inventory up to 10 units.
- If we end the day with fewer than 3 units, order enough to bring next day's beginning inventory up to 7 units.
- If we end the day with fewer than 8 units, order enough to bring next day's beginning inventory up to 15 units.

Use simulation to compare these policies with regard to expected daily costs, expected number of units short per day, and expected number of units spoiling each day. Assume that the hospital begins day 1 with 5 units of the drug on hand. (*Hint*: You will need to keep track of the age distribution of the units on hand at the beginning of each day. Assume that the hospital uses a FIFO (first in, first out) inventory policy. The trick is to get formulas that relate the age of each unit of the drug you have at the beginning of the day to the age of each unit you have at the end of the day.)

13.7 SUPPLY CHAIN MODELS

One of today's hottest areas of interest, both for academics and business managers, is the supply chain process. This refers to the entire process of getting materials from suppliers, transforming them into finished products, and ultimately getting the finished products to customers. With current computer technology and enterprise resource planning (ERP) software packages available from companies such as SAP, companies are able to interact with their customers and suppliers in a much more integrated manner, thus making their supply chains more efficient than ever before. Indeed, efficient supply chains have become a requirement in most industries. Without them, companies cannot compete successfully.

There are numerous interesting and difficult management science problems under the (very wide) supply chain umbrella. We consider one of these in the following example.[7] It is a problem faced by many companies in the fashion industry. When they introduce a new fashion, they are never sure whether it will sell well or not. Therefore, a reasonable strategy is to produce a limited amount early and see how things go. If the product sells well early, they can produce more later on—subject to capacity restrictions. If the product does poorly early, they can cut their losses short.

---

[7]This is an optimization model that requires the Evolutionary Solver discussed in Chapter 8.

EXAMPLE | 13.8

PLANNING PRODUCTION OF BLOUSES AT SHIRTTAILS

ShirtTails is a clothing manufacturer that operates its own chain of discount retail stores. At the beginning of November 2000, ShirtTails is trying to plan its production of a new blouse that is intended to be worn primarily in the warmer months. Based on production constraints from other products, the company knows it has two opportunities to produce this blouse—in November 2000 and later in April 2001. The production capacity (for this blouse) is 1200 in November. In April, the capacity will increase to 2500. By April, demand for the blouses produced in November will be known. Using this information, ShirtTails will then be able to plan its production in April.

The unit cost of producing a blouse is $12, and the selling price will be $14. These will remain constant. There is a $1 holding cost per blouse still in inventory after the pre-April demand. By November 2001, if there are any remaining blouses in inventory, they will be sold at a markdown price of $4. (This is because ShirtTails plans to introduce a new blouse the next year.) Demand for the blouses before April is not known with any certainty, but ShirtTails believes it should be somewhere between 100 and 1000. After April, the demand for blouses is expected to be anywhere from 3 to 7.5 times as large as the demand before April.

What production plan should the company use to maximize the expect profit from these blouses?

Solution

We first need to recognize that a production plan is really a *contingency plan*. This means that the company will determine a production quantity in November, but it will not commit to a production quantity in April until after it observes the pre-April demand. In other words, the contingency plan will specify a single production quantity in November and a production quantity in April for *each* pre-April demand that might be observed.

Before solving anything numerically, we must decide on probability distributions of demand. We will eventually try several, but we will initially assume "unimodal" symmetric discrete distributions—essentially the discrete analog of a normal distribution where the probabilities increase and then decrease. We will spell out the details shortly.

Finally, we want to point out explicitly that this is *not* a simulation model, despite the uncertainty. We plan to calculate an expected profit for any given production plan and then use the Evolutionary Solver to maximize this expected profit.

DEVELOPING THE SPREADSHEET MODEL

The completed model appears in Figures 13.19 and 13.20. (See the file FASH-ION.XLS.) It can be developed with the following steps.

1   Inputs. Enter the inputs in the shaded ranges in Figure 13.19. These include the given costs, the capacities, and the probability distributions we are initially assuming. Regarding these distributions, rows 13 and 14 indicate the distribution of pre-April demand, which can be any value from 100 to 1000 in increments of 100. Note that the probabilities increase gradually and then decrease—the "unimodal" property we mentioned. The table in rows 18–27 then specifies the distribution of post-April demand, given the pre-April demand. For example, if pre-April demand is 400 (in column E),

Two-stage production for a fashion product

Use the Tools/Scenarios menu item to view models that incorporate different types of probabilities. When any of these scenarios is "shown," you'll see the optimal production policy for that scenario.

Range names used:
UnitCost - B4
SalesPrice - B5
Markdown - B6
UnitHoldCost - B7
PenaltyCost - B8
EarlyCap - B9
LaterCap - B10
Probs1 - B14:K14
Probs2 - L18:L27
EarlyProd - B30
LaterProd - B32:K32
ProdCosts - B35:K35
HoldCosts - B37:K37
ExpRevs - B49:K49
ExpMarkdownRevs - B61:K61
ExpProfit - B68

Inputs

Unit production cost	$12	constant through both periods
Selling price	$14	constant through both periods
Markdown price	$4	for any items left over after later period
Holding cost	$1	charged per unit in inventory after early period
Overcapacity penalty	$500,000	
Early capacity	1200	
Later capacity	2500	

Demand during early period

Value	100	200	300	400	500	600	700	800	900	1000
Probability	0.05	0.05	0.05	0.10	0.25	0.25	0.10	0.05	0.05	0.05

Distribution of demand during later period (probabilities at right assumed valid for each column separately)

Multiple of early demand	Later demand (one column for each possible early demand)										Probability
3	300	600	900	1200	1500	1800	2100	2400	2700	3000	0.05
3.5	350	700	1050	1400	1750	2100	2450	2800	3150	3500	0.05
4	400	800	1200	1600	2000	2400	2800	3200	3600	4000	0.05
4.5	450	900	1350	1800	2250	2700	3150	3600	4050	4500	0.10
5	500	1000	1500	2000	2500	3000	3500	4000	4500	5000	0.25
5.5	550	1100	1650	2200	2750	3300	3850	4400	4950	5500	0.25
6	600	1200	1800	2400	3000	3600	4200	4800	5400	6000	0.10
6.5	650	1300	1950	2600	3250	3900	4550	5200	5850	6500	0.05
7	700	1400	2100	2800	3500	4200	4900	5600	6300	7000	0.05
7.5	750	1500	2250	3000	3750	4500	5250	6000	6750	7500	0.05

FIGURE 13.19 Inputs for Fashion Model

then post-April demand will be one of the values in the range E18:E27, with the corresponding probabilities in column L (which are also unimodal). This setup implies that the two periods have highly correlated demands. If pre-April demand is high, post-April demand is also likely to be high.

❷ **Production plan.** Moving to the optimization model in Figure 13.20, enter any production quantities in cell B30 and row 32. For example, the particular values in the figure (the optimal values) imply that ShirtTails will produce 600 blouses in November. Then if pre-April demand is 400 (column E), it will produce 1600 more blouses in April. In contrast, if pre-April demand is 600 or more (columns G–K), it will produce at capacity, 2500, in April.

❸ **Production cost.** The total production cost is proportional to the total number of blouses produced. Calculate it in row 35 by entering the formula

=UnitCost*(EarlyProd+B32)

in cell B35 and copying it across.

❹ **Holding cost.** The holding cost depends only on the November production quantity and pre-April demand. Calculate it in row 37 by entering the formula

=UnitHoldCost*MAX(EarlyProd-B13,0)

in cell B37 and copying it across.

❺ **Sales revenue.** The total sales revenue (not including markdown sales) depends on both production quantities and both pre-April and post-April demand. Therefore,

	A	B	C	D	E	F	G	H	I	J	K
29	**Production decisions**										
30	Early production	600									
31											
32	Later production	0	500	1050	1600	2150	2500	2500	2500	2500	2500
33											
34	**Costs, revenues for all scenarios**										
35	Production cost	$7,200	$13,200	$19,800	$26,400	$33,000	$37,200	$37,200	$37,200	$37,200	$37,200
36											
37	Holding cost	$500	$400	$300	$200	$100	$0	$0	$0	$0	$0
38											
39	Sales revenue	$5,600	$11,200	$16,800	$22,400	$28,000	$33,600	$39,200	$43,400	$43,400	$43,400
40		$6,300	$12,600	$18,900	$25,200	$31,500	$37,800	$43,400	$43,400	$43,400	$43,400
41		$7,000	$14,000	$21,000	$28,000	$35,000	$42,000	$43,400	$43,400	$43,400	$43,400
42		$7,700	$15,400	$23,100	$30,800	$38,500	$43,400	$43,400	$43,400	$43,400	$43,400
43		$8,400	$15,400	$23,100	$30,800	$38,500	$43,400	$43,400	$43,400	$43,400	$43,400
44		$8,400	$15,400	$23,100	$30,800	$38,500	$43,400	$43,400	$43,400	$43,400	$43,400
45		$8,400	$15,400	$23,100	$30,800	$38,500	$43,400	$43,400	$43,400	$43,400	$43,400
46		$8,400	$15,400	$23,100	$30,800	$38,500	$43,400	$43,400	$43,400	$43,400	$43,400
47		$8,400	$15,400	$23,100	$30,800	$38,500	$43,400	$43,400	$43,400	$43,400	$43,400
48		$8,400	$15,400	$23,100	$30,800	$38,500	$43,400	$43,400	$43,400	$43,400	$43,400
49	Expected sales revenues	$8,015	$14,980	$22,470	$29,960	$37,450	$42,560	$43,190	$43,400	$43,400	$43,400
50											
51	Markdown revenue	$800	$1,200	$1,800	$2,400	$3,000	$2,800	$1,200	$0	$0	$0
52		$600	$800	$1,200	$1,600	$2,000	$1,600	$0	$0	$0	$0
53		$400	$400	$600	$800	$1,000	$400	$0	$0	$0	$0
54		$200	$0	$0	$0	$0	$0	$0	$0	$0	$0
55		$0	$0	$0	$0	$0	$0	$0	$0	$0	$0
56		$0	$0	$0	$0	$0	$0	$0	$0	$0	$0
57		$0	$0	$0	$0	$0	$0	$0	$0	$0	$0
58		$0	$0	$0	$0	$0	$0	$0	$0	$0	$0
59		$0	$0	$0	$0	$0	$0	$0	$0	$0	$0
60		$0	$0	$0	$0	$0	$0	$0	$0	$0	$0
61	Expected markdown revenues	$110	$120	$180	$240	$300	$240	$60	$0	$0	$0
62											
63	**Expected values**										
64	Production cost	$31,500									
65	Holding cost	$105									
66	Sales revenue	$36,101									
67	Markdown revenue	$185									
68	Profit	$4,681									

FIGURE 13.20 Optimization Model

there is a whole matrix of these quantities, one for each possible combination of demands. Fortunately, these can be calculated with one general formula. To do so, enter the formula

=SalesPrice*MIN(B$13+B18,EarlyProd+B$32)

in cell B39 and copy it to the range B39:K48. Note that the first argument of the MIN is the total demand. The second argument is the total production. ShirtTails sells the smaller of these two quantities at the $14 price.

6 **Expected sales revenue.** For each possible pre-April demand—that is, each column from B to K—we need to calculate the expected total sales revenue, where the expected value is over the distribution of post-April demand. To do this, enter the formula

=SUMPRODUCT(B39:B48,Probs2)

in cell B49 and copy it across row 49. For example, if we are told that pre-April demand is 400 (column E), our best guess for total sales revenue is $29,960.

7 **Markdown revenue.** The calculation of markdown revenue is similar to the previous two steps. First, enter the formula

=Markdown*MAX((EarlyProd+B$32)-(B$13+B18),0)

in cell B51 and copy it to the range B51:K60. These cells show the markdown revenue for each demand combination. Then calculate the expected markdown revenues, given pre-April demand, by entering the formula

=SUMPRODUCT(B51:B60,Probs2)

in cell K61 and copying it across row 61.

8   **Expected revenues, costs, and profits.** At this point, rows 35, 37, 49, and 61 contain revenues and costs for each possible value of pre-April demand. To get overall expected values, we must "SUMPRODUCT" these with the row of pre-April demand probabilities. For example, calculate the overall expected sales revenue in cell B66 with the formula

=SUMPRODUCT(Probs1,ExpRevs)

The others are calculated similarly, and the expected profit is the sum of expected revenues minus the sum of expected costs. These are the values ShirtTails can expect as it looks ahead from November 2000—that is, before any demands have been observed.

USING THE EVOLUTIONARY SOLVER

We set up the Evolutionary Solver as shown in Figure 13.21. The target cell is the expected profit, the changing cells are the production quantities, and we must constrain them to be within capacity. Of course, the production quantities must also be nonnegative.

FIGURE 13.21
Solver Dialog Box
for Fashion Model

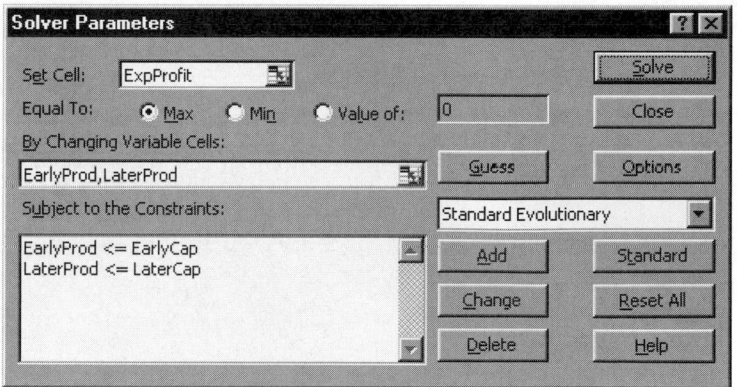

The solution in Figure 13.20 is fairly intuitive. ShirtTails could produce up to 1200 units in November, but it holds production to 600 because it is not sure whether these blouses will be popular. Once it observes pre-April demand, it then produces more or less, depending on the success of the blouses. If pre-April demand is its minimum value, 100, then there are already 500 of these "dogs" left in inventory, and the company does not produce any more. But if pre-April demand is sufficiently large, the company recognizes that it has a hot item and produces to capacity in April.

We finish this example by seeing how the shape of the demand distribution affects the optimal production plan. The distribution we have been using assumes a most likely demand in the middle, with less less likely demand values on either side—the unimodal property. We investigate two other possibilities, shown in Figures 13.22 and 13.23 on page 758. We call the first of these "U-shaped" because the probabilities are large on either end but decrease in the middle. This is reasonable if ShirtTails believes the blouse will be either very popular or very unpopular. The second distribution,

FIGURE 13.22 Results for a U-Shaped Probability Distribution

	A	B	C	D	E	F	G	H	I	J	K	L
12	**Demand during early period**											
13	Value	100	200	300	400	500	600	700	800	900	1000	
14	Probability	0.25	0.10	0.05	0.05	0.05	0.05	0.05	0.05	0.10	0.25	
15												
16	**Distribution of demand during later period (probabilities at right assumed valid for each column separately)**											
17	Multiple of early demand	Later demand (one column for each possible early demand)										Probability
18	3	300	600	900	1200	1500	1800	2100	2400	2700	3000	0.25
19	3.5	350	700	1050	1400	1750	2100	2450	2800	3150	3500	0.10
20	4	400	800	1200	1600	2000	2400	2800	3200	3600	4000	0.05
21	4.5	450	900	1350	1800	2250	2700	3150	3600	4050	4500	0.05
22	5	500	1000	1500	2000	2500	3000	3500	4000	4500	5000	0.05
23	5.5	550	1100	1650	2200	2750	3300	3850	4400	4950	5500	0.05
24	6	600	1200	1800	2400	3000	3600	4200	4800	5400	6000	0.05
25	6.5	650	1300	1950	2600	3250	3900	4550	5200	5850	6500	0.05
26	7	700	1400	2100	2800	3500	4200	4900	5600	6300	7000	0.10
27	7.5	750	1500	2250	3000	3750	4500	5250	6000	6750	7500	0.25
28												
29	**Production decisions**											
30	Early production	450										
31												
32	Later production	0	350	750	1150	1550	1950	2350	2500	2500	2500	
33												
63	**Expected values**											
64	Production cost	$22,470										
65	Holding cost	$122										
66	Sales revenue	$26,171										
67	Markdown revenue	$13										
68	Profit	$3,591										

FIGURE 13.23 Results for Equally Likely Probabilities

	A	B	C	D	E	F	G	H	I	J	K	L
12	**Demand during early period**											
13	Value	100	200	300	400	500	600	700	800	900	1000	
14	Probability	0.10	0.10	0.10	0.10	0.10	0.10	0.10	0.10	0.10	0.10	
15												
16	**Distribution of demand during later period (probabilities at right assumed valid for each column separately)**											
17	Multiple of early demand	Later demand (one column for each possible early demand)										Probability
18	3	300	600	900	1200	1500	1800	2100	2400	2700	3000	0.10
19	3.5	350	700	1050	1400	1750	2100	2450	2800	3150	3500	0.10
20	4	400	800	1200	1600	2000	2400	2800	3200	3600	4000	0.10
21	4.5	450	900	1350	1800	2250	2700	3150	3600	4050	4500	0.10
22	5	500	1000	1500	2000	2500	3000	3500	4000	4500	5000	0.10
23	5.5	550	1100	1650	2200	2750	3300	3850	4400	4950	5500	0.10
24	6	600	1200	1800	2400	3000	3600	4200	4800	5400	6000	0.10
25	6.5	650	1300	1950	2600	3250	3900	4550	5200	5850	6500	0.10
26	7	700	1400	2100	2800	3500	4200	4900	5600	6300	7000	0.10
27	7.5	750	1500	2250	3000	3750	4500	5250	6000	6750	7500	0.10
28												
29	**Production decisions**											
30	Early production	571										
31												
32	Later production	0	363	879	1285	1817	2228	2500	2500	2500	2500	
33												
63	**Expected values**											
64	Production cost	$26,740										
65	Holding cost	$136										
66	Sales revenue	$30,845										
67	Markdown revenue	$100										
68	Profit	$4,070										

in Figure 13.23, has equal probabilities for all demand values. This equally likely case is reasonable if ShirtTails has "no idea" how popular the blouses will be. In comparison with the unimodal scenario, we see some clear differences between the optimal solutions. The equally likely scenario calls for less production in November, generally less production in April, and a somewhat lower expected profit. This pattern is even more evident with the U-shaped scenario, which has the lowest production levels and the lowest expected profit.

These differences make intuitive sense. With a unimodal distribution, the company has the most assurance of what demand is likely to be, and it can plan accordingly. Planning is more difficult with the equally likely "no idea" distribution, and it is even worse with the U-shaped distribution. With this latter distribution, the company isn't sure whether to produce a lot in case demand is strong or to produce very little in case demand is weak. It stands to lose no matter what it does! Of course, the company cannot simply choose one distribution over another because one produces a larger expected profit. It should choose the distribution most in line with its realistic assessment of what demand is likely to be. ∎

Excel Tip   As the text box in Figure 13.19 indicates, we used Excel's Scenario feature to save each of the three scenarios under the names Unimodal, U-shaped, and Equally Likely. This feature is useful if you want to store several "named" scenarios in a single workbook. To do so, enter key inputs values in your spreadsheet that constitute a scenario. Then use the Tools/Scenarios menu item and click on Add. This gives you a chance to name a scenario and designate the cells (unfortunately called Changing Cells, but not the same concept as the Solver's Changing Cells) that include the key inputs. If you ever want to view this scenario later on, just use the Tools/Scenarios menu item, select the scenario you want from the list of scenarios, and click on View.

PROBLEMS

Skill-Building Problem

40. The problem in Example 13.8 assumes that the heaviest demand occurs in the second (post-April) phase of selling. It also assumes that capacity is higher in the second production opportunity than in the first. Suppose the situation is reversed, so that the higher capacity and most of the demand occur in the first phase. Make some reasonable assumptions for the resulting input parameters, and then solve for the optimal production plan. Do you get qualitatively different results? Which situation would you rather face if you were ShirtTails?

13.8   CONCLUSION

We have examined a variety of inventory/ordering models in this chapter. The general theme is the balance companies try to find between competing costs. If they order frequent, small quantities, they keep inventory low but they incur large setup costs. In contrast, if they order infrequent, large quantities, they minimize ordering costs, but they incur large holding costs. The basic EOQ model and its many variations we have discussed are able to find the right balance. These EOQ models are relatively straightforward and find many uses in today's business world. However, as we introduce complications that real companies face, such as multiple products, uncertain demand, uncertain delivery lead times, and complex supply chain considerations, the models can become extremely difficult. In this case simulation is often the best alternative. Indeed, it is sometimes the *only* feasible alternative.

PROBLEMS

Skill-Building Problems

41. Customers at Joe's Office Supply Store demand an average of 6000 desks per year. Each time an order is placed, an ordering cost of $300 is incurred. The annual holding cost for a single desk is 25% of the $200 cost of a desk. One week elapses between the placement of an order and the arrival of the order. In parts **a–d**, assume that no shortages are allowed.
  a. Each time an order is placed, how many desks should be ordered?
  b. How many orders should be placed each year?
  c. Determine the total annual costs (excluding purchasing costs) of meeting the customers' demands for desks.
  d. If the lead time is 5 weeks, what is the reorder point? (One year equals 52 weeks.)
  e. How do the answers to parts **a** and **b** change if shortages are allowed and a cost of $80 is incurred if Joe's is short 1 desk for 1 year?

42. A camera store sells an average of 100 cameras per month. The cost of holding a camera in inventory for a year is 30% of the price the camera shop pays for the camera. It costs $120 each time the camera store places an order with its supplier. The price charged per camera depends on the number of cameras ordered, as specified in Table 13.6. Each time the camera store places an order, how many cameras should it order?

TABLE 13.6	Data for Camera Problem
No. of Cameras Ordered	**Price per Camera**
1–10	$100
11–40	$90
41–100	$70
More than 100	$55

43. A hospital must order the drug Porapill from Daisy Drug Company. It costs $500 to place an order. Annual demand for the drug is normally distributed with mean 10,000 and standard deviation 3000, and it costs $5 to hold 1 unit in inventory for 1 year. (A unit is a standard container for the drug.) Orders arrive 1 month after being placed. Assume that all shortages are backlogged.
  a. What (R, Q) policy should the company use if it wants to meet 95% of all customer demand from existing inventory?

b. Suppose the company could pay C dollars per year to decrease its lead time per order from 1 month to half a month. What is the most it would be willing to pay to do this (and still have a 95% service level)?

44. Chicago's Treadway Tires Dealer must order tires from its national warehouse. It costs $10,000 to place an order. Annual tire sales are normally distributed with mean 20,000 and standard deviation 5000. It costs $10 per year to hold a tire in inventory, and the lead time for delivery of an order is normally distributed with mean 3 weeks and standard deviation 1 week. Assume that all shortages are backlogged.
  a. Find the (R, Q) policy the company should use to meet a service level where 96% of all demand is met with on-hand inventory.
  b. Assume that the company could pay C dollars per year to decrease the variability in lead times to essentially 0. That is, the lead time would then be a certain 3 weeks. What is the most it would be willing to pay (and still meet the service level in part **a**)?

Skill-Extending Problems

45. A newspaper has 500,000 subscribers who pay $4 per month for the paper. It costs the company $200,000 to bill all its customers. Assume that the company can earn interest at a rate of 20% per year on all revenues. Determine how often the newspaper should bill its customers. (*Hint*: Consider unpaid subscriptions as the inventoried good.)

46. A firm knows that the price of the product it is ordering is going to increase permanently by X dollars. It wants to know how much of the product it should order before the price increase goes into effect. Here is one approach to this problem. Suppose the firm places one order for Q units before the price increase goes into effect.
  a. What extra holding cost is incurred by ordering Q units now?
  b. How much in purchasing costs is saved by ordering Q units now?
  c. What value of Q maximizes purchasing cost savings less extra holding costs?
  d. Suppose that the annual demand is 1000 units, the holding cost per unit per year is $7.50, and the price of the item is going to increase by $10. How large an order should the firm place before the price increase goes into effect?

47. Based on Riccio et al. (1986). The borough of Staten Island has two sanitation districts. In district 1, street litter piles up at an average rate of 2000 tons per week, and in district 2, it piles up at an average rate of 1000 tons per week. Each district has 500 miles of streets. Staten Island has 10 sanitation crews and each crew can clean 50 miles per week of streets. To minimize the average level of the total amount of street litter in the two districts, how often should each district be cleaned? Assume that litter in a district grows at a constant rate until it is picked up, and assume that pickup is instantaneous. (*Hint:* Let p_i equal the average number of times that district i is cleaned per week. Then $p_1 + p_2 = 1$.)

48. A company inventories two items. The relevant data are shown in Table 13.7. Determine the optimal inventory policy if no shortages are allowed and if the average investment in inventory is not allowed to exceed $700. If this constraint could be relaxed by $1, by how much would the company's annual costs decrease? (*Hint:* Use the Solver.)

TABLE 13.7	**Data for Two-Item Inventory Problem**	
	Item 1	Item 2
Annual demand	6000	4000
Per-unit cost	$4.00	$3.50
Annual holding cost	30% per year	25% per year
Price per order	$35	$20

49. An **exchange curve** can be used to display the trade-offs between the average investment in inventory and the annual ordering cost. To illustrate the usefulness of a trade-off curve, suppose that a company must order two products with the attributes shown in Table 13.8.

TABLE 13.8	**Data for Exchange Curve Problem**		
	Order Cost	Annual Demand	Unit Purchase Cost
Product 1	$50	10,000	$200.00
Product 2	$80	20,000	$2.50

a. Draw a curve that displays annual order cost on the horizontal axis and average inventory investment on the vertical axis.

b. Currently the firm is ordering each product 10 times per year. Demonstrate that this is an unsatisfactory ordering policy.

c. Suppose management limits the company's average inventory investment to $10,000. Use the exchange curve to determine the best ordering policy.

50. A company currently has two warehouses. Each warehouse services half the company's demand, and the annual demand serviced by each warehouse is normally distributed with mean 10,000 and standard deviation 1000. The lead time for meeting demand is 1/10 year. The company wants to meet 95% of all demand on time. Assume that each warehouse uses the EOQ formula to determine its order quantity and that this leads to $Q = 2000$ for each warehouse.

a. How much safety stock must be held at each warehouse?

b. Show that if the company had only one warehouse, it would hold less safety stock than it does when it has two warehouses.

c. A young MBA argues, "By having one central warehouse, I can reduce the total amount of safety stock needed to meet 95% of all customer demands on time. Therefore, we can save money by having only one central warehouse instead of several branch warehouses." How might this argument be rebutted?

Modeling Problems

51. A trucking firm must decide at the beginning of the year on the size of its trucking fleet. If on a given day the firm does not have enough trucks, the firm will have to rent trucks from Hertz. Discuss how you would determine the optimal size of the trucking fleet?

52. A computer manufacturer produces computers for 40 different stores. To monitor its inventory policies, the manufacturer needs to estimate the mean and standard deviation of its weekly demand. How might it do this?

53. Based on Brout (1981). Planner's Peanuts sells 100 products. The company has been disappointed with the high level of inventory it keeps of each product and its low service level (percentage of demand met on time). Describe how you would help Planner's improve its performance on both these objectives. Pay close attention to the data you would need to collect and how the data would be used.

54. Austin (1977) conducted an extensive inventory analysis for the United States Air Force. He found that for over 250,000 items the annual holding cost was assumed to equal 32% of the item's purchase price. He also found that when an order was placed for most items, a fixed cost of over $200 was incurred. The Air Force held 1 month of safety stock for each item. Given this limited information, discuss how you could improve the Air Force's inventory policies.

Subway Token Hoarding

R iders of the subway system in the city of Metropolis must pay for the ride by purchasing a token. The same token can also be used to ride the buses in Metropolis. A single token is good for a trip to any destination served by the system. (Tokens are also used by millions of commuters for bridge, tunnel, and highway tolls in many areas of the country.)

Late in 1996 Metropolis transit officials announced that they were seeking a fare increase from $1.50 to $2.00. Later negotiations with politicians in the state capital reduced the requested increase to $1.75. It usually takes a few weeks between the announcement of a fare increase and the time that the increase goes into effect. Knowing that an increase will occur gives users of mass transit an opportunity to mitigate the effect of the increase by hoarding tokens—that is, by purchasing a large supply of tokens before the fare increase goes into effect.

There is a clear motivation for hoarding tokens—namely, the purchase of tokens before a fare increase offers a savings over purchasing the same tokens at a higher price after the change in fare. Why wouldn't riders wish to purchase a very large supply of tokens? The reason is the inventory cost that arises because of the time value of money.[8] The larger the supply that is hoarded, the longer the time until the tokens are used. Purchasing the supply of tokens represents an immediate cost, but the benefit is only realized over a longer period of time.

Thus, there is a trade-off between the immediate cost and the prolonged benefit. The optimal number of tokens to hoard balances these two effects to maximize the present value of the net benefit of the hoarding strategy.

Suppose that the current price of subway tokens is $p_1 = \$1.50$ and the fare is due to rise to $p_2 = \$1.75$. Suppose that you use the subway to commute twice per day, 5 days per week, 50 weeks per year. Also, suppose that you can purchase (or *hoard*) any number of tokens before the price increase takes effect. The hoarded tokens will be used by you during your normal usage of the mass transit system. After your hoard runs out, you will start purchasing tokens each day at the higher price. Suppose that your cost of capital is 15% per year. This means that you can borrow money to purchase your token supply, but the interest cost on the borrowed money is 15% per year.[9]

Questions

1. What is the optimal number of tokens to hoard?
2. What is the present value of the savings over not hoarding at all?
3. Suppose that the optimal quantity to hoard is Q^*. What is the present value of the savings if you decide to hoard only $0.8Q^*$?

---

[8]We are assuming that the hoarded tokens will be used by the hoarder for rides on the mass transit system, not for the immediate sale to other riders. In fact, such sales are illegal in Metropolis.

[9]Using 250 commuting days per year, you can assume that the daily interest cost is 0.05592% (= $1.15^{(1/250)} - 1$).

Retail Pricing Using Retailer[10]

etailer is an exercise designed to simulate the pricing decisions faced by the management of a large chain of retail clothing stores.[11] The simulation focuses on two important aspects of the pricing decision: *timing* and *magnitude* of price reductions. The retailer must decide when to take a price cut, if at all. If a price cut is taken, the magnitude of the cut must also be determined. These decisions are interrelated and further complicated because price reductions cannot be rescinded.

To place this problem in perspective, we give an overview of the fashion retail industry. Then we present a description of the production and distribution process, followed by a brief discussion of the technology and issues involved in pricing and markdowns. The implication of a markdown strategy for overall corporate earnings is illustrated for a specific company.

To help you develop a good pricing strategy for playing Retailer, historical data are provided in the file RETAIL.XLS. Specific instructions and suggestions for preparing to play Retailer are described in the final section.

The Fashion Retail Industry

The fashion retail industry is highly fragmented. Companies range in size from small boutiques operated as sole proprietorships to multinational specialty retailers such as Benetton, The Limited, and Gap Inc. Other important outlets include national department store chains, such as Macy's and Nordstrom's in the United States, Marks and Spencer in Europe, and the rapidly growing mail-order segment (Spiegel, J. Crew, and so on).

While many retailers serve only as intermediaries between producers and consumers, there is an increasing trend in the industry toward *private label* merchandise, which is manufactured exclusively for a particular retailer. Because it is exclusive, private label merchandise gives a store greater pricing power. It also helps differentiate a store's merchandise mix. Specialty retailers (Benetton, The Limited, etc.) have always manufactured (or subcontracted the manufacture of) their own exclusive designs. Recently, department stores such as Macy's are following this pattern by introducing their own private label lines.

While there is a tremendous variety in the range of merchandise sold by fashion retailers, from an operations standpoint the merchandise can be broken down into two main categories:

- **Staple Items.** Also known as *basic goods*, these are items that consumers purchase regularly and that do not become obsolete quickly. Socks, underwear, T-shirts, and core denim garments like 5-pocket jeans are considered staples. Also included in this category are "classic" garments, such as black gabardine skirts, khaki pants, white button-down Oxford shirts, and other items that are relatively immune to shifting fashion trends. Staple items are characterized by relatively stable and predictable demand.

- **Fashion Items.** These are items with a strong fashion component that quickly become obsolete or outdated. Fashion items are targeted for specific seasons (fall, spring, cruise, and holiday, for example) and in many cases are marketed over a series of "mini-seasons" lasting as short as 8 weeks. These items are used to enliven the presentation within a store and are frequently featured in its window display. In many ways, they also define the "style" of a store and help position the store relative to its competitors.

A range of garment types are found in the fashion category. Demand for fashion items is highly unpredictable and erratic; an item can be a hit and sell out in a matter of weeks, or consumers might utterly reject the style, resulting in only a fraction of the total stock selling during its targeted season.

Of course, a store's merchandise portfolio can be broken down in many different ways. For example, some stores categorize merchandise by fabric

[10]*Acknowledgment*: This case was coauthored with Garrett van Ryzin.

[11]The Retailer game is in the file RETAIL.EXE. It has never been updated to Windows format, but this DOS-based program still works well.

type (knits versus wovens) or department (sportswear, accessories, and so on). However, the staple-fashion classification turns out to be most useful in understanding the relationship between production, distribution, and pricing.

Production and Distribution

Garment production involves four major stages. First, and perhaps most important, is the design of the garments themselves. This is a highly creative process that, in most cases, begins one year in advance of the target season. Basic silhouettes, colors, and fabrics are chosen at this stage. Designs of individual garments or *styles* are often based on a particular theme (for example, the "Victorian look" or the "Western look") to form an entire *line* of clothes. The line projects a unified image and also helps ensure that garments coordinate well with each other.

Once designs are finalized, production quantities are determined. These quantities are based on very rough forecasts of the likely sales of individual styles. Given the vagaries of fashion trends and the long lead times involved, these forecasts are typically highly inaccurate.

Materials are then procured for production. Fabric is ordered from textile mills. Mills range in size from large national firms such as Burlington, Cone Mills, and Galey and Lord, to small specialty mills that produce silks and woolens. The lead time for fabric procurement can range from 1 to 2 weeks for standard in-stock fabrics to several months for special-order fabrics (for example, fabrics with custom colors or weaves). Buttons, zippers, and other accessories must also be ordered at this stage.

While materials are being ordered, production time is arranged either at a firm's own facilities or through subcontractors. Firms that specialize in particular fabric types, such as Italy's Benetton, with its core line of natural fiber knitwear, or Levi Strauss and Co., with its signature denim jeans, are more likely to own their own facilities; those without strong materials orientation often use subcontractors.

Subcontractors provide two key advantages to retailers: (1) flexible production capacity and (2) production expertise in particular fabric types. Both can be significant advantages when faced with fast moving fashion trends. For example, Ireland is well regarded as a source for high-quality woolen knits, whereas Hong Kong is the preferred source for silk garments because it is close to the sources of raw materials and has the machinery and skilled labor necessary to work with this delicate fiber. Denim and gabardine are relatively easy fabrics to work with, and garments made from these fabrics can be produced in a variety of locations, for example, Indonesia, Puerto Rico, or the United States. As a result, it is not uncommon for a retailer to have production contracts in dozens of countries in any given season. Lead times can range from under 4 weeks for an in-house domestic shop producing a simple garment to several months for an overseas contractor who requires advance production agreements.

Finally, once garments are cut and assembled, they are shipped to distribution centers and then from distribution centers to individual stores. The distribution process can be quick (1–2 weeks) for a domestic supplier, but in the case of overseas suppliers it can take 4–6 weeks if garments are transported in container ships. Overall, the total lead time for production is typically 6–12 weeks for a domestic contractor producing from standard fabric stock, 3–4 months for an overseas contractor using stock fabrics, and more than 6 months for an overseas contractor using a special-order fabric.

For staple items, periodic production runs can be scheduled to ensure a steady flow of merchandise from production facilities to stores. The management of this process is carried out using many of the traditional tools of inventory control. Indeed, the primary concern with staple items is reducing lead time and costs for reordering. This is accomplished through better communication via electronic data interchange (EDI)[12] and better materials handling technology.[13] Fashion items, however, are usually produced in a *single production run* because the fabrics and patterns change significantly from one season to the next and the lead times involved in

---

[12]EDI refers to a collection of technologies for computer-to-computer transmission of standard trading documents such as purchase orders and invoices. The technology is based on the ANSI X.12 standard, a detailed set of standards for protocols and message formats.

[13]The term "quick response" is often used in the industry to refer to lead-time reduction techniques.

production are usually too long to permit restocking within a tight 8–15 week sales season.

Pricing, Markdowns, and Leftovers

With perfect forecasts, merchandise is available in the exact quantities demanded by consumers and a store sells out its entire stock at full price. In practice, this is rarely the case. More often, a store finds itself short of stock on hit items, while selling only a fraction of its initial stock if a style proves unpopular. Items that remain unsold at the end of the selling season are typically sold in factory outlets (if available) or sold to discounters ("jobbers"). In the latter case, labels are often removed to prevent devaluation of the company's or designer's image.

Without the option to restock fashion items during a sales season, merchandise managers are left with few alternatives to match supply and demand for individual styles. One option is to transfer merchandise from stores where sales are weak to those where sales are strong. The second option is to change the price, usually by marking down styles that are not selling. The main decisions in taking a markdown are its timing and magnitude. For most retailers, the process of making markdown decisions is more of an art than a science. It is based mainly on the judgment of experienced merchandise managers.

POS Data and Markdown Control

A major technological trend in the retail industry is the development of point-of-sale (POS) technology. Essentially, a POS system links computerized cash registers (which are often equipped with laser scanners for automated reading of bar-coded tags) and scanners at distribution centers with a central computer in a retailer's home office. Local computers (usually PC-based) in the individual retail locations and distribution centers collect data on sales and inventories and are polled periodically by the central computer to update the status of each style in a store's line. Through a POS system, senior managers have a real-time view of the sales activities throughout their entire distribution chain.

Currently, most POS data are used only to identify ("flag") particular styles that are not performing up to expectations. For example, many retailers use an index of weekly sell-through percentage, defined as the ratio of a given week's sales to the in-store inventory at the start of that week. Each week items are sorted by sell-through percentages. These lists are used by merchandise managers to make markdown decisions. To date, however, very little analysis of POS data is performed beyond this simple exception reporting.

Financial Implications

To understand the financial impact of a markdown policy, it is useful to examine a specific company's earnings. Gap Inc. provides a good example. Gap Inc. has several subsidiaries: Gap Stores, Gap Kids, and Banana Republic. Each sells casual clothes and denim.

In the *New York Times* article shown in Figure 13.24 (page 766), a sharp earnings increase for Gap Inc. is partially attributed to its markdown strategy.[14] Financial information for Gap Inc. is shown in Tables 13.9–13.11 (pages 767–768). They show that in 1992, Gap had almost $3 billion in sales, producing a net income of approximately $210 million. With 144 million shares of stock outstanding in 1992, this represented earnings per share of $1.47.

Suppose that Gap could increase revenues 2% by changing its markdown strategy. This would represent a $59 million increase in sales. Since the cost of goods sold is not affected by the pricing strategy, pretax income would also increase by $59 million. This represents a 17% increase in pretax income and thus provides a 17% increase in net income and earnings per share. Likewise, a 2% decrease in revenue would decrease net income by 17%. *Relatively small changes in revenue can have a substantial impact on a company's bottom line.*

Preparation for Retailer

In the retailer simulation exercise, the player plays the role of upper management at a large chain of retail stores. The stores start with an initial stock of 2000 units of a fashion item initially priced at $60.

---

[14]The article does not contain enough information to determine whether Gap Inc.'s markdown strategy changed or whether items were simply selling faster so that fewer markdowns were required.

There are high hopes that the item will fly off the shelves, but only some items do. The length of the selling season is 15 weeks. Production and distribution costs for the item have been paid, so that cost is sunk. The goal is to maximize the revenue from the 2000 units during the selling season plus any salvage value. Management has decided to allow four price levels: full price ($60), 10% off ($54), 20% off ($48), and 40% off ($36). After observing sales for the current item (and historical data from roughly similar fashion items), in any given week management can leave the price the same or cut the price. Once the price is cut, company policy does *not* allow the price to be raised. If the price has been cut to 40% off, further markdowns are not possible in later weeks.

In the first week the price is set at $60. Thus, there are 14 weeks remaining for price cut decisions. All unsold inventory at the end of 15 weeks is sold for a salvage value of $25 per unit.

To make more informed markdown decisions, historical data for 15 different items are available in the file RETAIL.XLS. These are all fashion items, and some turned out to be very popular items while some did not sell so well.[15] Although the items are different, their responsiveness to price cuts are quite similar. The historical data in RETAIL.XLS have been "deseasonalized." That is, the data have been normalized to remove the predictable effects of seasons and holidays on sales figures. These effects are also removed from the Retailer simulation exercise.[16] Nevertheless, the unpredictable component of sales is quite significant. Even at the same price, sales can vary considerably from week to

---

[15] To generate the data, weekly demand for each item (at a given price) is sampled from a distribution with a mean that is different for each item. This "true mean" is unknown at the beginning of each selling season but can be estimated more accurately as additional weeks of sales are observed.

[16] In statistical terms, sales from one week to the next are independent. Sales are also identically distributed if the price is not changed.

TABLE 13.9 **Gap Inc.: Estimated Sales and Income by Division**

	1989	1990	1991	1992	1993E
Sales ($ millions)					
Gap Stores	$1,307	$1,554	$1,944	$2,185	$2,335
Gap Kids	$70	$140	$264	$375	$500
Banana Republic	$210	$240	$310	$400	$480
Total Sales	$1,587	$1,934	$2,518	$2,960	$3,315
% Change		21.9%	30.2%	17.6%	12.0%
Operating Income					
Gap Stores	$174	$223	$315	$278	$301
% of Sales	13.3%	14.4%	16.2%	12.7%	12.9%
Gap Kids	$6	$12	$29	$34	$45
% of Sales	8.6%	8.6%	11.0%	9.1%	9.0%
Banana Republic	($5)	$5	$31	$32	$43
% of Sales	−2.4%	2.1%	10.0%	8.0%	9.0%
Total Op. Income	$175	$240	$375	$344	$389
% of Sales	11.0%	12.4%	14.9%	11.6%	11.7%
Contribution to Sales					
Gap Stores	82.4%	80.4%	77.2%	73.8%	70.4%
Gap Kids	4.4%	7.2%	10.5%	12.7%	15.1%
Banana Republic	13.2%	12.4%	12.3%	13.5%	14.5%
Contribution to Profits					
Gap Stores	99.4%	92.9%	84.0%	80.8%	77.4%
Gap Kids	3.4%	5.0%	7.7%	9.9%	11.6%
Banana Republic	−2.9%	2.1%	8.3%	9.3%	11.1%

week because of weather, competitors, and a host of other factors. The historical data in RETAIL.XLS have also been normalized, so that the initial prices of all items are scaled to $60 and the initial quantities are scaled to 2000 units.

Before playing Retailer, you should carefully analyze the historical data and try to develop a sensible markdown strategy. You should work out any desired formulas in advance, so that necessary calculations can be done simply and quickly. In analyzing the historical data, you might want to attempt to answer the following questions:

- What is the average effect on sales of each size price cut? For example, for a price cut from $60 to $54, what is the average increase in weekly sales?

- How variable are sales from one item to the next?

In developing a strategy, you might want to consider the following:

- If demand were not variable, what would the optimal price cut strategy be? For example, suppose the demand at a price of $60 were a constant 80 items per week. Using your estimated demand sensitivities, to what level would you cut the price and when would you cut the price?

- How might your strategy be altered to account for uncertainty in demand?

- How would your strategy have performed on the historical data?

TABLE 13.10 Gap Inc.: Operating Statement Information

	1989	1990	1991	1992	1993E
Net Sales ($ millions)	$1,587.0	$1,934.0	$2,518.0	$2,960.0	$3,315.2
Cost of Goods Sold	1,046.2	1,241.2	1,568.0	1,955.6	2,182.3
S, G & A	364.1	454.2	575.7	661.3	743.8
Interest Expense	2.8	1.4	3.5	3.8	6.0
Pretax Income	162.7	237.1	370.8	339.8	383.0
Taxes	65.1	92.4	140.9	129.1	145.5
Net Income	97.6	144.7	229.9	210.7	237.5
EPS	$0.69	$1.02	$1.62	$1.47	$1.65
Shares Out (millions)	141.0	141.6	142.0	143.7	144.2
Sales % Change	26.8%	21.9%	30.3%	17.7%	16.0%
Comp-Stores	15.0	14.0	13.0	5.0	5.0
% of Sales					
Cost of Goods Sold	65.9	64.2	62.3	66.1%	65.8%
S, G & A	22.9	23.5	22.9	22.3	22.4
Interest Expense	0.2	0.1	0.1	0.1	0.2
Pretax Income	10.3	12.3	14.7	11.5	11.6
Tax Rate	40.0	39.0	38.0	38.0	38.0

Source: Company reports & C. J. Lawrence estimates.

TABLE 13.11 Gap Inc.: Estimated Store Profile

	1989	1990	1991	1992	1993E
Total					
Number of Stores	960	1,092	1,216	1,307	1,416
Average Store Size	4,226	4,361	4,637	4,980	5,390
Beginning Year Square Feet	3,843	4,067	4,762	5,638	6,509
Year-End Square Feet	4,057	4,762	5,638	6,509	7,632
% Change	5.6%	17.4%	18.4%	15.4%	17.3%
Average Square Feet	3,950	4,415	5,200	6,074	7,071
% Change	5.8%	11.8%	17.8%	16.8%	16.4%
Total Sales ($ million)	$1,587	$1,934	$2,518	$2,960	$3,315
% Change	27.9%	21.9%	30.2%	17.6%	12.0%
Sales/Average Square Foot	$402	$438	$484	$487	$469
% Change	20.9%	9.0%	10.5%	0.6%	−3.8%
Operating Income	$175	$240	$375	$344	$389
Operating Margin	11.0%	12.4%	14.9%	11.6%	11.7%
Comparable Store Sales	15.0%	14.0%	13.0%	5.0%	3.0%

Source: Company reports & C. J. Lawrence estimates.

## CHAPTER 14

Queueing Models

WAITING LINES AT LOURDES HOSPITAL AND L. L. BEAN

Long waiting lines in service organizations can be bad for business,
and the money spent to reduce these lines is often money well
spent. This is the conclusion of two studies reported in *Interfaces*,
one relating to the mail-order company L. L. Bean and the other to Lourdes
Hospital in New York State. Each study employed a queueing model to
determine the staffing levels necessary to reduce congestion to an
acceptable level.

The article "Staffing a Centralized Appointment Scheduling
Department in Lourdes Hospital," by Agnihothri and Taylor (1991),
describes how Lourdes Hospital decided to use a centralized system to
schedule, by phone, appointments for outpatients and inpatients and
ambulatory services requested by physicians, their staff, hospital personnel,
and patients. The decision to centralize certainly made sense. Instead of

having doctors and patients call many different departments for appointments and information, the system allowed them to call a well-trained and centrally located staff. However, a disadvantage quickly became obvious: the staff were not able to handle the large numbers of calls, particularly at peak periods during the day. Their goal of being able to answer 90% of all arriving calls was not being met, and all parties involved—doctors, patients, and staff—were frustrated with long waits and busy signals.

The authors collected data on the rates of incoming calls and the times required to "service" these calls. They found, among other things, that the pattern of calls was approximately the same each day of the week but the rate of calls differed during various times of the day. Therefore, they solved several queueing models, each for a different time of day, to determine staffing levels that would eliminate much of the congestion and many of the complaints. The study was a big success. As the authors state, "Prior to the study, three to four formal complaints were made each week about the busy phone lines. They fell to less than one per week immediately after the staffing changes, and since July 1988, complaints have been very infrequent and can usually be attributed to a known factor, such as an unexpected absence of a staff member."

The L. L. Bean study reported in the article "Establishing Telephone-Agent Staffing Levels through Economic Optimization," by Andrews and Parsons (1993), is similar to the hospital study in that L. L. Bean also experienced high levels of telephone congestion. Too many customers calling to order merchandise got a busy signal or had to wait a long time on line for an operator. The company had not ignored the problem in the past. In fact, it set a goal of having no more than 15% of the calls wait more than 20 seconds before reaching an operator, and it attempted to meet this goal with its rule-of-14: employ enough operators so that each handles about 14 calls per hour.

The problem was that there was little scientific basis for this rule-of-14; it was essentially an intuitive guideline. Worse yet, there was no guarantee that the company's goal of answering at least 85% of the calls within 20 seconds was a good one from an *economic* point of view. Before the study, L. L. Bean had never really analyzed the relevant costs, particularly the cost of lost business from fed-up customers who took their business elsewhere. After all, it was difficult to track customers who got busy signals or hung up after waiting a few minutes. Would they call L. L. Bean again or not? This study gathered data on lost business due to impatient customers, analyzed these data statistically, and then used a queueing model to determine the number of operators to employ (at various times of the day) to maximize expected profit. The authors report that for the first year it was used (1988) their new system resulted in an annualized profit gain of over $200,000. ■

14.1 INTRODUCTION

A basic fact of life is that we all spend a great deal of time waiting in queues. This occurs when we wait in line at a bank, at the supermarket, at a fast-food restaurant, at a stoplight, and many other situations. Of course, people are not the only entities that wait in queues. For example, televisions at a television repair shop, other than the one(s) being repaired, are essentially waiting in line to be repaired. Or when people submit computer jobs to a mainframe computer via remote terminals, these jobs typically wait in a queue (according to some priority system) until the computer has time to run them.

Mathematically, it does not really matter whether the entities waiting are people or televisions or computer jobs. The same type of analysis applies to all of these. The purpose of such an analysis is generally twofold. First, we want to examine an *existing* system to quantify its operating characteristics. For example, if a fast-food restaurant currently employs 12 people in various jobs, we might be interested in determining the amount of time a typical customer must wait in line or how many customers are typically waiting in line. The second purpose of queueing analysis is to learn how to make a system better. We might find, for example, that the fast-food restaurant would do better, from an economic standpoint, by employing only 10 workers and deploying them in a different manner.

The first objective, analyzing the characteristics of a particular system, is quite difficult from a mathematical point of view. There are two basic modeling approaches: analytical and simulation. With the analytical approach, we search for mathematical *formulas* that describe the operating characteristics of the system, usually in "steady state." With this approach, the mathematical models are typically too complex to solve unless we make simplifying (and possibly unrealistic) assumptions. For example, a commonly observed queueing situation occurs at a typical supermarket, where customers join one of several lines (probably the shortest), possibly switch lines if they see that another line is moving faster, and eventually get served by one of the checkout people. However, as common as this is—and as simple as it is to describe—it is *very* difficult to analyze analytically. The second approach, simulation, allows us to analyze much more complex systems, *without* making many simplifying assumptions. However, the drawback to queueing simulation, at least for many queueing systems, is that it requires specialized software packages.

In this chapter we will employ both the analytical approach and simulation. For the former, we will discuss several well-known queueing models that describe some—but certainly not all—queueing situations in the real world. For these we will see how to calculate such operating characteristics as the average waiting time per customer, the average number of customers in line, and the fraction of time servers are busy. As we stated, these analytical models generally require simplifying assumptions, and even then they remain a mystery to most nontechnical managers. Therefore, we will also discuss queueing simulations. Unfortunately, queueing simulations are not nearly as straightforward as the simulations we have developed in previous chapters. We typically need to generate random times between customer arrivals and random service times and then "play out" the events, and this playing out of events is far from easy in a spreadsheet. We will give only a taste of what can be done—and why commercial software packages are usually used instead of spreadsheets.

The second objective in many queueing studies is optimization, where we attempt to find the "best" system (in some sense). Of course, to find the best system, we need to be able to analyze each of several competing systems, either analytically or by simulation. But beyond this, we must make difficult choices. For example, if the fast-food restaurant is trying to decide how many employees to hire for various times of day, it must analyze the trade-off between more employees (better service) and fewer employees (lower wages). The cost of extra employees is easy to quantify—the marginal cost of one extra employee is the wage rate. However, it is difficult to estimate the "cost" of making a customer wait an extra 2 minutes in line. In terms of immediate out-of-pocket costs, it costs the restaurant nothing. But it might have long-range implications—fewer customers might bring their business to this restaurant if they have to wait a long time in line. Therefore, the restaurant manager must trade off better service versus higher employee wages when making the decision. To find the optimal number of employees, the restaurant must estimate the dollar cost of having a customer wait in line for some amount of time, such as a minute. Only by estimating this cost can it make an economic choice between the cost of waiting and the cost of more efficient service.

The examples in this chapter will highlight these two objectives. We will learn how to find important characteristics, such as expected waiting times, of specific systems, and we will also illustrate how to search for economically optimal systems.

This chapter is quite different from earlier chapters. This is due to the nature of queueing systems, not to any plan on our part. The models in previous chapters could almost always be developed from "first principles." By using relatively simple functions like SUM, SUMPRODUCT, IF, and so on, we were able to convert inputs into outputs in a way understandable to most nontechnical people. This is no longer possible in queueing models. The inputs are typically quantities such as mean arrival rates of customers and mean service times. The required outputs are typically mean waiting times in queues, mean queue lengths, the fraction of time servers are busy, and possibly others. Getting from the inputs to the outputs is mathematically *very difficult*, well beyond the level of this book. Therefore, there are many times in this chapter where you will have to "take our word for it." Nevertheless, the models we will illustrate are still very valuable for the important insights they provide.

14.2 ELEMENTS OF QUEUEING MODELS

We begin by listing some of the features of queueing systems that distinguish one system from another. Almost all queueing systems are alike in that customers enter a system, possibly wait in one or more queues, get served, and then depart.[1] This general description of a queueing system—customers entering, waiting in line, and being served—hardly suggests the variety of queueing systems that exist. We now discuss some of the key features and their variations.

Characteristics of Arrivals

First, we must specify the arrival process. This includes the timing of arrivals as well as the types of arrivals. Regarding timing, it is most common to specify **interarrival times**, the times between successive customer arrivals. It is possible that these interarrival times are known—that is, they are nonrandom. For example, the arrivals at some doctors' offices are scheduled fairly precisely. However, it is much more common that interarrival times are random with a probability distribution. In real applications, this probability distribution must be estimated from observed customer arrival times.

Regarding the types of arrivals, there are at least two issues. First, do customers arrive one at a time or in batches—carloads, for example? The simplest system is when customers arrive one at a time, as we will assume in all of the models in this chapter. Second, are all customers essentially alike, or can they be separated into priority classes? At a computer center, for example, certain jobs might receive higher priority and run first, while the lower-priority jobs go to the back of the line and run only after midnight. We will assume throughout this chapter that all customers have the same priority.

Another issue is whether (or how long) customers will wait in line. A customer might arrive at the system, see that too many customers are waiting in line, and decide not to enter the system after all. This is called **balking**. A variation of this is where the choice is made by the system, not the customer. In this case, we assume there is a

---

[1]From here on, we will refer to the entities requesting service as "customers," regardless of whether they are actually people. Also, we will refer to "servers" performing service on these customers, regardless of the type of work being performed and whether the servers are people or machines.

waiting room size such that if the number of customers in the system equals the waiting room size, newly arriving customers are not allowed to enter the system. We call this a **limited waiting room** system. Another type of behavior is called **reneging**. This is when a customer already in line becomes impatient and leaves the system before starting service.

Service Discipline

When customers enter the system, they might have to wait in line until a server becomes available. In this case we must specify the **service discipline**. The service discipline is the rule that states which customer, from all who are waiting, goes into service next. The most common service discipline is **first-come-first-served** (FCFS). Here customers are served in the order of their arrival. All of the models we will discuss will use the FCFS discipline. However, other service disciplines are possible, including **service-in-random-order** (SRO), **last-come-first-served** (LCFS), and various priority disciplines (if there are customer classes with different priorities). For example, a type of priority discipline used in some manufacturing settings is called the **shortest-processing-time** (SPT) discipline. In this case the jobs that are waiting to be processed are ranked according to their eventual processing (service) times, which are assumed to be known. Then the job with the shortest processing time is processed next.

One other aspect of the waiting process is whether there is a *single* line or *multiple* lines. For example, most banks now have a single line. An arriving customer joins the end of the line. When any teller finishes service, the customer at the head of the line then goes to that teller. In contrast, most supermarkets have multiple lines. When a customer goes to a checkout counter, he must choose which of several lines to enter. Presumably, he will choose the shortest line, but he might use other criteria in his decision. Once he joins a line (inevitably the slowest-moving one, from our experience!), he might decide to move to another line that seems to be moving faster.

Service Characteristics

Now we discuss the service itself. In the simplest systems, each customer is served by exactly one server, even though there might be multiple servers. For example, when you enter a bank, you are eventually served by a single teller, even though several tellers are working. The service times are typically random, although constant (nonrandom) service times are sometimes possible. When service times are random, we need to specify the probability distribution of a typical service time. This probability distribution can be the same for all customers and servers, or it can depend on the server and/or the customer. As with interarrival times, service time distributions must typically be estimated from service time data in real applications.

In a situation like the typical bank, where customers join a single line and are then served by the first available teller, we say the servers (tellers) are in **parallel**. (See Figure 14.1 on page 774.) A different type of service process is found in many manufacturing settings. For example, various types of parts (the customers) might enter a system with several types of machines (the servers). Each part type then follows a certain machine routing, such as machine 1, then machine 4, and then machine 2. Each machine has its own service time distribution, and a typical part might have to wait in line behind any or all of the machines on its routing. This type of system is called a **queueing network**. The simplest type of queueing network is a **series system**, where all parts go through the machines in numerical order: first machine 1, then machine 2, then machine 3, and so on. (See Figure 14.2.) We will examine mostly parallel systems in this chapter, but we will also illustrate a series system simulation.

FIGURE 14.1
Queueing System
with Servers in
Parallel

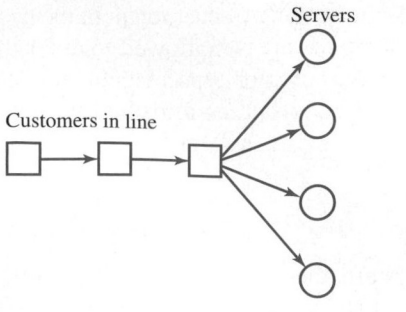

FIGURE 14.2
Queueing System
with Servers in Series

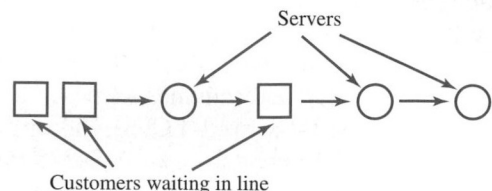

Short-Run Versus Steady-State Behavior

If you run a fast-food restaurant, you might be particularly interested in the queueing behavior during your peak lunchtime period. During this period, the customer arrival rate increases sharply, and you might employ more workers to meet the increased customer load. In this case your primary interest is in the "short-run" behavior of the system—the next hour or two. Unfortunately, short-run behavior is the most difficult to analyze, at least with analytical models. This is one reason, among others, for using simulation.

But how do we draw the line between the "short run" and the "long run"? The answer depends on how long the effects of initial conditions last. In the restaurant example, the initial conditions are determined by the number of customers already in line at the beginning of the lunch period—say, at 11:30. Suppose the restaurant manager is interested in the average number of customers waiting in line over a 2-hour peak period. The question then is whether this average is strongly affected by the number of customers in line at 11:30. In other words, do the effects of the initial conditions get "washed out" in a period as long as 2 hours, or do they persist? Ultimately, the only way to answer this question is with empirical evidence. We might compare a lunch period starting with no people in line at 11:30 with one where many people are already in line at 11:30. If the average levels of congestion over the entire 2-hour lunch period are approximately the same, then the initial conditions at 11:30 evidently make little difference, and a *long-run* analysis is permitted. However, if the lunch period that starts with many people in line is never quite able to overcome this initial load—that is, it tends to stay crowded—then the initial conditions are important, and a *short-run* analysis is required.

Analytical models are best suited for studying long-run behavior. This type of analysis is called **steady-state analysis** and will be the focus of the first part of this chapter. One requirement for any steady-state analysis is that the parameters of the system remain constant for the entire time period. In particular, the arrival rate must remain constant. In the restaurant example, if the objective is to study a 2-hour peak lunchtime period where the arrival rate is significantly larger than normal, and if we decide to employ steady-state analysis, we must be aware that the results of this 2-hour analysis do *not* apply to the rest of the day, when the arrival rate is much lower. If the parameters of the system change from one time period to another, then separate steady-state analyses are required for each time period. Alternatively, we can use simulation, where constant parameters are *not* required.

Another requirement for steady-state analysis is that the system must be **stable**. This means that the servers must serve fast enough to keep up with arrivals—otherwise, the queue could theoretically grow without limit. For example, in a single-server system where all arriving customers join the system, the requirement for system stability is that the arrival rate must be less than the service rate. If the system is not stable, the analytical models discussed in this chapter cannot be used. Again, however, we can use simulation, which does not require system stability.

14.3   THE EXPONENTIAL DISTRIBUTION

Queueing systems generally contain uncertainty. Specifically, times between customer arrivals (interarrival times) and customer service times are generally modeled as random variables. The most common probability distribution used to model these uncertain quantities is the **exponential** distribution. Many queueing models can be analyzed in a fairly straightforward manner, even on a spreadsheet, if we assume exponentially distributed interarrival times and service times. This exponential assumption buys us a lot in terms of simplified analysis, but it is quite strong. Therefore, it is important to understand the exponential distribution and some of its ramifications for queueing applications.

The random variable X has an exponential distribution with parameter λ (with $\lambda > 0$) if the density function for X has the form $f(x) = \lambda e^{-\lambda x}$ for $x > 0$. This exact form is not as important as the shape of the graph it implies, as shown in Figure 14.3.[2]

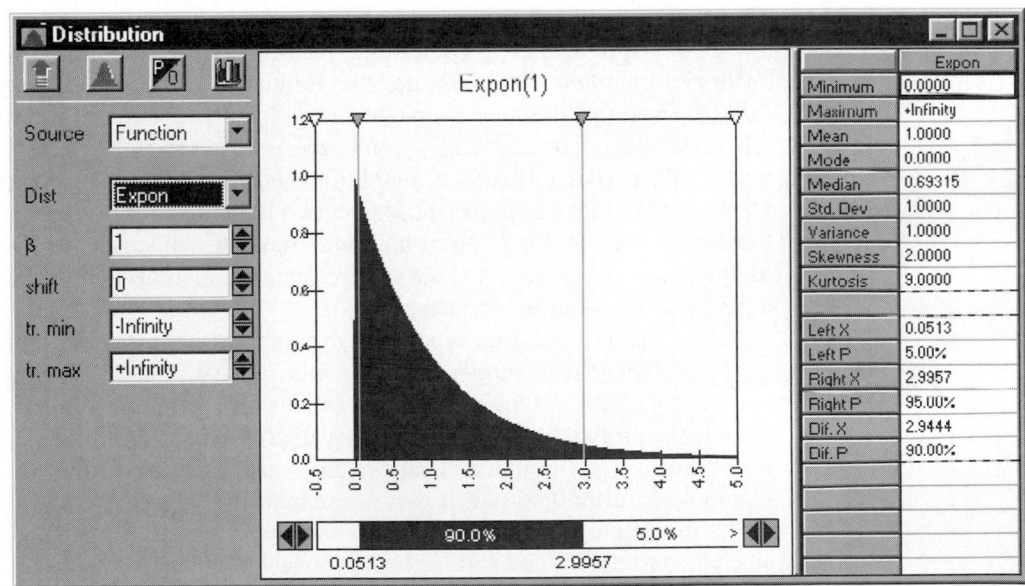

FIGURE 14.3 Typical Exponential Distribution

[2]You might want to compare this density to the more familiar bell-shaped, symmetric normal curve. In contrast to the normal distribution, the exponential is not bell-shaped, and has a heavy skew to the right.

(We obtained this graph from the @Risk Model window, a great place to explore shapes of different distributions.) Because this density decreases continually from left to right, its mode (the most likely value) is at 0. This means that X is more likely to be near 0 than any other value. Equivalently, if we collect many observations from an exponential distribution and draw a histogram of the observed values, then we expect it to resemble the smooth curve in Figure 14.3, with the tallest bars to the left. The mean and standard deviation of this distribution are easy to remember. They are both equal to the *reciprocal* of the parameter λ. For example, an exponential distribution with parameter $\lambda = 0.1$ has both mean and standard deviation equal to 10.

The random variable X will always be expressed in some time unit, such as minutes. For example, X might be the number of minutes it takes to serve a customer. Now, suppose that the mean service time is 3 minutes. Then $1/\lambda = 3$, so that $\lambda = 1/3$. For this reason, λ can be interpreted as a *rate*—in this case, 1 customer every 3 minutes (on average). Of course, the value of λ depends on the unit of time. If we switch from minutes to hours, say, λ changes from 1/3 (1 every 3 minutes) to $60(1/3) = 20$ (20 every hour). The corresponding mean is then $1/\lambda = 1/20$ hour.

The Memoryless Property

The property that makes the exponential distribution so useful in queueing models (and in other management science models) is called the **memoryless property**. It can be stated as follows. Let x and h be any positive numbers that represent amounts of time. Then if X is exponentially distributed, the following equation holds:

$$P(X > x + h | X > x) = P(X > h) \qquad \textbf{(14.1)}$$

The probability on the left is a conditional probability, the probability that X is greater than $x + h$, *given* that it is greater than x. The memoryless property states that this conditional probability is the same as the unconditional probability that X is greater than h. We now interpret this important property in several contexts.

First, suppose that X is the time, measured in hours, until failure of some item such as a lightbulb. Now consider two lightbulbs with the same exponential time to failure. The only difference is that the first lightbulb has already survived $x = 20$ hours, whereas the second lightbulb is brand new. We want the probabilities that lightbulbs 1 and 2 will survive at least $h = 5$ additional hours. The memoryless property says that these probabilities are the *same* for the two lightbulbs! This means that the lightbulb that has been in use for 20 hours has the same chance of surviving at least 5 more hours as the brand new lightbulb. For this reason, the memoryless property is sometimes called the "no wearout" property.

As a second example, suppose that X is the time, measured in minutes, until the next customer arrival. Suppose it is currently 3:00 P.M., and the previous arrival occurred at 2:57 P.M. Then we know that X is greater than 3 minutes. Given this information, what is the probability that the *next* arrival will occur after 3:05 P.M.? (Here $x = 3$ and $h = 5$, measured in minutes.) This is the same as the probability that the next arrival would occur after 3:05 P.M. if there were an arrival right now, at 3:00 P.M. That is, as far as the future (after 3:00 P.M.) is concerned, we can forget how long it has been since the last arrival and assume that an arrival just occurred, at 3:00 P.M. This example illustrates why the property is called the *memoryless* property.

These examples indicate why the exponential distribution is attractive from a mathematical point of view. If we observe a process at any time, all exponential times (interarrival times and service times, say) essentially "start over" probabilistically—we do not have to know how long it has been since various events (the last arrival or the beginning of service) occurred. The exponential distribution is the only continuous probability distribution with this property. On the negative side, however, this strong memoryless property makes the exponential distribution inappropriate for many real applications. In the lightbulb example, we might dismiss the exponential assumption immediately on the grounds that lightbulbs *do* wear out—a bulb that has been in continuous use for 20 hours is *not* as good as a brand new one. The ultimate test of appropriateness is whether sample data fit an exponential curve. We illustrate how to check this in the following example.

EXAMPLE   **14.1**

ESTIMATING INTERARRIVAL AND SERVICE TIME DISTRIBUTIONS AT A BANK

A bank manager would like to use an analytical queueing model to study the congestion at the bank's automatic teller machines (ATMs). A simple model of this system requires that the interarrival times (times between customer arrivals to the machines) and service times (times customers spend with the machines) are exponentially distributed. During a period of time when business is fairly steady, several employees use stopwatches to gather data on interarrival times and service times. These are listed in Figure 14.4. The bank manager wants to know, based on these data, whether it is reasonable to assume exponentially distributed interarrival times and service times. In each case he also wants to know the appropriate value of λ.

FIGURE 14.4
Interarrival and
Service Times for
ATM Example

	A	B	C	D	E
1	Interarrival times and service times at a bank (in seconds)				
2					
3	Averages of data below				
4		InterArrivalTime	ServiceTime		
5		25.3	22.3		
6					
7	Customer	InterArrivalTime	ServiceTime		
8	1	8	11		
9	2	33	20		
10	3	9	16		
11	4	11	8		
12	5	5	12		
13	6	24	17		
14	7	4	41		
15	8	46	7		
16	9	25	19		
17	10	10	43		
101	94	3	11		
102	95	14	16		
103	96	17	30		
104	97	17	24		
105	98	3	31		
106	99	42	59		
107	100	112	22		
108	101	17	40		
109	102	5	11		

Solution

To see whether these times are consistent with the exponential distribution, we plot histograms of the interarrival times and the service times. (See the file EXPONFIT.XLS.)

This can be done with StatPro's Histogram procedure. The histograms appear in Figures 14.5 and 14.6. The histogram of the interarrival times appears to be quite consistent with the exponential density shown in Figure 14.3. Its highest bar is at the left, and the remaining bars fall off gradually from left to right. On the other hand, the histogram of the service times is not shaped like the exponential density. Its highest bar is *not* the one farthest to the left but instead corresponds to the category from 15 to 30 seconds. Considering the way automatic teller machines operate, this is not surprising. There is some minimum time required to process *any* customer, regardless of the task, so that the most likely times are *not* close to 0. Therefore, the exponential assumption for interarrival times is reasonable, but it is questionable for service times.

FIGURE 14.5
Histogram of
Interarrival Times for
ATM Example

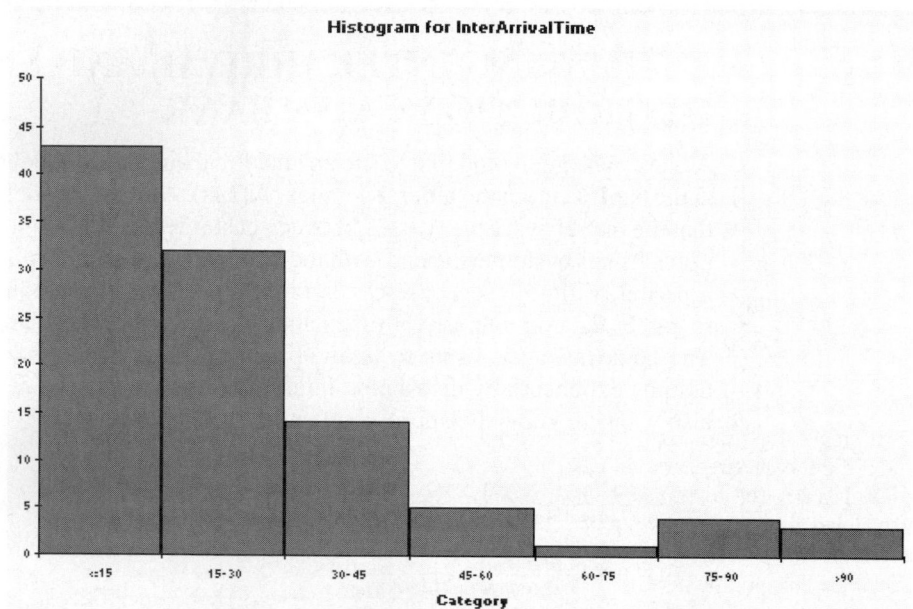

FIGURE 14.6
Histogram of Service
Times for ATM
Example

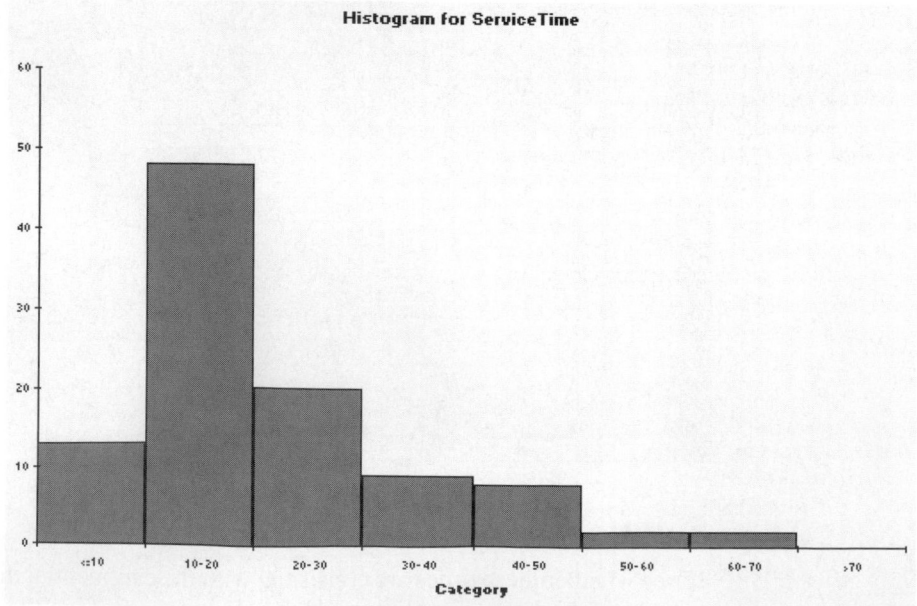

In either case, if the manager decides to accept the exponential assumption, the parameter λ is the rate of arrivals (or services) and is estimated by the reciprocal of the average of the observed times. For interarrival times, this estimate of λ is the reciprocal of the average in cell B5: $1/25.3 = 0.0395$—that is, 1 arrival every 25.3 seconds. For service times, the estimated λ is the reciprocal of the average in cell C5: $1/22.3 = 0.0448$—that is, 1 service every 22.3 seconds. ■

The Poisson Process Model

When the times between arrivals are exponentially distributed, we sometimes hear that "arrivals occur according to a Poisson process." There is a close relationship between the exponential distribution, which measures *times* between events such as arrivals, and the **Poisson distribution**, which counts the *number* of events in a certain length of time. The details of this relationship are beyond the level of this book, so we will not explore the topic any further here. However, if you hear, say, that customers arrive at a bank according to a Poisson process with rate 1 every 3 minutes, this means that the interarrival times are exponentially distributed with parameter $\lambda = 1/3$.

PROBLEMS

Skill-Building Problems

1. An extremely important concept in queueing models is the difference between rates and times. If λ represents a rate (customers per hour, say), then argue why $1/\lambda$ is a time and vice versa.

2. Explain the basic relationship between the exponential distribution and a Poisson process. Also, explain how the exponential distribution and the Poisson distribution are fundamentally different. (*Hint*: What type of data does each describe?)

3. It is possible to generate random numbers in a spreadsheet that have an exponential distribution with a given mean. For example, to generate 200 such numbers from an exponential distribution with $\lambda = 1/3$, enter the formula =**–3*LN(RAND())** in cell A4 and copy it to the range A5:A203. Then select the A4:A203 range, choose the Edit/Copy command, and choose the Edit/Paste Special command with the Values option. (This "freezes" the random numbers, so that they don't change each time the spreadsheet recalculates.) Explore the properties of these numbers as follows.
   a. Find the average of the 200 numbers with the AVERAGE function. What theoretical value should this average be close to?
   b. Find the standard deviation of the 200 numbers with the STDEV function. What theoretical value should this standard deviation be close to?
   c. Create a histogram of the random numbers, using about 15 categories, each of length 1, where the first category extends from 0 to 1. Does the histogram have the shape you would expect?
   d. Suppose that you collected the data in column A by timing arrivals at a store. The value in cell A4 is the time (in minutes) until the first arrival, the value in cell A5 is the time between the first and second arrivals, the value in cell A6 is the time between the second and third arrivals, and so on. How might you convince yourself that the interarrival times for this store are indeed exponentially distributed? What is your best guess for the arrival rate (customers per minute)?

Skill-Extending Problem

4. Do exponentially distributed random numbers have the memoryless property? Here is one way to find out. Generate many exponentially distributed random numbers with mean 3, using the formula in the previous problem. Find the fraction of them that are greater than 1. This estimates the probability $P(X > 1)$. Now find all random numbers that are greater than 4. Among these, find the fraction that are greater than 5. This estimates the probability $P(X > 4 + 1 | X > 4)$. According to the memoryless property, these two estimates should be nearly equal. Are they? Try to do this *without* freezing the random numbers, so that you can get repeated estimates of the two probabilities by pressing the F9 key.

14.4 IMPORTANT QUEUEING RELATIONSHIPS

As we stated, the calculations required in queueing models are neither simple nor obvious. Fortunately, there are several very useful and general relationships that hold for a wide variety of queueing models. We briefly discuss them here so that we can use them in the queueing models in later sections.

There are two general types of outputs we typically calculate in a queueing model: **time averages** and **customer averages**. Typical time averages are:[3]

- L_Q, the expected number of customers in the queue
- L_{Sys}, the expected number of customers in the system
- L_{Serv}, the expected number of customers in service
- P(all idle), the probability that all servers are idle
- P(all busy), the probability that all servers are busy

If you were going to estimate the quantity L_Q, for example, you might observe the system at many time points, record the number of customers in the queue at each time point, and then average these numbers. In other words, you would average this measure of the system over *time*. (To estimate a probability such as P(all busy), you would observe the system at many time points, record a 1 each time all servers are busy and a 0 each time at least one server is idle, and then average these 0's and 1's.)

In contrast, typical customer averages are:

- W_Q, the expected time a customer waits in the queue
- W_{Sys}, the expected time spent in the system (waiting in line or being served)
- W_{Serv}, the expected time spent in service

To estimate the quantity W_Q, for example, you would observe many customers, record the time in queue for each customer, and then average these times over the number of customers observed. Now you are averaging over *customers*.

Little's Formula

There is a famous formula that relates time averages and customer averages in steady state. This formula was first discovered by Little, and it is still called **Little's formula**.[4] The formula is easy to state, but not always easy to apply. Consider any queueing system. Let λ be the average rate at which customers enter this system, let L_{Sys} be the expected number of customers in the system, and let W_{Sys} be the expected time a typical customer spends in the system. Then Little's formula can be expressed as

$$L_{Sys} = \lambda W_{Sys} \qquad \textbf{(14.2)}$$

It can also be stated in terms of L_Q and W_Q or in terms of L_{Serv} and W_{Serv}. That is, two alternative versions of Little's formula are

$$L_Q = \lambda W_Q \qquad \textbf{(14.3)}$$

and

$$L_{Serv} = \lambda W_{Serv} \qquad \textbf{(14.4)}$$

---

[3]These quantities will appear several times throughout this chapter, and we will continue to use this notation.
[4]The original result was published in Little (1961). Numerous extensions of the basic result have been published since, including Brumelle (1971), Stidham (1974), and Heyman and Stidham (1980).

The reasoning behind Little's formula is actually very simple. For example, to see why equation (14.3) is true, consider a long time period of length T. During this period, we expect about λT customers to arrive (from the definition of λ as a rate), and each of these waits in queue for an expected time W_Q. Therefore, the expected total number of customer-minutes spent in queue is $\lambda T W_Q$. On the other hand, the expected number of customers in the queue at any time during this period is L_Q, so the total number of customer-minutes spent in the queue can also be calculated as $L_Q T$. Setting $\lambda T W_Q$ equal to $L_Q T$ and canceling T, we get equation (14.3). Strictly speaking, this argument is valid only for extremely large T, which is why Little's formula is a *steady-state* result. When we use simulation for relatively small values of time T, we will see that Little's formula is an approximation only.

Typically, we use analytical methods to find one of the L's and then appeal to Little's formula to find the corresponding W. Alternatively, we can find L from W. For example, suppose the arrival rate to a single-server queueing system is 30 customers per hour ($\lambda = 30$). Also, suppose we know (probably from an analytical model) that the expected number of customers in the system is $L_{\text{Sys}} = 2.5$. Then equation (14.2) implies that a typical customer spends an expected time

$$W_{\text{Sys}} = L_{\text{Sys}}/\lambda = 2.5/30 = 0.0833 \text{ hour} = 5 \text{ minutes}$$

in the system. If we also know that the average number of customers in the queue is $L_Q = 1.8$, then equation (14.3) implies that a typical customer's expected time in the queue is

$$W_Q = L_Q/\lambda = 1.8/30 = 0.06 \text{ hour} = 3.6 \text{ minutes}$$

Other Relationships

There are also two other formulas that relate these quantities. First, all customers are either in service or in the queue, so we have

$$L_{\text{Sys}} = L_Q + L_{\text{Serv}} \tag{14.5}$$

In the previous example, equation (14.5) implies that $L_{\text{Serv}} = 2.5 - 1.8 = 0.7$. (For a single-server system this means that exactly one customer is in service 70% of the time and no customers are in service 30% of the time.)

Second, we have

$$W_{\text{Sys}} = W_Q + W_{\text{Serv}} \tag{14.6}$$

Equation (14.6) follows because the time spent in the system is the time spent in the queue plus the time spent in service, and W_{Serv} is the expected time in service. In the previous example, equation (14.6) implies that the expected time a typical customer spends in service is $5.0 - 3.6 = 1.4$ minutes.

One final important queueing measure is called the **server utilization**. The server utilization, denoted by U, is defined as the long-run fraction of time a server is busy. In a multiple-server system, where there are s identical servers in parallel, server utilization is defined as

$$U = L_{\text{Serv}}/s$$

That is, it is the expected number of busy servers divided by the number of servers. For example, if $s = 3$ and $L_{\text{Serv}} = 2.55$, then $U = 0.85$. In this case the expected number of busy servers is 2.55, and each of the 3 servers is busy about 85% of the time.

PROBLEMS

Skill-Building Problems

5. Assume that parts arrive to a machining center at a rate of 60 parts per hour. The machining center is capable of processing 75 parts per hour—that is, the mean time to machine a part is 0.8 minute. If you are watching these parts *exiting* the machine center, what exit rate do you observe, 60 or 75 per hour? Explain.

6. Little's formula applies to an entire queueing system or to a subsystem of a larger system. For example, consider a single-server system composed of two "subsystems." The first subsystem is the waiting line, and the second is the service area, where service actually takes place. Let λ be the rate that customers enter the system and assume that $\lambda = 60$ per hour.

  a. If the expected number of customers waiting in line is 2.5, what does Little's formula applied to the first subsystem tell us?

  b. Let μ be the service rate of the server (in customers per hour). Assuming that $\lambda < \mu$ (so that the server can serve customers faster than they arrive), argue why the rate into the second subsystem must be λ. Then, letting $\mu = 80$ per hour, what does Little's formula applied to the

second subsystem tell us about the expected number of customers in service?

7. Consider a bank where potential customers arrive at rate 60 customers per hour. However, because of limited space, 1 out of every 4 arriving customers finds the bank full and leaves immediately (without entering the bank). Suppose that the average number of customers waiting in line in the bank is 3.5. How long will a typical *entering* customer have to wait in line? (*Hint*: In Little's formula, λ refers only to customers who join the system.)

Skill-Extending Problem

8. Consider a fast-food restaurant where customers enter at rate 75 per hour. There are 3 servers. Customers wait in a single line and go, in first-come-first-served fashion, to the first of the 3 servers who is available. Each server can serve 1 customer every 2 minutes on average. If you are standing at the exit, counting customers as they leave the restaurant, at what rate will you see them leave? On average, how many of the servers are busy?

14.5 ANALYTICAL MODELS

I n this section we discuss several analytical models for queueing systems. As we stated, these models cannot be developed without a fair amount of mathematical background—much more than we assume in this book. Therefore, we must rely on the queueing models that have been developed in the management science literature—and there are literally hundreds or even thousands of these. We will illustrate only the most basic models, and even for these, we will provide the key formulas. In some cases, we even automate these formulas with behind-the-scenes macros. This will enable you to focus on the aspects of practical concern: (1) the meaning of the assumptions and whether they are realistic, (2) the relevant input parameters, (3) interpretation of the outputs, and possibly (4) how to use the models for economic optimization.

The Basic Single-Server Model

We begin by discussing the most basic single-server model, labeled the $M/M/1$ model. This shorthand notation, developed by Kendall, implies three things. The first M implies that the distribution of interarrival times is exponential.[5] The second M implies that the distribution of service times is also exponential. Finally, the "1" implies that there is a *single* server. It is customary to let λ be the arrival rate and μ be the service rate. This

---

[5]The M actually stands for "Markov," a technical term that is synonymous with the exponential distribution.

means that $1/\lambda$ is the mean time between arrivals and $1/\mu$ is the mean service time per customer. The model in this section is sometimes called the "classical" $M/M/1$ queueing model, which means that all customers who arrive join the system and stay until they arc eventually served. An example of this model is the following.

EXAMPLE 14.2

QUEUEING AT A POSTAL BRANCH

The Smalltown postal branch employs a single clerk. Customers arrive at this postal branch according to a Poisson process at rate 30 customers per hour, and the average service time is exponentially distributed with mean 1.5 minutes. All arriving customers enter the branch, regardless of the number already waiting in line. The manager of the postal branch would ultimately like to decide whether to improve the system. To do this, she first needs to develop a queueing model that describes the steady-state characteristics of the current system.

Solution

To begin, we must choose a common unit of time and then express the arrival and service rates (λ and μ) in this unit. We could measure time in seconds, minutes, hours, or any other convenient time unit, as long as we are consistent. Here we will choose minutes. Then, because 1 customer arrives every 2 minutes, $\lambda = 1/2$. Also, because the mean service *time* is 1.5 minutes, the service *rate* is its reciprocal—that is, $\mu = 1/1.5 = 0.667$. For the $M/M/1$ model, it turns out that the server utilization equals λ/μ, the arrival rate divided by the service rate. To ensure that the system is stable, we must require that the server utilization is less than 1, so that the arrival rate is less than the service rate. Otherwise, waiting lines will tend to grow indefinitely in the long run.

Stability in $M/M/1$ model: Server utilitization $= \lambda/\mu < 1$

In general, the formulas for the $M/M/1$ model are somewhat complex. Therefore, we have implemented them in an $M/M/1$ "template" file. (See Figure 14.7 and the

	A	B	C	D	E	F	G	H	I
1	**M/M/1 queueing template**								
2									
3	**Inputs**								
4	Unit of time	minute							
5	Arrival rate	0.500	customers/minute						
6	Service rate	0.667	customers/minute						
7									
8	**Outputs**								
9	**Direct outputs from inputs**				**Distribution of number in system**			**Distribution of time in queue**	
10	Mean time between arrivals	2.000	minutes		n (customers)	P(n in system)		t (in minutes)	P(wait > t)
11	Mean time per service	1.500	minutes		4	0.079		2.000	0.537
12	Server utilization	0.750							
13									
14	**Summary measures**								
15	Expected number in system	2.999	customers						
16	Expected number in queue	2.249	customers						
17	Expected time in system	5.999	minutes						
18	Expected time in queue	4.499	minutes						
19	Percentage who don't wait in queue	25.0%							

FIGURE 14.7 Template for the $M/M/1$ Queue

file MM1_TEMPLATE.XLS.) We will not provide step-by-step instructions because we expect that you will use this as a template rather than enter the formulas yourself. However, we make the following points.

1. All you need to enter are the inputs in cells B4 through B6. Note that the rates in cells B5 and B6 are relative to the time unit you specify in cell B4.

2. You can enter *numbers* for the rates in cells B5 and B6, or you can base these on observed data. If you look at the MM1_TEMPLATE.XLS file, you will see that there is a Data sheet with data on interarrival times and services times that the postal branch manager might have collected. (See Figure 14.8.) Given such data, you would enter the formulas

   =1/Data!B5

   and

   =1/Data!C5

   in cells B5 and B6 of the Template sheet.

FIGURE 14.8
Interarrival and
Service Time Data

	A	B	C	D
1	**Data on interarrival times and service times**			
2				
3	**Summary measures from data below**			
4		Interarrival times	Service times	
5	Mean	2.188	1.564	
6				
7	**Data (all times in minutes)**			
8		Interarrival times	Service times	
9		0.091	0.213	
10		1.350	4.501	
11		1.699	5.343	
12		1.420	0.268	
13		5.361	0.261	
14		0.469	0.593	
98		0.786	0.946	
99		2.970	0.195	
100		0.159	1.716	
101		0.889	3.157	
102		0.771	1.956	
103		2.928	0.187	
104		0.823	4.275	
105		0.273	0.546	
106		0.078	2.743	
107		0.374	0.292	
108		1.099	0.818	
109		4.543	1.978	

3. The values in cells B5, B15, and B17 are related by the equation (14.2) version of Little's formula. Similarly, the values in cells B5, B16, and B18 are related by equation (14.3).

4. The template is set up so that you can enter any value for n in cell E11 to obtain the steady-state probability of n customers in the system in cell F11. (This is the same as the *fraction* of time where n customers are in the system.) You can even enter several values of n in cells E11, E12, and so on, and then copy the formula in cell F11 down for these values. Similarly, you can enter any time t in cell H11 and obtain the probability that a typical customer will wait in the queue at least time t in cell I11. The values of n and t shown in Figure 14.7 are for illustration only.

From Figure 14.7 we see, for example, that when the arrival rate is 0.5 and the service rate is 0.667, the expected number of customers in the queue is 2.25 and the expected time a typical customer spends in the queue is 4.5 minutes. However, 25% of all customers spend no time in the queue, while 53.7% spend more than 2 minutes in the queue. Also, just for illustration, we see that the steady-state probability of having exactly 4 customers in the system is 0.079. Equivalently, there are exactly 4 customers in the system 7.9% of the time.

The bank manager can experiment with other arrival rates or service rates in cells B5 and B6 to see how the various output measures are affected. One particularly important insight can be obtained through a data table, as shown in Figure 14.9. The current server utilization is 0.75, and the system is behaving fairly well, with short waits in queue on average. The data table, however, shows how bad things can get when the service rate is just barely above the arrival rate, so that the server utilization is just barely below 1. (The single output for this data table is the expected time in queue, from cell B18, and the column input cell is the service rate cell, B6.) The corresponding line chart shows that the expected time in queue increases extremely rapidly as the service rate approaches the arrival rate. Whatever else the bank manager learns from this model, she now knows that she does not want a service rate close to the arrival rate, at least not for extended periods of time.

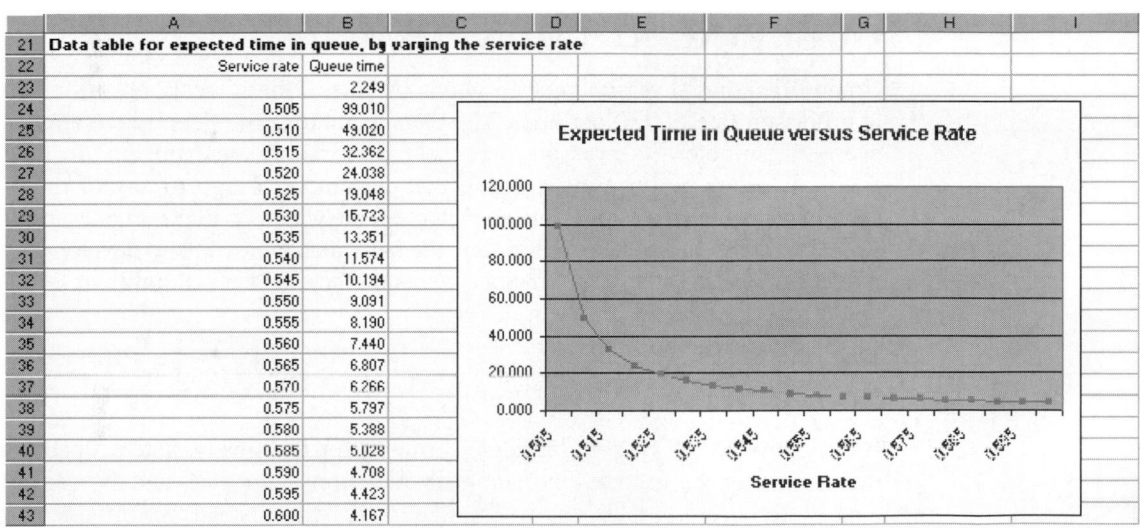

FIGURE 14.9 Effect of Varying Service Rate

The Basic Multiple-Server Model

Many service facilities such as banks and postal branches employ multiple servers. Usually, these servers work in parallel, so that each customer goes to exactly one server for service and then exits. In this section we will analyze the simplest version of this multiple-server parallel system, labeled the $M/M/s$ model. Again, the first M means that interarrival times are exponentially distributed. The second M means that the service time for *each* server is exponentially distributed. (We also assume that each server is identical to the others, in the sense that each has the same mean service time.) Finally, the s in $M/M/s$ denotes the number of servers. (Of course, if $s = 1$, the $M/M/s$ and $M/M/1$ models are identical.)

If you think about the multiple-server facilities you typically enter, such as banks, post offices, and supermarkets, you recognize that there are two types of waiting line configurations. The first, usually seen at supermarkets, is where each server has a separate line. Each customer must decide which line to join (and then either stay in that line or switch later on). The second, seen at most banks and post offices, is where there is a *single* waiting line, from which customers are served in FCFS (first-come-first-served) fashion. We will examine this second type only. (The first is much more difficult to analyze.)

There are three inputs to this system: the arrival rate λ, the service rate (per server) μ, and the number of servers s. To ensure that the system is stable, we must also assume that the server utilization, now given by $\lambda/(s\mu)$, is less than 1. In words, we require that the arrival rate λ be less than the *maximum* service rate $s\mu$ (which is achieved when all s servers are busy). If the server utilization is not less than 1, the length of the queue will eventually increase without bound.

$$\text{Stability in } M/M/s \text{ model:} \quad \text{Server utilitization} = \lambda/(s\mu) < 1$$

The following example illustrates that while the $M/M/s$ model is more complex than the $M/M/1$ model, it can still be analyzed on a spreadsheet.

EXAMPLE   14.3

QUEUEING AT COUNTYBANK

CountyBank has several branch locations. At one of these locations, customers arrive at a Poisson rate of 150 per hour. The branch employs 6 tellers. Each teller takes, on average, 2 minutes to serve a customer, and service times are exponentially distributed. Also, all tellers perform all tasks, so that customers can go to any of the 6 tellers. Customers who arrive and find all 6 servers busy join a single queue and are then served in FCFS fashion. As a first step, the bank manager wants to develop a queueing model of the current system. Then he wants to find the "best" number of tellers, given that tellers are paid $8 per hour.

Solution

As in the $M/M/1$ system, there are formulas for the steady-state probabilities, and these can then be used to find summary measures such as L and W. However, the details are fairly complex and will not be given here. Instead, we provide a template in the file MMS_TEMPLATE.XLS for performing the calculations. See Figure 14.10. All you need to do is enter the inputs in cells B4 through B7 and then click on the button. This button runs a macro that calculates all of the necessary outputs and places them in the appropriate cells. For this example the necessary inputs are the unit of time (we have chosen "hour"), the arrival rate (150), the service rate per server (30), and the number of servers (6). After clicking on the button, you will notice that all output cells contain *formulas* except for cell B16. This cell contains the probability that the system is empty (or, equivalently, the fraction of time the system is empty). All other output cells depend on this value and Little's formula. However, the corresponding formulas are quite complex, as you can see by browsing through the output cells.

From Figure 14.10 we see that when there are 6 tellers and the server utilization is 0.833, the expected number of customers in the system is 7.94 and the expected time a typical customer spends in the system is 0.053 hour (about 3.2 minutes). Also, about 41% of all arriving customers can go immediately into service, whereas about 32% of all customers must wait more than 0.02 hour (about 1.2 minutes) in the queue. Finally, we can find the expected fraction of time each teller is busy as L_{Serv}/s. (This

	A	B	C	D	E	F	G	H	I
1	M/M/s Queue - A "Template"				Directions:				
2					1. Enter the inputs in cells B4 through B7 (and in cells E12 and H12 if you like).				
3	Inputs				2. Click on the button below to perform the calculations.				
4	Unit of time	hour							
5	Arrival rate	150	customers/hour						
6	Service rate per server	30	customers/hour		Perform the				
7	Number of servers	6			calculations				
8									
9	Outputs								
10	Direct outputs from inputs				Distribution of number in system			Distribution of time in queue	
11	Mean time between arrivals	0.007	hours		n (customers)	P(n in system)		t (in hours)	P(wait > t)
12	Mean time per service	0.033	hours		3	0.0940		0.020	0.322
13	Server utilization	0.833							
14									
15	Summary measures								
16	P(system empty)	0.005							
17	Percentage who wait in queue	58.8%							
18	Expected number in system	7.938	customers						
19	Expected number in queue	2.938	customers						
20	Expected time in system	0.053	hours						
21	Expected time in queue	0.020	hours						
22	Percentage who don't wait in queue	41.2%							

FIGURE 14.10 Template for the $M/M/s$ Queue

calculation doesn't appear in the spreadsheet.) We find L_{Serv}, the expected number of busy tellers, from

$$L_{\text{Serv}} = L_{\text{Sys}} - L_Q = 7.938 - 2.938 = 5$$

Then the expected fraction of time each teller is busy is $L_{\text{Serv}}/s = 5/6 = 0.833$. If this number doesn't ring a bell, it should—it is the server utilization in cell B13. This is no coincidence. The server utilization in an $M/M/s$ system, calculated as the arrival rate divided by the maximum service rate, is always the expected fraction of time a typical server is busy.

We now turn to the economic analysis. There is a cost and a benefit from adding a teller. The cost is the wage rate paid to the extra teller, $8 per hour. The benefit is that customers wait less time in the bank. Adding an extra teller will make both W_{Sys} and W_Q decrease by the *same* amount because W_{Sys} is W_Q plus the expected service time per customer, and the latter does not change with extra tellers. That is, extra tellers decrease only the expected time in line, not the time in service. (The expected time in service would change only if we made each teller *faster*, rather than adding tellers.) To see how W_Q changes, try entering 7 and then 8 for the number of tellers in cell B7 of Figure 14.10 (and clicking on the button for each change). You should observe that the value of W_Q changes from 0.0196 hour (with 6 tellers) to 0.0054 hour (with 7 tellers) to 0.0019 hour (with 8 tellers). Because the arrival rate is 150 customers per hour, these waiting times translate to 2.94, 0.81, and 0.285 customer-hours spent waiting in line each hour.

The problem is evaluating the *cost* of waiting in line. This is not an "out-of-pocket" cost for the bank, but the bank realizes that it is an indirect cost in that customers who experience long waits might take their business elsewhere. In any case, the key to the trade-off is assessing a unit cost, c_Q, per customer per hour of waiting in the queue. If the manager can assess this unit cost, then the total expected cost per hour of customer waiting is $c_Q \lambda W_Q$. (The reasoning is that λ customers arrive per hour and each waits an expected time W_Q in the queue.) Then we can trade off this waiting cost against the cost of hiring extra tellers.

We provide another template in the file MMS_OPT_TEMPLATE.XLS that helps solve the problem. See Figure 14.11 (page 788). You now need to provide the arrival rate, the service rate per server, the wage rate per server, and the unit waiting cost per

FIGURE 14.11
A Template for
Queueing
Optimization

	A	B	C	D	E	F	G	H	I
1	M/M/s Queue - A "Template" for Optimizing				Directions:				
2					1. Enter the inputs in cells B4 through B8				
3	**Inputs**				2. Click on the button below to perform the calculations.				
4	Unit of time	hour							
5	Arrival rate	150	custs/hour						
6	Service rate per server	30	custs/hour			Perform the			
7	Wage rate per server	$8.00	$/hour			calculations			
8	Cost per customer for time in queue	$5.50	$/hour						
9									
10	Minimum number of servers	6							
11									
12	**Outputs**								
13	Number of servers	6	7	8					
14	Server utilization	0.833	0.714	0.625					
15	P(system empty)	0.005	0.006	0.006					
16	Percentage who wait in queue	0.588	0.324	0.167					
17	Expected time in queue	0.020	0.005	0.002					
18	Wages paid per hour	$48.00	$56.00	$64.00					
19	Queueing cost per hour	$16.16	$4.46	$1.53					
20	Total cost per hour	$64.16	$60.46	$65.53					
21									
22	Starting with the minimum number of servers in column B, the macro								
23	keeps increasing the number of servers until the total cost in row 20								
24	increases. Then the next to last total cost must be the minimum.								
25									

customer per unit time in line. You should *not* enter the number of servers as an input. Instead, the macro (again, run by clicking on the button) calculates selected summary measures of the system for several choices of the number of servers. Specifically, it begins by using the smallest number of servers required to keep the system stable. In this case, 6 servers are required, as seen in cell B10. Then it keeps adding a server and calculating the total expected cost for that number of servers—total wages plus total expected waiting cost—until the total expected cost starts to increase. Given the inputs in Figure 14.11, where the manager assesses customer waiting time at $5.50 per hour, the total expected cost when there are 6 tellers is $64.16. It then decreases to $60.46 with 7 tellers, and then it increases to $65.53 with 8 tellers. Because the total expected cost would only continue to increase with more than 8 tellers, the macro quits with 8, implying that 7 tellers is best.

This procedure requires a value for c_Q in cell B8. Because this value is probably very difficult for a bank manager to assess, we can instead use an indirect approach. We will find ranges for c_Q where a specific number of servers is economically optimal. To do this, first enter the largest reasonable value of c_Q in cell B8 and run the macro. For example, if the manager knows he would never value customer waiting time at more than $20 per hour, enter $20 in cell B8. Running the macro with this c_Q gives the results in Figure 14.12. They imply not only that a choice of 8 tellers is optimal when $c_Q = 20$, but also that no more than 8 tellers would ever be optimal for any *lower* value of c_Q. Given the output in Figure 14.12, we now ask, "When is 6 tellers better than 7?" The total cost comparison, using the values of W_Q in row 17, shows that 6 tellers is better than 7 when

$$6(8) + c_Q(150)(0.0196) < 7(8) + c_Q(150)(0.0054)$$

This reduces to $c_Q < 3.76$. Alternatively, 7 tellers is better than 8 when

$$7(8) + c_Q(150)(0.0054) < 8(8) + c_Q(150)(0.0019)$$

which reduces to $c_Q < 15.24$. These results imply that it is best to use 6 tellers when $c_Q < \$3.76$. Otherwise, if $c_Q < \$15.24$, it is best to use 7 tellers. Finally, for c_Q between $15.24 and $20, it is best to use 8 tellers.

	A	B	C	D	E	F	G	H	I
1	M/M/s Queue - A "Template" for Optimizing				Directions:				
2					1. Enter the inputs in cells B4 through B8				
3	Inputs				2. Click on the button below to perform the calculations.				
4	Unit of time	hour							
5	Arrival rate	150	custs/hour						
6	Service rate per server	30	custs/hour						
7	Wage rate per server	$8.00	$/hour			Perform the			
8	Cost per customer for time in queue	$20.00	$/hour			calculations			
9									
10	Minimum number of servers	6							
11									
12	Outputs								
13	Number of servers	6	7	8	9				
14	Server utilization	0.833	0.714	0.625	0.556				
15	P(system empty)	0.005	0.006	0.006	0.007				
16	Percentage who wait in queue	0.588	0.324	0.167	0.081				
17	Expected time in queue	0.0196	0.0054	0.0019	0.0007				
18	Wages paid per hour	$48.00	$56.00	$64.00	$72.00				
19	Queueing cost per hour	$58.75	$16.21	$5.58	$2.01				
20	Total cost per hour	$106.75	$72.21	$69.58	$74.01				
21									
22		Starting with the minimum number of servers in column B, the macro							
23		keeps increasing the number of servers until the total cost in row 20							
24		increases. Then the next to last total cost must be the minimum.							
25									

A Comparison of Models

Here is a question many of you have probably pondered while waiting in line. Would you rather go to a system with one fast server or a system with several slow servers? In the latter case, we will assume that only one waiting line forms, so that you can't get unlucky by joining the "wrong" line. The solution to the question is fairly straightforward, now that we know how to obtain outputs for $M/M/1$ and $M/M/s$ models. In the following example we will make the comparison numerically. For a fair comparison, we will assume that (1) the arrival rate is the same for both systems and (2) the service rate μ_{fast} for the single fast server is equal to s times μ_{slow}, where μ_{slow} is the service rate for *each* of the s slow servers.

EXAMPLE 14.4

COMPARING ONE FAST SERVER TO SEVERAL SLOW SERVERS

Which system has the better steady-state characteristics such as L_{Sys}, W_{Sys}, L_Q, and W_Q: a single-server system where the single server can serve 30 customers per hour, or a 5-server system where each of the servers can serve 6 customers per hour? For each system we will assume that customers arrive according to a Poisson process at rate 25 per hour.

Solution

First, note that the two models are comparable in the sense that $\mu_{fast} = s\mu_{slow}$ because $\mu_{fast} = 30$, $s = 5$, and $\mu_{slow} = 6$. Equivalently, the server utilization is 5/6 for each. The spreadsheets in Figures 14.13 and 14.14 answer our question. (They were formed from the MM1_TEMPLATE.XLS and MMS_TEMPLATE.XLS files simply by changing the inputs.) As you can see, the comparison is not entirely clear-cut. The $M/M/1$

	A	B	C	D	E	F	G	H	I
1	**M/M/1 queueing template**								
2									
3	**Inputs**								
4	Unit of time	hour							
5	Arrival rate	25.000	customers/hour						
6	Service rate	30.000	customers/hour						
7									
8	**Outputs**								
9	**Direct outputs from inputs**				**Distribution of number in system**			**Distribution of time in queue**	
10	Mean time between arrivals	0.040	hours		n (customers)	P(n in system)		t (in hours)	P(wait > t)
11	Mean time per service	0.033	hours		4	0.080		0.250	0.239
12	Server utilization	0.833							
13									
14	**Summary measures**								
15	Expected number in system	5.000	customers						
16	Expected number in queue	4.167	customers						
17	Expected time in system	0.200	hours						
18	Expected time in queue	0.167	hours						
19	Percentage who don't wait in queue	16.7%							

FIGURE 14.13 $M/M/1$ System with a Fast Server

	A	B	C	D	E	F	G	H	I
1	**M/M/s Queue - A "Template"**				**Directions:**				
2					1. Enter the inputs in cells B4 through B7 (and in cells E12 and H12 if you like).				
3	**Inputs**				2. Click on the button below to perform the calculations.				
4	Unit of time	hour							
5	Arrival rate	25	customers/hour						
6	Service rate per server	6	customers/hour		**Perform the**				
7	Number of servers	5			**calculations**				
8									
9	**Outputs**								
10	**Direct outputs from inputs**				**Distribution of number in system**			**Distribution of time in queue**	
11	Mean time between arrivals	0.040	hours		n (customers)	P(n in system)		t (in hours)	P(wait > t)
12	Mean time per service	0.167	hours		3	0.1191		0.250	0.178
13	Server utilization	0.833							
14									
15	**Summary measures**								
16	P(system empty)	0.010							
17	Percentage who wait in queue	62.0%							
18	Expected number in system	7.267	customers						
19	Expected number in queue	3.101	customers						
20	Expected time in system	0.291	hours						
21	Expected time in queue	0.124	hours						
22	Percentage who don't wait in queue	38.0%							

FIGURE 14.14 $M/M/s$ System with Slow Servers

system has a smaller L_{Sys} but a larger L_Q. Similarly, it has a smaller W_{Sys} but a larger W_Q. Finally, the $M/M/1$ system is worse in the sense that it has a smaller percentage of customers who experience no waiting in line (16.7% versus 38.0%) and a larger percentage who must wait in line at least 0.25 hour (23.9% versus 17.8%). The basic conclusion is that if you hate to wait in a queue, you should prefer the system with multiple slow servers. However, once it is your turn to be served, you will clearly prefer the system with the single fast server. In this latter system you will spend less *total* time in the system, but more of it will be spent waiting in line. Take your choice! ∎

The Effect of the Server Utilization

We have mentioned that for an $M/M/1$ or $M/M/s$ system to be stable, the server utilization must be less than 1. In words, the system must be able to service the customers faster than they arrive—otherwise, the queue length will eventually grow without limit. It is interesting to see, however, what happens to a system when the traffic intensity gets closer and closer to 1 but stays less than 1. As the following continuation of the CountyBank example will show, the effects can be disastrous. (We already saw this phenomenon for a single-server system in Example 14.2. It is worth seeing again, this time in a multiple-server setting.)

EXAMPLE 14.5

INCREASINGLY LONG LINES AT COUNTYBANK

Over a period of time, the CountyBank branch office from Example 14.3 has been experiencing a steady increase in the customer arrival rate. This rate has increased from the previous value of 150 customers per hour to 160, then to 170, and it is still increasing. During this time, the number of tellers has remained constant at 6, and the mean service time per teller has remained constant at 2 minutes. The bank manager has seen an obvious increase in bank congestion. Is this reinforced by the $M/M/s$ model? What will happen if the arrival rate continues to increase?

Solution

Because $s\mu$ has stayed constant at value $6(30) = 180$, the server utilization, $\lambda/(s\mu)$, has climbed from $150/180 = 0.833$ to $160/180 = 0.889$ to $170/180 = 0.944$—and it is still climbing. We know that λ must stay below 180 or the system will become unstable, but what about values of λ slightly below 180? We recalculated the spreadsheet in Figure 14.14 for several values of λ and obtained the results in Table 14.1. (W_{Sys} and W_Q are expressed in minutes.) Although each column of this table represents a stable system, the congestion is becoming unbearable. When $\lambda = 178$, the expected line length is over 80 customers, and a typical customer must wait about a half hour in line. Things are twice as bad when $\lambda = 179$.

TABLE 14.1	**Effects of Increasing Arrival Rate**					
	Customer Arrival Rate (λ)					
	150	**160**	**170**	**175**	**178**	**179**
Utilization	0.833	0.889	0.944	0.972	0.989	0.994
L_{Sys}	7.94	11.04	20.14	38.18	92.21	182.22
W_Q	2.94	5.71	14.47	32.35	86.28	176.25
W_{Sys}	3.18	4.14	7.11	13.09	31.08	61.08
W_Q	1.18	2.14	5.11	11.09	29.08	59.08

The conclusion should be clear to the bank manager. Something must be done to alleviate the congestion—probably extra tellers—and the bank will no doubt take such measures if it wants to stay in business. However, the point of the example is that systems moving toward the borderline of stability can become extremely congested. As the results in the table indicate, there is a huge difference between a system with a server utilization of 0.9 and one with a server utilization of 0.99! ■

Other Analytical Models

The basic $M/M/s$ model and its subcase, the $M/M/1$ model, represent only two of the hundreds or even thousands of analytical queueing models researchers have studied.

Some of these are relatively simple extensions of the models we have discussed, and others are much more complex. Two of the relatively simple extensions are the **limited waiting room** and **limited source** models. Both of these continue to assume exponential interarrival times and service times. In the limited waiting room model, we start with the basic $M/M/s$ model but assume that arrivals are turned away when the number already in the queue is at some maximum level. For example, we might prescribe that at most 10 customers can wait in line. If a customer arrives and there are already 10 customers in line, then this new customer must go elsewhere (to another bank branch, say).

In the limited source model we assume that there are only a finite (fairly small) number of customers in the entire population. The context is usually that the customers are machines. Then an "arrival" means that a machine breaks down and arrives to a repair center. A "service" means a machine repair. The unique aspect of this type of system is that the arrival rate to the repair center depends on the number of machines already there. When most of the machines are in repair, the arrival rate to the repair center is necessarily low—there are not very many machines left to break down because most of them are already broken down! Conversely, when the number in the repair shop is low, the arrival rate to the repair shop is much higher because most machines are candidates for imminent breakdowns.

We will not give examples of these two extensions. However, we have included templates for them in the files LIMITED_Q_TEMPLATE.XLS and LIMITED_SOURCE_TEMPLATE.XLS.

Another interesting variation of the $M/M/s$ model is to allow nonexponential interarrival and/or service times. Then we use the letter G (for general) instead of M. Specifically, the $G/G/s$ model allows *any* interarrival time distribution and *any* service time distribution. This more general model is important for two reasons. First, data on interarrival times or service times often indicate that the exponential distribution represents a poor approximation to reality. (This is especially true for service times in real applications.) Second, summary measures such as W_{Sys} or W_Q can be quite sensitive to the form of the interarrival time and/or service time distributions. Therefore, $M/M/s$ models, even those that use the actual *mean* interarrival time and *mean* service time, can give very misleading results when the correct distributions are not exponential.

Unfortunately, it is extremely difficult to obtain exact analytical results for the $G/G/s$ model. This is the bad news. The good news is that there is an approximation to this model that gives quite accurate results. In addition, it can be implemented fairly easily in a spreadsheet. This approximation is attributed to two researchers, Allen and Cunneen, and is referred to as the Allen–Cunneen approximation. [See page 218 of Tanner (1995).] We illustrate it in the following example.

EXAMPLE 14.6

REVISITING COUNTYBANK WITH NONEXPONENTIAL TIMES

The bank manager in Example 14.3 doubts that the exponential distribution provides a good approximation to the actual interarrival times and service times. Therefore, he collects data on successive interarrival times and service times on 127 consecutive customers. He then calculates the means and standard deviations of these, with the results shown in rows 5 and 6 of Figure 14.15. (See the Data sheet of the file GGS_TEMPLATE.XLS.) Are these data consistent with exponential interarrival times

FIGURE 14.15
Data for Estimating
Parameters of
Distributions

	A	B	C
1	**Data (in minutes) during peak periods**		
2			
3	**Summary of data below**		
4		Times between arrivals	Service times
5	Mean	0.0064	0.0364
6	Stdev	0.0069	0.0543
7	SqCV	1.1364	2.2243
8			
9	**Data**		
10	Customer	Times between arrivals	Service times
11	1	0.0028	0.0037
12	2	0.0043	0.0096
13	3	0.0015	0.0330
14	4	0.0098	0.0012
15	5	0.0235	0.0376
16	6	0.0090	0.0127
17	7	0.0025	0.0521
18	8	0.0021	0.0156
134	124	0.0048	0.0267
135	125	0.0046	0.0395
136	126	0.0051	0.0058
137	127	0.0039	0.0181

and service times? If not, how much do summary measures such as W_Q and L_Q change if we use the Allen–Cunneen approximation instead of the $M/M/s$ model? We again assume that there are 6 tellers at the bank.

Solution

First, note that the estimated arrival rate from the data is the reciprocal of the average interarrival time. Taking the reciprocal of the value in cell B5, we obtain an arrival rate of about 155 customers per hour. Similarly, taking the reciprocal of the average service time in cell C5, we obtain a service rate (per server) of about 27 customers per hour. These are nearly the same rates we used in Example 14.3. But are these times *exponentially* distributed?

One useful measure for a distribution of positive quantities is the **squared coefficient of variation**, defined as the squared ratio of the standard deviation to the mean and denoted by scv.

$$\text{Squared coefficient of variation} = scv = (\text{standard deviation/mean})^2$$

You might recall that the standard deviation of the exponential distribution equals the mean, so that $scv = 1$ for the exponential distribution. Researchers often characterize a distribution as being more or less variable than an exponential distribution by seeing whether its scv is greater than or less than 1. Intuitively, the reason is that if we fix the mean at some value, then scv increases as the standard deviation increases. So if we compare a nonexponential distribution to an exponential distribution, both of which have the same mean, then the nonexponential will exhibit more variability than the exponential if its scv is greater than 1, and it will be less variable if its scv is less than 1. As we will see, this scv measure is critical. It is not only required by the Allen–Cunneen approximation, but it also has a big impact on the behavior of the queueing system.

The scv values for the bank data appear in row 7 of Figure 14.15. For example, the formula in cell B7 is **=(B6/B5)^2**. We see that the interarrival times are slightly more variable, and the service times are considerably more variable, than they would be for exponentially distributed times. This indicates that the $M/M/s$ model might give misleading results. We check this by comparing the $M/M/s$ results with the $G/G/s$

results. To obtain the $M/M/s$ results, we enter the reciprocals of the averages in row 4 of Figure 14.15 as inputs to the MMS_TEMPLATE.XLS file to obtain Figure 14.16. In particular, we see that $L_Q = 13.793$ and $W_Q = 0.089$ (about 5.3 minutes per customer).

In contrast, the Allen–Cunneen approximation appears in Figure 14.17. Its inputs include not only the arrival and service rates (the reciprocals of the mean times), but also the scv values for indicating variability. As we indicate in the figure, these inputs in the shaded cells can be entered as numbers or as links to summary measures from data, as we have done here. (Compare cells B7 and B8 of Figure 14.17 to row 7 of Figure 14.15, for example.) Then the approximation uses rather complex formulas in rows 11 through 20, which we will not list here, to obtain the approximate summary measures in cells B17 through B20. (Note that no macro is required.) As for the results, we note that the values of L_Q and W_Q have changed considerably from the $M/M/s$ model. They are now $L_Q = 23.177$ and $W_Q = 0.149$ (or about 8.9 minutes per customer). The reason is that congestion in a queueing system typically *increases* as the interarrival time and service time distributions exhibit more variability, even if they retain the same means. In particular, the large value of scv for the service time distribution causes considerably longer queue lengths and waiting times in the queue than in a comparable exponential system.

	A	B	C	D	E	F	G	H	I
1	M/M/s Queue - A "Template"				Directions:				
2					1. Enter the inputs in cells B4 through B7 (and in cells E12 and H12 if you like).				
3	Inputs				2. Click on the button below to perform the calculations.				
4	Unit of time	hour							
5	Arrival rate	155.42	customers/hour						
6	Service rate per server	27.49	customers/hour		Perform the				
7	Number of servers	6			calculations				
8									
9	Outputs								
10	Direct outputs from inputs				Distribution of number in system			Distribution of time in queue	
11	Mean time between arrivals	0.006	hours		n (customers)	P(n in system)		t (in hours)	P(wait > t)
12	Mean time per service	0.036	hours		3	0.0324		0.020	0.699
13	Server utilization	0.942							
14									
15	Summary measures								
16	P(system empty)	0.001							
17	Percentage who wait in queue	84.6%							
18	Expected number in system	19.446	customers						
19	Expected number in queue	13.793	customers						
20	Expected time in system	0.125	hours						
21	Expected time in queue	0.089	hours						
22	Percentage who don't wait in queue	15.4%							

FIGURE 14.16 Results from $M/M/s$ Model

FIGURE 14.17
Allen–Cunneen
Approximation

	A	B	C	D	E	F
1	G/G/s template using the Allen-Cunneen approximation					
2						
3	Inputs					
4	Arrival rate	155.417		Enter numbers here, or (as in this file)		
5	Service rate per server	27.491		enter links to summary data from		
6	Number of servers	6		observed interarrival and service		
7	SqCV for interarrival times	1.136		times on another sheet.		
8	SqCV for service times	2.224				
9						
10	Calculations of intermediate quantities					
11	Ratio of arrival rate to service rate	5.653		The approximation is valid only when		
12	Server utilization	0.942		the utilization in cell B12 is less than		
13	A Poisson quantity	0.760		1. Otherwise, it gives nonsensical		
14	Erlang C-function	0.846		outputs.		
15						
16	Important outputs					
17	Expected wait in queue	0.149				
18	Expected queue length	23.177				
19	Expected wait in system	0.186				
20	Expected number in system	28.830				

The Allen–Cunneen approximation is evidently not well known, but we believe it is very important for the insights it can provide. We saw in the example that, as the variability increases in either the interarrival times or the service times, the congestion tends to increase. On the other side, it allows us to see how much better a system might behave if we could *reduce* the variability. For example, suppose the bank has the same means as in the example, but it is somehow able to schedule the arrivals at exactly 1 customer every 1/155.417 hour—no uncertainty whatsoever. The results appear in Figure 14.18. (The only change we had to make was to enter 0 in cell B7.) The change in the outputs is rather dramatic. The values of W_Q and L_Q were 0.149 and 23.177 in the example. Now they have decreased to 0.099 and 15.340. This is one more example of how variability is the enemy in queueing systems.

As we stated, researchers have shown that the Allen–Cunneen approximation provides very accurate estimates of quantities such as L_Q and W_Q for a wide variety of interarrival time and service time distributions in the $G/G/s$ model. The approximation appears to be equally accurate regardless of whether the scv values are less than 1 or greater than 1.[6] This is fortunate, because interarrival times and service times (especially service times) are *not* exponentially distributed in many real queueing systems.

FIGURE 14.18
Queueing System with No Variability in the Arrival Times

	A	B	C	D	E	F
1	*G/G/s* template using the Allen–Cunneen approximation					
2						
3	**Inputs**					
4	Arrival rate	155.417		Enter numbers here, or (as in this file)		
5	Service rate per server	27.491		enter links to summary data from		
6	Number of servers	6		observed interarrival and service		
7	SqCV for interarrival times	0.000		times on another sheet.		
8	SqCV for service times	2.224				
9						
10	**Calculations of intermediate quantities**					
11	Ratio of arrival rate to service rate	5.653		The approximation is valid only when		
12	Server utilization	0.942		the utilization in cell B12 is less than		
13	A Poisson quantity	0.760		1. Otherwise, it gives nonsensical		
14	Erlang C-function	0.846		outputs.		
15						
16	**Important outputs**					
17	Expected wait in queue	0.099				
18	Expected queue length	15.340				
19	Expected wait in system	0.135				
20	Expected number in system	20.993				

PROBLEMS

Skill-Building Problems

9. A fast-food restaurant has one drive-through window. An average of 40 customers per hour arrive at the window. It takes an average of 1 minute to serve a customer. Assume that interarrival and service times are exponentially distributed.
   a. On average, how many customers are waiting in line?
   b. On average, how long does a customer spend at the restaurant (from time of arrival to time service is completed)?
   c. What fraction of the time are more than 3 cars in line? (Here, the line includes the car, if any, being serviced.)

[6]Also, the approximation is *exact* if both scv values are equal to 1—that is, if the distributions are exponential.

10. The Decision Sciences Department is trying to determine whether to rent a slow or a fast copier. The department believes that an employee's time is worth $15 per hour. The slow copier rents for $4 per hour, and it takes an employee an average of 10 minutes to complete copying. The fast copier rents for $15 per hour, and it takes an employee an average of 6 minutes to complete copying. An average of 4 employees per hour need to use the copying machine. (Assume the copying times and interarrival times to the copying machine are exponentially distributed.) Which machine should the department rent to minimize expected total cost per hour?

11. The MM1_TEMPLATE.XLS file is now set up so that you can enter any integer in cell E11 and the corresponding probability of that many in the system appears in cell F11. Change this setup so that columns E and F specify the distribution of the number in the *queue* rather than the system. That is, set it up so that if you enter an integer in cell E11, the formula in cell F11 gives the probability of that many customers in the queue. (*Hint*: You don't even need to understand the current formula in cell F11. You only need to understand the relationship between the number in the queue and the number in the system. If there are n in the system, how many are in the queue?)

12. The MM1_TEMPLATE.XLS file is now set up so that when you enter any time value in cell H11, the formula in cell I11 gives the probability that the wait in queue will be greater than this amount of time. Suppose that you would like the information to go the other direction. That is, you would like to specify a probability, such as 0.05, in cell I11 and obtain the corresponding time in cell H11. Try doing this as follows with Excel's Goal Seek tool. Use the Tools/Goal Seek menu items to get to a dialog box. Then in this dialog box, enter I11 as the set cell, enter the desired probability such as 0.05 in the By Value box, and enter H11 as the changing cell. Use this procedure to answer the following. In an $M/M/1$ queue where customers are entering at rate 50 per hour and the mean service time is 1 minute, find the number of minutes t such that there is a 5% chance of having to wait in the queue more than t minutes.

13. Expand the MM1_TEMPLATE.XLS file so that the steady-state probability distribution of the number in the system is shown in tabular form and graphically. That is, enter values 0, 1, and so on (up to some upper limit you can choose) in the range from cell E11 down and copy the formula in cell F11 down accordingly. Then create a column chart using the data in columns E and F.

14. For an $M/M/1$ queueing system, it can be shown that $L_{Sys} = \lambda/(\mu - \lambda)$. Suppose that λ and μ are both doubled. How is L_{Sys} changed? How is W_{Sys} changed? How is W_Q changed? How is L_Q changed? (Remember the basic queueing relationships, including Little's formula.)

15. Suppose that you observe a sequence of interarrival times, such as 1.2, 3.7, 4.2, 0.5, 8.2, 3.1, 1.7, 4.2, 0.7, 0.3, and 2.0. For example, 4.2 is the time between the arrivals of customers 2 and 3. If you average these, what parameter of the $M/M/s$ model are you estimating? Use these numbers to estimate the arrival rate λ. If instead these numbers were observed service times, what would their average be an estimate of, and what would the corresponding estimate of μ be?

16. In the $M/M/s$ model, where μ is the service rate per server, explain why $\lambda < \mu$ is *not* the appropriate condition for steady state but $\lambda < s\mu$ is.

17. Expand the MMS_TEMPLATE.XLS file so that the steady-state probability distribution of the number in the system is shown in tabular form and graphically. That is, enter values 0, 1, and so on (up to some upper limit you can choose) in the range from cell E12 down and copy the formula in cell F12 down accordingly. Then create a column chart using the data in columns E and F.

18. Each airline passenger and his or her luggage must be checked to determine whether he or she is carrying weapons onto the airplane. Suppose that at Gotham City Airport, an average of 10 passengers per minute arrive, where interarrival times are exponentially distributed. To check passengers for weapons, the airport must have a checkpoint consisting of a metal detector and baggage X-ray machine. Whenever a checkpoint is in operation, two employees are required. These two employees work simultaneously to check a *single* passenger. A checkpoint can check an average of 12 passengers per minute, where the time to check a passenger is also exponentially distributed. Under the assumption that the airport has only one checkpoint, answer the following questions.
   a. Why is an $M/M/1$, not an $M/M/2$, model relevant here?
   b. What is the probability that a passenger will have to wait before being checked for weapons?
   c. On average, how many passengers are waiting in line to enter the checkpoint?
   d. On average, how long will a passenger spend at the checkpoint (including waiting time in line)?

19. A supermarket is trying to decide how many cash registers to keep open. Suppose an average of 18 customers arrive each hour, and the average checkout time for a customer is 4 minutes. Interarrival times and service times are exponentially distributed, and the system can be modeled as an $M/M/s$ system. (In contrast to the situation at most supermarkets, we assume that all customers wait in a single line.) It costs $20 per hour to operate a cash register, and a cost of $0.25 is assessed for each minute the customer spends in the cash register area (in line or being served). How many registers should the store open to minimize the expected hourly cost?

20. A small bank is trying to determine how many tellers to employ. The total cost of employing a teller is $100 per day, and a teller can serve an average of 60 customers per day. An average of 50 customers per day arrive at the bank, and both service times and interarrival times are exponentially distributed. If the delay cost per customer-day is $100, how many tellers should the bank hire?

21. In this problem, all interarrival and service times are exponentially distributed.
    a. At present, the finance department and the marketing department each has its own typists. Each typist can type 25 letters per day. Finance requires that an average of 20 letters per day be typed, and marketing requires that an average of 15 letters per day be typed. For each department, determine the average length of time that elapses between a request for a letter and completion of the letter.
    b. Suppose that the two typists are grouped into a typing pool; that is, each typist is now available to type letters for either department. For this arrangement, calculate the average length of time between a request for a letter and completion of the letter.
    c. Comment on the results of parts **a** and **b**.
    d. Under the pooled arrangement, what is the probability that more than 0.2 day will elapse between a request for a letter and start of the letter?

22. MacBurger's is attempting to determine how many servers to have available during the breakfast shift. During each hour, an average of 100 customers arrive at the restaurant. Each server can handle an average of 50 customers per hour. A server costs $5 per hour, and the cost of a customer waiting in line for one hour is $20. Assuming that an $M/M/s$ model is applicable, determine the number of servers that minimizes the sum of hourly delay and service costs.

23. An average of 100 customers arrive each hour at the Gotham City Bank. The average service time for each customer is 1 minute. Service times and interarrival times are exponentially distributed. The manager wants to ensure that no more than 1% of all customers will have to wait in line for more than 5 minutes. If the bank follows the policy of having all customers join a single line, how many tellers must the bank hire?

The following problems are optional. They are based on the limited queue and limited source models in the LIMITED_Q_TEMPLATE.XLS and LIMITED_SOURCE_TEMPLATE.XLS files.

24. A service facility consists of one server who can serve an average of two customers per hour (service times are exponential). An average of three customers per hour arrive at the facility (interarrival times are assumed to be exponential). The system capacity is three customers—two waiting and one being served.
    a. On average, how many potential customers enter the system each hour?
    b. What is the probability that the server is busy at a typical point in time?

25. An average of 40 cars per hour (interarrival times are exponentially distributed) are tempted to use the drive-through window at the Hot Dog King Restaurant. If a total of more than 4 cars are in line (including the car at the window), a car will not enter the line. It takes an average of 4 minutes (exponentially distributed) to serve a car.
    a. What is the average number of cars waiting for the drive-through window (not including the car at the window)?
    b. On the average, how many cars will be served per hour?
    c. I have just joined the line at the drive-through window. On average, how long will it be before I receive my food?

26. A laundromat has five washing machines. A typical machine breaks down once every 5 days. A repairer can repair a machine in an average of 2.5 days. Currently, three repairers are on duty. The owner of the laundromat has the option of replacing them with a superworker, who can repair a machine in an average of 5/6 of a day. The salary of the superworker equals the pay of the three regular employees. Breakdown and service times are exponential. Should the laundromat replace the three repairers with the superworker?

27. The limited source model can often be used to approximate the behavior of a computer's CPU (central processing unit). Suppose that 20 terminals (assumed to always be busy) feed the CPU. After the CPU responds to a user, he or she takes an average of 80 seconds before sending another request to the CPU (this is called the "think time"). The CPU takes an average of 2 seconds to respond to any request. On average, how long will a user have to wait before the CPU acts on his or her request? How will your answer change if there are 30 terminals? 40 terminals? Of course, you must make appropriate assumptions about the exponential distribution to answer this question.

Skill-Extending Problems

28. Consider an airport where taxis and customers arrive (exponential interarrival times) with respective rates of 1 and 2 per minute. No matter how many other taxis are present, a taxi will wait. If an arriving customer does not find a taxi, the customer immediately leaves.
    a. Model this system as an $M/M/1$ queue. (Hint: Think of the taxis as the customers.)
    b. Find the average number of taxis that are waiting for a customer.
    c. Suppose all customers who use a taxi pay a $2 fare. During a typical hour, how much revenue will the taxis receive?

29. A bank is trying to determine which of two machines to rent for check processing. Machine 1 rents for $10,000 per year and processes 1000 checks per hour. Machine 2 rents for $15,000 per year and processes 1600 checks per hour. Assume that machines work 8 hours a day, 5 days a week, 50 weeks a year. The bank must process an average of 800 checks per hour, and the average check processed is for $100. Assume an annual interest rate of 20%. Then determine the cost to the bank (in lost interest) for each hour that a check spends waiting for and undergoing processing. Assuming that interarrival times and service times are exponentially distributed, which machine should the bank rent?

30. A worker at the State Unemployment Office is responsible for processing a company's forms when it opens for business. The worker can process an average of 4 forms per week. In 1992 an average of 1.8 companies per week submitted forms for processing, and the worker had a backlog of 0.45 week. In 1993 an average of 3.9 companies per week submitted forms for processing, and the worker had a 5-week backlog. The poor worker was fired but later sued to get her job back. The court said that because the amount of work submitted to the worker had approximately doubled, the worker's backlog should also have doubled. Because her backlog increased by more than a factor of 10, she must have been slacking off, so the state was justified in firing her. Use queueing theory to defend the worker. (This is based on an actual case!)

31. For the $M/M/1$ queueing model, why do the following results hold? (Hint: Remember that $1/\mu$ is the mean service time. Then think how long a typical arrival must wait in the system or in the queue.)
    a. $W_{Sys} = (L_{Sys} + 1)/\mu$
    b. $W_Q = L_{Sys}/\mu$

32. Referring to Problem 18, suppose the airline wants to determine how many checkpoints to operate to minimize operating costs and delay costs over a 10-year period. Assume that the cost of delaying a passenger for one hour is $10 and that the airport is open every day for 16 hours per day. It costs $1 million to purchase, staff, and maintain a metal detector and baggage X-ray machine for a 10-year period. Finally, assume that each passenger is equally likely to enter a given checkpoint, so that the "effective" arrival rate to any checkpoint is the total arrival rate divided by the number of checkpoints. (Assume that each checkpoint has its own waiting line.)

33. The manager of a bank wants to use an $M/M/s$ queueing model to weigh the costs of extra tellers against the cost of having customers wait in line. The arrival rate is 60 customers per hour, and the average service time is 4 minutes. The cost of each teller is easy to gauge—it is the $8.50 per hour wage rate. However, because it is difficult to estimate the cost per minute of waiting time, the bank manager decides to hire the minimum number of tellers so that a typical customer has probability 0.05 of waiting more than 5 minutes in line.
    a. How many tellers will the manager use, given this criterion?
    b. By deciding on this many tellers as "optimal," the manager is implicitly using some value (or some range of values) for the cost per minute of waiting time. That is, a certain cost (or cost range) would lead to the same number of tellers as suggested in part a. What is this implied cost (or cost range)?

34. An average of 100 customers per hour arrive at Gotham City Bank. It takes a teller an average of 2 minutes to serve a customer. Interarrival and service times are exponentially distributed. The bank currently has 4 tellers working. The bank manager wants to compare the following two systems with regard to the average number of customers present in the bank and the probability that a customer will spend more than 8 minutes in line.
    ■ System 1: Each teller has his or her own line (and no moving between lines is permitted). Arriving customers are equally likely to choose any teller.
    ■ System 2: All customers wait in a single line for the first available teller.
      If you were the bank manager, which system would you prefer?

35. Consider the following two queueing systems.
    ■ System 1: An $M/M/1$ system with arrival rate λ and service rate 3μ
    ■ System 2: An $M/M/3$ system with arrival rate λ and each server working at rate μ
      Which system will have the smaller W_{Sys} and L_{Sys}?

The following problems are optional. They are based on the limited queue model in the LIMITED_Q_TEMPLATE.XLS file.

36. Two one-barber shops sit side by side in Dunkirk Square. Each can hold a maximum of 4 people, and

any potential customer who finds a shop full will not wait for a haircut. Barber 1 charges $11 per haircut and takes an average of 15 minutes to complete a haircut. Barber 2 charges $7 per haircut and takes an average of 10 minutes to complete a haircut. An average of 10 potential customers per hour arrive at each barber shop. Of course, a potential customer becomes an actual customer only if he or she finds that the shop is not full. Assuming that interarrival times and haircut times are exponential, which barber will earn more money?

37. The small mail-order firm Sea's Beginning has one phone line. An average of 60 people per hour call in orders, and it takes an average of 1 minute to handle a call. Time between calls and time to handle calls are exponentially distributed. If the phone line is busy, Sea's Beginning can put up to $c - 1$ people on hold. If $c - 1$ people are on hold, a caller gets a busy signal and calls a competitor (Air's End). Sea's Beginning wants only 1% of all callers to get a busy signal. How many people should it be able to put on hold, that is, what is the required value of c?

14.6 QUEUEING SIMULATION

A popular alternative to using the analytical models from the previous section is to develop queueing simulations. There are several advantages to using simulation. Probably the most important advantage is that we are not restricted to the assumptions required by the standard analytical queueing models. These models typically require that the interarrival times and service times are exponentially distributed, customers wait in a single queue and are served in FCFS fashion, all servers are identical in terms of their service time distributions, there are no customer types with higher priority than others, and so on.[7] When we use simulation, anything goes. If we want nonexponential service times, they are easy to build in. If we want customers to wait in several lines, one behind each server, and we even want to allow them to switch queues (as you might in a supermarket), simulation can handle it. If we want higher-priority customers to be able to "bump" lower-priority customers out of service, it is no problem with simulation. Just about any queueing situation can be simulated. A second advantage of queueing simulation is that we *see* the action through time. Simulation outputs typically include not only summary measures such as the average queue length for some period of time, but they can also include time series graphs of important quantities such as the number of servers busy or the number of customers waiting in line. In this way, we can see how queues build from time to time. In addition, we can run a simulation many times, each time using different random numbers, to see how one day might differ from another.

The downside of queueing simulation is that it has traditionally required either a clever computer programmer, a specialized software package, or both. The difficulty is not one of random number generation. It is easy to generate all the random quantities (interarrival times and service times, say) required by a simulation. The difficult part is essentially a bookkeeping problem. Imagine that you are given a list of customer arrival times and their corresponding service times. The question is whether you can "play out" the events as they would then occur through time. Say customer 17 arrives at 9:47, sees that 4 customers are ahead of her in line, and all 3 of the servers in the system are currently busy with customers. How do you know when customer 17 will enter service, and with which server? This is the biggest challenge in a queueing simulation—keeping track of the timing of events as they unfold through time. Special queueing software is available to do all of the bookkeeping for you, but this software

---

[7]There are indeed analytical models for many "nonstandard" queueing situations, but they are mathematically too complex for most users to understand.

is often expensive and far from trivial to master. Therefore, some people write their own programs, in FORTRAN, C, or Visual Basic, say, to keep track of the events. Unfortunately, even good programmers struggle when writing queueing simulations. There are numerous details to get straight. One "small" error can make a queueing simulation behave very differently than intended.

We know that most of you reading this book are not programmers. You want the insights that a simulation can provide, but you do not want to develop the simulations yourself. Therefore, we have developed two fairly general simulation models that you can run. Each of them is based on a program, written in Excel's VBA programming language, that runs in the background and does all of the simulation bookkeeping. All you need to do is enter the appropriate input parameters and click a button. The outputs will appear automatically.

It is also possible to develop spreadsheet simulations for some queueing situations *without* writing any computer programs. The bookkeeping is accomplished entirely with Excel formulas that incorporate the logic of the model. We will discuss briefly how this can be done. Admittedly, it is not easy (or even very natural) to develop queueing simulations in Excel worksheets, but it is an excellent exercise in logic that you might want to try.

A Multiple-Server Simulation

The first simulation model we will examine is a variation of the $M/M/s$ queueing model we discussed in the previous section. (It is in the file MULTSERVERSIM.XLS.) Customers arrive to a service center according to a Poisson process (exponential inter-arrival times), they wait (if necessary) in a single queue, and then they are served by the first available server. The simulation model is different in the following respects from the analytical $M/M/s$ model.

- The service times are not necessarily exponentially distributed. We allow three options: (1) constant (nonrandom) service times, (2) exponentially distributed service times, and (3) gamma distributed service times. This latter option uses the gamma distribution, which is typically shaped as in Figure 14.19. Because its mode

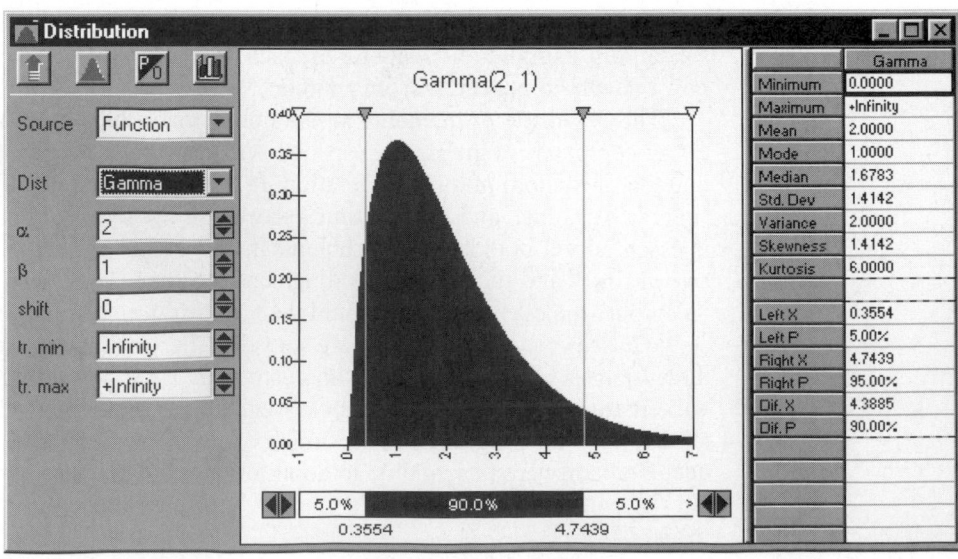

FIGURE 14.19 Typical Gamma Distribution

is *not* necessarily 0, as with the exponential distribution, it is often more realistic for service times. By allowing three different service time distributions, we can see how different amounts of variability in the service times affect outputs such as waiting times.

- The waiting room is of limited size, where this size is an input parameter. If the queue is already this long and another customer arrives, this new customer is not allowed to enter the system.

- The simulated run time is another user input. We might want to run a simulation for 100 hours (of *simulated* time) or only 1 hour. By varying the run time, we can see how long-run behavior might differ from short-run behavior. In addition, there is a "warmup time" input. The simulation always starts empty and idle, which might not be very realistic if we want to simulate a peak period, say, that is bound to start with some customers already in the system. Therefore, the purpose of the warmup period is to allow the system get to a "typical" busy state. However, no statistics are collected during the warmup period. Statistics are collected only during the run time period. As an example, suppose a bank opens at 9:00 A.M., empty and idle, and we are interested in the period from 11:30 A.M. until 1:30 P.M. Then the warmup period would be of length 2.5 hours, and the run-time period would be of length 2 hours.

- Every time we run the simulation, we are asked for a "random number seed." The actual number we enter is not important. The important part is that if we enter the *same* seed for two different runs, we get the same stream of random numbers. This is often useful for comparing different systems under "like" conditions (the same interarrival times or the same service times, say). Alternatively, if we enter *different* seeds for two different runs, we get a different stream of random numbers on each run. This is useful for seeing how much the system behavior can vary from one run to the next.

These last two points enable some very important insights into queueing systems in general. An analytical model such as the $M/M/s$ model provides summary measures, typically means, in steady state. It might say, for example, that the mean time in queue per customer is 4.85 minutes. But if we simulate such a system for 2 hours, say, and average the times in queue for the simulated customers, will the average be 4.85 minutes? The answer is a very definite "no." First, the average might not be the steady-state value because 2 hours might not be long enough to approximate steady state. Second, different runs using different random numbers will typically provide different averages. You might be surprised to see how much they can vary.

We now illustrate how the simulation works by revisiting the CountyBank queueing situation (see Examples 14.3 and 14.6) with simulation.

EXAMPLE   **14.7**

SIMULATING QUEUEING AT COUNTYBANK

CountyBank has already used analytical models to obtain steady-state measures of queueing behavior. However, it wonders whether these provide very realistic estimates of what occurs during a 2-hour peak period at the bank. During this peak period, arrivals occur according to a Poisson process of 2 per minute, there are 6 tellers employed, and each service time has a mean length of 2.7 minutes. The standard deviation of service times is estimated at 1.5 minutes, and a histogram of historical service times has a shape much like the shape in Figure 14.19, so that the gamma distribution is reasonable. What insights can the bank manager obtain from simulation?

Solution

If we use the $M/M/s$ model (ignoring the fact that service times are not really exponentially distributed), we obtain the results in Figure 14.20. (The value in cell B6 is $1/2.7$, the reciprocal of the mean service time.) For example, the mean wait in queue is $W_Q = 3.33$ minutes. If we use the $G/G/s$ model with the Allen–Cunneen approximation, we obtain the results in Figure 14.21. (The values in cells B5 and B8 are $1/2.7$ and $(1.5/2.7)^2$. The value in cell B7 is 1 because the exponential distribution has coefficient of variation 1.) The value of W_Q is now 2.18. Evidently, the gamma distribution, which has a much lower coefficient of variation, results in less time in the queue.

FIGURE 14.20
Results from the
$M/M/s$ Model

	A	B	C
1	**M/M/s Queue - A "Template"**		
2			
3	**Inputs**		
4	Unit of time	minute	
5	Arrival rate	2	customers/minute
6	Service rate per server	0.37037	customers/minute
7	Number of servers	6	
8			
9	**Outputs**		
10	**Direct outputs from inputs**		
11	Mean time between arrivals	0.500	minutes
12	Mean time per service	2.700	minutes
13	Server utilization	0.900	
14			
15	**Summary measures**		
16	P(system empty)	0.002	
17	Percentage who wait in queue	74.0%	
18	Expected number in system	12.061	customers
19	Expected number in queue	6.661	customers
20	Expected time in system	6.031	minutes
21	Expected time in queue	3.331	minutes
22	Percentage who don't wait in queue	26.0%	

FIGURE 14.21
Results from the
$G/G/s$ Model

	A	B	C	D	E	F
1	**G/G/s template using the Allen-Cunneen approximation**					
2						
3	**Inputs**					
4	Arrival rate	2.000				
5	Service rate per server	0.370		Enter numbers here, or (as in this file)		
6	Number of servers	6		enter links to summary data from		
7	SqCV for interarrival times	1.000		observed interarrival and service		
8	SqCV for service times	0.309		times on another sheet.		
9						
10	**Calculations of intermediate quantities**					
11	Ratio of arrival rate to service rate	5.400		The approximation is valid only when		
12	Server utilization	0.900		the utilization in cell B12 is less than		
13	A Poisson quantity	0.778		1. Otherwise, it gives nonsensical		
14	Erlang C-function	0.740		outputs.		
15						
16	**Important outputs**					
17	Expected wait in queue	2.179				
18	Expected queue length	4.359				
19	Expected wait in system	4.879				
20	Expected number in system	9.759				

The queueing simulation results appear in Figure 14.22. This sheet is set up with a nice user interface. By clicking on the top button, you see a couple of dialog boxes where you can enter the required inputs. These appear in Figures 14.23 and 14.24. (Alternatively, you can enter the inputs directly into the cells and click on the second

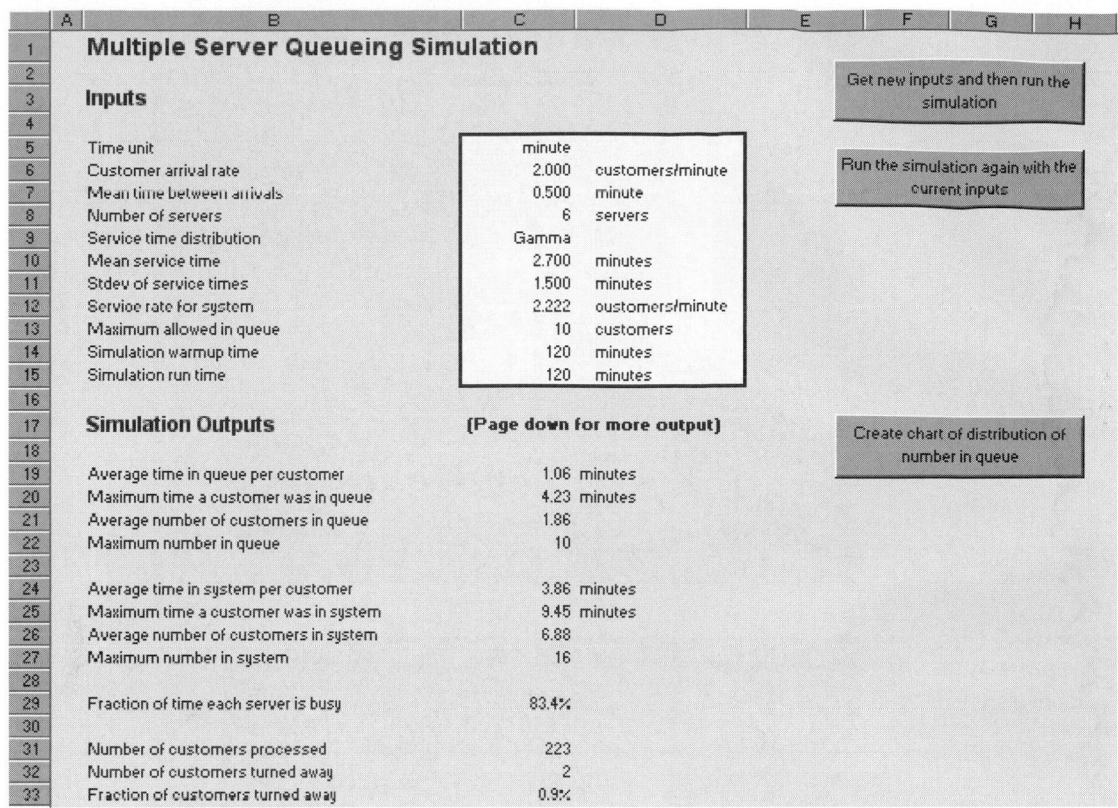

FIGURE 14.22 Simulation Results

FIGURE 14.23
First Input Dialog
Box

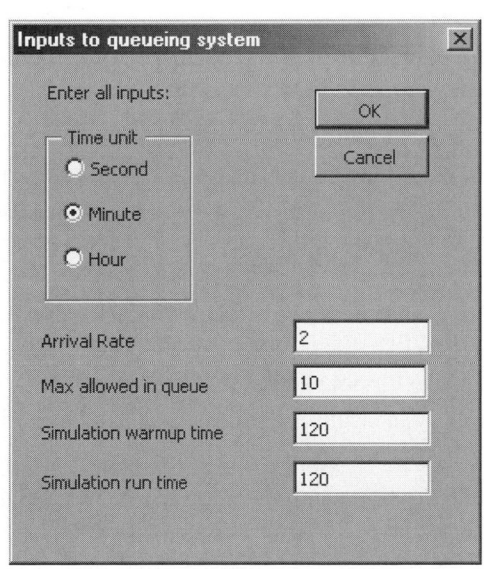

button to run the simulation.) Then you see the dialog box in Figure 14.25 (page 804), where you can designate a random number seed. After this is done, the simulation is run. (This one took about 2 seconds on our PC.)

FIGURE 14.24
Second Input Dialog
Box

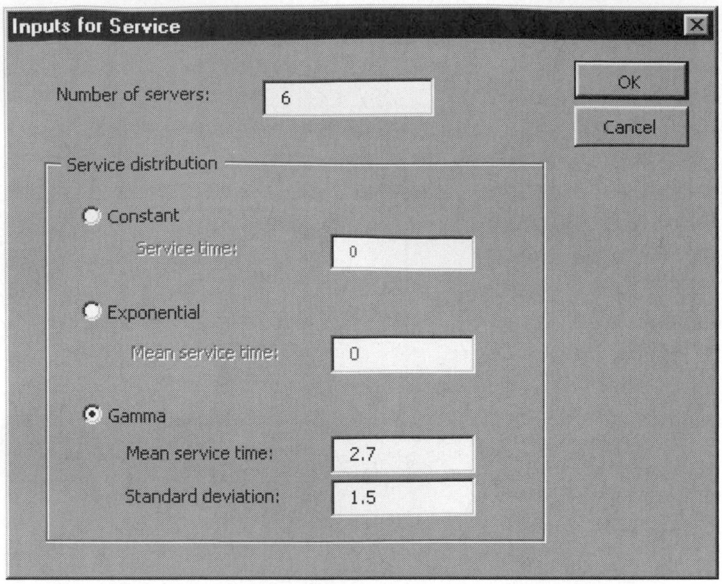

Inputs for Service

Number of servers: 6

OK
Cancel

Service distribution

○ Constant
Service time: 0

○ Exponential
Mean service time: 0

● Gamma
Mean service time: 2.7
Standard deviation: 1.5

FIGURE 14.25
Input Box for
Random Number
Seed

Microsoft Excel

Enter a starting seed (1 to 2147483646).

OK
Cancel

111

Again, we will not delve into all of the details, but when the simulation runs it does the following:

- It starts with an empty and idle system—no customers are in the bank.

- It keeps simulating customer arrivals and service times, and it keeps playing out the events, but it doesn't keep track of any customer statistics for the first 120 minutes, the warmup time. It keeps track of statistics only for the *next* 120 minutes, the run time.

- If a customer arrives and there are already 10 customers in line, this customer is turned away (or, if you like, the customer decides not to bother waiting). If we want to ensure that no one is turned away, we can choose a large value for this input.

- It reports the summary measures for this run, as shown in Figure 14.22.

The outputs in Figure 14.22 should be self-explanatory. During the 2-hour period, 223 customers entered the bank, and 2 were turned away. Each teller was busy, on average, 83.4% of the time, the average customer waited in the queue for 1.06 minutes, the average length of the queue was 1.86, the maximum queue length was 10, and so on. By clicking on the bottom button, we can also obtain a graph of the queue length distribution, as in Figure 14.26. Each bar represents the percentage of simulated time the queue length was any particular value. For example, the bar on the left shows that there was no queue at all about 45% of the time.

Clearly, the average time in queue, 1.06 minutes, is much smaller than W_Q from the $M/M/s$ and $G/G/s$ models. Which is the "correct" value for CountyBank's 2-hour

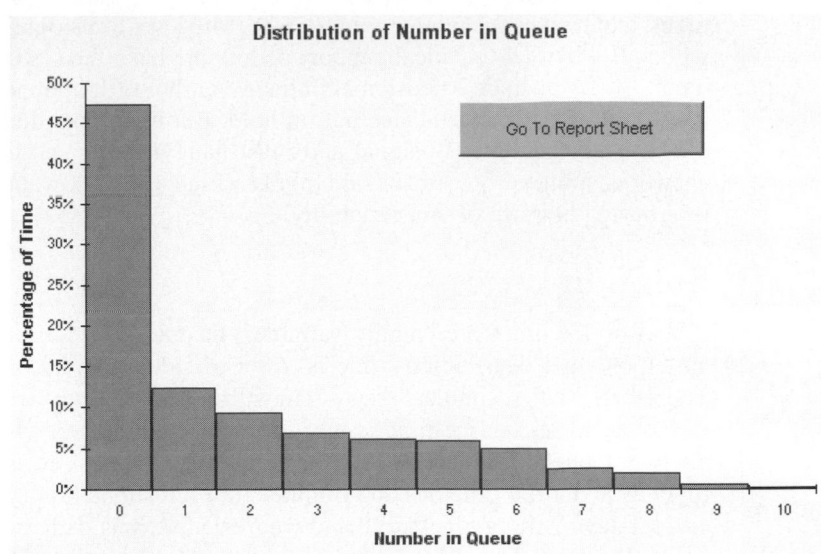

FIGURE 14.26
Chart of Queue
Length Distribution

peak period? This is not an easy question to answer. The 1.06 value from the simulation depends to a great extent on the random numbers we happened to simulate. To illustrate this, we ran the simulation several more times, each with a different random number seed, and we obtained values ranging from slightly under 0.7 to slightly over 2.1. This shows the bank manager that the average time in queue during any day's 2-hour peak period *depends on the day*. Some days she will get lucky and other days she won't. This variability from day to day—that is, from run to run—is possibly the most important insight we can gain from simulation.

Besides the variability from day to day, the simulation results can depend on the run time length, and they can be affected by the limited queue size. For example, we ran the simulation for 10,000 minutes. The average time in queue did not change much, but hundreds of customers were turned away. Then we changed the maximum queue size to 100 and ran the simulation again for 10,000 minutes. The average time in queue was now much larger (over 2 minutes) and no customers were turned away. This illustrates that if all customers are allowed to enter the system, the average time in queue increases, whereas if many are turned away, the average time in queue, *for those who enter*, is much smaller. ■

The next example uses the same simulation model (still the MULTSERVER-SIM.XLS file) but with different inputs. Specifically, we will see the effect on waiting for different service time distributions, all with the same mean. For a given mean, the exponential distribution has the most variability, the constant distribution has the least (none), and the gamma distribution is typically in the middle. We will see whether this ordering carries over to average times in the queue.

EXAMPLE 14.8

QUEUEING FOR HELP AT HYTEX

HyTex is a software company that offers technical support for its customers over the phone. The demand for help is fairly constant throughout the day, with calls arriving at a rate of approximately 10 per minute. HyTex keeps 35 technical support lines open at all times, and it takes 3.5 minutes, on average, to answer a customer's question. Customers who call when all technical support people are busy face two possible situations. If there are fewer than 20 customers already on hold (the phone version of waiting in line), then a new caller is also put on hold. But if 20 customers are already on hold, a new caller gets a busy signal and must hang up. The service times—the times to answer customers' questions—are highly variable. HyTex wants to know how much it is suffering because of this variability.

Solution

If the service times are "highly variable," then a histogram of them might resemble an exponential distribution—that is, a lot of short calls but a few really long ones. Therefore, we first simulate the system with exponential service times. The arrival rate is 10, the mean service time is 3.5, the number of servers is 35, and the maximum allowable queue size is 20. With these parameters, we used a warmup time of 1000 minutes and a run time of 2000 minutes for each simulation (you can think of this as several days "strung together"), and we made five runs with different random number seeds. We then changed the service time distribution to the gamma distribution with mean 3.5 and standard deviation 2.8. (This distribution has a squared coefficient of variation of 0.64, so it is not as variable as the exponential distribution, which has squared coefficient of variation 1.) Finally, we changed the service time distribution to be constant with value 3.5. For both the gamma and constant distributions, we made five runs, using the same seeds as in the exponential runs. (If you want to mimic our results, use the seeds 111, 222, 333, 444, and 555.)

Selected results appear in Table 14.2. For each simulation run, we list two quantities: the average time in queue for the customers who did not receive busy signals, and the fraction of callers who received busy signals and were therefore lost. If we look only at the average times in queue, the results sometimes go in the *opposite* direction than what we predicted. The most variable distribution, the exponential, sometimes has the smallest times, whereas the least variable distribution, the constant, always has the largest times. However, there is a reason. These averages are only for the customers who were able to enter the system. As the percentages of lost callers show, many more callers were lost with the exponential than the constant distribution, with the gamma distribution in the middle. (Over a period of 2000 minutes, with an arrival rate of 10 per minute, the system sees about 20,000 callers. An extra 1 percent lost therefore translates to about 200 callers—not insignificant.) With highly variable service times, customers might not wait quite as long in the queue because there are not as many customers to wait—many of them cannot get through at all!

TABLE 14.2	**Comparison of Models**					
	Average Time in Queue			**Percentage of Callers Lost**		
Seed	**Exponential**	**Gamma**	**Constant**	**Exponential**	**Gamma**	**Constant**
111	0.92	0.84	0.92	4.8	3.6	3.0
222	0.81	0.80	0.85	4.1	3.1	2.3
333	0.81	0.81	0.87	4.0	3.4	2.8
444	0.80	0.82	0.88	4.7	3.5	2.8
555	0.77	0.75	0.82	3.8	2.9	2.4

So we again see that variability is the enemy. HyTex hates to have unhappy customers, and customers who receive busy signals are probably the unhappiest. The company should try to reduce the variability of service times, even if it cannot reduce the *mean* service time. If this is not possible, there are two other possible remedies: (1) hire more technical support people, or (2) rent more trunk lines, so that more customers can be put on hold. ■

A Series System Simulation with Blocking

Outputs from one queue are often inputs to another queue. This is particularly true in many manufacturing environments, where a part has to pass through several "stations" in succession. At each station a machine does a certain operation and then passes the part to the next station. After the part has gone through each station, it goes into finished product inventory. If each part has to pass through station 1, then station 2, and so on, we call the system a **series** system. One possible series system appears in Figure 14.27. This system has three stations. Stations 1 and 3 each have a single machine (labeled M1 and M3), whereas station 2 has two machines (labeled M2,1 and M2,2). Each part has to be processed at M1, then at M2,1 *or* M2,2, and then at M3. There can also be limited **buffers** (spaces for queueing) in front of the stations. In the figure, there is no limit to the queue size in front of station 1 (which we will always assume), but there is room for only 3 parts in front of station 2 and room for only 4 parts in front of station 3. These limited buffers can create **blocking**. As an example, suppose the buffers in front of station 2 are all full and a part finishes processing at station 1. Then this part is blocked, which means that it cannot move from machine M1, and this prevents other parts from entering M1 for processing. There can even be a "cascading" effect, where blocking of a part at M2,1 or M2,2 eventually causes blocking at M1. This blocking can have a serious negative effect on overall operations.

FIGURE 14.27
A Series System with
Possible Blocking

3-station system with multiple machines at station 2

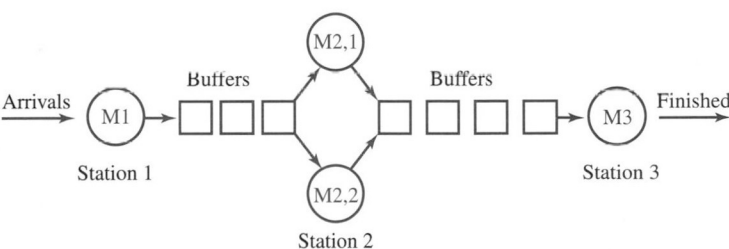

We have developed a simulation, again written in VBA, for this type of system. (See the file SERIESSIM.XLS.) It allows up to 10 stations in series with any number of machines per station and any numbers of buffers in front of the stations (after station 1, which always has unlimited buffers). Parts arrive to station 1 with a given arrival rate. We allow two possibilities: (1) a constant (nonrandom) arrival process, where parts arrive according to a precise nonrandom schedule, and (2) a Poisson arrival process, where times between arrivals are exponentially distributed. Similarly, the processing (service) times for the different stations can differ, and each can have either a constant (nonrandom) distribution or an exponential distribution. The simulation starts in the empty and idle state, there can be a warmup period where no statistics are collected, and then the simulation runs for a prescribed number of minutes.

It is very difficult to guess how this type of system might behave. In fact, this is the whole purpose of the simulation. It allows a manufacturer to analyze many "what-if" scenarios, without actually making changes to the physical system. We illustrate how this might work in the following example.

EXAMPLE 14.9

PROCESSING PARTS AT STREAMLINING

The Streamlining Company manufactures various types of automobile parts. Its factory has several production lines, all versions of the series system in Figure 14.27, with varying numbers of stations and machines. In an effort to improve operations, the company wants to gain some insights into how average throughput times and other output measures are affected by various inputs. (The throughput time is the elapsed time from when a part enters the system until it finishes processing at all stations.) Specific questions of interest are:

- Is it better to have a single fast machine at each station or multiple slower machines?
- How much does the variability of the arrival process to station 1 affect outputs? What about the variability of processing times at machines?
- The company has experimented with 0 buffers and has found that the resulting blocking can be disastrous. It now wants to create some buffers (which entails a significant cost). In front of which stations should it place the buffers?

Solution

The simulation model in the file SERIESSIM.XLS allows us to experiment as much as we like by changing inputs, running the simulation, and examining the outputs. The inputs section appears in Figure 14.28.[8] Note that 1 is the code for constant interarrival or processing times, whereas 2 is the code for exponentially distributed times. Also, cell B14 is black to indicate that the number of buffers in front of station 1 is always unlimited. When we run the simulation, we obtain outputs such as those in Figure 14.29. (These are for the inputs in Figure 14.28.) Perhaps the most important part of the outputs is in the range B18:B21. For this particular run, we see that the average part took 7.457 minutes to get through the system. Only 28.09% of this was in processing.

FIGURE 14.28
Inputs Section

	A	B	C	D	E	F
1	**Inputs for simulation**					
2						
3	**Arrival process of parts to station 1:**		Enter inputs in all of the input (shaded) cells, then click on the button to run the simulation.			
4	Distribution (1 for constant, 2 for exponential)	2				
5	Arrival rate to station 1 (parts/minute)	1.00				
6						
7	**Configuration of process (fill in the gray cells):**			Run the simulation		
8	Number of stations (<= 10)	3				
9						
10	Station	1	2	3		
11	Number of parallel machines at stations	1	1	1		
12	Distribution of processing time for each machine at station (1 for constant, 2 for exponential)	2	2	2		
13	Mean processing time (minutes) per machine	0.7	0.7	0.7		
14	Number of buffers in front of stations		5	5		
15						
16	**Simulation times (minutes)**					
17	Warmup time (no statistics collected)	1000				
18	Run time	10000				

[8]There are no dialog boxes as in the MULTSERVERSIM.XLS file. However, when you change the number of stations in cell B8, the shaded input range in rows 11–14 automatically resizes to accommodate the number of stations.

FIGURE 14.29
Simulation Outputs

	A	B	C	D	E
1	**Simulation Outputs**				
2					
3	Number of items processed	10090			
4	Number left at closing	16			
5					
6	**Part averages (minutes/part)**			**Time averages**	
7	Average time in queues			Average queue lengths	
8	Station 1	2.400		Station 1	2.42
9	Station 2	1.565		Station 2	1.58
10	Station 3	1.302		Station 3	1.31
11	Total in all stations	5.267			
12				Percent time processing	
13	Average times being blocked			Station 1	69.70%
14	Station 1	0.056		Station 2	71.38%
15	Station 2	0.039		Station 3	70.66%
16	Total in all stations	0.095			
17				Percent time blocked	
18	Average throughput time	7.457		Station 1	5.65%
19	Percent time in queue	70.63%		Station 2	3.95%
20	Percent time being blocked	1.28%			
21	Percent time being processed	28.09%			

The rest was spent in queues or being blocked at station 1 or 2. In addition, we see at the top of the output that 10,090 parts were completed during the run-time period (some of which entered the system during the warmup period), and 16 parts were left uncompleted at the end of the run time.

Turning to Streamlining's questions, we first examine the trade-off between fast and slow machines. The outputs in Figure 14.30 (page 810) are typical. (These results were obtained by making multiple runs and copying the outputs from each run to a "summary" sheet. For each set of inputs, we made three runs with random number seeds 111, 222, and 333.) We keep the arrival rate at 1 part per minute and the mean service rate at 1/0.6 parts per minute at each station. In the first set of runs, there is a single fast machine at each station. Each machine has an exponential processing time with mean 0.6 minute. In the second set of runs, we triple the number of machines at each station and also triple the mean processing time for each machine to achieve equivalent "slow" machines.

The use of three runs per configuration indicates that different random numbers can produce slightly different results. However, if average throughput time is of primary interest, it is clear that the fast machines are better. Even so, the results are probably not clear-cut to a manufacturer. For example, manufacturing companies typically like high utilization of their machines. The slow machines have much higher utilization than the fast ones. The fast machines tend to process the parts quickly, but then the parts are often passed to a queue. So it comes down to a trade-off between a lot of time in processing or a lot of time in queues.

This configuration might be described as "low utilization." Parts arrive at rate 1 per minute, and each mean processing time (for the fast machines) is only 0.6 minute. Figure 14.31 (page 811) shows the same type of results when the utilization is much higher. Here we increase the mean processing times for the fast machines to 0.9 (and triple them for the slow machines). We also increase the buffer sizes to 10. This system is a disaster—take a look at the average throughput times and the average times spent in queue in front of station 1, for example—but it does indicate a very interesting result. In terms of average throughput time, the slow machines are now *better* by quite a margin. Can you see why intuitively? The reason is that when utilization is high, one long processing time on a "fast" machine—which is always possible with an exponential distribution—can back up the whole system for quite a while. If there are multiple machines, however, parts can "move around" a machine experiencing a long

	A	B	C	D	E	F	G	H	I
1	Inputs (all use arrival rate of 1, exponential interarrival times, 3 stations, warmup time of 1000, run time of 10000)								
2									
3	Station	1	2	3		1	2	3	
4	Number of parallel machines at stations	1	1	1		3	3	3	
5	Distribution of processing time for each machine at station (1 for constant, 2 for exponential)	2	2	2		2	2	2	
6	Mean processing time/machine	0.6	0.6	0.6		1.8	1.8	1.8	
7	Number of buffers in front of stations	■	5	5		■	5	5	
8									
9	Counts of parts	Run 1	Run 2	Run 3		Run 1	Run 2	Run 3	
10	Number processed completely	10098	10045	10069		10094	10044	10067	
11	Number left at end only partially completed	7	2	5		14	5	11	
12									
13	Part averages (minutes/part)	Run 1	Run 2	Run 3		Run 1	Run 2	Run 3	
14	Average time in queues								
15	Station 1	0.978	1.057	1.138		0.526	0.584	0.690	
16	Station 2	0.913	0.916	0.864		0.530	0.533	0.496	
17	Station 3	0.822	0.801	0.827		0.500	0.486	0.497	
18	Total in all stations	2.713	2.774	2.829		1.555	1.604	1.683	
19									
20	Average times being blocked								
21	Station 1	0.021	0.023	0.019		0.040	0.043	0.038	
22	Station 2	0.017	0.017	0.015		0.032	0.031	0.029	
23	Total in all stations	0.037	0.040	0.034		0.071	0.074	0.066	
24									
25	Average throughput time	4.549	4.614	4.663		7.022	7.075	7.151	
26	Percent time in queue	59.65%	60.12%	60.67%		22.15%	22.66%	23.54%	
27	Percent time being blocked	0.82%	0.87%	0.72%		1.02%	1.05%	0.93%	
28	Percent time being processed	39.53%	39.01%	38.61%		76.83%	76.29%	75.53%	
29									
30	Time averages	Run 1	Run 2	Run 3		Run 1	Run 2	Run 3	
31	Average queue lengths								
32	Station 1	0.99	1.06	1.15		0.53	0.59	0.70	
33	Station 2	0.92	0.92	0.87		0.53	0.54	0.50	
34	Station 3	0.83	0.80	0.83		0.51	0.49	0.50	
35									
36	Percent time processing								
37	Station 1	59.79%	60.24%	60.04%		60.10%	60.57%	60.33%	
38	Station 2	61.20%	60.28%	60.08%		61.47%	60.55%	60.34%	
39	Station 3	60.61%	60.18%	61.19%		60.58%	60.16%	61.19%	
40									
41	Percent time blocked								
42	Station 1	2.09%	2.33%	1.87%		1.03%	1.10%	0.98%	
43	Station 2	1.69%	1.72%	1.52%		0.81%	0.79%	0.68%	

FIGURE 14.30 Fast Versus Slow Machines with Low Utilization

processing time, and the whole system is not as affected. We might have guessed this before running the simulation, but simulation confirms it.

Streamlining's next question concerns the variability of arrival and processing times. Here we examine a 3-station process, with 1 machine at each station and 5 buffers in front of stations 2 and 3. Parts arrive at rate 1 per minute, and the average service time is 0.7 minute at each machine. Figure 14.32 (page 812) lists some results. In columns B and C, interarrival times and processing times are exponential. In columns D and E, interarrival times are constant and processing times are exponential. This might be realistic if the company "releases" one part to the line every minute according to a nonrandom schedule. In columns F and G, interarrival times are exponential and processing times are constant. Finally, both are constant in column H. We made two runs for each of the random cases. Of course, only one run is necessary for the nonrandom case. By this time, these results should not come as a surprise. The more the company can do to wipe out variability, the better the manufacturing process will operate.

Finally, we analyze the effect of buffers and their placement. We now assume a 10-station process with a single machine at each station. The parts arrive at rate 1 per minute, each machine has a mean processing time of 0.5 minute, and all times are

	A	B	C	D	E	F	G	H	I
1	Inputs (all use arrival rate of 1, exponential interarrival times, 3 stations, warmup time of 1000, run time of 10000)								
2									
3	Station	1	2	3		1	2	3	
4	Number of parallel machines at stations	1	1	1		3	3	3	
5	Distribution of processing time for each machine at station (1 for constant, 2 for exponential)	2	2	2		2	2	2	
6	Mean processing time/machine	0.9	0.9	0.9		2.7	2.7	2.7	
7	Number of buffers in front of stations		10	10			10	10	
8									
9	Counts of parts	Run 1	Run 2	Run 3		Run 1	Run 2	Run 3	
10	Number processed completely	9962	9922	9965		10076	9950	10074	
11	Number left at end only partially completed	163	133	144		53	108	23	
12									
13	Part averages (minutes/part)	Run 1	Run 2	Run 3		Run 1	Run 2	Run 3	
14	Average time in queues								
15	Station 1	105.539	40.671	122.249		41.921	29.573	46.259	
16	Station 2	6.067	5.375	5.840		6.219	5.104	5.708	
17	Station 3	4.347	3.996	4.372		4.197	3.665	4.258	
18	Total in all stations	115.952	50.042	132.461		52.337	38.343	56.225	
19									
20	Average times being blocked								
21	Station 1	0.114	0.090	0.108		0.306	0.223	0.265	
22	Station 2	0.055	0.047	0.054		0.156	0.116	0.137	
23	Total in all stations	0.169	0.137	0.163		0.462	0.340	0.402	
24									
25	Average throughput time	118.644	52.780	135.160		60.850	46.674	64.799	
26	Percent time in queue	97.73%	94.81%	98.00%		86.01%	82.15%	86.77%	
27	Percent time being blocked	0.14%	0.26%	0.12%		0.76%	0.73%	0.62%	
28	Percent time being processed	2.13%	4.93%	1.88%		13.23%	17.12%	12.61%	
29									
30	Time averages	Run 1	Run 2	Run 3		Run 1	Run 2	Run 3	
31	Average queue lengths								
32	Station 1	106.39	41.07	122.72		42.28	29.87	46.64	
33	Station 2	6.04	5.34	5.82		6.27	5.08	5.76	
34	Station 3	4.33	3.96	4.36		4.23	3.65	4.29	
35									
36	Percent time processing								
37	Station 1	88.58%	89.42%	89.20%		93.38%	92.42%	93.59%	
38	Station 2	90.21%	89.23%	89.01%		93.32%	90.97%	91.87%	
39	Station 3	89.61%	89.04%	90.66%		90.68%	89.27%	91.80%	
40									
41	Percent time blocked								
42	Station 1	11.39%	8.96%	10.78%		6.43%	4.68%	5.55%	
43	Station 2	5.48%	4.64%	5.43%		3.31%	2.40%	2.91%	

FIGURE 14.31 Fast Versus Slow Machines with High Utilization

exponentially distributed. You might expect that when parts arrive only half as fast as the machines can process them, there should be no problem. This is not true, especially if buffers are severely limited. We made several runs, starting with 0 buffers in the system and gradually adding buffers. Selected results for average throughput times appear in Figure 14.33 (page 833). When there are no buffers, blocking kills the system. This might not be evident from the percentages listed, because each part spends only a small amount of time being blocked. But there is almost always blocking somewhere in the system, and the effect is that a long queue eventually builds in front of station 1.

Suppose Streamlining has enough funds to build exactly 1 buffer somewhere. Where should the buffer be placed? We made nine runs, placing the single buffer in front of each station, with the results in rows 19–22. It is clear that the single buffer should be placed in the *middle* of the line, in front of station 6. Placing it at the front or the back of the line does virtually no good. The reason is probably not intuitive, at least not until we provide the clue. The basic problem with this serial system is the interdependence between stations. A long processing time at one station can have negative effects throughout the entire line. Upstream stations (to the left) become blocked, and downstream stations (to the right) become starved for parts to process.

	A	B	C	D	E	F	G	H
1	**Constant versus exponential interarrival or service times**							
2								
3	Each run has arrival rate 1, 3 stations with 1 machine each, mean service time 0.7, 5 buffers at stations 2 and 3, warmup time 1000, and run time 10000							
4								
5		Exp arrivals, Exp services		Const arrivals, Exp services		Exp arrivals, Const services		Both const
6	**Counts of parts**	Run 1	Run 2	Run 1	Run 2	Run 1	Run 2	Only run
7	Number processed completely	10090	10039	10004	9999	10098	10042	10000
8	Number left at end only partially completed	16	8	4	5	3	2	2
9								
10	**Part averages (minutes/part)**	Run 1	Run 2	Run 1	Run 2	Run 1	Run 2	Only run
11	Average time in queues							
12	Station 1	2.400	2.935	0.587	0.631	0.789	0.838	0.000
13	Station 2	1.565	1.565	1.017	1.026	0.000	0.000	0.000
14	Station 3	1.302	1.244	1.065	1.048	0.000	0.000	0.000
15	Total in all stations	5.267	5.744	2.670	2.704	0.789	0.838	0.000
16								
17	Average times being blocked							
18	Station 1	0.056	0.062	0.013	0.015	0.000	0.000	0.000
19	Station 2	0.039	0.037	0.018	0.019	0.000	0.000	0.000
20	Total in all stations	0.095	0.100	0.031	0.034	0.000	0.000	0.000
21								
22	Average throughput time	7.457	7.941	4.799	4.837	2.889	2.939	2.100
23	Percent time in queue	70.63%	72.33%	55.63%	55.91%	27.29%	28.52%	0.00%
24	Percent time being blocked	1.28%	1.25%	0.65%	0.71%	0.00%	0.00%	0.00%
25	Percent time being processed	28.09%	26.42%	43.72%	43.39%	72.71%	71.48%	100.00%
26								
27	**Time averages**	Run 1	Run 2	Run 1	Run 2	Run 1	Run 2	Only run
28	Average queue lengths							
29	Station 1	2.42	2.95	0.59	0.63	0.80	0.84	0.00
30	Station 2	1.58	1.57	1.02	1.03	0.00	0.00	0.00
31	Station 3	1.31	1.25	1.07	1.05	0.00	0.00	0.00
32								
33	Percent time processing							
34	Station 1	69.70%	70.27%	69.16%	69.94%	70.69%	70.30%	70.01%
35	Station 2	71.38%	70.27%	70.58%	70.03%	70.69%	70.30%	70.01%
36	Station 3	70.66%	70.16%	70.01%	69.90%	70.69%	70.30%	70.01%
37								
38	Percent time blocked							
39	Station 1	5.65%	6.26%	1.30%	1.48%	0.00%	0.00%	0.00%
40	Station 2	3.95%	3.74%	1.82%	1.94%	0.00%	0.00%	0.00%

FIGURE 14.32 Constant Versus Exponential Times

By placing a buffer in the middle of the line, we do the most we can to break the line into two less dependent parts. This effect can be seen by continuing to add buffers one at a time. When there are 2 buffers, one should be placed about a third of the way down the line, and the other should be placed about two-thirds of the way down, breaking the line into 3 approximately equal sections. Similarly, when there are 3 buffers, they should be placed to break the line into 4 approximately equal sections.

The bottom section of Figure 14.33 indicates the "saturation" effect of adding more buffers. The company gets a lot from its money from the first few buffers, but after the first few, blocking becomes a minor problem and more buffers fail to make much of an improvement. If buffers entail significant costs, Streamlining must trade off these costs against lower average throughput times and possibly other considerations. ■

Spreadsheet Queueing Simulation Models

The simulation models in the previous two subsections rely on intricate VBA programs to take care of all of the details behind the scenes. There is an alternative way to develop queueing simulation models—right in Excel spreadsheets. These simulation models require no VBA code at all, only Excel formulas. However, they employ fairly difficult

	A	B	C	D	E	F	G	H	I	J	K
1	**Effect on throughput of adding buffers**										
2											
3	For each run, arrival process has rate 1, exponential interarrival times, warmup time 1000, and run time 10000										
4											
5	Station inputs are as follows, with only the buffers in row 10 changing from one run to the next										
6	Station	1	2	3	4	5					
7	Number of parallel machines at stations	1	1	1	1	1	1	1	1	1	1
8	Distribution of processing time for each machine at station (1 for constant, 2 for exponential)	2	2	2	2	2	2	2	2	2	2
9	Mean processing time/machine	0.5	0.5	0.5	0.5	0.5	0.5	0.5	0.5	0.5	0.5
10	Number of buffers in front of stations	0	0	0	0	0	0	0	0	0	0
11											
12	**No buffers**										
13	Average throughput time	837.302									
14	Percent time in queue	99.11%									
15	Percent time being blocked	0.43%									
16	Percent time being processed	0.47%									
17											
18	**Exactly 1 buffer in system**	At 2	At 3	At 4	At 5	At 6	At 7	At 8	At 9	At 10	
19	Average throughput time	774.887	717.163	668.415	645.790	637.323	646.021	689.034	736.138	781.783	
20	Percent time in queue	99.06%	98.95%	98.88%	98.85%	98.85%	98.88%	98.96%	99.05%	99.13%	
21	Percent time being blocked	0.48%	0.52%	0.54%	0.54%	0.52%	0.49%	0.45%	0.42%	0.41%	
22	Percent time being processed	0.46%	0.53%	0.58%	0.61%	0.63%	0.63%	0.59%	0.53%	0.46%	
23											
24	**Exactly 2 buffers in system**	At 2,10	At 3,9	At 4,8	At 5,7	Both at 6					
25	Average throughput time	710.386	577.575	470.710	441.238	542.693					
26	Percent time in queue	98.99%	98.76%	98.43%	98.34%	98.64%					
27	Percent time being blocked	0.47%	0.55%	0.66%	0.70%	0.59%					
28	Percent time being processed	0.54%	0.69%	0.91%	0.96%	0.77%					
29											
30	**Exactly 3 buffers in system**	At 2,6,10	At 3,6,9	At 4,6,8	At 5,6,7						
31	Average throughput time	479.545	344.361	272.953	324.105						
32	Percent time in queue	98.46%	97.86%	97.29%	97.74%						
33	Percent time being blocked	0.64%	0.86%	1.06%	0.92%						
34	Percent time being processed	0.90%	1.29%	1.64%	1.34%						
35											
36	**Many buffers**	1 at each	2 at each	5 at each	20 at each						
37	Average throughput time	12.787	10.399	9.997	9.986						
38	Percent time in queue	49.68%	46.89%	49.58%	50.02%						
39	Percent time being blocked	11.32%	5.13%	0.49%	0.00%						
40	Percent time being processed	39.01%	47.99%	49.92%	49.98%						

FIGURE 14.33 Buffers and Their Placement

logic. They also have their limits—it would take real ingenuity to model any but the simplest queueing situations in spreadsheets. Nevertheless, we have included several examples of spreadsheet queueing simulation models in the CD-ROM that accompanies this book.[9] (The files are called QSIM1.XLS, QSIM2.XLS, and so on.) We will not describe the details here, except to say that each row in the simulation corresponds to a particular customer. We simulate the customer's arrival time and service time and then use logical formulas to track this customer's stay in the system. After we develop the timing logic, it is then straightforward to calculate outputs of interest. For example, each customer row includes the customer's time in the queue in a particular column. To calculate the average time in queue, we simply average the numbers in this column.

To provide a taste of what is involved, we show part of the model from a three-server queue system in Figures 14.34 and 14.35 on page 814. (They come from the file QSIM2.XLS.) The first of these contains most of what we want—customer arrival times, service times, queueing times, starting times (in service), and departure times. However, the data about servers in Figure 14.35 are necessary so that we know when customers can go into service and which servers they will be assigned to. The logic

---

[9]We developed the method used in these files. However, similar methods for spreadsheet queueing simulation were developed independently by Savage (1998) and Grossman (1999).

	Customer	IA Time	Arrival Time	Service Time	Queue Time	Start Time	Depart Time
1	Multiple server queueing simulation (starting empty and idle)						
3	Customer	IA Time	Arrival Time	Service Time	Queue Time	Start Time	Depart Time
4	1	1	1	5	0	1	6
5	2	1	2	6	0	2	8
6	3	1	3	3	0	3	6
7	4	1	4	3	2	6	9
8	5	1	5	5	1	6	11
9	6	2	7	6	1	8	14
10	7	1	8	3	1	9	12
11	8	1	9	6	2	11	17
12	9	1	10	1	2	12	13
13	10	1	11	2	2	13	15
14	11	1	12	7	2	14	21
15	12	1	13	3	2	15	18
16	13	1	14	4	3	17	21
17	14	2	16	4	2	18	22
18	15	1	17	3	4	21	24
19	16	1	18	4	3	21	25
20	17	3	21	2	1	22	24
21	18	3	24	3	0	24	27
22	19	1	25	3	0	25	28
152	149	1	186	3	1	187	190
153	150	1	187	1	1	188	189

Range names used:
Service_Time - D4:D153
Queue_Time - E4:E153
NIQ_Before - AG4:AG153
NIQ_After - AH4:AH153

FIGURE 14.34 Multiple-Server Simulation Model, Part 1

	Work, right before customer entry, for server:										Server to	Work, right after customer entry, for server:										Number in queue	
	1	2	3	4	5	6	7	8	9	10	assign	1	2	3	4	5	6	7	8	9	10	Before entry	After entry
4	0	0	0								1	5	0	0								0	0
5	4	0	0								2	4	6	0								0	0
6	3	5	0								3	3	5	3								0	0
7	2	4	2								1	5	4	2								0	1
8	4	3	1								3	4	3	6								0	2
9	2	1	4								2	2	7	4								0	1
10	1	6	3								1	4	6	3								0	1
11	3	5	2								3	3	5	8								0	1
12	2	4	7								1	3	4	7								1	2
13	2	3	6								1	4	3	6								1	2
14	3	2	5								2	3	9	5								1	2
15	2	8	4								1	5	8	4								1	2
16	4	7	3								3	4	7	7								1	2
17	2	5	5								1	6	5	5								1	2
18	5	4	4								2	5	7	4								1	2
19	4	6	3								3	4	6	7								1	2
20	1	3	4								1	3	3	4								0	1
21	0	0	1								1	3	0	1								0	0
22	2	0	0								2	2	3	0								0	0
152	6	1	2								2	6	4	2								1	2
153	5	3	1								3	5	3	2								0	1

FIGURE 14.35 Multiple-Server Simulation Model, Part 2

in these figures is the difficult part. Once it is developed, we can easily obtain outputs such as in Figures 14.36–14.38. Also, because the random data in columns B and D of Figure 14.34 are "live," we can press the F9 button to recalculate everything and immediately see how the outputs change.

Spreadsheet queueing simulation has its place. By developing the logical formulas, you can gain a better insight into how queueing systems work, and you can definitely sharpen your spreadsheet skills. However, it is easy to get lost in the details and miss the main goal of queueing for business applications—namely, to gain insights. We caution you not to lose sight of this overriding goal.

FIGURE 14.36
Chart of Waiting
Times in Queue

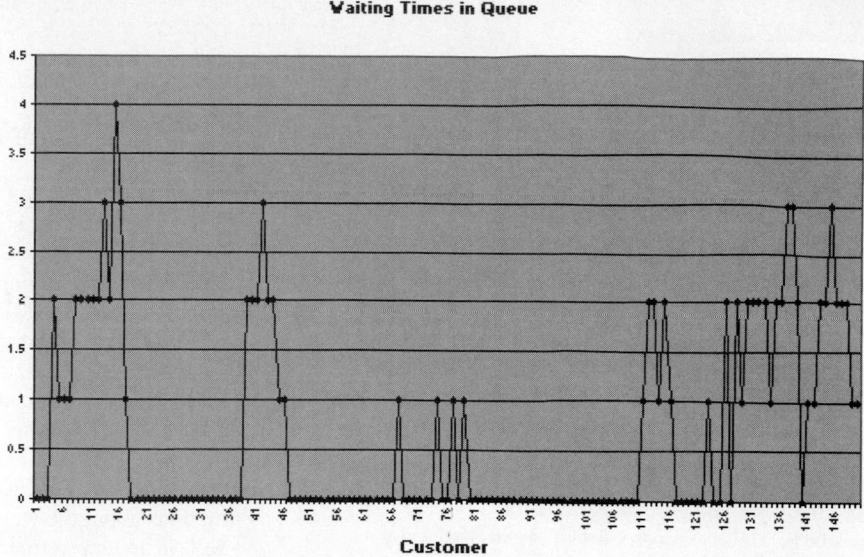

FIGURE 14.37
Chart of Queue
Lengths through Time

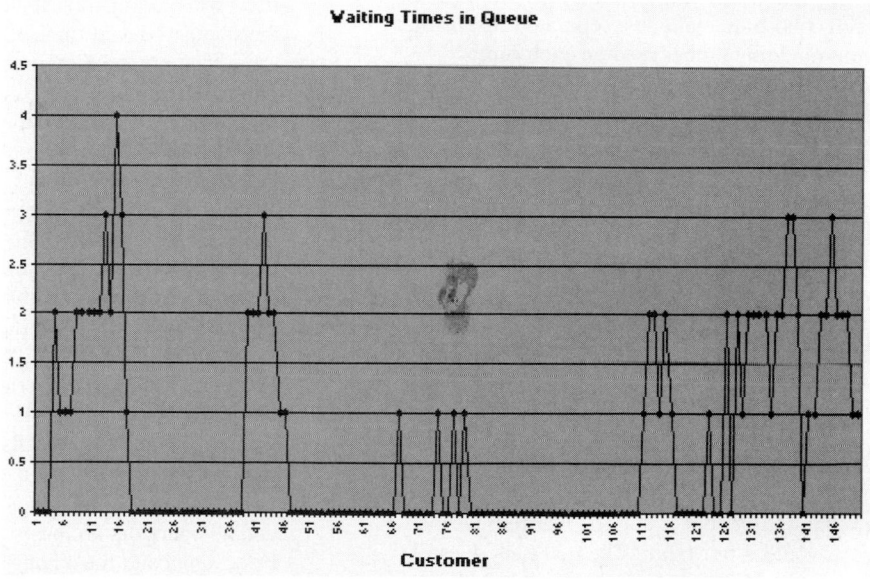

FIGURE 14.38
Summary Measures
for Multiple-Server
Simulation

	A	B	C	D	E	F
1	**Multiple server queue - Selected output measures**					
2						
3	Average queue time	0.667				
4	Average queue length	0.521				
5						
6	Max wait in queue	4				
7	Max queue seen by arrivals	2				
8	Max queue at any time	3				
9						
10	Fraction with no wait	0.627				
11						
12	Fraction waiting more than:					
13	Minutes	1	2	3	4	5
14	Fraction	0.240	0.047	0.007	0.000	0.000
15						
16	Average time in service	3.100				
17	Fraction of time busy per server	0.807				

14.6 Queueing Simulation **815**

Skill-Building Problems

38. The Smalltown Credit Union experiences its greatest congestion on paydays from 11:30 A.M. until 1:00 P.M. During these rush periods, customers arrive according to a Poisson process at rate 2.1 per minute. The credit union employs 10 tellers for these rush periods, and each takes 4.7 minutes to service a customer. Customers who arrive to the credit union wait in a single queue, if necessary, unless there are already 15 customers in the queue. In this latter case, arriving customers are too impatient to wait, and they leave the system. Simulate this system to find the average wait in queue for the customers who enter, the average number in queue, the percentage of time a typical teller is busy, and the percentage of arrivals who do not enter the system. Try this simulation under the following conditions and comment on your results. For each condition, make five separate runs, using a different random number seed on each run.

  a. Try a warmup time of 2 hours. Then try no warmup time. Use exponentially distributed service times for each.

  b. Try exponentially distributed service times. Then try gamma distributed service times, where the standard deviation of a service time is 2.4 minutes. Use a warmup period of 1 hour for each.

  c. Try 10 tellers, as in the statement of the problem. Then try 11, then 12. Use exponentially distributed service times and a warmup period of 1 hour for each.

  d. Why might the use of a long warmup time bias the results toward *worse* system behavior than would actually be experienced? If you could ask the programmer of the simulation to provide another option concerning the warmup period, what would it be? (*Hint*: The real rush doesn't begin until 11:30.)

39. How long does it take to reach "steady state"? Use simulation, with the MULTSERVERSIM.XLS file, to experiment with the effect of warmup time and run time on the key outputs. For each of the following, assume a five-server system with a Poisson arrival rate of 1 per minute and gamma distributed service times with mean 4.0 minutes and standard deviation 3.1 minutes. For each part, make five separate runs, using a different random number seed on each run.

  a. Use a warmup time of 0 and a run time of 30 minutes.

  b. Use a warmup time of 0 and a run time of 180 minutes.

  c. Use a warmup time of 120 minutes and a run time of 30 minutes.

  d. Use a warmup time of 120 minutes and a run time of 180 minutes.

  e. Repeat parts **a–d** when the mean and standard deviation of service times are 4.8 and 4.2 minutes, respectively. (This should produce considerably more congestion.)

40. Given the model in the MULTSERVERSIM.XLS file, what unit cost parameters should be used if we are interested in "optimizing" the system? Choose representative unit costs, and then illustrate how to use the simulation outputs to estimate total system costs.

41. Simulate the system in Problem 10. Make any assumptions about the warmup time and run time you believe are appropriate. Try solving the problem with exponentially distributed copying times. Then try it with gamma distributed copying times, where the standard deviation is 3.2 minutes. Do you get the same recommendation on which machine to purchase?

42. In Example 14.4 of Section 14.5, we examined whether an $M/M/1$ system with a single fast server is better or worse than an $M/M/s$ system with several slow servers. Keeping the same inputs as in the example, use simulation to see whether you obtain the same type of results as with the analytical models. Then repeat, using gamma distributed service times with standard deviation 6 minutes.

43. A telephone-order sales company must determine how many telephone operators are needed to staff the phones during the 9-to-5 shift. It is estimated that an average of 480 calls are received during this time period and that the average call lasts for 6 minutes. There is no "queueing." If a customer calls and all operators are busy, this customer receives a busy signal and must hang up. If the company wants to have at most 1 chance in 100 of a caller receiving a busy signal, how many operators should be hired for the 9-to-5 shift? Base your answer on an appropriate simulation. Does it matter whether the service times are exponentially distributed or gamma distributed? Experiment to find out.

44. US Airlines receives an average of 500 calls per hour from customers who want to make reservations, where the times between calls follow an exponential distribution. It takes an average of 3 minutes to handle each call. Each customer who buys a ticket contributes $100 to US Airlines profit. It costs $15 per hour to staff a telephone line. Any customer who receives a busy signal will purchase a ticket from another airline. How many telephone lines should US Airlines have? Base your answer on an appropriate simulation. Does it matter whether the service times are exponentially distributed or gamma distributed? Experiment to find out.

45. Consider a series system of the type in the SERIESSIM.XLS file. There are two stations. Each station has three machines, and the mean processing time for each machine is 3.1 minutes. Parts are arriving to station 1 at a Poisson rate of 0.8 per minute. The processing times at one station are constant. At the other they are exponentially distributed. Where would you rather have the constant processing times—at station 1 or station 2? Does the answer depend on the number of buffers in front of station 2? Experiment to find out.

Skill-Extending Problems

46. A company's warehouse can store up to 4 units of a good. Each month, an average of 10 orders for the good are received. The times between the receipts of successive orders are exponentially distributed. When an item is used to fill an order, a replacement item is immediately ordered, and it takes an average of 1 month for a replacement item to arrive. If no items are on hand when an order is received, the order is lost. Use simulation to estimate the fraction of all orders that will be lost due to shortage? (*Hint:* Let the storage space for each item be a "server" and think about what it means for a server to be busy. Then decide on an appropriate definition of "service" time.)

47. Referring to the multistation serial system in the SERIESSIM.XLS file, let s_i and $1/\mu_i$ be the number of machines and the mean processing time at station i. Then the mean processing rate at station i is $s_i\mu_i$. We might expect that the system will operate well only if each $s_i\mu_i$ is greater than λ, the arrival rate to station 1. This problem will ask you to experiment with the simulation to gain some insights into congestion. For each part below, assume a Poisson arrival rate of $\lambda = 1$ per minute, and assume that processing times are exponentially distributed. Each

part below can be answered independently. For each, you should discuss the most important outputs from your simulation.
   a. Each station has $s_i = 1$ and the μ_i's are constant from station to station. There are 100 (essentially unlimited) buffers in front of all stations after station 1. Each processing time has mean $1/\mu_i = 0.6$ minute and there are three stations.
   b. Same as part **a**, except that there are ten stations.
   c. Same as part **a**, except that each processing time has mean 0.9 minute.
   d. Same as part **c**, except that there are ten stations.
   e. Repeat parts **a–d**, but now assume there are only two buffers in front of each station.

48. Repeat the previous problem, but now assume that $s_i = 3$ at each station. Change the μ_i's so that the products $s_i\mu_i$ are the same as in the previous problem.

49. Continuing Problem 47, we might expect that the system will be only as good as the station with the smallest value of $s_i\mu_i$ (called the bottleneck station). This problem asks you to experiment with the simulation to gain some insights into bottlenecks. For each part below, assume a Poisson arrival rate of $\lambda = 1$ per minute, and assume that processing times are exponentially distributed. Each station has $s_i = 1$ and there are five stations. Each station, except for the bottleneck station, has a processing time mean of $1/\mu_i = 0.6$ minute. The bottleneck station has mean 0.9 minute. Each part below can be answered independently. For each, you should discuss the most important outputs from your simulation.
   a. Suppose there are 100 (essentially unlimited) buffers in front of all stations after station 1. Run the simulation when station 1 is the bottleneck. Repeat when it is station 2; station 3; station 4; station 5.
   b. Repeat part **a** when there are only two buffers in front of each station after station 1.
   c. Suppose station 3 is the bottleneck station and you have four buffers to allocate to the whole system. Experiment to see where they should be placed.

14.7 CONCLUSION

We have seen that there are two basic approaches for analyzing queueing models. The first is the analytical approach, where we attempt to find formulas (or possibly algorithms, implemented with macros) to calculate steady-state performance measures of the system. The second is the simulation approach, where we simulate the random elements of the system and then keep track of the events as they occur through time. The advantage of the analytical approach is that, at least for the simplest models, it provides summary measures such as L_Q and W_Q that are relatively simple to interpret. Also, if we have template files for these systems, we can easily vary the inputs to see how the outputs change. The main disadvantage of the analytical approach is that the mathematics becomes extremely complex unless we are willing to make simplifying assumptions, some of which can be unrealistic. For example, we must typically assume that service times are exponentially distributed, an unrealistic assumption in many real applications. Also, we must typically assume that the arrival rate remains constant through time and that we are concerned only with "steady state."

The simulation approach provides much more flexibility. For example, it is no more difficult to simulate nonexponential times than exponential times. Also, simulation lets us "see" how the system behaves and how queues can build up through time. The disadvantage of queueing simulation is that it is not well suited to spreadsheets. We have two basic choices: buy (and learn) specialized queueing software packages, or write our own queueing simulation in procedural languages such as VBA. Neither is an attractive possibility. However, the two general queueing simulation models we have provided in the MULTSERVERSIM.XLS and SERIESSIM.XLS files allow us to experiment with many system configuration to see how inputs and inherent randomness affect system outputs. The insights gained can be extremely valuable.

PROBLEMS

Skill-Building Problems

50. An average of 50 customers per hour arrive at a small post office. Interarrival times are exponentially distributed. Each window can serve an average of 25 customers per hour. Service times are exponentially distributed. It costs $25 per hour to open a window, and the post office values the time a customer spends waiting in line at $15 per customer-hour. To minimize expected hourly costs, how many postal windows should be opened?

51. An average of 300 customers per hour arrive at a huge branch of Bank 2. It takes an average of 2 minutes to serve each customer. It costs $10 per hour to keep a teller window open, and the bank estimates that it will lose $50 in future profits for each hour that a customer waits in line. How many teller windows should Bank 2 open?

52. Ships arrive at a port facility at an average rate of two ships every 3 days. On average, it takes a single crew 1 day to unload a ship. Assume that interarrival and service times are exponential. The shipping company owns the port facility as well as the ships using that facility. The company estimates that it costs $1000 per day for each day that a ship spends in port. The crew servicing the ships consists of 100 workers, each of whom is paid an average of $30 per day. A consultant has recommended that the shipping company hire an additional 40 workers and split the employees into two equal-sized crews of 70

each. This would give each crew an average unloading or loading time of 1.5 days. Which crew arrangement would you recommend to the company?

53. An average of 40 jobs per day arrive at a factory. The time between arrivals of jobs is exponentially distributed. The factory can process an average of 42 jobs per day, and the time to process a job is exponentially distributed.
   a. On average, how long does it take before a job is completed (measured from the time the job arrives at the factory)?
   b. What fraction of the time is the factory idle?
   c. What is the probability that work on a job will begin within 2 days of its arrival at the factory?

54. A printing shop receives an average of one order per day. The average length of time required to complete an order is half a day. At any given time, the print shop can work on at most one job. Interarrival times and service times are exponentially distributed.
   a. On average, how many jobs are present in the print shop?
   b. On average, how long will a person who places an order have to wait until it is finished?
   c. What is the probability that an order will begin work within 2 days of its arrival?

55. At the Franklin Post Office, patrons wait in a single line for the first open window. An average of 100 patrons per hour enter the post office, and each window can serve an average of 45 patrons per hour. The post office estimates a cost of $0.10 for each minute a patron waits in line and believes that it costs $20 per hour to keep a window open. Interarrival times and service times are exponential.

a. To minimize the total expected hourly cost, how many windows should be open?

b. If the post office's goal is to ensure that at most 5% of all patrons will spend more than 5 minutes in line, how many windows should be open?

56. The manager of a large group of employees must decide whether she needs another photocopying machine. The cost of a machine is $40 per 8-hour day whether or not the machine is in use. An average of 4 people per hour need to use the copying machine. Each person uses the copier for an average of 10 minutes. Interarrival times and copying times are exponentially distributed. Employees are paid $8 per hour, and we assume that a waiting cost is incurred when a worker is waiting in line or is using the copying machine. How many copying machines should be rented?

57. The Newcoat Painting Company has for some time been experiencing high demand for its automobile repainting service. Because it has had to turn away business, management is concerned that the limited space available to store cars awaiting painting has cost them in lost revenue. A small vacant lot next to the painting facility has recently been made available for rental on a long-term basis at a cost of $10 per day. Management believes that each lost customer costs $20 in profit. Current demand is estimated to be 21 cars per day with exponential interarrival times (including those turned away), and the facility can service at an exponential rate of 24 cars per day. Cars are processed on a FCFS basis. Waiting space is now limited to 9 cars but can be increased to 20 cars with the lease of the vacant lot. Newcoat wants to determine whether the vacant lot should be leased. Management also wants to know the expected daily lost profit due to turning away customers if the lot is leased. Only one car can be painted at a time. (Try using the LIMITED_Q_TEMPLATE.XLS file for an analytical solution and the MULTSERVERSIM.XLS file for a simulation solution.)

58. An average of 90 patrons per hour arrive at a hotel lobby (interarrival times are exponential) waiting to check in. At present there are 5 clerks, and patrons wait in a single line for the first available clerk. The average time for a clerk to service a patron is 3 minutes (exponentially distributed). Clerks earn $10 per hour, and the hotel assesses a waiting time cost of $20 for each hour that a patron waits in line.

a. Compute the expected cost per hour of the current system.

b. The hotel is considering replacing one clerk with an Automatic Clerk Machine (ACM). Management estimates that 20% of all patrons will use an ACM. An ACM takes an average of 1 minute to service a patron. It costs $48 per day (1 day equals 8 hours) to operate an ACM. Should the hotel install the ACM? Assume that all customers who are willing to use the ACM wait in a separate queue.

Skill-Extending Problem

59. The mail order firm of L. L. Pea receives an average of 200 calls per hour, where times between calls are exponentially distributed. It takes an L. L. Pea operator an average of 3 minutes to handle a call. If a caller gets a busy signal, L. L. Pea assumes that he or she will call a competing mail-order company, and L. L. Pea will lose an average of $30 in profit. The cost of keeping a phone line open is $9 per hour. How many operators should L. L. Pea have on duty? Use simulation to answer this question. Does the answer depend on whether the service times are exponentially distributed?

Modeling Problems

60. Bloomington Hospital knows that insurance companies are going to reduce the average length of stay of many types of patients. How can queueing models be used to determine how changes in insurance policies will influence the hospital?

61. Excessive delays have recently been noted on New York City's 911 system. Discuss how you would use queueing models to improve the performance of the 911 system.

62. Suppose that annually an average of λ library patrons want to borrow a book. A patron borrows the book for an average of $1/\mu$ years. Suppose we observe that the book is actually borrowed an average of R times per year. Expain how we can estimate λ, which is an unobservable quantity. (*Hint*: Let U be the expected number of times per year a patron wants to borrow the book and the book is out. Note that $\lambda = R + U$.)

63. Based on Quinn et al. (1991). Winter Riggers handles approximately $400 million in telephone orders per year. Winter Riggers' system works as follows. Callers are connected to an agent if one is available. Otherwise, they are put on hold (if a "trunk" or line is available). A customer can hang up at any time and leave the system. Winter Riggers would like to efficiently manage the telephone system (lines and agents) used to process these orders. Of course, orders are very seasonal and depend on the time of day.

a. What decisions must Winter Riggers make?

b. What would be an appropriate objective for Winter Riggers to minimize (or maximize)? What difficulties do you see in specifying the objective?

c. What data would Winter Riggers need to keep track of to improve its efficiency?

64. Zerox has 16 service centers throughout the United States. Zerox is trying to determine how many technicians it should assign to each service center. How would you approach this problem?

65. Based on Kolesar et al. (1974). Metropolis PD Precinct 88 needs to determine the minimum number of police cars required to meet its needs for the next 24 hours. An average call for service requires 30 minutes. The number of calls the police department expects to receive during each hour is shown in Table 14.3. The Metropolis PD standard of service is that there should be a 90% chance that a car is available to respond to a call. For each of the following, discuss how you might find a solution.

a. Suppose that patrol officer teams assigned to a car work an 8-hour shift beginning at either 12 A.M., 8 A.M., or 4 P.M. Officers get an hour off for a meal. This hour can be anytime between the second and fifth hour of their shift. The precinct wants to know how many teams are needed to meet daily demand.

b. Suppose that patrol officer teams assigned to a car begin their 8-hour shifts at 12 A.M., 8 A.M., 12 P.M., 4 P.M., and 8 P.M. An hour off for meals may be taken anytime during a shift. The precinct again wants to know how many teams are needed to meet daily demand.

TABLE 14.3	Calls for Metropolis PD Problem		
	Number of Calls		**Number of Calls**
12 A.M.–1 A.M.	9.8	12 P.M.–1 P.M.	4.3
1 A.M.–2 A.M.	9.6	1 P.M.–2 P.M.	5.0
2 A.M.–3 A.M.	8.7	2 P.M.–3 P.M.	5.9
3 A.M.–4 A.M.	7.6	3 P.M.–4 P.M.	6.6
4 A.M.–5 A.M.	6.7	4 P.M.–5 P.M.	7.8
5 A.M.–6 A.M.	5.3	5 P.M.–6 P.M.	8.6
6 A.M.–7 A.M.	4.1	6 P.M.–7 P.M.	9.4
7 A.M.–8 A.M.	3.2	7 P.M.–8 P.M.	9.8
8 A.M.–9 A.M.	2.5	8 P.M.–9 P.M.	10.2
9 A.M.–10 A.M.	2.5	9 P.M.–10 P.M.	10.4
10 A.M.–11 A.M.	2.9	10 P.M.–11 P.M.	10.2
11 A.M.–12 P.M.	3.8	11 P.M.–12 A.M.	10.0

The Catalog Company Problem

The Catalog Company is a mail- and phone-order company that sells generic brands of houseware items and clothing. Approximately 95% of customer orders are received by phone; the remaining 5% are received in the mail. Phone orders are accepted at Catalog Company's toll-free 800 number, 800-SAVE-NOW. The number is available 9 hours per day (8 A.M. to 5 P.M.), 5 days a week.

Sarah Walters, a recent graduate of Columbia Business School, has just been hired by Catalog to improve its operations. Sarah would like to impress her boss, Ben Gleason, the president of Catalog Company, with some ideas that would quickly improve the company's bottom line. After spending a week learning about Catalog's operations, Sarah feels that a substantial impact can be made by a closer evaluation of the phone order system.

Currently, Catalog employs a single full-time operator to take orders over the phone. Sarah wonders whether additional operators should be hired to take phone orders. Ben feels that Sarah's time might be better spent studying the catalog mailing lists. Ben reasons that the mailing lists are where customers are generated, and improving the list will bring in more revenue. And besides, Ben says, "Catalog's phone operator, Betty Wrangle, seems to be doing nothing more than half of the time that I walk by. Hiring more operators to do nothing will just waste more money." Although Sarah knows the mailing lists are important, she thinks that a study of the mailing lists will take far more time than a quick evaluation of the phone order system.

Forging ahead, Sarah discovered the following information about the phone order system. The phone operator, Betty Wrangle, is paid $9 per hour in wages and benefits. The average cost to Catalog for a completed 800 number call is $1.50. With only one phone line, any incoming calls that arrive when Betty is on the phone to another customer get a busy signal. The cost of the phone line is $40 per month. The phone company can immediately add up to four additional phone lines using the same 800 number, each at a cost of $40 per month per line. Catalog's phone system is such that it cannot be upgraded in the near future to allow incoming calls to be placed on hold. The average profit on an order (not including the cost of the operator or phone call) is 40% of the amount of the order. For example, an order of $100 brings a profit of $40 to Catalog.

Sarah decided that additional information needed to be collected about the frequency of incoming calls, the length of the calls, and so on. After talking to the phone company, Sarah learned that she could borrow equipment for one day that could detect when a call was coming in, even when Betty was on the phone. The caller would still get a busy signal and be lost, but Sarah would know that a call had been attempted. Sarah collected almost nine hours of data the next day; these data are presented in Table 14.4. Sarah believes that most of the callers who receive a busy signal take their business elsewhere and are totally lost to Catalog. Sarah does not feel that extending the hours of operation of the 800 number would be beneficial because the hours of operation are printed prominently in all of the catalogs.

The first call arrives 0.036 hour into the day. It takes Betty 0.054 hour to process the call and record the order for $65.21 worth of merchandise. Callers 5 and 6 get busy signals when they call, because Betty was still processing caller 4. Because calls 5 and 6 were lost, no call length information was available and no orders were placed. Data collection was stopped at call number 80.

Questions

Use the complete information in the file CATALOG.XLS to answer the following questions.

1. Approximately what fraction of the time is Betty idle? Is Ben's estimate correct?

2. Approximately how many calls are lost in an average hour due to a busy signal?

3. Use the data to estimate the average arrival rate of all attempted calls to Catalog. Give an approximate 95% confidence interval for the estimate. Plot a frequency histogram of interarrival

TABLE 14.4	Call Data for Catalog Case Study			
Call Number	Arrival Time (hours)	Busy Signal? (1 = busy, 0 = not)	Call Length (hours)	Order Size (dollars)
1	0.0359	0	0.0544	65.21
2	0.1564	0	0.0503	62.47
3	0.3066	0	0.0191	62.46
4	0.3609	0	0.0109	38.11
5	0.3610	1	N/A	N/A
6	0.3689	1	N/A	N/A
7	0.4094	0	0.0877	54.02
⋮	⋮	⋮	⋮	⋮
80	8.4890	0	0.0310	10.00

times. Does the distribution of interarrival times appear to be exponential?

4. Use the data to estimate the average service rate of all completed calls. Give an approximate 95% confidence interval for the estimate. Plot a frequency histogram of service times. Does the service time distribution appear to be exponential?

Give an approximate 95% confidence interval for the average revenue per call.

5. Would you recommend that Catalog acquire additional phone lines and operators? If so, how many? If not, why not? Justify your answer in enough detail so that Ben Gleason would be convinced of your recommendation.

15

Regression
Analysis

SITE LOCATION FOR LA QUINTA MOTOR INNS

Regression analysis is an extremely flexible tool that can aid
decision making in many areas. Kimes and Fitzsimmons (1990)
describe how it has been used by La Quinta Motor Inns, a
moderately-priced hotel chain oriented toward serving the business traveler,
to help make site location decisions. Location is one of the most important
decisions for a lodging firm. All hotel chains search for ideal locations and
often compete against each other for the same sites. A hotel chain that can
select good sites more accurately and quickly than its competition has a
distinct competitive advantage.

Kimes and Fitzsimmons, academics hired by La Quinta to model their
site location decision process, used regression analysis. They collected data
on 57 mature inns belonging to La Quinta during a 3-year business cycle.
The data included profitability for each inn (defined as operating margin

percentage—profit plus depreciation and interest expenses, divided by the total revenue), as well as a number of potential explanatory variables that could be used to predict profitability. These explanatory variables fell into five categories: competitive characteristics (such as number of hotel rooms in the vicinity and average room rates); demand generators (such as hospitals and office buildings within a 4-mile radius that might attract customers to the area); demographic characteristics (such as local population, unemployment rate, and median family income); market awareness (such as years the inn has been open and state population per inn); and physical considerations (such as accessibility, distance to downtown, and sign visibility).

The analysts then determined which of these potential explanatory variables were most highly correlated (positively or negatively) with profitability and entered these variables into a regression equation for profitability. The estimated regression equation was

$$\text{Predicted Profitability} = 39.05 - 5.41\text{StatePop} + 5.81\text{Price}$$
$$- 3.09\sqrt{\text{MedIncome}} + 1.75\text{ColStudents}$$

where StatePop is the state population (1000s) per inn, Price is the room rate for the inn, MedIncome is the median income ($1000s) of the area, ColStudents is the number of college students (1000s) within 4 miles, and all variables in this equation are standardized to have mean 0 and standard deviation 1. This equation predicts that profitability will increase when room rate and the number of college students *increase* and when state population and median income *decrease*. The R^2 value (to be discussed in this chapter) was a respectable 0.51, indicating a reasonable predictive ability. Using good statistical practice, the analysts validated this equation by feeding it explanatory variable data on a set of *different* inns, attempting to predict profitability for these new inns. The validation was a success—the regression equation predicted profitability fairly accurately for this new set of inns.

La Quinta management, however, was not as interested in predicting the exact profitability of inns as in predicting which would be profitable and which would be unprofitable. A cutoff value of 35% for operating margin was used to divide the profitable inns from the unprofitable inns. (Approximately 60% of the inns in the original sample were profitable by this definition.) The analysts were still able to use the regression equation they had developed. For any prospective site, they used the regression equation to predict profitability, and if the predicted value was sufficiently high, they predicted that this site would be profitable. They selected a decision rule—that is, how high was "sufficiently high"—from considerations of the two potential types of errors. One type of error, a false positive, was predicting that a site would be profitable when in fact it was headed for unprofitability. The opposite type of error, a false negative, was predicting that a site would be unprofitable (and rejecting the site) when in fact it would have been profitable. La Quinta management was more concerned about false positives, so it was willing to be conservative in its decision rule and miss a few potential opportunities for profitable sites.

Since the time of the study, La Quinta has implemented the regression model in spreadsheet form. For each potential site, it collects data on the relevant explanatory variables, uses the regression equation to predict the site's profitability, and applies the decision rule on whether to build or not. Of course, the model's recommendation is only that—a recommendation. Top management has the ultimate say on whether any site is used or not. As Sam Barshop, then chairman of the board and president of La Quinta Motor Inns stated, "We currently use the model to help us in our site-screening process and have found that it has raised the 'red flag' on several sites we had under consideration. We plan to continue using and updating the model in the future in our attempt to make La Quinta a leader in the business hotel market." ∎

15.1 INTRODUCTION

Regression analysis is the study of relationships between variables.[1] It is one of the most useful tools for a business analyst because it applies to so many situations. Some potential uses of regression analysis in business include the following:

- How do wages of employees depend on years of experience, years of education, and gender?

- How does the current price of a stock depend on its own past values, as well as the current and past values of a market index?

- How does a company's current sales level depend on its current and past advertising levels, the advertising levels of its competitors, the company's own past sales levels, and the general level of the market?

- How does the unit cost of producing an item depend on the total quantity of items that have been produced?

- How does the selling price of a house depend on such factors as the appraised value of the house, the square footage of the house, the number of bedrooms in the house, and perhaps others?

Each of these questions asks how a single variable, such as selling price or employee wages, depends on other relevant variables. If we can estimate this relationship, then we can not only better understand how the world operates, but we can also do a better job of predicting the variable in question. For example, we can not only understand how a company's sales are affected by its advertising, but we can also use the company's records of current and past advertising levels to predict future sales.

The branch of statistics that studies such relationships is called **regression analysis**, and is the subject of this chapter. Because of its generality and applicability, regression analysis is one of the most pervasive of all statistical methods in the business world.

There are several ways to categorize regression analysis. One categorization is based on the overall purpose of the analysis. As suggested above, there are two potential objectives of regression analysis: to understand how the world operates and to make predictions. Either of these objectives might be paramount in any particular application. If the variable in question is employee wages and we are using variables such as years of experience, years of education, and gender to explain wage levels, then the purpose of the analysis is probably to understand how the world operates—that is, to explain how the variables combine in any given company to determine wages. More specifically, the purpose of the analysis might be to discover whether there is any gender discrimination in wages, after allowing for differences in work experience and education level.

On the other hand, the primary objective of the analysis might be prediction. A good example of this is when the variable in question is company sales, and variables such as advertising and past sales levels are used as explanatory variables. In this case it is certainly important for the company to know how the relevant variables impact its sales. But the company's primary objective is probably to predict *future* sales levels, given current and past values of the explanatory variables. The company might also use a regression model for a what-if analysis, where it predicts future sales for many conceivable patterns of advertising and then selects its advertising level on the basis of these predictions.

---

[1]This chapter is a condensed version of Chapters 13 and 14 of Albright et al. (2000). An excellent treatment of regression, emphasizing business applications, is given by Mendenhall and Sincich (1993).

Fortunately, the same regression analysis enables us to solve both problems simultaneously. That is, it indicates how the world operates and it enables us to make predictions. So although the objectives of regression studies might differ, the same basic analysis always applies.

A second categorization of regression analysis is based on the type of data being analyzed. There are two basic types: cross-sectional data and time series data. Cross-sectional data are usually data gathered from approximately the same period of time from a cross section of a population. The housing and wage examples mentioned earlier are typical cross-sectional studies. The first concerns a sample of houses, presumably sold during a short period of time, such as houses sold in Florida during the first quarter of 1998. The second concerns a sample of employees observed at a particular point in time, such as a sample of automobile workers observed at the beginning of 1997. In contrast, time series studies involve one or more variables that are observed at several, usually equally-spaced, points in time. The stock price example mentioned earlier fits this description. We observe the price of a particular stock and possibly the price of a market index at the beginning of every week, say, and then try to explain the movement of the stock's price through time.

Regression analysis can be applied equally well to cross-sectional and time series data. In either case we might be attempting to understand how the world operates or to make predictions. However, there are technical reasons for treating time series analysis somewhat differently. The primary reason is that time series variables are usually related to their own past values. This property of many time series variables is called **autocorrelation**, and it complicates the analysis.

A third categorization of regression analysis involves the number of explanatory variables in the analysis. First, we need to introduce some terms. In every regression study there is a single variable that we are trying to explain or predict. This is called the **response** variable or the **dependent** variable. To help explain or predict the response variable, we use one or more **explanatory** variables. These explanatory variables are also called **predictor** variables or **independent** variables. If there is a single explanatory variable, the analysis is called **simple regression**. If there are several explanatory variables, it is called **multiple regression**.[2]

There are important differences between simple and multiple regression. The primary difference, as the name implies, is that simple regression is simpler. The calculations are simpler, the interpretation of output is somewhat simpler, and fewer complications can occur. We will begin with simple regression examples to introduce the ideas of regression. But we will soon see that simple regression is no more than a special case of multiple regression, and there is little need to single it out for separate discussion—especially when computer software is available to perform the calculations in either case.

In this chapter we will show how to estimate regression equations that describe relationships between variables. We will also discuss the interpretation of these equations, and we will explain numerical measures that indicate the goodness of fit of the equations we estimate. We will then extend the analysis to statistical inference of regression output. This will suggest sensible rules for including or excluding potential explanatory variables in a regression equation. Finally, we will discuss modeling possibilities for incorporating various types of variables into regression equations, and we will discuss predictions based upon regression.

---

[2]The traditional terms used in regression are *dependent* and *independent* variables. However, because these terms can cause confusion with probabilistic independence, a totally different concept, there has been an increasing use of the terms *response* and *explanatory* variables. We will use the latter terms in this book.

15.2 SCATTERPLOTS: GRAPHING RELATIONSHIPS

A good way to begin any regression analysis is to draw one or more scatterplots. A scatterplot is a graphical plot of two variables, an X and a Y. Consider a data set with n observations, where for each observation there are at least two variables. We choose two of these variables and label them X and Y. Then for each of the observations, we plot the X and Y values as a point on a two-dimensional graph. The scatterplot is the resulting scatter of points. If there is any relationship between the two variables, it is usually apparent from the scatterplot.

The following example, which we will carry throughout this chapter, illustrates the usefulness of scatterplots. It is a typical example of cross-sectional data.

EXAMPLE 15.1

SALES VERSUS PROMOTIONAL EXPENDITURES AT PHARMEX

Pharmex is a chain of drugstores that operate around the country. To see how effective its advertising and other promotional activities are, the company has collected data from 50 randomly selected metropolitan regions. In each region it has compared its own promotional expenditures and sales to those of the leading competitor in the region over the past year. There are two variables:

- Promote: Pharmex's promotional expenditures as a percentage of those of the leading competitor
- Sales: Pharmex's sales as a percentage of those of the leading competitor

Note that each of these variables is an "index," not a dollar amount. For example, if Promote equals 95 for some region, this tells us only that Pharmex's promotional expenditures in that region are 95% as large as those for the leading competitor in that region. The company expects that there is a positive relationship between these two variables, so that regions with relatively more expenditures have relatively more sales. However, it is not clear what the nature of this relationship is. The data are listed in the file PHARMEX.XLS. (See Figure 15.1 on page 828 for a partial listing of the data.) What type of relationship, if any, is apparent in a scatterplot?

Solution

First, we note that there are two ways to create a scatterplot in Excel. We can use Excel's Chart Wizard to create an X-Y chart, or we can use StatPro's Scatterplot procedure. The advantage of the latter is that the X variable (the one on the horizontal axis) doesn't need to be to the left of the Y variable in the data set, so we generally favor its use in regression applications.

Which variable should be on the horizontal axis? In regression we always put the explanatory variable on the horizontal axis and the response variable on the vertical axis. In this example, the store believes large promotional expenditures tend to "cause" larger values of sales, so we put Sales on the vertical axis and Promote on the horizontal axis. The resulting scatterplot appears in Figure 15.2.

This scatterplot indicates that there is indeed a positive relationship between Promote and Sales—the points tend to rise from bottom left to top right—but the rela-

FIGURE 15.1
Data for Drugstore
Example

	A	B	C	D	E	F
1	**Data on drugstore promotional expenditures and sales**					
2						
3	Note: each value is a percentage of what the leading competitor did					
4						
5	Region	Promote	Sales			
6	1	77	85			
7	2	110	103			
8	3	110	102			
9	4	93	109			
10	5	90	85			
11	6	95	103			
12	7	100	110			
13	8	85	86			
14	9	96	92			
15	10	83	87			
53	48	100	98			
54	49	95	108			
55	50	96	87			

FIGURE 15.2
Scatterplot of Sales
versus Promote

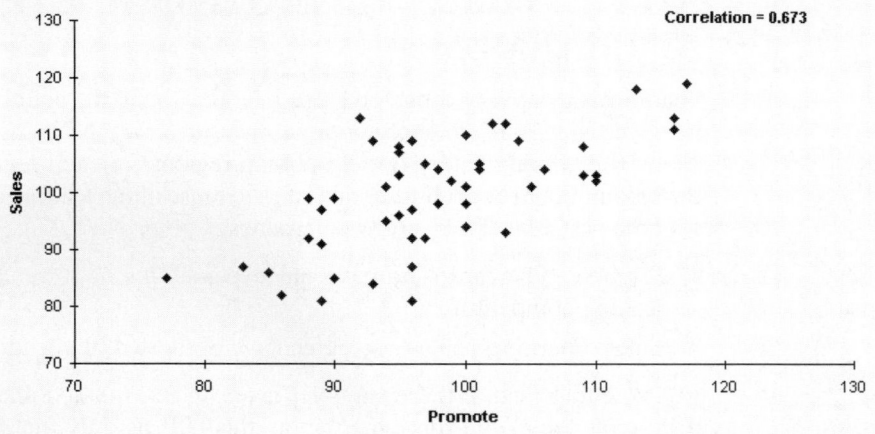

tionship is not perfect. If it were perfect, a given value of Promote would prescribe the value of Sales exactly. Clearly, this is not the case. For example, there are five regions with promotional values of 96 but different sales values. So the scatterplot indicates that while the variable Promote might be helpful for predicting the Sales value, it will not yield perfect predictions.

Note the correlation of 0.673 shown at the top of Figure 15.2. The StatPro add-in inserts this value automatically to indicate the strength of the linear relationship between the two variables. For now, just note that it is positive and its magnitude is moderately large. We will say more about correlations in the next section.

Finally, we say something about causation. There is a tendency for an analyst (such as a drugstore manager) to say that larger promotional expenses *cause* larger sales values. However, unless the data are obtained in a carefully controlled experiment—which is certainly not the case here—we can never make definitive statements about causation in regression analysis. The reason is that we can almost never rule out the possibility that some other variable is causing the variation in *both* of the observed variables. While this might be unlikely in this drugstore example, it is still a possibility. ■

The following example uses time series data to illustrate several other features of scatterplots. We will also follow this example throughout the chapter.

EXAMPLE 15.2

ANALYZING OVERHEAD EXPENSES AT BENDRIX

The Bendrix Company manufactures various types of parts for automobiles. The manager of the factory wants to get a better understanding of overhead costs. These overhead costs include supervision, indirect labor, supplies, payroll taxes, overtime premiums, depreciation, and a number of miscellaneous items such as insurance, utilities, and janitorial and maintenance expenses. Some of these overhead costs are "fixed" in the sense that they do not vary appreciably with the volume of work being done, whereas others are "variable" and do vary directly with the volume of work. The fixed overhead costs tend to come from the supervision, depreciation, and miscellaneous categories, whereas the variable overhead costs tend to come from the indirect labor, supplies, payroll taxes, and overtime premiums categories. However, it is not easy to draw a clear line between the fixed and variable overhead components.

The Bendrix manager has tracked total overhead costs over the past 36 months. To help "explain" these, he has also collected data on two variables that are related to the amount of work done at the factory. These variables are:

- MachHrs: number of machine hours used during the month
- ProdRuns: the number of separate production runs during the month

The first of these is a direct measure of the amount of work being done. To understand the second, we note that Bendrix manufactures parts in fairly large batches. Each batch corresponds to a production run. Once a production run is completed, the factory must "set up" for the next production run. During this setup there is typically some downtime while the machinery is reconfigured for the part type scheduled for production in the next batch. Therefore, the manager believes both of these variables might be responsible (in different ways) for variations in overhead costs. Do scatterplots support this belief?

Solution

The data appear in Figure 15.3. (See the BENDRIX.XLS file.) Each observation (row) corresponds to a single month. We want to investigate any possible relationship between the Overhead variable and the MachHrs and ProdRuns variables, but because these are time series variables, we should also be on the lookout for any relationships

FIGURE 15.3
Data for Bendrix
Overhead Example

	A	B	C	D
1	Monthly data on manufacturing overhead costs			
2				
3	Month	MachHrs	ProdRuns	Overhead
4	1	1539	31	99798
5	2	1284	29	87804
6	3	1490	27	93681
7	4	1355	22	82262
8	5	1500	35	106968
9	6	1777	30	107925
10	7	1716	41	117287
11	8	1045	29	76868
12	9	1364	47	106001
13	1U	1516	21	88738
37	34	1723	35	107828
38	35	1413	30	88032
39	36	1390	54	117943

between these variables and the Month variable. That is, we should investigate any time series behavior in these variables. This data set illustrates, even with a modest number of variables, how the number of potentially useful scatterplots can grow quickly. At the very least, we should examine the scatterplot between each potential explanatory variable (MachHrs and ProdRuns) and the response variable (Overhead). These appear in Figures 15.4 and 15.5. We see that Overhead tends to increase as either MachHrs increases or ProdRuns increases. However, both relationships are far from perfect.

To check for possible time series patterns, we can also create a time series plot for any of the variables. (Actually, this is equivalent to a scatterplot of the variable versus Month, with the points joined by lines.) One of these, the time series plot for Overhead, appears in Figure 15.6. It shows a fairly random pattern through time, with no apparent upward trend or other obvious time series pattern. You can check that time series plots of the MachHrs and ProdRuns variables also indicate no obvious time series patterns.

In summary, the Bendrix manager should continue to explore the positive relationship between Overhead and each of the MachHrs and ProdRuns variables. However, none of the variables appears to have any time series behavior, and the two potential explanatory variables do not appear to be related to each other.

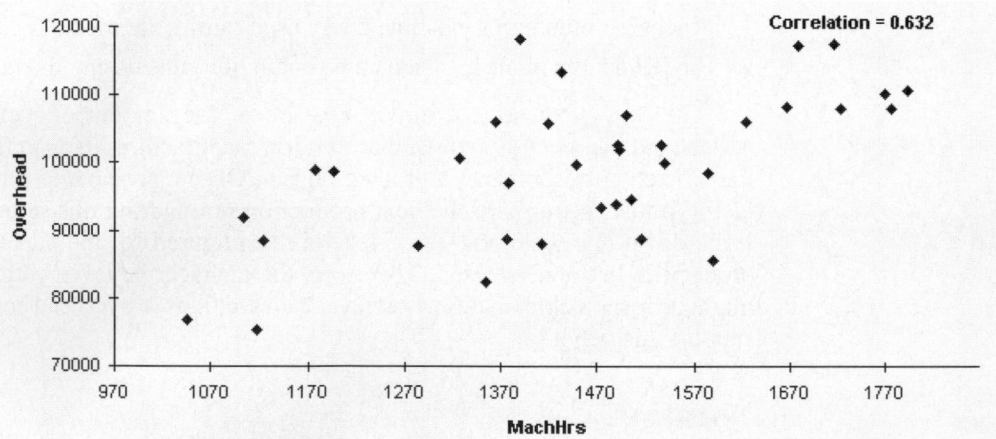

FIGURE 15.4 Scatterplot of Overhead versus Machine Hours

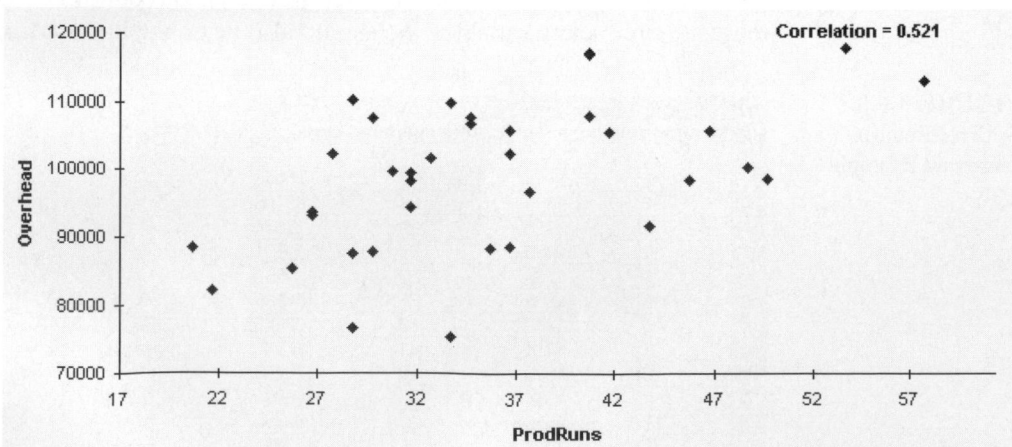

FIGURE 15.5 Scatterplot of Overhead versus Production Runs

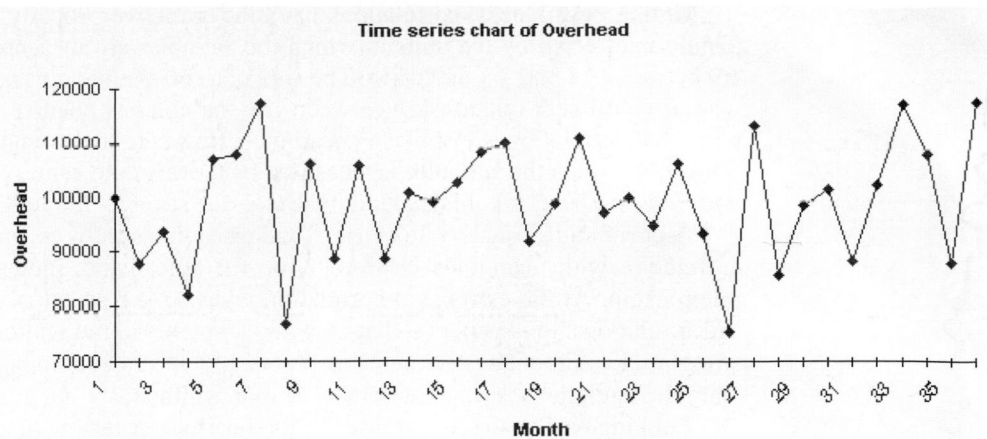

FIGURE 15.6 Time Series Plot of Overhead versus Month ■

Scatterplots are extremely useful for detecting behavior that might not be obvious otherwise. We illustrate some of these in the next few subsections. First, the typical relationship we hope to see is a straight-line, or *linear*, relationship. This does not mean that all points lie on a straight line—this is too much to expect in business data—but that the points tend to cluster around a straight line. The scatterplots in Figures 15.2, 15.4, and 15.5 all exhibit linear relationships, at least in the sense that no curvature is obvious.

15.3 CORRELATIONS: INDICATORS OF LINEAR RELATIONSHIPS

Scatterplots provide graphical indications of relationships, whether they be linear, nonlinear, or essentially nonexistent. Correlations are numerical summary measures that indicate the strength of relationships between pairs of variables. A correlation between a pair of variables is a single number that summarizes the information in a scatterplot. A correlation can be very useful, but it has an important limitation: it can only measure the strength of a *linear* relationship.

The usual notation for a correlation between two variables X and Y is r_{XY}. The subscripts can be omitted if the variables are clear from the context of the problem. The formula for r_{XY} is given below. It requires a considerable amount of computation, so that correlations are almost always computed by software packages.

$$r_{XY} = \frac{\sum(X_i - \overline{X})(Y_i - \overline{Y})/(n-1)}{s_X s_Y} \tag{15.1}$$

The numerator of equation (15.1) is also a measure of association between two variables X and Y. It is called the **covariance** between X and Y. Like a correlation, a covariance is a single number that measures the strength of the linear relationship between two variables. By looking at the sign of the covariance or correlation—plus or minus—we can tell whether the two variables are positively or negatively related. The drawback to a covariance, however, is that its magnitude depends on the units in which the variables are measured, making it difficult to interpret.

Unlike covariances, correlations have the attractive property that they are completely unaffected by the units in which the variables are measured. All correlations are between -1 and $+1$, inclusive. The sign of a correlation, plus or minus, determines whether the linear relationship between two variables is positive or negative. In this respect, a correlation is just like a covariance. However, the strength of the linear relationship between the variables is measured by the absolute value, or magnitude, of the correlation. The closer this magnitude is to 1, the stronger the linear relationship.

A correlation equal to 0 or near 0 indicates practically no linear relationship. A correlation with magnitude close to 1, on the other hand, indicates a strong linear relationship. At the extreme, a correlation equal to -1 or $+1$ occurs only when the linear relationship is perfect—that is, when all points in the scatterplot lie on a single straight line. Although such extremes practically never occur in business applications, "large" correlations, say, greater than 0.9 in magnitude, are not at all uncommon.

Looking back at the scatterplots for the Pharmex drugstore data in Figure 15.2, we see that the correlation between Sales and Promote is positive—as we would guess from the upward-sloping scatter of points—and that it is equal to 0.673. This is a moderately large correlation. It indicates what we see in the scatterplot, namely, that the points vary considerably around any particular straight line. Similarly, the scatterplots for the Bendrix manufacturing data in Figures 15.4 and 15.5 indicate moderately large positive correlations, 0.632 and 0.521, between Overhead and MachHrs and between Overhead and ProdRuns.

An obvious question is whether a given correlation is "large." This is a difficult question to answer directly. Clearly, a correlation such as 0.992 is quite large—the points tend to cluster very closely around a straight line. Similarly, a correlation of 0.034 is quite small—the points tend to be a shapeless swarm. But there is a continuum of in-between values, as exhibited in Figures 15.2, 15.4, and 15.5. We will give a more definite answer to this question when we examine the *square* of the correlation later in this chapter.

As for calculating correlations, there are two possibilities in Excel. To calculate a *single* correlation r_{XY} between variables X and Y, we can use Excel's CORREL function in the form

$$=\text{CORREL}(X\text{-range}, Y\text{-range})$$

Alternatively, we can use StatPro to obtain a whole table of correlations between a set of variables.

Finally, we reiterate the important limitation of correlations (and covariances), namely, that they apply only to *linear* relationships. If a correlation is close to 0, we cannot automatically conclude that there is no relationship between the two variables. We should look at a scatterplot first. The chances are that the points are a shapeless swarm and that no relationship exists. But it is also possible that the points cluster around some curve. In this case the correlation is misleading, and the nonlinear shape should be analyzed further.

15.4 SIMPLE LINEAR REGRESSION

In this section we will see how to quantify relationships when there is a *single* explanatory variable. We do so by fitting a straight line through the scatterplot of the response variable Y versus the explanatory variable X.

Least Squares Estimation

The scatterplot between Sales and Promote, repeated in Figure 15.7, hints at a linear relationship between these two variables. What straight line provides the best "fit" to these data? Consider the magnified graph in Figure 15.8. Here we show several points in the scatterplot, along with a line drawn through them. Note that the vertical distance from the horizontal axis to any point, which is just the value of Sales for that point, can be decomposed into two parts: the vertical distance from the horizontal axis to the line, and the vertical distance from the line to the point. The first of these is called the **fitted value**, and the second is called the **residual**. The idea is very simple. By using a straight line to estimate the relationship between Sales and Promote, we expect a given Sales to be at the height of the line above any particular value of Promote—that is, we expect Sales to equal the fitted value.

But the relationship is not perfect. Not all (perhaps not any) of the points lie exactly on the line. The differences are the residuals. They show how much the observed values differ from the fitted values. If a particular residual is positive, the corresponding point is above the line; if it is negative, the point is below the line. The only time a residual is zero is when the point lies directly on the line. The relationship between observed values, fitted values, and residuals is very general and is stated below.

$$\text{Observed value} = \text{Fitted value} + \text{Residual}$$

We can now explain how to choose the "best-fitting" line through the points in the scatterplot. We choose the one with the *smallest sum of squared residuals*. The resulting line is called the **least squares line**. Why do we use the sum of *squared*

FIGURE 15.7
Scatterplot with Possible Linear Fit Superimposed

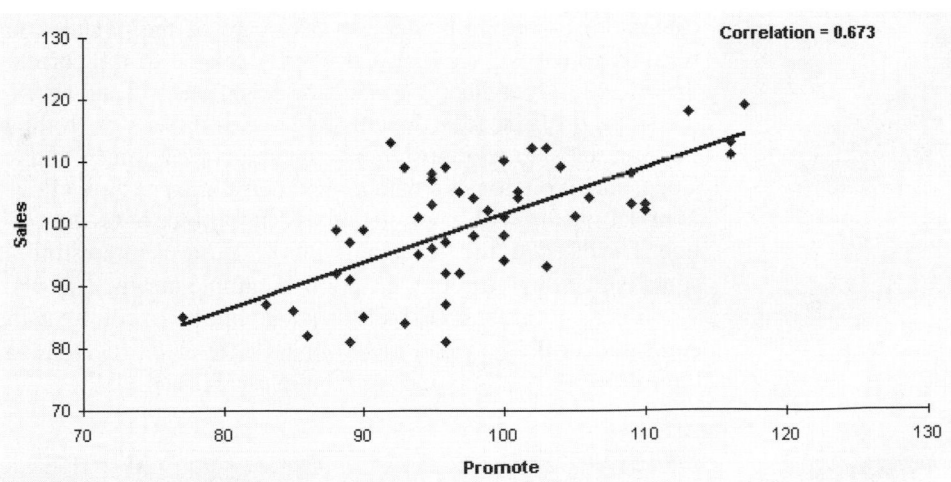

FIGURE 15.8
Fitted Values and Residuals

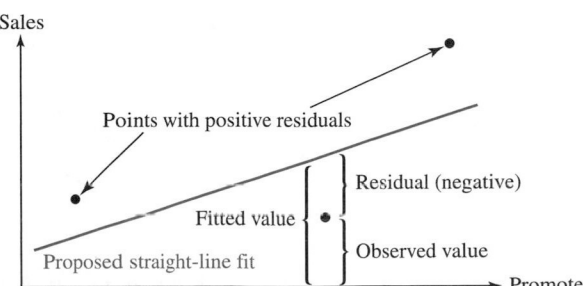

residuals? Why not minimize some other measure of the residuals? First, we do not simply minimize the sum of the residuals because the positive residuals would cancel the negative residuals. In fact, the least squares line has the property that the sum of the residuals is always exactly zero. To adjust for this, we could minimize the sum of the *absolute values* of the residuals, and this is a perfectly reasonable procedure. (It can be done with Solver.) However, for technical reasons it is not the procedure usually chosen. We settle on the sum of squared residuals because this method is deeply rooted in statistical tradition, and it works well.

The minimization problem itself is a calculus problem that we will not discuss here. Virtually all statistical software packages perform this minimization automatically, so we need not be concerned with the technical details. However, we will provide the formulas for the least squares line.

Recall from basic algebra that the equation for any straight line can be written as

$$Y = a + bX$$

Here, a is the Y-intercept of the line, the value of Y when $X = 0$, and b is the slope of the line, the change in Y when X increases by one unit. Therefore, to specify the least squares line, all we need to specify are the slope and intercept. These are given by

$$b = \frac{\sum(X_i - \overline{X})(Y_i - \overline{Y})}{\sum(X_i - \overline{X})^2} = r_{XY}\frac{s_X}{s_Y}$$

and

$$a = \overline{Y} - b\overline{X}$$

We have presented these formulas primarily for conceptual purposes, not for hand calculations—the computer can take care of the calculations. From the right-hand formula for b, we see that it is closely related to the correlation between X and Y. Specifically, if we keep the standard deviations, s_X and s_Y, of X and Y constant, then the slope b of the least squares line varies directly with the correlation between the two variables. A relationship with a large correlation (negative or positive) has a steep slope, and a relationship with a small correlation has a shallow slope. At the extreme, a nonrelationship with a correlation of 0 has a slope of 0—that is, it results in a horizontal line. The effect of the formula for a is not quite as interesting. It simply forces the least squares line to go through the point of sample means, $(\overline{X}, \overline{Y})$.

It is easy to obtain the least squares line in Excel, by using either Excel's built-in Analysis ToolPak or StatPro's Simple Regression procedure. We illustrate the latter in the following continuations of Examples 15.1 and 15.2.

EXAMPLE 15.1 (CONTINUED)

SALES VERSUS PROMOTIONAL EXPENDITURES AT PHARMEX

Find the least squares line for the Pharmex drugstore data, using Sales as the response variable and Promote as the explanatory variable.

Solution

We use the StatPro/Regression Analysis/Simple menu item. After specifying that Sales is the response (dependent) variable and that Promote is the explanatory (independent) variable, we see the dialog box in Figure 15.9. This gives us the option of creating several scatterplots involving the fitted values and residuals. We suggest checking the second option, as shown.

The regression output includes three parts. The first two are a list of fitted values and residuals, placed in columns next to the data set, and any scatterplots selected from the dialog box in Figure 15.9. The third part of the output is the most important. It appears in Figure 15.10.

FIGURE 15.9
Dialog Box for
Scatterplot Options
in Simple Regression
Procedure

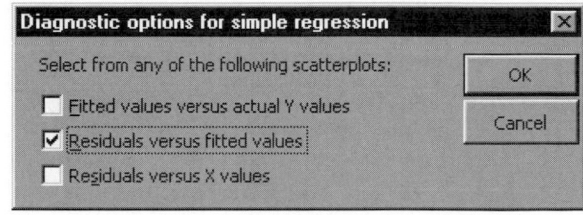

FIGURE 15.10
Regression Output
for Drugstore
Example

	A	B	C	D	E	F	G	H
1	Results of simple regression for Sales							
2								
3	Summary measures							
4		Multiple R	0.6730					
5		R-Square	0.4529					
6		StErr of Est	7.3947					
7								
8	ANOVA table							
9		Source	df	SS	MS	F	p-value	
10		Explained	1	2172.8804	2172.8804	39.7366	0.0000	
11		Unexplained	48	2624.7396	54.6821			
12								
13	Regression coefficients							
14			Coefficient	Std Err	t-value	p-value	Lower limit	Upper limit
15		Constant	25.1264	11.8826	2.1146	0.0397	1.2349	49.0179
16		Promote	0.7623	0.1209	6.3037	0.0000	0.5192	1.0054

We will eventually learn what most of the output in Figure 15.10 means, but for now, we will concentrate on only a small part of it. Specifically, we find the intercept and slope of the least squares line under the Coefficient label in cells C15 and C16. They imply that the equation for the least squares line is[3]

$$\text{Predicted Sales} = 25.1264 + 0.7623\,\text{Promote}$$

We can interpret this equation as follows. The slope, 0.7623, indicates that the sales index tends to increase by about 0.76 for each unit increase in the promotional expenses index. Alternatively, if we compare two regions, where region 2 spends one unit higher than region 1, we predict the sales index for region 2 to be 0.76 larger than the sales index for region 1. The interpretation of the intercept is less important. It is literally the predicted sales index for a region that does no promotions. However, no region in the sample has anywhere near a zero promotional value. Therefore, in a situation like this, where the range of observed explanatory variable values does not include 0, it is best to think of the intercept term as an "anchor" for the least squares line that allows us to predict Y values for the range of *observed* X values.

[3]We will always report the left side of the estimated regression equation as the *predicted* value of the response variable. It is not the *actual* value of the response variable because the observations do not all lie on the estimated regression line.

A useful graph in almost any regression analysis is a scatterplot of residuals (on the vertical axis) versus fitted values. This scatterplot for the Pharmex data appears in Figure 15.11. We typically examine such a scatterplot for any striking patterns. A "good" fit not only has small residuals, but it has residuals scattered *randomly* around 0 with no apparent pattern. This appears to be the case for the Pharmex data.

FIGURE 15.11
Scatterplot of
Residuals versus
Fitted Values in
Pharmex Example

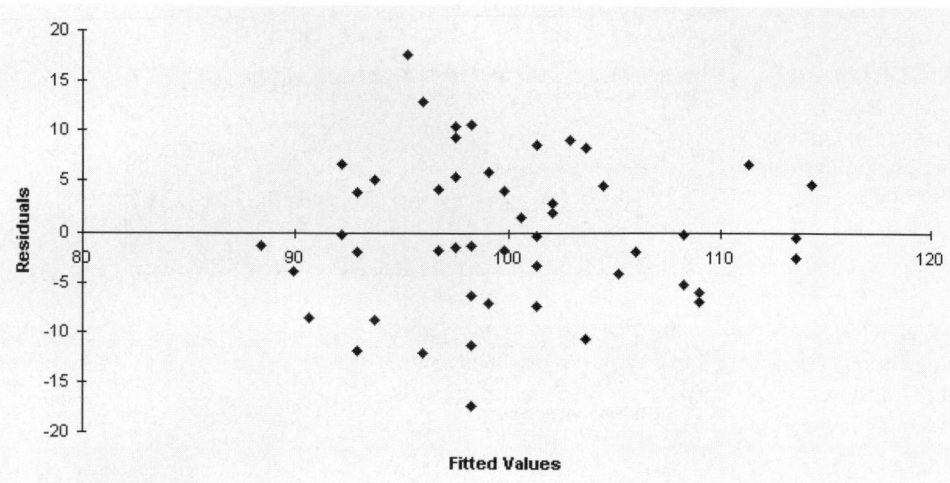

EXAMPLE 15.2 (CONTINUED)

ANALYZING OVERHEAD EXPENSES AT BENDRIX

The Bendrix manufacturing data set has two potential explanatory variables, MachHrs and ProdRuns. Eventually, we will estimate a regression equation with *both* of these variables included. However, if we include only one at a time, what do they tell us about overhead costs?

Solution

The regression output for Overhead with MachHrs as the single explanatory variable appears in Figure 15.12. The output when ProdRuns is the only explanatory variable appears in Figure 15.13. The two least squares lines are therefore

$$\text{Predicted Overhead} = 48,621 + 34.7\text{MachHrs} \qquad (15.2)$$

and

$$\text{Predicted Overhead} = 75,606 + 655.1\text{ProdRuns} \qquad (15.3)$$

Clearly, these two equations are quite different, although each effectively breaks overhead into a fixed component and a variable component. Equation (15.2) implies that the fixed component of overhead is about $48,621. Bendrix can expect to incur this amount even if zero machine hours are used. The variable component is the 34.7MachHrs term. It implies that the expected overhead increases by about $35 for each extra machine hour. Equation 15.13, on the other hand, breaks overhead into a fixed component of $75,606 and a variable component of about $655 per each production run.

	A	B	C	D	E	F	G	H
1	*Results of multiple regression for Overhead*							
2								
3	*Summary measures*							
4		Multiple R	0.6319					
5		R-Square	0.3993					
6		Adj R-Square	0.3816					
7		StErr of Est	8584.7393					
8								
9	*ANOVA Table*							
10		Source	df	SS	MS	F	p-value	
11		Explained	1	1665463468.0000	1665463468.0000	22.5986	0.0000	
12		Unexplained	34	2505723392.0000	73697746.8235			
13								
14	*Regression coefficients*							
15			Coefficient	Std Err	t-value	p-value	Lower limit	Upper limit
16		Constant	48621.3555	10725.3330	4.5333	0.0001	26824.8707	70417.8403
17		MachHrs	34.7022	7.2999	4.7538	0.0000	19.8671	49.5374

FIGURE 15.12 Regression Output for Overhead versus MachHrs

	A	B	C	D	E	F	G	H
1	*Results of multiple regression for Overhead*							
2								
3	*Summary measures*							
4		Multiple R	0.5205					
5		R-Square	0.2710					
6		Adj R-Square	0.2495					
7		StErr of Est	9457.2393					
8								
9	*ANOVA Table*							
10		Source	df	SS	MS	F	p-value	
11		Explained	1	1130248108.0000	1130248108.0000	12.6370	0.0011	
12		Unexplained	34	3040938752.0000	89439375.0588			
13								
14	*Regression coefficients*							
15			Coefficient	Std Err	t-value	p-value	Lower limit	Upper limit
16		Constant	75605.5156	6808.6104	11.1044	0.0000	61768.7637	89442.2675
17		ProdRuns	655.0707	184.2747	3.5549	0.0011	280.5797	1029.5616

FIGURE 15.13 Regression Output for Overhead versus ProdRuns

The difference between these two equations can be attributed to the fact that neither tells the whole story. If the manager's goal is to split overhead into a fixed component and a variable component, then the variable component should include *both* of the measures of work activity (and maybe even others) to give a more complete explanation of overhead. We will see how to do this when we reanalyze this example with multiple regression. ∎

Standard Error of Estimate

The magnitudes of the residuals provide a good indication of how useful the regression line is for predicting Y values from X values. However, because there are numerous residuals, it is useful to summarize them with a single numerical measure. This measure, called the **standard error of estimate** and denoted s_e, is essentially the standard deviation of the residuals. If e_i is a typical error, then s_e is given by

$$s_e = \sqrt{\frac{\sum e_i^2}{n-2}} \tag{15.4}$$

The usual rules of thumb for standard deviations can be applied to the standard error of estimate. For example, we expect about 2/3 of the residuals to be within one standard error of their mean (which is 0). Stated another way, we expect about 2/3 of the observed Y values to be within one standard error of the corresponding fitted values (usually denoted by $\widehat{Y}$). Similarly, we expect about 95% of the observed Y values to be within two standard errors of the corresponding fitted $\widehat{Y}$ values.[4]

The standard error for the Pharmex data appears in cell C6 of Figure 15.10. Its value, approximately 7.39, indicates the typical error we are likely to make when we use the fitted value (based on the regression line) to predict sales from promotional expenses. More specifically, if we use the regression equation to predict sales for many regions, based on the promotional expenses in each region, then about 2/3 of the predictions will be within 7.39 of the actual sales values, and about 95% of the predictions will be within two standard errors, or 14.78, of the actual sales values.

We can often use the standard error of estimate to judge which of several potential regression equations is the most useful. In the Bendrix manufacturing example we estimated two regression lines, one using MachHrs and one using ProdRuns. From Figures 15.12 and 15.13, their standard errors are approximately $8585 and $9457. These imply that MachHrs is a slightly better predictor of overhead. The predictions based on MachHrs will tend to be slightly more accurate than those based on ProdRuns. Of course, we might guess that predictions based on *both* predictors will yield even more accurate predictions, and this is definitely the case, as we will see when we discuss multiple regression.

R-Square: The Coefficient of Determination

We now discuss another important measure of the goodness of fit of the least squares line. This is called the **coefficient of determination**, or simply R^2. Along with the standard error of estimate s_e, it is the most frequently quoted measure in applied regression analysis. Its value is always between 0 and 1, and it can be interpreted as the *percentage of variation of the response variable explained by the regression line.*

The R^2 measure is based on this idea. Its formula is

$$R^2 = 1 - \frac{\sum e_i^2}{\sum (Y_i - \overline{Y})^2} \qquad (15.5)$$

Equation (15.5) indicates that when the residuals are small, then R^2 will be close to 1, but when they are large, R^2 will be close to 0.

We see from cell C5 of Figure 15.10 that the R^2 measure for the Pharmex drugstore data is 0.453. In words, the single explanatory variable Promote is able to explain only 45.3% of the variation in the Sales variable. This is not particularly good. There is still 54.7% of the variation left unexplained. Of course, we would like R^2 to be as close to 1 as possible. Usually, the only way to increase it is to use better and/or more explanatory variables.

Analysts often compare equations on the basis of their R^2 values. We see from Figures 15.12 and 15.13 that the R^2 values using MachHrs and ProdRuns as single explanatory variables for the Bendrix overhead data are 39.9% and 27.1%. These provide one more piece of evidence that MachHrs is a slightly better predictor of Overhead than ProdRuns. Of course, they also suggest that the percentage of variation

---

[4]This requires that the residuals be at least approximately normally distributed, a requirement we will discuss more fully later in this chapter.

of Overhead explained could be increased by including *both* variables in a single equation. This is true, as we will see shortly.

There is a good reason for the notation R^2. It turns out that R^2 is the square of the correlation between the observed Y values and the fitted $\widehat{Y}$ values. This correlation appears in all regression outputs. For the Pharmex data it is 0.673, as seen in cell C4 of Figure 15.10. Aside from rounding error, the square of 0.673 is 0.453, the R^2 value right below it. In the case of simple linear regression, when there is only a single explanatory variable in the equation, the correlation between the Y variable and the fitted $\widehat{Y}$ values is the same as the absolute value of the correlation between the Y variable and the explanatory X variable. For the Pharmex data, we already saw that the correlation between Sales and Promote is indeed 0.673.

PROBLEMS

Skill-Building Problems

1. Management of a home appliance store in Charlotte would like to understand the growth pattern of the monthly sales of VCR units over the past two years. The managers have recorded the relevant data in the file P15_1.XLS. Have the sales of VCR units been growing linearly over the past 24 months? Using simple linear regression, explain why or why not.

2. Do the sales prices of houses in a given community vary systematically with their sizes (as measured in square feet)? Attempt to answer this question by estimating a simple regression model where the sales price of the house is the response variable and the size of the house is the explanatory variable. Use the sample data given in P15_2.XLS. Interpret your estimated model and the associated coefficient of determination R^2.

3. The file P15_3.XLS contains observations of the American minimum wage during each of the years from 1950 through 1994. Has the minimum wage

been growing at roughly a *constant* rate over this period? Use simple linear regression analysis to address this question. Explain your results.

4. Based on the data in the file P15_4.XLS from the U.S. Department of Agriculture, explore the relationship between the number of farms (X) and the average size of a farm (Y) in the United States between 1950 and 1997. Specifically, generate a simple linear regression model and interpret it.

5. The management of Beta Technologies, Inc., is trying to determine the variable that best explains the variation of employee salaries using a sample of 52 full-time employees in the file P15_5.XLS. Estimate simple linear regression models to identify which of the following has the *strongest* linear relationship with annual salary: the employee's gender, age, number of years of relevant work experience prior to employment at Beta, number of years of employment at Beta, or number of years of post-secondary education. Provide support for your conclusion.

15.5 MULTIPLE REGRESSION

In general, there are two possible approaches to obtaining improved fits. The first is to examine a scatterplot of residuals for nonlinear patterns and then make appropriate modifications to the regression equation. We will discuss this approach later in this chapter. The second approach is much more straightforward—we simply add more explanatory variables to the regression equation. In the Bendrix manufacturing example we deliberately included only a single explanatory variable in the equation at a time so that we could keep the equations simple. But because scatterplots indicate that both explanatory variables are also related to Overhead, we ought to try including both in the regression equation. With any luck, the linear fit should improve.

When several explanatory variables are included in the equation, we move into the realm of multiple regression, so there are a few new ideas. First, assuming there are only two explanatory variables, the line we are fitting to the data is really a *plane* in three-dimensional space. There is one dimension for the response variable and one for each explanatory variable. Although we can imagine a flat plane passing through a swarm of points, it is difficult to graph this on a two-dimensional screen. If there are more than two explanatory variables, then we can only imagine the regression plane; drawing in four dimensions (or higher dimensions) is impossible. Nevertheless, it is still possible to find the least squares regression equation numerically. It is still the equation that minimizes the sum of squared residuals, and it is calculated by most statistical packages, including StatPro.

If Y is the response variable and X_1 through X_k are the explanatory variables, then a typical multiple regression equation has the form

$$Y = a + b_1 X_1 + b_2 X_2 + \cdots + b_k X_k \qquad \textbf{(15.6)}$$

Here, a is again the Y-intercept, and b_1 through b_k are the slopes. Collectively, we refer to a and the b's in equation (15.6) as the **regression coefficients**. The intercept a is the expected value of Y when all of the X's equal 0. Of course, this makes sense only if it is practical for all of the X's to equal 0. Each slope coefficient is the expected change in Y when this particular X increases by one unit and the other X's in the equation remain constant. For example, b_1 is the expected change in Y when X_1 increases by one unit and the other X's in the equation, X_2 through X_k, remain constant.

This extra proviso, "when the other X's in the equation remain constant," is very important for the interpretation of the regression coefficients. In particular, it means that the estimates of the b's depend on which other X's are included in the regression equation. We illustrate these ideas in the following continuation of the Bendrix manufacturing example.

EXAMPLE 15.2 (CONTINUED)

ANALYZING OVERHEAD EXPENSES AT BENDRIX

Estimate the regression equation and interpret the regression output for Overhead when both explanatory variables, MachHrs and ProdRuns, are included in the regression equation.

Solution

Unlike the situation with simple regression, we do not even attempt to provide formulas for the regression coefficients in multiple regression. These require matrix algebra and are best left for a more technical course. Instead, we rely on computer software such as the StatPro add-in. To obtain the output, we use the StatPro/Regression Analysis/Multiple menu item, select Overhead as the response (dependent) variable, and select MachHrs and ProdRuns as the explanatory (independent) variables. The dialog box shown in Figure 15.14 then gives us options of which scatterplots to obtain and whether we want columns of fitted values and residuals placed next to the data set. We filled it in as shown in the figure, selecting scatterplots of the fitted values versus the observed values and residuals versus fitted values, and requesting columns of fitted values and residuals.

The main regression output appears in Figure 15.15. The coefficients in the range C16:C18 indicate that the estimated regression equation is

$$\text{Predicted Overhead} = 3997 + 43.54\text{MachHrs} + 883.62\text{ProdRuns} \qquad \textbf{(15.7)}$$

FIGURE 15.14
Dialog Box of
Options with
Multiple Regression
Procedure

Diagnostic options for regression   ? ✕

You can select from any of the following scatterplots: [OK]

☑ Fitted values versus actual Y values   [Cancel]

☐ Fitted values versus X values (one plot for each X)

☑ Residuals versus fitted values

☐ Residuals versus X values (one plot for each X)

Note: If you select the following option, two new variables will be appended to your data set.

☑ Columns of fitted values and residuals

The interpretation of equation (15.7) is that if the number of production runs is held constant, then the overhead cost is expected to increase by \$43.54 for each extra machine hour, and if the number of machine hours is held constant, the overhead cost is expected to increase by \$883.62 for each extra production run. The Bendrix manager can interpret the intercept, \$3997, as the fixed component of overhead. The slope terms involving MachHrs and ProdRuns are the variable components of overhead.

It is interesting to compare equation (15.7) with the separate equations for Overhead involving only a single variable each. From the previous section these are

$$\text{Predicted Overhead} = 48{,}621 + 34.7\text{MachHrs}$$

and

$$\text{Predicted Overhead} = 75{,}606 + 655.1\text{ProdRuns}$$

Note that the coefficient of MachHrs has increased from 34.7 to 43.5 and the coefficient of ProdRuns has increased from 655.1 to 883.6. Also, the intercept is now lower than either intercept in the single-variable equations. In general, it is difficult to guess the changes that will occur when we introduce more explanatory variables into the equation, but it is likely that changes will occur.

The reasoning is that when MachHrs is the only variable in the equation, we are obviously *not* holding ProdRuns constant—we are ignoring it—so in effect the coefficient 34.7 of MachHrs indicates the effect of MachHrs *and* the omitted ProdRuns on

	A	B	C	D	E	F	G	H
1	*Results of multiple regression for Overhead*							
2								
3	*Summary measures*							
4		Multiple R	0.9308					
5		R-Square	0.8664					
6		Adj R-Square	0.8583					
7		StErr of Est	4108.9932					
8								
9	*ANOVA Table*							
10		Source	df	SS	MS	F	p-value	
11		Explained	2	3614020652.0000	1807010326.0000	107.0261	0.0000	
12		Unexplained	33	557166208.0000	16883824.4848			
13								
14	*Regression coefficients*							
15			Coefficient	Std Err	t-value	p-value	Lower limit	Upper limit
16		Constant	3996.6782	6603.6509	0.6052	0.5492	-9438.5612	17431.9176
17		MachHrs	43.5364	3.5895	12.1289	0.0000	36.2335	50.8393
18		ProdRuns	883.6179	82.2514	10.7429	0.0000	716.2760	1050.9598

FIGURE 15.15 Multiple Regression Output for Bendrix Example

Overhead. But when we include both variables, then the coefficient 43.5 of MachHrs indicates the effect of MachHrs only, holding ProdRuns constant. Because the coefficients of MachHrs in the two equations have different *meanings*, it is not surprising that we obtain different numerical estimates of them.

The multiple regression output in Figure 15.15 is very similar to simple regression output.[5] In particular, cells C5 and C7 again show R^2 and the standard error of estimate s_e. Also, the square root of R^2 appears in cell C4. We interpret these quantities almost exactly as in simple regression. The standard error of estimate is a measure of the prediction error we are likely to make when we use the multiple regression equation to predict the response variable. In this example about 2/3 of the predictions should be within one standard error, or $4109, of the actual overhead cost. By comparing this with the standard errors from the single-variable equations for Overhead, $8585 and $9457, we see that the multiple regression equation is likely to provide predictions that are more than twice as accurate as the single-variable equations—quite an improvement!

The R^2 value is again the percentage of variation of the response variable explained by the combined set of explanatory variables. For the Bendrix data we see that MachHrs and ProdRuns combine to explain 86.6% of the variation in Overhead. This is a big improvement over the single-variable equations that were able to explain only 39.9% and 27.1% of the variation in Overhead. Remarkably, the combination of the two explanatory variables explains a larger percentage than the *sum* of their individual effects. This is not common, but as this example shows, it is possible.[6]

Although the R^2 value is one of the most frequently quoted values from a regression analysis, it does have one serious drawback—it can only *increase* when extra explanatory variables are added to an equation. This can lead to "fishing expeditions," where we keep adding variables to an equation, some of which have no conceptual relationship to the response variable, just to inflate the R^2 value. To "penalize" the addition of extra variables that do not really belong, an **adjusted** R^2 value is typically listed in regression outputs. This adjusted value appears in cell C6 of Figure 15.15. Although it has no direct interpretation as "percentage of variation explained," it *can* decrease when extra explanatory variables that do not really belong are added to an equation. Therefore, it is a useful index that we can monitor. If we add variables and the adjusted R^2 *decreases*, then the extra variables are essentially not pulling their weight and should probably be omitted. ■

PROBLEMS

Skill-Building Problems

6. A trucking company wants to predict the yearly maintenance expense (Y) for a truck using the number of miles driven during the year (X_1) and the age of the truck (X_2, in years) at the beginning of the year. The company has gathered the data given in the file P15_6.XLS. Note that each observation corresponds to a particular truck. Estimate a multiple regression model using the given data. Interpret each of the estimated regression coefficients. Also, interpret the standard error of estimate s_e and the coefficient of determination R^2 for these data.

---

[5]One difference, however, is that the StatPro multiple regression output is not linked to the data by formulas. If the data change, you must rerun the Multiple Regression procedure to update the output.

[6]It is so uncommon, in fact, that neither of the authors realized that it could occur. However, we checked our figures—there are no errors in the calculations!

7. An antique collector believes that the price received for a particular item increases with its age and with the number of bidders. The file P15_7.XLS contains data on these three variables for 32 recently auctioned comparable items. Estimate a multiple regression model using the given data. Interpret each of the estimated regression coefficients. Is the antique collector correct in believing that the price received for the item increases with its age and with the number of bidders? Interpret the standard error of estimate s_e and the coefficient of determination R^2.

8. Stock market analysts are continually looking for reliable predictors of stock prices. Consider the problem of modeling the price per share of electric utility stocks (Y). Two variables thought to influence this stock price are return on average equity (X_1) and annual dividend rate (X_2). The stock price, returns on equity, and dividend rates on a randomly selected day for 16 electric utility stocks are provided in P15_8.XLS. Estimate a multiple regression model using the given data. Interpret each of the estimated regression coefficients. Also, interpret the standard error of estimate s_e, the coefficient of determination R^2, and the adjusted R^2.

9. The manager of a commuter rail transportation system was recently asked by her governing board to determine which factors have a significant impact on the demand for rides in the large city served by the transportation network.. The system manager has collected data on variables thought to be possibly related to the number of weekly riders on the city's rail system. The file P15_9.XLS contain these data.
   a. What are the expected signs of the coefficients of the explanatory variables in this multiple regression model. Provide reasoning for each of your stated expectations. (Answer this *before* using regression.)
   b. Estimate a multiple regression model using the given data. Interpret each of the estimated regression coefficients. Are the signs of the estimated coefficients consistent with your expectations as stated in part **a**?
   c. What proportion of the total variation in the number of weekly riders is *not* explained by this estimated multiple regression model?

10. Consider the enrollment data for *Business Week*'s top 50 U.S. graduate business programs in the file P15_10.XLS. Use these data to estimate a multiple regression model to assess whether there is a systematic relationship between the total number of full-time students and the following explanatory variables: the proportion of female students, the proportion of minority students, and the proportion of international students enrolled at these distinguished business schools.

   a. Interpret the coefficients of your estimated regression model. Do any of these results surprise you? Explain.
   b. How well does your estimated regression model fit the given data?

11. David Savageau and Geoffrey Loftus, the authors of *Places Rated Almanac* (published in 1997 by Macmillan) have ranked 325 metropolitan areas in the United States with consideration of the following aspects of life in each area: cost of living, transportation, jobs, education, climate, crime, arts, health, and recreation. The data are in the file P15_11.XLS.
   a. Use multiple regression analysis to explore the relationship between the metropolitan area's overall score and the set of potential explanatory variables.
   b. Interpret each of the estimated coefficients in the regression model. Are the signs of the estimated coefficients consistent with your expectations? If not, can you explain any discrepancies between your findings and expectations?
   c. Does the given set of explanatory variables do a good job of explaining changes in the overall score? Explain why or why not.

Skill-Extending Problems

12. The owner of a restaurant in Bloomington, Indiana, has recorded sales data for the past 19 years. He has also recorded data on potentially relevant variables. The data are listed in the file P15_12.XLS.
   a. Estimate a simple linear regression model involving annual sales (the explanatory variable) and the size of the population residing within 10 miles of the restaurant (the explanatory variable). Interpret R^2.
   b. Add another explanatory variable—annual advertising expenditures—to the regression model in part **a**. Estimate and interpret this expanded model. How does the R^2 value for this multiple regression model compare to that of the simple regression model estimated in part **a**? Explain any difference between the two R^2 values. Compute and interpret the *adjusted R^2* value for the revised model.
   c. Add one more explanatory variable to the multiple regression model estimated in part **b**. In particular, estimate and interpret the coefficients of a multiple regression model that includes the *previous* year's advertising expenditure. How does the inclusion of this third explanatory variable affect the R^2 and adjusted R^2 values, in comparison to the corresponding values for the model of part **b**? Explain any changes in these values.

13. A regional express delivery service company recently conducted a study to investigate the relationship between the cost of shipping a package (Y), the package weight (X_1), and the distance shipped (X_2). Twenty packages were randomly selected from among the large number received for shipment, and a detailed analysis of the shipping cost was conducted for each package. These sample observations are given in the file P15_13.XLS.

a. Estimate a simple linear regression model involving shipping cost and package weight. Interpret the slope coefficient of the least squares line as well as the value of R^2.

b. Add another explanatory variable—distance shipped—to the regression model in part **a**. Estimate and interpret this expanded model. How does the R^2 value for this multiple regression model compare to that of the simple regression model estimated in part **a**? Explain any difference between the two R^2 values. Compute and interpret the *adjusted* R^2 value for the revised model.

15.6 THE STATISTICAL MODEL

To this point, we have been "line fitting." That is, we have simply been finding the best-fitting line to a set of points. We now turn to statistical inference. We must first make several assumptions about the population. Throughout the analysis these assumptions remain *assumptions*, not facts. They represent an idealization of reality, and as such, they are never likely to be entirely satisfied for the population in any real study. From a practical point of view, all we can ask is that they represent a close approximation to reality. If this is the case, then the analysis is valid. But if the assumptions are grossly violated, we should be very suspicious of the statistical inferences that are based on these assumptions. Although we can never be entirely certain of the validity of the assumptions, there are ways to check for gross violations, and we will discuss some of these.

Regression Assumptions

1. There is a population regression line with intercept α and slopes β_1 through β_k (where k is the number of explanatory variables). This line joins the means of the response variable for all values of the explanatory variables. For any fixed values of the explanatory variables, the mean of the errors is 0.

2. For any values of the explanatory variables, the standard deviation of the response variable is a constant, the same for all such values.

3. For any values of the explanatory variables, the response variable is normally distributed.

4. The errors are probabilistically independent.

Because these assumptions are so crucial to the analysis that follows, it is important to understand exactly what they mean. Assumption 1 is probably the most important. It implies that for some set of explanatory variables, there is an exact linear relationship in the population between the *means* of the response variable and the values of the explanatory variables. The actual observations are scattered around this line so that the average of the vertical distances from the line is 0.

Assumption 2 concerns variation around the population regression line. Specifically, it states that the variation of the Y's about the regression line is the *same*, regardless of the values of the X's. A technical term for this property is **homoscedasticity**. We prefer a simpler term: **constant error variance**. In the Pharmex example, constant error variance implies that the variation in Sales values is the same regardless of the value of Promote. In the Bendrix example, constant error variance implies that overhead costs vary just as much for small values of MachHrs and ProdRuns as for large values—or any values in between.

There are many applications in which assumption 2 is questionable. The variation in Y often increases as X increases—a violation of assumption 2. We might see this in a scatterplot of AmountSpent (on some consumer products) versus Salary for a sample of a company's customers, as in Figure 15.16. Customers with small salaries have little disposable income, so they all tend to spend small amounts for consumer items. Customers with large salaries have more disposable income. Some of them spend a lot of it on consumer items and some spend only a little of it—hence a larger variation. Scatterplots with this "fan" shape are not at all uncommon in real studies, and they exhibit a clear violation of assumption 2. We say that the data in this graph exhibit **heteroscedasticity**, or more simply, **nonconstant error variance**.

Assumption 3 states that the errors are normally distributed. We can check this by forming a histogram of the residuals. If assumption 3 holds, then the histogram should be approximately symmetric and bell-shaped. But if there is an obvious skewness, too many residuals more than, say, two standard deviations from the mean, or some other nonnormal property, then this indicates a violation of assumption 3.

Finally, assumption 4 requires probabilistic independence of the errors. Intuitively, this assumption means that information on some of the errors provides no information on other errors. For example, if we are told that the overhead costs for months 1–4 are all above the regression line (positive residuals), we cannot infer anything about the residual for month 5 if assumption 4 holds.

For cross-sectional data there is generally little reason to doubt the validity of assumption 4 unless the observations are ordered in some particular way. For cross-sectional data we generally take assumption 4 for granted. However, for time series data assumption 4 is often violated. This is because of a property called **autocorrelation**. For now, we simply mention that one output given automatically in most regression packages is the **Durbin–Watson statistic**. The Durbin–Watson statistic is one measure of autocorrelation and thus it measures the extent to which assumption 4 is violated. We can usually ignore it in cross-sectional studies, but it is important for time series data.

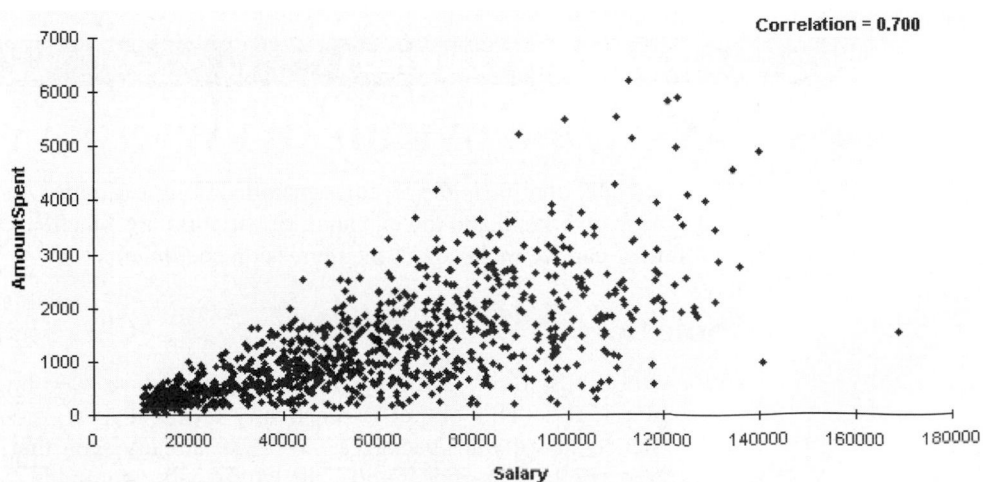

FIGURE 15.16 Scatterplot with Nonconstant Error Variance

15.7 INFERENCES ABOUT THE REGRESSION COEFFICIENTS

Deciding which explanatory variables to include in a regression equation is probably the most difficult part of any applied regression analysis. Available data sets frequently offer an overabundance of potential explanatory variables. In addition, it is possible and often useful to create new variables from original variables, such as their squares or logarithms. So where do we stop? One overriding principle is **parsimony**—explaining the most with the least. For example, if we can explain a response variable nearly as well with two explanatory variables as with ten explanatory variables, then the principle of parsimony says to use only two. Models with fewer explanatory variables are generally easier to interpret, so we prefer them whenever possible.

In our search for a "best" regression, it is useful to examine the estimates of the regression coefficients more closely. Our point of view now is that the estimates we obtain from any particular data set would change if we obtained different data. How much might the estimates change? We turn to that question in this section.

Recall that the sampling distribution of any statistic derived from sample data is the distribution of this statistic over all possible samples. This idea can be applied to the least squares estimate of a regression coefficient. For example, the sampling distribution of b_1, the least squares estimate of the "true" coefficient β_1, is the distribution of b_1's we would see if we observed many samples and ran a least squares regression on each of them.

Let β_i be any of the β's, and let b_i be the least squares estimate of β_i. Then if the regression assumptions hold, the standardized value $(b_i - \beta_i)/s_i$ has a t distribution with $n - k - 1$ degrees of freedom. Here, k is the number of explanatory variables included in the equation, and s_i is the **standard error of** b_i. The formula for s_i is not shown here, but its value is printed in all standard regression outputs. It measures how much the b_i's would vary from sample to sample. A small value of s_i is preferred—it means that b_i is a more accurate estimate of the true coefficient β_i.

We have stated this result for a typical coefficient of one of the X's. These are usually the coefficients of most interest. However, exactly the same result holds for the intercept term α. Now we will see how to use this result.

EXAMPLE 15.2 (CONTINUED)

ANALYZING OVERHEAD EXPENSES AT BENDRIX

This example continues the Bendrix manufacturing example. As before, the response variable is Overhead and the explanatory variables are MachHrs and ProdRuns. What inferences can we make about the regression coefficients?

Solution

When we use StatPro's Multiple Regression procedure, we obtain the output shown in Figure 15.17. (This output is practically identical to regression outputs from all other statistical software packages.) We have already seen that the estimates of the regression coefficients appear under the label Coefficient in the range C16:C18. These values estimate the true, but unobservable, population coefficients. The next column, labeled Std Err, shows the s_i's. Specifically, 3.590 is the standard error of the coefficient of MachHrs, and 82.251 is the standard error of the coefficient of ProdRuns.

	A	B	C	D	E	F	G	H
1	*Results of multiple regression for Overhead*							
2								
3	*Summary measures*							
4		Multiple R	0.9308					
5		R-Square	0.8664					
6		Adj R-Square	0.8583					
7		StErr of Est	4108.9932					
8								
9	*ANOVA Table*							
10		Source	df	SS	MS	F	p-value	
11		Explained	2	3614020652.0000	1807010326.0000	107.0261	0.0000	
12		Unexplained	33	557166208.0000	16883824.4848			
13								
14	*Regression coefficients*							
15			Coefficient	Std Err	t-value	p-value	Lower limit	Upper limit
16		Constant	3996.6782	6603.6509	0.6052	0.5492	-9438.5612	17431.9176
17		MachHrs	43.5364	3.5895	12.1289	0.0000	36.2335	50.8393
18		ProdRuns	883.6179	82.2514	10.7429	0.0000	716.2760	1050.9598

FIGURE 15.17 Regression Output for Bendrix Example

The b_i's represent point estimates of the β_i's, based on this particular sample. The s_i's indicate the accuracy of these point estimates. For example, the point estimate of β_1, the effect on Overhead of a one-unit increase in MachHrs, is 43.536. We are about 95% confident that the true β_1 is within two standard errors of this point estimate, that is, from 36.357 to 50.715. Similar statements can be made for the coefficient of ProdRuns and the intercept (Constant) term.

As with any population parameters, we can use the sample data to obtain confidence intervals for the regression coefficients. For example, the preceding paragraph implies that an approximate 95% confidence interval for the coefficient of MachHrs extends from 36.357 to 50.715. StatPro automatically provides 95% confidence intervals for the regression coefficients.

There is another important piece of information in regression outputs: the t-values for the individual regression coefficients. These are shown in the "t-value" column of the regression output in Figure 15.18. The formula for a t-value is simple. It is the ratio of the estimated coefficient to its standard error:

$$t\text{-value} = b_i/s_i$$

Therefore, it indicates how many standard errors the regression coefficient is from 0. For example, the t-value for MachHrs is about 12.13, so we know that the regression coefficient of MachHrs, 43.536, is over 12 standard errors to the right of 0. Similarly, the coefficient of ProdRuns is more than 10 of its standard errors to the right of 0.

A t-value can be used in an important hypothesis test for the corresponding regression coefficient. To motivate this test, suppose that we want to decide whether a particular explanatory variable belongs in the regression equation. A sensible criterion for making this decision is to check whether the corresponding regression coefficient is 0. If a variable's coefficient is 0, there is no point in including this variable in the equation; the 0 coefficient will cancel its effect on the response variable.

	A	B	C	D	E	F	G	H
14	*Regression coefficients*							
15			Coefficient	Std Err	t-value	p-value	**Lower limit**	**Upper limit**
16		Constant	3996.6782	6603.6509	0.6052	0.5492	**-9438.5612**	**17431.9176**
17		MachHrs	43.5364	3.5895	12.1289	0.0000	**36.2335**	**50.8393**
18		ProdRuns	883.6179	82.2514	10.7429	0.0000	**716.2760**	**1050.9598**

FIGURE 15.18 Confidence Intervals for Regression Coefficients

Therefore, it is reasonable to test whether a variable's coefficient is 0. This is usually tested versus a *two-tailed* alternative. The null and alternative hypotheses are of the form $H_0 : \beta_i = 0$ versus $H_a : \beta_i \neq 0$. If we can reject the null hypothesis and conclude that this coefficient is *not* 0, then we have an argument for including the variable in the regression equation. Conversely, if we cannot reject the null hypothesis, we might decide to eliminate this variable from the equation.

Most computer packages, including StatPro, make this test easy to run by reporting the corresponding p-value for the test. The p-value is the probability (in both tails) of being beyond the listed t-value. For example, referring again to Figure 15.18, the t-value for MachHrs is 12.13, and the associated p-value (rounded to four decimal places) is 0.0000. This means that there is virtually no probability of being beyond the observed t-value, so that we can definitely reject the null hypothesis that the coefficient of MachHrs is 0. In words, we are sure that the true coefficient of MachHrs is not 0. The same can be said for the coefficient of ProdRuns. ■

Making Include/Exclude Decisions

We now make further use of the t-values of regression coefficients. In particular, we will see how they can be used to make include/exclude decisions for explanatory variables in a regression equation. We know that a t-value can be used to test whether a population regression coefficient is 0. But does this mean that we should automatically include a variable if its t-value is significant and automatically exclude it if its t-value is not significant? The decision is not always this simple.

The bottom line is that we are always trying to get the best fit possible, and because of the principle of parsimony, we want to use the fewest number of variables. This presents a trade-off, where there are often no easy answers. On the one hand, more variables certainly increase R^2 and they usually reduce the standard error of estimate s_e. On the other hand, fewer variables are better for parsimony. Therefore, we present several guidelines. These guidelines are not hard and fast rules, and they are sometimes contradictory. In real applications there are often several equations that are equally good for all practical purposes, and it is rather pointless to search for a single "true" equation.

Guidelines for Including/Excluding Variables in a Regression Equation

1. Look at a variable's t-value and its associated p-value. If the p-value is above some accepted significance level, such as 0.05, then this variable is a candidate for exclusion.

2. Check whether a variable's t-value is less than 1 or greater than 1 in magnitude. If it is less than 1, then s_e will decrease (and adjusted R^2 will increase) if this variable is excluded from the equation. If it is greater than 1, the opposite will occur. These are mathematical facts. Because of them, some statisticians advocate excluding variables with t-values less than 1, and including variables with t-values greater than 1.

3. Look at t-values and p-values, rather than correlations, when making include/exclude decisions. An explanatory variable can have a fairly high correlation with the response variable, but because of *other* variables included in the equation, it might not be needed. This would be reflected in a low t-value and a high p-value, and this variable could possibly be excluded for reasons of parsimony. This often occurs in the presence of multicollinearity, discussed in the next section.

4. When there is a group of variables that are in some sense logically related, it is sometimes a good idea to include all of them or exclude all of them. In this case, their individual t-values should not be used. Instead, there is a "partial F test" that can be used to test whether the group as a whole is significant. (We will not discuss this test here.)

5. Use economic and/or physical theory to decide whether to include or exclude variables, and put less reliance on t-values and/or p-values. The idea is that some variables might really *belong* in an equation because of their theoretical relationship with the response variable, and their low t-values, possibly the result of an unlucky sample, should not disqualify them from being in the equation. Similarly, a variable that has no economic or physical relationship with the response variable might have gotten a significant t-value just by chance. This does not necessarily mean that it should be included in the equation. We should not use a computer package blindly to hunt for "good" explanatory variables. We should have some idea, before running the package, which variables belong and which do not.

Again, these guidelines can give contradictory signals. Specifically, guideline 2 bases the include/exclude decision on whether the magnitude of the t-value is greater or less than 1. However, analysts who base the decision on statistical significance at the usual 5% level, as in guideline 1, typically exclude a variable from the equation unless its t-value is at least 2 (approximately). This latter approach is more stringent—fewer variables will be retained—but it is probably the more popular approach. However, either approach is likely to result in "similar" equations for all practical purposes.

PROBLEMS

Skill-Building Problems

14. For this problem, refer to Problem 6 and the data in the file P15_6.XLS.
   a. Estimate a multiple regression model using the given data.
   b. Is there evidence of any violations of the key assumptions of regression analysis?
   c. Interpret the 95% confidence intervals for the regression coefficients of X_1 and X_2. Based on these interval estimates, which variables, if any, would you choose to remove from the model estimated in part **a**? Explain your decision.

15. For this problem, refer to Problem 4 and the data in the file P15_4.XLS.
   a. Estimate a simple linear regression model.
   b. Test whether there is sufficient evidence to conclude that the slope parameter is *less than* 0. Use a 5% significance level.
   c. Based on your finding in part **b**, is it possible to conclude that a linear relationship exists between the number of farms and the average farm size between 1950 and 1997? Explain.

15.8 MULTICOLLINEARITY

Recall that the coefficient of any variable in a regression equation indicates the effect of this variable on the response variable, provided that the other variables in the equation remain constant. Another way of stating this is that the coefficient represents the effect of this variable on the response variable *in addition to* the effects of the other variables in the equation. For example, if MachHrs and ProdRuns are included in the equation for Overhead, then the coefficient of MachHrs indicates the *extra* amount MachHrs explains about variation in Overhead, in addition to the amount already explained by ProdRuns. Similarly, the coefficient of ProdRuns indicates the extra amount ProdRuns explains about variation in Overhead, in addition to the amount already explained by MachHrs. Therefore, the relationship between an explanatory variable X and the response variable Y is not always accurately reflected in the coefficient of X; it depends on which *other* X's are included in the equation.

This is especially true when there is a linear relationship between two or more *explanatory* variables, in which case we have **multicollinearity**. By definition, multicollinearity is the presence of a fairly strong linear relationship between two or more explanatory variables, and it can make estimation difficult. Consider the following example. It is a rather trivial example, but it is useful for illustrating the potential effects of multicollinearity.

EXAMPLE 15.3

HEIGHT VERSUS FOOT LENGTH

We want to explain a person's height by means of foot length. The response variable is Height, and the explanatory variables are Right and Left, the length of the right foot and the left foot, respectively. What can occur when we regress Height on *both* Right and Left?

Solution

Admittedly, there is no need to include both Right and Left in an equation for Height—either one of them would do—but we include them both to make a point. Now, it is likely that there is a large correlation between height and foot size, so we would expect this regression equation to do a good job. For example, the R^2 value will probably be large. But what about the coefficients of Right and Left? Here there is a problem. The coefficient of Right indicates the right foot's effect on Height in addition to the effect of the left foot. This additional effect is probably minimal. That is, after the effect of Left on Height has already been taken into account, the extra information provided by Right is probably minimal. But it goes the other way also. The extra effect of Left, in addition to that provided by Right, is probably minimal.

To show what can happen numerically, we generated a hypothetical data set of heights and left and right foot lengths. (See the file HEIGHT.XLS.) We did this so that, except for random error, height is approximately 32 plus 3.2 times foot length (all expressed in inches). As shown in Figure 15.19, the correlation between Height and either Right or Left in our data set is quite large, and the correlation between Right and Left is very close to 1.

The regression output when both Right and Left are entered in the equation for Height appears in Figure 15.20. This tells a somewhat confusing story. The multiple R and the corresponding R^2 are about what we would expect, given the correlations between Height and either Right or Left in Figure 15.19. In particular, the multiple R is close to the correlation between Height and either Right or Left. Also, the s_e value is quite good. It implies that predictions of height from this regression equation will typically be off by only about 2 inches.

However, the coefficients of Right and Left are not at all what we might expect, given that we generated heights as approximately 32 plus 3.2 times foot length. In fact, the coefficient of Left has the wrong sign—it is *negative*! Besides this "wrong"

FIGURE 15.19
Correlations in
Height versus Foot
Length Example

	E	F	G	H	I
3	*Table of correlations*				
4			Height	Right	Left
5		Height	1.000		
6		Right	0.903	1.000	
7		Left	0.900	0.999	1.000

FIGURE 15.20
Regression Output
for Height versus
Foot Length Example

	A	B	C	D	E	F	G	H
1	*Results of multiple regression for Height*							
2								
3	*Summary measures*							
4		Multiple R	0.9042					
5		R-Square	0.8176					
6		Adj R-Square	0.8140					
7		StErr of Est	2.0041					
8								
9	*ANOVA Table*							
10		Source	df	SS	MS	F	p-value	
11		Explained	2	1836.3845	918.1923	228.6003	0.0000	
12		Unexplained	102	409.6916	4.0166			
13								
14	*Regression coefficients*							
15			Coefficient	Std Err	t-value	p-value	Lower limit	Upper limit
16		Constant	31.7603	1.9595	16.2087	0.0000	27.8737	35.6469
17		Right	6.8229	3.4285	1.9901	0.0493	0.0226	13.6233
18		Left	-3.6448	3.4411	-1.0592	0.2920	-10.4701	3.1806

sign, the tip-off that there is a problem is that the t-value of Left is quite small and the corresponding p-value is quite large. Judging by this, we might conclude that Height and Left are either not related or are related negatively. But we know from Figure 15.19 that both of these conclusions are false. In contrast, the coefficient of Right has the "correct" sign, and its t-value and associated p-value do imply statistical significance, at least at the 5% level. However, this happened mostly by chance. Slight changes in the data could change the results completely—the coefficient of Right could become negative and insignificant, or both coefficients could become insignificant.

The problem is that although both Right and Left are clearly related to Height, it is impossible for the least squares method to distinguish their *separate* effects. Note that the regression equation does estimate the combined effect fairly well—the difference between the coefficients of Right and Left is $6.823 - 3.645 = 3.178$. This is close to the coefficient 3.2 we used to generate the data. Also, the estimated intercept 31.760 is close to the intercept 32 we used to generate the data. Therefore, the estimated equation will work well for predicting heights. It just doesn't have reliable estimates of the individual coefficients of Right and Left. ■

This example illustrates an extreme form of multicollinearity, where two explanatory variables are very highly correlated. In general, there are various degrees of multicollinearity. In each of them, there is a linear relationship between two or more explanatory variables, and this relationship makes it difficult to estimate the individual effect of the X's on the response variable. The symptoms of multicollinearity can be "wrong" signs of the coefficients, smaller-than-expected t-values, and larger-than-expected (insignificant) p-values. In other words, variables that are really related to the response variable can look like they aren't related, based on their p-values, because their effects on Y are already explained by other X's in the equation.

Exact Multicollinearity

One other assumption is important for numerical calculations. We must assume that no explanatory variable is an *exact* linear combination of any other explanatory variables. Another way of stating this is that there is no exact linear relationship between any set of explanatory variables. This would occur, for example, if one variable were an exact multiple of another, or if one variable were equal to the sum of several other variables. More generally, it occurs if one of the explanatory variables can be written as a weighted sum of several of the others.

If such a relationship holds, it means that there is *redundancy* in the data. One of the *X*'s could be eliminated without any loss of information. A simple example is the following. Suppose that MachHrs1 is machine hours measured in hours, and MachHrs2 is machine hours measured in *hundreds* of hours. Then it is clear that these two variables contain exactly the same information, and either of them could be eliminated.

Generally, it is fairly simple to spot an exact linear relationship and then to eliminate it by excluding the redundant variable from the analysis. However, if we do *not* spot the relationship and try to run the regression analysis with the redundant variable included, regression packages will typically respond with an error message. If the package interrupts the analysis with an error message containing the words "exact multicollinearity" or "linear dependence," then we should look for a redundant explanatory variable. As an example, the message from StatPro in this case is shown in Figure 15.21. We got it by deliberately entering dummy variables from *each* category of a categorical variable (see Section 15.9)—something we should *not* do.

FIGURE 15.21
Error Message
from StatPro
Indicating Exact
Multicollinearity

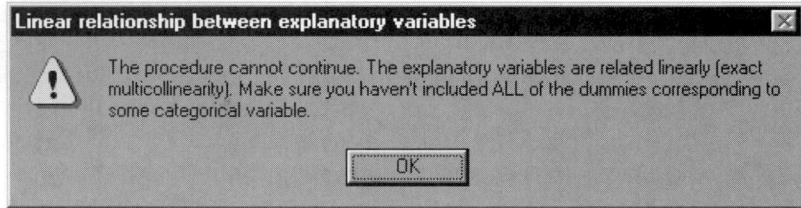

PROBLEMS

Skill-Building Problems

16. Using the data given in P15_2.XLS, estimate a multiple regression equation to predict the sales price of houses in a given community. Employ all available explanatory variables. Is there evidence of multicollinearity in this model? Explain why or why not.

17. For this problem, refer to Problem 10 and the data in the file P15_10.XLS.
   a. Determine whether each of the regression coefficients for the explanatory variables in this model is statistically different from 0 at the 5% significance level. Summarize your findings.
   b. Is there evidence of multicollinearity in this model? Explain why or why not.

18. For this problem, refer to Problem 9 and the data in the file P15_9.XLS.

   a. Estimate a multiple regression model using all of the available explanatory variables. Perform a test of significance for each of the model's regression coefficients. Are the signs of the estimated coefficients consistent with your expectations?
   b. Is there evidence of multicollinearity in this model? Explain why or why not. If multicollinearity appears to be present, explain how you could eliminate this problem.

19. For this problem, refer to Problem 11 and the data in the file P15_11.XLS. Use multiple regression analysis to explore the relationship between the metropolitan area's overall score and the set of numerical factors. Which explanatory variables should be included in a final version of this regression model? Justify your choices.

20. For this problem, refer to Problem 5 and the data in the file P15_5.XLS.

    a. Estimate a multiple regression model to explain the variation in employee salaries at Beta Technologies using all of the potential explanatory variables.

    b. Using your regression output, determine which of the explanatory variables should be excluded from the regression equation. Provide reasoning for your decision to remove each such variable.

21. For this problem, refer to Problem 12 and the data in the file P15_12.XLS.

    a. Estimate a multiple regression equation that includes annual sales as the response variable and the following explanatory variables: year, size of the population residing within 10 miles of the restaurant, annual advertising expenditures, and advertising expenditures in the *previous* year.

    b. Which of the explanatory variables have significant effects on sales at the 10% significance level? Do any of these results surprise you? Explain why or why not.

    c. Does multicollinearity appear to be present in the regression model? Why or why not?

15.9 MODELING POSSIBILITIES

Once we move from simple to multiple regression, the floodgates open. All types of explanatory variables are potential candidates for inclusion in the regression equation. In this section we will examine several new types of explanatory variables. These include "dummy" variables, interaction terms, and non-linear transformations. The techniques in this section provide us with many alternative approaches to modeling the relationship between a response variable and potential explanatory variables. In many applications these techniques produce much better fits than we could obtain without them.

As the title of this section suggests, these techniques are modeling *possibilities*. They provide a wide variety of explanatory variables to choose from. However, this does not mean that it is wise to include all or even many of these new types of explanatory variables in any particular regression equation. The chances are that only a few, if any, will significantly improve the linear fit. Knowing which explanatory variables to include requires a great deal of practical experience with regression, as well as a thorough understanding of the particular problem to be solved. The material in this section should *not* be an excuse for a mindless fishing expedition.

Dummy Variables

Some potential explanatory variables are categorical and cannot be measured on a quantitative scale. However, these categorical variables are often related to the response variable, so we need a way to include them in a regression equation. The trick is to use **dummy** variables, also called **indicator** or **0–1** variables. Dummy variables are variables that indicate the category a given observation is in. If a dummy variable for a given category equals 1, the observation is in that category; if it equals 0, the observation is not in that category.

There are basically two situations. The first and perhaps most common situation is when a categorical variable has only two categories. A good example of this is a "gender" variable that has the two categories "male" and "female." In this case we need only a *single* dummy variable, and we have the choice of assigning the 1's to either category. If we label the dummy variable Gender, then we can code Gender as 1 for males and 0 for females, or we can code Gender as 1 for females and 0 for males. We just need to be consistent and specify explicitly which coding scheme we are using.

The other situation is when there are more than two categories. A good example of this is when we have quarterly time series data and we want to treat the quarter of the year as a categorical variable with four categories, 1–4. Then we can create four dummy variables, Q1–Q4. For example, Q2 equals 1 for all second-quarter observations and equals 0 for all other observations. Although we can create four dummy variables, we will see that only three of them—*any* three—should be used in a regression equation.

The following example illustrates how we form, use, and interpret dummy variables in regression analysis.

EXAMPLE 15.4

CHECKING FOR SALARY DISCRIMINATION AT FIFTH NATIONAL BANK

The Fifth National Bank of Springfield is facing a gender discrimination suit.[7] The charge is that its female employees receive substantially smaller salaries than its male employees. The bank's employee database is listed in the file BANK.XLS. For each of its 208 employees, the data set includes the following variables:

- EducLev: education level, a categorical variable with categories 1 (finished high school), 2 (finished some college courses), 3 (obtained a bachelor's degree), 4 (took some graduate courses), 5 (obtained a graduate degree)

- JobGrade: a categorical variable indicating the current job level, the possible levels being 1–6 (6 is highest)

- YrHired: year employee was hired

- YrBorn: year employee was born

- Gender: a categorical variable with values "Female" and "Male"

- YrsPrior: number of years of work experience at another bank prior to working at Fifth National

- PCJob: a dummy variable with value 1 if the employee's current job is computer-related and value 0 otherwise

- Salary: current annual salary in thousands of dollars

Figure 15.22 lists a few of the observations. Do these data provide evidence that females are discriminated against in terms of salary?

Solution

A naive approach to this problem compares the average female salary to the average male salary. This can be done with an Excel pivot table or with a more formal hypothesis test. Using these methods, we find that the average of all salaries is $39,922, the female average is $37,210, the male average is $45,505, and the difference between the male and female averages is statistically significant at any reasonable level of significance—the females are definitely earning less than males. But perhaps there is a reason for this. They might have lower education levels, they might have been hired more recently, they might be working at lower job grades, and so on. The question is whether the difference between female and male salaries is still evident after taking these other attributes into account. This is a perfect task for regression.

---

[7]This example and the accompanying data set are based on a real case. Only the bank's name has been changed.

FIGURE 15.22
Selected Data for
Bank Example

	A	B	C	D	E	F	G	H	I
1	Bank salary data								
2									
3	Employee	EducLev	JobGrade	YrHired	YrBorn	Gender	YrsPrior	PCJob	Salary
4	1	3	1	92	69	Male	1	No	32
5	2	1	1	81	57	Female	1	No	39.1
6	3	1	1	83	60	Female	0	No	33.2
7	4	2	1	87	55	Female	7	No	30.6
8	5	3	1	92	67	Male	0	No	29
9	6	3	1	92	71	Female	0	No	30.5
10	7	3	1	91	68	Female	0	No	30
11	8	3	1	87	62	Male	2	No	27
12	9	1	1	91	33	Female	0	No	34
13	10	3	1	86	64	Female	0	No	29.5
209	206	5	6	63	33	Male	0	No	88
210	207	5	6	60	36	Male	0	No	94
211	208	5	6	62	33	Female	0	No	30

We first need to create dummy variables for the various categorical variables. We can do this manually with IF functions or we can use StatPro's Dummy Variable procedure. To do it manually, we can create a dummy variable Female based on Gender in column J by entering the formula

=IF(F4="Female",1,0)

in cell J4 and copying it down. Note that we are coding the females as 1's and the males as 0's. (The quotes are necessary when a nonnumerical value is used in an IF function.)

StatPro's Dummy Variable procedure is somewhat easier, especially when there are multiple categories. For example, to create five dummies, Ed_1–Ed_5, for each of the education levels, we can use the StatPro/Data Utilities/Create Dummy Variables menu item, select the "Create several dummies from a categorical variable" option, select the EducLev variable to base the dummies on, and (after the dummies have been created) change their default names to Ed_1–Ed_5. This procedure simply enters IF functions in the dummy cells, exactly as we would do manually. We can follow the same procedure to create six dummies, Job_1–Job_6, for the job grade categories.

Sometimes we might want to collapse several categories. For example, we might want to collapse the five education categories into three categories: 1, (2,3), and (4,5). The new second category includes employees who have taken undergraduate courses or have completed a bachelor's degree, and the new third category includes employees who have taken graduate courses or have completed a graduate degree. It is easy to do this. We simply add the Ed_2 and Ed_3 columns to get the dummy for the new second category, and similarly add the Ed_4 and Ed_5 columns for the new third category.

Once the dummies have been created, we can run a regression analysis with Salary as the response variable, using any combination of numerical and dummy explanatory variables. However, there are two rules we must follow:

- We should not use any of the *original* categorical variables, such as EducLev, that the dummies are based on.
- We should use *one less dummy* than the number of categories for any categorical variable.

This second rule is a technical one. If we violate it, the statistical software will give us an error message. For example, if we want to use education level as an explanatory variable, we should enter only five of the six dummies Ed_1–Ed_6. *Any* five of these can be used. The omitted dummy then corresponds to the **reference** category. As we will see, the interpretation of the dummy variable coefficients are all relative to this reference category. When there are only two categories, as with the gender variable, we typically name the variable with the category, such as Female, that corresponds to the 1's. If we create the dummy variables manually, we probably don't even bother to create a Male dummy. In this case "Male" automatically becomes the reference category.

To get used to dummy variables in regression, we will proceed in several stages in this example. We first estimate a regression equation with only one explanatory variable, Female. The output appears in Figure 15.23. The resulting equation is

$$\text{Predicted Salary} = 45.505 - 8.296\text{Female} \qquad \textbf{(15.8)}$$

FIGURE 15.23
Output for Bank Example with a Single Explanatory Variable

	A	B	C	D	E	F	G	H
1	*Results of multiple regression for Salary*							
2								
3	*Summary measures*							
4		Multiple R	0.3465					
5		R-Square	0.1201					
6		Adj R-Square	0.1158					
7		StErr of Est	10.5843					
8								
9	*ANOVA Table*							
10		Source	df	SS	MS	F	p-value	
11		Explained	1	3149.6346	3149.6346	28.1151	0.0000	
12		Unexplained	206	23077.4727	112.0266			
13								
14	*Regression coefficients*							
15			Coefficient	Std Err	t-value	p-value	Lower limit	Upper limit
16		Constant	45.5054	1.2835	35.4534	0.0000	42.9749	48.0360
17		Female	-8.2955	1.5645	-5.3024	0.0000	-11.3800	-5.2110

To interpret this equation, recall that Female has only two possible values, 0 and 1. If we substitute Female = 1 into equation (15.8), we obtain

$$\text{Predicted Salary} = 45.505 - 8.296(1) = 37.209$$

Because Female = 1 corresponds to females, this equation indicates the average female salary. Similarly, if we substitute Female = 0 into equation (15.8), we obtain

$$\text{Predicted Salary} = 45.505 - 8.296(0) = 45.505$$

Because Female = 0 corresponds to males, this equation indicates the average male salary. Therefore, the interpretation of the -8.296 coefficient of the Female dummy variable is straightforward. It is the average female salary relative to the reference (male) category—females get paid \$8296 less on average than males.

Equation (15.8) tells only part of the story. It ignores all information except for gender. We expand this equation by adding the experience variables YrsPrior and YrsExper, where YrsExper is years of experience with Fifth National and is calculated in a new column as 95 minus YrHired. (The data are from 1995.) The output with the Female dummy variable and these two experience variables appears in Figure 15.24. The corresponding regression equation is

$$\text{Predicted Salary} = 35.492 + 0.988\text{YrsExper} + 0.131\text{YrsPrior} - 8.080\text{Female}$$
$$\textbf{(15.9)}$$

It is again useful to write equation (15.9) in two forms: one for females (substituting Female = 1) and one for males (substituting Female = 0). After the arithmetic, they become

$$\text{Predicted Salary} = 27.412 + 0.988\text{YrsExper} + 0.131\text{YrsPrior}$$

and

FIGURE 15.24
Regression Output with Two Numerical ExplanatoryVariables Included

	A	B	C	D	E	F	G	H
1	*Results of multiple regression for Salary*							
2								
3	*Summary measures*							
4		Multiple R	0.7016					
5		R-Square	0.4923					
6		Adj R-Square	0.4848					
7		StErr of Est	8.0794					
8								
9	*ANOVA Table*							
10		Source	df	SS	MS	F	p-value	
11		Explained	3	12910.6678	4303.5559	65.9279	0.0000	
12		Unexplained	204	13316.4395	65.2767			
13								
14	*Regression coefficients*							
15			Coefficient	Std Err	t-value	p-value	Lower limit	Upper limit
16		Constant	35.4917	1.3410	26.4661	0.0000	32.8476	38.1357
17		YrsPrior	0.1313	0.1809	0.7259	0.4687	-0.2254	0.4881
18		Female	-8.0802	1.1982	-6.7438	0.0000	-10.4426	-5.7178
19		YrsExper	0.9880	0.0809	12.2083	0.0000	0.8284	1.1476

$$\text{Predicted Salary} = 35.492 + 0.988\text{YrsExper} + 0.131\text{YrsPrior}$$

Except for the intercept term, these equations are identical. We can now interpret the coefficient -8.080 of the Female dummy variable as the average salary "penalty" for females relative to males *after controlling for job experience*. Gender discrimination still appears to be a very plausible conclusion. However, note that R^2 is only 49.2%. Perhaps there is still more of the story to tell.

We next add job grade to the equation by including five of the six job grade dummies. Although *any* five could be used, we use Job_2–Job_6, so that the lowest level becomes the reference category. The resulting output appears in Figure 15.25.

FIGURE 15.25
Regression Output with Job Grade Dummies Included

	A	B	C	D	E	F	G	H
1	*Results of multiple regression for Salary*							
2								
3	*Summary measures*							
4		Multiple R	0.8616					
5		R-Square	0.7423					
6		Adj R-Square	0.7320					
7		StErr of Est	5.8275					
8								
9	*ANOVA Table*							
10		Source	df	SS	MS	F	p-value	
11		Explained	8	19469.1336	2433.6417	71.6627	0.0000	
12		Unexplained	199	6757.9736	33.9597			
13								
14	*Regression coefficients*							
15			Coefficient	Std Err	t-value	p-value	Lower limit	Upper limit
16		Constant	30.2296	1.1730	25.7705	0.0000	27.9164	32.5428
17		YrsPrior	0.1489	0.1320	1.1286	0.2604	-0.1113	0.4092
18		Female	-1.9622	1.0051	-1.9523	0.0523	-3.9442	0.0198
19		Job_2	2.5753	1.1821	2.1786	0.0305	0.2443	4.9063
20		Job_3	6.2947	1.1703	5.3786	0.0000	3.9869	8.6025
21		Job_4	10.4745	1.3676	7.6588	0.0000	7.7776	13.1715
22		Job_5	16.0114	1.5593	10.2681	0.0000	12.9364	19.0863
23		Job_6	27.6472	2.4176	11.4357	0.0000	22.8797	32.4146
24		YrsExper	0.4084	0.0778	5.2522	0.0000	0.2551	0.5617

The estimated regression equation is now

$$\text{Predicted Salary} = 30.230 + 0.408\text{YrsExper} + 0.149\text{YrsPrior} - 1.962\text{Female}$$
$$+ 2.575\text{Job\_2} + 6.295\text{Job\_3} + 10.475\text{Job\_4}$$
$$+ 16.011\text{Job\_5} + 27.647\text{Job\_6} \qquad \textbf{(15.10)}$$

Now there are two categorical variables involved, gender and job grade. However, we can still write a separate equation *for any combination* of categories by setting the dummies to the appropriate values. For example, the equation for females at the fifth job grade is found by setting Female = 1 and Job_5 = 1, and setting the other job dummies equal to 0. After combining terms, this equation becomes

$$\text{Predicted Salary} = 44.279 + 0.408\text{YrsExper} + 0.150\text{YrsPrior}$$

The intercept 44.279 is the intercept from equation (15.10), 30.230, plus the coefficients of Female and Job_5.

We can interpret equation (15.10) as follows. For either gender and any job grade, the expected increase in salary for one extra year of experience with Fifth National is $408; the expected increase in salary for one extra year of prior experience with another bank is $149. The coefficients of the job dummies indicate the average increase in salary an employee can expect relative to the reference (lowest) job grade. For example, an employee in job grade 4 can expect to earn $10,475 more than an employee in job grade 1, given that they have the same experience levels and are of the same gender. Finally, the key coefficient, the negative $1962 for females, indicates the average salary disadvantage for females relative to males, given that they have the same experience levels *and* are in the same job grade. Note that the R^2 value is now 74.2%, quite a bit larger than the R^2 value from equation (15.9).

Although the "penalty" for females in equation (15.10) is still substantial, it is less than a fourth of the penalty we saw in equations (15.8) and (15.9). It appears that females are paid less on average partly because they are in the lower job categories. We can check whether females are disproportionately in the lower job categories with a pivot table. We use Excel's pivot table tool, putting JobGrade in the row area, Gender in the column area and the count of *any* variable in the data area. If we express counts as percentages of the columns, we obtain the pivot table in Figure 15.26.

Clearly, females tend to be concentrated at the lower job grades. For example, 28.85% of all employees are at the lowest job grade, but 34.29% of all females are at this grade and only 17.65% of males are at this grade. The opposite is true at the higher job grades. This certainly helps to explain why females get lower salaries on average, but it does not explain why females are at the lower job grades in the first place. We will not be able to provide a thorough analysis of this issue, but we will add one more piece to the puzzle—for now—by adding education level (using the dummies Ed_2–Ed_5), age (calculated as 95 minus YrBorn), and PCJob to equation (15.10). The resulting output appears in Figure 15.27. The coefficients of this equation can be seen from the output. This equation does not appear to add much to equation (15.10). The R^2 value has increased only slightly to 76.5%, and the adjusted R^2 value has barely increased at all. The penalty for being a female, $2555, is now slightly greater than its previous value of $1962.

We can interpret the coefficients of the education dummies in this expanded equation as the benefit (or loss, if negative) of extra education relative to a high school diploma, the reference category. For example, the benefit of a bachelor's degree over a high school diploma is $528, given that all the other variables in the equation are held constant. However, because of their relatively high p-values, the coefficients of the education dummies Ed_2–Ed_4 are not very stable estimates, and we should not put too much faith in them. The coefficient of PCJob implies that an employee with

FIGURE 15.26
Pivot Table of Job
Grade Counts for
Bank Data

	A	B	C	D
1	Count	Gender		
2	JobGrade	Female	Male	Grand Total
3	1	34.29%	17.65%	28.85%
4	2	20.71%	19.12%	20.19%
5	3	25.71%	10.29%	20.67%
6	4	12.14%	16.18%	13.46%
7	5	6.43%	17.65%	10.10%
8	6	0.71%	19.12%	6.73%
9	Grand Total	100.00%	100.00%	100.00%

a computer-related job can expect an extra $4923 in salary relative to an employee without a computer-related job, provided that the other variables in the equation are the same for both employees. The Age coefficient is quite small and indicates that age has little effect—in addition to the effects of the other variables—on salary.

The main conclusion we can draw from the output in Figure 15.27 is that there is still a plausible case to be made for discrimination against females, even after including information on all of the variables in the database in the regression equation. We conclude this example for now, but there is still more we will say about it in the next two subsections.

FIGURE 15.27
Regression Output
with Other Variables
Added

	A	B	C	D	E	F	G	H
1	Results of multiple regression for Salary							
2								
3	Summary measures							
4		Multiple R	0.8748					
5		R-Square	0.7652					
6		Adj R-Square	0.7482					
7		StErr of Est	5.6481					
8								
9	ANOVA Table							
10		Source	df	SS	MS	F	p-value	
11		Explained	14	20070.2508	1433.5893	44.9390	0.0000	
12		Unexplained	193	6156.8564	31.9008			
13								
14	Regression coefficients							
15			Coefficient	Std Err	t-value	p-value	Lower limit	Upper limit
16		Constant	29.6899	2.4900	11.9236	0.0000	24.7788	34.6011
17		YrsPrior	0.1677	0.1404	1.1943	0.2338	-0.1093	0.4447
18		PCJob	4.9228	1.4738	3.3402	0.0010	2.0160	7.8297
19		Female	-2.5545	1.0120	-2.5242	0.0124	-4.5504	-0.5585
20		Ed_2	-0.4856	1.3987	-0.3472	0.7289	-3.2442	2.2731
21		Ed_3	0.5279	1.3575	0.3889	0.6978	-2.1496	3.2054
22		Ed_4	0.2852	2.4047	0.1186	0.9057	-4.4577	5.0281
23		Ed_5	2.6908	1.6209	1.6601	0.0985	-0.5061	5.8877
24		Job_2	1.5645	1.1858	1.3194	0.1886	-0.7742	3.9032
25		Job_3	5.2194	1.2624	4.1345	0.0001	2.7295	7.7092
26		Job_4	8.5948	1.4960	5.7451	0.0000	5.6442	11.5455
27		Job_5	13.6594	1.8743	7.2879	0.0000	9.9627	17.3561
28		Job_6	23.8324	2.7999	8.5119	0.0000	18.3101	29.3547
29		YrsExper	0.5156	0.0980	5.2621	0.0000	0.3223	0.7088
30		Age	-0.0090	0.0577	-0.1553	0.8767	-0.1228	0.1048

Interaction Terms

When we include *only* a dummy variable in a regression equation, we are allowing the intercepts of the two lines to differ, but we are *forcing* the lines to be parallel. Sometimes we want to allow them to have different slopes, in addition to possibly different intercepts. We can do this with an **interaction** variable. Algebraically, an interaction variable is the *product* of two variables. Its effect is to allow the effect on Y of one of the variables to depend on the value of the other variable.

Let X be a quantitative variable and let D be a dummy variable. Suppose we create the interaction variable XD (the product of X and D) and then estimate the equation

$$\widehat{Y} = a + b_1 X + b_2 D + b_3 XD$$

As usual, we can rewrite this equation as two separate equations, depending on whether $D = 0$ or $D = 1$. If $D = 1$, we combine terms to write

$$\widehat{Y} = (a + b_2) + (b_1 + b_3)X$$

If $D = 0$, the dummy and interaction terms drop out and we obtain

$$\widehat{Y} = a + b_1 X$$

The important part is that the interaction term, $b_3 XD$, allows the slope of the regression line to differ between the two categories.

The following continuation of the bank discrimination example illustrates one possible use of interaction variables.

EXAMPLE	15.4 (CONTINUED)

CHECKING FOR SALARY DISCRIMINATION AT FIFTH NATIONAL BANK

Earlier we estimated an equation for Salary using the numerical explanatory variables YrsExper and YrsPrior and the dummy variable Female. If we drop the YrsPrior variable from this equation (for simplicity) and rerun the regression, we obtain the equation

$$\text{Predicted Salary} = 35.824 + 0.981\text{YrsExper} - 8.012\text{Female} \qquad \textbf{(15.11)}$$

The R^2 value for this equation is 49.1%. If we decide to include an interaction variable between YrsExper and Female in this equation, what is its effect?

Solution

We first need to form an interaction variable that is the product of YrsExper and Female. This can be done in two ways in Excel. We can do it manually by introducing a new variable that contains the product of the two variables involved, or we can use the StatPro/Data Utilities/Create Interaction Variable(s) menu item. For the latter, we select Female and YrsExper as the variables to be used to create an interaction variable, and we do *not* check either of the boxes in the next dialog box—we do not want either to be treated as a categorical variable.[8]

Once the interaction variable has been created, we include it in the regression equation in addition to the other variables in equation (15.11). The multiple regression output appears in Figure 15.28. The estimated regression equation is

$$\text{Predicted Salary} = 30.430 + 1.528\text{YrsExper} + 4.098\text{Female}$$
$$-1.248\text{YrsExper*Female}$$

(where YrsExper*Female is StatPro's default name for the interaction variable). As

[8]See the Help screen for this data utility. It explains the StatPro options for creating interaction variables.

FIGURE 15.28
Regression Output
with an Interaction
Variable

	A	B	C	D	E	F	G	H
1	*Results of multiple regression for Salary*							
2								
3	*Summary measures*							
4		Multiple R	0.7991					
5		R-Square	0.6386					
6		Adj R-Square	0.6333					
7		StErr of Est	6.8163					
8								
9	*ANOVA Table*							
10		Source	df	SS	MS	F	p-value	
11		Explained	3	16748.8748	5582.9583	120.1620	0.0000	
12		Unexplained	204	9478.2324	46.4619			
13								
14	*Regression coefficients*							
15			Coefficient	Std Err	t-value	p-value	Lower limit	Upper limit
16		Constant	30.4300	1.2166	25.0129	0.0000	28.0314	32.8287
17		Female	4.0983	1.6658	2.4602	0.0147	0.8138	7.3827
18		YrsExper	1.5278	0.0905	16.8887	0.0000	1.3494	1.7061
19		Female*YrsExper	-1.2478	0.1367	-9.1296	0.0000	-1.5173	-0.9783

in the general discussion, it is useful to write this as two separate equations, one for females and one for males. The female equation (Female = 1) is

$$\text{Predicted Salary} = (30.430 + 4.098) + (1.528 - 1.248)\text{YrsExper}$$
$$= 34.528 + 0.280\text{YrsExper}$$

and the male equation (Female = 0) is

$$\text{Predicted Salary} = 30.430 + 1.528\text{YrsExper}$$

Graphically, these equations appear as in Figure 15.29. The Y-intercept for the female line is slightly higher—females with no experience with Fifth National tend to start out slightly higher than males—but the slope of the female line is much lower. That is, males tend to move up the salary ladder much more quickly than females. Again, this provides another argument, although a somewhat different one, for gender discrimination against females. By the way, note that the R^2 value with the interaction variable has increased from 49.1% to 63.9%. The interaction variable has definitely added to the explanatory power of the equation.

FIGURE 15.29
Nonparallel Female
and Male Salary
Lines

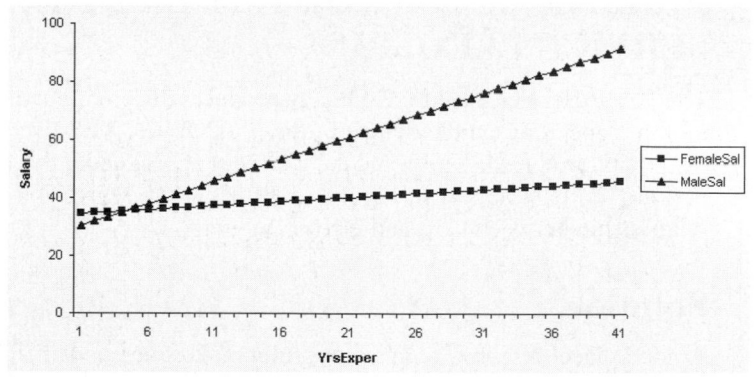

This example illustrates just one possible use of interaction variables. The product of any two variables, a numerical and a dummy variable, two dummy variables, or even two numerical variables, can be used. The trick is to interpret the results correctly, and the easiest way to do this is the way we have been doing it—by writing several separate equations and seeing how they differ.

There are pros and cons to adding interaction variables. On the plus side, they allow for more complex and interesting models, and they can provide significantly better fits. On the minus side, they can become difficult to interpret correctly. Therefore, we recommend that they be added only when there is good economic and statistical justification for doing so.

Nonlinear Transformations

The general linear regression equation has the form

$$\widehat{Y} = a + b_1 X_1 + b_2 X_2 + \cdots + b_k X_k$$

It is *linear* in the sense that the right-hand side of the equation is a constant plus a sum of products of constants and variables. However, there is no requirement that the response variable Y or the explanatory variables X_1 through X_k be *original* variables in the data set. Most often they are, but they are also allowed to be transformations of original variables. We already saw one example of this in the previous section with interaction variables. They are not original variables but are instead products of original (or even transformed) variables. We enter them in the same way as original variables; only the interpretation differs. In this section we will look at several nonlinear transformations of variables. These are often used because of curvature detected in scatterplots.. They can also arise because of economic considerations. That is, economic theory often leads us to particular nonlinear transformations.

We can transform the response variable Y or we can transform any of the explanatory variables, the X's. We can also do both. In either case there are a few nonlinear transformations that are typically used. These include the natural logarithm, the square root, the reciprocal, and the square. The point of any of these is usually to "straighten out" the points in a scatterplot. If several different transformations straighten out the data equally well, then we prefer the one that is easiest to interpret.

We begin with a small example where only the X variable needs to be transformed.

EXAMPLE 15.5

ANALYZING COST OF POWER AT PUBLIC SERVICE ELECTRIC

The Public Service Electric Company produces different quantities of electricity each month, depending on the demand. The file POWER.XLS lists the number of units of electricity produced (Units) and the total cost of producing these (Cost) for a 36-month period. The data appear in Figure 15.30. How can regression be used to analyze the relationship between Cost and Units?

Solution

A good place to start is with a scatterplot of Cost versus Units. This appears in Figure 15.31. It indicates a definite positive relationship and one that is nearly linear. However, there is also some evidence of curvature in the plot. The points increase slightly less rapidly as Units increases from left to right. In economic terms, there may be economies of scale, where the marginal cost of electricity decreases as more units of electricity are produced.

FIGURE 15.30
Data for Electric
Power Example

	A	B	C	D
1	Data on cost versus production level			
2				
3	Month	Cost	Units	
4	1	45623	601	
5	2	46507	738	
6	3	43343	686	
7	4	46495	736	
8	5	47317	756	
9	6	41172	498	
10	7	43974	828	
11	8	44290	671	
12	9	29297	305	
13	10	47244	637	
37	34	46295	667	
38	35	45218	705	
39	36	45357	637	

Nevertheless, we first use regression to estimate a *linear* relationship between Cost and Units. The resulting regression equation is

$$\text{Predicted Cost} = 23{,}651 + 30.53\text{Units}$$

The corresponding R^2 and s_e are 73.6% and \$2734. We also requested a scatterplot of the residuals versus the fitted values, always a good idea when nonlinearity is suspected. This plot is shown in Figure 15.32. The sign of nonlinearity in this plot is that the residuals to the far left and the far right are all negative, whereas the majority of the residuals in the middle are positive. Admittedly, the pattern is far from perfect—there are quite a few negative residuals in the middle—but the plot does hint at nonlinear behavior.

Quadratic Fit This negative–positive–negative behavior of residuals suggests a *parabola*—that is, a quadratic relationship with the *square* of Units included in the equation. We first create a new variable Sqr(Units) in the data set. This can be done manually (with the formula **=C4^2** in cell D4, copied down) or with the StatPro/Data Utilities/Transform Variables menu item. This latter method is easier to use and allows us to transform several variables simultaneously. Then we use multiple regression to

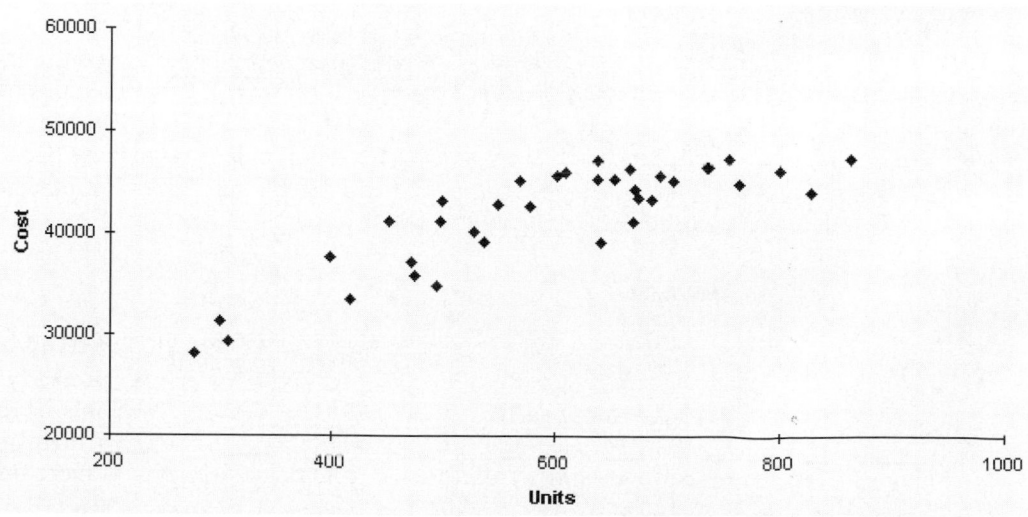

FIGURE 15.31 Scatterplot of Cost Versus Units for Electricity Example

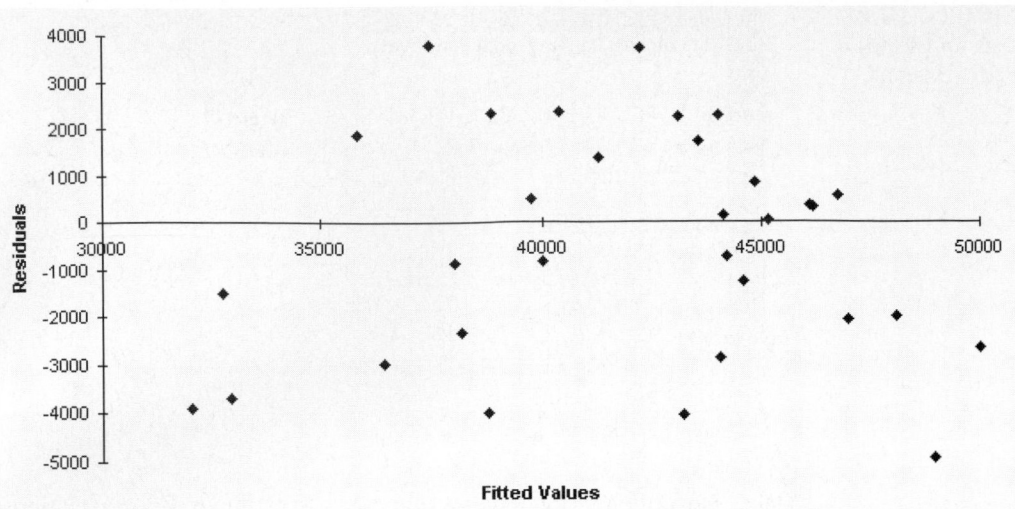

FIGURE 15.32 Residuals from a Straight-Line Fit

estimate the equation for Cost with *both* explanatory variables, Units and Sqr(Units), included. The resulting equation, as shown in Figure 15.33, is

$$\text{Predicted Cost} = 5793 + 98.35\text{Units} - 0.0600\text{Sqr(Units)} \qquad (15.12)$$

Note that R^2 has increased to 82.2% and s_e has decreased to \$2281.

One way to see how this regression equation fits the scatterplot of Cost versus Units (in Figure 15.31) is to use Excel's trendline option. To do so, activate the scatterplot, click on any point, use the Chart/Add Trendline menu item, click on the Type tab, and select the Polynomial type of order 2, that is, a quadratic. (This is for Excel 97 and 2000. For Excel 5 and 95, use the Insert/Trendline menu item instead.) A graph of equation (15.12) is superimposed on the scatterplot, as shown in Figure 15.34. It shows a reasonably good fit, plus an obvious curvature.

The main disadvantage of a quadratic regression equation is that there is no easy way to interpret the coefficients of Units and Sqr(Units). In particular, we cannot conclude from the 98.35 coefficient of Units that Cost increases by 98.35 dollars when Units increases by 1. The reason is that when Units increases by 1, Sqr(Units) *also*

FIGURE 15.33
Regression Output
with Squared Term
Included

	A	B	C	D	E	F	G	H
1	*Results of multiple regression for Cost*							
2								
3	*Summary measures*							
4		Multiple R	0.9064					
5		R-Square	0.8216					
6		Adj R-Square	0.8108					
7		StErr of Est	2280.7998					
8								
9	*ANOVA Table*							
10		Source	df	SS	MS	F	p-value	
11		Explained	2	790511520.9722	395255760.4861	75.9808	0.0000	
12		Unexplained	33	171667568.0000	5202047.5152			
13								
14	*Regression coefficients*							
15			Coefficient	Std Err	t-value	p-value	Lower limit	Upper limit
16		Constant	5792.7983	4763.0586	1.2162	0.2325	-3897.7249	15483.3216
17		Units	98.3504	17.2369	5.7058	0.0000	63.2816	133.4192
18		Sqr(Units)	-0.0600	0.0151	-3.9806	0.0004	-0.0906	-0.0293

increases. All we can say is that the terms in equation (15.12) combine to explain the nonlinear relationship between units produced and total cost.

Logarithmic Fit Instead of a quadratic fit, we can try a logarithmic fit. In this case we create a new variable, Log(Units), the natural logarithm of Units, and then regress Cost against the *single* variable Log(Units). To create the new variable, we can either use Excel's LN function or StatPro/Data Utilities/Transform Variables menu item. Also, we can superimpose a logarithmic curve on the scatterplot of Cost versus Units by using Excel's trendline feature with the logarithmic option. This curve appears in Figure 15.35. To the naked eye, it appears to be similar, and about as good a fit, as the quadratic curve in Figure 15.34.

The resulting regression equation is

$$\text{Predicted Cost} = -63{,}993 + 16{,}654\text{Log(Units)} \tag{15.13}$$

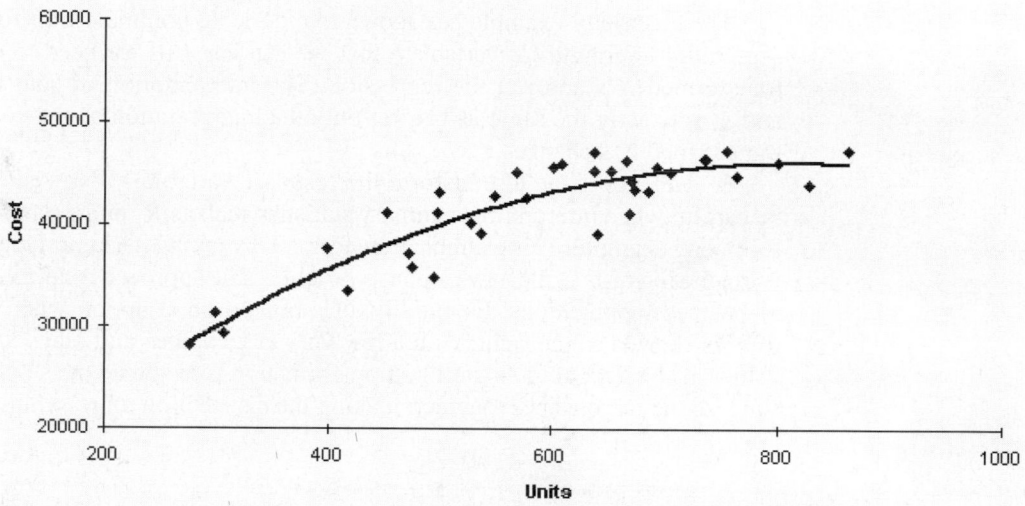

FIGURE 15.34 Quadratic Fit in Electricity Example

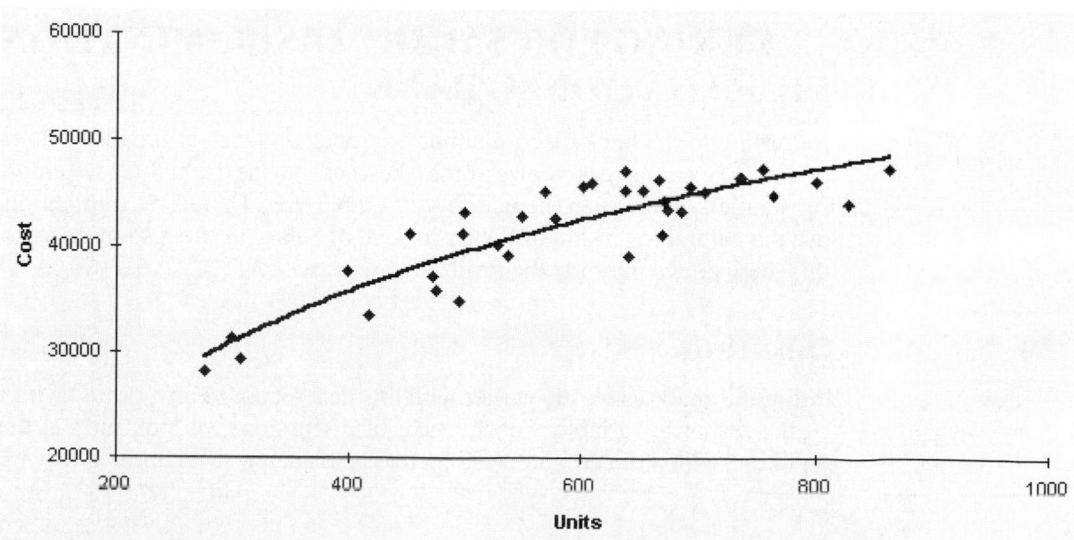

FIGURE 15.35 Logarithmic Fit to Electricity Data

and the R^2 and s_e values are 79.8% and 2393. These latter values indicate that the logarithmic fit is not quite as good as the quadratic fit. However, the advantage of the logarithmic equation is that it is easier to interpret. In fact, one reason logarithmic transformations of variables are used as widely as they are in regression analysis is that they are fairly easy to interpret.

In the present case, where the log of an *explanatory* variable is used, we can interpret its coefficient as follows. Suppose that Units increases by 1%—from 600 to 606, for example. Then equation (15.13) implies that the expected cost will increase by approximately $0.01(16,654) = 166.54$ dollars. In words, every 1% increase in Units is accompanied by an expected $166.54 increase in expected cost.[9] Note that for larger values of Units, a 1% increase represents a larger absolute increase (from 700 to 707 instead of from 600 to 606, say). But each such 1% increase entails the *same* increase in expected cost. This is another way of describing the "decreasing marginal cost" property. ∎

The electricity example has shown two possible nonlinear transformations of the *explanatory* variable (or variables) that we can use. All we need to do is create the transformed X's and run the regression. The interpretation of statistics such as R^2 and s_e is exactly the same as before; only the interpretation of the coefficients of the transformed X's changes.

It is also possible to transform the response variable Y. Now, however, we must be careful when interpreting summary statistics such as R^2 and s_e, as we explain in the following example. This example transforms Y by taking its natural logarithm and then using the log of Y as the new response variable. This approach is taken in a wide variety of business applications. Essentially, it is often a good option when the distribution of Y is skewed to the right, with a few very large values and many small to medium values. The effect of the logarithm transformation is to spread the small values out and squeeze the large values together, making the distribution more symmetric.

EXAMPLE   15.4 (CONTINUED)

CHECKING FOR SALARY DISCRIMINATION AT FIFTH NATIONAL BANK

Returning to the bank discrimination example, a glance at the distribution of salaries of the 208 employees shows some skewness to the right—a few employees make substantially more than the majority of employees. Therefore, it might make sense to use the natural logarithm of Salary instead of Salary as the response variable. If we do this, how do we interpret the results?

Solution

All of the analyses we did earlier with this data set could be repeated with Log(Salary) as the response variable. For the sake of discussion, we look only at the regression equation with Female and YrsExper as explanatory variables. After we create the

---

[9]In general, if b is the coefficient of the log of X, then the expected change in Y when X increases by 1% is approximately 0.01 times b.

Log(Salary) variable and run the regression, we obtain the output in Figure 15.36. The estimated regression equation is

$$\text{Predicted Log(Salary)} = 3.5829 + 0.0188\text{YrsExper} - 0.1616\text{Female} \qquad \textbf{(15.14)}$$

The R^2 and s_e values are 42.4% and 0.1794. For comparison, when this same equation was estimated with Salary as the response variable, R^2 and s_e were 49.1% and 8.070.

We first interpret R^2 and s_e. Neither is directly comparable to the R^2 or s_e value with Salary as the response variable. Recall that R^2 in general is the percentage of the response variable explained by the regression equation. The problem here is that the two R^2 values are percentages explained of *different* response variables, Log(Salary) and Salary. The fact that one is smaller than the other (42.4% versus 49.1%) does not necessarily mean that it corresponds to a "worse" fit. They simply are not comparable.

The situation is even worse with s_e. Each s_e is a measure of a typical residual, but the residuals in the Log(Salary) equation are in "log dollars," whereas the residuals in the Salary equation are in dollars. These units are completely different. For example, the log of $1000 is only 6.91. Therefore, it is no surprise that s_e for the Log(Salary) is *much* smaller than s_e for the Salary equation. If we want comparable standard errors for the two equations, we must take antilogs of fitted values from the Log(Salary) equation to convert them back to dollars, subtract these from the original Salary values, and take the standard deviation of these "residuals." (The EXP function in Excel can be used to take antilogs.) You can check that the resulting standard deviation is 7.774.[10] This is somewhat smaller than s_e from the Salary equation, an indication of a slightly *better* fit.

FIGURE 15.36
Regression Output with Log(Salary) as Response Variable

	A	B	C	D	E	F	G	H
1	Results of multiple regression for Log(Salary)							
2								
3	Summary measures							
4		Multiple R	0.6514					
5		R-Square	0.4243					
6		Adj R-Square	0.4187					
7		StErr of Est	0.1794					
8								
9	ANOVA Table							
10		Source	df	SS	MS	F	p-value	
11		Explained	2	4.8613	2.4307	75.5556	0.0000	
12		Unexplained	205	6.5950	0.0322			
13								
14	Regression coefficients							
15			Coefficient	Std Err	t-value	p-value	Lower limit	Upper limit
16		Constant	3.5829	0.0280	128.0326	0.0000	3.5277	3.6381
17		Female	-0.1616	0.0265	-6.0936	0.0000	-0.2139	-0.1093
18		YrsExper	0.0188	0.0018	10.5556	0.0000	0.0153	0.0224

Finally, we interpret equation (15.14) itself. Fortunately, this is fairly easy. When the response variable is Log(Y) and a term on the right-hand side of the equation is of the form bX, then whenever X increases by 1 unit, $\widehat{Y}$ changes by a constant *percentage*, and this percentage is approximately equal to b (written as a percentage). For example, if $b = 0.035$, then when X increases by 1 unit, $\widehat{Y}$ increases by approximately 3.5%. Applied to equation (15.14), this means that for each extra year of experience with Fifth National, an employee's salary is expected to increase by about 1.88%. To interpret the Female coefficient, note that the only possible increase in Female is 1 unit, from 0

---

[10]To make the two "standard deviations" comparable, we use the denominator $n - 3$ in each.

for male to 1 for female. When this occurs, the expected percentage *decrease* in salary is approximately 16.16%. In other words, equation (15.14) implies that females can expect to make about 16% less than men with comparable years of experience. ∎

We are not necessarily claiming that the bank data are fit better with Log(Salary) as the response variable than with Salary—it appears to be a virtual toss-up. However, the lessons from this example are important in general. They are as follows:

1. The R^2 values with Y and Log(Y) as response variables are not directly comparable. They are percentages explained of *different* variables.

2. The s_e values with Y and Log(Y) as response variables are usually of totally different magnitudes. To make the s_e from the log equation comparable, we must calculate residuals in the *original* units, as described in the example.

3. To interpret any term of the form bX in the log equation, we first express b as a percentage. For example, $b = 0.035$ becomes 3.5%. Then when X increases by 1 unit, the expected *percentage* change in Y is approximately b.

Multiplicative Relationships

A particular type of nonlinear relationship that has firm grounding in economic theory is called a **multiplicative** relationship. It is also called a **constant elasticity** relationship. It has the form

$$Y = aX_1^{b_1} X_2^{b_2} \cdots X_k^{b_k} \tag{15.15}$$

One property of this type of relationship is that the effect of a change on any explanatory variable X_i on Y depends on the levels of the other X's in the equation. This is not true for the *additive* relationships

$$Y = a + b_1 X_1 + b_2 X_2 + \cdots + b_k X_k$$

that we have been discussing. For additive relationships, when any X_i increases by one unit, Y changes by b_i units, regardless of the levels of the other X's.

The term "constant elasticity" comes from economics. Economists define the elasticity of Y with respect to X as the percentage change in Y that accompanies a 1% increase in X. Often this is in reference to a demand–price relationship. Then the "price elasticity" is the percentage decrease in demand when price increases by 1%. Usually, the elasticity depends on the current value of X. For example, the price elasticity when the price is $35 might be different than when the price is $50. However, when the relationship is of the form

$$Y = aX^b$$

then the elasticity is *constant*, the same for any value of X. Moreover, it is approximately equal to the exponent b. For example, if $Y = 2X^{-1.5}$, then the constant elasticity is approximately -1.5, so that when X increases by 1%, Y decreases by approximately 1.5%.

The constant elasticity property carries over to the multiple-X relationship in equation (15.15). Then each exponent is the approximate elasticity for its X. For example, if $Y = 2X_1^{-1.5} X_2^{0.7}$, then we can make the following statements:

- When X_1 increases by 1%, Y decreases by approximately 1.5%, regardless of the current values of X_1 and X_2.

- When X_2 increases by 1%, Y increases by approximately 0.7%, regardless of the current values of X_1 and X_2.

We can use linear regression to estimate the nonlinear relationship in equation (15.15) by taking natural logarithms of *all* variables. Here we exploit two properties of logarithms: (1) the log of a product is the sum of the logs, and (2) the log of X^b is b times the log of X. Therefore, taking logs of both sides of equation (15.15) gives

$$\text{Log}(Y) = \text{Log}(a) + b_1\text{Log}(X_1) + \cdots + b_k\text{Log}(X_k)$$

This equation is *linear* in the log variables $\text{Log}(Y)$ and $\text{Log}(X_1)$ through $\text{Log}(X_k)$, so it can be estimated in the usual way with multiple regression. We can then interpret the coefficients of the explanatory variables directly as elasticities. The following example illustrates the method.

EXAMPLE 15.6

DEMAND FOR AUTOMOBILES IN THE UNITED STATES

The file CARDEMAND.XLS contains annual data (1970–1987) on domestic auto sales in the United States. The data are listed in Figure 15.37. The variables are defined as

- Quantity: annual domestic auto sales (in number of units)
- Price: real price index of new cars
- Income: real disposable income
- Interest: prime rate of interest

FIGURE 15.37
Data for Automobile Demand Example

	A	B	C	D	E
1	Car demand data				
2					
3	Year	Quantity	Price	Income	Interest
4	1970	7,115,270	107.6	1668.1	7.91%
5	1971	8,676,410	112	1728.4	5.72%
6	1972	9,321,310	111	1797.4	5.25%
7	1973	9,618,510	111.1	1916.3	8.03%
8	1974	7,448,340	117.5	1896.6	10.81%
9	1975	7,049,840	127.6	1931.7	7.86%
10	1976	8,606,860	135.7	2001	6.84%
11	1977	9,104,930	142.9	2066.6	6.83%
12	1978	9,304,250	153.8	2167.4	9.06%
13	1979	8,316,020	166	2212.6	12.67%
14	1980	6,578,360	179.3	2214.3	15.27%
15	1981	6,206,690	190.2	2248.6	18.87%
16	1982	5,756,610	197.6	2261.5	14.86%
17	1983	6,795,230	202.6	2331.9	10.79%
18	1984	7,951,790	208.5	2469.8	12.04%
19	1985	8,204,690	215.2	2542.2	9.93%
20	1986	8,222,480	224.4	2645.1	8.33%
21	1987	7,080,890	232.5	2676.1	8.22%

Estimate and interpret a multiplicative (constant elasticity) relationship between Quantity and Price, Income, and Interest.

Solution

We first take natural logs of all four variables. (This can be done in one step with the StatPro/Data Utilities/Transform Variables menu item or we can use Excel's LN function.) We then use multiple regression, with Log(Quantity) as the response variable and

Log(Price), Log(Income), and Log(Interest) as the explanatory variables. The resulting output is shown in Figure 15.38. The corresponding equation for Log(Quantity) is

$$\text{Predicted Log(Quantity)} = 4.675 - 1.185\text{Log(Price)} + 2.183\text{Log(Income)}$$
$$- 0.191\text{Log(Interest)}$$

If we like, we can convert this back to original variables, that is, back to multiplicative form, by taking antilogs. The result is

$$\text{Predicted Quantity} = 107.198\text{Price}^{-1.185}\text{Income}^{2.183}\text{Interest}^{-0.191}$$

where the constant 107.198 is the antilog of 4.675 (and can be calculated in Excel with the EXP function).

In either form, the equation implies that the elasticities are approximately equal to -1.185, 2.183, and -0.191. When Price increases by 1%, Quantity tends to decrease by about 1.185%; when Income increases by 1%, Quantity tends to increase by about 2.183%; and when Interest increases by 1%, Quantity tends to decrease by about 0.191%.

Does this multiplicative equation provide a better fit to the automobile data than an additive relationship? Without doing considerably more work, it is difficult to answer this question with any certainty. As we discussed in the bank salary example, it is *not* sufficient to compare R^2 and s_e values for the two fits. Again, the reason is that one has Log(Quantity) as the response variable, while the other has Quantity, so the R^2 and s_e measures are not comparable. We will simply state that the multiplicative relationship provides a reasonably good fit—a scatterplot of its fitted values versus residuals shows no unusual patterns—and it makes sense economically.

FIGURE 15.38
Regression Output for Multiplicative Relationship

	A	B	C	D	E	F	G	H
1	*Results of multiple regression for Log(Quantity)*							
2								
3	*Summary measures*							
4		Multiple R	0.8445					
5		R-Square	0.7132					
6		Adj R-Square	0.6517					
7		StErr of Est	0.0887					
8								
9	*ANOVA Table*							
10		Source	df	SS	MS	F	p-value	
11		Explained	3	0.2738	0.0913	11.6043	0.0004	
12		Unexplained	14	0.1101	0.0079			
13								
14	*Regression coefficients*							
15			Coefficient	Std Err	t-value	p-value	Lower limit	Upper limit
16		Constant	4.6747	3.2631	1.4326	0.1739	-2.3240	11.6733
17		Log(Price)	-1.1845	0.3619	-3.2732	0.0056	-1.9606	-0.4083
18		Log(Income)	2.1828	0.6584	3.3151	0.0051	0.7706	3.5950
19		Log(Interest)	-0.1906	0.0811	-2.3501	0.0340	-0.3646	-0.0167

PROBLEMS

Skill-Building Problems

22. Suppose that a regional express delivery service company wants to estimate the cost of shipping a package (Y) as a function of cargo type, where cargo type includes the following possibilities: fragile, semifragile, and durable. Costs for 15 randomly chosen packages of approximately the same weight and same distance shipped, but of different cargo types, are provided in P15_22.XLS.

a. Formulate an appropriate multiple regression model to predict the cost of shipping a given package.

b. Estimate the formulated model using the given sample data, and interpret the estimated regression coefficients.

c. According to the estimated regression model, which cargo type is the *most* costly to ship? Which cargo type is the *least* costly to ship?

d. How well does the estimated model fit the given sample data? How might the model be improved?

e. Given the estimated regression model, predict the cost of shipping a package with semifragile cargo.

23. For this problem, refer to Problem 3 and the data in the file P15_3.XLS.

a. Generate a scatterplot diagram for these data. Comment on the observed behavior of the minimum wage over time.

b. Estimate an appropriate regression model to explain the variation of the American minimum age over the given time period. Interpret the estimated regression coefficients.

c. Analyze the estimated model's residuals. Is the estimated regression model adequate? If not, return to part **b** and revise the model. Continue to revise the model until your results are satisfactory.

24. An insurance company wants to determine how its annual operating costs depend on the number of home insurance (X_1) and automobile insurance (X_2) policies that have been written. The file P15_24.XLS contains relevant information for 10 branches of the insurance company. The company believes that a multiplicative model might be appropriate because operating costs typically increase by a constant percentage as the number of either type of policy increases by a given percentage. Use the given data to estimate a multiplicative model for this insurance company. Interpret your results. Does a multiplicative model provide a good fit to these data?

25. For this problem, refer to Problem 8 and the data in the file P15_8.XLS.

a. Estimate a multiple regression model using the given data. Include linear terms as well as an interaction term involving the return on average equity (X_1) and annual dividend rate (X_2).

b. Which of the three explanatory variables (X_1, X_2, and X_1X_2) should be included in a final version of this regression model? Explain. Does your conclusion make sense in light of your knowledge of corporate finance?

Skill-Extending Problems

26. Suppose that you are interested in predicting the price of a laptop computer based on its various features. The file P15_26.XLS contains observations on the sales price and a number of potentially relevant variables for a randomly chosen sample of laptop computers.

a. Formulate a multiple regression model that includes all potential explanatory variables and estimate it with the given sample data.

b. Interpret the estimated regression equation. Indicate the impact of each attribute on the computer's sales price. For example, what impact does the monitor type have on the average sales price of a laptop computer?

c. How well does the estimated regression model fit the data given in the file P15_26.XLS?

d. Use the estimated regression equation to predict the price of a laptop computer with the following features: a 60-megahertz processor, a battery that holds its charge for 240 minutes, 32-megabytes of RAM, a DX chip, a color monitor, a mouse pointing device, and a 24-hour, toll-free customer service hotline.

27. Continuing Problem 7, suppose that the antique collector believes that the *rate of increase* of the auction price with the age of the item will be driven upward by a large number of bidders. How would you revise the multiple regression model developed previously to model this feature of the problem?

a. Estimate your revised model using the data in the file P15_7.XLS.

b. Interpret each of the estimated coefficients in your revised model.

c. Does this revised model fit the given data better than the original multiple regression model? Why or why not?

28. Continuing Problem 8, revise the multiple regression model developed previously to include an interaction term between the return on average equity (X_1) and annual dividend rate (X_2).

a. Estimate your revised model using the data provided in the file P15_8.XLS.

b. Interpret each of the estimated coefficients in your revised model. In particular, how do you interpret the coefficient for the interaction term in the revised model?

c. Does this revised model fit the given data better than does the original multiple regression model? Why or why not?

29. Continuing Problem 13, suppose that one of the managers of this regional express delivery service company is trying to decide whether to add an interaction term involving the package weight (X_1) and the distance shipped (X_2) in the multiple regression model developed previously.

a. Why would the manager want to add such a term to the regression equation?

b. Estimate the revised model using the data given given in the file P15_13.XLS.

c. Interpret each of the estimated coefficients in your revised model. In particular, how do you interpret the coefficient for the interaction term in the revised model?

d. Does this revised model fit the given data better than the original multiple regression model? Why or why not?

15.10 PREDICTION

Once we have estimated a regression equation from a set of data, we might want to use this equation to predict the value of the response variable for *new* observations. As an example, suppose that a retail chain is considering opening a new store in one of several proposed locations. It naturally wants to choose the location that will result in the largest revenues. The problem is that the revenues for the new locations are not yet known. They can be observed only after stores are opened in these locations, and the chain cannot afford to open more than one store at the current time. An alternative is to use regression analysis. Using data from *existing* stores, the chain can run a regression of the response variable revenue on several explanatory variables such as population density, level of wealth in the vicinity, number of competitors nearby, ease of access given the existing roads, and so on.

Assuming that the regression equation has a reasonably large R^2 and, even more important, a reasonably small s_e, the chain can then use this equation to predict revenues for the proposed locations. Specifically, it will gather values of the explanatory variables for each of the proposed locations, substitute these into the regression equation, and look at the predicted revenue for each proposed location. All else being equal, it will probably choose the location with the highest predicted revenue.

We generally want a **point prediction** and a **prediction interval**. The point prediction is a best guess, obtained by substituting the new X values into the regression equation. That is, the point prediction is the fitted value $\widehat{Y}$. The prediction interval, generally quoted at the 95% level, provides an interval around the point prediction where we are 95% sure the actual Y value will fall. Although the exact formulas for the lower and upper limits of a 95% prediction interval are complicated, it usually suffices to approximate them by going out $2s_e$ on each side of $\widehat{Y}$, where s_e is the standard error of estimate:

$$\text{Approximate 95\% prediction interval: } \widehat{Y} \pm 2s_e$$

To see how this can be implemented in Excel, we revisit the Pharmex drugstore data set, where a sales index is regressed on a promotional expenditures index for a sample of 50 regions.

EXAMPLE | **15.1 (CONTINUED)**

SALES VERSUS PROMOTIONAL EXPENDITURES AT PHARMEX

Besides the 50 regions in the data set, Pharmex does business in five other regions, which have promotional expenses indices of 114, 98, 84, 122, and 101. Find a point prediction for Sales and a 95% prediction interval for each of these regions.

Solution

This example cannot be solved directly with StatPro, but it is relatively easy with Excel's built-in functions. We illustrate the procedure in Figure 15.39. The original data appear in columns B and C. We use the range names SalesOld and PromoteOld for the data in these columns. The new regions appear to the right in rows 9–13. Their given values of Promote are in the range G9:G13, which we name PromoteNew. To obtain the predicted sales for these regions, we use Excel's TREND function by highlighting the range H9:H13, typing the formula

=TREND(SalesOld,PromoteOld,PromoteNew)

and pressing Ctrl-Shift-Enter. This substitutes the new values of the explanatory variable (in the third argument) into the regression equation based on the data from the first two arguments.

We then calculate the limits of a 95% prediction interval for each new region in columns I and J by going out two standard errors on each side of the predicted values in column H. This uses the standard error of estimate, 7.395, that we calculated earlier for this example. We see from the wide prediction intervals how much uncertainty remains. For example, the prediction interval for a region with Promote equal to 114 extends from 97.24 to 126.82. This implies that the point prediction for this region, 112.03, contains a considerable amount of uncertainty. The reason is the relatively large standard error of estimate, s_e. If we could reduce s_e, the length of the prediction interval would be reduced accordingly. Contrary to what you might expect, this is *not* a sample size problem. A larger sample size would almost surely *not* produce a smaller value of s_e. The problem is that Promote is not highly correlated with Sales. The only way to decrease s_e and obtain more accurate predictions is to find other explanatory variables that are more closely related to Sales.

	A	B	C	D	E	F	G	H	I	J	K
1	Pharmex drugstore data										
2											
3	Original data (used to estimate regression)										
4											
5	Region	Promote	Sales			Predictions for individual customers					
6	1	77	85			Approximate std err		7.395			
7	2	110	103								
8	3	110	102			Region	Promote	Pred Sales	Std Err	Lower limit	Upper limit
9	4	93	109			51	114	112.03	7.395	97.24	126.82
10	5	90	85			52	98	99.83	7.395	85.04	114.62
11	6	95	103			53	84	89.16	7.395	74.37	103.95
12	7	100	110			54	122	118.13	7.395	103.34	132.92
13	8	85	86			55	101	102.12	7.395	87.33	116.91
14	9	96	92								
15	10	83	87								
52	47	98	104								
53	48	100	98								
54	49	95	108								
55	50	96	87								

FIGURE 15.39 Prediction in Simple Regression ∎

Prediction When *Y* Is Transformed This method of obtaining a point prediction and then going out two standard errors on each side for a 95% prediction interval can be always be used. However, if we have transformed *Y*, say, by using Log(*Y*) as the response variable, then we need to apply the method to the *appropriate* point prediction and standard error. Specifically, suppose Log(*Y*) is used as the response variable, and we want to predict *Y*. The following procedure is often used.

1. Run a regression in the usual way with Log(Y) as the response variable, and request a list of the fitted values.

2. Take EXP of each of the fitted values. These represent predictions of the Y's. (Remember that EXP is Excel's "antilog" function. It transforms log dollars, say, into dollars.)

3. Calculate the absolute percentage errors between Y's and the predictions from step 2.

4. Average the absolute percentage errors in step 3, and multiply this average by 1.25. This approximates the standard deviation of the *percentage* errors, labeled s_{pe}. For example, s_{pe} might be 4.7%. This indicates the magnitude of typical prediction errors.

5. For each *new* observation, substitute its X's into the regression equation and take EXP of the result. This provides a point prediction. Now go out $2s_{pe}$ on each side of the point prediction in a percentage sense. For example, if the point prediction is 120 and s_{pe} is 4.7%, then a 95% prediction interval extends from 9.4% below 120 to 9.4% above 120—from 108.72 to 131.28.

We will present an example of this procedure in Section 16.6 of the next chapter, when we consider exponential trends.

PROBLEMS

Skill-Building Problems

30. For this problem, refer to Problem 26 and the data in the file P15_26.XLS.
  a. Estimate a multiple regression model that includes all available explanatory variables.
  b. Use the estimated regression equation to predict the price of a laptop computer with the following features: a 50-megahertz processor, a battery that holds its charge for 180 minutes, 20 megabytes of RAM, a DX chip, a color monitor, a trackball pointing device, and a 24-hour, toll-free customer service hotline.
  c. Find a 95% prediction interval for the price of a laptop computer as characterized in part **b**.

31. Suppose that a power company located in southern Alabama wants to predict the peak power load (i.e., Y, the maximum amount of power that must be generated each day to meet demand) as a function the daily high temperature (X). A random sample of

25 summer days is chosen, and the peak power load and the high temperature are recorded on each day. The file P15_31.XLS contain these observations.
  a. Use the given data to estimate a simple linear regression model. How well does the estimated regression model fit the given data?
  b. Examine the residuals of the estimated regression equation. Do you see evidence of any violations of the assumptions regarding the errors of the regression model?
  c. Given your result in part **b**, do you recommend modifying the original regression model in this case? If so, how would you revise it?
  d. Use the final version of your regression model to predict the peak power load on a summer day with a high temperature of 90 degrees.
  e. Find a 95% prediction interval for the peak power load on a summer day with a high temperature of 90 degrees.

15.11 CONCLUSION

In this chapter we have seen how useful regression analysis can be for a variety of business applications and how statistical software such as the StatPro add-in in Excel enables us to obtain relevant output—both graphical and numerical—with very little effort. However, we have also seen that there are many concepts that need to be understood well before regression analysis can be used appropriately. Given the user-friendly software currently available, it is all too easy to generate enormous amounts of regression output and then misinterpret or misuse much of it.

At the very least, you should (1) be able to interpret the standard regression output, including statistics on the regression coefficients and summary measures such as R^2 and s_e, (2) know what to look for in the many available scatterplots, (3) know how to use dummy variables, interaction terms, and nonlinear transformations to improve a fit, and (4) be able to spot clear violations of the regression assumptions. However, we have not covered everything. Indeed, many entire books are devoted exclusively to regression analysis. Therefore, you should recognize when you do *not* know enough to handle a regression problem such as nonconstant error variance or autocorrelation appropriately. In this case it is best to consult a statistical expert.

PROBLEMS

Skill-Building Problems

32. Management of a home appliance store in Charlotte would like to understand the growth pattern of the monthly sales of VCR units over the past 2 years. Managers have recorded the relevant data in the file P15_1.XLS. The question is whether the sales of VCR units have been growing *linearly* over the past 24 months.
  a. Generate a scatterplot diagram for these data. Comment on the observed behavior of monthly VCR sales at this store over time.
  b. Formulate and estimate an appropriate regression model to explain the variation of monthly VCR sales over the given time period. Interpret the estimated regression coefficients.
  c. Analyze the estimated model's residuals. Is your estimated regression model adequate? If not, return to part **b** and revise your model. Continue to revise the model until your results are satisfactory.

33. Chipco, a small computer chip manufacturer, wants to be able to forecast monthly operating costs as a function of the number of units produced during a month. The company has collected the 16 months of data in the file P15_33.XLS.
  a. Determine an equation that can be used to predict monthly production costs from units produced. Are there any outliers?
  b. How could the regression line obtained in part **a** be used to determine whether the company was efficient or inefficient during any particular month?

34. The "beta" of a stock is found by running a regression with the monthly return on a market index as the explanatory variable and the monthly return on the stock as the response variable. The beta of the stock is then the slope of this regression.
  a. Explain why most stocks have a positive beta.
  b. Explain why a stock with a beta with absolute value greater than 1 is more volatile than the market and a stock with a beta with absolute value less than 1 is less volatile than the market.
  c. Use the data in the file P15_34.XLS to estimate the beta for Ford Motor Company.
  d. What percentage of the variation in Ford's return is explained by market variation? What percentage is unexplained by market variation?
  e. Verify (using Excel's COVAR and VAR functions) that the beta for Ford is given by

$$\frac{\text{Covariance between Ford and Market}}{\text{Variance of Market}}$$

  Also, verify that the correlation between Ford return and Market return is the square root of R^2.

35. The file P15_35.XLS contains monthly returns on Anheiser-Busch (AB) and a market index for the period 1988–1993. Use these data to answer the following questions.
  a. What percentage of the variation in the return in AB is explained by variation in the market? What percentage is unexplained by variation in the market?
  b. Predict the change in AB during a month in which the market goes up by 2%.
  c. Use Excel's CORREL functions to determine the correlation between the return on AB and the market. Verify that this correlation between AB and the market is equal to the square root of R^2 from the regression output.
  d. Estimate the beta for AB by using regression. (See the previous problem for a definition of

beta.) Then verify that it can also be found (using Excel's COVAR and VAR functions) from

$$\frac{\text{Covariance between AB and Market}}{\text{Variance of Market}}$$

36. The file P15_36.XLS contains monthly sales (in thousands) and price of a popular candy bar.
   a. Describe the type of relationship between price and sales (linear, nonlinear, strong, weak).
   b. What percentage of variation in monthly sales is explained by variation in price? What percentage is unexplained?
   c. If the price of the candy bar is $0.55, predict monthly candy bar sales.
   d. Use the regression output to determine the correlation between price and candy bar sales.
   e. Are there any outliers?

37. The file P15_37.XLS contains the amount of money spent advertising a product (in thousands of dollars) and the number of units sold (in millions) for 8 months .
   a. Assume that the only factor influencing monthly sales is advertising. Fit the following three curves to these data: linear $(Y = a + bX)$, exponential $(Y = ab^X)$, and power $(Y = aX^b)$. Which equation best fits the data?
   b. Interpret the best-fitting equation.
   c. Using the best-fitting equation, predict sales during a month in which $60,000 is spent on advertising.

38. Callaway Golf is trying to determine how the price of a set of clubs affects the demand for clubs. The file P15_38.XLS contains the price of a set of clubs (in dollars) and the monthly sales (in millions of sets sold).
   a. Assume the only factor influencing monthly sales is price. Fit the following three curves to this data: linear $(Y = a + bX)$, exponential $(Y = ab^X)$, and power $(Y = aX^b)$. Which equation best fits the data?
   b. Interpret your best-fitting equation.
   c. Using the best-fitting equation, predict sales during a month in which the price is $470.

39. The file P15_39.XLS contains the databit power per chip for computers. Use regression to estimate how databit power per chip has changed over time. (This result is called Moore's law.) Also predict the databit power per chip in the year 2000. Do you think Moore's law can continue indefinitely? (*Source: One World Ready or Not,* by William Greider, 1996)

40. The file P15_40.XLS contains the cost of building (in hundreds of millions of dollars) a plant to produce RAM chips for PC's. Use regression to estimate how (or whether) the cost of building a RAM plant has increased over time. Predict the cost of building a RAM plant in the year 2000. (*Source: One World Ready or Not,* by William Greider, 1996)

41. The auditor of Kiely Manufacturing is concerned about the number and magnitude of year-end adjustments that are made annually when the financial statements of Kiely Manufacturing are prepared. Specifically, the auditor suspects that the management of Kiely Manufacturing is using discretionary write-offs to manipulate the reported net income. To check this, the auditor has collected data from 25 firms that are similar to Kiely Manufacturing in terms of manufacturing facilities and product lines. The cumulative reported third quarter income and the final net income reported are listed in the file P15_41.XLS for each of these 25 firms. If Kiely Manufacturing reported a cumulative third quarter income of $2,500,000 and a preliminary net income of $4,900,000, should the auditor conclude that the relationship between cumulative third quarter income and the annual income for Kiely Manufacturing differs from that of the 25 firms in this sample? Why or why not?

42. For 12 consecutive weeks, you have observed the sales (in number of cases) of canned tomatoes at Mr. D's. Each week you kept track of the following:
   ▪ Was a promotional notice placed in all shopping carts for canned tomatoes?
   ▪ Was a coupon given for canned tomatoes?
   ▪ Was a price reduction (none, 1 or 2 cents off) given?
   The file P15_42.XLS contains these data.
   a. Use multiple regression to determine how the above factors influence sales.
   b. Discuss whether your final equation has any problems with heteroscedasticity or multicollinearity.
   c. Predict sales of canned tomatoes during a week in which Mr. D's uses a shopping cart notice, a coupon, and a 1-cent price reduction.

43. The file P15_43.XLS contains data on pork sales. Price is in dollars per hundred pounds, quantity sold is in billions of pounds, per capita income is in dollars, U.S. population is in millions, and GNP is in billions of dollars.
   a. Use the data to develop a regression equation that could be used to predict the quantity of pork sold during future periods. Does heteroscedasticity or multicollinearity appear to be a problem?
   b. Suppose that during each of the next two quarters, price is 45, U.S. population is 240, GNP is 2620, and per capita income is 10,000. (These are in the units described above.) Predict the quantity of pork sold during each of the next 2 quarters.

44. The file P15_44.XLS contains the quarterly revenues (in millions of dollars) of Washington Gas and Light for the years 1980–1986. We want to use these data to build a multiple regression model that can be used to forecast future revenues.

a. Which variables should be included in the regression? Be sure to explain your rationale for including or excluding variables.

b. Interpret the coefficients of your final equation.

c. Make a forecast for revenues during the first quarter of 1987. Also, estimate the probability that 1987 Quarter 1 revenues will be at least $150 million dollars. (*Hint*: Use the standard error of prediction and the fact that the errors are approximately normally distributed.)

45. The belief that larger majorities for a president in a presidential election help the President's party increase its representation in the House and Senate is called the "coattail" effect. The file P15_45.XLS gives the percent by which each president since 1948 won the election and the number of seats in the House and Senate gained (or lost) during each election. Are these data consistent with the idea of presidential coattails? (*Source*: *Wall Street Journal*, September 10, 1996)

46. When potential workers apply for a job that requires extensive manual assembly of small intricate parts, they are initially given three different tests to measure their manual dexterity. The ones who are hired are then periodically given a performance rating on a 0–100 scale that combines their speed and accuracy in performing the required assembly operations. The file P15_46.XLS lists the test scores and performance ratings for a randomly selected group of employees. It also lists their seniority (months with the company) at the time of the performance rating.

a. Look at a matrix of correlations. Can you say for certainty (based only on these correlations) that the R^2 value for the regression will be at least 35%? Why or why not?

b. Is there any evidence (from the correlation matrix) that multicollinearity will be a problem? Why or why not?

c. Run the regression of JobPerf versus all four independent variables. List the equation, the value of R^2, and the value of s_e. Do all of the coefficients have the signs you would expect? Briefly explain.

d. Referring to the equation in part **c**, if a worker (outside of the 80 in the sample) has 15 months of seniority and test scores of 57, 71, and 63, give a prediction and an approximate 95% prediction interval for this worker's JobPerf score.

e. One of the t-values for the coefficients in part **c** is less than 1. Does it mean that this variable is not related to JobPerf?

f. Arguably, the three test measures provide overlapping (or redundant) information. For the sake of parsimony (explaining "the most with the least"), it might be sensible to regress JobPerf versus only two explanatory variables, Sen and AvgTest, where AvgTest is the average of the three test scores, that is, AvgTest = (Test1+Test2+Test3)/3. Run this regression and report the same measures as in part **c**: the equation itself, R^2, and s_e. Would you argue that this equation is "just as good as" the equation in part **c**? Explain briefly.

47. Nicklaus Electronics manufactures electronic components used in the computer and space industries. The annual rate of return on the market portfolio and the annual rate of return on Nicklaus Electronics stock for the last 36 months are shown in the file P15_47.XLS. The company wants to calculate the "systematic risk" of its common stock. (It is systematic in the sense that it represents the part of the risk that Nicklaus shares with the market as a whole.) The rate of return Y_t in period t on a security is believed to be related to the rate of return m_t on a market portfolio by the equation

$$Y_t = a + bm_t + e_t$$

Here, a is the risk-free rate of return, b is the security's systematic risk, and e_t is an error term. Using the data available, estimate the systematic risk of the common stock of Nicklaus Electronics. Would you say that Nicklaus stock is a "risky" investment? Why or why not?

48. The auditor of Kaefer Manufacturing uses regression analysis during the analytical review stage of the firm's annual audit. The regression analysis attempts to uncover relationships that exist between various account balances. Any such relationship is subsequently used as a preliminary test of the reasonableness of the reported account balances. The auditor wants to determine whether a relationship exists between the balance of accounts receivable at the end of the month and that month's sales. The file P15_48.XLS contains data on these two accounts for the last 36 months. It also shows the sales levels 2 months prior to month 1.

a. Is there any statistical evidence to suggest a relationship between the monthly sales level and accounts receivable?

b. Referring to part **a**, would the relationship be described any better by including this month's sales and the previous month's sales (called lagged sales) in the equation for accounts receivable? What about adding the sales from more than a month ago to the equation? For this problem, why might it make accounting sense to include lagged sales variables in the equation? How do you interpret their coefficients?

c. During month 37, which is a fiscal year-end month, the sales were $1,800,000. The reported accounts receivable balance was $3,000,000. Does this reported amount seem consistent with past experience? Explain.

Skill-Extending Problems

49. An economic development researcher wants to understand the relationship between the size of the monthly home mortgage or rent payment for households in a particular middle-class neighborhood and the following set of household variables: family size, approximate location of the household within the neighborhood, an indication of whether those surveyed own or rent their home, gross annual income of the first household wage earner, gross annual income of the second household wage earner (if applicable), average monthly expenditure on utilities, and the total indebtedness (excluding the value of a home mortgage) of the household. Observations on each of these variables for a large sample of households are recorded in the file P15_49.XLS.

   a. Beginning with family size, iteratively add one explanatory variable and estimate the resulting regression equation to explain the variation in the monthly home mortgage or rent payment. If adding any explanatory variable causes the *adjusted* R^2 measure to fall, do not include that variable in subsequent versions of the regression model. Otherwise, include the variable and consider adding the next variable in the set. Which variables are included in the final version of your regression model?

   b. Interpret the final estimated regression equation you obtained through the process outlined in part **a**. Also, report and interpret the standard error of estimate s_e, the coefficient of determination R^2, and the adjusted R^2 for the final estimated model.

50. (Based on an actual court case in Philadelphia) In the 1994 congressional election, the Republican candidate outpolled the Democratic candidate by 400 votes (excluding absentee ballots). The Democratic candidate outpolled the Republican candidate by 500 absentee votes. The Republican candidate sued (and won), claiming that vote fraud must have played a role in the absentee ballot count. The Republican's lawyer ran a regression to predict (based on past elections) how the absentee ballot margin could be predicted from the votes tabulated on voting machines. Selected results are given in the file P15_50.XLS. Show how this regression could be used by the Republican to prove his claim of vote fraud. (*Hint*: Is the 1994 result an outlier?)

51. The file P15_51.XLS contains data on the price of new and used Taurus sedans. All used prices are from 1995. For example, a new Taurus bought in 1985 cost $11,790 and the wholesale used price of that car in 1995 was $1700. A new Taurus bought in 1994 cost $18,680 and it could be sold used in 1995 for $12,600.

   a. You want to predict the resale value (as a percentage of the original price of the vehicle) as a function of the vehicle's age. Find an equation to do this. (You should try at least two different equations and choose the one that fits best.)

   b. Suppose all police cars are Ford Tauruses. If you were the business manager for the New York Police Department , what use would you make of your findings from part **a**?

52. (The data for this problem are fictitious, but they are not far off.) For each of the top 25 business schools, the file P15_52.XLS contains the average salary of a professor. Thus, for Indiana University (number 15 in the rankings), the average salary is $46,000. Use this information and regression to show that IU is doing a great job with its available resources.

53. Suppose the correlation between the average height of parents and the height of their firstborn male child is 0.5. You are also told that:
   ■ The average height of all parents is 66 inches.
   ■ The standard deviation of the average height of parents is 4 inches.
   ■ The average height of all male children is 70 inches.
   ■ The standard deviation of the height of all male children is 4 inches.

If a mother and father are 73 and 80 inches tall, respectively, how tall do you predict their son to be? Explain why this is called "regression toward the mean."

54. Do increased taxes increase or decrease economic growth? The file P15_54.XLS contains tax revenues as a percentage of Gross Domestic Product (GDP) and the average annual percentage growth in GDP per capita for nine countries during the years 1970–1994. Do these data support or contradict the dictum of supply-side economics? (*Source: The Economist*, August 24, 1996)

55. The file P15_55.XLS contains monthly cost accounting data on overhead costs, machine hours, and direct material costs. This problem will help you explore the meaning of R^2 and the relationship between R^2 and correlations.

   a. Create a table of correlations between the individual variables.

   b. If you ignored the two explanatory variables MachHrs and DirMatCost and predicted each OHCost as the *mean* of all OHCosts, then a typical "error" would be OHCost minus the mean of all OHCosts. Find the sum of squared errors using this form of prediction, where the sum is over all observations.

   c. Now run three regressions: (1) OHCost versus MachHrs, (2) OHCost versus DirMatCost, and (3) OHCost versus both MachHrs and DirMatCost. (The first two are simple regressions, the third is a multiple regression.)

For each, find the sum of squared residuals, and divide this by the sum of squared errors from part **b**. What is the relationship between this ratio and the associated R^2 for that equation? (Now do you see why R^2 is referred to as the percentage of variation explained?)

d. For the first two regressions in part **c**, what is the relationship between R^2 and the corresponding correlation between the response and explanatory variables? For the third regression, it turns out that the R^2 can be expressed as a complicated function of all three correlations in part **a**, that is, not just the correlations between the response variable and each explanatory variable, but also the correlation between the explanatory variables. Note that this R^2 is not just the sum of the R^2 values from the first two regressions in part **c**. Why do you think this is true, intuitively? However, R^2 for the multiple regression is still the square of a correlation, namely, the correlation between the observed and predicted values of OHCost. Verify that this is the case for these data.

56. The file P15_56.XLS contains hypothetical starting salaries (in $1000s) for MBA students directly after graduation. The file also lists their years of experience prior to the MBA program and their class standing in the MBA program (on a 0-100 scale).

a. Estimate the regression equation with Salary as the response variable and Exper and Class as the explanatory variables. What does this equation imply in words? What does the standard error of estimate s_e tell you? What about R^2?

b. Repeat part **a**, but now include the interaction term Exper*Class (the product) in the equation as well as Exper and Class individually. Answer the same questions as in part **a**. What evidence is there that this extra variable (the interaction variable) is worth including? How do you interpret this regression equation?

57. Confederate Express is attempting to determine how its monthly shipping costs depend on the number of units shipped during a month. The file P15_57.XLS contains the number of units shipped and total shipping costs for the last 15 months.

a. Use regression to determine a relationship between units shipped and monthly shipping costs.

b. Plot the errors for the predictions in order of time sequence. Is there any unusual pattern?

c. We have been told that there was a trucking strike during months 11–15, and we believe that this might have influenced shipping costs. How could the answer to part **a** be modified to account for the effects of the strike? After accounting for the effects of the strike, does the unusual pattern in part **b** disappear?

58. You are trying to determine the effects of three packaging displays (A, B, and C) on sales of toothpaste. The file P15_58.XLS contains the number of cases of toothpaste sold for 9 consecutive weeks. The type of store (GR = grocery, DI = discount, and DE = department store) and the store location (U = urban, S = suburban, and R = rural) are also listed.

a. Run a multiple regression to determine how the type of store, display, and store location influence sales. Which potential explanatory variables should be included in the equation? Be sure to explain your rationale for including or excluding variables.

b. What type of store, store location, and display appears to maximize sales?

c. For the type of store in your part **b** answer, estimate the probability that 80 or more cases of toothpaste will be sold during a week. (*Hint*: Use the standard error of prediction and the fact that the errors are approximately normally distributed.)

59. You want to determine the variables that influence bus usage in major American cities. For 24 cities, the following data are listed in the file P15_59.XLS:
- Bus travel (annual, in thousands of hours)
- Income (average per capita income)
- Population (in thousands)
- Land area (in square miles)

a. Use these data to fit the equation

$$\text{BusTravel} = \alpha \ \text{Income}^{\beta_1} \ \text{Population}^{\beta_2} \ \text{LandArea}^{\beta_3}$$

b. Are all variables significant at the 0.05 significance level?

c. Interpret the estimates of β_1, β_2, and β_3.

60. The file P15_60.XLS contains the following information for the years 1970–1987:
- Domestic auto sales (in thousands)
- Real price index for new car prices (where 1967 = 100 is the base index)
- Real disposable income (in 1982 dollars)
- Interest rate

a. Fit a multiplicative model that can be used to predict domestic auto sales. Make sure all variables are significant at the 0.10 significance level.

b. Are there any outliers? If so, what happens if you omit them? *Should* they be omitted?

c. Interpret the coefficients of your final equation.

d. During a year in which the real price index is 250, the interest rate is 12%, and real disposable income per person is $3500, there is a 5% chance that car sales will be less than or equal to what value? (*Hint*: Use the standard error of prediction and the fact that the errors are approximately normally distributed.)

61. The capital asset pricing model (CAPM) is a cornerstone of finance. To apply the CAPM, we assume that each stock has a risk measure (called the beta of the stock) associated with it. Then the CAPM asserts that
  - The expected return on $1 invested in a stock is a linear function of the stock's beta.
  - $1 invested in a stock with a 0 beta will earn an annual return equal to the risk-free interest rate (r_f) on 90-day treasury bills.
  - $1 invested in a stock with a beta of 1 will yield an annual return equal to the annual return (r_m) on the market portfolio.
  a. Formulate a population regression model incorporating the above features of the CAPM. The explanatory variable is the stock's beta and the response variable is the annual return on $1 invested in the stock.
  b. Given the data in Table 15.1, test the adequacy of the model developed in part **a**. Assume $r_f = 0.09$ and $r_m = 0.18$.

TABLE 15.1	Stock Returns and Betas	
Company	**Beta**	**Annual Return**
AT&T	0.56	0.14
IBM	1.07	0.19
GM	0.76	0.16
Polaroid	2.17	0.28
Chrysler	1.04	0.18

62. How does inflation in a country affect exchange rates? The file P15_62.XLS contains the following information for 11 countries.
  - Ratio of percentage increase in prices in local country from 1973–1995 to percentage increase in U.S. prices from 1973–1995.
  - Ratio of 1995 units of local currency per dollar to 1973 units of local currency per dollar.

Use these data to explain how inflation affects exchange rates. How can you explain these results? (*Source: The Economist*, January 20, 1996)

63. The file P15_63.XLS shows the "yield curve" (at monthly intervals) for the years 1985–1992. For example, in January 1985 the annual rate on a 3-month T-bill was 7.76% and the annual rate on a 30-year government bond was 11.45%. Use regression to determine which interest rates tend to move together most closely? (*Source*: International Investment and Exchange Database developed by Craig Holden, Indiana University School of Business)

64. The file P15_64.XLS contains sample data on annual sales for Prozac, a drug produced by Eli

Lilly. For each year, the file lists the price per day of therapy (DOT) charged for Prozac and total Prozac sales (in millions of DOT) for the year. Assuming that price is the only factor influencing Prozac sales, determine the number of DOT of Prozac that Lilly should produce for the year to ensure that there is only a 1% chance that Lilly runs out of Prozac. Assume the current price of Prozac is $1.75. (*Hint*: Use the standard error of prediction and the fact that the errors are approximately normally distributed.)

65. Suppose that an economist has been able to gather data on the demand/price relationship for a particular product. After analyzing scatterplots and using economic theory, the economist decides to estimate an equation of the form $Q = aP^b$, where Q is quantity demanded and P is price. An appropriate regression analysis is then performed, and the estimated parameters turn out to be $a = 1000$ and $b = -1.3$. Now consider two scenarios: (1) the price increases from $10 to $12.50; (2) the price increases from $20 to $25.
  a. Do you expect the percentage decrease in demand to be the same in scenario (1) as in scenario (2)? Why or why not?
  b. What is the expected percentage decrease in demand in scenario (1)? In scenario (2)? Be as exact as possible. (*Hint*: Remember from economics that an elasticity shows directly what happens for a "small" percentage change in price. These changes are not that small, so you will have to do some calculating.)

66. A human resources analyst believes that in a particular industry, the wage rate ($/hr) is related to seniority by an equation of the form $W = ae^{bS}$, where W equals wage rate and S equals seniority (in years). However, the analyst suspects that both parameters, a and b, might depend on whether the workers belong to a union or not. Therefore, the analyst gathers data on a number of workers, both union and nonunion, and estimates the following equation with regression:

$$\ln(W) = 2.14 + 0.027S + 0.12U + 0.006SU$$

Here $\ln(W)$ is the natural log of W, U is 1 for union workers and 0 for nonunion workers, and SU is the product of S and U.
  a. According to this model, what is the predicted wage rate for a nonunion worker with 0 years of seniority? What is it for a union worker with 0 years of seniority?
  b. Explain exactly what this equation implies about the predicted effect of seniority on wage rate for a nonunion worker; for a union worker.

67. Pernavik Dairy produces and sells a wide range of dairy products. Because most of the dairy's costs and prices are set by a government regulatory board, most of the competition between the dairy and its competitors takes place through advertising. The controller of Pernavik has developed the sales and advertising levels for the last 52 weeks. These appear in the file P15_67.XLS. Note that the advertising levels for the three weeks prior to week 1 are also listed. The controller wonders whether Pernavik is spending too much money on advertising. He argues that the company's contribution-margin ratio is about 10%. That is, 10% of each sales dollar goes toward covering fixed costs. This means that each advertising dollar has to generate at least $10 of sales or the advertising is not cost-effective. Use regression to determine whether advertising dollars are generating this type of sales response. (*Hint*: It is very possible that the sales value in any week is affected not only by advertising this week, but also by advertising levels in the past one, two, or three weeks. These are called "lagged" values of advertising. Try regression models with lagged values of advertising included, and see whether you get better results.)

68. Danielson Electronics manufactures color television sets for sale in a highly competitive marketplace. Recently Ron Thomas, the marketing manager of Danielson Electronics, has been complaining that the company is losing market share because of a poor-quality image, and he has asked that the company's major product, the 25-inch console model, be redesigned to incorporate a higher quality level. The company general manager, Steve Hatting, is considering the request to improve the product quality but is not convinced that consumers will be willing to pay the additional expense for improved quality.

As the company controller, you are in charge of determining the cost effectiveness of improving the quality of the television sets. With the help of the marketing staff, you have obtained a summary of the average retail price of the company's television set and the prices of 29 competitive sets. In addition, you have obtained from *The Shoppers' Guide*, a magazine that evaluates and reports on various consumer products, a quality rating of the television sets produced by Danielson Electronics and its competitors. The file P15_68.XLS summarizes

these data. According to *The Shoppers' Guide*, the quality rating, which varies from 0 to 10 (10 being the highest level of quality), considers such factors as the quality of the picture, the frequency of repair, and the cost of repairs. Discussions with the product design group suggest that the cost of manufacturing this type of television set is $125 + Q^2$, where Q is the quality rating.

a. Regress AvgPrice versus QualityRating. Does the regression equation imply that customers are willing to pay a premium for quality? Explain.

b. Given the results from part **a**, is there a preferred level of quality for this product? Assume that the quality level will affect only the price charged and not the level of sales of the product.

c. How might you answer part **b** if the level of sales is also affected by the quality level (or alternatively, if the level of sales is affected by price)?

69. The file P15_69.XLS contains 1987 data on gasoline consumption and several economic variables. The variables are: gasoline consumption for passenger cars (GasUsed), service station price excluding taxes (SSPrice), retail price of gasoline including state and federal taxes (RPrice), Consumer Price Index for all items (CPI), Consumer Price Index for public transportation (CPIT), number of registered passenger cars (Cars), average miles traveled per gallon (MPG), and real per capita disposable income (DispInc). (Sources: *Basic Petroleum Data Book*, published by the American Petroleum Institute, 1989, and *Economic Report of the President*, 1988)

a. Regress GasUsed linearly versus CPIT, Cars, MPG, DispInc, and DefRPrice, where DefRPrice is the deflated retail price of gasoline (RPrice divided by CPI). What signs would you expect the coefficients to have? Do they have these signs? Which of the coefficients are statistically significant at the 0.05 significance level?

b. The government made the claim that for every one cent of tax on gasoline, there would be a $1 billion increase in tax revenue. Use the estimated equation in part **a** to support or refute the government's claim.

Quantity Discounts at the FirmChair Company

The FirmChair Company manufactures customized wood furniture and sells the furniture in large quantities to major furniture retailers. Jim Bolling has recently been assigned to analyze the company's pricing policy. He has been told that quantity discounts were usually given. For example, for one type of chair, the pricing changed at quantities of 200 and 400—that is, these were the quantity "breaks," where the marginal cost of the next chair changed. For this type of chair, the file FIRMCHAIR.XLS contains the quantity and total price to the customer for 81 orders. Use regression to help Jim discover the pricing structure that FirmChair evidently used. (*Note*: A linear regression of TotPrice versus Quantity will give you a "decent" fit, but you can do much better by introducing appropriate variables into the regression.)

Demand for French Bread at Howie's

Howie's Bakery is one of the most popular bakeries in town, and the favorite at Howie's is French bread. Each day of the week, Howie's bakes a number of loaves of French bread, more or less according to a daily schedule. To maintain its fine reputation, Howie's gives to charity any loaves not sold on the day they are baked. Although this occurs frequently, it is also common for Howie's to run out of French bread on any given day—more demand than supply. In this case, no extra loaves are baked that day; the customers have to go elsewhere (or come back to Howie's the next day) for their French bread. Although French bread at Howie's is always popular, Howie's stimulates demand by running occasional 10% off sales.

Howie's has collected data for 20 consecutive weeks, 140 days in all. These data are listed in the file HOWIES.XLS. The variables are Day (Monday–Sunday), Supply (number of loaves baked that day), OnSale (whether French bread is on sale that day), and Demand (loaves actually sold that day). Howie's would like you to see whether regression can be used successfully to estimate Demand from the other data in the file. Howie reasons that if these other variables can be used to predict Demand, then he might be able to determine his daily supply (number of loaves to bake) in a more cost-effective way.

How successful is regression with these data? Is Howie correct that regression can help him determine his daily supply? Is any information "missing" that would be useful? How would you obtain it? How would you use it? Is this extra information *really* necessary?

Investing for Retirement

Financial advisors offer many types of advice to customers, but they generally agree that one of the best things people can do is invest as much as possible in tax-deferred retirement plans. Not only are the earnings from these investments exempt from income tax (until retirement), but the investment itself is tax-exempt. This means that if a person invests, say, $10,000 of his $100,000 in a tax-deferred retirement plan, he pays income tax that year on only $90,000 of his income. This is probably the best method available to most people for avoiding tax payments. However, which group takes advantage of this attractive investment opportunity: everyone, people with low salaries, people with high salaries, or who?

The file RETIREPLAN.XLS lets you investigate this question. It contains data on 194 couples: number of dependent children, combined annual salary of husband and wife, current mortgage on home, average amount of other (nonmortgage) debt, and percentage of combined income invested in tax-deferred retirement plans (assumed to be limited to 15%, which is realistic). Using correlations, scatterplots, and regression analysis, what can you conclude about the tendency to invest in tax-deferred retirement plans in this group of people?

Heating Oil at Dupree Fuels Company[11]

Dupree Fuels Company is facing a difficult problem. Dupree sells heating oil to residential customers. Given the amount of competition in the industry, both from other home heating oil suppliers and from electric and natural gas utilities, the price of the oil supplied and the level of service are critical in determining a company's success. Unlike electric and natural gas customers, oil customers are exposed to the risk of running out of fuel. Home heating oil suppliers therefore have to guarantee that the customer's oil tank will not be allowed to run dry. In fact, Dupree's service pledge is, "50 free gallons on us if we let you run dry." Beyond the cost of the oil, however, Dupree is concerned about the perceived reliability of his service if a customer is allowed to run out of oil.

To estimate customer oil use, the home heating oil industry uses the concept of "degree days." A degree day is equal to the difference between the average daily temperature and 68 degrees Fahrenheit. So if the average temperature on a given day is 50, the degree days for that day will be 18. (If the degree day calculation results in a negative number, the degree days number is recorded as 0.) By keeping track of the number of degree days since the customer's last oil fill, by knowing the size of the customer's oil tank, and by estimating the customer's oil consumption as a function of the number of degree days, the oil supplier can estimate when the customer is getting low on fuel and then resupply the customer.

Dupree has used this scheme in the past but is disappointed with the results and the computational burdens it places on the company. First, the system requires that a consumption-per-degree-day figure be estimated for each customer to reflect that customer's consumption habits, size of home, quality of home insulation, and family size. Because Dupree has over 1500 customers, the computational burden of keeping track of all of these customers is enormous. Second, the system is crude. The consumption per degree day for each customer is computed by dividing the oil consumption during the preceding year by the degree days during the preceding year. This approach has proved to be very unreliable. Customers have tended to use less fuel than estimated during the colder months and more fuel than estimated during the warmer months. This means that Dupree is making more deliveries than necessary during the colder months and customers are running out of oil during the warmer months.

Dupree wants to develop a consumption estimation model that is practical and more reliable. The following data are available in the file DUPREE.XLS:

- The number of degree days since the last oil fill and the consumption amounts for 67 customers.

- The number of people residing in the homes of each of the 67 customers. Dupree thinks that this might be important in predicting the oil consumption of customers using oil-fired hot water heaters because it provides an estimate of the hot-water requirements of each customer. Each of the customers in this sample uses an oil-fired hot-water heater.

- An assessment, provided by Dupree sales staff, of the home type of each of these 67 customers. The home type classification, which is a number between 1 and 5, is a composite index of the home size, age, exposure to wind, level of insulation, and furnace type. A low index implies a lower oil consumption per degree day, and a high index implies a higher consumption of oil per degree day. Dupree figures that the use of such an index will allow them to estimate a consumption model based on a sample data set and then to apply the same model to predict the oil demand of each of his customers.

Use regression to see whether a statistically reliable oil consumption model can be estimated from the data.

---

[11]Case Studies 15.4 and 15.5 are based on problems from *Advanced Management Accounting*, 2nd edition, by Robert S. Kaplan and Anthony A. Atkinson, Prentice Hall, 1989.

Forecasting Overhead at Wagner Printers

Wagner Printers performs all types of printing including custom work, such as advertising displays, and standard work, such as business cards. Market prices exist for standard work, and Wagner Printers must match or better these prices to get the business. The key issue is whether the existing market price covers the cost associated with doing the work. On the other hand, most of the custom work must be priced individually. Because all custom work is done on a job-order basis, Wagner routinely keeps track of all the direct labor and direct materials costs associated with each job. However, the overhead for each job must be estimated. The overhead is applied to each job using a predetermined (normalized) rate based on estimated overhead and labor hours. Once the cost of the prospective job is determined, the sales manager develops a bid that reflects both the existing market conditions and the estimated price of completing the job.

In the past the normalized rate for overhead has been computed by using the historical average of overhead per direct labor hour. Wagner has become increasingly concerned about this practice for two reasons. First, it hasn't produced accurate forecasts of overhead in the past. Second, technology has

changed the printing process, so that the labor content of jobs has been decreasing, and the normalized rate of overhead per direct labor hour has steadily been increasing. The file WAGNER.XLS shows the overhead data that Wagner has collected for its shop for the past 52 weeks. The average weekly overhead for the last 52 weeks is $54,208, and the average weekly number of labor hours worked is 716. Therefore, the normalized rate for overhead that will be used in the upcoming week is about $76 (= 54,208/716) per direct labor hour.

Questions

1. Determine whether you can develop a more accurate estimate of overhead costs.

2. Wagner is now preparing a bid for an important order that may involve a considerable amount of repeat business. The estimated requirements for this project are 15 labor hours, 8 machine hours, $150 direct labor cost, and $750 direct material cost. Using the existing approach to cost estimation, Wagner has estimated the cost for this job as $2040 (= 150 + 750 + (76 × 15)). Given the existing data, what cost would you estimate for this job?

## CHAPTER 16

Time Series Analysis and Forecasting

FORECASTING AT TACO BELL

How much quantitative analysis occurs at fast-food restaurants? At Taco Bell, a lot! This is described in an article by Huerter and Swart (1998), who explain the approach to labor management that has occurred at Taco Bell restaurants over the past decade. Labor is a large component of costs at Taco Bell. Approximately 30% of every sales dollar goes to labor. However, the unique characteristics of fast-food restaurants make it difficult to plan labor utilization efficiently. In particular, the Taco Bell product—food—cannot be inventoried; it must be made fresh at the time the customer orders it. Because of shifting demand throughout any given day, where the lunch period accounts for approximately 52% of a day's sales and as much as 25% of a day's sales can occur during the busiest hour, labor requirements vary greatly throughout the day. If too many workers are on hand during slack times, they are paid for doing practically nothing. Worse than that, however, are the lost sales (and unhappy customers) that occur if too few workers are on hand during peak times. Prior to 1988, Taco Bell made very little effort to manage the labor problem in an efficient, centralized manner. It simply allocated about 30% of each store's sales to the store managers and let them allocate it as best they could—not always with good results.

In 1988 Taco Bell initiated its "value meal" deals, where certain meals were priced as low as 59 cents. This increased demand to the point where management could no longer ignore the labor allocation problem. Therefore, in-store computers were installed, data from all stores were collected, and a team of analysts was assigned the task of developing a cost-efficient labor allocation system. This system, which has now been fully integrated into all Taco Bell stores since 1993, is composed of three subsystems: (1) a forecasting subsystem that, for each store, forecasts the arrival rate of customers by 15-minute interval by day of week; (2) a simulation subsystem that, for each store, simulates the congestion and number of lost customers that will occur for any customer arrival rate, given a specific number (and deployment) of workers; and (3) an optimization subsystem that, for each store, indicates the minimum cost allocation of workers, subject to various constraints, such as a minimum service level and a minimum shift length for workers. Although all three of these subsystems are important, the forecasting subsystem is where it all starts. Each store must have a reasonably accurate forecast of future customer arrival rates, broken down by small time intervals (such as 11:15 A.M. to 11:30 A.M. on Friday), before labor requirements can be predicted and labor allocations can be made in an intelligent manner. Like many real-world forecasting systems, Taco Bell's has two important characteristics: (1) it requires extensive data, which have been made available by the in-store computer systems, and (2) the eventual forecasting method used is mathematically a fairly simple one, namely, 6-week moving averages, which we will study in this chapter.

Simple or not, the forecasts, as well as the other system components, have enabled Taco Bell to cut costs and increase profits considerably. In its first four years, 1993–1996, the labor management system is estimated to have saved Taco Bell approximately $40.34 million in labor costs. Because the number of Taco Bell stores is constantly increasing, the annual company-wide savings from the system will certainly grow in the future. In addition, the focus on quantitative analysis has produced other side benefits for Taco Bell. Its service is now better and more consistent across stores, with many fewer customers leaving because of slow service. Also, the quantitative models developed have enabled Taco Bell to evaluate the effectiveness of various potential productivity enhancements, including self-service drink islands, customer-activated touch screens for ordering, and smaller kitchen areas. So the next time you order food from Taco Bell, you can be assured that there is definitely a method to the madness! ■

16.1 INTRODUCTION

Many decision-making applications depend on a forecast of some quantity. Here are several examples.

- When a service organization, such as a fast-food restaurant, plans its staffing over some time period, it must forecast the customer demand as a function of time. This might be done at a very detailed level, such as the demand in successive half-hour periods, or at a more aggregate level, such as the demand in successive weeks.

- When a company plans its ordering or production schedule for a product it sells to the public, it must forecast the customer demand for this product so that it can stock appropriate quantities—neither too much nor too little.

- When an organization plans to invest in stocks, bonds, or other financial instruments, it typically attempts to forecast movements in stock prices and interest rates.

- When government representatives plan policy, they attempt to forecast movements in macroeconomic variables such as inflation, interest rates, and unemployment.

Unfortunately, forecasting is a very difficult task, both in the short run and in the long run. Typically, we base forecasts on observations made in the past. We investigate past behavior, search for patterns or relationships, and then we make forecasts. There are two problems with this approach. The first is that it is not always easy to uncover historical patterns or relationships. In particular, it is often difficult to separate the "noise" (random behavior) from the underlying patterns. Some forecasts can even overdo it, by attributing importance to patterns that are in fact random variations and are unlikely to repeat themselves.

The second problem is that there are no guarantees that past patterns will continue in the future. The OPEC countries could raise their oil prices again, a company's competitor could introduce a new product into the market, the bottom could fall out of the stock market, and so on. Each of these shocks to the system being studied could drastically alter the future in a highly unpredictable way. This partly explains why forecasts are almost always wrong. Unless they have inside information to the contrary, forecasters must assume that history will repeat itself. But we all know that history does *not* always repeat itself. Therefore, there are many famous forecasts that turned out to be way off the mark, even though the forecasters made reasonable assumptions and used standard forecasting techniques. Nevertheless, forecasts are required constantly by businesses, so we have to give it our best effort.

There are many forecasting methods available, and all practitioners have their favorites. To say the least, there is little agreement among practitioners or theoreticians as to the best forecasting method. The methods can generally be divided into three groups: (1) **judgmental** methods, (2) **extrapolation** (or **time series**) methods, and (3) **econometric** (or **causal**) methods. The first of these is basically nonquantitative and will not be discussed here; the last two are quantitative. In this section we will describe extrapolation and econometric methods in some generality. In the rest of the chapter, we will go into more detail, particularly about the extrapolation methods.

Extrapolation methods are quantitative methods that use past data of a time series variable—and nothing else, except possibly time itself—to forecast future values of the variable. The idea is that we can use past movements of a variable, such as company sales or U.S. exports to Japan, to forecast its future values. There are many extrapolation methods available, including trend-based regression, exponential smoothing, moving averages, and autoregression models. Some of these methods are relatively simple, both conceptually and in terms of the calculations required, whereas others are quite complex.

All of these extrapolation methods search for *patterns* in the historical series and then extrapolate these patterns into the future. Some try to track long-term upward or downward trends and then project these. Some try to track the seasonal patterns (sales up in November and December, down in other months, for example) and then project these. Basically, the more complex the method, the more closely it tries to track historical patterns. Researchers have long believed that it is an asset of a method to be able to track the ups and downs—the zigzags on a graph—of a time series. This has led to voluminous research and increasingly complex methods. But is complexity always better?

Surprisingly, empirical evidence shows that it is sometimes worse. This is documented in the quarter-century review article by Armstrong (1986) and the article by Schnarrs and Bavuso (1986). They document a number of empirical studies on literally thousands of time series forecasts where complex methods fared no better, and often worse, than simple methods. In fact, the Schnarrs and Bavuso article presents evidence that a naive forecast from a "random walk" model often outperforms all of the more sophisticated extrapolation methods.[1]

Econometric models, also called **causal** models, use regression to forecast a time series variable by means of other explanatory time series variables. For example, a company might use a causal model to regress future sales on its advertising level, the population income level, the interest rate, and possibly others. Because we have already discussed regression models in some depth, we will not devote much time to econometric models in this chapter; the mechanics are largely the same as in any regression analysis.

16.2 GENERAL CONCEPTS

Before proceeding, we introduce a bit of notation and discuss some concepts common to most forecasting methods. In general, we let Y denote the variable we want to forecast. Then Y_t denotes the observed value of Y at time t. Typically, the first observation (the most distant one) corresponds to period $t = 1$, and the last observation (the most recent one) corresponds to period $t = T$, where T denotes the number of historical observations of Y. The periods themselves might be weeks, months, quarters, years, or any other convenient unit of time.

Suppose we have just observed Y_{t-k} and want to make a "k-period-ahead" forecast; that is, we want to use the information until time $t - k$ to forecast Y_t. Then we denote the resulting forecast by $F_{t-k,t}$. The first subscript denotes the period in which the forecast is made, and the second subscript denotes the period being forecasted. As an example, if the data are monthly and September 1999 corresponds to $t = 67$, then a forecast of Y_{69}, the value in November 1999, would be labeled $F_{67,69}$. The **forecast error** is the difference between the actual value and the forecast. It is denoted by E with appropriate subscripts. Specifically, the forecast error associated with $F_{t-k,t}$ is $E_{t-k,t}$:

$$E_{t-k,t} = Y_t - F_{t-k,t}$$

This double-subscript notation is necessary to specify when the forecast is being made and which period is being forecasted. However, the former is generally clear from context. Therefore, to simplify the notation, we will usually drop the first subscript and write F_t and E_t to denote the forecast of Y_t and the error in this forecast.

There are actually two steps in any forecasting procedure. The first step is to build a model that fits the historical data well. The second step is to use this model to forecast the future. Most of the work goes into the first step. For any trial model we see how well it "tracks" the known values of the time series. Specifically, we calculate the one-period-ahead forecasts F_t (or more precisely, $F_{t-1,t}$) from the model and compare these to the known values, Y_t, for each time period t in the historical period. We attempt

---

[1] With this naive model we forecast that the next period's value will be the same as this period's value. So if today's closing stock price is 51.375, we forecast that tomorrow's closing stock price will be 51.375.

to find a model that produces small forecast errors, E_t. We expect that if the model forecasts the *historical* data well, it will also forecast *future* data well.

Forecasting software packages typically report several summary measures of the forecast errors. The most important of these are MAE (mean absolute error), RMSE (root mean square error), and MAPE (mean absolute percentage error). These are defined below. Fortunately, models that make any one of these measures small tend to make the others small, so that we can choose whichever measure we want to minimize. In the following formulas, N denotes the number of terms in each sum. This value is typically slightly less than T, the number of historical observations, because it is not usually possible to provide a forecast for each historical period.

$$\text{MAE} = \left(\sum_{t=1}^{N} |E_t| \right) / N \tag{16.1}$$

$$\text{RMSE} = \sqrt{\left(\sum_{t=1}^{N} E_t^2 \right) / N} \tag{16.2}$$

$$\text{MAPE} = 100\% \times \left(\sum_{t=1}^{N} |E_t / Y_t| \right) / N \tag{16.3}$$

RMSE is similar to a standard deviation in that the errors are squared. Because of the square root, its units are the same as those of the forecasted variable. The MAE is similar to the RMSE, except that absolute values of errors are used instead of squared errors. The MAPE is probably the most easily understood measure because it does not depend on the units of the forecasted variable; it is always stated as a percentage. For example, the statement that the forecasts are off on average by 2% has a clear meaning.

Some forecasting software packages are able to choose the best model from a given class—the best exponential smoothing model, for example—by minimizing MAE, RMSE, or MAPE. However, because the details of the package are not always given, we might not be absolutely sure which of these measures is being minimized. Fortunately, this is probably not too important. A model with a small RMSE typically has a small MAPE and a small MAE. In any case, small values of these measures guarantee only that the model forecasts the *historical* observations well. There is still no guarantee that the model will forecast *future* values accurately.

We will now examine a number of useful forecasting models. You should be aware that more than one of these models can be appropriate for any particular time series data. For example, a random walk model and an autoregression model might be equally effective for forecasting stock price data. We will try to give some insights into choosing the best type of model for various types of time series data. However, the ultimate choice depends on the experience of the user.

16.3 RANDOM SERIES

The simplest time series model is the **random** model. In a random model the observations vary around a constant mean, have a constant variance, and are probabilistically independent of one another. Intuitively, a random time series has no time series pattern whatsoever. The observations do not tend to trend upward or downward, the variance does not increase through time, and the observations in one period do not tend to be larger than those in any other periods.

It is probably easier to understand the random model by seeing time series that are *not* random. The time series plots in Figures 16.1–16.5 illustrate some common nonrandom patterns. In Figure 16.1, there is an upward trend. In Figure 16.2, the variance is increasing through time (larger zigzags to the right). Figure 16.3 exhibits seasonality, where observations in certain months are consistently larger than those in other months. There is a "meandering" pattern in Figure 16.4, where large observations tend to be followed by other large observations, and small observations tend to be followed by other small observations. Finally, the opposite behavior of Figure 16.4 is illustrated in Figure 16.5. Here, there are too *many* zigzags—large observations tend to follow small observations, and small observations tend to follow large observations.

A random model can be written as

$$Y_t = \mu + \varepsilon_t \tag{16.4}$$

FIGURE 16.1
A Series with Trend

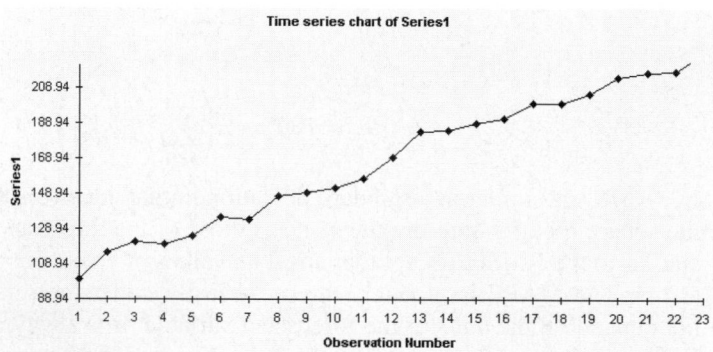

FIGURE 16.2
A Series with Increasing Variance Through Time

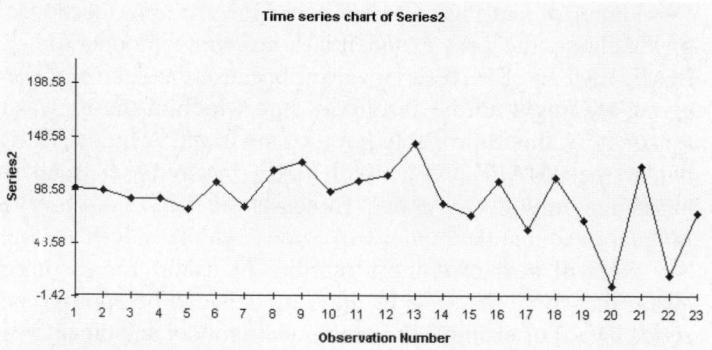

FIGURE 16.3
A Series with Seasonality

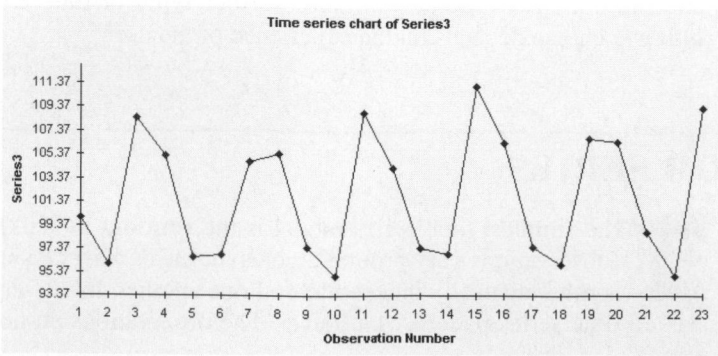

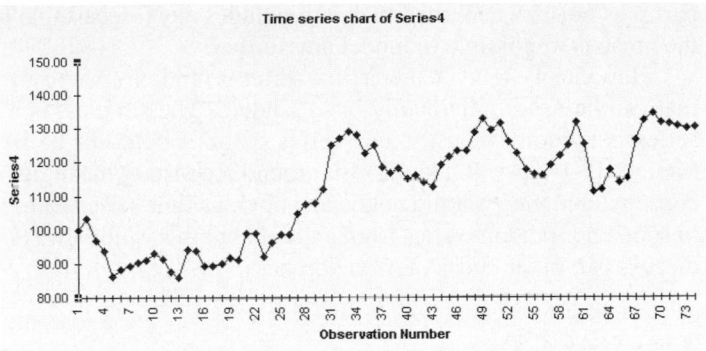

FIGURE 16.4
A Series That
Meanders

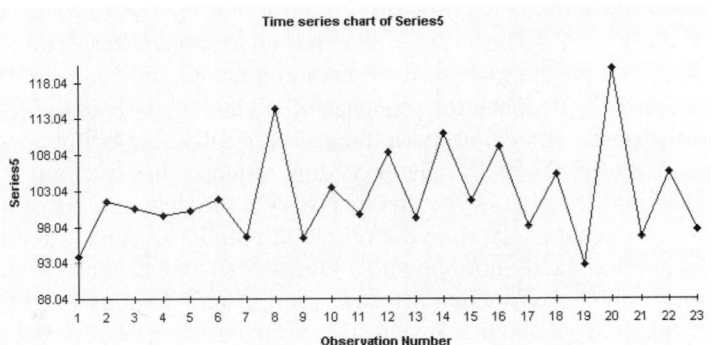

FIGURE 16.5
A Series That
Zigzags Frequently

Here, μ is a constant, the mean of the Y_t's, and ε_t is the residual (or error) term. We assume that the residuals have mean 0, variance σ^2, and are probabilistically independent of one another. In words, the observations vary around the mean μ and have variance σ^2. If the residuals are normally distributed (which is *not* an assumption of the random model), then about 2/3 of the observations will be within the interval $\mu \pm \sigma$, and about 95% of the observations will be within the interval $\mu \pm 2\sigma$.

There are two situations where random time series occur. The first is when the *original* time series is random. For example, when studying the time pattern of diameters of individual parts from a manufacturing process, we might discover that the successive diameters behave like a random time series. In this case we can essentially ignore the fact that the observations are being collected through time, and treat them as a random sample from a distribution with mean μ and standard deviation σ. In forecasting terms, this means that the best forecast of any future observation is simply μ, and a corresponding 95% forecast interval is approximately $\mu \pm 2\sigma$. That is, we can expect 95% of future observations to be within this interval. If we do not know μ or σ, we can instead use the sample mean $\overline{Y}$ and the sample standard deviation s from the historical data.

The second situation where a random series occurs is more common. This is when we fit a model to a time series to obtain an equation of the form

$$Y_t = \text{fitted part} + \text{residual} \tag{16.5}$$

Although the fitted part varies from model to model, its essential feature is that it describes any underlying time series pattern in the original data. The residual is then whatever is left, and we hope that the series of residuals is random with mean $\mu = 0$. The fitted part is used to make forecasts, and the residuals, often called noise, are forecasted to be zero. Indeed, the primary goal in this chapter is to model Y_t as a fitted part plus noise, where the fitted part includes any forecastable pattern in the series, and the noise is impossible to model any further.

How can we tell whether a time series is random? There are several possible checks that can be used individually or in tandem. The simplest is a visual check. If a time series is random, then its time series graph should *not* be like any of the graphs in Figures 16.1–16.5. It should vary around a constant mean, its variance should remain constant, and there should not be any obvious time series patterns. Sometimes it is easy to spot a nonrandom series from a graph, but this is not always the case. Therefore, we discuss two other checks for randomness.

The Runs Test

One check uses the **runs test**. For each observation Y_t we associate a 1 if $Y_t \geq \overline{Y}$ and a 0 if $Y_t < \overline{Y}$.[2] The Y_t series then has an associated series of 0's and 1's. For example, suppose that the successive observations are 87, 69, 53, 57, 94, 81, 44, 68, and 77, with mean $\overline{Y} = 70$. Then the sequence of 0's and 1's is 1, 0, 0, 0, 1, 1, 0, 0, 1. Four of the nine observations are above the mean and five are below it. A **run** is a sequence of consecutive 0's or 1's. The preceding sequence has five runs: 1; 0 0 0; 1 1; 0 0; and 1. The runs test checks whether this is about the right number of runs for a random series.

In general, let R be the observed number of runs. Then it can be shown that R is approximately normal with a given mean and standard deviation when the series is random. By subtracting the mean from R and dividing the difference by the standard deviation, we obtain a Z value that is the basis for the test. For example, if the absolute value of Z is greater than 1.96, then we can reject the null hypothesis of randomness at the 5% significance level.

Note that if Z is large and positive, then there are *more* runs than expected. This means there is too much zigzagging in the time series graph. On the other hand, if the magnitude of Z is large but Z is negative, then there are *fewer* runs than expected. This situation is more common. Here the observations tend to stay above the mean (or below the mean) for longer stretches than we would expect in a random series.

We can perform the runs test easily with StatPro, as illustrated in the following example.

EXAMPLE 16.1

FORECASTING STEREO SALES

Monthly sales for a chain of stereo retailers are listed in the file STEREO.XLS. They cover the period from the beginning of 1995 to the end of 1998, during which there was no upward or downward trend in sales and no clear seasonal peaks or valleys. This behavior is apparent in the time series chart of sales in Figure 16.6. It is possible that this series is random. Does a runs test support this conjecture?

Solution

We use the StatPro Runs Test procedure, found under the StatPro/Statistical Inference/Runs Test menu item. We must specify the time series variable (Sales) and the

---

[2]The runs test can also be based on the sample median of the Y's instead of the sample mean. In fact, it could be based on *any* cutoff value.

FIGURE 16.6
Time Series Plot of
Stereo Sales

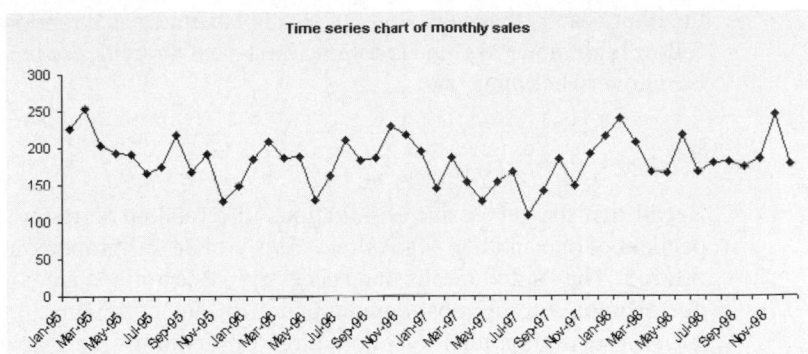

cutoff value for the test, which can be the mean, the median, or even a user-specified value. For this example we select the mean and obtain the output shown in Figure 16.7. Note that StatPro adds two new variables, Sales_High and Sales_NewRun, as well as the elements for the test. The values in the Sales_High are 1 or 0, depending on whether the corresponding sales values are above or below the mean. The values in the Sales_NewRun column are also 1 or 0, depending on whether a *new* run starts in that month.

FIGURE 16.7
Runs Test for
Randomness

	A	B	C	D	E	F	G	H	I
1	Monthly stereo sales (in $1,000s)								
2									
3	Month	Sales		Sales_High	Sales_NewRun			*Runs Test Results for Sales*	
4	Jan-95	226		1	1				
5	Feb-95	254		1	0			Number of obs	48
6	Mar-95	204		1	0			Number above cutoff	26
7	Apr-95	193		1	0			Number below cutoff	22
8	May-95	191		1	0			Number of runs	20
9	Jun-95	166		0	1				
10	Jul-95	175		0	0			E(R)	24.833
11	Aug-95	217		1	1			Stdev(R)	3.403
12	Sep-95	167		0	1			Z-value	-1.420
13	Oct-95	192		1	1			p-value (2-tailed)	0.155
14	Nov-95	127		0	1				
15	Dec-95	148		0	0				
48	Sep-98	175		0	0				
49	Oct-98	185		1	1				
50	Nov-98	245		1	0				
51	Dec-98	177		0	1				

The rest of the output is fairly straightforward. We find the number of observations above the mean as the sum of column D and the number of runs as the sum of column E. Cells I10 and I11 contain the mean and standard deviation of R, assuming randomness, and cell I12 contains the Z value for the test. Finally, we find the two-sided p-value in cell I13 with the formula

=2*(1-NORMSDIST(ABS(Z)))

It is the probability beyond Z under the standard normal curve. We use the factor 2 to obtain the probability in *both* tails.

The output indicates some evidence of nonrandomness—not enough runs. The expected number of runs under randomness is 24.833, and there are only 20 runs for this series. However, the evidence is certainly not overwhelming—the p-value is only 0.155. If we ran this test as a one-tailed test, checking only for too *few* runs, then the appropriate p-value would be 0.078, half of the value shown in cell I12. The conclusion in either case is that sales do not "zigzag" as much as a random series—highs tend to follow highs and lows tend to follow lows—but the evidence in favor of nonrandomness is not overwhelming. ■

Autocorrelation

Recall that the successive observations in a random series are probabilistically independent of one another. Many time series violate this property and are instead **autocorrelated**. The "auto" means that successive observations are correlated with one other. For example, in the most common form of autocorrelation, *positive* autocorrelation, large observations tend to follow large observations, and small observations tend to follow small observations. In this case the runs test is likely to pick it up, because there will be fewer runs than expected and the corresponding Z-value for the runs test will be significantly negative. Another way to check for the same nonrandomness property is to calculate the autocorrelations of the time series.

To understand autocorrelations it is first necessary to understand what it means to **lag** a time series. This concept is easy to understand in spreadsheets. We again use the monthly stereo sales data for 1995–1998 in the STEREO.XLS file. To lag by 1 month, we simply "push down" the series by one row. See column C of Figure 16.8. Note that there is a blank cell at the top of the lagged series (in cell C4). We can continue to push the series down one row at a time to obtain other lags. For example, the lag 3 version of the series appears in the range E7:E54. Now there are three missing observations at the top. Note that in December 1995, say, the first, second, and third lags correspond to the observations in November 1995, October 1995, and September 1995, respectively. That is, lags are simply previous observations. In general, the lag k observation corresponding to period t is Y_{t-k}. These lagged columns can be obtained by copying and pasting the original series or by using the StatPro/Data Utilities/Create Lagged Variable(s) menu item.

The **autocorrelation of lag** k, for any integer k, is the correlation between the original series and the lag k version of the series. For example, in Figure 16.8 the lag 1 autocorrelation is the correlation between the observations in columns B and C. Similarly, the lag 2 autocorrelation is the correlation between the observations in columns B and D.

We have shown the lagged versions of Sales in Figure 16.8 to help motivate the concept of autocorrelation. However, we can use StatPro's Autocorrelation procedure directly, *without* forming the lagged variables, to calculate autocorrelations. This is illustrated in the following continuation of Example 16.1.

FIGURE 16.8
Lags and Autocorrelations for Stereo Sales

	A	B	C	D	E	F	G	H	I	J
1	Illustration of lagging and autocorrelation									
2										
3	Month	Sales	Sales_Lag1	Sales_Lag2	Sales_Lag3			Autocorrelations		
4	Jan-95	226	*	*	*			Lag	Autocorr	StErr
5	Feb-95	254	226	*	*			1	**0.3492**	0.1443
6	Mar-95	204	254	226	*			2	0.0772	0.1443
7	Apr-95	193	204	254	226			3	0.0814	0.1443
8	May-95	191	193	204	254			4	-0.0095	0.1443
9	Jun-95	166	191	193	204			5	-0.1353	0.1443
10	Jul-95	175	166	191	193			6	0.0206	0.1443
11	Aug-95	217	175	166	191					
12	Sep-95	167	217	175	166					
48	Sep-98	175	181	179	168					
49	Oct-98	185	175	181	179					
50	Nov-98	245	185	175	181					
51	Dec-98	177	245	185	175					

EXAMPLE   16.1 (CONTINUED)

FORECASTING STEREO SALES

The runs test on the stereo sales data suggests that the pattern of sales is not completely random. Large values tend to follow large values, and small values tend to follow small values. Do autocorrelations support this conclusion?

Solution

We use StatPro's Autocorrelation procedure, found under the StatPro/Summary Stats/ Autocorrelations menu item. It requires us to specify the time series variable (Sales), the number of lags we want (we chose 6), and whether we want a chart of the autocorrelations. This chart is called a **correlogram**. The resulting autocorrelations and correlogram appear in Figures 16.8 and 16.9. A typical autocorrelation of lag k indicates the relationship between observations k periods apart. For example, the autocorrelation of lag 3, 0.0814, indicates that there is very little relationship between observations separated by 3 months.

FIGURE 16.9
Correlogram for
Stereo Sales

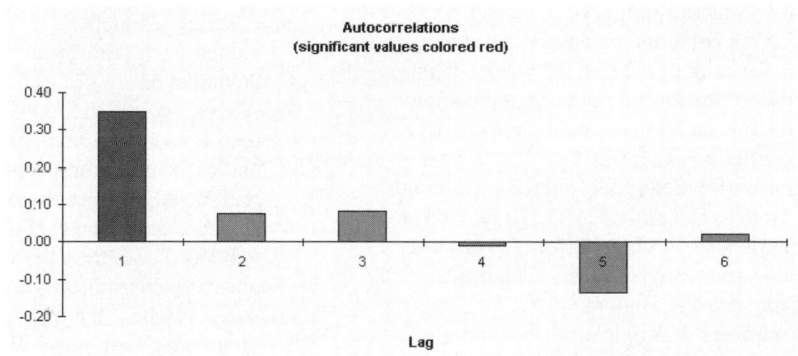

How large is a "large" autocorrelation? Under the assumption of randomness, it can be shown that the standard error of any autocorrelation is approximately $1/\sqrt{T}$, in this case $1/\sqrt{48} = 0.1443$. (Recall that T denotes the number of observations in the series.) If the series is truly random, then only an occasional autocorrelation should be larger than two standard errors in magnitude. Therefore, any autocorrelation that *is* larger than two standard errors in magnitude is worth our attention. These significantly nonzero autocorrelations are boldfaced in the numerical output and shown in red in the chart. The only "large" autocorrelation for the sales data is the first, or lag 1, autocorrelation of 0.3492. The fact that it is *positive* indicates once again that there is some tendency for large sales values to follow large sales values and for small to follow small. The autocorrelations for other lags are less than two standard errors in magnitude and can be considered "noise." ■

Typically, we can ask for autocorrelations up to as many lags as we like. However, there are several practical considerations to keep in mind. First, it is common practice to ask for no more lags than 25% of the number of observations. For example, if there are 48 observations, we should ask for no more than 12 autocorrelations (lags 1–12). Second, the first few lags are typically the most important. Intuitively, if there is any relationship between successive observations, it is likely to be between nearby observations. The June 1996 observation is more likely to be related to the May 1996 observation than to the October 1995 observation. It sometimes happens that there is a fairly large spike in the correlogram at some large lag, such as lag 9, but this can often be ignored as a random "blip" unless there is some obvious reason for its occurrence. The one exception to this is a *seasonal* lag. For example, for monthly data an autocorrelation at lag 12 corresponds to a relationship between observations a year apart, such as May 1996 and May 1995. If this autocorrelation is significantly large, it probably should not be ignored.

PROBLEMS

Skill-Building Problems

1. The file P16_1.XLS contains the number of airline tickets sold by the CareFree Travel Agency each month from January 1995 to December 1998. Is this time series *random*? Perform a runs test and compute a few autocorrelations to support your answer.

2. The file P16_2.XLS contains the weekly sales at a local bookstore for each of the past 25 weeks. Is this time series *random*? Perform a runs test and compute a few autocorrelations to support your answer.

3. The number of employees on the payroll at a food processing plant is recorded at the start of each month from January 1996 to December 1998. These data are provided in the file P16_3.XLS. Perform a runs test and compute a few autocorrelations to determine whether this time series is random.

4. The quarterly numbers of applications for home mortgage loans at a branch office of Northern Central Bank from the first quarter of 1993 to the fourth quarter of 1998 are recorded in the file P16_4.XLS. Perform a runs test and compute a few autocorrelations to determine whether this time series is random.

Skill-Extending Problems

5. Determine whether the RAND() function in Excel actually generates a random stream of numbers.

Generate at least 100 random numbers to perform this test. Summarize your findings.

6. Use a runs test and calculate autocorrelations to decide whether each random series explained below is random. For each part, simulate at least 100 random numbers in the series.
   a. A series of independent normally distributed values, each with mean 70 and standard deviation 5.
   b. A series where the first value is normally distributed with mean 70 and standard deviation 5, and each succeeding value is normally distributed with mean equal to the *previous* value and standard deviation 5. (For example, if the fourth value is 67.32, then the fifth value will be normally distributed with mean 67.32.)
   c. A series where the first value, Y_1, is normally distributed with mean 70 and standard deviation 5, and each succeeding value, Y_t, is normally distributed with mean $(1 + a_t)Y_{t-1}$ and standard deviation $5(1 + a_t)$, where the a_t's are independent, normally distributed values with mean 0 and standard deviation 0.2. (For example, if $Y_{t-1} = 67.32$ and $a_t = -0.2$, then Y_t will be normally distributed with mean $0.8(67.32) = 53.856$ and standard deviation $0.8(5) = 4$.)

16.4 THE RANDOM WALK MODEL

Random series are often building blocks for other time series models. The model we now discuss, the **random walk** model, is an example of this. In a random walk model, the series itself is not random. However, its *differences*—that is, the changes from one period to the next—are random. This type of behavior is typical of stock price data (as well as various other time series data). For example, the graph in Figure 16.10 shows monthly Dow Jones averages from January 1988 through

FIGURE 16.10
Time Series Plot of
Dow Jones Index

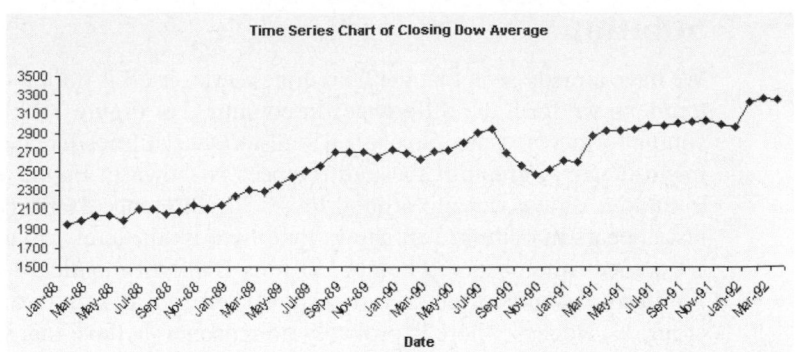

March 1992. This series is not random, as can be seen from its gradual upward trend. (Although the runs test and autocorrelations are not shown for the series itself, they confirm that the series is not random. There are significantly *fewer* runs than expected, and the autocorrelations are significantly *positive* for many lags.)

If we were standing in March 1992 and were asked to forecast the Dow Jones average for the next few months, it is intuitive that we would not use the average of the historical values as our forecast. This forecast would probably be too low because the series has an upward trend. Instead, we might base our forecast on the most recent observation. This is exactly what the random walk model does.

An equation for the random walk model is

$$Y_t = Y_{t-1} + \mu + \varepsilon_t$$

where μ is a constant and ε_t is a random series (noise) with mean 0 and some standard deviation σ. If we let $DY_t = Y_t - Y_{t-1}$, the change in the series from time $t - 1$ to time t (where D stands for difference), then we can write the random walk model as

$$DY_t = \mu + \varepsilon_t$$

This implies that the differences form a random series with mean μ and standard deviation σ. An estimate of μ is the average of the differences, labeled $\overline{Y}_D$, and an estimate of σ is the sample standard deviation of the differences, labeled s_D.

In words, a series that behaves according to this random walk model has random differences, and the series tends to trend upward (if $\mu > 0$) or downward (if $\mu < 0$) by an amount μ each period. If we are standing in period t and want to make a forecast F_{t+1} of Y_{t+1}, then a reasonable forecast is

$$F_{t+1} = Y_t + \overline{Y}_D$$

That is, we add the estimated trend to the current observation to forecast the next observation.

We illustrate this method in the following example of the Dow Jones data.

EXAMPLE   16.2

FORECASTING THE DOW JONES INDUSTRIAL AVERAGE

Given the monthly Dow Jones data in the file DOW.XLS, check that it satisfies the assumptions of a random walk, and use the random walk model to forecast the value for April 1992.

Solution

We have already seen that the Dow Jones series itself is not random, due to the upward trend, so we form the differences in column C of Figure 16.11. (We can do this with simple formulas, or we can use the StatPro/Data Utilities/Create Difference Variable(s) menu item.) A graph of these differences is shown in Figure 16.12. It appears to be a random series, varying around the mean difference 26.00 (in cell C58). The runs test appears in column J. It shows that there is absolutely no evidence of nonrandom differences; the observed number of runs is almost identical to the expected number. Similarly, the autocorrelations (not shown here) are all small except for a random "blip" at lag 11. Because there is probably no reason to believe that values 11 months apart really *are* related, we would tend to ignore this autocorrelation.

Assuming that the random walk model is adequate, the forecast of April 1992 made in March 1992 is the observed March value, 3247.42, plus the mean difference, 26.00, or 3273.42. A measure of the forecast accuracy is provided by the standard deviation, $s_D = 84.65$, of the differences in cell C59. We can be 95% certain that our forecast is off by no more than $2s_D$, or about 170.

If we want to forecast farther into the future, say, 3 months ahead, based on data through March 1992, we would add the most recent value, 3247.42, to 3 times the mean difference, 26.00. That is, we just project the trend that far into the future. The corresponding standard deviation turns out to be $\sqrt{3}s_D$. However, we caution about forecasting too far into the future, especially for such a volatile series such as the Dow. In reality, the whole nature of the *future* series can change. For example, the Dow

FIGURE 16.11
Differences for Dow Jones Data

	A	B	C	D	E	F	G	H	I	J
1	Monthly Dow Jones average closing index, Jan 88 to Mar 92									
2										
3	A random walk?									
4										
5	Date	Dow	Diff		Diff_High	Diff_NewRun			Runs Test Results for Diff	
6	Jan-88	1947.35	·		·	·				
7	Feb-88	1980.65	33.3		1	1			Number of obs	50
8	Mar-88	2044.31	63.66		1	0			Number above cutoff	26
9	Apr-88	2036.13	-8.18		0	1			Number below cutoff	24
10	May-88	1988.91	-47.22		0	0			Number of runs	26
11	Jun-88	2104.94	116.03		1	1				
12	Jul-88	2104.22	-0.72		0	1			E(R)	25.960
13	Aug-88	2051.29	-52.93		0	0			Stdev(R)	3.494
14	Sep-88	2080.06	28.77		1	1			Z-value	0.011
15	Oct-88	2144.31	64.25		1	0			p-value (2-tailed)	0.991
16	Nov-88	2099.04	-45.27		0	1				
17	Dec-88	2148.58	49.54		1	1				
56	Mar-92	3247.42	-9.85		0	1				
57										
58	Means	2585.64	26.00							
59	Stdevs	373.80	84.65							

FIGURE 16.12
Time Series Plot of Dow Differences

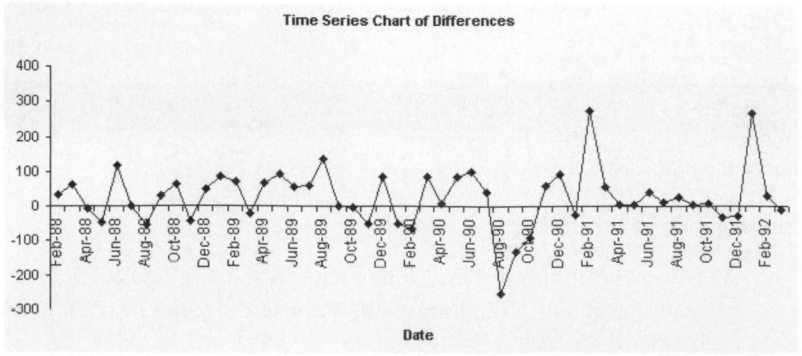

went through the roof shortly after the period in this example. It is unlikely that *any* automatic forecasting model could have predicted the dramatic upward trend in the Dow we saw through the mid to late 1990s. ∎

Skill-Building Problems

7. The file P16_7.XLS contains the daily closing prices of American Express stock from July 21, 1997, through July 20, 1998.
  a. Use the random walk model to forecast the closing price of this stock on July 21, 1998.
  b. We can be 95% certain that the forecast made in part **a** is off by no more than what dollar value?

8. The closing value of the AMEX Airline Index for each trading day from July 21, 1997, through July 21, 1998, is given in the file P16_8.XLS.
  a. Use the random walk model to forecast the closing price of this stock on July 22, 1998.
  b. We can be 68% certain that the forecast made in part **a** is off by no more than what dollar value?

9. The closing value of the Dow Jones Industrial Index for each trading day from March 31, 1998, through July 21, 1998, is provided in the file P16_9.XLS.
  a. Use the random walk model to forecast the closing price of this stock on July 22, 1998.
  b. Use the random walk model to forecast the closing price of this stock on July 29, 1998.
  c. Would it be wise to use the random walk model to forecast the closing price of this stock for a trading day approximately *one month* after July 21, 1998? Explain why or why not.

10. Continuing the previous problem, consider the differences between consecutive closing values of the Dow Jones Industrial Index for the given set of trading days. Do these differences form a random series? Demonstrate why or why not.

11. The purpose of this problem is to get you used to the concept of autocorrelation in a time series. You could do it with any time series, but here you should use the series of Wal-Mart daily stock prices from the beginning of 1992 through the end of July 1992. The data are in the file P16_11.XLS.
  a. First, do it the easy way. Use the Autocorrelations procedure in StatPro to get a list of autocorrelations and a corresponding correlogram. You can choose the number of lags.
  b. Now do it the "hard" way. Create columns of lagged versions of the Close variable—3 or 4 lags will suffice. Next, look at scatterplots of Close

versus its first few lags. If the autocorrelations are large, you should see fairly tight scatters—that's what autocorrelation is all about. Also, generate a correlation matrix to see the correlations between Close and its first few lags. These should be just about the same as the autocorrelations you found in part **a**. (Autocorrelations are calculated slightly differently than regular correlations, which accounts for any slight discrepancies you might notice, but these discrepancies should be minor.)
  c. Create the first differences of Close in a new column. (You can do this manually with formulas, or you can use StatPro's Differences procedure under Utilities.) Now repeat parts **a** and **b** with the differences instead of the original closing prices. That is, examine the autocorrelations of the differences. They should be small, and the scatterplots of the differences versus lags of the differences should be "swarms." This illustrates what happens when the differences of a time series variable have "insignificant" autocorrelations.
  d. Write a short report of your findings.

Skill-Extending Problems

12. Consider a random walk model with the following equation: $Y_t = Y_{t-1} + 500 + \varepsilon_t$, where ε_t is a random series with mean 0 and standard deviation 10.
  a. Use Excel to simulate a time series that behaves according to this random walk model.
  b. Use the time series you constructed in part **a** to forecast the next observation.

13. The file P16_13.XLS contains the daily closing prices of Procter & Gamble stock from July 21, 1997, through July 20, 1998. Use only the data from the beginning of the period through June 19, 1998, to estimate the trend component of the random walk model (i.e., assume that it is currently June 19, 1998, and you seek to forecast this time series from this point onward). Next, use the estimated random walk model to forecast the behavior of the time series from June 22 through July 20 of 1998. Comment on the accuracy of the generated forecasts over this period. How could you improve the forecasts as you progress through these next 20 trading days?

16.5 AUTOREGRESSION MODELS

A regression-based extrapolation method is to regress the current value of the time series on past (lagged) values. This is called **autoregression**, where the "auto" means that the explanatory variables in the equation are lagged values of the response variable, so that we are regressing the response variable on lagged versions of itself. This procedure is fairly straightforward on a spreadsheet. We first create lags of the response variable and then use a regression procedure to regress the original column on the lagged columns. Some trial and error is generally required to see how many lags are useful in the regression equation. The following example illustrates the procedure.

EXAMPLE 16.3

FORECASTING HAMMER SALES

A retailer has recorded its weekly sales of hammers (units purchased) for the past 42 weeks. (See the file HAMMERS.XLS.) A graph of this time series appears in Figure 16.13. It reveals a "meandering" behavior. The values begin high and stay high awhile, then get lower and stay lower awhile, then get higher again. (This behavior could be caused by any number of things, including the weather, increases and decreases in building projects, and possibly others.) How useful is autoregression for modeling these data and how would it be used for forecasting?

FIGURE 16.13
Time Series Plot of
Sales of Hammers

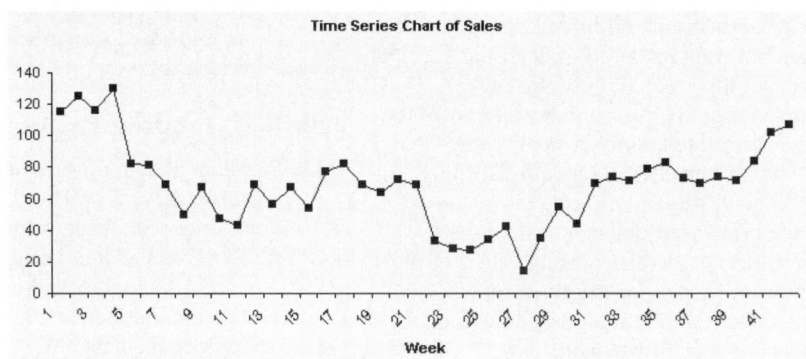

Solution

A good place to start is with the autocorrelations of the series. These indicate whether the Sales variable is linearly related to any of its lags. The first six autocorrelations are shown in Figure 16.14. The first three of them are significantly positive, and then they decrease. Based on this information, we create three lags of Sales and run a regression of Sales versus these three lags. The output from this regression appears in Figure 16.15. We see that R^2 is fairly high, about 57%, and that s_e is about 15.7. However, the p-values for lags 2 and 3 are both quite large. It appears that once the first lag is included in the regression equation, the other two are not really needed.

Therefore, we reran the regression with only the first lag included. (Actually, we first omitted only the third lag. But the resulting output showed that the second lag was still insignificant, so we then omitted it, too.) The regression output with only the first

FIGURE 16.14
Correlogram for
Hammer Sales Data

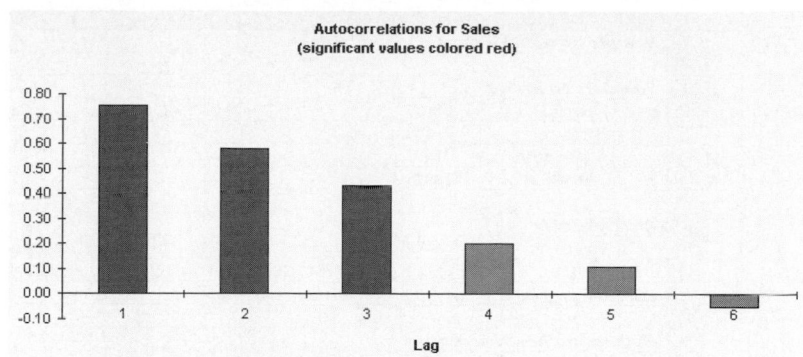

FIGURE 16.15
Autoregression
Output with Three
Lagged Variables

	A	B	C	D	E	F	G	H
1	*Results of multiple regression for Sales*							
2								
3	*Summary measures*							
4		Multiple R	0.7573					
5		R-Square	0.5736					
6		Adj R-Square	0.5370					
7		StErr of Est	15.7202					
8								
9	*ANOVA Table*							
10		Source	df	SS	MS	F	p-value	
11		Explained	3	11634.2001	3878.0667	15.6927	0.0000	
12		Unexplained	35	8649.3896	247.1254			
13								
14	*Regression coefficients*							
15			Coefficient	Std Err	t-value	p-value	Lower limit	Upper limit
16		Constant	15.4986	7.8820	1.9663	0.0572	-0.5027	31.5000
17		Sales_Lag1	0.6398	0.1712	3.7364	0.0007	0.2922	0.9874
18		Sales_Lag2	0.1523	0.1987	0.7665	0.4485	-0.2510	0.5556
19		Sales_Lag3	-0.0354	0.1641	-0.2159	0.8303	-0.3686	0.2977

lag included appears in Figure 16.16 (page 904). In addition, a graph of the response and fitted variables, that is, the original Sales variable and its forecasts, appears in Figure 16.17. The estimated regression equation is

$$\text{Forecasted Sales}_t = 13.763 + 0.793\text{Sales}_{t-1}$$

The associated R^2 and s_e values are approximately 65% and 15.4. The R^2 value is a measure of the reasonably good fit we see in Figure 16.17, whereas s_e is a measure of the likely forecast error for short-term forecasts. It implies that a short-term forecast could easily be off by as much as two standard errors, or about 31 hammers.

To use the regression equation for forecasting *future* sales values, we substitute known or forecasted sales values in the right side of the equation. Specifically, the forecast for week 43, the first week after the data period, is

$$\text{Forecasted Sales}_{43} = 13.763 + 0.793\text{Sales}_{42} = 13.763 + 0.793(107) = 98.6$$

Here we use the *known* value of sales in week 42. However, the forecast for week 44 requires the *forecasted* value of sales in week 43:

$$\text{Forecasted Sales}_{44} = 13.763 + 0.793\text{Forecasted Sales}_{43}$$
$$= 13.763 + 0.793(98.6) = 92.0$$

Perhaps these two forecasts of future sales values are on the mark, and perhaps they are not. The only way we will know for certain is by observing future sales

FIGURE 16.16
Autoregression
Output with a Single
Lagged Variable

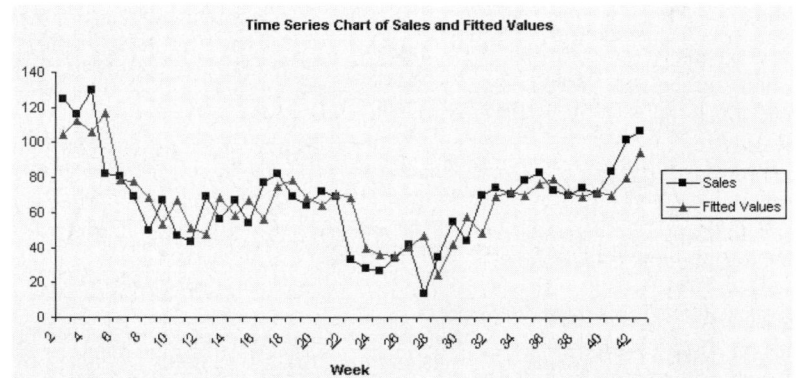

	A	B	C	D	E	F	G	H
1	*Results of multiple regression for Sales*							
2								
3	*Summary measures*							
4		Multiple R	0.8036					
5		R-Square	0.6458					
6		Adj R-Square	0.6367					
7		StErr of Est	15.4476					
8								
9	*ANOVA Table*							
10		Source	df	SS	MS	F	p-value	
11		Explained	1	16969.9761	16969.9761	71.1146	0.0000	
12		Unexplained	39	9306.5117	238.6285			
13								
14	*Regression coefficients*							
15			Coefficient	Std Err	t-value	p-value	Lower limit	Upper limit
16		Constant	13.7634	6.7906	2.0268	0.0496	0.0281	27.4987
17		Sales_Lag1	0.7932	0.0941	8.4329	0.0000	0.6029	0.9834

FIGURE 16.17
Forecasts from
Autoregression

Time Series Chart of Sales and Fitted Values

values. However, it is interesting that in spite of the *upward* movement in the series in the last 3 weeks, the forecasts for weeks 43 and 44 are for *downward* movements. This is a combination of two properties of the regression equation. First, the coefficient of $Sales_{t-1}$, 0.793, is positive. Therefore, the equation forecasts that large sales will be followed by large sales—that is, positive autocorrelation. Second, however, this coefficient is less than 1, and this provides a dampening effect. The equation forecasts that a large will follow a large, but not *that* large. ■

PROBLEMS

Skill-Building Problems

14. Consider the Consumer Price Index, which provides the annual percentage change in consumer prices, for the period from 1914 through 1996. The data are in the file P16_14.XLS.
   a. Compute the first six autocorrelations of this time series.
   b. Use the results of part **a** to specify one or more autoregression models. Estimate each model with the available data. Which model provides the best fit to the given data?

   c. Use the best autoregression model found in part **b** to produce a forecast of the CPI in 1997. Also, provide a measure of the likely forecast error in this case.
15. Consider the proportion of Americans under the age of 18 living below the poverty level for each of the years beginning in 1959 and proceeding through 1996. The data are in the file P16_15.XLS.
   a. Compute the first six autocorrelations of this time series.
   b. Use the results of part **a** to specify one or more autoregression models. Estimate each model

with the available data. Which model provides the best fit to the given data?

c. Use the best autoregression model found in part **b** to produce a forecast of the proportion of American children living below the poverty level in 1997. Also, provide a measure of the likely forecast error in this case.

16. Examine the trend in the annual average values of the discount rate for the period 1977–1996. The data are in the file P16_16.XLS.

a. Specify one or more autoregression models based on autocorrelations of this time series. Estimate each model with the available data. Which model provides the best fit to the given data?

b. Use the best autoregression model found in part **a** to produce forecasts of the discount rate in 1997 and 1998.

17. Consider the average annual interest rates on 30-year fixed mortgages in the United States during the period from 1972 through 1996. The data are recorded in the file P16_17.XLS.

a. Specify one or more autoregression models based on autocorrelations of this time series. Estimate each model with the available data. Which model provides the best fit to the given data?

b. Use the best autoregression model found in part **a** to produce forecasts of the average annual interest rates on 30-year fixed mortgages in 1997, 1998, and 1999.

18. The file P13_18.XLS lists the monthly unemployment rates for the last 10 years. A common way to forecast time series is by using regression with lagged variables.

a. Predict future monthly unemployment rates using some combination of the unemployment rates for the last 4 months. For example, you might use last month's unemployment rate and the unemployment rate from 3 months ago as explanatory variables. Make sure all variables

that you finally decide to keep in your equation are significant at the 0.15 level.

b. Do the residuals in your equation exhibit any autocorrelation?

c. Predict the December 1997 unemployment rate.

d. There is a 5% chance that the December 1997 unemployment rate will be less than what value?

e. What is the probability the December 1997 unemployment rate will be less than 5%?

19. The unit sales of a new drug for the first 25 months after its introduction into the marketplace are recorded in the file P16_19.XLS. Specify one or more autoregression models based on autocorrelations of this time series. Estimate each model with the available data. Which model provides the best fit to the given data? Finally, use the best autoregression model you found to forecast the sales of this new drug in month 26.

Skill-Extending Problem

20. The file P16_13.XLS contains the daily closing prices of Procter & Gamble stock from July 21, 1997, through July 20, 1998.

a. Use only the data from the beginning of the period through June 19, 1998, to estimate an appropriate autoregression model (i.e., assume that it is currently June 19, 1998, and you seek to forecast the given time series from this point onward).

b. Next, use the estimated autoregression model to forecast the behavior of the time series from June 22 through July 20 of 1998. Comment on the accuracy of the generated forecasts over this period.

c. How well does the autoregression model perform in comparison to the random walk model with respect to the accuracy of these forecasts? Explain any significant differences between the forecasting abilities of the two models.

16.6 REGRESSION-BASED TREND MODELS

Many time series follow a long-term trend except for random variation. This trend can be upward or downward. A straightforward way to model this trend is to estimate a regression equation for Y_t, using time t as the *single* explanatory variable. In this section we will discuss the two most frequently used trend models, **linear** trend and **exponential** trend.

Linear Trend

A linear trend means that the time series variable changes by a constant *amount* each time period. The relevant equation is

$$Y_t = \alpha + \beta t + \varepsilon_t \tag{16.6}$$

where, as in previous regression equations, α is the intercept, β is the slope, and ε_t is an error term. The interpretation of β is that it represents the expected change in the series from one period to the next. If β is positive, the trend is upward; if β is negative, the trend is downward. The intercept term α is less important. It literally represents the expected value of the series at time $t = 0$. If time t is coded so that the first observation corresponds to $t = 1$, then α is where we expect the series to have been one period before we started observing. However, it is possible that time is coded in another way. For example, we might have annual data that start in 1985. Then the first value of t might be entered as 1985, which means that the intercept α corresponds to a period 1985 years earlier! Clearly, we would not take its value literally in this case.

As always, the graph of the time series is a good place to start. It indicates whether a linear trend model is likely to provide a good fit. Generally, the graph should rise or fall at approximately a constant rate through time, without too much random variation. But even if there is a lot of random variation—a lot of zigzags—fitting a linear trend to the data might still be a good starting point. Then the *residuals* from this trendline, which should have no remaining trend, could possibly be modeled by some other method in this chapter.

EXAMPLE 16.4

FORECASTING QUARTERLY SALES AT REEBOK

The file REEBOK.XLS includes quarterly sales data for Reebok from first quarter 1986 through second quarter 1996. The time series plot of these data is shown in Figure 16.18. Sales increase from \$174.52 million in the first quarter to \$817.57 million in the final quarter. How well does a linear trend fit these data? Are the residuals from this fit random?

Solution

The plot in Figure 16.18 indicates an obvious upward trend with little or no curvature. Therefore, a linear trend is certainly plausible. We use regression to estimate the linear fit, where Sales is the response variable and Time is the single explanatory variable. Note in the file that we have two columns that indicate time. The Time variable is coded

FIGURE 16.18
Time Series Plot of Reebok Sales

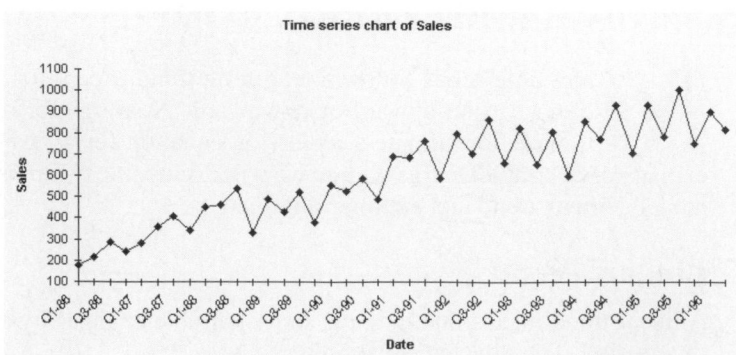

1–42 and is used as the explanatory variable in the regression. The Quarter variable simply labels the quarters (Q1-86–Q2-96) and is used only to label the horizontal axis in Figure 16.18; it is not used for any numerical calculations. The regression output in Figure 16.19 shows that the estimated equation is

$$\text{Forecasted Sales} = 244.82 + 16.53\text{Time}$$

with R^2 and s_e values of 83.8% and $90.38 million. The linear trendline, superimposed on the sales data in Figure 16.20, appears to be a decent fit. It implies that sales are increasing by about $16.53 million per quarter during this time period.[3]

The fit is far from perfect, however. First, the s_e value, $90.38 million, is an indication of the typical forecast error. This is substantial, approximately equal to 11% of the final quarter's sales. Furthermore, there is some regularity to the forecast errors, shown in Figure 16.21. They zigzag more than a random series. There is possibly some seasonal pattern in the sales data, which we might be able to pick up with a more sophisticated forecasting method. However, the basic linear trend is sufficient as a first approximation to the behavior of sales.

FIGURE 16.19
Regression Output for Linear Trend

	A	B	C	D	E	F	G	H
1	*Results of multiple regression for Sales*							
2								
3	*Summary measures*							
4		Multiple R	0.9152					
5		R-Square	0.8377					
6		Adj R-Square	0.8336					
7		StErr of Est	90.3844					
8								
9	*ANOVA Table*							
10		Source	df	SS	MS	F	p-value	
11		Explained	1	1686121.5556	1686121.5556	206.3964	0.0000	
12		Unexplained	40	326773.3750	8169.3344			
13								
14	*Regression coefficients*							
15			Coefficient	Std Err	t-value	p-value	Lower limit	Upper limit
16		Constant	244.8154	28.3989	8.6206	0.0000	187.4192	302.2117
17		Time	16.5304	1.1506	14.3665	0.0000	14.2049	18.8559

FIGURE 16.20
Time Series Plot with Linear Trend Superimposed

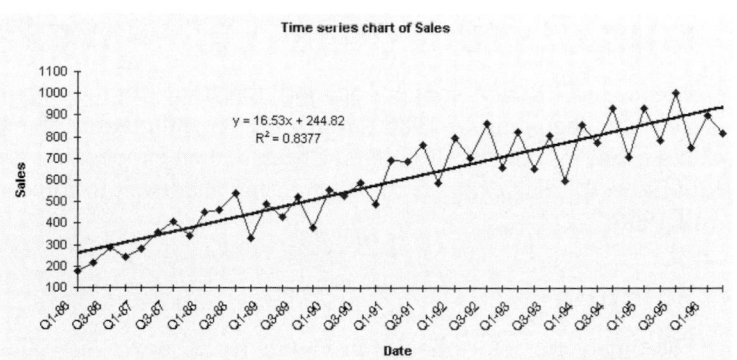

[3]To get this chart in Excel, first create a scatterplot of Sales versus Time, using the option to connect the dots. Then use the Chart/Add Trendline menu item, choose the Linear type, and choose to display the equation and R^2 value under Options.

FIGURE 16.21
Time Series Plot of
Forecast Errors

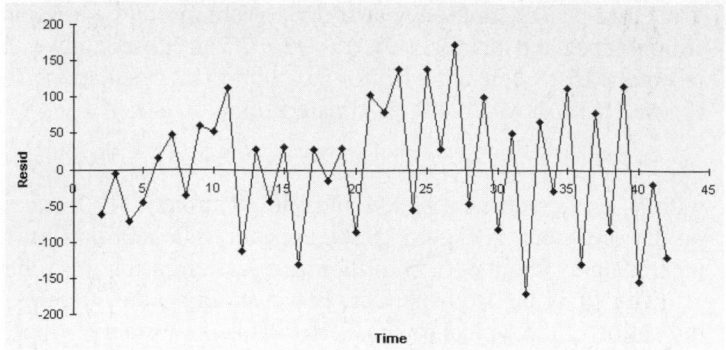

Exponential Trend

In contrast to a linear trend, an exponential trend is appropriate when a time series changes by a constant *percentage* (as opposed to a constant dollar amount) each period. The equation for an exponential trend is

$$Y_t = \alpha e^{\beta t} \tag{16.7}$$

where α and β are constants. It can be shown that the coefficient β (expressed as a percentage) is approximately the percentage change per period. For example, if $\beta = 0.05$, the series is increasing by approximately 5% per period.[4] On the other hand, if $\beta = -0.05$, the series is decreasing by approximately 5% per period.

To estimate an exponential trend, we note that by taking logarithms of both sides, the log of Y_t is linear in t:

$$\ln(Y_t) = \alpha' + \beta t$$

where $\alpha' = \ln(\alpha)$. This implies that we can estimate the parameters of equation (16.7) by regressing $\ln(Y_t)$ on time t. The estimated slope of the regression equation is an estimate of β, whereas the antilog of the estimate of the intercept is an estimate of α. We illustrate the procedure in the following example.

EXAMPLE | **16.5**

FORECASTING QUARTERLY SALES AT INTEL

The file INTEL.XLS contains quarterly sales data for the chip manufacturing firm Intel from the beginning of 1986 through the second quarter of 1996. Each sales value is expressed in millions of dollars. Check that an exponential trend fits these sales data fairly well. Then estimate the relationship and use it to forecast the next two quarters of 1996.

Solution

The time series plot of sales in Figure 16.22 shows that sales are clearly increasing at an *increasing* rate, which a linear trend would not capture. The smooth curve in

---

[4]A more accurate estimate of this percentage change is $e^{\beta} - 1$. For example, when $\beta = 0.05$, this is $e^{\beta} - 1 = 5.13\%$.

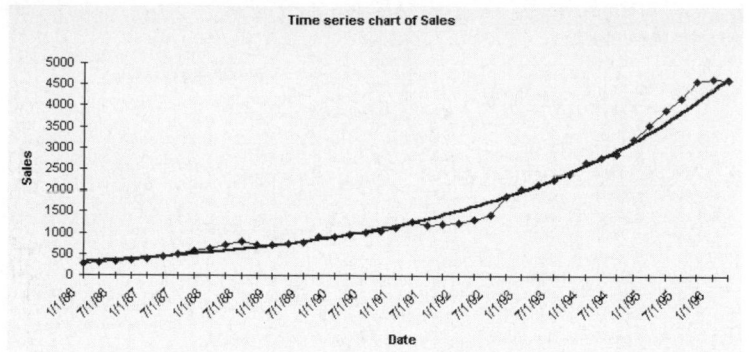

this figure is an exponential trendline, which appears to be an adequate fit. (We get it by choosing Add Trendline from the Chart menu, then choosing the Exponential type.) Alternatively, we can try to "straighten out" the data by taking the log of sales with Excel's LN function. A time series plot of the log data, with a *linear* trendline superimposed, appears in Figure 16.23. These two figures go together logically in the sense that if an exponential trendline fits the original data well, then a linear trendline will fit the transformed data well, and vice versa. Either is evidence of an exponential trend in the sales data.

FIGURE 16.23
Time Series Plot
of Log Sales with
Linear Trend
Superimposed

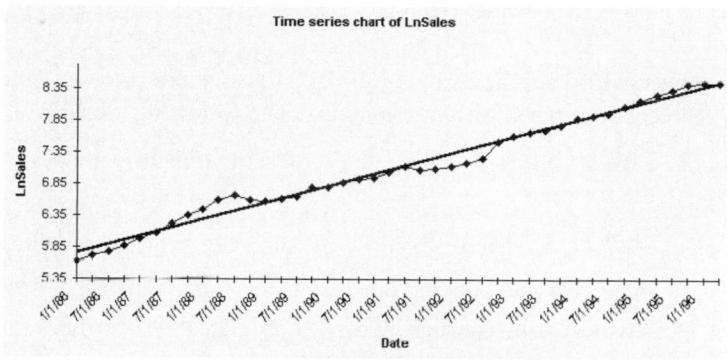

To estimate the exponential trend, we run a regression of the log of sales, LnSales, versus Time. The resulting data and output appear in Figure 16.24 (page 910). The regression output shows that the estimated log of sales is given by

$$\text{Forecasted LnSales} = 5.6883 + 0.0657\text{Time}$$

Alternatively, by taking antilogs we obtain an estimated equation for Sales:

$$\text{Forecasted Sales} = 295.377e^{0.0657\text{Time}}$$

(Note that the antilog of the constant 5.6883 appears in cell J22. We can calculate it with Excel's EXP function.) Looking at the coefficient of Time, we see that Intel's sales are increasing by approximately 6.6% per quarter during this period. This translates to an annual percentage increase of about 29%! Perhaps the slight tailing off that we see at the right of Figure 16.22 indicates that Intel cannot keep up this fantastic rate forever.

	A	B	C	D	E	F	G	H	I	J	K	L	M	N
1	Quarterly data on Intel sales ($ millions)													
2														
3	Time	Date	Sales	LnSales	FittedSales	AbsPctError		*Results of multiple regression*						
4	1	1/1/86	280.05	5.6350	315.45	12.64%								
5	2	4/1/86	305.18	5.7209	336.88	10.39%		*Summary measures*						
6	3	7/1/86	324.14	5.7812	359.77	10.99%			Multiple R	0.9917				
7	4	10/1/86	355.64	5.8739	384.21	8.03%			R-Square	0.9834				
8	5	1/1/87	394.53	5.9777	410.31	4.00%			Adj R-Square	0.9830				
9	6	4/1/87	438.96	6.0844	438.19	0.17%			StErr of Est	0.1060				
10	7	7/1/87	501.13	6.2169	467.96	6.62%								
11	8	10/1/87	572.49	6.3500	499.76	12.70%		*ANOVA Table*						
12	9	1/1/88	635.81	6.4549	533.71	16.06%			Source	df	SS	MS	F	p-value
13	10	4/1/88	726.68	6.5885	569.97	21.56%			Explained	1	26.6625	26.6625	2373.2787	0.0000
14	11	7/1/88	784.94	6.6656	608.70	22.45%			Unexplained	40	0.4494	0.0112		
15	12	10/1/88	727.34	6.5894	650.06	10.63%								
16	13	1/1/89	713.08	6.5696	694.22	2.64%		*Regression coefficients*						
17	14	4/1/89	747.34	6.6165	741.39	0.80%				Coefficient	Std Err	t-value	p-value	
18	15	7/1/89	771.44	6.6483	791.76	2.63%			Constant	5.6883	0.0333	170.8029	0.0000	
19	16	10/1/89	894.97	6.7968	845.56	5.52%			Time	0.0657	0.0013	48.7163	0.0000	
20	17	1/1/90	894.46	6.7962	903.01	0.96%								
21	18	4/1/90	968.30	6.8755	964.36	0.41%		**Summary measures in original units**						
22	19	7/1/90	1012.44	6.9201	1029.88	1.72%			Antilog of intercept	295.38				
23	20	10/1/90	1046.07	6.9528	1099.85	5.14%			MAPE	7.44%				
24	21	1/1/91	1132.78	7.0324	1174.58	3.69%			Stdev of pct error	9.30%				
25	22	4/1/91	1252.69	7.1330	1254.38	0.14%								
44	41	1/1/96	4644.00	8.4433	4373.62	5.82%								
45	42	4/1/96	4621.00	8.4384	4670.78	1.08%								
46														
47	Forecasts for future quarters and 95% forecast intervals													
48	Time	Date	Forecast	Lower limit	Upper limit									
49	43	7/1/96	4988.12	4060.22	5916.02									
50	44	10/1/96	5327.03	4336.08	6317.97									

FIGURE 16.24 Estimation of Exponential Trend

Forecasting the Future Figure 16.24 also shows how to develop forecasts and 95% forecast intervals for future quarters. The following steps are required.[5]

1. **Fitted values.** Calculate the forecasts of historical sales in column E by entering the formula

=$J$22*EXP($J$19*A4)

in cell E4 and copying down. This is formula is based directly on equation (16.7).

2. **Absolute percentage errors.** Calculate the absolute values of the percentage forecast errors in column F by entering the formula

=ABS((E4-C4)/C4)

in cell F4 and copying down.

3. **MAPE and standard deviation of percentage errors.** Calculate the mean absolute percentage error in cell J23 with the formula

=AVERAGE(F4:F45)

Then approximate the standard deviation of the percentage errors, s_{pe}, in cell J24 with the formula

=1.25*J23

4. **Forecasts.** For any future period in row 49, calculate a forecast in cell C49 with the formula

=$J$22*EXP($J$19*A49)

and copy it down for any other future periods.

[5]This uses the procedure outlined at the end of the previous chapter.

5. **Forecast intervals.** To obtain 95% forecast intervals, enter the formulas

=C49*(1-2*$J$24)

and

=C49*(1+2*$J$24)

in cells D49 and E49, and copy them down for any other future periods.

In summary, we forecast Intel's future sales by projecting that its current sales (as of 4/1/96) will continue to increase by about 6.6% per quarter. However, the wide forecast intervals (so wide as to be practically useless in this example) indicate the high level of uncertainty that exists for future sales. ■

Whenever we observe a time series that is increasing at an increasing rate (or decreasing at a decreasing rate), an exponential trend model is worth trying. The key to the analysis is to regress the *logarithm* of the time series variable versus time. It is somewhat more difficult than in the linear case to use the regression for forecasting, but it can be accomplished with the above step-by-step procedure.

PROBLEMS

Skill-Building Problems

21. The file P16_1.XLS contains the number of airline tickets sold by the CareFree Travel Agency each month from January 1995 to December 1998.
    a. Does a linear trend appear to fit these data well? If so, estimate and interpret the linear trend model for this time series. Also, interpret the R^2 and s_e values.
    b. Provide an indication of the typical forecast error generated by the estimated model in part **a**.
    c. Is there evidence of some seasonal pattern in these sales data? If so, characterize the seasonal pattern.
22. The file P16_22.XLS contains the daily closing prices of Wal-Mart stock from July 21, 1997, to July 20, 1998. Does an exponential trend fit these data well? If so, estimate and interpret the exponential trend model for this time series. Also, interpret the R^2 and s_e values.
23. This file P16_23.XLS contains annual data on the amount of life insurance in force in the United States from 1945 to 1981. Fit an exponential growth curve to these data. Use it to forecast values for the next 3 years, including 95% forecast intervals.
24. The file P16_24.XLS contains 5 years of monthly data on sales (number of units sold) for a particular company. The data set begins in January 1995. The company suspects that except for random noise, its sales are growing by a constant *percentage* each month and that they will continue to do so for at least the near future.

a. Explain briefly whether the plot of the series visually supports the company's suspicion.
b. Fit the appropriate regression model to the data. Report the resulting equation and state explicitly what it says about the percentage growth per month.
c. What are the RMSE and MAPE for the forecast model in part **b**? In words, what do they measure? Considering their magnitudes, does the model seem to be doing a good job?
d. In words, how does the model make forecasts for future months? Specifically, if you had the forecast value for December 1999 (the last month in the data set), what simple arithmetic could you use to obtain forecasts for the next few months?
25. The data in the file P16_25.XLS contains quarterly data on GDP from 1966-I to 1991-IV. (The data are expressed in billions of current dollars, they are seasonally adjusted, and they represent annualized rates.)
    a. Look at a time series plot of GDP. Does it suggest a linear relationship? An exponential relationship?
    b. Use regression to estimate an exponential relationship between GDP and Time. Interpret the associated "constant" term and the "slope" term. Would you say that the fit is good? Use the exponential trend model to forecast values for the next 4 quarters, including 95% forecast intervals.

Skill-Extending Problem

26. The file P16_26.XLS contains monthly time series data on corporate bond yields from January 1975 to March 1992. These are averages of daily figures, and each is expressed as an annual rate. The variables are:

- Yield—average yield on corporate bonds
- YieldAAA—average yield on AAA bonds
- YieldAA—average yield on AA bonds
- YieldA—average yield on A bonds
- YieldBAA—average yield on BAA bonds

If you examine the Yield variable, you will notice not only that the autocorrelations of the series are large for many lags, but that the lag-1 autocorrelation of the *differences* is significant. This is very common. It means that the series is not a random walk and that it is probably possible to provide a better forecast than the "naive" forecast from the random walk model. Here is the idea. The large lag-1 autocorrelation of the differences means that the differences are related to the first lag of the differences. This relationship can be estimated by creating the difference variable and a lag of it, then regressing the former on the latter, and finally using this information to forecast the original Yield variable.

a. Verify that the autocorrelations are as described above, and form the difference variable and the first lag of it. Call these DYield and L1DYield (where D is for difference, L1 is for first lag).

b. Run a regression with DYield as the response variable and L1DYield as the single explanatory variable. In terms of the original variable Yield, this equation can be written as

$$\text{Yield}_t - \text{Yield}_{t-1} = a + b(\text{Yield}_{t-1} - \text{Yield}_{t-2})$$

Solving for Yield_t, this is equivalent to the following equation that can be used for forecasting:

$$\text{Yield}_t = a + (1 + b)\text{Yield}_{t-1} - b\text{Yield}_{t-2}$$

Try it—that is, try forecasting April 1992 from the known February and March 1992 values. How might you forecast the May 1992 and June 1992 values? (*Hint*: If you do not have an *observed* value to use in the right side of the equation, use a forecasted value.)

c. The autocorrelation structure led us to the equation in part **b**. That is, the autocorrelations of the original series took a long time to die down, so we looked at the autocorrelations of the differences, and the large spike at lag 1 led to regressing L1DYield on DYield. In turn, this led ultimately to an equation for Yield_t in terms of its first two lags. Now see what you would have obtained if you had tried regressing Yield_t on its first two lags in the first place, that is, if you had used regression to estimate the equation

$$\text{Yield}_t = a + b_1\text{Yield}_{t-1} + b_2\text{Yield}_{t-2}$$

When you use multiple regression to estimate this equation, do you get the same equation as in part **b**?

16.7 MOVING AVERAGES

Perhaps the simplest and one of the most frequently used extrapolation methods is the method of **moving averages**. To implement the moving averages method, we first choose a **span**, the number of terms in each moving average. Let's say the data are monthly and we choose a span of 6 months. Then the forecast of next month's value is the average of the most recent 6 months' values. For example, we average January–June to forecast July, we average February–July to forecast August, and so on. This procedure is the reason for the term *moving* averages.

The role of the span is important. If the span is large—say, 12 months—then many observations go into each average, and extreme values have relatively little effect on the forecasts. The resulting series of forecasts will be much smoother than the original series. (For this reason, the moving average method is called a **smoothing** method.) In contrast, if the span is small—say, 3 months—then extreme observations have a larger effect on the forecasts, and the forecast series will be much less smooth. In the extreme, if the span is 1, there is no smoothing effect at all. The method simply forecasts next month's value to be the same as the current month's value. (This is often called the **naive** forecasting model. It is a special case of the random walk model we discussed earlier, with the mean difference equal to zero.)

What span should we use? This requires some judgment. If we believe the ups and downs in the series are random noise, then we don't want future forecasts to react too quickly to these ups and downs, and we should use a relatively large span. But if we want to track every little zigzag—under the belief that each up or down is predictable—then we should use a smaller span. We should not be fooled, however, by a plot of the (smoothed) forecast series superimposed on the original series. This graph will almost always look better when a small span is used, because the forecast series will appear to track the original series better. Does this mean it will always provide better future forecasts? Not necessarily. There is little point in tracking random ups and downs closely if they represent unpredictable noise.

The following example, a continuation of Example 16.2, illustrates the use of moving averages on the Dow Jones index.

EXAMPLE | **16.2 (CONTINUED)**

FORECASTING THE DOW JONES INDUSTRIAL AVERAGE

We again look at the Dow Jones monthly data from January 1988 through March 1992. How well do moving averages track this series when the span is 3 months; when the span is 12 months? What about future forecasts, that is, beyond March 1992?

Solution

Although the moving averages method is quite easy to implement in Excel—we just form an average of the appropriate span and copy it down—it can be tedious. Therefore, we instead use the Forecasting procedure of StatPro. Actually, this procedure is fairly general in that it allows us to forecast with several methods, either with or without taking seasonality into account. Since this is our first exposure to this procedure, we will go through it in some detail in this example. In later examples, we will mention some of its other capabilities.

We use the StatPro/Forecasting menu item and eventually choose Dow as the variable to analyze. We then see several dialog boxes, the first of which appears in Figure 16.25. Here we specify the timing. Are the data annual, quarterly, and so on, and (if relevant) what year and period do they begin? We can also elect to "hold out" a subset of the data for validation purposes, and we can specify how many periods to forecast into the future. (If we hold out several periods at the end of the data set for validation, then any model is estimated only for the non-hold-out observations, and summary measures are reported for the non-hold-out and hold-out subsets separately.) Figure 16.25 shows that the Dow data are monthly, they begin in the first month of 1988, we do not hold out any data for validation, and we want to forecast 12 months into the future.

In the next dialog box, shown in Figure 16.26, we specify which forecasting method to use and any parameters of that method. Here we are using the moving averages method with a span of 3. Also, we indicate in this dialog box that the data are *not* seasonal. We next see a dialog box that allows us to request various time series plots, and finally we get the usual choice of whether to report the output on the current worksheet or a new worksheet.

FIGURE 16.25
Timing Dialog
Box for StatPro
Forecasting
Procedure

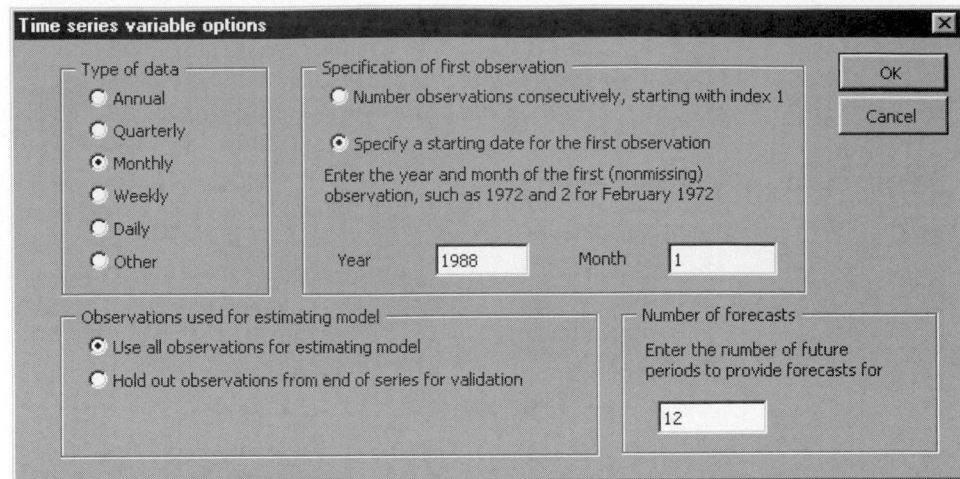

FIGURE 16.26
Method Dialog
Box for StatPro
Forecasting
Procedure

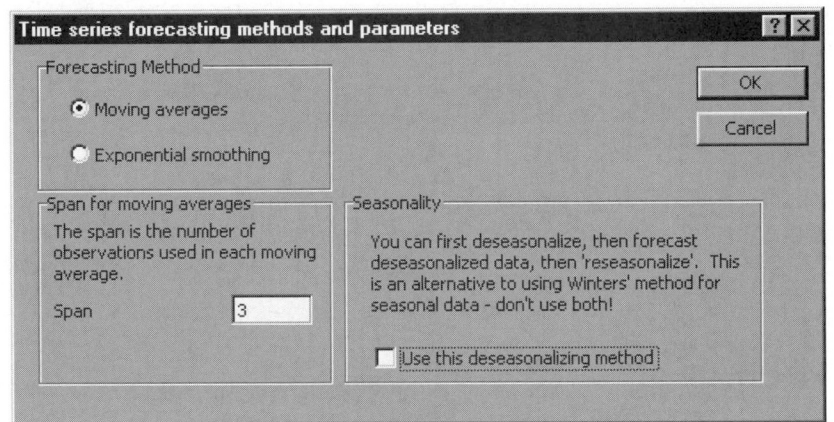

The output consists of several parts, as shown in Figures 16.27–16.30.[6] First, the forecasts and forecast errors are shown for the historical period of the data. Actually, with moving averages we lose some forecasts at the beginning of the period. For example, we lose three when the span is 3 because we don't have enough *previous* data to calculate these early averages. If we ask for *future* forecasts, they are shown in red at the bottom of the data series. Of course, there are no accompanying forecast errors because we do not yet have observations for these future periods. To the left of all this, we see the summary measures MAE, RMSE, and MAPE of the forecast errors. Finally, if we ask for any time series plots, these appear on separate sheets.

The essence of the forecasting method is very simple and is captured in column F of Figure 16.27 (for a span of 3). It uses the formula

=AVERAGE($E2:$E4)

in cell F5, which is then copied down. The forecast errors are then just the differences between columns E and F. For the future periods, the forecast formulas use observations

---

[6]The outputs for StatPro's forecasting procedure are tied to the data by formulas and range names created by StatPro. If you make multiple runs on the same data (using different spans, say), you should put their outputs on separate sheets. Otherwise, some of the outputs for the early runs will be based on range names for the latest run—and will be wrong.

FIGURE 16.27
Moving Averages
Output with Span 3

	A	B	C	D	E	F	G
1	*Forecasting results for Dow*			Date	Observation	Forecast	Error
2				Jan-88	1947.350		
3	**Moving averages**			Feb-88	1980.650		
4				Mar-88	2044.310		
5	Span	3		Apr-88	2036.130	1990.770	45.360
6				May-88	1988.910	2020.363	31.453
7	**Estimation period**			Jun-88	2104.940	2023.117	81.823
8				Jul-88	2104.220	2043.327	60.893
9	MAE	94.9825		Aug-88	2051.290	2066.023	-14.733
10	RMSE	121.8219		Sep-88	2080.060	2086.817	-6.757
11	MAPE	3.57%		Oct-88	2144.310	2078.523	65.787
12				Nov-88	2099.040	2091.887	7.153
13				Dec-88	2148.580	2107.803	40.777
49				Dec-91	2958.640	3005.403	-46.763
50				Jan-92	3227.060	2988.167	238.893
51				Feb-92	3257.270	3057.273	199.997
52				Mar-92	3247.420	3147.657	99.763
53				Apr-92		3243.917	
54				May-92		3249.536	
55				Jun-92		3246.957	
56				Jul-92		3246.803	
57				Aug-92		3247.765	
58				Sep-92		3247.175	
59				Oct-92		3247.248	
60				Nov-92		3247.396	
61				Dec-92		3247.273	
62				Jan-93		3247.306	
63				Feb-93		3247.325	
64				Mar-93		3247.301	

FIGURE 16.28
Moving Averages
Output with Span 12

	A	B	C	D	E	F	G
1	*Forecasting results for Dow*			Date	Observation	Forecast	Error
2				Jan-88	1947.350		
3	**Moving averages**			Feb-88	1980.650		
4				Mar-88	2044.310		
5	Span	12		Apr-88	2036.130		
6				May-88	1988.910		
7	**Estimation period**			Jun-88	2104.940		
8				Jul-88	2104.220		
9	MAE	210.5725		Aug-88	2051.290		
10	RMSE	226.5329		Sep-88	2080.060		
11	MAPE	7.71%		Oct-88	2144.310		
12				Nov-88	2099.040		
13				Dec-88	2148.580		
49				Dec-91	2958.640	2900.355	58.285
50				Jan-92	3227.060	2929.332	297.728
51				Feb-92	3257.270	2982.620	274.650
52				Mar-92	3247.420	3015.473	231.948
53				Apr-92		3042.748	
54				May-92		3052.516	
55				Jun-92		3062.857	
56				Jul-92		3070.750	
57				Aug-92		3078.463	
58				Sep-92		3084.495	
59				Oct-92		3090.673	
60				Nov-92		3096.584	
61				Dec-92		3105.790	
62				Jan-93		3118.052	
63				Feb-93		3108.968	
64				Mar-93		3096.610	

FIGURE 16.29
Moving Averages
Forecasts with
Span 3

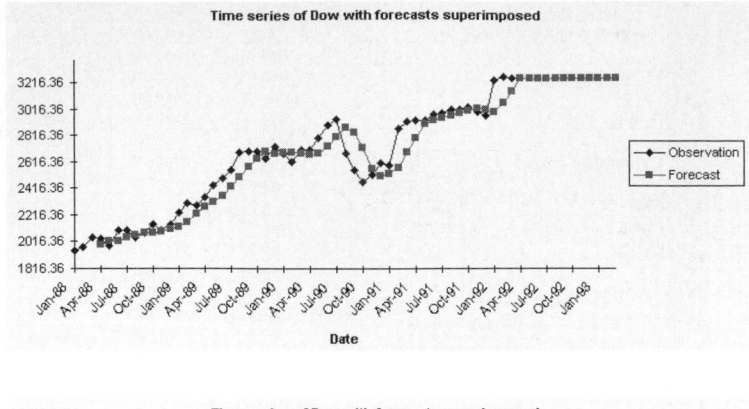

FIGURE 16.30
Moving Averages
Forecasts with
Span 12

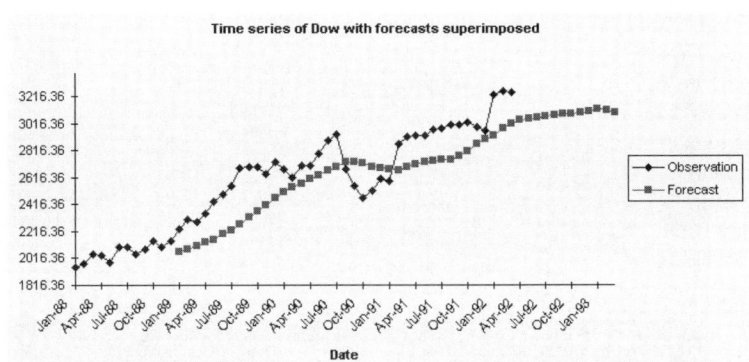

when they are available. If they are not available, previous forecasts are used. For example, the value in cell F54, the forecast for May 1992, is the average of the *observed* values in February and March and the *forecasted* value in April. Finally, the summary formulas in the range B9:B11 implement equations (16.1), (16.2), and (16.3).[7]

The plots in Figures 16.29 and 16.30 show the behavior of the forecasts. The forecasts with span 3 appear to track the data better, whereas the forecast series with span 12 is considerably smoother—it reacts less to the ups and downs of the series. The summary measures MAE, RMSE, and MAPE confirm that moving averages with span 3 forecast the *known* observations better. For example, the forecasts are off by about 3.6% with span 3, versus 7.7% with span 12. Nevertheless, there is no guarantee that a span of 3 is better for forecasting *future* observations. ■

The moving average method we have presented is the simplest of a group of moving average methods used by professional forecasters. We *smoothed* exactly once; that is, we took moving averages of several observations at a time and used these as forecasts. More complex methods smooth more than once, basically to get rid of random noise. They take moving averages, then moving averages of these moving averages, and so on for several stages. This can become quite complex, but the objective is quite simple—to smooth the data so that we can see underlying patterns.

---

[7]If you want to learn some interesting features of Excel, take a close look at the formulas in these three cells. The formulas with curly brackets around them are *array* formulas. To enter them, type the formula without the curly brackets and then press Ctrl-Shift-Enter.

Skill-Building Problems

27. The file P16_7.XLS contains the daily closing prices of American Express stock from July 21, 1997, through July 20, 1998.

    a. Using a span of 3 days, forecast the price of this stock on July 21, 1998, with the method of moving averages. How well does the moving average method with span 3 forecast the known observations in this data set?

    b. Using a span of 10 days, forecast the price of this stock on July 21, 1998, with the method of moving averages. How well does the moving average method with span 10 forecast the known observations in this data set?

    c. Which of these two spans appears to be more appropriate? Explain your choice.

28. The closing value of the Dow Jones Industrial Index for each trading day from March 31, 1998, through July 21, 1998, is provided in the file P16_9.XLS.

    a. Using a span of 2 days, forecast the price of this stock on July 22, 1998, with the method of moving averages. How well does the moving average method with span 2 forecast the known observations in this data set?

    b. Using a span of 5 days, forecast the price of this stock on July 22, 1998, with the method of moving averages. How well does the moving average method with span 5 forecast the known observations in this data set?

    c. Using a span of 15 days, forecast the price of this stock on July 22, 1998, with the method of

moving averages. How well does the moving average method with span 15 forecast the known observations in this data set?

    d. Which of these three spans appears to be most appropriate? Explain your choice.

29. The file P16_22.XLS contains the daily closing prices of Wal-Mart stock from July 21, 1997, through July 20, 1998. Use the method of moving averages with a carefully chosen span to forecast this time series on July 21 through July 24 of 1998. Defend your choice of the span.

Skill-Extending Problems

30. Consider the file P16_30.XLS, which contains total monthly U.S. retail sales data for the years 1993–1996. Use the method of moving averages with a carefully chosen span to forecast U.S. retail sales in 1997. While retaining the final 6 months of observations for validation purposes, use the method of moving averages with a carefully chosen span to forecast U.S. retail sales in 1997. Comment on the performance of your model. What makes this time series more challenging to forecast?

31. Consider a random walk model with the following equation: $Y_t = Y_{t-1} + \varepsilon_t$, where ε_t is a random series with mean 0 and standard deviation 1. Specify a moving averages forecasting model that is equivalent to this random walk model. In particular, what is the appropriate size of the span in the equivalent moving averages model? Describe the smoothing effect of this span choice.

16.8 EXPONENTIAL SMOOTHING

There are two possible criticisms of the moving averages method. First, it puts equal weight on each value in a typical moving average when making a forecast. Many people would argue that if next month's forecast is to be based on the previous 12 months' observations, then more weight ought to be placed on the more recent observations. The second criticism is that the moving averages method requires a lot of data storage. This is particularly true for companies that routinely make forecasts of hundreds or even thousands of items. If 12-month moving averages are used for 1000 items, then 12,000 values are needed for next month's forecasts. This may or may not be a concern, considering today's relatively inexpensive computer storage capabilities.

Exponential smoothing is a method that addresses both of these criticisms. It bases its forecasts on a weighted average of past observations, with more weight put on the more recent observations, and it requires very little data storage. In addition, it is not difficult for most business people to understand, at least conceptually. Therefore, this method finds widespread use in the business world, particularly when frequent and automatic forecasts of many items are required.

There are many versions of exponential smoothing. The simplest is called, surprisingly enough, **simple** exponential smoothing. It is relevant when there is no pronounced trend or seasonality in the series. If there is a trend but no seasonality, then **Holt's** method is applicable. If, in addition, there is seasonality, then **Winters'** method can be used. This does not exhaust the list of exponential smoothing models—researchers have invented many other variations—but these three models will suffice for us.

Simple Exponential Smoothing

We now examine simple exponential smoothing in some detail. We first introduce two new terms. Every exponential model has at least one **smoothing constant**, which is always between 0 and 1. Simple exponential smoothing has a single smoothing constant denoted by α. (Its role will be discussed shortly.) The second new term is L_t, called the **level** of the series at time t. This value is not observable but can only be estimated. Essentially, it is where we think the series would be at time t if there were no random noise. Then the simple exponential smoothing method is defined by the following two equations, where F_{t+k} is the forecast of Y_{t+k} made at time t:

$$L_t = \alpha Y_t + (1 - \alpha)L_{t-1} \qquad \textbf{(16.8)}$$

$$F_{t+k} = L_t \qquad \textbf{(16.9)}$$

You should understand what these equations say. Equation (16.8) shows how to update the estimate of the level. It is a weighted average of the current observation, Y_t, and the previous level, L_{t-1}, with respective weights α and $1 - \alpha$. Equation (16.9) shows how forecasts are made. It says that the k-period-ahead forecast, F_{t+k}, made of Y_{t+k} in period t, is the most recently estimated level, L_t. This is the *same* for any value of $k \geq 1$. The idea is that in simple exponential smoothing, we believe that the series is not really going anywhere. So as soon as we estimate where the series ought to be in period t (if it were not for random noise), we forecast that this is where it will also be in any future period.

The smoothing constant α is analogous to the span in moving averages. There are two ways to see this. The first way is to rewrite equation (16.8), using the fact that the forecast error, E_t, made in forecasting Y_t at time $t - 1$ is $Y_t - F_t = Y_t - L_{t-1}$. A bit of algebra then gives

$$L_t = L_{t-1} + \alpha E_t \qquad \textbf{(16.10)}$$

This says that the next estimate of the level is adjusted from the previous estimate by adding a multiple of the most recent forecast error. This makes sense. If our previous forecast was too high, then E_t is negative, and we adjust the estimate of the level downward. The opposite is true if our previous forecast was too low. However, equation (16.10) says that we do not adjust by the entire magnitude of E_t, but only by a fraction of it. If α is small, say $\alpha = 0.1$, then the adjustment is minor; if α is close to 1, the adjustment is large. So if we want to react quickly to movements in the series, we choose a large α; otherwise, we choose a small α.

Another way to see the effect of α is to substitute recursively into the equation for L_t. If you are willing to go through some algebra, you can verify that L_t satisfies

$$L_t = \alpha Y_t + \alpha(1 - \alpha)Y_{t-1} + \alpha(1 - \alpha)^2 Y_{t-2} + \alpha(1 - \alpha)^3 Y_{t-3} + \cdots \qquad \textbf{(16.11)}$$

where this sum extends back to the first observation at time $t = 1$. Equation (16.11) shows how the exponentially smoothed forecast is a weighted average of previous observations. Furthermore, because $1 - \alpha$ is less than 1, the weights on the Y's decrease from time t backward. Therefore, if α is close to 0, then $1 - \alpha$ is close to 1 and the weights decrease very slowly. In other words, observations from the distant past continue to have a large influence on the next forecast. This means that the graph of the forecasts will be relatively smooth, just as with a large span in the moving averages method. But when α is close to 1, the weights decrease rapidly, and only very recent observations have much influence on the next forecast. In this case forecasts react quickly to sudden changes in the series.

What value of α should you use? There is no universally accepted answer to this question. Some practitioners recommend always using a value around 0.1 or 0.2. Others recommend experimenting with different values of α until a measure such as RMSE or MAPE is minimized. Some packages even have an optimization feature to find this optimal value of α. (This is the case with StatPro.) But just as we discussed in the moving averages section, the value of α that tracks the historical series most closely does not necessarily guarantee the most accurate *future* forecasts.

EXAMPLE   16.6

FORECASTING QUARTERLY SALES AT EXXON

The file EXXON.XLS contains data on quarterly sales (in millions of dollars) for the period from 1986 through the second quarter of 1996. A time series chart of these sales in Figure 16.31 shows that there is some evidence of an upward trend in the early years, but that there is no obvious trend during the 1990s. Does a simple exponential smoothing model track these data well? How do the forecasts depend on the smoothing constant α?

FIGURE 16.31
Time Series Plot of
Exxon Sales

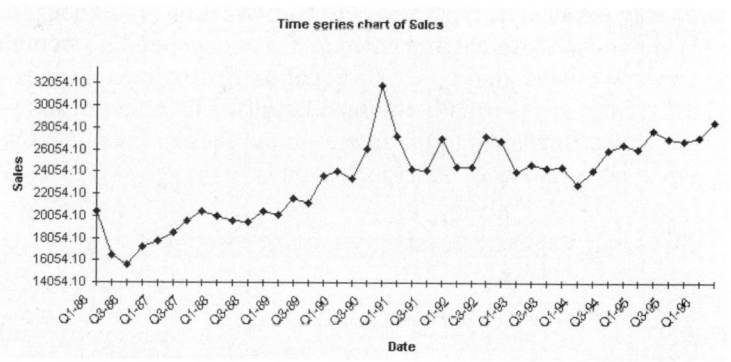

Solution

We will use StatPro to implement the simple exponential smoothing model, specifically equations (16.8) and (16.9). We do this again with the StatPro/Forecasting menu item.[8] We first specify that the data are quarterly, beginning in quarter 1 of 1986, we do not hold out any of the data for validation, and we ask for 8 quarters of future forecasts. We then fill out the next dialog box as shown in Figure 16.32. That is, we select the

[8]We make the same comment as in the previous section. If you make multiple runs on the same data with StatPro's forecasting procedure, you should put the outputs on separate worksheets.

FIGURE 16.32
Method Dialog
Box for StatPro
Forecasting
Procedure

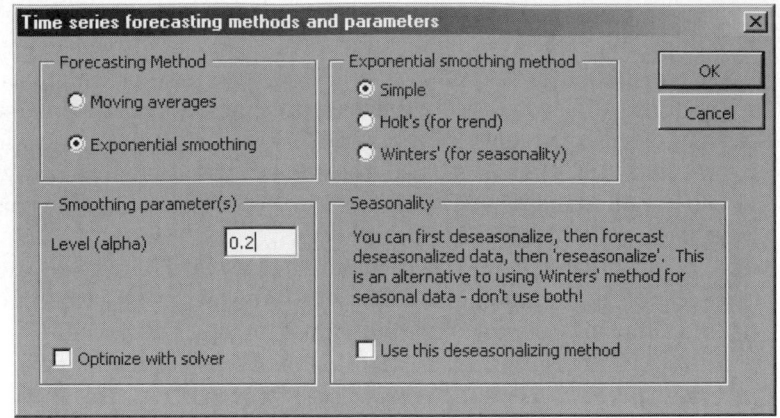

exponential smoothing option in the upper left, select the Simple option, choose a smoothing constant (0.2 was chosen here, but any other value could be chosen) and elect not to optimize, and specify that the data are not seasonal. On the next dialog sheet we ask for time series charts of the series with the forecasts superimposed and the series of forecast errors. The results appear in Figures 16.33, 16.34, and 16.35. The heart of the method takes place in columns F, G, and H of Figure 16.33. Column F calculates the smoothed levels (L_t) from equation (16.8), column G calculates the forecasts (F_t) from equation (16.9), and column H calculates the forecast errors (E_t) as the observed values minus the forecasts. For example, the formula in cell F6 is

=Alpha*E6+(1-Alpha)*F5

Initialization One exception to this scheme is in row 2. Every exponential smoothing method requires *initial* values, in this case the initial smoothed level in cell F2. There is no way to calculate this value, L_1, from equation (16.8) because the *previous* value, L_0, is unknown. Different implementations of exponential smoothing initialize in different ways. We have simply set L_1 equal to Y_1 (in cell E2). The effect of initializing in different ways is usually minimal because any effect of early data is usually washed out as we forecast into the future. In the present example, data from 1986 have little effect on forecasts of 1996 and beyond.

FIGURE 16.33
Simple Exponential
Smoothing Output

	A	B	C	D	E	F	G	H
1	*Forecasting results for Sales*			Date	Observation	SmLevel	Forecast	Error
2				Q1-86	20468.003	20468.003		
3	**Simple exponential smoothing**			Q2-86	16529.003	19680.203	20468.003	-3939.000
4				Q3-86	15673.003	18878.763	19680.203	-4007.200
5	Smoothing constant(s)			Q4-86	17218.003	18546.611	18878.763	-1660.760
6	Level	0.200		Q1-87	17781.003	18393.489	18546.611	-765.608
7				Q2-87	18588.003	18432.392	18393.489	194.514
8	**Estimation period**			Q3-87	19600.003	18665.914	18432.392	1167.611
9				Q4-87	20447.003	19022.132	18665.914	1781.089
10	MAE	1730.2410		Q1-88	20045.003	19226.706	19022.132	1022.871
11	RMSE	2324.5773		Q2-88	19614.003	19304.166	19226.706	387.297
12	MAPE	7.37%		Q3-88	19465.003	19336.333	19304.166	160.837
13				Q4-88	20433.003	19555.667	19336.333	1096.670
43				Q2-96	28561.000	26855.615	26429.269	2131.731
44				Q3-96			26855.615	
45				Q4-96			26855.615	
46				Q1-97			26855.615	
47				Q2-97			26855.615	
48				Q3-97			26855.615	
49				Q4-97			26855.615	
50				Q1-98			26855.615	
51				Q2-98			26855.615	

FIGURE 16.34
Plot of Forecasts
from Simple
Exponential
Smoothing

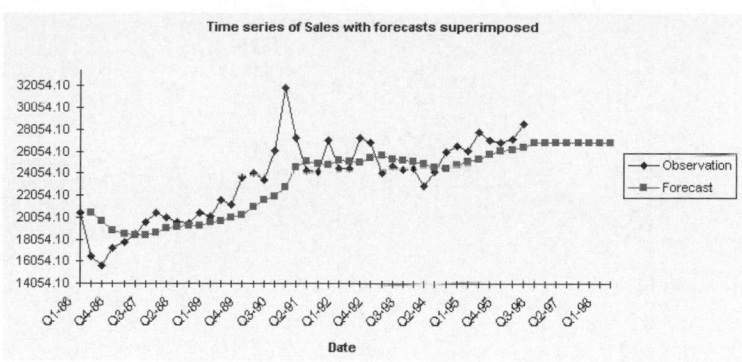

FIGURE 16.34
Plot of Forecasts
from Simple
Exponential
Smoothing

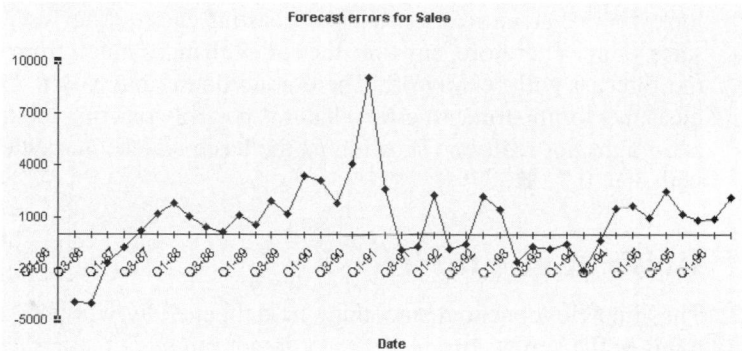

FIGURE 16.35
Plot of Forecast
Errors from Simple
Exponential
Smoothing

Note that the 8 future forecasts (rows 44 down) are all equal to the last calculated smoothed level, the one for second quarter of 1996 in cell F43. The fact that these remain constant is a consequence of the assumption behind *simple* exponential smoothing, namely, that the series is not really going anywhere. Therefore, the last smoothed level is the best indication of future values of the series.

Figure 16.34 shows the forecast series superimposed on the original series. We see the obvious smoothing effect of a relatively small α level. The forecasts do not track the series very well, but if the various zigzags in the original series are really random noise, then perhaps we don't want the forecasts to track these random ups and downs too closely. Perhaps we instead prefer a forecast series that emphasizes the basic underlying pattern. Figure 16.35 shows the time series of forecast errors. Although these errors are sometimes quite large, they do appear to be fairly random.

We see several summary measures of the forecast errors from Figure 16.33. The RMSE and MAE indicate that the forecasts from this model are typically off by a magnitude of about 2300 ($2.3 billion), and the MAPE indicates that this magnitude is about 7.4% of sales. This is a fairly sizable error. One way to try to reduce it is to use a different smoothing constant. We can either experiment with the value of α in cell B6, or we can run the procedure again and check the "optimize" box.[9] The optimal α for this example is somewhere between 0.8 and 0.9, although RMSE is relatively constant for any α between these two values. Figure 16.36 shows the forecast series with $\alpha = 0.85$. Its values of RMSE, MAE, and MAPE, not shown, are 1885, 1355, and 5.74%. The forecast series now appears to track the original series very well—or does it? A closer

---

[9]This runs Excel's Solver to find the value of α that minimizes RMSE, subject to $0 \leq \alpha \leq 1$. Sometimes, as in the current example, the Solver will not converge to any solution if we start at the default value $\alpha = 0.1$. In this case it is best to try a different initial value of α.

FIGURE 16.36
Plot of Forecasts
with a Larger
Smoothing Constant

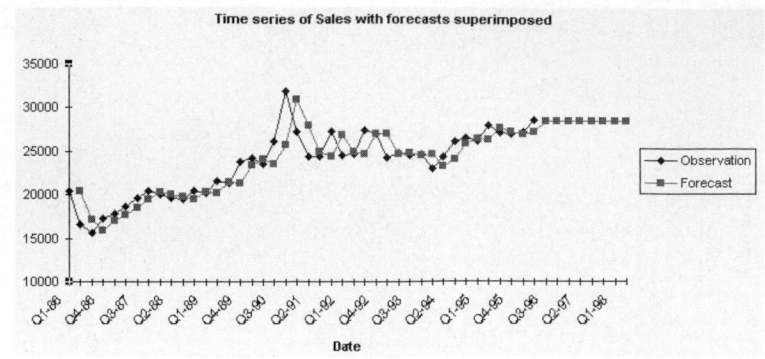

look shows that we are essentially forecasting each quarter's sales value by the *previous* sales value. Therefore, any time the series changes much from one quarter to the next, the forecast will be way off. There is no doubt that $\alpha = 0.85$ gives lower summary measures for the forecast errors, but it is possibly reacting too quickly to random noise and might not really be showing us the basic underlying pattern of sales that we see with $\alpha = 0.2$. ∎

Holt's Model for Trend

The simple exponential smoothing model generally works well if there is no obvious trend in the series. But if there is a trend, then this method consistently lags behind it. For example, if the series is constantly increasing, simple exponential smoothing forecasts will be consistently low. Holt's method rectifies this by dealing with trend explicitly. In addition to the level of the series, L_t, Holt's method includes a trend term, T_t, and a corresponding smoothing constant β. The interpretation of L_t is exactly as before. The interpretation of T_t is that it represents an estimate of the change in the series from one period to the next. The equations for Holt's model are as follows.

$$L_t = \alpha Y_t + (1 - \alpha)(L_{t-1} + T_{t-1}) \qquad \text{(16.12)}$$
$$T_t = \beta(L_t - L_{t-1}) + (1 - \beta)T_{t-1} \qquad \text{(16.13)}$$
$$F_{t+k} = L_t + kT_t \qquad \text{(16.14)}$$

These equations are not as bad as they look. (And don't forget that the computer does all of the calculations for you.) Equation (16.12) says that the updated level is a weighted average of the current observation and the previous level plus the estimated change. Equation (16.13) says that the updated trend term is a weighted average of the difference between two consecutive levels and the previous trend term. Finally, equation (16.14) says that the k-period-ahead forecast made in period t is the estimated level plus k times the estimated change per period.

Everything we said about α for simple exponential smoothing applies to both α and β in Holt's model. The new smoothing constant β controls how quickly the method reacts to perceived changes in the trend. If β is small, the method reacts slowly. If it is large, the method reacts more quickly. Of course, there are now two smoothing constants to select. Some practitioners suggest using a small value of α (0.1 to 0.2, say) and setting β equal to α. Others suggest using an optimization option (available in StatPro) to select the "best" smoothing constants. We illustrate the possibilities in the following example.[10]

---

[10]StatPro's initialization for Holt's method bases the initial level, L_0, on the first observation, and the intial trend, T_0, on the average of all of the one-period differences for the non-holdout observations.

EXAMPLE   16.2 (CONTINUED)

FORECASTING THE DOW JONES INDUSTRIAL AVERAGE

We return to the Dow Jones data from Example 16.2. Again, these are average monthly closing prices from January 1988 through March 1992. Recall that there is a definite upward trend in this series. In this example we investigate whether simple exponential smoothing can capture the upward trend. Then we see whether Holt's exponential smoothing method can make an improvement.

Solution

The graph in Figure 16.37 shows how a simple exponential smoothing model handles this trend, using $\alpha = 0.2$. Its summary error measures are not bad (MAPE is 5.38%, for example), but the forecast series is clearly lagging behind the original series. Also, the forecasts for the next 12 months are constant, because no trend is built into the model. In contrast, the graph in Figure 16.38 shows forecasts from Holt's model with $\alpha = \beta = 0.2$. The forecasts are still far from perfect (MAPE is now 4.01%), but at least the upward trend has been captured. This model appears likely to make better future forecasts than the simple exponential smoothing model.

FIGURE 16.37
Plot of Forecasts from Simple Exponential Smoothing

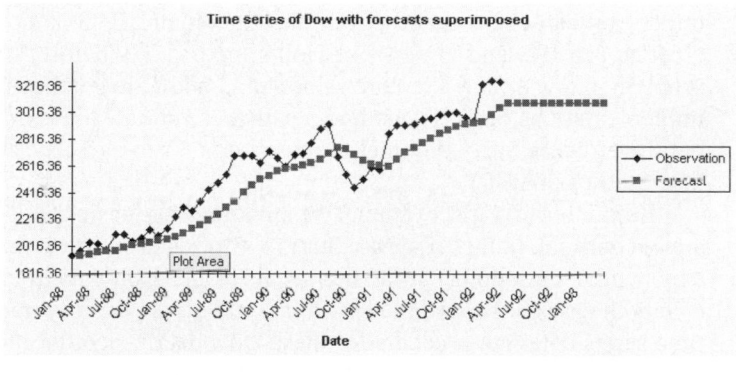

FIGURE 16.38
Plot of Forecasts from Holt's Method

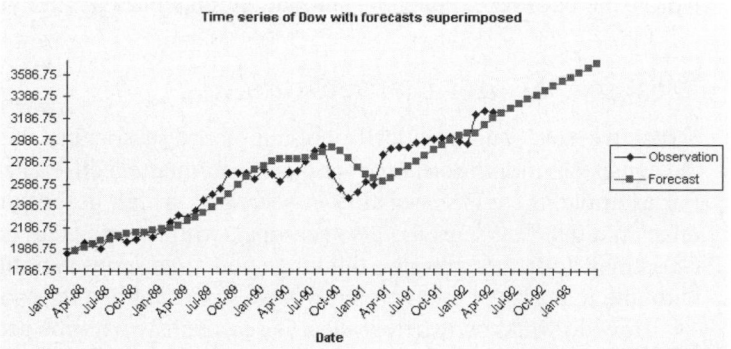

To produce the output from Holt's method with StatPro (part of which is shown in Figure 16.39 on page 924), we proceed exactly as with the simple exponential smoothing procedure. The only difference is that we now get to choose two smoothing parameters. The output in Figure 16.39 is also very similar to simple exponential smoothing output, except that there is now an extra column (column G) for the estimated

	A	B	C	D	E	F	G	H	I
1	*Forecasting results for Dow*			Date	Observation	SmLevel	SmTrend	Forecast	Error
2				Jan-88	1947.350	1947.350	25.492		
3	**Holt's exponential smoothing**			Feb-88	1980.650	1974.403	25.804	1972.842	7.808
4				Mar-88	2044.310	2009.028	27.568	2000.207	44.103
5	Smoothing constant(s)			Apr-88	2036.130	2036.503	27.549	2036.596	-0.466
6	Level	0.200		May-88	1988.910	2049.024	24.544	2064.052	-75.142
7	Trend	0.200		Jun-88	2104.940	2079.842	25.799	2073.567	31.373
8				Jul-88	2104.220	2105.356	25.742	2105.640	-1.420
9	**Estimation period**			Aug-88	2051.290	2115.137	22.549	2131.098	-79.808
10				Sep-88	2080.060	2126.161	20.244	2137.686	-57.626
11	MAE	106.3884		Oct-88	2144.310	2145.986	20.161	2146.405	-2.095
12	RMSE	136.9544		Nov-88	2099.040	2152.725	17.476	2166.147	-67.107
13	MAPE	4.01%		Dec-88	2148.580	2165.877	16.611	2170.202	-21.622
14				Jan-89	2234.680	2192.927	18.699	2182.489	52.191
49				Dec-91	2958.640	3035.074	26.527	3054.182	-95.542
50				Jan-92	3227.060	3094.693	33.146	3061.601	165.459
51				Feb-92	3257.270	3153.725	38.323	3127.839	129.431
52				Mar-92	3247.420	3203.122	40.538	3192.048	55.372
53				Apr-92				3243.660	
54				May-92				3284.198	
55				Jun-92				3324.736	
56				Jul-92				3365.274	
57				Aug-92				3405.811	
58				Sep-92				3446.349	
59				Oct-92				3486.887	
60				Nov-92				3527.425	
61				Dec-92				3567.963	
62				Jan-93				3608.500	
63				Feb-93				3649.038	
64				Mar-93				3689.576	

FIGURE 16.39 Output from Holt's Method

trend. You can check that the formulas in columns F, G, and H implement equations (16.12), (16.13), and (16.14) for Holt's method. As before, there is an initialization problem in row 2. These require values of L_1 and T_1 to get the method started. Different implementations of Holt's method obtain these initial values in slightly different ways, but the effect is fairly minimal in most cases. (You can check cells F2 and G2 to see how StatPro does it.)

Before leaving this example, we mention that the smoothing constants used above are *not* optimal. In fact, if we use StatPro's optimize option to find the best α (for simple exponential smoothing) or the best α and β (for Holt's method), we find that the best α in both cases is 1.0 and the best β is 0.0. This is certainly not always the case for all time series data, but it occurs for these Dow data. According to these parameters, the best forecast of next month's value is this month's value plus a constant trend. In other words, the optimal exponential smoothing model is again a random walk model! ∎

Winters' Model for Seasonality

So far we have said practically nothing about seasonality. Seasonality is defined as the consistent month-to-month (or quarter-to-quarter) differences that occur each year. For example, there is seasonality in beer sales—high in the summer months, lower in other months. Toy sales are also seasonal, with a huge peak in the months preceding Christmas. In fact, if you start thinking about time series variables that you are familiar with, the majority of them probably have some degree of seasonality.

How do we know whether there is seasonality in a time series? The easiest way is to check whether a plot of the time series has a *regular* pattern of ups and/or downs in particular months or quarters. Although random noise can sometimes obscure such a pattern, the seasonal pattern is usually fairly obvious. (Some time series software packages have special types of graphs for spotting seasonality, but we won't discuss these here.)

There are basically two extrapolation methods for dealing with seasonality. We can either use a model that takes seasonality into account explicitly and forecasts it, or we can first **deseasonalize** the data, then forecast the deseasonalized data, and finally adjust the forecasts for seasonality. The exponential smoothing model we discuss here, Winters' model, is of the first type. It attacks seasonality directly. In the next section we will see how to deseasonalize data so that the second approach can be used.

Seasonal models are usually classified as **additive** or **multiplicative**. Suppose that we have monthly data, and that the average of the 12 monthly values for a typical year is 150. An additive model finds seasonal indices, one for each month, that we *add* to the monthly average, 150, to obtain a particular month's value. For example, if the index for March is 22, then we expect a typical March value to be $150 + 22 = 172$. If the seasonal index for September is -12, then we expect a typical September value to be $150 - 12 = 138$. A multiplicative model also finds seasonal indices, but we *multiply* the monthly average by these indices to get a particular month's value. Now if the index for March is 1.3, we expect a typical March value to be $150(1.3) = 195$. If the index for September is 0.9, then we expect a typical September value to be $150(0.9) = 135$.

Either an additive or a multiplicative model can be used to forecast seasonal data. However, because multiplicative models are somewhat easier to interpret (and often work well in applications), we will focus on them. Note that the seasonal index in a multiplicative model can be interpreted as a percentage. Using the figures in the previous paragraph, March tends to be 30% above the monthly average, whereas September tends to be 10% below it. Also, the seasonal indices in a multiplicative model should sum to the number of seasons (12 for monthly data, 4 for quarterly data). Computer packages typically ensure that this happens.

We now turn to Winters' exponential smoothing model. It is very similar to Holt's model—it again has level and trend terms and corresponding smoothing constants α and β—but it also has seasonal indices and a corresponding smoothing constant γ (gamma). This new smoothing constant γ controls how quickly the method reacts to perceived changes in the pattern of seasonality. If γ is small, the method reacts slowly. If it is large, the method reacts more quickly. As with Holt's model, there are equations for updating the level and trend terms, and there is one extra equation for updating the seasonal indexes. For completeness, we list these equations below, but they are clearly too complex for hand calculation and are best left to the computer. In equation (16.17), S_t refers to the multiplicative seasonal index for period t. In equations (16.15), (16.17), and (16.18), M refers to the number of seasons ($M = 4$ for quarterly data, $M = 12$ for monthly data).

$$L_t = \alpha \frac{Y_t}{S_{t-M}} + (1 - \alpha)(L_{t-1} + T_{t-1}) \tag{16.15}$$

$$T_t = \beta(L_t - L_{t-1}) + (1 - \beta)T_{t-1} \tag{16.16}$$

$$S_t = \gamma \frac{Y_t}{L_t} + (1 - \gamma)S_{t-M} \tag{16.17}$$

$$F_{t+k} = (L_t + kT_t)S_{t+k-M} \tag{16.18}$$

To see how the forecasting in equation (16.18) works, suppose we have observed data through June and want a forecast for the coming September, that is, a 3-month-ahead forecast. (In this case t refers to June and $t + k = t + 3$ refers to September.) Then we first add 3 times the current trend term to the current level. This gives a forecast for September that would be appropriate if there were no seasonality. Next, we multiply this forecast by the most recent estimate of September's seasonal index (the one from the *previous* September) to obtain the forecast for September. Of course, the computer does all of the arithmetic, but this is basically what it is doing. We illustrate the method in the following example.[11]

EXAMPLE   16.7

FORECASTING QUARTERLY SALES AT COCA-COLA

The data in the COCACOLA.XLS file represent quarterly sales (in millions of dollars) for Coca-Cola from quarter 1 of 1986 through quarter 2 of 1996. As we might expect, there has been an upward trend in sales during this period, and there is also a fairly regular seasonal pattern, as shown in Figure 16.40. Sales in the warmer quarters, 2 and 3, are consistently higher than in the colder quarters, 1 and 4. How well can Winters' method track this upward trend and seasonal pattern?

FIGURE 16.40
Time Series Plot of Coca-Cola Sales

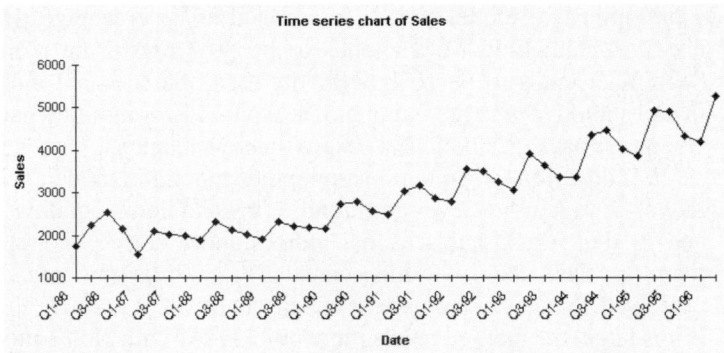

Solution

To use Winters' method with StatPro, we proceed exactly as with any of the other exponential smoothing methods. In particular, we fill out the second main dialog box as shown in Figure 16.41. Note that the "Use this deseasonalizing method" option at the bottom right has been disabled. It wouldn't make much sense to deseasonalize *and* use Winters' method; we use one or the other. Also, we have elected to optimize the smoothing constants, but this is optional.

Parts of the output are shown in Figure 16.42. The following points are worth noting. (1) The optimal smoothing constants (those that minimize RMSE) are $\alpha = 1.0$, $\beta = 0.0$, and $\gamma = 0.244$. Intuitively, these mean that we react right away to changes in level, we never react to changes in trend (which is *not* the same as saying that there is no trend!), and we react fairly slowly to changes in the seasonal pattern. (2) If we ignore seasonality, the series is trending upward at a rate of 67.107 per quarter (see column G). This is our initial estimate of trend and, because $\beta = 0$, we never change it. (3) The seasonal pattern stays constant throughout this 10-year period. The seasonal indices, shown in column H, are 0.879, 1.096, 1.064, and 0.961. For example, quarter 1 is about 12% below the yearly average, and quarter 2 is almost 10% above the yearly

---

[11]StatPro's initialization for Winters' method is rather complicated. Basically, it uses the method in the next section to obtain initial seasonal indices. Then it obtains the initial level and trend exactly in Holt's method, except from the deseasonalized data.

FIGURE 16.41
Method Dialog Box
from StatPro
Forecasting
Procedure

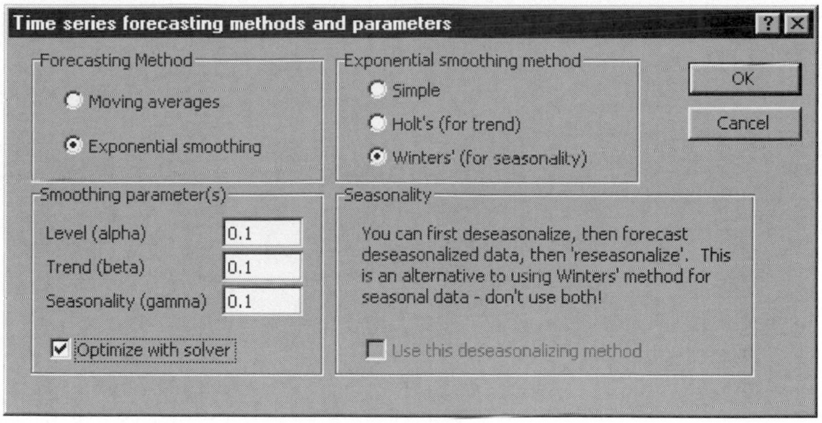

Time series forecasting methods and parameters

Forecasting Method
○ Moving averages
◉ Exponential smoothing

Exponential smoothing method
○ Simple
○ Holt's (for trend)
◉ Winters' (for seasonality)

OK
Cancel

Smoothing parameter(s)
Level (alpha)   0.1
Trend (beta)   0.1
Seasonality (gamma) 0.1
☑ Optimize with solver

Seasonality
You can first deseasonalize, then forecast deseasonalized data, then 'reseasonalize'. This is an alternative to using Winters' method for seasonal data - don't use both!
☐ Use this deseasonalizing method

average. (4) The forecast series tracks the actual series quite well. For example, MAPE is 3.95%, meaning that on average our forecasts are only about 4% in error.

The plot of the forecasts superimposed on the original series, shown in Figure 16.43 (page 928), indicates that Winters' method clearly picks up the seasonal pattern and the upward trend and projects both of these into the future. (We asked for forecasts of 8 future quarters.)

One final comment is that we are not obligated to find the *optimal* smoothing constants. Some analysts might suggest using more "typical" values such as $\alpha = \beta = 0.2$ and $\gamma = 0.5$. (We often choose γ larger than α and β because each season's seasonal index gets updated only once per year.) To see how these smoothing constants would affect the results, we can simply substitute their values in the range B6:B8 of Figure 16.42. As we would expect, MAE, RMSE, and MAPE all get worse (they increase to 141, 191, and 5.48%, respectively), but a plot of the forecasts superimposed on the original sales data still indicates a very good fit.

	A	B	C	D	E	F	G	H	I	J
1	*Forecasting results for Sales*			Date	Observation	SmLevel	SmTrend	SmSeason	Forecast	Error
2				Q1-1986	1734.827	1973.930	67.107	0.879		
3	**Winters' exponential smoothing**			Q2-1986	2244.961	2048.133	67.107	1.096	2237.183	7.778
4				Q3-1986	2533.805	2380.639	67.107	1.064	2251.331	282.474
5	Smoothing constant(s)			Q4-1986	2154.963	2243.139	67.107	0.961	2351.527	-196.564
6	Level	1.000		Q1-1987	1547.819	1761.147	67.107	0.879	2030.406	-482.587
7	Trend	0.000		Q2-1987	2104.412	1919.907	67.107	1.096	2003.952	100.460
8	Seasonality	0.244		Q3-1987	2014.363	1892.597	67.107	1.064	2114.855	-100.492
9				Q4-1987	1991.747	2073.245	67.107	0.961	1882.670	109.077
10	**Estimation period**			Q1-1988	1869.050	2126.652	67.107	0.879	1881.091	-12.041
11				Q2-1988	2313.632	2110.784	67.107	1.096	2404.582	-90.950
12	MAE	101.2270		Q3-1988	2128.320	1999.666	67.107	1.064	2318.012	-189.692
13	RMSE	136.0574		Q4-1988	2026.829	2109.762	67.107	0.961	1985.529	41.300
14	MAPE	3.95%		Q1-1989	1910.604	2173.933	67.107	0.879	1913.185	-2.581
15				Q2-1989	2331.165	2126.779	67.107	1.096	2456.407	-125.242
40				Q3-1995	4895.000	4599.103	67.107	1.064	4864.389	30.611
41				Q4-1995	4333.000	4510.297	67.107	0.961	4482.784	-149.784
42				Q1-1996	4194.000	4772.039	67.107	0.879	4022.942	171.058
43				Q2-1996	5253.000	4792.442	67.107	1.096	5304.193	-51.193
44				Q3-1996					5172.203	
45				Q4-1996					4732.993	
46				Q1-1997					4388.867	
47				Q2-1997					5547.226	
48				Q3-1997					5457.903	
49				Q4-1997					4990.870	
50				Q1-1998					4624.782	
51				Q2-1998					5841.452	

FIGURE 16.42 Output from Winters' Method

FIGURE 16.43
Plot of Forecasts
from Winters'
Method

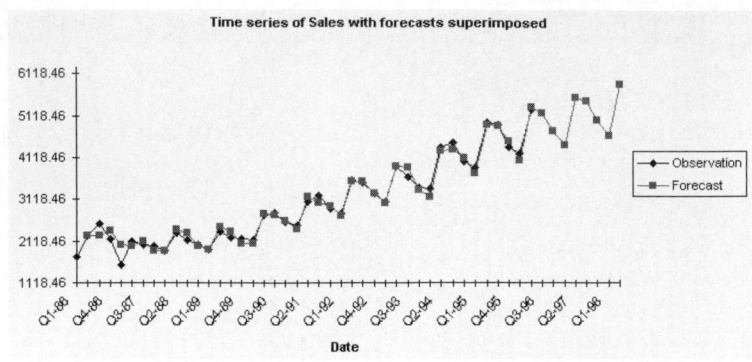

The three exponential smoothing methods we have examined are not the only ones available. For example, there are linear and quadratic models available in some software packages. These are somewhat similar to Holt's model except that they use only a single smoothing constant. There are also "adaptive" exponential smoothing models, where the smoothing constants themselves are allowed to change through time. Although these more complex models have been studied thoroughly in the academic literature and are used by some practitioners, they typically offer only marginal gains in forecast accuracy over the models examined here.

PROBLEMS

Skill-Building Problems

32. Consider the airline ticket data from Problem 1 in the file P16_1.XLS. Put the outputs for the following questions on *separate* sheets.
   a. Create a time series chart of the data. Based on what you see, which of the exponential smoothing models do you think will provide the best forecasting model? Why?
   b. Use simple exponential smoothing to forecast these data, using no hold-out period and requesting 12 months of future forecasts. Use the default smoothing constant of 0.1.
   c. Repeat part **b**, optimizing the smoothing constant. Does it make much of an improvement?
   d. Repeat parts **b** and **c** twice, first using Holt's method and then Winters' method. That is, for each of these methods, use the default smoothing constants of 0.1, then use optimal smoothing constants.
   e. Write a short report to summarize your results.
33. Consider the applications for home mortgages data from Problem 4 in the file P16_4.XLS. Put the outputs for the following questions on *separate* sheets.
   a. Create a time series chart of the data. Based on what you see, which of the exponential smoothing models do you think will provide the best forecasting model? Why?

b. Use simple exponential smoothing to forecast these data, using no hold-out period and requesting 4 quarters of future forecasts. Use the default smoothing constant of 0.1.
c. Repeat part **b**, optimizing the smoothing constant. Does it make much of an improvement?
d. Repeat parts **b** and **c** twice, first using Holt's method and then Winters' method. That is, for each of these methods, use the default smoothing constants of 0.1, then use optimal smoothing constants.
e. Write a short report to summarize your results.
34. Consider the American Express closing price data from Problem 7 in the file P16_7.XLS. Put the outputs for the following questions on *separate* sheets and focus only on the closing prices.
   a. Create a time series chart of the data. Based on what you see, which of the exponential smoothing models do you think will provide the best forecasting model? Why? (*Note*: The data are currently sorted from most recent to most distant in the past. Sort them in the opposite order first.)
   b. Use Holt's exponential smoothing to forecast these data, using no hold-out period and requesting 20 days of future forecasts. Use the default smoothing constant of 0.1.
   c. Repeat part **b**, optimizing the smoothing constant. Does it make much of an improvement?

d. Repeat parts **b** and **c**, this time using a hold-out period of 50 days.

e. Write a short report to summarize your results.

35. Consider the poverty level data from Problem 15 in the file P16_15.XLS. Put the outputs for the following questions on *separate* sheets. Focus on the Percent variable.

a. Create a time series chart of the data. Based on what you see, which of the exponential smoothing models do you think will provide the best forecasting model? Why?

b. Use simple exponential smoothing to forecast these data, using no hold-out period and requesting 3 years of future forecasts. Use the default smoothing constant of 0.1.

c. Repeat part **b**, optimizing the smoothing constant. Make sure you request a chart of the series with the forecasts superimposed. Does the optimal smoothing constant make much of an improvement?

d. Write a short report to summarize your results. Considering the chart in part **c**, would you say the forecasts are "good?"

Problems 36–39 ask you to apply the exponential smoothing formulas. These do not require StatPro. In fact, they do not even require Excel. You can do them with a hand calculator (or with Excel).

36. The University Credit Union is open Monday through Saturday. Winters' method is being used (with $\alpha = \beta = \gamma = 0.5$) to predict the number of customers entering the bank each day. After incorporating the arrivals of 16 October 1996, $L_t = 200$, $T_t = 1$, and the "seasonalities" are as follows: Monday, 0.90; Tuesday, 0.70; Wednesday, 0.80; Thursday, 1.1; Friday, 1.2; Saturday, 1.3. For example, the number of customers entering the bank on a typical Monday is 90% of the number of customers entering the bank on an average day. On Tuesday, 17 October 1996, 182 customers enter the bank. At the close of business on 17 October 1996, make a forecast for the number of customers who will enter the bank on 25 October 1996.

37. Last National Bank is using Winters' method (with $\alpha = 0.2$, $\beta = 0.1$, and $\gamma = 0.5$) to forecast the number of customers served each day. The bank is open Monday through Friday. At present, the following "seasonalities" have been estimated: Monday, 0.80; Tuesday, 0.90; Wednesday, 0.95; Thursday, 1.10; Friday, 1.25. A seasonality of 0.80 for Monday means that on a Monday, the number of customers served by the bank tends to be 80% of average. Currently, the level is estimated to be 20 customers, and the trend is estimated to equal 1 customer. After observing that 30 customers are served by the bank on Monday, forecast the number of customers who will be served by the bank on Wednesday.

38. We have been assigned to forecast the number of aircraft engines ordered each month by Commins Engine Company. At the end of February, the forecast is that 100 engines will be ordered during April. During March, 120 engines are ordered.

a. Using $\alpha = 0.3$, determine a forecast (at the end of March) for the number of orders placed during April. Answer the same question for May. Use simple exponential smoothing.

b. Suppose at the end of March, MAE = 16. At the end of March, Commins can be 68% sure that April orders will be between what two values?

39. Suppose that Winters' method is used to forecast quarterly U.S. retail sales (in billions of dollars). At the end of the first quarter of 1997, $L_t = 300$, $T_t = 30$, and the seasonal indices are as follows: quarter 1, 0.90; quarter 2, 0.95; quarter 3, 0.95; quarter 4, 1.20. During the second quarter of 1997, retail sales are $360 billion. Assume $\alpha = 0.2$, $\beta = 0.4$, and $\gamma = 0.5$.

a. At the end of the second quarter of 1997, develop a forecast for retail sales during the fourth quarter of 1997.

b. At the end of the second quarter of 1997, develop a forecast for the second quarter of 1998.

Skill-Extending Problems

40. Simple exponential smoothing should work well for a times series that varies randomly around some mean level μ. That is, it should work well when $Y_t = \mu + \varepsilon_t$, where μ is fixed and ε_t is a random series with mean 0 and standard deviation σ. For this problem, assume in addition that ε_t is normally distributed. Using the values $\mu = 100$ and $\sigma = 15$, simulate a series of 150 observations, Y_1 to Y_{150}. (Don't freeze the random numbers.) Then run StatPro's simple exponential smoothing procedure on these simulated data, using smoothing constant 0.1. (Make sure you request a chart of the time series with the forecasts superimposed.) Because the random numbers are not frozen, all results should change appropriately when you press the F9 key. Discuss whether simple exponential smoothing with this smoothing constant appears to be doing a good job.

41. Redo the previous problem, but now assume that the Y_t process follows a random walk, so that $Y_t = Y_{t-1} + \mu + \varepsilon_t$. Assume that $Y_0 = 100$, $\mu = 1$, and $\sigma = 4$. See whether Holt's method, with smoothing constants 0.1 and 0.1, works any better than simple exponential smoothing for this type of process. (*Note*: Put your outputs from simple exponential smoothing and from Holt's method on *separate* sheets.)

42. Holt's exponential smoothing method should work well for a times series that varies randomly around some trend line. That is, it should work well when

$Y_t = a + bt + \varepsilon_t$, where a and b are fixed and ε_t is a random series with mean 0 and standard deviation σ. For this problem, assume in addition that ε_t is normally distributed. Using the values $a = 100$, $b = 5$, and $\sigma = 15$, simulate a series of 150 observations, Y_1 to Y_{150}. (Don't freeze the random numbers.) Then run Holt's procedure on these simulated data, using smoothing constants 0.1 and 0.1. (Make sure you request a chart of the time series with the forecasts superimposed.) Because the random numbers are not frozen, all results should change appropriately when you press the F9 key. Discuss whether Holt's method with these smoothing constants appears to be doing a good job. Then see whether simple exponential smoothing, with smoothing constant 0.1, can track this type of process well. (*Note*: Put your outputs from simple exponential smoothing and from Holt's method on *separate* sheets.)

43. Holt's method assumes an additive trend. For example, a trend of 5 means that the level will increase by 5 units per period. Suppose there is actually a **multiplicative trend**. Thus, if the current estimate of the level is 50 and the current estimate of the trend is 1.2, we would predict demand to increase by 20% per period. So we would forecast the next period's demand to be 50(1.2) and forecast the demand two periods in the future to be $50(1.2)^2$. If we want to use a multiplicative trend in Holt's method, we should use the following equations:

$$L_t = \alpha y_t + (1 - \alpha)(I)$$

$$T_t = \beta(II) + (1 - \beta)T_{t-1}$$

a. Determine (I) and (II).
b. Suppose we are working with monthly data and month 12 is December, month 13 January, and so on. Also suppose that $L_{12} = 100$ and $T_{12} = 1.2$. Suppose $Y_{13} = 200$. At the end of month 13, what is the prediction for Y_{15}? Assume $\alpha = \beta = 0.5$.

44. In our discussion of Winters' method, a monthly seasonality of 0.80 for January, say, means that during January, air conditioner (AC) sales are expected to be 80% of the sales during an average month. An alternative approach to modeling seasonality (called an **additive model**) is to let the seasonality factor for each month represent how far above average AC sales will be during the current month. For instance, if $s_{\text{Jan}} = -50$, then AC sales during January are expected to be 50 less than AC sales during an average month. (This is 50 ACs, not 50%.) If $s_{\text{July}} = 90$, then AC sales during July are expected to be 90 more than AC sales during an average month. Let

s_t = Seasonality for month t after observing month t demand

L_t = Estimate of level after observing month t demand

T_t = Estimate of trend after observing month t demand

Then the Winters' method equations given in the text should be modified as follows:

$$L_t = \alpha(I) + (1 - \alpha)(L_{t-1} + T_{t-1})$$
$$T_t = \beta(L_t - L_{t-1}) + (1 - \beta)T_{t-1}$$
$$s_t = \gamma(II) + (1 - \gamma)s_{t-12}$$

a. Determine (I) and (II).
b. Suppose that month 13 is January, $L_{12} = 30$, $T_{12} = -3$, $s_1 = -50$, and $s_2 = -20$. Let $\alpha = \gamma = \beta = 0.5$. Suppose 12 ACs are sold during month 13. At the end of month 13, what is the prediction for AC sales during month 14?

45. A version of simple exponential smoothing can be used to predict the outcome of sporting events. To illustrate, consider pro football. We first assume that all games are played on a neutral field. Before each day of play, we assume that each team has a rating. For example, if the rating for the Bears is +10 and the rating for the Bengals is +6, we would predict the Bears to beat the Bengals by $10 - 6 = 4$ points. Suppose that the Bears play the Bengals and win by 20 points. For this game, we "underpredicted" the Bears' performance by $20 - 4 = 16$ points. The best α for pro football is $\alpha = 0.10$. After the game, we therefore increase the Bears' rating by $16(0.1) = 1.6$ and decrease the Bengals's rating by 1.6 points. In a rematch, the Bears would be favored by $(10 + 1.6) - (6 - 1.6) = 7.2$ points.

a. How does this approach relate to the equation $L_t = L_{t-1} + \alpha e_t$?
b. Suppose that the home field advantage in pro football is 3 points; that is, home teams tend to outscore visiting teams by an average of 3 points a game. How could the home field advantage be incorporated into this system?
c. How could we determine the best α for pro football?
d. How might we determine ratings for each team at the beginning of the season?
e. Suppose we tried to apply the above method to predict pro football (16-game schedule), college football (11-game schedule), college basketball (30-game schedule), and pro basketball (82-game schedule). Which sport would have the smallest optimal α? Which sport would have the largest optimal α?
f. Why would this approach probably yield poor forecasts for major league baseball?

16.9 DESEASONALIZING: THE RATIO-TO-MOVING-AVERAGES METHOD

Y ou have probably seen references to time series data that have been *deseasonalized*. In this section we will discuss why and how this is done. We will also see how it can be used to forecast seasonal time series.[12] First, data are often published in deseasonalized form so that readers can spot trends more easily. For example, if we see a time series of sales that has not been deseasonalized, and it shows a large increase from November to December, we might not be sure whether this represents a real increase in sales or a seasonal phenomenon (Christmas sales). However, if this increase is really just a seasonal effect, then the deseasonalized version of the series will show no such increase in sales.

Government economists and statisticians have a variety of sophisticated methods for deseasonalizing time series data, but they are all variations of the **ratio-to-moving-averages** method described here. This method is applicable when we believe that seasonality is multiplicative, as described in the previous section. Our job is to find the seasonal indices, which can then be used to deseasonalize the data. For example, if we estimate the index for June to be 1.3, this means that June's values are typically about 30% larger than the average for all months. Therefore, to deseasonalize a June value, we divide it by 1.3 (to make it smaller). Similarly, if February's index is 0.85, then February's values are 15% below the average for all months. So to deseasonalize a February value, we divide it by 0.85 (to make it larger).

To find the seasonal index for June 91 (or any other month) in the first place, we essentially divide June's observation by the average of the 12 observations surrounding June. (This is the reason for the term "ratio" in the name of the method.) There is one minor problem with this approach. June 91 is not exactly in the middle of any 12-month sequence. If we use the 12 months from January 91 to December 91, June 91 is in the *first* half of the sequence; if we use the 12 months from December 90 to November 91, June 91 is in the *last* half of the sequence. Therefore, it is best to compromise by averaging the January-to-December and December-to-November averages to obtain what is called a **centered** average. Then the seasonal index for June is June's observation divided by this centered average. The following equation shows more specifically how it works.

$$\text{Jun91 index} = \frac{\text{Jun91}}{\left(\frac{\text{Dec90} + \cdots + \text{Nov91}}{12} + \frac{\text{Jan91} + \cdots + \text{Dec91}}{12} \right) / 2}$$

The only remaining question is how to combine all of the indices for any specific month such as June. After all, if we have data for several years, the above procedure produces several June indices, one for each year. The usual way to combine them is simply to average them. This single average index for June is then used to deseasonalize *all* of the June observations.

Once the seasonal indices are obtained, we divide each observation by its seasonal index to deseasonalize the data. The deseasonalized data can then be forecasted by any of the methods we have described (other than Winters' method, which wouldn't make much sense). For example, we could use Holt's method or the moving average method to forecast the deseasonalized data. Finally, we "reseasonalize" the forecasts by *multiplying* them by the seasonal indices.

---

[12]This method is an alternative to Winters' method for dealing with seasonality. The two methods usually, but not always, give similar forecasts.

As this description suggests, the method is not meant for hand calculations! However, it is straightforward to implement in StatPro, as we illustrate in the following example.

EXAMPLE 16.7 (CONTINUED)

FORECASTING QUARTERLY SALES AT COCA-COLA

We return to the Coca-Cola sales data. Is it possible to obtain the same forecast accuracy with the ratio-to-moving-averages method as we obtained with Winters' method?

Solution

The answer to this question depends on which forecasting method we use to forecast the *deseasonalized* data. The ratio-to-moving-averages method is only a means for deseasonalizing the data and providing seasonal indices. Beyond this, any method can be used to forecast the deseasonalized data, and some methods typically work better than others. For this example, we compared two possibilities: the moving averages method with a span of 4 quarters, and Holt's exponential smoothing method optimized. We show the results only for the latter. Because the deseasonalized series still has a clear upward trend, we would expect Holt's method to do well, and we would expect the moving averages forecasts to lag behind the trend. This is exactly what occurred. For example, the values of MAPE for the two methods are 6.97% (moving averages) and 3.78% (Holt's).

To implement this latter method in StatPro, we proceed exactly as before, but this time we check the "Use this deseasonalizing method" box in the dialog box in Figure 16.41. (Now Holt's option will be checked, so the deseasonalizing option will be enabled.) By checking the deseasonalizing option, we then get a larger selection of optional charts. We can see charts of the deseasonalized data and/or the original "reseasonalized" data.

FIGURE 16.44
Summary Measures for Forecast Errors

	A	B	C
1	*Forecasting results for Sales*		
2			
3	**Holt's exponential smoothing**		
4			
5	Smoothing constant(s)		
6	Level	0.898	
7	Trend	0.000	
8			
9	**Estimation period**		
10		Deseas	Actual
11	MAE	98.7705	97.1839
12	RMSE	141.5835	135.3411
13	MAPE	3.78%	3.78%

Selected outputs are shown in Figures 16.44–16.47. Figures 16.44 and 16.45 show the numerical output. In particular, Figure 16.45 shows the seasonal indices from the ratio-to-moving averages method in column G. These are virtually identical to the seasonal indices we found using Winters' method, although the methods are mathematically different. Column H contains the deseasonalized sales (column F divided by column G), columns I–L implement Holt's method on the deseasonalized data, and columns M and N are the "reseasonalized" forecasts and errors.

	E	F	G	H	I	J	K	L	M	N
1	Date	Observation	SeasIndex	DeseasObs	SmLevel	SmTrend	DeseasFCast	DeseasError	Forecast	Error
2	Q1-86	1734.827	0.879	1973.930	1973.930	67.107				
3	Q2-86	2244.961	1.096	2048.133	2047.409	67.107	2041.037	7.095	2237.184	7.777
4	Q3-86	2533.805	1.064	2380.639	2353.512	67.107	2114.517	266.122	2250.561	283.244
5	Q4-86	2154.963	0.961	2243.139	2261.231	67.107	2420.620	-177.480	2325.467	-170.504
6	Q1-87	1547.819	0.879	1761.148	1818.963	67.107	2328.338	-567.190	2046.305	-498.486
7	Q2-87	2104.412	1.096	1919.906	1916.457	67.107	1886.070	33.836	2067.324	37.088
8	Q3-87	2014.363	1.064	1892.597	1901.869	67.107	1983.565	-90.968	2111.184	-96.821
9	Q4-87	1991.747	0.961	2073.215	2002.617	67.107	1968.977	104.268	1891.577	100.170
10	Q1-88	1869.050	0.879	2126.965	2126.965	67.107	2129.724	-3.072	1871.750	-2.700
11	Q2-88	2313.632	1.096	2110.783	2119.273	67.107	2194.073	-83.290	2404.926	-91.294
12	Q3-88	2128.320	1.064	1999.665	2018.698	67.107	2186.380	-186.715	2327.048	-198.728
13	Q4-88	2026.829	0.961	2109.762	2107.320	67.107	2085.805	23.958	2003.813	23.016
41	Q4-95	4333.000	0.961	4510.297	4525.823	67.107	4662.610	-152.313	4479.326	-146.326
42	Q1-96	4194.000	0.879	4772.039	4753.782	67.107	4592.930	179.109	4036.587	157.413
43	Q2-96	5253.000	1.096	4792.440	4795.340	67.107	4820.889	-28.450	5284.184	-31.184
44	Q3-96		1.064				4862.447		5175.288	
45	Q4-96		0.961				4929.555		4735.777	
46	Q1-97		0.879				4996.662		4391.414	
47	Q2-97		1.096				5063.769		5550.405	
48	Q3-97		1.064				5130.877		5460.988	
49	Q4-97		0.961				5197.984		4993.654	
50	Q1-98		0.879				5265.091		4627.329	
51	Q2-98		1.096				5332.199		5844.631	

FIGURE 16.45 Ratio-to-Moving-Averages Output

FIGURE 16.46
Forecast Plot of
Deseasonalized
Series

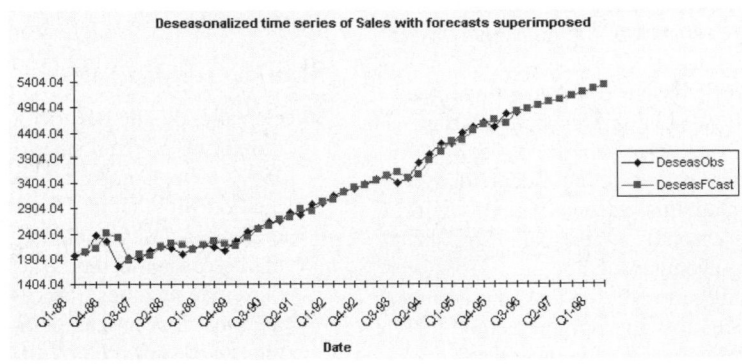

FIGURE 16.47
Forecast Plot of
Reseasonalized
(Original) Series

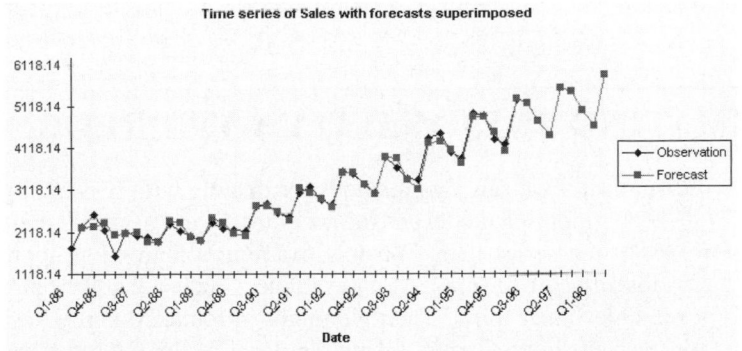

The deseasonalized data, with forecasts superimposed, appear in Figure 16.46. Here we see only the smooth upward trend with no seasonality, which Holt's method is able to track very well. Then Figure 16.47 shows the results of reseasonalizing. Again, the forecasts track the actual sales data very well. In fact, we see that the summary measures of forecast errors (in Figure 16.44, range C11:C13) are comparable to those from Winters' method. The reason is that both arrive at virtually the same seasonal pattern. ∎

Skill-Building Problems

46. Examine the provided monthly time series data for total U.S. retail sales of building materials (which includes retail sales of building materials, hardware and garden supply stores, and mobile home dealers). The data are in the file P16_46.XLS.
  a. Is seasonality present in these data? If so, characterize the seasonality pattern and then deseasonalize this time series using the ratio-to-moving-averages method.
  b. If you decided to deseasonalize this time series in part **a**, forecast the deseasonalized data for each month of 1997 using the moving averages method with an appropriate span.
  c. Does Holt's exponential smoothing method optimized outperform the moving averages method employed in part **b**? Demonstrate why or why not.

47. The file P16_47.XLS consists of the monthly retail sales levels of U.S. gasoline service stations from January of 1993 through December of 1996.
  a. Is there a seasonal pattern in these data? If so, how do you explain this seasonal pattern? Also, if necessary, deseasonalize these data using the ratio-to-moving-averages method.
  b. Forecast this time series for the first four months of 1997 using the most appropriate method for these data. Defend the use of your preferred forecasting method.

48. The file P16_1.XLS contains the number of airline tickets sold by the CareFree Travel Agency each month from January of 1995 to December of 1998.
  a. Is there a seasonal pattern in these data? If so, how do you explain this seasonal pattern? Also, if necessary, deseasonalize these data using the ratio-to-moving-averages method.
  b. Forecast this time series for the first four months of 1999 using the most appropriate method for these data. Defend the use of your preferred forecasting method.

49. Continuing Problem 46, how do your answers change when you employ Winters' method to handle seasonality in this time series? Explain. Which forecasting method do you prefer, Winters' method or a method used in Problem 46? Defend your choice.

Skill-Extending Problem

50. Consider the file P16_50.XLS, which contains total monthly U.S. retail sales data for the years 1993–1996. Compare the effectiveness of Winters' method with that of the ratio-to-moving-averages method in deseasonalizing this time series. Using the deseasonalized time series generated by each of these two methods, forecast U.S. retail sales with the most appropriate method for these data. Defend the use of your preferred forecasting method.

16.10 ESTIMATING SEASONALITY WITH REGRESSION

Earlier we saw two methods for dealing with seasonality: Winters' exponential smoothing model and the ratio-to-moving-averages method for deseasonalizing time series data. We now examine a regression approach that uses dummy variables for the seasons. As an example, suppose that the data are quarterly data with a possible linear trend. Then we might introduce dummy variables Q_1, Q_2, and Q_3 for the first three quarters (using quarter 4 as the reference quarter) and estimate the equation

$$\widehat{Y}_t = a + bt + b_1 Q_1 + b_2 Q_2 + b_3 Q_3$$

Then the coefficients of the dummy variables, b_1, b_2 and b_3, indicate how much each quarter differs from the reference quarter, quarter 4.

For example, if the estimated equation is

$$\widehat{Y}_t = 130 + 25t + 15Q_1 + 5Q_2 - 20Q_3$$

then the average increase from one quarter to the next is 25 (the coefficient of t). This is the trend effect. However, quarter 1 averages 15 units higher than quarter 4, quarter 2 averages 5 units higher than quarter 4, and quarter 3 averages 20 units lower than quarter 4. These coefficients indicate the effect of seasonality.

It is also possible to estimate a *multiplicative* model using dummy variables for seasonality (and possibly time for trend). Then we would estimate

$$\widehat{Y}_t = ae^{bt}e^{b_1 Q_1}e^{b_2 Q_2}e^{b_3 Q_3}$$

or, after taking logs,

$$\ln \widehat{Y}_t = \ln a + bt + b_1 Q_1 + b_2 Q_2 + b_3 Q_3$$

One advantage of this approach is that it provides a model with *multiplicative* seasonal factors. It is also fairly easy to interpret the regression output, as illustrated in the following continuation of the Coca-Cola example.

EXAMPLE | **16.7 (CONTINUED)**

FORECASTING QUARTERLY SALES AT COCA-COLA

Returning to the Coca-Cola sales data, does a regression approach provide forecasts that are as accurate as those provided by the other seasonal methods in this chapter?

Solution

We illustrate the multiplicative approach, although an additive approach is also possible. Figure 16.48 illustrates the data setup. Besides the Sales and Time variables, we need dummy variables for three of the four quarters, and a Log_Sales variable. We then use multiple regression, with Log_Sales as the response variable, and Time, Q1, Q2, and Q3 as the explanatory variables.

FIGURE 16.48
Data Setup for Multiplicative Model with Dummies

	A	B	C	D	E	F	G
1	Coca Cola quarterly sales						
2							
3	Quarter	Sales	Time	Q1	Q2	Q3	Log_Sales
4	Q1-86	1734.83	1	1	0	0	7.45866298
5	Q2-86	2244.96	2	0	1	0	7.71644343
6	Q3-86	2533.80	3	0	0	1	7.8374774
7	Q4-86	2154.96	4	0	0	0	7.67552883
8	Q1-87	1547.82	5	1	0	0	7.34460212
9	Q2-87	2104.41	6	0	1	0	7.65179137
10	Q3-87	2014.36	7	0	0	1	7.60805829
11	Q4-87	1991.75	8	0	0	0	7.59676742
42	Q3-95	4895.00	39	0	0	1	8.49596955
43	Q4-95	4333.00	40	0	0	0	8.37401542
44	Q1-96	4194.00	41	1	0	0	8.34141021
45	Q2-96	5253.00	42	0	1	0	8.56655462

The regression output appears in Figure 16.49. Of particular interest are the coefficients of the explanatory variables. Recall that for a log response variable, these coefficients can be interpreted as *percentage* changes in the original sales variable. Specifically, the coefficient of Time means that deseasonalized sales increase by about 2.4% per quarter. Also, the coefficients of Q1, Q2, and Q3 mean that sales in quarters 1, 2, and 3 are, respectively, about 8.0% below, 13.7% above, and 10.4% above sales in the reference quarter, quarter 4. This pattern is comparable to the pattern of seasonal indices we saw earlier for these data.

FIGURE 16.49
Regression Output
for Multiplicative
Model

	A	B	C	D	E	F	G	H
1	*Results of multiple regression for Log_Sales*							
2								
3	*Summary measures*							
4		Multiple R	0.9697					
5		R-Square	0.9404					
6		Adj R-Square	0.9340					
7		StErr of Est	0.0823					
8								
9	*ANOVA Table*							
10		Source	df	SS	MS	F	p-value	
11		Explained	4	3.9538	0.9884	145.9732	0.0000	
12		Unexplained	37	0.2505	0.0068			
13								
14	*Regression coefficients*							
15			Coefficient	Std Err	t-value	p-value	Lower limit	Upper limit
16		Constant	7.3946	0.0348	212.6519	0.0000	7.3241	7.4650
17		Time	0.0242	0.0010	23.0503	0.0000	0.0220	0.0263
18		Q1	-0.0795	0.0360	-2.2110	0.0333	-0.1524	-0.0066
19		Q2	0.1368	0.0360	3.8056	0.0005	0.0640	0.2097
20		Q3	0.1042	0.0368	2.8315	0.0075	0.0296	0.1788

To compare the forecast accuracy of this method with earlier examples, we must go through several steps manually. The multiple regression procedure in StatPro provides (as an option) the fitted values and residuals for the log of sales, as shown in columns H and I of Figure 16.50. Then we need to take antilogs in column J to obtain forecasts of the original sales data, and subtract these from the sales data to obtain forecast errors in column K. Using these errors in column K, we can then use the formulas that were used in StatPro's forecasting procedure to obtain the summary measures MAE, RMSE, and MAPE. As we see, the forecasts are not quite as accurate as before. For example, MAPE is 5.36% as compared to earlier MAPEs of about 3.8%. However, a plot of the forecasts superimposed on the original data, shown in Figure 16.51, shows that the method again tracks the data very well.

FIGURE 16.50
Forecast Errors and
Summary Measures

	A	B	H	I	J	K	L	M	N
1	Coca Cola quarterly sales								
2									
3	Quarter	Sales	Fitted logs	Resids logs	FCasts	FCast Errors		Summary stats	
4	Q1-86	1734.83	7.339	0.119	1539.52	195.31			
5	Q2-86	2244.96	7.580	0.137	1958.13	286.83		MAE	286.83
6	Q3-86	2533.80	7.571	0.266	1941.72	592.09		RMSE	186.07
7	Q4-86	2154.96	7.491	0.184	1792.30	362.67		MAPE	5.36%
8	Q1-87	1547.82	7.436	-0.091	1695.77	-147.95			
9	Q2-87	2104.41	7.676	-0.025	2156.87	-52.46			
10	Q3-87	2014.36	7.668	-0.060	2138.79	-124.43			
11	Q4-87	1991.75	7.588	0.009	1974.21	17.54			
42	Q3-95	4895.00	8.441	0.055	4634.78	260.22			
43	Q4-95	4333.00	8.361	0.013	4278.12	54.88			
44	Q1-96	4194.00	8.306	0.036	4047.72	146.28			
45	Q2-96	5253.00	8.546	0.020	5148.35	104.65			

FIGURE 16.51
Plot of Forecasts for
Multiplicative Model

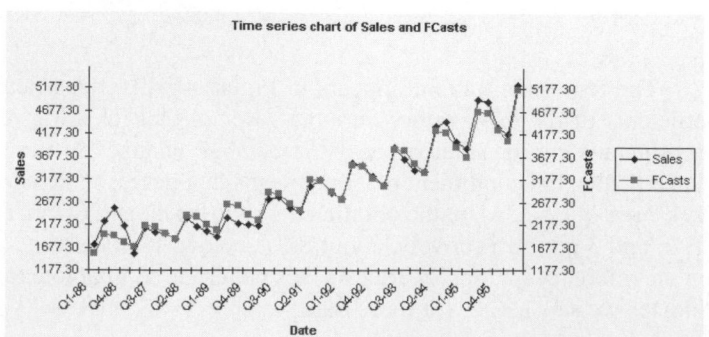

This method of detecting seasonality by using dummy variables in a regression equation is always an option. The other variables included in the regression equation could be time t, lagged versions of Y_t, and/or current or lagged versions of other explanatory variables. These variables would capture any time series behavior other than seasonality. Just remember that there is always one less dummy variable than the number of seasons. If the data are quarterly, then three dummies are needed; if the data are monthly, then eleven dummies are needed. If the coefficients of any of these dummies turn out to be statistically insignificant, they can be omitted from the equation. Then the omitted terms are in effect combined with the reference season. For example, if the Q_1 term above were omitted, then quarters 1 and 4 would essentially be combined and treated as the reference season, and the other two seasons would be compared to them through their dummy variable coefficients.

PROBLEMS

Skill-Building Problems

51. Suppose that a time series consisting of 6 years (1993–1998) of quarterly data exhibits definite seasonality. In fact, assume that the seasonal indices turn out to be 0.75, 1.45, 1.25, and 0.55.
  a. If the last four observations of the series (the four quarters of 1998) are 2502, 4872, 4269, and 1924, calculate the deseasonalized values for the four quarters of 1998.
  b. Suppose that a plot of the deseasonalized series shows an upward linear trend, except for some random noise. Therefore, a linear regression of this series versus time is estimated, and it produces the equation

  Deseasonalized value $= 2250 + 51$Quarter

  Here the time variable "Quarter" is coded so that Quarter $= 1$ corresponds to first quarter 1993, Quarter $= 24$ corresponds to fourth quarter 1994, and the others fall in between. Forecast the actual (not descasonalized) values for the four quarters of 1999.
52. The file P16_52.XLS contains monthly data on federal receipts of taxes from January 1985 through March 1992. There are two variables: IndTax (taxes from individuals) and CorpTax (corporate taxes). For this problem, work only with IndTax.
  a. What evidence is there that seasonality is important for this series? Find seasonal indices and state briefly what they mean.
  b. Forecast the next 12 months by using a linear trend on the seasonally adjusted data. State briefly the steps you go through to get this type of forecast, give the final RMSE, MAPE, and forecast for April 1992. Then show numerically how you could replicate this forecast; i.e., show

on paper how the package uses its estimated model to get the April 1992 forecast. (Substitute in specific numbers, and do the arithmetic.)
53. Quarterly sales for a department store over a 6-year period are given in the file P16_53.XLS.
  a. Use multiple regression to develop a model that can be used to predict future quarterly sales. (*Hint*: Use dummy variables and an explanatory variable for the quarter number, 1–24.)
  b. Letting Y_t be the sales during quarter t, discuss how to fit the following model to these data:

$$Y_t = \alpha\beta_1^t\beta_2^{X_1}\beta_3^{X_2}\beta_4^{X_3}$$

  Here $X_1 = 1$ if t is a first quarter, $X_2 = 1$ if t is a second quarter, and $X_3 = 1$ if t is a third quarter. (*Hint*: Take logarithms of both sides.)
  c. Interpret the answer to part **b**.
  d. Which model appears to yield better predictions for sales, the one in part **a** or the one in part **b**?
54. Confederate Express Service is attempting to determine how its shipping costs for a month depend on the number of units shipped during a month. The number of units shipped and total shipping cost for the last 15 months are given in the file P16_54.XLS.
  a. Determine a relationship between units shipped and monthly shipping cost.
  b. Plot the errors for the predictions in order of time sequence. Is there any unusual pattern?
  c. We have been told that there was a trucking strike during months 11–15, and we believe that this may have influenced shipping costs. How could the answer to part **a** be modified to account for the effects of the strike? After accounting for the effects of the strike, does the unusual pattern in part **b** disappear?

Skill-Extending Problems

55. Consider the file P16_55.XLS, which contains total monthly U.S. retail sales data for the years 1993–1996. In this case, does a regression approach for estimating seasonality provide forecasts that are as accurate as those provided by (a) Winters' method and (b) the ratio-to-moving-averages method? Compare the summary measures of forecast errors associated with each method for deseasonalizing the given time series. Summarize and explain your findings upon performing these comparisons.

56. Examine the provided monthly time series data for total U.S. retail sales of building materials (which includes retail sales of building materials, hardware and garden supply stores, and mobile home dealers). The data are in the file P16_56.XLS. In this case, does a regression approach for estimating seasonality provide forecasts that are as accurate as those provided by (a) Winters' method and (b) the ratio-to-moving-averages method? Compare the summary measures of forecast errors associated with each method for deseasonalizing the given time series. Summarize and explain your findings upon performing these comparisons.

16.11 CONCLUSION

We have covered a lot of ground in this chapter. Because forecasting is such an important activity in business, it has received a tremendous amount of attention by both academicians and practitioners. All of the methods discussed in this chapter—and more—are actually used, often on a day-to-day basis. There is really no point in arguing which of these methods is best. All of them have their strengths and weaknesses. The most important point is that when they are applied properly, they have all been found to be useful in real business applications.

PROBLEMS

Skill-Building Problems

57. The file P16_57.XLS contains quarterly revenues of Toys 'R Us for the years 1992–1995. Discuss the seasonal and trend components of the growth of Toys 'R Us revenues. Also, use any reasonable forecasting method to forecast quarterly revenues for 1996. Explain your reason for using the method you use.

58. The file P16_58.XLS contains 1991–1997 quarterly revenues and earnings per share (EPS) for the following companies: Mattel, McDonald's, Eli Lilly, General Motors, Microsoft, AT&T, Nike, GE, Coca-Cola, and Ford. (*Source*: Standard and Poor's 500 Guide: 1998)
   a. For each company, use a regression model with trend and seasonal components to forecast revenues and EPS.
   b. For each company, use Winters' method to forecast revenues and EPS.
   c. For each company, which method appears to be more accurate?

59. The file P16_59.XLS contains the sales in (millions of dollars) for Sun Microsystems for the years 1987–1993.
   a. Use these data to predict 1994 and 1995 Sun sales. You need consider only a linear and exponential trend, but you should justify the equation you choose.
   b. In words, how will your predictions of sales increase from year to year?
   c. Are there any outliers?

60. The file P16_60.XLS contains the sales in (millions of dollars) for Procter and Gamble for the years 1984–1993.
   a. Use these data to predict 1994 and 1995 P&G sales. You need consider only a linear and exponential trend, but you should justify the equation you choose.
   b. Use your part **a** answer to explain in words how your predictions of P&G sales will increase from year to year.
   c. Are there any outliers?
   d. You are 95% sure that 1995 P&G sales will be between what two values?

61. The file P16_61.XLS lists the 1984–1995 sales of Nike. Forecast 1996 and 1997 sales with a linear or exponential trend. Are there any outliers in your predictions for 1984–1995?

62. The file P16_62.XLS contains data on pork sales. Price is in dollars per hundred pounds sold, quantity sold is in billions of pounds, per capita income is in dollars, U.S. population is in millions, and GNP is in billions of dollars.

   a. Use these data to develop a regression equation that could be used to predict the quantity of pork sold during future periods. Is autocorrelation, heteroscedasticity, or multicollinearity a problem?

   b. Suppose that during each of the next two quarters, price is $45, U.S. population is 240, GNP is 2620, and per capita income is $10,000. Predict the quantity of pork sold during each of the next two quarters.

   c. We expect our prediction of pork sales to be accurate within what value 68% of the time?

   d. Use Winters' method to develop a forecast for pork sales during the next two quarters.

63. The file P16_63 contains data on a motel chain's revenue and advertising.

   a. Use these data and multiple regression to make predictions of the motel chain's revenues during the next four quarters. Assume that advertising during each of the next four quarters is $50,000. (*Hint*: Try using advertising, lagged by one period, as an explanatory variable.)

   b. Use Holt's method to make forecasts for the motel chain's revenues during the next four quarters.

   c. Use simple exponential smoothing to make predictions for the motel chain's revenues during the next four quarters.

   d. Use Winters' method to determine predictions for the motel chain's revenues during the next four quarters.

   e. Which forecasts would you expect to be the most reliable?

64. The file P16_64.XLS contains data on monthly U.S. housing sales (in thousands of houses) for 1967–1972.

   a. Using Winters' method, find values of α, β, and γ that yield a RMSE as small as possible.

   b. Although we have not discussed autocorrelation for smoothing methods, good forecasts derived from smoothing methods should exhibit no autocorrelation. Do the forecast errors for this problem exhibit autocorrelation?

   c. It has been stated that if only trend and seasonality are important factors, then α should be at most 0.5. Explain why this problem produced $\alpha > 0.5$.

   d. At the end of December 1972, what is the forecast of housing sales during the first 3 months of 1973?

65. Let Y_t be the sales during month t (in thousands of dollars) for a photography studio, and let P_t be the price charged for portraits during month t. The data are in the file P16_65.XLS. Use regression to fit the following model to these data:

$$Y_t = \alpha + \beta_1 Y_{t-1} + \beta_2 P_t + \varepsilon_t$$

This equation indicates that last month's sales and the current month's price are explanatory variables. The last term, ε_t, is an error term.

   a. If the price of a portrait during month 21 is $10, what would we predict for sales in month 21?

   b. Does there appear to be a problem with autocorrelation, heteroscedasticity, or multicollinearity?

66. The file P16_66.XLS gives quarterly auto sales, GNP, interest rates, and unemployment rates.

   a. With all but the most recent 2 years of data, use regression to forecast auto sales. Carefully interpret the coefficients in your final equation.

   b. Use all but the most recent 2 years of data to develop an exponential smoothing model to forecast future auto sales.

   c. To *validate* your model, determine which model does the better job of forecasting for the most recent 2 years of data. It is usually recommended to hold back some of your data to validate any forecast model. This helps avoid "overfitting."

Skill-Extending Problems

67. The file P16_67.XLS gives monthly exchange rates (dollars per unit of local currency) for 25 countries. Technical analysts believe that by charting past changes in exchange rates, it is possible to predict future changes of exchange rates. After analyzing the autocorrelations for the given data, do you believe that technical analysis has potential?

68. The file P16_68.XLS contains 5 years of monthly data, starting in January 1995, for a particular company. The first variable is Time (1–60). The second variable, Sales1, has data on sales of a product. Note that Sales1 increases linearly throughout the period, with only a minor amount of "noise." (The third variable, Sales2, will be discussed and used in the next problem.) For this problem use the Sales1 variable to see how the following forecasting methods are able to track a linear trend.

   a. Forecast this series with the moving average method with various spans such as 3, 6, and 12. What can you conclude?

b. Forecast this series with simple exponential smoothing with various smoothing constants such as 0.1, 0.3, 0.5, and 0.7. What can you conclude?

c. Now repeat part **b** with Holt's exponential smoothing method, again for various smoothing constants. Can you do significantly better than in parts **a** and **b**?

d. What can you conclude from your findings in parts **a**, **b**, and **c** about forecasting this type of series?

69. The Sales2 variable in the file from the previous problem was created from the Sales1 variable by multiplying by monthly seasonal factors. Basically, the summer months are high and the winter months are low. This might represent the sales of a product that has a linear trend and seasonality.

a. Repeat parts **a**, **b**, and **c** from the previous problem to see how well these forecasting methods can deal with trend *and* seasonality.

b. Now use Winters' method, with various values of the three smoothing constants, to forecast the series. Can you do much better? Which smoothing constants work well?

c. Use the ratio-to-moving-average method, where you first do the seasonal decomposition and then forecast (by any appropriate method) the deseasonalized series. Does this do as well as, or better than, Winters' method?

d. What can you conclude from your findings in parts **a**, **b**, and **c** about forecasting this type of series?

Arrivals at the Credit Union

The Indiana University Credit Union Eastland Plaza branch was having trouble getting the correct staffing levels to match customer arrival patterns. On some days, the number of tellers was too high relative to the customer traffic, so that tellers were often idle. On other days, the opposite occurred; long customer waiting lines formed because the relatively few tellers could not keep up with the number of customers. The credit union manager, James Chilton, knew that there was a problem, but he had little of the quantitative training he believed would be necessary to find a better staffing solution. James figured that the problem could be broken down into three parts. First, he needed a reliable forecast of each day's number of customer arrivals. Second, he needed to translate these forecasts into staffing levels that would make an adequate trade-off between teller idleness and customer waiting. Third, he needed to translate these staffing levels into individual teller work assignments—who should come to work when.

The last two parts of the problem require analysis tools (queueing and scheduling) that we will not pursue here. However, you can help James with the first part—forecasting. The file CREDITUNION.XLS lists the number of customers entering this credit union branch each day of the past year. It also lists other information: the day of the week, whether the day was a staff or faculty payday, and whether the day was the day before or after a holiday. Use this data set to develop one or more forecasting models that James could use to help solve his problem. Based on your model(s), make any recommendations about staffing that appear reasonable.

Forecasting Weekly Sales at Amanta

Amanta Appliances sells two styles of refrigerator at over 50 locations in the Midwest. The first style is a relatively expensive model, whereas the second is a standard, less expensive model. Although weekly demand for these two products is fairly stable from week to week, there is enough variation to concern management at Amanta. There have been relatively unsophisticated attempts to forecast weekly demand, but they haven't been very successful. Sometimes demand (and the corresponding sales) are lower than forecasted, so that inventory costs are high. Other times the forecasts are too low. When this happens and on-hand inventory is not sufficient to meet customer demand, Amanta requires expedited shipments to keep customers happy—and this nearly wipes out Amanta's profit margin on the expedited units.[13] Profits at Amanta would almost certainly increase if demand could be forecasted more accurately.

Data on weekly sales of both products appear in the file AMANTA.XLS. A time series chart of the two sales variables indicates what Amanta management expected—namely, there is no evidence of any upward or downward trends or of any seasonality. In fact, it might appear that each series is an unpredictable sequence of random ups and downs. But is this really true? Is it possible to forecast either series, with some degree of accuracy, with an extrapolation method (where only past values of *that* series are used to forecast current and future values)? What method appears to be best? How accurate is it? Also, is it possible, when trying to forecast sales of one product, to somehow incorporate current or past sales of the *other* product in the forecast model? After all, these products might be "substitute" products, where high sales of one go with low sales of the other, or they might be complementary products, where sales of the two products tend to move in the *same* direction.

---

[13] Because Amanta uses expediting when necessary, its sales each week are equal to its customer demands. Therefore, we use the terms *demand* and *sales* interchangeably.

References

Aarvik, O., and P. Randolph. "The Application of Linear Programming to the Determination of Transmission Line Fees in an Electrical Power Network. *Interfaces* 6 (1975): 17–31.

Agnihothri, R., and P. Taylor. "Staffing a Centralized Appointment Scheduling Department in Lourdes Hospital." *Interfaces* 21, no. 5 (1991): 1–15.

Albright, S.C., W. Winston, and C. Zappe. *Managerial Statistics.* Pacific Grove: Duxbury Press, 2000.

Altman, E. *Handbook of Corporate Finance.* New York: Wiley, 1986.

Andrews, B., and H. Parsons. "Establishing Telephone-Agent Staffing Levels through Economic Optimization." *Interfaces* 23, no. 2 (1993): 14–20.

Armstrong, S. "Research on Forecasting: A Quarter-Century Review, 1960–1984." *Interfaces* 16, no. 1 (1986): 89–103.

Armstrong, S. *Long-Range Forecasting.* New York: Wiley, 1985.

Armstrong, S. "Forecasting by Extrapolation: Conclusions from 25 Years of Research." *Interfaces* 14, no. 6 (1984): 52–66.

Arntzen, B., G. Brown, T. Harrison, and L. Trafton. "Global Supply Chain Management at Digital Equipment Corporation." *Interfaces* 25, no. 1 (1995): 69–93.

Austin, L. "Project EOQ: A Success Story in Implementing Academic Research." *Interfaces* 7, no. 4 (1977): 1–14.

Babich, P. "Customer Satisfaction: How Good Is Good Enough?" *Quality Progress* 25 (Dec. 1992): 65–68.

Balson, W., J. Welsh, and D. Wilson. "Using Decision Analysis and Risk Analysis to Manage Utility Environmental Risk." *Interfaces* 22, no. 6 (1992): 126–139.

Baumol, W. "The Transactions Demand for Cash: An Inventory Theoretic Approach." *Quarterly Journal of Economics* 16 (1952): 545–556.

Bean, J., C. Noon, S. Ryan, and G. Salton. "Selecting Tenants in a Shopping Mall." *Interfaces* 18, no. 2 (1988): 1–10.

Bean, J., C. Noon, and G. Salton. "Asset Divestiture at Homart Development Company." *Interfaces* 17, no. 1 (1987): 48–65.

Benninga, S. *Numerical Methods in Finance.* Cambridge, MA: MIT Press, 1989.

Bernstein, R., D. Sokal, S. Seitz, B. Auvert, J. Stover, and W. Naamara. "Simulating the Control of a Heterosexual HIV Epidemic in a Severely Affected East African City." *Interfaces* 28, no. 3 (1998): 101–126.

Black, F., and M. Scholes. "The Pricing of Options and Corporate Liabilities." *Journal of Political Economy* 81 (1973): 637–654.

Borison, A. "Oglethorpe Power Corporation Decides about Investing in a Major Transmission System." *Interfaces* 25, no. 2 (1995): 25–36.

Boykin, R. "Optimizing Chemical Production at Monsanto." *Interfaces* 15, no. 1 (1985): 88–95.

Brigandi, A., D. Dargon, M. Sheehan, and T. Spencer. "AT&T's Call Processing Simulator (CAPS) Operational Design for Inbound Call Centers." *Interfaces* 24, no. 1 (1994): 6–28.

Brout, D. "Scientific Management of Inventory on a Hand-Held Calculator. *Interfaces* 11, no. 6 (1981): 57–69.

Brown, G., et al. "Real-Time Wide Area Dispatch of Mobil Tank Trucks." *Interfaces* 17, no. 1 (1987): 107–120.

Brown, G., A. Geoffrion, and G. Bradley. "Production and Sales Planning with Limited Shared Tooling at the Key Operation." *Management Science* 27 (1981): 247–259.

Brumelle, S. "On the Relation between Customer and Time Averages in Queues." *J. of Applied Probability* 8 (1971): 508–520.

Callen, J. "DEA: Partial Survey and Applications for Managerial Accounting." *Journal of Management Accounting Research* 3 (1991): 35–56.

Calloway, R., M. Cummins, and J. Freeland. "Solving Spreadsheet-Based Integer Programming Models: An Example from International Telecommunications." *Decision Sciences* 21 (1990): 808–824.

Carino, H., and C. Lenoir. "Optimizing Wood Procurement in Cabinet Manufacturing." *Interfaces* 18, no. 2 (1988): 11–19.

Caulkins, J., E. Kaplan, P. Lurie, T. O'Connor, and S. Ahn. "Can Difficult-to-Reuse Syringes Reduce the Spread of HIV Among Injection Drug Users?" *Interfaces* 28, no. 3 (1998): 23–33.

Cebry, M., A. DeSilva, and F. DiLisio. "Management Science in Automating Postal Operations: Facility and Equipment Planning in the United States Postal Service." *Interfaces* 22, no. 1 (1992): 110–130.

Charnes, A., and L. Cooper. "Generalization of the Warehousing Model." *Operational Research Quarterly* 6 (1955): 131–172.

Cheung, H., and J. Auger. "Linear Programming and Land Use Allocation." *Socio-Economic Planning* 10 (1976): 43–45.

Chrisman, J., T. Fry, G. Reeves, H. Lewis, and R. Weinstein. "A Multiobjective Linear Programming Methodology for Public Sector Tax Planning." *Interfaces* 19, no. 5 (1989): 13–30.

Cournot, A. *Mathematical Principles of the Theory of Wealth*. New York: Macmillan, 1897.

Cox, J., and M. Rubinstein. *Options Markets*. Englewood Cliffs, NJ: Prentice Hall, 1985.

Cox, J., S. Ross, and M. Rubinstein. "Option Pricing: A Simplified Approach." *Journal of Financial Economics* 7 (1979): 229–263.

Dantzig, G. "The Diet Problem." *Interfaces* 20, no. 4 (1990): 43–47.

Davis, L. *Handbook of Genetic Algorithms*. Van-Nostrand Reinhold (1991).

Deming, E. *Out of the Crisis*. Cambridge, MA: MIT Center for Advanced Engineering Study, 1986.

Denardo, E., U. Rothblum, and A. Swersey. "Transportation Problem in Which Costs Depend on Order of Arrival." *Management Science* 34 (1988): 774–784.

DeWitt, C., L. Lasdon, A. Waren, D. Brenner, and S. Melhem. "OMEGA: An Improved Gasoline Blending System for Texaco." *Interfaces* 19, no. 1 (1989): 85–101.

Dijkstra, M., L. Kroon, M. Salomon, J. van Nunen, and L. Wassenhove. "Planning the Size and Organization of KLM's Aircraft Maintenance Personnel." *Interfaces* 24, no. 6 (1994): 47–65.

Dobson, G., and S. Kalish. "Positioning and Pricing a Product Line." *Marketing Science* 7 (1988): 107–126.

Dolan, Robert J. & Simon, Hermann, *Power Pricing*. The Free Press, New York, 1996.

Eaton, D., et al. "Determining Emergency Medical Service Vehicle Deployment in Austin, Texas." *Interfaces* 15, no. 1 (1985): 96–108.

Efroymson, M., and T. Ray. "A Brand-Bound Algorithm for Plant Location." *Operations Research* 14 (1966): 361–368.

Ellis, P., and R. Corn. "Using Bivalent Integer Programming to Select Teams for Intercollegiate Women's Gymnastics Competition." *Interfaces* 14, no. 3 (1984): 41–46.

Engemann, K., and H. Miller. "Operations Risk Management at a Major Bank." *Interfaces* 22, no. 6 (1992): 140–149.

Eppen, G., K. Martin, and L. Schrage. "A Scenario Approach to Capacity Planning." *Operations Research* 37, no. 4 (1989): 517–527.

Evans, J. "The Factored Transportation Problem." *Management Science* 30 (1984): 1021–1024.

Fabian, T., "A Linear Programming Model of Integrated Iron and Steel Production." *Management Science* 4 (1958): 415–449.

Feinstein, C. "Deciding Whether to Test Student Athletes for Drug Use." *Interfaces* 20, no. 3 (1990): 80–87.

Fitzsimmons, J., and L. Allen. "A Warehouse Location Model Helps Texas Comptroller Select Out-of-State Audit Offices." *Interfaces* 13, no. 5 (1983): 40–46.

Franklin, A., and E. Koenigsberg. "Computer School Assignments in a Large District." *Operations Research* 21 (1973): 413–426.

Garvin, W., W. Crandall, J. John, and R. Spellman. "Applications of Linear Programming in the Oil Industry." *Management Science* 3 (1957): 407–430.

Gene Hunter. Ward Systems Group, Frederick, Maryland, 1995.

Geoffrion, A., and G. Graves. "Better Distribution Planning with Computer Models." *Harvard Business Review* (July–August 1976).

Glassey, R., and V. Gupta. "A Linear Programming Analysis of Paper Recycling." *Studies in Mathematical Programming*. Ed. H. Salkin and J. Saha. New York: North-Holland, 1978.

Glover, F., et al. "The Passenger-Mix Problem in the Scheduled Airlines." *Interfaces* 12 (1982): 873–880.

Glover, F., G. Jones, D. Karney, D. Klingman, and J. Mote. "An Integrated Production, Distribution, and Inventory System." *Interfaces* 9, no. 5 (1979): 21–35.

Glover, F., and D. Klingman. "Network Applications in Industry and Government." *AIIE Transactions* 9 (1977): 363–376.

Goldberg, D. *Genetic Algorithms in Search Optimization and Machine Learning*. Addison-Wesley (1989).

Golden, B., E. Wasil, and P. Harker. *The Analytic Hierarchy Process*. New York: Springer-Verlag, 1989.

Gorman, M. "Santa Fe Railway Uses an Operating-Plan Model to Improve Its Service Design." *Interfaces* 28, no. 4 (1998): 1–12.

Grossman, S., and O. Hart. "An Analysis of the Principal Agent Problem." *Econometrica* 51 (1983): 7–45.

Grossman, T. "Spreadsheet Modeling and Simulation Improves Understanding of Queues." *Interfaces* 29, no. 3 (1999): 88–103.

Hansen, P., and R. Wendell. "A Note on Airline Commuting." *Interfaces* 11, no. 12 (1982): 85–87.

Hauser, J., and S. Gaskin. "Application of the Defender Consumer Model." *Marketing Science* 3, no. 4 (1984): 327–351.

Heady, E., and A. Egbert. "Regional Planning of Efficient Agricultural Patterns." *Econometrica* 32 (1964): 374–386.

Hertz, D. "Risk Analysis in Capital Investment." *Harvard Business Review* 42 (Jan.–Feb. 1964): 96–108.

Hess, S. "Swinging on the Branch of a Tree: Project Selection Applications." *Interfaces* 23, no. 6 (1993): 5–12.

Heyman, D. and S. Stidham. "The Relation between Customer and Time Averages in Queues." *Operations Research* 28 (1980): 983–984.

Holland, J. *Adaptation in Natural and Artificial Systems*. University of Michigan Press (1975).

Holmer, M. "The Asset-Liability Management Strategy System at Fannie Mae." *Interfaces* 24, no. 3 (1994): 3–21.

Hoppensteadt, F., and C. Peskin. *Mathematics in Medicine and the Life Sciences*. New York: Springer-Verlag, 1992.

Howard, R. "Heathens, Heretics, and Cults: The Religious Spectrum of Decision Aiding." *Interfaces* 22, no. 6 (1992): 15–27.

Huerter, J., and W. Swart. "An Integrated Labor-Management System for Taco Bell." *Interfaces* 28, no. 1 (1998): 75–91.

Hull, J. *Options, Futures, and Other Derivative Securities*. 2nd edition. Englewood Cliffs, NJ: Prentice Hall, 1993.

Ignall, E., and P. Kolesar. "Operating Characteristics of a Simple Shuttle under Local Dispatching Rules." *Operations Research* 20 (1972): 1077–1088.

Jacobs, W. "The Caterer Problem." *Naval Logistics Research Quarterly* 1 (1954): 154–165.

Jarrow and Turnbull. *Derivative Securities*. Cincinnati: South-Western College Publishing, 1996.

Johnson, R., and D. Wichern. *Applied Multivariate Statistical Analysis*, 4th edition. Prentice Hall (1998).

Kahn, J., M. Brandeau, and J. Dunn-Mortimer. "OR Modeling and AIDS Policy: From Theory to Practice." *Interfaces* 28, no. 3 (1998): 3–22.

Kelly, J. "A New Interpretation of Information Rate." *Bell System Technical Journal* 35 (1956): 917–926.

Kimes, S., and J. Fitzsimmons. "Selecting Profitable Hotel Sites at La Qunita Motor Inns. *Interfaces* 20 no. 2 (1990): 12–20.

Kirkwood, C. "An Overview of Methods for Applied Decision Analysis" *Interfaces* 22, no. 6 (1992): 28–39.

Klingman, D., and N. Phillips. "Topological and Computations Aspects of Preemptive Multicriteria Military Personnel Assignment Problems." *Management Science* 30, no. 11 (1984): 1362–1375.

Klingman, D., N. Phillips, D. Steiger, and W. Young. "The Successful Deployment of Management Science throughout Citgo Petroleum Corporation." *Interfaces* 17, no. 1 (1987): 4–25.

Kolesar, P., and E. Blum. "Square Root Laws for Fire Engine Response Distances." *Management Science* 19 (1973): 1368–1378.

Kolesar, P., T. Crabill, K. Rider, and W. Walker. "A Queueing Linear Programming Approach to Scheduling Police Patrol Cars." *Operations Research* 23 (1974): 1045–1062.

Krajewski, L., L. Ritzman, and P. McKenzie. "Shift Scheduling in Banking Operations: A Case Application." *Interfaces* 10, no. 2 (1980): 1–8.

Krumm, F., and C. Rolle. "Management and Application of Decision and Risk Analysis in Du Pont." *Interfaces* 22, no. 6 (1992): 84–93.

Lancaster, L. "The Evolution of the Diet Model in Managing Food Systems." *Interfaces* 22, no. 5 (1992): 59–68.

Lanzenauer, C., E. Harbauer, B. Johnston, and D. Shuttleworth. "RRSP Flood: LP to the Rescue." *Interfaces* 17, no. 4 (1987): 27–40.

Lee, H., C. Billington, and B. Carter. "Hewlett-Packard Gains Control of Inventory and Service through Design for Localization." Interfaces 23, no. 4 (1993): 1–11.

Lee, S., and L. Moore. "Optimizing University Admissions Planning." *Decision Sciences* 5 (1974): 405–414.

Liggett, R. "The Application of an Implicit Enumeration Algorithm to the School Desegregation Problem." *Management Science* 20 (1973): 159–168.

Lin, W., T. Mock, and A. Wright. "The Use of AHP as an Aid in Planning the Nature and Extent of Audit Procedures." *Auditing: A Journal of Practice and Theory* 4, no. 1 (1984): 89–99.

Little, J.D.C. "A Proof for the Queuing Formula $L = \lambda W$." *Operations Research* 9 (1961): 383–387.

Littlechild, S. "Marginal Pricing with Joint Costs." *Economic Journal* 80 (1970): 323–334.

Lodish, L., et al. "Salesforce Sizing and Deployment Using a Decision Calculus Model at Syntex Laboratories." *Interfaces* 18, no. 1 (1986): 5–20.

Love, R., and J. Hoey. "Management Science Improves Fast-Food Operations." *Interfaces* 20, no. 2 (1990): 21–29.

Love, R., and L. Yerex. "An Application of a Facilities Location Model in the Prestressed Concrete Industry." *Interfaces* 6, no. 4 (1976): 45–49.

Luenberger, D. *Investment Science*. Oxford University Press (1997).

Machol, R. "An Application of the Assignment Problem." *Operations Research* 18 (1970): 745–746.

Magoulas, K., and D. Marinos-Kouris. "Gasoline Blending LP." *Oil and Gas Journal* (July 1988): 44–48.

Makuch, W., J. Dodge, J. Ecker, D. Granfors, and G. Hahn. "Managing Consumer Credit Delinquency in the US Economy: A Multi-Billion Dollar Management Science Application." *Interfaces* 22, no. 1 (1992): 90–109.

Marcus, A. "The Magellan Fund and Market Efficiency." *Journal of Portfolio Management* (Fall 1990): 85–88.

Martin, C., D. Dent, and J. Eckhart. "Integrated Production, Distribution, and Inventory Planning at Libbey-Owens-Ford." *Interfaces* 23, no. 3 (1993): 68–78.

Maxwell, W., and R. Wilson. "Dynamic Network Flow Modelling of Fixed Path Material Handling Systems." *AIIE Transactions* 13, no. 1 (1981): 12–21.

Mellichamp, J., D. Miller, and O. Kwon. "The Southern Company Uses a Probability Model for Cost Justification of Oil Sample Analysis." *Interfaces* 23, no. 3 (1993): 118–124.

Mendenhall, W., and T. Sincich. *A Second Course in Business Statistics: Regression Analysis, 4th edition*. New York: Dellen Publishing Company, 1993.

Miser, H. "Avoiding the Corrupting Lie of a Poorly Stated Problem." *Interfaces* 23, no. 6 (1993): 114–119.

Montgomery, D., and E. Del Castillo. "A Nonlinear Programming Response to the Dual Response Problem." *Journal of Quality Technology* 25, no. 3 (1993): 199–204.

Morrison, D., and R. Wheat. "Pulling the Goalie Revisited." *Interfaces* 16, no. 6 (1984): 28–34.

Morton, T. "Planning Horizons for Dynamic Programming." *Operations Research* 27 (1979): 730–743.

Muckstadt, J., and R. Wilson. "An Application of Mixed Integer Programming Duality to Scheduling Thermal Generating Systems." *IEEE Transactions on Power Apparatus and Systems* (1968): 1968–1978.

Mulvey, J. "An Asset-Liability Investment System." *Interfaces* 24, no. 3 (1994): 22–33.

Mulvey, M. "Strategies in Modeling: A Personnel Example." *Interfaces* 9, no. 3 (1982): 66–75.

Myers, R. *Classical and Modern Regression with Applications*. Belmont, CA: Duxbury Press, 1990.

Myers, R., A. Khuri, and W. Carter. "Response Surface Methodology: 1966–1988." *Technometrics* 3 (1989): 137–157.

Nicholson, T. *Optimization in Industry: Volume 2 Applications*. Chicago: Aldine-Atherton, 1971.

Norton, R. "Which Offices or Stores Perform Best? A New Tool Tells." *Fortune* October 31 (1994).

Norton, R. "A New Tool to Help Managers." *Fortune* (May 30, 1994): 135–140.

Oliff, M., and E. Burch. "Multiproduct Production Scheduling at Owens-Corning Fiberglass." *Interfaces* 15, no. 5 (1985): 25–34.

Owens, D., M. Brandeau, and C. Sox. "Effect of Relapse to High-Risk Behavior on the Costs and Benefits of a Program to Screen Women for Human Immunodeficiency Virus." *Interfaces* 28, no. 3 (1998): 52–74.

Paltiel, A., and K. Freedberg. "The Cost-Effectiveness of Preventing Cytomegalovirus Disease in AIDS Patients." *Interfaces* 28, no. 3 (1998): 34–51.

Porteus, E. "Investing in Reduced Setups in the EOQ Model." *Management Science* 31, no. 8 (1985): 998–1010.

Quinn, P., B. Andrews, and H. Parsons. "Allocating Telecommunications Resources at L. L. Bean, Inc." *Interfaces* 21, no. 1 (1991): 75–91.

Ravindran, A. "On Compact Book Storage in Libraries." *Opsearch* 8 (1971): 245–252.

Reichheld, F. *The Loyalty Effect*. Harvard Business School Press (1996).

Riccio, L., J. Miller, and A. Little. "Polishing the Big Apple." *Interfaces* 16, no. 1 (1986): 83–88.

Robichek, A., D. Teichroew, and M. Jones. "Optimal Short-Term Financing Decisions." *Management Science* 12 (1965): 1–36.

Robinson, P., L. Gao, and S. Muggenborg. "Designing an Integrated Distribution System at DowBrands, Inc." *Interfaces* 23, no. 3 (1993): 107–117.

Rohn, E. "A New LP Approach to Bond Portfolio Management." *Journal of Financial and Quantitative Analysis* 22 (1987): 439–467.

Rothstein, M. "Hospital Manpower Shift Scheduling by Mathematical Programming." *Health Services Research* (1973).

Saaty, T. *The Analytic Hierarchy Process*. New York: McGraw-Hill, 1988.

Salkin, H., and C. Lin. "Aggregation of Subsidiary Firms for Minimal Unemployment Compensation Payments via Integer Programming." *Management Science* 25 (1979): 405–408.

Sartoris, W., and M. Spruill. "Goal Programming and Working Capital Management." *Financial Management* 3 (1974): 67–74.

Savage, S. *Insight.xla, Business Analysis Software for Microsoft Excel*. Pacific Grove: Duxbury Press, 1998.

Schindler, S., and T. Semmel. "Station Staffing at Pan American World Airways." *Interfaces* 23, no. 3 (1993): 91–106.

Schnarrs, S., and J. Bavuso. "Extrapolation Models on Very Short-Term Forecasts", *Journal of Business Research* 14 (1986): 27–36.

Schrage, L. *Optimization Modeling Using LINDO*. ITP Publishing (1997).

Schrage, L., *WHAT'S BEST! Release 2.0*. Belmont, CA: Duxbury Press, 1996.

Sexton, T., S. Sleeper, and R. Taggart. "Improving Pupil Transportation in North Carolina." *Interfaces* 24, no. 1 (1994): 87–103.

Shanker, R., and A. Zoltners. "The Corporate Payments Problem." *Journal of Bank Research* (1972): 47–53.

Sherman, H. D., and G. Ladino. "Managing Bank Productivity Using Data Envelopment Analysis (DEA)." *Interfaces* 25, no. 2 (1995): 60–80.

Silver, E., D. Pyke, and R. Peterson. *Inventory Management and Production Planning and Scheduling*, 3rd ed., New York: Wiley, 1998.

Smith, S. "Planning Transistor Production by Linear Programming." *Operations Research* 13 (1965): 132–139.

Sonderman, D., and P. Abrahamson. "Radiotherapy Design Using Mathematical Programming." *Operations Research* 33, no. 4 (1985): 705–725.

Spencer, T., A. Brigandi, D. Dargon, and M. Sheehan. "AT&T's Telemarketing Site Selection System Offers Customer Support. *Interfaces* 20, no. 1 (1990).

Steuer, R. "Sausage Blending Using Multiple Objective Programming." *Management Science* 30 (1984): 1376–1384.

Stidham, S. "A Last Word on $L = \lambda W$." *Operations Research* 22 (1974): 417–421.

Strong, R. "LP Solves Problem: Eases Duration Matching Process." *Pension and Investment Age* 17, no. 26 (1989): 21.

Sullivan, R., and S. Secrest. "A Simple Optimization DSS for Production Planning at Dairyman's Cooperative Creamery Association." *Interfaces* 15, no. 5 (1985): 46–54.

Swart, W., and L. Donno. "Simulation Modeling Improves Operations, Planning and Productivity of Fast-Food Restaurants." *Interfaces* 11, no. 6 (1981): 35–47.

Tanner, Mike. *Practical Queueing Analysis.* Berkshire, England: McGraw-Hill International (UK) Ltd., 1995.

Taylor, P., and S. Huxley. "A Break from Tradition for the San Francisco Police: Patrol Officer Scheduling Using an Optimization-Based Decision Support Tool." *Interfaces* 19, no. 1 (1989): 4–24.

Taylor, B., and A. Keown. "Planning Urban Recreational Facilities with Goal Programming." *Journal of Operational Research Society* 29, no. 8 (1984): 751–758.

Ulvila, J. "Postal Automation (ZIP+4) Technology: A Decision Analysis." *Interfaces* 17, no. 2 (1987): 1–12.

Vasko, F., J. Wolfe, and K. Stott. "Optimal Selection of Ingot Sizes via Set Covering." *Operations Research* 35 no. 3 (1955): 346–353.

Volkema, R. "Managing the Process of Formulating the Problem." *Interfaces* 25, no. 3 (1995): 81–87.

Waddell, R. "A Model for Equipment Replacement Decisions and Policies." *Interfaces* 13, no. 4 (1983): 1–8.

Walker, W. "Using the Set Covering Problem to Assign Fire Companies to Firehouses." *Operations Research* 22 (1974): 275–277.

Weber, S. "A Modified Analytic Hierarchy Process for Automated Manufacturing Decisions." *Interfaces* 23, no. 4 (1993): 75–84.

Welling, P. "A Goal Programming Model for Human Resource Allocation in a CPA Firm." *Accounting, Organizations and Society* 2 (1977): 307–316.

Westerberg, C., B. Bjorklund, and E. Hultman. "An Application of Mixed Integer Programming in a Swedish Steel Mill." *Interfaces* 7, no. 2 (1977): 39–43.

Winston, W. L. *Operations Research: Applications and Algorithms.* 3rd ed. Belmont, California: Duxbury Press, 1994.

Winston, W. *Decision Making Under Uncertainty with RISKOptimizer.* Palisade Corporation, 1999.

Zahedi, F. "The Analytic Hierarchy Process—A Survey of the Method and Its Applications." *Interfaces* 16, no. 4 (1986): 96–108.

Zangwill, W. "The Limits of Japanese Production Theory." *Interfaces* 22, no. 5 (1992): 14–25.

Index

IMPORTANT
**If the CD-ROM packaging has been opened,
the purchaser cannot return the book for a refund!
The CD-ROM is subject to this agreement!**

LICENSING AND WARRANTY AGREEMENT

Notice to Users: Do not install or use the CD-ROM until you have read and agreed to this agreement. You will be bound by the terms of this agreement if you install or use the CD-ROM or otherwise signify acceptance of this agreement. If you do not agree to the terms contained in this agreement, do not install or use any portion of this CD-ROM.

License: The material in the CD-ROM (the "Software") is copyrighted and is protected by United States copyright laws and international treaty provisions. All rights are reserved to the respective copyright holders. No part of the Software may be reproduced, stored in a retrieval system, distributed (including but not limited to over the www/Internet), decompiled, reverse engineered, reconfigured, transmitted, or transcribed, in any form or by any means—electronic, mechanical, photocopying, recording, or otherwise—without the prior written permission of Duxbury Press, an imprint of Brooks/Cole (the "Publisher"). Adopters of Winston & Albright's *Practical Management Science, Second Edition* may place the Software on the adopting school's network during the specific period of adoption for classroom purposes only in support of that text. The Software may not under any circumstances, be reproduced and/or downloaded for sale. For further permission and information, contact Brooks/Cole, 511 Forest Lodge Road, Pacific Grove, California 93950.

The DecisionTools® Suite software in the CD-ROM is copyrighted by Palisade Corporation of Newfield, NY, and may be used for academic purposes only. Any nonacademic use of the DecisionTools® Suite software contained herein is strictly forbidden and represents a violation of this license agreement. For information on purchasing and using the DecisionTools® Suite software for nonacademic purposes, contact the Technical Sales Department, Palisade Corporation, 31 Decker Road, Newfield, NY, 14867.

Limited Warranty: The warranty for the media on which the Software is provided is for ninety (90) days from the original purchase and valid only if the packaging for the Software was purchased unopened. If, during that time, you find defects in the workmanship or material, the Publisher will replace the defective media. The Publisher provides no other warranties, expressed or implied, including the implied warranties of merchantability or fitness for a particular purpose, and shall not be liable for any damages, including direct, special, indirect, incidental, consequential, or otherwise.

For Technical Support:
 Voice:1-800-423-0563   Fax:1-606-647-5045   E-mail: support@kdc.com